COMPLETE
OUTDOORS
ENCYCLOPEDIA

COMPLETE OUTDOORS ENCYCLOPEDIA

by Vin T. Sparano

UNIVERSE

Published by Universe Publishing
A Division of Rizzoli International Publications, Inc.
300 Park Avenue South
New York, NY 10010
www.rizzoliusa.com

This is the fifth edition of *Complete Outdoors Encyclopedia*.
Previous editions were published in 1972, 1980, 1988, and 1998.

Disclaimer: While all of the information in this book—both in text and illustrations—has been fact
checked and field tested, the publisher and author make no warranty, express or implied, that the
information is appropriate for every individual, situation, or purpose, and assume no responsibility
for errors or omissions. All information in this book is presented for entertainment value only, and
for an adult audience. Before attempting any new activity, make sure that you are aware of your own
limitations and all applicable risks. This book is not intended to replace sound judgment or professional
advice from an experienced instructor or outdoor guide.

Always follow any and all manufacturer's instructions when using any equipment featured in
this book. If the manufacturer of your equipment does not recommend the use of the equipment in the
manner herein described or depicted, you should comply with the manufacturer's recommendations.
You assume all risk and full responsibility for all of your actions, and the publisher and author will
not be held responsible for any loss, damage, or injury of any sort, whether consequential, incidental,
special, or otherwise, that may result from the information presented in this book.

In addition, masculine pronouns were used throughout the text in this book. This was done for
the sake of simplicity only, and was not intended to exclude female outdoors enthusiasts.

Project Editor: Candice Fehrman
Book Design: Lori S. Malkin
Text: Vin T. Sparano

2014 2015 2016 2017 / 10 9 8 7 6 5 4 3 2 1

Printed in China

ISBN-13: 978-0-7893-2705-5

Library of Congress Catalog Control Number: 2013949708

■ ■ ■

To my wife and partner, Betty,
who demands so little
from a man who chases
the seasons.

■ ■ ■

Contents

Preface

It's hard to believe that *Complete Outdoors Encyclopedia* is more than 40 years old. The first edition was published in 1972 and it quickly won the Library Association Award for an Outstanding Reference Work. That award and recognition set the stage, and my motivation and love for the outdoors inspired me to move ahead with the second edition in 1980, the third edition in 1988, and the fourth edition in 1998. Each edition had to be totally revised and expanded to keep in step with the never-ending changes in outdoor sports.

Complete Outdoors Encyclopedia spans three generations of sportsmen and has become a one-book library that continues to guide sportsmen through the growing maze of outdoor technology. I've watched outboard motors grow from 50 to 350 horsepower, recurve bows change to complicated compound crossbows, small center-console boats transformed into 35-footers with four monster outboard engines on the transom. I have also seen the invention of inline muzzleloaders, and the introduction of modern sporting rifles and fishing reels that don't backlash and look like sports cars.

We have all witnessed the boom in fishing kayaks, paddleboards, and electronics that find fish and keep us from getting lost. The changes have not only been in better equipment and gear. Over the years, we have also learned how to be safer in the woods and waters. We have learned about new advice, ranging from removing a fishhook in your hand to treating a snakebite. The changes are truly amazing.

The biggest change in this fifth edition is the introduction of four-color photography from cover to cover. Now you will know what a rainbow trout and a Brittany spaniel really look like. This newest revision took one full year of work and I can't claim credit for doing it all. A special thanks goes to Candice Fehrman, my editor at Rizzoli/Universe. Candice's computer skills made life easier for this writer in dealing with the monumental task of selecting more than a thousand photos and illustrations. I also want to thank Lori S. Malkin, who designed this book page by page. When I asked Lori to do the impossible, she did it!

A special thanks goes to my son Matt Sparano, an exceptional sportsman, who I asked to volunteer for most of the casting and shooting photos.

Finally, there's Jim Muschett, my publisher at Rizzoli/Universe, who became a close friend as we worked through the massive task of networking with writers, photographers, and the outdoor industry.

There are many more people to thank for their help in creating this new edition, including photographers William Hartley, Len Rue Jr., Tim Christie, Dick McLaughlin, Dusan Smetana, and Denver Bryan. Special people in the outdoor industry also played an important role, including Katie Mitchell and Kim Phillips at Bass Pro, Tom Rosenbauer at Orvis, Isaiah James at Windsor Nature Discovery, Mac McKeever at L.L. Bean, Tammy Sapp at Bass Pro Shops, Joe Arterburn and Kellie Mowery at Cabela's, Joan Wulff and Sheila Hassan from the Wulff School of Fly Fishing, and many others who answered my requests for photos and data.

Now you are holding the fifth edition of *Complete Outdoors Encyclopedia*, the most colorful of all previous editions, and the result of a massive effort to bring you the most valuable guide to the outdoors ever published. For those new to the outdoors, this edition will teach you skills to be safe and knowledgeable. For experienced sportsmen, this edition will keep you up-to-date on the latest achievements that will continue to guide you whenever you go afield.

I hope I have succeeded in bringing you the ultimate guide to the outdoors.

—**Vin T. Sparano**
Editor Emeritus/Senior Field Editor
Outdoor Life

Section One
HUNTING AND SHOOTING

- RIFLES · SHOTGUNS · HANDGUNS ·
- CARTRIDGES · SHOTSHELLS ·
- TRAPSHOOTING · SKEETSHOOTING ·
- COMPETITION SHOOTING ·
- FIELD CARE OF GAME ·

RIFLE ACTIONS

Popular rifle actions used today fall into two broad classifications: the repeating action and the single-shot action. An older action design is the double-barreled rifle. The double-barreled rifle is extremely limited in use for a number of reasons that will be discussed in some detail later.

Among the repeaters, the most popular is the bolt-action rifle, which uses a manually operated steel bolt assembly to chamber and seal a cartridge in the breech. Two other repeating-rifle mechanisms are the lever and pump, or slide, actions, which are also manually operated to chamber and seal cartridges for firing. Fourth and last of the repeating rifles is the semi-automatic or autoloader, an action that requires only a pull of the trigger to fire a cartridge, eject the spent case, chamber a new cartridge, and cock the rifle for the next shot.

Single-shot rifles come in three designs: the single-shot bolt action, which differs from the repeating bolt action in that it has no magazine or clip; the break action, which, in the simplest terms, uses a lever (usually a thumb lever) to break open the rifle and expose the chamber for loading; and the falling-block action, an old design that for all practical purposes was considered dead and obsolete a few decades ago. Sturm, Ruger and Company brought the strong falling-block design back to life in 1966 with the introduction of the Ruger No. 1 Single Shot. Browning followed with its Model 1885, another single-shot rifle using the falling-block system. The Ruger No. 1 is available in a variety of calibers from varmint to big-game loads. The Browning Model 1885, which was also available in a variety of calibers, is no longer made.

Parts of the Bolt-Action Rifle

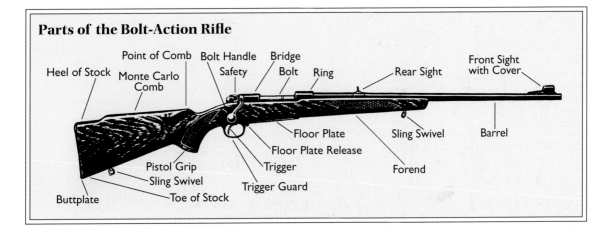

Bolt-Action Rifles

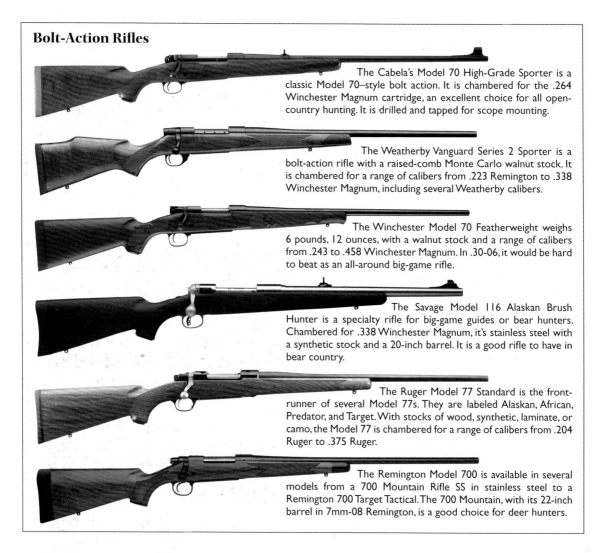

The Cabela's Model 70 High-Grade Sporter is a classic Model 70–style bolt action. It is chambered for the .264 Winchester Magnum cartridge, an excellent choice for all open-country hunting. It is drilled and tapped for scope mounting.

The Weatherby Vanguard Series 2 Sporter is a bolt-action rifle with a raised-comb Monte Carlo walnut stock. It is chambered for a range of calibers from .223 Remington to .338 Winchester Magnum, including several Weatherby calibers.

The Winchester Model 70 Featherweight weighs 6 pounds, 12 ounces, with a walnut stock and a range of calibers from .243 to .458 Winchester Magnum. In .30-06, it would be hard to beat as an all-around big-game rifle.

The Savage Model 116 Alaskan Brush Hunter is a specialty rifle for big-game guides or bear hunters. Chambered for .338 Winchester Magnum, it's stainless steel with a synthetic stock and a 20-inch barrel. It is a good rifle to have in bear country.

The Ruger Model 77 Standard is the front-runner of several Model 77s. They are labeled Alaskan, African, Predator, and Target. With stocks of wood, synthetic, laminate, or camo, the Model 77 is chambered for a range of calibers from .204 Ruger to .375 Ruger.

The Remington Model 700 is available in several models from a 700 Mountain Rifle SS in stainless steel to a Remington 700 Target Tactical. The 700 Mountain, with its 22-inch barrel in 7mm-08 Remington, is a good choice for deer hunters.

These various actions all have advantages and disadvantages. Only by examining each action in detail can hunters and target shooters select the most practical and effective rifle for their particular uses.

▉ Bolt Action

The most widely used rifle in the field and on the range is the bolt action, and there are several good reasons for this fact. The bolt action is strong and simple. It disassembles easily for cleaning, an important factor for the hunter in the field. The bolt on most modern rifles can be easily slipped out of the receiver and wiped clean of dirt, sand, or wet snow. With the bolt removed, a hunter who has just taken a fall can simply glance through the breech to check for obstructions in the bore.

Because the bolt affords strong hand leverage, this action is also best for the shooter who handloads his own ammunition. The powerful pull of the bolt is an advantage when extracting dirty or stuck cases. Likewise, cases that are slightly oversize can usually be chambered with a bit more than normal pressure on closing the bolt. Because the bolt locks a cartridge at the head, the cases are not subjected to stretch when fired and only the necks of the cases generally need to be resized during the reloading process.

How a Bolt-Action Rifle Works

1 • Raising the bolt handle un-locks the bolt head from the bar-rel chamber. At the same time, the notch at the bottom of the bolt handle catches and pushes up the protruding finger of the firing-pin head, pushing the firing pin to the rear.

2 • Moving the bolt assembly back ejects the empty case. A circu-lar spring in the end of the bolt (see detail) exerts pressure on the claw, holding the case tightly. When the mouth of the fired case clears the chamber, the spring-loaded ejector flips the case clear. The pressure of the magazine spring now raises a new cartridge to the loading position.

3 • Moving the bolt handle for-ward and turning it downward locks the bolt in the chamber and seals in the cartridge. The sear engages the notch on the firing-pin head, cocking the rifle. (Detail shows how the bolt locks into the barrel chamber.)

4 • Pulling the trigger disengages the sear from the notch on the firing-pin head. The main spring forces the firing pin forward, deto-nating the cartridge.

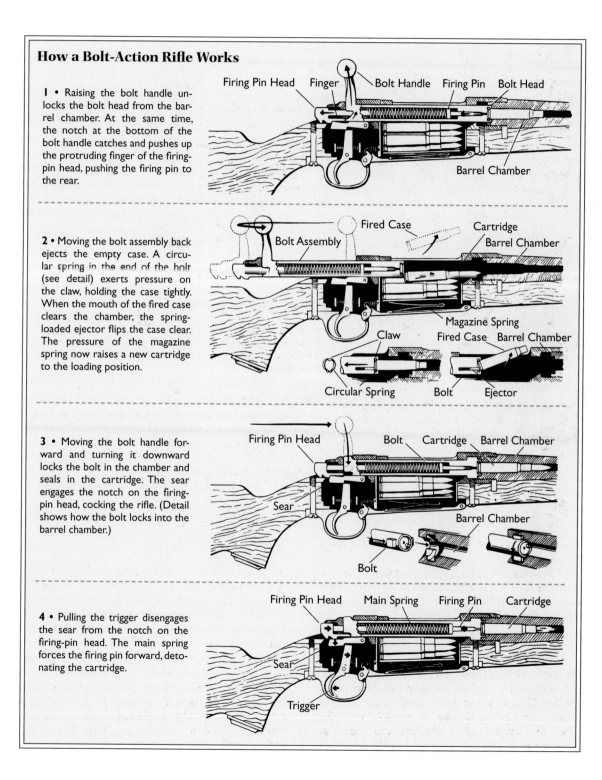

Firing Pin Head — Finger — Bolt Handle — Firing Pin — Bolt Head — Barrel Chamber

Bolt Assembly — Fired Case — Cartridge — Barrel Chamber — Magazine Spring — Claw — Fired Case — Barrel Chamber — Circular Spring — Bolt — Ejector

Firing Pin Head — Bolt — Cartridge — Barrel Chamber — Sear — Barrel Chamber — Bolt

Firing Pin Head — Main Spring — Firing Pin — Cartridge — Sear — Trigger

The bolt gun also has a one-piece stock that makes for better bedding of the action and barrel and produces greater accuracy than nearly all other rifle designs.

Who should use the bolt action? Because of its reliability and simplicity, the bolt-action rifle is the logical choice for hunters who prefer to hunt in remote areas, where gunsmiths and spare parts are scarce. Because of its superior accuracy, and the fact that it is chambered for nearly all flat-shooting, high-velocity cartridges, the bolt gun is a favorite among mountain and prairie hunters who are generally forced to take game at long ranges.

The bolt action also comes into its own as a target and benchrest rifle. The solid-locking action and one-piece stock produces accuracy, and the entire rifle is the most adaptable to alterations to satisfy the fancy of the serious target shooter.

Not all bolt-action rifles look alike and handle the same, however. Let's take a look at some typical factory models and learn the reasoning behind their designs.

The Ruger Model 77 and Winchester Model 70 are typical of the bolt actions built for hunting. Depending on the model, these Rugers and Winchesters are chambered for a variety of calibers, including the .204 Ruger, .25-06 Remington, 6.5 Creedmoor, .22-250, .243, .308, .270, .257 Roberts, .280 Remington, .30-06, 7mm Remington Magnum, .300, .338, .458 Winchester Magnums, 9.3x62mm, and .375 and .416 Ruger. This range of calibers fills the bill for all North American, European, and African game. Other gun companies, such as Remington, Browning, Savage, Kimber, and Sako, have comparable bolt-action models in many of these calibers.

The .460 Weatherby Magnum rifle fires one of the world's most powerful cartridges. The .460 Weatherby Magnum cartridge, using a 500-grain bullet, produces a muzzle energy of 7,507 foot-pounds. By comparison, the popular .30-06, with a 180-grain bullet, has a muzzle energy of about 2,910 foot-pounds. Though the .460 Weatherby Magnum is generally limited to the world's largest and most dangerous game, this rifle and caliber combination does prove that the bolt action's strong design can handle the most potent loads. Weatherby makes several models in a range of calibers.

One of the more specialized bolt actions is the Remington Model 700 SPS Varmint, designed for shooting woodchucks, coyotes, foxes, and any other varmints at long ranges. Its most distinguishing characteristic is the 26-inch, heavy-contour barrel, which affords steadier holding and consequently better accuracy. The rifle weighs about 8½ pounds with a synthetic stock and is chambered for a range of calibers from .17 Remington Fireball to .308 Winchester. The Model 700 Varmint comes without front and rear sights, as do most varminters, since these rifles invariably are mounted with scopes up to 24x. Bolt guns designated as varmint models are built for maximum range and precision shooting with high-velocity cartridges.

For the target shooter, the Anschutz Model 1907 ISU Standard Match is typical of a finely designed target rifle. It is suitable for all National Rifle Association matches and meets the requirements of the International Shooting Union. The 1907 Match weighs 11 pounds and has a fully adjustable trigger pull. Chambered for .22 Long Rifle only, the rifle's receiver is grooved for micrometer iron sights. Rifles of this type are used in Olympic and World Championship shooting. Available in both rimfire and centerfire calibers, such rifles usually have a heavy barrel, adjustable buttplate with hook, and an adjustable palm rest. A free rifle is drilled and tapped for receiver sights.

A shooter looking for a .22 bolt action for informal shooting and small-game hunting will have little trouble finding a model to fill his needs. There are three basic designs for the popular rimfire and the differences deal mainly with cartridge capacity.

The Henry Repeating Arms Acu-Bolt, for example, is a single-shot rifle ideal for beginners and youngsters. It is extremely safe. When the bolt is operated, the safety goes on automatically. Closing the bolt cocks it, of course, but the safety must then be moved to the off position before the rifle can be fired.

For those who want more ammunition in their guns, there are rifles such as the Ruger Model 77/22, which has a detachable rotary clip magazine with a capacity of 10 cartridges. The bolt is simply operated to eject the spent cartridge and chamber a new round. Another type of repeating bolt-action .22 employs a tubular magazine. Here again, the bolt is operated to eject the empty case and chamber a new round.

Repeating rifles, such as the Marlin and Ruger models, are well suited for small game, varmint shooting, and plinking. The single shot, which admittedly has limitations, comes into its own as a youngster's first rifle. All of these .22 rifles have a lot going for them. The rimfire cartridge has almost no recoil or loud muzzle blast to unnerve the shooter, making it easy for beginners to learn proper trigger squeeze and sight picture. Since the ammunition is relatively inexpensive, the .22 is also an intelligent investment for anyone who wants a rifle for informal target shooting and plinking.

■ Lever Action

The lever-action rifle is deeply embedded in American history. Its design produced the first successful repeating rifle in America. It has been labeled "the gun that won the West," and it has become a favorite among deer hunters in the East and Northeast. Today, the smooth and fast lever gun has earned a permanent niche for itself in the hunting clan. Like any rifle design, however, the lever action has advantages and disadvantages. Let's examine the advantages first.

Though the lever gun is not as strong or as accurate as the bolt-action rifle, it is faster to operate and easier to carry. Its narrow action and smooth lines make it an ideal scabbard gun for western hunters on horseback.

Combine the lever gun's quick handling for snap shots at moving game with the fact that most lever actions are generally chambered for medium-range deer cartridges and it's easy to understand why these rifles have also become a favorite among eastern and northeastern hunters, who get practically all their shots within 50 yards.

Another obvious advantage is that left-handed shooters can operate a lever action just as fast as right-handed shooters. This is an important factor for the southpaw woods hunter to consider. Though he may have his heart set on a bolt action, he'd be better off with a lever gun, with which he can get off a second or third shot without lowering the rifle from his shoulder. There are left-handed bolt-action rifles available, but they still cannot be handled from the shoulder as fast as a lever action. The left-handed bolt, however, is a good compromise for the woods hunter who may want to handload his own ammunition and supplement his deer trips with some varmint hunting and target shooting.

There is another advantage, though minor, that should at least be mentioned. The older-type lever actions, such as the Winchester 94 and the Marlin 336, offer an exposed hammer with a half-cock safety. The safety is engaged by thumbing the hammer back halfway, where it locks in place. This is a convenient feature for cold-weather hunters who must wear heavy gloves and for left-handed shooters who find other safeties

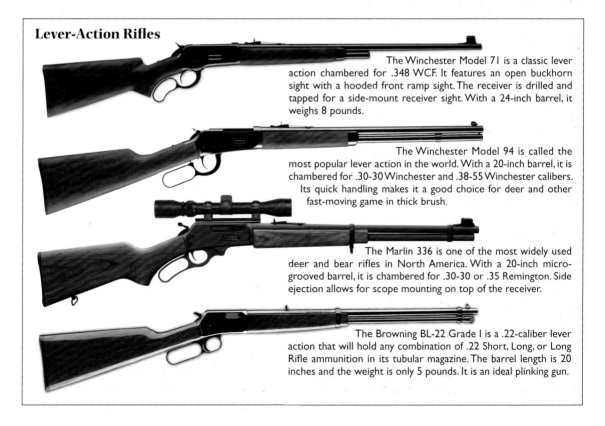

Lever-Action Rifles

The Winchester Model 71 is a classic lever action chambered for .348 WCF. It features an open buckhorn sight with a hooded front ramp sight. The receiver is drilled and tapped for a side-mount receiver sight. With a 24-inch barrel, it weighs 8 pounds.

The Winchester Model 94 is called the most popular lever action in the world. With a 20-inch barrel, it is chambered for .30-30 Winchester and .38-55 Winchester calibers. Its quick handling makes it a good choice for deer and other fast-moving game in thick brush.

The Marlin 336 is one of the most widely used deer and bear rifles in North America. With a 20-inch micro-grooved barrel, it is chambered for .30-30 or .35 Remington. Side ejection allows for scope mounting on top of the receiver.

The Browning BL-22 Grade I is a .22-caliber lever action that will hold any combination of .22 Short, Long, or Long Rifle ammunition in its tubular magazine. The barrel length is 20 inches and the weight is only 5 pounds. It is an ideal plinking gun.

How a Lever-Action Rifle Works

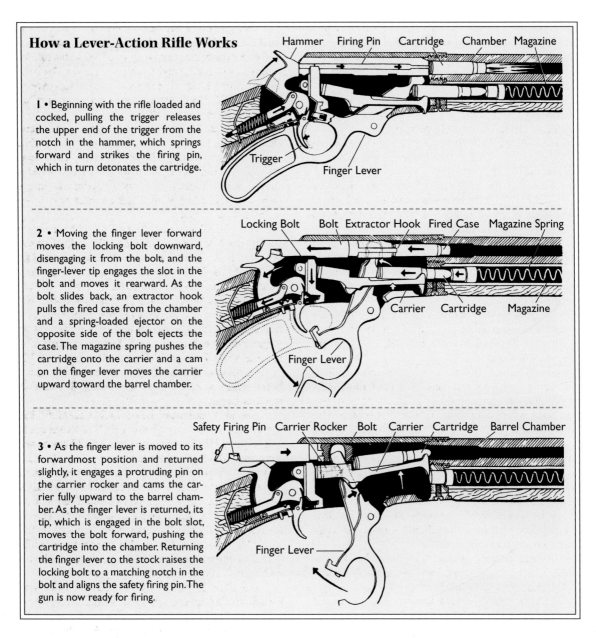

Hammer   Firing Pin   Cartridge   Chamber   Magazine

1 • Beginning with the rifle loaded and cocked, pulling the trigger releases the upper end of the trigger from the notch in the hammer, which springs forward and strikes the firing pin, which in turn detonates the cartridge.

Trigger   Finger Lever

Locking Bolt   Bolt Extractor Hook Fired Case Magazine Spring

2 • Moving the finger lever forward moves the locking bolt downward, disengaging it from the bolt, and the finger-lever tip engages the slot in the bolt and moves it rearward. As the bolt slides back, an extractor hook pulls the fired case from the chamber and a spring-loaded ejector on the opposite side of the bolt ejects the case. The magazine spring pushes the cartridge onto the carrier and a cam on the finger lever moves the carrier upward toward the barrel chamber.

Carrier   Cartridge   Magazine

Finger Lever

Safety Firing Pin Carrier Rocker Bolt Carrier Cartridge Barrel Chamber

3 • As the finger lever is moved to its forwardmost position and returned slightly, it engages a protruding pin on the carrier rocker and cams the carrier fully upward to the barrel chamber. As the finger lever is returned, its tip, which is engaged in the bolt slot, moves the bolt forward, pushing the cartridge into the chamber. Returning the finger lever to the stock raises the locking bolt to a matching notch in the bolt and aligns the safety firing pin. The gun is now ready for firing.

Finger Lever

---

awkward to reach. The Winchester Model 94 has a top-tang safety.

To fully cock the gun, the hammer is thumbed back all the way and the rifle is ready to be fired. If a hunter decides to pass up a shot, he simply holds the hammer with his thumb, depresses the trigger, and eases the hammer forward to half-cock safety. The simplicity of the exposed hammer design is a distinct advantage to sportsmen who hunt only a few weeks a year and it's also a safety feature to look for when shopping for a youngster's first deer rifle.

The fast lever-action rifle, however, does have its shortcomings. Most lever guns are fitted with two-piece stocks, and, in general, they are not as accurate as rifles with one-piece stocks. With some exceptions, the older-type lever actions are not strong enough to handle the high pressures of some modern cartridges, and they do not have the camming power to chamber and extract dirty or oversize cartridges.

The breech bolts in most lever guns don't lock at the head of the cartridge and the brass cases invariably stretch on firing. This makes lever actions a poor choice for handloaders. While these faults are of little concern to the occasional hunter, they are important factors to the more avid rifle shooter.

Now that the advantages and disadvantages of lever-action rifles have been discussed, let's talk about some of these typical guns presently on the market and how they may vary slightly in design.

The Winchester Model 94 is the most familiar lever action to hunters. It features a slide loading gate, tubular magazine, and exposed hammer with a half-cock safety. In the carbine version, it measures 38 inches long and weighs about 6¾ pounds. It is chambered for the .30-30 Winchester, a medium-class deer cartridge that can generally be expected to group at about 3½ inches at 100 yards. The model 94 is also available in .38-55 and .450 Marlin.

The Winchester 94 makes a fine saddle gun where long ranges aren't encountered, and it is a handy, light-weight deer gun in the wooded areas of the East and Northeast, where most shots are within 100 yards. The .30-30 is adequate for game the size of whitetails.

The handy little Model 94 that everyone loves to handle and shoot does have some drawbacks, though. It is not a long-range weapon and is not chambered for most modern high-velocity, flat-shooting cartridges. Since cases tend to stretch in the action, it is not a good choice for a hunter who plans to handload his own ammunition. All these factors should be taken into consideration when making a selection.

In lever actions, Winchester also makes Models 1892, 1886, and the much-loved historical Model 71, chambered for the .348 Winchester cartridge.

Another popular lever action is the Marlin Model 336C. It is chambered for the .30-30 Winchester and .35 Remington, both good brush cartridges that do their work well at medium ranges. In weight, length, and features, the Marlin 336C is similar to the Winchester Model 94. There is, however, one difference. The Marlin has a solid top receiver and ejects its empty cases from the side. This feature permits low scope mounting over the receiver.

The Marlin 336C has roughly the same drawbacks as the Winchester 94. While it is an ideal saddle rifle

and deer gun for brush hunters who get most shots at medium-size big game at short ranges, it is not a good choice for the hunter who may want to use his rifle for long shots in prairie and mountain country. Also, the Marlin 336C is not chambered for cartridges recommended for big North American game, such as grizzlies, brown bears, moose, and elk.

The Marlin Model 444 should be mentioned here, since it is the world's most powerful lever-action rifle. Using the basic Marlin 336 action design, the rifle is chambered for the .444 Marlin, a shoulderless cartridge that uses a 240-grain bullet and develops a muzzle energy of 2,942 foot-pounds and a muzzle velocity of 2,350 feet per second.

Up to 100–150 yards, the Marlin 444 is deadly on the biggest North American game. At longer ranges, however, both velocity and energy drop rapidly. This addition to the Marlin line of lever actions falls into a peculiar position. While it is certainly capable of flattening any vitally hit deer that crosses its path, the awesome cartridge is needlessly powerful for most deer hunters. Because the velocity and energy drop off at longer ranges, it does not meet the requirements of a mountain rifle. Perhaps the Marlin 444 is most suitable in such places as Alaska and Canada, where big brown bears, grizzlies, and moose are frequently taken at medium ranges.

Also worth discussion here is the Savage Model 99, a lever-action rifle that, unfortunately, is no longer made and is quite different from the Marlin and Winchester lever guns. The Savage 99 used a rotary magazine and cartridges loaded from the top, much like a bolt action. In the late 1960s, however, Savage introduced one of its Model 99s with a clip magazine that could be removed from the rifle by pushing a release button on the side of the receiver. The Model 99 ejected spent cartridges to the side, which made the rifle suitable for scope use. While it was a hammerless lever action, the Model 99 had a cocking indicator forward of the tang safety.

The Model 99 had a very strong action and it was perhaps the first lever action to be offered in a range of calibers that would push bullets faster and flatter than the typical, round-nose deer cartridges. As early as 1914, the Model 99 offered hunters the .250 Savage, which drove an 87-grain bullet at 3,000 feet per second, a sensational speed at that time. The Savage Model 99 was also chambered for the .243 and the .308 cartridges. The .243 Winchester cartridge, for example, made it suitable for medium game in plains or mountain country where flat trajectory and high velocity are assets.

In the 1970s, Browning introduced its BLR, a lever action with a detachable box magazine. Like the Savage, it could be chambered for a wider variety of cartridges than the more traditional lever actions that employ tubular magazines. A centerfire tubular-magazine lever action is not intended to handle cartridges with pointed bullets because of the possibility, however slim, that such a bullet could strike the cartridge ahead of it in the magazine and cause an accidental discharge if the rifle were dropped or severely jolted.

Moreover, the BLR has a rotary bolt with a very strong locking system that makes possible the chambering of modern high-velocity cartridges. It is now available in more calibers than any other lever action, ranging from .223 Remington to .450 Marlin.

It is sufficient to say there are many good .22 lever-action rifles on the market. While they cannot be considered fine target rifles, the .22 lever guns are enjoyable to use for small-game hunting, plinking, and informal target shooting. The choice is largely a matter of personal preference and the price tag.

■ Slide (or Pump) Action

Stated simply, the slide (or pump) action is operated by a quick backward and forward movement of the forend. This action ejects the spent case, rechambers a fresh cartridge, and cocks the rifle for the next shot.

The pump's obvious advantages are that it can be reloaded manually from the shoulder and that it is faster than a lever action. It is also a handy brush and timber rifle. The hunter accustomed to pump shotguns will also find this type of rifle a natural to use.

The pump has drawbacks, however. It has a two-piece stock and is therefore not as accurate as a bolt action. In addition, the pump's mechanism is not strong enough to chamber and eject handloaded ammunition with cases that have not been resized to original tolerances.

The pump is not a good choice for a hunter looking for maximum accuracy and a rifle that will really take all handloads.

The pump is a good choice, though, for a deer hunter who puts a great deal of faith in getting off a fast second shot in heavy cover, does not use handloaded ammunition, and uses a pump shotgun on game birds and small game.

Remington produces the Model 7600 pump-action rifle in a variety of calibers: the .243, .270, .280 Remington, .30-06, and .308. With these calibers, the Model 7600 is suitable for game ranging from coyotes to moose. It has a detachable four-shot clip magazine and weighs about 7½ pounds. The 7600 also features a solid top and ejects cases from the side, two features that make it good for scope mounting.

In the .22 class, the pump action has definitely made a place for itself among small-game hunters and plinkers. While it is definitely outclassed on the target range by bolt actions, the little .22 pump and its firepower has taken more than its share of cottontails, squirrels, pests, and other small game.

Nearly all of the modern .22 pumps have tubular magazines and side ejection, and are grooved for tip-off scope mounting. These pumps are an excellent choice for hunters who want to add an all-purpose .22 to their gun racks.

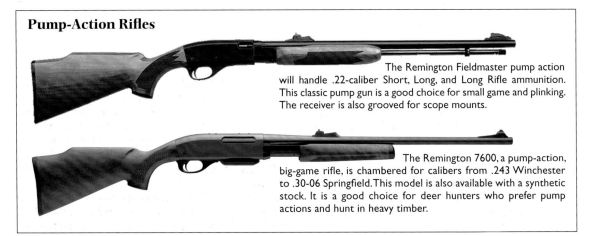

Pump-Action Rifles

The Remington Fieldmaster pump action will handle .22-caliber Short, Long, and Long Rifle ammunition. This classic pump gun is a good choice for small game and plinking. The receiver is also grooved for scope mounts.

The Remington 7600, a pump-action, big-game rifle, is chambered for calibers from .243 Winchester to .30-06 Springfield. This model is also available with a synthetic stock. It is a good choice for deer hunters who prefer pump actions and hunt in heavy timber.

How a Pump-Action Rifle Works

1 • Moving the forend rearward pushes back the action bar and the bolt assembly, which in turn moves the hammer downward and ejects the empty case. Ejection is accomplished by a circular spring in the end of the bolt (see detail, showing top view) with a claw that hooks under the rim of the cartridge and pulls it out of the chamber. When the case clears the chamber, the ejector spring in the bolt flips the case out. Then, the magazine spring moves a new cartridge upward.

2 • Moving the forend forward locks the cartridge in the barrel chamber. The notch in the sear holds the hammer so that the rifle is cocked. As the bolt carrier is moved forward, the threads on the bolt contact the locking lugs (see detail). Continued movement of the bolt carrier causes the cam pin on the carrier to engage a curved slot in the bolt, turning the bolt and threading it into locking lugs.

3 • Pulling the trigger disengages the sear from the notch on the hammer. The main spring forces the hammer against the firing pin, detonating the cartridge. The safety lock and a disconnecting device, which prevents the rifle from going off until the action is closed, is not shown.

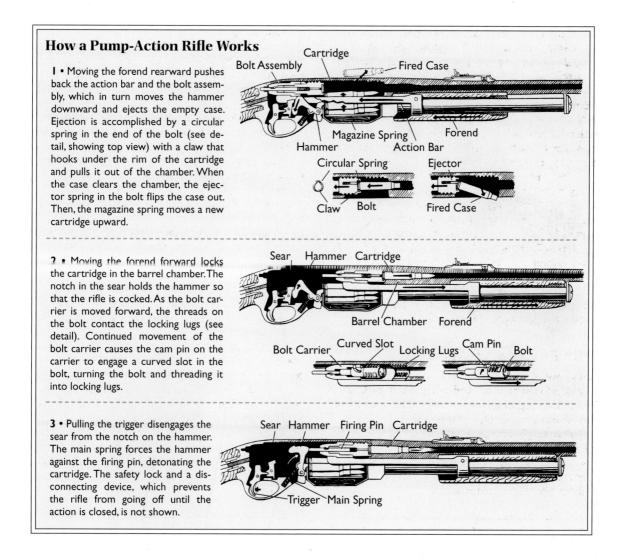

▣ Semi-Automatic or Autoloading Rifle

In discussing semi-automatics and autoloaders, let's simply refer to them as automatics, since this is what they are most often called by shooters. It should be made clear, however, that semi-automatics and autoloaders are not fully automatic, which means that they do not continue to fire as long as the trigger is held back. Such a rifle would, in effect, be a machine gun. Fully automatic rifles are not on the sporting market today and their possession by unauthorized personnel is prohibited by federal law.

Since no manual operation of any lever, bolt, or slide is required with an automatic after the first shot, the biggest advantage of such a rifle has to be firepower. Those quick second or third shots can sometimes mean meat in the pot for hunters in heavy timber or brushy areas.

The advantage of firepower can also be a double-edged sword. A big-game hunter, knowing he has only to squeeze the trigger again to send another bullet on its way, may well present a dangerous situation in the woods. For reasons not to be analyzed here, there is a tendency for some users of automatics to empty their

Autoloading Rifles

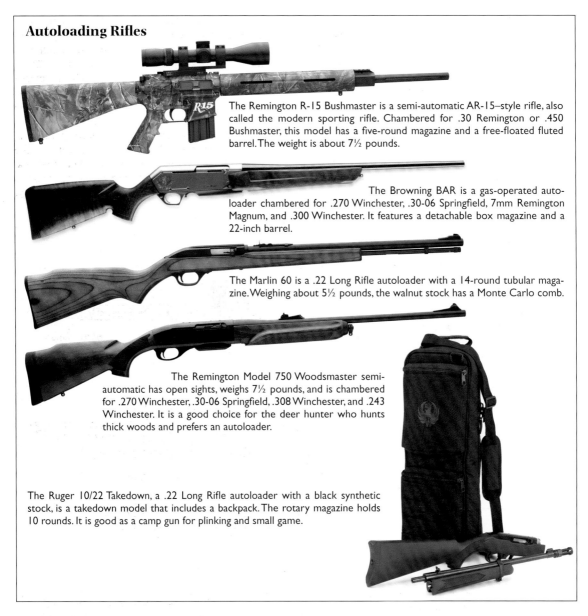

The Remington R-15 Bushmaster is a semi-automatic AR-15–style rifle, also called the modern sporting rifle. Chambered for .30 Remington or .450 Bushmaster, this model has a five-round magazine and a free-floated fluted barrel. The weight is about 7½ pounds.

The Browning BAR is a gas-operated autoloader chambered for .270 Winchester, .30-06 Springfield, 7mm Remington Magnum, and .300 Winchester. It features a detachable box magazine and a 22-inch barrel.

The Marlin 60 is a .22 Long Rifle autoloader with a 14-round tubular magazine. Weighing about 5½ pounds, the walnut stock has a Monte Carlo comb.

The Remington Model 750 Woodsmaster semi-automatic has open sights, weighs 7½ pounds, and is chambered for .270 Winchester, .30-06 Springfield, .308 Winchester, and .243 Winchester. It is a good choice for the deer hunter who hunts thick woods and prefers an autoloader.

The Ruger 10/22 Takedown, a .22 Long Rifle autoloader with a black synthetic stock, is a takedown model that includes a backpack. The rotary magazine holds 10 rounds. It is good as a camp gun for plinking and small game.

clips at fleeing big game after missing that first important shot. This, obviously, is dangerous in thickly wooded areas where other hunters are around.

The automatic design is tough on cases and tosses them far from the shooter, so it is also a poor choice for the handloader. The gas-operated automatic is not a simple mechanism and is more likely to have malfunctions than other type of rifle action. A hunter heading into a remote area for an extended hunt would be better off with a bolt action.

While there are some variations on the design of the automatic, these rifles still rely on one of two sources of power for their operation: recoil or gas. Both systems will be explained here very briefly, but readers interested in a detailed treatment of automatic-rifle design can find this information in any specialized gun book.

The recoil system, or blowback, uses a breechblock that is held against the head of the case by a spring. When a cartridge is fired, the breechblock moves to the rear, against the spring tension, and ejects the fired case. As the spring moves the breechblock forward, it cocks the rifle and picks up and chambers a fresh round.

One example of a modern rifle that uses the recoil, or blowback, mechanism is the Ruger 10/22, a small-game and plinking rifle that features a 10-shot detachable rotary magazine that fits flush into the stock. The rifle is an effective field gun in the hands of those familiar with firearms. An automatic is not recommended as a young shooter's first gun; it is not for beginners.

Since the blowback system used in these and nearly all other .22 automatics does not have a locking breechblock, the design is somewhat limited to rimfire and centerfire cartridges that develop low pressures. There are some modified blowback designs, such as retarded blowback, short-recoil, and long-recoil systems. It is sufficient to say here, however, that they all rely on the same basic principle for their operation.

Gas-operated centerfire automatics are quite different in design. In these rifles, a hole is drilled through the barrel to channel off gas from the first shot to provide power to work the action. After that first bullet passes over the hole in the barrel, gasses enter the hole and go

How an Autoloading Rifle Works

1 • Beginning with the rifle loaded and cocked, pulling the trigger disengages the sear from the notch on the hammer. The hammer spring forces the hammer against the firing pin, exploding the cartridge. After the bullet passes the port, residual gasses are metered downward through the barrel opening into the impulse chamber located in the forend.

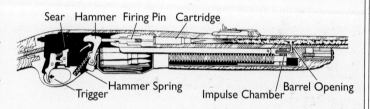

2 • Gases force the action bar and bolt assembly rearward, compressing the action spring, pushing down the hammer and ejecting the empty case. Further rearward travel of the bolt permits the next cartridge to raise into the path of the returning bolt. The ejection mechanism (see detail, showing top view) is the same as in the pump action.

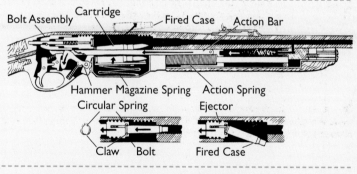

3 • The compressed action spring moves the action bar and bolt assembly forward, causing multiple lugs to lock the bolt into place (see detail), sealing the cartridge tightly in the barrel chamber. The notch in the sear holds the hammer in the cocked position. Pulling the trigger sets the weapon in motion as in the first illustration. The safety lock and a disconnecting device, which prevents the rifle from going off until the action is closed, is not shown.

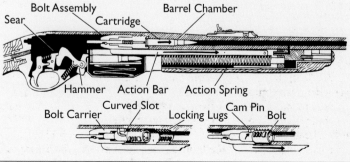

into a piston chamber in the forend. The piston forces a rod that unlocks the breech bolt and pushes it to the rear to eject the spent case and recock the rifle. At this point, a recoil spring takes over. The spring drives the breech bolt, rod, and piston forward. On this forward movement, a new cartridge is picked up and chambered for the next shot.

Because these gas-operated automatics have a breech bolt with lugs that lock at the head of the case, they can handle cartridges that develop very high pressures. One example is the Browning BAR Models, which are chambered for a range of calibers from .243 to .338 Winchester Magnum. Remington's Model 750 Woodsmaster is another example of an autoloader designed for high-pressure, big-game cartridges. It is chambered for the .270, .243, and .308 Winchester, and the old standard .30-06. Like the Browning, it features a detachable box magazine.

Relatively new gas-operated automatics are the AR-type rifles, which cosmetically look like military rifles. The National Shooting Sports Foundation uses the label "modern sporting rifle" to identify these automatics, which are based on the AR-15 platform. "AR" stands for Armalite Rifle, named after the company that developed it in the 1950s. "AR" does not stand for assault rifle or automatic rifle. These AR-15–style rifles may look like military rifles, but they function like any other semi-automatic sporting firearm, firing only one round with each pull of the trigger. Modern sporting rifles have proven accuracy and ruggedness in the field.

A good example of a modern sporting rifle is the Remington R-25, a gas-operated rifle chambered for the .308 Winchester, .243 Winchester, and 7mm-08

Remington. With a camouflaged synthetic stock, it weighs 7½ pounds and has a four-round detachable magazine. The Smith & Wesson entry into these modern sporting rifles is its M&P15 Sporter. With a synthetic stock and a 16-inch barrel, it weighs just 6½ pounds and is chambered for the 5.56mm NATO. If you're looking for a plinker in this type of rifle, Mossberg has the Tactical .22 Autoloader, which will give you firepower with low-cost ammunition. Other gun companies building AR-type rifles include Barrett, Bushmaster, Colt, and Heckler & Koch.

If you are choosing an automatic rifle for big game, after weighing all the advantages and disadvantages, you can't go wrong by selecting one of the rifles covered in this section. All are as reliable and accurate as an automatic can be. Among the various models, you'll also find a range of calibers from flat-shooting, high-velocity loads to the big magnums.

▪ Single-Shot Rifle

The single shot fills many outdoor needs and it is disappointing to see that so little attention is given to these firearms in the typical gun book. True, the single shot may never find a place among most hunters of deer and bigger game, but this type of rifle has many uses—and it should be remembered that such activities as one-shot antelope hunts have gained well-deserved prestige and popularity.

Most, but not all, single-shot rifles are either .22 Rimfire bolt actions or break actions. These .22s come into their own as a beginner's gun, a utility gun, a plinking gun, a trapper's and farmer's gun, or, where the laws allow, as part of a camper's gear. Because they are not

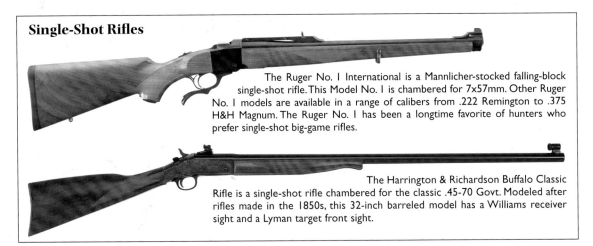

Single-Shot Rifles

The Ruger No. 1 International is a Mannlicher-stocked falling-block single-shot rifle. This Model No. 1 is chambered for 7x57mm. Other Ruger No. 1 models are available in a range of calibers from .222 Remington to .375 H&H Magnum. The Ruger No. 1 has been a longtime favorite of hunters who prefer single-shot big-game rifles.

The Harrington & Richardson Buffalo Classic Rifle is a single-shot rifle chambered for the classic .45-70 Govt. Modeled after rifles made in the 1850s, this 32-inch barreled model has a Williams receiver sight and a Lyman target front sight.

specialized guns, they fill a variety of needs. Moreover, they are inexpensive. The exceptions to the last two statements are the very specialized and usually expensive .22 single-shot bolt actions used for international target competitions—chiefly, free-rifle matches. (The word "free" here refers to a lack of restrictions on sophisticated features, such as an adjustable buttstock, palm rest, barrel weights, light trigger pull, and so on.)

Of more interest to average American shooters are the ordinary, inexpensive single shots, some with full-size stocks for adults and others in scaled-down versions for youngsters. Some of these rifles cock when a round is chambered; others must be cocked manually after the action is closed; and some have automatic safeties. Chipmunk Rifles makes a single-shot bolt-action rifle chambered for the .22 Rimfire. Some good choices are available for young shooters and plinkers.

Another type of single shot manufactured in the United States is the break action, or top-breaking action. Few single shots of this sort are available today. One is the Thompson/Center Encore Centerfire, a single-shot, break-open rifle available in calibers ranging from .22 Long Rifle to .45-70 Govt. These rifle calibers provide more power and a longer range than rimfires, of course, so this model fares well as a versatile gun for a variety of game animals.

Depending on the caliber, a single shot can take small game, pronghorns, deer, sheep, and bears—in fact, quite a few species of game, big and small. The demand for good single shots in a wide range of calibers was recognized by Sturm, Ruger and Company back in 1966, when Bill Ruger introduced the No. 1 Single-Shot Rifle. Inspired by the fine old Farquharson action, the Ruger No. 1 has an underlever that operates a falling-block action. It is chambered for calibers ranging from .223 Remington to .30-06 Springfield.

Models like the Ruger are rugged, accurate rifles. Mounted with carefully selected scope sights, such arms are more than adequate for big game, as well as varmint species. Traditionally, sheep hunters favor bolt-action repeaters, but some hunters have found these single shots to be very handy for mountain hunting because, with game such as sheep, the first shot should count.

▪ Air Guns

The growth of air guns had its start in the late 1800s when Clarence Hamilton in Plymouth, Michigan, built the first all-metal air gun. Hamilton's general manager L. C. Hough test fired the gun and exclaimed, "Boy, that's a daisy." The name has now become a trademark. Probably millions of shooters grew up with a Daisy Red Ryder BB gun.

Over the years, air rifles and pistols have grown from BB guns to serious sporting arms for hunters and competition shooters. Several air-gun companies, particularly the Crosman Corporation, have taken the lead in this industry. Crosman introduced the first pneumatic pump air gun in 1924, followed by the Benjamin pre-charged air rifle in 2008. In 2011, Crosman unveiled the Benjamin Rogue, a .357-caliber hunting rifle, the first air gun of its kind for bigger game.

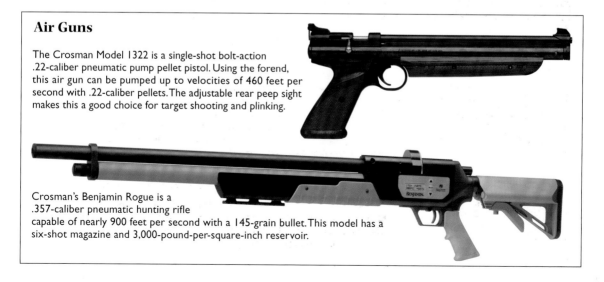

Air Guns

The Crosman Model 1322 is a single-shot bolt-action .22-caliber pneumatic pump pellet pistol. Using the forend, this air gun can be pumped up to velocities of 460 feet per second with .22-caliber pellets. The adjustable rear peep sight makes this a good choice for target shooting and plinking.

Crosman's Benjamin Rogue is a .357-caliber pneumatic hunting rifle capable of nearly 900 feet per second with a 145-grain bullet. This model has a six-shot magazine and 3,000-pound-per-square-inch reservoir.

Today, a variety of game can be hunted with these newer air guns, ranging from wild boar to small game. Air guns are available in .177, .22, and .25 calibers, as well as the new .357. The .22 and .25 are the choice calibers for small game. For bigger game, hunters should choose the .357. Large calibers carry more mass and, if traveling at the same velocity, will deliver more energy. The .177 can travel at tremendous speeds and achieves greater accuracy at long distances. The .177 is a favorite for target and competition shooters. Air guns today are also produced by Browning, Ruger, Beeman, Winchester, and Gamo.

■ Doubles and Combination Guns

The double rifle, in the simplest terms, is a double-barreled shotgun action with a strengthened frame, two rifle barrels, and iron sights. It can and has been chambered for a wide range of calibers, from .22 to .600. Because it has no long receiver, the double is short, handy, and fast. In fact, it is the fastest two-shot high-power rifle made.

These features would appear to make the double a dream gun for North American big game taken at medium ranges, but such is not the case. It is extremely

unlikely that a double-barreled rifle will ever be manufactured in the United States. Even in England, where most double-barreled rifles are made, they are generally available only on special order. And in Africa and India, where the double rifle earned its reputation for stopping dangerous game, it has been on the wane for some time. It is being replaced by strong bolt actions, such as the Winchester Model 70 and Remington Model 700, chambered for the .458 Winchester Magnum and the .416 Remington Magnum.

The biggest reason for the decrease in popularity of the double rifle is its high cost of manufacture. Getting both barrels aligned so that they place their bullets at the same point of aim, usually 80 or 100 yards, is a tedious and expensive task. It is done by repeated shooting and regulating of a wedge between the barrels until the bullets from both barrels have the same point of impact. The double is also two rifles with two sets of locks and two triggers. What all this means to the hunter is that a good double-barreled rifle may have a price tag ranging anywhere from $5,000 to $35,000.

In addition to the high cost, the double has other drawbacks. The ejectors frequently lack the power to pull or toss out stretched or dirty cases. And once a double is sighted for one particular load, other loads cannot

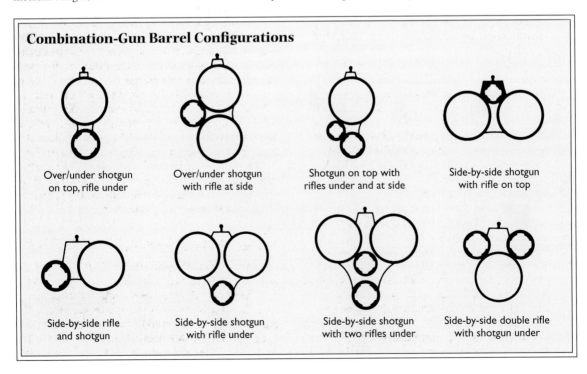

Combination-Gun Barrel Configurations

Over/under shotgun on top, rifle under

Over/under shotgun with rifle at side

Shotgun on top with rifles under and at side

Side-by-side shotgun with rifle on top

Side-by-side rifle and shotgun

Side-by-side shotgun with rifle under

Side-by-side shotgun with two rifles under

Side-by-side double rifle with shotgun under

Doubles and Combination Guns

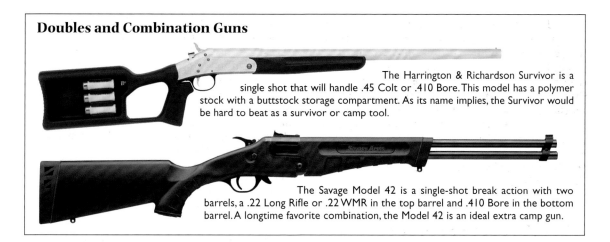

The Harrington & Richardson Survivor is a single shot that will handle .45 Colt or .410 Bore. This model has a polymer stock with a buttstock storage compartment. As its name implies, the Survivor would be hard to beat as a survivor or camp tool.

The Savage Model 42 is a single-shot break action with two barrels, a .22 Long Rifle or .22 WMR in the top barrel and .410 Bore in the bottom barrel. A longtime favorite combination, the Model 42 is an ideal extra camp gun.

be effectively used. As for accuracy, the doubles cannot compete with the comparatively new strong bolt-action repeaters built today. The double rifle has a romantic background, but it cannot be considered a practical fire-arm for the American hunter.

Combination guns are an interesting breed of rifle and shotgun. Longtime favorites in Europe, they are slowly becoming more popular in the United States. In areas where hunting seasons overlap and laws permit, the combination gun can be a good choice. It can also fill in as an off-season gun for plinking, woodchuck hunting, and so on.

Basically, there are eight types of combination guns: a rifle barrel under two shotgun barrels; an over/under shotgun and rifle combination; a shotgun barrel and two rifle barrels below and to the side; a four-barreled model with two shotgun barrels side by side and two rifle barrels underneath; a double-barreled rifle with a shotgun barrel underneath; an over/under shotgun with a rifle barrel to the side; a side-by-side double-barreled shotgun with a rifle barrel on top; and a side-by-side shotgun and rifle combination.

Several of these combination guns are of uncommon design and rarely seen today. They are generally of European origin, most being built in Germany. Unfortunately, nearly all European combination guns are quite expensive. Ferlach, for example, manufactures an over/under offering a choice of three shotgun gauges in the top barrel and more than seven rifle calibers in the bottom barrel. This particular Ferlach can be ordered with 12-gauge barrels on top and a .30-06 barrel underneath. Such a rifle could be quite useful to a deer hunter who may also want to take a grouse or two on the same

hunt. Or the shotgun barrel could be loaded with buckshot for the big buck that often bursts out of the brush and offers only a fast snap shot. The chief drawback is that imported combination guns like the Ferlach cost about four times as much as an average American rifle or shotgun. Ferlach and a few other European firms also build typical drillings—three-barreled combinations, usually with two smoothbores side by side and a rifle barrel underneath.

At one time, drillings were made in the United States, but the manufacture of combination guns in this country has always been limited to very few companies. Savage Arms was the only major American firm that built an over/under rifle-shotgun combination. Savage produced a series of these guns, the Model 24s, with the rifle barrel chambered for .22 Rimfire, .22 Hornet, .223 Remington, and .30-30 Winchester. The lower, smoothbore barrel was made in 12 and 20 gauge. These models made good camp guns, providing small game and birds for the pot. For the farmer, it kept pests under control. And, if the occasion arose, it could fill in as an ideal survival weapon. Savage now makes the Model 42, a rifle-shotgun combination much like the Model 24.

■ Muzzleloading Rifle

Muzzleloaders were pushed into obsolescence by breech-loaders long before the end of the 19th century, yet the old "frontloaders" were never quite buried by progress. Their revival began in the 1930s, gained staggering momentum in the 1960s, and is still growing at a phenomenal rate. One reason is the interest of many Americans in the ways of our forefathers. Another is

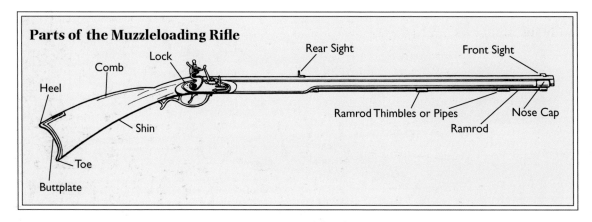

Parts of the Muzzleloading Rifle

the challenge of using primitive firearms. Probably most important of all is a kind of sporting contagion—word-of-mouth promotion by people who have discovered the fun of shooting muzzleloaders.

These shooters have their own organization, the National Muzzle Loading Rifle Association, with several hundred affiliated clubs. National and international club competitions include offhand shooting, shooting from a rest, flintlock matches, and even precision shooting with the big benchrest muzzleloading rifles like those of the late 1800s. In addition to rifle matches, there are events for muskets, shotguns, and handguns. Most colorful of all are the primitive matches, in which competitors dress in frontier clothing and test not

only their shooting ability but also other skills, such as tomahawk throwing and fire building with flint and steel.

Another form of competition is promoted by the North-South Skirmish Association, which holds regional and national matches. Teams from both sides of the Mason-Dixon Line name themselves after military units that fought during the Civil War. There are individual matches, but the most colorful and interesting are the team events. At the bigger shoots, hundreds of participants all fire at the same time, working against the clock to hit a specified number of breakable targets. Cannon competition is a bonus that leaves spectators gaping. The din and smoke are unforgettable.

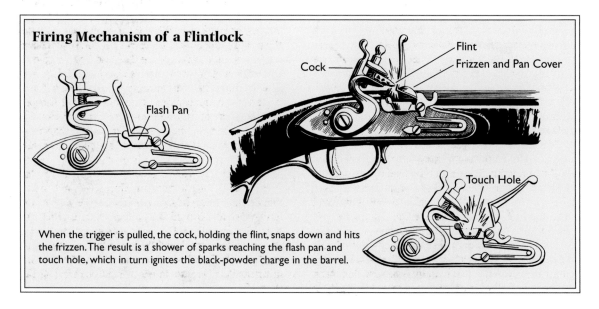

Firing Mechanism of a Flintlock

When the trigger is pulled, the cock, holding the flint, snaps down and hits the frizzen. The result is a shower of sparks reaching the flash pan and touch hole, which in turn ignites the black-powder charge in the barrel.

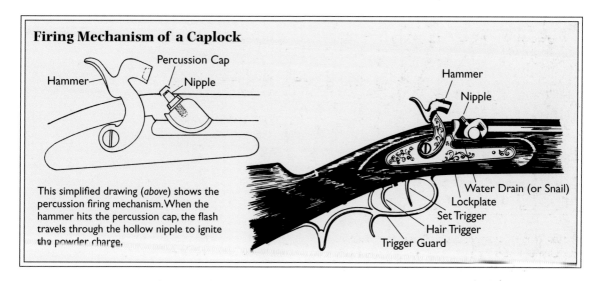

Firing Mechanism of a Caplock

Percussion Cap

Hammer

Nipple

Hammer

Nipple

Water Drain (or Snail)

Lockplate

Set Trigger

Hair Trigger

Trigger Guard

This simplified drawing (*above*) shows the percussion firing mechanism. When the hammer hits the percussion cap, the flash travels through the hollow nipple to ignite the powder charge.

Hunting with muzzleloaders has also gained immense popularity. Nearly all the states have special deer seasons for muzzleloaders, and other states permit their use during the regular deer season. Many other kinds of game are also hunted with these old-fashioned guns. The muzzleloaders now available are capable of taking all North American game. However, the smaller calibers (.30 to .45) should be limited to small game. Bores from .50 up are best for deer and heavier game, such as bears, elk, and moose. Many states stipulate a minimum bore size for deer or big game.

In accuracy, a good muzzleloading rifle is the equal of a cartridge rifle at moderate range, but trajectory is a problem. A typical muzzleloader for deer hunting has a muzzle velocity of about 2,000 feet per second when a .50-caliber ball is seated over 110 grains of black powder. With the rifle sighted-in to zero at 50 yards, this ball will be about 4 inches low at 100 yards. Sighted to hit 2 inches high at 50 yards, it will be a close 2 inches low at 100 yards.

Three basic types of muzzleloaders are in general use today: the flintlock, the caplock or percussion cap, and the in-line ignition system. To load a flintlock, the proper charge of black powder is first poured down the bore. The shooter then seats a precut, lubricated patch and ball over the muzzle. Using a starter—typically a short dowel with a round handle—the patched ball is moved down into the barrel. With a ramrod, it is pushed the rest of the way down until it is seated firmly against the powder. A small amount of very fine black powder (usually the granulation designated as FFFFg) is

dropped into the pan; this is the primer. The pan cover, or frizzen, is closed. Instead of the more modern hammer, this action employs a flint held in a cock. When the cock is pulled all the way back, it is ready to fire. At the pull of the trigger, the cock is released and the flint strikes the frizzen a glancing blow, producing a shower of sparks to ignite the fine powder in the flash pan. The flash goes through a small touch hole to ignite the main charge and fire the piece.

With a caplock gun, the percussion cap performs the same function as a modern primer in a cartridge. The cap is seated on a nipple at the end of a little tube leading into the barrel. When the hammer falls, it ignites the priming compound in the cap, driving sparks down the tube to the powder charge. The loading process with a percussion gun is the same as with a flintlock, except that the cap replaces the loose priming charge and flash-pan and the hammer replaces the cock and flint. Caplock rifles are more popular for hunting than flintlocks. The caps are faster and more convenient to use than loose priming powder, there is no need to replace flints, and ignition is faster and surer with a caplock.

The big change in muzzleloaders came in the 1980s when Tony Knight introduced the first in-line muzzleloader. Knight's design moved the nipple and ignition system behind the powder charge. When the muzzleloader is fired, the spark goes in a direct line to the powder charge. Knight's design pretty much took the "primitive" label out of muzzleloading. These in-line muzzleloaders became, in effect, high-powered, single-shot rifles.

Muzzleloading Rifles

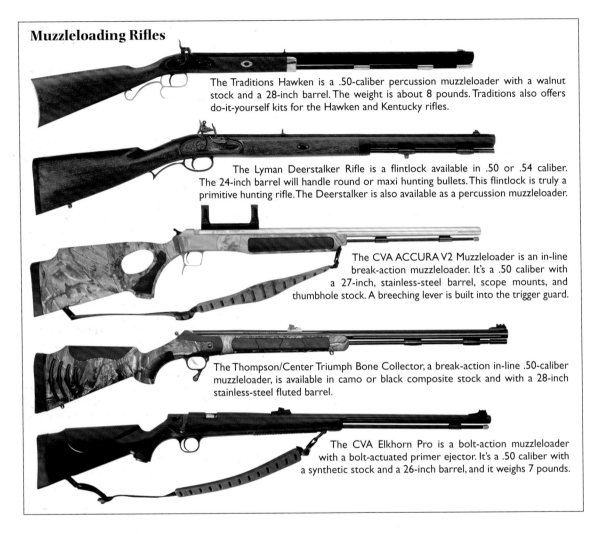

The Traditions Hawken is a .50-caliber percussion muzzleloader with a walnut stock and a 28-inch barrel. The weight is about 8 pounds. Traditions also offers do-it-yourself kits for the Hawken and Kentucky rifles.

The Lyman Deerstalker Rifle is a flintlock available in .50 or .54 caliber. The 24-inch barrel will handle round or maxi hunting bullets. This flintlock is truly a primitive hunting rifle. The Deerstalker is also available as a percussion muzzleloader.

The CVA ACCURA V2 Muzzleloader is an in-line break-action muzzleloader. It's a .50 caliber with a 27-inch, stainless-steel barrel, scope mounts, and thumbhole stock. A breeching lever is built into the trigger guard.

The Thompson/Center Triumph Bone Collector, a break-action in-line .50-caliber muzzleloader, is available in camo or black composite stock and with a 28-inch stainless-steel fluted barrel.

The CVA Elkhorn Pro is a bolt-action muzzleloader with a bolt-actuated primer ejector. It's a .50 caliber with a synthetic stock and a 26-inch barrel, and it weighs 7 pounds.

Several decades ago, most of the muzzleloaders in use were originals, reconditioned and tested for safety and functional reliability. But antique arms are often too valuable to be taken into the field, and the supply of shootable originals dwindled as muzzleloading gained unprecedented popularity. During the 1960s, a few imported replicas became available, and in the United States custom and semicustom makers were busy filling orders for new muzzleloaders.

Dixie Gun Works can be called a pioneer in this field. The company started importing muzzleloaders in the 1950s. Today, the Dixie catalog is crammed with everything a muzzleloading enthusiast would ever need, including accessories, parts, kits, and finished guns.

By the early 1970s, muzzleloaders were being mass-produced both here and abroad. Today, the array is staggering. Moreover, many of the guns are available either finished or in kit form for budget-minded do-it-yourselfers. And the custom makers are still producing finely crafted muzzleloaders—both replicas and new but authentically traditional designs. The in-line muzzleloader market, however, has pretty much taken over the field.

Among the mass-produced models, the Deerstalker, made by Lyman, is representative of black-powder guns made in traditional cap or flint versions. It's available in .50 or .54 caliber and features a 24-inch octagonal barrel. It weighs about 10 pounds. Cabela's builds the

Traditional Hawken Percussion Rifle in .40 and .54 calibers. This model, also available in cap or flint versions, has a walnut stock and weighs 9 pounds. It also has adjustable double-set triggers.

Lyman's Great Plains Rifle, though not billed as a Hawken replica, is a percussion half-stock that's quite representative of the guns once used by the men engaged in the western fur trade. It has browned-steel hardware and comes in .50 or .54 calibers.

A good example of the newer in-line ignition muzzleloaders is the Thompson/Center Triumph Bone Collector, a break-action rifle, which comes in .50 caliber. Most in-line muzzleloaders are available as break-action or bolt-action rifles. The break actions are more popular and easier to use.

The muzzleloading rifles described here are only a sampling of currently popular models available in traditional flint, percussion cap, and in-line versions. Companies that make or import muzzleloaders include Thompson/Center, Shiloh Sharps, Traditions, Cabela's, Savage, and CVA.

MUZZLELOADING PRECAUTIONS: Safety is a paramount concern when using any firearm, and extra precautions are mandatory with muzzleloaders. If the shooter wishes to use an old muzzleloader rather than a new one, it should not be fired until it has been inspected for safety—and serviced, if necessary—by a gunsmith who is familiar with black-powder guns. Otherwise, such a gun may be unsafe.

In addition to possibly dangerous defects, an old gun may be encountered with a load left in the barrel. This has even been known to happen with modern muzzleloaders. Because the load is unknown, it should **never** be fired. The bullet or ball should be pulled and the charge removed.

A common practice with percussion guns is to fire a cap, without any powder or ball, to clear the nipple of excess oil, but this should be done only after the barrel is cleared to the breech.

POWDER FOR MUZZLELOADERS: Another precaution concerns the proper powder. Nothing but black powder or Pyrodex should be used in a muzzleloader. The term "black powder" in this context does not refer to color in the usual sense, because most gunpowder is black or gray. The modern powders used in cartridges can be extremely dangerous in a muzzleloader. The kind to use is the powder that comes in cans labeled "black powder" by the manufacturer.

The one exception is Pyrodex, a propellant developed for use in black-powder guns. Its burning rate and pressure curve closely follow the characteristics of black powder, but Pyrodex is safer to ship and store, and it has become more readily available through retail outlets. Its only disadvantage is that it doesn't ignite well in flintlocks. Black powder comes in various granulations. The letters "Fg" identify the coarsest black powder available. The granulations most commonly used in muzzleloaders are "FFg" and "FFFg." The finest granulation, "FFFFg," ignites rapidly and is therefore used to prime the pan of a flintlock.

ACCESSORIES: Since a cartridge is literally assembled in a muzzleloader for each shot, a shooter must carry tools and equipment. A small toolbox or tackle box can

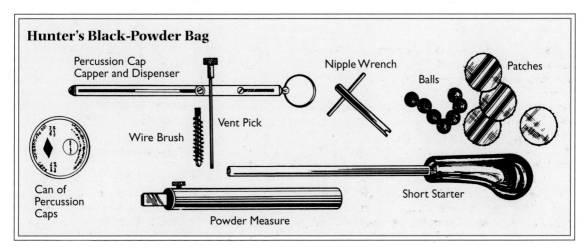

Hunter's Black-Powder Bag

Percussion Cap Capper and Dispenser

Nipple Wrench

Patches

Balls

Vent Pick

Wire Brush

Can of Percussion Caps

Short Starter

Powder Measure

hold what's needed on a rifle range. Its contents should include:

- Rifle balls or other suitable projectiles
- Percussion caps or flints
- Patches or patch material
- Patch lubricant
- Black powder of suitable granulation or Pyrodex
- Priming powder for a flintlock
- Extra nipples for a caplock
- Adjustable powder measure
- Knife for trimming patches
- Short starter
- Ramrod (extralong for range use)
- "Worm" for pulling lost patches from the bore
- Ball or bullet puller
- Cleaning patches
- Cleaning solvent
- Rust-preventative oil
- Pliers
- Screwdrivers
- Brass or copper drift for sight adjustments
- Light hammer
- Nipple wrench for a caplock

The muzzleloading hunter seldom carries all these items. He wants to travel light, and he's better off carrying

Muzzleloading Information

Any newcomer to the muzzleloading clan should seek reliable advice and read the loading data available from manufacturers and in black-powder handbooks. An excellent source of information about muzzleloading skills, products, competitions, hunting news, and so on is the National Muzzle Loading Rifle Association (www.nmlra.org).

his equipment in a shoulder pouch, called a "possibles bag." What it contains is up to the hunter, but only the real necessities should be carried. These include enough balls or other projectiles for the day's hunt, a few caps in a capper for a percussion gun, an extra flint or two for a flintlock, patching for both ball and cleaning, a patch knife, and a short starter. In addition, the hunter should have a powder measure and a small powder horn or flask.

With a caplock, a nipple wrench should be added to this list. It's possible (though hardly smart) to forget to put in the powder charge before loading a ball. If this happens, you can remove the nipple and sift in enough powder to blow the "dead ball" out of the barrel.

Gun Cleaning Made Easy

The length of time involved in cleaning your gun depends on the kind of day you've had. If it was dry with moderate temperatures, your rifle or shotgun may only need to be wiped down with a silicone gun cloth.

If you're a duck hunter, however, and your shotgun is subject to rain and salt spray, you will have to break the gun down and clean it thoroughly when you get home. In fact, I don't even wait until I get home. Before I put my shotgun back in the case, I spray the action and metal parts with WD-40 or a similar formula.

Never leave guns stored in a gun case unless the interior of the case has been treated. Most gun cases will hold moisture and produce rust, especially leather cases. If you don't have a gun cabinet or gun vault, leave the gun exposed in the back of a closet. It will gather dust, but it can be easily wiped off. If there are children in the house, make sure your rifle or shotgun is made inoperable until the next time you use it.

Cleaning a rifle or shotgun should not take more than 10 or 15 minutes. Break the gun down and clean all metal surfaces with a cloth dipped in gun solvent, especially the breech and face of the bolt. Using a cleaning rod, run a solvent-dipped wire brush, preferably bronze, through the bore. This will loosen dirt, carbon, and light rust. Next, run several dry patches through the bore until they come out clean. Then, run a patch soaked in gun oil through the bore until it is thoroughly coated. Finally, put a few drops of oil on your fingers and spread it evenly over all metal parts, especially moving mechanisms.

If your gun has a synthetic stock, you don't have to do anything. If you have a varnished stock, wipe it clean and coat it with car or furniture wax.

How to Load a Percussion Cap Muzzleloader

The procedure of loading a muzzleloader can be difficult and time consuming to hunters not familiar with their use. The margin of error is greater than with modern centerfire rifles—and it may cost you a trophy if you don't load your muzzleloader correctly. Follow each of the steps here in proper sequence. If your muzzleloader is new, read the manufacturer's specific directions for that gun. Demonstrating loading procedures is Nathan Figley, Hunter Safety Instructor and Senior Biologist for the New Jersey Division of Fish and Wildlife. Figley's muzzleloaders are a .50-caliber Thompson/Center Triumph and a New Englander.

Step 1 • Check to see if there is a charge in your muzzleloader by springing a rod. This can be done by dropping a range/ramrod down the barrel. The rod should bounce up and down and make a metal-on-metal pinging noise if unloaded. If there is a charge in the barrel, it will not bounce and there will be a dull thud when dropped. After firing a percussion cap or two to burn out any excess oil from your unloaded rifle, use a powder measure to determine the exact charge you want to use.

Step 2 • Next, pour the powder charge directly from the powder measure down the barrel of your muzzleloader. Keep your hands away from the open bore.

Step 3 • With the powder charge in place, now load the round ball (or a bullet) by placing it on a greased patch, centering it on the muzzle and pressing it into the bore. Some bullets, such as Maxi-Balls, do not need the greased patch. When they are molded, they have lubricating grooves in which a shooting paste is applied for the gas seal.

Step 4 • Use a ball short starter to start the projectile down the barrel. Always keep the muzzle away from your face.

Step 5 • Now, place the buttstock on the ground and, using your long ramrod, ram the ball firmly all the way down so that it is resting tightly against the powder charge. Do not leave any air space between it and the ball or you could bulge your barrel upon firing. Using your ramrod, continue to push the ball down the barrel, with short hand-over-hand strokes until the ball is firmly seated against the powder charge. Use short strokes and do not place your hand over the top of the ramrod for two reasons: a wood or fiber rod can bend and snap, and, with the downward force, the rod can go right through your hand (an aluminum rod will bend), and, if the gun fires while loading, the rod will slip out of your hands instead of blowing a hole through your palm.

Step 6 • The final step is to place a percussion cap firmly on the nipple. Use a No. 11 percussion or musket cap, depending on the nipple used. Wearing both eye and ear protection, you can now fire your muzzleloader.

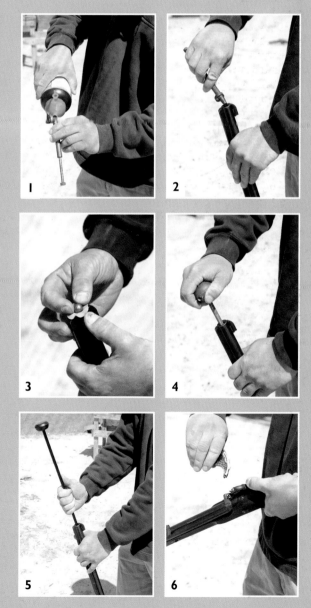

How to Load an In-Line Muzzleloader

1

2

3

4

5

6

Step 1 • Check to see if there is a charge in your muzzleloader by springing a rod. This is done by dropping a ramrod down the barrel. The rod should bounce up and down and make a metal-on-metal pinging noise if unloaded. If there is a charge in the barrel, the rod will not bounce and there will be a dull thud when dropped. Next, fire one or two caps to burn out any residual moisture or excess oil from your unloaded firearm. You can now proceed to load your in-line muzzleloader. In these photos, the shooter is using Pyrodex pellets, which generally come in 30- and 50-grain increments. This shooter uses a pipe cleaner to pick up the pellets from the box and place them in the muzzle.

Step 2 • Next, the shooter places a bullet into the muzzle. Modern technology has produced a number of excellent bullets for in-line muzzleloaders. Test several brands and designs until you find the one that gives you the best accuracy.

Step 3 • Use a ball short starter to start the bullet down and firmly into the barrel.

Step 4 • Next, using the long ramrod, seat the bullet against the pellet powder charge. Make sure the bullet is against the powder charge with no space between it and the powder charge. Once the bullet is seated, do not thump down hard on the bullet, as it may crush the pellet. The hole in the center of the pellet is designed to allow spark from the primer to travel up the entire length of the pellet, igniting it all at once.

Step 5 • Break open the muzzleloader and install a cap or a type 209 primer in the breech. Depending on when the in-line muzzleloader was produced, you may have other options. This shooter's gun can accept 209 primers, No. 11, and musket caps. The nipples must be changed in order to use each type.

Step 6 • Wearing both eye and ear protection, you can now fire your in-line muzzleloader.

RIFLE STOCKS

The purpose of a well-designed rifle stock is to put the shooter's eye quickly in line with the sights, enable him to hold the rifle as steady as possible in any position, and keep the effect of recoil to a minimum. The results are all achieved when the various parts of a rifle stock work in conjunction with one another, and when the shooter feels that the stock fits him comfortably.

How can a shooter select a stock that fits him? First, most factory stocks are well designed for shooters of average build, and tall and short shooters can easily compensate for a stock that does not feel exactly right. Most shooters, therefore, are satisfied with a mass-produced stock right from the factory.

Shooters who are more concerned about stock fit can make a selection by following the recommended stock measurements and tolerances that are discussed later in this section. There are also the problems of specialized stocks for target shooters and benchrest shooters. But first, let's look at the typical rifle stock and explain the function of each part.

Basically, four parts of the rifle stock determine the fit and feel to the shooter. These are the comb, cheekpiece, pistol grip, and forend. All four parts come in direct contact with the shooter's face and hands.

The comb should be of a height and thickness to ensure that the pressure of the cheek against it steadies the shooter's hold and quickly puts his eye in line with the sights. A comb that is too high and too thick will force a shooter to squeeze his cheek down on the comb to get his eye in line with the sights, and the result is an unnecessary whack on the cheek from the recoil.

The Monte Carlo comb is designed to raise and support the shooter's cheek and eye to bring the latter in line with the telescopic sights, which are a bit higher than open sights. A Monte Carlo comb may run level toward the butt, then drop rather sharply near the heel of the stock, or it may slope upward toward the butt. The Monte Carlo that slopes slightly upward from the front to rear is a good design, because the comb will recoil away from the face. A good Monte Carlo will help a shooter who uses telescopic sights. On rifles used exclusively with open sights, the Monte Carlo is of little value.

The slope of a comb also determines the drop at heel, which is the distance measured from an imaginary line from the line of sight down to the heel of the stock. In simple words, the greater the drop at heel, the more the recoil will be felt. Likewise, the less the drop at heel, the less the recoil will be felt. A straight stock, with little or no drop at heel, will bring the recoil straight back against the shoulder, minimizing the kick. Excessive drop at heel will cause the stock to thrust upward upon firing and bruise or hit the shooter's cheek.

In terms of actual measurements, the drop at heel for an average shooter using open sights should be 2½ to 2¾ inches. When the drop at heel is 3 inches or more on big-bore rifles, the recoil will be uncomfortable. A rifle used with scope sights should have a straighter stock and comb, with less "slope" and less drop at heel—about 2 to 2½ inches is good for the average shooter.

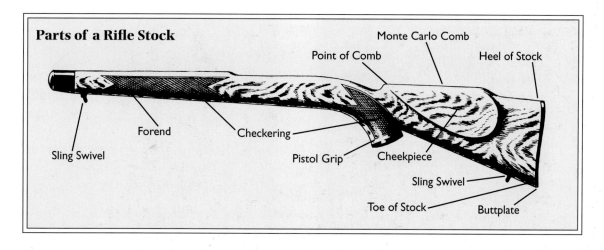

Parts of a Rifle Stock

Sling Swivel — Forend — Checkering — Pistol Grip — Point of Comb — Monte Carlo Comb — Cheekpiece — Heel of Stock — Sling Swivel — Toe of Stock — Buttplate

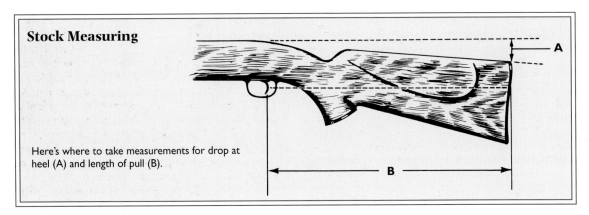

Stock Measuring

Here's where to take measurements for drop at heel (A) and length of pull (B).

The cheekpiece is an additional aid in supporting the face. Cheekpieces come in all sizes and shapes, but a well-designed and functional cheekpiece is simple and has clean lines. The bottom of the cheekpiece should not extend more than ½ to ⅝ inch from the stock. The forward portion should flow or merge smoothly into a well-rounded comb. It should be flat, giving support to a good portion of the face.

Another important part of a stock is the pistol grip, which should be shaped to enable the shooter to brace the butt against his shoulder while leaving the trigger finger free to squeeze off the shot. It should be curved so that the shooter has no stress or strain on the trigger. One rule of thumb in determining a properly curved grip is that the point of the comb should be directly and vertically over the center of the pistol-grip cap.

The circumference of the pistol grip should afford a firm and comfortable hold, without cramping the fingers. For the average shooter, a pistol grip should be round and about 4½ inches in circumference. Shooters with large hands may prefer a grip closer to 5 inches, but more than 5 inches is too much wood for comfortable and steady shooting.

The butt of the stock should be wide and flat to distribute recoil over a large area of the shoulder. The curved narrow butts, frequently seen on muzzleloaders and early breechloaders, can make the recoil of big-bore rifles quite painful.

The forend of a rifle stock has two purposes: to provide control over the rifle and to keep fingers away from a hot barrel. To accomplish these two objectives, the forend should be rounded to fit the contour of the

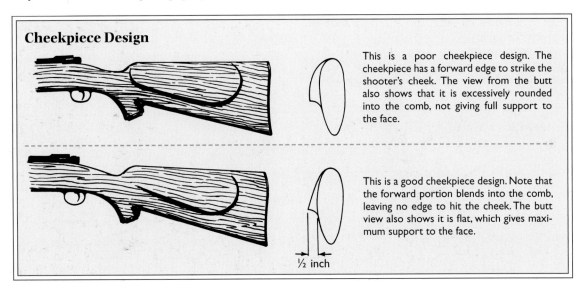

Cheekpiece Design

This is a poor cheekpiece design. The cheekpiece has a forward edge to strike the shooter's cheek. The view from the butt also shows that it is excessively rounded into the comb, not giving full support to the face.

This is a good cheekpiece design. Note that the forward portion blends into the comb, leaving no edge to hit the cheek. The butt view also shows it is flat, which gives maximum support to the face.

½ inch

Forend Design

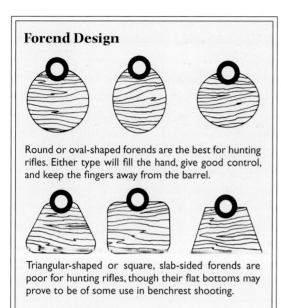

Round or oval-shaped forends are the best for hunting rifles. Either type will fill the hand, give good control, and keep the fingers away from the barrel.

Triangular-shaped or square, slab-sided forends are poor for hunting rifles, though their flat bottoms may prove to be of some use in benchrest shooting.

a shooter will be able to shoulder his rifle firmly and reach the trigger with his finger. Because all men and women are not the same size with arms the same length, the length of pull varies. It should be emphasized here, however, that factory stocks generally have a length of pull of 13½ inches, which is a good compromise for average shooters for all-around use. With the exception of very big shooters with long arms or very short shooters, a pull of 13½ inches should prove adequate. For the more serious shooter who may want to alter his factory rifle or is planning to invest in a custom-built rifle, the accompanying chart will be helpful.

Checkering on a rifle stock definitely has a function, in addition to making a stock attractive. For the hunter, checkering means a nonslip grip on his rifle in wet weather or while wearing gloves. It keeps both hands from sliding or moving on the pistol grip and forend, making for a more rigid hold.

Unfortunately, most modern factory stocks now come with checkering that is not really checkering

cupped hand and full to keep fingers from making contact with the barrel.

When the palm and fingers of the hand are turned inward, as if to grip a baseball bat or tennis racket, they naturally form a circle or oval—this shape, therefore, is undoubtedly the best for a forend. The forend can be held fully, the shooter has maximum control, and there are no gaps between the wood and hand. Forends that are triangular in cross section, or have squared jutting "jaws" or slab sides, are not only unappealing to the eye, but are awkward to hold.

Length of pull, the measurement between the trigger and butt, is another very important factor in stock design since it determines how quickly and comfortably

Recommended Length of Pull for Custom Rifles

Size	Recommended Length of Pull (inches)
Tall men (6'1" to 6'3")	13¾ to 14
Average men (5'8" to 6')	13¼ to 13½
Short men, average women	13 to 13¼
Short women, youngsters	12¾

Rifle Scopes

I put scopes on all rifles I use for big game, but it's important to pick the right scope model. If you hunt the Northeast woods, for example, stick with low power scopes and their generous field of view. The scope on my Ruger gives me a 45-foot field of view at 100 yards with the power set at 2x. Under most conditions, I leave the scope at 2x. Select a scope that will give you the biggest field of view at the lowest power setting. I also use only detachable sling swivels on my deer rifles and remove the sling when I start still-hunting. A sling can get in the way and snag brush when you are trying to be as quiet as possible.

Rifle-Stock Design

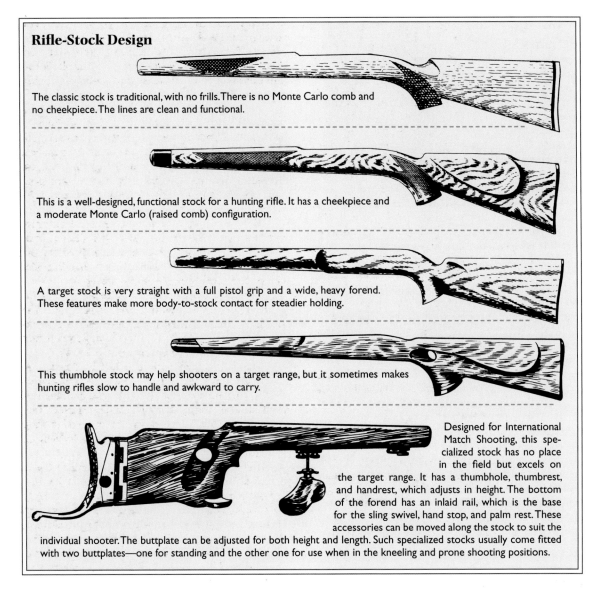

The classic stock is traditional, with no frills. There is no Monte Carlo comb and no cheekpiece. The lines are clean and functional.

This is a well-designed, functional stock for a hunting rifle. It has a cheekpiece and a moderate Monte Carlo (raised comb) configuration.

A target stock is very straight with a full pistol grip and a wide, heavy forend. These features make more body-to-stock contact for steadier holding.

This thumbhole stock may help shooters on a target range, but it sometimes makes hunting rifles slow to handle and awkward to carry.

Designed for International Match Shooting, this specialized stock has no place in the field but excels on the target range. It has a thumbhole, thumbrest, and handrest, which adjusts in height. The bottom of the forend has an inlaid rail, which is the base for the sling swivel, hand stop, and palm rest. These accessories can be moved along the stock to suit the individual shooter. The buttplate can be adjusted for both height and length. Such specialized stocks usually come fitted with two buttplates—one for standing and the other one for use when in the kneeling and prone shooting positions.

at all. It is merely a design impressed into the wood by a machine. This is a step down from the earlier factory stocks that had true checkering, even though most of the work was carelessly done. In those days, most factory stocks were checkered from 14 to 18 lines to the inch.

Custom rifle builders today still do all their checkering by hand. It is long, tedious work, which is one reason for the high cost of custom firearms. These men, who use good, hard wood, checker about 24 to 26 lines to the inch. Precision checkering with sharp diamonds is one

indication that the stockmaker is a master of his trade.

The features of a rifle stock mentioned thus far pertain to a sporter or hunting rifle. There are exceptions, such as target stocks, thumbhole stocks, stocks with rollover cheekpieces, and so on. Some of these exceptions are legitimate and aid the shooter, but most just make the rifle awkward to handle. Any hunter who sticks to the functional stock design described in this section is sure to find himself with a comfortable and good-handling field rifle.

Woods for Rifle Stocks

The strength and "eye appeal" of a finished stock depends on several factors. A stock that has considerable figure or "burl" generally comes from a piece of wood cut from where roots and limbs branch out from the trunk of a tree. While this wood may look attractive, it is not necessarily the best wood for a rifle stock, particularly a one-piece stock. Because there is considerable figure in the wood, it is prone to warping with climatic changes and such warping in the forend of a rifle can throw off accuracy under hunting conditions. Such wood is better for shotgun stocks.

The one-piece rifle stock should be straight grained, with the grain running parallel to the direction of the grip and the grain in the forend slightly diagonal to the barrel. This keeps warping in the forend to a minimum. The grip should never be cut cross grain, since this would dangerously weaken the stock at a critical point.

It is sufficient to say here that a good stock should have a drying-out period of about four or five years—that is, from the time it is cut from the tree until it is finally turned into a finished gunstock. The drying period, naturally, allows the wood to lose all its moisture, keeping warping to a minimum in the finished product.

The most common wood used for factory gunstocks is American walnut. Though it generally lacks the fancy figure of other woods, it is a good stock wood. It is most often straight grained, but occasionally a factory stock of American walnut will show up with attractive burl figure. The configuration depends upon from which part of the tree the stock blank is cut. If cut from the crotch of limbs or roots, the finished stock will nearly always have a fancy figure. American walnut, though not as hard a stock material as European walnut, holds checkering well.

There are many other woods used to make gunstocks. Some are soft; some are hard. Some have good figure; others are straight grained.

Finishing the Wood Gunstock

The best finish for a wood rifle stock is a straight oil finish, nearly always with boiled linseed oil. It is a durable finish and one that can be easily maintained by simply handrubbing on another coat of oil. And it does not crack or peel, which can and does happen with factory stocks finished with varnish or lacquer.

Sanding is the first step to putting a good oil finish on a bare stock. Before any oil is applied, the wood must be made as smooth as possible. After an initial sanding with 180-grit sandpaper, wet the wood with a cloth. The moisture will cause the grain to raise and become rough. After the wood has dried, use 180-grit sandpaper again and sand the stock as smooth as possible. Follow this same procedure, still using the 180-grit sandpaper, one more time.

The next step is to progress to a finer sandpaper, such as 240 grit. Once again, wet the stock, allow the grain to raise and the wood to dry, then sand as smooth as possible with the 240-grit paper. When this is done, follow the same procedure again, only this time use 320-grit sandpaper. Continue to wet and sand with the 320-grit paper until the grain will no longer raise when wet.

When sanding is complete, the actual oil finish can be applied. If the wood appears quite porous, however, a filler should be used before the oil is rubbed on. Commercial fillers are available, but an excellent filler can be concocted by mixing equal parts of white shellac and alcohol. This should be applied with a brush or cloth, allowed to dry, then sanded off. Depending on the wood, several coats of filler may be necessary. Remember to always allow the filler to dry thoroughly and sand between coats. The stock is now ready for the oil.

There are several commercial oil finishes on the market and any one of them will do a good job if directions are followed carefully. Some of the finishing kits available also provide shortcuts for the refinisher. One method is to add a bit of spar varnish to the oil to bring a fast sheen to the wood. Lacquer and plastic finishes are also available for a fast finishing job.

Let's assume here, however, that a straight boiled linseed-oil finish is desired. Properly done, a pure oil finish is extremely durable and, most important, easily maintained. The first step is to apply a fairly heavy coat of linseed oil to the wood and set the stock aside for a day or two, allowing the wood to absorb the oil and dry thoroughly. When this is done, rub the stock down with fine steel wool. You'll note that the wood is taking on a light satin sheen.

Now comes the hard part. Start to apply thin coats of the oil and rub them well into the wood. The harder the oil is rubbed into the stock, the better. After each thin coat of oil is rubbed into the wood, wipe off the excess oil and allow the remaining oil to dry thoroughly. If this is not done, the coats of oil that are not dry will begin to build up gummy deposits on the wood. If this happens, the only alternative is to sand the stock down to the bare wood and start the job all over again. It is, therefore, **very** important for a coat of oil to dry thoroughly before another is applied. There is no set number of coats of oil to be rubbed into a stock. The process is simply repeated until the desired finish is obtained. The idea is to build up many thin coats of oil on the wood until the stock takes on a rich satin finish that will resist rain, snow, heat, and so on.

One of the biggest advantages to a good oil finish is that if the stock is lightly scratched in the field or marred in any way, another coat of oil, applied as described here, will bring the finish back to its original condition.

Naturally, the above method is for a stock of bare wood with no finish at all. If it is a factory stock that is to be refinished, the old factory finish, usually varnish or lacquer, must first be removed and the bare wood made as smooth as possible. This is done simply by brushing the stock with commercial varnish remover and waiting for the stock to blister and peel. The old finish can then be scraped off with a knife or razor blade. This is a messy but necessary job and it is not uncommon to use more than one coat of varnish remover to get all of the old finish off the wood. Once this is done, start with the sanding process described above to get a new oil finish.

Getting a good oil finish on a gunstock is not a difficult job, but it is a long and tedious project. The results, however, make the effort worthwhile.

■ Synthetic Gunstocks

Although wood is the traditional material for making gunstocks, synthetic materials have come on strong. There are many advantages to these space-age materials. Fiberglass and Kevlar, for example, are tough and light. They resist weather and freezing temperatures without swelling or warping and pushing the barrel and action enough to shift a rifle's zero. These stocks are also strong enough to take the hard knocks and falls of mountain hunting.

The early synthetic stocks included Charter's AR-7 with a plastic called Cycolac. Back in 1959, Remington introduced its Model 66 rifle, which has a stock of structural nylon. These stocks can be made in any color and checkering is molded in.

In the mid-1980s, synthetic stocks began to show up on big-game rifles from other manufacturers, too. Currently, nearly all gunmakers offer models in a variety of synthetic stock styles and colors, including camouflage. These stocks are durable and unaffected by climate or weather conditions. Synthetic stocks combined with stainless-steel mechanisms and barrels are totally weatherproof and are a good choice for hunters who care more about ruggedness than aesthetics.

RIFLE BARRELS

The modern rifle barrel has come a long way since the time of the twist or Damascus barrels of the 19th century. During those early years, barrels were made by twisting and welding strips of iron around a mandrel to form a hollow tube. Such barrels were fine during the black-powder era when pressures were comparatively low and lead bullets were used. But then came smokeless powder and with it higher temperatures and higher pressures than the black-powder barrels could handle. The high-velocity, smokeless-powder cartridges also used metal-jacketed bullets, which caused too much abrasion in barrels made of iron or mild steel, a low-carbon alloy.

Progress by steelmakers and a great deal of experimenting by gun companies resulted in the steel rifle barrel of today. The modern rifle barrel is tough, but it can still be machined easily. It can resist erosion and withstand the stresses and strains created by high pressures.

The steel is tough enough that rifling holds up under the abrasion of metal-jacketed bullets.

The majority of barrels for high-power rifles are made of chrome molybdenum steel. Some barrels are made of stainless steel, which meets all the requirements of a good barrel material and has the additional virtue of being rustproof. One reason stainless steel is not used for all barrels is that it is difficult to machine.

Gun manufacturers get their barrels in the form of long steel bars, which are cut to desired lengths. The bar is then ready for drilling and reaming. Drilling is done by a deep-hole drill, a long rod with a V-cut running its entire length. One edge of this V does all the cutting. The barrel rotates at high speed while the deep-hole drill, which remains stationary and does not spin, bores a hole from breech to muzzle.

Once the initial hole is cut, a series of reamers, usually three or more, are used to ream the hole to the desired bore diameter. These reamers make the bore as smooth as possible and ready the barrel for rifling.

Rifling

Rifling, simply put, is a system of spiral grooves cut into the bore to make the bullet spin and stabilize it on its way to the target.

Before discussing the various forms of rifling, let's first learn the meaning of bore diameter, groove diameter, and lands. These terms will make rifling and rifling methods easier to understand.

Grooves are the spiral cuts running the length of the barrel. The distance from the bottom of one groove to the bottom of the opposite groove is called groove diameter. Lands refers to the portion of the bore left between the rifling grooves. The measurement between lands is called bore diameter.

There are various forms of rifling, but the type most commonly used today has square-cut lands and grooves. These grooves, which spiral to the right and are always cut opposite one another, usually number four or six in most factory guns. One exception is Marlin's MicroGroove barrel, which has 16 shallow grooves cut into the bore. The theory behind having many shallow grooves is that it minimizes bullet distortion and increases accuracy.

There are several other forms of rifling, but none, to this writer's knowledge, are used today. One type of rifling, called either segmental or Metford, has lands and grooves with rounded-off edges. It was used in Europe for black-powder guns because it made barrels easier to keep clean. The black powder was not apt to foul the barrel quickly since there were no sharp edges in the rifling to catch particles. Another form of rifling is the oval bore, which, as its name implies, has an out-of-round bore. The oval actually turns as it moves down the length of the barrel and spins the bullet. At one time, oval-bore rifling was used both in England and the United States. Still another type of rifling is the parabolic pattern, which gives a pinwheel appearance when looking down the barrel. This type of rifling was used in some rifles around 1920.

Methods of putting rifling into a barrel vary, and this has been particularly true within the past 30 years. At one time, all manufacturers cut rifling into a barrel by the same process, and that was cutting one groove at a time. The cutter bit made one complete pass through the barrel, while at the same time the barrel rotated at a predetermined speed to give the rifling the desired

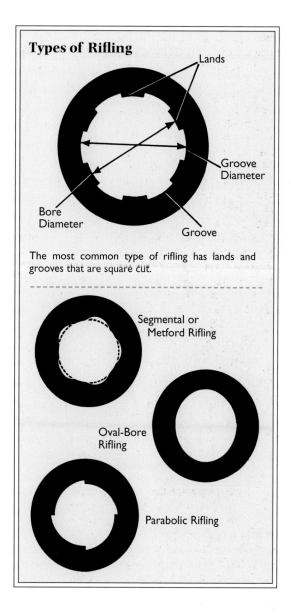

Types of Rifling

Lands

Groove Diameter

Bore Diameter

Groove

The most common type of rifling has lands and grooves that are square cut.

Segmental or Metford Rifling

Oval-Bore Rifling

Parabolic Rifling

amount of twist. Then, if the barrel was to have four-groove rifling, the barrel was given a quarter turn and another groove was cut. These steps continued until all grooves were cut. It is important to note here that the bit could not cut a groove to its proper depth on a single pass, so a number of shallow cuts had to be made until the groove reached the correct depth.

Cutting one groove at a time was obviously slow, and this brought about the use of broaches. A broach is a steel tool with several cutting edges. When the tool is pushed or pulled through the bore, each cutting edge removes slightly more steel than the one preceding it. All the rifle grooves are cut in a single operation. Though these broaching tools are expensive and costly to repair, this method is certainly much faster than cutting one groove at a time.

Still another method of putting rifling in a barrel, called cold forming, was developed during World War II. This procedure involves placing the barrel over a mandrel or carbide die that has the reverse impression of rifling on it. The barrel and mandrel are then placed in a forging machine that pounds the outside of the barrel until the rifling is formed inside the barrel.

One last rifling process involves the use of a carbide rifling button to form the rifling in a bore. The torpedo-like carbide button has reverse spiral grooves machined into it. When pushed or pulled through a bore, the button compresses and forms rifling rather than cutting it. The operation is done by one pass through the barrel and production goes much faster. Most manufacturers now use this button-rifling method. Most important to the shooter is the fact that button-rifled barrels tend to be more accurate than those rifled by other methods.

■ Rates of Twist

The rate of twist of the rifling is directly related to the bullet weight (and velocity) that particular firearm can handle with accuracy. Heavier (longer) bullets in a given caliber require a faster rifling twist.

A good example of this is the .30-06 and the .308 Winchester. Both rifles use bullets of the same diameter (.308 inch), which are available in a wide assortment of weights ranging from 110 grains up to 220 grains. While both of these rifles turn in excellent results with all of the medium-weight (150- and 180-grain) bullets, their abilities differ when it comes to the very heavy or the very light.

The .30-06 will handle 220-grain bullets better because it has a faster twist of one turn in 10 inches. On the other hand, the .308 Winchester turns in better results with the light 110-grain bullets due to its slower twist of one turn in 12 inches.

When extremely light bullets are used in a barrel with a fast twist, they may accelerate too rapidly and deform themselves. The weight, length, and shape of the bullet are important to accuracy. The length of the projectile must be compatible with the rifling twist and velocity or the bullet may become erratic in flight.

Keep in mind that you may obtain good results in your firearm with a supposedly less-than-optimum bullet weight simply by reducing or increasing the velocity a bit. Don't be discouraged from experimenting with various bullet weights. However, stay within safe pressure limits.

■ Chamber

The oversize portion at the breech end of the barrel is called the chamber of the rifle. It is designed to hold the cartridge that is to be fired. The chamber must be

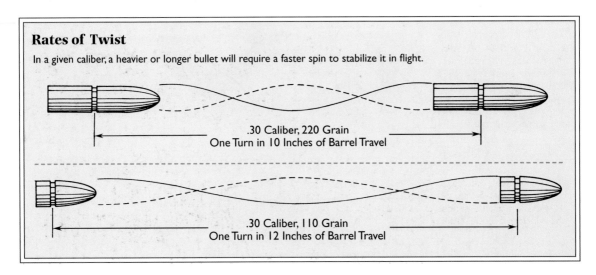

Rates of Twist

In a given caliber, a heavier or longer bullet will require a faster spin to stabilize it in flight.

.30 Caliber, 220 Grain
One Turn in 10 Inches of Barrel Travel

.30 Caliber, 110 Grain
One Turn in 12 Inches of Barrel Travel

slightly bigger than the cartridge to allow the brass case to expand slightly from the pressure of the exploding powder and contract sufficiently for ejection of the spent case from the chamber.

The throat or neck of the chamber, which encircles the case neck, should likewise be oversize to allow the case neck to expand enough to release the bullet for its flight through the barrel.

Headspace

Any definition or description of a chamber automatically leads into the subject of headspace. To make headspace easier to understand, let's first define a couple of terms. Headspace is the distance between the head of a cartridge case and the face of a closed and locked bolt. Headspace measurement is the distance between the face of a closed bolt and the point of contact on the cartridge case that controls the distance the case will go into the chamber. Consequently, headspace measurement determines headspace.

Headspace measurement would be simple if all cartridges were chambered the same way, but there are four types of cartridges (rimmed, rimless, belted, and rimless pistol), and headspace is measured differently for each type. The accompanying illustrations clearly show the headspace measurement for each class or type of cartridge. They also illustrate how each type

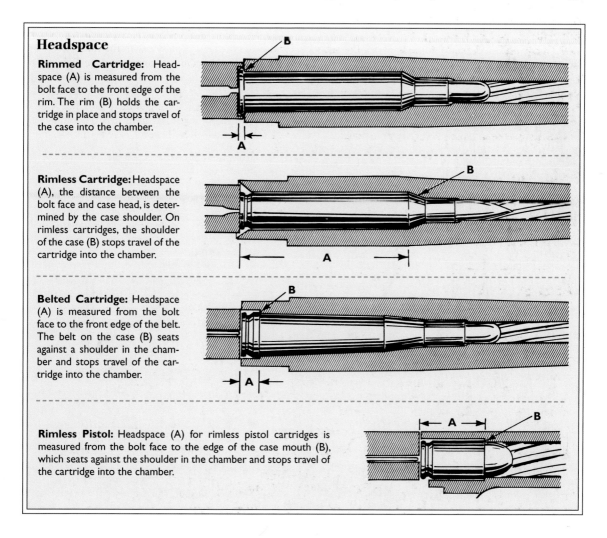

Headspace

Rimmed Cartridge: Headspace (A) is measured from the bolt face to the front edge of the rim. The rim (B) holds the cartridge in place and stops travel of the case into the chamber.

Rimless Cartridge: Headspace (A), the distance between the bolt face and case head, is determined by the case shoulder. On rimless cartridges, the shoulder of the case (B) stops travel of the cartridge into the chamber.

Belted Cartridge: Headspace (A) is measured from the bolt face to the front edge of the belt. The belt on the case (B) seats against a shoulder in the chamber and stops travel of the cartridge into the chamber.

Rimless Pistol: Headspace (A) for rimless pistol cartridges is measured from the bolt face to the edge of the case mouth (B), which seats against the shoulder in the chamber and stops travel of the cartridge into the chamber.

of cartridge fits in the chamber, showing the contact points between the case and chamber that hold the cartridge in place.

Obviously, since all chambers and cartridges cannot be made exactly alike, there is always some space between the bolt face and the head of the cartridge. In modern high-power rifles, the acceptable tolerance between the bolt face and head of a maximum gauge used to determine headspace is six thousandths of an inch.

If there is too much space between the cartridge head and bolt face, a condition known as excessive headspace exists. If there is not enough space between the cartridge head and bolt face, the problem of insufficient headspace exists. Either of these conditions in a rifle handling high-powered cartridges can be dangerous if it goes unchecked.

How does a shooter determine whether his rifle has excessive or insufficient headspace? There are several symptoms to look for: When a shooter has difficulty chambering a cartridge or getting the bolt to close or lock, his rifle may have insufficient headspace. Another indication is shiny score marks on the head of the case, which may be the result of the bolt closing too tightly on the cartridge and creating friction between the head of the case and the bolt face. Any of these signs may indicate insufficient headspace. This means pressures may run abnormally high when the rifle is fired.

However, a shooter who recognizes these signs should not automatically assume his rifle has an insufficient headspace problem. The chamber may be normal and the problem may lie with the cartridges being used, particularly with reloaded ammunition. As mentioned above, it is almost impossible for all cartridges of one caliber to have exactly the same dimensions.

If insufficient headspace is suspected, it is best to take the rifle to a gunsmith and have it checked with headspace gauges. If the problem does exist, it can often be corrected by reaming out the chamber to an acceptable tolerance.

In rifles with excessive headspace, there is too much room between the head of the cartridge and the bolt face. When such a rifle is fired, the head of the cartridge face comes back against the bolt face and the case expands beyond normal limits. The case may stretch or crack near the head or pull itself apart completely.

Determining the possibility of excessive headspace in a rifle is done by examining the spent cases for the following telltale signs:

1. A partial crack or rupture is visible near the head of the case.

2. A stretched ring mark is visible on the brass near the head of the case. This can be considered a warning sign of possible complete separation of the head from the case.

3. When firing reduced loads in a rimless case, a protruding primer is an indication of excessive headspace.

4. In rimfire cartridges, excessive headspace will produce a bulge near the rim.

5. Total case separation—in this extreme situation, the cartridge pulls apart completely, usually near the head, and only the rear section of the case ejects.

Here again, signs of excessive headspace may not necessarily mean a chamber problem. A full-length resizing die, for example, may shorten a case and create excessive headspace in a normal chamber. The best bet is to take both the rifle and ammunition to a gunsmith and have him check the firearm with headspace and case gauges. Sometimes the problem can be corrected by changing ammunition or resizing it.

CARTRIDGES

L et's get off to a good start by calling a cartridge by its right name. It's a cartridge, and calling it anything else is wrong. It's not a bullet, a slug, a shell, nor anything else that does not adequately describe a cartridge. A cartridge is not a single item or unit, but a combination of various components, which include a bullet, case, powder, and primer. Put these four basic components together and you have a cartridge.

It's not all that simple, however, since cartridges are broken down into types. Among metallic rifle cartridges, there are two basic categories—rimfires and centerfires.

The common rimfire cartridge has its primer sealed in and around the entire rim. The firing pin striking the rim anywhere around the edge of the cartridge will ignite the charge. Examples of rimfire cartridges are the .22 Short, .22 Long, .22 Long Rifle, .22 Magnum, and 5mm Remington Rimfire Magnum.

Centerfire cartridges have a primer in the center of

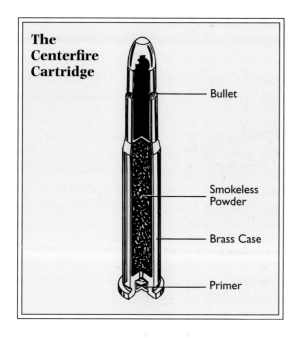

The Centerfire Cartridge

- Bullet
- Smokeless Powder
- Brass Case
- Primer

the base of the cartridge case. The firing pin striking the primer ignites the primer and sets off the powder charge via a flash hole in the brass case. Centerfires make up the bulk of modern sporting ammunition.

The Case

Just about all modern rifle cartridge cases are made of brass, which is most suitable for reloading. There are still some plated steel cases in use, but brass is still the first choice. The cartridge case has a number of important jobs. It houses the powder charge, and it holds the primer and bullet firmly in place. Upon firing a cartridge, the case also seals off gases from escaping from the breech.

Cartridge cases fall into five categories or types: rimmed, semi-rimmed, rebated, rimless, and belted case.

Rimmed cases are an old design and are still very much in use today. The .30-30 Winchester, for example, uses a rimmed cartridge case. The rim of the cartridge is the contact point that keeps the cartridge from entering the chamber.

A semi-rimmed case is one that has a rim a bit bigger in diameter than the body of the case, and the extraction groove is cut under the rim. Semi-rimmed cases are not too common today and the .225 Winchester may be the only current cartridge using this type of case.

The rebated cartridge case is one of the easiest to spot. The rim is smaller in diameter than the base of the case body. The extraction groove is cut under the rim. An old design, it was apparently revived in the .284 Winchester cartridge.

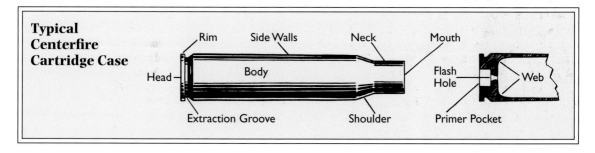

Typical Centerfire Cartridge Case

Rim · Side Walls · Neck · Mouth · Head · Body · Flash Hole · Web · Extraction Groove · Shoulder · Primer Pocket

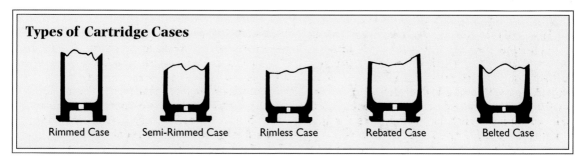

Types of Cartridge Cases

Rimmed Case · Semi-Rimmed Case · Rimless Case · Rebated Case · Belted Case

The rimless case is the design most widely used today. The rim diameter and the diameter of the case body are nearly identical and the extraction groove is cut into the head of the case. The classic .30-06 uses the rimless case.

The belted case has become synonymous with magnum calibers. The purpose of the belt is to provide sufficient headspace. The belt acts as a rim on what is essentially a rimless case. The extractor groove is cut into the belt just as it is cut into the case of a rimless case.

▪ The Bullet

A bullet is simply a component of a cartridge and a nonspherical projectile that is fired through a rifle barrel. But there the simplicity ends. Bullet design varies, depending on whether the bullet is to be used for long-range varmint shooting, brush hunting for whitetails, bear hunting, or hunting thick-skinned dangerous game.

For example, bullets designed for varmint shooting, generally in the .17- to .24-caliber class, are constructed with soft lead cores, thin metal jackets, and can be either soft or hollow pointed. They are usually sharp pointed to enable them to retain velocity better, which means a flatter trajectory. This design, however, causes them to expand quickly and disintegrate when they hit.

Such varmint bullets are fine for long-range shooting where there are no obstructions, but they rank a poor second on bigger game because they are easily deflected by the smallest twig in their path and they go to pieces before good penetration occurs. While it is true that varmint cartridges have taken numerous heads of big game, the fact remains that these bullets are not suitable for that purpose.

For thin-skinned big game, ranging from deer to moose, bullets are larger in diameter, heavier in weight,

and made with soft lead cores and thin jackets. They differ from varmint bullets in that plenty of lead is exposed at the point to give good even expansion or "mushrooming" and reliable penetration. Major ammunition companies, including Winchester, Remington, Federal, Hornaday, and Weatherby, produce a variety of bullet designs to maximize penetration and controlled expansion. Winchester and Remington have gone a step further and also produce ammunition with lead-free bullets in big-game calibers.

Finally, there are bullets built for thick-skinned dangerous game. These bullets are invariably full jacketed with no lead exposed. Their purpose is to penetrate thick hides and smash bone. No appreciable mushrooming is expected of them. These solid bullets are best jacketed in steel and have round or flattened points. Such bullets are for massive African game, such as Cape buffalo and elephants, where a hunter may need fast and deep penetration to stop a charge. They are not practical for any North American big-game animals.

A bullet designed with a point at both ends would be best aerodynamically since it would reduce wind resistance and air drag, but such a bullet, for obvious reasons, is not feasible. The closest to it, however, is the boat-tail bullet, which tapers slightly at the rear. This is the best choice for long-range shooting. Combine the boat-tail design with a spire point or spitzer point, and the result is a bullet with top flight characteristics.

Such pointed bullets, however, have disadvantages. First, they cannot be safely used in rifles with tubular magazines, because recoil may drive the sharp nose of such a bullet into the primer of the cartridge in front of it. Second, sharp-pointed bullets have less shocking power on big game than round-nose bullets, because tissue, like air, offers less resistance to sharp-pointed bullets. For this reason, the sharp-pointed bullets designed for hunting will nearly always have soft or hollow points.

A term that is often mentioned when the subject of bullets comes up is sectional density, which is the ratio of a bullet's diameter to its weight. The sectional density of a bullet is figured by dividing the bullet's weight in pounds by the square of the diameter. Unless a shooter is good at math, he'll have trouble with the formula. It is important to remember, however, that bullets with a low sectional density are short and fat and the velocity is lower than bullets with a high sectional density. Bullets with a high sectional density are long, slim, and retain velocities well over long ranges.

What does this mean to the average hunter? In simple terms, a bullet with a high sectional density, such as

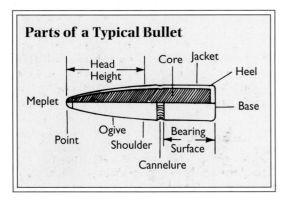

Parts of a Typical Bullet

Head Height • Core • Jacket • Heel • Meplet • Base • Point • Ogive • Shoulder • Bearing Surface • Cannelure

Modern Bullet Designs

This is a full-jacketed or non-expanding solid bullet. The only opening in the jacket is at the base of the bullet.

This is an expanding bullet with a round nose and soft point. A large area of lead is exposed at the tip with a one-piece jacket covering the sides and bases of the bullet. The cannelure aids in crimping the cartridge case neck into the bullet.

This is an expanding bullet with a round nose and soft point. The one-piece jacket has slits in the forward portion to weaken the nose and bring on quick-controlled expansion.

This is a hollow-point expanding bullet. The jacket encloses the sides and base, but is weakened by knurling near the tip to promote quick expansion.

The Nosler Partition bullet has a metal jacket open at both ends to expose lead. The partition strengthens the base of the bullet and the jacket decreases in thickness toward the tip. It is one of the best expanding-bullet designs.

The boat-tail bullet is tapered at the base to reduce air drag. It is a top bullet design for long-range shooting.

The Winchester Silvertip has a copper jacket that covers the side and base of the bullet. The tip is covered with a soft aluminum case that extends back and under the copper jacket. The Silvertip has good expanding qualities.

The Remington Bronze Point has a bronze wedge in the tip that produces good expansion when it is driven to the rear of the bullet on impact.

The Remington Core-Lokt is a soft-point, round-nose bullet. The forward edge of the jacket has a scalloped edge to ensure uniform mushrooming. The bullet is strengthened by increased jacket thickness near the base.

The Hornady pointed soft-point expanding bullet has a lead core exposed at the tip. The one-piece jacket covers the base and side of the bullet. Note the pronounced thinning of the jacket in the nose section.

The RWS H-Mantel bullet is a semi-fragmenting bullet design. The outer jacket is steel covered with cupro-nickel alloy. The tip cap enclosing the internal cavity is copper. The jacket is indented at the halfway point to separate the frangible forward section from the base.

The Remington hollow-point Core-Lokt has a shallow tip cavity to lessen quick expansion. The jacket is purposely thin at the nose to weaken it.

---

a 130-grain .270 would be fine for game taken at long ranges. For the brush hunter, however, a chunky .35-caliber deer-class bullet with a low sectional density would be OK in wooded areas where ranges are not extreme.

Still another term that frequently gets tossed around is ballistic coefficient, which is a complicated principle that relates a bullet's sectional density to its shape and measures its ability to overcome air resistance.

Unless a shooter plans to get involved in handloading his own ammunition for hunting, there is really no need to learn the aerodynamic principles and formulas of bullet design and weight. Firearms manufacturers have done extensive research to produce the best bullets for various hunting conditions. Before buying ammunition for a hunting trip, take a look at the accompanying Modern Bullet Designs illustrations to see the various options.

■ The Primer

The primer is frequently referred to as the spark plug of the cartridge, and one would be hard put to find a better description. The primer contains a highly explosive

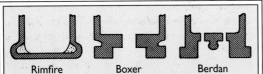

Rimfire   Boxer   Berdan

These cutaways of cartridge case heads show three basic designs for primers. The **rimfire primer** has priming compound completely around the rim. The firing pin striking the rim anywhere ignites the cartridge. **Boxer primer** fits into the primer pocket. The firing pin striking the primer ignites the mixture and sets off the cartridge via the flash hole. The case for the **Berdan primer** has a built-in anvil. When the firing pin strikes the primer, the cartridge is set off via flash holes around the anvil.

compound that, when struck by the firing pin, ignites the cartridge's powder charge via a flash hole in the brass case.

Thanks to modern manufacturing techniques, the chances of primer malfunction are rather remote. When a malfunction does occur, it is generally because of a weak firing pin or because oil, grease, or water has worked its way into the primer. If you're a handloader, keep the primer dry and clean and don't handle it if your fingers have even a trace of lubricant.

The typical American primer for a centerfire cartridge is actually an assembly of several components, including an anvil, cup, paper, and the priming mixture. The paper lies between the mixture and the anvil. The primer ignites when the firing pin crushes the explosive mixture against the anvil. Just about all primers made in the United States use chemicals that are noncorrosive and nonmercuric.

Types of Boxer Primers

Primer	Diameter (inches)
Large rifle	.210
Large rifle magnum	.210
Large pistol	.210
Large pistol magnum	.210
Small rifle	.175
Small rifle magnum	.175
Small pistol	.175
Small pistol magnum	.175

There are basically two types of primers in use today: Boxer and Berdan. The Boxer primer has a built-in anvil, which means it can be punched out of a spent case with a decapping pin. This is a great advantage to handloaders. The Berdan primer does not have a built-in anvil. Instead, the anvil is an integral part of the cartridge case. This makes removal of the primer difficult, which accounts for the increased usage of the Boxer primer throughout the world. To a limited degree, the Berdan primer is still used in Europe.

The difference in reliability between the Boxer and the Berdan primers is almost nonexistent—both are dependable. Cartridge cases using the Boxer primer use one large flash hole in the primer pocket, while the Berdan primer ignites the powder charge through several small holes around the built-in anvil in the case. The Boxer primer is the most widely used because it is a boon to handloaders.

Boxer primers are made in two different sizes and eight different types (see accompanying chart). The large rifle primers are used with cartridges such as the .270, .308, .30-06, and similar calibers. The large pistol primers are used in such calibers as the .45 Auto, .44 Special, and so on.

The small rifle primers are used in the .22 Hornet, .222 Remington, and similar cartridges. The small pistol primers are used in the .32 Smith & Wesson, .38 Special, and similar cartridges.

The magnum primers, as the accompanying chart indicates, are the same in diameter as the other primers. The difference lies in their chemical structure. Magnum primers are built to provide long sustained heat to ensure complete ignition when large quantities of powder are used.

There are at least eight manufacturers producing dependable primers for handloaders. If you're going to try handloading, you'll find that all handloading manuals will list the correct primer size for your cartridge.

Rimfire cartridges, such as the .22s, use a much different priming design. The priming mixture in these small cartridges is distributed completely around the rim of the case. The firing pin, striking anywhere around the rim, will ignite the priming mixture and fire the cartridge.

■ The Powder

When was the first time a gunpowder was used in a firearm? That's a tough, if not impossible, question to

Finger-Pointing Phenomenon

Try extending your index finger parallel to the forend of your shotgun next time you're on a claybird range. It may look awkward at first, but stick with it and it may well improve your shooting. Pointing your finger at a target is much more accurate than pointing a shotgun barrel. In fact, if you point at a flying target with your finger, you will probably be on target every time. Extending your index finger along the forend is a simple extension of this finger-pointing phenomenon.

answer. It's generally accepted that the Chinese developed black powder (a mixture of sulphur, charcoal, and potassium nitrate) for use in fireworks and a man named Roger Bacon adapted it to firearms around 1265.

During the pioneer era, before the advent of smokeless powder, black powder was used in muzzleloading rifles and cap-and-ball pistols. Black powder is not an ideal propellant and no factory cartridges today are loaded with it. Small batches are still produced, however, for the growing number of gun enthusiasts who enjoy shooting and hunting with muzzleloaders.

Black powder has more than a few disadvantages, which should be explained before discussing the development of smokeless powder. First, black powder is explosive and consequently presents a potential danger to the user. If a spark or hot ash should hit a pound of black powder on your reloading bench, it could result in a serious explosion. And in spite of the fact that it is an explosive, it burns at a constant rate and it takes a great deal of it to produce enough gas to get a bullet up to the acceptable velocity. This was one reason the old muzzleloaders had long barrels; they were needed to give the black powder enough time to burn and build up pressure. Black powder also gives off great clouds of smoke from the muzzle of an old front-loading gun and fouls a barrel badly. To maintain any kind of accuracy, muzzleloaders have to be cleaned frequently.

So, unless you're a muzzleloading enthusiast, forget black powder. It was used at a time when there was nothing else to do the job. Now smokeless powder is available, which is far superior in all respects.

Modern smokeless powders stem from the discovery of nitroglycerin and guncotton. Nitroglycerin is a liquid that results from the action of nitric and sulphuric acids on glycerin. Guncotton is formed by the action of the same acids on various kinds of cellulose and cotton. It is difficult to categorize smokeless powders because they come in almost endless varieties and shapes, but they are basically separated into powders for rifles, shotguns, and handguns. Perhaps the single most important fact about smokeless powder is that the rate of burning can be controlled so that its use can be boosted to maximum efficiency in various types of firearms.

To control the burning rate of smokeless powder, you can use one of two methods—size of granulation of the powder or coating the grains with a retardant substance. Either of these two methods produces progressive-burning powder. To put it simply, the smaller the grains of powder, the faster the burning rate; the bigger the grains, the slower the burning rate. When a retardant coating is used, this coating must first be burned off before the powder burns. The purpose is to get the powder to start burning slowly, and then increase the rate of burning as the bullet starts its trip through the barrel. The result is a continuous accelerating thrust pushing the bullet.

How can this progressive-burning principle be applied to cartridges? A few examples should make it clear. Light bullets require less gas pressure to start moving in a barrel than heavier bullets. Using the .308 as an example, a fast-burning powder can be used with the 110-grain bullet, but a slow-burning powder should be used with the heavier 200-grain bullet.

Let's carry this a step further and take a look at rifle and handgun ammunition. A rifle may have a barrel up to 22 or 24 inches, which means more time is available for a powder to build up pressure, so one of the slower-burning powders can be used. In a handgun, however, where peak velocity must be reached quickly because of the short barrel, a very fast powder must be used.

If you're a handloader, the importance of correct powder selection cannot be overemphasized, since it will have a direct bearing on velocity. You'll be confronted with powder in various forms, including circular flakes, small cylinders, and small spheres. A good handloading manual, however, will recommend what kind of powder to use and what velocity you can expect with various bullet weights.

If you're not a handloader but an average hunter, there's no need to worry about the gunpowder in the factory ammunition you buy at your favorite gun shop. If it's from a reputable manufacturer, you can be sure you're getting the right powder.

CARTRIDGE SELECTION

It is just about impossible to talk about cartridge selection without also covering the subject of ballistics (velocity, trajectory, and energy), since a shooter must obviously know how a particular cartridge will perform before he makes his choice.

Let's first start out with a basic premise. Game is killed by a good combination of rifle, cartridge, and shooter. The most important is the shooter. The most efficient rifle and cartridge is nearly worthless unless the hunter can comfortably handle his gun and confidently place his bullet in a vital area. If a hunter can't kill a deer with a .30-30, there is no reason to believe he will do much better with a .338 Winchester Magnum.

When a hunter using a deer-class cartridge finds himself wounding and missing game with any amount of frequency, the problem is usually with the hunter behind the gun, not the gun itself. The solution to such a problem is more time on the range, where a shooter can find where his bullets are going and make the necessary sight adjustments. He should also put in as much practice as possible to develop a steady hold and good smooth trigger squeeze.

■ Deer Hunting in Brush

There are some guidelines a hunter can follow in selecting a cartridge for his brand of hunting. If he's a typical deer hunter who takes his game in wooded country where ranges are not extreme, he'd be wise to pick a caliber between .25 and .35, handling bullets weighing from 120 to 200 grains. This would give him a fairly heavy bullet pushed along at a not-too-fast velocity that would give it good timber qualities. You don't want a very high-velocity bullet that will go through a deer at short range and exit before it can properly expand. A heavy, medium-velocity bullet would also be less apt to be deflected by brush and, if properly constructed, would not disintegrate on impact. A bullet that goes to pieces when it strikes is all right for varminters, but not for big-game hunters who need bullets that will provide good penetration.

Another fact to keep in mind is that the typical deer hunter, unless he plans to hunt moose or bears as well, should not overpower himself with the mighty magnums, such as the .300 and .338 Winchester cartridges. These big, belching berthas can be a definite handicap. Because of their uncomfortable recoil and muzzle blast,

these rifles are not fired as often as a hunting rifle should be and the result is that the shooter does not become familiar with his rifle and may also develop a flinch or become afraid of his rifle—something that is sure to mean missed or wounded game.

So if you're a deer hunter in brush country, stick to the calibers you can handle comfortably and confidently. A well-placed shot with a .30-30 will kill cleaner than a sloppy shot with one of the big magnums.

As mentioned earlier, the deer-class cartridges between .25 and .35 calibers are good choices. A few excellent cartridges for brush hunting are the old-time .308 Winchester, 7mm-08, .35 Remington, .30-06, and .300 Savage.

■ Western Deer Hunting

The deer hunter in the West has a different problem. He needs a cartridge that will produce high velocity and flat trajectory for the long, 200-yard-plus shots he will encounter in mountain and prairie country. He also needs a quick-expanding bullet that is fairly light.

Generally, the western hunter chooses from the .25- to .30-caliber range of cartridges. Because of the

First Deer Gun

I rank the Marlin 336C, chambered for both the .30-30 Winchester and the .35 Remington, among the top deer guns for eastern woods. The .30-30 Winchester has only 10½ foot-pounds of recoil, light enough to be shot comfortably at a range or in the field, and it weighs only 7 pounds. The .30-30 is enough gun to bring down a big buck with a well-placed shot. Recoil with the .35 Remington is a bit more than with the .30-30, but easily manageable. For sights, I would mount a compact scope with the lowest power setting I could find. At 1x, for example, the field of view at 100 yards would be about 100 feet. I would recommend this Marlin in either .35 Remington or .30-30 Winchester as an ideal starter rifle for young and beginning deer hunters.

long shooting distances involved, bullet weights are more important here, since they will affect trajectory and bullet drop. The proven cartridges for western hunting include the .270 with a 150-grain bullet, .243 with a 100-grain bullet, .25-06 with a 120-grain bullet, .264 Winchester Magnum with a 140-grain bullet, 7mm-08 Remington with a 140-grain bullet, 7mm Remington Magnum with a 175-grain bullet, .280 Remington with a 165-grain bullet, .30-06 with a 180-grain bullet, and any of the .300 Magnums.

It certainly is not unusual for western hunters to include such game as antelope, sheep, and goats in some of their hunts. These medium-size game animals all have one thing in common: they are generally taken at long range. Any of the cartridges and bullet weights listed above for the western hunter will do the job on these animals.

Big Game/Varmint Cartridges

Cartridges for deer-size game in the West and East have been covered, but how about hunters looking for a big-game cartridge that can also be used during the off-season for varmints? If this is the case, any selection will have to be a compromise. The ideal deer cartridge can never be a top-flight woodchuck or varmint load. The best solution is to favor the lighter, high-velocity cartridges that will reach out for chucks but also be adequate for deer. Such compromise cartridges include the .243 Winchester with the 80-grain bullet for varmints and the 100-grain bullet for deer or the .25-06 Remington with the 90-grain bullet for varmints and the 120-grain bullet for deer. Similar combinations include the .257 Roberts, .270, and 6mm Remington. In a pinch, the .308 and .30-06 with light bullets can also prove adequate for long-range woodchuck shooting.

This assumes, of course, that a shooter following these recommendations is shopping for a rifle that will work on both deer and varmints. If a hunter, however, already owns a .270 or .30-06, it would be poor economics for him to unload it and buy another rifle that would be closer to a deer-and-varmint combination gun. It would be much wiser to simply use lighter bullets on varmints and heavier bullets on deer-size game. The .30-06, for example, offers a range of bullet weights from 110 to 220 grains. The .308 offers nearly the same range of bullet weights.

Perhaps another point to keep in mind before swapping your rifle is that most hunters who suddenly become addicted to varmint shooting will invariably end up with one of the specialized high-velocity, flat-shooting varmint cartridges, such as the .17 Remington, .222 Remington, .223 Remington, or .22-250 Remington.

One of the most perplexing yet interesting problems is the search for the all-around cartridge, one that can fill in during the summer months for chucks, take deer on those annual hunts, and also be put to use on occasional trips for such big game as elk, moose, caribou, and brown and grizzly bears. Such an all-around cartridge has to be a compromise. No single cartridge does the job well on all game, from chucks to moose. If you choose a powerful cartridge, you must cope with heavy recoil, muzzle blast, and noise, even if you just want to hunt chucks on a Saturday afternoon. If you choose a lighter cartridge, it may fall slightly short of the acceptable power for game such as elk or moose.

But if a hunter can afford just one gun for all game, the old .30-06 is most often recommended. With a 110-grain bullet, it produces a velocity of 3,370 feet per second, which makes it a more than adequate varmint load. The deer or sheep hunter can use the 180-grain bullet, which leaves the muzzle at 2,700 feet per second. For bigger game, the 220-grain bullet leaves the muzzle at 2,410 feet per second and packs 2,830 foot-pounds of energy.

If the .30-06 is the best all-around cartridge, it isn't the only one. The .308 Winchester is available with bullets weighing 110, 125, 150, 180, and 200 grains. Bullets for the .270 Winchester come in 100, 130, and 150 grains. The .280 Remington and 7mm Mauser can also do far more than one job—as can the 7mm Remington Magnum for a hunter who can take recoil. All these cartridges have a good variety of bullet weights and good retention of velocity and energy.

Cartridges for Dangerous Game

For heavy and dangerous game, the choice of a cartridge is not difficult because there are not that many American-made cartridges available for such animals. For Alaskan bears, Cape buffalo, and the big Asian and African cats, a hunter can use such cartridges as the .300 Holland & Holland, .338 Winchester Magnum, .300 and .340 Weatherby Magnums, or .375 Holland & Holland. For the toughest game, such as elephant and rhino, a hunter should use solid bullets in such cartridges as the .378 Weatherby Magnum, .375 Holland & Holland, .458 Winchester Magnum, .460 Weatherby Magnum, .416 Rigby, .470 Nitro Express, and .416 Remington Magnum.

BALLISTICS

Ballistics, which is a study of what happens to a bullet in flight when it leaves the muzzle of a rifle, is an extremely valuable aid to a shooter in selecting and comparing the pros and cons of various cartridges. Without getting too technical, ballistics covers trajectory, velocity, and muzzle energy of a cartridge. Before going any further, you should know what these terms mean.

Trajectory is the curved path the bullet takes from muzzle to target. No bullet will travel a flat path to the target—even if velocity were pushed to more than 4,000 feet per second and the range was only 10 yards. A bullet, because of gravitational pull, begins to drop the instant it leaves the barrel. It is the degree of the trajectory curve that is of key importance to the shooter, and this is determined by the initial muzzle velocity and bullet shape.

The faster a bullet leaves the muzzle, the shallower the trajectory curve or, in other words, the "flatter" the path of the bullet. As mentioned above, bullet shape also has an effect on the trajectory curve. Long, sharp-pointed bullets handle wind resistance better, retain velocity longer than chunky round-nose bullets, and produce a flatter bullet path.

Velocity is simply the speed at which a bullet travels, and this is usually measured in feet per second. (Generally, the abbreviation "fps" is used after the digits.) On nearly all published ballistic charts, figures on velocity are given at the muzzle and at ranges of 100, 200, and 300 yards. The purpose is to tell how well or how poorly a particular cartridge retains its speed. Such figures are valuable in cartridge and bullet weight selection.

Muzzle energy is a measurement expressed in foot-pounds of the impact by a bullet as it leaves the muzzle of a rifle. Ballistic charts nearly always give energy figures for bullets at the muzzle and at ranges of 100, 200, and 300 yards. These figures are useful in determining how rapidly various loads and bullets lose impact power in flight.

What do trajectory, velocity, and energy mean to a hunter or target shooter? The answer is the difference between missing and hitting. Trajectory figures will tell you which cartridges shoot flatter than others, though there is really no such thing as a flat-shooting cartridge. The trajectory curve (flight path of a bullet) has often been compared to a baseball player throwing a ball. The farther he must toss a ball, the higher he must throw it to make it reach its target. The same applies to a bullet. The farther the target, the higher the muzzle of a rifle must be raised, by adjusting the rear sight upward, to make the bullet travel a greater distance.

Published ballistic tables also almost always show trajectory figures, which indicate a bullet's flight path from muzzle to target. The figures, given in inches, indicate the rise or drop of a bullet from the line of sight.

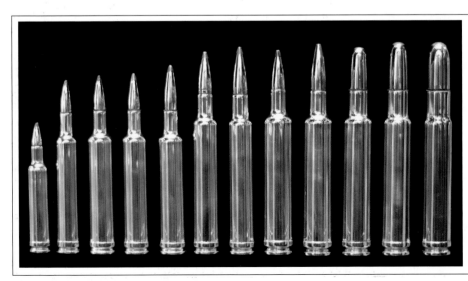

The Weatherby cartridge lineup—from .224 to .460 calibers—illustrates the size comparisons of modern centerfire calibers. Ammunition from other manufacturers would show size proportions similar to Weatherby.

Recommended Calibers and Bullet Weights for Game

FOR VARMINTS

Cartridge	Bullet Weight (grains)	Muzzle Velocity (feet/second)	Cartridge	Bullet Weight (grains)	Muzzle Velocity (feet/second)
.17 Remington	25	4,020	.257 Weatherby	87	3,825
5mm Remington Magnum	38	2,100	.220 Swift	48	4,110
.22 Long Rifle	40	1,145	.225 Winchester	55	3,650
.22 Long Rifle	40	1,335	.243 Winchester	80	3,500
.22 Long Rifle HP	37	1,365	.25-06 Remington	90	3,500
.22 WRF (.22 Remington Special)	45	1,450	.25-06 Remington	100	3,300
.22 Winchester Automatic	45	1,055	6mm Remington	80	3,544
.22 Winchester Magnum Rimfire	40	2,000	.25-20 HV	60	2,250
.218 Bee	46	2,860	.256 Winchester Magnum (rifle)	60	2,000
.22 Hornet	45	2,690	.250 Savage	87	3,030
.22 Hornet	46	2,690	.257 Roberts	87	3,200
.222 Remington	50	3,200	.264 Winchester Magnum	100	3,700
.222 Remington Magnum	55	3,300	.270 Weatherby	100	3,760
.22-250 Remington	55	3,810	.270 Winchester	100	3,480
.223 Remington	55	3,300	.284 Winchester	125	3,200
.224 Weatherby	50	3,750	.308 Winchester	110	3,340
.240 Weatherby	70	3,850	.30-06 Springfield	110	3,370

FOR BIG GAME

Cartridge	Bullet Weight (grains)	Muzzle Energy (foot-pounds)	Cartridge	Bullet Weight (grains)	Muzzle Energy (foot-pounds)
†.243 Winchester	100	2,090	.30 Remington	170	1,700
.250 Savage	100	1,760	*.30-40 Krag	180	2,440
†6mm Remington	100	2,260	*.30-40 Krag	220	2,360
†.25-06 Remington	120	2,590	*.300 Savage	180	2,240
.25-35 Winchester	117	1,370	†*.30-06 Springfield	180	2,910
†6.5mm Remington Magnum	120	2,780	*.30-06 Springfield	220	2,830
†.240 Weatherby	100	2,554	†*.300 Winchester Magnum	180	3,770
.257 Roberts	117	1,820	†*.300 Weatherby	180	4,201
†.264 Winchester Magnum	140	3,180	.303 Savage	190	1,650
†*.270 Weatherby	150	3,501	*.303 British	180	2,580
†*.270 Winchester	150	2,800	.307 Winchester	150	2,760
†*.280 Remington	165	2,910	.307 Winchester	180	2,510
†*.284 Winchester	150	2,800	†*.308 Winchester	180	2,720
*7mm Mauser	175	2,410	*.308 Winchester	200	2,670
7-30 Waters	120	1,940	.32 Winchester Special	170	1,960
7mm/08 Remington	140	2,542	.32 Remington	170	1,700
†*7mm Remington Magnum	175	3,660	*8mm Mauser (8x57, or 7.9)	170	2,490
†*7mm Weatherby	154	3,406	8mm Remington Magnum	185	3,896
.30-30 Winchester	170	1,860	†*.338 Winchester Magnum	200	4,000

(continued on page 52)

Recommended Calibers and Bullet Weights for Game (continued)

FOR BIG GAME (continued)

Cartridge	Bullet Weight (grains)	Muzzle Energy (foot-pounds)	Cartridge	Bullet Weight (grains)	Muzzle Energy (foot-pounds)
*.338 Winchester Magnum	300	4,000	.375 Winchester	200	2,150
†*.340 Weatherby	200	4,566	*.375 Holland & Holland	270	4,500
*.348 Winchester	200	2,840	*.375 Holland & Holland	300	4,330
.35 Remington	200	1,950	*.416 Rigby Solid	410	2,370
.350 Remington Magnum	200	3,261	*.416 Rigby Trophy Bonded		
.351 Winchester Self Loading	180	1,370	Sledgehammer	400	2,370
.356 Winchester	200	2,460	.44 Magnum	240	1,630
.356 Winchester	250	2,160	*.444 Marlin	240	3,070
*.358 Winchester	200	2,840	.45-70 Govt	405	1,570
*.358 Winchester	250	2,810	*.470 Nitro Express	500	2,150

*Suitable for heavy game, such as elk or moose, as well as for lighter species, such as deer.
†Suitable for long-range plains or mountain hunting where flat trajectory is important (game such as sheep and goats).

FOR DANGEROUS GAME

Cartridge	Bullet Weight (grains)	Muzzle Energy (foot-pounds)	Cartridge	Bullet Weight (grains)	Muzzle Energy (foot-pounds)
*7mm Remington Magnum	175	3,660	*.375 Holland & Holland	270	4,500
*.30-06 Springfield	220	2,830	**.375 Holland & Holland	300	4,330
*.300 Holland & Holland	180	3,400	†.375 Holland & Holland	300 Solid	4,330
**.300 Holland & Holland	220	3,350	†.378 Weatherby	300 Solid	5,700
*.300 Winchester Magnum	180	3,770	‡.416 Rigby	410 Solid	2,370
**.300 Weatherby	220	4,123	.416 Remington	400 Solid	2,400
8mm Remington Magnum	220	3,912	*.444 Marlin	240	3,070
*.338 Winchester Magnum	250	4,050	**.458 Winchester Magnum	510	5,140
**.338 Winchester Magnum	300	4,000	‡.458 Winchester Magnum	500 Solid	5,040
**.340 Weatherby	200	4,566	‡.460 Weatherby	500 Solid	8,095
*.350 Remington Magnum	250	3,220	‡.470 Nitro Express	500 Solid	2,150
*.358 Winchester	250	2,810			

*Only for such North American species as Alaskan bear and moose.
**Not for elephants or rhino, but suitable for large Asiatic and African cats.

†Adequate for elephant, rhino, and buffalo.
‡Recommended for the toughest, most dangerous game.

Let's take, for example, the .30-06 with a 180-grain bullet. Sighted-in at 200 yards, the bullet will hit 2.4 inches high at 100 yards and 9 inches low at 300 yards. Obviously, the midrange figures are valuable when trying to figure out the best range to sight-in your hunting rifle, and they also tell you where to hold at ranges closer or farther than the distance for which your rifle is sighted.

The Recommended Calibers and Bullet Weights for Game chart is a compilation of ballistic figures from various ammunition makers. Studying this chart will give you a good insight into how various cartridges perform and how they compare with one another. Use it when trying to pick a varmint load that shoots the flattest, or when trying to find the load that offers the widest range of bullet weights for all-around hunting.

RIFLE SIGHTS

■ Iron Sights

Mass-produced rifles usually come with a plain open rear sight and bead-type front sight. Few hunters are satisfied with these sights, which really are suitable only for auxiliary use in case a scope becomes inoperative. However, many manufacturers have improved the sights they install. In former years, a low semi-buckhorn rear sight came on almost all rifles, even if the stock had a high Monte Carlo comb for use with a scope. Today, most factory rifles with high combs have appropriately higher open sights, and many of these sights also feature adjustments that permit more precise alignment. The improvements are welcome, but for most purposes open sights still can't match a telescopic sight or an aperture (peep) sight. These rifles are drilled and tapped for scope mounting, and big-game models are rarely seen in the field without a scope.

There are two basic types of open sights: the V- or U-notch and the patridge, which has a square notch used with a square blade front sight.

In the first category, there is some controversy about the shape and size of the V- or U-notch, which may take the form of a shallow V, a deep V, or a V with "ears," which is called the buckhorn. The worst of the lot is the buckhorn with "ears" that blot out more than half of the target when the sights are lined up. Fortunately, very few guns now come equipped with buckhorn sights, but there are still enough around to cause problems. One can replace it, of course, but the sight can also be partly fixed or improved by filing down the ears to the top of the V.

The deep V is a big improvement over the buckhorn sight, but it also has a drawback. A hunter will most likely sight-in his rifle by carefully placing the front bead down into the V-notch, which is the correct way to do it. This works well on the range, where the shooter has plenty of time to zero in, but problems come up in the field. Shooting at game during the poor light of dusk or dawn, the hunter may not seat the front bead as deep or as carefully in the V as he did on the range. This means he will shoot high and miss his target.

The shallow V is the best compromise for an open rear sight. The absence of any kind of ears means at least half of the target can be seen. The shooter has more light to work with, and the shallow V-notch literally doesn't leave much room for error in seating the bead. Some manufacturers place a white diamond or triangle at the bottom of the V, and this certainly helps to quickly center the bead. If an open sight must be used, the shallow V is the best choice.

Front bead sights for the above, incidentally, come in a variety of colors, including gold, ivory, or red plastic. Some show up better than others under certain lighting conditions, but the gold bead has been proven the best for all conditions.

Assuming you're a target shooter and not a hunter, the patridge sight, with its square-cut notch rear sight and square blade front sight, is actually more accurate and a better choice than the sights using a bead front sight. With this sight, the front blade is centered in the square notch of the rear sight and a six o'clock hold is

---

Basic Types of Iron Sights

Buckhorn

Shallow V

Aperture or Peep

Patridge

The buckhorn is the worst of the lot since it covers too much of the animal. The shallow V is an improvement, as it allows a hunter to see more of the game at which he's shooting. The aperture or peep sight is the best choice for hunting because it's fast, lets in plenty of light and landscape, and the hunter simply puts the bead where he wants to hit and squeezes off. The patridge sight is actually the most accurate, but it's a difficult one to use on game and should be used only for target shooting.

Sights

▶ The Lyman 66A Receiver "Peep" Sight is designed for flat receivers, such as Winchester and Marlin lever actions or shotguns. It has audible ¼-minute clicks for elevation and windage. The peep sight is faster and superior to open iron sights and is a good choice for deer hunting in heavy timber.

▼ The Lyman 93 Match Globe Front Sight is designed for any rifle and mounts on a standard dovetail base. This target front sight comes with several Anschutz-size inserts to match various target or hunting conditions.

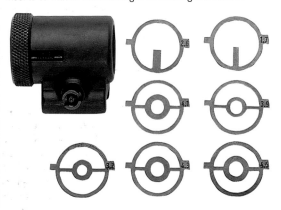

▼ Lyman introduced the Marlin Tang in 1995 for most Marlin lever actions. Similar tang sights are also available for Winchester lever actions. The tang peep sight will help the shooter sharpen the front sight. It allows a clear view of the target and front sight.

taken. That is, the front blade is placed at the bottom edge of the bull's-eye. The sight picture should look like an apple sitting on a fence post. This sight combination is surprisingly accurate for target work, but a difficult one to use on game.

The biggest problem with open sights is adjustment—that is, lack of dependable adjustment. If bullets consistently hit left, the rear sight in its dovetail mount must be tapped to the right—not a very precise technique. If bullets consistently hit high or low, the rear sight must be moved accordingly on the notched bar, to a lower notch to lower the point of impact and to a higher notch to raise it. Sometimes a rifle will shoot high with the sight in its lowest notch. This leaves you with two choices: file down the notch or look for a better sight.

Another problem with open sights is that they require the shooter to focus on three things at once: the

rear sight, the front bead, and the target. This is not a simple trick even for the best pair of eyes. A shooter trying to keep everything in focus at the same time will find himself shifting focus back and forth between the rear and front sights and his target, and such an arrangement will mean misses.

APERTURE OR PEEP SIGHT: The peep sight is far superior to the best open sight ever designed. The peep is mounted on the receiver of the rifle, only a few inches from the eye, and the shooter looks through it, not at it. The peep sight works on the principle that the eye will automatically center the front bead in the hole. Many hunters and shooters find this hard to believe, but there is no doubt that it works.

It's important to remember to try not to focus on the aperture itself. It's supposed to look slightly blurred. Simply look through the hole and pick up the front bead.

Your eye will automatically center it in the hole and all you have to do is put the bead on your target.

The peep sight also offers the important feature of positive adjustment. The aperture can be adjusted for both windage and elevation by means of screws that provide corrections of ¼ to ½ inch at 100 yards.

All peep sights come with insert discs for target shooting. The hole through these discs is generally very small, and they're fine for shooting at paper on the range. Hunters, however, should take this disc and throw it away. It's not needed and only decreases the size of your sight picture. The peep sight is the fastest of all iron sights for hunting. It lets you see plenty of light, landscape, and nearly all of a game animal when shooting. It may be hard to believe, but a hunter can pick up a running whitetail faster through a peep sight than an open sight—then it's just a matter of putting the bead on the animal and squeezing off.

▪ Telescopic Sights

Most hunting rifles today have telescopic sights mounted on them. Hunters and shooters have come to realize that these riflescopes are not the fragile optical instruments they were in the 1920s. The modern scope is a rigid dependable sight that under almost all conditions is far superior to any other sight.

Hunters who are getting on in years and beginning to have difficulty with iron sights when trying to focus the rear sight, front sight, and target at the same time can eliminate this problem with a scope. With a scope, the image of the target or game is placed right on the crosshairs, and when the hunter focuses on the crosshairs he will find his target is also automatically in focus.

Elderly hunters with failing eyesight can often stretch their hunting years by using a scope.

Another advantage is that game that may ordinarily go unnoticed in protective cover can often be picked up in the magnification of a riflescope. Scopes also add a margin of safety to hunting. What may look like a deer with the naked eye may well turn out to be another hunter through a 4x scope. A scope will also lengthen the hunting day by enabling a hunter to see well enough to shoot in the poor light of dawn and dusk.

Disadvantages of the scope are few. A scope will add weight to a rifle, anywhere from 6 ounces to maybe more than a pound. A scope also adds bulk, which sometimes creates a minor problem when carrying the rifle. Rain or snow can also put a scope temporarily out of commission, unless it is equipped with scope caps of some sort. A scope can also be a handicap for short-range snap shooting at game in thick cover. But all these problems can be solved to a degree.

Scopes are perhaps best classified by their type: hunting scopes, scopes for .22 rifles, and target and varmint scopes.

HUNTING SCOPES: A few fixed power scopes are still available, but variable power scopes dominate the market with scopes offering a variety of magnifications of 1.5x–4x and up to 6x–42x. In buying a scope, the shooter has to decide what power to choose and the answer depends on the hunting to be done. The highest-powered scopes listed above may be wanted for varmint hunting, but are not really suitable for most hunting.

High magnification can actually be a drawback. The greater the magnification, the smaller the field of view (the width of the area visible through the scope at

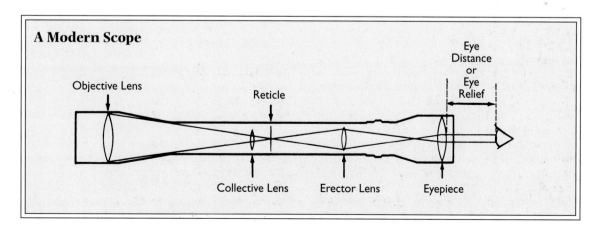

A Modern Scope

Objective Lens

Reticle

Eye Distance or Eye Relief

Collective Lens   Erector Lens   Eyepiece

Scopes

▼ The Leopold Model VX-R rifle scope features a FireDot Reticle, which is activated from standby mode whenever the rifle is moved. The model shown is the 2x–7x compact that measures 11.3 inches and weighs 12.7 ounces.

◀ Nikon Monarch scopes have BDC reticles that compensate for trajectory to provide aiming points for various distances up to 600 yards. Models range from 2.5x–10x to 6x–24x.

◀ The Swarovski Z3 Scope is a lightweight scope. The 3x–10x model weighs about 12 ounces and measures 12½ inches. A 4x–12x version of the Z3 measures 14 inches.

◀ The Redfield Revenge scopes range in powers from 2x–7x to 6x–18x. Some models of this scope feature Redfield's Accu-Ranger Ballistics System. The 2x–7x is a compact scope that measures only 11.3 inches.

▼ The Pursuit X1 is an electronic red-dot sight that has various reticle options, as well as dots in red, blue, or green. The sight measures 4½ inches and has five brightness settings. The Pursuit is powered by one 3-volt lithium battery.

▼ The Burris AR-132 has a 4-MOA red dot with 1x magnification and ballistic reticle with bullet drop compensation points. This model can be mounted on the Picatinny rail-mounting brackets.

100 yards). Moreover, high power increases the apparent tremors in the sight picture. With a smaller field of view plus the problem of holding steady, lining up on moving game can be difficult. Sometimes a shooter can't even find the game in his scope before it disappears into thick cover.

If your hunting is mostly in woods and brush, your best bet is a variable in the 1.5x–5x class. Many of the newer scopes, including variable models, feature an extrawide field of view. With a wide-field 1.5x–5x scope cranked down to the lowest setting, the field of view is about 70 feet at 100 yards. At the top setting, it's about 27 feet. For all-around hunting, a 2x–7x compact variable is probably best. Although the 3x–9x is extremely popular, its slightly increased magnification isn't really

worth the extra bulk and weight if the scope is to be used for a wide variety of hunting. If you use just one rifle and your hunting ranges from eastern whitetails to Colorado mule deer, a 2x–7x variable would be your best choice. If your hunting is strictly eastern, you want a wide field of view and you don't need as much power, so your best bet is a 1.5x–5x variable or as close as you can get to this power range.

SCOPES FOR .22s: Most .22 rifles are used for plinking and hunting small game and it's hard to imagine such a rimfire gun without a scope. The bulk of the .22s available today come equipped with cheap iron sights that can rarely be adjusted for accurate shooting. A receiver or peep sight is certainly an improvement, but a scope will turn most .22s into accurate firearms.

There are not many scopes specifically designed for .22s. Cabela's makes a rimfire scope in 3x–9x that sells for under $100. Cost should not be a critical factor here, since scopes for .22 rifles generally run up to $150 and they are a good investment. It's wise here to mention that under no circumstances should some of these scopes be mounted on a high-powered rifle, since it could result in a serious eye injury. These inexpensive scopes for .22s usually have an eye relief (the distance between the eye and ocular lens that gives the shooter maximum field of view) of about 3 inches. A .22 has just about no recoil, so the eye being this close to the ocular lens presents no problems. Put the same scope on a high-powered rifle with heavy recoil, however, and the scope tube could be driven into the shooter's eye.

Don't shortchange your .22 rifle with an inexpensive scope if you have doubts about its quality. Most .22s deserve the best scope you can afford and with a solid mounting system. The best power for a scope to be used on a .22 is not as important as it is with big-game rifles. For target shooting and small-game hunting, a 4x or a 3x–9x variable power scope is fine.

TARGET AND VARMINT SCOPES: Scopes for long-range varmint shooting and for benchrest and other serious target competitions are a special breed. Years ago, the necessary accuracy was obtained only with scopes that were more than 2 feet long with fragile adjustments in the mounts. Now, with very few exceptions, powerful and precise target scopes employ internal adjustments, and they measure no more than about 18 inches long. Bushnell, Leupold & Stevens, Nikon, Redfield, and a few others offer rugged, precise, internally adjusted target scopes that look like hunting models.

The field of view is smaller than the field in a lower-powered hunting scope, but this doesn't matter in a scope to be used strictly for varmint hunting or target work. Serious varmint shooters generally use scopes with 10x–30x magnification, though some of them favor even greater power. For target shooting, 15x and 20x scopes are preferred, and bench shooters use 20x and even 25x scopes.

▉ Electronic Sights

Electronic red-dot sights solve a lot of problems for hunters and it has been proven that this type of reticle is the fastest on medium-range and moving targets. All a hunter has to do is put the red dot on his target and pull the trigger. There's no need to align the rear and front iron sights. A hunter shoots with both eyes open and these sights work equally well in both poor light and bright sunlight.

The Bushnell Trophy Red Dot is a good example of the electronic red-dot sights available today. With unlimited eye relief, you can mount it on handguns, rifles, and shotguns. With its Zoom Dot feature, the shooter can zoom from a 3-MOA red dot to a 10-MOA red dot, as well as crosshairs and a 65-MOA circle with a 3-MOA red dot. This Bushnell model measures only 5½ inches and has multiple brightness levels.

Other companies making electronic sights include Pursuit, Burris, Leupold & Stevens, Pentax, Nikon, Pulsar, Redfield, and Vortex.

▉ The Scope Reticle

A scope reticle is simply a fixed or suspended device in a scope tube that marks the aiming point. Reticles come in many sizes and shapes, and they can be confusing to a hunter who is worried about laying out considerable cash for a scope and then discovering that the reticle is wrong for him.

The accompanying illustrations show most reticle types, including the traditional plain crosshair, post and crosswire, dot, range-finders, and dual-thickness (heavy and thin) crosswire. Most reticles are wire, though some makers in the past used animal hairs, etched glass, or spider silk.

The simpler the reticle, the easier it is to aim with. A sight picture cluttered with multiple crosshairs or other range-finding devices can sometimes be more trouble than it's worth. As with scope power, the best type of reticle depends on the hunting for which it's most often used.

For years, the most popular reticle was the standard crosshair, sometimes tapered toward the center but usually of uniform thickness. This type was and still is offered with fine wire for target or varmint shooting or heavier wire for big game.

For aiming at moving game in woods and brush, a good variation is the post and crosswire. The vertical post is usually tapered and flat topped. In variable-power scopes, it generally comes up exactly to the horizontal crosswire. In fixed-power scopes, it generally extends a trifle above the horizontal wire. In either case, its top is the aiming point. The crosswire is merely a horizontal reference line to help the hunter keep from canting his rifle. Such a reticle works well for relatively

Reticle Options

There is a wide range of scope reticles shown here, from American reticles to those by European and Japanese makers. These represent most of the types available today. Some of the reticles are shown both in standard form and wide-view models. The bottom scope assists in range determination.

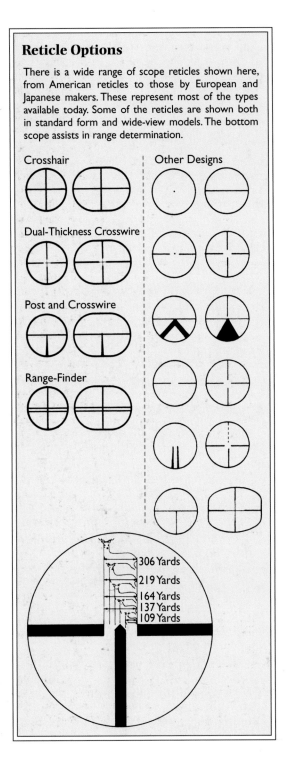

Crosshair

Other Designs

Dual-Thickness Crosswire

Post and Crosswire

Range-Finder

306 Yards
219 Yards
164 Yards
137 Yards
109 Yards

fast shooting in poor light, because the thick-bottomed post is so easy to see.

But at long range, a post covers too much of the target—as do the coarse crosshairs that have been traditional in many big-game scopes. One solution is the use of fine crosshairs, and another is the combination of a center dot and fine or tapered crosshairs. Many target and varmint shooters like the dot and fine crosshairs. For big game in open country, a suspended dot (without crosshairs) was at one time quite popular. It's fast to use, but this type of dot isn't good for target work, as it covers the bull's-eye. Even in hunting, the size of the dot is important. A 2-minute dot, for example, covers 2 inches at 100 yards, a 4-minute dot covers 4 inches, and so on. Choose one that won't cover too much of the target in your type of hunting, and remember that knowing its size will help you estimate its range. A varmint hunter with a 6x or 8x scope wouldn't want more than a 1-minute dot, but a big-game hunter in open country might want a 2- or even 4-minute dot.

The standard crosshair, post, and dot reticles are no longer as popular as they once were, because a relatively new type has gained eminence for many shooting purposes. This is the dual-thickness crosswire. Leupold introduced it in the late 1960s and called it the Duplex. Now, many makers offer it under different names.

This type of reticle employs rather heavy vertical and horizontal crosswires that abruptly become fine near the center. Even in poor light, the shooter's eye quickly picks up the coarse wires, and the fine center wires allow precise aiming—even at a small target. If there's one all-around hunting reticle, this is it.

With a bit of practice, such a reticle also permits fast range estimation. Let's say, for instance, that you're hunting deer with a wide-view scope, either 4x or 1.5x–4.5x variable at the high setting. In either case, the space between the point of the heavy outer wires at 100 yards is 22 inches. A mature deer's body is only about 18 inches deep, from the top of the back to the belly (a fact that seems to surprise many hunters). If the deer's body, from top to bottom, fills the vertical space between the wires, the deer is about 80 yards away. If it fills half the space, it's 160 yards away. To get the knack of judging range with your reticle, just practice on stationary targets of known sizes at known distances.

The dual-thickness reticle is so practical and popular that it has replaced the ordinary crosshair as the "standard" type. If you order a scope without specifying the reticle, chances are you'll get the dual design.

■ Mounting the Scope

There are several factors to consider before mounting a scope. By reading about the various types of mounts, you can determine which is the best scope mount for your gun and use.

BRIDGE OR TOP MOUNT: The bridge mount is chiefly for a hunter who plans to stick a scope on his rifle and leave it there. It's a sturdy mount, suitable for saddle-scabbard carrying and other jolting treatment. One major disadvantage is that the mounting blocks are screwed into the top of the receiver so that, with many rifles, the iron sights can't be used if the scope is damaged and has to be removed. The mount bases hide the open sights. However, this is no longer a problem on many modern rifles that have higher-than-normal factory-installed sights for use with a high-combed stock. Also, some mounts are grooved to allow sighting with the scope removed. With or without these improvements, a sturdy top mount is a good choice for target shooting or hunting in which a scope is just as important as an accurate rifle.

SEE-THROUGH MOUNT: The see-through mount is an old but recently revived idea. This is essentially a bridge mount with a peep hole through the bases so the shooter can also use his iron sights in a pinch. The see-through mount should be particularly appealing to the brush hunter who is never quite sure whether he'll need a scope for a long shot or iron sights for a close quick shot. It does have disadvantages, however. For one thing, the scope must necessarily be mounted high, which means the shooter will have to crane his neck upward slightly to get a good sight picture through the tube. This is a good reason for only putting these mounts on rifles with Monte Carlo combs or fairly high rollover cheekpieces. Also, because the scope is mounted high, it makes a bulky package and the sight is more accident prone. Some of these mounts, however, are designed to permit easy sighting through especially low see-through designs.

All factors considered, the see-through mount is a fair compromise for the hunter who wants an instant choice of scope or iron sights. But he will have to accept the fact that the scope will not be mounted in the best possible position, which is as low as possible and directly over the receiver.

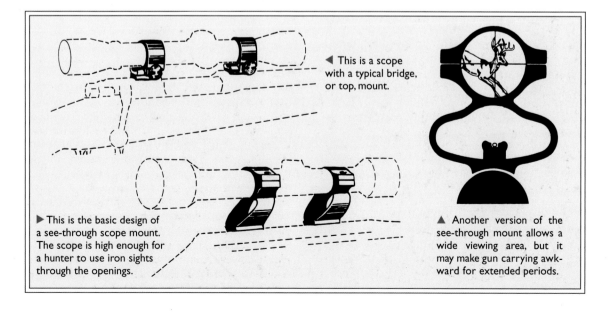

◄ This is a scope with a typical bridge, or top, mount.

▶ This is the basic design of a see-through scope mount. The scope is high enough for a hunter to use iron sights through the openings.

▲ Another version of the see-through mount allows a wide viewing area, but it may make gun carrying awkward for extended periods.

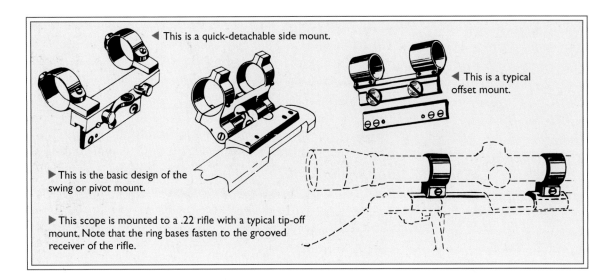

◄ This is a quick-detachable side mount.

◄ This is a typical offset mount.

► This is the basic design of the swing or pivot mount.

► This scope is mounted to a .22 rifle with a typical tip-off mount. Note that the ring bases fasten to the grooved receiver of the rifle.

QUICK-DETACHABLE MOUNT: This mount is the best and only choice for a hunter who occasionally wants to remove his scope and use the iron sights, or who wants to use his scope in conjunction with a receiver or peep sight. The base portion of this mount is generally screwed and pinned to the side or top of the receiver, so that when the scope and ring portion of the mount is removed, there are no obstructions along the top of the barrel and iron sights can be used.

As mentioned above, the quick-detachable mount can also be effectively used in conjunction with a receiver or peep sight that has a removable slide. The scope can quickly be removed and the slide of the receiver sight slipped in. This makes it a fine choice for the hunter heading into a remote area. If the scope should accidentally get knocked out of commission, he can remove it and have a reliable receiver sight to fall back on.

SWING OR PIVOT MOUNT: Still another version of the side mount is the swing mount, which is basically a hinged bracket screwed to the side or top of the receiver. With this arrangement, a hunter confronted with a quick shot at close range has only to swing the scope out of the way and use the iron sights. Makers claim a scope will maintain its zero when swung back and forth.

OFFSET MOUNT: This mount, which is literally offset to the side of the receiver, has only one practical application—and that's for rifles that eject fired cases from the top of the receiver. It is somewhat awkward to use, since the shooter must cock his head over the comb to see through

the scope. But if a hunter has a top-ejection rifle and wants to put a scope on it, he doesn't have much choice and he must consider the offset mount. It does, however, also offer the instant choice of iron or scope sights.

PICATINNY RAIL MOUNT: This scope mount, sometimes called the tactical rail, was designed to standardize a mounting system for scopes and accessories, such as tactical lights, night-vision devices, and lasers. The rail is a series of T-shaped ridges with flat slots. Scopes and accessories are mounted by sliding them on the rail from either side and then clamped to the rail with screws or levers. The Picatinny rail seems to lend itself more readily to modern sporting rifles and tactical firearms.

TIP-OFF MOUNT: The tip-off mount, because it is not designed as rigidly as other mounts, is relegated to the .22 rifles. The tip-off mount should not be cut short, however. It works fine, is inexpensive, and can be clamped on a .22 rifle in minutes by someone who knows almost nothing about guns.

Whereas most modern high-power rifles come factory drilled and tapped for scope bases, the .22s have the male portion of a dovetail machined into the top of the receivers. The female portion of the tip-off mount, which holds the scope, is simply fastened in place on the receiver with coin-slotted screws.

Generally, the cost of putting a scope on a .22 is nonexistent, since nearly all new .22s have grooved receivers and the inexpensive .22 scopes come equipped with the complete tip-off mount.

Sighting-In a Rifle

Sighting-in a rifle isn't difficult, just time consuming, and shortcuts will only work against you. Follow the correct step-by-step procedure and you'll reap the rewards in the field.

Start by bore sighting the rifle. This gives you a baseline from which all other adjustments can be made. Bore sighting is best done at 25 yards. You'll find this relatively short range is particularly helpful when sighting-in a new rifle or a gun you're using for the first time. It

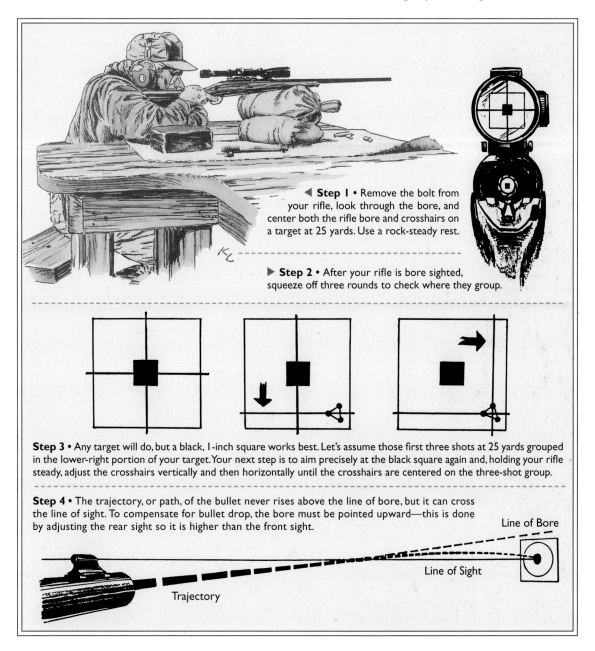

Step 1 • Remove the bolt from your rifle, look through the bore, and center both the rifle bore and crosshairs on a target at 25 yards. Use a rock-steady rest.

Step 2 • After your rifle is bore sighted, squeeze off three rounds to check where they group.

Step 3 • Any target will do, but a black, 1-inch square works best. Let's assume those first three shots at 25 yards grouped in the lower-right portion of your target. Your next step is to aim precisely at the black square again and, holding your rifle steady, adjust the crosshairs vertically and then horizontally until the crosshairs are centered on the three-shot group.

Step 4 • The trajectory, or path, of the bullet never rises above the line of bore, but it can cross the line of sight. To compensate for bullet drop, the bore must be pointed upward—this is done by adjusting the rear sight so it is higher than the front sight.

Line of Bore

Line of Sight

Trajectory

virtually ensures that you'll at least put your first bullet on the paper.

With that first bullet on target, it's easy to subsequently adjust for windage and elevation, and to fine-tune your sights for any range you choose. Conversely, when you attempt to sight-in at 100 or 200 yards, you can use up a lot of ammunition and patience trying to find out where your bullets are going.

Bore sighting is simple with a bolt-action rifle. You have to use some sort of benchrest—a cardboard carton with notches carved at both ends will do. Remove the bolt from the rifle and put it securely on your rest, or cradle it in the notches of the cardboard box. Look through the bore at the target and move the rifle—and rest—until the target is centered in the bore.

Then, look through your scope and see where the crosshairs fall. If the crosshairs don't intersect on the target center, adjust the windage and elevation until

they do. When the crosshairs and bore are both perfectly centered, you've created a proper baseline. (The procedure is similar for iron sights: just remember that the goal is to get the sight picture and the bore sight both centered on the target.)

How do you bore sight a lever-action pump gun or autoloader? You have to use a "boresighter," a device that aligns either the scope or iron sights without the need for looking down the bore. You might be able to beg or borrow one from a local gun shop, but consider buying your own. The cost is usually under $100 and having a boresighter can be invaluable, particularly when you need to double-check the sights after a rifle has suffered some hard knocks on a plane or in a saddle scabbard. Laser boresighters make this task amazingly easy.

With your rifle bore sighted, squeeze off three shots at the center of the target. Note the location of your

Bullet Impact with Rifle Sighted-In at 25 Yards (inches)

Caliber	Bullet Weight (grains)	25 Yards	50 Yards	100 Yards	200 Yards	250 Yards
.222 Remington	50	0	+¾	+2¼	+½	-2½
.243 Winchester	100	0	+¾	+2	+1¾	-½
6mm Remington	100	0	+¾	+1¾	+2	0
.256 Winchester Magnum	60	0	+¾	+1¼	-3	-8½
6.5mm Remington Magnum	120	0	+¾	+2	+½	-2¼
.264 Winchester Magnum	140	0	+¾	+2½	+2	0
.270 Winchester	150	0	+1	+1¾	-½	-4
.284 Winchester	150	0	+1	+2½	+1¼	-1
7mm Remington Magnum	150	-¼	+¾	+1¾	+1¼	-½
7mm Remington Magnum	175	0	+½	+1¼	0	-2½
.30-30 Winchester	150	0	+1	+2¾	-¾	-5
.30-30 Winchester	170	+¼	+1¼	+2¾	-2½	-10
.30-06	150	0	+1	+2¼	+1¼	-1½
.30-06	180	0	+1	+2¼	+¾	-2½
.300 Winchester Magnum	150	0	+¾	+2¼	+1¾	0
.300 Savage	150	0	+1	+1¾	-½	-4
.300 Savage	180	0	+1¼	+2¾	-½	-5½
.308 Winchester	150	0	+1	+2¼	+½	-2½
.308 Winchester	180	0	+1	+1¾	-½	-4
.308 Winchester	200	0	+1	+2	-1	-7
.338 Winchester Magnum	200	0	+¾	+2½	+1½	-2
.35 Remington	200	+¼	+1½	+3	-3	-13
.358 Winchester	250	0	+1¼	+2½	0	-4½
.44 Remington Magnum	240	+½	+2	+2¾	-10½	—
.444 Marlin	240	+¼	+1½	+2½	-2	-9½

Sighting-in a new hunting or target rifle is easy with the use of a laser boresighter, which will align crosshairs in a scope with the bores of a rifle. A boresighter will get your bullets on the paper, and then scope settings are fine-tuned.

three-shot group and aim again at the center of the target, but this time don't shoot. Hold the rifle as steady as possible on the center of the target and move the crosshairs both vertically and horizontally until they're centered on your shot group. Once you've done this, you've effectively moved the sights to where the rifle is shooting. Three more rounds should confirm that you are sighted-in at 25 yards or very close to it.

Why 25 yards? The typical centerfire rifle sighted-in at 25 yards will also be sighted-in for about 200 yards because of the bullet's trajectory, at about 2 to 3 inches high at 100 yards, which is perfect for most deer hunters. Trajectory and point of impact will vary slightly depending on the specific ammunition and bullet weight you select. Once you're happy with a brand of ammunition and bullet weight, try to stick with the combination.

When necessary, manufacturers provide ballistic charts to help in switching between ammo for different types of hunting.

The final step of sighting-in is shooting at 100 yards and 200 yards to confirm the actual point of impact and make your final click adjustments for elevation and windage. These adjustments might vary depending on the brand of scope you use, but generally one click will move the point of impact ¼ inch at 100 yards.

As a practical rule, sight-in for the longest possible range that won't cause midrange misses (because of the arc of the bullet's trajectory). If you're planning a hunt that will require long-range shooting, it's a good idea to fire a few additional shots at targets set at 250, 275, and 300 yards to get a precise idea of where the bullets are hitting and what your aiming point should be.

The SiteLite SL-150 is a laser boresighter that will help shooters sight-in their rifles by aligning crosshairs of a scope with bores of a rifle. The SiteLite will fit all calibers from .22 to .50, plus 12- and 20-gauge shotguns. Some boresighters will also fit on most muzzleloaders.

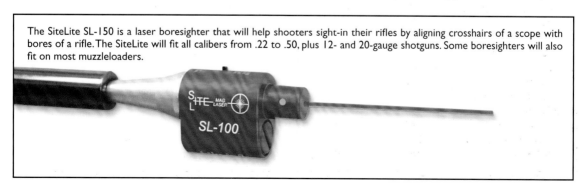

RIFLE ACCESSORIES

When a hunter finally feels that he has put together a winning combination of cartridge, rifle, and sights, he'll find there are a few extra items he'll need to round out his rig. The most important items will be covered here in detail.

■ Slings

Anyone who has ever hunted with a rifle knows the value of a sling, whether it's a simple carrying sling or a military-type target sling. A sling means a rifle can be carried on the shoulder or across the back, leaving both hands free for climbing, dragging out game, and so on. And, of course, the sling is used to help steady your hold for a shot.

Three types of slings are available to the hunter: the military sling, the Whelen-type sling, and the carrying sling.

The military sling is fine for match shooting, but it is generally too heavy and wide (1¼ inches) for most hunting rifles. If you're turned on by the military sling, however, there are some that are manufactured to be lighter and narrower.

A better choice for a hunting rifle is the one-piece Whelen sling, which has a single claw hook to lengthen or shorten it. This sling is about 50 to 55 inches long and measures ¾ to 1 inch wide, just about right for a hunting

rifle. The Whelen sling can be adjusted to a comfortable carrying length that will also work out well if the hunter wants to use the "hasty sling" position to steady his rifle.

Most hunting rifles have a simple carrying sling or strap. There are two basic versions—a straight strap and the popular "cobra" sling, which widens at the forend, like a cobra's hood, so that it won't dig into the shoulder. A lining patch of suede, sheepskin, or rough leather prevents it from slipping. Some straight slings have a sliding pad that works like the cobra design does to distribute the load and prevent the strap from slipping off the shoulder. Fastenings on both straight and cobra slings include claws, leather thongs, buckles, and even Velcro hook-and-pile closures. The cobra type is excellent for general use on a hunting rifle, and a plain one works just as well as an expensive one with decorative tooling.

■ Swivels

Swivels come in two basic types: those that mount permanently to the rifle and quick-detachable models.

The permanent types are fine if you're going to put a sling on a rifle and leave it there. But for a few extra dollars, the quick-detachable swivels are a better bargain. The bases of the swivels are mounted on the rifle and the sling-holding portion of the swivel has a spring catch that quickly detaches from the base. This means a hunter can have bases installed on several rifles and use the same sling on all of them. Another advantage is that the brush hunter who finds his sling getting in the way in thick cover can remove the sling and carry it in his pocket. When he's walking out on a woods road, he can snap it back on.

These are some basic sling designs: military sling, Whelen sling, plain carrying strap, cobra sling, and straight strap with sliding shoulder pad.

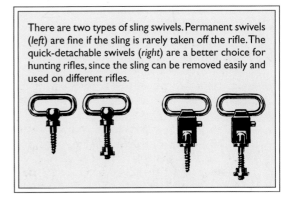

There are two types of sling swivels. Permanent swivels (*left*) are fine if the sling is rarely taken off the rifle. The quick-detachable swivels (*right*) are a better choice for hunting rifles, since the sling can be removed easily and used on different rifles.

There are three recoil pad designs. The vented pad (*left*) is preferred when the stock is to be lengthened. The slip-on pad (*middle*) has a detachable as well as recoil-absorbing feature. The solid pad (*right*) is preferred for rifles with magnum recoil.

Recoil Pads

Nearly all factory rifles in magnum calibers come equipped with rubber recoil pads to cushion the jolt of the gun's recoil. Most other high-power rifles, however, come with steel, aluminum, or plastic buttplates. These are fine, but do nothing to soften recoil. The hunter who uses his rifle during cold-weather hunting seasons when he's wearing heavy clothing does not need a rubber recoil pad, but a shooter who uses his rifle year-round would be well advised to have one installed on his rifle. Recoil can easily bruise a shooter's shoulder while target shooting or varmint hunting during the summer months while wearing only a light shirt.

Recoil pads also serve another purpose. They can shorten or lengthen a stock by as much as an inch or so. If you're a 6-footer with long arms, have the pad installed without the stock being cut. This will lengthen the stock an inch or more than the standard 13½-inch length of pull on most factory rifles. If you're a short person with short arms and the butt catches under your arm when you are mounting the gun, have the stock cut and a recoil pad installed for a length of pull from 12 to 12½ inches.

There are three types of recoil pads and selection is mostly a matter of personal preference. All three types serve the same function—they absorb recoil.

The side-vented pad, which is generally found on more shotguns than rifles, is good and perhaps a preferred choice if a stock is to be lengthened. The solid rubber pad is usually factory installed on guns that pack a magnum recoil. The slip-on pad can be put on and taken off a rifle butt in seconds. It's a good bet for a youngster who is beginning to outgrow his youth's model rifle. The slip-on pad will lengthen the stock and he can get a few more years of use out of the gun.

Gun Cases and Scabbards

It's poor economics to put a $1,200 rifle and scope rig in a cheap plastic case and expect it to survive unscathed the bumps and jolts of a rough trip. The better protected a rifle and sights, the more likely the sights will remain zeroed in. The rifle itself will also be saved from unnecessary scratches and gouges.

The type of case depends on the hunting to be done. The average hunter who almost always uses his car to get to his hunting grounds can get by with a good-grade gun case made of canvas, vinyl, Cordura nylon, or leather. Pick a case that has a heavy rubber tip protector at the muzzle and one that's lined with flannel or fleece. Leather is the best protector in this type of case, but is also the most expensive. A good compromise is a lined heavy-duty vinyl or nylon case that has a zipper at least one-third of the way down from the butt end. If it has a compartment for a cleaning rod, all the better.

If a hunter travels to far-off places, he should pick one of the hard plastic or aluminum gun cases lined with polyurethane foam. The rifle and scope are held firmly in place while it bumps its way through airline and train depots. Here again, cost is a factor. The best cases of this

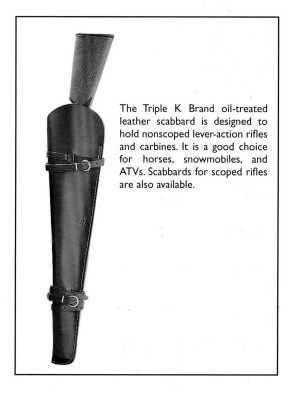

The Triple K Brand oil-treated leather scabbard is designed to hold nonscoped lever-action rifles and carbines. It is a good choice for horses, snowmobiles, and ATVs. Scabbards for scoped rifles are also available.

type are expensive. Generally, however, one can get a good multiribbed hard-plastic case with foam lining for about $150. And remember that these same cases can also be used for fishing tackle during the off-season.

Hunters who seek their game from the back of a horse need saddle scabbards. Always made of a good-grade thick leather because of the rugged use they get on mountain trails, these scabbards also make good cases for transporting guns in cars, buses, trains, and so on. Since scabbards are expensive, select one carefully.

Nylon scabbards are also available and are considerably less expensive than leather. They are constructed of Cordura nylon with a closed-cell foam and nylon lining. This nylon-foam laminate, unlike leather, will not absorb moisture, so a rifle can be carried for days, or even stored, without danger of rust or chemical reaction to the gun's bluing.

A good scabbard should cover the rifle completely, but still leave enough of the rifle butt exposed so that it can be hauled out for a quick dismount and shot. It should also have a boot that can be buckled on during transportation and bad weather, yet can be easily removed during the hunt. The two straps that hold it to the saddle should be 40 to 45 inches long and strong.

This is a cleaning rod with attachments for holding a cloth patch and for a wire brush.

The Rifle Cleaning Kit

The cost of a cleaning kit is minimal when compared to the price of a good rifle, yet such a kit could keep a rifle from rusting and perhaps from becoming inoperable. The basic cleaning kit should contain the following:

- A cleaning rod of proper size to fit the bore diameter
- A bristle brush, either brass or hard nylon
- Cloth cleaning patches
- Gun solvent
- Gun oil
- Linseed oil

Any centerfire rifle using jacketed bullets should be cleaned after each shooting session. First, run the bristle brush, soaked with solvent, through the bore. Follow with about two dry cleaning patches, then one clean patch coated with oil. It doesn't take long, but it will keep your bore in top shape.

If you're shooting a .22 Rimfire with waxed or grease-coated bullets, there's no need to clean the rifle. The bullet's coating is actually a rust preventative and the rifle can be fired indefinitely without cleaning.

Once the bore has been taken care of, wipe all metal parts with an oily rag or a silicone-treated gun cloth. This will keep rust from forming on exposed parts.

A lightly oiled rag can also be used on the stock to remove fingerprints or smudges, since such stocks are generally varnished or lacquered.

If the stock is deeply scratched, however, rub the wood with linseed oil. The oil will help coat the scratch. This oil coating is the next best thing to refinishing the entire stock.

HUNTING/COMPETITION SHOOTING

Competition shooting knows no boundaries. It pits man against man, state against state, and nation against nation. It is a worldwide activity. Matches are governed by the rules and regulations of such organizations as the National Rifle Association and the International Shooting Union.

The variety of events in these matches are many and diversified, but most include shooting from the basic positions of standing, prone, kneeling, and sitting.

The photos in this section illustrate in detail the techniques of getting into and shooting from the accepted positions. The hunter would also do well to study each position carefully and adapt his shooting style to them. The human body is a shaky shooting platform at best and these positions have been internationally proven to be the steadiest.

◼ Benchrest Shooting

The idea behind benchrest target shooting is simple. The shooter tries to put each bullet into the hole made by its predecessor—five shots, but only one hole. Needless to say, that's easier said than done; and that's where the simplicity of benchrest ends and the challenge begins.

The name "benchrest" comes from the fact that the rifle is supported on a bench during shooting. Two sandbags, one at the forend and one at the toe of the stock, hold it steady.

Benchrest shooting has several classes of competition, each with different rules on what guns may be used. The most popular division is the Heavy Varmint Class. Rifles used in this class must be of a centerfire caliber and weigh a maximum of 13½ pounds. The rules are intended to restrict contestants to a gun that could very well be used for varmint hunting.

The most exotic form is called Benchrest Unlimited Class. Rifles in this class are often called "shooting machines" because they are very heavy and usually mounted on steel rails, which are in turn mounted on a short and very sturdy tripod. The favorite calibers in this class are .222 Remington and .308 Winchester, although any caliber may be used. Other classes include Light Varmint and Sporter, which place additional restrictions on rifle weight and caliber.

Scoring is done on the basis of group size. There is no bull's-eye per se; the idea is that all shots are close together and not necessarily in the middle of the target. The shooter producing the smallest average group resulting from five shots at five different targets at a given range wins. Targets are shot at 100 and 200 yards; the average groups at 100 yards are now running ¼ inch or less. There is one class that does use a bull's-eye target—but the bull's-eye is a ¹⁄₁₆-inch dot at 100 yards!

For more information about this type of shooting, visit the National Benchrest Shooters Association website: www.nbrsa.org.

Recreational shooting is not limited to hunters or competitive target shooters. It's for everyone and can be a safe family recreational activity.

RIFLE SHOOTING POSITIONS

The photos in this section illustrate in detail the techniques of getting into and shooting from the accepted positions.

The Prone Position

▼ This is an oblique view of the prone position. The angle made by the shooter's spine and rifle will vary from less than 30 degrees up to 45 degrees, depending on the type of rifle and shooter's conformation. The shooter's body should be straight, with feet spread out and heels flat for solid support. The position should be adjusted for comfort. Comfort is the key.

▼ In this view, note that the shooter has elected to draw his right leg up. This frequently improves comfort. Also, when firing points are inclined, the drawn-up right leg elevates the right shoulder.

The Standing Position

▶ In the standing position, the shooter faces about 85 degrees from the line of aim. The feet are spread comfortably apart. The left hand grasps the forend at a point giving the steadiest feel. The butt is tucked into the pocket of the shoulder. The left arm should be under the forend of the rifle, but not so far under that the arm feels strained or twisted.

▼ This is a familiar position among competition shooters, but it's also valuable for hunters when there is no other shooting support available. Here the left elbow rests on the hip for extra support. The weight of the rifle is supported by the fingertips of the left hand with the thumb under the trigger guard and the rest of the fingers contacting the bottom of the stock. Note that the left elbow is not directly under the stock, contrary to an old rule that fortunately has died. Otherwise, to cock the elbow under the forend of the rifle, the shooter would be also twisting his shoulder, which would cause discomfort while failing to provide stability.

The Sitting Position

◄ The sitting position is often preferred to the prone position in hunting situations where vegetation can otherwise block the line of sight. In the sitting position, the shooter bends slightly forward from the waist. The right elbow is positioned against the inside of the right knee. The left elbow should rest comfortably against the left knee. The feet are spread slightly farther apart than the knees.

► The cross-legged sitting position is sometimes preferred by shooters with lighter and thinner physical frames. Note that the elbows are positioned solidly against the knees, and the legs are crossed and braced solidly. The shooter is in solid contact with the ground.

The Kneeling Position

◄ The kneeling position is not as steady as the sitting position, which is preferred by hunters. In the kneeling position, the shooter keeps his left elbow braced over his left knee. The torso is slightly forward with most of the weight resting on the left knee. The left leg is nearly vertical under the rifle to provide maximum support. The left toe should either be pointing in the same direction as the muzzle or turned slightly inward.

The Hasty Sling Position

Many hunters have slings on their rifles, but surprisingly few use the hasty sling technique, which greatly steadies a rifle. Here's how to use the hasty sling in three easy steps.

◀ **Step 1** • Put your arm through the sling as shown. Place the sling midway between the elbow and the shoulder.

▶ **Step 2** • Next, bring the left hand around the sling and between the sling and forend of the rifle.

▼ **Step 3** • Finally, shoulder the rifle. If the sling is adjusted properly, the rifle will come up snug and steady. The left hand should be against the sling and swivel.

▉ Ear Protection

According to the Occupational Safety and Health Administration (OSHA), any sound over 90–95 decibels (dBs) can result in hearing loss. Shotguns and rifles, depending on the firearms, can have noise levels of 140 to 190 decibels. Pain and permanent hearing loss begins at 125 decibels. By comparison, a roaring jet on takeoff only reaches a level of 100 decibels and a thunderclap can register 110 decibels.

Here are some statistics that should scare any target shooter or hunter: A study in the Archive of Family Medicine concluded that hunting and target shooting are the two recreational pursuits most hazardous to hearing. And target shooters are twice as likely to damage their ears as hunters.

How does a shotgun or rifle blast damage ears? Without getting too technical, sound pressure is measured in decibels. The average person can hear sounds down to zero decibels. People with exceptional hearing can hear sounds at -15 decibels, but as the decibels increase in number, so does the risk of hearing loss. There's little danger of permanent hearing loss until the noise level reaches 90–95 decibels. Obviously, the impact of a rifle or shotgun blast of 140 decibels will inflict hearing loss unless the ear is protected.

Repeated exposure to 90–95 decibels over an extended period of time will damage the microscopic hair cells found inside the cochlea or inner ear. These cells respond to mechanical sound vibrations by sending an electrical signal to the brain, where it translates into sound. Different groups of hair cells are responsible for different frequencies or rates of vibrations. With extended exposure to levels over 90–95 decibels, these hair cells in the inner ear are damaged and permanent hearing loss occurs.

There are various ways to protect your ears when you're target shooting or hunting. You can use earmuffs, foam plugs, electronic muffs, or combinations of ear protection and sound-amplification aids. Selection should be based on a Noise Reduction Rating (NRR), which is required by law to be shown on the label of every hearing protector sold in the United States. If an ear protector has a rating of 29 decibels, for example, the protector would reduce a rifle blast of 150 decibels down to 121 decibels. NRR ratings, however, are based on optimized lab tests and may bear little resemblance to what users get in practice. Some units labeled as a 20–30-decibel reduction may only achieve a 10–20-decibel reduction when poorly fitted.

There's a simple way for shooters to determine their bad ear. If you shoot right-handed, your left ear is closer and faces the muzzle and it is likely to be the ear that suffers more hearing loss than the right ear. If you shoot left-handed, the right ear takes the brunt of the muzzle blast.

Several manufacturers produce products with a combination of ear protection and sound amplification. They are effective and can add many years of active hunting for sportsmen who are experiencing hearing loss. This technology is also available in electronic earmuffs and they tend to be less costly. Most of these electronic muffs have NRR ratings of about 25 decibels.

It's important to remember that hearing aids are not ear protectors. Most hearing aids are vented, making them useless as hearing protectors. In fact, hearing aids should not be used in high-noise areas whether they are turned on or off.

If you're looking for a simple economical solution to protecting your ears, use foam plugs. Most plugs are made of expandable foam. Properly inserted, foam plugs offer among the best protection available and are comfortable for most wearers. Many shooters, however, still don't know how to use them. The plug must be rolled into a very thin cylinder and inserted well into the ear canal. Foam earplugs can have an NRR rating of 30 decibels. The very best protection is to use the foam plugs in combination with earmuff protectors. Keep in mind that the object is to obtain a solid and comfortable seal against noise; any ear protector that has a "leak" will not protect your hearing.

There's a wide choice of ear protection available to shooters. If your hearing is still good and you want to keep it that way, it's critical that you use ear protection whenever target shooting or hunting. If you've been negligent like older shooters, the damage has probably already been done, but you can still protect what's left of your hearing by always using ear protection, even if you're only a bystander at a range.

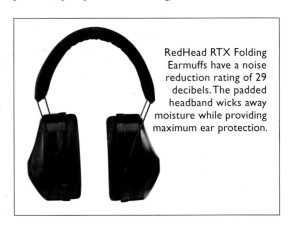

RedHead RTX Folding Earmuffs have a noise reduction rating of 29 decibels. The padded headband wicks away moisture while providing maximum ear protection.

SHOTGUN ACTIONS

The modern shotgun of today falls into one of four basic designs: the break action, which includes the single shot, the side-by-side double, and the over/under double; the pump action; the autoloader, which includes gas- and recoil-operated models; and finally the bolt action.

Selection of a shotgun differs slightly from that of a rifle in that personal preference and cost play more important roles, but there are still some guidelines to follow when choosing one of these smoothbore shotguns.

■ Break-Action Single Shot

The break-action single shot is the cheapest and simplest shotgun available today. But, like a good ax or knife, it can do many jobs. Made with or without an exposed hammer and in all popular gauges and chokes, the single shot has taken game from squirrels with No. 6 shot to black bears with rifled slugs.

While not the ideal shotgun for hunting, it makes a fine first shotgun for youngsters. Safe and simple to use, a youngster can use it to break his first clay pigeon, bag his first cottontail, and even accompany Dad with it on his first deer hunt.

There are some factors to consider, however. The single shot is a light weapon and has a fair amount of recoil in the bigger gauges. If the gun is for a youngster, pick a 20 gauge with a 26-inch Modified choke barrel. The recoil of a 12 gauge may be too much for some youngsters to handle. The 20 gauge also gets the nod over the .410 as a hunting load. With a bit of practice, a youngster can knock over rabbits consistently with a

20 gauge, but with a .410 it generally takes a good shot, and this is especially true on winged game.

It seems to be a popular idea to buy a .410 for a youngster's first shotgun, but I wonder how many fathers would want to take out after pheasants and grouse with a .410? So why harness a youngster with such a gauge? The .410 shotgun can be an effective hunting arm, but only in the hands of an exceptionally skilled shot. The 20 gauge is a better choice and if the gun is fitted with a recoil pad, the recoil can generally be handled by youngsters of average build.

The single-shot break action also makes a good camper's gun and is a longtime favorite of the farmer. The camper can use the gun for claybird shooting or taking a rabbit for the pot, if he's camping during small-game season. The break action has a quick takedown feature, which means the gun can be stored conveniently in a camper. For the farmer, such a gun becomes more of a tool than a sporting arm. He uses it to kill marauding crows or a fox raiding his chicken house. The farmer is better off with a 12 gauge, since he can also use it come deer season. The camper, however, would do well to stick to a 20 gauge, so the entire family can comfortably shoot the gun.

As for safety, the break action can't be beat. Simply break it open and you can carry it around with no fear of an accidental discharge.

Another type of single-shot break action is the specially designed trap gun. These guns are fitted with ventilated ribs and are precision bored. They are very expensive and should only be considered by the serious trapshooter. Prices could range up to $20,000.

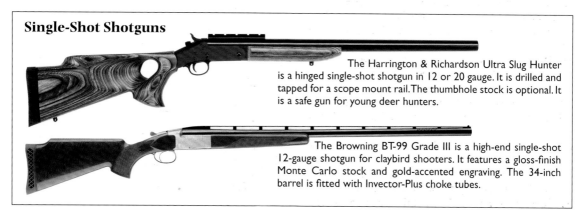

Single-Shot Shotguns

The Harrington & Richardson Ultra Slug Hunter is a hinged single-shot shotgun in 12 or 20 gauge. It is drilled and tapped for a scope mount rail. The thumbhole stock is optional. It is a safe gun for young deer hunters.

The Browning BT-99 Grade III is a high-end single-shot 12-gauge shotgun for claybird shooters. It features a gloss-finish Monte Carlo stock and gold-accented engraving. The 34-inch barrel is fitted with Invector-Plus choke tubes.

■ Side-by-Side and Over/Under Double

The side-by-side and over/under doubles are so similar in basic design that they should be discussed together. The side-by-side double, as its name indicates, wears its barrels next to each other. The over/under double has its two barrels stacked vertically, one on top of the other.

As a good, safe, and dependable hunting arm, the double is near the top of the list. The traditional doubles have two triggers, one for each barrel, or a nonselective single trigger. On the models with single nonselective triggers, the barrel with the more open choke always fires first. On a double-choked Modified and Full, for example, the trigger will always fire the Modified barrel first. Incidentally, these doubles, which are not too expensive, also have a matted rib and extractors, which means the fired shell must be removed manually.

The better and more expensive doubles have single selective triggers, which means the hunter can choose the barrel he wants to fire first. These doubles are generally equipped with automatic ejectors and frequently with ventilated ribs, particularly on the over/unders.

As mentioned above, the double is a traditional hunting arm and a top choice for small game, upland game, and waterfowl. Its advantages are many. First, it is the safest hunting gun. To tell if it is loaded, simply break it and take a glance. When hunting in wet and sloppy weather, you can also tell at a glance if the bores are obstructed in any way. You also have the choice of two chokes to control the shot pattern. And another factor to keep in mind is that for the same barrel length, the overall length of the double is a few inches shorter than autoloaders and pumps. It also balances better because there is more weight between the hands.

Doubled-Barreled Shotguns

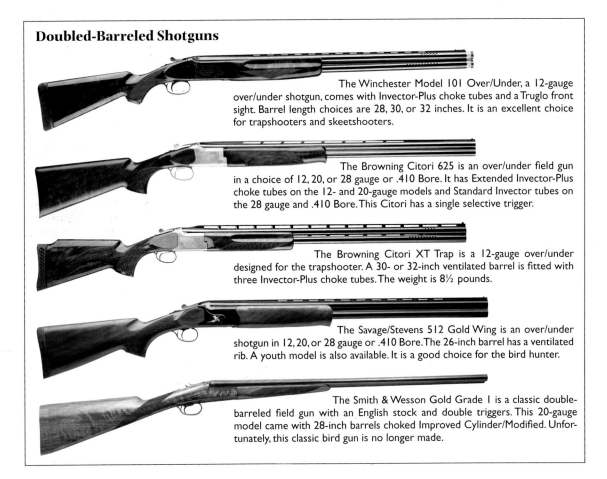

The Winchester Model 101 Over/Under, a 12-gauge over/under shotgun, comes with Invector-Plus choke tubes and a Truglo front sight. Barrel length choices are 28, 30, or 32 inches. It is an excellent choice for trapshooters and skeetshooters.

The Browning Citori 625 is an over/under field gun in a choice of 12, 20, or 28 gauge or .410 Bore. It has Extended Invector-Plus choke tubes on the 12- and 20-gauge models and Standard Invector tubes on the 28 gauge and .410 Bore. This Citori has a single selective trigger.

The Browning Citori XT Trap is a 12-gauge over/under designed for the trapshooter. A 30- or 32-inch ventilated barrel is fitted with three Invector-Plus choke tubes. The weight is 8½ pounds.

The Savage/Stevens 512 Gold Wing is an over/under shotgun in 12, 20, or 28 gauge or .410 Bore. The 26-inch barrel has a ventilated rib. A youth model is also available. It is a good choice for the bird hunter.

The Smith & Wesson Gold Grade 1 is a classic double-barreled field gun with an English stock and double triggers. This 20-gauge model came with 28-inch barrels choked Improved Cylinder/Modified. Unfortunately, this classic bird gun is no longer made.

The Lovely 28

The late Bob Brister, an expert wingshooter and former *Field & Stream* gun editor, once said, "It's not how much shot you throw up in the air, it's where the shot goes that's important." Bob was on target. I've learned to tolerate recoil, but lately I've fallen in love with skeetshooting with my 28-gauge SKB over/under. The gun is lighter, kicks less, handles easier with a slimmer design, and my scores are even a tad better than when I use my 20-gauge double. For bird hunting over dogs, the 28 gauge is a great choice.

Actual selection of a double depends a great deal on your budget. The better doubles with the more desirable features cost more. There are some basic guidelines to follow, however. If you're an average hunter who gets out about a half-dozen times a year and who sticks mainly to small game and game birds, one of the cheaper doubles should fill the bill. If the choice of barrel chokes to be fired first is important to you, get a double-trigger model. You may have to look hard for a double-trigger model today. Not many are available and they tend to be expensive. Otherwise, a single nonselective trigger will work just as well.

Some hunters claim the single nonselective trigger is a handicap, since you have no choice of which barrel to shoot first. But, looking at the problem realistically, nine times out of 10 a hunter will want to shoot the open-choke barrel first anyway, since small game and birds are likely to be close when he gets that first shot. The double-trigger model does have one edge over the

single nonselective trigger, and that's for the hunter who occasionally shoots trap with the tighter-choked barrel.

If you can afford the extra cash, you can avoid making the above decision by getting a double with a single selective trigger. Then, by manipulating a button near the tang safety, you have a quick choice of which barrel to shoot first—open or tight choke. If you do a great deal of small-game hunting, from cottontails to waterfowl, with some trap and skeet tossed in, it would be worth the extra money to pick a shotgun with a selective trigger.

Should your gun be a side-by-side or an over/under? Here again, it's largely a matter of personal preference. Some shooters like the single sighting plane of the over/under. If you have spent a great deal of time shooting a rifle or pump shotgun, you may also prefer the over/under. Other hunters like the traditional quick-handling feel of a side-by-side. Your best bet is to handle both types of guns and let "feel" be the deciding factor.

A number of companies, including Browning, SKB, Beretta, Krieghoff, Ljutic, Perazzi, and Winchester, also make over/unders with interchangeable barrels. Nearly all include screw-in choke tubes.

■ The Pump Shotgun

The pump gun is likely the most popular shotgun for hunting, though in the past decade it has been getting some stiff competition from the increasing number of over/unders and, to a lesser degree, side-by-side doubles introduced to the shooting public.

This manually operated repeater, however, has some distinct advantages. Since it is cheaper to manufacture, the pump can be sold at a lower price—usually less than a good double. Some hunters, particularly waterfowlers, like the magazine capacity of three or more

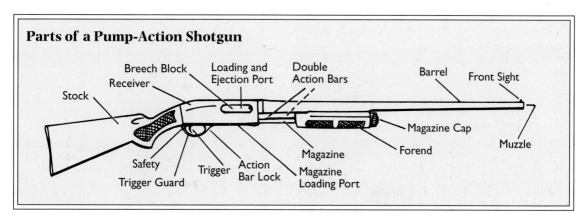

Parts of a Pump-Action Shotgun

Stock · Receiver · Breech Block · Loading and Ejection Port · Double Action Bars · Barrel · Front Sight · Magazine Cap · Muzzle · Forend · Magazine · Safety · Trigger · Action Bar Lock · Magazine Loading Port · Trigger Guard

How a Pump-Action Shotgun Works

1 • With the gun loaded and cocked, pulling the trigger trips the sear, releasing the hammer to strike the firing pin and fire the shell.

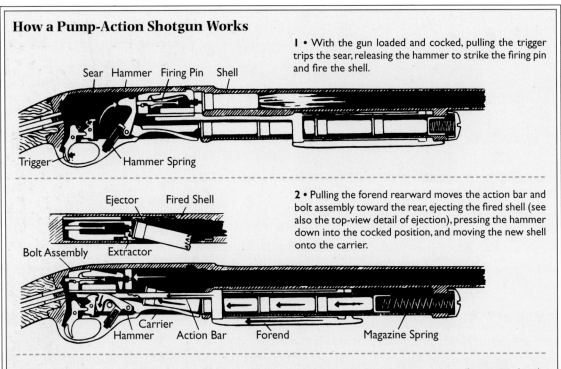

Sear   Hammer   Firing Pin   Shell

Trigger   Hammer Spring

2 • Pulling the forend rearward moves the action bar and bolt assembly toward the rear, ejecting the fired shell (see also the top-view detail of ejection), pressing the hammer down into the cocked position, and moving the new shell onto the carrier.

Ejector   Fired Shell

Bolt Assembly   Extractor

Carrier
Hammer   Action Bar   Forend   Magazine Spring

3 • A detail of the carrier mechanism shows how the bolt assembly at its rearmost position engages the carrier dog. As the bolt assembly moves forward, it moves the carrier dog downward, pivoting the carrier and new shell up into loading position. At the same time, the shell latch moves to the right to hold the remaining shells in the magazine.

Bolt Assembly

Carrier
Carrier Dog

Carrier
Carrier Dog   Shell Latch

4 • As the forend action bar and bolt assembly continue to move forward, the new shell is pushed into the chamber, and the sear engages the hammer, locking it. At the final movement of the forend, the slide continues forward, pushing the locking block up to lock the action for firing.

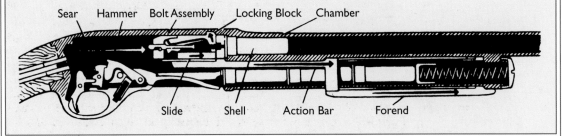

Sear   Hammer   Bolt Assembly   Locking Block   Chamber

Slide   Shell   Action Bar   Forend

Pump-Action Shotguns

The Weatherby PA-08 is a pump shotgun that comes in several models chambered for 12 and 20 gauge. A waterfowl version is camouflaged and a slug gun model is available with scope mounts and a rifled barrel.

The Remington 870 Wingmaster, a long-time favorite of sportsmen, is available in several models in 12, 20, and 28 gauge and .410 Bore. The 870 comes in a tactical design as well as pump guns for waterfowlers, turkey hunters, and claybird shooters.

The Mossberg 510 Mini, a pump shotgun in 20 gauge and .410 Bore, is a good choice for young shooters. With a synthetic stock and an 18½-inch barrel, the weight is only 5 pounds.

The Winchester SXP Turkey Hunter, a 12-gauge pump, has a 3½-inch chamber to give a maximum range for turkeys. It has an Invector-Plus Extra Full turkey choke tube. This specialized model has a 24-inch barrel and Truglo fiber-optic adjustable sights. The receiver is also drilled and tapped for scope bases.

shells. It's also fast and offers a single sighting plane. Most well-known manufacturers produce shotguns with screw-in choke tubes, so the choke on your shotgun can be changed quickly and easily in the field. If you don't like any choke device in or on your muzzle, you can always get a pump that will take interchangeable barrels. A pump with a couple of interchangeable barrels makes a dandy combination. For example, there isn't much that a shotgun hunter can't handle if he has one 28-inch Full choke barrel and one 26-inch Improved Cylinder barrel. By simply switching barrels, he'll do well on the trap range with the tight choke and do equally well with the open choke on upland game.

Those who prefer doubles will point out that pumps are too long, the muzzle too heavy, and they don't have the slim feel and handling qualities of a fine double. This is all true to a degree, but it actually all boils down to the fact that you can get an extremely well-made pump shotgun for the price of a fair double.

■ The Autoloader

The autoloading, or automatic, shotgun works on one of two principles: recoil or gas. The accompanying illustrations show step by step how each type of mechanism works. Both types work well and both are equally acceptable in the field. Remington uses gas operation in its Model 1100, as does Browning with its Silver Models.

The autoloading shotgun has all the advantages and disadvantages of the pump. The only difference is that manual operation after each shot is eliminated with the autoloader, which means faster firepower.

When is this fast firepower really needed? It's difficult to say. The average small-game hunter can get by without an automatic and, actually, he's better off with a gun that requires some manual manipulation between shots for safety's sake. The small-game and bird hunter rarely gets the chance to cut loose with more than two shots and the speed with which he gets off those two shots is not as critical as some hunters believe.

Parts of an Autoloading Shotgun

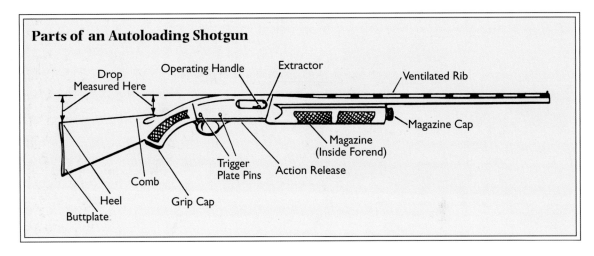

The autoloader, however, may be preferred by waterfowlers and skeetshooters. Duck hunters often have the chance to get off extra shots and they want to fire those second and third shots fast when a mallard discovers he's been had and retreats. And the skeet-shooter who is having trouble breaking doubles will appreciate the autoloader since all he has to do is squeeze the trigger to get off a second shot.

Autoloading Shotguns

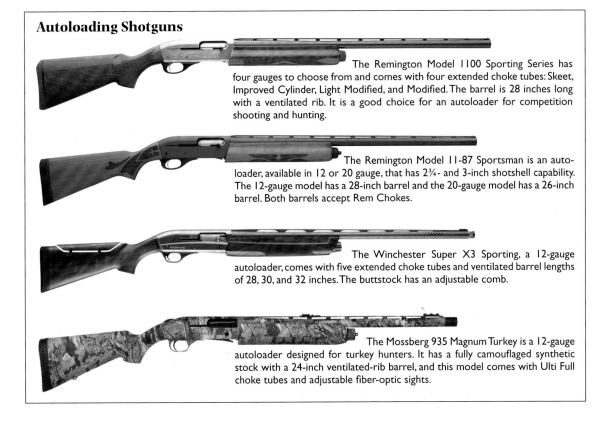

The Remington Model 1100 Sporting Series has four gauges to choose from and comes with four extended choke tubes: Skeet, Improved Cylinder, Light Modified, and Modified. The barrel is 28 inches long with a ventilated rib. It is a good choice for an autoloader for competition shooting and hunting.

The Remington Model 11-87 Sportsman is an auto-loader, available in 12 or 20 gauge, that has 2¾- and 3-inch shotshell capability. The 12-gauge model has a 28-inch barrel and the 20-gauge model has a 26-inch barrel. Both barrels accept Rem Chokes.

The Winchester Super X3 Sporting, a 12-gauge autoloader, comes with five extended choke tubes and ventilated barrel lengths of 28, 30, and 32 inches. The buttstock has an adjustable comb.

The Mossberg 935 Magnum Turkey is a 12-gauge autoloader designed for turkey hunters. It has a fully camouflaged synthetic stock with a 24-inch ventilated-rib barrel, and this model comes with Ulti Full choke tubes and adjustable fiber-optic sights.

How a Gas-Operated Shotgun Works

1 • Starting with the gun cocked and loaded, squeezing the trigger releases the hammer, which strikes the firing pin and fires the shell.

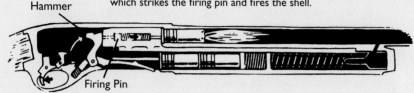

2 • The gas generated by the fired shell is metered down through the gas port in the barrel into the cylinder. The pressure of the gas in the cylinder then pushes the piston and connecting rod rearward, moving the bolt from the chamber. As the bolt travels rearward, it recocks the hammer and opens the carrier lock.

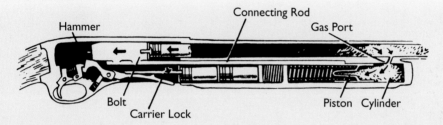

3 • Further rearward travel of the bolt ejects the spent shell through the side opening, and the magazine spring pushes a fresh shell onto the carrier.

4 • The piston spring starts the piston forward, moving the bolt forward, and pivoting the carrier to bring the new shell into loading position. As the bolt moves all the way forward, it loads the new shell into the chamber. Spent gas escapes through the port.

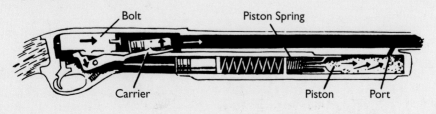

How a Recoil-Operated Shotgun Works

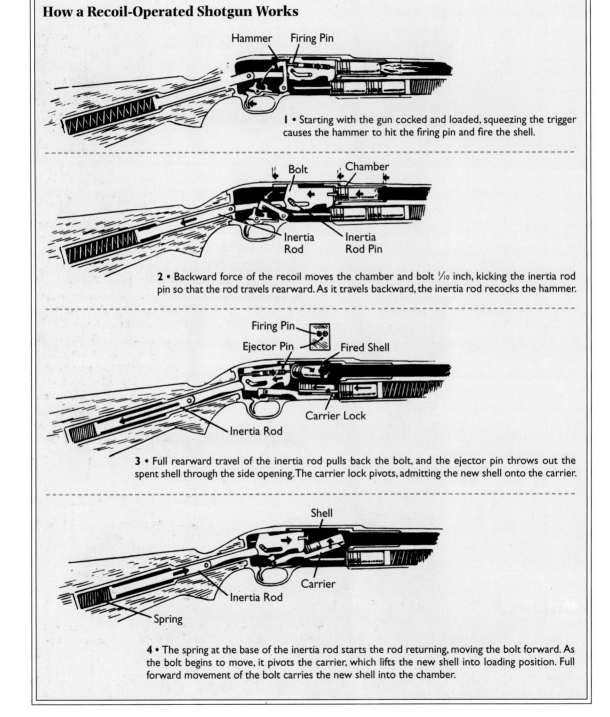

1 • Starting with the gun cocked and loaded, squeezing the trigger causes the hammer to hit the firing pin and fire the shell.

2 • Backward force of the recoil moves the chamber and bolt $1/10$ inch, kicking the inertia rod pin so that the rod travels rearward. As it travels backward, the inertia rod recocks the hammer.

3 • Full rearward travel of the inertia rod pulls back the bolt, and the ejector pin throws out the spent shell through the side opening. The carrier lock pivots, admitting the new shell onto the carrier.

4 • The spring at the base of the inertia rod starts the rod returning, moving the bolt forward. As the bolt begins to move, it pivots the carrier, which lifts the new shell into loading position. Full forward movement of the bolt carries the new shell into the chamber.

The Bolt Action

As far as fast-handling qualities on small game and birds go, bolt actions are at the bottom of the list and this may be the reason very few are even built today. They work out best where fast shooting isn't involved. Hunters in states where rifles are not allowed for deer hunting, for example, may find a bolt action a good choice if it's fitted with iron sights or a scope and used with shotgun slugs. It's also a more than adequate choice for farmers who want an inexpensive shotgun to protect crops and stock from predators and pests.

Muzzleloading Shotgun

Muzzleloading shotguns, though not as popular as muzzleloading rifles and handguns, have claimed a growing number of enthusiasts in recent years. Quite a few shooters hunt with them—though such guns are slow to load—and quite a few shooters compete in muzzleloading trap and skeet matches. The supply of shootable antiques began to dwindle quite some time ago, and most of the muzzleloading smoothbores in use today are new, factory-made guns. Now and then you may see a flintlock, but caplocks are the general rule.

A few are single barreled, which means they're single shots, of course, but most are side-by-side doubles. Quality varies widely, and it's true that you get what you pay for. Good ones, mostly imported, cost no more (and sometimes less) than breechloading shotguns of comparable quality, and are available from Cabela's, Davide Pedersoli, and a few other companies.

For Upland Hunters

If you hunt pheasants and grouse and you can't make up your mind about shot size, pick No. 7½. In either 12 or 20 gauge, it's a good all-around shot size for most upland species. For quail and woodcock in thick alders, try No. 8 field loads in a skeet-choked gun. For rabbit hunters, No. 6 shot will do the job.

Before loading such a shotgun, all oil should be removed with a dry patch, and the nipple—or nipples, if it's a double—should be cleared by firing several caps to remove any residual oil from the breech area. Then, pour the powder charge down the barrel. If you're using a 12 gauge for upland hunting, this would be a 3-dram charge of FFg black powder or a bulk charge of Pyrodex from the same measure setting. Most shotgunning is done with loads measured in drams, but, in case you're wondering, 82 grains is the same as 3 drams. The traditional wad column consists of an over-powder card, a couple of filler wads, the load of shot, and an over-shot wad. In this upland load, 1 to 1¼ ounces of shot will work well.

Some shooters use one-piece plastic wads, but you'll get better results with the traditional wad column or a combination of the traditional and contemporary. If you choose the latter, use the over-powder wad and fillers for a cushion, but top them with a plastic shot pouch. This will tighten your pattern. After pouring in the shot, still use an over-powder wad to hold the load in. Then, with the nipples capped, just cock the gun and fire away.

Double-Barreled Shotguns

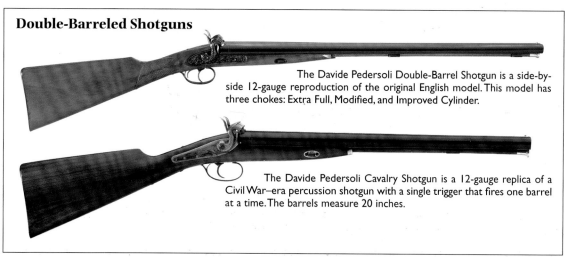

The Davide Pedersoli Double-Barrel Shotgun is a side-by-side 12-gauge reproduction of the original English model. This model has three chokes: Extra Full, Modified, and Improved Cylinder.

The Davide Pedersoli Cavalry Shotgun is a 12-gauge replica of a Civil War–era percussion shotgun with a single trigger that fires one barrel at a time. The barrels measure 20 inches.

GAUGE AND SHOT SIZE

The system of referring to shotguns by gauges was started many years ago. The inside diameter of a shotgun's bore was designated by the number of lead balls that would fit the bore and would make up 1 pound. For example, a round lead ball that would fit the bore of a 12 gauge would weigh ½2 pound, and 12 of these balls would weigh 1 pound. A 20 gauge would take 20 lead balls that would weigh 1 pound, and so on. The .410 is the only departure from this system. The .410 is not a gauge at all, but the actual measurement in inches of the diameter of the bore.

The accompanying illustrations show in actual size the diameters of shotgun bores in the common gauges. Gauge is also converted into measurement in inches.

■ The 12 Gauge, An All-Around Shotgun

The typical hunter looks for one shotgun that he can shoot well and use on everything from small game to deer. There is no doubt that such an all-around shotgun has to be a 12 gauge. In the early 1900s, the 10 gauge with 1¼ ounces of shot was a hot item and considered a good choice for an all-around gauge, but modern shotshells have changed the scene. Today, the 12 gauge can do anything the 10 gauge did, and sometimes do it better.

Gunning for small game and upland birds, a hunter can get by very well with the standard 2¾-inch, 12-gauge shotshell loaded with 1¼ ounces of shot. The waterfowl hunter who takes his birds at greater range should use the 12-gauge, 2¾-inch magnum load with 1½ ounces of shot or the 3-inch magnum load with 1⅜

to 1⅞ ounces of shot. If it's deer you're after, use the 2¾-inch magnums loaded with 12 pellets of 00 buckshot, or the 3-inch magnum with 15 pellets of 00 buckshot or 10 pellets of 000 buckshot. Shotgun slugs are another option.

The 12-gauge shotgun, however, is heavier and bulkier than guns in the smaller gauges. The ammunition is also bigger and heavier to carry. This may not mean much to the duck hunter sitting in a blind, but the upland gunner who carries his shotgun all day may find the smaller gauges more suitable.

■ The 16 Gauge

The 16 gauge shotgun simply refuses to die, even though the 12 gauge has it beat as an all-around gauge and the 20 gauge comes off as a better choice for a light, quick-handling shotgun for small game and birds. Some hunters claim the 16 gauge is a good compromise between the 12 and 20 gauge, but this is a tough argument to prove.

The standard 16-gauge load carries 1⅛ ounces of shot, exactly the same as the 2¾-inch, 20-gauge magnum load, and ⅛ ounce less than the standard 12-gauge load. The 2¾-inch, 16-gauge magnum shell has 1¼ ounces of shot, the same as the standard 12-gauge field load and the 20-gauge, 3-inch magnum.

True, the 16-gauge gun is a bit lighter than the 12 gauge, but it's not as light as a 20 gauge. What does all this mean? If you have a 16 gauge, keep it and you will be happy with it. But if you're buying a new shotgun, you're better off narrowing your selection down to the 12 or 20 gauge.

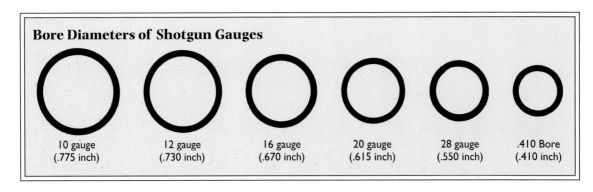

Bore Diameters of Shotgun Gauges

| 10 gauge (.775 inch) | 12 gauge (.730 inch) | 16 gauge (.670 inch) | 20 gauge (.615 inch) | 28 gauge (.550 inch) | .410 Bore (.410 inch) |

The 20 Gauge

The 20-gauge shotgun makes the grade as a top choice for all-around upland gunning and waterfowl shooting over decoys. It's lighter and slimmer than the 12 gauge, which makes it a faster-handling gun and a more comfortable one to carry in pheasant fields and through briar patches. The ammunition is also lighter to carry.

And it's a fact that most upland game is shot at under 30 yards, so the 20 gauge has more than adequate killing range. The standard 20-gauge load carries 1 ounce of shot, which is enough for just about all upland hunting. If a hunter expects to take birds under tougher conditions, he can use the 20-gauge, 2¾-inch magnum load with 1⅛ ounces of shot. For ducks over decoys, the 20-gauge, 3-inch magnum is the ticket. In fact, the 3-inch magnum load will also do the job at pass shooting.

Hunters who have both 12- and 20-gauge guns in their racks admit that most often they will pick the 20 gauge when heading for favorite rabbit patches and grouse covers.

The 28 Gauge and .410

The 28 gauge seems to have a growing number of fans and it's with good reason. The 28-gauge shotgun is slim and light with not much recoil. On a skeet range, it is a pure joy to shoot. For the average upland gunner, the 28 gauge may not be big enough. The skilled shooter, however, should take a closer look. The 28 gauge is available in a load with ⅞ ounce of shot, which makes it adequate for woodcock, quail, doves, and similar birds. If you're shooting over dogs, the 28 gauge is more than enough gun.

The .410 is another load that has limited use. It's fine for the smaller species that can be taken at close range, but it's not recommended for anything else. True, at one time or another, a hunter has been seen knocking down pheasants with a .410—but these men are generally skilled shotgunners. The average hunter would be far better off with a 12 or 20 gauge. The same reasoning can be used to discourage a parent from buying his child a .410. A wiser choice for a youngster would be a light 20 gauge.

Gauges for Trap and Skeet

When it comes to shooting claybirds, whether on official trap and skeet ranges or in a wooded area with a buddy tossing the birds out with a hand trap, almost any shotgun can be pressed into service for fun and practice. But serious trapshooters and skeetshooters stick to proven combinations.

On the trap range, for example, nearly all shooting is done with a 12-gauge gun. The barrel is 30 inches long, bored Full choke, and wears a ventilated rib.

The skeetshooter goes to the opposite extreme. He generally starts with a 12-gauge gun, the most popular for the beginner at skeet. But he can vary his gauges, since regulated skeet matches are broken down into four events: the 12 gauge, the 20 gauge, the 28 gauge, and the .410. As the skeetshooter improves at the game, he feels obliged to go to the smaller gauges.

The most common skeet gun has a 26-inch barrel that is bored Skeet, which is a choke that falls between Improved Cylinder and Cylinder.

Selecting Shot Size: Lead Shot

Shot (the pellets in a shotshell) is normally made of lead, a relatively cheap metal and one that's soft enough that it won't score gun barrels or damage choke construction. Being heavy, it has good ballistic qualities. It's an ideal metal for the pellets used in most types of shotgunning. Everyone agrees about that, but the subject of the best shot size for a given type of game often starts arguments. Some grouse hunters, for example, prefer shot as large as No. 7½ or even No. 6, claiming the larger sizes plow through foliage well. Others prefer shot as small as No. 9 since a lot more No. 9s go into a shell, and a dense pattern of shot is more likely to put some pellets into the mark.

Shotgun Guidelines

With any gauge, shotshells of a given nominal length should not be fired in a gun the chamber length of which is shorter than the fired shell length, such as a 3-inch shell fired in a 2¾-inch chamber. In a shotgun chambered for .410 Bore, do not use any centerfire metallic cartridges.

In Shotgun Chambered For	Do Not Use These Shells
10 gauge	12 gauge
12 gauge	16 gauge
12 gauge	20 gauge
16 gauge	20 gauge
20 gauge	28 gauge

An accompanying chart, Shotshell Selector, offers advice formulated by experts. Other charts show the comparative shot sizes, plus the average number of pellets per ounce.

Selecting Shot Size: Steel Shot, Bismuth, and Tungsten

Lead shot has one serious drawback. The fired pellets fall into marshes and fields, where they are picked up as grit by feeding waterfowl. The ingested lead is poisonous. Retained in the gizzards of the birds, it kills large numbers of ducks and geese. In some areas, the problem is insignificant. The diet of the birds is one factor. The hardness of the marsh is another, since lead sinks into soft mud and the birds cannot get it. All the same, widespread poisoning of waterfowl by lead shot has mandated the use of a substitute material in shotshells for duck and goose shooting. No truly ideal nontoxic substitute has yet been found, but steel shot—the subject of research and development programs at ammunition companies for a number of years—has been significantly improved and is now supplied by the major manufacturers in waterfowl loads.

Since steel is only about 70 percent as heavy as lead, it requires more space in a shell than an equal amount of lead. Whereas an average of 135 No. 4 lead pellets make an ounce, you need about 192 steel pellets of the same size to make an ounce. A 1¼-ounce load of steel shot takes up so much more space in a shotshell that the makers have developed new powders that take up less space, as well as a special plastic wad that merely acts as a gas seal and shot cup. There is no cushion section, and the shot cup is long enough to cover the entire length of the shot column. This protects the walls of the gun barrel from the hard steel pellets as they travel through the bore.

Because steel is lighter than lead, it is less efficient ballistically. To offset the loss of retained velocity and energy, larger shot must be used. Manufacturers have developed roughly equivalent steel loads in which there is only a small sacrifice in the number of pellets. In an ounce of No. 4 lead shot, for instance, there are 135 pellets; in an ounce of No. 2 steel shot there are 125. A 2¾-inch, 12-gauge shell has an average of 169 pellets in a 1¼-ounce No. 4 lead load, 156 pellets in a 1¼-ounce No. 2 steel load. Laboratory and field tests by Remington, Winchester, and Federal have shown that appropriate steel loads (No. 2 steel as a substitute for No. 4 lead, for instance) lose more velocity and energy than lead shot at 40 and 50 yards, but the difference isn't drastic. In addition, 3-inch magnum 12-gauge shells with steel shot have become available, but you need not switch to long magnum steel loads in a situation that would call for 2¾-inch lead-shot loads. Assuming you have a gun chambered for 3-inch shells, you use such steel-shot

Shotshell Selector (Lead Shot Unless Indicated as Steel)

Game	Type of Shell	Size
Ducks	Magnum or Hi-Power	4, 5, 6, Steel 2, 4
Geese	Magnum or Hi-Power	BB, 2, 4, Steel BB, 1, 2
Pheasants	Magnum or Hi-Power	5, 6, 7½
Quail	Hi-Power or Field Load	7½, 8, 9
Ruffed grouse and Hungarian partridge	Hi-Power or Field Load	6, 7½, 8
Other grouse, chukar partridge	Hi-Power or Field Load	5, 6, 7½
Doves and pigeons	Hi-Power or Field Load	6, 7½, 8, 9
Rabbits	Hi-Power or Field Load	4, 5, 6, 7½
Woodcock, snipe, rail	Field Load	7½, 8, 9
Squirrels	Hi-Power or Field Load	4, 5, 6
Wild turkey	Magnum or Hi-Power	2, 4, 5, 6
Crows	Hi-Power or Field Load	5, 6, 7½
Fox	Magnum or Hi-Power	BB, 2, 4

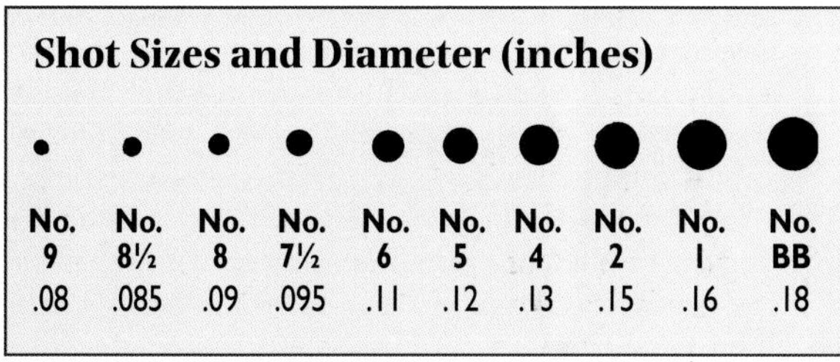

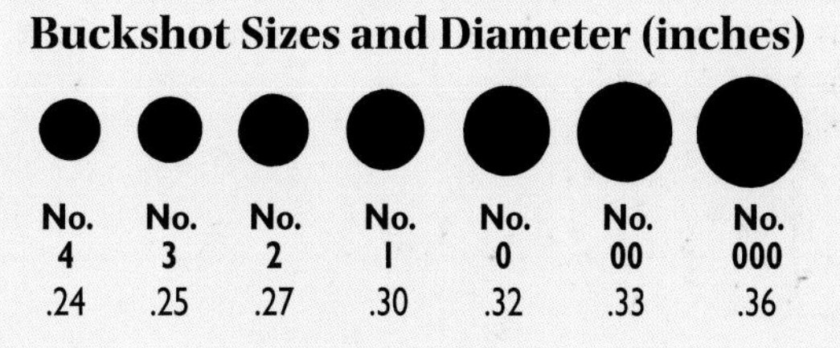

Shot Sizes and Diameter (inches)

No. 9	No. 8½	No. 8	No. 7½	No. 6	No. 5	No. 4	No. 2	No. 1	No. BB
.08	.085	.09	.095	.11	.12	.13	.15	.16	.18

Buckshot Sizes and Diameter (inches)

No. 4	No. 3	No. 2	No. 1	No. 0	No. 00	No. 000
.24	.25	.27	.30	.32	.33	.36

Approximate Number of Pellets in a Given Charge

The exact number of pellets can vary depending upon the brand and lot.

Shot Size	2 oz.	1⅞ oz.	1⅝ oz.	1½ oz.	1⅜ oz.	1¼ oz.	1⅛ oz.	1 oz.	⅞ oz.	¾ oz.	½ oz.
No. 2	180	169	146	135	124	113	102	90	79	68	45
No. 4	270	253	221	202	185	169	152	135	118	101	67
No. 5	340	319	277	255	234	213	192	170	149	128	85
No. 6	450	422	396	337	309	281	253	225	197	169	112
No. 7½	700	656	568	525	481	437	393	350	306	262	175
No. 8	820	769	667	615	564	513	462	410	359	308	205
No. 9	1,170	1,097	951	877	804	731	658	585	512	439	292

loads only where you would use 3-inch magnum loads of lead shot. Where standard lead-shot loads are used, standard steel-shot loads have enough power.

However, the appropriate shot size obviously differs with steel. From tests done by the manufacturers, rules of size have been formulated for switching to steel shot. Essentially, you go up one size for a given use. Shells are commonly available with several sizes of steel shot—No. 4, 2, 1, and BB. The three smallest sizes—No. 4, 2, and 1—are most often used. Generally speaking, the BB size is used for ultralong-range pass shooting at geese. That makes the guidelines easy: where you would use No. 5 or 6 lead shot, use No. 4 steel; where you would use No. 4 lead shot, use No. 2 steel; where you would use No. 2 lead shot, use No. 1 steel. To put it another way, use No. 4 steel for ducks over decoys; No. 2 steel for close-range shooting at geese over decoys and for longer-range pass shooting at ducks; and No. 1 or BB size for pass shooting at geese.

Although steel is ballistically inferior to lead, it has one advantage. Because the pellets are so hard, they suffer very little deformation as they pass through a gun's bore. Therefore, they produce slightly tighter patterns than lead. Some hunters have found that they get

better results with steel by switching from Full to Modified choke for pass shooting, except when the range is quite long. As for the power of steel shot at waterfowling ranges, field tests have proved that it will bring down ducks and geese at 50 yards or so just as well as lead if the pattern is properly centered on the target. The average shotgunner shouldn't be trying for ducks or geese at ranges beyond 50 yards.

A widely publicized drawback is the supposed harm that steel shot will do to a shotgun barrel. It is true that double-barreled guns and even some of the older repeaters with relatively thin or soft-steel barrels can suffer minor damage—either the barrel rings or bulges in the choke area. While these effects aren't hazardous, such guns should be reserved for other kinds of hunting. Most modern guns will not be harmed by steel shot. If in doubt, consult the manufacturer of your shotgun.

Tungsten and bismuth are two developments in the search for a nontoxic shot with ballistics comparable to lead. Tungsten shot was introduced by Federal Cartridge Company in 1997. It is actually tungsten-iron shot, a blend of two metal powders, 40 percent tungsten and 60 percent iron, pressed into the shape of a sphere. The pellets are then sintered or bonded together by a heating process. The shot is then coated with a rust inhibitor. Tungsten is harder than lead, steel, and bismuth. Tungsten-iron shot is 30 percent denser than steel, 94 percent as dense as lead, and 10 percent denser than bismuth.

Bismuth shot is another nontoxic shot available to waterfowl hunters. Bismuth shot is formed from an alloy composed of 97 percent bismuth and 3 percent tin. Bismuth is found in deposits with tin, copper, tungsten, gold, silver, and lead, and then is separated during a refining process. Bismuth shot is 91 percent as dense as lead, a considerable improvement over steel's 71 percent. Bismuth is no longer available in commercial shotshells, but some manufacturers still sell bismuth shot for reloaders.

Remington's search for effective nontoxic shot led to the development of Hevi-Shot, which is a mixture of tungsten, nickel, and iron. Hevi-Shot is the heaviest of all the nontoxic shot and it's even heavier than lead. Hevi-Shot should only be used in shotguns built for steel shot.

SHOTGUN BARREL AND CHOKE

▨ The Barrel

Many years ago, the most popular shotgun had a 30-inch Full choke barrel. Today, because of modern shotshells with plastic shot collars and protectors that give tighter patterns, the No. 1 choice is a 28-inch barrel with Modified choke. And upland gunners are even switching to 24- and 26-inch barrels with Improved Cylinder choke. All this makes sense. A shorter barrel means a lighter gun that is easier to carry and faster to shoot in thick upland cover.

Years ago, most shotgunners believed that barrels 36 inches and longer shot harder and farther than shorter barrels. This was true in the black-powder days when long barrels were required for full velocity to develop before the shot reached the muzzle. Now, with modern smokeless powder, full velocity is reached in less than 24 inches. In fact, velocity in a 36-inch barrel is slowed down a bit because once the powder is burned and full velocity is reached within 24 inches, friction takes over between the shot charge and bore, which decreases velocity.

If some hunters are still convinced they can knock down more game with long barrels, it is only because such barrels give a longer sighting plane and afford better balance and steadiness of swing. This is one reason for the popularity of 30- and 32-inch barrels on the trap range. Velocity has nothing to do with it.

As a general rule, a hunter is better off using as short a barrel as possible without sacrificing balance. Manufacturers know this and build their guns accordingly. (See accompanying Recommended Barrel Lengths chart.)

▨ The Choke

The choke on a shotgun is the amount of constriction in the bore of the barrel that is used to control the spread of the shot charge. The greater the constriction, which starts about 3 inches from the muzzle, the tighter the concentration of pellets during flight. Likewise, the less the constriction, the greater or wider the spread of pellets in flight.

The choke principle is easily understood by comparing it to a garden hose. Tighten the garden-hose nozzle and you'll get a narrow, heavy stream of water. Open it up and you'll get a wide spray. The choke and the garden-hose nozzle work on basically the same principle.

Chokes on today's shotgun barrels range from Full choke, which has the most constriction and

Recommended Barrel Lengths for Various Types of Shooting

Types of Shooting	Barrel Length (inches)
Long-range duck or goose	30 to 32
Waterfowl over decoys	28 to 30
Pheasant or grouse	25 to 28
Rabbits or squirrels	25 to 28
Quail, doves, or woodcock	24 to 28
Turkey	28 or 30
Deer	22 to 28
Trapshooting	30 to 32
Skeetshooting	25 to 28
All-around shooting	28
Sporting clays	28 to 32

Determining a Barrel's Choke

Choke	Percentage of Shot in 30-Inch Circle at 40 Yards
Full	70–80
Improved Modified	65–70
Modified	55–60
Quarter	50–55
Improved Cylinder	45–50
Skeet No. 2	50–60
Skeet No. 1 (Cylinder)	35–40

consequently throws the tightest concentration of shot, to Cylinder, which means no choke at all—that is, no constriction at any point in the bore. Listing them by their common names, the popular range of chokes includes Full, Modified, Improved Modified, Improved Cylinder, Skeet, and Cylinder.

The constriction in the bore is generally accomplished by reaming or swagging, but much more important than the method is the amount of constriction and its effect on shot spread and pattern. Choke is the difference between bore diameter and muzzle diameter measured in one-thousandths of an inch. This measurement is also referred to as points. For example, the bore of a 12-gauge barrel will measure .730 inch and a constriction of .035 inch near the muzzle will make it a Full choke barrel. You can also say the barrel has a 35-point constriction.

Unfortunately, bore diameters and constriction diameters often vary from manufacturer to manufacturer. For example, two 20-gauge guns, both stamped Modified choke but turned out by two different gunmakers, may have a constriction difference of as much as .025 inch, or 25 points. The result is, of course, that not all guns of the same choke will shoot identical patterns. One manufacturer's Full choke may throw a Modified pattern and vice versa. The only foolproof way of determining the choke of a shotgun is to pattern it.

Before patterning a shotgun, you should know that the choke of a shotgun is determined by the percentage of pellets from the particular shotshell load that falls within a 30-inch circle at 40 yards. The figures in the accompanying chart are generally accepted as standard guidelines in determining a barrel's choke.

So if you're having trouble with your shotgun, either missing birds with it or getting more than your share of cripples, it would be wise to pattern your gun and see exactly what choke you have and whether your pattern is too dense or sparse for the ranges at which you're shooting.

To pattern a shotgun, simply tack up a piece of paper that is 4 feet by 4 feet. Draw a small bull's-eye in the center of the paper, and then inscribe a 30-inch circle around it. Now, check the shotshell load you normally use and compute the number of pellets in it. Take a shot at 40 yards at the bull's-eye, count the pellet holes within the circle, and figure out the percentage that landed in the circle. Check this figure with the accompanying chart and you'll be able to determine the true choke of your shotgun, regardless of the size hole in the barrel or what is stamped on the barrel. Patterning your shotgun and knowing exactly what pattern it throws can be just as important as sighting-in a rifle, and no deer hunter should go afield without sighting-in his rifle.

It's important to note that these patterns are taken at 40 yards and that most game is taken at considerably closer ranges. In fact, the majority of small game and upland birds are shot at 30 yards or less. So that Full choke spread that looks great on paper at 40 yards would actually be much smaller and the pellets much more concentrated at, say, 25 yards. To the grouse hunter who rarely shoots birds at more than 25 yards, this would mean two things: a lot of misses, or, if he was an excellent shot, birds shot to pieces. What all this means is that the choke you select depends on the game you're hunting.

The hunter after grouse, rabbits, quail, and woodcock—which are all taken in fairly heavy cover—should use a Modified or Improved Cylinder choke, preferably the latter. If he's a waterfowl gunner, he should use a Modified or Full choke. Though most duck hunters would feel handicapped with a Modified choke, this would probably be a better choice.

For game such as turkeys, usually taken at greater ranges, a Full choke is the top choice. For all-around small-game and bird hunting, the Improved Cylinder or Modified choke comes off as the best compromise. With today's screw-in chokes, most shotguns are supplied with chokes covering the entire range of choke sizes.

■ How to Pattern a Shotgun

Imagine this upland hunting situation: A bird dog locks up on point and a pheasant hunter moves in for the shot. When he gets within 10 feet or so of the dog, a ringneck flushes straight up. Startled, the hunter immediately nails the bird with his shotgun. At such short range, the bird catches the full load of pellets from a Modified choke barrel or a screw-in choke labeled Modified. The result? The pheasant is raked so badly with pellets that it cannot be salvaged for the table.

This situation occurs all too frequently and pretty much for the same reason—many hunters simply do not know how their shotguns will pattern at various ranges. The result is that they will either miss long shots at game or blast birds apart at close ranges. They also assume that a barrel or a screw-in choke will throw a Modified pattern because it is stamped Modified. This isn't always true. There is only one way to find out what your shotgun will do at different ranges and that is to take your gun out and pattern it on paper. It's a simple job, and the results may surprise you.

As a reminder, the choke on a shotgun is the amount of constriction in the muzzle of the barrel or the screw-in choke that is used to control the spread of the shot charge. The greater the constriction, the tighter the concentration of pellets during flight. The less the constriction, the greater the spread of pellets during flight. And the degree of choke is determined by the percentage of pellets from a particular shotshell load that hit within a 30-inch circle at 40 yards.

The range to begin patterning is 40 yards. The only exceptions are the 28 gauge, the .410, and skeet chokes of all gauges—which should be patterned at 25 yards. To pattern your shotgun, you'll also have to know the approximate number of pellets in the shotshells you're using. You should always pattern your shotgun with the hunting loads you ordinarily use. You can get the number of pellets from most firearm catalogs or you can actually cut open a couple of shotshells and count them.

Targets are available with a printed 30-inch circle and a claybird for an aiming point. Such targets, however, are not necessary. Any sheet of paper measuring 4 feet by 4 feet will do. Just mark a spot in the center of the paper to use as an aiming point. You can make the frame of your target from 6-foot firing strips. The two uprights, which are sharpened and driven into the ground, measure a full 6 feet. The three cross members are 45 inches across. Use ordinary bulletin-board pushpins to hold the target in place.

Actual patterning is simple. Mark each target with the range and pertinent data about the hunting load you're using. For example, mark your targets as follows: 40 yards, Remington Express, 12 gauge, Modified, No. 6, 1¼ ounces.

Fire at least five shots, at a new target each time, at 40, 30, and 15 yards. Do this with each choke. After all the shooting is done, use a felt-tip marker and mark and count each pellet hole within the 30-inch circle. When you get this figure, divide it by the number of pellets in the shot charge and multiply it by 100. The answer will be your pattern percentage. Next, figure the average percentage of your five shots with each choke.

Another important factor should be mentioned here. The 30-inch circle must encompass the most pellet holes on the paper. If you're lucky, the aiming point on your target will result in putting the most pellets in the printed circle. If the densest part of your pattern is **not** within the circle, you must make a second circle encompassing the most pellet holes. Count the holes within this second circle and figure out the percentage.

For example, take the Remington Express 12-gauge loads with 1¼ ounces of No. 6 shot. The ammo maker says that this load has 276 pellets. When tested at 40 yards, the Modified barrel put 131 pellets into a 30-inch circle. Divide 276 into 131, multiply the answer by 100, and you'll get 47 percent.

Now this is where the whole patterning business gets tricky and why it is so important to pattern your own gun. According to firearm manufacturers, a Modified choke throws a 55–60 percent pattern at 40 yards, yet this particular barrel patterned 47 percent at 40 yards, roughly 10 percent less. Your Modified barrel may pattern at exactly 55 percent, or it may throw a denser pattern. Patterns will vary among the same chokes and even when you change shot size.

Actual Results of Patterning

Using 12-gauge Remington Express loads with 1¼ ounces of No. 6 shot

Range (yards)	Choke	Percentage
40	Modified	47
40	Improved Cylinder	40
40	Cylinder	37
30	Modified	80
30	Improved Cylinder	58
30	Cylinder	47
15	Modified	96
15	Improved Cylinder	95
15	Cylinder	95

For the results of my test with the Remington Express, see the accompanying chart. It's obvious, by comparing percentages, that these barrels do not jibe with some of the percentages listed by firearm manufacturers. At 40 yards, for example, the Modified and Improved Cylinder patterned more open than anticipated. This was especially surprising, because the Remington loads used the Power Piston wad and shot collar, which protects the shot from deformation as it travels through the barrel. These shot collars will frequently make a Modified choke throw a tight Modified or Full pattern. This, however, does not happen in all cases.

What conclusions can you draw from this patterning session? First, don't shoot game too close or you will needlessly load birds with too many pellets. If you shoot a lot of game over dogs, stick with Improved Cylinder or even Cylinder choke and let the birds get out at least 30 yards before shooting. And you can gain a great deal of new respect for Cylinder choke. It threw a good pattern and put only 11 pellets less than the Improved Cylinder in a 30-inch circle at 30 yards. And the 20-inch Cylinder barrel will make the gun a charm to handle in grouse country.

At 40 yards, which is a long shot in anyone's book, both the Modified and Improved Cylinder chokes threw killing patterns. This means that occasional misses at long ranges are probably the shooter's fault and not the gun's. The reason for misses on those long shots is easy to figure out: the shooter is not leading the birds enough and the shot charge is passing harmlessly behind them.

What all this means is that you are probably hunting with guns choked too tight. Most shooters should use their Modified barrels for claybird shooting and pass shooting at waterfowl. For pheasants, where a hunter has a chance to let the birds get out to 30 yards, stick with the Improved Cylinder barrel. When hunting grouse and woodcock in thick cover, use the 20-inch Cylinder barrel.

If you take the time to pattern your shotgun, you will know what your barrels and chokes will do. I strongly recommend that you go out and see how your shotgun stacks up on paper. There may be some surprises in store for you.

Mastering Shotgun Lead

A good wingshot will usually know when he is going to miss a bird or clay target the instant that he pulls the trigger. There are a whole bunch of reasons for missing, but they can all be boiled down to this: the shot simply doesn't feel right. Similarly, when the shot does feel right, you'll bust that bird nearly every time.

Always remember that your sight picture with a shotgun will never be better than the first time you pick up that bird with your swing. If you hesitate and then try to recover your lead or swing, you will likely miss.

There are three basic wingshooting techniques that can work for you, and the one that you choose depends on field conditions and your own shooting preference. Most shotgunners call them snap shooting, swing through, and sustained lead.

Snap Shooting: This technique relies on instinct and the hand/eye coordination of the shooter. Theoretically, a good quarterback should make an excellent wingshot. He throws the football where his receiver will intercept it. A snap shooter uses the same technique. Pick a spot where you think the bird will be and shoot. You must focus, point, and fire the instant the buttstock hits your shoulder. Snap shooting is a good technique for most upland gunning when quail and grouse flush close.

Swing Through: The easiest to master, the swing-through technique is also the most natural. The shooter focuses on the bird, swings the muzzle smoothly from behind and past the target, fires when the bead covers the target, and then follows through, continuously swinging. The shooter does not estimate lead. The lead becomes automatic with the swing through and the trigger pull. For this reason, there must be no hesitation in swing speed and trigger pull.

Sustained Lead: For high-flying birds such as ducks and geese, the sustained lead technique can be effective. The shooter estimates lead and swings well ahead of the target. Sustaining the swing, the shooter fires when he feels he has locked into the proper lead. Because the shotgun's muzzle is not moving as quickly as in the swing-through method, more lead is essential with this technique.

Pattern Your Shotgun for Turkeys

Turkeys make a tough target. They are difficult to see and even harder to kill. The head and neck are the only vital areas that ensure a fast, clean kill, but this will only happen if your shotgun throws a tight, dense shot pattern.

The best shotgun choice for turkeys is a 12-gauge magnum, though the 10 gauge is gaining some ground among turkey hunters. The best shot sizes are No. 2, 4, 5, or 6. The best shotgun chokes are Full, Extra Full, and Super Full.

Patterning your shotgun for turkey hunting is simply a matter of shooting your shotgun with various shot sizes at different ranges to determine the most effective combination.

To pattern your shotgun, you will need two loads of each shot size and six targets that show the full-size head and neck of a gobbler. Start by taking one shot at each target at 15, 25, and 40 yards.

With each load and choke combination, count the number of pellets in the vital area of the gobbler's head. Opinions vary on the number of pellets you will need in a vital area to put a turkey down, but you will need at least six to kill a turkey. Some experienced hunters, however, claim that a turkey hunter will need up to 30 pellets in a vital area to kill a gobbler quick and clean.

After you have tried all the different loads at 15, 25, and 40 yards, analyze your targets and count the pellets in the vital area. Determine which load gives you the densest pattern in the gobbler's head and neck. That's the load to use.

Remember that 40 yards is about the maximum shotgun range on gobblers, regardless of your choke and load combination. Any turkey farther than 40 yards is not in killing range and you should not take the shot.

There was a time when duck hunting was considered the most dangerous form of hunting. That's no longer true. Turkey hunting now accounts for most accidents. There are some good rules for turkey hunters to keep in mind:

- Never wear red, white, black, or light-blue clothing that could be visible to other hunters. These are the colors of a spring gobbler. Wear full camouflage, but avoid white socks or T-shirts, which might look like the white part of a gobbler.

- Use your turkey call in terrain where you can see at least 50 yards in every direction.

- Keep your back against a tree trunk, stump, or boulder that is higher than your head.

- If you see another turkey hunter approaching, stay still and whistle or shout loudly.

- Never sneak in on a turkey that is gobbling, and avoid using a call when hunters are nearby.

- If you use a decoy, position it so that you are not in any possible line of fire with it. Position the decoy so it can be seen from the sides, not from in front of or behind you. Use only hen decoys, never a fake gobbler.

This Winchester patterning target shows the head and neck of an adult gobbler. Vital and nonvital areas are based on an X-ray of an actual turkey.

Vital Areas

■ Bony skull and vertebrae (penetration will immobilize)

Ⓧ Aiming point and center of pattern

Non-Vital Areas

A Esophagus (gullet)	**D** Snood (dew bill)
B Trachea (windpipe)	**E** Loose neck skin
C Wattles	

■ Solving Shotgun Problems

Knowing the right barrel length and choke for your hunting is fine if you're in the process of buying a new gun. But what about the chap who already has a gun and is dissatisfied because the barrel is too long or the pattern it throws is too dense or too sparse? Suppose his favorite grouse gun has a 26-inch barrel with Improved Cylinder choke and he suddenly decides he wants to take up duck hunting. How does he get a tighter pattern out of it? Or suppose he wants to take his Full choke duck gun grouse hunting and wants a wider pattern, but is unwilling to have the shotgun bored out to Improved Cylinder. All of these problems can be solved one way or another. Let's take them one by one.

First, let's talk about the fellow who was told that a 30-inch barrel and Full choke was the greatest combination, but now he discovers that his barrel is hanging up on limbs and brush in heavy cover while hunting rabbits and grouse and that he's either missing his target or shooting it to pieces. He knows he needs a shorter barrel and a more open choke. There are a few ways he can solve his problem. One way that would involve no expense is to use brush loads (also called scatter loads), a special shotshell that has dividers separating the shot charge. At one time, manufacturers supplied these loads, but they are now hard to find. They can, however, be handloaded. Such a shotshell would open his choke

in one step. That means his Full choke could be turned into a Modified choke by simply changing ammunition. But, unfortunately, brush loads are usually only available in one shot size, generally No. 8. And the hunter still has the problem of the long barrel.

A better alternative would be to have his barrel cut down to 28 inches and bored Improved Cylinder or Modified. Generally, taking 2 inches off a barrel will still leave enough constriction to enable a gunsmith to open the choke. If the hunter wants to cut his 30-inch barrel down to 26 inches, he has a bigger problem. Taking 4 inches off a barrel will remove all constriction and he'll have a Cylinder bore, which may or may not be too open for his kind of hunting. It should be mentioned here that some hunters who have chopped 4 inches off their shotguns have found them to be deadly on upland game, probably because they were consistently shooting their game a lot closer than they realized. But if a hunter finds that a complete loss of choke in his gun is a handicap, he has no choice but to install a variable-choke device or have the barrel fitted for screw-in choke tubes.

As for the grouse hunter who has a 26-inch barrel with an Improved Cylinder choke and wants to start duck hunting, he has no choice but to install a variable-choke device. The same applies to the duck hunter with a Full choke gun who wants a more open choke for upland game, but still wants to be able to fall back on a

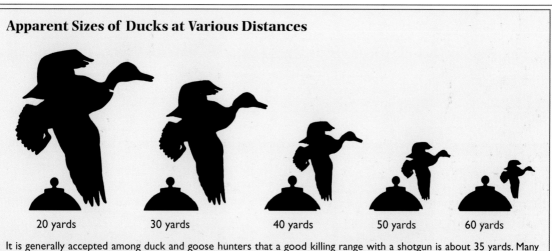

Apparent Sizes of Ducks at Various Distances

| 20 yards | 30 yards | 40 yards | 50 yards | 60 yards |

It is generally accepted among duck and goose hunters that a good killing range with a shotgun is about 35 yards. Many hunters, however, have difficulty judging distance. These illustrations, courtesy of Browning Arms, show what a duck looks like over your shotgun barrel at 20, 30, 40, 50, and 60 yards. Another good rule of thumb is that if your shotgun bead obliterates the duck's head or if the bead looks bigger than the duck's head, the bird is probably out of effective killing range.

Full choke for ducks. This explains the enormous popularity of the screw-in choke tubes that are now available on nearly all shotguns.

The only exception to the above cases are the shotguns produced to accept interchangeable barrels. With these, a hunter can buy a variety of barrels to suit his needs until his money runs out.

■ Shotgun Chokes

Variable-choke selectors, which are rarely seen today, are mechanical devices fitted to the muzzle of a shotgun that enable the shooter to quickly and simply change the choke from Extra Full to Cylinder, with a variety of choices in between.

The Cutts Compensator, which is no longer made, was a typical example of the interchangeable tube-type choke device. The main body of the device, which also served as a muzzle brake and reduced recoil, was fitted to the muzzle. A hunter who wanted to change his choke merely screwed in tubes of various degrees of constriction to give different patterns.

The collet-type variable chokes, which are rarely used today, used an adjustable nozzle-like affair on the muzzle to change the choke setting. The hunter simply turned a knurled ring to increase or decrease the constriction at the muzzle to change his choke and pattern.

The newer screw-in choke tubes have become enormously popular and most major gunmakers now offer them on shotguns under a variety of names. Winchester calls its choke-tube system Invector-Plus and Remington calls its system Rem Choke. All systems work basically the same way. The choke tube is threaded and seated in the muzzle with a wrench. Extra tubes with different chokes can be easily carried and replaced quickly in the field.

Hunters who can't make up their minds about the best choke for their gun, or who are determined to use one gun for all game, will find these choke tubes a good deal. With screw-in tubes, hunters can use the same gun for pass shooting at waterfowl at 50 yards and quail gunning at 20 yards.

These screw-in chokes offer another advantage as well. They give the hunter the option of having his barrel cut down to as much as 24 or 26 inches. This is

Shotgun Chokes

◀ Remington Rem Choke screw-in tubes offer a range of chokes, including Turkey Super Full, Turkey Extra Full, Modified, Improved Cylinder, Skeet, and Rifled Rem, which adds rifling and rotational stability to smoothbore barrels.

▶ Kick's High Flyer choke tube is a diagonally ported choke tube to reduce recoil by 25 percent. Designed for steel shot, this screw-in tube can also be used for all upland game. It installs easily without a wrench.

▼ The Remington Rem Choke Wingmaster HD (Heavy Density) is built to handle nontoxic shot and steel shot. This pass-shooting tube is choked Full. Other tubes include flooded timber choked Improved Cylinder, over decoys choked Modified, and turkey/predator choked Extra Full.

▶ RedHead choke tubes are made of stainless steel and are designed to screw in flush with the muzzle. Chokes include Full, X-Full Turkey, Skeet, Improved Cylinder, and Modified.

a definite asset, since there is no reason for a pump or autoloader to have a barrel longer than 26 inches. And a 24-inch barrel is fast and deadly on game such as quail and woodcock.

Even though these choke devices have the settings clearly indicated on them, it's still a good idea to check the pattern to make sure that it is doing the job it is supposed to do.

SHOTGUN STOCKS

The shotgunner—unlike the rifle shooter, who generally has plenty of time to snuggle up comfortably to his stock and squeeze off a careful shot—has a different set of problems to cope with. His game is almost always moving—running on the ground or taking to the air in a burst of wingbeats. He rarely has time to mount his gun carefully and shoot slowly. He is forced to focus on his target, snap the shotgun to his shoulder, start his swing, determine lead, and slap the trigger. Human reaction time, from the point of mounting the gun to pulling the trigger, has been clocked at ¼ second. For the average gunner, that's fast shooting.

What all this means is that the stock fit of a shotgun is very important, perhaps more so than with a rifle. It seems strange then that many hunters will go to great lengths to get a rifle stock that fits their physical frame, yet will grab any shotgun out of the rack and take it out for a day of grouse shooting.

Shotgunners should take the fit of their guns more seriously. You should first understand that a skilled wing shot actually "points" with the position of his feet and

head before he even brings the shotgun to his shoulder. If the stock fits his frame, the gun will almost automatically be on target when he mounts it. If it's a poor fit, he'll likely shoot over, under, in front of, or behind the bird.

If you're a wealthy shooter who can afford to have shotguns custom built and stocks shaped to exacting dimensions by means of a complicated "try gun," your solution is simple. The custom gun builder will see that your stock fits properly. But the majority of hunters have to solve their own problems of shotgun stock fit and the first step is a basic understanding of the various measurements and how they will affect shooting in the field.

■ Length of Pull

Length of pull is the distance between the butt and trigger. If this measurement is too long, the shooter will catch the heel of the stock on his clothes or under his armpit. If the length of pull is too short, the shooter will find that he will be smacking his nose with the thumb of his right hand when he pulls the trigger and the gun recoils. The proper

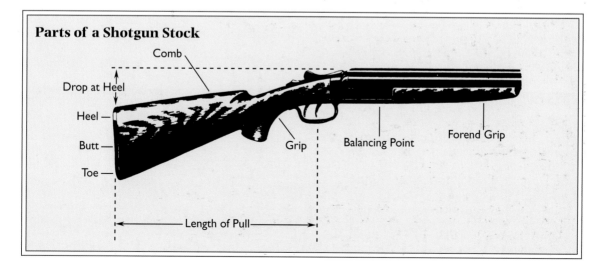

Parts of a Shotgun Stock

Comb

Drop at Heel

Heel

Butt

Toe

Grip

Balancing Point

Forend Grip

Length of Pull

length of pull, then, is one that will enable a shooter to mount the gun easily, clearing his clothes and keeping his thumb a safe distance from his nose.

The typical factory shotgun comes off the line with a length of pull of about 14 inches, which is usually all right for men 5 feet, 8 inches to 5 feet, 10 inches tall. A man taller than 6 feet will generally do better with a length of pull of 14¼ to 14½ inches. A boy, woman, or short man about 5½ feet tall, should look for a length of pull of about 13½ inches. The important factor is that the shooter should be able to mount his gun quickly and comfortably.

Drop at Comb

Drop at comb is the distance from the top of the forward edge of the comb and the line of sight. This is an important measurement since the comb, in a sense, is the rear sight of a shotgun because it positions and lines up the eye with the front bead sight. If the comb is too high, it will raise the eye of the shooter. This means he will see more barrel and point the barrel up. When this happens, the shot charge will go higher and he'll likely shoot over his birds. If the drop at comb is too low, the reverse happens—the gunner will shoot under his birds.

The typical factory-made shotgun has a drop at comb of 1½ inches, which is suitable for a man 5 feet, 7 inches to 5 feet, 11 inches tall. A 6-footer, however, needs less drop at comb. Thickness of the comb is also a factor. A thick comb will position the eye higher than a low comb.

This business of comb height is perhaps the most common reason for misses. If a hunter sees too much barrel when he quickly mounts his gun and feels he is getting more than his share of misses, it's a good bet that he's overshooting his target. If a hunter feels he must raise his cheek a bit to get a clear view of the front bead, chances are the comb is too low and he'll shoot under some of his birds.

The one exception to this is the trapshooter, who consistently shoots at a fast-rising target and wants to keep the claybird in sight at all times. He uses a special trap stock with a drop at comb of about 1⅜ inches. This will give him a high comb, which means his shot charge will fly higher. In effect, he has a built-in lead when he shoots directly at a claybird tossed straightaway.

The hunter, however, gets most of his shots at 20 to 25 yards and frequently prefers to blot out his game at closer ranges. If his gun has a high comb, like the trapshooter's, he'll shoot over the bird.

Firearm manufacturers have accounted for these differences and have turned out shotguns labeled field models and trap models. The difference lies mainly in stock dimensions.

Drop at Heel

Drop at heel is the distance between the heel of the stock and the line of sight. Here again, this measurement depends on the shooter's physical frame. The typical factory shotgun has a drop at heel of 2½ inches, which is fine for all-around use. A squarely built man, however, might prefer less drop at heel—which means a straighter stock. A round-shouldered and bull-necked shooter would be better off with a greater drop at heel. It's a generally accepted fact that the less drop at heel (the straighter the stock), the easier the gun will be to mount and shoot. Recoil is also felt less with a straight stock, since the gun will recoil more directly into the shoulder.

Pitch

Pitch is the angle of the buttplate on the butt and is measured from the muzzle. To determine pitch, a shotgun is stood on its butt with the action touching a wall. The measurement is then taken from the muzzle to the wall (see accompanying illustration).

Pitch is important in shotguns, since the point of impact can be raised or lowered by changing the butt solidly against the shooter's shoulder. With too little downward pitch, the butt may slip down and point the gun up, which will make the shot charge fly high. With too much downward pitch, the stock may ride up the shoulder and the shot charge will fly low. A pitch of 2 to 3 inches is about right for a shotgun with a 28-inch barrel.

Cast-Off

Hunters who stick to American-made guns need not be concerned with cast-off, since guns made in the United

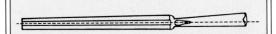

This illustration shows proper cast-off on a double-barreled shotgun for a right-handed shooter. Note that the butt angles to the right of the line of sight. Cast-off is rarely designed into American-made guns.

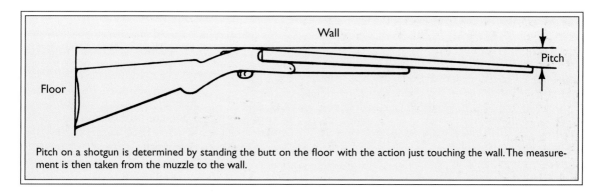

Pitch on a shotgun is determined by standing the butt on the floor with the action just touching the wall. The measurement is then taken from the muzzle to the wall.

States rarely have this feature. Cast-off means that, for a right handed shooter, the butt is angled slightly to the right of the line of sight (or slightly to the left for a left-handed shooter). Cast-off is supposed to make the gun easier to mount and swing. It is common on British-made shotguns.

Stock Style

Shotgun stocks come in two basic designs: pistol-grip stock and English straight stock. The English straight stock looks neater and has a trimmer appearance. This straight-stock design is popular in Europe, and it also seems to have periods of popularity in North America.

The modern American shotgun has a pistol grip, which puts the wrist in a comfortable position and affords better control when swinging the gun and shooting. The original purpose of the straight stock was to allow the hand to flow more quickly when pulling the second trigger on a double-barreled shotgun, but this

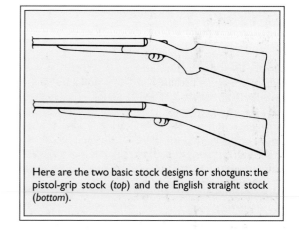

Here are the two basic stock designs for shotguns: the pistol-grip stock (*top*) and the English straight stock (*bottom*).

is not needed with a single-trigger gun. Some shooters feel they have better control with a pistol grip. Still, the appearance of the straight stock is again winning favor among some shooters.

SHOTSHELL SELECTION AND BALLISTICS

The changes in shotshell construction over the years have been phenomenal. Older hunters can probably remember when just about all shotshells were made of paper impregnated with wax. A look inside these shells was often bewildering. They generally had about 10 to 12 components, including a brass cup, primer, paper case, base wad, shot, over-powder wad, filler wads, over-shot wad, and so on.

In those days, ammunition makers ran those components through a complicated process before turning out the finished shell. The shells had several drawbacks. They could not be reloaded more than several times, water would eventually get into the paper body and the case would slowly deteriorate, and the shot charge would frequently deform when it came into contact with the bore.

Things started to change around 1960, when Remington introduced the plastic shell, which was waterproof and offered longer case life for those shooters who handloaded their own shotshells. Then came the plastic shot sleeve or collar, which surrounded and protected the pellets from becoming deformed as the shot charge traveled through the barrel. Many plastic shot sleeves now also form the over-powder wad. Winchester made shotshell construction even simpler when it designed its plastic shells in such a way that made even base wads unnecessary. The over-shot wad was eliminated when the star crimp came into standard use. The star crimp uses the shell case itself to seal off the top of the completed shotshell. This type of crimp also makes reloading easier and less expensive.

The shotshells of today are more durable and uniform, produce denser patterns, and can be reloaded many more times at less cost than the shotshells of a couple of decades ago.

Standard Shells

American-made shotguns are chambered for the standard 2¾-inch shotshell. It should be mentioned here, however, that the shell labeled "2¾ inches" is not actually 2¾ inches long, but about ¼ inch shorter. The 2¾-inch measurement is taken when the case is open, before crimping. The chamber of the shotgun, on the other hand, *is* 2¾ inches. This difference in measurement is to allow enough room in the gun's chamber for the crimp to unfold completely.

The difference in shell length and chamber length should make it obvious that hunters should not attempt to shoot 3-inch magnum shotshells in guns chambered for the 2¾-inch standard loads, in spite of what some shotgunners claim. It's all right to shoot a shell that is shorter than the gun is chambered for, but it is dangerous to shoot long shells in guns chambered for shorter shells. The chamber does not allow enough room for the crimp to unfold completely and excessive pressure can build up when the shot charge forces its way through a crimp that is not completely open.

The Magnums

Magnum shotshells are available in 2¾-, 3-, and 3½-inch size. Just about all shotguns chambered for the 2¾-inch standard shells will take the 2¾-inch magnum shells. The 3- and 3½-inch magnum shells, however, need guns chambered to handle the longer shells.

Magnum shotshells have more powder and shot than standard field loads do, but do not expect them to perform miracles. The extra powder and shot will increase the effective range on game because of the extra number of pellets, but the muzzle velocity of a magnum shell is nearly the same as that of a standard high-velocity load.

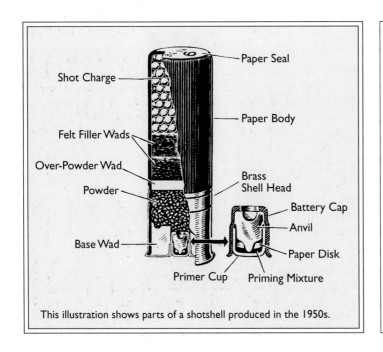

Shot Charge

Paper Seal

Felt Filler Wads

Paper Body

Over-Powder Wad

Powder

Brass Shell Head

Battery Cap

Anvil

Base Wad

Paper Disk

Primer Cup   Priming Mixture

This illustration shows parts of a shotshell produced in the 1950s.

This cutaway shows Winchester's rifle slug construction. This shotshell, the Razorback XT, is designed for hog hunting with a 1-ounce segmented slug. The load achieves a velocity of 1,600 feet per second.

Magnums, however, do give the hunter an extra edge when gunning for deer and tough game, such as turkeys and geese.

Special Loads

Brush loads, also called scatter or spreader loads, are shotshells that have a divider of sorts separating the shot charge into three or four separate sections. When the shell is fired, these partitions spread the shot charge into a more open pattern, in spite of the gun's designated choke. Generally, a brush load will, in effect, open the choke of a gun one setting. Fired in a Full choke gun, for example, a brush load will throw a Modified pattern. Used in a Modified choke barrel, a brush load will produce an Improved Cylinder pattern, and so on.

These brush loads are sometimes difficult to find. Not all manufacturers make them. They can, however, be handloaded by using a spreader device in the shot charge, usually a partitioned piece of cardboard forming an X.

The Remington Duplex Magnum, another unique shotshell, is loaded with both large- and medium-size pellets. The theory is that the large pellets retain maximum energy for long range and the smaller pellets make the pattern denser at close range. The duplex shotshell

Winchester Blind Side 12-gauge shells use cube-shaped HEX pellets in waterfowl and pheasant loads. The pellets stack easier and attain velocities of 1,675 feet per second.

loads are usually designed for turkey hunters with a mix of No. 4 and 6 shot sizes. Some hunters can get the same results by first loading their gun with a smaller pellet size load for a close-range dense pattern, and following up with a larger shot size load for retained energy and longer range.

Rifled Slugs

Shotgun slug loads were developed to give the shotgunner big-game capability at short range in areas that were too densely populated for safe use of rifles. Originally, slugs didn't really enjoy a great reputation for accuracy, but that has all changed.

Slugs, in their variations, are elongated (conical) projectiles. The best way to make such projectiles shoot accurately is to fire them from a rifled barrel. However, shotguns many years ago were smoothbored and had no rifling. This one factor had automatically limited shooters to close- or medium-range shooting. Today, many shotguns are manufactured with rifled barrels specifically for rifle slugs and modern slug loads are capable of 2-inch groups at 100 yards.

A brief explanation of interior ballistics points out the general lack of understanding of what is needed, in principle, to obtain optimum accuracy. Basically, a slug must be kept centered in the barrel without being tilted, deformed, or similarly abused. Wadding beneath the slug should fully seal the bore and provide a rigid base for the slug to rest upon.

Often, a slug will be considerably undersize for the barrel through which it is fired. In this case, the slug literally bounces from side to side as it travels toward the muzzle. After every contact with the bore wall, the slug sustains a bit of deformation and tilts to a new angle before going over to bounce against the other side of the bore.

The Brenneke slug is specially designed for shotgun hunting of big game. The slug and wad are joined to form one long projectile, which increases ballistic performance and accuracy. Keyholing is eliminated.

However, the worst happens at the muzzle as the slug departs. Since its wanderings within the bore are of a random nature, a slug will contact the choke taper of the muzzle in a different spot nearly every shot. You can imagine how the point of impact is affected by the first shot, which strikes the choke at six o'clock, the second, which strikes it at twelve o'clock, and so on.

The worst offenders, generally speaking, are those slugs that are not securely attached to their wad columns and thus centered in the bore. When fired in standard shotgun barrels (not special slug barrels), the over-powder felt cushion wad topped by a thick nitro card tends to seal the bore pretty well and keep propellant gases where they belong—behind the projectile. However, nothing keeps the slug centered and stationary in the bore's center and so the slug bounces from side to side on the way out the muzzle.

Although the common slug has a hollow base and is cast of soft lead, there seems to be a real advantage to protecting the hollow base from damage due to wads forcing themselves into the base—that's why a sturdy nitro card often proves to be a real group-tightener when seated over the felt cushion wad. The nitro card keeps the felt wad out of the slug base, minimizing projectile deformation.

Projectiles like the Brenneke slug, which has the over-powder wad or plastic obturating cup securely attached to the slug proper, seem to perform consistently well. No doubt part of this can be attributed to the relative stability of the slug atop the wads, but the "weathervane" effect of the attached wads is perhaps the prime stabilizing agent.

When a shooter thinks of a shotshell slug, the first image that comes to mind is that of a fat chunk of lead with a hollow base only slightly greater in length than width. The shooter probably sees this slug with deep grooves on its exterior that strongly resemble rifling marks, although smooth-sided projectiles are also available to the casting reloader.

This slug derives any performance from the "shuttlecock" weight distribution—a heavy nose pulling along the rest of the body. Once it is clear of the gun muzzle, the slug settles down and flies with fine stability. The Brenneke slug works on the same general shuttlecock principle, but relies on the attached base wad to "weathervane" and further prevent gross deviation in flight.

When the early slugs proved somewhat less than accurate, the firearms industry pondered on the problem, and among other things, the rifled slug was announced. The fairly logical reasoning was that, through the use of rather large spiral lands and grooves, the slug would be spun by air resistance during flight. Thus stabilized, the slug would be notably more accurate.

Rifled slugs can be a benefit, though, particularly when the "lands" extend from the projectile circumference. These lands, acting like fenders, serve to keep the slug centered in the bore and thus produce a more accurate shot.

The Brenneke slug features projectiles that are nearly bore size. Not only does this stabilize the slug better, but slug contact with the bore wall is reduced and thus the friction, pressure, and bore leading are also reduced.

In the final analysis, experimentation is the only answer. There are specially bored shotguns and special barrels made for slug shooting, however many older or "regular" shotguns will do an excellent job. Try slug loads in your gun. If you have several sets of barrels, change off and duplicate the test. Experiment with various slug loads. Winchester has the XP3 Sabot slug, which is designed specifically for rifled shotgun barrels. Remington has the AccuTip Bonded Sabot slug, also designed for rifled shotgun barrels.

Once you have a gun, regardless of choke, printing a reasonable group (say, 2 inches at 50 yards), the next step is to fit good rifle sights—either metallic or a low-powered scope. In almost all cases, a shotgun will

Why did you miss that claybird or pheasant? Too high? Low? Behind? The Winchester AA TrAAcker is a non-pyrotechnic shotshell loaded with a plastic colored wad that tracks in the shot cloud, making it clearly visible on the range and in the field. The TrAAcker comes with multi-colored wads for various shooting conditions—black for clear skies and blaze orange for overcast skies.

Rifled Slugs

Approximate ballistics courtesy of Federal Cartridge Company

Gauge	Weight (ounces)	Velocity (feet per second)		Energy (foot-pounds)		Drop (inches)		Barrel Length (inches)*
		Muzzle	50 Yards	Muzzle	50 Yards	50 Yards	100 Yards	
10	1¾	1,280	1,080	2,785	1,980	2.9	13.2	32
12	1¾	1,490	1,240	2,695	1,865	2.3	9.8	30
12	1	1,560	1,175	2,365	1,340	2.0	9.0	30
16	⅘	1,600	1,175	1,990	1,070	2.1	10.4	28
20	¾	1,600	1,270	1,865	1,175	1.9	9.5	26
.410	⅕	1,830	1,335	650	345	1.6	8.2	26

*All calculations were based on full choke barrels of this length.

throw slugs to a different impact point than shot, and the shooter should be able to properly zero the gun.

Finally, as hunting season rolls around, load up on a good number of slugs and head for the range. Sight-in off the bench, and then expend the remaining rounds in either the offhand or sitting position. Get to know the gun and what it will do up to 100 yards and beyond.

■ Powder

The designation "dram equivalent" on a box of shot-shells still confuses some shooters. The term is actually a throwback to the old black-powder days, when the standard load had a powder charge of about 3 drams. Today, of course, shotshells are loaded with modern smokeless powder. The dram equivalent label, however, is still used by many manufacturers. When you pick up a box of shotshells and see it stamped "3¼ dram equivalent," this means that the amount of smokeless powder in the loads will produce the same amount of pressure and velocity as the designated drams of black powder. It's worth noting here that a charge of smokeless powder may be less than half the weight of the dram equivalent.

Rifle shooters, realizing the importance of velocity, energy, and trajectory, take a great interest in ballistics, but most shotgunners pay little attention to how hard a shot charge moves once it leaves the barrel. Such information provides a better understanding of how a gun and ammunition will perform at typical or long ranges and on various kinds of game.

With regard to steel shot for waterfowling, published figures have been controversial—even contradictory in some cases—as manufacturers have continually sought to improve the powders and other components

Buckshot

Courtesy of Federal Cartridge Company

Gauge	Per Box	Length (inches)	Dram Equivalent	Shot Sizes
10	5	3½	Magnum	00 Buck/18 Pellets
10	5	3½	Magnum	4 Buck/54 Pellets
12	5	3	Magnum	000 Buck/10 Pellets
12	5	3	Magnum	00 Buck/15 Pellets
12	5	3	Magnum	1 Buck/24 Pellets
12	5	3	Magnum	4 Buck/41 Pellets
12	25	3	Magnum	4 Buck/41 Pellets
12	5	2¾	Magnum	00 Buck/12 Pellets
12	5	2¾	Magnum	1 Buck/20 Pellets
12	5	2¾	Magnum	4 Buck/34 Pellets
12	25	2¾	Magnum	4 Buck/34 Pellets
12	5	2¾	Maximum	000 Buck/8 Pellets
12	5	2¾	Maximum	00 Buck/9 Pellets
12	5	2¾	Maximum	0 Buck/12 Pellets
12	5	2¾	Maximum	1 Buck/16 Pellets
12	5	2¾	Maximum	4 Buck/27 Pellets
16	5	2¾	Maximum	1 Buck/12 Pellets
20	5	3	Magnum	2 Buck/18 Pellets
20	5	2¾	Maximum	3 Buck/20 Pellets

Lead and Steel Pellet Energy Comparison

Courtesy of Federal Cartridge Company

Muzzle velocity of lead pellets is figured at 1,330 feet per second. Muzzle velocity of steel pellets is figured at 1,365 feet per second.

PELLET ENERGY IN FOOT-POUNDS AT RANGE (yards)

Shot Type/Size	30	40	50
Lead No. 6	3.0	2.3	1.7
Steel No. 4	3.5	2.5	1.8
Lead No. 4	5.6	4.4	3.4
Steel No. 2	6.0	4.4	3.4
Lead No. 2	9.5	7.5	6.1
Steel No. BB	11.6	9.0	7.1

PELLETS PER OUNCE

Shot Size	Steel	Lead
No. BB	72	50
No. 1	103	N/A
No. 2	125	87
No. 4	192	135
No. 6	315	225

Shot sizes should be adjusted to compensate for steel's lighter weight. When switching from lead to steel, larger shot sizes should be selected. With the increased initial velocity of steel, this will provide adequate downrange pellet energy. However, hunters have their own preferred shot size and load and should experiment with different loads to determine which is the best for their type of hunting.

EXTREME RANGES

Waterfowl hunting usually involves the longest distances for shotgun shooting. The practical range for taking ducks and geese is 35 to 50 yards. Individual pellets,

Shot Size	Yards
00 Buck	610
No. 2 Shot	337
No. 6 Shot	275
No. 9 Shot	225

however, may travel great distances. For safety when hunting, consider these possible extreme ranges.

Shotgun Shell Ballistics

Gauge	Type Load	Shot Size	Muzzle Velocity (feet per second)	Pellet Muzzle Energy (foot-pounds of 1 pellet)	Velocity (60 yards)
10	High Velocity	No. 4	1,330	12.7	685
12	Standard Velocity	No. 6	1,255	6.8	610
12	High Velocity	No. 6	1,330	7.6	630
12	High-Velocity 3-Inch Magnum	No. 6	1,315	7.4	625
16	Standard Velocity	No. 6	1,185	6.0	595
16	High Velocity	No. 6	1,295	7.2	620
20	Standard Velocity	No. 6	1,165	5.8	590
20	High Velocity	No. 6	1,220	6.4	605
20	High-Velocity 3-Inch Magnum	No. 6	1,315	7.4	625
28	High Velocity	No. 6	1,300	7.3	620
.410	High-Velocity 3-Inch	No. 6	1,260	6.8	612

The above ballistics are average. There is some variation between brands and different sizes and weights of shot. The heavier the pellet, the greater the remaining energy and velocity at 60 yards.

Average Pellet Count: Lead Shot

Weight of shot in ounces (grams); 3 percent antimony

Shot Size	½ (14.17)	¹¹/₁₆ (19.49)	¾ (21.25)	⅞ (24.80)	I (28.35)	1⅛ (31.89)	1¼ (35.44)	1⅜ (38.98)	1½ (42.52)	1⅝ (46.06)	1⅞ (53.15)	2 (56.70)	2¼ (63.78)
No. 9	292	402	439	512	585	658	731	804	877	951	1,097	1,170	1,316
No. 8½	249	342	373	435	497	559	621	683	745	808	932	994	1,118
No. 8	205	282	307	359	410	461	512	564	615	666	769	820	922
No. 7½	175	241	262	306	350	394	437	481	525	569	656	700	787
No. 6	112	155	169	197	225	253	281	309	337	366	422	450	506
No. 5	85	117	127	149	170	191	212	234	255	276	319	340	382
No. 4	67	93	101	118	135	152	169	186	202	219	253	270	304
No. 2	43	60	65	76	87	98	109	120	130	141	163	174	196
No. BB	25	34	37	44	50	56	62	69	75	81	94	100	112

Average Pellet Count: Steel Shot

Weight of shot in ounces (grams)

Shot Size	¾ (21.25)	¹⁵/₁₆ (26.58)	I (28.35)	1⅛ (31.89)	1¼ (35.44)	1⅜ (38.98)	1½ (42.52)	1⁹/₁₆ (44.30)	1⅝ (46.06)
No. 7	316	395	422	475	527	580	633	659	685
No. 6	236	295	315	354	394	433	472	492	512
No. 5	182	228	243	273	304	334	364	380	395
No. 4	144	180	192	216	240	264	288	300	312
No. 3	118	143	158	178	197	217	237	247	257
No. 2	94	117	125	141	156	172	187	195	203
No. 1	77	97	103	116	129	142	154	161	167
No. BB	54	67	72	81	90	99	108	112	117
No. BBB	46	58	62	70	77	85	93	97	101
No. T	39	49	52	58	65	71	78	81	84
No. F	30	37	40	45	50	55	60	62	65

Steel Shot Velocities

Gauge	Length (inches)	Dram Equivalent	Ounces Shot	Shot Sizes	Muzzle Velocity (feet per second)
10	3½	4¼	1⅝	No. BB, 2	1,350
12	3	3½	1⅜	No. BB, 1, 2, 4	1,265
12	3	Maximum	1¼	No. BB, 1, 2, 4	1,450
12	2¾	3¾	1¼	No. BB, 1, 2, 4	1,325
12	2¾	3¾	1⅛	No. 2, 4, 6	1,365
20	3	3¼	1	No. 4, 6	1,330
20	2¾	3¼	¾	No. 4, 6	1,425

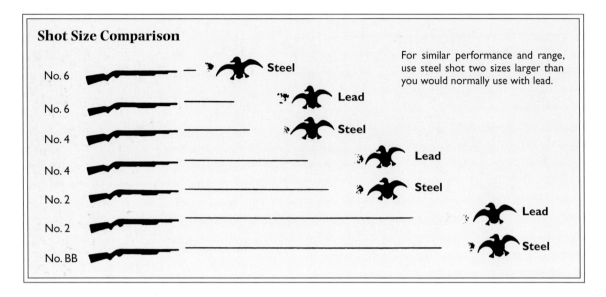

Shot Size Comparison

For similar performance and range, use steel shot two sizes larger than you would normally use with lead.

No. 6 — Steel
No. 6 — Lead
No. 4 — Steel
No. 4 — Lead
No. 2 — Steel
No. 2 — Lead
No. BB — Steel

used with steel pellets. As explained in the Gauge and Shot Size section, steel No. 2s are the correct substitute for lead No. 4s.

For the waterfowler, exact figures on steel shot velocity and energy are less important than the knowledge that steel does slow down at a considerably greater rate than lead, and it packs less energy at equal range. Although very skillful gunners can kill geese at more than 60 yards even with steel, the average hunter should not attempt shots at ranges much beyond 50 yards. Even

at that distance—and here's an important fact that seems to have eluded many hunters—it's necessary to swing the gun farther ahead of a duck or goose when using steel shot than when using lead in order to compensate for the relatively slow travel of the shot string.

Slug shooters seem to devote more time to studying the performance of their loads than do other shotgunners, but they too would do well to pay more attention to ballistics. The accompanying charts provide data for rifled slugs as well as standard lead- and steel-shot loads.

TRAPSHOOTING

A trap field consists of a trap situated in a trap house and five shooting positions spaced 3 yards apart. All five positions are 16 yards from the trap. Five shots are taken by each shooter at each of the five positions. This makes a total of 25 shots and this is referred to as a round of trap. Each shooter takes his turn in shooting and, upon completion of his five shots, moves to the next position. Each time the shooter on the fifth position completes his five shots, he goes to the first position, and so on.

Targets are thrown from the trap and must go a minimum of 48 yards and not more than 52 yards. The targets must be thrown between 8 to 12 feet high at

10 yards in front of the trap. Each of these traps moves automatically to a position unknown to the shooter; therefore, the shooter never knows where the target will be thrown. In singles shooting, the trap is adjusted so that within the normal distribution of angles as thrown by the trap, the right angle is not less than straightaway from position one.

There are three different events held in trapshooting. The first type is known as the "16-yard event." This event is held in classes and each shooter is placed in a class according to his ability.

The second event, probably the most popular, is known as "handicap shooting." Each shooter is given

Trapshooting at Each Station

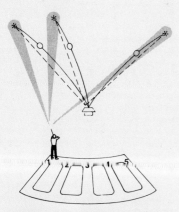 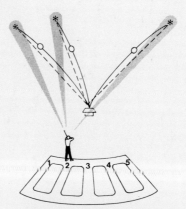 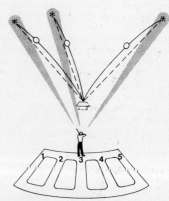

At Station 1: Your feet should be placed as shown, with your left foot pointed toward the left corner of the trap house. Your gun should also point at the left corner of the trap house. Solid lines indicate the flight angles of three typical targets you may encounter; dotted lines indicate the swing and follow-through of your gun as well as the target breaking point.

At Station 2: Your feet should be placed as indicated, with your left foot pointed one-quarter of the way in from the left corner of the trap house. Point the gun halfway between the left corner and center of the trap house.

At Station 3: Your left foot should be pointed slightly to the left of the center of the trap house. Your gun should be pointed toward the center of the trap house.

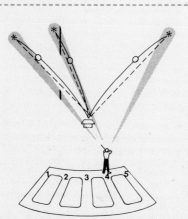 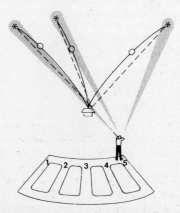

At Station 4: Your feet should be placed as indicated, with your left foot pointed one-quarter of the way in from the right corner of the trap house. Point your gun halfway between the center and right corner of the trap house.

At Station 5: Your feet should be placed as shown, with your left foot pointed toward the right corner of the trap house. Point your gun at the right corner of the trap house.

a shooting position at a certain distance from the trap. These distances are from 18 to 27 yards, depending on the shooter's ability. The intent of this handicapping is to make the shooters compete on an equal basis. There are no classes in these events and all shooters are competing against each other.

The third type of shooting is known as "doubles." This is the most difficult event, as two targets are thrown simultaneously. Unlike 16-yard and handicap shooting, the flight of these targets is fixed, and the left and right targets follow the path of the extreme left and right 16-yard targets.

Almost all shooting is done with a 12-gauge gun. There are no minimum restrictions, but the maximum is no more than 1⅛ ounces of shot and no more than 3 drams of powder. No shot larger than 7½ nor any gun larger than a 12 gauge may be used.

All traps must throw unknown angles. Some do this by mechanical means and are powered by electrical motors. The most modern traps load the targets and reset the angles automatically.

Clay pigeons are all of a standard size. They are basically black with a yellow, orange, or white trim. Some are made all black. These color variations are used depending on which has the best visibility. This varies at different gun clubs based on the background of each field.

An area of 1,000 feet deep by 1,000 feet wide is sufficient for safety purposes for a trap field.

■ Techniques of Trapshooting

To be a fine trapshooter, you must point the shotgun. Some people believe that because of the pattern the shot throws, this should be fairly simple. Once you have tried it, you will discover there is a lot of room around the moving target.

Targets are thrown at varying angles; consequently, the shooter must be prepared to shoot anywhere within that given area. The first thing to do as you prepare to shoot is plant your feet properly. You must be able to turn to the right or left with ease in order to hit targets flying in different directions. When shooting at the first station, you will get no more than a straightaway target for your extreme right. You can also get an extremely wide angle to the left. Knowing this, you should face halfway in between both extremes. Obviously, a shooter should face in the center of both extreme right and left targets on all five stations. If for some reason or another you face too far in one direction, you will find your body winding up like a spring when you try to move in the opposite

direction. This will cause you to slow down or even stop your swing, and you'll miss or barely hit the target.

The next step in shooting is to start your gun in the proper place. The gun should be started halfway between the two extreme angles of the targets. At Station 1, the gun should be pointed at the left corner of the trap house; at Station 2, halfway between the left corner and the center of the trap house; at Station 3, the center of the trap house; at Station 4, halfway between the center and the right corner of the trap house; and at Station 5, at the right corner of the trap house. Under certain wind conditions, it is advisable to start the gun higher. A target will sometimes climb considerably even though it is thrown from the trap at the legal height. The amount the gun should be raised is determined by the shooter based on the amount of climb of the target. There are many shooters who normally start higher simply because they have to move the gun less to get to the target and it is easier for them to shoot in this manner.

Most new shooters are more concerned with the recoil of the gun than anything else. Their first thought is to get the gun on their shoulder comfortably so it won't kick. They place the gun on their shoulder, and then try to bring their head down on the stock of the gun. This tends to stretch the neck muscles and pulls the head off the stock. The proper way is to bring the gun up to the face and line up the gun with the eye. Then, the shoulder is raised to the gun. With constant practice, this becomes a natural act.

When you have accomplished the foregoing, call for the target. As you will not know in which direction the target will fly, you must let it get a sufficient distance from the trap house before starting to move the gun. You must never try to guess where the target is going. Once the direction of the target is determined, the next step is to visualize where you want to point the gun in order to break the target. The gun should be held firmly but not tightly by your hand on the grip. Your other hand should grip the forend lightly, and your arms should be relaxed. Too tight a grip causes a jerky swing on the target. Trap targets take very little lead and the amount of this lead can only be determined by the shooter through experience. Of course, the targets flying straightaway from the shooter take no lead at all. I have known some very fast shooters who claim they do not lead any target.

Never try to hold a certain lead on the target. The instant you have the gun pointed where you want it, pull the trigger. If you stay with the target, it will drop away from you and you will shoot over it. Try to swing the gun smoothly up to the target.

Eventually, you will develop a sense of timing and you will shoot at your targets with a fairly consistent rate of speed. This varies with each person, depending on how well coordinated you may be. Most beginning shooters shoot too slow, but by shooting with faster shots, they will eventually increase their speed. Unlike upland game birds, trap targets are moving at their fastest rate of speed when they leave the trap house. This does not leave much time to think about a shot. Game birds start slowly and increase their speed as they go, giving the shooter more time.

One of the most common errors is to raise your head off the gunstock. Sometimes this is caused by shooters wanting to get a better look at the target and sometimes by not bringing the **gun tight** enough into the face. In either case, it will cause you to shoot over the target.

Handicap trap is the same as 16-yard trap except the ranges are greater—depending on the shooter's ability. Everything that applies to 16-yard shooting applies to handicap. The gun is moved to a lesser degree, but you have to point finer on the targets. You can be a little sloppy in your 16-yard shooting and still get some fair hits, but that same sloppiness will cost you targets when shooting at the longer ranges. The more your skill increases, the farther back you will want to shoot. The wind, if it is a strong one, can even blow the target away from where you pointed before the shot even gets there. Most good handicap shooters who shoot from 23 to 27 yards are fast shooters. Their speed gives them better chances at these long ranges. As you increase your range yard by yard in handicap, you have to learn to make slight changes in your shooting. Your mental attitude may become a problem, too, just because you know it's tougher to shoot from the new distance than it was a yard closer. Handicap shooting takes a lot of practice and most regular trapshooters realize this and do most of their practicing there.

Shooting doubles is the most challenging phase of trapshooting. First of all, you must face in a direction equally distant from both targets. You have the advantage of knowing where both of these targets are going so you are able to do this without any difficulty. Because you know where the target will be, you can start your gun much higher, which will give you a very short swing. This enables you to move to your second target much faster than you would if you started your gun where you would when shooting singles on that particular station. All of the top doubles shooters are fast shooters. Remember, you are shooting at two targets both going away from you, and the more time you take in shooting, the farther away they will be. Most doubles shooters widen their stance and point their toes farther apart. This prevents their knees from locking their body and preventing their swing to either side.

International Trap

Virtually everywhere except in the United States, the so-called "international" methods, equipment, procedures, and rules govern trapshooting. International Trap differs in three primary ways from the American version. First, you get two shots at each bird, and if you miss with the first but hit with the second, it counts as a hit. That may make the international version sound easier, but in reality it's much harder. The second and third differences are the reasons why.

The trap mechanism for the international game is set to fling targets through the air at a significantly greater velocity than in the American version. Try hitting a claybird as it zips through the air at about 100 miles per hour and you will begin to appreciate the second difference.

The third involves angle and height. In International Trap, targets go out at random angles, as in American trap, and you may get some straightaway birds, but the trap mechanism is also set to throw them at much more acute angles—much farther to the left or right. And it may throw one about as low as a fleeing rabbit. You never know whether your next target will be a towering one, or will go out at moderate height, or will be a "grasscutter" streaking away just a few inches off the ground.

Americans trying this competition for the first time invariably find it extremely difficult—and disconcerting. They very quickly come to understand why a second shot is permitted. And that second shot can be all the tougher because the speeding target is so far away by then. Expect embarrassingly low scores at first.

By the way, a good international trapshooter always fires his second shot, even if he doesn't need it. This is because he develops a very helpful rhythm, or sense of timing, in getting off two shots. Failing to fire the second shot breaks the rhythm.

A great many renowned shotgun experts feel that the international version is closer to field shooting because of the angle and height variations, and it is thus a better way to improve your wing shooting for hunting purposes.

SKEETSHOOTING

Skeet fields were originally a full semicircle, but it was necessary to make some changes for the safety of the shooters. The fields are now altered slightly and the targets are thrown at a slight angle from each trap house. A target must travel a minimum of 55 yards.

There are two trap houses. One is known as the high house and is located immediately behind Station 1. The targets emerge from this trap house at a height of 10 feet. The other trap is known as the low house and the target emerges from a height of 3½ feet.

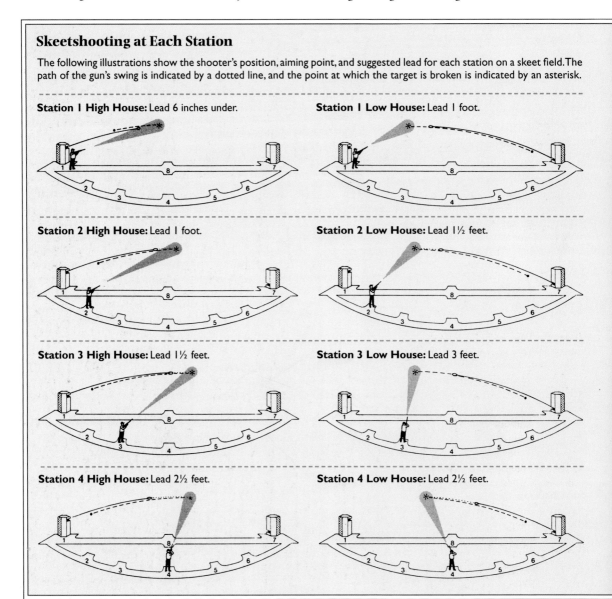

Skeetshooting at Each Station

The following illustrations show the shooter's position, aiming point, and suggested lead for each station on a skeet field. The path of the gun's swing is indicated by a dotted line, and the point at which the target is broken is indicated by an asterisk.

Station 1 High House: Lead 6 inches under.

Station 1 Low House: Lead 1 foot.

Station 2 High House: Lead 1 foot.

Station 2 Low House: Lead 1½ feet.

Station 3 High House: Lead 1½ feet.

Station 3 Low House: Lead 3 feet.

Station 4 High House: Lead 2½ feet.

Station 4 Low House: Lead 2½ feet.

There are eight stations marked out on the field. Seven are an equal distance apart (26 feet, 8 inches) and are placed on the semicircle. The eighth station is in the center of the field midway between the two trap houses. Each shooting station is 3 feet square. Any part of both of the shooter's feet must touch the station.

A single shot is taken at targets from both houses on all eight stations. A target from the high house is always shot first. After finishing the single shots, doubles are fired. At Stations 1, 2, 6, and 7, two targets are thrown simultaneously and the going-away target is fired upon with the first shot and the incoming target with the second shot. This makes a total of 24 shots. The 25th shot is taken immediately following the first target missed and the identical shot must be made. If no misses occur, the shot is taken from the Station 8 Low House. Each group

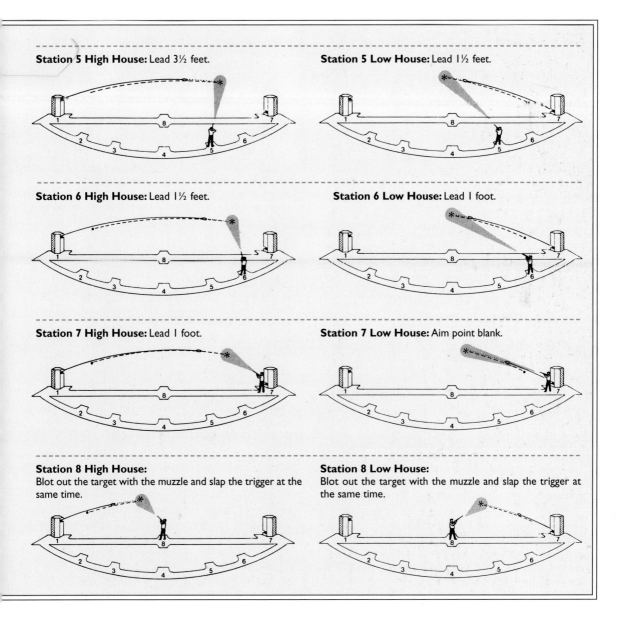

Station 5 High House: Lead 3½ feet.

Station 5 Low House: Lead 1½ feet.

Station 6 High House: Lead 1½ feet.

Station 6 Low House: Lead 1 foot.

Station 7 High House: Lead 1 foot.

Station 7 Low House: Aim point blank.

Station 8 High House:
Blot out the target with the muzzle and slap the trigger at the same time.

Station 8 Low House:
Blot out the target with the muzzle and slap the trigger at the same time.

Skeet Doubles

In doubles, targets emerge from both houses, requiring that you decide which to shoot first.

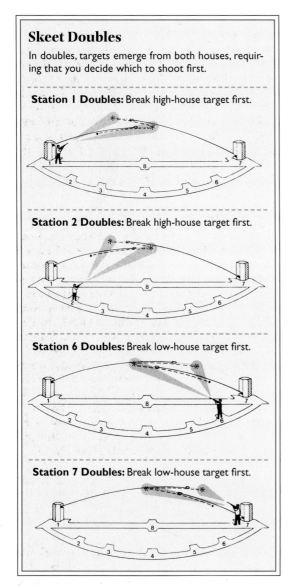

Station 1 Doubles: Break high-house target first.

Station 2 Doubles: Break high-house target first.

Station 6 Doubles: Break low-house target first.

Station 7 Doubles: Break low-house target first.

of 25 shots is known as a round and is also the amount of shells in each box.

Shooting is conducted with groups of five persons or less. Each group is known as a squad. Each shooter takes his turn on each station in the order in which they are signed up and continue in that order.

For safety reasons, it is considered necessary to have an area of 1,000 feet deep and 2,000 feet long for a skeet field. No. 9 shot cannot travel this far and this amount of room is more than ample.

There are two types of traps available. One type is handloaded and the other is automatically loaded. Most targets that are used are black with a yellow, orange, or white band.

■ Techniques of Skeetshooting

Skeet offers a greater variety of shots than any other shotgun game. You know where each target is going, but, in spite of that advantage, you still have to hit them. Beginners have to learn that they cannot break targets by shooting at them. After you learn to break a few, you'll get the general idea that you must shoot in front of each target in order to break it. Lead is the common term for this. The next step is to learn just how much lead is needed for each shot. This will come from practice and from the help of other shooters. Try to learn to master one shot at a time, but this is possible only if you can get a skeet field to yourself.

It is reasonable to assume that a target flying at a given rate of speed and a load of shot fired from a shotgun at a given range will meet if the proper amount of lead is given. The confusing thing to many new shooters is the amount of lead necessary for each shot. Years ago, shooters' reaction times were checked by one of the universities and they found that it took approximately two-fifths of a second from the time the mind registered it was the proper time to pull the trigger to the time the shot left the end of the shotgun barrel. Obviously, a fast-swinging shooter is going to move that gun barrel farther in that period of time than a slow-swinging shooter. Because of this, you'll get different answers from different shooters on just how much a target must be led.

Although getting the proper lead on each target is the ultimate objective, you must pay attention to stance and proper gun mounting. Position the feet correctly for each shot by facing the general area where you expect to break the target. The next step is to place the gun at a position in front of the trap house. Many new shooters will place the gun directly even with the trap house. This results in having to move the gun too fast in order to catch up with the target and you'll end up with very poor control of the shotgun. As a rule of thumb, a spot approximately one-third of the distance from the trap house to Station 8 would be about right. Some youngsters with very fast reactions can come in a little closer to the trap house, whereas those who are considerably older and their reactions slowing down must do just the opposite. The height of the gun should be approximately a couple of feet below the path of the target. This will allow ample room to see a target go downward if the wind happens to push it below its regular flight. Going up with a target that rises presents no problem, but if the target gets below the gun, you'll lose sight of it entirely.

After you get your feet placed right for the shot you are making and the gun started in the right place in relation to the trap house, the last thing that comes to mind is to get the correct lead for the shot you are about to make. These three steps—foot placement, gun placement, and lead—are the basic steps for each shot.

Next, you must call for the target; the word "pull" is used by most shooters. Do not start the gun moving until the target appears. Bring the gun up to the shoulder at the same time you are moving the gun after the target. It is best to try to keep the gun moving with the target and continue moving out to the correct lead. The instant this lead is reached, pull the trigger. Never try to hold a lead in order to break a target at a certain spot on the field. Pull that trigger the instant that lead is reached. One of the two most common faults of shooters is to stop swinging their gun after the lead is reached. You are not apt to make this mistake if you do not try to hold the lead. It is always best to "follow through" with your swing just like golfers, tennis players, and baseball players do. Beware of the shooter who advises you that the shot you just missed was the result of shooting behind the target. This leads you to believe you did not have enough lead when in reality you stopped swinging your gun.

The other common fault of the shooter is that sometimes he does not "get his head down on the stock." This means he is looking above the barrel instead of down the barrel. This results in shooting over the top of the target.

It is impossible to learn all of these steps at one time. If you try, you will only confuse yourself. Learn them one at a time. These are the basic steps of becoming a good shooter. Try to memorize the leads for each shot and in time you will automatically remember them. This will also help tremendously with your field shooting. Every shot you make at skeet—with the exception of those at Station 8—are identical to shots you will make in upland bird shooting. It will surprise you how much your field shooting will improve after a few rounds of skeet.

■ International Skeet

International Skeet, like International Trap, is unquestionably more demanding than the American form. For one thing, the trap spring is set to throw the bird considerably faster—and just think what that does to a Station 8 shot! For another, you cannot shoulder the gun before calling for the bird. You must keep the stock down at waist level, as if you were hunting and about to mount the gun while your dog points. The butt must touch your hipbone.

Finally—and probably most disconcerting of all for Americans unfamiliar with the international competition—a target does not necessarily fly out the instant you call, "Pull!" It may go out on the instant of demand, but it may also be delayed for an unknown time, up to three full seconds. That makes it very much like a live bird flushing, and the game in general is enormously beneficial in improving your performance in the field.

CLAY TARGET GAMES

In recent years, shotgunners (and their gun clubs) have developed a great number of variations on trap and skeet—plus some target games with little or no resemblance to those traditional shoots. The unconventional exercises and competitions have several special attractions. In some instances, the necessary equipment and layout may be inexpensive compared to the investment needed to set up a regulation trap or skeet field. In other instances, the attraction is informality or a chance for gunners of unequal skill to compete on a more or less equal footing. One very strong appeal is the similarity of some of the games to field shooting. Artificial situations are concocted that imitate real hunting situations—the sudden and unexpected sight of game, an explosive flush, shots made at tough angles, and variations in target speed. All of this adds up to great practice, a lot of misses, plenty of fun, and occasional hilarity. Here are some of the more common nontraditional games, beginning with sporting clays—the most popular of all.

■ Sporting Clays

This is a clay target game designed to simulate shooting situations and target angles encountered when hunting with a shotgun. It is a flexible, easily changed game aimed at duplicating the hunting shots and angles most commonly encountered while hunting. Shooting stations are often in woods or brush where the target must be broken quickly before it disappears from view. In short, it is truly a hunter's game where shooters can gather and have fun while improving their hunting skills.

Although it began and has evolved into the most popular clay target game in England, it has also become highly popular in the United States. It is difficult because, as in hunting, the shooter is never sure precisely when the target will appear. Some targets are very high overhead incomers, simulating doves, ducks, or other high-flying game. Others are fast, going-away challenges resembling upland birds. No two sporting clays ranges need be quite the same, and competition can be made as difficult or as easy as desired by location of the shooting positions relative to the location of the trap machines (which ideally are out of view of the shooter).

Ordinary clay targets are used, and shooters move in squads from one shooting location, or "stand," to the next. Each shooter faces the same basic challenge and will receive essentially the same targets at the same approximate speed, angle, and height. But variations of wind, slight differences in how a target may be placed on the throwing arm of the trap, and time of appearance of the target offer many of the variables of field hunting.

Normally, squads of six shooters go from one stand to the next. They are told by the referee what basic target to expect (singles, doubles, high, low, or waiting), and each shooter has the opportunity to view at least one set of targets, either in advance if he is the squad leader or by watching other shooters perform.

The largest layouts typically involve 100 targets shot at from 10 stands, while small shooting layouts sometimes have as few as three stands, and 25 or 30 targets can make up the contest. But invariably the shooter will be confronted by some very high or long shots and some close, fast ones. Some will be going away; some will be incoming.

One shooter at a time stands at the shooting station with the gun in a "low gun" position, similar to the way the gun is carried when hunting. When the shooter calls "Pull," the target may appear instantly or at any time up to three seconds later. He may not shoulder the gun until the target appears. No more than two targets will appear at one time, and guns may contain no more than two shotgun shells. Two shots are permitted at singles, one each at doubles. Hits or misses are scored by the referee; to score a hit, the target must be broken. Sporting clays is a difficult game, intentionally so because it simulates the difficulties of hunting. Properly set up, competent

Rabbit Run

If your gun club has trap houses with roofs strong enough to support a shooter's weight, here's a good game to lend variety to your program. Shooters stand atop the house and fire at targets that skim a foot or so above the ground. They appear underfoot and depart at various angles at great speed. The trap-throwing angle is depressed and spring tension is increased to pitch targets low to the ground that will reach out 40 yards or more from the trap house.

shooters can expect to score on only about 80 to 85 percent of the targets attempted.

There is virtually no angle encountered in field shooting that cannot, to a very realistic degree, be simulated by sporting clays. As a result, shooters gain not only the excitement and fun of the shooting, but also become much better game shots.

Perhaps more important than the competitive angle is the excellent game-shooting practice at informal "fun shoots" arranged by the participants to suit their own needs. Regularly used field-hunting shotguns and a minimum of equipment expense can lead to much better game shooting the next hunting season.

Almost anywhere it is safe to hunt or to fire a shotgun, some sort of sporting clays layout can be accommodated. The important requirement is that there be a "safety zone" of at least 300 yards in the direction the shooter must fire from each shooting station. Farms, ranches, gun clubs, hunting clubs, and even unused areas around golf courses can be used as long as there is no danger of pellets striking people, livestock, buildings, or other objects.

The best and most attractive layouts are usually in wooded areas featuring some hill or ridge from which high targets can be launched. If the terrain is suitable, the trap machines that launch the targets should be hidden from the shooter's view. It is much more like game shooting when a target suddenly appears over trees or from behind a clump of brush.

On flat land, some sort of tower is usually required to house one or two trap machines. The high target is a very important part of sporting clays because it simulates a situation so often encountered in dove and waterfowl hunting and because the high incomer or crosser is not effectively simulated by trap or skeet. If building a tower is not possible, barns, windmills, or water tanks may substitute or the shooter can be down on a riverbed with the trap on a high bank above him.

Several shooting stations can be set up to use a single tower. Situated in front of the tower, the shooter gets the high overhead incomer. Moved to the right or left, he gets high crossing targets. Moved directly beneath the tower, he gets high going-away "birds" similar to the angles presented by high ducks passing over from behind the blind. On flat land, it is often possible to obscure the origin of low targets by putting up trees, brush, hay bales, or some sort of cover around each shooting station, in effect making it more like a blind.

It is important, if manually operated traps are used, that the trap operator be protected from pellets. This can be done by situating the traps behind a ridge or hill or by erecting some sort of protection for the trapper. Bales of hay are often effective, as are corrugated heavy metal sheets. Operators of traps, like competitors, should wear shooting glasses for added protection against the odd "flyer" or stray pellet.

Trap machines can be simple, inexpensive devices that are manually operated or the most sophisticated automatic-loading, oscillating types. The only real requirement is that the machine be capable of throwing a target sufficiently fast so that it is not a cinch to hit. In the United States, a leading trap company is developing new models capable of throwing the fast targets best used at sporting clays. However, there is no rule that specifies target speed or distance because, as yet, there are no hard-and-fast rules. But even inexpensive traps throwing relatively slow targets can offer better practice than none at all. A number of manual traps from various countries are available for less than $400 each and will throw targets almost 100 yards. In general, a target that will travel 75 yards is considered ideal.

The amount and type of equipment needed depends upon the size of the layout and how many shooting stations will be set up. Ideally, there should be a minimum of five stations, and some more elaborate layouts might offer 10 or more. But that doesn't mean a separate trap is needed for each station. By drawing up the course in such a way that a shooter fires at the same target, but from a different angle, the effect is of an entirely different "bird." A minimum of three traps is usually recommended; these can be turned to throw a different direction or angle and can accommodate up to 10 shooting stations.

The most effective trap to use in a tower is an oscillating machine (like the ones used in American trapshooting) and preferably an autoloading model. This eliminates the need for a trapper in the tower and the problem of protecting him from shot pellets. However, manual traps mounted in towers and operated by the trapper at the sound of the referee's whistle or call are perfectly feasible. The trap boys can be protected by corrugated metal shields.

There are many inexpensive portable trap machines on the U.S. market and, if mounted on an automobile spare tire and wheel, they can be rolled to different locations. The spare tire, laid flat on the ground, then serves as a sturdy base for the trap and helps protect it from the jolts and vibrations of operation. A wooden pallet can also make an inexpensive, easily moved base for traps, as can a steel oil drum filled with concrete.

The only other major item of equipment is some form of enclosure for the shooter (usually made of chicken wire with wooden framework), which prevents him from swinging around to the rear and thus possibly endangering spectators. Sporting clays is an interesting spectator sport, and the gallery is perfectly safe if the shooter is enclosed. On individual farm or hunting club layouts, however, such protective "cages" may not be necessary. Much depends upon the experience of the shooter and the nature of the layout. If possible, the "cages" should be portable for the times when other angles and shooting positions are desired.

The important thing is to get hunters improving their shooting skills in the off-season. Hunting and shooting clubs can and should set up their own shoots with their own rules and have fun. Simulate your own game-shooting situations and keep practicing with your favorite hunting shotgun. You'll be amazed at the improvement in your shooting skill during the hunting season.

Anyone with access to sufficient land and financing for enough traps can set up a sporting-clays layout. It can be as simple or as elaborate as desired. Sporting clays is a natural for hunting clubs, particularly those in areas where waterfowl hunting is permitted on mornings only. Sporting-clays practice can be an excellent way to use those open afternoons and also make better duck and goose hunters of the membership. The improvement in hitting long crossing and high overhead shots can be phenomenal, mainly because no other target game in the United States (other than a few club tower shoots) has offered the opportunity to practice these shots. But any hunting club can improve interest and off-season use of the club (as well as in-season use, too) with a sporting-clays setup.

Walk-Up Skeet (or Trap)

In this game, the shooter takes his place at Station 4 and starts to walk toward Station 8. He may receive a target from either the high or low house at the puller's option, and unknown to the shooter. The target is thrown at any time during the shooter's walk toward Station 8, but before he reaches that post.

A similar game is played on a standard trap field, with the gunner beginning the long walk toward the trap house at the 27-yard marker. Targets fly at unknown angles, of course, appearing at the option of the puller. At some clubs, walk-up skeet or trap is played with doubles being thrown. A club that has its trap field superimposed on its skeet field can add still more variety to the game using all three machines.

Sporting clays are an ideal "interest builder" for a trap or skeet club with some space not being used. Since a sporting-clays shoot requires from 25 to 100 shells—unlike big trap- and skeetshoots, which require up to 500—it can be an excellent way of getting new hunter-members out to use club facilities. Sporting clays is also an excellent way of attracting potential new members to the club. An "open shoot" just prior to the beginning of bird-hunting season is almost certain to bring out hunters and spectators, and some of those spectators may ultimately become members. A special "Hunter's Division" for visitors who don't compete at trap or skeet could be a big incentive to getting new shooters interested.

Sporting clays can also be an excellent means of providing corporate entertainment on a farm, ranch, or hunting lease. And since the only permanent facility required is a tower (and often not even that), the investment is virtually nil except for a few relatively inexpensive traps.

One of the concerns about hunter safety in America today is that many hunters have so little opportunity to learn the safe ways of gun handling, the instant decisions that must be made as to whether to shoot or not shoot. These things cannot be learned on a skeet or trap range, where guns are never carried loaded even from one station to the next.

But shooting sporting clays can involve walking with a loaded gun (in the walk-up event only), and it also deals with shooting in wooded areas, possibly from positions of somewhat unsure footing, and, in short, simulates many of the situations of field shooting where safety is a major consideration.

Practice at walking with other hunters (or walking from one sporting-clays station to the next) is a good way to learn very quickly if one has careless gun-handling habits. Sporting-clays participants are sticklers for gun safety and proper gun-carry positions.

Sporting-clays layouts are used by state shooting-program instructors because they offer a more realistic environment than a classroom or traditional skeet and trap fields. Proper field procedures can be demonstrated and practiced with the help and direction of hunting-safety instructors.

CRAZY QUAIL: This is an exciting clay target game that was developed in Texas. It is a great fun game where shooters can easily make up their own rules and create new versions of the game. It is also an excellent warm-up for the hunting season. Targets are thrown from a single trap in a 360-degree circle, where there are safe distances.

No shooter can outguess the person operating the trap. He deliberately tries to confuse the shooter by changing the angle of rotation after each shot. Also, he may use one-second or 10-second delays in releasing after the shooter yells, "Pull."

Crazy Quail is a combination of skeet and trap. For instance, a target may be thrown back at the shooters similar to a skeet Station 8, or a target may be thrown away from the shooter similar to regulation trap. The setup is also convenient for teaching a beginning shooter, as spring tension can be eased for a slower target and the trap held at a constant angle; also, the shooter can move close to the release point.

Crazy Quail is most often set up with the trap in a pit. A mound of dirt is usually built to act as a safe barrier between the releaser and the shooter. Where there is poor drainage, the trap can be set up at ground level and a higher mound built for safety purposes.

A practice trap is welded onto a vertical shaft. A seat for the releaser, attached to the shaft, swings in a complete circle. The shooters usually stand 16 yards behind the trap, but they may wish to vary this. Be sure that in any direction you will be shooting there is safe clearance for 300 yards.

RIVERSIDE SKEET: This clay target game was developed in 1948 by shooters at the Riverside Yacht Club in Riverside, Connecticut. It is known in southern Connecticut as that "Blankity Blank Riverside Skeet." There are five stations, arranged similarly to standard trap. A trap is safely located at each end of the line. The traps are angled so that when doubles are thrown the targets cross at about 25 yards.

The shooter at Station 1 gets a left-hand single, then a right-hand single. His third shot is a single at the option of the releaser, the idea being to confuse the shooter. After the third shot, the shooting rotates to Station 2 and the other stations. After each shooter has fired three rounds, the shooter at Station 1 then fires a double. After all stations have fired a double, which totals five shots per person, all shooters rotate the same as in standard trap.

Shooters can work out many variations of the game. The trap angles can be varied to make the shooting more difficult. Since the game was first started at the Riverside Yacht Club, there have been only 12 scores of 25 out of 25.

Riverside Skeet can easily be set up at an existing trap or skeet club. Ideally, the shooters would face north or northeast, as this is the optimum direction to keep the sun out of their eyes. The traps are controlled electrically by the releaser, who stands behind the shooters. Manual traps can be used, but in the long run it might be cheaper to use autoloading traps.

FIVE-STAND SPORTING: Another version of sporting clays is five-stand sporting. Usually set up in a five-station trap field format, this game uses six to eight automatic traps at different locations. There are three levels of difficulty: Level I, five single targets with full use of the gun for scoring; Level II, three single targets and a simultaneous pair; and Level III, one single target and two simultaneous pairs. Shooters, usually a squad of five, can move from station to station with a predetermined menu of shots and combinations. Five-stand sporting can also be shot without the shooters knowing any claybird sequence or pattern.

■ National Sporting Clays Association

The first rule of the National Sporting Clays Association is that shooting be made as near as possible to game shooting. The whole idea is to simulate local hunting and the shots most frequently encountered while in

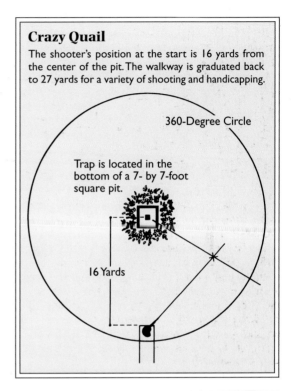

Crazy Quail

The shooter's position at the start is 16 yards from the center of the pit. The walkway is graduated back to 27 yards for a variety of shooting and handicapping.

360-Degree Circle

Trap is located in the bottom of a 7- by 7-foot square pit.

16 Yards

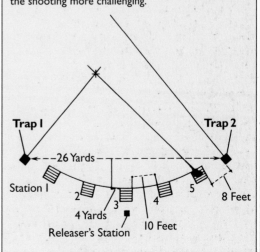

Riverside Skeet

The stations are located 3 to 4 yards apart. For your installation, refer to the illustration below for a start. You may wish to try variations periodically to make the shooting more challenging.

Trap 1   Trap 2

←—26 Yards—→

Station 1

2   5   8 Feet

3   4

4 Yards   10 Feet

Releaser's Station

the field. Shooting stands or "stations" are preferably located in woods or brush or using terrain in such a way that the trap machines that launch targets are hidden from the shooter's view.

Squads of up to six shooters move from one shooting stand to another, and one shooter at a time stands waiting with the toe of the butt touching his waistline. At his call of "ready," the target may be launched instantly or up to three seconds later; the shooter may not shoulder the gun until the target appears.

Twelve-gauge guns or smaller, loaded with no more than 1¼ ounces of shot, are used. No special spreader loads are permitted.

Shooters must not load until they are in position at the shooting stand, and the gun must be unloaded and open any time the shooter turns toward the referee or crowd. The sequence of targets at each shooting station is announced in advance and is the same for each shooter. Normally, each shooter finishes his single targets; then, in the same squad order, shoots doubles if that particular station offers doubles.

Guns may be loaded with no more than two shells. On single targets, two shots are permitted, and scoring is the same whether the bird is broken on the first or second shot. On doubles, the shooter may fire twice at the same target (if he misses the first shot) or may switch to the other. Should both targets break with one shot, they are scored as both dead, exactly as would be the case if two game birds were taken with one shot.

The number of targets shot at each shooting station varies, but a big shoot will usually be 10 targets from each of 10 stations. For informal shooting, it's up to the group, as long as everyone shoots the same number of birds from the same station.

HANDGUN ACTIONS

■ Mechanisms

Before discussing the various sporting uses of the handgun, let's talk about the different types of actions. Apart from a few single-shot models, there are only two basic designs: the semi-automatic and the revolver. The semi-automatic comes in two versions—the blowback and breechblock designs—which are similar to the mechanisms used in semi-automatic rifles.

Briefly, the semi-automatic uses gas pressure from the powder to operate the mechanism. The first step in firing an automatic is to pull the slide back and then release it. As the slide moves forward, it will pick up and chamber a cartridge from the magazine, as well as cock the handgun. When the trigger is pulled and that first round is fired, the energy from the explosion drives the slide backward, ejecting the empty case. As the slide automatically moves forward again, it picks up and chambers the next round and the gun is ready to fire again.

The revolver also comes in two versions: the single action and double action. The single action, put simply, means the hammer must be pulled back for every shot. In effect, it must be cocked manually each time. While cocking the single action, a spur also engages a notch in the cylinder, rotating it to the next loaded chamber. The double action only requires the trigger to be pulled each time to fire the cartridges in the cylinder. Pulling the trigger moves the hammer back to full cock, rotates the cylinder, releases the sear, and fires another round.

■ Revolver or Semi-Automatic?

Revolver and semi-automatic handguns seem to have an equal number of fans. Ask the owner of a revolver what kind of handgun to buy and he'll tell you a revolver. And the owner of a semi-automatic pistol will swear by his type of gun. There are some basic distinctions between the two designs, however.

The revolver is inherently safer because more manual operation is required between shots. But the semi-automatics, which will be called automatics from here on, fire more rapidly. The automatics have a larger magazine capacity and are more compact than the typical revolver of the same caliber, but revolvers will handle some ammunition interchangeably. The .357 Magnum, for example, will accept the .38 Special, but not conversely. The automatic may be faster to reload, but the revolver is more rugged and requires little maintenance.

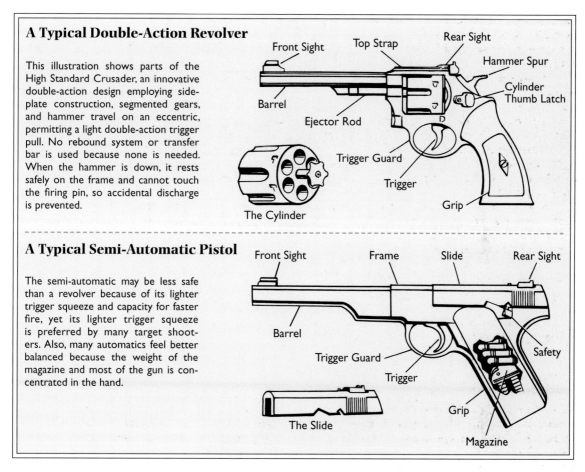

A Typical Double-Action Revolver

This illustration shows parts of the High Standard Crusader, an innovative double-action design employing side-plate construction, segmented gears, and hammer travel on an eccentric, permitting a light double-action trigger pull. No rebound system or transfer bar is used because none is needed. When the hammer is down, it rests safely on the frame and cannot touch the firing pin, so accidental discharge is prevented.

Front Sight — Top Strap — Rear Sight — Hammer Spur — Cylinder Thumb Latch — Barrel — Ejector Rod — Trigger Guard — Trigger — Grip — The Cylinder

A Typical Semi-Automatic Pistol

The semi-automatic may be less safe than a revolver because of its lighter trigger squeeze and capacity for faster fire, yet its lighter trigger squeeze is preferred by many target shooters. Also, many automatics feel better balanced because the weight of the magazine and most of the gun is concentrated in the hand.

Front Sight — Frame — Slide — Rear Sight — Barrel — Trigger Guard — Trigger — Safety — Grip — Magazine — The Slide

Examining these comparisons, it does become apparent that the revolver makes a better handgun for hunting, plinking, and informal target shooting. It is dependable, needs little care, and has some built-in safety features. A fairly hard trigger pull is needed to cock, rotate the cylinder, and fire additional rounds.

With an automatic, once the first shot is fired, only a light trigger pull will discharge another round. The revolver is obviously safer. The revolver is also easier for the novice to understand and learn how to shoot. Granted, the automatic provides more rapid firepower, but there is no outdoor sport where such firepower is really necessary.

The automatic does have its fans, however. Roughly half of all handgun matches are won with automatics and the military forces of the United States, and most others, use the automatic. This is probably so for a number of reasons. When it comes to target shooting, the automatic is a better balanced firearm, since most of the weight of the gun and the loaded magazine is concentrated in the hand. A target shooter who competes in rapid-fire matches will find he can get his shots off quicker and more smoothly with an automatic. As for the military, its main concern is defense, and rapid firepower is an important consideration. The same is true for law-enforcement agencies. Nearly all law-enforcement officers now carry automatics. Automatics also offer larger magazine capacities.

This all boils down to a few basic conclusions. For hunting and plinking, the revolver is the best choice. The serious target shooter, who gets involved in official matches, should look to the automatic. If a shooter is involved in all three—hunting, plinking, and target shooting—the choice will have to be one of personal preference. Select the handgun with which you feel most safe and comfortable.

This is the correct way to hold and load a single-action revolver. In some models, the hammer is in half-cock position, so the cylinder will rotate. In other models, such as this Ruger Single-Six, the hammer must be down and the loading gate opened before the cylinder can be rotated for loading. With the hinged loading gate opened, the cylinder can be rotated as cartridges are placed in the cylinders.

This is the correct and safe way to hold and load a double-action revolver. Place the fingers through the frame and around the cylinder as cartridges are loaded into the cylinders. If you should be required to leave your revolver unattended at a shooting range, always leave it with the cylinder swung out for safety.

SELECTING THE HANDGUN

Now that you know the basic mechanics of revolvers and semi-automatic handguns, the questions of sights, barrel length, and caliber arise. A shooter may have decided on a revolver, for example, but now he must select a caliber, sights, and so on. If he wants to hunt squirrels, he certainly wouldn't choose a .357 Magnum. And if target shooting is his primary interest, he'll obviously steer clear of fixed sights. The best way to handle this problem of selection is to choose the gun to fit the sport. Let's discuss them one by one.

■ Hunting

It takes a skilled marksman to master the handgun, so anyone who decides to hunt with a sidearm needs all the help he can get. One of the important differences between a handgun for hunting and a precision target pistol is weight. The hunter's gun should be lighter, simply because he has to carry it around with him.

Weight, however, helps any shooter to maintain a steadier hold, so the problem is a bit of a double-edged sword. A good rule is to pick a hunting handgun that

Revolvers

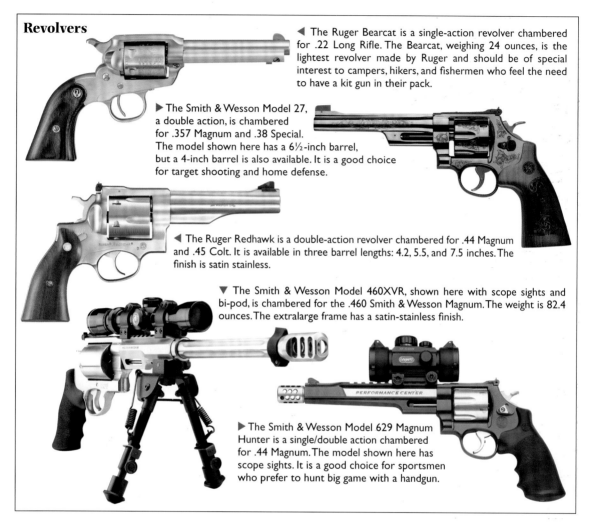

◀ The Ruger Bearcat is a single-action revolver chambered for .22 Long Rifle. The Bearcat, weighing 24 ounces, is the lightest revolver made by Ruger and should be of special interest to campers, hikers, and fishermen who feel the need to have a kit gun in their pack.

▶ The Smith & Wesson Model 27, a double action, is chambered for .357 Magnum and .38 Special. The model shown here has a 6½-inch barrel, but a 4-inch barrel is also available. It is a good choice for target shooting and home defense.

◀ The Ruger Redhawk is a double-action revolver chambered for .44 Magnum and .45 Colt. It is available in three barrel lengths: 4.2, 5.5, and 7.5 inches. The finish is satin stainless.

▼ The Smith & Wesson Model 460XVR, shown here with scope sights and bi-pod, is chambered for the .460 Smith & Wesson Magnum. The weight is 82.4 ounces. The extralarge frame has a satin-stainless finish.

▶ The Smith & Wesson Model 629 Magnum Hunter is a single/double action chambered for .44 Magnum. The model shown here has scope sights. It is a good choice for sportsmen who prefer to hunt big game with a handgun.

is not in the featherweight class, but is not excessively heavy either. For a .22 handgun, one that weighs from 25 to 35 ounces is about right. For the heavier calibers, such as the .357, .41, .454 Casull, and .44 Magnum, a handgun should weigh between 40 and 50 ounces.

Sights, as indicated earlier, should be the best available and always with a rear sight that is adjustable for windage and elevation. Micrometer sights usually found on quality target pistols work fine in the game field. A handgun hunter, like a rifle shooter, must sight-in his firearm and know the point of impact at various ranges. This is only possible with adjustable sights. Fixed sights, such as those generally found on service revolvers, have no place in the field.

The handgun hunter does have another choice when it comes to sights. He can mount a scope on the gun. In addition to magnification, a scope on a handgun serves a very important function. It puts the crosshairs and target in one optical plane so that both are in sharp focus. Without the scope, it is impossible for shooters to bring both the sights and target into sharp focus, and this problem gets more acute as handgunners get on in years. Handgun scopes solve this frustrating problem. These special scopes have long eye relief, generally 10 to 24 inches. Magnification is usually 1.3x–4x, fixed, and variable 1.5x–4x.

Barrel length is still another factor to consider. The handgun used for hunting should have a long barrel,

Semi-Automatic Handguns

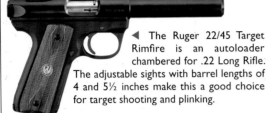

◀ The Ruger 22/45 Target Rimfire is an autoloader chambered for .22 Long Rifle. The adjustable sights with barrel lengths of 4 and 5½ inches make this a good choice for target shooting and plinking.

◀ The Browning Hi-Power Standard, an autoloader, is chambered for 9mm. The polished blue barrel is 4.6 inches and the weight is 32 ounces. The magazine capacity is 10 rounds.

◀ The Para Expert 1445, an autoloader, is chambered for the .45 ACP. This stainless-steel model has a fiber-optic front sight on its 5-inch barrel. It is a good choice for home defense.

◀ The Browning Buck Mark Camper is a stainless autoloader chambered for .22 Long Rifle. It is available in three barrel lengths: 4, 5½, and 7¼ inches. It is ideal for campers, hikers, and for hunting small game.

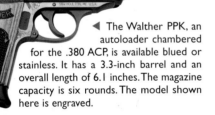

◀ The Walther PPK, an autoloader chambered for the .380 ACP, is available blued or stainless. It has a 3.3-inch barrel and an overall length of 6.1 inches. The magazine capacity is six rounds. The model shown here is engraved.

◀ The Ruger KP95, chambered for the 9mm Luger, has three-dot fixed sights on a 3.9-inch barrel and weighs 27 ounces. This gun is also available in a stainless-steel model.

Black-Powder Handguns

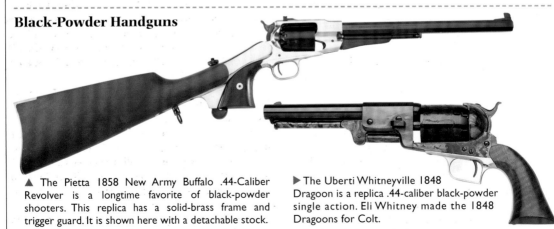

▲ The Pietta 1858 New Army Buffalo .44-Caliber Revolver is a longtime favorite of black-powder shooters. This replica has a solid-brass frame and trigger guard. It is shown here with a detachable stock.

▶ The Uberti Whitneyville 1848 Dragoon is a replica .44-caliber black-powder single action. Eli Whitney made the 1848 Dragoons for Colt.

and one from 6 to 10 inches is a good handling length. There are several reasons for avoiding the short-barreled models. First, and most important, is that they do not give a long enough sight radius for good accuracy. It's an accepted fact that the longer the distance between the front and rear sights, the greater the accuracy potential. In the magnum calibers, the short barrels also give off greater muzzle flash and noise, both of which could bring on a case of flinches.

With short-barreled handguns in the big calibers, there is also the problem of loss of velocity. A .41 Magnum cartridge, for example, will leave the muzzle of an 8⅜-inch barrel at 1,500 feet per second, but only 1,250 feet per second from the muzzle of a 4-inch barrel. A short barrel is simply not long enough for full thrust to take place behind the bullet. This situation is particularly important if the shooter handloads his ammunition to maximum charges.

Picking the right caliber depends on the size of the game being hunted. For small game, such as rabbits, squirrels, sitting grouse, and the smaller varmints, a handgun chambered for the .22 Long Rifle is adequate. It's accurate and ammunition is inexpensive (which means plenty of practice shooting at low cost). Revolvers are also available chambered for the .22 Winchester Magnum, which is nothing more than a souped-up .22. The .22 Magnum gives an edge to the hunter who is after slightly larger small game, such as raccoons, bobcats, or possibly foxes. The one drawback is that the .22 Magnum is not interchangeable with the .22 Long Rifle. Buying a handgun chambered for the .22 Magnum means ammunition will be more expensive and the gun will likely not be used often for extended shooting sessions and practice. But if the idea of a .22 Magnum appeals to you, there is a solution. Ruger's Single-Six Convertible is equipped with two interchangeable cylinders, one chambered for the standard .22, the other for the .22 Magnum. The shooter uses the .22 Magnum cylinder for hunting and switches to the standard .22 cylinder for target practice and plinking.

Another interesting development in recent years has been the revival of single-shot pistols. They've become particularly popular for varminting at longer ranges than the usual handgunning distances, so their owners often scope them. The best known are the Thompson/Center Contender and Encore, which come in a wide variety of calibers, from .22 Rimfire, both standard and magnum, to powerful centerfire calibers suitable for big game. Included are a number of good varminting cartridges such as .223 Remington and .17

HMR. A few big-game hunters use single shots, but most prefer repeaters. Revolvers are the favorites, at least partly because they come in a wide range of very popular calibers.

For big game, the centerfire magnums take the lead, though other calibers will do in a pinch. The .45 Auto, .44 Special, and .45 Colt will work on deer-size animals if the range is not excessive, say 100 feet or so. Beyond that range, you're pushing your luck and it's best to rely on the magnums.

The big four magnums are the .357, .41, .44, and .454 Casull. The .357 Magnum, the smallest of the big four with its 158-grain bullet, develops a muzzle energy of 845 foot-pounds and a muzzle velocity of 1,550 feet per second. The recoil is heavy, but not enough to shake up the average shooter. The .357 is fine for deer, mountain lions, coyotes, and bobcats. It also makes a dandy rig for varmints. The .357 has taken bigger game, such as bears, but using it on animals weighing more than 200 pounds is stretching the cartridge beyond its limits.

One very big advantage in selecting a .357 Magnum is that the handgun will also accept the .38 Special, a popular target load. (Caution: The .38 Special can be fired in guns chambered for the .357 Magnum, but the .357 Magnum **cannot** be fired in a gun chambered for the .38 Special.) The .357 Magnum, then, is a good combination rig for hunting. The magnum loads are adequate for deer and smaller game. Switch to the .38 Special cartridge and the gun can be used for target shooting and plinking. This is a particularly good combination for the reloader, since the .38 Special is an inexpensive round to reload.

Next in size is the .41 Magnum, which would probably be considered an excellent load for big game if the .44 Magnum wasn't around. The .41 Magnum was designed to fill the gap between the .357 and .44 Magnums, but it hasn't quite turned out that way. The .41 offers slightly less velocity and energy than the .44, but recoil is still considerable.

The .44 Remington Magnum takes top honors for big-game hunting. Its big bullet doesn't travel quite as fast as the .357 Magnum, but it has a muzzle velocity in excess of 1,450 feet per second, and it develops nearly double the foot-pounds of energy of the .357 Magnum.

Out to 100 yards, a skilled shooter can take big game with any of these cartridges. All are ideal for deer and black bears. They would also be good insurance when traveling in grizzly country. However, these very hefty magnums are not for inexperienced or weak-handed shooters. They're the most powerful factory-loaded handgun cartridges made, and they produce the recoil and muzzle blast that must be expected from such cartridges.

Target Shooting

The shooter who wants to take up target shooting with a handgun should definitely start out with a .22 Rimfire. Because recoil is almost nonexistent with a .22, the shooter can concentrate on developing good shooting habits, such as proper trigger squeeze, grip, stance, and so on. Theoretically, after a training period with a .22 Rimfire, a shooter should be able to progress to larger calibers without letting heavier recoil and muzzle blast affect his shooting style.

As mentioned earlier, the revolver is simpler and safer to use. But since the safety factor is not as critical on a supervised target range as it is in the field, a shooter can select either a revolver or an automatic. Both are accurate handguns and, under target-range conditions, both are equally reliable.

Barrel length for a target pistol should not be less than 6 inches. The only exceptions to this barrel-length rule are the few specially designed target pistols, such as the .45-caliber Colt Gold Cup National Match, but it's best to stick to barrels that fall between 6 and 9 inches for serious target shooting.

Target guns should be heavier than sidearms used for hunting. Target shooters do not have to carry their guns great distances, so weight is not a burden. A heavier gun means a steadier hold on the range and this is important in competition. Generally, a target handgun should weigh between 38 and 48 ounces, but a handgun chambered for the .38 Special or .45 Auto usually weighs a bit more.

When a shooter moves from the .22 Rimfire to the bigger calibers, he'll have to choose between a revolver and automatic. The two most popular centerfire target cartridges are the .38 Special and the .45 Auto. One factor to keep in mind is that you'll have a wider selection of handguns to choose from with the .38 Special. The .38 Special also kicks less than the .45 Auto.

And if you want to get involved in both hunting and target shooting, the .38 Special is by far a better choice since it can also be fired in .357 Magnum revolvers. A good combination, then, would be a match-grade .357 Magnum. The .357 Magnum cartridges can be used for

A good example of a handgun that works well for target shooting and plinking is the Ruger GP100 (*top*) chambered for the .357 Magnum. Used for hunting, the .357 is more than capable of bringing down medium-size game, such as wild hogs. The less expensive .38 Special cartridges can also be fired in the same handgun. If you decide to try handloading, you can load economical .38 Special wadcutters for target shooting and plinking. Ideally, the .22-caliber rimfire makes the perfect plinking handgun. A good choice is the Ruger .22-caliber Single-Six (*bottom*) with an interchangeable .22 Magnum cylinder. Choose .22 Long Rifle ammunition for plinking and you also have the option of changing cylinders and shooting .22 Magnum cartridges for small-game hunting.

both hunting and target work. If you find the .357 too much gun for the target range, simply switch to the .38 Special loads and use the same gun.

Needless to say, all target handguns must have the best sights available, and these are generally micrometer sights with solid adjustments for windage and elevation.

In addition to these conventional target handguns, there are more specialized types that are useful only for specific—and very sophisticated—target events. There are .22 Long Rifle free pistols (single shots called "free" in reference to the lack of restrictions on weight, sight radius, trigger pull, types of grips, and so on). There are .22 Long Rifle automatics with adjustable grips, weights, and other features for standard international matches. For rapid fire international matches, there are special automatics chambered for the .22 Short. And there are specially modified revolvers for Police Course matches, as well as revolvers and automatics for other combat-style target competitions.

Among rifles, too, there are specialized models for sophisticated matches—game-silhouette rifles, free rifles, highly tuned sporters for running-game targets, and so on. Two good sources of information on competitive shooting with both handguns and rifles are the National Rifle Association of America (www.nra.org) and National Shooting Sports Foundation (www.nssf.org).

▪ Plinking

Plinking means shooting at tin cans, paper targets, stationary claybirds, or any other safe target. Plinking has also turned beginners into skilled shooters. In short, it's an ideal and informal way of learning how to safely handle and shoot guns.

The ideal handgun for plinking is the .22 Rimfire, since ammunition is cheap and plinking usually involves a lot of shooting. The .22's recoil is nil, which means the entire family can get involved. A revolver is the best bet for this type of informal shooting, since it is the safest gun to handle.

Adjustable sights are advisable even on guns for plinking, though fixed sights are sometimes adequate for busting tin cans.

Theoretically, any gun you happen to have in your hand at the moment can be used for plinking. If you can stand the cost of the more expensive centerfire ammunition, that's fine, but the .22 Rimfire is the ideal plinker and also a good choice for the camper who can legally take a handgun along on his trips.

▪ Muzzleloading Handgun

Among muzzleloading handguns, there are replica and nonreplica revolvers, as well as replica and nonreplica single shots. Of the replica revolvers, copies of the old Colts exceed all others in number. Most of them are used for plinking or informal target shooting. A few shooters also use such guns for hunting.

For shooters who want truly authentic Colts of the colorful 1850–1870 era, they're now available from at least a half dozen makers. The 1860 Army, the Dragoons, and the 1851 Navy are some of the currently available models.

The revolvers are all percussion guns, of course. Single shots come in flintlock as well as percussion versions. The flintlocks are less popular, but they're available from Traditions, Lyman, and a few other companies. These pistols are replicas or near-replicas of late 18th- and early 19th-century guns. They're mostly used for plinking, although flintlock target matches are sometimes conducted. Some models are available in kit form as well as finished.

Some of the same single-shot pistols, or guns very much like them, are available in caplock versions from the same makers or importers, as well as from most of the other companies engaged in the muzzleloading business. A flintlock pistol is loaded in the same manner as a flintlock rifle (see the Muzzleloading Rifle section), except that a pistol charge is considerably lighter than the charge for a rifle of the same caliber. The charge for a percussion pistol is also much lighter than for a rifle of the same caliber, and the loading procedure requires a few words of advice here.

First, clean all the oil from the bore—and from the cylinder if the gun is a revolver. Then, fire a couple of caps to clear the nipple (or each nipple of a revolver) to clear out any residual oil. From this point on, the procedures differ for the single shot and the revolver. Let's take a look at the single shot first.

Place the hammer at half cock and pour the correct measure of powder down the barrel. Follow it with a patched ball of the correct caliber. Good patch material is tightly woven cotton, 0.15 inch thick. You'll have to give the starter a good bump with the heel of your hand, but a tight-fitting ball is vital for accuracy. After starting it, use the ramrod to push it all the way to the powder. Seat it firmly, but don't pound on it. Now, when you seat a percussion cap over the nipple, the gun is ready to fire.

Loading a cap-and-ball revolver begins in the same way—by cleaning out the oil and clearing the nipples. Next, move the hammer to half cock. The cylinder can then be turned by hand. From a powder measure, drop a proper charge into one chamber and place an unpatched ball over the powder at the mouth of the chamber. Cap-and-ball revolvers have built-in ramming systems, and you now turn the cylinder until the loaded chamber is under the rammer. Lower the ramming level to seat the ball against the powder. Repeat these operations until all the chambers are loaded, and then fill the mouth of each chamber with grease. Lubricants are available for this, but ordinary vegetable shortening works well, as does automotive water-pump grease. Plugging the chamber mouths with grease is insurance against a multiple

discharge, and it also softens fouling. Having done this, just cap the nipples and the gun is ready to fire.

Black-powder guns require a thorough cleaning after a firing session and, for best results, quick cleanings during a session. With a single shot, just use a damp patch followed by a dry one after each shot and your score will improve. With a revolver, you should use the same treatment after firing the full cylinder.

As with muzzleloading long guns, the National Muzzle Loading Rifle Association (www.nmlra.org) provides members with news and information regarding matches, gun shows, and other activities, as well as products.

SHOOTING THE HANDGUN

Of all sporting arms, the handgun is the most difficult to master. An outstretched arm, with a couple of pounds of gun at the end, becomes a shaky mass of nerves and muscle. And the short sight radius of the handgun doesn't help matters.

Perhaps the most common mistake made by novice handgunners is that they try too hard to steady their arm. They squeeze the grip harder, which only results in a worse case of the trembles and makes matters worse. The handgun should be held firmly, but not tightly. Don't fight the wandering front sight; let it move back and forth across the target. The secret is the trigger squeeze. First, take a deep breath, let out half of it, and then aim. When the sights cross the bull's-eye, start the trigger squeeze. When it wanders past the bull's-eye, stop the squeeze but maintain pressure on the trigger. Continue the squeeze when the sights cross the target again. Continue to do this and, eventually, the gun will fire at a point when the sights are on target. You should not be aware of when the gun will go off. Just concentrate on a slow, determined trigger squeeze.

In all likelihood, your handgun will have the common patridge sight. The correct way to use this sight is to center the post of the front sight in the square notch of the rear sight. The top of the front post should be level with the top of the rear notch. The accompanying illustration shows the correct sight picture with the patridge sight. The bull's-eye should look like an apple sitting on a fence post.

Novice handgunners also make the mistake of trying to keep both the sights and target in focus at the same time, which is impossible. When shooting a handgun,

keep the sights in focus. The target should and will be slightly blurred.

The serious target shooter will stick to his one-hand hold, because it is traditional among paper-target shooters and also because regulated competition matches may require it. But the hunter is not shooting at paper. He is shooting at game and a poor shot may well mean a wounded animal or a miss. The handgun hunter needs all the help he can get to steady his hold. In the field, he should always use a two-hand hold, and steady his sights even more by using a rest whenever possible.

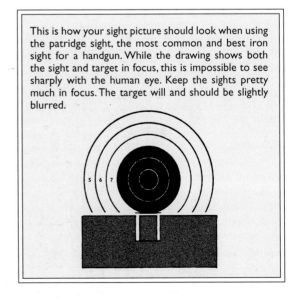

This is how your sight picture should look when using the patridge sight, the most common and best iron sight for a handgun. While the drawing shows both the sight and target in focus, this is impossible to see sharply with the human eye. Keep the sights pretty much in focus. The target will and should be slightly blurred.

HANDGUN SHOOTING POSITIONS

The photos in this section illustrate the various handgun grips and shooting positions that have proven the steadiest under most conditions.

The Grip

This is the correct one-hand hold for a double-action revolver. Hold the grip firmly, but not tightly.

This is the correct two-hand hold for revolvers. This is the hold hunters should learn well, since it's foolish to use the less steady one-hand hold when shooting at targets or live game.

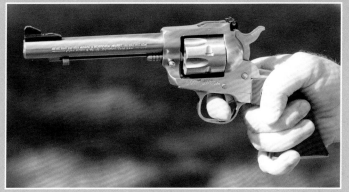

This is the correct grip for a heavy single-action revolver with factory grips. Note the little finger is curled and braced under the grip. Though this grip may look awkward, the little finger provides additional support.

Offhand Handgun Standing Positions

▲ This offhand position is for target shooting at paper only. Space your feet comfortably, with your arm extended straight at the target. Lean slightly toward the target, inserting your free hand in your pocket, rather than letting it dangle freely at your side. Under controlled conditions, a shooter can fire amazing offhand groups, but a hunter has no business shooting at game from this position.

▼ This is the offhand handgun position for hunters when no other rest is available. Cup your left hand slightly around the gun butt, which should be resting in the palm of your left hand. Extend your arms, but not so straight that you begin to shake. Relax and get comfortable.

The Sitting Position

▶ The sitting position is best for high grass when no rest is available. Facing the target, lean forward, and rest your elbows on your knees. Keep both arms relatively straight if possible, but a slight bend in the arms is OK. The most important thing is to support both elbows comfortably on your knees. Note that the feet are spread farther apart than the knees and the shooter uses a two-hand grip with the left hand cupped around the right hand. The gun butt is supported in the palm of the left hand.

◀ This is an excellent position for hunters on stand in wooded areas. Sit facing the target and rest your back against the support, usually a tree, so that your elbows are supported by both knees and you can extend your arms.

Sitting with Arm Rest

▶ Though this sitting position may look strange at first, it is very steady when no other rest is available. This position has become popular with long-range silhouette shooters. Note that every part of the body is supported and braced. The buttocks are on the ground, the gun hand rests on the knee, and the shooter's back is braced by the left arm on the ground. This unique shooting position clearly shows that the shooter can relax and squeeze off his shot comfortably. No part of his body is strained or twisted.

The Prone Position

▶ This is the steadiest of all handgun positions. Simply lie flat on the ground, with your feet comfortably spaced, arms almost fully extended, and elbows resting on the ground. The line of sight should run directly down the center of your back. A handgun hunter should use this position whenever possible.

Supported Handgun Positions

◀▲ As a handgun hunter, you owe it to the game you hunt to make sure your shot counts. Use every rest or prop. If there's a tree available, brace your left arm against it as shown, and support your gun hand on your left wrist. Use posts, stumps, rocks, anything that will steady your handgun. Always hold the gun with two hands.

HANDLOADING

This section on reloading metallic cartridges and shotshells is intended to introduce hunters and target shooters to the fascinating and money-saving hobby of reloading your own ammunition. Before you invest in equipment, you should begin with buying and studying a reloading manual, including the data tables. I recommend the Lyman manuals, and you should also visit the Lyman website (www.lymanproducts.com). I reloaded my own ammunition for years, and it's a fascinating way to improve your shooting on the range and in the field.

simple basics. However, for the benefit of the uninitiated, let's begin at this point.

Each factory-loaded cartridge that you purchase and fire represents extensive thought and care on the part of its manufacturer. If you are to reload a fired cartridge, and duplicate, if possible, the original factory loading, you must first learn to appreciate some of the intricacies of ammunition design. The information, photos, and instructional illustrations in this section are provided courtesy of Lyman, a major manufacturer of reloading equipment for rifle, handgun, and shotshell ammunition.

■ Rifle Cartridges

If you are considering reloading, it is safe to assume that you have already had considerable shooting experience. Certainly, you have purchased and fired a good many rounds of factory-loaded ammunition. Hence, you are equipped with a working knowledge of various caliber designations and cartridge shapes, and you have learned to recognize the correct cartridge for your particular rifle. Probably many readers will have an overall understanding of shooting that extends beyond these

■ Reloading Rifle Cartridges

The mechanics of each reloading step are quite simple. However, there are several important considerations to be given to each step. Observing these considerations will help ensure that all ammo you assemble is safe, will function reliably, and will be accurate. This information is important and must be read and understood before actually beginning to assemble ammunition.

The following step-by-step descriptions deal with assembling fired bottleneck (shouldered) cartridges with

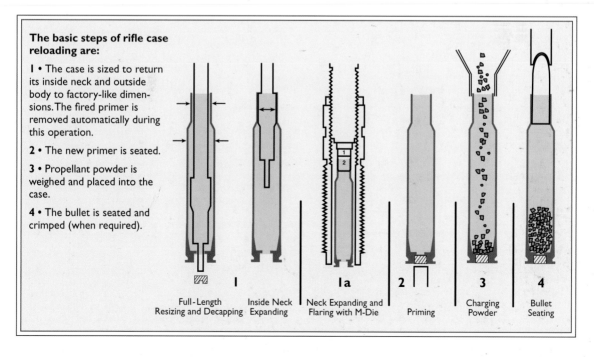

The basic steps of rifle case reloading are:

1 • The case is sized to return its inside neck and outside body to factory-like dimensions. The fired primer is removed automatically during this operation.

2 • The new primer is seated.

3 • Propellant powder is weighed and placed into the case.

4 • The bullet is seated and crimped (when required).

1		1a	2	3	4
Full-Length Resizing and Decapping	Inside Neck Expanding	Neck Expanding and Flaring with M-Die	Priming	Charging Powder	Bullet Seating

13 Steps for Reloading Jacketed-Bullet Bottleneck Cartridge Ammo

1 • Selection of load and components

2 • Case inspection

3 • Case cleaning

4 • Inside neck brushing (not required when using new, unfired cases)

5 • Case lubrication

6 • Case resizing and fired primer removal (not required when using new, unfired cases)

7 • Lubricant removal and second inspection

8 • Case length measuring

9 • Case trimming and deburring (not always required)

10 • Primer seating

11 • Powder weighing and charging

12 • Bullet seating and, if required, crimping

13 • Final inspection

jacketed bullets intended for use in either rifles or handguns. Slight deviations from these steps are required when reloading ammo with lead bullets for rifle or handgun cartridges having a straight case (no shoulder), or when loading new, unfired cases.

Reloading a fired cartridge generally requires 13 basic steps. The sequence or actual number of these can vary depending on the specific equipment used and the reloader's preference. The sequence described here is based on the method that is most often favored by knowledgeable handloaders. Again, not every step is always required.

STEP 1 ■ SELECTION OF LOAD AND COMPONENTS: At first, the selection of components may seem like a difficult and confusing task. This is especially true if you have not yet acquired a general knowledge of basic ammunition details. Nonetheless, you soon will find that component selection quickly becomes an easy and fun part of reloading. The learning process can be hastened along by developing as much ammo knowledge as

leisure reading time will allow. There are many excellent shooting and hunting magazines that will be a great help in this regard.

■ Selecting Cartridge Cases

The selection of fired cartridge cases, or new brass, presents no special challenge. If you have saved your fired cases you need only separate them into specific groups by brand and lot number. Lot numbers appear on the factory ammo box. This number may be on an inside flap or the back of the box. Keeping brass segregated by lots will maximize accuracy potential and ballistic uniformity. If you purchase new, unfired cases, they must, of course, be of the appropriate caliber. Purchasing bulk-packaged cases (in lots of 50, 100, or more) is the least expensive way of obtaining new brass. Caution: Never load cartridge cases from an unknown source, (i.e., cases picked up at the range or sold as once-fired brass). Use only brand-new brass or cases obtained as the result of firing factory ammo in your firearm.

■ Selecting Primers

The proper primer size is listed at the beginning of the data for each cartridge, (e.g., large rifle, large rifle magnum, small rifle, etc.). For your first loads, you should use the exact primer used for the development of the Lyman data. As an alternate, match the primer brand and correct size to the brand of the case you are reloading. Do not use magnum primers unless the data specifically calls for these, as doing so can alter ballistic uniformity and the safety of the data.

Do not allow cartridge nomenclature to enter into the selection of primers. For example, the .222

Test Components

Cases	Remington
Trim-To Length	1.400 inches
Primers	Remington 7½
Primer Size	Small Rifle
Lyman Shell Holder	No. 26
Jacketed Bullets Used	Hornady V-Max #22004, 32 grains
	Hornady V-Max #22006, 40 grains
	Hornady SP #22008, 45 grains

Primer size and the specific primer used is clearly shown at the beginning of the data for each caliber.

Remington Magnum never requires the use of a magnum primer and the .416 Rigby always requires the use of a magnum primer. Always follow the primer size and type as listed in the data tables.

■ Selecting Propellant Powders

Propellant powders are available in about 100 different types. The burning speed of each and the ballistics obtained can vary tremendously. Powders are designed to suit specific applications, such as bullet weight, case size and shape, pressure level, and other specific ballistic and firearm needs. As a result, only certain propellants are suitable for specific applications. When selecting a powder for your first reloading efforts, you should use the propellant listed for the accuracy load. Caution: Always start with the exact powder charge weight shown under the starting grains column. Heavier loads should not be used until the reloader has gained some experience and fully understands proper load development.

■ Selecting Jacketed Bullets

Bullet selection may at first seem confusing. To simplify the process, select a bullet weight to duplicate the factory ammo you favor. Many calibers use the same diameter bullet. For example, .300 Savage, .30-40 Krag, .308 Winchester, .30-06 Springfield, .300 Winchester Magnum, and others all use a .308-inch diameter (30-caliber) bullet.

There is another consideration when selecting bullets. The muzzle velocity of a cartridge may require a specific bullet jacket strength and construction. For example, the .30 M1 Carbine uses a .308-inch bullet, but because of its very low velocity, it requires a bullet having a very soft jacket in order to properly expand. The .30-30 has a modest velocity and it also needs a relatively soft bullet, albeit stronger than those for the .30 M1 Carbine. Still other calibers require a bullet designed for a midrange velocity bullet, e.g., the .222 Remington. Bullets that are ideal for this cartridge often are designated with nomenclature that suggests rapid bullet expansion: Blitz, Expander, Super Explosive (SX), and so on. Often bullets for specific applications will be so marked on the package. Some examples are .22 Hornet, .30-30, and .32 Winchester Special.

Most data specifies the bullet manufacturer's product number for each tested bullet weight. Each of the listed bullets will work fine for target shooting. However, for proper expansion on varmints or big game, you will need to make certain that the bullet you select is properly designed and suitable for the velocity range of your cartridge. If you are loading for hunting, avoid the use of bullets designated as Match or Target style, as these may not expand properly on game.

Often you will be able to purchase the identical bullet used in your favorite factory loads. Some of these include the Nosler Partition, Nosler Ballistic Tip, and Swift A-Frame bullets. Many other factory bullet types are available to the handloader.

Selecting a Propellant

20-grain Jacketed V-Max Ballistic Coefficient: .185
1.830 inches overall length Sectional Density: .097

Powder	Suggested Starting Grains	Velocity (feet per second)	Pressure (pounds per square inch)	Max Load Grains	Velocity (feet per second)	Pressure (pounds per square inch)
IIMR-4198	15.3	3,556	35,800	17.0+	3,999	50,800
N133	17.0	3,526	35,500	19.0	3,973	51,400
RX10	16.8	3,607	36,600	18.5	3,954	49,100
H-322	17.5	3,463	33,800	19.5+	3,920	49,400
Benchmark	18.0	3,611	38,700	20.0+	3,990	51,900
X-Terminator	18.0	3,594	39,400	20.0	3,975	51,800
AA-2230	18.5	3,649	36,800	20.5+	4,016	50,500
H-335	18.7	3,541	36,500	20.6	4,036	52,600

The selection of a propellant for your first loads is easily made by referencing the bullet weight you are using, the accurate powder, and the starting load (all highlighted here) as shown in the data.

Other important bullet selection criteria are the possible need for a cannelure or the requirement for a blunt-nosed bullet.

■ The Loading Sequence

The use of two loading blocks is suggested. As each step is performed, the case should be removed from one loading block, processed, and then placed in the second loading block. This will keep the process orderly and prevent many common bench errors. Note: Lyman strongly suggests that the reloader follow the batch method of ammo making. That is, perform a single operation on all cases to be reloaded before proceeding to the next step.

STEP 2 ■ CASE INSPECTION: Fired cartridge cases have a finite life. Depending upon the firearm used, caliber of the firearm, internal ballistics of the load, and other considerations, it is reasonable to expect two to 15 firings from each case. Six firings are average for the typical bottleneck rifle cartridge, such as the .270 Winchester or .30-06 Springfield. Belted magnum cases such as the 7mm Remington Magnum, .300 Winchester Magnum, and .338 Winchester Magnum typically last for only three firings. Low-pressure cartridges fired in strong actions, such as the .416 Rigby, generally offer the greatest number of firings. All else equal, cases fired in semi-automatic rifles will have a shorter reloading life than cases fired in bolt-action rifles.

All cases reach a point when further reloading becomes unsafe. The keeping of careful reloading records, and the performing of visual inspections on each case before, during, and after reloading, are essential to ensure that you use only suitably safe fired cases.

Begin your inspection by wiping each case with a cloth to remove excess fouling, dirt, and any foreign material that could scratch your resizing die or the case itself. Turn each case mouth down and tap it lightly on the bench to dislodge anything that may have entered the case after firing.

Now, look for split necks or bodies, signs of incipient case separation (a bright partial or complete ring around the case at the point where the case's solid base joins the wall of the cartridge), corrosion, or burn-through perforations. Also look for any signs of gas leakage around the primer pocket. Eliminate all cases with any visual defect or abnormality. To prevent later inadvertent use of a rejected case, crimp its mouth shut with a pair of pliers before discarding it. Then, place each case, mouth up, in a loading block.

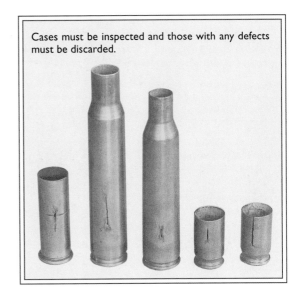

Cases must be inspected and those with any defects must be discarded.

STEP 3 ■ CASE CLEANING: Case cleaning is an important step to protect your reloading dies and firearm chambers. If you also want your reloads to look like new, now is the time to put all your cases into a Lyman tumbler. Follow the instructions that come with it. After removing the cases from the tumbler, tap the mouth of each case on the bench to ensure that no tumbling media remains in it. Then, wipe each case lightly with a clean cloth.

STEP 4 ■ INSIDE NECK BRUSHING: This is a step that some reloaders omit. However, it is a simple one that takes very little time and it will improve the performance of your ammunition. Brushing the inside case neck will rid it of excess firing residue, enhance the ease of pulling the expanding button through the case neck (when withdrawing the case from the sizing die), and extend the useful life of the sizing die's expanding button. It will also enhance accuracy by helping to maintain uniform bullet pull.

This operation simply involves three or four passes of a brush through the case mouth. Place the brushed case into the second loading block, mouth down, to allow any loosened crud to fall free of the case. To prevent the accumulation of debris in the second loading block, many reloaders tap the case mouth on the bench before placing it in the block.

STEP 5 ■ CASE LUBRICATION: When a cartridge is fired, it expands. The expanded dimensions are not compatible

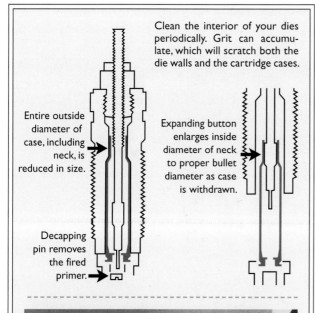

Clean the interior of your dies periodically. Grit can accumulate, which will scratch both the die walls and the cartridge cases.

Entire outside diameter of case, including neck, is reduced in size.

Expanding button enlarges inside diameter of neck to proper bullet diameter as case is withdrawn.

Decapping pin removes the fired primer.

The first die usage step of reloading requires that the lubricated case be completely run into the full-length resizing die. This will return the case to factory-like dimensions and remove the old primer.

with holding a new bullet with proper tension (bullet pull), and are not conducive to easy chambering. To avoid these and other difficulties, all fired cases must be resized.

Roll a case lightly across your lubricant pad. Do not fail to lubricate each case or it will stick solidly in the resizing die, creating a problem that is very difficult to correct. Do not use excessive lubricant, as doing so will cause cases to dent during the resizing step. Use only enough lubricant to ensure the case enters and leaves the resizing die without difficulty. Be neat. Do not get lubricant into the primer pocket or case mouth. Do not get lube on the case shoulder or it will dent, or possibly collapse, during resizing. Dipping the case mouth in mica, a dry powder lubricant, will help the expander button pass smoothly through the case neck. Place the case in the loading block mouth up.

STEP 6 ▪ CASE RESIZING AND FIRED PRIMER REMOVAL: Place a lubed case into the shell holder and run the case into the full-length resizing die. Follow the instructions for proper die adjustment as explained in the material supplied with your die set. After the first case is resized, wipe off the lubricant with a clean cloth. Then, place the case into a cartridge headspace gauge. If a die adjustment is needed, now is the time. The resizing die generally is adjusted so that the shell holder, at the top of its travel, will contact the resizing die and create a slight cam action against the die. During this operation, the fired primer will automatically be ejected from the case. Withdraw the case from the sizing die and place the case into the loading block mouth down. Visually inspect each case as it is placed in the loading block to ensure the fired primer has been removed. Note: The decapping rod should be adjusted just low enough to ensure the primer is pushed free of the case. If the decapping rod is too low, it will impact the inside bottom of the case and be damaged. Proceed until all cases have been lubed and sized.

STEP 7 ▪ LUBRICANT REMOVAL AND SECOND INSPECTION: Carefully wipe each case with a clean cloth to remove all traces of sizing lubricant. Use a clean section of the cloth for each case. Next, carefully inspect the case for any flaws. Repeated case resizing and firings can cause case mouths and bodies to become brittle and split when fired or during resizing. Also watch for signs of incipient case separation. It is a good idea at this time to drop the resized case into a cartridge headspace gauge as a worthwhile inspection step. This will ensure that your sizing die is correctly adjusted to give the case the proper headspace length. Place cleaned and inspected cases in your loading block mouth up. Should you find any defects, this is the time to discard the entire lot of cases. Important: Case lubricant can ruin a primer, resulting in delayed ignition or a failure to fire. To avoid potential primer contamination, this is the point to stop the reloading process and thoroughly wash and dry your hands.

■ **Special Step for Straight Cases or When Using Lead Bullets**

Straight cases cannot be properly neck expanded in a resizing die. Such cases must now be expanded in a special expanding die, such as the Lyman M die. This extra die is supplied in all appropriate caliber die sets. If you wish to load lead bullets, the case mouth must have a two-step expansion. This is also done with an M die. Follow the instructions that come with all three die straight case sets or with the M die when purchased as an accessory for loading lead bullets into bottleneck cases.

STEP 8 ■ CASE LENGTH MEASURING: Case measuring is an important step both for safety and proper ammunition functioning. Cases stretch when fired and during the resizing step. If they become too long, they will be difficult, if not impossible, to chamber. Excessive chamber pressure can also be caused by exceeding maximum case length. Therefore, each case must be carefully measured at this point. A dial indicator or digital caliper is the best tool for this process.

The data section illustration for each cartridge clearly indicates the maximum allowable length for the resized case. If one or more cases are found to be at maximum or greater length, trim all cases to a uniform length as described in the next step.

STEP 9 ■ CASE TRIMMING AND DEBURRING: As stated previously, cases must be trimmed when they exceed the maximum allowable length. Additionally, case trimming is recommend whenever starting to load new or once-fired brass, as such cases will not be of a uniform length. Trimming cases to a uniform length will enhance accuracy and ballistic uniformity. Note: If you will be crimping cases to bullets (required for ammo to be used in

Test Components	
Cases	Hornady
Trim-To Length	1.840 inches
Primers	Remington 7½
Primer Size	Small Rifle
Lyman Shell Holder	No. 26
Jacketed Bullets Used	Hornady V-Max #21710, 20 grains Hornady HP #1710, 25 grains

semi-automatic and pump-action rifles, or for ammo to be used in tubular magazines), the crimping process will be less than satisfactory if the cases are not of a uniform length. Many reloaders who crimp cases trim after every firing/resizing cycle.

The proper trim-to length for cases is clearly shown in the data for each cartridge. Adjust your trimmer according to the manufacturer's instructions. When trimming, allow for some dwell time—that is, for a number of rotations of the cutter after the case has been trimmed to length. This will help ensure the maximum uniformity of finished lengths.

After trimming, remove the burrs (formed by the trimmer cutter) from both the inside and outside of the case mouth using a Lyman deburring tool. A few twists of the tool is all that is needed. Do not deburr the case to a sharp edge. Tap the case mouth on the bench to dislodge any brass chips from inside the case. Place the case, mouth down, in your loading block.

Caution: The material trimmed from a case flows from the junction of the case head and wall. As brass continues to flow and is trimmed away, this section of the case becomes thinner until it reaches a point where the case is severely weakened. Therefore, never trim a case more than four times (keep careful records). When a case needs its fifth trimming, it must be discarded. The initial trim of new cases is not counted when determining the number of times a case is trimmed, as this trim is done not because of case stretch but rather to create a uniform length.

STEP 10 ■ PRIMER SEATING: While not absolutely essential, it is advisable to clean primer pockets before seating a new primer. This is a simple operation requiring only a few twists of the pocket cleaning tool. As each case's primer pocket is cleaned, place the case in the loading block mouth up.

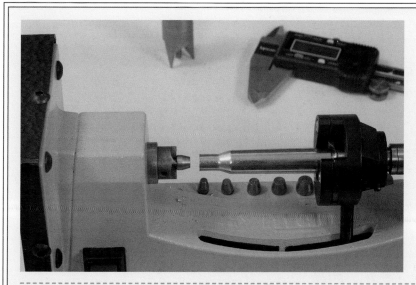

Case trimmers are miniature lathes that quickly restore a case to a safe and accurate overall length.

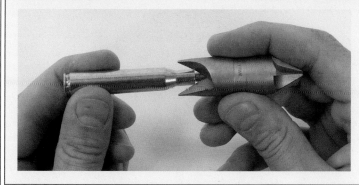

After trimming, all cases must be lightly deburred on the inside and outside of the case mouth.

Bring a box of 100 primers to the bench and read the label aloud to ensure that you have the correct brand and size. Then double check again. You must use the primer size and type called for in the data.

Caution: Safety glasses should be worn whenever handling primers. It's also important to wash and thoroughly dry your hands before starting to prime.

Place a quantity of primers (never more than 100—or a lesser amount as needed) onto a primer flipper tray. Gently rotate the primer tray until all primers are anvil side up.

Most loading tools come equipped with a basic primer seating tool that primes the case at the normal shell-holder position. Follow the instructions supplied with the tool. Place a primer, anvil up, into the priming post, push the post under the shell holder, and then lower the shell holder over the post to seat the primer. On many loading tools, this requires a "feel" method to seat the primer to the correct depth. Some tools will have a rudimentary stop to adjust primer seating depth.

A better method for primer seating is to use a ram-prime tool that mounts into the tool's die station. Primer seating depth then can be controlled by adjustment of the ram-prime body combined with using the press handle's solid stop at the end of the priming stroke. This method produces a very uniform primer seating depth. Generally, primers should be seated 0.003 inch to 0.005 inch below flush of the case head—a nominal of 0.004 inch below flush.

Caution: Primers seated too high (above flush) are a needless hazard. It is possible that such primers can be ignited before the firearm action is closed, causing

Primer seating may be accomplished in many ways and with differing tools. One of the best methods is to use a Ram Prime unit mounted in the reloading tool's die station.

a serious accident. High primers are also prone to misfires. Primers seated too deeply (below flush) can become erratic in performance or misfire. Primers are also explosive and require special care in storage and handling.

Place the primed case in the loading block mouth down. When all cases have been primed, verify proper priming depth by running a finger over each case head. The novice should use a caliper to verify proper primer seating depth and then run a finger over several of these. This will teach the correct "feel" so that you can verify all remaining seating depths by feel. After you check primer depth, return the case, mouth up, to the loading block.

After priming, return any unused primers to their original container and replace them in your storage area.

STEP 11 ▪ POWDER WEIGHING AND CHARGING:
Weighing powder must be done with great care and accuracy. Set up your powder scale carefully, following the instructions supplied with it. It is good practice to verify the scale's accuracy by using a weight check set.

Bring only one powder can to the loading bench. Read the label aloud. You must use the exact powder called for in the data. Then double check again. The inadvertent use of the wrong powder can cause a catastrophic accident.

Bring a box of bullets to the loading bench and read aloud the label on your bullet box to make certain the bullets are the correct weight (matched to the data you are using). Then, measure the diameter and weigh a few bullets to be certain that what is in the box is the same as the label. Factory packaging errors have occurred. (A bullet will be seating immediately after a case is charged with powder.)

Pour some powder into the powder trickler and position the trickler alongside the scale pan. Also pour some powder into an open container (or preferably into a powder measure). Use a scoop of appropriate size to place a quantity of powder, somewhat less than a full charge, onto the scale pan.

If using a powder measure, adjust the measure to dispense somewhat less powder than you require. The metered charge will vary so be certain that the heaviest charges will not exceed the desired weight. (It is nettlesome to try and remove excess powder from the scale pan.) Dispense a metered charge directly onto the scale pan and then place the pan on the scale hanger.

Note: A handy powder scoop can be made by cutting off a fired case at an appropriate length and twisting a wire handle into the case rim's undercut. Straight cases such as the .30 M1 Carbine, .44 Magnum, and .45-70 make the best scoops.

Bring the scale into perfect balance, using the powder trickler to add one kernel of powder at a time to the scale pan. Now, pour the weighed powder charge into a case using a powder funnel. Make certain that the scale poises are not inadvertently moved during the loading process.

Caution: Powder is highly flammable and requires care in storage and handling. In addition, Lyman lab technicians have observed a potential serious phenomenon involving mechanical powder scales, plastic loading blocks, Styrofoam packaging, and other objects made of plastic. These materials sometimes retain a static electric charge, enough to create an electrostatic field of varying radii. This electrostatic field has proven capable of causing radical defection of uncharged and zeroed scales. Dependent upon circumstances, powder in the scale pan tends to dampen the amount of deflection by varying degrees.

Notes on Using a Powder Measure

After metering a powder charge, it should be checked and brought into perfect balance using a scale and powder trickler. If you are loading ammunition for a noncritical application, in order to save time you may opt to pour a metered powder charge directly into a case (without the scale check and trickler balance). Caution: This method should never be used with maximum loads or by novices at any time. When using a powder measure in this manner, always check at least every 10th load on the scale to ensure that the measure has not gone out of adjustment and that you are using a uniform metering technique. Keep in mind that fine (small) grain or spherical powders lend themselves to more uniform metering, as opposed to course (large) grain propellants. Be sure you are capable of metering uniform charges before using this method. Verify your uniformity by weighing 20 or more consecutive metered charges.

Lyman strongly urges reloaders to clear the loading bench before setting up the scale. Then, replace equipment one piece at a time while observing the scale pointer. Any item that causes a scale deflection should be removed from the loading bench. Do this at every loading session.

Novices should avoid the use of compressed powder charges (where the powder level in the case is so high as to require compression of the powder in order to seat a bullet to the correct depth).

STEP 12 ▪ BULLET SEATING AND CRIMPING: Next, immediately transfer the charged case to the loading tool and seat a bullet to the correct overall length. Follow the die manufacturer's instructions to properly seat the bullet to the correct depth. The maximum overall length for a loaded round is clearly listed in the data for each cartridge. Dependent upon the bullet and equipment used, the finished individual overall cartridge length may vary by plus or minus 0.005 inch.

Note: Generally, bullets should be seated to the overall length shown at the top of each data panel. Do

check to see that ammo so assembled will feed through the magazine of your rifle and that it chambers properly. Do this testing out of doors with the muzzle pointed at a safe backstop. Or better yet, make a dummy round (no powder or primer) to check overall length. Circumstances, which include magazine length, chamber dimensions, and bullet give, may make it necessary to use a different length.

When all cases are charged and bullets seated, return all powder (from trickler, open container, or powder measure) to the original container and return the container to its remote storage area.

Bullet crimping is required whenever there is a possibility of the bullet striking a firearm surface (during the feed/chamber cycle) with sufficient force to push the bullet deeper into the case. This means that ammunition for almost all semi-automatic and pump actions should have the case crimped to the bullet. Also, if there is a danger

Immediately after adding powder to the case, seat the bullet to have a finished cartridge of the correct overall length.

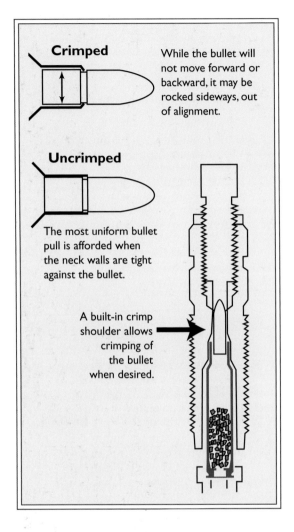

Crimped

While the bullet will not move forward or backward, it may be rocked sideways, out of alignment.

Uncrimped

The most uniform bullet pull is afforded when the neck walls are tight against the bullet.

A built-in crimp shoulder allows crimping of the bullet when desired.

you first back off the bullet seating screw substantially. Then, screw the die down far enough to turn the case mouth slightly inward into the bullet cannelure when the loaded round is fully raised into the die. Be certain the bullet seating screw is backed off far enough to prevent it from touching the bullet.

Note: The crimping operation may be combined with bullet seating, but the best results are obtained when it is done as a separate operation.

STEP 13 ▪ FINAL INSPECTION: The final inspection should be done with great care. Start by looking for imperfections. These may include, but are not limited to, case necks that split during bullet seating, and case shoulders that buckled during crimping (most often due to a poor bullet cannelure or improper die adjustment). A second check of primer depth should be made by running your finger over each case head. Dropping the loaded round into a case headspace gauge is also recommended to help ensure it will chamber properly. Also, measure a sampling of the loaded rounds to check for proper overall length. Should any round be found abnormal, discard it in a safe manner.

Place loaded rounds into a suitable container. Clearly mark the container with the date loaded, primer used, times trimmed, powder and charge, bullet brand, weight and type, and overall ammo length. Then, enter all this information into your reloading log. Your log should also include the lot numbers of all the components used.

▪ Reloading Shotshells on a Single-Stage Press

There are many makes and models of shotshell reloading presses on the market. Press types range from very basic nonprogressive models to very elaborate, progressive ones. The cost can range from less than $50 for a basic unit to hundreds of dollars for the most elaborate type. Nonprogressive tools usually provide a production rate of 125 to 200 rounds per hour.

A production rate of approximately 100 shells per hour will allow the beginner time to learn what is happening. As experience is gained, the reloader will be able to increase output to about 150 rounds per hour without sacrificing the time necessary to keep a constant vigil over each loading step.

This section will familiarize the reader with the basic steps of ammo assembly. For purposes of demonstration, the loading procedure is described as it occurs when using a MEC 600 Jr. Mark V reloading tool. The 600 Jr., like

of the bullet creeping forward out of the case (loads with very heavy recoil) while in the magazine, ammunition should be crimped. All ammunition to be used in tubular magazines must be crimped to prevent bullets from being driven deeper into the case during recoil. All ammo to be used in a revolver also should be crimped. Because crimping has a somewhat detrimental effect on accuracy, crimping should be limited to ammo intended for one or more of the previously mentioned applications.

Keep in mind that your bullets must have a cannelure (a groove around the bullet) in order to crimp. Such bullets must first be seated to a depth that will align the case mouth with the center of the bullet cannelure. Adjusting your seating/crimping die requires that

almost all quality shotshell reloading tools, completes the essential loading procedure in a concise sequence.

As packaged from the factory, most shotshell reloading presses are adjusted to properly assemble a loaded round. However, depending upon the specific case and load you wish to assemble, some die adjustment or powder bushing/shot bar replacement may be necessary. Some tools are not packaged with a powder bushing, requiring this to be purchased separately. Generally, once the tool is adjusted to load shells, only the crimp start and final crimp stations may need occasional readjustment. This may be necessary when switching from one specific set of components to another, such as changing from the older Winchester compression-formed case to the newer high-strength hull. Most adjustments are relatively easy once you become familiar with the press.

Note: While there are 11 steps in shotshell assembly, there are only five station positions on the 600 Jr. loading press. Some of the steps, such as verification of powder bushing and shot bar, are not actual loading sequences and are performed only once at the beginning of each loading session. Case inspections are also done "off-machine." Finally, the 600 Jr. combines powder charging, wad seating, and shot charging into one press station.

STEP 1 ▪ BUSHING AND BAR VERIFICATION:

At the beginning of each loading session, you must ensure that the right powder bushing and shot bar are installed on the loading press. Carefully check the number on the powder bushing against the number listed in your loading records, or in the manufacturer's bushing tables. Often, you will be able to see the powder bushing's number through an opening in the loading tool/metering bar (positioned directly beneath the powder hopper). Also, check the nomenclature on the left end of the shot bar to be certain you will meter the correct shot charge. Keep in mind that the actual weights of the metered powder and shot charges must be verified on a scale as the loading process begins. You may have to substitute the powder bushing you first selected for a smaller or larger one.

STEP 2 ▪ COMPONENT SELECTION, VERIFICATION, AND HOPPER FILLING:

Refer to the data pages of a reloading manual to select the load you wish to use. Bring the required components (primers, powder, wads, and shot) to the loading bench. It is vital that you use only the components listed in the recipe for the load you wish to

11 Steps for Reloading on a Single-Stage Press

1 • Bushing and bar verification

2 • Component selection, verification, and hopper filling

3 • Case inspection

4 • Case resizing and fired primer removal

5 • Primer seating

6 • Powder charging

7 • Wad seating (with appropriate pressure)

8 • Shot metering (from the tool's built-in measure)

9 • Crimp starting

10 • Final crimp

11 • Loaded round inspection

assemble. Verify that you have placed the right components on the bench by reading aloud from the labels of the primer, powder, and wad containers, while you once again compare the nomenclature with your data.

Place only one box of 100 primers on the loading bench. Position your primers on the right side of the press, alongside the priming station. You should never

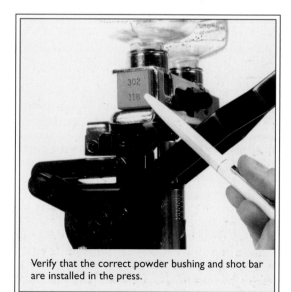

Verify that the correct powder bushing and shot bar are installed in the press.

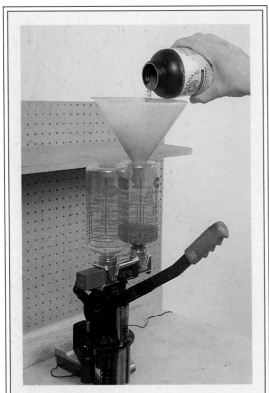

After verifying that you have selected the proper powder and shot for the desired load, fill the respective hoppers.

have more than 100 primers on the bench at one time, as this will minimize the potential danger if the primers are accidentally ignited.

Next, fill the powder hopper with the appropriate propellant. Never bring more than 1 pound of powder to the bench at one time. Continue your setup by placing your wads to the left of the press, preferably in a wad dispenser. The dispenser will keep the wads in place without letting them roll around and off the bench. Finally, fill the shot hopper with the shot size you wish to load.

STEP 3 ▪ CASE INSPECTION: It will prove convenient to inspect all of your cases at one time. Such a batch inspection will help keep your mind on the task without the potential distraction of loading a shell between each inspection. Carefully discard any case that has a defect. Some of the defects you may encounter include splits, tears, and leaky primer pockets. Make certain that all

cases to be reloaded are of one type, and that this type matches the data listing you are using.

When you finish the inspection, place your fired cases to the right side of the press. It will prove useful to place them in a shallow container to keep them from rolling around or possibly off the bench. Some reloaders use a second wad dispenser for this purpose.

STEP 4 ▪ CASE RESIZING AND FIRED PRIMER REMOVAL: Lyman strongly recommends that reloaders wear a pair of safety glasses or goggles while assembling ammunition. With your right hand, place a fired case directly below the resizing and decapping die. This is the station located to the right and rear of the press. (Alternately, some reloaders prefer to slip the fired case partway up into the die body.) With the left hand, pull the tool handle all the way down. This will cause the sizing die to reduce the enlarged metal head of the fired case down to a diameter closely duplicating that of new factory ammo, thus ensuring that the shell will chamber smoothly in your shotgun.

As you resize the fired case, the decapping rod, which is centrally located in the die body, forces the fired primer out of the case. Return the press handle to its full upright position in order to partially eject the sized and decapped case from the die. The case is now ready to be removed from the die.

Before advancing the case to the next operation, give it a visual inspection to ensure that it has not developed any defects. For example, has a split occurred in the resized metal case head?

STEP 5 ▪ PRIMER SEATING: Using your right hand, place a new primer into the priming station located at the front right of the loading tool. Next, place the case to be primed onto the priming ram. With your left hand, pull down the tool handle to force the case over the primer. Be certain to pull down far enough to fully seat the primer. Its battery cup should be flush with the case head. Visually inspect the new primer to ensure that it is fully seated. Now you are ready to advance the primed case to the next press station.

STEP 6 ▪ POWDER CHARGING: With your right hand, place the primed case onto the station located at the middle front of the press base. Using your left hand, pull down the press handle and hold it in this position. Now, with your right hand, push the right end of the powder and shot metering bar fully to the left side. This

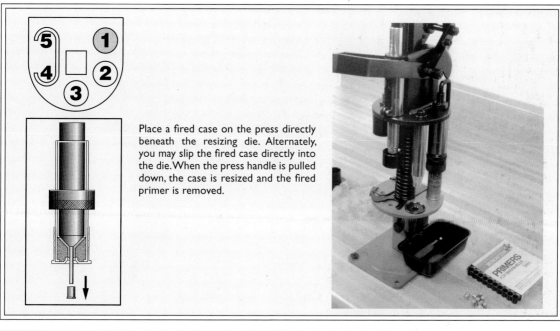

Place a fired case on the press directly beneath the resizing die. Alternately, you may slip the fired case directly into the die. When the press handle is pulled down, the case is resized and the fired primer is removed.

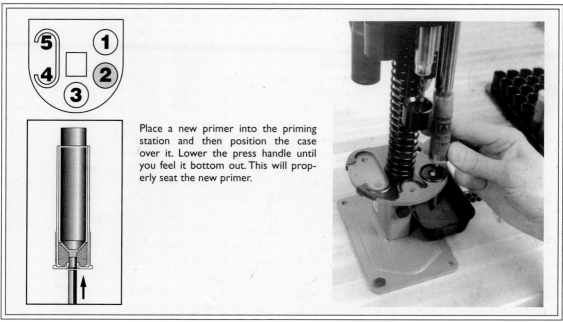

Place a new primer into the priming station and then position the case over it. Lower the press handle until you feel it bottom out. This will properly seat the new primer.

will place a powder charge into your case. Now, raise the press handle.

Note: The powder charge must be verified with a powder scale. Check at least 10 sequential loads.

The average charge weight must be as specified per the data listing. If it is not, try smaller or larger bushings until it is exact or within a -5 percent grain tolerance. Powder charge verification needs to be done

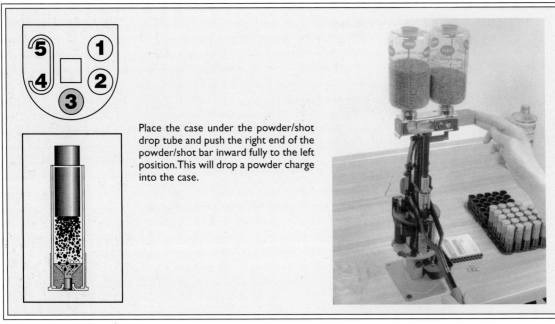

Place the case under the powder/shot drop tube and push the right end of the powder/shot bar inward fully to the left position. This will drop a powder charge into the case.

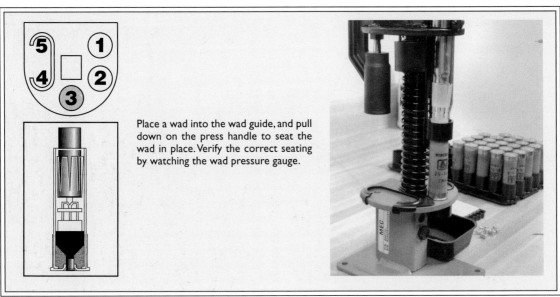

Place a wad into the wad guide, and pull down on the press handle to seat the wad in place. Verify the correct seating by watching the wad pressure gauge.

only once at the beginning of each loading session and whenever a new lot of powder is put to use. **Never** simply push the powder bar back and forth to obtain charge weights. All powder weight checking **must** be done with charges obtained during a normal loading sequence.

STEP 7 ■ WAD SEATING: Without moving the case, use your left hand to place a wad in the wad guide. (The wad guide will automatically be held in position on the case mouth as a result of moving the powder-metering bar during the previous step.) Pull the press handle fully down, this time with the right hand, and the wad will be

The components of a reloaded shotshell are a case, primer, powder, wad, and shot.

seated on the powder charge. Allow the press handle to move upward slightly, just enough to raise the bottom of the wad ram about ½ inch off the wad. Hold the press handle in this position.

Note: The amount of wad pressure required to obtain a perfect crimp is adjusted at this station. Also, verify proper wad seating by watching the wad seating height and pressure gauge as the press handle reaches the bottom of its stroke. For example, if the pressure gauge shows too little pressure, the wad may not be seated on the powder charge (perhaps because of a missing or incomplete powder charge). If the gauge shows too much pressure, something is wrong (perhaps a cocked wad, wrong wad, wrong case, or too much powder)

Be sure the wad enters the case without damaging its cup-shaped base. Ensure that the petals of the wad are fully seated against the case wall. Also be sure the wad comes into firm contact with the powder charge. Use at least 20 pounds of wad-seating pressure.

STEP 8 ▪ SHOT METERING: Push the left end of the shot metering bar fully to the right. This will cause a shot charge to fall into the case. Return the press handle to its upright position.

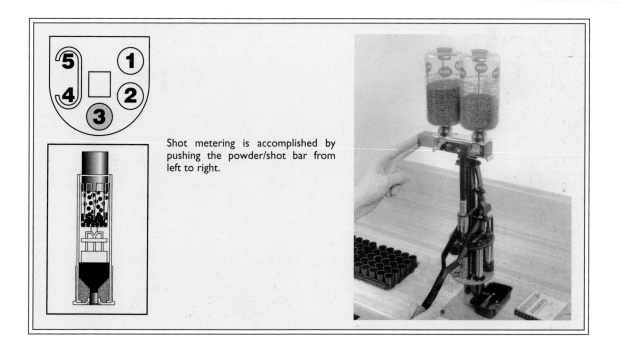

Shot metering is accomplished by pushing the powder/shot bar from left to right.

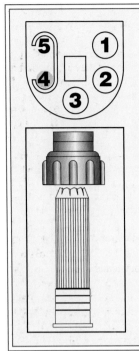

The crimp is started using a crimp starter that matches the original number of crimp folds (six or eight).

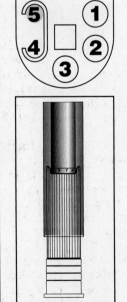

At the last loading station, the crimp is closed. The depth of the finished crimp should be very similar to that of the original factory round.

Note: Shot charge weight must be verified at this point in the same manner as the powder charge. A weight as specified in the data with a -5 percent tolerance is acceptable. This verification needs to be done only at the beginning of each loading session, or whenever a new bag of shot is put to use. Never use a shot charge that exceeds the weight listed in the data. It is possible for a shot charge to partially jam (or bridge) in the shot drop tube. Therefore, visually inspect the shell to be certain that a full shot charge has been placed in the case. If only a partial shot charge is in the case, try lowering the shot drop tube back into the case and lightly tapping on the shot drop tube. The tapping will often allow a jammed shot charge to fall free. Once a complete shot charge is in the case, you are now ready for the next step.

STEP 9 ▪ CRIMP STARTING: Place the charged shotshell case at the crimp starting station at the front and left of the tool. Move the press handle fully downward to start the case mouth crimp. The started crimp should close the case about one-third to halfway. The crimp starter is adjustable and can be raised or lowered to provide the proper amount of crimp start. Raise the press handle.

Note: The crimp starter must match the fired case's original 6- or 8-point crimp.

STEP 10 ▪ FINAL CRIMP: Position the partially crimped shell under the final crimping die at the rear and left of the press. Pull the press handle downward smoothly until it stops. This will form the final crimp.

Note: The crimping die of the 600 Jr. can be adjusted to put more or less taper on the end of a case. This crimping die also may require adjustment to compensate for different styles of cases or loading specifications. If crimps are incomplete, dished, or excessively spiraled, refer to your press's instruction manual for the proper die-adjustment procedure. Crimp depth should duplicate or be as close as possible to that of the original factory crimp.

STEP 11 ▪ LOADED ROUND INSPECTION: At this point, you should have a fully loaded shotshell that looks and performs as good as a factory-loaded round. Give the finished product a thorough inspection. Safely discard any rounds that show the slightest imperfections. A case ring gauge at this final inspection is a good idea, as this will ensure that cases are properly resized. That is all there is to the steps of assembling shotshells.

FROM FIELD TO TABLE

▪ Where to Hit Big Game

The most important factor in killing big game quickly and cleanly is bullet placement. Even a .375 Magnum won't knock down a small whitetail for keeps unless the deer is hit in a vital organ. Caliber means little if a hunter doesn't put the bullet where it will be most effective. You'll minimize chances of losing wounded game if you take time to study the animals you hunt and learn the location of vital organs.

The accompanying illustrations show the anatomy of popular big game and the aiming points that are important. The information should also benefit the bowhunter, whose arrow kills by hemorrhage. He should note especially the location of main arteries.

Though the most vital organ in any animal is the brain, you should rule out a brain shot 98 percent of the time. The brain is a small target and easy to miss. A brain shot is also a poor choice for a trophy hunter. A brain shot on a deer, for example, will shatter the base of the skull, making a head mount nearly

impossible. Bears are scored by skull dimensions, and any head shot on a bruin will smash the skull and make scoring impossible. When is a brain shot justified? Only on dangerous game when it is charging. In North America, this means bears. Aim to hit 2 inches above the center of the eyes of a bear, and you should hit the brain.

Neck shots involve some risk of wounding antlered game because the spinal column in the neck is only about 2 inches in diameter. If you hit neck muscles and arteries but miss the spine, your deer may run a fair distance before dropping. A neck shot is a fair choice only at close range, where you can be reasonably sure of putting your bullet into the spinal column.

What is the best shot? Let's talk in terms of vital areas as opposed to vital organs. The forward one-third of a deer is a vital area since it houses the heart, lungs, several major arteries, spine, and shoulder. Any bullet hitting these areas will bring down a big-game animal.

The best shot, then, is at a vital organ in a vital

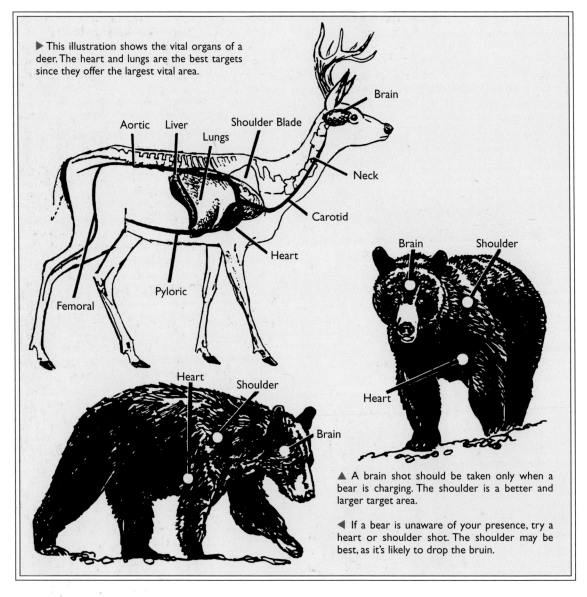

▶ This illustration shows the vital organs of a deer. The heart and lungs are the best targets since they offer the largest vital area.

Brain

Aortic   Liver   Shoulder Blade

Lungs

Neck

Carotid

Heart

Pyloric

Femoral

Brain   Shoulder

Heart

Heart   Shoulder

Brain

Heart

▲ A brain shot should be taken only when a bear is charging. The shoulder is a better and larger target area.

◀ If a bear is unaware of your presence, try a heart or shoulder shot. The shoulder may be best, as it's likely to drop the bruin.

area—specifically the heart. Though a heart shot frequently will not drop an animal in its tracks, it is always a fatal shot, and tracking a heart-shot animal is not difficult. One big advantage of aiming for the heart is that a miss will generally still hit some other vital organ. A shot at the heart, for example, will likely put the bullet into the lungs also. A hit in the lungs may knock a deer down through shock. If not, the animal will eventually die through hemorrhaging.

No animal can survive a bullet through the lungs, but it may sometimes travel a good distance. If you spot blood on brush a few feet off the ground and to the side of the tracks, blood is coming from the sides of the deer—a good indication of a lung hit. The deer will be bleeding freely, and tracking should not be difficult. Frothy blood is another sign of a lung hit.

Recognizing blood and hair signs can be useful to a hunter. Bright-red blood generally means a heart or lung shot. A deer shot in the heart, however, may not start to bleed immediately, so follow the tracks until you can confirm a miss or hit. If you spot brown-yellow blood, particularly if there are bits of white hair in it, you can be reasonably sure that the deer is gutshot. This is unfortunate since a gutshot animal can travel a great distance before dying. If you've gutshot an animal, stick with the track. You'll get it eventually, but it won't be easy.

The track itself can be a tip-off to the location of a wound. A broken leg will show as drag marks in snow or mud. Blood in or right next to the tracks may mean a leg wound.

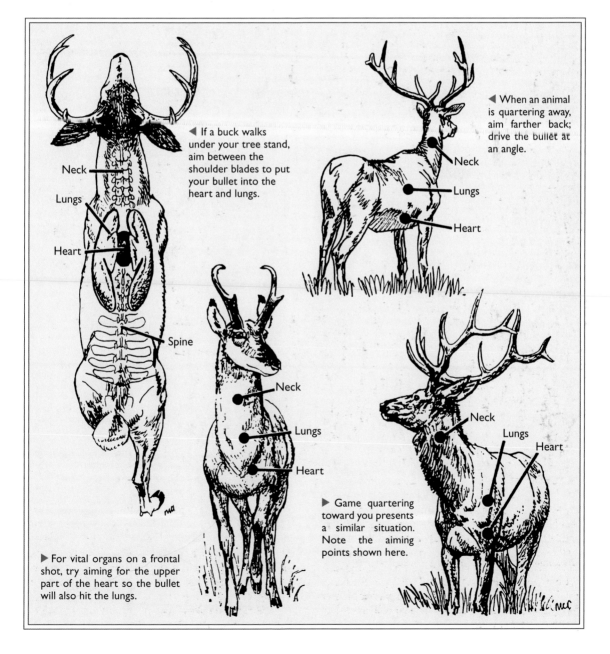

◀ If a buck walks under your tree stand, aim between the shoulder blades to put your bullet into the heart and lungs.

Neck

Lungs

Heart

Spine

◀ When an animal is quartering away, aim farther back; drive the bullet at an angle.

Neck

Lungs

Heart

Neck

Lungs

Heart

▶ Game quartering toward you presents a similar situation. Note the aiming points shown here.

Neck

Lungs

Heart

▶ For vital organs on a frontal shot, try aiming for the upper part of the heart so the bullet will also hit the lungs.

If your initial shot is high, missing both the heart and lungs, your bullet may still hit a vital spot. Such a shot may shatter the shoulder, breaking the animal down and rendering it helpless.

The only time a hunter should intentionally aim for the shoulder is on dangerous game. A bear hunter, for example, wants to knock down and immobilize a bruin quickly, especially if it's charging. A shoulder shot will accomplish it (if a brain shot is considered too risky), and the hunter can then put in a killing shot with little danger.

Once you know where the vital organs are, you must also know where to put your rifle sights in relation to the animal's position.

To hit the heart when an antlered animal is broadside, put your sights just above where the foreleg joins the body. Aim a bit high, so that if you miss the top portion of the heart you will still hit the lungs.

If a buck is facing you, put your sights just below dead center on its chest. If your shot is a good one, you'll hit the top of the heart as well as the lungs.

If you are in a tree stand and a buck walks under you, a somewhat different problem arises. Since less heart and lung area is available, the best aim is right between the shoulder blades for a hit in the heart and lungs. Remember that you are shooting from above and various angles must be taken into account.

Quartering animals present some problems. Excited hunters frequently assume that a quartering animal presents the same target as a broadside, but on a deer quartering away, your points of aim should be farther back on the body.

■ Getting Big Game Home

If you're one of the lucky big-game hunters, you will have to haul a sizable animal out of the woods and get it safely home.

Handling big game requires some planning. First, make sure you are carrying the right gear. In a small daypack or in your pockets, you should be carrying a 10- or 12-foot length of rope, a small bone saw, and a knife. If you're planning to hunt elk or moose in a remote area where you might have to quarter an animal to carry it out, you should also include a small pulley and a hand ax.

The easiest and best way to get a deer out of the field is to drag it out. On snow or leaves, a deer will slide easily. If the terrain is rough, however, drag your deer out on a small piece of tarp. Make sure the head or rack is securely tied to one end of the tarp, which will act as a sled.

Two men can easily drag out a deer, but you can do it alone if you don't rush and make sure to stop to rest often. After you have field dressed the deer, tie the front legs behind the head with your drag line and then loop it around the deer's muzzle. When you pull your deer, it will be more streamlined and slide without hanging up on rocks and shrubs.

If you're alone, make a loop in your drag line and wrap it around your body like a harness. You will get more leverage if you use your body rather than your arms to drag a deer. Your drag line should also be short enough to lift the deer's head off the ground when you're dragging it.

A small, field-dressed deer will weigh under 100 pounds and can probably be carried out by one hunter. Simply lash all four feet together and carry it on one shoulder with the head to the rear. With your hand on the opposite side, reach around, grab the head, and hold it to your side. For safety, always wrap a red bandanna or a blaze-orange vest around the carcass when carrying it out.

When you have a heavy deer or a black bear, tie its legs together and then run a thick tree limb between its legs and as close to the body as possible. Two men can place the pole on their shoulders and carry it out. Always remember to tie a red or orange bandanna to the carcass. If you and a friend are carrying out a deer, talk loudly so other hunters will hear you. If you're alone, whistle as loud as you can.

Once you get your deer to your car, you will have a different set of problems. The best place to put a deer is in the trunk because it's unheated. With the threat of Lyme disease from deer ticks, it's also a good idea to keep the carcass away from car heaters and your own body. If you must transport a deer outside your vehicle, wrap it in blankets and tie it on the roof of your car. Never haul it on a fender or hood, where engine heat may "cook" the meat by the time you get home.

When you're forced to quarter an animal, leave the hide on. If you want to save the hide for tanning, you should make sure someone has some plastic bags to protect the meat in transit.

Once you get to camp, however, take the meat out of the plastic bags and hang it to air dry. If there are flies around, sprinkle the meat with black pepper. In fact, any game meat hanging in camp during warm weather should be coated with black pepper to keep the bugs off.

The Game Processors

Every fall, hunters spend thousands of dollars on big-game hunts. If they are lucky, they will take a trophy whitetail or an elk or moose. Whatever the trophy, these hunters will look for a reliable butcher to process and ship their meat home.

The average bull elk may weigh from 500 to 600 pounds. That's a lot of meat and it represents a sizable investment. When you turn it over to a butcher, make sure it's the right man. First, don't be taken in by the processor who advertises the most. Many good game processors don't advertise at all. Based on their good reputation, word-of-mouth recommendations produce more business than they can handle.

It's important to remember that wild-game processing is basically exempt from USDA regulations, which means that temperature control, cleanliness, and packing are pretty much left to the discretion of the processor or butcher. You will have to determine the cleanliness of the cutting tables, knives, grinders, saws, and other equipment.

If you're planning to hunt out of state, plan to arrive a couple of days before your hunt. In addition to scouting and setting up camp, the extra time will give you a chance to find the right processor. Start by inquiring at sporting-goods stores, game wardens, gas stations, and cafés. If one person is recommended by different people, pay him a visit.

Use common sense. If a processing plant has a foul smell, find out why, but be fair. The smell may be coming from meat that was already contaminated before it was brought into the place. Look around the floor. Are there fresh meat scraps on the floor or have they been there a while? Check the saw. If it's not cleaned regularly, it will smell. Brown stains around a meat grinder are a good sign that the processor doesn't clean his place regularly.

It is not unreasonable to ask a processor to see his cooler. If game is skinned and field dressed properly, the meat doesn't smell, so be suspicious of a cooler that has a questionable odor. If a cooler is overloaded with game, it will run several degrees warmer than the preferred 36°F to 38°F. If you're not sure, don't leave your animal there. Remember that the stench of overaged (rotting) meat can't be disguised.

If you have to rely on an outfitter, ask him for the name of his processor long before your hunt. Call him and ask for references. If he procrastinates or refuses to cooperate, look elsewhere. In the West, you will be charged by hanging weight, so insist that any processor weighs your meat in front of you, and stay there until he tags the carcass with your name before placing it in cold storage.

If you're not sure how you want the meat cut, tell your processor to butcher it into steaks, chops, and roasts, and leave the tenderloin whole. The burger trim should be ground into hamburger or made into sausage (fresh, summer, or smoked).

The Best Venison

It's true that venison should be allowed to cure for at least a week before eating, but this is not true of the tenderloins and liver, which can be eaten soon after a deer or elk is brought into camp. Prepared properly, the tenderloins and liver can be turned into delicious dinners in camp or at home.

The tenderloins are two small strips of meat, measuring 1 to 2 inches in diameter and about 12 to 15 inches long. They are located on both sides of the backbone inside the upper chest cavity. The tenderloins can only be removed from inside the chest cavity. Don't confuse the tenderloins with the backstraps, which are cut away from both sides of the backbone from outside the carcass. Backstraps, incidentally, produce your venison filet mignon. But even the backstraps cannot compare with the tenderloins, the tenderest part of a deer.

As soon as you field dress that deer, cut out the tenderloins. Do it before the air has a chance to toughen the meat's surface. Use a small knife to separate the tenderloins from the cavity. Once the initial cut is made, you may be able to pull the tenderloins free, but do it carefully because the meat is so tender it may tear.

Cooking the tenderloins back in camp or at home is easy. Because the meat is tender and tasty, a simple recipe that will not alter the flavor is best. In deer camp, where you want to keep cooking time down to a minimum, cut the tenderloins into medallions about ½ inch thick and coat them with salt, pepper, and a touch of garlic powder. Then, sauté the pieces in a hot skillet greased with butter until the meat is rare and pink inside.

At home, marinate the tenderloins in Italian salad dressing for an hour or so, then put them on a hot grill and only allow the charcoal to sear the exterior. When the inside of the tenderloins are pink, take them off the grill and slice them into medallions. The tenderloins are a perfect first fare for those people who have traditionally refused to eat venison.

In deer camp, the tenderloins are always the appetizer and the liver is the main course. When you take the liver out of your deer during the field-dressing

Field Dressing Your Buck

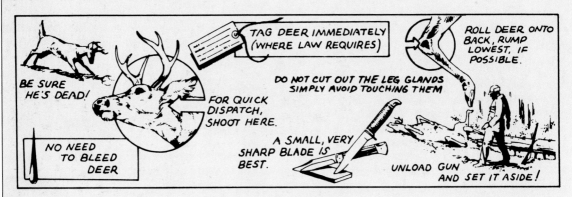

BE SURE HE'S DEAD!

NO NEED TO BLEED DEER

TAG DEER IMMEDIATELY (WHERE LAW REQUIRES)

FOR QUICK DISPATCH, SHOOT HERE.

DO NOT CUT OUT THE LEG GLANDS SIMPLY AVOID TOUCHING THEM

A SMALL, VERY SHARP BLADE IS BEST.

ROLL DEER ONTO BACK, RUMP LOWEST, IF POSSIBLE.

UNLOAD GUN AND SET IT ASIDE!

Step 1 • Remove the penis and scrotum with shallow cuts. Do not pierce the body cavity. ▪ **Step 2 •** With the tip of the knife, cut completely around the rectum to free it from the rest of the skin. ▪ **Step 3 •** Pull the rectum outside of the body and tie it off to prevent feces from reaching the meat.

Step 4 • Open the abdomen from the rear to the sternum (where the last ribs join). Hold the intestines down with your fingers and the back of your hand so that you do not cut or pierce the intestinal tract or paunch. ▪ **Step 5 •** Cut the bladder out very carefully. Try not to spill urine.

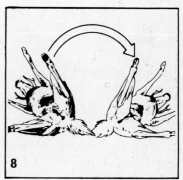

Step 6 • Pull the rectum inside the cavity and cut the tissue holding it in place. ▪ Step 7 • With the deer lying on one side, cut all tissues that hold the intestines in place all the way down to the animal's spine. ▪ Step 8 • The next step is to rotate the deer over so that you can free the intestines from the other side.

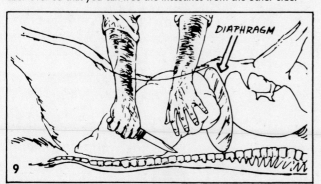

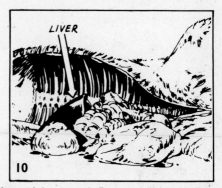

Step 9 • Repeat step 7; little cutting is needed. Then, sever the gullet in front of the stomach. Do not spill the contents. If you do, wipe clean. ▪ Step 10 • The contents of the abdomen come out in one big mass. Retrieve the liver and cool it quickly in open air or water.

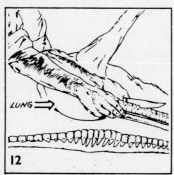

Step 11 • Cut out the diaphragm (wall from abdomen to chest). ▪ Step 12 • Reach up inside the chest and sever the gullet and windpipe. Pull them out with the lungs and heart. ▪ Step 13 • Wipe dry. If it's hot, it's better to split the breast, open the neck, and cut out the rest of the windpipe and gullet to avoid spoilage. If, however, the head is to be mounted, "cape out" (skin) the neck first.

Skinning Your Deer

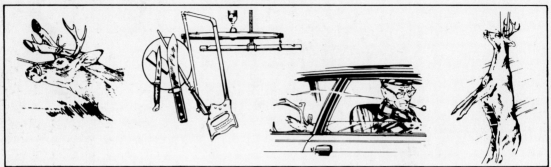

After field dressing, tie the forefeet over the neck. Drag out with rope around the antlers and half hitch around the upper jaw. Never subject the carcass to heat. Don't use the car heater; keep the windows open. Hang the deer in a cool place (41°F to 45°F) for a week with the hide still on to tenderize the meat and enhance the flavor before skinning. The methods shown here result in rawhide suitable for tanning. For a head-and-shoulders mount, see step 13.

Step 1 • With the point of the knife, cut the hide from the abdominal cut to just below both joints. Don't touch the leg glands. ▪ **Step 2** • Skin out both thighs. Try not to cut meat or the inner side of the skin. ▪ **Step 3** • With the deer still lying on the floor, skin out the thighs to the top of the legs. ▪ **Step 4** • Saw off the lower legs just below the joints. Use a meat-cutting saw or crosscut wood saw.

Step 5 • Hang the deer with a gambrel or stick in each leg between the bone and tendon. ▪ **Step 6** • If it wasn't done during field dressing, cut the H-bone of the pelvis with your saw. ▪ **Step 7** • Continue skinning. Leave the tail on the hide by tunneling under it between the hide and back. ▪ **Step 8** • Hide in this area usually comes off quite easily. Pull on the hide and then cut.

Step 9 • Sever the tail near the body inside the hide. This avoids cutting the hair, which you'd have to pick off the meat. ▪ **Step 10** • Use a knife to separate the hide from the thin muscles near the abdominal lengthwise incision. ▪ **Step 11** • Hoist the deer higher. Pull with one hand and "fist" the hide. ▪ **Step 12** • Saw off the forelegs. Split the breast and neck and cut out the gullet.

Step 13 • Slit the skin of the forelegs to the breast cut. (If you want the deer head mounted by a taxidermist, the inset shows cuts for caping out the neck. Unless you are skilled enough for meticulous skinning of eyes, ears, and nose, cut off the head. Refrigerate or freeze if there is a delay in delivery to the taxidermist. ▪ **Step 14** • Skin out the legs and neck. The neck is the hardest area to skin. ▪ **Step 15** • Pull the hide down and then use a knife. Continue to the base of the skull. ▪ **Step 16** • Saw off the head. Again, doing it this way avoids cutting the hair.

Step 17 • Remove dirt and debris. Cut out and discard the bloodshot meat around the bullet holes. Pick off all deer hair, which otherwise lends a bad taste to the meat when cooked. ▪ **Step 18** • The hide still has the head and tail attached. Cut the head off. Wipe the inside of the hide dry with a cloth. ▪ **Step 19** • Sprinkle borax or salt on the inside of the hide. Fold lengthwise, hair out, roll it up, and tie. Send the hide to a taxidermist or tanner at once or store in refrigerator or freezer until you can do so.

Butchering Your Deer

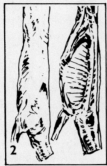

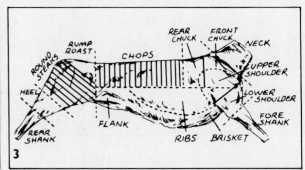

Step 1 • Cut the spine in half lengthwise. The cut can be corrected if it wanders. ▪ **Step 2** • With a meat-cutting saw or fine carpenter's saw, cut the carcass into two sides. Start where the tail was severed. ▪ **Step 3** • Dotted lines show the major cuts. Solid lines indicate secondary cuts that divide roasts into two or separate steaks and chops. This illustration shows the right-hand side. After cutting the whole side, repeat cuts on the left side.

Step 4 • Divide the haunch from the loin. With all cuts, use a knife first. If you hit bone, use a saw to complete the cut. A cleaver is handy but not essential. ▪ **Step 5** • Cut the rump roast off the haunch. Make a neat, straight cut because it determines the angle of cuts for round steaks. ▪ **Step 6** • Cut thin or thick round steaks as you prefer, but keep the cuts parallel. ▪ **Step 7** • Down toward the joint, the meat is tough. There, take off a chunk called the heel, usually used for stew.

Step 8 • Now for the front part: cut the entire shoulder and foreleg off the side where the shoulder joins the body. The knife blade is horizontal. ▪ **Step 9** • There is no ball-and-socket joint, so this cut is easy. ▪ **Step 10** • Separate the shoulder from the shank at the joint or close to it. You need the saw for this cut. The shank is used as chop meat. ▪ **Step 11** • The shoulder is usually divided into two separate pieces for pot roasts or stew meat.

Step 12 • Cut off the neck. The neck is tough like the shank or shoulder and is best used as chop or stew meat. ▪ **Step 13** • Saw the ribs off. This long, angled cut is made where the thin meat between the ribs thickens toward the spine. ▪ **Step 14** • Separate the chuck (under the meat cutter's left hand) from the loin. The loin is cut into chops; chuck is usually cut into two roasts. ▪ **Step 15** • Cut the loin into chops, as thick as you like. They resemble lamp chops. These cuts are started with the knife and completed with the saw.

Step 16 • Trim the thick fat off the chops. Heavy fat should be trimmed off all cuts. It has an unpleasant flavor. ▪ **Step 17** • Cut the chuck into two equal portions. It's too big to cook whole (usually as a pot roast) unless you have a big family. ▪ **Step 18** • This long cut starts parallel to the first rib and outside it and then circles around the tips of the ribs. ▪ **Step 19** • The cut is completed. It separates the brisket and flank from the ribs. Brisket and flank go into chop meat.

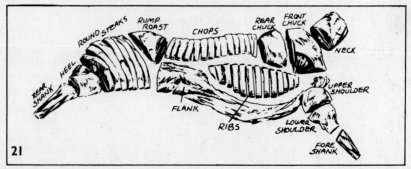

Step 20 • Separate the ribs. The knife slides along the bone to one side so all the meat between the two ribs stays attached to a single rib. ▪ **Step 21** • Here are all the cuts from the right side, properly trimmed. If you do mangle a piece, remember that you can always bone it out and grind it up for chop meat or mince meat or chop it up into chunks for stew.

Boning Your Deer

Step 1 • Begin the boning process by cutting the neck off the skinned carcass. Be sure to first cut off the meatless lower legs. ■ **Step 2** • Split the neck and unroll the meat from the neck bone. A small knife will help. Neck meat makes good stew and roasts. ■ **Step 3** • The next cut, to remove the backstrap, should be made from in front of the pelvic bone to the shoulder. Cut along the spine, 2 inches deep.

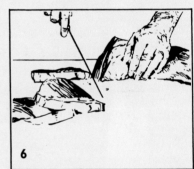

Step 4 • To extract the backstrap, cut along the side of the ribs over the point where the ribs curve down to join the backbone. Loosen with fore and aft cross cuts. ■ **Step 5** • Repeat the procedure to extract the second fillet. Pull and rip the layer of fat and tissue from the fillet. ■ **Step 6** • Many claim that this is the finest meat on the deer. Cut the trimmed loin into steaks about ¾ to 1 inch thick.

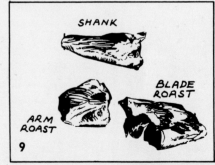

Step 7 • Remove the shoulders by working your knife through the tissue between the leg and ribs. ■ **Step 8** • Bone the shoulder for use as stew meat or rolled for roast, or simply cut into three pieces. ■ **Step 9** • Remove the shoulder roast from the leg by severing at the upper joint. Separate the arm roast from the shank with a saw. The shank makes excellent venison soup.

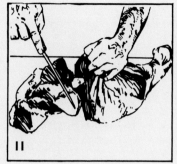

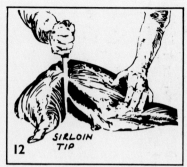

Step 10 • To detach the ham, start your cut near the tail bone. Slice the tissue and tendons, and then detach with a saw or by twisting the ball joint. ■ **Step 11** • The rump roast is at the top part of the ham. To remove it, make your cut as vertical as possible, leaving enough meat for a meal. ■ **Step 12** • Lay the hind leg on the table and remove the sirloin tip by using the leg bone to guide the knife. Start at the kneecap and work up.

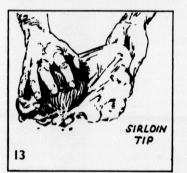

Step 13 • Once the sirloin tip has been removed, trim the scrap and tissue. This piece, resembling a football, makes a great roast or can be cut into steaks. ■ **Step 14** • In removing bone from the remaining piece (round), cut tissue separating the shank from the round and bone. ■ **Step 15** • Shave and cut the meat loose from the leg bone. This will take maneuvering around the joints, but keep cutting.

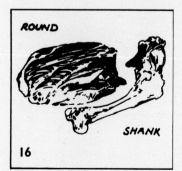

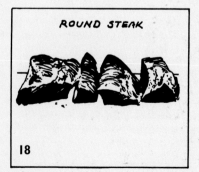

Step 16 • Here's what the finished product should look like. Now, separate the round into its individual muscle pieces, each encased in tissue. ■ **Step 17** • Divide by cutting the connective membrane. Avoid cutting into the meat. Trim the scrap for grinding or stew. ■ **Step 18** • Chunks of trimmed round can be sliced thin for use as steaks and made on the barbecue or cooked whole as roasts.

Cooking A Cottontail

Let's start with the basic premise that if a rabbit is to taste good it must be field dressed with the same promptness and care as a deer. A deer must be field dressed on the spot with all internal organs removed. The same care should be taken with cottontails to ensure good game flavor. When your cottontail is ready for the pot, the one recipe that will do justice to any rabbit is Hasenpfeffer, an old-time German dish. Here's how to prepare it.

INGREDIENTS:

I rabbit, cut into serving pieces
¾ teaspoon pepper
I teaspoon salt
I sliced onion
3 garlic cloves
2 bay leaves
8 ounces vinegar
8 ounces water
I cup sweet or sour cream
¼ cup butter or margarine

INSTRUCTIONS:

First, marinate the rabbit pieces in the measured ingredients of pepper, salt, onion, garlic cloves, bay leaves, vinegar, and water. Use an earthenware crock, placed in a refrigerator for 48 hours, turning the pieces occasionally. Remove the pieces and brown them in butter, adding a little marinade from time to time. Allow the meat to simmer for about one hour or until tender. Remove the pieces and add the cream to make gravy. Pour the gravy generously over the rabbit into a serving dish. If you wish to experiment a bit, substitute wine for the equal parts of water and vinegar. Another variation is making the marinade with equal parts of water and beer or ale. Hasenpfeffer is usually served with potato pancakes or potato dumplings. Though the recipe is traditionally a rabbit dish, it works equally well with venison or any other game.

operation, wipe it clean and put it in a plastic bag. Back in camp, soak it in a pan of water with a cup of salt. Keep changing the water until the liver is thoroughly purged of blood, and then pat dry.

Preparing the liver is just as easy as the tenderloins. All you need is about a pound of bacon, four or five onions, flour, and butter. First, fry the bacon in a skillet. In a second skillet, sauté the sliced onions with butter until the onions are soft and transparent. When both the bacon and onions are done, set them aside. Now, flour the liver, which you've already cut into pieces ½ inch thick, and fry them in the skillet with the bacon drippings. Serve the bacon and onions over the liver.

■ Venison Jerky

When frontiersmen headed west and mountain men ran traplines in the Rockies, these adventurers had a common problem: no refrigerators or freezers. The only way they could preserve meat was to dry it. Those problems no longer exist today, but sportsmen still enjoy making and eating dried meat.

Jerky is nothing more than lean raw meat with all the moisture removed. Round steak from a deer, elk, moose, caribou, or antelope makes the best jerky. Fatty meat, such as bear and wild boar, does not make very good jerky.

You can also use domestic beef to make jerky. Just make sure the meat is very lean. You must also trim away all fat, sinew, and gristle—too much fat in jerky can cause rancid meat.

You can use the sun to dry meat, but it's safer and more convenient to use your kitchen oven or a fruit dehydrator. Always remember that you are drying the meat and not cooking it.

First, cut the venison with the grain into strips about 6 inches long, 1 inch wide, and ¼ inch thick. Next, coat the meat with salt and pepper, then brush heavily with liquid smoke, which you can find in any supermarket. Let the meat marinate overnight in your refrigerator.

The next day, drain the meat on paper towels and place the strips in your oven. It's best to run a toothpick through the end of a strip and hang it from your oven rack. Put a tray under the meat to catch the drippings. Most ovens will handle about two dozen strips.

Now, set your oven at about 130°F or its lowest setting. Use a meat thermometer to make sure the oven stays at 130°F. Drying time may vary slightly, but most of the time it takes about 10 to 12 hours. It's important to leave the oven door slightly open to allow moisture to escape.

If it has dried properly, the meat will be dark with no moisture in its center. You should also be able to bend the strips of meat without breaking them.

You can store the meat in any moisture-proof containers. Any jar with a tight lid or a ziplock plastic bag will do. You can eat jerky anytime. Just bite off a piece and start chewing. The saliva from your mouth will reconstitute the dried meat into tasty food.

There are all kinds of variations to making jerky. If you don't like the liquid smoke taste, marinate the venison in equal parts of soy sauce and Worcestershire sauce and ¼ teaspoon of garlic powder. If you like it hot, substitute cayenne pepper for the garlic powder. You can also rub the meat with a sugar cure before drying, and then coat the meat completely after drying with steak sauce.

There is also no need to limit yourself to venison. You can just as easily make turkey or pheasant jerky. Because you will need strips, the meat must come from the breasts of these birds. Cut the strips 2 or 3 inches long with the grain of the meat running lengthwise. Season the breast meat the same as the venison meat. The drying process, however, may take less time. Depending on the thickness of the cuts, four to six hours in your oven, set on the lowest temperature, should do it.

■ Field Care of Game Birds

Many pheasants, grouse, chukars, and other game birds are ruined between the time of the kill and the time they reach the table. Some hunters will put a bird into a hot, rubber-lined game pocket, leaving it there to "cook" and perhaps spoil by the day's end.

Other hunters may field dress a bird, let it hang a couple of days, and then try to pluck it. The usual result is that pieces of the skin are torn away and the bird is a big mess.

Here's some sound advice from more than a few shooting-preserve operators who have literally cleaned thousands of pheasants and other game birds. These experts agree on the right way to handle a bird in the field.

Obviously, a pheasant should be field dressed soon after it is shot, particularly in warm weather. Field dressing is a simple operation. First, lay the bird on its back and pull the feathers off from below the breastbone to the anal opening, clearing the area for the first cut. Make the cut from the soft area below the breastbone down to the anal opening. Make this cut carefully so that no organs are cut or broken, which can taint the meat. First, cut the skin, and then cut through the meat. Reach in and take out the viscera, pulling down toward the anal opening. Now, remove the windpipe and crop.

During warm weather, pack the empty cavity with dry grass and then press the sides of the opening tightly together. The grass will absorb blood in the cavity and will keep insects from entering it. This is not necessary in cold weather, when you can leave the cavity open and let the meat cool, free of insects. You can expedite cooling in winter by placing some snow in the body cavity. Both dry grass and snow can also be used with equal effectiveness on furred small game, such as rabbits and squirrels.

Many hunters believe it is a crime to skin a bird, but some prefer to skin pheasants. One reason for skinning is because of the critical conditions necessary for effective plucking. You can easily pluck a bird immediately after it is shot and the body is warm. The feathers will pull out with little trouble, and the skin will not tear. But some hunters dislike stopping a hunt after each kill so that you can pluck a bird. Also, once a bird is plucked in the field, the bare skin is exposed to dirt and bacteria.

Once the body has cooled, a pheasant cannot be dry plucked without being torn up. It must be dipped in hot water (180°F). If the water is cooler or warmer than 180°F, the skin will tear. Because of the difficulty in maintaining the correct water temperature, this method isn't recommended. If you plan to pluck pheasants, though, remember this temperature factor.

The best bet is to field dress the bird as soon as possible after it is shot and skin it when you get home. If you prefer, you can hang your birds in a cool, dry place for a couple of days before skinning. This aging process has some merit for slightly tenderizing old cock birds, but you will generally be unable to detect any difference in taste between birds skinned at once and those skinned a few days later.

Skinning a bird is easy. Slit the skin lengthwise, keeping the cutting edge along the center of the breastbone. Now, peel the skin away from the breast, down to the legs, and up to the neck. Work the skin over each thigh and upper leg, stopping when you reach the leg joint. At this point, bend each leg backward until the joint cracks, and then cut off the leg. With the breast and both legs now free of skin, cut the tail off at its base.

Now, take each wing and bend it backward at the first joint until it cracks. Cut off the wing tips and the head. Finally, peel the skin down toward the neck and off the bird.

If you freeze your birds after skinning, make sure there are no air pockets in the package, since these air traps can cause freezer burn. When you plan to eat a bird, let it thaw slowly in the refrigerator. Don't rush it on the kitchen counter.

The absence of skin on your birds should not bother you, and it doesn't affect the table quality of the birds. Game birds are generally dry and must be basted frequently while cooking. Cover the birds with bacon strips. The bacon creates a "skin" for the birds, retaining body juices and adding moisture and taste.

Section Two

GAME ANIMALS AND BIRDS

BIG-GAME ANIMALS

Grizzly Bear *(Ursus arctos)*

RANGE: This bear is found mostly in inland Alaska, though there are also small herds of grizzlies in the Rocky Mountains. A variety of the grizzly, the Alaska brown bear—once considered to be a separate species—inhabits the Alaska Peninsula to its southernmost point. Limited sections of British Columbia, the Yukon Territory, and nearby islands are also inhabited by the brown bear.

IDENTIFICATION: The grizzly bear has a compact, powerful frame, with long, thick hair ranging from dark brown to shades of tan to almost yellow. The tips of the hairs are grizzled—hence the bear's name. The grizzly has sharply curved claws, 3¾ inches long, which it uses for fighting and digging. The grizzly has a prominent shoulder hump, a feature that distinguishes it from black and polar bears.

SIZE: The typical grizzly is 6 to 8 feet long; the distance from its foot to the top of its hump is about 3½ feet. The average weight is 800 pounds, though some grizzlies weigh as much as 1,100 pounds.

The world-record grizzly, whose skull was picked up in Lone Mountain, Alaska, in 1976, scored $27^{13}/_{16}$ points in the Boone and Crockett Club competition. The record skull measured $17^{9}/_{16}$ inches long and $10^{9}/_{16}$ inches wide.

The brown bear, the largest of the carnivorous, land-based mammals, reaches 8 to 10 feet in length and stands 4½ feet from the top of its shoulder. The average male weighs 1,000 pounds, the female rarely more than 800. Some browns on record have weighed more than 1,500 pounds.

The world-record Alaska brown bear, killed by Roy Lindsley on Kodiak Island in 1952, scored $30^{12}/_{16}$ points in the Boone and Crockett Club competition. The record male's skull measured $17^{15}/_{16}$ inches long and $12^{13}/_{16}$ inches wide.

FOOD: The grizzly is classified as a carnivore, but because grasses, sedges, roots, and tubers of plants are readily available, the grizzly has omnivorous tendencies. Salmon, mice, snakes, and frogs also supplement this bear's diet.

EDIBILITY: Indians and outdoorsmen used to eat the flesh in early times, but the grizzly bear is primarily a trophy animal today.

Grizzly Bear

Black Bear

■ Black Bear *(Ursus americanus)*

RANGE: Every Canadian province, as well as Alaska, is populated with black bears, as is a substantial portion of the United States from Montana south through Arizona and New Mexico. Sections of the northeastern, northwestern, and Gulf Coast states are inhabited by the species, along with northern Mexico and northeastern Arkansas.

IDENTIFICATION: Shiny black hair covers a major part of the body, but it turns lighter around the eyes and muzzle. A blaze of white adorning the chest is a distinguishing characteristic, as is the absence of the conspicuous shoulder hump of the Alaska brown bear and the grizzly bear.

SIZE: A prime male weighs between 300 and 400 pounds; a female far less. Some black bears on record have weighed more than 600 pounds. The average animal stands 3 feet high at the shoulder and measures 5½ feet in length.

The world-record bear, a skull picked up in Sanpete County, Utah, in 1975, scored 23¹⁰/₁₆ points in the Boone and Crockett Club competition. The skull measured 14¹²/₁₆ inches long and 8¹³/₁₆ inches wide.

FOOD: The black bear tends to be omnivorous, eating grasses, fruits, berries, buds, fish, rodents, and sedges. Dead bears, ants, and bees are also on its menu.

EDIBILITY: The meat is dark and tends to be coarse, but it is very good when handled and prepared properly.

■ Polar Bear *(Ursus maritimus)*

RANGE: Polar bears are found predominantly in regions of the Arctic coast, ranging from Labrador west to Alaska's Seward Peninsula and south along the Hudson Bay and James Bay shore.

IDENTIFICATION: The polar bear's body is almost completely covered by long, thick, yellow-white fur during the entire year. Only the lips, eyes, nose, and toenails are black. The head is small and tapering, the neck long and muscular, and the body somewhat pear-shaped.

SIZE: Though the male averages 1,000 pounds, some bears have been reported as heavy as 1,600 pounds. A prime male stands 4 feet high at the shoulder, usually measuring 8 feet in length. Females tend to be smaller.

The world-record polar bear was taken by Shelby Longoria in 1963 off Kotzebue, Alaska. The male had a Boone and Crockett Club score of 29¹⁵/₁₆ points, with a skull measuring 18⁸/₁₆ inches in length and 11⁷/₁₆ inches in width. The polar bear is currently ineligible, until further notice, for the North American Big Game competition.

Polar Bear

FOOD: The most carnivorous bear of all, the polar bear dines on seals, foxes, mollusks, lemmings, birds, caribou, and dead or helpless whales. Often, however, this species eats seaweed, grasses, and roots.

EDIBILITY: Polar bear meat is the main staple of the diet of the Eskimos, but the liver can be poisonous due to the excessive amounts of vitamin A within.

Whitetail Deer
(Odocoileus virginianus)

RANGE: The whitetail deer inhabits a vast section of North America, from southern Canada down through the southern border of the United States. Only a few dry regions of western North America are devoid of whitetails.

IDENTIFICATION: In spring, the whitetail sports a bright, brownish-red coat made up of thin hair. With the coming of winter, a new coat grows, with long, kinky hair varying in color from brownish gray to blue. The nose is pure black with two white bands behind it. The face is brown and the eyes are circled with white. The darkest part of the body is the middle of the back. Though gradually lighter on other parts of the body, the coloring turns abruptly white at the stomach. The antlers consist of two main beams that grow outward, backward, and then sweep forward.

SIZE: A typical whitetail is slightly taller than 3 feet at the shoulder, measures 5 to 6 feet in length, and weighs about 150 pounds. The largest whitetail ever recorded, however, weighed 425 pounds.

Whitetail Deer

The world-record whitetail deer, according to the Boone and Crockett Club ratings, scored 213⅝ points. Taken by Milo Hanson on November 3, 1993, in Saskatchewan, the rack's inside spread was 27⅝ inches.

FOOD: Most types of vegetation are included in the whitetail's diet, which changes with both the season and the area of the country inhabited. Favorites on the menu are white cedar, white acorns, witchhazel, pine, red maple, apples, dogwood, oak, sweetfern, sumac, wintergreen, bearberry, Oregon grape, hemlock, willow, greenbriar, snowberry, and arborvitae. Among the cultivated crops it seeks out are soybeans, trefoil, rye, alfalfa, corn, rape, cabbage, clover, and lespedeza.

EDIBILITY: Whitetail venison, if treated like good beef, will taste delicious. Prompt and proper field dressing ensures fine meat.

Mule Deer

Mule Deer (Odocoileus hemionus)

RANGE: The overall area encompassed by the mule deer extends from southeastern Alaska to Mexico, and east to west Texas, Minnesota, and the Hudson Bay. Those muleys inhabiting the coastal area from Alaska to mid-California are properly termed blacktail deer.

IDENTIFICATION: The mule deer's basic coloring in summer is a brownish red, changing to a brownish gray in winter. The nose and the band around the muzzle are black; the face and a section around the eyes are white. The deer's throat has two white patches separated by a dark bar, its belly and the inside of its legs are whitish, and its hoofs are jet black. The tail is round and white, but becomes black about 2 inches from the tip. The ears often reach 11 inches in total length. A buck's antlers, very large and heavy, divide into two main beams. Each beam forks into two tines.

Though closely related to the mule deer, the blacktail does have some distinctions. The ears measure 6½ inches and are narrower, and the tail is dark on top with a white underside. But like the muley, the blacktail's coloring is brownish red in summer and brownish gray in winter.

SIZE: This species stands about 3½ feet high at the shoulder, measures close to 6½ feet in length, and averages between 175 and 200 pounds in weight. The blacktail is slightly smaller on average. One mule deer that was recorded weighed 480 pounds.

The world-record mule deer, according to the Boone and Crockett Club records, was killed in Dolores County, Colorado, in 1972 by Doug Burris Jr. Scoring 226⅘ points, the rack's right main beam, sporting 6 points, measured 30⅛ inches; its left beam, sporting 5 points, measured 28⅞ inches. The rack's inside spread was 30⅞ inches.

FOOD: In summer, grasses play an important role in the mule deer's diet: ricegrass, needlegrass, grama grass,

Elk

wheatgrass, bluegrass, fescue grass, and bromegrass. In winter, when grasses are scarce, browse takes over: mountain mahogany, cliffrose, sagebrush, poplar, bitterbrush, jack pine, sunflower, cedar, oak, snowberry, bearberry, fir, and serviceberry. Although the deer eats almost any vegetation, it prefers fungus, nuts, cactus fruits, acorns, wildflowers, ferns, and berries.

Rating high on the blacktail's menu are wild oats, manzanita, ceanothus, chamise, buckthorn, buttercup, bromegrass, and fescue grass. Cactus fruit, nuts, wildflowers, acorns, fungus, berries, and acorns are also preferred foods.

EDIBILITY: Deer venison, though it is drier than beef, is quite delicious.

Elk *(Cervus canadensis)*

RANGE: The bulk of the elk population is in the Rocky Mountains, ranging from British Columbia to New Mexico and Arizona. Herds are also found in some midwestern and eastern states. Alberta, Saskatchewan, and Manitoba also have fair-size elk populations.

IDENTIFICATION: The elk's normal winter coat is brownish gray with long chestnut-brown hair on its head and neck. Its legs are dark and its belly nearly black. The rump patch and short tail are yellowish white. Cow elk are lighter than bulls. In summer, the elk's coat turns a reddish color.

SIZE: Bull elk range in weight from 600 pounds to as much as 1,000 pounds. Cows are smaller, averaging about 600 pounds. A good-size bull may stand 5 feet tall at the shoulder and measure 10 feet in length. Antlers of a prime bull grow up to 5 feet above its head, with each antler sporting from 5 to 7 points and measuring 60 inches or more along the beam.

The world-record head, taken in 1968 in White Mountains, Arizona, had a Boone and Crockett Club score of 442⅝ points. Both beams measured 56⅔ inches long. The right beam had 6 points, the left 7 points. The inside spread measured 47⅛ inches.

FOOD: The diet consists mainly of grasses and browse. Some of the prime foods are pinegrass, bluegrass, blue bunchgrass, sweet vernal grass, and wheatgrass. Elk eat nearly all the conifers, aspen, and willows. Their diet may also include alder, maple, blackberry, and serviceberry.

EDIBILITY: The meat is dark and much like beef in taste and texture. Elk is generally considered to be very good eating.

Moose *(Alces alces)*

RANGE: The Alaska-Yukon moose is found in the Alaska and Yukon Peninsulas; the Canada moose is found in every Canadian province and in sections of northern Minnesota, Wisconsin, and Maine; the Wyoming, or Shiras, moose inhabits the area from the Rocky Mountain region of northern Colorado and Utah north to the border between Canada and the United States.

IDENTIFICATION: The moose is a large, antlered, ungraceful-looking creature. The primary color is black, though shades of dark brown and russet have been spotted. The nostrils, circles around the eyes, inner parts of the ear, and lower portions of the legs are whitish gray. The hindquarters are much more tapered than the forequarters, and together they hold the moose's belly approximately 40 inches from the ground. The immense antlers weigh around 90 pounds and often reach 6 feet in length. The tail is 3 inches long and stub-like. The ears are large, and the long face finishes up in a wide, downturned muzzle.

Moose

SIZE: A typical large bull is from 6½ to 7½ feet tall at the shoulder, measures 8½ to 10½ feet in length, and weighs between 1,300 and 1,400 pounds. Several recorded bulls have weighed in at as high as 1,800 pounds.

The world-record Alaska-Yukon moose scored 261⅝ points in the Boone and Crockett Club competition. Killed by John A. Crouse in Fortymile River, Alaska, in 1994, the trophy's greatest spread measured 65⅛ inches.

The world-record Canada moose, according to the Boone and Crockett Club rating system, scored 242 points. Killed by Michael E. Laub in 1980 near Grayling River, British Columbia, the trophy had a right palm measuring 44⅝ inches with 15 points and a left palm measuring 45 inches with 16 points. The greatest spread was 63 inches.

The world-record Wyoming moose, killed by John M. Oakley in Green River Lake, Wyoming, in 1952, scored 205⅝ points in the Boone and Crockett Club competition. Its greatest spread was 53 inches; its right palm was 38⅝ inches and its left palm was 38⅝ inches. Both palms sported 15 points.

FOOD: A favorite food is dwarf willow, as is white birch, aspen, and balsam fir in forested sections. In summer, the moose seeks shelter from the heat and insects at lakes, where it dines on eelgrass, sedges, pondweeds, and water lilies. Red osier, alder, honeysuckle, chokecherry, striped maple, spiraea, snowberry, dwarf birch, current, elder, cranberry, mountain ash, and cottonwood are also preferred items.

EDIBILITY: Though a bit darker and drier than beef, moose meat is very similar in taste.

Bighorn Sheep *(Ovis canadensis)*

RANGE: The Rocky Mountain bighorn is found in remote areas from central British Columbia down through the northern Rocky Mountains. The desert bighorn inhabits a good portion of the southeastern United States and northern Mexico.

IDENTIFICATION: The bighorn has a well-muscled, finely proportioned body set atop stout, strong legs. The head and heavy majestic horns are supported by a rather sturdy neck. The horns, dark brown in color, have conspicuous growth rings and may weigh more than 20 pounds. The Rocky Mountain bighorn is dark brown, the desert bighorn pale buff, but the tail on both is black.

Bighorn Sheep

White is the color of the animal's muzzle, a patch around the eye, a rump patch, and an edging running along the back of each leg. The ears, though small, are alert.

SIZE: An average ram stands 3 to 3½ feet tall at the shoulder, measuring 5 to 6 feet in length. The ram weighs about 200 pounds, although some on record have surpassed 300 pounds. Ewes are usually a bit less than three-quarters the size of rams.

The world-record Rocky Mountain bighorn sheep, according to the Boone and Crockett Club records, was taken by Guinn D. Crousen in Luscar Mountain, Alberta, in 2000 and scored 208⅜ points.

The world-record desert bighorn scored 205⅛ points in the Boone and Crockett Club competition. Taken by a Native American in Lower California, Mexico, in 1940, the trophy's right horn measured 43⅝ inches and the left measured 43⅜ inches. The greatest spread came to 25⅝ inches.

FOOD: Grasses comprise the bulk of the bighorn's diet. They include fescue grass, wheatgrass, sedges, rushes, horsetail, little ricegrass, penstemon, June grass, and vetch. When the grasses are covered by snow in winter, browse—sagebrush, willow, alder, chokeberry, bitterbrush, rabbitbrush, greasebrush, and mountain mahogany—takes a prominent place on the menu.

EDIBILITY: Many big-game hunters rate bighorn sheep as the finest of all wild-game meat.

Dall Sheep *(Ovis dalli)*

RANGE: This species inhabits the mountainous regions of northern Alaska east to the western Mackenzie Mountain range.

IDENTIFICATION: Dall rams and ewes are practically snow white except for a few black hairs in their tails. The horns, a bit lighter than those of the Stone ram, have a conspicuous flare that keeps them away from the ram's eyes. Also, the light-yellow horns show well-defined yearly growth marks that reveal the animal's age. Ewes have horns that usually resemble thin spikes and rarely grow beyond 15 inches in length. In winter, the waxy hair covering the body reaches 3 inches in length, but this hair is shed before summer and replaced by a shorter coat.

SIZE: A typical Dall ram weighs between 180 and 200 pounds, stands slightly above 3 feet high at the shoulder, and measures approximately 6 feet in length.

The world-record Dall sheep, killed by Harry L. Swank Jr. in Alaska's Wrangell Mountains in 1961, scored 189⅞ points in the Boone and Crockett Club competition. The right and left horns measured 48⅜ and 47⅞ inches respectively. The greatest spread was 34⅜ inches.

FOOD: Forbes and grasses make up the bulk of the Dall sheep's diet, though it will also eat browse, especially the dwarf willow.

EDIBILITY: Most hunters rate the meat far better than

Dall Sheep

that of domestic sheep. In fact, they consider it to be the finest in the world.

Stone Sheep *(Ovis dalli stonei)*

RANGE: This subspecies of the Dall sheep is found in northern British Columbia.

IDENTIFICATION: Stone sheep have colorings varying from grayish blue to bluish black to black. Stones do, however, have a light belly, a white rump patch, and a white edging down the rear of each leg. There is also a sort of whitish blotch near the face, which tends to enlarge with age. The horns of the Stone ram are a bit heavier than those of the Dall ram. The coat covering the body measures 3 inches, but it is shed when summer approaches and is replaced by a shorter coat.

SIZE: An average Stone ram weighs between 180 and 200 pounds, measures 6 feet in length, and stands just above 3 feet tall at the shoulder.

The world-record Stone sheep, killed by L. S. Chadwick on the Muskwa River of British Columbia in 1936, scored 196⅛ points in the Boone and Crockett Club competition. The right horn was 50⅛ inches long and the left was 51⅝ inches long. The greatest spread was 31 inches.

FOOD: Grasses and forbes comprise the major portion of the Stone sheep's diet. The sheep does dine on browse, however, especially the dwarf willow.

EDIBILITY: The meat of the domestic sheep can't compare with that of this fine specimen. Many hunters rate its meat as the finest in the world.

Rocky Mountain Goat *(Oreamnos americanus)*

RANGE: This species inhabits the steep slopes of the western mountains from Washington and Idaho up through central Yukon and southern Alaska.

IDENTIFICATION: The mountain goat's body is a short, blunt, boxlike structure, and except for the bottom 8 inches of each leg, it is covered by an abundance of hair. The shoulders are humped and the head is long and narrow. Its lengthy hair is pure white save for a yellow

Rocky Mountain Goat

tint, but pure black is the color of its horns, nose, eyes, and hoofs. The horns, rising from the rear of the head, are slender and curve backward. Both the billy and the nanny sport horns and beards. For the billy, the horns average 12 inches; for the nanny, 9 inches.

SIZE: A typical mountain goat stands just higher than 3 feet at the shoulder and measures 5 to 6 feet in length. Though the species averages between 150 and 300 pounds, the heaviest mountain goat on record weighed more than 500 pounds.

The world-record mountain goat was killed by Troy M. Sheldon in 2011 in Stikine River, British Columbia. It scored 57⅛ points in the Boone and Crockett Club competition. Its right and left horns both measured 11⅜ inches.

FOOD: In summer, the goat's diet consists of grasses, browse, and forbes, specifically bluegrass, wheatgrass, purple milk vetch, green lily, strawberry, alpine sorrel, and alpine equisetum. In winter, goats switch to aspen, red osier, bearberry juniper, willow, dwarf birch, and balsam fir. Lichens and mosses are year-round favorites.

EDIBILITY: The meat of a trophy billy is usually rather tough, as the animal is getting on in years. The meat of the younger animals, though, is used for food.

Caribou *(Rangifer tarandus)*

RANGE: There are four varieties of caribou, formerly classified as subspecies but now considered to be of the same species, for which *Rangifer tarandus* is the accepted scientific name. The mountain caribou inhabits the tundra and coniferous forests of Canada and Alaska. The Barren Ground caribou summers from Canada

Caribou

and northern Alaska to the far north until the land runs out. In winter, it migrates to the south as far as Saskatchewan and northern Manitoba. The woodland caribou is found in forested areas between northern Idaho and Great Slave Lake and from Newfoundland to the Alaska-Yukon border. The fourth variety is the Quebec-Labrador caribou.

IDENTIFICATION: The caribou has a dark neck and a long mane running under the neck from chin to chest. In the summer, the fur is dark brown, but becomes brownish gray in winter. The belly, rump patch, feet, and short tail vary in color from pale gray to yellowish white throughout the year. A wide muzzle circled with white hairs, long fur, and a main beam that sweeps backward, upward, and outward, finishing in a flat palm, typify the species. The mountain caribou is the largest and darkest of the four types. The Barren Ground is the smallest and palest; its neck is a very bright white. Both the male and female of the species have antlers; the male sheds his in December or January, the female during the fawning period in May or June.

SIZE: An average mountain caribou bull measures 7 1/2 to 8 feet in length, close to 4 feet from foot to shoulder, and weighs between 500 and 600 pounds. Some recorded mountain caribou have weighed in the vicinity of 700 pounds. Females are smaller and lighter. The world-record mountain caribou, killed by Paul T. Deuling in 1988 in Pelly Mountains, Yukon Territory, scored 459 3/8 points in the Boone and Crockett Club competition. The right beam had 18 points and measured 51 7/8 inches; the left had 20 points and measured 48 7/8 inches. The greatest inside spread measured 40 inches.

A typical Barren Ground bull is 6 1/2 feet long, 3 1/2 feet high from foot to shoulder, and averages 375 pounds. Females are smaller and weigh less. The world-record Barren Ground caribou, killed by Daniel L. Dobbs in Iliamna Lake, Alaska, in 1999, scored 477 points in the Boone and Crockett Club competition. The right beam measured 55 5/8 inches and had 17 points; the left measured 57 7/8 inches and had 25 points. The greatest inside spread between beams was 38 3/8 inches.

A typical woodland caribou bull is about 8 feet long, measures 4 feet from foot to shoulder, and weighs approximately 400 pounds. Females tend to be smaller in both total weight and size. The world-record woodland caribou was killed sometime prior to 1910 in Newfoundland, scoring 419 5/8 points in the Boone and Crockett Club competition. The left beam measured 47 3/8 inches and had 18 points, the right 50 1/8 inches and 19 points. The greatest inside spread was 43 2/8 inches in between beams.

Another category has been added to the Boone and Crockett Club listings—the Quebec-Labrador caribou—because racks from that region are so impressive. The world record, taken in 1931 by Zack Elbow in Nain, Labrador, scored 474 6/8 points. Its right beam was 60 4/8 inches and had 22 points. Its left was 61 1/8 inches and had 30 points. The inside spread was 58 2/8 inches.

FOOD: Caribou favor lichens as their main food, but also eat grasses, twigs, shrubs, flowers, moss, and practically any other plant matter available.

EDIBILITY: Caribou meat is rated excellent.

Pronghorn Antelope
(Antilocapra americana)

RANGE: The pronghorn is located in the region from southern Saskatchewan south through the western United States to the Mexican plains.

IDENTIFICATION: The pronghorn is similar to a small deer in body structure and coloring. Both the males and females have similar markings—two black horns (both of which are longer than the ears) and a bright tannish-red hue on the upper body and the outside of the legs. The inside of the legs and underparts are a strong white, as is the rump patch. The necks of both sexes are streaked by two thick, brown bands. The buck, however, has a wide, black band that extends from the nose to just below the eyes.

SIZE: A full-grown male may reach 3½ feet in height at the shoulder, and 5 feet in length, with an average weight of between 100 and 140 pounds. Does usually peak at 80 pounds. There is a tie for the world-record pronghorn. The first was taken in Coconino County, Arizona, in 2000 by Dylan M. Woods and scored 95 points in the Boone and Crockett Club competition. The right horn measured 19⅜ inches, the left 18⅝ inches, and the inside spread was 11⅞ inches. The second—which also scored 95 points—was taken in Mohave County, Arizona, in 2002 by David Meyer. The right and left horns both measured 17⅜ inches and the inside spread was 10⅛ inches.

FOOD: The diet consists chiefly of vegetable substances, such as saltbrush, onion, western juniper, sagebrush, and bitterbrush.

EDIBILITY: Hunters rate the meat very good.

▮ Bison *(Bison bison)*

RANGE: The wild bison no longer exists in the United States, and those of the species that remain are located in national parks, wildlife refuges, and private ranches in North America. Yellowstone National Park and South Dakota's Wind Cave National Park, Montana's National Bison Range, and Oklahoma's Wichita Wildlife Refuge all have bison, as do Big Delta, Alaska, and northern Alberta's Wood Buffalo Park.

IDENTIFICATION: The bison has a humped back, and is the largest wild animal on the North American continent. Lengthy hair, reaching 8 inches in winter and 4 inches in summer, covers its head, neck, shoulders, and forequarters. The hair on the rear section of the bison usually measures one-half the length of the hair on the front section. Hair color ranges from dark brown to black, but the sun often bleaches it to a dark tan. Both males and females have two thick horns, both of which are sharply upturned.

Pronghorn Antelope

SIZE: A large bull measures 11½ to 12 feet in length and stands 6 feet high from his foot to the apex of his hump. Bulls usually weigh about 2,000 pounds, while cows are much smaller, weighing 800 to 900 pounds. Records indicate that some bison have reached weights of nearly 3,000 pounds.

The world-record bison, killed by Sam T. Woodring in Yellowstone National Park, Wyoming, in 1925, scored 136⅛ points in the Boone and Crockett Club competition. Its right horn measured 21⅞ inches; its left 23⅜ inches. The greatest spread between the record's horns was 35⅜ inches.

Bison

FOOD: As the bison hasn't any teeth in the front of its upper jaw, its diet consists of grasses, such as tumbleweed, grama grass, dropseed grass, and buffalo grass. Using its tongue and lower incisors, the bison snips off the grasses.

EDIBILITY: When bison weren't as scarce, people raved about the fine flavor of their meat. The bison's tongue and hump meat were considered delicacies. Some bison meat is available today from specimens killed on private ranches.

Mountain Lion *(Felis concolor)*

RANGE: This species, which is also known as the cougar, puma, painter, panther, catamount, and American lion, is distributed throughout western North America from northern British Columbia south to Mexico, east to the Rocky Mountains and Saskatchewan, and along the Gulf Coast states to Mississippi. The mountain lion is also found in southern Florida.

IDENTIFICATION: The body color is practically uniform, though it may vary from russet to nearly gray. The fur measures a uniform inch all over the body, dark near the eyes and upper muzzle and off-white at the forepart of the mouth, lower flanks, and belly. The eyes are frequently yellow, the ears pronounced but well rounded. Its prominent whiskers tend to be white. The tail, measuring from 2 to 3 feet, has a dark tip. The rounded head appears small in comparison to the body.

SIZE: The mountain lion is the largest North American unspotted cat. A mature adult measures 7 to 9½ feet in length, stands 26 to 31 inches at the shoulder, and weighs up to 275 pounds. Most lions are far lighter, and females are usually two-thirds the weight of males. The heaviest cat weighed more than 300 pounds before evisceration.

The world-record cougar, according to the Boone and Crockett Club records, was taken by Douglas E. Schuk in Tatlayoko Lake, British Columbia, in 1979. Scoring 16⁴⁄₁₆ points, the skull measured 9⁵⁄₁₆ inches long and 6¹¹⁄₁₆ inches wide.

FOOD: Mule deer in particular are the staple of the mountain lion's diet, though it enjoys all species of deer. Horses and steers are also preyed upon, colts being a favorite. Chickens, pigs, goats, turkeys, and sheep also have their place on the menu.

Mountain Lion

EDIBILITY: The meat is reminiscent of lamb or veal in flavor, texture, and taste. The relative lack of fat, however, makes it somewhat dry.

Jaguar *(Felis onca hernandesii)*

RANGE: Though quite rare in the United States, the jaguar is located from Mexico southward to Central and South America.

IDENTIFICATION: The body, compact and enormously muscled, is coated with spots. This coat, basically yellow shading to tawny, features small spots around the head, large spots on the legs, and an intermixing of the two across the chest. The spots are actually rosettes, square in shape. The back and sides are covered with large, black rosettes with yellow middles and a black spot in the center. The tail measures just 30 inches long, shorter than the cougar's. The predominantly white feet have tiny black spots. The head is round, the ears short and finely rounded, and the whiskers long, white, and highly prominent.

SIZE: The jaguar is the Western Hemisphere's largest cat, usually measuring 6 to 9 feet in overall length, 2⅓ feet high at the shoulder, and weighing from 200 to 250 pounds. Some specimens have been reported at more than 350 pounds.

The world-record skull scored 18⁷⁄₁₆ points in the Boone and Crockett Club competition. Taken by C. J. McElroy in 1965 in Sinaloa, Mexico, the jaguar's skull measured 10¹⁵⁄₁₆ inches in length and 7⁵⁄₁₆ inches in width.

Collared Peccary

FOOD: Monkeys, parrots, coatis, and turkeys form a part of the jaguar's diet, as do peccaries, cattle, sea turtles, and man himself.

EDIBILITY: Jaguars and other big cats are generally not hunted for meat and there is little information on their edibility. However, research indicates that the meat of big cats is reported as "sweet" with very little fat content.

Collared Peccary *(Tayassu tajacu)*

RANGE: The peccary, or javelina, resides in arid, brushy regions and scrub oak forests along the border between the United States and Mexico, extending from eastern Texas west to Arizona.

IDENTIFICATION: The collared peccary resembles a pig in that it has a lengthy snout with a tough disc at its tip, along with a very short neck, short but stout legs, and a somewhat arched back. Also, its ears are small, erect, and pointed. Though the eyelids have long lashes, the eyes themselves are small. The body is covered with 2-inch-long, bristly, salt-and-pepper gray hair. A thin, white band begins under the animal's throat and joins on its back. About 8 inches above its short tail, on the center of its back, is a gaping musk gland.

SIZE: A typical member of this species is 2½ feet in length, measures 22 inches high at the shoulder, and averages between 40 and 65 pounds in weight.

FOOD: Prickly pears—fruit and spines—are the peccary's favorite food. It also eats roots, tubers, acorns, nuts, fruits, and berries. Being omnivorous, the species also dines on insects and the young and eggs of ground-nesting birds, amphibians, and reptiles. Snake meat is a special treat.

EDIBILITY: Peccary meat, dry in texture and light in color, is considered tasty by some people; others tend to disagree.

European Wild Hog *(Sus scrofa)*

RANGE: This species is far from numerous in the United States. To find European wild hogs, hunters must go to the areas of initial releases (e.g., Tennessee's Great Smoky Mountains and North Carolina's Hooper's Bald) .

IDENTIFICATION: Thin and muscular (unlike its domesticated relative), the wild hog has tusks measuring up to 9 inches in length. Its snout is long and saucerlike, its eyes rather small, and its always-erect ears about 5 inches long. The wild hog is usually pure black, but, on occasion, its bristly guard hairs may be white. Its long legs give it nearly the swiftness of a deer.

SIZE: A typical adult measures 30 inches in height at the shoulder and is 4 to 5 feet long. In North America, a big hog may weigh from 300 to 350 pounds. Some European wild hogs, however, have been recorded at close to 600 pounds.

FOOD: During the warmer months, wild hogs feed on roots, tubers, fruits, berries, and grasses. Their menu also ranges from fawns to nuts, including rabbits, mice, frogs, beechnuts, and even rattlesnakes (the wild hog appears to be immune to its poison).

EDIBILITY: The wild hog is hunted chiefly for sport and trophies, as its meat is reputed to be tough.

European Wild Hog

KNOW YOUR BIG-GAME TRACKS

It's hard to imagine a big-game hunter in the woods not scanning the ground carefully for animal tracks. Even during the off-season, it's a wise use of time to study tracks. They will tell you what big-game animals live in your favorite hunting areas.

The animal tracks shown here will help you identify big game. The dimensions given will also be helpful, but regard them only as benchmarks. The track sizes here are for average adult animals. Obviously, smaller tracks are made by young animals and oversize tracks by exceptionally large ones.

Identifying tracks is largely a process of elimination. For example, if you find a single-file pad track, you can eliminate all hoofed animals and animals that leave a double or side-by-side track. Animals that leave a single-file track include wolves and lions. Also, if the track has claw prints, you can probably eliminate the mountain lion, which normally keeps its claws retracted. After you have

narrowed tracks down to a couple of species, final identification should be easy.

When you've identified the species, you may also be able to determine its size by the depth of the track. If possible, compare the tracks to others of the same species over the same terrain. If one deer track is an inch deep and another of the same size is 2 inches deep, it follows that the deeper track belongs to a heavier deer—possibly a big buck.

Study animal tracks every time you're in the woods, and learn to identify the animals that left them. It will lend you insight into the wildlife around you and make you a better hunter.

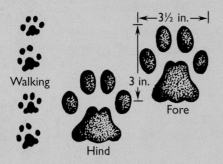

▲ **Mountain Lion:** A mountain lion's forepaws are larger than its hind feet; its claws are retracted and rarely show in the track.

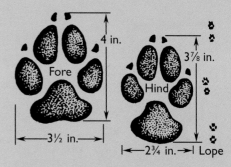

▲ **Wolf:** Wolf tracks are similar to a large dog's. The forepaw is typically wider than the rear paw.

▼ **Bighorn Sheep:** A bighorn has blunt toes and a slight hollow on the outer edges of a widely split hoof.

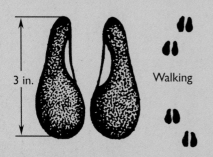

▶ **Mountain Goat:** Look for a widely splayed hoof and soft-edged print from the rubberlike hoof.

◄ **Whitetail Deer:** A buck's tracks are longer and wider than a doe's tracks. Dewclaws seldom show.

Walking

3 in.

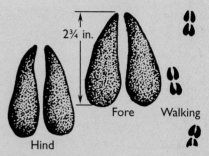

2¾ in.

Fore   Walking

Hind

▲ **Antelope:** Dewclaws are absent in the track of a pronghorn antelope. The forehoof is also wider than the hind hoof.

▶ **Mule Deer:** The track of the mule deer is very similar to that of the whitetail.

3 in.

Walking

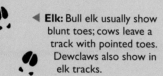

◄ **Elk:** Bull elk usually show blunt toes; cows leave a track with pointed toes. Dewclaws also show in elk tracks.

4 in.

Walking

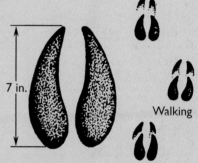

7 in.

Walking

▲ **Moose:** Moose have pointed hooves; hind hooves often overlap tracks of front hooves.

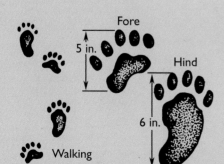

Fore

5 in.

Hind

6 in.

Walking

▲ **Black Bear:** The black bear's claws are shorter than a grizzly's (about 1½ inches) and rarely show in tracks.

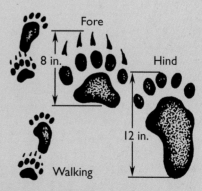

Fore

8 in.

Hind

12 in.

Walking

▲ **Grizzly:** The grizzly's forepaws have exceptionally long claws—sometimes more than 3 inches long in a full-grown adult.

SMALL-GAME ANIMALS

▧ Cottontail Rabbit *(Sylvilagus)*

RANGE: Combined, the four species of the cottontail, which include the Eastern cottontail (*Sylvilagus floridanus*), mountain cottontail (*S. nuttali*), desert cottontail (*S. auduboni*), and New England cottontail (*S. transitionalis*), inhabit much of the United States, except for some sections of the Far West.

IDENTIFICATION: The body pigment is basically brown with the possibility of a reddish or buff cast. Guard hairs with black tips are scattered throughout, but the belly, chin, and undersides of the legs are white. The underside of the tail is also white, resembling a cotton ball when the rabbit is scampering around—hence its name. The majority of cottontails have a white spot on the forehead between the eyes. The whiskers, though long, are light and relatively inconspicuous. The ears, 2½ to 3 inches long, are bare on the inside but lightly furred on the outside.

SIZE: The cottontail is from 14 to 19 inches long and stands from 6 to 7 inches at the shoulder. Females tend to be a bit larger than males. Weights vary from 2½ to 3½ pounds, the latter being the top weight that has ever been recorded.

FOOD: The diet of the cottontail consists of crabgrass, bluegrass, and other grasses; all kinds of fruits and berries; such cultivated crops as clover, alfalfa, lettuce, beans, wheat, soybeans, and cabbage; weeds such as

Cottontail Rabbit

Varying Hare

yarrow and goldenrod; sheep sorrel; wild cherry; and wild shrubs. Sumac is a favorite food in winter.

EDIBILITY: The meat, lightly colored and finely textured, is delicious.

▧ Varying Hare *(**Lepus americanus**)*

RANGE: The varying hare inhabits the tree limits of Alaska and Canada, south through New England and the Appalachians to Tennessee in the east. In the Rockies, it ranges to northern New Mexico and to mid-California.

IDENTIFICATION: The hare's coat acts as excellent camouflage. Though brown in summer, the coat is shed in winter for a white one. A dark line runs down the center of its back, ending in a dark rump and tail top. The chin, belly, and undersides of the tail are white, but the throat is a brownish red. The feet are huge and hairy.

SIZE: A typical member of this species stands 8 to 9 inches at the shoulder and measures 21 inches in length. Though weights vary from 3 to 4½ pounds, the heaviest varying hare ever recorded weighed 5¼ pounds.

FOOD: Almost any vegetation appeals to the hare, but it has its preferences—succulent grasses and the tender tips of woody plants in summer, and dead grasses, buds, and bark in winter. White cedar is also a favorite.

EDIBILITY: As the varying hare usually lacks any fat, the meat is dry.

▪ Jackrabbit *(Lepus)*

RANGE: The whitetail jackrabbit (*Lepus townsendii*) inhabits the sagebrush regions and grasslands from northern New Mexico north to southern Alberta, and from Lake Michigan west to the Sierras. The blacktail jackrabbit (*Lepus californicus*) lives in the deserts and open grasslands of the western United States from mid-Arkansas to the Pacific coast, north to southeastern Washington in the west and mid-South Dakota in the east.

IDENTIFICATION: The whitetail jackrabbit's tail is white on both top and bottom. Its conspicuous ears measure 5 to 6 inches in length. In summer, the coat is a light grayish brown over the sides and back, but the belly is lighter. The ear tips are black. When winter arrives, the coat is completely white or, on occasion, buff white. The blacktail's rump is black, as is the top of its tail. Its ears are longer than the whitetail's by an inch or so. The underside of the tail is white, as is the belly. The ears are white outside, brown inside, and black-tipped. Though the whitetail sheds twice annually, the color change is relatively insignificant.

SIZE: A typical whitetail jackrabbit measures between 22 and 26 inches long and weighs from 6 to 10 pounds. The average blacktail jackrabbit is 18 to 24 inches long and weighs between 4 and 7½ pounds. The heaviest jackrabbit on record was a whitetail that tipped the scales at 13 pounds.

Jackrabbit

FOOD: Though jackrabbits eat practically all kinds of vegetation in their diets, shrubs, weedy plants, and grasses make up the bulk of it. Main food items include spiderling, snakeweed, mesquite, grama grass, rabbitbrush, sagebrush, greasewood, filaree, prickly pears, eriogonum, and saltbrush.

EDIBILITY: Whitetail meat is said to be far preferable to the meat of the blacktail. Younger jackrabbits are more palatable than their elders.

▪ Arctic Hare *(Lepus arcticus)*

RANGE: The Arctic hare is found in the tundra region of northern Canada, from Newfoundland to the Mackenzie River. The Alaskan hare (*Lepus othus*) inhabits the area west of the Mackenzie Delta along the coast of Alaska to the Alaska Peninsula.

IDENTIFICATION: The hare's fur is pure white in winter, except for the black-tipped ears. In summer, the hare's coat becomes brown. There is no lag in the transition of the coat from white to brown in relation to the land. For example, when patches of white and brown are mixed on the coat, the ground is still covered with snow patches.

SIZE: The largest of the North American hares, the Arctic hare measures up to 28 inches long, stands close to 1 foot high at the shoulder, and weighs from 6 to 12 or more pounds.

FOOD: The basic food of the Arctic hare is the dwarf willow—its buds, leaves, catkins, bark, and even roots. Berries, mosses, herbs, and grasses are also eaten.

EDIBILITY: All those who have eaten Arctic hare meat regard it highly.

▪ European Rabbit *(Oryctolagus cuniculus)*

RANGE: Sometimes called the San Juan rabbit after the islands off the coast of Washington where it still runs wild, the European rabbit is more commonly found in captivity today. As a game animal, it has been a failure.

IDENTIFICATION: Somewhat similar to the cottontail in pigmentation, the European rabbit's hair is a light brown, intermingled with black. The nape of this rabbit's neck is buff, however, while the cottontail has a reddish nape. The tail, belly, and insides of the legs are white, but the tips of the 3½-inch ears are black.

SIZE: Larger than the cottontail, this species can reach some 18 inches in length and 5 pounds in weight.

FOOD: The preferred foods are herbs and grasses, but the European rabbit won't turn away from coarse vegetation when its favorites are scarce.

EDIBILITY: The meat, light in color, is quite tasty.

■ Gray Squirrel *(Sciurus carolinensis)*

RANGE: The eastern gray squirrel (*Sciurus carolinensis*) is located in hardwood forests from eastern Texas and eastern Saskatchewan to the Atlantic coast, and from the Gulf of Mexico to southern Canada. The Arizona gray squirrel (*Sciurus arizonensis*) inhabits pine and oak forests in southeastern and central Arizona. The western gray squirrel (*Sciurus griseus*) is also found in oak and pine forests, but in the region from southern California north to Washington.

IDENTIFICATION: The gray squirrel's coloring is salt-and-pepper gray. The body's underfur is solid gray with guard hairs that go from gray at the base to buff brown to black, and finish off in a white tip. The small hairs of the face, muzzle, and ears are a yellow tan, while those

Gray Squirrel

Fox Squirrel

under the throat, its underparts, and the insides of its legs are a rich white.

SIZE: A large adult measures between 17 and 20 inches depending upon its range, the tail taking up approximately 8 to 8½ inches of that length. Males and females tend to weigh the same—slightly more than 1 pound. The heaviest gray squirrel recorded weighed 1½ pounds.

FOOD: Nuts are a staple in the squirrel's diet and are cached for later use. The squirrel also feeds on buds, berries, tree blossoms, fruits, fungi, and field corn, as well as eggs and baby birds.

EDIBILITY: The quality and flavor of squirrel meat is generally regarded as excellent.

■ Fox Squirrel *(Sciurus niger)*

RANGE: The eastern fox squirrel (*Sciurus niger*) inhabits the open woods from the Canadian border to the Gulf of Mexico, and from the Atlantic coast to eastern Colorado. New England is free of the species. The Apache fox squirrel (*Sciurus apache*) resides in southeastern Arizona's Chiricahua Mountains and in Mexico.

IDENTIFICATION: Northeastern squirrels are frequently gray, and resemble oversize gray squirrels except for the rusty flank markings. In the West, bright rust is the dominant color, while black is the main pigment in the South. The hair tips of the tail are an orange color. The ears are round and large, the whiskers long and conspicuous. The plane from the ear to the nose is straighter than that of the gray squirrel.

SIZE: The typical fox squirrel weighs from 1½ to 3 pounds, the latter being exceptional for the species. Females tend to weigh a bit more than males. The total length is usually 28 inches (1 foot of which is a plumed tail), and the height at the shoulder is between 3½ and 4 inches.

FOOD: Like the gray squirrel, the fox squirrel rates nuts—especially acorns—as an important item in its diet. The most important are the nuts of the white oak, black oak, and red oak. Hickory nuts, beechnuts, hazelnuts, black walnuts, butternuts, and pecans are runners-up. Osage oranges are a wintertime treat, and blossoms, the fruit of maples, domesticated and wild fruits and berries, and fungi are favorites during other seasons. The fox squirrel also has a penchant for field corn.

EDIBILITY: The meat of the fox squirrel is rated as highly palatable.

■ Raccoon *(Procyon lotor)*

RANGE: The raccoon inhabits nearly all of the United States, parts of Mexico, and also extreme southern Canada, northward along the border between Saskatchewan and Alberta.

IDENTIFICATION: Though this species varies in size and color depending on its location, two conspicuous features distinguish it—the black mask across the eyes and the ringed tail. The latter is usually 10 inches long. The dense underfur is brownish red. Guard hairs are tipped with white, but come in shades of black, red, yellow, and gray. The white face and ears offer sharp contrast to the black nose and mask. The soles of the feet are jet black, the tops light.

SIZE: An average male measures 34 inches in length and stands from 9 to 12 inches high at the shoulder. A typical adult weighs from 12 to 16 pounds, but some males exceed 25 pounds. The heaviest coon ever recorded tipped the scales at 62 pounds, 6 ounces, and measured 55 inches from tail tip to nose tip.

FOOD: Wild raccoons eat snakes, eggs, baby birds, baby mice, baby rabbits, mussels, fish, frogs, grapes, berries, apples, and acorns. Crayfish is a delicacy to the raccoon, and both sweet corn and field corn are very important in the diet.

EDIBILITY: Hunters have long considered raccoon meat a delicacy.

■ Woodchuck/Groundhog *(Marmota monax)*

RANGE: About 500 million woodchucks are said to inhabit North America, ranging from eastern Alaska to Labrador, south in the central and eastern United States to Arkansas and Alabama, respectively, and to northern Idaho in the western United States.

IDENTIFICATION: The round, barrel-like body is supported by short but powerful legs. Brown is the basic body color, but shades of red to nearly black are fairly common. The guard hairs are silver-tipped, giving the animal a grizzled look. The ears are short and round, and the black eyes stick out above its flattened skull.

SIZE: A large male measures up to 26 inches in length (5 or 6 inches of which is its tail), often stands 6 to 7 inches high at the shoulder, and averages 10 pounds in weight. Females tend to be a bit smaller. The heaviest recorded chuck weighed 15¾ pounds.

FOOD: Woodchucks are 99 percent vegetarian, feeding on soybeans, corn, alfalfa, beans, peas, clover, and lettuce among the cultivated crops. Bark, twigs, and buds

Raccoon

Woodchuck/Groundhog

of low-growing bushes like sumac and wild cherry are also part of the diet. Fruits and berries of all types are frequently consumed.

EDIBILITY: Woodchuck meat, particularly that of the young, makes very good eating.

■ Prairie Dog *(Cynomys)*

RANGE: The whitetail species (*Cynomys gunnisoni, C. leucurus,* and *C. parvidens*) are found in mountainous

Prairie Dog

valleys from central Arizona and New Mexico to southern Montana. The blacktail prairie dog (*Cynomus ludovicianus*)—though once found in the high plains from southern Alberta and Saskatchewan to the Mexican border, and from the eastern Rocky Mountains to eastern Kansas and Nebraska—is relatively extinct. A small number of them, however, are located in national parks and monuments.

IDENTIFICATION: Unlike its name suggests, the prairie dog is a rodent rather than a dog. The tag comes from its yapping bark. The head comes to a flat surface, and the whiskers are prominent. The ears are short and rounded, and the black eyes are encircled in white. The body hair tends to be short, ranging in color from dark, brownish red to light gray. The animal's underparts are light. The slender tail differentiates the blacktail and whitetail prairie dogs. In the former, the tail has a black terminal tip and measures about 3½ inches in length. The latter's tail is a bit shorter (perhaps 2½ inches long) with a white tip.

SIZE: An adult measures some 15 inches in length, stands 5 inches high at the shoulder, and weighs between 1½ and 3 pounds.

FOOD: Vegetation is readily available to the prairie dog, and it takes advantage of it. The blacktail favors grama grass, wheatgrass, fescue grass, Russian thistle, bromegrass, and bluegrass. The whitetail also dines on Russian thistle and wheatgrass, but adds saltbrush, sagebrush, wild onion, dandelion, and nightshade to the menu. Insects, especially grasshoppers, whet the prairie dog's appetite. It also eats meat (e.g., ground-nesting birds) once in a while.

EDIBILITY: Though the Indians enjoyed the meat, today's hunters dislike the "earthy" flavor.

■ Opossum *(Didelphis marsupialis)*

RANGE: The opossum is found in woods and agricultural regions from Ontario west to eastern Colorado and east to Florida. Many inhabit the Pacific coast stretch from Canada through California.

IDENTIFICATION: This species is the only marsupial (pouched animal) in North America, housing its somewhat underdeveloped young in a pouch where they are

Opossum

nourished through the mother's nipples until they can seek out their own food. The animal's ears are black, though often white-rimmed, as are the eyes, legs, and feet. The face and toes are white, while the nose is pink. Because of the silver-tipped guard hairs, the opossum's fur appears salt-and-pepper gray, but the underfur is cotton white. A white-yellow stain is apparent on the throat due to a gland secretion. The lengthy, whitish tail tends to be practically bare of hair.

SIZE: A typical opossum may measure up to 3 feet in length, 12 to 15 inches of which is the animal's tail. Though this marsupial generally weighs 5 or 6 pounds, one recorded male weighed 14 pounds.

FOOD: Persimmons are one of the opossum's favorite treats, but its diet ranges from mice, ground-nesting birds, moles, shrews, and rabbits to dead and crippled game to fruits and green vegetation. Earthworms, grains, reptiles, and amphibians round out the menu.

EDIBILITY: Those hunters who have eaten opossum meat claim it is tasty.

PREDATORS

▉ North American Wolf (Canis)

RANGE: The gray wolf (*Canis lupus*) is located in the tundra and forests in a major portion of Canada from the United States border north to the Arctic and Alaska, and also in the northern sections of Michigan, Minnesota, and Montana. The red wolf (*Canis niger*) recently clung to existence in western Louisiana and eastern Texas, but the populations died off there. Efforts are under way to stock red wolves elsewhere.

IDENTIFICATION: The wolf is large and doglike in appearance, so much so that its head somewhat resembles that of a German shepherd. There is an immense color range that may run the gamut from practically pure white to coal black. The legs and underparts are lighter than the remainder of the body. A scent gland is found at the base of the wolf's tail above its anus.

SIZE: A mature male stands up to 38 inches high at the shoulder, measures 6 feet in length, and weighs 100 pounds or more. The heaviest recorded male tipped the scales at 175 pounds. Females tend to be lighter than males.

FOOD: The wolf preys on large game such as caribou, mountain sheep, moose, and deer, as well as marmots, varying hares, grouse, ptarmigan, small birds, eggs, mice, ducks, and geese. During the salmon runs, the wolf may be found in the vicinity.

North American Wolf

Coyote

▪ Coyote *(Canis latrans)*

RANGE: This species is located throughout western North America from the Arctic Ocean to Mexico, east to James Bay, southern Quebec, and Vermont, and south to the Mississippi River. Other eastern states either have the coyote naturally or through introduction.

IDENTIFICATION: The face of the coyote is sharp, reminiscent of a wild dog with a shaggy coat and erect ears. The nose is black, but the upper face, the top of the head, and the outer portion of the ears are a sandy grayish red with black hairs intermingled. The area around the mouth and throat is white, as are the inside of the ears. The eyes are yellow, the pupils black. The body color varies from gray to dull yellow. The rough-textured pelage is dark on the back, but gets whiter on the belly. The tail is 2 inches in length and ¼ inch in width, ending in a dark tip.

SIZE: An average male coyote weighs between 18 and 30 pounds, stands approximately 2 feet tall at the shoulder, and measures 44 to 54 inches in length (12 to 16 inches of which is its tail). Females tend to be four-fifths the weight and size of the males. The heaviest coyotes on record have weighed as much as 75 pounds.

FOOD: The coyote preys on rabbits, antelope, ground squirrels, mice, rats, prairie dogs, livestock, and poultry.

Rating second to the initial list are fruits, berries, and melons, both domesticated and wild.

▪ Bobcat *(Lynx rufus)*

RANGE: Bobcats are found from the Maritime provinces westward across southern Canada to southern British Columbia, and southward from the latter to Mexico and the Gulf of Mexico. Except for the area along the Mississippi and Ohio Rivers and in the Appalachian Mountains, the cat, which is also called the wildcat, catamount, tiger cat, bay lynx, lynx cat, or red lynx, is absent from a considerable portion of the eastern and central United States.

IDENTIFICATION: The bobcat varies in coloration depending upon its location. The cats in the southwestern desert regions are the palest, while those in the northern, forested regions are the darkest. The nose is a pinkish red, and the base color of the face, back, and sides is yellowish, gray, or brownish red. A checkering of black or a darker color than that of the base accompanies the face and the body. White is the color under the chin, throat, belly, and tail, and also around the eyes. The 4- to 7-inch tail, however, has a black spot over the tip. The fur, although brittle, is quite long and luxurious. This predator's face seems wide due to its face ruff, and slight tufts of hair stand up from the tips of its ears. The eyes are yellow, the pupils black. In comparison to its body size, the bobcat's legs are long, its large paws well furred.

SIZE: A typical bobcat measures approximately 50 inches in length, stands 22 inches high at the shoulder, and weighs between 18 and 25 pounds. Female cats tend to be a bit smaller and lighter than their male coun-

Bobcat

terparts. Bobcats in the North are larger than those in the South. Though there are many cases of these predators weighing in the 40- to 45-pound class, one of 76 pounds and another of 69 pounds have been recorded.

FOOD: The main staples in the diet of this species are the rabbit and the hare. The animal also preys readily on squirrels, rats, mice, porcupines, and chipmunks. Ruffed grouse is its favorite among the ground-nesting birds, though all types are eligible for its menu. Deer and wild turkeys at times make this list.

Lynx *(Lynx lynx)*

RANGE: The lynx, also known as the Canadian lynx, lucivee, wildcat, catamount, and loup-cervier, is distributed from Newfoundland west to the Arctic Ocean in Alaska, south to the northern United States in Minnesota, Wisconsin, Michigan, and New England, and in the Rocky Mountain areas of Wyoming and Utah. It resides as far south as mid-Washington and Oregon and western Montana. *Lynx subsolanus*, another subspecies, is found solely on the island of Newfoundland.

IDENTIFICATION: This predator's main features are its large, padded feet and its 2-inch-long, black ear tufts. A smoky gray is the lynx's basic color, often intermixed with tan shading. The large face ruff is white with black barring, and the sharp tips practically meet under its chin. White also appears around the animal's muzzle, inside its ears, beneath its eyes, and on the insides of its legs. The body, though compact, is supported by unusually long legs, and is spotted or barred with a black coloring. The tail, often 4 inches long, is light in color and has a jet-black tip.

Lynx

SIZE: A typical adult lynx measures between 3 and 3⅓ feet in length, stands between 1½ and 2 feet high at the shoulder, and tips the scale between 12 and 25 pounds. The heaviest lynx on record weighed 40 pounds.

FOOD: The varying hare is at the top of this predator's menu, with squirrels, mice, voles, lemmings, beavers, and both spruce and ruffed grouse taking relatively minor roles. According to records, the lynx's predatory link with the varying hare is so intense that the former's population is uncannily proportional to that of the latter.

Gray Fox

Gray Fox *(Urocyon cinereoargenteus)*

RANGE: This species inhabits the open forests and brush country across the southern United States, northward in the West to the state of Washington and northern Colorado and to southern Canada in eastern and central North America. *Urocyon littoralis*, a second species, is found on a couple of the Channel Islands off the coast of southern California.

IDENTIFICATION: The top of the animal's head and back is salt-and-pepper gray, but the flanks, the ears, and the area just below them are a rust-red color. The belly, chest, throat, and inner side of the legs are whitish. The 12- to 15-inch tail is gray with a prominent black mane running to the black tip. A 4½-inch musk gland is visible on the top of the tail.

SIZE: A typical adult stands 15 inches high at the shoulder, is up to 45 inches from nose tip to tail tip, and weighs between 8 and 11 pounds. The heaviest recorded gray fox weighed 19 pounds.

Red Fox

FOOD: Gray foxes prey heavily upon rabbits and ruffed grouse, and, depending on the abundance of the prey animal, fish, snakes, rats, mice, and insects. Dead and crippled animals are easy game for the wary gray fox.

Red Fox *(Vulpes vulpes)*

RANGE: The red fox is distributed from Alaska and northern Canada south to the Gulf of Mexico (except under the fall line of the southeastern states). Though it is found southward to the border of Mexico in places in the West, it is absent in the high plains from Mexico to central Alberta.

IDENTIFICATION: The red fox is slightly built, and resembles a domesticated dog. There are considerable color variations. This species ranges from a dark russet red to a light yellowish blond. The nose pad and the outside of the ear tips are black, the upper face rusty, the throat and cheeks white. The bushy tail, somewhat cylindrical in shape, is usually colored the same as the back (the darkest part of the animal) and has a light underside and a huge white tip. The belly tends to be white.

SIZE: A mature red fox is 3 to 3½ feet long (13 to 15 inches of which is its tail), stands 16 inches high at the shoulder, and weighs from 6 to 15 pounds. The latter is the top weight recorded.

FOOD: Ranking at the top of the list is the meadow mouse, a plentiful and nutritious animal. The red fox also favors rabbits, ruffed grouse, quail, pheasants, muskrats, squirrels, hares, chipmunks, and groundhogs. Preying on poultry yards is frequent. Weasels, snakes, shrews, beetles, moles, crickets, and grasshoppers are also part of this fox's menu, along with corn, melons, berries, and fruits.

Common Crow *(Corvus brachyrhynchos)*

RANGE: Breeding takes place from northern British Columbia, northern Saskatchewan, northern Manitoba, northern Ontario, central Quebec, and southern Newfoundland south to northern Baja California, central Arizona, central New Mexico, Colorado, central Texas, the Gulf Coast, and southern Florida.

IDENTIFICATION: The common crow is a large, predominantly black bird with a purple gloss. The sturdy bill, the long, thick legs, and the large, strong feet are also black. The bird's nostrils are hidden by bristlelike feathers that rise from its forehead. The tail is gently rounded, but has a somewhat square tip.

SIZE: The crow measures from 17 to 21 inches in length.

FOOD: More than 650 different items have been discovered in the crow's diet, 70 percent of which is vegetable matter—large amounts of corn and other cultivated crops, as well as wild fruits and seeds. The remainder consists of insects, spiders, reptiles, amphibians, snails, birds and their eggs, carrion, and crustaceans, as well as small mammals.

FLIGHT SPEED: Though the crow usually averages between 20 and 30 miles per hour in flight, it has been known to attain speeds of 40 to 45 miles per hour.

Northwestern Crow *(Corvus caurinus)*

RANGE: Found along the coasts and islands from Kodiak Island to western Washington, the Northwestern crow wanders inland in Washington and Oregon.

IDENTIFICATION: The Northwestern crow tends to be a small replica of the common crow, also having a predominantly black body with a purple gloss. Its nostrils are barely visible due to the bristlelike feathers that rise from its forehead. It has large, strong feet, a sturdy bill, and long, thick legs. All are black.

SIZE: The Northwestern crow rarely grows longer than 16 or 17 inches.

FOOD: The diet consists of shellfish, other invertebrates, insects, offal, seashore carrion, seeds, and berries.

FLIGHT SPEED: The normal speed is from 20 to 30 miles per hour, but crows have been known to reach speeds of 40 to 45 miles per hour.

Fish Crow *(Corvus ossifragus)*

RANGE: The locale for this bird is from the coast of Rhode Island to the coast of southern Florida, west along the Gulf Coast to southeast Texas, and inland along the major waterways.

IDENTIFICATION: The fish crow highly resembles the common crow in that it is also mostly black with a purple gloss, has feathers rising from its forehead that tend to hide its nostrils, and has a sturdy bill, long, thick legs, and large, strong feet, all of which are black. The fish crow, however, is smaller and slimmer than the common crow, and its wings are broader at the base and more pointed at the tips. The tail is gently rounded.

SIZE: This predator averages between 16 and 20 inches in length.

FOOD: Being omnivorous, the diet of the fish crow ranges from primarily marine invertebrates, offal, bird's eggs, seashore carrion, and insects to seeds, fruits, and berries.

FLIGHT SPEED: Though the crow can reach speeds of 40 to 45 miles per hour in flight, its usual speed ranges from 20 to 30 miles per hour.

UPLAND GAME BIRDS

A NOTE ON EDIBILITY: All upland game birds are edible, but some are better than others. Wild turkey, quail, ruffed grouse, and pheasant all rate high on the edibility list.

Ruffed Grouse *(Bonasa umbellus)*

RANGE: Locales for this bird include the Yukon and Porcupine River Valleys of Alaska and the Yukon. In addition, it is found throughout Canada and the U.S. Pacific Northwest, northern Rocky Mountain states, and the Mid-Atlantic region.

IDENTIFICATION: The ruffed grouse has a large, square, reddish-brown or gray tail with thin, dark barring, followed by narrow, light barring, followed by a broader black band, and terminating in a light band. A ruff composed of blackish feathers appears on both sides of the bird's neck. The upper parts range in color from gray to brown, mottled with darker colors. The undersides tend to be lighter, on occasion buffy, and are barred with

Ruffed Grouse

black and dark brown. The head is crested, and a small, bare, red patch appears above each eye. The West Coast members of this species are reddish, while those of the Rocky Mountains are grayish. Eastern ruffed grouse are brownish. Females and young are duller in color, with less prominent ruffs.

SIZE: An adult ruffed grouse is usually 16 to 19 inches in length.

FOOD: About 90 percent of the diet consists of leaves, buds, fruits, seeds, and nuts. The remaining 10 percent is made up of insects.

Blue Grouse
(Dendragapus obscurus)

RANGE: This game bird is found from southeastern Alaska down through western Canada and California to northwest New Mexico.

IDENTIFICATION: This game bird has distinctive large feet, short legs, and a short, stout bill. Its plumage tends to be dusky or grayish blue in color, and its tail is square-tipped and black. Some members of the species have a wide terminal band of light color on their tails, while others have a narrow band or no band at all. The male has whitish feathers under its tail and on its throat. Above the eyes is a small bare patch of orange or yellow skin. The female is black with brown bars and mottling and sports a dark though light-tipped tail. The male has small inflatable air sacs at the sides of his throat to assist in vocalization.

SIZE: This western grouse measures from 15½ to 21 inches in length.

FOOD: A major portion (approximately 90 percent) of the diet is composed of leaves, seeds, and berries. The remainder consists of animal matter, such as insects and spiders.

Blue Grouse

Spruce Grouse

Spruce Grouse
(Canachites canadensis)

RANGE: This bird, also called Franklin's grouse, is found in Alaska, Canada, and along the entire U.S.-Canadian border from Washington to Maine.

IDENTIFICATION: On the male, this game bird's throat, undersides, and tail are black. The upperparts are brown, barred with darker brown, and marked with white at the flanks and the sides of the throat. A small, bright-red patch of bare skin is found just above the eyes of the male. The female lacks this red spot, and the black coloring of the male is replaced by brown in the female.

SIZE: The spruce grouse averages between 15 and 17 inches in length.

FOOD: Its diet consists of buds and needles of the spruce and other conifers, along with berries and vegetable matter. Some insects are included.

Greater Prairie Chicken
(Tympanuchus cupido)

RANGE: Western Canada and the southern United States are the two areas where this game bird may be found.

IDENTIFICATION: In general, the prairie chicken, or pinnated grouse, is brown, buff, and barred dark brown above, and a lighter brown and whitish below. On each side of the bird's throat is a cluster of slender black pinnate feathers. In the vicinity of this cluster, on the male, are large, orange air sacs that are inflatable. The tail is short, rounded, and very dark.

SIZE: The prairie chicken measures from 16½ to 18 inches in length.

FOOD: About 85 percent of the diet consists of all forms of vegetable matter. Insects, particularly grasshoppers, comprise the remainder.

Sage Grouse
(Centrocercus urophasianus)

RANGE: This species is found in parts of the western United States and minute sections of southeastern Alberta and southwestern Saskatchewan.

IDENTIFICATION: This game bird is the only grouse that has a black belly. Its tail feathers are long and pointed, its throat black with a tiny white necklace. The white breast features prominent feathers, and the remainder of the plumage is mottled or barred with white, black, dark brown, and light brown. Yellow is the color of the small, bare-skinned patch above the eye. The hen is mottled and barred in black, brown, and white over most of its body, but, as in the male, the belly is black, flanked by white.

SIZE: The sage grouse is the largest of all grouse, measuring 22 to 30 inches in length. The average female is 22 inches, the average male 28 inches.

FOOD: This grouse's diet consists of tender, succulent vegetation and some insects. Adults eat the leaves of the sage, but their gizzards and stomachs are not constructed to accept harsh foods.

Sharp-Tailed Grouse
(Pedioecetes phasianellus)

RANGE: This species is located in vast sections of southern Canada, and in several parts of the northern United States south through Nevada, Utah, and Colorado.

IDENTIFICATION: This game bird has a long, pointed tail, and its body is barred light brown with dark brown and black above. Below, it is whitish. The breast is scaled with brown and the flank is barred with brown and black. The wings are grayish on top, spotted with white. The long, central tail feathers are the same color as the bird's back; the remainder of the tail is white. An air sac and a small crest appear on the throat, but the side of the neck is devoid of long feathers.

SIZE: The sharp-tailed grouse measures from 15 to 20 inches in length. Though the same size as the ruffed grouse, it is a bit slimmer.

FOOD: About 90 percent of the menu consists of leaves, grass, fruits, and seeds. Grasshoppers and other insects comprise the rest.

Chukar Partridge
(Alectoris chukar)

RANGE: The semiarid mountain regions of the western United States, specifically parts of Washington, Idaho, Nevada, Wyoming, Colorado, and California, are this bird's haunts.

IDENTIFICATION: The chukar partridge has a short tail that is brownish gray above. The wings are the same color. Two black lines begin at the forehead, run through the eyes, and then turn downward, forming a V on the

Chukar Partridge

upper breast that fully encloses the yellow throat and cheeks. The lower breast is gray; the rest of the underside (the dark-barred flanks inclusive) is yellowish. Red or pink is the color of the legs, bill, and feet. Immature birds are usually duller in color.

SIZE: This game bird, on average, measures 13 inches in length.

FOOD: Fruits, seeds, and leaves comprise 60 percent of the diet, the rest being insects and spiders.

Hungarian Partridge
(Perdix perdix)

RANGE: This game bird breeds in large sections of southern Alberta and southern Saskatchewan, plus small sections of Manitoba and Ontario. Practically every northern state in the United States has border representatives of this species, down through the northern portions of California, Nevada, Utah, Iowa, Illinois, and Indiana.

IDENTIFICATION: The Hungarian partridge has a gray nape and breast, and a brownish-red face and throat. Its cape, wings, and tail are black. The back, also black, is barred with a brownish red. The wings have white spots. The undersides are buffy; the flanks are buffy gray, barred with a reddish brown. In the center of the breast, a dark brown spot is conspicuous. Gray is the color of the bill, feet, and legs.

SIZE: This species measures between 12 and 14 inches in length.

FOOD: Leaves and shoots of grasses and clover, seeds, berries, grains, spiders, and insects all are part of this game bird's diet.

Ring-Necked Pheasant
(Phasianus colchicus)

RANGE: The ring-necked pheasant ranges from southern Canada down through Baja California and northern Mexico, and can be found in parts of Texas, Oklahoma, Kansas, Missouri, Illinois, Indiana, Ohio, and Maryland.

IDENTIFICATION: The cock is more colorful than the hen. It has a head and neck that are a dark metallic

Ring-Necked Pheasant

green. A bright-red patch of bare skin is conspicuous around the eye and on the cheek. The lengthy feathers above the eye form a double crest. The plumage of the underparts, upper back, and shoulders is a rich, bronzy red brown with dark-brown, black, and white markings. The feathers of the rump and up the lower back are grayish green; the flank feathers are a light golden brown with dark-brown streaks. The slender, pointed feathers of the tail are dull bronze barred with dark brown, and cover more than half the length of the body. The legs and feet are gray; the bill is yellowish. The hen is brownish and much paler below, marked with darker brown and black above. Darker brown and whitish bars streak the lengthy yellow-brown tail.

SIZE: This game bird measures between 21 and 36 inches in length, depending upon its sex. The cock tends to be about 10 inches longer than the hen.

FOOD: About 25 percent of the diet consists of insects, the remainder being shoots, nuts, and fruits.

FLIGHT SPEED: The ring-necked pheasant flies at speeds between 35 and 40 miles per hour.

Bobwhite Quail
(Colinus virginianus)

RANGE: This species is sparse out West, located only in parts of southern British Columbia, Washington, Oregon, Idaho, Arizona, and Mexico. But moving eastward, this bird is far more abundant and is found from southeast Wyoming, eastern Colorado, and eastern New Mexico all the way to the Atlantic, save for the New England states.

Bobwhite Quail

IDENTIFICATION: The bobwhite quail is a chicken-like bird with strong, lengthy legs, a stout bill, and a short, dark, strong tail. Its color tends to vary depending upon its range, but in general the bird is brownish, barred with white and lighter below. Above, it has brown marked with darker brown; frequently, these dark-brown areas have random whitish spots. The dark-brown head is slightly crested, featuring white eye stripes. Many—but not all—members of the species have a white throat as well. The female tends to be dull yellow or buff in color.

SIZE: Measuring 8½ to 10½ inches in length, this game bird is smaller than the average quail.

FOOD: About 85 percent of the bobwhite's diet consists of all types of plant life; the remainder is primarily insects.

FLIGHT SPEED: Over short distances, the bobwhite's flight is strong and rapid, often reaching speeds of 40 to 45 miles per hour.

Harlequin Quail
(Cyrtonyx montezumae)

RANGE: This game bird, also known as Mearn's quail, inhabits the far southwestern United States, ranging from Arizona, New Mexico, and Texas down through the less arid and more mountainous areas of southern Mexico.

IDENTIFICATION: The breast and undersides of the harlequin quail are reddish brown; the flanks and sides of the neck are gray with conspicuous round, white spots. Long, buff feathers comprise the head's large appearance. The stocky bird's head is white, and is separated from the breast by a black ring at the neck. Mustaches, earmarks, and a black throat patch are additional features. The wings, tail, and back are variegated designs of black, white, and brown. On the distaff side, the browns are duller, and the female is more lightly colored below and on the throat and head. In addition, there are dark markings behind the eye and at the lower edge of the throat.

SIZE: Measuring 8 to 9½ inches in length, the harlequin is similar in size to the bobwhite quail.

FOOD: Acorns, piñon nuts, other seeds, and grasses and leaves comprise the harlequin quail's diet. Insects are rarely eaten.

FLIGHT SPEED: The harlequin quail clocks 40 to 45 miles per hour, but can sustain this speed only over rather short distances.

Gambel's Quail
(Lophortyx gambelii)

RANGE: The arid Southwest is this bird's haunt, from New Mexico, Colorado, Utah, and Nevada through northeastern Baja California.

IDENTIFICATION: The males of the species feature a black forehead that lacks the white spots of the California quail. They also have a buff-colored belly with a big, centrally located black spot. The flank feathers are reddish brown with white streaks and slashes. The hens are similar to the males in that they also have a buff-colored belly and white streaks across their reddish-brown flanks.

SIZE: The Gambel's quail reaches lengths of 10 to 11½ inches.

FOOD: A mere 2 percent of the diet consists of insects; the major portion consists of leaves, seeds, plant shoots, fruits, and grains.

FLIGHT SPEED: The speed of this quail is 40 to 45 miles per hour. Though strong and rapid, its flight is usually over short distances.

■ Mountain Quail *(Oreortyx pictus)*

RANGE: This upland bird resides on the coastal ranges from southern Vancouver Island in British Columbia down to northern Baja California, and in the Sierra Nevada and other ranges of eastern Nevada and California. Introductions into the western states of Washington, Idaho, Oregon, and Nevada have been successful.

IDENTIFICATION: The mountain quail's head, shoulders, lower breast, and crest are a grayish blue. A long, pointed, stiff plume rises from its head. The upper breast and throat are reddish brown. The neck, also a grayish blue, is separated from the upper breast by a white line. There is also some white around the eyes and around much of the face. The flanks are colored reddish brown with an upper edging of white, and a series of wide, rounded bars (also white) cover the bottom part of the back. The wings and tail are a neutral brown.

SIZE: The mountain quail measures 10½ to 11½ inches in length.

Scaled Quail

FOOD: Buds, seeds, fruits, flowers, leaves, and plant shoots comprise most of the diet. An insignificant number of insects is also consumed.

FLIGHT SPEED: Though it has a strong, rapid 40- to 45-mile-per-hour speed, this quail usually only flies short distances.

■ Scaled Quail *(Callipepla squamata)*

RANGE: This bird is found only in Texas north to Colorado, west to Arizona, and south to Mexico.

IDENTIFICATION: Dark-edged gray-and-white scales appear to coat the breast, neck, and shoulders of this species. A white topknot caps the gray head. A medium brownish gray colors the back, wings, and tail; the feet and legs are a bluish gray. Both sexes are alike in coloration.

SIZE: This species measures 10 to 12 inches in length, this being generally a couple of inches longer than the bobwhite quail.

FOOD: Insects comprise approximately 30 percent of the diet, with buds, seeds, leaves, and other plant material making up the rest.

FLIGHT SPEED: The scaled quail moves rapidly and strongly over short distances, hitting speeds of 40 to 45 miles per hour.

■ California Quail *(Lophortyx californicus)*

RANGE: This quail ranges from southwestern British Columbia to the southern tip of Baja California, and inland from the Pacific to western Nevada. In recent years, the species has been introduced in parts of Utah, Nevada, Idaho, Oregon, and Washington.

IDENTIFICATION: The adult male of this species has a long, large-tipped black plume that curves forward from the forepart of its dark, reddish-brown cap. The forehead, as well as a line that extends from it to the back of the head above the eye, is white. The necklace beginning behind the eye and bordering the black throat and face is also white. The breast is grayish blue, as is the back of the neck, the nape of which is spotted with white. The

California Quail

IDENTIFICATION: The wild version of the turkey is slimmer and has longer legs than the domestic variety. Its wattles, neck, and head are reddish, grading to a blue. The attractive plumage is an iridescent bronze with black bars; the tail tips are buff. The male has a long hank, consisting of hairlike feathers hanging from its breast; the hen usually lacks this "beard." The wings are round and short; the feet and legs are large and strong. The large, sturdy bill appears to be hooked.

SIZE: This game bird measures from 36 to 48 inches long, with the hen usually averaging some 10 inches shorter than the cock. The average weight of these gobblers is between 15 and 20 pounds.

FOOD: Twigs, fruits, seeds, and nuts make up 85 percent of the wild turkey's menu; insects make up the rest.

FLIGHT SPEED: Though this species cannot fly long distances, it can attain speeds of 30 to 35 miles per hour when it does take flight.

belly feathers are white with black edging, save for the middle of the abdomen—there, they are reddish brown. The back and tail are medium brown; so, too, are the flanks, which feature white slashes. The hen does not have the reddish-brown patches and the white-and-black patterned head. Her plume tends to be browner and her face whitish with dull-brown marks and spots. Otherwise, she highly resembles the male.

SIZE: From 9½ to 11 inches in length, the California quail is just a bit larger than the bobwhite.

FOOD: Leaves, grains, fruits, seeds, and grass make up about 95 percent of the diet, with insects and other animal matter comprising the remainder.

FLIGHT SPEED: Though frequently attaining speeds of 40 to 45 miles per hour, the quail usually travels only very short distances.

Wild Turkey *(Meleagris gallopavo)*

RANGE: The wild turkey has six subspecies: the eastern (most of the eastern United States), the Florida (basically Florida), the Merriam (mostly western United States), the Mexican (central Mexico), the Rio Grande (southwestern United States), and the Gould (northwestern Mexico).

Band-Tailed Pigeon *(Columba fasciata)*

RANGE: The band-tailed pigeon breeds from southwest British Columbia to the mountains of Baja California and northern Nicaragua. It winters from California, Arizona, and New Mexico southward.

IDENTIFICATION: The band-tailed pigeon's head, foreneck, and complete breast are pinkish gray. A conspicuous narrow white bar separates the head from the cape. The latter is a metallic, black-bordered grayish yellow

Wild Turkey

that fades into a greenish-gray black. Its rump and wings are gray and its flight feathers are almost totally black. The gray-green tail is centrally barred with dark gray. The undertail plumage and belly are white, while the legs, feet, and bill (which ends in a black tip) are yellow. The red-rimmed eyes are also yellow.

SIZE: This game bird averages between 14 and 15½ inches in length.

FOOD: This species favors nuts, especially acorns, but berries, flowers, fruits, grains, and other seeds and vegetables make their way into its diet.

■ Willow Ptarmigan
(*Lagopus lagopus*)

RANGE: Large groups are found in the wide-open areas of Canada and Alaska, though some have also wandered down into the northern United States east of the Rocky Mountains.

IDENTIFICATION: In summer, the male's belly, feet, legs, and wings are white. Its rather small tail and its bill are black, and the remainder of its plumage is a reddish brown, including the throat. A "comb," or tiny patch of bare skin located above the eye, is a strong scarlet. The hen, on the other hand, is mottled a buff brown and is

Mourning Dove

white above. Her feet, legs, and belly are whitish; the rest of the undersides are wavy-barred with whitish, buff, and brown colorings. In winter, however, both the male and female are totally white save for the tail and bill, which remain black.

SIZE: The willow ptarmigan measures from 15 to 17 inches in length.

FOOD: Fruits, buds, leaves, and insects are consumed through the warmer months; in winter, the twigs of shrubs and trees are added to the diet.

■ Mourning Dove
(*Zenaidura macroura*)

RANGE: This species breeds throughout North America and southern Canada, and winters from the Great Lakes south to Panama.

IDENTIFICATION: The mourning dove has a smallish black spot behind and below its dark eyes. The tail is wedge-shaped and slender, the feathers being white-tipped except for the longer central ones. The plumage is buff brown with a metallic purplish sheen at the side of the neck. The wings are gray with a purple tinge to them, though the flight feathers are somewhat darker. Occasionally, the back will be sparsely covered with very dark brown spots.

SIZE: The mourning dove averages between 11 and 13 inches in length.

FOOD: Seeds (mainly those of weeds) practically make

Willow Ptarmigan

up this bird's entire menu. Minute amounts of other vegetable matter are also eaten.

FLIGHT SPEED: The mourning dove has been clocked between 60 and 65 miles per hour.

White-Winged Dove
(Zenaidura asiatica)

RANGE: Though this bird is found mainly in the Southwest, there are members of the species throughout the continental United States and parts of southern Canada.

IDENTIFICATION: The plumage is predominantly buff brown, with some purplish tinges (particularly around the head). A conspicuous white patch is visible on the wing. The flight feathers are practically black, and white patches are evident on the partly rounded tail. The orange eye features a minute black spot behind and below it. The feet and legs are red; the bill is black.

SIZE: The white-winged dove measures from 11 to 12½ inches in length.

FOOD: Shrubs and cacti, the fruit of trees, grains, and other vegetable matter comprise this game bird's diet.

American Woodcock
(Philohela minor)

RANGE: In warmer weather, this bird is found from southeastern Manitoba down through the eastern tip of

American Woodcock

Texas, and throughout the entire eastern United States. In winter, it is concentrated in the southeastern United States, spreading a bit farther into Texas, Oklahoma, Arkansas, Alabama, Georgia, and Florida.

IDENTIFICATION: The American woodcock has a straight bill that is twice the size of its head. Its neck is rather short, as is its tail. Above the coloring is a variegated pattern of black, gray, and brown; below, it is rufous. There is a trio of wide, black bands separated both from one another and from the gray forehead by thin, rufous bands. The legs, feet, and bill are a dark-flesh color.

SIZE: This species measures 10 to 12 inches in length.

FOOD: Earthworms make up the bulk of the diet, but occa seeds, berries, and insect larvae are significant components of the diet.

WATERFOWL

Barnacle Goose *(Branta leucopsis)*

RANGE: This species is located along the coastal regions of North America from Labrador down to North Carolina, as well as inland as far as Ohio.

IDENTIFICATION: The barnacle goose's head, bill, and chest are black; in contrast, its face, cheeks, and upper

throat are white. The remainder of the bird's upperparts are dark slate or brownish. Its underparts are white. The bird's neck, also black, is rather long.

SIZE: Medium size for a goose, this bird averages between 24 and 27 inches in length.

FOOD: Grass is the primary dish on the menu.

Flight Statistics for Waterfowl

According to Ducks Unlimited, the fastest duck ever recorded was a red-breasted merganser that reached a top speed of 100 miles per hour. This beat the previous record held by a canvasback clocked at 72 miles per hour. Blue-winged and green-winged teal, thought by many hunters to be the fastest, are actually among the slowest, having speeds of only 30 miles per hour. Most waterfowl fly at speeds of 40 to 60 miles per hour.

How high do ducks fly? Ducks usually migrate at an altitude of 200 to 4,000 feet, but are capable of reaching greater heights. A jet plane over Nevada struck a mallard at 21,000 feet.

The long-distance champion is the black brant, which migrates nonstop from Alaska to Baja California, a journey of 3,000 miles, in just 60 to 72 hours.

■ Blue Goose *(Chen caerulescens)*

RANGE: The Gulf Coast of eastern Texas and Louisiana is the habitat of this bird.

IDENTIFICATION: The blue goose features a white head, upper neck, and throat. Its back and a major portion of its body are a dark, brownish gray. The flight feathers on the wing are black; the tail and the feathers below the wing are white. Though the edge of the bill is black, the rest of the bill and legs are pinkish. Immature blue geese have dark bills and lack the white heads of their parents.

SIZE: This species is medium size, measuring from 25 to 30 inches long.

FOOD: The menu consists of sedges, grains, grasses, and waterweeds.

■ Common Canada Goose *(Branta canadensis)*

RANGE: The breeding range is from northern Canada down to central California. There are a couple of colonies south of this line. In the winter, the species travels down to the southern United States and even into northeastern Mexico.

IDENTIFICATION: The body is brownish, while the head, tail, neck, feet, and bill are black. Several white patches are apparent on the cheeks. The throat and underrump are also white.

SIZE: This species varies widely in size, measuring from 22 to 40 inches in length.

FOOD: The common Canada goose feasts on aquatic vegetation, grains, and grass.

■ Emperor Goose *(Philacte canagica)*

RANGE: Winters are spent primarily in the Aleutian Islands, but Hawaii and California are also home to the species. On rare occasions, some will be found in Oregon.

IDENTIFICATION: The main body coloring is a grayish blue, but the bird's head and rear portion of its neck are white. The throat is black. The wings and the body feathers are dark-edged, giving this species a scaly appearance. The very young birds have a grayish-blue coloring spotted with white on their heads and necks.

Common Canada Goose

SIZE: Medium size for a goose, this bird is from 26 to 28 inches in length.

FOOD: Shellfish and seaweed comprise the bulk of the diet. In tundra regions, however, berries and grasses are also eaten.

Snow Goose

Snow Goose *(Chen hyperborea)*

RANGE: The most abundant of all North American geese, this species inhabits northern Baja California, Mexico, the Gulf Coast, and the Atlantic coast from New Jersey down through the Carolinas.

IDENTIFICATION: Though predominantly white, the snow goose has black flight feathers. The black-edged bill and the legs of the species are pink. Immature snow geese are gray above, with somewhat blackish bills.

SIZE: The snow goose is medium size, measuring 25 to 38 inches long.

FOOD: Waterweeds, sedges, grains, and grasses rank high on the menu.

Ross's Goose *(Chen rossii)*

RANGE: Though it breeds in a tiny section of the coastal tundra in northwestern Keewatin and northeastern Mackenzie, the Ross's Goose relocates in winter to California's Central Valley.

IDENTIFICATION: The Ross's goose resembles the snow goose in that it is white and has black flight feathers on the wings. It differs, however, in that its pink bill is not black-edged. The legs are pink. The bill is relatively rough, and has warts at its base.

SIZE: At 20 to 26 inches in length, this is the smallest American goose.

FOOD: The menu consists of grasses, sedges, grains, and waterweeds.

White-Fronted Goose *(Anser albifrons)*

RANGE: The western United States breeds most of these birds. They are also found occasionally along the Atlantic coast.

IDENTIFICATION: The body coloring is a grayish brown. The feet tend to be either orange or yellow, the forward section of the face white. Young white-fronted geese do not have white faces, although they do have light-colored bills.

SIZE: Ranging from medium to large among geese, this species measures between 26 and 34 inches long.

FOOD: The bulk of the diet is composed of berries, nuts, leaves, grains, and grasses. On occasion, aquatic insects are consumed.

Brant *(Branta bernicla)*

RANGE: The brant usually spends its winters along the Pacific coast from Baja California north to British

Brant

Columbia, and along the Atlantic coast from North Carolina up through Massachusetts. However, this far-ranging species is often found farther north or south of these haunts.

IDENTIFICATION: The brant's short neck is black, as is its head, bill, and chest. On the upper neck of the adult, there appears a partial white necklace. The remainder of the upperparts are brownish or a dark-slate color. The American subspecies has small, light-gray markings on the front section of its white underparts.

SIZE: About 20 to 24 inches in length, the brant is small-ish to medium size among geese.

FOOD: Sea lettuce and eelgrass are the main foods. Small insects are also occasionally consumed.

■ Black Brant *(Branta nigricans)*

RANGE: The breeding area includes the coasts of the Canadian Arctic east to longitude 110° west. Winters are spent on the Pacific coast south to Baja California and inland to Nevada.

IDENTIFICATION: The black brant has a black breast that extends into a blackish belly. Unlike the brant, this species has a complete, rather than partial, white collar around its neck. The forepart of the undersides is also much darker, making the bird appear blacker.

SIZE: A typical member of this species is about 24 inches in length.

FOOD: Like the brant, this species primarily eats eel-grass, but also dines on sea lettuce.

■ Black Duck *(Anas rubripes)*

RANGE: The breeding range includes central Canada east to northern Labrador and Newfoundland, and down to the Great Lakes region and eastern North Carolina. In winter, the bird ranges from the southern edge of the breeding area to the Gulf Coast and southern Florida. Its distribution is rather spotty.

IDENTIFICATION: Both sexes appear similar, having very dark brown bodies with paler cheeks and throats. The

Black Duck

black-bordered speculum is purple. The yellowish-to-greenish bill has a black knob at its tip. The legs are red or dusky. The underparts appear nearly black when the duck is in flight.

SIZE: The typical black duck measures from 21 to 26 inches in length.

FOOD: Three-quarters of the black duck's diet is vegetable matter, mainly grasses and aquatic plants. The remainder consists of animal matter—specifically crustaceans, insects, mollusks, and small fish.

■ Black-Bellied Tree Duck *(Dendrocygna autumnalis)*

RANGE: Though native to southern Texas, this bird has strayed into Arizona and California.

IDENTIFICATION: The bill of this species is bright pink, the legs pale pink. The breast is brownish, as are the upperparts. The black-bellied tree duck, as its name indicates, has a black belly. The throat and cheeks are gray, the wings mantled dark.

SIZE: The black-bellied duck reaches from 20 to 22 inches in length.

FOOD: Black-bellied tree ducks eat about 90 percent plant material, including sorghum, Bermuda grass, smartweeds, millets, and water stargrass. They sometimes also eat insects and mollusks.

Bufflehead
(Bucephala albeola)

RANGE: The bufflehead breeds across much of Canada and Alaska, but it winters in Mexico and along the Gulf Coast.

IDENTIFICATION: The male has a large, blackish head that is overlaid with a purplish-green iridescence. Above and behind the eye, a white quarter-circle patch is conspicuous. The tail and back are black; the rest of the plumage is white, including a prominent upper-wing patch that is very noticeable when the duck is swimming. The female features a grayish-brown back and head, and lighter-colored flanks that are whitish below. On the lower rear quarter of the head, a tiny white spot can be seen.

SIZE: The smallest of the diving ducks, the bufflehead measures 12 to 16 inches long.

FOOD: About 80 percent of the menu is fish, mollusks, insects, and crustaceans. Aquatic plants make up the remainder.

Canvasback *(Aythhya valisineria)*

RANGE: This species winters in British Columbia, Montana, Colorado, the eastern Great Lakes, and eastern Massachusetts down to central Mexico, the Gulf Coast states, and northern Florida. Breeding takes place from central Alaska to Manitoba and south through California, Utah, Colorado, Nebraska, and Minnesota.

IDENTIFICATION: The back and flanks of the male are whitish, and the head and bill appear longer than those of the redhead. Where the head and bill merge, there is a slight concave curvature. The female has a brownish breast and head, a whitish belly and flanks, and a light-gray back.

SIZE: The canvasback averages between 19 and 24 inches in length.

FOOD: About 80 percent of the diet is composed of vegetable matter—primarily aquatic plants and wild celery of the genus *Vallisneria*. Fish, insects, and mollusks are sometimes eaten.

American Coot

American Coot *(Fulica americana)*

RANGE: The main breeding area extends in Canada from New Brunswick to British Columbia. In addition, there are colonies in Florida, along the Gulf Coast, and in Panama, Nicaragua, and Baja California. In winter, the bird relocates in southern British Columbia, the American Southwest, the Ohio River Valley, and Maryland down to Panama, the Greater Antilles, and the Bahamas.

IDENTIFICATION: The plumage of the American coot is a darkish gray that becomes a bit larger below. Beneath the short tail, a patch of white is visible. The eye is red; the feet and legs are a shade of green. The bill, on the stout side and conical, is the color of white china. The downy young are blackish and feature an orange bill; in addition, the feathers around the shoulders, neck, and head are either orange or orange-tipped.

SIZE: Similar in size to a small chicken, this species is 13 to 16 inches long.

FOOD: Being omnivorous, the American coot dines on all classes of vegetable matter, as well as crustaceans, worms, snails, tadpoles, and fish.

European Coot *(Fulica atra)*

RANGE: Breeding occurs throughout Europe, save for the northernmost areas. Some stragglers have been sighted in Greenland, Labrador, and Newfoundland.

IDENTIFICATION: The European coot is almost an exact replica of the American coot, except for the fact that the feathers located below the tail are slate gray in color instead of white.

SIZE: Similar in size to the American coot, this species is from 14 to 16 inches long.

FOOD: This species feeds on plant food and tiny animals. In shallow-water regions, the European coot dives for water plants, which it picks clean of snails and other small aquatic animals.

■ Common Eider (*Somateria dresseri*)

RANGE: The Aleutian Islands, southwestern Alaska, most of Canada, and Maine comprise the breeding range of this species. Winters are spent at the southern tip of the ice pack and southward to British Columbia, Washington, and the Mid-Atlantic states.

IDENTIFICATION: There is a conspicuous amount of white on the back and wings of the male. The white head features a black cap and a pair of pale-green patches at the rear. The flight feathers of the wings, the rump, the tail, and the undersides are black; the breast is pinkish. The feet are greenish gray. The bill tends to be either orange or yellow. The female's bill, however, is grayish, and her body color is light brown with black and dark-brown barrings.

SIZE: The largest of the eiders, the common eider measures 21 to 27 inches in length.

FOOD: Mollusks make up 80 percent of the American eider's diet. Tiny crustaceans, fish, echinoderms (sea urchins and starfish), and small amounts of plant food are also eaten.

■ King Eider (*Somateria spectabilis*)

RANGE: This species breeds on the islands and Arctic coasts from northwestern Alaska to Hudson and James Bays and northern Labrador. In winter, this eider is located in the Aleutian Islands, southern Alaska, California, the Great Lakes, New Jersey, and Newfoundland.

IDENTIFICATION: From a distance, the forward half of the male king eider seems white, the rear half black. The crown is gray, the breast pinkish. Traces of pale green are visible on the face, and there is a tiny black crescent beneath each eye. A prominent white patch can be seen on the wing and also on the bottom part of the rump. A black-edged frontal knob at the tip of the orange bill flares out over the forehead. The hen is a browner red than the American eider hen.

SIZE: The king eider is 18 to 24 inches long.

FOOD: The menu includes mollusks (predominantly mussels), starfish, sea urchins, crustaceans, and insects. A small percentage of the diet is composed of seaweeds and eelgrass.

■ Spectacled Eider (*Lampronetta fischeri*)

RANGE: The principal breeding region is the Aleutians, but some members of the species are found on rare occasions on Kodiak Island.

IDENTIFICATION: The male spectacled eider's neck, throat, and upperparts are white; its underparts are black. The head is a pale green, and a large white area edged with black—the spectacles—appears around the eyes. The female has brownish plumage and lighter-brown spectacles.

SIZE: This species is 20 to 23 inches long.

FOOD: This diving duck feasts on crowberries, sedges, pondweeds, and algae (seaweeds).

■ Steller's Eider (*Polysticta stelleri*)

RANGE: The breeding area includes the Arctic coasts and islands of Alaska. A number of these eiders are also found in Maine and Quebec.

IDENTIFICATION: This bird has a thick body and a rather short neck. The drake features a white head with a tiny gray crest at the back. The throat is black, as is the eye-ring. The back, tail, feathers beneath the tail, and neck-ring are black. The breast and remainder of the undersides are reddish brown. The flank, as well as a major portion of the wing feathering visible from the sides, is

Gadwall

white. The feet and bills of both sexes are blackish. The female has a whitish and dark-brown eye-ring and a white-bordered blue wing speculum.

SIZE: From 17 to 19 inches in length, the Steller's eider is small for a diving duck.

FOOD: A major portion of the diet consists of fish, worms, insects, mollusks, and crustaceans. The remaining percentage is made up of plant food—algae and pondweeds.

■ Fulvous Tree Duck
(Dendrocygna bicolor)

RANGE: This duck resides in California, New Mexico, Texas, and southern Louisiana. Some strays have also been sighted around the Great Lakes as far north as Nova Scotia.

IDENTIFICATION: This species has a grayish bill and grayish feet; its head, breast, and underparts are tawny brown, or fulvous, in color. The back and rear of the neck are dark brown. The throat features a buffy patch and a series of white slashes that are underlined with dark brown at the side.

SIZE: The smallest of the tree ducks, the fulvous tree duck measures 18 to 21 inches in length.

FOOD: The diet consists primarily of grasses, seeds, and weeds. On several occasions, however, this duck has been sighted gleaning cornfields.

■ Gadwall *(Anas strepera)*

RANGE: Breeding occurs in most of western North America and in some of the Mid-Atlantic states. For winter, gadwalls usually migrate to southern Mexico or to Florida.

IDENTIFICATION: The breeding plumage of the male is gray; the neck and head are brownish. Black feathers are apparent above and below the gray tail. The prominent white speculum is bordered with black. At the bend of the wing, there is a chestnut-brown patch. The belly is white, the feet yellowish, and the bill dark. The female's body is almost completely dull brown save for the whitish upperparts and white speculum.

SIZE: The gadwall is from 19 to 23 inches long.

FOOD: Approximately 90 percent of the diet consists of aquatic plants, grasses, grains, nuts, and acorns. The remaining 10 percent is animal matter, primarily insects and crustaceans.

■ Common Goldeneye
(Bucephala clangula)

RANGE: This duck breeds in the northern coniferous forest, from the tree line down, in southern Alaska and along the entire U.S.-Canadian border. The bird winters from the bottom edge of the breeding region to the southern United States.

IDENTIFICATION: The drake features a glossy dark-green head with a circular white patch just before, and

Common Goldeneye

slightly under, its golden eyes. The breast, neck, flanks, and underside are white. The dark-gray back is broadly hatched with white at the sides. The young and the females have red-brown heads, and their necks, breasts, and undersides are white. The flanks and a bar across the top of the breast are gray, as is the back. The white on the wing of the drake is more prominent than on the wing of the hen.

SIZE: The common, or American, goldeneye measures 15 to 21 inches in length.

FOOD: Animal matter predominantly comprises this duck's diet—mollusks, insects, fish, and crustaceans. During the breeding seasons, plants are also consumed.

■ Barrow's Goldeneye
(Bucephala islandica)

RANGE: The breeding area in western North America is shaped like an inverted V, beginning in south-eastern Alaska and northwestern British Columbia; one arm extends south to California's High Sierras, the other arm southeast to the Colorado mountains. Some breeding also takes place in northern Quebec. Winters are spent on the Pacific shores from southern Alaska to central California, and on the Atlantic shores from Long Island, New York, to the mouth of the St. Lawrence River.

IDENTIFICATION: The Barrow's goldeneye is remark-ably similar to the American goldeneye, except for the fact that the female has a shorter bill. The head of the drake is glossed with purple, and there is a white cres-cent between the bill and the eye.

SIZE: This species is 16 to 20 inches in length.

FOOD: About 75 percent of the diet is animal mat-ter, principally mollusks. This species consumes more insects than the American goldeneye.

■ Harlequin Duck
(Histrionicus histrionicus)

RANGE: The breeding area extends from south-central and southern Alaska (including the Aleutian Islands) south and southeast to British Columbia, the mountains of California, and Colorado. Some breeding takes place in Quebec and Labrador, as well as in Maryland.

IDENTIFICATION: The body of the drake is medium blue gray except for the reddish-brown flanks. A patch of white is conspicuous in front of the eyes. Behind the eyes, there is a tiny circular spot and a vertical white line. There are also a pair of white slashes radiating from the back onto the breast. A heavy white bar followed by smaller white bars is visible on the wing when the bird is at rest. There is also a reddish-brown streak on the crown. Both the male and female have legs, feet, and bills that are grayish blue. The female's body is medium brown save for the lighter belly and a trio of white spots on the head—two in front, one behind.

SIZE: The harlequin duck's length range is from 14½ to 21 inches.

FOOD: Animal matter—insects, crustaceans, fish, mollusks, and sea urchins—comprises 97 percent of the diet. The rest is vegetation.

■ Red-Breasted Merganser
(Mergus serrator)

RANGE: Breeding occurs near the tree line in Canada, Alaska, and along the U.S.-Canadian border. In winter, this merganser stays in the coastal regions from south-eastern Alaska to Baja California, as well as along the Atlantic coast.

IDENTIFICATION: Both sexes have ragged crests, with eyes, bills, legs, and feet that are red. The drake features a metallic-green head. The forward and lateral sections of the neck are white, as are the undersides and breast.

Hooded Merganser

The breast is crossed by a wide, dark-buff band that is haphazardly streaked with dark brown. The back and parts of the wings are black, the speculum white. There are some white patches on the wings that, like the tail, are shaded dark gray. The flanks and the feathers above and below the tail are finely barred with black.

SIZE: The red-breasted merganser is 19 to 26 inches long; it is smaller than the common merganser.

FOOD: The bird's diet consists of fish, crustaceans, mollusks, and aquatic insects.

Common Merganser
(Mergus merganser)

RANGE: Breeding occurs in southern Alaska, across Canada, in the mountains of central California, Arizona, and New Mexico, and east to the Great Lakes region and northern New England. Wintering spots are southerly to New Mexico, the western Gulf Coast, northern Georgia, and South Carolina.

IDENTIFICATION: The drake lacks a crest; its neck and head are dark metallic green. Its bill is bright red, its back black, its tail gray, its feet orange, and its breast white. The undersides and the flanks usually have a bright-pink tinge to them. The female, on the other hand, has a rough crest at the back of its reddish-brown head. The neck is the same color as the head, while the throat is white. The tail and back are medium gray, the flanks light gray. The black-and-gray wings feature a white speculum. The undersides tend to be whitish.

SIZE: Relatively large for a duck, the common merganser measures 21 to 27 inches in length.

FOOD: A major section of the diet consists of fish, but tiny mollusks, insects, aquatic plants, and crustaceans are also eaten.

Hooded Merganser
(Lophodytes cucullatus)

RANGE: This species breeds from southeastern Alaska and southern Canada down through the whole of the United States save the southwestern quarter. Winters are passed in the region encompassed by southern British Columbia and Massachusetts south through mid-Mexico, the Gulf Coast, and Florida.

IDENTIFICATION: The drake features a large crest; its head, neck, back, and tail are black. A white quarter-circle is very conspicuous just below and to the rear of the eye. The breast and underparts are white, and a pair of black fingers stretches from the back over to the breast. The feet are dusky yellow, the bill blackish, and the eyes yellow. The female has a smaller crest. Her back, tail, and wings are dark gray; in addition, each wing is patched with white. The flanks and upper breast are medium gray; the remainder of the upperparts is whitish. The face is a dusky grayish red that fades to a dusky brownish red at the crest and at the back of the head. The female's bill and feet are dusky yellow and her eyes are yellow.

SIZE: The smallest and slimmest of the mergansers, the hooded merganser measures 16 to 20 inches long.

FOOD: The hooded merganser primarily eats animal matter—fish, insects, crustaceans, and amphibians. Small amounts of grasses, pondweeds, grains, and other vegetables make up the rest of the menu.

Green-Winged Teal
(Anas carolinensis)

RANGE: This bird's breeding area is enclosed in a triangular region of North America from west-central Alaska and northwestern Mackenzie south to lower California and east to Newfoundland. Winters are spent in southern British Columbia and throughout most of the United States.

IDENTIFICATION: Both the male and female feature bright, glossy-green speculums. The male's head is a bright, reddish brown with a wide, bright-green band beginning around the eyes and continuing to the back of the head. The buffy breast is spotted with black. The feathers below the tail are buffy and edged with black. The belly is white; the remainder of the plumage is grayish. The female is grayish brown, though lighter below. Her feet and bill are grayish.

SIZE: This teal measures 12 to 16 inches in length.

FOOD: Plants (chiefly the aquatic type, but including grasses) comprise 8 percent of the green-winged teal's diet. Insects, mollusks, and maggots dining on rotting fish are also consumed.

Blue-Winged Teal
(Anas discors)

RANGE: Breeding occurs throughout most of Canada and also throughout the southwestern and Mid-Atlantic states of the United States.

IDENTIFICATION: Many of the tiny feathers atop the wing are a very pale blue. Both sexes feature lengthy, bright-green speculums. The drake has a large, white face crescent that can be at times indistinct. His bill is blue black, his head blue purple. The breast, flanks and underparts are dullish brown; the back is darker brown. Feathers above and below the tail are black, and just forward of the tail is a white patch. The female is brownish; her dusky bill is edged with pink. Her legs are yellowish.

SIZE: This teal measures 14 to 17 inches long.

FOOD: Though primarily a mix of aquatic plants, rice, corn, and grasses, the diet does include about 30 percent animal matter—mollusks, crustaceans, and insects.

Cinnamon Teal
(Anas cyanoptera)

RANGE: The breeding range is from southwestern Canada and Wyoming south to northern Mexico. In winter, this teal is found from the southwestern United States through Central America and northwestern South America. Some members of this species are occasionally found in the eastern United States.

IDENTIFICATION: The hens and drakes are so similar in appearance that they are nearly impossible to tell apart. Practically all of the plumage is a rich cinnamon-brown hue. The back and wings lack such coloring, and instead resemble those of the blue-winged teal.

SIZE: This duck measures 16 inches in length.

FOOD: About 80 percent of the diet consists of grasses, weeds, and aquatic plants; the remainder consists of insects and mollusks.

Common Teal (Anas crecca)

RANGE: Found mainly in Africa and Eurasia, the common teal is also found along the eastern coast of North America as far south as South Carolina.

IDENTIFICATION: The male common teal resembles its green-winged counterpart in almost every way. There are two main differences: the common drake has a horizontal white stripe on its back above the folded wings, and it does not have the vertical white crescent behind the breast. The female is indistinguishable from the female green-winged teal.

SIZE: This species measures 13 to 16 inches in length.

FOOD: About 80 percent of the diet is plant matter—mainly aquatic, but some grasses. This teal also eats insects, mollusks, and the maggots that dine on rotting fish.

American Widgeon
(Mareca americana)

RANGE: Breeding occurs in Alaska, western Canada, and the American Northwest. Wintering spots reach from southern Alaska, the central United States, and New England south to Costa Rica and the West Indies.

IDENTIFICATION: The male of the species features a gray head with a glaring white cap and a metallic-green band that extends from just in front of each eye to the rear of the head. The breast is pink, while the flanks tend to be whitish. The wings are dark, and each wing has a bright-green speculum and a conspicuous white patch on top. The gray tail has black feathers both above and

American Widgeon

Wood Duck

back of the head. Red, black, and white colorings comprise the variegated bill. The neck and breast are a bright, reddish brown. The back is of a dark iridescence, and the flanks are a creamy buff with black-and-white vertical lines separating them from the breast. The upperparts are whitish. The female of the species has a grayish head that features a whitish ring around the eye. Her throat is white and her back is a moderate brown gray. The breast and flanks are brownish.

SIZE: The wood duck is 17 to 21 inches long.

FOOD: Mainly a vegetarian, this species dines on shrubs and tree seeds, grasses, and aquatic plants. Some insects and tiny spiders are also consumed.

below. Preceding these feathers is a white mark that extends up from the belly. The female widgeon is recognized by her grayish head, brownish back, and tannish-red flanks and breast. The white patch on the male wing is, on the female, light gray. The feet and bills of both sexes are blue gray.

SIZE: Somewhat larger than the European widgeon, the American widgeon measures 18 to 23 inches long.

FOOD: More than 90 percent of the diet consists of vegetable matter, with the remainder consisting of insects and mollusks.

Wood Duck *(Aix sponsa)*

RANGE: Breeding ranges stretch from central British Columbia to central California, and are also located in such disparate areas as the Great Lakes, New England, Northeast Canada, the Gulf Coast, and Cuba. Winters are spent in the United States, and as far south as mid-Mexico.

IDENTIFICATION: This species is considered one of the most beautiful of all native American ducks. It has a big crest and a chunky body. The drake's head is a mix of iridescent green and blackish purple. On each side of the head there is a pair of thin white lines—one curving over the eye from the bill to the terminal point of the crest, and the other running parallel to it, but beginning behind the eye. The throat is white, with one finger stretching to just beneath the eyes and the other to the

Masked Duck *(Oxyura dominica)*

RANGE: This species is found in Vermont, Massachusetts, Maryland, Louisiana, Wisconsin, Florida, and Texas.

IDENTIFICATION: The drake has a reddish-brown head and a black mask around the entire face. The upperparts are buffy and there are dark spots on the flanks. The wings and tail are dark, and the wings feature a large, white speculum. The black back has red-brown spots. The hen is dark buff in color, with dark-brown spots and scales. She sports a cap, as well as a pair of streaks below it. Her wings and tail are the same color as the male's.

SIZE: The masked duck measures 9 to 11 inches long.

FOOD: Masked ducks eat seeds, roots of aquatic plants, aquatic insects, and crustaceans.

Mottled Duck *(Anas fulvigula)*

RANGE: This species inhabits the Gulf Coast from Texas to Mississippi, as well as the Florida Peninsula.

IDENTIFICATION: True to its name, the mottled duck is pale brown, mottled with black, and its speculum is a bluish green.

SIZE: The mottled duck, also called the dusky duck, is about 20 inches long.

FOOD: Though the majority of the diet consists of

acorns, berries, grains, grasses, sedges, and aquatic vegetables, tiny amounts of insect material and mollusks are also consumed.

■ Oldsquaw *(Clangula hyemalis)*

RANGE: Breeding takes place in the Arctic tundra from western Alaska through northern Canada. Winters are spent along the coasts from the breeding places to California in the West and North Carolina in the East. An additional wintering area is the Great Lakes.

IDENTIFICATION: The drake alternates between a pair of distinct, rich plumages every year. The hen also has differing summer and winter plumages. In summer, the male's head, neck, breast, and tail are a dull-glossed black; in addition, there is a large, pale-gray patch above the eyes. The dark feathers of the back are bordered with a light brown. The upperparts and huge areas of the wings are white, the feet a grayish blue. The pinkish bill has a dark tip, a white edge, and a blue patch in the vicinity of its base. In winter, the upper breast, neck, and head become white, with a black patch under and to the back of the eye. The forecrown is a buffy yellow. The rest of the tail, breast, and most of the back, as well as several wing feathers, are black. The remainder of the undersides and the wings are white. All plumages feature distinctively long tail feathers.

SIZE: The oldsquaw measures 14 to 23 inches in length, approximately one-third of which is its tail.

FOOD: Mostly mollusks, crustaceans, insects, and fish are consumed, along with tiny amounts of pondweeds and grasses.

■ Mallard *(Anas platyrhynchos)*

RANGE: This surface-feeding species is located throughout a major portion of the temperate Northern Hemisphere (save for northeastern Canada).

IDENTIFICATION: The adult male features a metallic-green head and neck that are separated from its bright-chestnut breast by a thin, white ring. The underparts are a light gray, the upperparts a dark gray. The tail is both black and white, with conspicuously curled feathers on top. The dark wings have a band of rich iridescent blue; the band is edged on each side first by a thin, black band and then a thin, white band. These bands, called speculums, are partly visible when the bird is at rest. The female also has a speculum, but it is predominantly dark or mottled brown and bordered by white. She has a tiny dark cap and an eye stripe, and lacks the curled tail feathers of the male. The male's bill is yellow, the female's orange. Orange feet are common to both sexes.

SIZE: The mallard ranges from 16 to 27 inches in length.

FOOD: Aquatic vegetables, acorns, berries, sedges, grains, and grasses are consumed, as well as small amounts of mollusks and insects.

■ Ring-Necked Duck *(Aythya collaris)*

RANGE: Breeding takes place from southern British Columbia to the Maritime provinces and in the northern parts of the United States. Winters are spent along the coasts to Massachusetts and southwestern British Columbia.

IDENTIFICATION: The ring-necked duck features a glossy purple head, a black breast, a dark, greenish-glossed back, gray flanks, and white upperparts. The grayish bill has a black tip; the two colors are separated by a thin, white ring. The breast and neck are separated by a brown ring. The female is brownish and has a white ring above the eye and a slender, white line leading from this ring to the back of the head. The male and female both have a conspicuous pale-blue patch on the wing.

Mallard

SIZE: This species measures 14 to 18½ inches in length.

FOOD: Four-fifths of the diet revolves around vegetable matter—mainly sedges, grasses, and aquatic plants. The remainder consists of mollusks and insects.

Ruddy Duck (Oxyura jamaicensis)

RANGE: Breeding extends from central British Columbia and the Canadian Prairie provinces down to Guatemala and the Bahamas. In winter, the ducks relocate to south-ern British Columbia, south-central United States, Penn-sylvania, and Massachusetts.

IDENTIFICATION: In summer, the drake has a reddish-brown back, neck, and flanks. His cheeks are white, but his cap, spikelike tail, and the flight feathers on the wing are blackish. The bill is a rich blue; the upperparts are whitish and barred lightly with browns. In winter, the drake is similar to the female, but he retains the white cheeks. The hen features a dark brownish-gray cap, neck, upper breast, back, wings, and tail. Horizontal brown streaks run through her whitish cheeks. The feet, legs, and bill are gray, the undersides whitish, and the flank and lower breast excessively barred with black.

SIZE: The ruddy duck is from 14 to 17 inches long.

FOOD: Approximately 75 percent of the ruddy duck's diet consists of wild celery, sedges, pondweeds, and grasses; the remainder includes such animal matter as insects and tiny shellfish.

Pintail (Anas acuta)

RANGE: This bird breeds in western and north-central North America, New England, and eastern Canada. Winters are spent in southeastern Alaska, along the Gulf Coast, and in Massachusetts.

IDENTIFICATION: The male features a rather long, pointed tail, which, when in full plumage, accounts for his large size range. The lengthy, slender tail and neck are quite distinctive. His back and flanks are grayish, but he is blackish beneath the tail and on the wing. The head and throat are a bright, purplish brown; this color also proceeds down the rear of the neck. The forward part of the neck and the undersides are white, as well as a

Pintail

finger that extends from the throat first into the brown area of the head and then to behind the eye. A patch at the rear of the flanks is also white. The feet and the bill are bluish gray.

SIZE: As mentioned above, the pintail's length var-ies extensively, depending on tail size. Adults average between 20 and 29 inches in length.

FOOD: The menu for the pintail reads as follows: aquatic plants, weeds, small mollusks, grasses, crustaceans, grains, and insects.

Redhead (Aythya americana)

RANGE: The breeding range encompasses a triangular area from eastern British Columbia south to lower Cali-fornia, and from there east to the Great Lakes. In winter, the redhead resides from southwestern British Columbia east to Maryland, and south to lower Baja California, central Mexico, the Gulf Coast, and Florida.

IDENTIFICATION: The male's back, wings, flanks, and tail are gray; the breast is blackish; the head is reddish brown. The bill and legs of both sexes are grayish blue. The bill's black tip is separated from the remainder of the bill by a thin, whitish line. The male breast is white. The female is buffy brown and also has a white breast.

SIZE: The redhead is 18 to 22 inches in length.

Redhead

FOOD: About 90 percent of the diet is aquatic plants; the remainder is mollusks and insects.

Greater Scaup *(Aythya marila)*

RANGE: The scaup breeds in central and south-central Alaska through the Yukon into western Mackenzie. In winter, it relocates from southeastern Alaska down to southern California, and from the eastern Great Lakes and the Canadian Maritime provinces south to Florida and the Gulf Coast.

IDENTIFICATION: The greater scaup is quite similar to the redhead in appearance except for the fact that the male of this species features a metallic-green head with a purplish cast, and the female greater scaup has a dark-brown head with a conspicuous white feather patch. Also, at the bottom of the blue-hued bill, the whiteness extends farther into the wing as a gradually thinning, blurry line. The "nail" at the bill's tip is much larger in the greater scaup than in the lesser scaup.

SIZE: This species measures from 15 to 21 inches in length.

FOOD: The menu is an omnivorous one, being 50 percent vegetables (aquatic plants and grasses) and 50 percent animals (crustaceans, insects, and mollusks).

Lesser Scaup *(Aythya affinis)*

RANGE: This scaup breeds from central Alaska and the tree limits of Mackenzie and Keewatin, east of the Coast Ranges to central British Columbia and Idaho, and east of the Rocky Mountains to Colorado, Nebraska, and Iowa, and a bit farther east. In winter, it is found northerly along the coasts to British Columbia and Connecticut, and in the interior to southern Arizona, southern New Mexico, central Texas, Missouri, and the southern Great Lakes area.

IDENTIFICATION: This species has less white in the wing than does the greater scaup, and has a smaller dark-colored "nail" at the tip of the bill. The head is often glossy purple rather than green, giving the scaup the appearance of having a slight crest.

SIZE: The lesser scaup measures between 14 and 19 inches in length.

FOOD: Being more of a vegetarian than the greater scaup, the lesser scaup favors aquatic plants and grasses. It does, however, also consume crustaceans, insects, and mollusks.

Common Scoter *(Oidemia nigra)*

RANGE: Breeding areas include western and southern Alaska and the Aleutian Islands. In winter, the species relocates to the Great Lakes and along the Atlantic coast from Newfoundland to South Carolina.

IDENTIFICATION: The common scoter's entire plumage is slightly glossy and blackish. The bright-orange bill features a grayish "lip." The feet and legs are gray green. The female is dark brown, but has whitish cheeks and a whitish throat; her bill is a gray blue. The immature scoter looks like the female, but is lighter below. The eyes of this species are dark.

SIZE: Moderate size for a diving duck, this scoter measures 17 to 21 inches long.

FOOD: Mollusks are the preferred dish, with crustaceans, fish, and insects the runners-up. About 10 percent of the diet is made up of plant matter.

■ Surf Scoter (*Melanitta perspicillata*)

RANGE: Breeding occurs from northeastern Alaska to the western half of Mackenzie and on islands in James Bay. Some have also been seen in central Labrador. In winter, this scoter resides along the Pacific coast from the eastern Aleutians to Baja California and on the Atlantic Seaboard from Nova Scotia to North Carolina.

IDENTIFICATION: The male's plumage is black, but there is one white patch at the back of the head and another at the forehead. The large, swollen bill consists of white, red, bluish gray, and yellow colorings in a variegated pattern. The eyes are white. Both sexes have dusky-yellow feet and no trace of white at all on the wings. The female is dark brown, and has white patches on the head not unlike those of the white-winged scoter. The surf scoter, however, has an additional white patch at the back of the head.

SIZE: Medium size among diving ducks, this scoter measures between 17 and 21 inches.

FOOD: About 60 percent of this bird's diet consists of mollusks, and another 10 percent consists of vegetable matter. Scallops and oysters are also consumed.

■ White-Winged Scoter (*Melanitta deglandi*)

RANGE: This species breeds in west-central Alaska, northwestern Mackenzie, and along the Rocky Mountains. In summer, the bird ranges from eastern Canada south to Massachusetts. In winter, it moves on to the Great Lakes and along the temperate Atlantic and Pacific coasts.

IDENTIFICATION: This scoter features a glossy, purplish plumage that is punctuated by a white speculum and a tiny patch of white around the eyes. The bill is orange, lightening to yellow at the tip. There is a black knob at the base of the bill. The female's body is dark brown, her upperparts white. A pair of white spots is located beneath the eyes, one is forward, the other at the back. Her bill is gray blue. The feet of both sexes are a dusky pink, the eyes white. Immature scoters resemble the female.

SIZE: A medium-size diving duck, this scoter measures between 19 and 23 inches in length.

FOOD: Approximately 75 percent of the scoter's diet is composed of mollusks, mussels, clams, and oysters. The remainder is crustaceans, a small amount of plant matter, and insects.

■ Shoveler (*Spatula clypeata*)

RANGE: The breeding area encompasses Alaska, central and southeastern Canada, both coasts, and the Great Lakes area. In winter, the species spreads eastward.

IDENTIFICATION: This species has a wide spatulate bill that is quite distinct among North American birds; this bill is longer than the bird's head. The drake's breeding plumage consists of a metallic green head and neck. The breast, upperparts, tail, and the forepart of the back are white. A wide, red-brown band stretches across the belly from flank to flank. The remainder of the back and the feathers above and below the tail are blackish green or black. The female is reminiscent of the female cinnamon teal, even to the horizontal, pale-blue line above the wing. The eye of the hen is dull brown, that of the drake rich yellow.

SIZE: The shoveler averages some 20 inches in length.

FOOD: The shoveler eats primarily grasses and aquatic plants, as well as large amounts of vegetable debris, which are strained from the ooze at marsh and pond bottoms. Small amounts of mollusks, aquatic insects, and fish are also eaten.

Shoveler

SHOREBIRDS

A NOTE ON EDIBILITY: Shorebirds are not known for their edibility. The flavor of the flesh of the Wilson's snipe is, as its scientific name implies, delicate, but it may be the only shorebird that is palatable.

■ Purple Gallinule
(Porphyrula martinica)

RANGE: Mainly inhabiting coastal lowlands and large river basins in the triangle formed by Tennessee, Louisiana, and South Carolina, this shorebird has also found its way throughout most of the United States and into southeastern Canada.

IDENTIFICATION: The purple gallinule sports extremely flamboyant colors. A deep, rich purple coats the head, neck, and undersides, while the back, wings, and upper tail feathers are dark greenish with a bronze-like sheen. The feathers below the short tail are white, while the feet and legs are a prominent yellowish green. The bill is bright red at the base and bright yellow at the tip. A tough, fleshy casque begins at the bottom of the upper bill and flares out to the middle of the head. Immature gallinules are light gray and white below, dark gray above. Their casques and bills are a dull gray. The chicks are glossy black with white bristles on their cap, cheeks, chin, and forehead.

SIZE: Medium size for a rail, the purple gallinule measures 13 inches in length (the same size as the Florida gallinule).

FOOD: The menu consists of rice, grains, seeds, insects, small mollusks, and amphibians.

■ Common Gallinule
(Gallinula chloropus)

RANGE: This bird is found in southern Canada, throughout much of the United States, and in such South American countries as Peru, Argentina, and Brazil.

IDENTIFICATION: The common gallinule resembles the purple gallinule in general appearance, but it is dark gray instead of purple. The yellow-tipped bill and the casque are bright red, and the legs and feet are greenish yellow. The top edge of the flank is white, and it appears as a white streak down the side when the bird is swimming. The central feathers of the undertail are dark gray. The downy young are glossy black, and the skin at the bottom of the black-tipped, reddish bill is a bright red. The chin feathers are curled and stiff, the forehead white.

SIZE: Like the purple gallinule, this shorebird is about 13 inches in length.

FOOD: Though consisting primarily of underwater plants, the diet also features herbs, grasses, seeds, and berries. This gallinule also eats insects, snails, and worms.

■ Carolina Rail
(Porzana carolina)

RANGE: The Carolina rail breeds throughout lower Canada, Saskatchewan, and Manitoba. In the United States, the rail can be found in the Southwest, Plains states, and the Midwest.

IDENTIFICATION: Typically, this rail has a body that is compressed laterally. Its cap, nape, tail, back, and wings are brown. In addition, the back and wings are spotted and marked with black and buff coloring. There is irregular barring below that is composed of thin, white lines on medium gray. The rest of the head and breast are a warmish gray, but the face and bib are black. The short, yellowish bill features a blackish tip; the feet and legs are a greenish yellow. The adult's eye is vermilion, but the eye is yellow in the duller, browner, immature bird. The downy young are a glossy black with curled, stiff chin feathers of a rich orange. Their yellowish bills are enlarged and reddish at the base.

SIZE: A smallish rail, this bird—also called the sora—is only 8 to 10 inches long.

FOOD: The sora eats more vegetation than is the norm for a rail. The diet consists primarily of aquatic plants, but the consumption of small mollusks, insects, and worms is also high, particularly in the spring.

Greater Yellowlegs

Virginia Rail *(Rallus limicola)*

RANGE: This shorebird breeds from Guatemala north to southern Canada.

IDENTIFICATION: The Virginia rail has a long bill and very gray cheeks. On its underparts, there are wide, black lines that alternate with thin, wavy white lines. The feet, legs, and bill of the rail are pink. The young are nearly black.

SIZE: A medium-size rail, this bird measures from 8½ to 10½ inches in length.

FOOD: The diet consists of worms, mollusks, aquatic insects, amphibians, and small fish. On occasion, seeds are included.

Greater Yellowlegs *(Totanus melanoleucus)*

RANGE: The breeding grounds are from central Alaska east to Labrador and Newfoundland; the wintering areas are from southwestern British Columbia through the West Indies and Latin America.

IDENTIFICATION: The greater yellowlegs has a slender but sturdy, slightly upturned, blackish bill that is approx-imately 50 percent longer than the head. The upperparts are dark brown, the outer flight feathers black. The tail (lightly barred) and the back are also black. The bill of this species is proportionately longer and stockier than the bill of the lesser yellowlegs.

SIZE: This shorebird is 12½ to 15 inches long.

FOOD: This bird's menu consists of small fish, insects (primarily aquatic), worms, small mollusks, and crustaceans.

Lesser Yellowlegs *(Totanus flavipes)*

RANGE: This species breeds from north-central Alaska east to Quebec. Winters are spent along the coastal low lands from Mexico, the Gulf Coast, and South Carolina down through Central America and the West Indies.

IDENTIFICATION: The lesser yellowlegs is practically identical to the greater yellowlegs, except for the fact that the bill of this species is much more slender and, lacking the upturn, much straighter.

SIZE: This shorebird is smaller than the greater yellowlegs, measuring 9½ to 11 inches in length.

FOOD: Like the greater yellowlegs, the lesser yellowlegs consumes insects, small fish, mollusks, and crustaceans.

Wilson's Snipe *(Gallinago delicata)*

RANGE: Though this shorebird breeds in the Arctic tundra down to New York and the mountains of California, it winters from the Gulf Coast states southward to Brazil and Columbia.

IDENTIFICATION: The upperparts of this—the only North American species of snipe—are blackish with buff mottling. A pair of conspicuous buff stripes are located along the back, and another down the center of the crown. The body is whitish below, but has brown spots on the throat and tail. The latter is black with a red tip.

SIZE: The Wilson's snipe measures some 11 inches in length, 3 inches of which is its tail.

FOOD: Its menu consists of worms, snails, and insects.

Section Three
FISHING

SPINNING

Spinning became popular in America in the late 1940s. It is unique because the reel is mounted on the underside of the rod—rather than on top, as in other methods—and because the reel spool remains stationary (does not revolve) when the angler is casting and retrieving.

In operation, the weight and momentum of the lure being cast uncoils line (usually monofilament, fluorocarbon, or braid) from the reel spool. Unlike conventional revolving-spool reels, in which the momentum of the turning spool can cause backlashes, the spinning-reel user has no such problem, for the line stops uncoiling at the end of the cast. A beginner can learn to use spinning gear much faster than conventional tackle. Still another advantage of spinning gear is that it permits the use of much lighter lines and smaller, lighter lures than can be cast with conventional equipment.

▪ The Reel

On a standard open-face spinning reel, the pickup mechanism is usually of a type called the bail—a metal arm extending across the spool's face. To cast a lure or bait, the angler opens the bail by swinging it out and down. This frees the line, which, as a rule, the angler momentarily controls with his index finger. He casts and then cranks the reel handle—not a full turn but just a small fraction of a turn. This snaps the bail closed, engaging the line.

Other devices on a spinning reel include the drag and the antireverse lock. The drag, an adjustable mechanism usually consisting of a series of discs and friction washers, is fitted on the outer (forward) face of the spool or at the rear of the gear housing in most reels. The drag

permits a hooked fish to take out line without breaking off, while the reel handle remains stationary. The antireverse lock, usually a lever mounted on the gear-housing cover, prevents the reel handle from turning in reverse at such times as when a hooked fish is running out or when you are trolling.

Spinning reels are designed for all types of fishing. How does the beginner select the right one for his particular needs? A reel's weight and line capacity are the major determining factors. For ultralight fishing with tiny lures (1/16 to 5/16 ounce), a reel weighing 5 to 8 ounces and holding about 100 yards of 2- to 4-pound-test line is the ticket. Reels for light freshwater use weigh 8 to 10 ounces and hold up to 200 yards of 6- or 8-pound-test line. Reels for general freshwater and light saltwater use weigh 12 to 16 ounces and hold up to 250 yards of 8- to 15-pound-test line. Heavy offshore and surf-spinning reels weigh upwards of 25 ounces and hold a minimum of 250 yards of 15-pound-test line. These yardage capacities are for monofilament or fluorocarbon line. Smaller-diameter braid line will usually increase these capacities on most reels.

In addition to the open-face spinning reel, there is a closed-face design. This type, too, is mounted under the rod. Its spool and working parts are enclosed in a hood, with the line running through an opening at the front. The pickup mechanism is normally an internal pin, and there's no need for a bail since the line control is accomplished by other means. In some of these reels, which were fairly common at one time, line was disengaged from the pickup by backing the handle a half turn. In others, it was accomplished by pushing a button, working a lever or disc, or pressing the front reel plate. Closed-face reels are still available, but are no longer common.

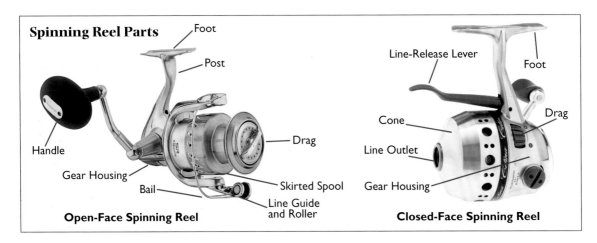

Spinning Reel Parts

Foot
Post
Handle
Gear Housing
Bail
Drag
Skirted Spool
Line Guide and Roller

Open-Face Spinning Reel

Line-Release Lever
Foot
Cone
Drag
Line Outlet
Gear Housing

Closed-Face Spinning Reel

Besides eliminating the bail, closed-faced reels give the spool and other parts some protection from the elements and help to keep out sand, dirt, and the like. Some fishermen, however, dislike the fact that the line is choked through the constriction at the point of the cone, feeling that this arrangement somewhat limits casting range and accuracy. Another drawback is that the hood enclosing the spool hides the line from the angler's view, preventing him from seeing line tangles and whether or not the line is uncoiling smoothly.

Mainly because of the simplicity of spinning reels, there has been little gadgeteering by manufacturers. However, some unusual features have appeared over the years. These have included bails that open automatically, self-centering (self-positioning) bails, rear drags,

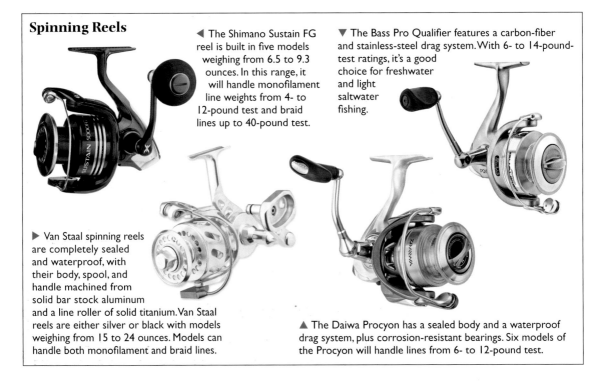

Spinning Reels

◀ The Shimano Sustain FG reel is built in five models weighing from 6.5 to 9.3 ounces. In this range, it will handle monofilament line weights from 4- to 12-pound test and braid lines up to 40-pound test.

▼ The Bass Pro Qualifier features a carbon-fiber and stainless-steel drag system. With 6- to 14-pound-test ratings, it's a good choice for freshwater and light saltwater fishing.

▶ Van Staal spinning reels are completely sealed and waterproof, with their body, spool, and handle machined from solid bar stock aluminum and a line roller of solid titanium. Van Staal reels are either silver or black with models weighing from 15 to 24 ounces. Models can handle both monofilament and braid lines.

▲ The Daiwa Procyon has a sealed body and a waterproof drag system, plus corrosion-resistant bearings. Six models of the Procyon will handle lines from 6- to 12-pound test.

How to Match Up Spinning Tackle

This chart is meant only as a general guide aimed at helping you put together, in proper balance, the basic elements of a spinning outfit tailored for fish of a particular weight category. Specific conditions—and your ability and personal preferences—should also be considered.

Species of Fish	Reel	Rod Action, Length (feet)	Line (pound test)	Lure Weights (ounces)
Trout, small bass, grayling, panfish	Ultralight	Ultralight, 4 to 6	2, 3	1/16 to 5/16
Smallmouth, largemouth, and white bass, pickerel, trout, grayling	Light	Light, 5½ to 6½	4 to 8	¼ to ⅜
Large bass and trout, walleye, pickerel, pike, snook, landlocked salmon	Medium	Medium, 6 to 7½	6 to 10	⅜ to ⅝
Salmon, lake trout, muskellunge, pike, bonefish, tarpon, striped bass, bluefish	Heavy	Heavy, 7 to 8½	10 to 15	½ to 1½
General saltwater use (surf and boat)	Extraheavy	Extraheavy, 9 to 13	12 and up	1 and up

and skirted spools, which prevent line from getting behind the spool.

The Rod

There are spinning rods designed for every conceivable kind of sport fishing. They come in lengths from 4 to 13 feet and weigh from 2 to 30 ounces. Most are constructed of fiberglass, graphite, carbon, or Kevlar. Construction is usually one, two, or three pieces; however, some spinning rods designed for backpackers may have as many as a half-dozen sections.

Spinning rods fall into five general categories: ultralight, light, medium, heavy, and extraheavy. They are further broken down according to the type of reel and design of the hand grip.

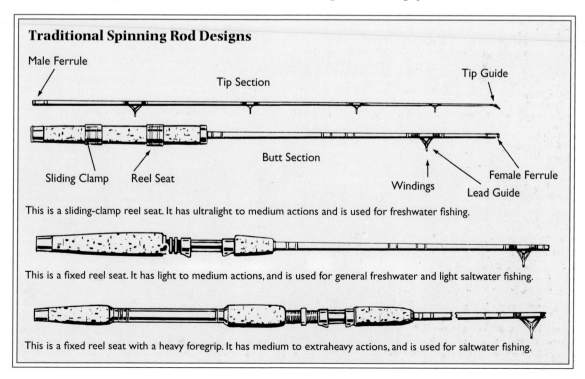

Traditional Spinning Rod Designs

This is a sliding-clamp reel seat. It has ultralight to medium actions and is used for freshwater fishing.

This is a fixed reel seat. It has light to medium actions, and is used for general freshwater and light saltwater fishing.

This is a fixed reel seat with a heavy foregrip. It has medium to extraheavy actions, and is used for saltwater fishing.

How to Cast with Spinning Tackle

The Grip • Proper grip for open-face spinning reels puts two fingers on each side of the reel's supporting post. The index finger holds the line until the cast is made. With a closed-face spinning reel, the grip is similar except the index finger is used to control and release the line with a trigger release.

The Straightaway Cast • Here are the three steps in making a straightaway cast with an open-face spinning reel. Starting with your rod at a 45-degree angle, with your index finger holding the line, bring the rod backward smoothly until you feel the rod loaded with the weight of your lure or bait. The rod is powered forward, the line is released, and the rod is held at the angle shown, while the lure or bait sails to the target. A sidearm cast, generally used to avoid overhead foliage, is similar to the straight-away cast, except the rod is held parallel to the ground during the cast.

The Underhand Lob • The underhand lob or underhand cast, usually used to clear brush or to cope with the wind, starts with the rod tip low to the ground and high on the upward swing. A lure with the underhand lob will sail in a high, soft arc *(right)* and will hit the water gently. It is a good cast for clear, shallow runs, where a splashy cast would scare fish.

The Bow-and-Arrow Cast • This is a trick that anglers use to shoot a lure through holes in streamside brush. The photos show the same cast from two different positions. Holding the rod low and parallel to the water will clear the cast from overhead brush. Holding the rod high will clear low brush and likely give you more distance. The technique is the same. Grasp the bend of the lowest hook on the lure so that it will clear your fingers smoothly and safely. Then, release the line, shooting the lure like an arrow.

FLY FISHING

The art of fly fishing dates back to at least the third century AD and so is one of the oldest forms of sport fishing. Its adherents—and they are legion—say that it is also the most artistic form of the sport.

Fly fishing is unique in two basic ways. In all other forms of fishing, the weight of the lure or bait is what enables the angler to cast; in fly fishing, the weight of the line itself enables the cast. In spinning, spincasting, and baitcasting, a natural bait or a lure or plug imitating a natural bait is offered to the fish; a fly fisherman's offering is a near-weightless bit of feathers and hair that imitates an insect in one of its forms of life (though some flies—streamers and bucktails—imitate baitfish).

■ The Reel

It is generally agreed that the reel, with the exception of saltwater fly fishing, is the least important item of fly-fishing tackle, and yet without it, the angler would find himself amid a tangle of line and leader. The fly reel is mounted below the rod grip and close to the butt end of the rod. In most kinds of fishing, the reel's main function is to store line that is not being used. In handling large fish, however, the workings and drag of the fly reel come into play.

There are two basic types of fly reels: the single action and the automatic.

The single-action reel, which is best when the quarry is either small or quite heavy fish, is so named because the spool makes one complete turn for each turn of the handle. The spool is deep and narrow. A beginner should make sure that the reel has a strong click mechanism to prevent the line from overrunning, and if he'll be tangling with sizable, strong-running fish, such as striped bass, tarpon or salmon, he should get a reel with a good smooth adjustable drag.

The standard (trout size) single-action fly reel weighs 3 to 5 ounces and has a spool diameter of 3 to 4 inches. The spool should be filled with enough line (the fly line itself, usually 30 yards, plus sufficient "backing" line) to reach within about ⅜ inch of the reel's cross braces. Many of the best fly fishermen like 15- to 30-pound-test braid or monofilament line as backing. For most freshwater fishing, 20-pound-test braid backing is fine, but 30-pound test is recommended for species such as striped bass, bonefish, and salmon. The chief advantages of the single-action fly reel are that it weighs considerably less than the automatic and it can hold much more backing, an important factor in handling large fish.

The automatic fly reel has a spring-operated spool

How to Match Up Fly Tackle

This chart is meant only as a general guide aimed at helping you put together, in proper balance, the basic elements of a fly-fishing outfit tailored for fish of a particular weight category. Specific conditions—and your ability and personal preference—should also be considered. The line sizes below are meant only as a general guide, and a newcomer to fishing should note that there is a wide range of conditions and circumstances that determines the correct line weight for a given rod. Level and double-taper fly lines may still be available, but the best advice for easy casting is to use weight-forward lines.

Species of Fish	Reel	Rod Length (feet)	Lines		
			Level	Double-Taper	Weight-Forward
Trout, small bass, grayling, panfish	Single-action, automatic	6½ to 7½	L4 or L5	DT4F or DT5F; DT6S	WF4F; WF6S
Smallmouth, largemouth, and white bass, pickerel, trout, grayling	Single-action, automatic	7½ to 8½	L6 or L7	DT6F or DT7F; DT8S	WF6F; WF8S
Large bass and trout, landlocked salmon, walleye, pickerel, pike	Single-action	8½ to 9	L8 or L9	DT8F or DT9F; DT9S	WF9F; WF10S
Salmon, lake trout, muskellunge, pike, bonefish, tarpon, striped bass, bluefish	Single-action	9½	L10	DT10F	WF10F; WF10S

KEY TO LINE DESIGNATIONS: L—LEVEL DT—DOUBLE TAPER WF—WEIGHT FORWARD F—FLOATING S—SINKING

Basic Types of Fly Reels

◄ The Orvis Battenkill Bar Stock is a typical fly reel design. Depending on the Orvis model, the Battenkill can handle any species from trout to billfish with line weights of 1 to 11.

▶ The Pflueger Automatic fly reel has a spring-operated spool that retrieves line automatically when an angler activates the lever. A one-time favorite with some fly fishermen, it has decreased in popularity.

▲ The World Wide Sportsman Gold Cup is a fly reel designed for big fish. Two models are built for fly lines up to WF12F with 300 yards of 30-pound backing. It features a heat-resistant carbon drag.

▲ The Sage 1600 is an all-aluminum fly reel with a quick-release spool change and a sealed graphite drag. It is built for line weights of 4 to 9. In the model with a line weight range of 4 to 6, the Sage 1600 weighs only 5⅞ ounces. It is a good freshwater choice.

▲ The White River Kingfisher fly reel, machined from cold-forged aluminum with a sealed drag system, has an open-frame design and offers a wide range of models for freshwater and saltwater fishing. These models handle fly line weights from 3 to 10 with room for backing.

that retrieves line automatically when the angler activates the spool-release lever. The spring is wound up as line is pulled from the reel, but line may be stripped from the reel at any time, even when the spring is tightly wound.

Though heavier than the single action (the weight range is 5 to 10 ounces), the automatic greatly facilitates line control. Instead of having to shift the rod from the right to the left hand (assuming the user is right-handed) to reel in line—as the user of the single-action reel must do—the automatic user simply touches the release lever with the little finger of his right hand.

Fly Rod Parts

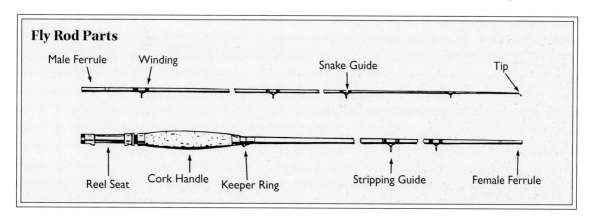

Male Ferrule   Winding   Snake Guide   Tip

Reel Seat   Cork Handle   Keeper Ring   Stripping Guide   Female Ferrule

How to Wade a River

Wading looks easy enough, but it can turn into a dangerous situation if you are swept off your feet in the swift current. The rules for safe wading are simple. First, never take a step in any direction unless your rear or anchor foot is firmly planted. Next, slide your lead foot forward until it is secure. When your lead foot is firmly planted, then slide your anchor foot ahead. Never try to wade by lifting your feet. The current will swing your leg out from under you and throw you off balance. Avoid wading big, wide stretches of river. It is safer to wade from pool to pool, taking advantage of slower current to rest.

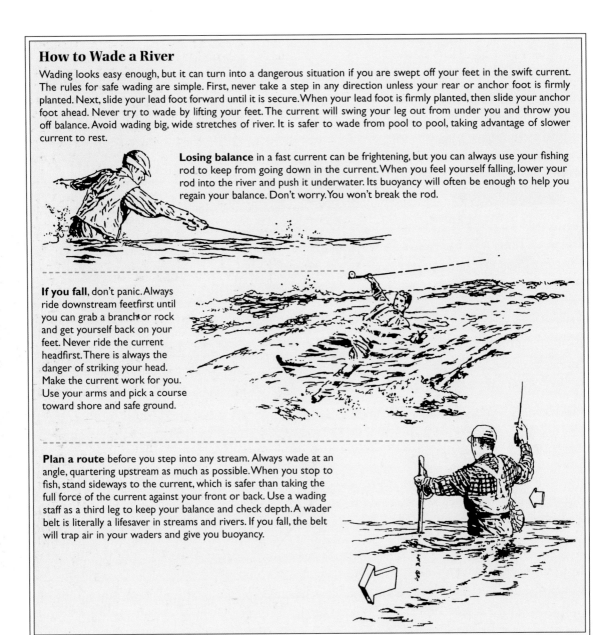

Losing balance in a fast current can be frightening, but you can always use your fishing rod to keep from going down in the current. When you feel yourself falling, lower your rod into the river and push it underwater. Its buoyancy will often be enough to help you regain your balance. Don't worry. You won't break the rod.

If you fall, don't panic. Always ride downstream feetfirst until you can grab a branch or rock and get yourself back on your feet. Never ride the current headfirst. There is always the danger of striking your head. Make the current work for you. Use your arms and pick a course toward shore and safe ground.

Plan a route before you step into any stream. Always wade at an angle, quartering upstream as much as possible. When you stop to fish, stand sideways to the current, which is safer than taking the full force of the current against your front or back. Use a wading staff as a third leg to keep your balance and check depth. A wader belt is literally a lifesaver in streams and rivers. If you fall, the belt will trap air in your waders and give you buoyancy.

■ The Rod

The rod is of paramount importance to the fly caster. It must be suited to the kind of fishing he does (saltwater, trout, bass bugging, and so on), and it must be matched with the proper fly line.

Fly rods are made of fiberglass, graphite, or bamboo. Graphite fly rods are faster and more sensitive than fiberglass rods. And, ounce for ounce, graphite is twice as strong as glass. What length rod should the beginner select?

According to the recommendations of casting instructors and tackle manufacturers, a good all-purpose length is 8 to 8½ feet with a weight of about 5 ounces. Such a rod should have fast action.

Action, briefly, is a measure of a rod's flexibility, and it determines the use for which the rod is suited. In fast-action rods, best suited for dry-fly fishing, most of the flex (or bend) is at the tip. Medium-action rods bend down to the middle and are designed to perform over a wide range of conditions. They are probably the best choice for an all-purpose fly rod. Slow-action rods, a traditional design that works well for fishing streamers, bass bugs, and the like, bend well down to and even into the butt.

Good fly rods have a screw-lock reel seat, which holds the reel securely. Line guides are usually made of stainless steel, except that the tip guide and sometimes the stripper guide (the one nearest to the reel) may be chrome or highly durable carboloy steel. The largest fly rods, those designed for taking tarpon and other large saltwater fish, have an extension butt or a fore-end grip, which gives the angler more leverage.

How to Use Fly Tackle

Sheila M. Hassan (*right*) is a Federation of Fly Fishers Master Certified casting instructor. She is the director at the Wulff School of Fly Fishing and an IGFA world-record holder for bonefish and bluefish. Joan Wulff (*left*) is a fly-fishing legend and a National Casting Champion with a record distance cast of 161 feet. Joan, elected to the IGFA Hall of Fame, is the founder of the Wulff School of Fly Fishing. The photos and techniques described in this section are from *Fly Casting: A Systematic Approach* by Sheila Hassan.

The Grip • The thumb on top of the cork handle is the strongest grip for most people. With your thumb on top, the index finger is on the opposite side of the rod butt. You want the thumb and index finger to balance the rod, with your lower three fingers gently wrapped around the rod butt. A key feature of your grip is to be sure the heel of your hand sits on top of the cork grip. Your lower three fingers cradle the rod butt low in the fingers, like when you lift a suitcase handle. The primary points of pressure are your thumb and index finger, and your lower two fingers. Your middle finger is less important for controlling the rod, so it is available to help manage your fly line with shooting and stripping.

How to Use Fly Tackle *(continued)*

Wrist Action • The wrist can be very helpful in your casting, but must be used in moderation. The wrist has two positions: bent down, which is a zero-degree angle to your forearm *(left)*, and straight, which is a 45-degree angle to your forearm. This change in angle occurs when you stop and the rod unloads. It is useful for the forward cast stop. Every backcast starts with your wrist in the bent-down position and ends with your wrist in the straight position, with the rod butt at an approximately 45-degree angle to your forearm.

Basic Cast • The basic cast is the classic fly cast. It has both a backcast and a forward cast. Each cast is separate. Stand in a vertical stance with your feet, shoulders, and hips facing your target. Starting with your line straight on the water, use your rod hand and forearm as a unit to lift the line off the water. Remember that all casts start slowly and build acceleration gradually. Lift the line off the water with just enough speed so you lift inch by inch. If you lift too fast, you will see the water spray as it rips off the surface. If you lift too slowly, you will run out of stroke length. The correct speed is determined by watching your line and lifting inch by inch. You should see a small, V-shaped wake as you lift the line. This wake shows you have the right speed.

Next, you must focus on timing. Timing is the pause after the cast while the loop unrolls behind you but maintains the line under tension. Remember that the cast

must bend and unbend the rod. This can only happen when the line is under tension. When your backcast has unrolled, it is time for the forward cast. Look to your target and think of aiming the cast. Move your rod arm toward the target area, leading with the elbow and finishing with the hand. Start the forward cast slowly and build acceleration gradually to load the rod. With the line under tension and the rod loaded, you are ready for the forward cast wrist rotation to stop the rod. Push forward with your thumb and pull back with your lower fingers. Watch your loop unroll and follow through with the rod tip down to the water. The cast is complete.

1

2

False Cast • False casting is making a series of backcasts and forward casts without letting the line touch the water. False casting is used to dry your dry fly. Dry flies are designed to sit on top of the water, but can become waterlogged as you fish. False casting is also used to change direction, from downstream to upstream, and to measure the distance of your cast. Steps 1 through 5 show the sequence—elbow lifts and lowers, forearm moves back and forth. It's critical to maintain line tension between your rod and fly line in your left hand. Make sure there is no slack between the line hand and the stripping guide of the rod. False casting also allows you to add length to your cast by adding the technique of shooting line.

3

4

5

How to Use Fly Tackle *(continued)*

Shooting Line • After you learn to false cast, the next step is shooting line. Shooting line means you can extend the range of your fishing without having to carry that extra line in the air during your cast.

Before you get in the starting position, make sure you have enough line available to shoot. Start with a small amount, about 4 feet. You will have the rod in one hand and the line in the other hand. Make sure there is no slack between the line hand and the stripping guide of the rod. The extra line for shooting will be in a loose loop between your rod hand and line hand. Start by making two or three false casts. Watch for the casting loop to be formed after the stop on the forward

cast. When you see the loop has formed, you can release the line from your fingers and the loop will pull the extra line out.

When you are practicing shooting line, you may need to work on your timing of the shoot. If you release your line too soon, the loop will not have formed and you will not be able to shoot line. If you wait too long, your loop will unroll completely and there will be no energy left to shoot extra line. The rod must be stopped effectively, which means a smooth acceleration to an abrupt stop. This is what gives you a good loop with enough energy to shoot line. Practice shooting line on your third false cast and work on the timing until you can shoot all 4 feet.

Headwind • For most fly fishermen, wind is a challenge. In all wind situations, you will want high line speed to control your fly line. To handle a headwind, you will want a tight loop with more speed. To get a tighter loop, adjust your casting arc so it is only as wide as needed, and cast along a straight line, directly to the target. You will want to cast on a steeper downward angle and have your loop unroll inches above the water. Use a higher rate of acceleration and cast a little faster to get higher line speed. Crouching down low with your body may help you get that lower angle and greater speed. This combination of adjustments helps your loop cut into the wind better and helps you cast in headwinds.

Tailwind • A good technique for dealing with tailwinds is to make two forward casts. Turn to stand sideways to your target. Make a forward cast to your right side. While the cast is unrolling, rotate your hand and forearm to make a forward cast in the other direction, toward your left side. After the hand and forearm rotate, bring the elbow back in by your side and complete your forward cast to the left side. This is a very effective technique for tailwinds, as it uses the strength of your muscles in the forward direction to cast into the tailwind.

Single Haul • To learn the single haul, start with a single haul on the backcast. Move your line hand and rod hand in the same direction to start the casting stroke. When you reach the line leader connection, the rod hand will execute the stop, while the line hand accelerates in an opposite direction for the haul. Be sure to stop the line hand haul when the rod hand completes the stop.

As you lift the line off the water, if your rod hand is relaxed, you can feel the rod bending. The haul should feel like you are pulling into this bend, creating a deeper bend. Think of the backcast haul as helping to lift the fly off the water. Within the casting stroke, the loading move is the longest part. The stop and haul are relatively short in comparison. The wrist rotation and haul are very brief; they last just long enough to lift the fly off the water. As the fly leaves the water, your haul is complete and the rod is stopped. Your rod and line hands maintain their positions while the loop unrolls. On the next forward cast, as you move your rod arm forward, your line hand pivots to maintain its position relative to the rod hand. Make sure there is no slack between the line hand and rod hand and present the fly.

How to Use Fly Tackle *(continued)*

Double Haul • The key to the double haul is that it adds the power of the left hand to the work of the rod hand to increase the load in the rod. Start the backcast as usual with the rod hand and line hand moving in the same direction. When the rod hand is ready to execute the stop, the line hand accelerates in the opposite direction, with a crisp acceleration to a stop. While the line unrolls on the backcast, the line hand gives back the line it has just hauled out. The line hand will return to a position near the reel. It is crucial to be sure there is no slack in the line as the line hand gives back the line. When the loop has unrolled and the forward cast begins, the line hand and rod hand move forward. When the rod hand starts the forward cast wrist rotation for the stop, the line hand accelerates away from the rod hand. While the forward cast loop unrolls, the line hand gives back the line it has hauled out. You can either shoot the line or return the line hand to a position near the reel.

Roll Cast • The easily learned roll cast pays off heavily when the fisherman has some barrier behind him that prevents a normal backcast. In fact, the roll cast is a quick way to make a new cast under almost any circumstance. To execute this cast, tilt your arm at a slight angle away from your body as you lift your hand up toward your temple. Allow the line to slide behind the rod tip to create a D-shaped loop. Stop and allow the line to settle. Check your hand height and the angle of your rod butt to your forearm to be sure it is not greater than 45 degrees. Line

up your elbow with your target area. Execute the forward cast by slowly lowering your elbow to move your rod hand in line with your target area. Continue the acceleration to the target. When your thumb pad is opposite the target area, use hand movement to execute the forward cast wrist rotation and stop the rod. Lower the rod tip as the loop unrolls.

BAITCASTING

Baitcasting is a method of fishing distinguished by the use of a revolving-spool reel. Originally intended by its 19th-century creators as a means of casting live baitfish, baitcasting tackle today is used to present all sorts of offerings—from worms and minnows to spoons and huge jointed plugs—to game fish in both fresh and salt water. This method is also known as plugcasting.

Before the advent of spinning gear, baitcasting was the universally accepted tackle for presenting baits or lures. Even today, many anglers—especially those who grew up with a baitcasting outfit in their hands—prefer this method, even though the revolving-spool reel is more difficult to use than fixed-spool spinning and spincasting reels. The baitcaster feels that his gear gives him more sensitive contact with what is going on at the end of his line. He feels that he can manipulate a lure better on baitcasting gear and have better control over a hooked fish. Most fishermen agree that when the quarry is a big, strong fish such as a muskie, pike, or saltwater fish, baitcasting outfits get the nod over spinning or spincasting tackle.

Baitcasting tackle is often preferred for trolling, too, for the revolving-spool reel makes it easy to pay out line behind the moving boat, and the rod has enough backbone to handle the big, water-resistant lures used in many forms of trolling.

■ The Reel

The reel is by far the most important part of a baitcasting outfit, and the budding baitcaster would do well to buy the best reel he can afford.

The main distinguishing feature of baitcasting reels is that the spool revolves when line is cast out or reeled in, while in spinning and spincasting reels the spool remains stationary.

Baitcasting reels have a relatively wide, shallow spool, and most have multiplying gears that cause the

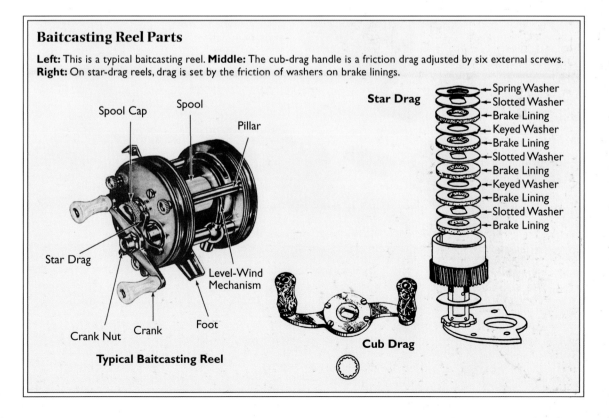

Baitcasting Reel Parts

Left: This is a typical baitcasting reel. **Middle:** The cub-drag handle is a friction drag adjusted by six external screws. **Right:** On star-drag reels, drag is set by the friction of washers on brake linings.

Spool Cap
Spool
Pillar
Spring Washer
Slotted Washer
Brake Lining
Keyed Washer
Brake Lining
Slotted Washer
Brake Lining
Keyed Washer
Brake Lining
Slotted Washer
Brake Lining
Star Drag
Star Drag
Level-Wind Mechanism
Crank Nut
Crank
Foot
Cub Drag

Typical Baitcasting Reel

How to Match Up Baitcasting Tackle

This chart is meant only as a general guide aimed at helping you put together, in proper balance, the basic elements of a baitcasting outfit. Specific conditions—and your ability and personal preferences—should also be considered.

Species of Fish	Reel	Rod Action, Length (feet)	Line (pound test)	Lure Weights (ounces)
Panfish, small bass, pickerel, trout	Multiplying gear with level-wind	Ultralight, 6 to 6½	6 to 8	⅛ to ¼
Bass, pickerel, walleye, small pike, trout	Multiplying gear with level-wind	Light, 5½ to 6½	6 to 12	¼ to ½
Large bass, walleye, pike, lake trout, muskie, striped bass	Multiplying gear with star drag	Medium, 5 to 6	10 to 20	⅝ to ¾
Muskie, steelhead, lake trout, salmon, striped bass, bluefish, tarpon, snook	Multiplying gear with star drag	Heavy, 4½ to 7	18 to 25	¾ and up

Baitcasting Reels

▶ The Johnny Morris Signature Series Baitcast Reel is built on a solid aluminum frame with a carbon-titanium finish. This reel has an 11-bearing system and a carbon drag with up to 14 pounds of drag pressure. Five different models weigh from 8.3 to 9.6 ounces. The line capacity is 160 yards of 12-pound-test monofilament.

▶ The Daiwa PX Type-R Baitcast Reel is a lightweight reel at 5.8 ounces. It's designed for light lures on light lines, and the capacity is 95 yards of 6-pound-test monofilament. The maximum drag is 13 pounds.

▲ The Abu Garcia Revo MGX is a featherweight baitcasting reel for light-tackle freshwater fishing. Weighing only 5.4 ounces with a gear ratio of 7:1 and a maximum drag pressure of 24 pounds, the reel features 10 stainless-steel bearings and a line capacity of 115 yards of 12-pound-test monofilament.

▲ The Browning Midas Low-Profile Baitcast Reel has a one-piece aluminum frame, a V-shaped spool of forged aluminum, and nine stainless-steel bearings. It also has a magnetic cast control and heavy thumb-bar release. It will hold 120 yards of 12-pound-test line.

▲ The Abu Garcia 5600 is designed to handle most species of freshwater and inshore saltwater fish. A familiar reel for generations, the Abu Garcia Ambassadeur series features stainless-steel ball bearings, a carbon star-drag system, and line capacities up to 245 yards of 14-pound-test monofilament.

spool to revolve several times (usually four) for each complete turn of the reel handle. There is also some kind of drag mechanism, which is helpful in fighting big fish. These range from a simple click mechanism to a screw-down nut to a star drag. Some older reels have what is called a cub drag, which is adjusted by turning six screws on the base of the handle.

Almost all of today's good baitcasting reels have an important device called a level-wind. It usually takes the form of a U-shaped loop of heavy wire attached to a base that travels from one side of the spool to the other by means of a wormlike gear. The device permits line to be wound evenly on the spool and thus is a big help in preventing backlashes, which are often caused by line "lumping up" on the spool. A backlash occurs when the speed of the revolving spool is faster than that of the outgoing line, resulting in a "bird's nest."

Most baitcasting reels are being made with anti-backlash devices. These employ either centrifugal force or pressure on the spool axle or flange to slow down the spool during a cast. Some reels use magnets to accomplish this process. However, though these antibacklash devices are helpful, the user of a baitcasting reel must still learn to apply thumb pressure to the spool if he is to prevent backlashes under all conditions. Only experience can teach how much thumb pres-sure is needed under any given set of circumstances.

Another development in baitcasting is the free-spool reel. Without this feature, the cast lure not only pulls out line and turns the spool, but also turns the gears, the level-wind, and the reel handle. All these moving parts tend to shorten the cast. But in the free-spool reel, most of the gearing is disconnected from the spool before a cast is made, and only the spool (and sometimes the level-wind) turns. This makes it easier to start and stop the turning of the spool and so permits the use of lighter lures than can be cast with a standard baitcasting reel. Longer casts are also possible. A turn of the handle reengages the gears of the free-spool reel so that the retrieve can be made.

▪ The Rod

Most baitcasting rods are now made of fiberglass or graphite. Rod lengths range from about 4 to more than 7 feet. Some, obviously, are more suitable for specific purposes. The most popular length—because it works well for many kinds of fishing—is about 6 feet. Manufacturers generally classify their rods according to their action, which refers to the lure weights that a rod handles efficiently. Generally, ultralight rods can handle lures weighing ¼ ounce or less. Light rods can handle ¼ to ½ ounce.

Typical Casting Rod Designs

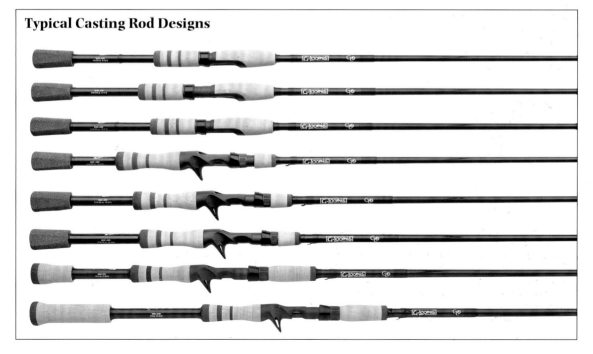

These are typical casting rod handles. The pistol grip (*top*) is for one-handed casting, while the straight grip (*bottom*) is for two-handed casting. The longer handle, originally built for bigger fish, is now finding favor with bass fishermen. Two-handed casting is less tiring and makes longer casts possible.

Heavy Muskie Rod with Foregrip

Popping Rod with Straight-Grip Handle

Medium rods are better at handling ⅝ to ¾ ounce, and heavy rods are for ¾ ounce or more.

Baitcasting rods have either a straight handle or a pistol-grip handle. No longer common is the double-offset handle, in which the reel seat is depressed and the butt grip is canted downward. Other features of baitcasting rods are a finger hook on the underside of the reel seat and a reel-holding screw lock.

Baitcasting rods are of one- or two-piece construction. Some have ferrules about midway up the rod, while others may have a detachable handle. The most popular baitcasting rods have a straight handle, a long butt section, a foregrip usually made of cork, and a rubber butt cap. These rods, sometimes called popping rods, have become so popular that lighter-action models are now commonly used for freshwater fishing. The longer straight handle makes it more comfortable and less tiring for casting and fighting fish. Well suited for freshwater and light saltwater use, these rods can also handle an extensive range of lure weights for various species of fish.

Fishing Pliers

For many years, the only tool on a fisherman's belt was a small pair of pliers with spring-loaded handles and a wire cutter on the side of the jaws. To make mine slip-proof, I put pieces of surgical tubing over the handles. The pliers measured only 4½ inches long, probably too short when dislodging big hooks from big fish with sharp teeth. I used mine mostly to pull knots tight, cut monofilament and wire, and rig baits. These pliers worked fine for one or two seasons, but then the cutters got dull and the spring-loaded handles always had to be oiled regularly to keep them working freely.

A lot has happened over the years! Today, fishermen now have a choice of dozens of fishing tools to hang on their belts, ranging from pliers made from titanium and aircraft aluminum to plastic. The new multipurpose pliers will also do a variety of jobs. Most models will crimp, cut braid and wire, and are totally corrosion proof. And those long-nose models will keep your fingers safely away from sharp teeth and hooks.

The price tags on some of these pliers are a real enigma. They range from $12 to more than $300. Are the inexpensive models good? Can fishermen justify dropping hundreds of dollars on a pair of pliers? Are they worth the money? Is it easier to buy $12 pliers and throw them away at the end of the season? Those expensive titanium pliers may well outlive you. These are tough questions to answer. Let your fishing budget be your guide.

Offshore Angler 7½-inch aluminum pliers have double-coated carbon steel jaws and tungsten replaceable cutters that cut tough fishing lines, including braid.

How to Use Baitcasting Tackle

How to Plug Cast • The grip should be relaxed and natural. The thumb on the reel spool controls the line during a cast. The reel is tipped so the spool is almost vertical with the handles up. This cuts down on spool friction.

Basic Forward Cast • Never take your eyes off your target. Let your rod tip whip down to a horizontal position behind you, and then drive it forward with speed and power. Thumb pressure used to hold the reel spool is released as the rod points toward the target. Very light thumbing on the spool will control the lure's flight and avoid a backlash. Most conventional reels have braking systems or magnetic cast controls to avoid backlashes.

Lure Retrieve • After the lure hits the water, assuming you are casting with your right hand, quickly move the rod to your left hand for the retrieve with your hand comfortably cupping the sideplate of the reel. Raise the rod to about 45 degrees and keep the butt against your body. This will keep the outfit steady and ready for a quick strike.

How to Use Baitcasting Tackle *(continued)*

Backhand Cast • The backhand cast is used to get your lure or bait out when some obstacle behind you prevents a routine backswing. Start with the rod horizontally in front of you. Bring the rod sharply rearward until you feel the weight of the lure and your rod loads. Immediately, with a strong snap of the wrist, bring your rod forward and release the line to complete the cast.

Sidearm Cast • The sidearm cast is a powerful toss that is good for long-range work and casting into the wind. It also saves the day when overhead foliage prevents a vertical backswing. The casting motion follows a one-two pattern. Sight the target, swing the rod back, and whip it forward. The casting arm remains straight and the rod tip points at the target until the lure is well on its way.

Flipping

Flipping is an effective technique for bass fishermen. It's a simple but deadly approach for presenting a lure in and around brush, standing timber, grass, logs, lily pads, and heavy vegetation.

For flipping, most bass fishermen prefer 7- to 8-foot casting rods with 25- to 30-pound-test line. Lure selections are usually sparse—jigs and plastic worms. The fisherman ties on a black, blue, or brown ½-ounce "living rubber" jig. He protects the large hook with a fiber guard, and tips it with an Uncle Josh Pork Frog. This is especially deadly in the cooler springtime waters.

Flipping allows you to keep the lure close to cover constantly, thus allowing the fish to bite with very little effort or movement. Start with about 8 to 9 feet of line from rod tip to lure. Then, strip off an arm's length of line. Using your wrist and not your shoulder or elbow, begin swinging the lure like a pendulum. Never let the lure come too far back. The swing should be smooth. When the lure reaches the back of its arc closest to you, a slight flick of the wrist (pretend you're only using the rod tip to do the work) will aim the lure toward the target. At this point, the line should be allowed to slide through your hand and the rod tip should be lowered to steer the lure to the desired spot.

A silent entry is essential. Never release the line until the lure reaches the water, because you want to control the lure. Once in the water, the jig or worm should fall freely to the bottom. Then, your task is to climb and wriggle the lure up and over every limb, root, and stem, carefully watching the line for the slightest nibble.

Flipping is simple yet deadly when fishing shorelines or heavy vegetation. Silent entry of your lure is essential.

SPINCASTING

Spincasting is a method of fishing that, in effect, combines a push-button type of spinning reel with a baitcasting rod. This tackle efficiently handles lures and baits of average weights from ¼ to ¾ ounce. With lighter or heavier lures, its efficiency falls off sharply. Spincasting is ideal for newcomers to fishing, for it is the easiest casting method to learn and is the ticket for lots of trouble-free sport.

The Reel

Spincasting reels, like spinning reels, operate on the fixed-spool principle—that is, the weight of the lure or bait being cast uncoils the line from the stationary spool. Most spincasting reels are of the closed-face type, the spool and gearing being enclosed in a cone-shaped hood.

The major factor distinguishing the spincasting reel from the spinning reel is that spincasting action is controlled by a thumb-activated "trigger," a push button mounted on the reel. In operation, the spincaster holds his thumb down on the trigger until the rod is about halfway through the forward-cast motion. He then releases thumb pressure on the trigger, which frees the line and feeds it through a small hole in the center of the cone, sending the lure on its way.

There are two kinds of spincasting reels, those mounted atop the rod and those mounted below it. Most

The Pflueger Cetina, a typical spincast reel, comes in five models with pre-spooled monofilament ranging from 6- to 10-pound test.

The grip for the spincasting reel is similar to the grip used for the baitcasting reel. The thumb depresses the control lever during the backcast, checking the line, and releases pressure as the rod whips forward.

spincasting reels are of the top-mounted type and are designed for rods having an offset reel seat. They can be mounted on straight-grip rods, but this combination is uncomfortable to use since the caster must reach up with his thumb to activate the reel trigger.

Below-the-rod spincasting reels are a much different design. They combine the balance of a spinning reel with the ease of a spincast reel. The line aperture in the cone is also larger than on a spincast reel. A lever activates the casting mechanism, much the same as on a push-button spincast reel.

Spincasting reels have various kinds of adjustable drag mechanisms. In one kind, the drag is set by rotating the cone that surrounds the spool. Other reels have star drags like those found on baitcasting reels. The drag in still other reels is activated by turning the reel handle.

Spincast reels are ideal for night fishing because of their trouble-free operation. However, besides the fact that they can handle a rather limited range of lure weights, if very light line is used on these reels, the line has a tendency to foul in the housing.

▉ The Rod

Spincasting rods are basically the same as those designed for baitcasting, but there are a few differences. In general, spincasting rods average a bit longer than baitcasting rods. (The most popular lengths are 6 and 6½ feet.) They have flexible tips that are more responsive, and guides that are usually of the larger, spinning-rod type.

Typical Spincasting Rod

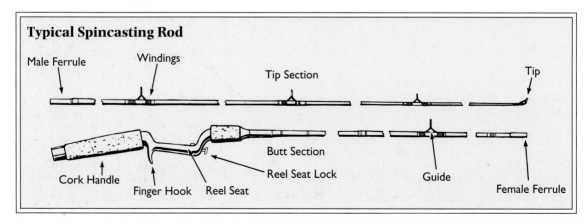

Male Ferrule   Windings   Tip Section   Tip

Cork Handle   Finger Hook   Reel Seat   Butt Section   Guide   Female Ferrule
                                          Reel Seat Lock

How to Match Up Spincasting Tackle

This chart is meant only as a general guide aimed at helping you put together, in proper balance, the basic elements of a spincasting outfit tailored for fish of a particular weight category. Specific conditions—and your ability and personal preferences—should also be considered.

Species of Fish	Reel	Rod Action, Length (feet)	Line (pound test)	Lure Weights (ounces)
Panfish, small trout and bass, pickerel	Light	Light, 6½ to 7	4 to 8	⅛ to ⅜
Trout, bass, pickerel, pike, landlocks, walleye	Medium	Medium, 6 to 7	6 to 12	⅜ to ⅝
Pike, lake trout, steelhead, muskie, salmon, striped bass, snook, bonefish	Medium-Heavy, with star drag	Medium-Heavy, 6 to 6½	10 to 15 ⅛	½ to ¾

CONVENTIONAL TACKLE FOR SALTWATER TROLLING AND CASTING

A host of saltwater game fish—from half-pound snapper bluefish to 40-pound yellowtails to bluefin tuna weighing nearly a ton—draws millions of fishermen to the briny each year. They stand in crashing surf and on jetties and piers, and they sail for deeper waters aboard boats of almost every description.

Because of the great differences in weights of saltwater fish, it is important for the fisherman to be armed with balanced tackle that is suited for the particular quarry he is after. Just as the freshwater muskie angler wouldn't use bluegill tackle, the person who is trolling for, say, blue marlin wouldn't use a jetty outfit designed for striped bass.

Balanced tackle—in which the rod, reel, line, and other items are all in reasonable proportion to one another—is important. A properly balanced outfit—for example, a 9-foot surf rod with a good casting reel and 15- to 25-pound-test line—is a joy to use. Conversely, if you substituted a 5-foot boat rod for the 9-footer in the above outfit and tried to cast, you would soon be turning the air blue. Besides the casting advantage, properly balanced gear makes hooking and playing a fish easier and more effective.

Let's take a detailed look at the various kinds of conventional saltwater gear and how to match up the component parts.

How to Match Up Saltwater Casting Tackle

This chart is meant only as a general guide aimed at helping you put together, in proper balance, the basic elements of a spincasting outfit tailored for fish of a particular weight category. Specific conditions—and your ability and personal preferences—should also be considered.

Species of Fish	Reel	Rod Type, Length (feet)	Line (pound test)	Lure Weights (ounces)
Small stripers, bluefish, weakfish, snook, bonefish, redfish, salmon, pompano, jacks	Light, with star drag	Popping, 6 to 7	8 to 15	½ to 1
Stripers, big bluefish, school tuna, albacore, bonito, salmon, dolphin, wahoo	Medium	Medium, 6½ to 8	12 to 30	¾ to 3
Channel bass, black drum, tarpon, dolphin, big kingfish, sharks	Heavy, with star drag	Heavy, 7 to 8½	15 to 40	1½ to 3
Surf species (bluefish, stripers, drum, channel bass, etc.)	Squidding (surf casting)	Surf, 7 to 10	15 to 45	1½ to 6

■ Trolling Reels

Trolling is a method of fishing in which a lure or bait is pulled along behind a moving boat. It is also a method in which the reel is of paramount importance.

At one time, saltwater trolling reels were designated by a simple but not completely reliable numbering system. This system employed a number followed by a diagonal (/) and then the letter O, which merely stood for "ocean." The numbers ran from 1 to 16, with each one representing the line capacity of the reel. The higher the number, the larger the reel's line capacity. It should be noted, however, that these numbers were not standardized—that is, one manufacturer's 4/O trolling reel may have had a smaller capacity than another maker's 4/O.

Trolling reels today are typically classified by line class and line capacity. For example, reels are classified as 12-pound test, 20-pound test, 50-pound test, 80-pound test, and so on. Weighing from 18 ounces up to nearly 10 pounds, these reels are designed primarily for handling the largest game fish (sailfish, marlin, bluefin tuna, and swordfish), but are also effective for bluefish, striped bass, channel bass, albacore, dolphins, and the like. Generally, 12- and 20-pound class is considered light tackle, 30- to 50-pound class is medium

weight, and 80- to 130-pound class is for the heaviest saltwater species.

These reels have no casting features (such as anti-backlash devices) since their sole function is trolling. Spools are smooth running, usually operating on ball bearings. The reels are ruggedly built and, of course, corrosion resistant. Unique features include lugs on the upper part of the sideplate for the attachment of a big-game fishing harness worn by the fisherman, a U-shaped clamp for a more secure union of rod and reel, and, in the largest reels, a lug-and-brace arrangement for extra rigidity.

By far the most important feature on a trolling reel is the drag. If a reel is to handle the sizzling runs and line-testing leaps of fish weighing hundreds of pounds, its drag must operate smoothly at all times. And the drag must not overheat or it may bind, causing the line to break.

Inexpensive reels of this type have the star type of drag consisting of a series of alternating metal and composition (or leather) washers. In some trolling reels, the drag is an asbestos composition disc that applies pressure directly to the reel spool.

Some expensive trolling reels have not one but two drag controls. One is a knob-operated device that lets you preset drag tension to a point below the breaking strength of the line being used. The other is a lever, mounted on the sideplate, that has a number of positions and permits a wide range of drag settings, from very light up to the safe maximum for the line in use. This lever, when backed off all the way, throws the reel into a free spool.

Trolling-reel spools are made of metal, usually either machined bronze or anodized aluminum, and range in width from 1⅝ inches to 5 inches (for the 80- to 180-pound-test outfits).

Some trolling reels are designed especially for wire and lead-core lines. They have narrow but deep spools and extrastrong gearing.

Other features of trolling reels include a free-spool lever mounted on the sideplate, a line-counting feature, a single oversize handle grip, and high-speed gear ratios ranging to as much as 40 inches of line retrieved for every single turn of the handle.

■ Trolling Rods

Big-game trolling rods have the strength and fittings to withstand the power runs and magnificent leaps of such heavyweights as marlin, sailfish, and giant tuna. The

---

Saltwater Reel Parts

The Daiwa Seagate is a typical saltwater conventional reel for general offshore fishing. Various models of the Seagate weigh from 14 to 21 ounces. The heaviest model will hold 630 yards of 50-pound-test braid line and 310 yards of 40-pound-test monofilament. For unlimited big-game fishing, reels get bigger and stronger to withstand powerful runs. They also cost more.

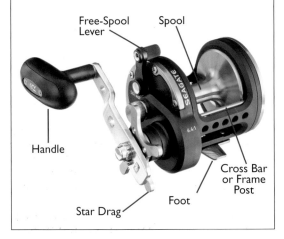

Free-Spool Lever

Spool

Handle

Cross Bar or Frame Post

Star Drag

Foot

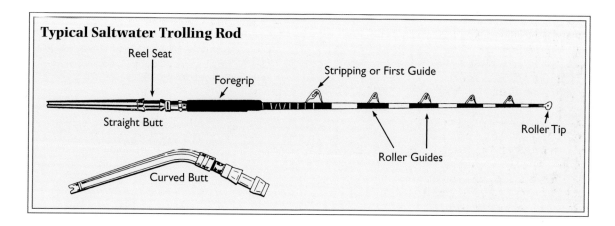

Typical Saltwater Trolling Rod

Reel Seat

Foregrip

Stripping or First Guide

Straight Butt

Roller Tip

Roller Guides

Curved Butt

great majority of these rods are of fiberglass and graphite composite construction.

Almost all blue-water rods have a butt section and a tip section—that is, they seldom have ferrules fitted midway along the working length of the rod. In most rods, the tip section is about 5 feet long, while butt lengths vary from 14 to 27 inches, depending on the weight of the tip. Tip sections are usually designated by weight, ranging from about 3 ounces to as heavy as 40 ounces, depending on the line that is being used and the fish that is being sought.

Trolling rods are rated according to the line-strength classes of the International Game Fish Association. The 11 IGFA classes are: 2-pound-, 4-pound-, 6-pound-, 8-pound-, 12-pound-, 16-pound-, 20-pound-, 30-pound-, 50-pound-, 80-pound-, 130-pound-, and 180-pound-test line. No rod used in catching a fish submitted for an IGFA record can have a tip length of less than 40 inches and the rod butt cannot exceed 27 inches in length. These measurements do not apply to surfcasting rods.

The fittings on trolling rods include strong, high-quality guides. The first guide above the reel (called the stripping guide) and the tip guide are of the roller type (either single-roller or double-roller). The middle guides, usually numbering four or five, are of the ring type and are made either of heavily chromed stainless steel or of tungsten carbide (carboloy), which is the most durable material. In some rods, all of the guides are rollers. Most roller guides have self-lubricating bearings that can be disassembled for cleaning.

Other features of trolling rods include extrastrong, locking reel seats, and gimbal fittings in the end of the butt that enable the rod to be fitted into a socket on a

boat's fighting chair or into a belt harness worn by the fisherman.

Casting and Boat Reels

Conventional (revolving-spool) reels in this category are widely used by saltwater fishermen who cast lures and baits from piers, bridges, jetties, and in the surf, and by sinker-bouncers (bottom fishermen) in boats. Actually an outgrowth and refinement of freshwater baitcasting reels, these reels fill the gap between those freshwater models and big-game trolling reels.

Many surf and jetty casters, especially those who are after big fish, prefer a conventional reel (and rod) over a spinning outfit because the conventional rig is better able to handle heavy lures and sinkers. And a vast majority of experienced bottom fishermen lean toward the revolving-spool reel.

Conventional reels designed for casting, often called squidding reels, have wide, light spools (a heavy spool makes casting difficult) of either metal or plastic (metal is preferred for most uses), and gear ratios ranging from 2:1 to 6:1. Weights range from about 12 to 22 ounces. In most models, the drag is of the star type and there is a free-spool lever mounted on the sideplate. Some of these reels have level-wind mechanisms.

Depending on the model, line capacities can range from about 250 yards of 12-pound-test monofilament to 350 yards of 30-pound-test mono. Line capacity can also be dramatically increased with braided line. For most surf, jetty, and pier situations, 250 yards of line is sufficient.

Most of these reels have a mechanical brake, magnets, or a device to help prevent the spool from overrun-

Saltwater Casting and Boat Reels

◀ The Shimano Tiagra is a two-speed reel with a ratcheting drag lever. It is machined from 7-millimeter aluminum pipe stock for maximum strength. The Tiagra reels are built for the biggest saltwater fish. The smallest model weighs 38 ounces. The biggest Tiagra weighs 115 ounces and can hold 950 yards of 80-pound test.

▼ The PENN International VSX is a series of blue-water reels for big fish. Five models are available and will handle a range of lines from 300 yards of 4-pound-test mono-filament to 650 yards of 150-pound-test braid. Like most big-game reels, the Internationals have lever drag systems.

▶ The Ocean Master is a saltwater casting reel for both inshore and light offshore fishing. The six-disc drag handles up to 15 pounds of drag pressure. It weighs 10½ ounces and will hold 175 yards of 14-pound-test monofilament. Reels of this size are ideal for fishing from piers and jetties, as well as for surf and bottom fishing from boats.

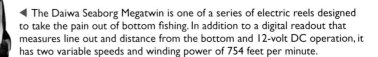

◀ The Daiwa Seaborg Megatwin is one of a series of electric reels designed to take the pain out of bottom fishing. In addition to a digital readout that measures line out and distance from the bottom and 12-volt DC operation, it has two variable speeds and winding power of 754 feet per minute.

ning during a cast and causing a backlash. In all models, however, as in freshwater baitcasting reels, thumb pressure against the spool is required to control the cast.

Conventional reels designed for deep-sea bottom fishing are quite similar to the casting models, but they are sometimes heavier and have deeper spools. They may also have larger capacities and take heavier lines.

■ Casting and Boat Rods

In choosing a conventional casting rod, more so than with a boat (bottom-fishing) rod, the type of fishing to be done and the fish being sought are critical factors. For casting in the surf, for example, the rod must be long enough so that the fisherman can make lengthy casts and hold the line above the breakers. A rod for jetty use, on the other hand, need not be so long. And if you'll be fishing mainly from piers and bridges, you'll need a rod with enough backbone to lift heavy fish from the water and up over the rail.

However, a beginning fisherman can get a casting rod that will handle most of the situations he'll be facing. A good choice would be one that is 8 to 9 feet in overall length and has a rather stiff tip. The stiff tip of a conventional rod lets the angler use a wide range of lure weights and enables him to have more control over big fish.

Conventional casting rods are available in lengths from 8 to 12 feet and even longer. Developments in graphite show that rods of this material can carry an exceptionally wide range of lure weights. In tests, weights of 18 ounces were cast with graphite rods. A majority of these rods are of two-piece construction, breaking either at the upper part of the butt or about midway up the working length of the rod.

These rods are distinguished by the number and arrangement of their guides. In most models, there are only three or four guides, including the tip guide, and all are located in the upper half of the tip section. Why this arrangement? Since these rods are stiffer than most others, fewer guides are required to distribute the strain along the length of the rod. The guides are bunched near the tip because that's where most of the bend occurs when a fish is being played.

Boat, or bottom-fishing, rods, as their name implies, are designed for noncasting use aboard boats—party

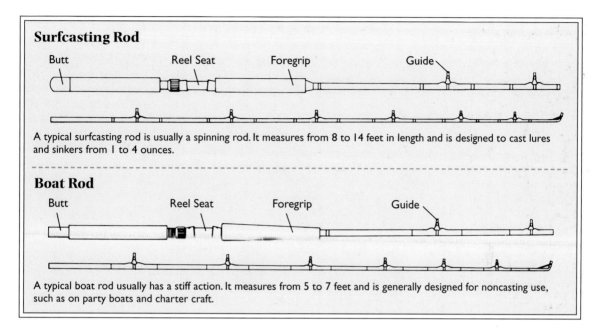

Surfcasting Rod

Butt   Reel Seat   Foregrip   Guide

A typical surfcasting rod is usually a spinning rod. It measures from 8 to 14 feet in length and is designed to cast lures and sinkers from 1 to 4 ounces.

Boat Rod

Butt   Reel Seat   Foregrip   Guide

A typical boat rod usually has a stiff action. It measures from 5 to 7 feet and is generally designed for noncasting use, such as on party boats and charter craft.

boats, charter craft, and private boats. They are also used on piers and bridges in situations in which a lure or bait is simply dropped down to the water.

Boat rods are considerably shorter than casting rods, running from about 5 to 7 feet in overall length, with a good average length being about 6 feet. Their shortness makes them highly maneuverable, a factor of more than a little importance aboard a crowded party boat, and makes it easier to handle, say, a 30-pound cod while trying to remain upright on a pitching deck.

As with most other modern rods, boat rods are mostly made of fiberglass or graphite. Most are one-piece or two-piece construction with a tip section and detachable butt. The number of guides on a boat rod depends on the length, but there are seldom more than six or eight. Some of these rods designed for large fish have a roller tip. Other boat-rod features are similar to those of casting rods.

Who Was Responsible for the First Circle Hook?

Circle hooks have been around since the turn of the century, but commercial longline fishermen brought them into worldwide use. It's ironic that the circle hook, developed for longline fishing because of its deadly hooking ability, would also become one of the most effective catch-and-release devices to come along in decades. Because of its unique design, fish will be hooked in the corner of the mouth, making release easy and without harm to the fish. What makes this hook so effective is the fact that fish will hook themselves, an important factor for longliners who leave their baited gear unattended. For recreational fishermen, it's important to remember not to try to set the hook when a fish takes the bait. Leaving your rod in a rod holder on a boat (dead sticking) is sometimes the best technique with circle hooks. Let the fish run and it will hook itself in the corner of the mouth. Circle hooks have proven effective for all species, including billfish.

How to Surf Cast

▼ **Fit of Rod and Reel** • This photo shows how the butt of a surf rod should just reach your armpit when held with your hand at the reel spool. A shorter butt section will lack the leverage to handle a long rod, while too long a butt adds needless weight. Proper butt length allows for comfortable and powerful two-handed casts.

▼ **The Casting Motion** • With feet set in a wide stance for balance, pull the rod butt powerfully with your left hand and push the grip behind the reel with your right hand, driving the rod tip forward. With both spinning tackle and conventional revolving-spool reels, the line is released when your rod is about 45 degrees in front of you.

▶ **"Fishing" the Cast** • When your lure or bait hits the water, the reel is engaged and you can begin your retrieve. If your lure comes in close to you without being hit by a fish, the rod is gradually angled to the right. This is to allow rod spring and a safe striking position if a fish hits in the final feet of a retrieve. The danger in striking at fish close in with the rod in front of you is that the lure may jerk loose and sail straight back into your face. The typical surf lure is heavy enough to do considerable damage with its sharp hooks. With your rod held to one side, a missed strike with a short line will only send the lure flying harmlessly back on the beach behind you.

▼ **Starting the Cast** • Start your cast from the stance shown. Your lure and bait should be dangling just above the sand as the rod is held parallel to the beach. If you are using a spinning reel, your index finger is extended to hold the line running between the spool and guides. When the rod snaps forward, the line is allowed to slip off your finger as the lure drives out over the water.

    With a conventional revolving-spool reel, your thumb should be on the spool with firm pressure at the start of the cast to hold the spool during the casting motion. As the rod is powered forward, the thumb is lifted to let the weight of the lure or sinker take out line. Very light thumbing of the spool as the line goes out will prevent backlashes.

HOW TO SET DRAG

Drag is what keeps a fish from breaking your line. That sounds simple, but fishermen sometimes lose big fish because they do not know or understand a few basic facts about the drag on their reel. Many anglers, for example, tighten their drag when a big fish makes a long run and strips off a lot of line. This is wrong. The drag should actually be lightened, because a lot of line in the water as well as a smaller spool diameter will increase the drag. Often the result is a lost trophy.

Drag is the resistance of a reel against the fighting pull of a fish, and it is set at a strain the line can endure without breaking. The drag mechanism usually consists of a series of metal (stainless steel, aluminum, or chromed brass) and composition (leather, cork, plastic, or fiber) washers. The washers are stacked, alternating metal and composition, and the friction between the surface areas of the washers creates "drag."

When an angler tightens the drag on his reel, he compresses these washers, creates more friction, and increases drag. Conversely, when he backs off the drag, he lessens friction and decreases drag.

If the size of a fish was the only factor in setting drag, the job would be easy. But there are other considerations, such as the friction of the line against the rod guides, resistance of the line being pulled through the water, and the amount of line remaining on the reel spool after a long run.

In addition, not all drags are created equal. They should be smooth, but many are sticky and jerky. In fact, it often takes as much as double the force of the drag setting to get the drag moving. For example, a drag set at 5 pounds may actually take up to 10 pounds of pull before the drag starts moving. It's obvious, therefore, that if you're using 8-pound-test line you should set your drag at about 2 pounds to allow for "starting your drag."

The amount of line on your spool is another factor. When the outside diameter of line on your spool is reduced by half, the drag tension is doubled. For example, if your drag is set at 2 pounds with a full spool, it will be increased to 4 pounds when a fish makes a long run and strips off half your line.

Long, fast runs will also generate friction and heat between the drag washers. This will frequently tighten a drag and add even more tension.

It's also important to remember that a rod held at about 45 degrees will add about 10 percent to the drag you get with the rod pointed directly at the fish. This

Minimum and Maximum Range of Drag		
Line	Minimum Drag (pounds)	Maximum Drag (pounds)
6-pound test	1½	4
8-pound test	2	5
10-pound test	3	6
12-pound test	4	8
20-pound test	6	12
30-pound test	8	15
50-pound test	12	25
80-pound test	20	40
130-pound test	30	50

increased drag is due to friction between your line and the rod guides. If the rod is held at about 90 degrees, drag will increase to about 35 percent of the initial setting.

This is why it is important to lighten the drag and, when possible, point the rod at the fish when it is about to be netted or gaffed. If you hold your rod high and keep a tight drag, a sudden lunge by a fish could break your line. But if you point the rod tip at the fish, the line will run off the spool more easily, even with the same drag setting.

This technique of lowering the rod is also used when handling thrashing or jumping fish, such as tarpon and marlin. Lowering the rod will lighten drag tension and "cushion" the line from the shock of a jumping fish. This is called "bowing." It's part of the technique that makes it possible to land 100-pound tarpon on 10-pound-test line.

Taking all the above factors into consideration, how does an angler set his drag so that he can feel reasonably secure when he hooks a trophy fish? The first step is to determine the minimum and maximum range of drag for the various pound-test lines (see accompanying chart). By minimum drag, I mean "starting drag," the amount of pull needed to get the drag moving. If the minimum drag seems light for the pound-test line, remember that there will be other factors increasing your drag beyond this setting, such as rod angle, spool diameter, and the amount of line in the water. Maximum drag means the heaviest setting you should use while fighting a fish. Never go beyond the maximum for your line class.

Let's take 12-pound-test line and see what factors come into play. Minimum drag is set at 4 pounds, but 8 pounds of pull will likely be required to get that drag started. If the angler holds his rod at 45 degrees or higher, he can add another 10 percent, which brings the drag to 9 pounds. To this figure you also have to add water resistance or line drag, which varies according to the amount of line in the water, line diameter, and the speed of the fish. With 12-pound-test line and a fast fish, it can amount to as much as 2 pounds, which brings the total up to 11 pounds of drag on 12-pound-test line. With only 1 pound of drag to spare, a big fish would likely break the line. It's obvious that you're far better off with a very light drag setting.

The first step is to set your drag at the minimum setting. This is easily done at dockside with a reliable fish scale and the help of a friend. Run your line through the guides and tie it to the scale. Ask your friend to hold the scale and back off about 30 feet. Tighten your drag and begin to apply pressure as you would when fighting a fish. Now, adjust the drag so that it comes into play when the scale reads the correct minimum drag weight. For example, if you're using 12-pound-test line, the drag should begin to slip when you apply enough pressure to pull the scale indicator to the 4-pound mark.

Now, with your drag set at 4 pounds, slowly tighten your drag until it comes into play at 8 pounds, which is the maximum setting. Note how many turns of the star drag or spool cap are required to bring your drag to the maximum setting. Play with the drag, setting it back and forth from 4 to 8 pounds. Do this several times and get the feel of the resistance and pressure you're putting on the line. With enough practice, you'll be able to safely lighten and tighten the drag while fighting a fish.

An easier technique is to leave your drag set at the minimum setting and use your hand or fingers to apply more drag. This is a method many anglers use and it works well. You can practice with your buddy and the scale. With drag at the minimum setting, cup your hand around the spool (assuming you're using an open-face spinning reel), grip it so that the drag does not slip, and apply just enough pressure to pull the scale indicator to the maximum figure. Practice this technique and you'll soon be able to bear down on a fish and gain line without even touching the drag knob.

As mentioned above, you can also cup your hand around the spool of an open-face spinning reel to apply more drag. With conventional reels, use your thumb against the spool and hold the lines against the rod. Make sure you lift your finger when a big fish begins to run, or else you'll get a bad line burn.

Learn to combine this hand technique with "pumping" and you will be able to land big fish on light lines. Pumping a big fish in is not difficult. Let's assume you're

Left: Setting drag on your reel is easy with the help of a friend. The angler puts pressure on a 30-pound-test outfit while his friend checks the indicator on a fish scale. For 30-pound-test line, the drag should be set at a minimum of 8 pounds and a maximum of 15 pounds. **Right:** Any fishing scale can be used to set drag as well as weigh fish. The indicator and numbers should be large enough to read without getting close.

using an open-face spinning reel with a light drag. Put your hand around the spool, apply pressure, and ease your rod back into a vertical position. Now, drop the rod tip and quickly reel in the slack. Repeat the process and you'll eventually have your fish at boatside. Always be ready, however, to lower the rod tip and release hand pressure from the spool when you think the fish is about to make a run. When it stops, you begin to pump once again.

One last point: At the end of the day, back off the drag and release all pressure on the washers, or they will lose their physical characteristics and take a set. If this happens, the drag will become jerky and unpredictable. If the washers do take a set, replacing them is the only solution.

ICE FISHING

Ice fishing differs greatly from open-water fishing, and it is a demanding sport. It requires an understanding of and an ability to cope with winter weather, knowledge of the cold-weather habits of the fish, and the use of an unusual assortment of gear, most of it unique to ice fishing.

There are two basic ice-fishing methods: tip-up fishing and jigging. In general, tip-ups are usually used on larger fish—pike, pickerel, walleyes, trout, and such—that prefer bait and require the angler to play the waiting game. Jigging is usually preferred for smaller fish that tend to school up—bluegills, perch, crappies, and the like. But these are merely generalizations, not hard-and-fast rules. For example, jigging (sometimes called chugging) is often quite productive on big lake trout and salmon in the Great Lakes.

◾ Tip-Ups

Also called tilts, these come in various styles, but they all perform two basic functions: they hold a baited line leading from a revolving-type reel spool, and they signal the bite of a fish. The most common type of tip-up consists of three strips of wood, each about 18 inches long. Two are cross pieces that form an X as they span the hole. The third piece is an upright; at its bottom end is attached a simple line-holding spool, while the upper end holds the signaling device. The signal is usually a piece of very flexible spring steel with a red (some anglers prefer black) flag on the end. After the hook is baited and lowered to the desired depth, the steel arm is "cocked"—bent over and down and hooked onto a "trigger." When a fish strikes, an arm on the revolving spool releases the steel arm and it flies erect.

In this type of tip-up, the reel is positioned underwater. In other variations, the reel is positioned above

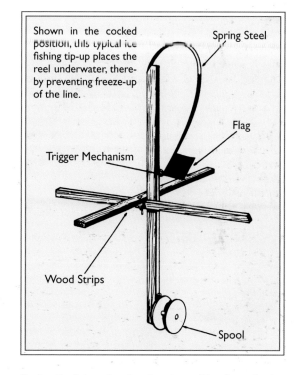

Shown in the cocked position, this typical ice fishing tip-up places the reel underwater, thereby preventing freeze-up of the line.

Spring Steel

Flag

Trigger Mechanism

Wood Strips

Spool

the ice. Each type has its advantages. The above-the-ice reel can be more sensitively adjusted for light-biting fish, but the line tends to freeze on the reel once it gets wet. The underwater reel largely eliminates the problem of freezing, but the fisherman must remove the tip-up from the hole before he can grab the line.

Baits for tip-up fishing are usually live. In general, it pays to match the size of the bait to the size of the fish you're after. Baits range from tiny maggots (often called mousies) and grubs for panfish, to worms and small minnows for walleyes, and up to 6-inch baitfish for pike.

Jigging Rods

There are two types of ice-fishing jigging rods. The top rod uses two wire hooks on a handle to hold the line. The bottom rod uses an inexpensive reel on a short, baitcasting type of rod.

■ Jigging Rods

As done by ice fishermen, jigging is simply a method of imparting an up-and-down movement to a lure or bait. Jigging can be—and is—done with any sort of line-holding rod or stick.

Some jigging rods—more appropriately called sticks—are simply pieces of wood 18 inches or so long, with U-shaped notches in each end. The line—10-pound-test monofilament is very popular—is wound lengthwise onto the stick around the U-shaped notches and is paid out as needed. There are other types of jigging sticks of varying designs, and many ice anglers use standard spinning or spincast rods or the butt half of a fly rod.

Rods made specially for ice jigging are simple affairs consisting of a fiberglass tip section that is 2 or 3 feet long seated in a short butt. The butt may have a simple revolving-spool reel or merely a pair of heavy-wire pro-jections around which the line is wound. The tip section may have two to four guides, including the tip guide. The shortness of such a rod lets the user fish up close to the hole and have better control over the lure or bait at the end of his line.

■ Jigging Lures and Baits

There are many and varied jigging lures and baits, but flashiness is built into most of them. Others produce best when "sweetened" with bait. Two popular jigging lures are: an ungainly looking critter with a heavy body shaped and painted to resemble a baitfish, a hook at each end and a treble hook in the middle of its underside, and a line-tie ring in the middle of its upper surface; and a long, slim, three- or four-sided, silvery model with a treble hook at one end and a line-tie ring at the other.

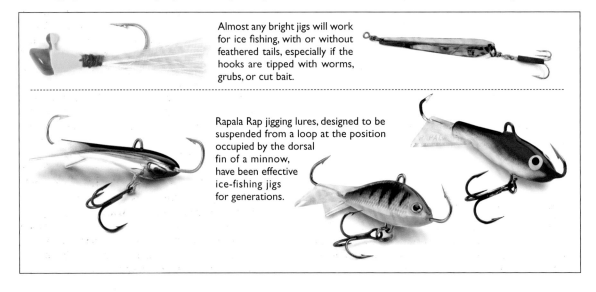

Almost any bright jigs will work for ice fishing, with or without feathered tails, especially if the hooks are tipped with worms, grubs, or cut bait.

Rapala Rap jigging lures, designed to be suspended from a loop at the position occupied by the dorsal fin of a minnow, have been effective ice-fishing jigs for generations.

Ice-Fishing Accessories

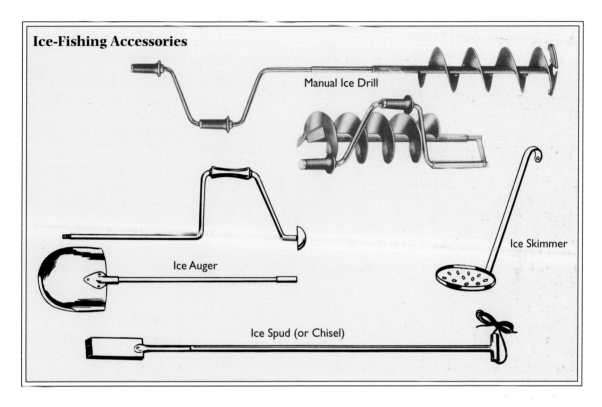

Manual Ice Drill

Ice Skimmer

Ice Auger

Ice Spud (or Chisel)

Jigging methods vary with the fisherman and with the fish being sought. However, a productive way to fish many jigging lures, especially flashier types, is to twitch the lure slightly and then jerk it suddenly upward with a quick upward movement of the arm. The proper interval between jerks is learned with experience.

Popular jigging baits include a single perch eye (either impaled on a small hook or used to sweeten a tiny hair or rubber-bodied ice fly), worms, grubs, maggots, insect larvae, minnows, and cut bait (pieces of skin or flesh that are cut from the tail or body of such fish as smelt and perch).

Jiggers tend to move around more than tip-up fishermen, boring holes in different areas until they find a productive spot.

■ Other Equipment

Like most other forms of fishing, ice angling requires some auxiliary equipment. Most ice anglers prefer to keep such gear to a minimum, for they have to haul it with them wherever they go on the ice.

If you're going to fish through holes in the ice, you need something to make those holes. The ice auger is a popular tool for this job. Augers come in different designs. One has a long handle with a U-shaped bend at the top, and a rounded cutting blade at the bottom. The handle is turned much like that of a manual drill, and the blade cuts a round hole through the ice. Another type looks like a giant ice drill with sharp, widely spaced threads. It is used in the same way. Gasoline-powered ice drills are also available.

Then there's the ice spud or chisel. This is a heavy metal handle with a large, chisel-type blade at the bottom. The spud's weight helps the angler punch down through the ice, but the user must shape the hole once he has broken through.

An indispensable item of accessory gear is the ice skimmer, a ladle-type device that is used to keep the hole clear of ice chips and chunks and to skim ice.

Many ice anglers like to use an attached spring clip. It is attached to the fishing line and used to determine the water depth—an important factor because in winter most game fish are found on or near the bottom. A heavy sinker will serve the same purpose.

■ Ice Safety

Winter is the time of year when ice fishermen venture out onto frozen waters. Most will have fun, but a few will get into trouble because they don't know how to make sure that the ice is safe. The first rule is never take chances. There are two periods when accidents are likely to happen: early in the season when slush ice doesn't freeze uniformly and late in the season when ice melts at an uneven rate. It takes prolonged periods of freezing to make ice safe. Here are some rules to remember:

- Be cautious of heavy snowfalls while ice is forming. Snow acts as an insulator. The result is a layer of slush and snow on top of treacherous ice.

- Clear, solid river ice is 15 percent weaker than clear lake ice.

- River ice is thinner midstream than near the banks.

- River mouths are dangerous because currents create pockets of unsafe ice.

Ice Safety Guidelines

These guidelines—courtesy of the Minnesota Department of Natural Resources—are for new, clear, solid ice only. White ice or "snow ice" is only about half as strong as new, clear ice. When traveling on white ice, double the thickness guidelines below.

Ice Thickness	Maximum Safe Load
2 inches or less	Stay off the ice!
4 inches	Ice fishing or other activities on foot
5 inches	Snowmobile or ATV
8 to 12 inches	Car or small pickup truck
12 to 15 inches	Medium truck

- When walking with friends, stay 10 yards apart.

- Lakes that have a lot of springs will have weak spots of ice.

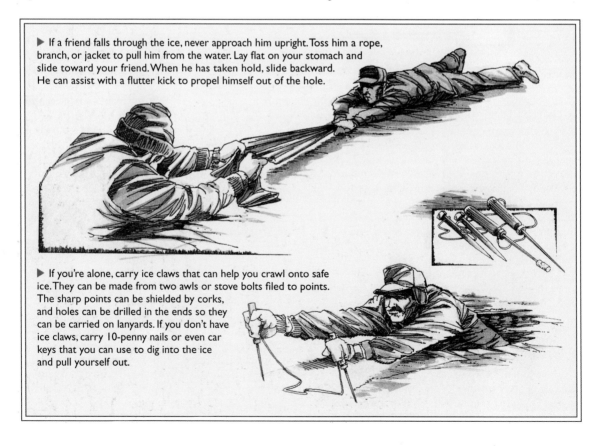

▶ If a friend falls through the ice, never approach him upright. Toss him a rope, branch, or jacket to pull him from the water. Lay flat on your stomach and slide toward your friend. When he has taken hold, slide backward. He can assist with a flutter kick to propel himself out of the hole.

▶ If you're alone, carry ice claws that can help you crawl onto safe ice. They can be made from two awls or stove bolts filed to points. The sharp points can be shielded by corks, and holes can be drilled in the ends so they can be carried on lanyards. If you don't have ice claws, carry 10-penny nails or even car keys that you can use to dig into the ice and pull yourself out.

LINES

No fisherman is stronger than the line that connects him and his quarry. Fishing lines are made of a wide variety of natural and synthetic materials and, as a result, differ widely in their characteristics and the uses to which they can be put. No two types of lines, for example, have the same degree of elasticity, abrasion resistance, water absorption, weight, and diameter.

Let's take a look at the physical characteristics of the various types of lines and the uses for which they are best suited.

MONOFILAMENT (SINGLE-STRAND NYLON): By far the most widely used fishing line today, monofilament is suitable for everything from blue-water trolling to surf-casting to freshwater spinning, and it is the universal material for leaders in both fresh water and salt because of its near-invisibility in water. It is extremely strong and light for its diameter, and it absorbs very little water (3 to 12 percent of its own weight). About the only drawback of monofilament is its relatively high rate of stretch (15 to 30 percent when dry, 20 to 35 percent when wet). For that reason, it is not the best choice for such uses as deep-water bottom fishing, during which large fish must be reeled up from considerable depths.

FLUOROCARBON: Fluorocarbon looks like monofilament, but it has different features. First, it's stiffer than monofilament and makes a better leader material. It also does not absorb water and is more resistant to oils, sun-

Fishing Line Troubleshooting

This chart was designed to help you quickly find and correct line troubles when you can least afford to have them—on the water. Copy this page and keep this handy chart in your tackle box.

Symptoms	Possible Causes	Recommended Cures
Unexplained line breaks under low-stress loads.	a. Nicks or abrasions. If the surface is smooth and shiny, failure may be line fatigue.	a. Strip off worn line or re-tie line more frequently.
	b. If surface is dull, faded, and fuzzy, failure is due to sunlight or excessive wear.	b. Replace line.
	c. Wear or stress points on guides or reel.	c. Replace worn guides.
Line is unusually sticky and stretchy.	Line stored in area of high heat or damaged by chemicals.	Replace line and change storage areas.
Line has kinks and flat spots.	a. Line spooled under excessive tension.	a. Use lower spooling tension. Make one final cast and rewind under low tension.
	b. Line stored on reel too long without use.	b. Strip out and soak last 50 yards in water.
Excessive curls and backlashes.	Using mono that is too heavy for reel spool diameter.	Use a more flexible mono or one with a lower pound test or smaller diameter.
Mono is stiff and brittle, and has a dry, powdery surface.	Improper storage in either wet or too warm conditions.	Replace line and change storage area.
Line looks good, but is losing too many fish.	Faulty or improperly set reel drag. Using too light a breaking strength for conditions.	Check reel drag. Lubricate or replace washers. Refill with line of higher breaking strength.
Reel casts poorly.	Not enough line on spool or line is too heavy for reel.	Fill spool with additional line. Use lighter, more limp monofilament.
Line is hard to see.	a. Line has faded due to excessive exposure to sunlight.	a. Replace line.
	b. Using wrong color line.	b. Switch to high-visibility line.

screen, and other substances that may deteriorate mono-filament. Fluorocarbon is actually a product of fluorine, carbon, and hydrogen. It's also tougher, sinks faster, and is more resistant to abrasion than monofilament.

DACRON: A DuPont trademark for a synthetic fiber that is made into a braided line, Dacron is nearly as strong as monofilament but does not stretch so much (about 10 percent). It has virtually the same characteristics whether wet or dry. Its visibility in water is greater than that of monofilament. Dacron's widest use is as trolling line.

LINEN: This is a braided line made from natural fibers and rated according to the number of threads, with each thread having a breaking strength of 3 pounds (six-thread linen has a breaking strength of 18 pounds, 15-thread linen has a breaking strength of 45 pounds, and so on). This material absorbs considerable amounts of water and is stronger when wet. Linen line is subject to deterioration and is heavy and bulky. Very little linen fishing line is made or used today.

CUTTYHUNK: This is a braided linen line originally cre-ated in the 1860s for the Cuttyhunk Fishing Club on Cuttyhunk Island, Massachusetts. The word Cuttyhunk is often used to denote any linen line.

SILK: Before World War II, fly-fishing lines were made of silk and had an oily coating to make them water resis-tant. Modern materials have made the silk line obsolete, and very few are in use today.

LEAD-CORE: This type of line is made by sheathing a flexible lead core in a tightly braided nylon sleeve. It's suitable for deep trolling in both fresh and salt water, and is especially useful for quickly getting a bait or lure down deep without bulky, heavy sinkers or planers. It's color-coded in 10-yard segments for precise depth control.

WIRE: These lines, too, are designed for deep trolling in both fresh and salt water. They're made of stainless steel, Monel (nickel alloy), bronze, or copper. Wire is popular for downrigger fishing, but because it's heavy enough to sink on its own, it's also used without downriggers and in many cases eliminates the need for a cumber-some drail weight or planer. Since it has no stretch, the angler can jig the rod and give movement to a bait or lure. However, wire is somewhat tricky until a fisherman gets used to it. Kinks can develop, causing weak spots or possibly cutting an unwary angler's hand. Wire line is generally available in a wider range of test weights than lead-core line. Wire leaders, usually sleeved in plastic, are widely used to prevent line cutting when fishing for such toothy battlers as pike, muskellunge, and many saltwater species.

Braided Fishing Lines

Braided fishing line has a small diameter, minimum stretch, and a good knot strength. The new, high-tech synthetic braided lines get a high score on all counts. There are more than a dozen manufacturers of these new space-age braided lines, and they all claim their lines are three times as strong as monofilament lines of the same diameter. This means, of course, that you can get three times as much line on your reel, which is one of the biggest advantages of braided line. You no longer need big reels to make sure you have enough line, an important consideration for saltwater fisher-men. The smaller diameter also means easier casting with lighter lures.

Braided lines have a stretch factor of less than 5 percent and some manufacturers even claim zero stretch. Monofilament has a stretch factor of about 25 percent, depending on the manufacturer. Minimal stretch is a big deal in fishing. It means sensitivity and fast hook-ups.

Braided lines have a lot going for them, including the sensitivity to transmit the slightest nibble. Braided lines are also sharp and hard. But they do present some problems. Nearly all braided lines float and easily get tan-gled in rigs and lures. In fact, many party or head boats prohibit braided lines because of tangles and the danger of cut fingers from these small-diameter, tough lines. If a caster gets a serious backlash and braided line digs into the spool, it may be nearly impossible to free the line.

Fly Lines

Ever since the time of Izaak Walton, anglers have been using special lines designed to present insect imitations to trout, salmon, and other fish. The earliest fly lines were made of braided horsehair. Then came oiled silk lines, which were standard until the late 1940s.

Today's fly lines are basically a synthetic coating over a braided core. They are made in various shapes and weights. Some are constructed so that they float (primar-ily for dry-fly fishing), and others are made to sink (for streamer and nymph fishing). Another development is

Choosing the Correct Fly Line

Rod Length	Proper Line
7½	DT4F or WF4F to WF6F
8	DT5F or WF5F to WF8F
8½	DT6F or WF6F to WF9F
9 and 9½	DT8F or WF8F to WF12F

Type of Water	Suitable Line Weights
Very small streams	4 to 5
Small and medium streams	5 to 8
Large streams	7 to 11
Lakes (light outfits)	5 to 7
Lakes (heavy outfits)	8 to 11
Salt water	9 to 15

is too heavy for the rod causes sloppy casts, poor presentation of the fly, and lack of accuracy, and it makes it difficult to manipulate the fly once it is on the water. An angler who uses a line that's too light for his rod must flail the rod back and forth during repeated backcasts in order to get out enough line to make his cast, and even then his forward cast might not "turn over" and the line may fall onto the water in a jumbled mass of coils.

Before 1961, fly lines were identified by a system of letters—A to I—with each letter representing a line diameter. For example, an A line measured .060 inch in diameter, and an I line measured .020 inch. But when modern fly lines replaced silk after World War II, weight, rather than diameter, became the critical factor in matching a fly line with a rod. So, in 1961, manufacturers adopted a universally accepted fly-line identification code. Its three elements give a complete description of a fly line.

The first part of the code describes the line type: L means level, DT means double taper, and WF means weight forward. The second element, a number, denotes the weight of the line's first 30 feet. The third element tells whether the line is floating (F), sinking (S), or floating-sinking (F/S). Therefore, a DT6F, for example, is a double-taper, weight-6 floating line.

Many fly-rod manufacturers today are eliminating the angler's problem of proper line choice by imprinting on the rod itself, usually just above the butt, the proper line size for that particular rod. However, there are other general ways to pick the right fly line. The general recommendations in the accompanying chart may help.

the floating-sinking, or intermediate, line, the first 10 to 30 feet of which sinks while the rest of it floats. Several manufacturers offer fly lines designed with special tapers for various conditions and species. Tarpon, bonefish, and billfish anglers now have access to fly lines that make casting to these species easier.

It is impossible to overemphasize the importance to the fly fisherman of balanced tackle, and the most vital element in a fly-fishing outfit is the line. It must "fit" the rod if casting is to be accurate and efficient. A line that

When making a cast with a fly rod, it's important to remember not to aim directly at the point where you want the fly to land. Aim a few feet above that point, so the fly will stop above the target and fall gently to the surface.

TAPER DESIGN: THE KEY TO CASTING PERFORMANCE

The fly line's shape, otherwise known as taper, determines how energy is transmitted and dissipated during the casting motion. By varying the lengths and diameters of the various parts of the line, specific performance attributes can be accentuated.

Parts of the Taper

Tip: This is the short (usually 6-inch) level front-end section of line primarily intended to protect the front taper. When changing leaders, a small part of the fly line is cut off. The level tip allows changes to be made without shortening the front taper and thus altering the way the line casts.

Front Taper: In conjunction with the diameter of the line's tip, the length of a line's front taper determines how powerfully or delicately a fly is delivered. Longer tapers dissipate more casting energy, enabling a more delicate presentation, while shorter tapers provide a much more powerful delivery.

Belly: The belly, the line section with the greatest diameter and length, carries most of the casting energy.

Rear Taper: This section decreases in diameter from the belly to the much thinner running section of the line in a weight-forward line. It is this transition that is the key to casting smoothness. Lines with short rear tapers cast quickly, but casting smoothness and control are sacrificed. Longer tapered lines cast more smoothly and are easier to control.

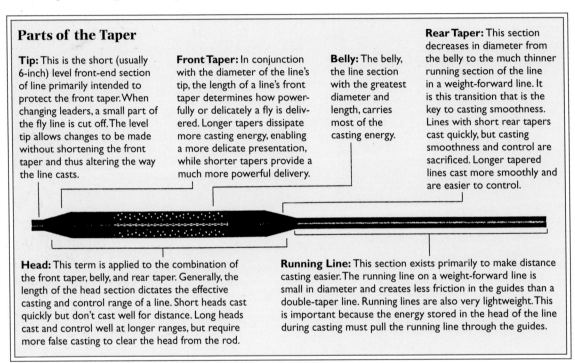

Head: This term is applied to the combination of the front taper, belly, and rear taper. Generally, the length of the head section dictates the effective casting and control range of a line. Short heads cast quickly but don't cast well for distance. Long heads cast and control well at longer ranges, but require more false casting to clear the head from the rod.

Running Line: This section exists primarily to make distance casting easier. The running line on a weight-forward line is small in diameter and creates less friction in the guides than a double-taper line. Running lines are also very lightweight. This is important because the energy stored in the head of the line during casting must pull the running line through the guides.

■ Taper Types

Fly lines are typically tapered so that they will deliver a leader and a fly appropriately. There are four basic taper types: level (L), double taper (DT), weight forward (WF), and shooting taper (ST).

LEVEL: These untapered lines are the same diameter from end to end. The lack of a taper makes them more difficult to cast accurately and control on the water.

DOUBLE TAPER: Best for short to medium casts in the 20- to 50-foot range, these lines have extralong bellies with identical tapers at either end. The tapers serve to dissipate casting energy, resulting in a delicate presentation. They don't, however, cast long distances as easily as weight-forward lines.

WEIGHT FORWARD: These lines are designed to fish well at short to long ranges. They cast farther and more easily than double-taper lines because their small-diameter running line offers less resistance in the rod guides.

SHOOTING TAPER: These tapers are best to use when maximum distance is needed, and control and accu-

racy are less important. Also called "shooting heads," they are commonly 30 to 35 feet long. They attach to a very small-diameter "shooting line" that offers less resistance in the rod guides. This results in maximum-length casts. The total length of the fly line ranges from around 100 to 120 feet.

■ Specialty Tapers

In addition to standard fly line tapers, there is a wide range of specialty tapers. These lines are designed to increase your effectiveness by providing performance characteristics to match situations you will encounter when fishing for specific species, ranging from trout and largemouth bass to tarpon and sailfish. Generally, when any large flies are used, more powerful tapers work best.

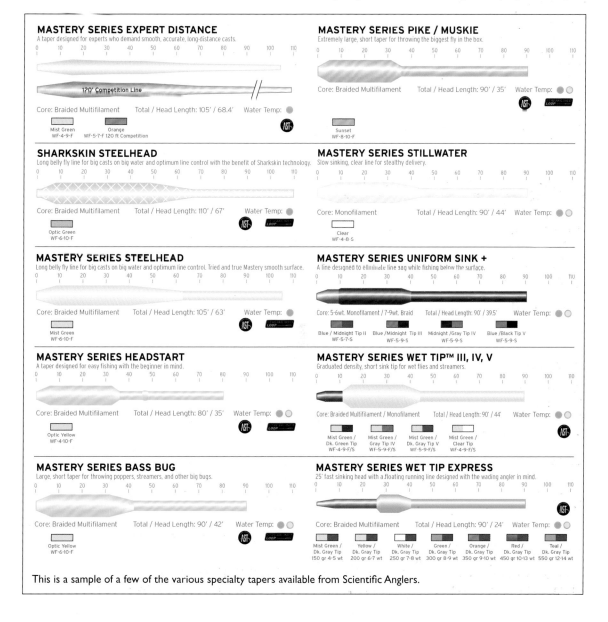

This is a sample of a few of the various specialty tapers available from Scientific Anglers.

■ Leaders

There are three basic leader materials: wire, monofilament (single-strand nylon), and fluorocarbon.

Wire leaders—either piano wire (high carbon or stainless steel) or braided wire—are used generally to protect the line from sharp underwater obstacles and from the teeth, gill plates, and other sharp appendages of both freshwater and saltwater fish. Some wire leaders, particularly the braided type, are enclosed in a sleeve of nylon, which prevents the wire strands from fraying and eliminates kinking.

Some monofilament and fluorocarbon leaders per-

Recommended Fly-Fishing Tippet Strength for Various Species

FRESH WATER

Species	Tippet	Species	Tippet
Bream, sunnies, other small fish	3-pound test	Sea-run brook trout	6-pound test
Smallmouth black bass	4- to 6-pound test	Cutthroat trout	3-pound test
Largemouth black bass	6- to 8-pound test	Sea-run cutthroat (bluebacks), harvest trout	4-pound test
Brown trout	3-pound test	Grayling	3-pound test
Brown trout (using streamers)	5-pound test	Rainbow trout	4-pound test
Sea-run brown trout	10-pound test	Steelhead (sea-run rainbow trout)	10-pound test
Brook trout	3-pound test	Winter steelhead	12-pound test
Brook trout (using streamers)	5-pound test		

SALT WATER

Species	Tippet	Species	Tippet
Mangrove or gray snapper	8-pound test	Jack crevalle	10-pound test
Bonefish	6- or 8-pound test	Horse-eye jack	10-pound test
Tarpon, baby (under 20 pounds)	8-pound test	Ladyfish	8-pound test
Tarpon, big (more than 20 pounds)	12-pound test	Snook	12-pound test
Channel bass (redfish)	10-pound test	Spotted seatrout	10-pound test
Striped bass (up to 10 pounds)	8-pound test	Barracuda	12-pound test
Striped bass (more than 10 pounds)	12-pound test		

SALTWATER FISH IN DEEP WATER, BY CHUMMING OR SIGHTING

Species	Tippet	Species	Tippet
Dolphin	10-pound test	Grouper	10-pound test
Mackerel	10-pound test	Yellowtail	10-pound test
False albacore	10-pound test	Bermuda Chub	10-pound test
Bonito	10-pound test		

SPECIAL LEADERS FOR FISH THAT MIGHT BITE OR FRAY THROUGH LEADER TIPPET

Species	Tippet and Leader
Bluefish	10-pound test with 12-inch, #4 wire leader added
Sailfish	12-pound test with 12-inch, 80-pound-test nylon added
Marlin	12-pound test with 12-inch, 100-pound-test nylon added
Tarpon	12-pound test with 12-inch, 100-pound-test nylon added
Tuna	12-pound test with 12-inch, 100-pound-test nylon added
Barracuda	12-pound test with 12-inch, #5 wire leader added
Sharks	12-pound test with 12-inch, #5 or #7 heavier wire leader added

form a similar function. Called shock tippets, they are short lengths (6 feet or shorter in most cases) of strong monofilament or fluorocarbon testing up to about 100 pounds depending on the size of the fish being sought. Shock tippets protect the line from sharp objects and teeth, but they are also able to withstand the sledge-hammer strikes of large fish. Shock tippets are especially important to fishermen targeting tarpon and billfish, such as sailfish and marlin.

The main purpose of most leaders, however, is to provide an all-but-invisible link between the end of the line and the lure, bait, or fly. Anglers using monofilament or fluorocarbon line might not need a leader, for the line itself is a leader material. But if highly visible braided line is sometimes used, a monofilament or fluorocarbon leader at least 6 feet long is a big advantage.

Fly fishing is perhaps the form of the sport in which the leader is most critical. Today's trout, salmon, and other fly-caught fish—both stocked and wild—are far more wise to the ways of the angler than they once were. When you go for these fish, a sloppy cast, a too-short leader, or an improperly presented fly will seldom bring a strike.

Though some fly fishermen feel that they can get by with a level leader (one with a diameter that is the same throughout its entire length), a tapered leader makes casting far more pleasant and efficient and brings far more strikes.

A tapered leader must be designed to transmit the energy of the cast from the line right down to the fly.

But because the fly fisherman's offerings range from dry flies and wet flies to streamers and bucktails to bass bugs, tapered leaders differ, too. The proper leader is also determined by water conditions and the size of the fish.

The makeup of a tapered leader starts with the butt section, which is tied to the end of the fly line. The diameter of the tapered leader should be approximately one-half to two-thirds the diameter of the end of the line. The leader then proceeds through progressively lighter (and thinner) lengths down to the tippet, to the end of which the fly is itself tied.

The most popular leader lengths are 7½ and 9 feet, but under some conditions—such as when casting to trout in low, clear water—leaders of 12, 15, or more feet may be necessary.

You can buy tapered leaders, either knotless or with the various sections knotted together. Each time you change flies, however, you must snip off a bit of the tippet, so it pays to carry small spools of leader material in various strengths so that you can tie on a new tippet when necessary. You can also tie your own tapered leaders.

Leader material is classified according to X designations (1X, 2X, 3X, and so on), with the number sometimes representing the pound test of the line. The X designations, however, rarely indicate the exact pound test of the leader, and these labels vary among manufacturers. Always check labels for the exact pound test before making a choice. Tapered leaders are classified the same way.

FISHHOOKS

Modern hook design and manufacturing has come a long way since the first Stone Age bone hooks found by archaeologists and dating back to more than 5,000 BC. Today's fishhooks come in hundreds of sizes, shapes, colors, and special designs. They're made from carbon steel, stainless steel, or some rust-resistant alloy. They're hardened and tempered, then plated or bronzed to meet special specifications. Some are thin steel wire for use in tying artificial flies; others are thick steel for big-game fish that prowl offshore waters.

There is no such thing as an all-purpose hook. Fishermen must carry a variety of patterns and sizes to match both the tackle and size of fish being hunted. Let's start from the beginning by learning the basic

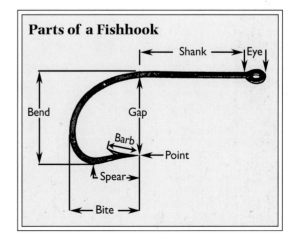

Parts of a Fishhook

nomenclature of a typical fishhook (see accompanying illustration).

Even the parts of a typical fishhook may vary in design to meet certain requirements. There are sliced shanks to better hold bait on the hook, forged shanks for greater strength in marine hooks, tapered eyes to reduce the weight of hooks used in tying dry flies, and so on.

Hook Wire Size

The letter X and the designations "Fine Wire" or "Heavy Wire" are used to indicate the weight or diameter of a hook. For example, a 2X Heavy Wire means the hook is made of the standard diameter for a hook two sizes larger, and a 3X Heavy Wire is made of the standard diameter for a hook three sizes larger.

For lightweight hooks, the designations are reversed. For example, a 2X Fine Wire means that the hook is made of the standard diameter for a hook two

sizes smaller, and so on. These designations, however, vary from manufacturer to manufacturer.

Obviously, an angler seeking a big fish should lean toward the heavy hooks, which are not apt to bend or spring when striking the larger fish that swim the waters, particularly salt water.

Fishermen who use live bait will want to use fine-wire hooks, which will not weigh down the bait. The use of flies, particularly dry flies, also requires fine-wire hooks, since their light weight will enable a fly to float more easily.

Shank Length

The letter X and the designations "Long" or "Short" are used to specify the shank length of a hook. One manufacturer lists shank lengths from extrashort to extralong. The formula for determining shank length is similar to that used for wire sizes. A 2X Long means the

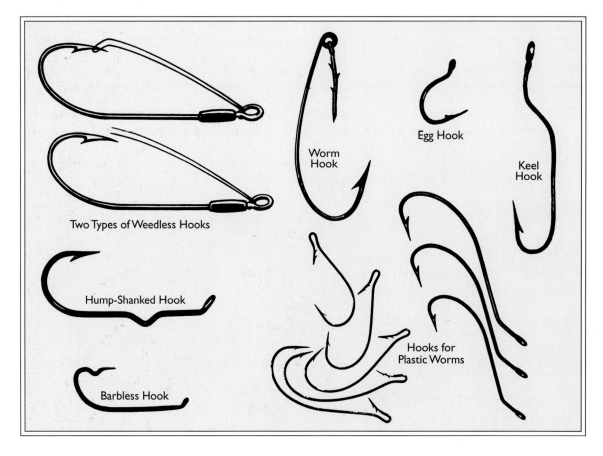

Two Types of Weedless Hooks

Hump-Shanked Hook

Barbless Hook

Worm Hook

Egg Hook

Keel Hook

Hooks for Plastic Worms

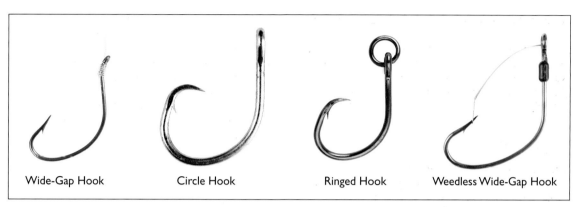

Wide-Gap Hook   Circle Hook   Ringed Hook   Weedless Wide-Gap Hook

Hook Part Variations

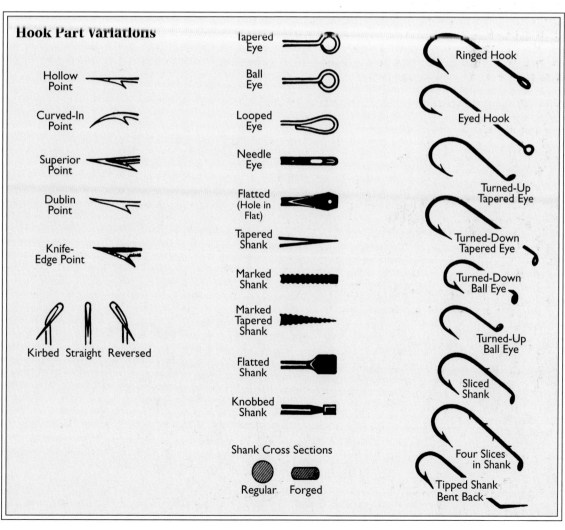

Hollow Point

Curved-In Point

Superior Point

Dublin Point

Knife-Edge Point

Kirbed Straight Reversed

Tapered Eye

Ball Eye

Looped Eye

Needle Eye

Flatted (Hole in Flat)

Tapered Shank

Marked Shank

Marked Tapered Shank

Flatted Shank

Knobbed Shank

Shank Cross Sections

Regular Forged

Ringed Hook

Eyed Hook

Turned-Up Tapered Eye

Turned-Down Tapered Eye

Turned-Down Ball Eye

Turned-Up Ball Eye

Sliced Shank

Four Slices in Shank

Tipped Shank Bent Back

Hooks for Fly Fishing

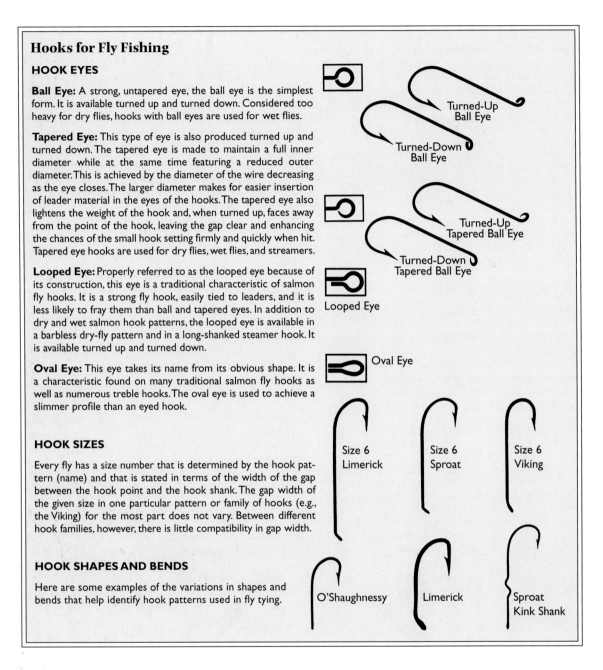

HOOK EYES

Ball Eye: A strong, untapered eye, the ball eye is the simplest form. It is available turned up and turned down. Considered too heavy for dry flies, hooks with ball eyes are used for wet flies.

Tapered Eye: This type of eye is also produced turned up and turned down. The tapered eye is made to maintain a full inner diameter while at the same time featuring a reduced outer diameter. This is achieved by the diameter of the wire decreasing as the eye closes. The larger diameter makes for easier insertion of leader material in the eyes of the hooks. The tapered eye also lightens the weight of the hook and, when turned up, faces away from the point of the hook, leaving the gap clear and enhancing the chances of the small hook setting firmly and quickly when hit. Tapered eye hooks are used for dry flies, wet flies, and streamers.

Looped Eye: Properly referred to as the looped eye because of its construction, this eye is a traditional characteristic of salmon fly hooks. It is a strong fly hook, easily tied to leaders, and it is less likely to fray them than ball and tapered eyes. In addition to dry and wet salmon hook patterns, the looped eye is available in a barbless dry-fly pattern and in a long-shanked steamer hook. It is available turned up and turned down.

Oval Eye: This eye takes its name from its obvious shape. It is a characteristic found on many traditional salmon fly hooks as well as numerous treble hooks. The oval eye is used to achieve a slimmer profile than an eyed hook.

HOOK SIZES

Every fly has a size number that is determined by the hook pattern (name) and that is stated in terms of the width of the gap between the hook point and the hook shank. The gap width of the given size in one particular pattern or family of hooks (e.g., the Viking) for the most part does not vary. Between different hook families, however, there is little compatibility in gap width.

HOOK SHAPES AND BENDS

Here are some examples of the variations in shapes and bends that help identify hook patterns used in fly tying.

shank of the hook is the standard length for a hook two sizes larger, and a 4X Long is the standard length for a hook four sizes larger. A 2X Short has a shank as short as the standard length of a hook two sizes smaller, and a 4X Short for a hook four sizes smaller, and so on. Again, these designations might vary from manufacturer to manufacturer.

Picking a hook with the correct shank length depends on the type of fishing you plan to undertake. A short-shank hook is preferred for baitfishing, since it can be hidden in the bait more easily. A long-shank hook is at its best when used for fish with sharp teeth. A bluefish, for example, would have a tough time getting past the long shank and cutting into the leader. Long-shank hooks are also used in tying streamers and bucktails.

Hook Characteristics

In addition to size and shank length, there are other characteristics to consider when selecting a hook for a specific purpose. The barb, obviously, is a critical part of the hook. A short barb is quick to set in the mouth of a fish, but it also gives a jumping fish a greater chance of dislodging it. A long barb, on the other hand, is more difficult to set but it also makes it a lot tougher for a fish to shake it loose.

So what guidelines should an angler follow? Let's list some basic recommendations. The all-around saltwater fisherman can't go wrong with the O'Shaughnessy, Kirby, Wide Gap, or Circle Hook patterns. And if you happen to have some salmon hooks, they're perfectly all right to use with a wire leader for barracuda and other toothy fish.

If you're a flounder fisherman, you'll find that the Chestertown and Carlisle patterns are your best bet. The long-shanked Chestertown makes it especially easy to unhook flounders.

If you're a bait fisherman, use the sliced-shanked Mustad-Beak or Eagle Claw patterns. Those extra barbs on the shanks do a good job of keeping natural baits secured to the hook.

Fishermen can also become confused when they see hooks with straight-ringed eyes, turned-up eyes, and turned-down eyes. This should not present a problem. If you're replacing hooks on lures or attaching hooks to spinners, use a straight-ringed eye. If you're tying short-shanked artificial flies, pick the turned-up eye, which will provide more space for the hook point to bite into the fish. The turned-down eye is the best bet for standard flies and for baitfishing, since it brings the point of the hook closest to a straight line of penetration when striking a fish.

Curved shanks also lead to some confusion. A curved shank—curved right or left—has its place in baitfishing. The offset point has a better chance of hitting flesh when a strike is made. When you are casting or trolling with artificial lures or spinners, however, the straight-shanked hook is a better choice, since it does not have a tendency to spin or twist, which is often the case with curved-shanked hooks.

ARTIFICIAL LURES

Fishing with bait is enjoyable, certainly, but there's something about fooling a fish with an artificial lure that gives most anglers a special charge.

A neophyte fisherman who visits a well-stocked sporting-goods store or tackle shop is confronted with a bewildering array of plugs, spoons, spinners, jigs, flies, bugs, and others. Some artificials look like nothing that ever swam, crawled, or flew, and yet they catch fish.

Let's look at each type of artificial lure and see how and why it works and how it should be fished.

Plugs

Plugs are lures designed to imitate small fish for the most part, though some plugs simulate mice, frogs, eels, and other food on which game fish feed. Plug action—meaning the way the lure moves when retrieved by the angler—is important and is something on which manufacturers expend much money and time. These lures are called crankbaits because every crank of the reel handle imparts some sort of diving or darting action.

The type, size, and weight of the plug you select is determined by the fish you are after and the kind of fishing tackle you are using. The charts found at the beginning of the Fishing section on how to match up various kinds of fishing tackle will help the beginner choose the right weight plugs.

There are five basic types of plugs: popping, surface, floating-diving, sinking (deep running), and deep diving.

POPPING: These plugs float on the surface and have concave, hollowed-out faces. The angler retrieves a popping plug by jerking the rod tip back so that the plug's face digs into the water, making a small splash, bubbles, and a popping sound. Some make a louder sound than others. This sound is especially attractive to largemouth bass, pike, muskies, and some inshore saltwater species, such as striped bass and bluefish. Most popping plugs (and

Freshwater vs. Saltwater Lures

A long time ago, I stopped labeling lures as "freshwater" and "saltwater." There is really no difference. Size no longer matters. I've caught 40-pound dolphin on 1-ounce bucktails and a 10-inch farm pond bass on a 7-inch Rapala. My favorite Creek Chub darter caught dozens of pike and so many bluefish that I retired the lure. The same is true for flies. My Clouser Minnows are equally productive on rainbow trout as they are on striped bass. Some lures have corrosion-resistant hooks and some have bronze hooks that will rust, but I never worry about hooks rotting away because they are easy to replace. With very few exceptions, all lures will work both in fresh and salt water.

most other plugs) have two sets of treble hooks. Popping plugs are most productive when the water surface is calm or nearly so. They should usually be fished slowly.

SURFACE: These plugs float on the surface, but they can be fished with various kinds of retrieves and create a different kind of surface disturbance than poppers do. Designed with an elongated, or bullet-shaped,

head, they create surface disturbance by various means, including propellers (at the head or at both head and tail), a wide metal lip at the head, or hinged metal "wings" just behind the head. They can be twitched so that they barely nod, retrieved steadily so that they chug across the water, or skimmed across the top as fast as the angler can turn his reel handle. The proper retrieve depends on the lure's design and, of course, on the mood

Popping Plugs

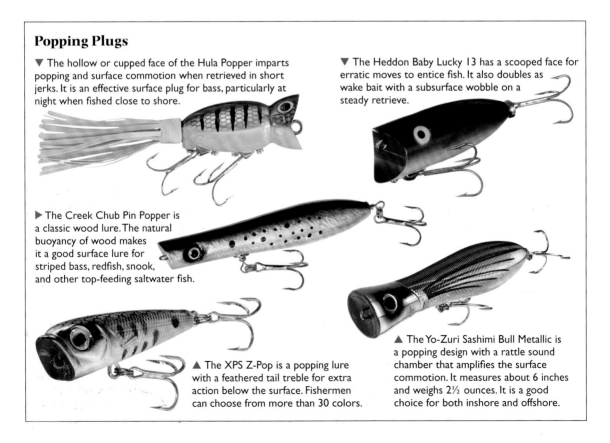

▼ The hollow or cupped face of the Hula Popper imparts popping and surface commotion when retrieved in short jerks. It is an effective surface plug for bass, particularly at night when fished close to shore.

▼ The Heddon Baby Lucky 13 has a scooped face for erratic moves to entice fish. It also doubles as wake bait with a subsurface wobble on a steady retrieve.

▶ The Creek Chub Pin Popper is a classic wood lure. The natural buoyancy of wood makes it a good surface lure for striped bass, redfish, snook, and other top-feeding saltwater fish.

▲ The XPS Z-Pop is a popping lure with a feathered tail treble for extra action below the surface. Fishermen can choose from more than 30 colors.

▲ The Yo-Zuri Sashimi Bull Metallic is a popping design with a rattle sound chamber that amplifies the surface commotion. It measures about 6 inches and weighs 2½ ounces. It is a good choice for both inshore and offshore.

Surface Plugs

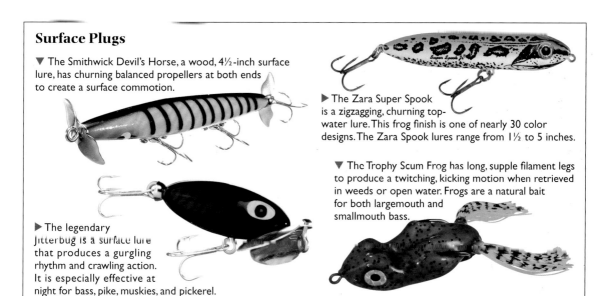

▼ The Smithwick Devil's Horse, a wood, 4½-inch surface lure, has churning balanced propellers at both ends to create a surface commotion.

► The Zara Super Spook is a zigzagging, churning top-water lure. This frog finish is one of nearly 30 color designs. The Zara Spook lures range from 1½ to 5 inches.

▼ The Trophy Scum Frog has long, supple filament legs to produce a twitching, kicking motion when retrieved in weeds or open water. Frogs are a natural bait for both largemouth and smallmouth bass.

► The legendary Jitterbug is a surface lure that produces a gurgling rhythm and crawling action. It is especially effective at night for bass, pike, muskies, and pickerel.

Floating-Diving Plugs

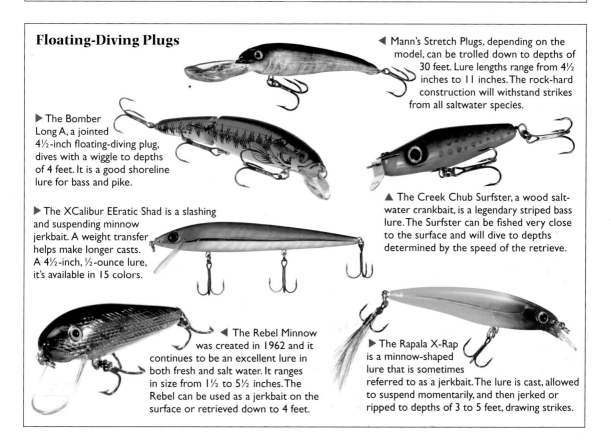

◄ Mann's Stretch Plugs, depending on the model, can be trolled down to depths of 30 feet. Lure lengths range from 4½ inches to 11 inches. The rock-hard construction will withstand strikes from all saltwater species.

► The Bomber Long A, a jointed 4½-inch floating-diving plug, dives with a wiggle to depths of 4 feet. It is a good shoreline lure for bass and pike.

► The XCalibur EEratic Shad is a slashing and suspending minnow jerkbait. A weight transfer helps make longer casts. A 4½-inch, ½-ounce lure, it's available in 15 colors.

▲ The Creek Chub Surfster, a wood salt-water crankbait, is a legendary striped bass lure. The Surfster can be fished very close to the surface and will dive to depths determined by the speed of the retrieve.

◄ The Rebel Minnow was created in 1962 and it continues to be an excellent lure in both fresh and salt water. It ranges in size from 1½ to 5½ inches. The Rebel can be used as a jerkbait on the surface or retrieved down to 4 feet.

► The Rapala X-Rap is a minnow-shaped lure that is sometimes referred to as a jerkbait. The lure is cast, allowed to suspend momentarily, and then jerked or ripped to depths of 3 to 5 feet, drawing strikes.

of the fish. It's best to try different retrieves until you find one that produces.

FLOATING-DIVING: These plugs are designed to float when at rest and dive when retrieved. Some float horizontally, while others float with the tail hanging down beneath the surface. They are made to dive by an extended lip at the head. The speed of the retrieve determines the depth of the dive. The faster the retrieve, the deeper the dive. Most of these plugs have a side-to-side wobbling action. An erratic retrieve—dive, surface, dive, surface—is often productive, and these plugs are also effective when made to swim just above a submerged weed bed, rock pile, and so on.

SINKING (DEEP RUNNING): These plugs sink as soon as they hit the water and are designed for deep work. Some sink slower than others and can be fished at various depths, depending on how long the angler waits before starting his retrieve. Most of these plugs have some

sort of wobbling action, and some fairly vibrate when retrieved. Some have propellers fore and aft.

These plugs are excellent fish-finders: the fisherman can start by bouncing them along the bottom, and if that doesn't work, he can work them at progressively shallower depths until he finds at what depth the fish are feeding. It should be remembered that deep-running plugs don't have to be fished in deep water; for example, in small sizes they're great for river smallmouths.

DEEP DIVING: These plugs may float or sink, but they all are designed with long or broad lips of metal or plastic that cause the plugs to dive to depths of 30 feet or more as the angler reels in. As with other diving plugs, the faster the retrieve, the deeper the dive. Most of these lures have some sort of wobbling action. They are ideally suited for casting or trolling in deep lakes and at the edges of drop-offs, and they work best in most waters when the fish are holding in deep holes, as fish usually do during midday in July and August.

Deep-Diving Plugs

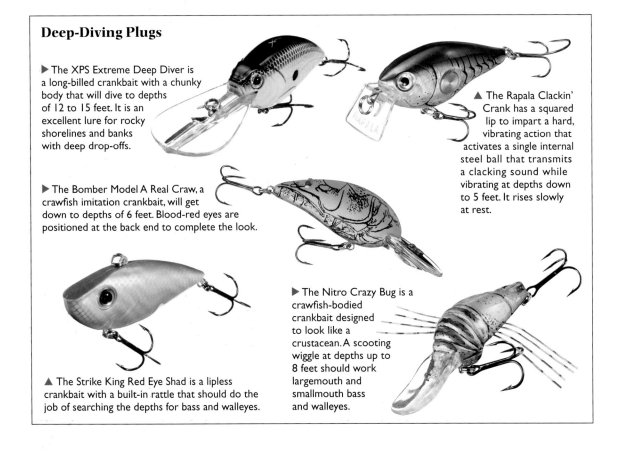

▶ The XPS Extreme Deep Diver is a long-billed crankbait with a chunky body that will dive to depths of 12 to 15 feet. It is an excellent lure for rocky shorelines and banks with deep drop-offs.

▲ The Rapala Clackin' Crank has a squared lip to impart a hard, vibrating action that activates a single internal steel ball that transmits a clacking sound while vibrating at depths down to 5 feet. It rises slowly at rest.

▶ The Bomber Model A Real Craw, a crawfish imitation crankbait, will get down to depths of 6 feet. Blood-red eyes are positioned at the back end to complete the look.

▶ The Nitro Crazy Bug is a crawfish-bodied crankbait designed to look like a crustacean. A scooting wiggle at depths up to 8 feet should work largemouth and smallmouth bass and walleyes.

▲ The Strike King Red Eye Shad is a lipless crankbait with a built-in rattle that should do the job of searching the depths for bass and walleyes.

Saltwater Diving and Trolling Lures

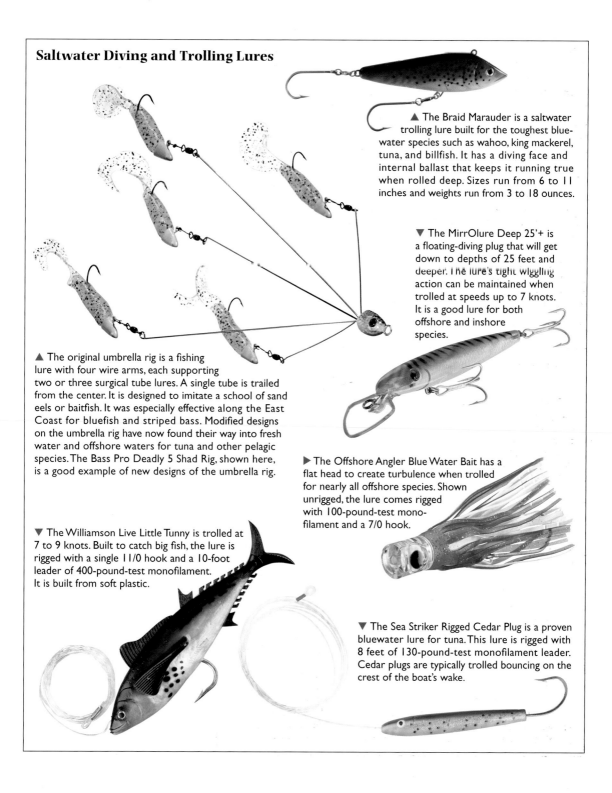

▲ The Braid Marauder is a saltwater trolling lure built for the toughest blue-water species such as wahoo, king mackerel, tuna, and billfish. It has a diving face and internal ballast that keeps it running true when rolled deep. Sizes run from 6 to 11 inches and weights run from 3 to 18 ounces.

▼ The MirrOlure Deep 25'+ is a floating-diving plug that will get down to depths of 25 feet and deeper. The lure's tight wiggling action can be maintained when trolled at speeds up to 7 knots. It is a good lure for both offshore and inshore species.

▲ The original umbrella rig is a fishing lure with four wire arms, each supporting two or three surgical tube lures. A single tube is trailed from the center. It is designed to imitate a school of sand eels or baitfish. It was especially effective along the East Coast for bluefish and striped bass. Modified designs on the umbrella rig have now found their way into fresh water and offshore waters for tuna and other pelagic species. The Bass Pro Deadly 5 Shad Rig, shown here, is a good example of new designs of the umbrella rig.

▶ The Offshore Angler Blue Water Bait has a flat head to create turbulence when trolled for nearly all offshore species. Shown unrigged, the lure comes rigged with 100-pound-test mono-filament and a 7/0 hook.

▼ The Williamson Live Little Tunny is trolled at 7 to 9 knots. Built to catch big fish, the lure is rigged with a single 11/0 hook and a 10-foot leader of 400-pound-test monofilament. It is built from soft plastic.

▼ The Sea Striker Rigged Cedar Plug is a proven bluewater lure for tuna. This lure is rigged with 8 feet of 130-pound-test monofilament leader. Cedar plugs are typically trolled bouncing on the crest of the boat's wake.

Spoons

▼ The Bass Pro Nitro Flash is a 5-inch spoon that can be cast and retrieved at different speeds. The lure can also be cast, allowed to drop, then jerked up to the surface much like a jig. It is a good lure for bass, pike, and muskies.

▲ The Kastmaster, machined from solid brass with weights ranging from $\frac{1}{12}$ ounce to 1 ounce, is a proven lure for fresh and salt water. This lure will cast like a bullet. A jerk retrieve is best on inshore species.

▶ The Clarkspoon has been around for generations. The smaller sizes, tipped with a strip of pork rind, are excellent lures for bass, pike, and muskies. In the bigger sizes, it's an effective lure for striped bass, bluefish, barracuda, king mackerel, and a host of inshore species.

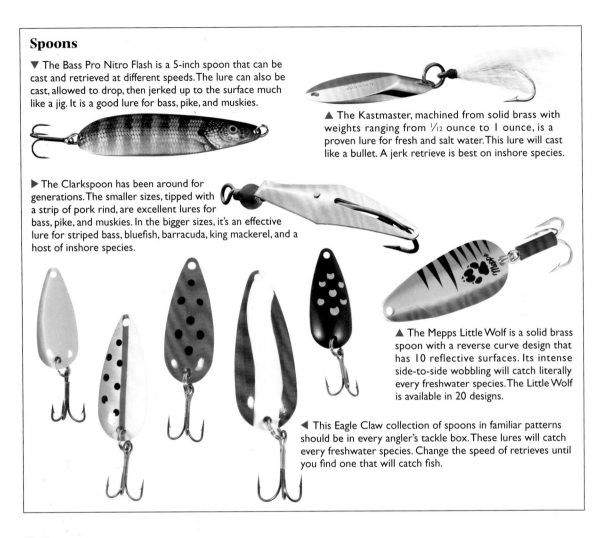

▲ The Mepps Little Wolf is a solid brass spoon with a reverse curve design that has 10 reflective surfaces. Its intense side-to-side wobbling will catch literally every freshwater species. The Little Wolf is available in 20 designs.

◀ This Eagle Claw collection of spoons in familiar patterns should be in every angler's tackle box. These lures will catch every freshwater species. Change the speed of retrieves until you find one that will catch fish.

■ Spoons

Spoons are among the oldest of artificial lures. If you cut the handle off a teaspoon, you'd have the basic shape of this lure.

Spoons are designed to imitate small baitfish of one kind or another, so flash is an important feature in many of these lures. Most spoons have a wobbling, side-to-side action when retrieved.

Many spoons have a silver or gold finish, while others are painted in various colors and combinations of colors. Most have a single free-swinging treble hook at the tail; others have a single fixed hook. Weedless arrangements are becoming more and more popular on both types.

In general, the smaller spoons are better in streams and ponds, while the larger ones are a good choice for lakes. However, the angler must remember that with two spoons of equal weight but different sizes, the smaller one will cast easier in wind and sink faster, while the larger one will sink slower and swim at shallower depths.

What's the best retrieve for a spoon? Again, that depends on weather and water conditions and other circumstances, including the mood of the fish. But generally, an erratic retrieve, with twitches and jerks of the rod tip, is better than a steady retrieve because it makes the spoon look like an injured baitfish. Attaching a strip of pork rind to a spoon often adds to its fish appeal.

■ Spinners

Spinners, like spoons, are designed to imitate baitfish, and they attract game fish by flash and vibration. A spinner is simply a metal blade mounted on a shaft by means of a revolving arm or ring called a clevis. Unlike a spoon, which has a wobbling action, a spinner blade rotates around the shaft when retrieved.

Other parts of a simple spinner include a locking device to accommodate a hook at one end of the shaft,

a metal loop to which the line is tied at the other end of the shaft, and a series of metal or plastic beads that separate the blade from the locking device and loop. In some spinners, notably the Colorado, the blade is mounted on a series of swivels instead of on a shaft.

Most spinners have either one or two blades. However, in some forms of fishing, particularly deep-water trolling for lake trout, eight or more spinner blades are mounted in tandem on a length of wire.

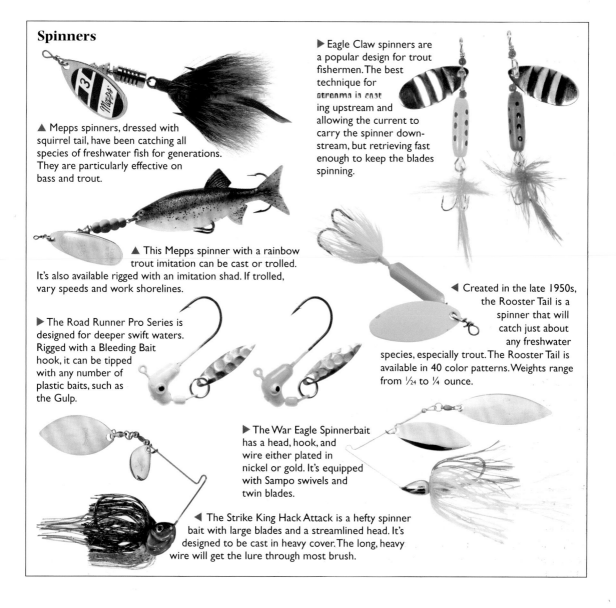

Spinners

▲ Mepps spinners, dressed with squirrel tail, have been catching all species of freshwater fish for generations. They are particularly effective on bass and trout.

▲ This Mepps spinner with a rainbow trout imitation can be cast or trolled. It's also available rigged with an imitation shad. If trolled, vary speeds and work shorelines.

► The Road Runner Pro Series is designed for deeper swift waters. Rigged with a Bleeding Bait hook, it can be tipped with any number of plastic baits, such as the Gulp.

► Eagle Claw spinners are a popular design for trout fishermen. The best technique for streams is casting upstream and allowing the current to carry the spinner downstream, but retrieving fast enough to keep the blades spinning.

◄ Created in the late 1950s, the Rooster Tail is a spinner that will catch just about any freshwater species, especially trout. The Rooster Tail is available in 40 color patterns. Weights range from $\frac{1}{24}$ to $\frac{1}{4}$ ounce.

► The War Eagle Spinnerbait has a head, hook, and wire either plated in nickel or gold. It's equipped with Sampo swivels and twin blades.

◄ The Strike King Hack Attack is a hefty spinner bait with large blades and a streamlined head. It's designed to be cast in heavy cover. The long, heavy wire will get the lure through most brush.

Buzz Baits

Booyah Counter Strike buzz baits have counter-rotating blades for stability and to create a distinct sound. Vary the retrieves with these lures to create a bubble trail.

Most spinner blades have either a silver or gold finish. Some, however, are painted in various colors, including black, yellow, and white, while others are striped and still others are made of simulated pearl. In general, the brighter finishes are best in shaded or discolored water and on overcast days, while the darker finishes are better in very clear water under bright skies.

Spinner blades have various shapes and other physical characteristics. Both shape and thickness determine how the blade reacts when retrieved. To illustrate this point, let's take a look at a few types of simple spinners, often used with bait, that have proven their worth over the years.

COLORADO: This spinner has a wide, nearly round blade that rotates well out from the shaft. Because it has considerable water resistance and spins relatively slowly, it is best suited for use in lakes and in streams with slow currents. A Colorado spinner used with a worm is a proven taker of trout, walleyes, and other fish.

WILLOW LEAF: This spinner has a long, narrow blade that spins fast and close to the shaft. Having minimum water resistance, it is well suited for use in fast-flowing water. A willow-leaf spinner is often used with a worm, minnow, or other natural baits.

JUNE BUG: Unusual in that the blade is attached directly to the shaft (there is no clevis), this spinner has a sort of "leg" that braces the blade against the shaft, and has a hole in the middle. A June Bug spinner with its hook sweetened by a night crawler is a potent combination for trout, walleyes, and many other game fish. The June Bug comes in various designs.

Spinner-blade sizes are usually classified by numbers, but the numbers vary with the manufacturers and are not a reliable guide for the buyer. It's easy enough to simply look over a selection of spinners and select the size that seems right for your particular purpose.

Many spinner-type lures are produced today and are extremely popular, especially among freshwater fishermen. In all of them, the basic attracting element is a revolving spinner blade. Most have some sort of weight built in along the shaft and a treble hook at the tail. In many, the treble hook is hidden or at least disguised with bucktail, feathers, squirrel tail, or a skirt of rubber or plastic strands. Weedless hooks are also becoming increasingly popular on these lures.

■ Buzz Baits

Buzz baits are spinner baits that incorporate a wide propeller and jig that churn a substantial commotion as the bait is retrieved across the surface, leaving a bubble trail. Buzz baits can be fished fast or slow, depending on water conditions and the mood of the fish. Try various retrieves until you find one that catches fish.

■ Jigs

Generally speaking, a jig is any lure with a weighted head (usually lead), a fixed hook, and a tail of bucktail, feathers, nylon, or similar material. Jigs are made in sizes of

Jigs

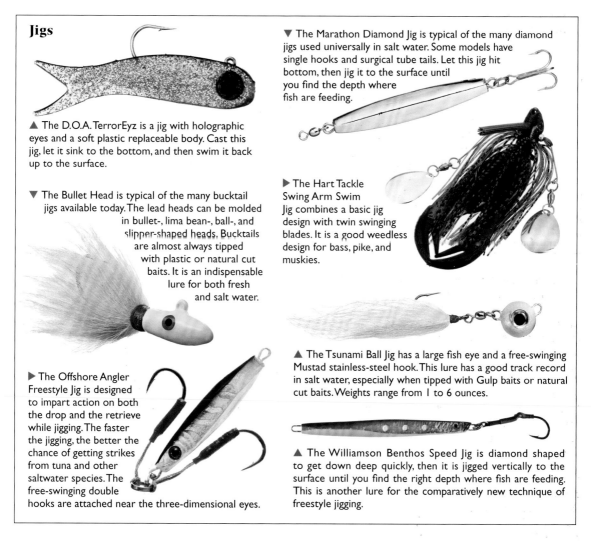

▲ The D.O.A. TerrorEyz is a jig with holographic eyes and a soft plastic replaceable body. Cast this jig, let it sink to the bottom, and then swim it back up to the surface.

▼ The Bullet Head is typical of the many bucktail jigs available today. The lead heads can be molded in bullet-, lima bean-, ball-, and slipper-shaped heads, Bucktails are almost always tipped with plastic or natural cut baits. It is an indispensable lure for both fresh and salt water.

▶ The Offshore Angler Freestyle Jig is designed to impart action on both the drop and the retrieve while jigging. The faster the jigging, the better the chance of getting strikes from tuna and other saltwater species. The free-swinging double hooks are attached near the three-dimensional eyes.

▼ The Marathon Diamond Jig is typical of the many diamond jigs used universally in salt water. Some models have single hooks and surgical tube tails. Let this jig hit bottom, then jig it to the surface until you find the depth where fish are feeding.

▶ The Hart Tackle Swing Arm Swim Jig combines a basic jig design with twin swinging blades. It is a good weedless design for bass, pike, and muskies.

▲ The Tsunami Ball Jig has a large fish eye and a free-swinging Mustad stainless-steel hook. This lure has a good track record in salt water, especially when tipped with Gulp baits or natural cut baits. Weights range from 1 to 6 ounces.

▲ The Williamson Benthos Speed Jig is diamond shaped to get down deep quickly, then it is jigged vertically to the surface until you find the right depth where fish are feeding. This is another lure for the comparatively new technique of freestyle jigging.

¹⁄₁₆ ounce to 6 ounces and even heavier, and they will take just about any fish that swims in fresh water or salt. Jigs imitate baitfish, crustaceans, and other game-fish forage. In some jigs, the hook rides with the point up to minimize the chance of snagging. Jigs, and related lures, take many forms. Here's a look at the most popular types.

FEATHERED JIG: Often called Japanese feathers, this jig is commonly used in saltwater trolling and casting. It consists of a heavy metal head with eyes. Through the head runs a wire leader, to the end of which the hook is attached. Running from the head down to the hook is a long tail, usually of feathers. A plastic sleeve covers the feathers for about half their length. This jig is typically used in trolling for tuna, billfish, dolphin, and other pelagic species.

BUCKTAIL JIG: This jig consists of a lead head, embedded hook, and trailing tail of bucktail. The head is painted, with the most popular colors being white, red, yellow, or combinations of these colors. The most popular member of the jig family, bucktail jigs are used on a wide variety of freshwater and saltwater game fish, especially largemouth and smallmouth bass, walleyes, pike, striped bass, bluefish, and many other bottom-feeders.

SHAD DART: This is a small jig (usually weighing about ¼ ounce) with a relatively long, narrow head, flat face, and short tail of bucktail or similar material. It is usually painted in two colors, with the most popular combi-nations being red and white, yellow and white, and red and yellow. It is an extremely popular lure for American (white) shad in East Coast rivers.

METAL (BLOCK-TIN) SQUIDS: Falling under the general category of jigs are these lures, which are used mostly in salt water for striped bass, bluefish, tuna, and the like. Made to resemble baitfish, they have a long, narrow body of block tin, stainless steel, chrome, or nickel-plated lead and either a single fixed hook or a free-swinging treble hook, with or without a tail of bucktail. Most metal squids range in length from 3 to 6 inches. All have bright finishes, usually silvery; in some, the finish is smooth, while others have a hammered finish that gives a scale-like appearance. Among the most popular metal squids are types such as the Hopkins (which has a hammered finish, a long, narrow, flat body, and a free-swinging tre-ble hook), the diamond jig (which has a four-sided body and a treble hook), and the sand eel (which has a long, rounded, undulating body). A strip of pork rind often adds to the effectiveness of metal squids.

JIG AND EEL: This jig consists of a small metal squid on which is rigged a common eel, either the real McCoy (usually dead and preserved) or a plastic artificial. These rigged eels range in length from about 6 inches up to a foot or longer. The jig and eel is a deadly combination for striped bass, big snook, redfish, and sea trout. The best retrieve depends on various conditions, but usually a slow, slightly erratic swimming motion is best.

Vertical jigging is a productive technique for a variety of species, especially in salt water. The most effective jigging method is to cast, let the jig drop to the bottom, and then begin retrieving with an up-and-down jigging motion. Once you determine where the fish are, concentrate on jigging at that depth. Most fish will strike when the jig is fluttering down to the bottom. Jigging speed will range from very rapid to slow and works best with braided line. Vertical jigging can be deadly on all species, especially striped bass, tuna, and grouper.

Hot Lures for Salmon

The most consistent key to catching salmon is color! Millions of salmon return each year to their birthplace to deposit billions of salmon eggs. Some of these eggs will eventually become salmon, but most will sink to the bottom and provide a food source for all Alaska game fish. Salmon eggs vary in color from pink to shades of red and orange. It's these reddish hues that trigger a feeding response.

What should be in your tackle box? A spin fisherman needs only spoons and jig heads with red or pink swimming plastic tails. Curly tails seem to work best. Cover the hook of the jig head and fish it slow with occasional twitches.

For fishermen who prefer to cast spoons, the same color rule applies. For several years, I've used Pixie spoons in weights from ¼ to ½ ounce. These chromed spoons have red or orange plastic insets molded to look like salmon egg clusters.

Alaska is a great proving ground for fly fishermen. Again, the color rule applies. When I arrived in Alaska, Chris Batin gave me a handful of his special flies. He calls them BBLs, which stands for Batin Bunny Leeches. The fly is a bright fuchsia-colored streamer with a barbell lead eye. Chris ties it on a 2X strong 1/0 hook with dyed rabbit fur. There's also enough weight with the barbell eyes to make it easy to cast with light spinning tackle. Chris's fly consistently proved deadly.

▲ Pixie Spoon
▼ Chris Batin's BBL

■ Plastic Lures

Hundreds of years from now the history books may refer to our era as the Age of Plastic. And fishermen haven't escaped the gaze of plastic manufacturers.

On the market today are soft-plastic lures that imi-tate just about anything a fish will eat. There are plastic worms, eels, snakes, crickets, crawfish, minnows, shrimp,

Rigging Plastic Worms

The plastic worm can be fished on the bottom, above the bottom, on the surface, and through thick weeds. It comes in different lengths, shapes, colors, flavors, and scents. The fake night crawler is so versatile it has spawned specialized hooks and a separate vocabulary. Here's how to tie the basic worm rigs, as well as when and where to fish them—and, just so there's no confusion, what they're called.

Floating Worm Rig: This is the simplest of all worm rigs. Thread a worm on a hook, push it up to the hook eye, and the rig is complete. You can buy floating worms (usually molded with air chambers), or you can make any worm a floater by threading a piece of cork on your line in front of the hook. You can also try "larding" the worm with bits of Styrofoam (cut from a plate or coffee cup). Some fishermen buy injectors—they look like miniature basketball pumps—to float worms, lizards, or any other soft-plastic lure. A floating worm works best at dusk or dawn. It's especially effective during spawning season, when bass are protective of their beds: cast the worm near a bass bed, swim it slowly, pause, and allow it to hang directly above the bed . . . and hang on.

Cork 3/0 Hook

Carolina Rig: This rig is designed to be fished deep, but not on the bottom. The principal difference between the Carolina and Texas rigs is that in the Carolina the sinker, usually a slip sinker, is placed 2 and 3 feet ahead of a floating worm. The sinker is held in position with a swivel (and often a bead). Use a bullet- or egg-shaped sinker; either will slide over most obstructions. The rig allows a bass to pick up the bait without immediately feeling the weight of a sinker, and it makes the worm more visible to suspended fish. The Carolina rig is another good summer lure for deep water. Depending on the amount of vegetation, the hook can be left exposed or buried in the worm.

Swivel   3/0 Hook

Slip Sinker (½ to 1 ounce)   Leader (2 to 3 feet)

Texas Rig: The Texas rig is a brush-buster. In its most common variant, a bullet-shaped sinker is threaded on the line just ahead of the worm, and the point of the hook is buried in it. This requires that the worm be carefully measured so it will hang straight when the hook point is inserted (it takes some practice). If the worm is "scrunched" on the shank of the hook, it won't be nearly as effective. The Texas rig is designed to be fished through weeds and brush and around stumps, and crawled along snag-infested bottoms. It's particularly effective on hot summer days when bass seek out brushy, shaded shorelines or hang very deep in cool water.

3/0 Hook

Slip Sinker (½ to 1 ounce)

Worm Hooks

This hook has a weighted shank with a free-swinging keeper at the eye to hold the worm.

This is a wide-gap hook with a weighted keeper. The worm is snugged against the eye; the point is buried.

The kink in the shank of this hook holds the worm securely and helps it hang straight.

The worm is treaded on the keeper. The ultrawide gap reduces the chance of a thrown hook.

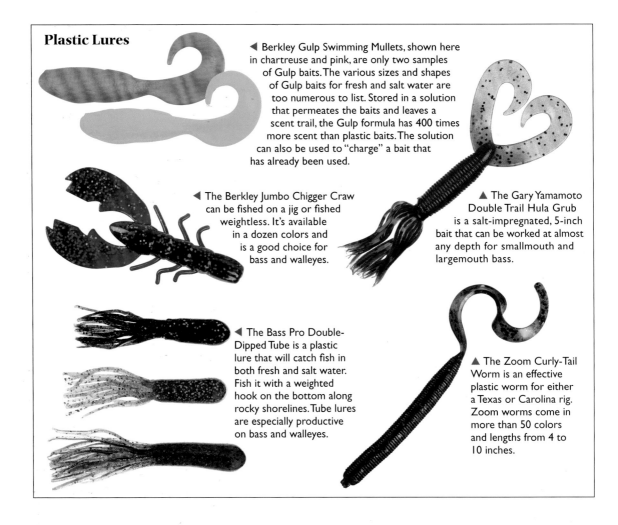

Plastic Lures

◄ Berkley Gulp Swimming Mullets, shown here in chartreuse and pink, are only two samples of Gulp baits. The various sizes and shapes of Gulp baits for fresh and salt water are too numerous to list. Stored in a solution that permeates the baits and leaves a scent trail, the Gulp formula has 400 times more scent than plastic baits. The solution can also be used to "charge" a bait that has already been used.

◄ The Berkley Jumbo Chigger Craw can be fished on a jig or fished weightless. It's available in a dozen colors and is a good choice for bass and walleyes.

▲ The Gary Yamamoto Double Trail Hula Grub is a salt-impregnated, 5-inch bait that can be worked at almost any depth for smallmouth and largemouth bass.

◄ The Bass Pro Double-Dipped Tube is a plastic lure that will catch fish in both fresh and salt water. Fish it with a weighted hook on the bottom along rocky shorelines. Tube lures are especially productive on bass and walleyes.

▲ The Zoom Curly-Tail Worm is an effective plastic worm for either a Texas or Carolina rig. Zoom worms come in more than 50 colors and lengths from 4 to 10 inches.

hellgrammites, mullet, flies, beetles, grasshoppers, frogs, and many, many more. Even salmon eggs! Many manufacturers impregnate these lures with secret formulas, attractants, and scents, claiming fish will strike these baits and not let go.

Surprisingly, a good many of these synthetic creations catch fish. A prime example is the plastic worm, which came into its own in the mid- and late 1960s. It has accounted for some eye-popping stringers of largemouth bass, especially in big southern lakes. A plastic worm threaded on a weedless hook and slithered through lily pads or an underwater weed bed is a real killer. Some plastic worms come with a weighted jig-type head or a spinner at the front.

■ Pork Rind

Pork rind, as used by fishermen, is the skin from the back of a hog. It is sold in jars containing a liquid preservative to prevent spoilage and to retain the rind's flexibility.

It used to be that pork rind was used only as an addition to a spoon or other lure. For example, a single-hook spoon with a 2- or 3-inch strip of pork rind was—and still is—a popular combination for pickerel, pike, and the like.

Pork rind is still widely used that way today. It is sold in many shapes and sizes, from tiny half-inch V-strips for panfish up to 6-inch strips for muskies and saltwater game fish. Pork-rind baits come in many colors and shapes, such as lizards, frogs, worms, and eels.

Pork Rind Designs

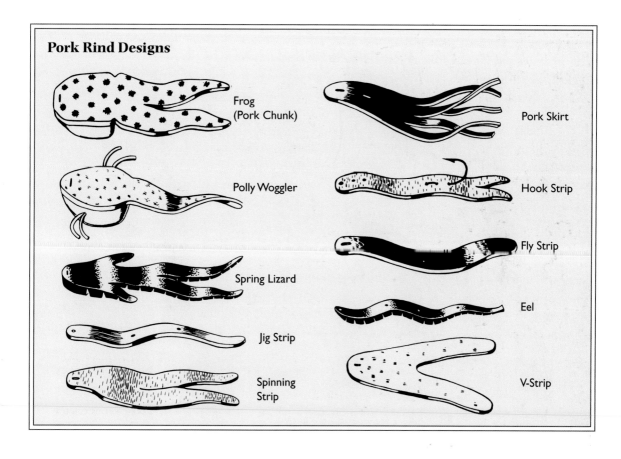

Frog (Pork Chunk)

Pork Skirt

Polly Woggler

Hook Strip

Spring Lizard

Fly Strip

Jig Strip

Eel

Spinning Strip

V-Strip

◾ Flies

An artificial fly is a combination of feathers, hair, floss, tinsel, and other materials tied to a hook to imitate a natural insect (dry and wet flies, including nymphs) or a baitfish (streamer flies and bucktails). Flies are used to take many freshwater and saltwater game fish, but most were originally designed for trout and salmon. There are four basic kinds of artificial flies: dry, wet (including nymph), streamer, and bucktail.

DRY FLIES: The dry fly, designed to imitate a floating insect, is tied so that the fibers of the hackles (feathers) stick out at approximately right angles to the shank of the hook. A properly tied dry fly sits high and lightly on the tips of its hackles, riding the surface of the water.

There are countless dry-fly patterns, but almost all of them fall into one of 10 basic types. Here is a brief description of each type:

Typical Parts of a Fly

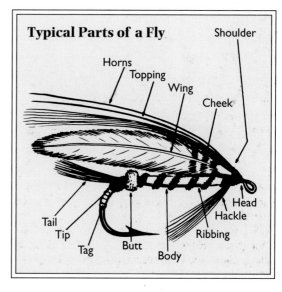

Shoulder

Horns

Topping

Wing

Cheek

Head

Hackle

Tail

Tip

Tag

Butt

Body

Ribbing

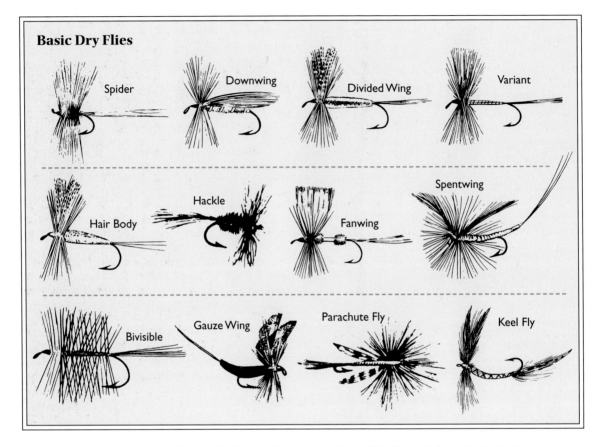

Basic Dry Flies

- **Downwing (or Sedge):** This fly has a built-up body, hackle, and wings lying flat along the shank of the hook. It floats with the hook underwater.

- **Divided Wing:** This is the standard dry-fly type. It has two erect separated wings of feather fibers, hackle, tapered body, and a stiff, slender tail. It floats with the hook above or partly underwater.

- **Hairwing:** This fly has upright wings made of deer hair, as well as hackle, a tapered body, and stiff tail. It floats with the hook above or partly underwater.

- **Fanwing:** This fly has large, flat, erect wings, hackle, body, and a stiff tail. It floats with the hook above or partly underwater. The large wings make this fly readily visible to an angler.

- **Bivisible:** This fly has no wings. White hackle is wound on the body at the fly's head, and hackle of another color (brown, gray, or black are the most popular) covers most of the remainder of the body. The

tail is stiff. It floats high, with the hook above water, and is highly visible to an angler.

- **Spentwing:** This fly has slender wings that stick out horizontally from the tapered body, hackle, and stiff tail. It floats on its wings and body with the bend of the hook underwater.

- **Spider:** This fly has no wings. The hackle is extralong and stiff. There is no body in the smaller sizes, a tinsel or herl body in the larger sizes. It has a stiff, extralong tail. It floats on its hackle tips and tail with the hook well out of the water.

- **Variant:** This fly has upright divided wings, extralong and stiff hackle, a very light body (or none at all), and a stiff, extralong tail. It floats on its hackle tips and tail with the hook well out of the water.

- **Hair Body:** This fly has upright divided wings, hackle, a body of clipped deer hair or similar material, and a stiff tail. It floats with the hook partly underwater.

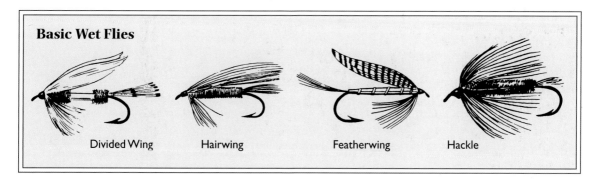

Basic Wet Flies

Divided Wing   Hairwing   Featherwing   Hackle

■ **Keel Fly:** The shank of the hook is weighted, causing the fly to ride upright in the water. The keel principle also has been applied to wet flies and streamers.

The budding fly fisherman who walks into a fishing-tackle store is sure to be overwhelmed by the display of artificial flies. Which patterns are best for his particular needs? Only experience can answer that question. However, here are 10 basic dry-fly patterns—and the most productive sizes—that should be found in every trout fisherman's fly box:

◦ Light Cahill, Size 16
◦ Gray Midge Hackle, Size 20
◦ Black Flying Ant, Size 20
◦ Red Variant, Size 14
◦ Black Gnat, Size 12

◦ Gray Wulff, Size 10
◦ Blue Dun, Size 16
◦ Adams, Size 12
◦ Quill Gordon, Size 14
◦ Jassid, Size 20

WET FLIES: Wet flies are tied to imitate submerged insects, either those that have fallen to the surface and drowned or those that are rising from the stream or lake bottom to the surface to hatch. Nymphs, which are classified as wet flies, are imitations of the larval or nymphal states of underwater insects that rise to the surface before hatching.

As with dry flies, there is a bewildering number of wet-fly patterns. However, most of them fall into one of four basic types. Here's a brief description of each type:

■ **Divided Wing:** Two prominent separated wings are tied at about a 30-degree angle from the shank of the hook. This type also has a wisp of hackle, body, and a stiff tail.

■ **Hairwing:** A wing of deer hair extends over the shank of the hook, a wisp of hackle, body, and a tail.

■ **Featherwing:** This type of fly has a swept-back wing of feather fibers, soft hackle, tapered body, and a sparse tail.

■ **Hackle:** This fly has soft hackle tied on at the head, which extends back over the built-up body all around the fly. It has a sparse tail.

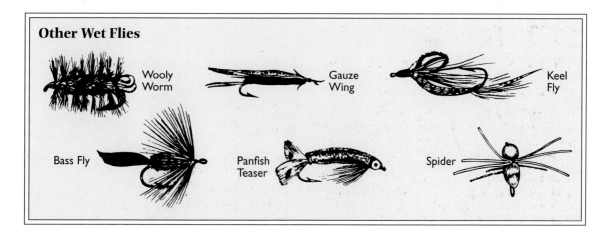

Other Wet Flies

Wooly Worm   Gauze Wing   Keel Fly

Bass Fly   Panfish Teaser   Spider

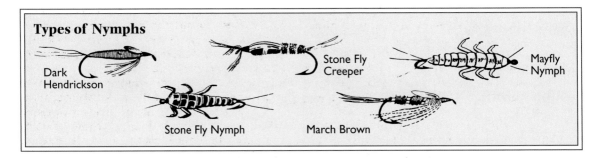

Types of Nymphs

Dark Hendrickson

Stone Fly Creeper

Mayfly Nymph

Stone Fly Nymph

March Brown

Here are 10 wet-fly patterns that should produce well for the trout fisherman:

- Gray Hackle, Yellow Body, Size 10
- Brown Hackle, Size 10
- Coachman, Size 12
- Royal Coachman, Size 12
- Black Gnat, Size 14
- Quill Gordon, Size 14
- Blue Dun, Size 16
- Light Cahill, Size 16
- March Brown, Size 12
- Ginger Quill, Size 16

NYMPHS: It is impossible to break down the various nymph patterns into broad classifications. However, most nymphs have the following basic characteristics: no wings, wisps of soft hackle at the head, a tapered body, usually of dubbed fur, and a sparse tail of a few feather fibers.

Here are 10 nymph patterns that no trout fisherman should be without:

- March Brown, Size 12
- Ginger Quill, Size 14
- Yellow May, Size 12
- Freshwater Shrimp, Size 8
- Light Mossback, Size 6
- Large Stone Fly, 2X Long shank, Size 8
- Large Mayfly, 2X Long shank, Size 10
- Caddis, 2X Long shank, Size 10
- Dark Olive, 2X Long shank, Size 12
- Montana, Size 4

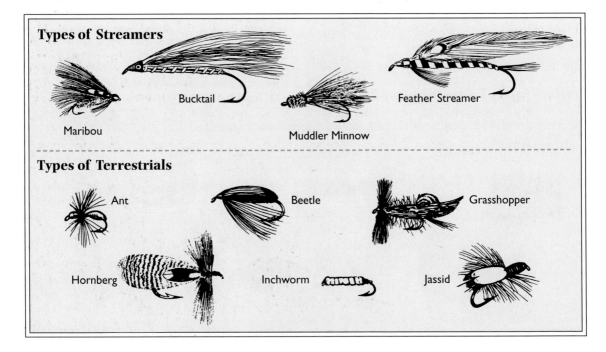

Types of Streamers

Maribou

Bucktail

Muddler Minnow

Feather Streamer

Types of Terrestrials

Ant

Beetle

Grasshopper

Hornberg

Inchworm

Jassid

STREAMERS AND BUCKTAILS: Streamer flies and bucktails are tied to imitate a minnow or other baitfish on which game fish feed. They are widely used in both fresh and salt water. Many saltwater streamers and bucktails, and some used in fresh water, have two hooks—the main hook, on which the dressings are tied, and a trailer hook. Streamers and bucktails are well known for producing big fish.

Streamers are tied with long wings of feathers. Bucktails are similar, but more durable, flies tied with wings of hair, usually deer hair. Most streamers and bucktails are tied on Size 8 and Size 10 long-shank hooks. Some have bodies that hide the shank of the hook, but in others the bare shank shows.

Here is a list of 10 of the most productive streamer patterns and 10 top bucktail patterns (best hook sizes are 6 to 12, unless otherwise noted):

Streamers	Bucktails
○ Black Ghost	○ Black Prince
○ Gray Ghost	○ Brown and White
○ Supervisor	○ Black and White
○ Mickey Finn	○ Red and White
○ Black-Nosed Dace	○ Mickey Finn
○ Red and Yellow	○ Platinum Blonde, Size 1/0
○ Clouser Minnow	○ Strawberry Blonde, Size 1/0
○ Red and White	○ Brown Muddler Minnow,
Multiwing, Size 1	Sizes 1/0 to 10
○ Black Marabou	○ Black Woolly Bugger,
○ White Marabou	Sizes 6 to 10
	○ White Marabou Muddler,
	Sizes 1/0 to 6

TERRESTRIALS: A class of artificial flies that is unique and deserves special mention is terrestrials—a group of flies, both wet and dry, that are tied to imitate insects that are born on land and then fly, jump, fall, crawl, or are blown into the water and become food for trout and other fish. Such insects include ants, grasshoppers, inchworms, beetles, houseflies, and others.

Among the most popular and productive terrestrial patterns are the Inchworm, the Black Ant (especially in very small sizes), and the Jassid, a fly that was developed in Pennsylvania and is particularly effective in limestone streams. It is tied on tiny hooks, with the best sizes being 18, 20, and 22.

BASS BUGS: If any form of fly fishing approaches the thrill of taking a wary trout on a dry fly, it is having a belligerent largemouth or smallmouth bass burst through the surface and engulf an enticingly twitched bass bug.

Bass bugs are fly-rod lures created to imitate such bass morsels as frogs, bees, dragonflies, mice, and anything else that looks like it would taste good to a bass or pike. Because of the size of a bass's mouth, these surface lures are tied on large hooks—size 4 to 2/0 in most cases. However, smaller versions of these bugs are made for panfish.

Most bass bugs fall into one of two categories: those with solid bodies (usually of cork, plastic, or balsa wood) and those with bodies of deer hair.

Many cork or balsa bugs have some hackle or bucktail at the tail to partly disguise the hook. Some have a perpendicular, hollowed-out surface so that when the angler jerks the rod tip the bug makes a popping sound that often brings a bass charging out of its lair. These bugs are called poppers. Others have a more streamlined body and are really designed to be twitched slowly rather than jerked.

Bass Bugs and Poppers

Classic Frog

Sneaky Pete Popper

Hair Bass Bug

Bluegill Bug

NATURAL FOODS AND THEIR IMITATIONS

Fly tying is the art of imitating or suggesting numerous food forms—insects, minnows, crustaceans, and similar forage eaten by fishes—by dressing hooks with feathers, fur, wool, tinsel, latex, wire, and other suitable materials.

The following text provides a breakdown of the basic food forms fly tiers try to imitate. Get to know them, how they act in their own environment and for which fishes they form partial or principal diets. You don't have to be an entomologist to be a successful fly fisherman, but the more you know about these basic foods, the more fish you are going to find in your creel or live box.

Larva • A larva is the immature, wingless, and often worm-like form in which certain insects hatch from the egg, and in which they remain until the pupa or chrysalis stage. Grubs, caterpillars, and maggots are examples. Wet-fly larval imitations are fished underwater.

Pupa • A pupa is the intermediate, usually dormant, form assumed by insects after the larva stage, and is maintained until the beginning of the adult (dun or subimago) stage. Wet-fly pupa imitations are fished underwater.

Nymphs • The nymph, in the strictest sense, is the stage in the development of an insect when the rudimentary wings of the adult (imago or spinner) become visible. It is common practice, however, to use the word "nymph" to cover all forms of developing underwater insects. Normally fished below the surface as a wet fly, some nymph patterns are dressed to float.

Adult Insects • Imitations of adult insects (imagoes or spinners) generally have wings and are tied in dry-fly patterns for surface fishing and in wet-fly patterns for use underwater. Wets also are dressed to resemble small fishes and other natural foods.

Terrestrials • Among the lesser fish foods, terrestrials are land insects that, through one misadventure or another, wind up in the water to become forage for hungry fish. As a group, they include grasshoppers, beetles, ants, crickets, crane flies, inchworms, leafhoppers, and spiders. Imitations are fished on or in the surface film.

Midges • Entomologists use the word "midge" to identify a special order (*Diptera*) of minute, two-winged insects that include flies, mosquitoes, jassids, and gnats. To a fly fisherman, however, it refers to any very small artificial fly. Thus, it becomes a catch-all term for tiny caddis nymphs, mayflies, some of the terrestrials, and other minutiae. Midges are dressed in both wet and dry patterns.

Crustaceans • Since they form an important part of the diet of a number of fresh- and saltwater fish, these little creatures deserve attention. They include crabs, crayfish, prawns, scuds, sandbugs, shrimps, and sowbugs. Imitations are fished underwater.

Baitfish • Baitfish fall into the collective term "minnows," which include shiners, chubs, dace, silversides, darters, and sculpins. They are an extremely important source of food for sport and game fish. Bucktail and streamer imitations are built on hooks running from standard length to size 8 extralong shanks. Although some patterns can be worked on the surface with good results, they are normally fished underwater.

Other Fish Foods • This category is a smorgasbord of such goodies as mice, moths, frogs, eels, bloodsuckers, worms, dragonflies, and bees. Imitations are made of hollow deer, elk, and caribou hair, cork, balsa wood, pre-cast plastic, and Mylar tubing. For the most part, these are fished on the surface.

This Muddler Minnow streamer (*top*) was created to imitate a real live minnow (*bottom*). Normally fished underwater, the popular Muddler Minnow can also be worked on the surface.

Deer-hair bugs are, as you might expect, made of deer hair that is wound onto a hook and clipped to form the body shape of a mouse, large insect, and the like. These bugs are best fished very slowly. Weedless arrangements, usually stiff monofilament or light wire, are sometimes used.

CHOOSING THE RIGHT FLY: Selecting the correct fly to use at any given time is a problem that has both delighted and dumbfounded anglers since the dawn of this sport. Dry fly, wet, or streamer? What color? What size?

The answers to these questions can often be found in the water at your feet. Study it carefully, both at the surface and underneath. If insects are flying from the surface, you are in the middle of a hatch, and you should select a dry fly that imitates as closely as possible the color and size of the natural insects. If you see subsurface insects, choose a wet fly or nymph of similar size and color.

However, spotting and identifying the natural insect may be difficult, due to water conditions, the minute size of the insects, and the sparseness of the hatch. (A "hatch" occurs when aquatic insects rise from the stream or lake bottom and change from the larval stage to winged adult flies.) Also, the fisherman may not have the right size and color of artificials in his fly box.

TYING FLIES AND BUGS

There are few pleasures in the sport of fishing that can match that of taking a trout, salmon, or other fish on a fly of your own creation. And there are other reasons for taking up this ancient art. On winter evenings, with the snow piled high outside and a bitter wind rattling the shutters, you can sit at the tying bench, reliving past fishing experiences and putting together the ingredients for future ones. And, of course, once you get the hang of it, you can tie respectable flies for a very small fraction of what you would pay for them in a store.

The following information from the late, well-known fisherman and expert fly tyer Tom McNally, and the accompanying illustrations, show the simple step-by-step procedures involved in tying the basic flies—streamers, wet flies, nymphs, and dry flies.

Writing of fly tying, a friend of mine described this ancient art as "the technique of fastening various materials on a hook to suggest real or fancied insects or food for the purpose of deceiving fish." That definition clears fly tying of the mysticism with which many would like to bury it. Actually, it's not difficult to turn out handsome, fish-catching flies. Anyone with a desire to learn can become a reasonably accomplished fly tyer. People with special aptitude can learn how to do it almost overnight.

Many years ago, I taught my wife to tie flies after three evening sessions at my worktable. Today, she shows me a trick or two. Some years ago, I taught my mother—who was looking for a hobby—to make shad flies and popping bugs. The ones she produced were sold in tackle stores. I don't know how many friends I've introduced to fly tying, and none failed to eventually turn out flies that were both attractive and fishable.

Fly tying was going on in Macedonia 2,000 years ago. A wasplike insect called hippuras was imitated by dressing a hook with purplish yarn and creamy hackles. The flies were floated, dry-fly fashion, on the Astraeus River. Ever since then, anglers have been using artificial flies—and many of those anglers have been tying their own. Judging from the growing interest in fly tying, fishermen will continue dressing their own hooks so long as there's fishing to be done. One doesn't have to be a watchmaker, surgeon, or engineer to tie flies. All that's needed is a little common sense and practice.

To become a professional or recognized fly tyer, of course, takes experience, and the intricacies of producing masterful flies would require a book-length treatise. But any beginner who absorbs the details here and studies the illustrations should be able to tie the simpler flies. Once big streamers and wet flies are mastered, and once you get the "feel" of the materials, the smaller and more complicated nymphs and dry flies can be attempted. The techniques are basically the same.

Why is fly tying growing in popularity? Because tyers save money? No, it's because fly tying is fun. Fishermen get more personal satisfaction out of gilling a bonefish or netting a trout with a hook they stuck into a vise and dolled up with feathers, tinsel, and fur.

That said, dollars can be saved by tying flies at home. A fly that would cost $4 at the tackle shop can

FRESHWATER FLIES

▼ Woolly Bugger

▲ Tunghead
Soft Hackle
Pheasant Tail

▼ Sparkle Dun

▲ Royal Wulff

▼ Red Quill

▼ Schultzy's Red Eyes Leech

▶ Quill
Gordon

▶ Royal Coachman

▼ Mega Clouser

▼ Muddler Minnow

▼ Zonker

◀ Cone-Head
Muddler
Minnow

◀ Egg-Sucking
Hornberg

▶ Mosquito
Dry Fly

▶ Light
Hendrickson

▶ March Brown

▶ Black Gnat

▼ Gold-Ribbed
Hare's Ear Wet

▶ Light Cahill

▶ Gray Fox
Variant

▶ Hard Body
Ant Wet

▼ Bead-Head Zug Bug

▶ Blue Dun

▶ Adams

▶ Bully Bluegill
Spider

SALTWATER FLIES

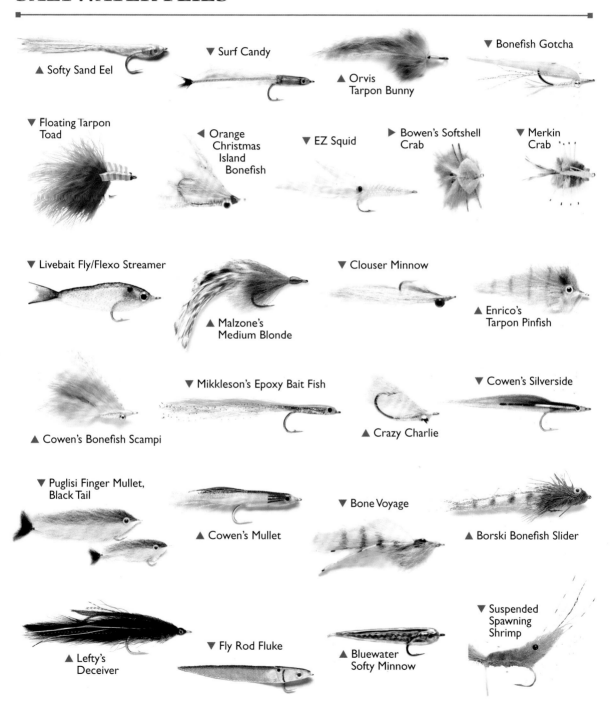

▲ Softy Sand Eel

▼ Surf Candy

▲ Orvis Tarpon Bunny

▼ Bonefish Gotcha

▼ Floating Tarpon Toad

◄ Orange Christmas Island Bonefish

◄ EZ Squid

► Bowen's Softshell Crab

▼ Merkin Crab

▼ Livebait Fly/Flexo Streamer

▼ Clouser Minnow

▲ Malzone's Medium Blonde

▲ Enrico's Tarpon Pinfish

▼ Mikkleson's Epoxy Bait Fish

▼ Cowen's Silverside

▲ Cowen's Bonefish Scampi

▲ Crazy Charlie

▼ Puglisi Finger Mullet, Black Tail

▼ Bone Voyage

▲ Cowen's Mullet

▲ Borski Bonefish Slider

▼ Suspended Spawning Shrimp

▲ Lefty's Deceiver

▼ Fly Rod Fluke

▲ Bluewater Softy Minnow

be made for less than $1. You can get a start in the fly-tying game for less than $150. Your hunting friends will add duck, goose, turkey, pheasant, and grouse feathers to your stock of materials, as well as rabbit, fox, squirrel, and skunk fur. Deer, moose, elk, and bear skins are also useful. The hair or feathers from almost any wildlife can be used by a fly tyer.

The tyer's mainstay, however, is the common barnyard chicken. Its hackles are used in nearly every fly. The great bulk of fly-tying materials comes from material houses, but even direct purchase is inexpensive. If you wind up like most tyers, thoroughly wrapped up in the hobby, you'll take on enough materials in a few years to open your own supply house. But like other fly tyers, you wouldn't part with a hair of your motley assortment.

To begin, you'll need a few basic tools: a vise, hackle pliers, scissors, and a razor blade. In the early days, flies were tied by holding the hook between one's fingers, but in 1897, D. H. Thompson ended this by producing a lever-and-cam type vise—the style most widely used and copied today. The vise is your single most important piece of equipment, and you should purchase a good one. Fine-pointed scissors will run about $10; the hackle pliers will be about $7. You may also want a bobbin to hold your spool of tying thread. It's inexpensive, frequently replaces hackle pliers, saves thread, and generally makes fly tying easier.

A beginner's basic materials should include thread (size 00 nylon), lacquer or head cement, hooks, hackles (neck, back, and breast feathers from roosters or gamecocks), duck-wing quills, mallard breast feathers, golden pheasant tippets, assortments of silk floss and chenille (a kind of tufted cord), tinsel, peacock herl from the "eyed" tail feathers of peacocks, and Mylar, a shiny metallic material that comes in narrow strips and in tube form. These materials, and more, usually are stocked by better sports and hobby stores. Some firms that deal in fly-tying materials supply catalogs, generally with photographs, that describe and price materials. The hook is the single most important factor in fishing, so tie your flies with the best.

■ Tools

A fly tyer needs only a few inexpensive tools. Let's take a look at each one and its use:

VISE: The most important device in the fly tyer's workshop, the vise is used to hold a hook securely and in the best position for the tyer to work around it. The most popular vise is the lever-and-cam type.

HACKLE PLIERS: These pliers are used to hold the tips of hackle feathers so that the tyer can wind the feathers onto the hook. Squeezing the sides of the pliers opens

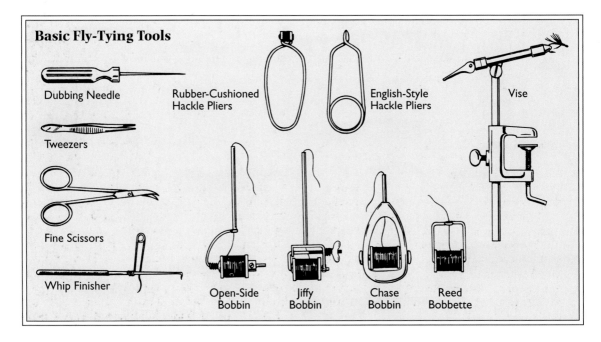

Basic Fly-Tying Tools

Dubbing Needle

Rubber-Cushioned Hackle Pliers

English-Style Hackle Pliers

Vise

Tweezers

Fine Scissors

Whip Finisher

Open-Side Bobbin

Jiffy Bobbin

Chase Bobbin

Reed Bobbette

the jaws. There are two types: rubber cushioned and English style. Both work well. A surgeon's artery forceps also make adequate hackle pliers.

SCISSORS: Scissors are used to cut thread and other dressing materials and to perform other auxiliary duties. The best type is a pair of sharp, fine-pointed scissors with either straight or curved blades. Larger scissors are helpful for making hair bugs.

BOBBIN: A bobbin is a device that holds the spool of tying thread and hangs down from the hook, providing necessary tension on the thread while the tyer is at work. Most bobbins have a tube through which the thread is fed. The bobbin saves thread, and it is especially useful to tyers who have rough hands that tend to fray the thread.

DUBBING NEEDLE: A large, fairly heavy, sharp steel needle set in a handle of wood or plastic, a dubbing needle performs many duties, including picking out fur bodies to make them fuzzier, picking out wound-under hackle, dividing wings, separating strands of floss and the like, applying head lacquer, and making a whip finish.

Other helpful fly-tying tools and auxiliaries include tweezers, hackle gauge, magnifying glass, hackle cutter, hackle clip, hackle guards, whip finisher, head lacquer, and thread wax.

Streamers

Although you may have no use for large streamer flies, they are easy-to-tie jobs that are ideal for your first lessons in fly tying. Stick to streamers until you get the knack of handling the tools and materials. It won't be necessary to follow a standard pattern in tying one of these big streamers, so the need for specific materials is lessened.

Always prepare your working area, tools, and materials before starting a fly. Rig a bright lamp on your desk, and place a large sheet of white cardboard or white paper under your vise to provide a white background while you work on the fly. This makes the fly easier to see and the materials simpler to locate. You'll need a short length of chenille, floss, or wool for the body of your streamer. The preferred colors are black, white, yellow, or red. About six hackles 3 to 4 inches long will make the wing, which can be one of the colors mentioned, mixed colors, or natural brown or barred-grizzly feathers from Plymouth Rock chickens. Two or three extra hackles, colored differently than ones used in the wing, also will be needed.

Mount your vise at a comfortable height and clamp a size 2 hook on it. The tying thread must be started on the hook. Most tyers first wax the thread since this waterproofs it, helps it hold to the hook, and generally produces a stronger fly. However, waxing takes time, and I doubt that it's vital to the durability of a fly. I haven't waxed thread for years, and my flies stay together. I apply a generous portion of fly-tying cement to the hook shank, then wind the tying thread from the hook eye to the bend. The cement waterproofs the thread and locks it to the hook.

When you've reached the hook bend with your thread, cut off any excess, and then tie in one end of the chenille (floss or wool) by looping the tying thread over it tightly. Wind the thread back to the hook eye, and let the bobbin hang or attach hackle pliers to the thread to keep it taut. The body material can be wound to within ¹⁄₁₆ inch of the hook eye, and tied off with the thread. The thread is looped in tight turns over the material to keep it in place. Be careful not to bring the body material all the way out to the hook eye or you'll have no room to tie off other materials or to form the fly's head. The excess body material is clipped off. Next comes the most difficult part of fly tying—attaching wings. Whether the fly is a streamer, nymph, wet, or dry, beginners usually have the most trouble with wings.

Choose from four to six hackles and use your fingernails to clean off some of the fuzzy fibers from the stems at the butt end of the feathers. Then, group the feathers in streamer-wing fashion and—holding them securely between two fingers of the left hand—place them in position on top of the hook, with the webby butts extending beyond the eye. Tie them in with tight loops of thread. Be sure to hold them tightly while tying. Otherwise, the hackles will turn on the hook and go in cockeyed. After making several tight turns over the butts, you can clip off the surplus.

The final step is hackling the head of the fly. The hackle feather (two or more may be needed to make a bushy fly) is wound around the hook so that the separate fibers flare outward like bristling hairs. This is the technique used in putting hackles on wet and dry flies. Good hackles are especially important on a dry fly because they make it float. Strip the web from the hackle feather, place it against the head of the fly at an angle, and secure with a few tight loops of thread. The hackle, gripped at the loose end by hackle pliers, should be turned around the fly two or three times. Then the thread can be wound over it once or twice, and the hackle tips can be cut off. The fly head is finished with several turns of tying

Tying a Streamer Fly

1 • Tying thread held in the bobbin is first wrapped on the shank of a vise-held hook.

2 • Yarn (floss or wool) that will form the body is tied in place with tight half hitches of thread.

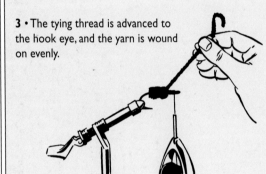

3 • The tying thread is advanced to the hook eye, and the yarn is wound on evenly.

4 • The body yarn is wound to within 1/16 inch of the hook eye and is tied off with several wraps of nylon thread.

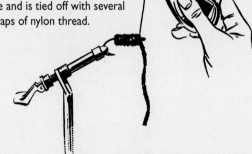

5 • After the thread tie-off, surplus yarn is snipped off close with fine-pointed scissors.

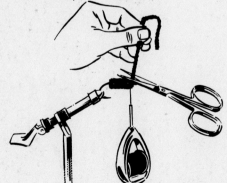

6 • Next, matched streamer feathers (four in this case) are tied in as shown here.

7 • After making several tight turns over the feather butts, clip off excess butts. The weight of the bobbin holds the thread taut.

8 • Hackle feathers make flies float. Two are needed for a bushy fly. Tie them in securely.

9 • Holding the hackle feather edgewise with the hackle pliers, wind the feather around the hook.

10 • Give the hackle feather two or three turns, tie end once or twice, and cut off surplus hackle tips.

11 • Use wraps of thread to create a streamer head. Cinch the head with half hitches or a whip finish.

12 • A light coat of lacquer on the fly head serves both to cement the thread and to waterproof it.

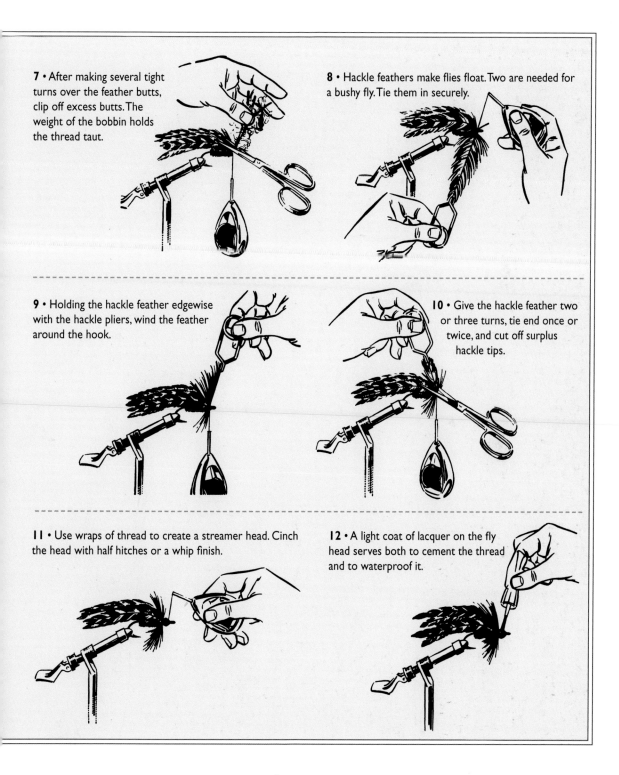

thread, and the thread is knotted off with a series of half hitches. Cement the head of the fly to waterproof it and keep knots secure. The whip-finish knot—identical to the one rod makers use in attaching guides—is better than half hitches, but it's a little beyond the beginner stage. Actually, half hitches, properly knotted and cemented, will keep a fly together indefinitely. The whip finish can be executed either manually or with the aid of a device called a whip finisher. For a look at both methods, see the end of this section.

The streamer is now finished, unless you'd like to paint "eyes" on it. This is easy to do with red, yellow, white, or black lacquer. You can buy small bottles of lacquer that have tiny brushes fixed to the caps. Most fly tyers paint their fly heads black. Lacquer dries in a few minutes. The fly's "eyes" are put on over the black base by dipping the blunt end of a fishing nail or wood match in light-colored lacquer and touching it to the head of the fly. As soon as that dries, a dark "pupil" is added. It's my opinion that such dolling up adds nothing to a fly's fish appeal, but it makes the fly more attractive to fishermen.

When you can tie one of these large streamers so it's proportioned correctly and won't come apart if you tug at a feather, you have mastered the fundamentals of fly tying. The methods you've learned in making this fly apply to any other pattern, including wets, nymphs, and dries.

The better streamers have tails, tinsel bodies, tinsel over chenille, wool, or floss, and perhaps colorful "cheeks" and "topping." The tying in of all these extras can be learned by following an advanced book on fly tying or watching an experienced tyer. Large streamers can be made with marabou feathers, bucktail hair, or saddle hackles. Either way, they're good for large trout, black bass, pike, walleyes, and saltwater species such as bonefish, striped bass, snook, and tarpon.

Wet Flies

A wet fly, whether bass- or trout-size, is tied much like a streamer, except that the wing material is usually cut from duck-wing quills or large turkey quills. (Refer to step-by-step illustrations for tying a streamer.) Other materials are red duck quill, silver tinsel, black silk floss, and red hackles.

Start your tying thread the same way you did when tying a streamer, only continue wrapping it around the hook to build up a tapered body. Cut a small section from the red duck quill and bind it down at the bend of the

hook with a few turns of thread. Be sure the tail is tied in tightly and is centered on top of the hook. Next, tie in a length of silver tinsel and several strands of black floss. The tying thread should be brought to the eye of the hook, and then the floss should be wrapped over the body, followed by the tinsel. The floss and tinsel are secured by thread at the head of the fly, and the surplus is trimmed off.

Attaching the wing is next. Select a pair of turkey quills and cut sections, one from each side of a feather, approximately half an inch wide. Place the two wing sections together, tips matched, curved sides facing. Grasp them firmly between your thumb and forefinger and place them on the shank behind the eye. (Pinching the wings firmly during the tying-on can't be over-emphasized. When wings are poorly done, it's usually because they were not held firmly while being tied.) Bring the tying thread over the wings and down on the opposite side, sliding it slightly back between the fingers. Pinching the wings tightly, pull the thread down, following with several turns over the butts. The wing should appear, with the butts ready to be trimmed. The final step is tying soft red hackle behind the fly head, just like the big streamer.

Nymphs

Nymphs are the best flies for catching trout, and they're also good for smallmouth bass and panfish. One of the simplest nymphs to make is the "attractor" type, which doesn't imitate any particular live nymph but suggests several kinds of real nymphs.

Begin the nymph by tying a tail. Tail material can be fibers from a feather, sections of peacock herl or deer, or boar hairs. Pig bristle makes an excellent tail because it isn't broken easily by fish. A narrow section cut from a turkey feather, or olive or black duck quill, will serve to make the nymph's back or wing case. Tie it in just above the tail. A short length of tinsel and some wool yarn, chenille, or floss (drab colors) is put on next. Wind the tying thread back and forth over the shank, making a tapered body form, and then wind on the body material and tinsel, tying them off near the hook eye. The quill section is brought forward, covering the top half of the nymph's body, and is tied down at the hook eye with a few tight turns of thread. The surplus is trimmed. Spin a small, webby hackle around the head, tie off, and trim so fibers extend only from the underside of the nymph to simulate legs. I usually lacquer a nymph's head, but some tyers lacquer the body, too.

Tying a Nymph

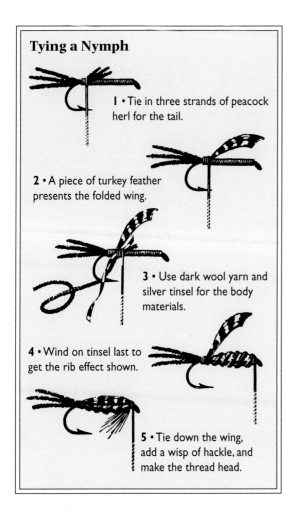

1 • Tie in three strands of peacock herl for the tail.

2 • A piece of turkey feather presents the folded wing.

3 • Use dark wool yarn and silver tinsel for the body materials.

4 • Wind on tinsel last to get the rib effect shown.

5 • Tie down the wing, add a wisp of hackle, and make the thread head.

■ Dry Flies

The bivisible—invented by the late Edward R. Hewitt—is the easiest dry fly to build. The bivisible is made by winding stiff, dry-fly quality rooster neck hackles along the shank of a hook. Usually two or three hackles are needed to give a bivisible enough bulk to float well. The simplest way to start a bivisible is by tying the tip sections of a couple of hackles at the bend of a hook, allowing the tips to extend backward to form a tail. The tying thread is then brought forward to the hook eye, the hackles are turned around the hook tightly, and finally tied down at the hook eye. That's all there is to this all-hackle dry fly. You'll find that it's a fish-catcher, too.

Excluding salmon flies, dry flies with upright wings are the most difficult flies to tie. Don't attempt them until you've had experience at tying the other types, and then start by making simple patterns. If you concentrate on large dries, no smaller than hook size 6 or size 8, the work will come to you faster.

The materials used for dry flies are selected for flotation, and for resistance to water absorption. Chenille, for example, becomes heavy with water, so it's never used in a good dry fly. The hackles and tail are what float a fly, so the finest quality gamecock or rooster neck hackles should be used. Common dry-fly body materials include floss, raffia (fiber from the raffia palm), deer or moose hair, quill, peacock herl, and muskrat fur.

To make a basic Black Gnat dry fly, start the tying thread as usual. Cut a narrow section from each side of a matched, slate-colored, duck-wing quill. Place the wing sections together, curved sides out. Grasping them firmly

Tying a Dry Fly

1 • Wrap the hook shank with thread and then tie on the wings.

2 • Turns of thread anchor the wings. After that, tie on the tail.

3 • Next, tie in black yarn and wind it forward to the wings.

4 • Tie on the hackle feather and wind it on edgewise.

5 • Trim off the surplus hackle, and tie and lacquer the fly head.

Tying a Cork Bug

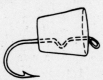  

1 • Make a slit in the cork body, fill the slit with cement, and press the cork into position on the hook shank.

2 • Tie four to six neck hackles behind the cork body.

3 • Wind on two or three soft hackles to form the collar, tie them off, and cement the windings.

---

between the thumb and forefinger, place them on the hook over the eye and bring the thread over the sections and down, making several tight turns. Still holding the sections firmly between the fingers, raise them erect, bring the tying thread in front of them, and make enough turns against the wing bases to keep them upright. Spread the wings

---

Tying the Whip Finish

Budding fly tyers that are confronted with illustrations of how to tie a whip finish may be inclined to switch to golf. Though this knot looks complicated, it can be mastered in about 10 minutes of practice once the basic steps have been learned. The whip finish is undoubtedly the neatest way to finish off a fly. It is practically invisible, even on tiny dry flies.

There are two ways to make the whip finish—manually (that is, with the fingers alone) or with the aid of an ingenious little device called the whip finisher.

Without the Tool: Here's how to do it manually (for purposes of clarity, the accompanying illustrations show the knot itself, without the finger manipulations, which are impossible to show in detail and which the tyer will pick up with a bit of practice).

Grasp the thread (which is hanging down from the hook) with the last three fingers of the left hand, about 6 inches below the hook. Position the right hand so that its back is facing the tyer, and grasp the thread 2 inches down from the hook with the first two fingers and thumb. Twist the right hand to the right and forward so that the palm is facing upward. There is now a loop in the thread (Step 1).

With the left thumb and forefinger (which are free), grasp the left-hand side of the loop, and begin to wind it around both the hook and the return portion of the loop (Step 2). Use the right hand to help the left in making one complete turn around the hook (Step 3).

Make about six complete turns around the hook and the return part of the loop, making the first half of each turn with the left hand and the last half with the right hand.

After the last turn is completed, hold the loop

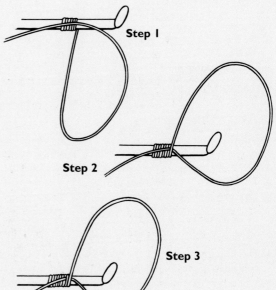

apart and wrap thread between them to the opposite side of the hook, reversing to describe a figure eight between the sections. Tie in a few stiff black hairs or some suitable hackle fibers for a tail. Cut off the excess tail fibers, then tie in black silk floss and bring the tying thread forward to the front of the wings. A glossy black hackle feather (two may be needed) is tied in front of the wings. Secure the hackle feather with several turns of thread. Then, use hackle pliers to grasp the tip of the hackle and take a turn or two in front of the wings and two or three turns in back. Catch the hackle tip with tying thread and bind it down. Cut off the surplus end of the hackle feather. Finish the fly with a small, neat head made with the tying thread. Lacquer the head. That's all—your first winged dry fly is finished. Your second dry fly will be easier than the first, the third easier still, and so on until you begin to feel skilled.

Cork Bug

You can buy cork bodies in many different shapes and sizes, or you can shape and size your own from a large piece of cork, using a razor blade and an emery board or small file. Be sure to sand the body smooth so that you get a good finish when you paint it. Here are the basic steps in making a cork-bodied bug:

Place a hump-shanked hook (available at most tackle-supply outlets) in the vise, coat the shank with liquid cement, and wrap the part that is to be covered by the cork body with tying thread.

With a razor blade, make a slit in the cork body, fill the slit with cement, and press the cork into position on the hook shank. Give the cork body two coats of liquid cement, clear enamel, or wood sealer, and let it dry.

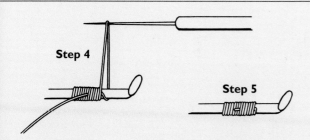

vertically taut with the left hand, and with the right hand insert into the loop, parallel to the hook, a dubbing needle (or a toothpick). Raise the dubbing needle until the loop is held taut by it (Step 4).

Then, with the left hand, pull on the free end of the thread, contracting the loop until the needle rests on the head of the fly. Remove the needle, pull the thread tight, and clip it off close (Step 5). The whip finish is now complete. The winding should be coated with head cement.

With the Tool: The whip finisher ties the same exact knot but eliminates the somewhat complicated finger manipulations. Here is how to use it:

Take the tool in the right hand, and place it near the hook and parallel to the hook shank. Run the thread from the hook around the spring retainer (Step 1).

Bring the end of the thread back near the fly, and with the tool's nose hook pick up the thread between the fly and the retainer (Step 2).

Now, keeping the thread taut with the left hand and in line with the fly, position the nose of the tool as close to the fly hook as possible—in fact, the fly hook can rest in the curve at the base of the tool's nose hook.

Rotate the tool clockwise around the hook shank, causing the thread to wind around both the hook and itself. Try to keep the windings tight up against one another. Make about six such turns (Step 3).

Keeping the thread taut, remove it from the tool's nose hook, and pull the thread with your left hand until the spring retainer is drawn up to the hook. Remove the retainer, pull the thread tight, and trim it off close to the windings. Apply head cement.

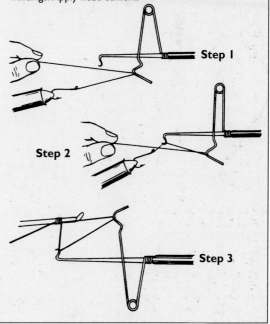

Tie to the shank of the hook, behind the cork body, four or six neck hackles (badger is a good choice) so that they flare out well and thus give a lifelike action when on the water.

Wind on two or three soft hackle feathers to form the collar, tie them off, and cement the windings. Paint the cork body with enamel of whatever color suits you, and paint on the eyes.

NATURAL FRESHWATER BAITS

Live bait is the real thing! Even the most avid purist would concede that live bait, when properly presented, is one of the deadliest of all lures. Many times, however, live bait is incorrectly rammed onto a hook. When this happens, the bait does not act naturally, may die quickly, and will likely turn away lunkers that grew big by learning how to recognize food that doesn't look right.

Live bait will only appear natural if placed on the hook correctly, and this depends on how you plan to fish it. You wouldn't, for example, hook a minnow behind the dorsal fin if you plan on trolling. Minnows just don't swim backward. Let's take a look at the popular baits and learn how to hook them.

Even though garden worms and night crawlers will take most species of fish, they must still be presented differently. A worm washed into a stream, for example, would drift with the current, so it should be fished that way. Hook it once through the collar or girdle with both ends free to drift naturally, fish it with no line drag, and let the current do the work. The worm should look strung out, bouncing along quickly through riffles and slowly through pools.

Using worms for panfish requires a different tack. Generally, the panfish angler is still-fishing, so natural presentation is less important. A single worm should be used and threaded about three times on the hook. If you're bothered by nibblers, use only a piece of worm and thread it on the hook, covering the point and barb completely.

Night crawlers are effective on bass, and many fishermen still-fish for bass with the big worms the same way they would for panfish. Actually, bass prefer a moving bait and anglers would catch more big bass if they cast and retrieved night crawlers slowly along the bottom. Hook the worm by running the point of the hook into its head, bringing the point and barb out an inch below the head. Rigged this way and retrieved slowly, a night crawler will appear to be crawling on the bottom.

Next on the list of most common live baits are minnows, from 1-inchers for panfish to 8-inchers for big fish.

There are two ways of hooking a live minnow, and how an angler intends to fish determines which one to use.

When trolling or fishing from a drifting boat, run the hook upward and through both lips of the minnow. The lip-hooked bait will move through the water on an even keel and look natural.

If you're still-fishing from an anchored boat or shoreline, hook the minnow just behind the dorsal fin. Be careful not to run the hook too deep or it will hit the spine and kill the bait. Hooked just behind the fin, a minnow can swim freely and for a surprisingly long time. There is no hook weight near its head or tail to throw off its balance.

Frogs rank as another excellent bait. Stick with the small frogs, however, such as leopard and green frogs. An old sock makes a fine frog carrier, and frogs are easy to find along any shoreline or riverbank during the summer. There is only one good way to hook a live frog and that is under the jaw and up through both lips. Cast it out and let the frog swim freely, or use a twitch-and-pause retrieve. A lip-hooked frog will stay alive for a long time. A frog can also be hooked through one of its hind legs. A hook through a frog's leg, however, will destroy some leg muscles, limiting its natural movement.

The crayfish, often called crawfish, is another top bait for bass and trout. The problem is that crayfish are often difficult to find. The best way to hunt them is at night in shallow water that has a rocky or gravel bottom. A crayfish's eyes will glow reddish in the beam of a flashlight. The light seems to freeze them and they can be easily picked up. The best way to hook a crayfish is to run the hook up, through, and out the top of its tail. Cast into rocky shorelines or streams, they'll account for big trout, bass, and walleyes.

Salamanders or newts also take bass, trout, and similar species. Finding salamanders isn't hard. They like small springs and streams. They're active at night and easily spotted with a flashlight. Salamanders are fragile and must be hooked carefully. Use a fine-wire hook and run it through the lips or the tail. Salamanders produce best when drifted along stream and river bottoms.

Natural Freshwater Baits

Natural Baits	Species of Fish
Minnows	Largemouth and smallmouth bass, trout, pickerel, pike, walleyes, perch, crappies, rock bass
Earthworms	Trout, white bass, rock bass, perch, crappies, catfish, sunfish, whitefish
Night crawlers	Largemouth and smallmouth bass, trout, pickerel, pike, walleyes, muskies, catfish, sturgeon
Crickets	Trout, crappies, perch, rock bass, sunfish
Grubs	Trout, crappies, perch, rock bass, sunfish
Caterpillars	Trout, largemouth and smallmouth bass, crappies, perch, rock bass, sunfish
Crayfish	Smallmouth bass, walleyes, trout, catfish
Hellgrammites	Trout, largemouth and smallmouth bass, walleyes, catfish, rock bass
Nymphs (mayfly, caddis fly, stone fly, and others)	Trout, landlocked salmon, perch, crappies, sunfish
Grasshoppers	Trout, largemouth and smallmouth bass, perch, crappies
Newts and salamanders	Largemouth and smallmouth bass, trout, pickerel, rock bass, walleyes, catfish
Frogs	Largemouth and smallmouth bass, pickerel, pike, muskies, walleyes
Wasp larvae	Perch, crappies, sunfish, rock bass
Suckers	Pike, muskies, smallmouth and largemouth bass
Mice	Largemouth and smallmouth bass, pike, muskies
Freshwater shrimp (scud)	Trout, smallmouth and largemouth bass, perch, crappies, rock bass, sunfish
Dragonflies	Largemouth and smallmouth bass, crappies, white bass, rock bass
Darters	Trout, largemouth and smallmouth bass, walleyes, pickerel, crappies, rock bass
Sculpins	Largemouth and smallmouth bass, walleyes, pickerel, rock bass
Salmon eggs	Trout, salmon
Cut bait (perch belly, etc.)	Pickerel, pike, muskies, largemouth and smallmouth bass, walleyes
Doughballs	Carp, catfish

The most popular live baits have been covered here, but there are still others worth mentioning. The hellgrammite, for example, ranks high with bass and trout. Water insects, hellgrammites average 1 to 2 inches long and can be caught in most streams by simply turning over rocks and holding a net just downstream from the rock. The hellgrammite has a hard collar just behind the head and this is where the hook should be inserted.

The nymph, an underwater stage of the aquatic fly, is still another top bait, particularly for trout. Nymphs differ in the way they behave. Some crawl on rocks, others climb shoreline growths, and still others float downstream. They will all eventually hatch into flies, but it is during this nymphal period that they can be effectively used as bait. There are two ways to put nymphs on a hook. They can be completely threaded—running the hook from the rear, through the body, and up to the head—or they can be simply hooked once just behind the head.

Grasshoppers also work well, and finding them is no problem. Most grassy fields are loaded with 'hoppers. Using a butterfly net, you should be able to fill a box quickly. It's easier to catch them at dawn and dusk. During midday, they are most active and spooky. There are several varieties of grasshoppers and nearly all of them take fish. It's best to use a fine-wire hook, running it down and through, behind the head.

Baiting Game

Worms, earthworms, and night crawlers are the most popular baits. Night crawlers come to the surface at night. They like warm and damp and dewy weather. Prowl around your lawn, a golf course, or a park after dark. Use a flashlight, but not one with a bright beam, which will spook worms. Cover the lens with red cellophane if necessary. Usually worms you will spot will only be partly out of their holes. Quickly press your finger at the spot where the tail enters the ground and grab the worm with the other hand.

Natural Freshwater Baits

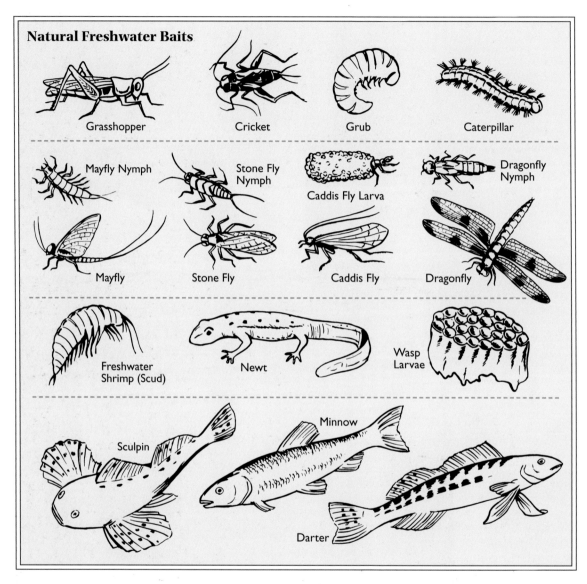

Grasshopper

Cricket

Grub

Caterpillar

Mayfly Nymph

Stone Fly Nymph

Caddis Fly Larva

Dragonfly Nymph

Mayfly

Stone Fly

Caddis Fly

Dragonfly

Freshwater Shrimp (Scud)

Newt

Wasp Larvae

Sculpin

Minnow

Darter

Crayfish and Hellgrammite Rigs

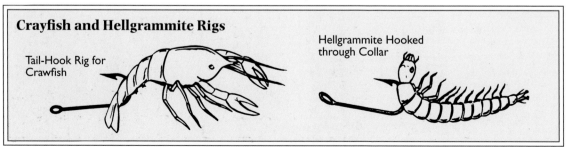

Tail-Hook Rig for Crawfish

Hellgrammite Hooked through Collar

Worm Rigs

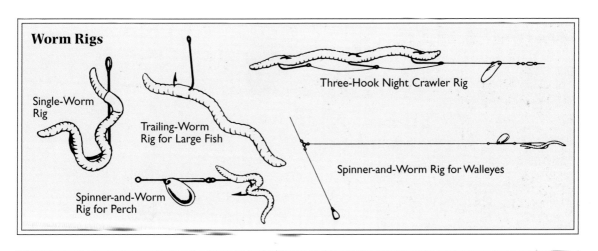

Single-Worm Rig

Trailing-Worm Rig for Large Fish

Three-Hook Night Crawler Rig

Spinner-and-Worm Rig for Walleyes

Spinner-and-Worm Rig for Perch

Minnow Rigs

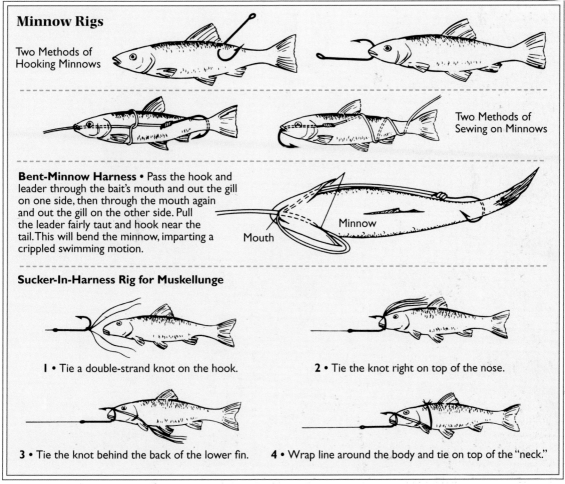

Two Methods of Hooking Minnows

Two Methods of Sewing on Minnows

Bent-Minnow Harness • Pass the hook and leader through the bait's mouth and out the gill on one side, then through the mouth again and out the gill on the other side. Pull the leader fairly taut and hook near the tail. This will bend the minnow, imparting a crippled swimming motion.

Mouth   Minnow

Sucker-In-Harness Rig for Muskellunge

1 • Tie a double-strand knot on the hook.

2 • Tie the knot right on top of the nose.

3 • Tie the knot behind the back of the lower fin.

4 • Wrap line around the body and tie on top of the "neck."

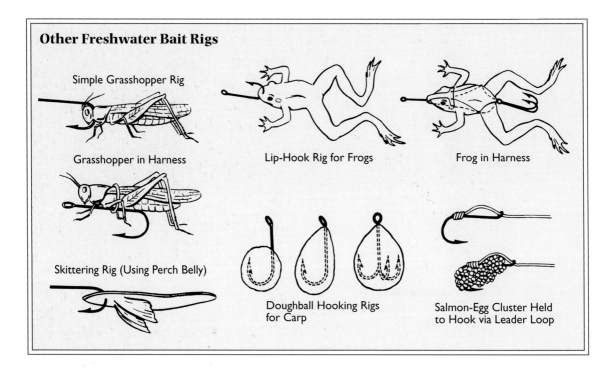

Other Freshwater Bait Rigs

Simple Grasshopper Rig

Lip-Hook Rig for Frogs

Frog in Harness

Grasshopper in Harness

Skittering Rig (Using Perch Belly)

Doughball Hooking Rigs for Carp

Salmon-Egg Cluster Held to Hook via Leader Loop

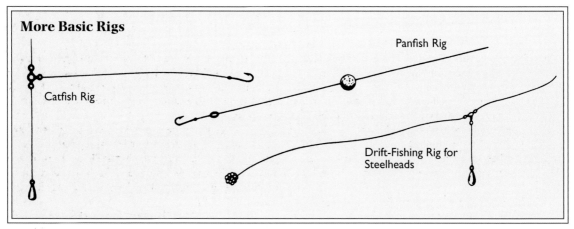

More Basic Rigs

Panfish Rig

Catfish Rig

Drift-Fishing Rig for Steelheads

Big Shiners for Big Bass

Nearly all bass experts agree that fishing a live shiner is one of the most effective ways to catch the biggest bass of your life. Like most things, however, it's not as easy as it sounds.

Your first problem may be finding 10- to 12-inch shiners. If your bait shop doesn't have them, you'll have to catch them in back bays and river pools. You can chum for shiners with oatmeal and bread crumbs and catch them with doughballs on a No. 12 or 14 hook. You'll need at least two dozen for a day of bass fishing.

Shiners are most productive when fished along shorelines or close to floating vegetation such as lily pads or hyacinths. The standard rig will have two hooks—a treble hook through the lips of the shiner, and a trailing single or treble hook in the tail of the bait or held along-

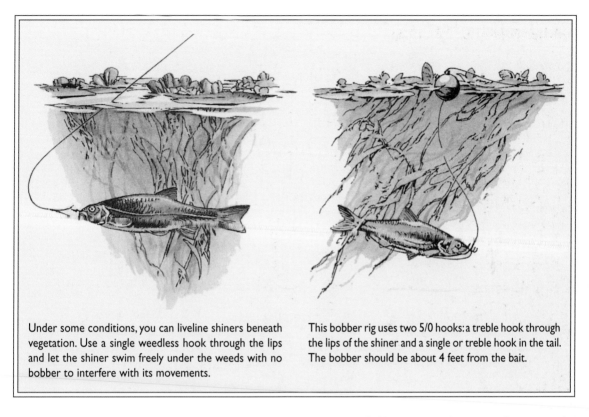

Under some conditions, you can liveline shiners beneath vegetation. Use a single weedless hook through the lips and let the shiner swim freely under the weeds with no bobber to interfere with its movements.

This bobber rig uses two 5/0 hooks: a treble hook through the lips of the shiner and a single or treble hook in the tail. The bobber should be about 4 feet from the bait.

side the tail with a rubber band. A bobber big enough to keep an active shiner from dragging it under water should be placed 3 to 4 feet above the bait.

Don't try to cast this half-pound bait overhand. Lob it underhand against shoreline vegetation and let the shiner take over. The fish will try to seek cover in the growth, and its movements will be telegraphed through the action of the bobber. When your shiner is motionless, jerk it back into action with a twitch or two of your rod tip.

The Best Tracking Line

Here's a neat trick: You may find it easier to track a shiner if you use a leader and a white level floating fly line with some backing on your conventional reel. The white fly line will be much more visible than monofilament. It will also be easier to track a bass when it picks up your bait.

If the bobber starts to bounce and jump on the surface, you'll know a big bass is after the shiner. Do nothing until that bobber goes down and stays down. A bass will grab the shiner around the middle and slowly swim away.

Begin counting as you watch your line move toward open water. As you count, slowly begin to reel in all slack until your rod tip is pointing in the direction the line is moving. Use your judgment here, but when your count is between 20 and 30 and all slack is out of your line, set the hook solidly.

Don't try to set the hook too quickly—you'll jerk the bait away from the bass. You have to allow enough time for the bass to pick up the shiner, swim away from the weed growth, and turn the shiner around in its mouth. Bass, like most other fish species, will swallow a live bait headfirst. You can also use circle hooks and you won't have to set the hook. As your line tightens, just lift your rod and the bass will hook itself.

You're after big bass, so leave your light tackle at home. Your best bet is a medium-weight rod with a conventional reel loaded with 20- to 30-pound-test line.

NATURAL SALTWATER BAITS

Natural baits are no less important in salt water than they are in fresh water. That fact is well known to anyone who has seen a school of blue-fish slash viciously into a horde of mossbunkers or a tuna or sailfish ravaging a ballyhoo bait.

What natural saltwater baits should you use and when? Those are questions that only time and experience can help you answer accurately. Generally, you will find that it pays to use any bait that is prevalent when and where you are fishing. A few discreet questions at a bait shop in the fishing area will go a long way toward helping you choose a productive bait.

How you rig a saltwater bait can be a vital factor. The primary consideration in rigging most baits is to make them appear as lifelike as possible, whether they are to be trolled, cast out and retrieved, or bounced on the bottom.

The accompanying illustrations show proven ways to prepare and rig the most popular baits used in salt water.

Florida Bait Bomb

One of the most exciting and productive ways to fish the inshore waters of Florida is to chum the patches of coral for yellowtail snappers, groupers, or the dozens of other species that live and hunt for food in these reefs. Every catch is a colorful surprise.

Captain Glen Miller, a charter captain for more than 30 years in the Florida Keys, and his mate, Brooks Gregory, are masters at chumming these patches. Glen knows how to position and anchor his boat so that the current will carry his chum to the fish living on the coral. If the current is too strong, the chum might pass over the patch and might not get close enough to pull fish into the chum. Once Glen has his position and current figured out, he starts to chum with a mixture of sand, chum, and oats. Within 10 or 15 minutes, small fish begin to appear, darting in and out of the chum.

Glen cautions about over-chumming. Put out too much chum and you will end up feeding the fish instead of catching them. Ladle out a handful of chum, and then wait until all the chum is out of sight before tossing out more. You can also place a frozen chum block in a mesh bag and hang it near the transom. Wave action will gradually thaw and release the chum automatically.

Now is the time to use Florida bait bombs. Some Florida captains call them bait balls or chum balls instead. Call them whatever you want, but these bombs are deadly and catch fish. Once Glen has a good slick working, he puts a piece of cut bait on a hook and centers it in the mixture of water, sand, chum, and oats. The mix is now formed into a snowball shape and packed firmly. The bait bomb is ready for fish.

Glen strips off about 12 yards of line from the reel, so there is no drag when he tosses the bait ball into the slick. The ball is allowed to drop slowly back into the slick. The ball puts out a small cloud of chum with the piece of cut bait in the middle. The fish will follow the chum and find the bait when the ball finally breaks apart in the current. A fish, usually a yellowtail snapper or one of many species of grouper, will invariably hit the bait. These Florida reefs harbor a great variety of fish. It is not uncommon to catch a dozen different species on one coral patch.

The bait bomb is only one trick Florida captains use to bring fish to the boat. While building a chum slick, some fishermen will also have two live grunt baits on the bottom and two live pilchards, one off an outrigger and another on a kite rod. More often than not, a big grouper will take a grunt on the bottom rig near the surface and a kingfish will nail the live pilchards.

This technique for using bait or chum balls is a strategy that should work anywhere a fisherman is trying to entice fish into a chum slick. It's so effective that commercial yellowtail fishermen use it in Florida. In northern coastal waters, weakfish and bluefish are two good targets for the Florida bait bomb.

Natural Saltwater Baits

Species of Fish	Natural Baits and Lures	Recommended Methods	Hooks
Albacore	Feather lures	Trolling	7/0
Amberjack	Strip baits, feathers, spoons, plugs	Trolling, casting	6/0 to 9/0
Barracuda	Baitfish, plugs, feathers, spoons	Trolling, casting	1/0 to 8/0
Bass, channel	Mullet, mossbunker, crabs, clams, spoons, plugs	Casting, still-fishing, trolling	6/0 to 10/0
Bass, sea	Squid, clams, sea worms, crabs, killie	Drifting, still-fishing	1/0 to 5/0
Bass, striped	Sea worms, clams, eels, metal squids, plugs, jigs, live mackerel	Casting, trolling, drifting, still-fishing	2/0 to 8/0
Billfish (sailfish, marlin, swordfish)	Balao, mackerel, squid, bonito, strip baits, feathered jigs	Trolling	4/0 to 12/0
Bluefish	Rigged eel, cut bait, butterfish, plugs, spoons, feathers	Trolling, casting, drifting, still-fishing	3/0 to 8/0
Bonefish	Cut bait (mainly sardines and conch), flies, plugs, spoons	Casting, drifting, still-fishing	1/0 to 4/0
Bonito	Feather lures, spoons	Trolling	4/0 to 6/0
Codfish	Clams, crabs, cut bait	Still-fishing, drifting	7/0 to 9/0
Dolphin	Baitfish, feather lures, spoons, plugs, streamer flies	Trolling, casting	2/0 to 6/0
Eel	Killie, clams, crabs, sea worms, spearing	Still-fishing, drifting, casting	6 to 1/0
Flounder, summer	Squid, spearing, sea worms, clams, killie, smelt	Drifting, casting, still-fishing	4/0 to 6/0
Flounder, winter	Sea worms, mussels, clams	Still-fishing	6 to 12 (long shank)
Grouper	Squid, mullet, sardines, balao, shrimp, crabs, plugs	Still-fishing, casting	4/0 to 12/0
Haddock	Clams, conch, crabs, cut bait	Still-fishing	1/0 to 4/0
Hake	Clams, conch, crabs, cut bait	Still-fishing	2/0 to 6/0
Halibut	Squid, crabs, sea worms, killie, shrimp	Still-fishing	3/0 to 10/0
Jack Crevalle	Baitfish, cut bait, feathers, metal squid, spoons, plugs	Trolling, still-fishing, casting, drifting	1/0 to 5/0
Mackerel	Baitfish, tube lures, jigs, spinners, streamer flies	Trolling, still-fishing, casting, drifting	3 to 6
Perch, white	Sea worms, shrimp, spearing, flies, spoons	Still-fishing, casting	2 to 6
Pollack	Squid strip, clams, feather lures	Still-fishing, trolling	6/0 to 9/0
Pompano	Sand bugs, jigs, plugs, flies	Trolling, casting, drifting, still-fishing	1 to 4
Porgy	Clams, squid, sea worms, crabs, mussel, shrimp	Still-fishing	4 to 1/0
Rockfish, Pacific	Herring, sardine, mussels, squid, clams, shrimp	Still-fishing, drifting	1/0 to 8/0
Snapper, mangrove	Cut bait, shrimp	Trolling, still-fishing, drifting	1/0 to 6/0
Snapper, red	Shrimp, mullet, crabs	Trolling, still-fishing, drifting	6/0 to 10/0
Snapper, yellowtail	Shrimp, mullet, crabs	Trolling, still-fishing	4 to 1/0
Snook	Crabs, shrimp, baitfish, plugs, spoons, spinners, feathers	Casting, drifting, still-fishing	2/0 to 4/0
Sole	Clams, sea worms	Still-fishing	4 to 6
Spot	Crabs, shrimp, baitfish, sea worms	Still-fishing	8 to 10
Tarpon	Cut bait, baitfish, plugs, spoons, feathers	Trolling, casting, drifting, still-fishing	4/0 to 10/0
Tautog (blackfish)	Clams, sea worms, crabs, shrimp	Still-fishing	6 to 2/0
Tomcod	Clams, mussels, shrimp	Still-fishing	6 to 1/0
Tuna, bluefin	Mackerel, flying fish, bonito, squid, dolphin, herring, cut bait, feathered jigs	Trolling	6/0 to 14/0
Wahoo	Baitfish, feathered jigs, spoons, plugs	Trolling, casting	4/0 to 8/0
Weakfish	Shrimp, squid, sea worms	Still-fishing, casting, drifting, trolling	1 to 4/0
Whiting, northern	Sea worms, clams	Still-fishing, drifting, casting	4 to 1/0
Yellowtail	Herring, sardine, smelt, spoons, metal squids, feather lures	Trolling, casting, still-fishing	4/0 to 6/0

How to Rig Saltwater Baits

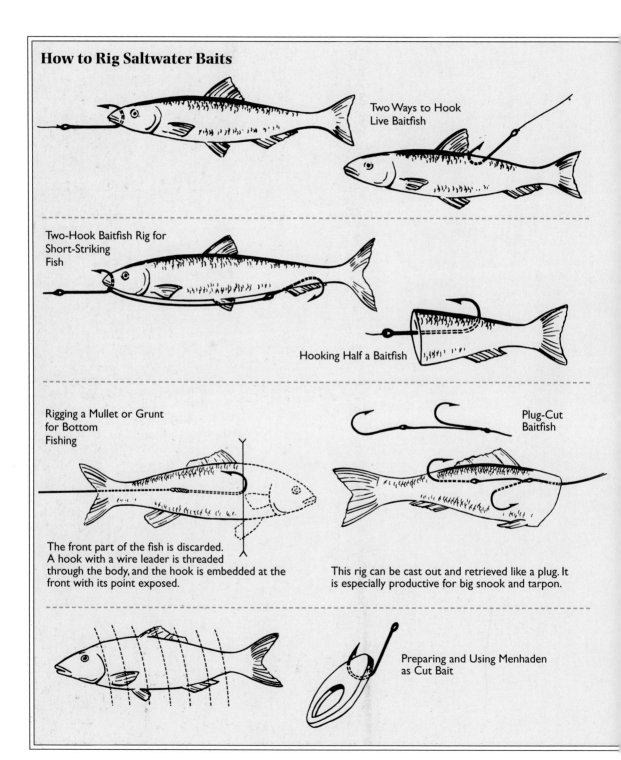

Two Ways to Hook Live Baitfish

Two-Hook Baitfish Rig for Short-Striking Fish

Hooking Half a Baitfish

Rigging a Mullet or Grunt for Bottom Fishing

Plug-Cut Baitfish

The front part of the fish is discarded. A hook with a wire leader is threaded through the body, and the hook is embedded at the front with its point exposed.

This rig can be cast out and retrieved like a plug. It is especially productive for big snook and tarpon.

Preparing and Using Menhaden as Cut Bait

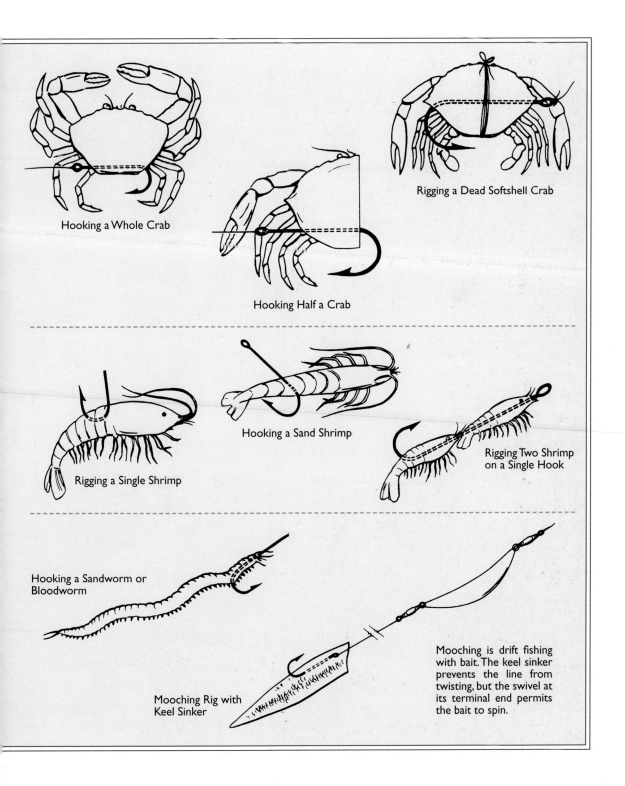

Hooking a Whole Crab

Hooking Half a Crab

Rigging a Dead Softshell Crab

Rigging a Single Shrimp

Hooking a Sand Shrimp

Rigging Two Shrimp on a Single Hook

Hooking a Sandworm or Bloodworm

Mooching Rig with Keel Sinker

Mooching is drift fishing with bait. The keel sinker prevents the line from twisting, but the swivel at its terminal end permits the bait to spin.

Saltwater Bait Rigs

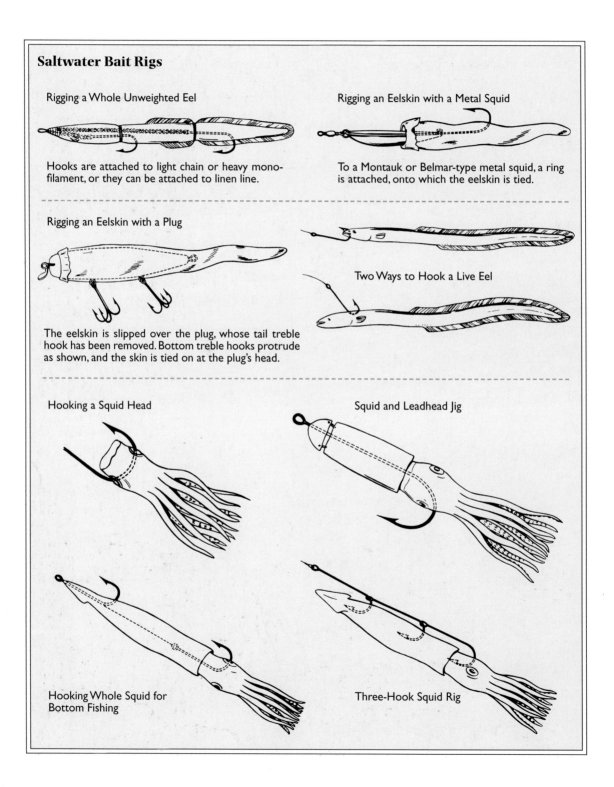

Rigging a Whole Unweighted Eel

Hooks are attached to light chain or heavy monofilament, or they can be attached to linen line.

Rigging an Eelskin with a Metal Squid

To a Montauk or Belmar-type metal squid, a ring is attached, onto which the eelskin is tied.

Rigging an Eelskin with a Plug

The eelskin is slipped over the plug, whose tail treble hook has been removed. Bottom treble hooks protrude as shown, and the skin is tied on at the plug's head.

Two Ways to Hook a Live Eel

Hooking a Squid Head

Squid and Leadhead Jig

Hooking Whole Squid for Bottom Fishing

Three-Hook Squid Rig

Saltwater Trolling Rigs

Rigging a Mullet for Trolling

Herring for Trolling

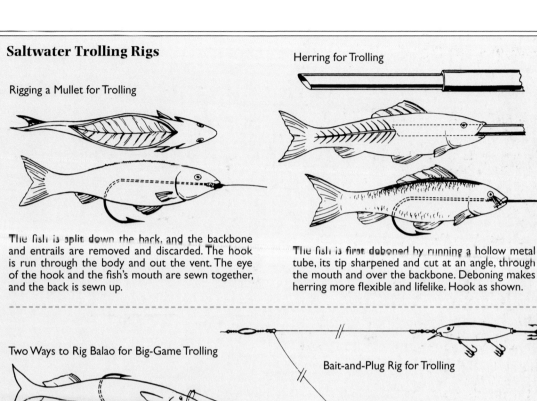

The fish is split down the back, and the backbone and entrails are removed and discarded. The hook is run through the body and out the vent. The eye of the hook and the fish's mouth are sewn together, and the back is sewn up.

The fish is first deboned by running a hollow metal tube, its tip sharpened and cut at an angle, through the mouth and over the backbone. Deboning makes herring more flexible and lifelike. Hook as shown.

Two Ways to Rig Balao for Big-Game Trolling

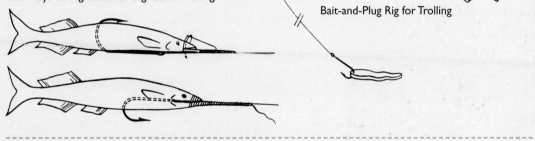

Bait-and-Plug Rig for Trolling

Rigging a Whole Eel with Tin Squid for Trolling and Casting

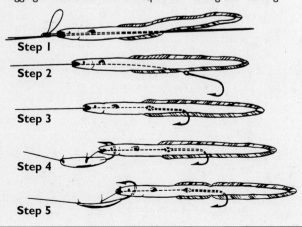

Step 1

Step 2

Step 3

Step 4

Step 5

To rig an eel this way, you'll need a long needle with an eye. Form a loop in some relatively heavy line (about 36-pound test) and run the loop through the needle's eye. Run the needle through the eel from mouth to vent (Step 1). Pull the loop all the way through the eel, and attach to it a 6/0 to 8/0 hook (Step 2). Draw the protruding line and hook shank into the eel (Step 3). Take a small block-tin squid, run its hook through the eel's head (or lips) from bottom to top, and tie the line to the eye on the flat surface of the squid (Step 4). With light line, tie the eel's mouth shut, make a tie around its head where the hook protrudes to prevent the hook from ripping out, and make a similar tie around the vent (Step 5).

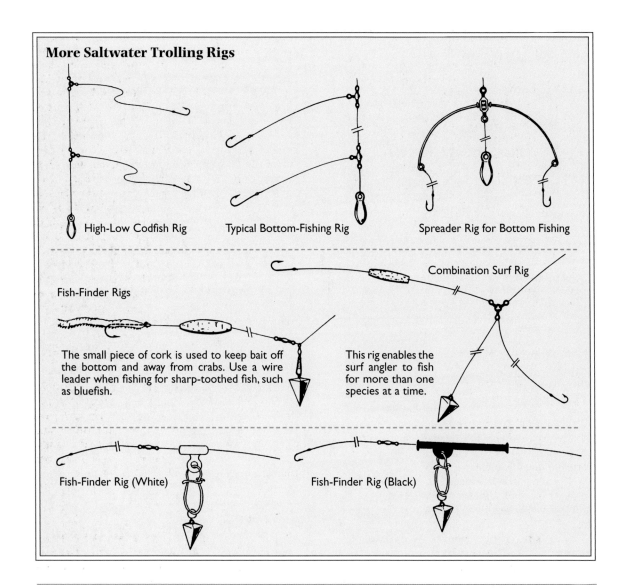

More Saltwater Trolling Rigs

High-Low Codfish Rig

Typical Bottom-Fishing Rig

Spreader Rig for Bottom Fishing

Combination Surf Rig

Fish-Finder Rigs

The small piece of cork is used to keep bait off the bottom and away from crabs. Use a wire leader when fishing for sharp-toothed fish, such as bluefish.

This rig enables the surf angler to fish for more than one species at a time.

Fish-Finder Rig (White)

Fish-Finder Rig (Black)

HOW TO CATCH BAIT AND KEEP IT FRESH

Anglers are often puzzled if they have to catch and keep something other than a dozen worms for a day's fishing. Catching the various baits and keeping them alive and kicking is not difficult, and sometimes catching bait is as much fun as the fishing. Only the popular baits are covered here. As you collect these, you'll soon discover that there are other baits available, such as grasshoppers, crickets, hellgrammites, lizards, and so on.

■ Worms

Worms, whether earthworms or night crawlers, are the most popular live baits. Night crawlers get their name from the fact that they come to the surface at night. They like warm and wet weather. Wait until it has been dark at least two to three hours, then prowl around your lawn, a golf course, or a park. Use a flashlight, but not one with a bright beam. If the beam is too bright, cover

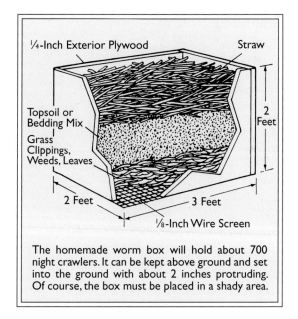

1/4-Inch Exterior Plywood   Straw

Topsoil or
Bedding Mix

Grass
Clippings,
Weeds, Leaves

2 Feet   3 Feet

2
Feet

1/8-Inch Wire Screen

The homemade worm box will hold about 700
night crawlers. It can be kept above ground and set
into the ground with about 2 inches protruding.
Of course, the box must be placed in a shady area.

the lens with red cellophane. When you spot a worm,
grab it by the head (the thicker end) with your fingers.
If the worm tries to shoot back into the hole, hold onto
one end until the worm releases tension and is free of
the hole.

If you can't find night crawlers at night, it's probably too dry for them to come to the surface. You can
wait for rain or water your lawn in the afternoon and go
worm hunting that night.

If you're after the common earthworm, which is
smaller than a night crawler, you'll have to dig for them.
Concentrate on compost heaps, vegetable gardens, and
stream banks.

A day's supply of worms can be carried in a few
inches of damp soil in a coffee can from which both
ends have been removed. Punch holes in the plastic lids
that come with the cans. With two of these lids in place,
it can be opened from either end for easy access to the
worms on the bottom. If you keep this container in a
burlap pouch and dip it occasionally in a cool creek, the
worms will stay fresh all day.

Commercial boxes for worms, as well as other baits,
are available. Most are made of porous fiberboard, which
insulates the box and keeps the inside cool and humid.

If you want to keep a good supply of worms on
hand, you can build a worm box. In a box of 2 feet by 3
feet by 2 feet, you can house 600 or 700 night crawlers.
Sink the box in a shady spot, allowing 2 inches of it to be

above ground. Damp and cool are the key words in keeping worms fresh. A wet burlap bag over some straw will
work well. You might also try spreading out a few hand-
fuls of ice cubes on the straw every two or three days. The
ice will keep the soil damp and cool as it melts. Food is no
problem, since worms eat almost anything. You can feed
them coffee grounds, breadcrumbs, and cornmeal.

Ice cubes, incidentally, can also be used effectively
when transporting and keeping worms on an extended
fishing trip. Try the following method on your next trip. In
the center of your bait box, which should measure about
12 inches by 12 inches by 8 inches if you're carrying 400
or so worms, clear a space in the bedding. Next, fill a glass
jar or plastic container with ice cubes, screw the cap back
on, and put it in a plastic bag. Place the container in the
center of the box and push the bedding or soil around it.
The ice will keep the soil cool and damp and it will stay
that way until the cubes melt. In hot weather, worms will
actually crowd around the jar. The purpose of the plastic is to seal in condensation. Without the plastic, the soil
would become too soggy for the worms.

■ Sea Worms

Sea worms, such as bloodworms and sandworms, are
delicate and should be kept in damp seaweed. If they
are to be kept for a week or so, spread them out in seaweed and keep them refrigerated. Bloodworms and
sandworms are enemies and should be kept separate.
Use a wood partition to divide your bait box into two
compartments.

■ Minnows

Minnows rank as the second-most popular bait, and
they can be caught almost as easily as worms. There are
several ways to collect minnows: minnow traps, drop or
umbrella nets, minnow seines, or cast nets.

Caution: A fishing license is usually required to
take bait in fresh water, and many states set limits on the
number of baitfish that may be kept. Check the fishing
regulations of your state before netting or trapping.

The minnow trap requires the least skill to use. It
works on the principle that a small fish will swim into
the funnel-like openings after food and be unable to find
its way out. For bait, you should wet oatmeal or cornmeal and roll it into balls the size of golf balls. The
meal will break up gradually in the trap and provide bait for
long periods. The best place to set the trap is in shallow

water near a dock or boathouse. On streams, set it near the head or side of a pool where the current is slow.

The drop or umbrella net, which measures 36 by 36 inches, gets more immediate results but may be more difficult to use. Lower it into the water just deep enough so that you can still lift it fast. Sprinkle breadcrumbs over it and let them sink. When minnows begin to feed on the crumbs, lift the net fast. With practice, you'll make good hauls every time.

A minnow seine not only produces a lot of bait, but also is fun to use, especially in bays and tidal rivers. A seine is usually 4 feet high and anywhere from 10 to 50 feet long, with lead weights along the bottom and floats on top. A 20-footer is a good size for most purposes. Seining is easy. Two people carry the seine about 100 feet from the shore or until the depth hits 4 feet or so. Keeping the weighted end of the seine on the bottom, the people sweep toward shore. The seine will belly out, catching everything in its path and carrying bait up on shore, where it can be picked up.

The cast net is one of the most useful tools of both the freshwater and saltwater angler, because he can use it to get the bait that he can't buy and to obtain forage baitfish native to the waters that he's fishing—which is the best bait to use under most circumstances. Monofilament nets, because their nylon strands are stiff, open better than nets made of braided threads. Mono nets also sink faster and are less visible after they're thrown into the water. Generally, they catch more fish, but they're also more expensive. Cast nets are available in various sizes and types. Experts throw 16-foot and larger nets, but anglers who would only use them occasionally are better off getting one that measures 8 to 10 feet. Bridge nets, popular in the Florida Keys, are short nets with extra lead weights around the bottom. When the net is dropped off a bridge into deep water, its added weight allows it to sink quickly and hold baitfish before they dive and escape. A plastic bucket is the best storage container for a net. All nets should routinely be rinsed with clean, fresh water and cleared of debris.

The next problem is keeping the minnows alive and fresh. The water must be aerated to keep enough oxygen in the bucket for survival, and this can be done in several ways. Water can be aerated by battery-powered devices, or you can aerate the water manually with a tin can. Scoop up a canful of water and pour it back into the bucket from a height of 2 feet. Doing this a dozen times every 15 minutes should provide sufficient oxygen for a couple dozen minnows.

If you plan to troll, keep bait in a bucket designed for trolling. This bucket, built to float on its side, will take water at an angle and aerate it.

If you're still-fishing, use the traditional bucket, which is actually two buckets. The outer bucket is used when transporting minnows. When you start fishing, lift out the insert and lower it into the water. The insert, which floats upright, is vented so that water is constantly changed.

Bait water must be kept at a constant temperature. In summer, add ice cubes to the water before transporting it. As the ice melts, it will cool the water and add oxygen. Take care, however, not to cool the water too fast. It is important to avoid abrupt temperature changes, which will kill minnows.

Crayfish and minnow traps are easy to use. Minnows and crayfish swim into the funnel-like openings at either end, but can't find their way out. Place the trap near docks or wherever the current is weak. Bait it with a paste mix of oatmeal and water rolled into balls the size of golf balls.

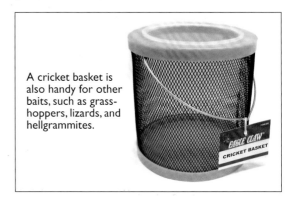

A cricket basket is also handy for other baits, such as grasshoppers, lizards, and hellgrammites.

How to Throw a Cast Net

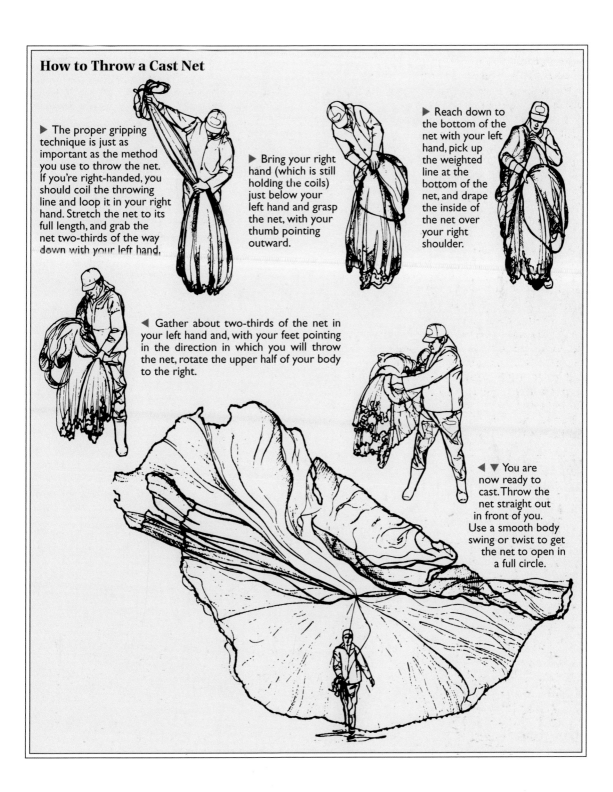

▶ The proper gripping technique is just as important as the method you use to throw the net. If you're right-handed, you should coil the throwing line and loop it in your right hand. Stretch the net to its full length, and grab the net two-thirds of the way down with your left hand.

▶ Bring your right hand (which is still holding the coils) just below your left hand and grasp the net, with your thumb pointing outward.

▶ Reach down to the bottom of the net with your left hand, pick up the weighted line at the bottom of the net, and drape the inside of the net over your right shoulder.

◀ Gather about two-thirds of the net in your left hand and, with your feet pointing in the direction in which you will throw the net, rotate the upper half of your body to the right.

◀▼ You are now ready to cast. Throw the net straight out in front of you. Use a smooth body swing or twist to get the net to open in a full circle.

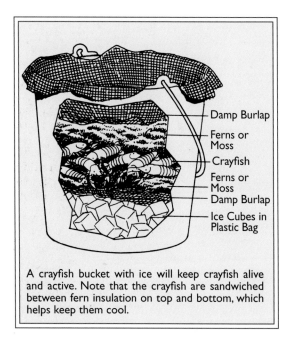

Damp Burlap
Ferns or Moss
Crayfish
Ferns or Moss
Damp Burlap
Ice Cubes in Plastic Bag

A crayfish bucket with ice will keep crayfish alive and active. Note that the crayfish are sandwiched between fern insulation on top and bottom, which helps keep them cool.

Crayfish

Crayfish make excellent bait, but they can sometimes be difficult to find. You'll do best at night along gravel shorelines. Crayfish feed in the shallows and you can spot them with a flashlight. Their eyes reflect reddish in the beam. When you locate one, hold a dip net behind it and touch its head with your hand or a stick. If you are lucky, it will swim backward into the net. If you are fast, you can try grabbing a crayfish from behind with your hand.

Keeping crayfish fresh in hot weather can be a problem. You can use an ice-bucket setup. In the bottom of a pail, place two dozen ice cubes in a plastic bag. Cover the ice with a layer of burlap, followed by a few inches of moss or ferns. Next, spread out the crayfish and cover them with another layer of moss or ferns. Cover this top layer with another piece of wet burlap. Crayfish will stay in fine shape in this insulated pail during the hottest weather. Keep the top piece of burlap wet.

Frogs

Few anglers will question the value of a lively frog as a bait. Look for frogs along the grassy banks of creeks, ponds, and lakes. Catching them is not hard. You can catch a fair number during the day, but you can collect more at night with a flashlight and a long-handled, small-mesh net. Frogs will remain still in the beam of a flashlight and you should have no trouble netting them. Keeping a day's supply of frogs is no problem. Commercial frog boxes are available, or you can make your own (see accompanying illustration).

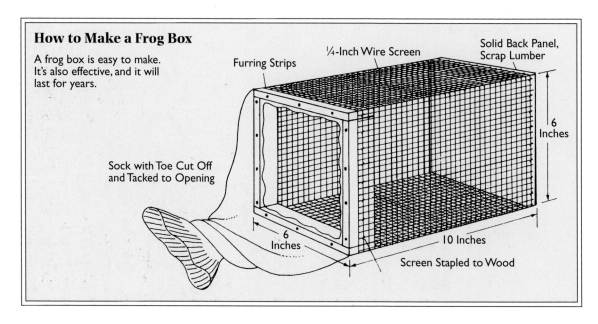

How to Make a Frog Box

A frog box is easy to make. It's also effective, and it will last for years.

Furring Strips

¼-Inch Wire Screen

Solid Back Panel, Scrap Lumber

6 Inches

Sock with Toe Cut Off and Tacked to Opening

6 Inches

10 Inches

Screen Stapled to Wood

TERMINAL-RIG ACCESSORIES

The items of fishing gear covered in this section are various components of the rigs shown in previous sections. These accessories are as important as links in a chain, so buy the best you can afford. A well-constructed snap swivel of the correct size, for example, won't come apart at the seams under the surge of a big fish.

Swivels come in many forms and sizes, but basically a swivel consists of two or three round metal eyes connected in such a way that each eye can rotate freely and independently of the others. Swivels perform such func-

tions as preventing or reducing line twist, enabling the angler to attach more than one component (sinker and bait, for example) to his line, and facilitating lure changes.

Sinkers, like swivels, come in many shapes and weights. Usually made of lead, they are used to get a bait (or lure) down to the desired depth.

Floats are lighter-than-water devices that are attached to the line. They keep a bait at a predetermined distance above the bottom and signal the strike of a fish. Floats are usually made of cork or plastic and come in many forms.

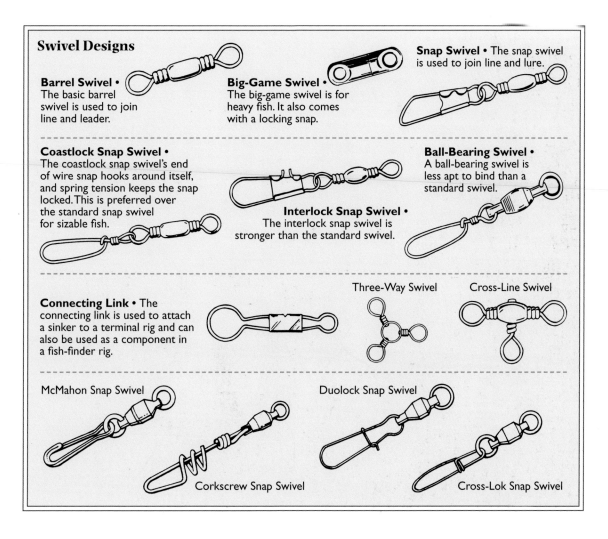

Swivel Designs

Barrel Swivel • The basic barrel swivel is used to join line and leader.

Big-Game Swivel • The big-game swivel is for heavy fish. It also comes with a locking snap.

Snap Swivel • The snap swivel is used to join line and lure.

Coastlock Snap Swivel • The coastlock snap swivel's end of wire snap hooks around itself, and spring tension keeps the snap locked. This is preferred over the standard snap swivel for sizable fish.

Interlock Snap Swivel • The interlock snap swivel is stronger than the standard swivel.

Ball-Bearing Swivel • A ball-bearing swivel is less apt to bind than a standard swivel.

Connecting Link • The connecting link is used to attach a sinker to a terminal rig and can also be used as a component in a fish-finder rig.

Three-Way Swivel

Cross-Line Swivel

McMahon Snap Swivel

Duolock Snap Swivel

Corkscrew Snap Swivel

Cross-Lok Snap Swivel

Sinker Designs

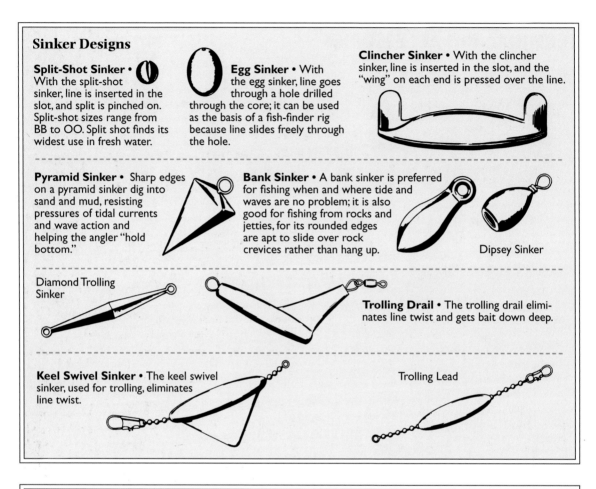

Split-Shot Sinker • With the split-shot sinker, line is inserted in the slot, and split is pinched on. Split-shot sizes range from BB to OO. Split shot finds its widest use in fresh water.

Egg Sinker • With the egg sinker, line goes through a hole drilled through the core; it can be used as the basis of a fish-finder rig because line slides freely through the hole.

Clincher Sinker • With the clincher sinker, line is inserted in the slot, and the "wing" on each end is pressed over the line.

Pyramid Sinker • Sharp edges on a pyramid sinker dig into sand and mud, resisting pressures of tidal currents and wave action and helping the angler "hold bottom."

Bank Sinker • A bank sinker is preferred for fishing when and where tide and waves are no problem; it is also good for fishing from rocks and jetties, for its rounded edges are apt to slide over rock crevices rather than hang up.

Dipsey Sinker

Diamond Trolling Sinker

Trolling Drail • The trolling drail eliminates line twist and gets bait down deep.

Keel Swivel Sinker • The keel swivel sinker, used for trolling, eliminates line twist.

Trolling Lead

Trolling Devices

The trolling planer is a heavily weighted device with metal or plastic "wings" that permit trolling at considerable depths. The bait-walker sinker keeps the bait moving near, but not dragging on, the bottom. The downrigger assembly shown has a terminal rig with a cable, cannonball, and release mechanism.

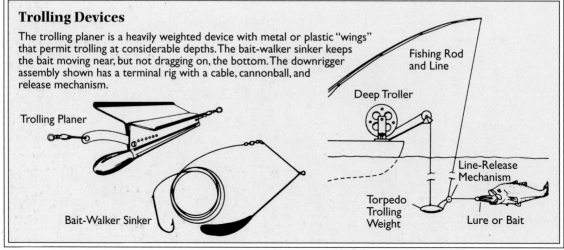

Trolling Planer

Bait-Walker Sinker

Fishing Rod and Line

Deep Troller

Line-Release Mechanism

Torpedo Trolling Weight

Lure or Bait

Float Designs

Cork Ball Float

Plastic Ball Float • In the plastic ball float, a spring-loaded top section, when depressed, exposes a small, U-shaped "hook" at the bottom into which line is placed. Releasing the top section reseats the "hook," holding the line fast.

The Caro-line cork float has a doubled length of line running through it lengthwise. The fishing line is run through the loop, and then the loop is pulled through the cork body, seating the line. The Caro-line float is generally used in surf fishing to keep a bait off the bottom and away from crabs.

Plastic Porcupine Float • The plastic porcupine float is light and highly sensitive to the strike of a fish.

Teeter Float • The teeter float has a slender section that floats perpendicular to the water and is highly sensitive to the strike of a fish.

Pencil Float • With the pencil float, line is attached at both ends. A strike causes one end to lift from the surface.

Panfish Are For Big People, Too

Every fisherman agrees that panfish are a perfect species for children. I agree, but I also think it's a great fish for big people, too. Bluegills and crappies are not difficult to catch and they are literally everywhere. In fact, many waters are overpopulated and overrun with stunted panfish. My favorite technique is with a fly rod and almost any kind of black or brown dry fly or small popper. Whether you're in a boat or fishing from shore, cast the fly as close as you can to the edge of a dock and twitch it a few times. If you don't get a hit, don't waste your time. Move to the next dock.

Not into fly fishing? You can do just as well with spinning tackle. You can catch panfish on small jigs and spoons, but, as a rule, bait works better than most lures. Worms and small minnows, especially for crappies, are the most consistent baits. Other baits that work include crickets, grubs, caterpillars, grasshoppers, and hellgrammites. Stick with ultralight tackle and 2- or 4-pound-test line. You can fish these baits deep with some split shot or with a bobber about 2 or 3 feet above your bait. With children, the bobber is probably more effective in shallow water close to shore. It's also fun for children to watch a bobber dance when a bluegill begins its attack.

Bluegills will eat just about anything you put in front of them, and you can find them in any shallow area of a lake or near structures such as docks and stumps. If you're looking for platter-size bluegills and crappies, there are a couple of factors to keep in mind. If you're fishing from shore, cast out a little farther and fish your bait deeper. Small bluegills will take bait anytime, but those bigger panfish concentrate their feeding at dawn and dusk.

Cleaning and cooking bluegills is easy. Fillet the two small slabs of meat from both sides of the fish. Dip the fillets in flour, egg, and bread crumbs, and then fry them golden brown in peanut or olive oil. It's that simple!

KNOTS

Anyone who aspires to competence as a fisherman must have at least a basic knowledge of knots. Most anglers know and use no more than half a dozen knots. However, if you fish a lot, you are sure to run into a situation that cannot be solved efficiently with the basic ties. The aim of this section is to acquaint you with knots that will help you handle nearly all line-tying situations.

All knots reduce—to a greater or lesser degree, depending on the particular knot—the breaking strength of the line. Loose or poorly tied knots reduce line strength even more. For that reason, and to avoid wasting valuable fishing time, it is best to practice tying the knots at home. In most cases, it's better to practice with cord or rope; the heavier material makes it easier to follow the tying procedures.

It is important to form and tighten knots correctly. They should be tightened slowly and steadily for best results. In most knots requiring the tyer to make turns around the standing part of the line, at least five such turns should be made.

Now let's take a look at the range of fishing knots. Included are tying instructions, as well as the uses for which each knot is suited.

■ BLOOD KNOT

This knot is used to connect two lines of relatively similar diameter. It is especially popular for joining sections of monofilament in making tapered fly leaders.

I • Wrap one strand around the other at least four times, and run the end into the fork thus formed.

2 • Make the same number of turns, in the opposite direction, with the second strand, and run its end through the opening in the middle of the knot, in the direction opposite that of the first strand.

3 • Hold the two ends so they do not slip (some anglers use their teeth). Pull the standing part of both strands in opposite directions, tightening the knot.

4 • Tighten securely, clip off the ends, and the knot is complete. If you want to tie on a dropper fly, leave one of these ends about 6 to 8 inches long.

■ STU APTE IMPROVED BLOOD KNOT

This knot is excellent for joining two lines of greatly different diameter, such as a heavy monofilament shock leader and a light leader tippet.

I • Double a sufficient length of the lighter line, wrap it around the standing part of the heavier line at least five times, and then run the end of the doubled line into the fork thus formed.

2 • Wrap the heavier line around the standing part of the doubled lighter line three times in the opposite direction, and run the end of the heavier line into the opening in the direction opposite that of the end of the doubled line.

3 • Holding the two ends to keep them from slipping, pull the standing parts of the two lines in opposite directions. Tighten the knot completely, using your fingernails to push the loops together if necessary, and clip off the ends.

DOUBLE SURGEON'S KNOT

This knot is used to join two strands of greatly unequal diameter.

1 • Place the two lines parallel, with the ends pointing in opposite directions. Using the two lines as a single strand, make a simple overhand knot, pulling the two strands all the way through the loop, and then make another overhand knot.

2 • Holding both strands at each end, pull the knot tight, and clip off the ends.

IMPROVED CLINCH KNOT

This knot is used to tie flies, bass bugs, lures, and bait hooks to line or leader. This knot reduces line strength only slightly.

1 • Run the end of the line through the eye of the lure, fly, or hook, and then make at least five turns around the standing part of the line. Run the end through the opening between the eye and the beginning of the twists, and then run it through the large loop formed by the previous step.

2 • Pull slowly on the standing part of the line, being careful that the end doesn't slip back through the large loop and that the knot snugs up against the eye. Clip off the end.

DOUBLE-LOOP CLINCH KNOT

This knot is the same as the improved clinch knot except that the line is run through the eye twice at the beginning of the tie.

DOUBLE IMPROVED CLINCH KNOT

This is the same as the improved clinch knot except that the line is used doubled throughout the entire tie.

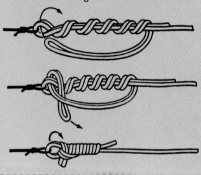

TRILENE KNOT

Used in joining line to swivels, snaps, hooks, and artificial lures, the Trilene knot is a strong, all-purpose knot that resists slippage and premature failures. It is easy to tie and retains 85 to 90 percent of the original line strength. The double wrap of monofilament line through the eyelet provides a protective cushion for added safety.

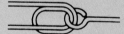

1 • Run the end of the line through the eye of the hook or lure and double back through the eye a second time.

2 • Loop around the standing part of the line five or six times.

3 • Thread the tag end back between the eye and the coils as shown.

4 • Pull up tight and trim the tag end.

SHOCKER KNOT

This knot is used to join two lines of unequal diameter.

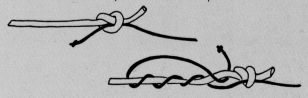

ARBOR KNOT

The arbor knot provides the angler with a quick, easy connection for attaching line to the reel spool.

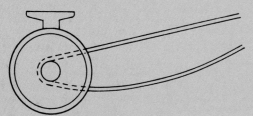

1 • Pass line around the reel arbor.

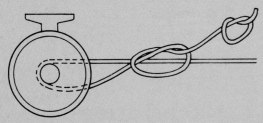

2 • Tie an overhand knot around the standing line. Tie a second overhand knot in the tag end.

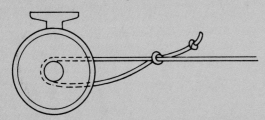

3 • Pull tight and snip off the excess. Snug down the first overhand knot on the reel arbor.

MULTIPLE CLINCH KNOT

This knot is used to join line and leader, especially in baitcasting. This knot slides through rod guides with a minimum of friction.

A loop is tied in the end of the line. Then, the leader is run into the loop, around the entire loop four times, and then back through the middle of the four wraps.

PALOMAR KNOT

This is a quick, easy knot to use when tying your line directly to a hook.

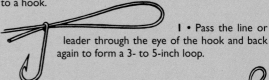

1 • Pass the line or leader through the eye of the hook and back again to form a 3- to 5-inch loop.

2 • Hold the line and hook at the eye. With the other hand, bring the loop up and under the double line and tie an overhand knot, but do not tighten.

3 • Hold the overhand knot. With the other hand, bring the loop over the hook.

4 • Hold the overhand knot. With the other hand, bring the loop over the hook.

PERFECTION LOOP KNOT

This knot is used to make a loop in the end of line or leader.

1 • Make one turn around the line and hold the crossing point with your thumb and forefinger.

2 • Make a second turn around the crossing point, and bring the end around and between loops A and B.

3 • Run loop B through loop A.

4 • Pull upward on loop B.

5 • Tighten the knot.

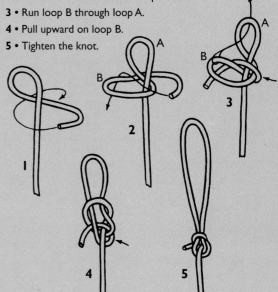

KING SLING KNOT

This knot offers the angler an easy-to-tie end loop knot that is used primarily as a connection for crankbaits. This knot allows the lure to work freely, making it more lifelike, and resulting in more strikes.

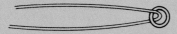

1 • Insert the tag end of the line through the artificial bait so that it extends 8 to 10 inches.

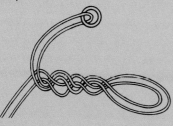

2 • Hold the tag end and the standing line in your left hand and form a loop.

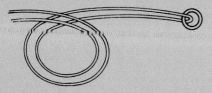

3 • With the bait in your right hand, make four turns around the tag end and the standing line above the loop.

4 • Bring the bait down and through the loop.

5 • To tighten, hold the line above the bait at the desired loop length and pull the tag end and the standing line at the same time. Trim the tag end.

DOUBLE SURGEON'S LOOP

This is a quick, easy way to tie a loop in the end of a leader. It is often used as part of a leader system because it is relatively strong.

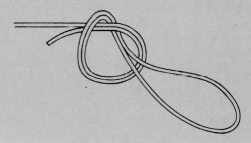

1 • Double the tag end of the line. Make a single overhand knot in the double line.

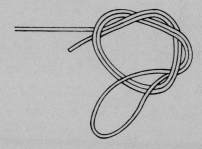

2 • Hold the tag end and standing part of the line in your left hand and bring the loop around and insert through the overhand knot again.

3 • Hold the loop in your right hand. Hold the tag end and standing line in your left hand. Moisten the knot (don't use saliva) and pull to tighten.

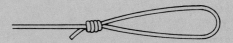

4 • Trim off the tag end.

WORLD'S FAIR KNOT

This is an easy-to-tie terminal tackle knot for connecting line to swivel or lure.

1 • Double a 6-inch length of line and pass the loop through the eye.

2 • Bring the loop back next to the doubled line and grasp the double line through the loop.

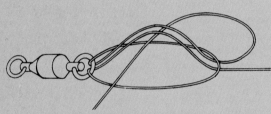

3 • Put the tag end through the new loop formed by the double line.

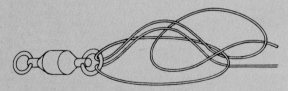

4 • Bring the tag end back through the new loop created by Step 3.

5 • Pull the tag end snug, and slide the knot up tight. Clip the tag end.

TUCKED SHEET BEND

This knot joins fly line and leader when the leader has an end loop.

1 • Run the fly line through the leader loop and around the loop as shown.

2 • Run the line back through the loops.

3 • Smoothly start to draw up the knots.

4 • Pull on both ends until the knot is tight.

DROPPER LOOP KNOT

This knot is frequently used to put a loop in the middle of a strand of monofilament.

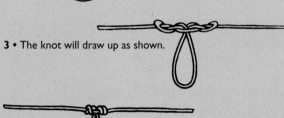

1 • Make a loop in the line and wrap one end overhand several times around the other part of the line. Pinch a small loop in the middle and thrust it between the turns as shown by the simulated, imaginary needle.

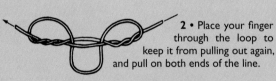

2 • Place your finger through the loop to keep it from pulling out again, and pull on both ends of the line.

3 • The knot will draw up as shown.

4 • The finished loop knot will appear as shown.

OFFSHORE SWIVEL KNOT

This knot is used to attach your line to a swivel.

1 • Slip a loop of double-line leader through the eye of the swivel. Rotate the loop a half turn to put a single twist between the loop and swivel eye.

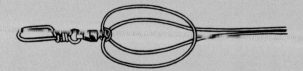

2 • Pass the loop with the twist over the swivel. Hold the loop end, together with both strands of double-line leader, with one hand. Let the swivel slide to the other end of the double loops now formed.

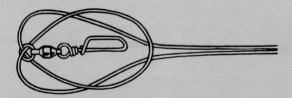

3 • Still holding the loop and lines, use your other hand to rotate the swivel through the center of both loops. Repeat at least five times.

4 • Continue holding the strands of double-line leader tightly, but release the end of the loop. As you pull on the swivel, loops of line will begin to gather.

5 • To draw the knot tight, grip the swivel with pliers and push the loops toward the eye with your fingers, still keeping the strands of leader pulled tight.

NAIL KNOT

This is the best knot for joining the end of a fly line with the butt end of a fly leader. The knot is smooth, streamlined, and will run freely through the guides of the fly rod. Caution: This knot is designed for use with modern synthetic fly lines; do not use it with an old silk fly line, for the knot will cut the line.

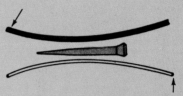

1 • Place the end of the fly line and the butt end of the leader—pointing in opposite directions—along the length of a tapered nail. Allow sufficient overlap.

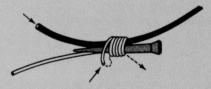

2 • Wrap the leader five or six times around itself, the nail, and the fly line, keeping the windings up against one another. Run the butt end of the leader back along the nail, inside the wraps.

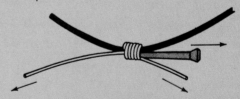

3 • Pull both ends of the leader tight, and then remove the nail and tighten again by pulling on both ends of the leader.

4 • Pull on both line and leader to test the knot, and clip off the ends, completing the knot.

NAIL KNOT (Alternate)

Tying procedures for this knot are the same as for the standard nail knot, except that in place of the nail, use an air-inflation needle like those used to inflate basketballs and footballs. The tip of the needle must be cut or filed off so that the tube is open at both ends. A large hypodermic needle with its point snipped off also works well. In tying Step 3 (third illustration from the top), the butt end of the leader—after having been wrapped five or six times around the fly line, leader, and tube—is simply run back through the tube (needle). Then, the knot is tightened, the tube is removed, and the final tightening is done.

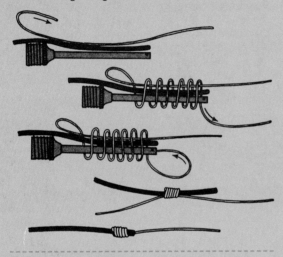

DOUBLE NAIL KNOT

This knot is used to join leader sections of the same or slightly different diameters. This is especially useful in salt-water fly fishing and in making heavy salmon leaders.

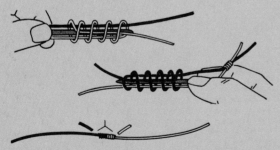

The tying procedure involves making two nail knots, one around each of the two leader sections. As each knot is formed, it is tightened only enough to prevent it from unraveling. When both are formed, each leader is pulled slowly so that the knots tighten together securely.

TURLE KNOT

This knot is used to tie a dry or wet fly to a leader tippet. It is not as strong as the improved clinch knot, but it allows a dry fly's hackle points to sit high and jauntily on the surface of the water.

1 • Run the end of the leader through the eye of the hook toward the bend, and tie a simple overhand knot around the standing part of the line, forming a loop.

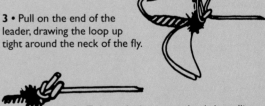

2 • Open the loop enough to allow it to pass around the fly, and place the loop around the neck of the fly, just forward of the eye.

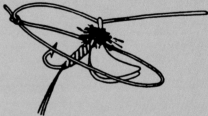

3 • Pull on the end of the leader, drawing the loop up tight around the neck of the fly.

4 • Tighten the knot completely by pulling on the main part of the leader.

LOOP KNOT

This knot is used to tie on a lure.

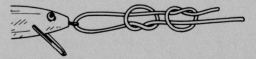

Tie an overhand knot in the line, leaving the loop loose and a sufficient length of line below the loop to tie the rest of the knot. Run the end through the hook eye and back through the loop in the line, and then tie another overhand knot around the standing part. Pull tight.

END LOOP

This knot is used to form a loop in the end of a line.

1 • Double the end of the line for about 6 or 8 inches.

2 • Wrap the double line around itself at least six times.

3 • Take the end of the doubled line and pass it through the first loop as shown.

4 • Now, tighten the knot by pulling on the loop and the tag end at the same time.

BUFFER LOOP

This knot is used to attach a lure to line or leader via a nonslip loop.

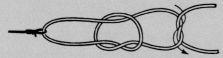

1 • Tie a simple overhand knot in the line, leaving the loop loose and leaving the end long enough to complete the knot, and then run the end through the eye of the lure.

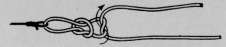

2 • Run the end back through the loose loop and make another overhand knot, using the end and standing part of the line.

3 • Tighten the overhand knot nearest to the lure eye, and then tighten the second overhand knot, which, in effect, forms a half hitch against the first knot.

4 • The finished knot appears as shown.

KNOTTING BACKING LINE TO FLY LINE

This knot is used to join backing line to fly line.

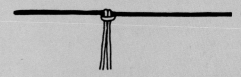

1 • Double the end of the backing line, make one wrap around the fly line, and pull all of the backing line through the loop at its doubled end so the lines appear as shown.

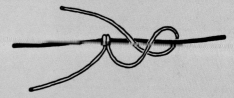

2 • With the end of the backing line, make a half hitch around the fly line, and pull it tight against the original knot.

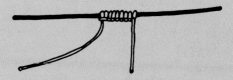

3 • Continue making such half hitches (eight or 10 should be enough) until the tie appears as shown.

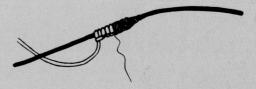

4 • Wrap the entire tie with nylon thread, including part of the end of the backing line. This step is simplified by placing the fly line in a fly-tying vise.

5 • Give the entire tie a good coat of lacquer.

■ ALBRIGHT KNOT (MONO TO MONO)

This knot is used to join lines of dissimilar diameter, such as a fly line to a leader or heavy shock leader to a finer leader tippet.

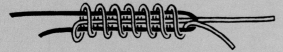

1 • Double the end of the heavier line, forming a long U shape. Bring the lighter line up into the U, and make about 10 wraps—in the direction of the bottom of the U—around the U and the standing part of the lighter line, bringing the end of the lighter line out of the bottom of the U.

2 • Pull slowly and evenly until the knot is tight.

■ ALBRIGHT KNOT (MONO TO WIRE)

This knot is used when a short length of wire leader is needed below monofilament leader tippet to prevent sharp-toothed fish from biting through the leader. The fly is attached to the wire leader with a brass crimping sleeve. It is also used to tie mono leader to wire or lead-core line so that the knot will pass through guides and tip tops smoothly. It eliminates the need for a swivel.

1 • Bend the end of a wire leader into a U or open-end loop. Run the end of monofilament into the tip of the U, make about seven wraps around the doubled wire, and run the end of the monofilament back out through the tip of the U.

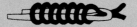

2 • Hold both leaders to prevent the knot from slipping, and slowly draw the wraps of monofilament tight.

3 • Clip off the ends, and the knot is finished.

■ FLY-LINE SPLICE

This splice is used to join two fly lines.

1 • Remove the coating from 2¼ inches of the end of each line, and fray about 1 inch.

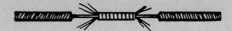

2 • Enmesh the frayed ends of one line with those of the other, and wrap most of this joint with nylon thread.

3 • Make another series of wrappings over the entire splice. Finish the job with coats of varnish.

■ HAYWIRE TWIST

This knot is used to tie wire to the hook, lure, or swivel, or make a loop in the end of the wire.

1 • Run about 4 inches of the end of the leader wire through the eye of the hook, lure, or swivel, and then bend the end across the standing part of the wire.

2 • Holding the two parts of the wire at their crossing points, bend the wire around itself, using hard, even, twisting motions. Both wire parts should be twisted equally.

3 • Then, using the end of the wire, make about 10 tight wraps around the standing part of the wire.

4 • Break off or clip the end of the wire close to the last wrap so that there is no sharp end, and the job is complete.

BIMINI TWIST

This knot is used to create a loop or double line without appreciably weakening the breaking strength of the line. It is especially popular in bluewater fishing for large saltwater fish. Learning this knot requires practice.

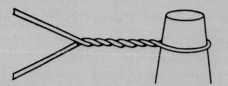

1 • Double the end of the line to form a loop, leaving yourself plenty of line to work with. Run the loop around a fixed object, such as a cleat or the butt end of a rod, or have a partner hold the loop and keep it open. Make 20 twists in the line, keeping the turns tight and the line taut.

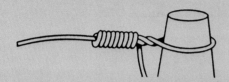

2 • Keeping the twists tight, wrap the end of the line back over the twists until you reach the V of the loop, making the wraps tight and snug up against one another.

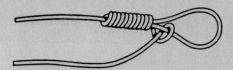

3 • Make a half hitch around one side of the loop and pull it tight.

4 • Then, make a half hitch around the other side of the loop, and pull this one tight, too.

5 • Now, make a half hitch around the base of the loop, tighten it, clip off excess line at the end, and the bimini twist is complete.

SPIDER HITCH

This knot serves the same function as the bimini twist, but many anglers prefer the spider hitch because it's easier and faster to tie—especially with cold hands—and requires no partner to help, nor any fixed object to keep the loop open. Plus, it's equally strong.

1 • Make a long loop in the line. Hold the ends between your thumb and forefinger, with the first joint of the thumb extending beyond your finger. Then, use your other hand to twist a smaller reverse loop in the doubled line.

2 • Slide your fingers up the line to grasp the small reverse loop together with the long loop. Most of the small loop should extend beyond your thumb tip.

3 • Wind the doubled line from right to left around both your thumb and the small loop, taking five turns. Then, pass the remainder of the doubled line (large loop) through the small loop.

4 • Pull the large loop to make the five turns unwind off the thumb, using a fast, steady pull—not a quick jerk.

5 • Pull the turns around the base of the loop tight and then trim off the tag end.

The Uni-Knot System

The Uni-Knot System consists of variations on one basic knot that can be used for most needs in fresh water and salt water. The system was developed by Vic Dunaway, editor of *Florida Sportsman* magazine and author of numerous books. Here's how each variation is tied, step by step.

■ TYING TO TERMINAL TACKLE

1 • Run the line through the eye of the hook, swivel, or lure at least 6 inches and fold it back to form two parallel lines. Bring the end of the line back in a circle toward the eye.

2 • Turn the tag end six times around the double line and through the circle. Hold the double line at the eye and pull the tag end to snug up turns.

3 • Pull the running line to slide the knot up against the eye.

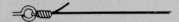

4 • Continue pulling until the knot is tight. Trim the tag end flush with the last coil of the knot. This basic Uni-Knot will not slip.

■ LOOP CONNECTION

Tie the same basic Uni-Knot as shown above—up to the point where the coils are snugged up against the running line. Then, slide the knot toward the eye only until the desired loop size is reached. Pull the tag end with pliers to tighten. This gives a lure or fly free, natural movement in the water. When a fish is hooked, the knot slides tight against the eye.

■ JOINING LINES

1 • With two lines of about the same diameter, overlap ends for about 6 inches. With one end, form a Uni-Knot circle and cross the two lines at about the middle of the overlap.

2 • Tie a basic Uni-Knot, making six turns around the lines.

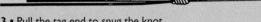

3 • Pull the tag end to snug the knot.

4 • Use the loose end of the overlapped line to tie a second Uni-Knot and snug it up in the same manner.

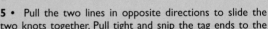

5 • Pull the two lines in opposite directions to slide the two knots together. Pull tight and snip the tag ends to the outermost coils.

■ JOINING LEADER TO LINE

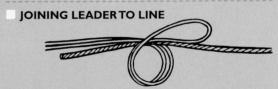

1 • Using a leader no more than four times the pound test of the line, double the end of the line and overlap with the leader for about 6 inches. Make a Uni-Knot circle with the doubled line.

2 • Tie a Uni-Knot around the leader with the doubled line, but use only three turns. Snug up.

3 • Now, tie a Uni-Knot with the leader around the doubled line, again using only three turns.

4 • Pull knots together tightly. Trim the tag ends and loop.

JOINING SHOCK LEADER TO LINE

1 • Using a leader of more than four times the pound test of the line, double the ends of both leader and line back about 6 inches. Slip the line loop through the leader loop far enough to permit tying a Uni-Knot around both strands of the leader.

2 • With doubled line, tie a Uni-Knot around the doubled leader, using only four turns.

3 • Put a finger through the loop of line and grasp both the tag end and running line to pull the knot snug around the leader loop.

4 • With one hand, pull the long end of the leader (not both strands). With the other hand, pull both strands of line. Pull slowly until the knot slides to the end of the leader loop and slippage is stopped.

DOUBLE-LINE SHOCK LEADER

1 • As a replacement for a bimini twist or spider hitch, first clip off the amount of line needed for the desired length of loop. Tie the two ends together with an overhand knot.

2 • Double the end of the running line and overlap it 6 inches with the knotted end of the loop piece. Tie a Uni-Knot with the tied loop around the double running line, using four turns.

3 • Now, tie a Uni-Knot with the doubled running line around the loop piece, again using four turns.

4 • Hold both strands of double line in one hand, both strands of loop in the other. Pull to bring the knots together until they barely touch.

5 • Tighten by pulling both strands of the loop piece, but only the main strand of running line. Trim off both loop tag ends, eliminating the overhand knot.

SNELLING A HOOK

1 • Thread line through the hook eye for about 6 inches. Hold the line against the hook shank and form a Uni-Knot circle. Make as many turns as desired through the loop and around the line and shank. Close the knot by pulling on the tag end.

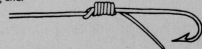

2 • Tighten by pulling the running line in one direction and the hook in the other. Trim off the tag end.

AVOIDING LINE TWIST

Winding new line on your reel is a fairly simple job, but if you do it wrong you'll end up with twists that will pose big problems from your first cast.

■ Open-Face Spinning Reel

First, attach the reel to a rod. Any rod will do, but never try winding line on a spool by holding the reel in your hands. Next, string the line through the guides, open the bail, and knot the line to the spool. Finally, flip the bail closed.

The line should spiral off the supply spool in the same direction it is going onto the reel spool. Keep the rod tip several feet from the supply spool and maintain tension on the line by holding it between the thumb and forefinger of your rod-holding hand.

If you're alone, place the spool label side up on the floor and wind about 10 feet of line under tension on your reel. Now, drop the rod tip. If the slack line between the rod tip and reel immediately starts to twist, you're putting the line on wrong. Flip the spool label side down and start again. The line should now wind on your reel correctly.

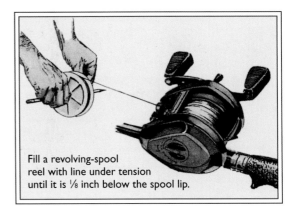

Fill a revolving-spool reel with line under tension until it is ⅛ inch below the spool lip.

You should fill an open-face spinning reel slightly below the spool lip. When the line drops more than ¼ inch below the spool lip, it's time to put on new line.

■ Revolving-Spool Reel

If you're filling a revolving spool reel, start by pushing a pencil through the center of the supply reel. Have a friend hold both ends of the pencil and exert pressure

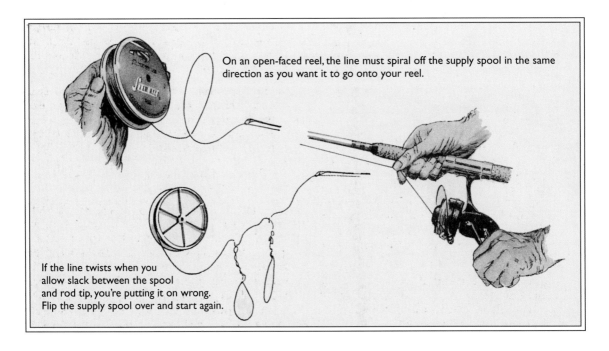

On an open-faced reel, the line must spiral off the supply spool in the same direction as you want it to go onto your reel.

If the line twists when you allow slack between the spool and rod tip, you're putting it on wrong. Flip the supply spool over and start again.

inward on the supply spool with his hand to put tension on the line.

The line will go on evenly from side to side if the reel has a level-wind. If not, make sure you wind the line on evenly. You can also use your index finger and thumb of your holding hand to maintain additional tension. Fill the spool to within ⅛ inch of the spool lip.

■ Spincast Reel

With closed-face spincast reels, use nearly the same method as for open-face spinning reels, except remove the nose cone and hold it in front of the reel while winding on line. Most spincast reels have narrow, deep spools,

which means you'll lose casting distance if the line level drops below ⅛ inch on the spool.

When filling a spincast reel, slip the nose cone forward as you wind line, exposing the spool. Don't overfill the spool.

CARE AND REPAIR OF FISHING TACKLE

There's more than a germ of truth in the old saying, "A fisherman is no better than his tackle." It pays in more ways than one to keep your gear in good working order. For one thing, proper maintenance can add a good many years to the working life of rods, reels, and other tackle on which hard-earned money has been spent. And legions of fishermen have discovered, to their chagrin, that un-oiled reels can "freeze up," neglected rods can snap, and rusty lure hooks can give out—just when that record-breaking fish comes along. The following tackle-care tips should help to prevent such problems.

■ Care of Rods

Today's rods are designed for long life, but they still require some basic maintenance. The steps recommended below should keep any rod in good working order. How often they should be applied depends upon how often the rods are used and whether they are used in fresh or salt water. Remember that saltwater rods—in fact, all saltwater gear—require much more care than freshwater rods. Even the best of tackle cannot withstand the corrosive action of salt.

I. Wash the rod, including the guides, thoroughly with soap and fresh water, rinse it with hot water, and let it dry completely. If the rod is used in salt water, this step should be taken after each use.

2. If the rod is two pieces or more, thoroughly clean the ferrules. If the ferrules are metal, give them a very light coating of grease to help prevent oxidation.

3. Apply a light coating of wax (automobile wax does a good job) to the entire rod—excluding the cork handle, if the rod has one, and guides.

4. If your rod is starting to show signs of wear, you may want to varnish it. Two thin coats are better than one heavy coat. To avoid creating bubbles in the varnish, apply it with a finger or a pipe cleaner.

5. Store your rod in a dry, safe place. If the rod is bamboo, it must be placed so that it lays flat; if stored on end, it may develop a "set" or permanent bend. Caution: Never store a wet cork-handled rod in a rod case. Mildew will surely form on the cork.

■ Care of Lines

Check each line for cracking, aging, wear, and rot. If the entire line is no longer serviceable, discard it. If one end has taken all the use, reverse the line. Fly lines tend to crack at the business end after considerable use. If the cracking is confined to the last foot or so, clip off the damaged section or, if the line is a double taper, reverse it. If the damage is more widespread, replace the line.

Check particularly for nicks and other weak spots in monofilament and fluorocarbon, and test the line's breaking strength. If it's weak, replace it. With braided line, check for dark spots, which signify rot, and test the breaking strength. Replace if weak.

◾ Care of Reels

Reels are the most important item of fishing gear and must be cared for properly. The following checklist should be followed:

1. Rinse the reel thoroughly with hot, fresh water. If used in salt water, do this after each trip and use soap. Let dry completely.

2. Oil sparingly.

3. Release drag tension to eliminate spring fatigue.

4. Check the reel's operation. Replace worn or missing parts, and send the reel to the manufacturer for repair if necessary.

5. Cover the reel with a very light coating of oil, and store it in a safe, dry place, preferably in a cloth bag (cloth permits air to enter and escape). Leather cases lock out air.

◾ Care of Tackle Accessories

Accessory equipment deserves equal time from the fisherman. Saltwater lures, for example, are expensive, so take a few minutes to rinse them off with soapy, fresh water after each use so that they don't corrode. The same applies to swivels, hooks, and other saltwater accessories.

The following checklist covers a general overhaul of a tackle box and its contents:

1. Remove the contents of the box, and place the items in some kind of order on a table rather than simply dumping them in a pile. This will help you remember where everything goes when it's time to put your accessories away after cleaning.

2. Use a vacuum cleaner to remove dust and dirt and other loose particles. If the box is metal, wipe the inside with an oily rag, and lubricate the hinges. If it is plastic, wash it with soap and water.

3. Examine the hooks and lures, and discard rusty hooks and all lures that are beyond repair. Make a list of those lures you'll need to restock the box while they are fresh in your mind.

How to Wrap Guides

1 • Start by wrapping over the end of the thread toward the guide so the thread end is held down by the wrapping. Using the tension from whatever type of tension device you are using to hold the wrapping tight, continue to turn the rod so that each thread lies as close as possible to the preceding turn.

2 • About five to eight turns from the finish of the wrap, insert the loop of the tie-off thread. (This can be 6 inches of heavier thread or a fine piece of nylon leader material.) Finish the wrap over this tie-off loop.

3 • Holding the wrap tightly, cut the wrapping thread about 4 inches from your rod. Insert this cut end through the tie-off loop. Still holding onto the wrapping thread, pull the cut-off thread under the wraps with the tie-off loop.

4 • With a razor blade, trim the cut-off end as close as possible to the wrap. With the back of a knife or your fingernail, push the wrapping up tight so that it appears solid, and none of the rod or guide shows through.

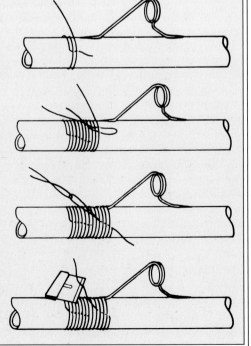

4. Repair salvageable lures. A soft-wire soap pad can be a great help in sprucing up dingy crankbait blades and spoons. Check for broken, rusty, or dull lure hooks, replacing the hooks if necessary or sharpening them with a small whetstone.

5. Sharpen all hooks, and give them a light coating of oil to prevent rust.

6. Wash the bag of your landing net with a mild detergent.

7. Patch all holes and weak spots in hip boots and waders, and store them in a dark, cool spot. The best way to store boots is to hang them upside down by the boot feet. A sturdy, heavy-wire coat hanger, cut in the middle of the bottom section and bent judiciously, makes an excellent and inexpensive boot-hanger.

■ Rod-Wrapping Tricks of the Trade

GUIDES AND TENSION: Guides should be purchased in matched sets to ensure uniformity. The feet of guides should be dressed with a file to a fine taper. Next, sight your rod. If you notice a slight bend or offset, apply guides opposite the bend; this will bring it into a straight position. Guides should be affixed with snug wrapping tension, so that you may sight after wrapping and make slight guide adjustments before applying the color preserver. Do not wrap guides to the absolute breaking point of the thread. Remember, 10 or 20 wraps of thread exert very heavy pressure on the feet of the guides. It is possible to damage a blank by wrapping too tight.

THREADS: Sizes 2/0 to E are the most commonly used threads. Sizes 2/0 or A are used for fly, casting, or spinning rods. Sizes D or E are used for the heavier freshwater spinning or saltwater rods. Naturally, the finer size 2/0 thread will make a neater job, but, being lighter, it is not quite as durable.

TRIM: You may trim the basic color of your wrap with five to 10 turns of another color of thread. This is done just as outlined in the instructions for a basic wrap.

COLOR PRESERVER AND ROD VARNISH: Good color preserver has plastic in it, and should be quite thin in order to penetrate the wrappings. Good-grade varnish is essential to the durability of the finish. Most custom rod builders prefer two-part rod finishes. A brush may be used to apply both the color preserver and rod varnish; however, air bubbles are usually present when a brush is used. To maintain a smooth finish, make certain these bubbles are out. A very satisfactory method of minimizing air bubbles is to apply both the color preserver and rod varnish with your index finger. This will prevent any clouding of the wrapping color.

■ Selecting the Tip Top and Other Guides

The rod builder, like just about everyone else, gets what he pays for. It doesn't pay to skimp on rod guides, especially if the rod is to be used in salt water or for heavy freshwater fish such as pike, muskies, and salmon.

Guides are made of various metals, including hardened stainless steel, chrome (or chrome-plated Monel), Fuji Hardloy, agate, and tungsten carbide, with the carbide types being the most durable. Silicone carbide or titanium carbide are recommended for abrasive lines, such as braid or Dacron. Roller guides for heavy saltwater fishing are usually made of stainless steel, Monel, or nickel alloy. The rod builder should note that guides are available in sets tailored to particular rod types and lengths.

The tip top must fit snugly over the end of the rod, and so its selection is sometimes a problem. The accompanying chart will help the rod builder overcome this problem. It shows the actual sizes, in 64ths of an inch, of the inside diameters of a wide range of tip-top guides.

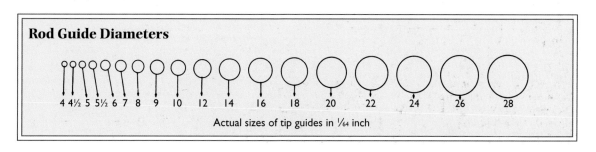

Rod Guide Diameters

4 4½ 5 5½ 6 7 8 9 10 12 14 16 18 20 22 24 26 28

Actual sizes of tip guides in 1/64 inch

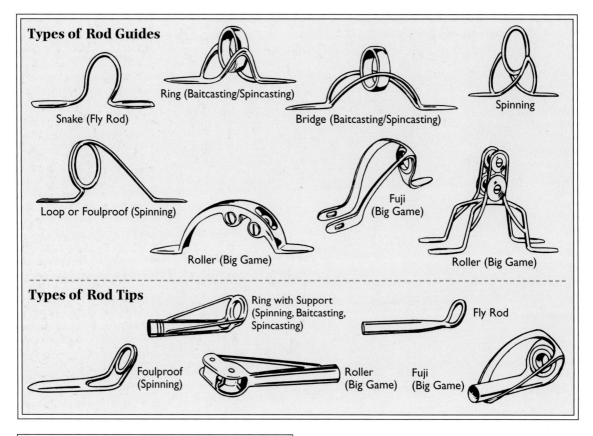

Types of Rod Guides

Snake (Fly Rod)

Ring (Baitcasting/Spincasting)

Bridge (Baitcasting/Spincasting)

Spinning

Loop or Foulproof (Spinning)

Roller (Big Game)

Fuji (Big Game)

Roller (Big Game)

Types of Rod Tips

Ring with Support (Spinning, Baitcasting, Spincasting)

Fly Rod

Foulproof (Spinning)

Roller (Big Game)

Fuji (Big Game)

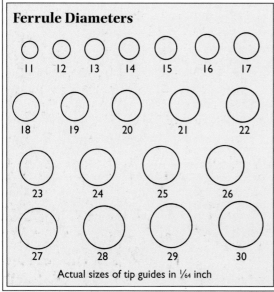

Ferrule Diameters

11 12 13 14 15 16 17

18 19 20 21 22

23 24 25 26

27 28 29 30

Actual sizes of tip guides in 1/64 inch

To determine what size tip top you need, simply place the end of the rod tip over the circles until you find the correct size.

■ Selecting Rod Ferrules

Most rods today that break down into two or more pieces avoid any kind of ferrule, preferring to use the tapers themselves to form a smooth integral connection and an action that comes close to a one-piece rod. Some rods, however, still use a ferrule system—joint-like devices inserted along the working length of a fishing rod that enables the rod to be dismantled into two or more sections. Ferrules are generally made of metal (nickel, brass, or aluminum), or a synthetic material. A ferrule set consists of two parts, the male ferrule and the female ferrule. The male section should fit snugly into the female section.

What size ferrule do you need for your rod? The accompanying chart will help you find out. It shows

Suggested Guide Spacing

All measurements are from the tip of the rod down. Figures indicate measurements at the guide ring.

	Rod Length	Lure-Weight Range (ounces)	Fly-Line Weights	Measurements at the Guide Ring (inches)							
				1st	2nd	3rd	4th	5th	6th	7th	8th
SPINCASTING, BAITCASTING	5½ ft.	⅛ to ⅓		4½	12	23	36				
	6 ft.	⅛ to ⅜		4	10	18	28	40			
	6 ft.	¼ to ¾		4	8¼	13	18	24½	32⅛	42	
	6 ft.	⅜ to 1¼		3½	7½	12	17⅜	23⅝	31⅞	42½	
	6 ft., 4 in.	¹⁄₁₆ to ¼		4	10	18½	28½	41			
	6 ft., 4 in.	⅜		4	10	18½	28½	41			
	6 ft., 4 in.	⅛ to ½		4	10	18½	28½	41			
	6 ft.	⅜ to ⅝		4	10	18	28	40			
	6 ft., 4 in.	¼ to ⅝		4	10	18½	28½	41			
FLY RODS	5 ft., 5 in.		5F, 6S	5	13	25	40				
	6 ft.		5F, 6S	3	7½	12	17¾	25	33	42½	
	7½ ft.		6F, 7S	6	13	21	30	41½	60		
	7 ft., 8 in.		6 or 7F, 7S	6	13	21	30	43	62		
	8 ft.		6 or 7F, 7S	6	13	21	30	41	52	66	
	8 ft.		7F, 7S	6	13	21	30	40	53	66	
	8 ft.		7 or 8F, 7 or 8S	6	13	21	30	41	53	66	
	8½ ft.		7 or 8F, 7 or 8S	6	13	21	30	40	56	73	
	8½ ft.		7F, 7S	6	13	21	30	40	56	73	
	8½ ft.		8 or 9F, 8 or 9S	6	13	21	30	40	56	73	
	9 ft.		7 or 8F, 7 or 8S	5	11	18	26	35	45	58½	73
	9 ft.		8 or 9F, 8 or 9S	5	11	18	26	35	45	58½	73
	10 ft.		9 or 10F, 9 or 10S	6	13	22	32	43	54½	66½	80½
SPINNING ROD	6 ft.	up to ¼		5½	15½	27½	40½				
	6 ft.	up to ⅜		3½	10	19	29¼	41½			
	6½ ft.	¹⁄₁₆ to ¼		3½	8½	15	23	33	46		
	6½ ft.	⅛ to 1		5	10⅜	16⅜	23⅜	31⅞	44		
	6½ ft.	⅛ to ⅜		3½	8½	15	23	33	46		
	6½ ft.	¼ to ⅝		3½	8½	15	23	33	46		
	7 ft. *	¹⁄₁₆ to ⅜	5 or 6F, 6S	4	10	18	27½	38½	52½		
	7 ft.	¹⁄₁₆ to ⅜		4	10	18	27½	38½	52½		
	7 ft.	up to 1½		4	10	18	27½	38	51		

KEY: F—FLOATING S—SINKING *—COMBINATION SPIN/FLY ROD

the actual sizes, in 64ths of an inch, of the inside diameters of a wide range of ferrules. To determine the correct ferrule for your rod, simply place the upper end of the butt section (if it is a two-piece rod) over the circles until you find the right fit.

■ Spacing of Rod Guides

Whether you are building a fishing rod from scratch (that is, taking a fiberglass blank and adding a butt, reel seat, and guides) or refinishing an old favorite, you must pay close attention to the placement of the guides along the working length of the rod.

Putting too many or too few guides on a rod, or placing them improperly along the rod, may detract from proper rod action and put undue strain on the line and the rod.

The accompanying chart gives the correct number of guides—and exact spacing measurements—for most spinning, baitcasting, spincasting, and fly rods.

ESTIMATING FISH WEIGHT

You've just caught a big pike. In fact, it measures 40 inches, according to the stick-on tape measure you received free from the bait shop. Now you want to know how much the pike weighs, but you don't have a scale.

Over the years, fishermen have come up with several ways to estimate fish weight without a scale. Some have proved to be fairly accurate; some didn't even come close. Eventually, the generally accepted formula became:

Length times Girth squared divided by 800 equals Weight,
or L x G² ÷ 800 = W

Using this formula is supposed to bring you within 10 percent of a fish's actual weight. The only problem is that the formula doesn't differentiate between fat fish (such as bass or tuna) and elongate fish (such as pike or barracuda).

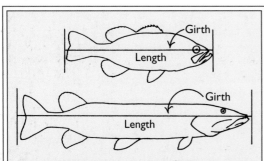

The traditional formula for determining the weight of a fish didn't take into account its shape—either elongate or round. The old equation could be off by as much as 10 percent.

Doug Hannon, a renowned Florida bass fisherman, has developed a more precise calculation specifically for bass and similarly shaped round fish. In addition to being more accurate, it requires only one measurement. Hannon's formula is:

Length cubed divided by 1,600 equals Weight,
or L³ ÷ 1,600 = W

If you caught a 20-inch bass, for example, the math would be 20 times 20 times 20 (8,000), divided by 1,600. Congratulations, that's a nice 5-pounder.

With the widespread adoption of catch-and-release fishing, fishermen have developed modifications of the length-cubed formula that work well with other species, too. For pike, muskies, and other elongate fish, use this formula:

$$L^3 ÷ 3,500 = W$$

In other words, that 40-inch pike that you caught would weigh about 18.3 pounds. (Actually, it's 18.28 pounds, but any fisherman is allowed to round up to the higher tenth.)

If you're a panfish specialist, the formula to use is:

$$L^3 ÷ 1,200 = W$$

An 8-inch bluegill, for example, would weigh 0.42 pounds. And if walleyes are your target, the formula changes slightly to:

$$L^3 ÷ 2,700 = W$$

This means the 22-inch walleye you boasted was a 10-pounder really only weighed about 4 pounds.

FIELD CARE AND DRESSING OF FISH

If you sit down at the dinner table and bite into a poor-tasting bass or walleye fillet from a fish you caught, there's a good chance that the second-rate taste is your own fault. In all probability, the fish was not handled properly from the moment it came out of the water. Fish spoil rapidly unless they are kept alive or quickly killed and put on ice.

Here are the necessary steps involved in getting a fresh-caught fish from the water to the table so that it will retain its original flavor.

First, the decision to keep a fish dead or alive depends on conditions. For example, if you're out on a lake and have no ice in your boat, you'll want to keep all fish alive until it's time to head home. Under no circumstances

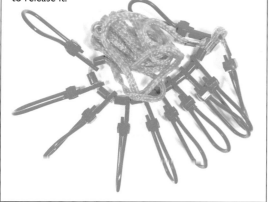

With safety-pin type stringers, run the clip through the thin membrane behind the lower lip. This lets the fish swim freely and won't injure the fish should you decide to release it.

should you toss fish into the bottom of the boat, let them lie there in the sun, and then gather them up at the end of the day. If you try that stunt, the fillets will reach your table with the consistency of mush and a flavor to match. Instead, put your fish on a stringer as quickly as possible and put them back into the water, where they can begin to recover from the shock of being caught.

Use the safety-pin type stringer and run the wire up through the thin, almost-transparent membrane just behind the fish's lower lip. This will enable the fish to swim freely, and the fish will recover from this minor injury should you decide to release it at the end of the day.

Do **not** shove the stringer under the gill cover and out of the mouth. This damages the gills and kills fish fast. Also, avoid cord stringers, where all fish are bunched in a clump at the end of the cord. This is perhaps acceptable on short trips for small panfish, which are generally caught in big numbers and quickly cleaned, but if you're after bigger fish and want to keep them alive and fresh—either for the table or release at the end of the day—use the safety-pin stringer. It does its job well.

If you're rowing or trolling slowly, you can probably keep the stringer in the water. If you have a big boat and motor, however, it's a good idea to take the stringer into the boat for those fast runs to other hotspots. If the run is fairly long, wet down the fish occasionally, but don't tow a fish in the water at high speed—you'll drown it.

If you're several miles from camp, use the following technique to get fish back alive. When returning to camp with a stringer of fish, stop your boat every half

mile or so and ease the fish over the side. Let the fish swim around for five minutes or so before hauling them back into the boat and continuing the trip to camp. This way, you should have no trouble reaching camp with lively walleyes to be put in your shoreline live box. Keeping fish alive is especially important on extended trips to remote areas, where ice in sufficient quantities isn't generally available.

On the subject of lengthy fishing trips to remote areas where ice is not available, you can still keep fish alive for a week or more. Your best bet is to use a home-made collapsible fish box, which can be weighted with a rock in a foot of water onshore or floated in deep water. Either way, the fish will stay alive until the end of the trip. Keeping fish alive for lengthy periods in remote areas is impossible without such a box. Keeping fish on a stringer at dockside will **not** work for long periods. With some wood and wire mesh, a fish box is easy to build. This assumes, of course, that a fish has been unhooked and is placed in the fish box in good condition. If it has been deeply hooked and appears to be dying slowly, however, it's best to kill the fish immediately, gut it, and keep it on ice.

Killing a fish quickly is simple. Holding the fish upright, impale it between the eyes with the point of your knife or rap it on the head with a heavy stick. The important factor is killing it quickly, since the more slowly it dies the more rapidly the flesh will deteriorate.

A wicker creel still does its job well. Lined with wet ferns, grass, or wet newspapers, it will keep fish reasonably cool on the hottest days. Canvas creels are also readily available and simple to use. Occasionally dipping the entire creel in a stream, wetting it thoroughly, will keep the fish inside in good shape during a daylong trip. If you're a surf fisherman, you can bury your fish in damp sand. This will keep your fish cool and out of the sun.

How to Field Dress a Fish

Step 1 • With the fish belly up, make a cut from the anal opening to the gills.

Step 2 • Make two cuts at the gills, one below and one above the gills where they form a V.

Step 3 • Next, stick a finger into the gullet as shown and begin to pull downward. The gills and entrails should come out easily.

Step 4 • With the entrails out, run your thumbnail along the backbone to break and clean the blood sac. Wash the fish. Once is enough—the less water coming into direct contact with the meat, the firmer the flesh will be when you eat it.

If you're a stream fisherman, it's wise to carry your catch in a canvas or wicker creel. The canvas creel works fine, so long as it is occasionally immersed in water. The traditional wicker creel will work just as well, but it should be lined with ferns, leaves, or wet newspaper.

If you're a surf fisherman, you can bury your catch in the damp sand. Just remember to mark the spot. A burlap sack occasionally doused in the surf also makes a practical fish bag. The important factor is to keep the fish cool and out of the sun.

Regardless of the various ways to keep fish cool, they should first be cleaned properly. With a bit of practice and a sharp knife, the job can be done in less than a minute.

Take a sharp knife and insert it in the anal opening on the underside of the fish. Slit the skin forward from there to the point of the V-shaped area where the forward part of the belly is attached to the gills. Put your finger into the gills and around that V-shaped area, and pull sharply to the rear. You will thus remove the gills and all or most of the entrails. Then, with the fish upside down, put your thumb into the body cavity at the anal opening, and press your thumbnail against the backbone. Keeping your nail tight against the bone, run your thumb forward to the head, thereby removing the dark blood from the sac along the backbone.

One more tip: More good fish meat is probably ruined during the drive home than during any other

How to Fillet Pickerel and Other Bony Fish

Too many fish in the pickerel family are being wasted because anglers do not know how to cope with the Y-bones. Bone-free fillets of pickerel, pike, and muskellunge are delicious. Give it a try!

To bake the fish whole, first scale the fish; then follow Steps 1 through 4, but leave the fillets attached to the skin. Then, skewer or sew the skin together to form a pocket for stuffing.

For pan frying or baking, there's no need to scale the fish, just wet the scales and work scaleside down on dry newspapers. Don't slip. Follow Steps 1 through 4; then with a thin, flexible knife, press the blade flat against the skin and, with a sawing motion, slide the knife along, freeing fillets from the skin. Your efforts should result in four bone-free fillets ready for the frying pan or for dusting with prepared baking mix before placing them in the oven.

The narrow strips along each side of the back can be rolled up in pinwheel fashion and held together with a toothpick inserted horizontally. If you like this system, strip the flank flesh and make pinwheels of all of it. The pinwheels come out with a handle for easy eating or dipping in sauces.

Caution: Cuts shown in the accompanying illustrations are made only down to the tough skin, not through it.

Notes on the Y-Bone Cuts: Until you have dressed a few, run the tip of an index finger along the fish to locate the line of the butts of the Y-bones. Ease the knife through the flesh on these cuts, slightly twisting the blade away from the bones. The knife is pushed through, as opposed to regular cutting action. It will follow the bone line easily.

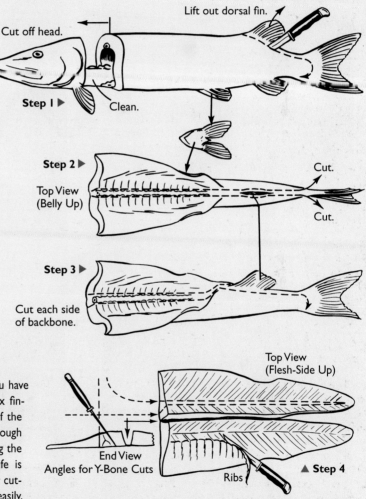

Lift out dorsal fin.

Cut off head.

Step 1 ▶ Clean.

Step 2 ▶ Top View (Belly Up)   Cut.   Cut.

Step 3 ▶ Cut each side of backbone.

Top View (Flesh-Side Up)

End View
Angles for Y-Bone Cuts

Ribs   ▲ **Step 4**

If it catches a bone, back up, increase the angle, and continue. The Y-bone strip and backbone will rip out in single strips if pinched between the thumb and index finger next to the skin to lift the head end from the skin. Grasp the lifted portion and rip out toward the tail.

How to Fillet a Fish

Step 1 • Using a sharp knife, make two initial cuts, one behind the gill plate (as shown) and another at the base of the tail down to the backbone or spine. The cut at the base of the tail is optional. Some fishermen prefer to extend the final fillet cut through the tail.

Step 2 • Next, make a cut on one side of the dorsal fin lengthwise from the first two initial cuts, starting behind the head and cutting down to the base of the tail. As you extend the cut, carefully begin to separate the fillet from the backbone.

Step 3 • Your slice downward will begin to separate the fillet from the backbone. A good fillet knife should have a 7- or 8-inch blade with some flex. A stainless-steel blade may be easier to maintain and will not rust, but carbon-steel fillet knives are easier to sharpen and will take an edge faster.

Step 4 • As you continue to separate the fillet, make sure you avoid the stomach and organs. Note that on this fillet there are no broken organs, digestive juices, or blood to taint the fillet.

Step 5 • Now, carefully begin to cut the fillet free from the fish. Keeping the blade as flat as possible will avoid damaging the fillets.

Step 6 • The final cut will free the clean fillet from the fish. If you prefer to skin your fillets, place them flesh side up, flat on the table. Work your knife blade between the skin and the meat, holding the skin down with your fingers. With a sawing motion, holding the blade flat and down against the skin, cut the meat free of the skin. The fillet and skin will separate easily.

Step 7 • This is how the fillet should look when cut from one side of the fish. Next, turn the fish over and remove the fillet from the other side of the fish exactly the same way. The next step (not shown here) is to remove the pinbones, which are in the forward third of the fillet. You can feel them easily with your fingers. Using needle-nose pliers, pull them out of the fillet. With a slight wiggle, they should slide out easily.

Step 8 • This is the final product—two clean salmon fillets. With the exception of flatfish, this technique will work on all other species with similar body types, such as striped bass, grouper, largemouth bass, and walleyes.

Easy Fish Release

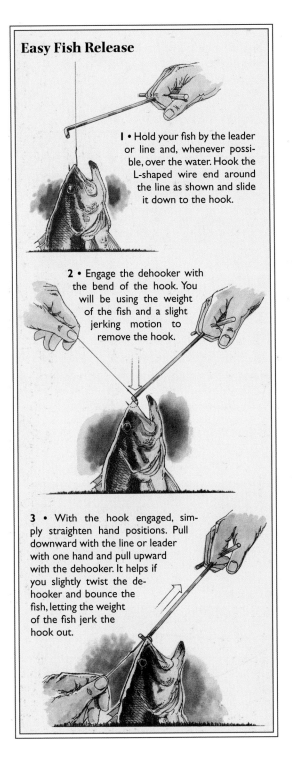

1 • Hold your fish by the leader or line and, whenever possible, over the water. Hook the L-shaped wire end around the line as shown and slide it down to the hook.

2 • Engage the dehooker with the bend of the hook. You will be using the weight of the fish and a slight jerking motion to remove the hook.

3 • With the hook engaged, simply straighten hand positions. Pull downward with the line or leader with one hand and pull upward with the dehooker. It helps if you slightly twist the dehooker and bounce the fish, letting the weight of the fish jerk the hook out.

point in the trip from the water to the plate. Take the time to ice the fish properly for the trip home. Don't pack the fish in direct contact with the ice. The ice is sure to melt, and the fish, lying in the water, might well deteriorate, becoming soft and mushy. It's far better to put the fish in plastic bags, seal the bags so that they are watertight, and then pack the bags in ice. The fish will stay cool—and dry—until you get home.

When you get the fish home, scale or skin them. If they are freshwater fish, wash them thoroughly, inside and out, in cool tap water. If they are saltwater fish, prepare a heavy brine solution, and brush them thoroughly (a pastry-type brush works well) with the brine until they are clean.

Separate the fish into lots, each of which will make a meal for yourself or your family, and wrap each lot in freezer paper or plastic wrap. Then, package them in sealable plastic bags, sealing as tightly as possible to prevent freezer burn. Freeze the fish as quickly as possible.

Some fishermen prefer not to field dress their fish, but to fillet and skin them. This method, which appears difficult but is actually quite simple, has a number of advantages. First, gutting the fish is not necessary since entrails are left intact and never touched with a knife. Second, messy scaling is also an eliminated step because the fillet is skinned and the skin discarded, scales and all. Finally, and perhaps most important, the fillets are bone-free.

Filleting fish is also a good idea for fishermen on extended trips, where sizable quantities of fish are to be packed out or transported home. The head, entrails, fins, and skin are left behind and only clean and meaty fillets are brought home. If you're fishing in another country and have to transport fillets across a border (Canada, for example), leave the skins attached to the fillets for identification to avoid fines.

■ Easy Fish Release

Effective catch-and-release fishing is a critical factor for the future of fish stocks in both fresh and salt water. A simple wire dehooker device is amazingly effective in releasing lip-hooked fish without harm and in a matter of seconds. The device, shown in the accompanying illustrations, is a wire with an L-shaped hook formed on the end. Using this type of dehooker, you can release a fish over water without touching it. The fish will drop safely back into the water.

If you must touch or net a fish, wear wet cotton gloves and always avoid touching the gills. If you regularly net your fish before release, use a smooth rubber mesh net,

How to Hold a Fish

You want to release the fish you just caught unharmed, but do you know where to hold it without damaging any of its vital organs so that you can remove the hook safely?

It really depends on the fish. Some have sharp teeth, while others have gill plates that will cut you like a knife. Fin spines are other obstacles to avoid. Bass—including stripers and members of the black bass family—are the easiest to hold because their lower jaws make perfect handles. You should lift a bass with your thumb inside its lower lip, and your curled index finger pinching firmly against it from the outside. Big crappies also can be handled in the same manner.

Unlike bass and crappies, walleyes have very sharp teeth and sharp gill plates. Don't even think about trying a lip hold on a walleye—you'll regret it. Instead, grab it behind the head and across the back. Always start your grip in front of the dorsal fin and carefully slide your hand to the rear, pushing down the sharp dorsal spines with the heel of your hand.

Panfish and some varieties of perch likewise have sharp dorsal spines and should be held in the same manner as walleyes. The dorsal fin of a bluegill can inflict a painful puncture if it's not held down with your hand.

Trout and salmon might not have sharp dorsal fins, but they do have mouths full of teeth. When you hold a trout or salmon, first wet your hands and then cradle the fish in the palms of both hands. Trout are slippery, so you will need a firm grip. Don't squeeze too tight, however, if you plan to release the fish. Squeeze a trout too hard and you might rupture its organs, which is fatal.

Many species of freshwater and saltwater fish have sharp teeth and require special handling. Bluefish and barracuda, for example, can inflict painful bites if not handled carefully. The best way to hold one of these toothy critters is to get a firm grip behind the top of its head and hold on tightly while you remove hooks with needle-nose fishing pliers. You're holding the fish in an area of its body that is virtually impervious to injury. The same technique will work for muskies, pike, and pickerel.

Catfish have spines in the dorsal and pectoral fins that can puncture skin and inflict a nasty wound. When you hold a catfish, grip it from the front and slide your hand carefully toward the tail, pushing down the fins and sharp spines. Catfish are tough and can usually survive a firmer grip than might be employed for trout.

Barracuda

Bass

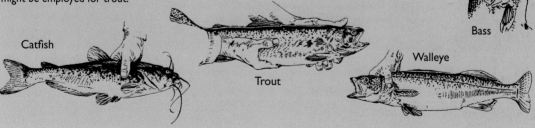

Catfish

Trout

Walleye

such as the nets used in fish hatcheries. Avoid nets with knots, which will break through the fish's protective coat of slime and make it vulnerable to fungus infection.

You can make your own catch-and-release device for lip-hooked fish from a length of heavy wire or you can buy one of the many inexpensive dehookers available from your local tackle dealer.

■ Smoking Your Fish

Smoking your catch is simple, and you can easily turn out great-tasting smoked fish of a variety of species, from salmon to tuna. You can make your own smoker, but it may be more practical to buy a manufactured model. The method described here is "hot" smoking, which produces smoked fish that should be eaten within several days.

Smoker

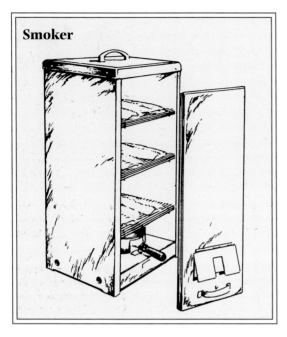

Best Woods for Smoking

Alder: This is the sportsman's favorite. It is a good flavor for all fish and seafood.

Cherry: This type of wood is distinctive and delicious. It is excellent for all dark meats and game. Combine it with other woods for new flavors.

Apple: This is the sweetest and mildest of all flavors. It has a subtle, velvety flavor.

Hickory: The commercial favorite, hickory is famous for flavoring hams and bacons.

Mesquite: A Western favorite, mesquite has a hearty, clean, smoky flavor. It is especially good for meat and poultry.

Before any fish is smoked, it must be brined. The brine solution will put salt in your fish to increase preservation, leech out blood, and intensify the smoke flavoring. Commercial brine solutions are available, or you can mix your own.

Fish fillets are the easiest to smoke. Make sure all the bones are removed, cut the fillets into sections, and rinse them off with water. Commercial brine solutions are available, but you can make a basic do-it-yourself mix with 1 gallon of water, 4 cups of salt, 2 cups of brown sugar, 2 tablespoons of crushed black pepper, and 2 tablespoons of crushed bay leaves. Next, soak the fillets in brine for four to six hours in your refrigerator. If the fillets are thick, keep them in the brine for up to 10 hours. Use a glass, stainless-steel, or plastic bowl. Do **not** use aluminum, which will affect the flavor.

After brining, pat the fillets dry and let them air-cool for 30 minutes or so. When a glaze forms on the surface, the fillets are ready to smoke. Use good-

Wrapper Freezing

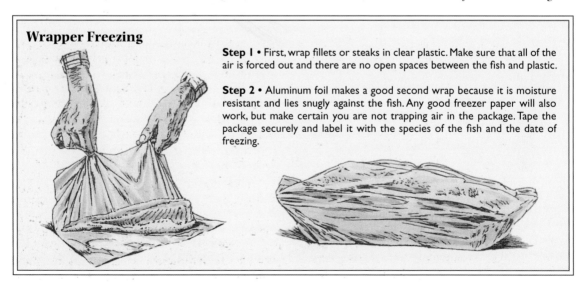

Step 1 • First, wrap fillets or steaks in clear plastic. Make sure that all of the air is forced out and there are no open spaces between the fish and plastic.

Step 2 • Aluminum foil makes a good second wrap because it is moisture resistant and lies snugly against the fish. Any good freezer paper will also work, but make certain you are not trapping air in the package. Tape the package securely and label it with the species of the fish and the date of freezing.

Container Freezing

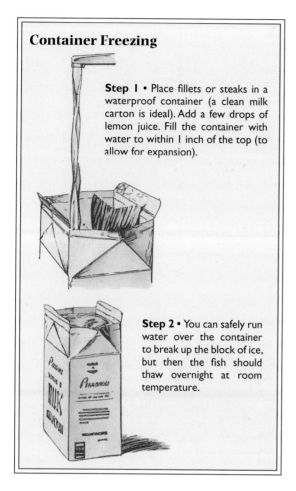

Step 1 • Place fillets or steaks in a waterproof container (a clean milk carton is ideal). Add a few drops of lemon juice. Fill the container with water to within 1 inch of the top (to allow for expansion).

Step 2 • You can safely run water over the container to break up the block of ice, but then the fish should thaw overnight at room temperature.

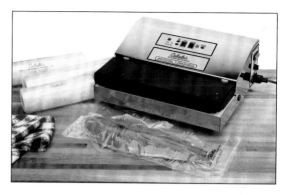

The Cabela's Pro Series Vacuum Sealer is an affordable solution to freezing quantities of fish and game. This machine will prevent freezer burn and extend freezer life. It will keep fish fresh for up to two years.

The Foodsaver Game Saver Deluxe is designed to vacuum seal food for long-term storage. Vacuum sealers literally suck all the oxygen out of a package before it is placed in a freezer. Freezer burn is eliminated because fish and game no longer come in contact with cold, dry air.

flavor wood and keep your smoker at about 160°F to 180°F. Your smoked fish should be ready in six to eight hours.

■ How to Freeze Fish

The biggest problem in freezing fish is preventing "freezer burn." That's when all of the moisture has been drawn out of the flesh and you are left with dried-out fillets. It is more likely to occur in "frost-free" freezers because they are designed to pull moisture from the air inside the freezer.

One way to guard against freezer burn is to freeze your fish in a block of ice. When your fish is completely encased in ice, no air can get at it. Freezing fish in this manner ensures maximum storage life for your fish. You can keep fish frozen in ice for up to two years without much flavor loss. The only disadvantage of container freezing is that it's bulky, awkward, and takes up more freezer space than wrapped packages. If freezer space is at a premium, double-wrap your fish tightly in plastic wrap and tightly wrap again in aluminum foil, which will maintain quality and flavor up to six months.

Unfortunately, trapped oxygen, which is virtually impossible to eliminate completely with traditional packaging, will promote bacteria that will spoil the quality of the fish and this will show up in odor and color. The best solution is vacuum packaging. Vacuum-packaging machines have proven their worth to sportsmen, who can now safely freeze and preserve fish for longer periods of time than with traditional methods. Vacuum-packaging machines work on a simple principle. They literally suck all the oxygen out of a package before it is placed in a freezer. Freezer burn is virtually eliminated because the fish no longer comes in contact with cold, dry air. In an oxygen-free environment, such as vacuum packaging produces, the bacterium that causes spoilage does not multiply fast and loss of food quality is slowed down drastically. The major advantage, of course, is the length of time vacuum-packaged fish can be safely frozen in your freezer. Vacuum-packed fish, depending on the fish species, can be safely stored in a freezer for up to two years.

■ Skin a Fish for Mounting

You're on a remote river in Alaska and you've just caught a giant sockeye salmon that's perfect for your wall back home. Freezers are in short supply and the closest taxidermist is unknown to you, expensive, and may get around to your fish when things get slow at his day job. You've got a problem.

Here's the solution: If you decide you want a skin mount of your fish, you can preserve your trophy by skinning and salting it in the field. Once home, you'll have plenty of time to find a reputable taxidermist, since the salted skin can be frozen indefinitely.

Some planning is required. You'll need to pack a few plastic trash bags, some cotton, cardboard, and paper clips. Anything else you need—such as table salt (2 to 4 pounds) and scissors—can be found in most fishing camps.

It's a good idea to practice this method before you go. Lay the fish on a piece of cardboard and position it exactly as you want it mounted. Trace the outline of the fish on the cardboard with a pencil. Then, at three spots along the length of the fish, measure its girth (or cut exact lengths of mono wrapped around it at these points). Save these dimensions with the outline. Also, take a few color photos of your catch as soon as possible, to help your taxidermist re-create true-to-life colors.

In these days of the catch-and-release mentality, most fishermen wisely opt to release their trophy fish unharmed and prefer to get a replica fiberglass mount of their fish instead. To ensure an accurate fiberglass replica, make sure you take a good color photo of the fish as well as an overall length measurement. The big advantage, aside from releasing your fish to fight another day, is that fiberglass mounts, which are hollow, are surprisingly lightweight, will never fade, and can also be hung outdoors.

How to Skin a Fish for Mounting

Step 1 • Make a lateral cut along the back side of the fish, where it will not show. Cut through the skin from the gill plate to the tail. Use scissors to cut cleanly through the bony substance at the gill plate.

Step 2 • Using a small knife, pare the skin away from the body. Work slowly, being careful not to tear the skin. Be particularly careful in the area around the gills.

Step 3 • At the fins, working from the inside with the scissors, cut the meat free. At the base of the tail, turn the knife and cut directly through the flesh. Take care not to cut the skin on the other side.

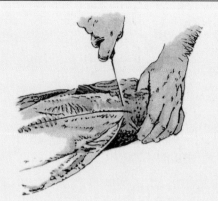

Step 4 • Working back from tail to head, cut the skin away from the body on the other side. When the skin is completely freed, sever the backbone, leaving the head attached to the skin.

Step 6 • Free the gills and remove all flesh from inside the head, including the eyes. During the entire skinning process, make sure you don't break or split any fins.

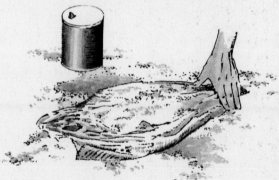

Step 5 • Holding the skin with one hand, use a spoon to gently scrape the remaining meat from the skin. Remove all the cartilage from below and behind the gill plates.

Step 7 • Rub liberal amounts of table salt into the skin, inside the head, and into the base of all fins. Use plenty of salt and work it in thoroughly, but gently.

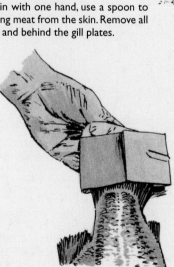

Step 8 • Wrap the fins in wet cotton. Place pieces of cardboard, held by paper clips, over the cotton. Wrap the fish in a plastic bag. Your trophy is now ready for the taxidermist.

WATER TEMPERATURE AND FISH

There is no doubt left in anglers' minds of the importance of water temperature and its direct bearing on the activities of fish. Water temperature will tell you where the fish gather and where they feed at various times of the year.

It is a scientifically proven fact that every species of fish has a preferred temperature zone or range and it will stay and generally feed in this zone. Smallmouth bass, for example, prefer water that is 65 to 68°F. During spring, this temperature range may be in shallow water, and in hot, midsummer weather, this range may be in depths of 30 feet or more. In other words, locate the depth that reads 65 to 68°F and you're sure to find smallmouths.

Taking temperature readings of water is not difficult, whether you use a sophisticated electronic thermometer or an inexpensive water thermometer lowered into the water on a fishing line. One electronic thermometer has a probe attached to a cable that is marked at regular intervals, so depth and temperature can be read simultaneously.

The inexpensive water thermometers can also do the job, and many also indicate depth by inserting a water pressure gauge in the thermometer tube. With these thermometers, allow at least 30 seconds to one minute for a reading. Also, the fishing line attached to it should be marked off in regular intervals, say 5 feet, so you can determine just how deep you are lowering the thermometer in the water.

The accompanying chart shows popular fresh- and saltwater game fish and baitfish and their preferred temperature zones. Look up the fish you are seeking and the water temperature it prefers. Then, begin taking temperature readings from the surface on down, at 5-foot intervals, until you locate the correct zone and depth. Concentrate your efforts at that depth and you'll soon come to discover how important this water temperature business is.

Preferred Temperature

Note: Celsius temperatures are rounded to the nearest degree.

FRESHWATER GAME FISH			
Species	**Lower Avoidance**	**Optimum**	**Upper Avoidance**
American shad (*Alosa sapidissima*)		66°F (19°C)	86°F (30°C)
Atlantic salmon (*Salmo salar*)		62°F (17°C)	
Atlantic sturgeon (*Acipenser oxyrhynchus*)	56°F (13°C)	66°F (19°C)	70°F (21°C)
Black crappie (*Pomoxis nigromaculatus*)	60°F (16°C)	70°F (21°C)	75F° (24°C)
Bloater (*Coregonus hoyi*)	43°F (6°C)		50°F (10°C)
Bluegill (*Lepomis macrochirus*)	58°F (14°C)	69°F (21°C)	75°F (24°C)
Brook trout (*Salvelinus fontinalis*)	44°F (7°C)	59°F (15°C)	70°F (21°C)
Brown bullhead (*Ictalurus nebulosus*)		74°F (23°C)	
Brown trout (*Salmo trutta*)	44°F (7°C)	55–65°F (13–18°C)	75°F (24°C)
Buffalo species (*Ictiobus sp.*)	81°F (27°C)		94°F (34°C)
Burbot (*Lota lota maculosa*)		52°F (11°C)	
Carp (*Cyprinus carpio*)	75°F (24°C)	84°F (29°C)	88°F (31°C)
Chain pickerel (*Esox niger*)	60°F (16°C)	66°F (19°C)	74°F (23°C)
Channel catfish (*Ictalurus punctutatus*)	55°F (13°C)	82–89°F (28–32°C)	
Chinook salmon (*Oncorhynchus tshawytscha*)	44°F (7°C)	54°F (12°C)	60°F (16°C)
Chum salmon (*Oncorhynchus keta*)		57°F (14°C)	
Cisco (*Coregonus artedii*)		52–55°F (11–13°C)	
Coho salmon (*Oncorhynchus kisutch*)	44°F (7°C)	54°F (12°C)	60°F (16°C)

FRESHWATER GAME FISH (continued)

Species	Lower Avoidance	Optimum	Upper Avoidance
Flathead catfish (*Pylodictis olivaris*)	81°F (27°C)		90°F (32°C)
Freshwater drum (*Aplodinotus grunniens*)		74°F (23°C)	
Grass pickerel (*Esox americanus vermiculatus*)		78°F (26°C)	
Grayling (*Thymallus arcticus*)			64°F (18°C)
Green sunfish (*Lepomis cyanellus*)	73°F (23°C)	87°F (31°C)	91°F (33°C)
Goldeye (*Hiodon alosoides*)	72°F (22°C)		83°F (28°C)
Kamloops trout (*Salmo gairdneri*)	46°F (8°C)	47–54°F (8–12°C)	
Kokanee (*Oncorhynchus nerka*)		52–55°F (11–13°C)	
Lake trout (*Salvelinus namaycush*)	42°F (6°C)	50–59°F (10–15°C)	
Lake whitefish (*Coregonus clupeaformis*)	43°F (6°C)	51°F (11°C)	
Landlocked Atlantic salmon (*Salmo salar sebago*)		50–58°F (10–14°C)	65°F (18°C)
Largemouth bass (*Micropterus salmoides*)	60°F (16°C)	80°F (27°C)	
Longnose gar (*Lepisosteus osseus*)		92°F (33°C)	
Longnose sucker (*Catostomus catostomus*)		53°F (12°C)	
Mooneye (*Hiodon tergisus*)	72°F (22°C)		81°F (27°C)
Muskellunge (*Esox masquinongy*)	55°F (13°C)	63°F (17°C)	72°F (22°C)
Northern pike (*Esox lucius*)	56°F (13°C)	63°F (17°C)	74°F (23°C)
Pink salmon (*Oncorhynchus gorbuscha*)		49°F (9°C)	
Pumpkinseed (*Lepomis gibbosus*)		82°F (28°C)	
Rainbow trout (*Salmo gairdneri*)	44°F (7°C)	48–65°F (9–18°C)	75°F (24°C)
Redhorse suckers (*Moxostoma sp.*)	72°F (22°C)		79°F (26°C)
Rock bass (*Ambloplites rupestris*)		70°F (21°C)	
Round whitefish (*Prosopium cylindraceum*)		63°F (17°C)	
Sauger (*Stizostedion canadense*)	55°F (13°C)	67°F (19°C)	74°F (23°C)
Shortnose gar (*Lepisosteus platostomus*)	81°F (27°C)		94°F (34°C)
Smallmouth bass (*Micropterus dolomieui*)	60°F (16°C)	65–68°F (18–20°C)	73°F (23°C)
Sockeye salmon (*Oncorhynchus nerka*)		55°F (13°C)	
Spotted bass (*Micropterus punctulatus*)	71°F (22°C)	75°F (24°C)	80°F (27°C)
Steelhead trout (*Salmo gairdneri*)	38°F (3°C)	48–52°F (9–11°C)	
Sunfishes (*Centrarchidae*)	50°F (10°C)	58°F (14°C)	68°F (20°C)
Tench (*Tinca tinca*)			79°F (26°C)
Walleye (*Stizostedion vitreum*)	50°F (10°C)	67°F (19°C)	76°F (24°C)
White bass (*Morone chrysops*)	62°F (17°C)	70°F (21°C)	78°F (26°C)
White crappie (*Pomoxis annularis*)		61°F (16°C)	
White perch (*Morone americana*)		89°F (32°C)	
White sucker (*Catostomus commersoni*)		72°F (22°C)	
Yellow bass (*Morone mississippiensis*)		81°F (27°C)	
Yellow bullhead (*Ictalurus natalis*)		83°F (28°C)	
Yellow perch (*Perca flavescens*)	58°F (14°C)	65°F (18°C)	74°F (23°C)

FRESHWATER BAITFISH

Species	Lower Avoidance	Optimum	Upper Avoidance
Alewife (*Alosa pseudoharengus*)	48°F (9°C)	54°F (12°C)	72°F (22°C)
Bitterling (*Rhodeus sericeus*)		77°F (25°C)	

FRESHWATER BAITFISH (continued)

Species	Lower Avoidance	Optimum	Upper Avoidance
Bluehead chub (*Nocomis leptocephalus*)	50°F (10°C)	59°F (15°C)	63°F (17°C)
Bluntnose minnow (*Pimephales notatus*)	70°F (21°C)	84°F (29°C)	88°F (31°C)
Desert pupfish (*Cyprinodon macularius*)	71°F (22°C)		78°F (26°C)
Emerald shiner (*Notropis atherinoides*)		61°F (16°C)	
Fathead minnow (*Pimephales promelas*)	77°F (25°C)	84°F (29°C)	90°F (32°C)
Fourhorn sculpin (*Myoxocephalus quadricornis*)	39°F (4°C)		
Gizzard shad (*Dorosoma cepedianum*)		69°F (21°C)	
Golden shiner (*Notemigonus crysoleucas*)		70°F (21°C)	
Goldfish (*Carassius auratus*)		77°F (25°C)	
Guppy (*Poecilia reticulata*)		84°F (29°C)	
Lake chub (*Couesius plumbeus*)		48–52°F (9–11°C)	
Longjaw mudsucker (*Gillichthys mirabilis*)	48°F (9°C)	72°F (22°C)	
Moapa dace (*Moapa coriacea*)		85°F (29°C)	
Mosquitofish (*Gambusia affinis*)		81°F (27°C)	85°F (29°C)
Mottled sculpin (*Cottus bairdi*)		48–52°F (9–11°C)	
Mozambique mouthbrooder (*Tilapia mossambica*)		83°F (28°C)	92°F (33°C)
Ninespine stickleback (*Pungitius pungitius*)		48–52°F (9–11°C)	
Quillback (*Carpiodes cyprinus*)		72°F (22°C)	
Rainbow smelt (*Osmerus mordax*)	43°F (6°C)	50°F (10°C)	57°F (14°C)
River carpsucker (*Carpoides carpio*)	79°F (26°C)		94°F (34°C)
Rosyface shiner (*Notropis rubellus*)	70°F (21°C)	80°F (27°C)	88°F (31°C)
Slimy sculpin (*Cottus cognatus*)	39°F (4°C)		43°F (6°C)
Spotfin shiner (*Cyprinella spiloptera*)	79°F (26°C)	85°F (29°C)	95°F (35°C)
Spottail shiner (*Notropis hudsonius*)		54°F (12°C)	
Stonecat (*Notorus flavus*)		59°F (15°C)	
Stoneroller (*Campostoma anomalum*)	75°F (24°C)	84°F (29°C)	91°F (33°C)
Trout-perch (*Percopsis omiscomaycus*)	50°F (10°C)		61°F (16°C)
White River killfish (*Crenichthys baileyi*)		85°F (29°C)	

SALTWATER GAME FISH

Species	Lower Avoidance	Optimum	Upper Avoidance
Albacore (*Thunnus alalunga*)	59°F (15°C)	64°F (18°C)	66°F (19°C)
Amberjack (*Seriola dumerili*)	60°F (16°C)	65°F (18°C)	72°F (22°C)
Atlantic bonito (*Sarda sarda*)	60°F (16°C)	64°F (18°C)	80°F (27°C)
Atlantic cod (*Gadus morhua*)	31°F (-1°C)	44–49°F (7–9°C)	59°F (15°C)
Atlantic croaker (*Micropogon undulatus*)			100°F (38°C)
Atlantic mackerel (*Scomber scombrus*)	45°F (7°C)	63°F (17°C)	70°F (21°C)
Barracuda (*Sphyraena barracuda*)	55°F (13°C)	75–79°F (24–26°C)	82°F (28°C)
Bigeye tuna (*Thunnus obesus*)	52°F (11°C)	58°F (14°C)	66°F (19°C)
Blackfin tuna (*Thunnus atlanticus*)	70°F (21°C)	74°F (23°C)	82°F (28°C)
Black marlin (*Makaira indica*)	68°F (20°C)	75–79°F (24–26°C)	87°F (31°C)
Bluefin tuna (*Thunnus thynnus*)	50°F (10°C)	68°F (20°C)	78°F (26°C)
Bluefish (*Pomatomus saltatrix*)	50°F (10°C)	66–72°F (19–22°C)	84°F (19°C)
Blue marlin (*Makaira nigricans*)	70°F (21°C)	78°F (26°C)	88°F (31°C)

SALTWATER GAME FISH *(continued)*

Species	Lower Avoidance	Optimum	Upper Avoidance
Bonefish (*Albula vulpes*)	64°F (18°C)	75°F (24°C)	88°F (31°C)
Dolphinfish (*Coryphaena hippurus*)	70°F (21°C)	75°F (24°C)	82°F (28°C)
Fluke or summer flounder (*Paralichthys dentatus*)	56°F (13°C)	66°F (19°C)	72°F (22°C)
Haddock (*Melanogrammus aeglefinus*)	36°F (2°C)	47°F (8°C)	52°F (11°C)
Horn shark (*Heterodontus francisci*)		75°F (24°C)	
Kelp bass (*Paralabrax clathratus*)	62°F (17°C)	65°F (18°C)	72°F (22°C)
King mackerel (*Scomberomorus cavalla*)	70°F (21°C)		88°F (31°C)
Opaleye (*Girella nigricans*)		79°F (26°C)	86°F (30°C)
Permit (*Trachinotus falcatus*)	65°F (18°C)	72°F (22°C)	92°F (33°C)
Pollock (*Pollachius virens*)	33°F (1°C)	45°F (8°C)	60°F (16°C)
Red drum (*Sciaenops ocellatus*)	52°F (11°C)	71°F (22°C)	90°F (32°C)
Red snapper (*Lutjanus blackfordi*)	50°F (10°C)	57°F (14°C)	62°F (17°C)
Sailfish (*Istiophorus platypterus*)	68°F (20°C)	79°F (26°C)	88°F (31°C)
Sand seatrout (*Cynoscion arenarius*)	90°F (32°C)	95°F (35°C)	104°F (40°C)
Sea catfish (*Arius felis*)			99°F (37°C)
Skipjack tuna (*Euthynnus pelamis*)	50°F (10°C)	62°F (17°C)	70°F (21°C)
Snook (*Centropomus undecimalis*)	60°F (16°C)	70–75°F (21–24°C)	90°F (32°C)
Spotted seatrout (*Cynoscion nebulosus*)	48°F (9°C)	72°F (22°C)	81°F (27°C)
Striped bass (*Morone saxatilis*)	61°F (16°C)	68°F (20°C)	77°F (25°C)
Striped marlin (*Tetrapturus audax*)	61°F (16°C)	70°F (21°C)	80°F (27°C)
Swordfish (*Xiphias gladius*)	50°F (10°C)	66°F (19°C)	78°F (26°C)
Tarpon (*Megalops atlantica*)	74°F (23°C)	76°F (24°C)	90°F (32°C)
Tautog (*Tautoga onitis*)	60°F (16°C)	70°F (21°C)	76°F (24°C)
Weakfish (*Cynoscion regalis*)		55–65°F (13–18°C)	78°F (26°C)
White marlin (*Tetrapturus albidus*)	65°F (18°C)	70°F (21°C)	80°F (27°C)
White sea bass (*Cynoscion nobilis*)	58°F (14°C)	68°F (20°C)	74°F (23°C)
Winter flounder (*Pseudopleuronectes americanus*)	35°F (2°C)	48–52°F (9–11°C)	64°F (18°C)
Yellowfin tuna (*Thunnus albacares*)	64°F (18°C)	72°F (22°C)	80°F (27°C)
Yellowtail (*Seriola dorsalis*)	60°F (16°C)	65°F (18°C)	70°F (21°C)

SALTWATER BAITFISH

Species	Lower Avoidance	Optimum	Upper Avoidance
Atlantic silverside (*Menidia menidia*)			90°F (32°C)
Atlantic threadfin (*Polydactylus octonemus*)			92°F (33°C)
Bay anchovy (*Anchoa mitchilli*)		82°F (28°C)	92°F (33°C)
California grunion (*Leuresthes tenuis*)	68°F (20°C)	77°F (25°C)	93°F (34°C)
Gulf grunion (*Leuresthes sardina*)	68°F (20°C)	89°F (32°C)	98°F (37°C)
Gulf menhaden (*Brevoortia patronus*)			86°F (30°C)
Pacific silversides (jacksmelt and topsmelt) (*Atherinopsis sp.*)	72°F (22°C)	77°F (25°C)	82°F (28°C)
Rough silverside (*Membras martinica*)			91°F (33°C)
Skipjack herring (*Alosa chrysochloris*)	72°F (22°C)		84°F (29°C)
Spot (*Leiostomus xanthurus*)			99°F (37°C)
Tidewater silverside (*Menidia beryllina*)			93°F (34°C)

Section Four
GAME FISH

• FRESHWATER SPECIES •
• SALTWATER SPECIES •

FRESHWATER SPECIES

■ Atlantic Salmon *(Salmo salar)*

DESCRIPTION: Atlantic salmon are anadromous fish, meaning that they are spawned in freshwater rivers and then migrate to the ocean to spend most of their lives before returning to fresh water to spawn themselves. When fresh from the sea, Atlantics are steel blue on top and silver on the sides and belly, and have dark spots on their sides. As their stay in fresh water lengthens, the colors become darker, with the sides taking on a pinkish hue as spawning time arrives. Very young salmon are called parrs. Parrs have distinctive dark vertical bars called parr markings. Unlike Pacific salmon, all of which die after spawning, about 15 percent of Atlantic salmon survive the spawning act and return to sea.

RANGE: The highly prized Atlantic salmon once ranged from Delaware north through Quebec and the Canadian Maritime provinces to Greenland, and in the western Atlantic Ocean to the British Isles and parts of Scandinavia. But today, because of "progress"—meaning dams, pollution, and urban and suburban sprawl—the range of the Atlantic salmon in the United States is restricted to a handful of rivers in Maine, though efforts are being made to restore this fine game fish to the Connecticut River and other northeastern rivers.

HABITAT: In fresh water, the Atlantic salmon must have clean, flowing, cold water. In upstream spawning areas, shallow water over a gravel bottom is a must so that the fish can create "redds," or spawning beds. When in the ocean, these salmon range over vast areas but tend to concentrate on feeding grounds, which are only recently being discovered.

SIZE: Mature Atlantic salmon weigh from 9 to 75 pounds, with the average being 12 pounds. Their size depends on how many years they have spent in the sea, where their growth is fast. Salmon that return to fresh water after only one or two years at sea are called grilse and weigh up to about 6 or 8 pounds.

FOOD: These fish feed on small baitfish and the like when in the ocean, but upon entering fresh water, they stop feeding almost completely. And yet they can be induced to strike an artificial lure, particularly dry and wet flies.

■ Landlocked Salmon
(Salmo salar sebago)

COMMON NAMES: Landlocked salmon, Sebago salmon, landlock, and ouananiche

DESCRIPTION: The landlocked salmon is very similar in coloration and general appearance to the Atlantic salmon, of which the landlock is a subspecies. It is assumed that the subspecies descended from Atlantic salmon trapped in freshwater lakes thousands of years ago. As their name suggests, landlocks do not spawn in the sea. They either spawn in their home lakes or descend to outlet streams to spawn.

Atlantic Salmon

RANGE: Landlocks range over much of New England (they are most numerous in Maine), Quebec and other parts of eastern Canada, and north to Labrador. They have been introduced in New York and other eastern states and in South America.

HABITAT: The landlock survives best in deep, cold lakes that have a high oxygen content.

SIZE: Most landlocks average 2 to 3 pounds, but a 6-pounder is not unusual and an occasional 10-pounder is caught. The maximum weight is about 30 pounds.

FOOD: Landlocks feed mostly on small baitfish, particularly smelt.

■ Chinook Salmon
(Oncorhynchus tshawytscha)

COMMON NAMES: Chinook salmon, king salmon, tyee salmon, and blackmouth (immature stage)

DESCRIPTION: The chinook, like all other Pacific salmon, is anadromous and seems to prefer the largest of Pacific coast rivers for spawning. Chinooks have a dark-blue back that shades to silver on the sides and white on the belly. Small, dark spots, barely noticeable in fish fresh from the sea, mark the upper part of the body.

RANGE: Chinook salmon range from southern California to northern Alaska, being more numerous in the northern part of that area. They often travel enormous distances upriver to spawn; in the Yukon River, for example, chinooks have been seen 2,000 miles from the sea.

HABITAT: Chinooks prefer large, clean, cold rivers, but often enter small tributary streams to spawn in shallow water over gravel bottoms.

SIZE: The chinook is the largest of the Pacific salmon, reaching weights of more than 100 pounds. Rarely, however, does a sport fisherman catch one of more than 60 pounds, and the average size is about 18 pounds.

FOOD: Chinook salmon eat ocean baitfish (herring, sardines, candlefish, and anchovies), freshwater baitfish, and fish roe.

■ Dog Salmon (Oncorhynchus keta)

COMMON NAMES: Dog salmon and chum salmon

DESCRIPTION: The dog salmon closely resembles the chinook salmon, but has black-edged fins and lacks the chinook's dark spots on the back, dorsal fin, and tail. During spawning, the male dog salmon often exhibits red or green blotches on its sides. The dog salmon is rarely taken by sport fishermen.

RANGE: One of five species of Pacific salmon, the dog salmon is found from central California north to Alaska, but is far more numerous in Alaska than farther south. In their sea migrations, dog salmon travel as far as the Aleutians, Korea, and Japan.

HABITAT: Like all other salmon, the dog spawns in gravel in freshwater rivers, usually in the lower reaches of the parent streams, but occasionally far upstream.

SIZE: Dog salmon reach weights of 30 pounds or a bit more, but they average 6 to 18 pounds.

FOOD: The diet of dog salmon consists mainly of baitfish and crustaceans.

■ Sockeye Salmon
(Oncorhynchus nerka)

COMMON NAMES: Sockeye salmon, red salmon, and blueback salmon

DESCRIPTION: The sockeye is similar to the chinook, but it has a small number of gill rakers and tiny spots along its back. When spawning, sockeye males turn dark red, with the forward parts of their body being greenish. Females range in color from olive to light red. Sockeyes are more often caught by sport fishermen than dog salmon, and they will take artificial flies and are good fighters.

RANGE: Sockeyes are found from California to Japan, but few are encountered south of the Columbia River. A landlocked strain of the sockeye (see Kokanee Salmon), originally found from British Columbia south to Oregon and Idaho, is being stocked in freshwater lakes in various areas of the United States.

HABITAT: This species spawns over gravel in freshwater lakes, especially those fed by springs.

SIZE: Sockeyes reach a maximum weight of about 15 pounds, but the average weight is 4 to 9 pounds.

FOOD: Sockeyes feed mainly on crustaceans, but also eat small baitfish.

Humpback Salmon
(Oncorhynchus gorbuscha)

COMMON NAMES: Humpback salmon and pink salmon

DESCRIPTION: Similar to other salmon but smaller, the humpback has small scales and its caudal fin (tail) has large, oval, black spots. At maturity, or at spawning time, the males develop a large, distinctive hump on their backs. The humpback is among the most commercially valuable of the Pacific salmon and is becoming more popular with sport fishermen.

RANGE: The humpback is found from California to Alaska and as far away as Korea and Japan.

HABITAT: This species spawns over gravel in freshwater rivers, usually near the sea.

SIZE: The smallest of the Pacific salmon, the humpback averages 3 to 6 pounds, attaining a maximum weight of about 10 pounds.

FOOD: Humpbacks subsist largely on a diet of crustaceans, baitfish, and squid.

Coho Salmon *(Oncorhynchus kisutch)*

COMMON NAMES: Coho salmon, silver, and hooknose

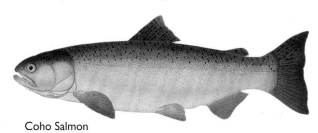

Coho Salmon

DESCRIPTION: The coho is generally silvery with a bluish back and has small, dark spots along the upper part of the sides and tail. When the spawning urge takes hold, the males assume a reddish coloration, but when they enter fresh water they become almost black. The coho is highly prized as a sport fish, striking artificials readily and leaping breathtakingly when hooked.

RANGE: The coho is found from California to Alaska and as far from the West Coast of the United States as Japan. It has also been transplanted with unprecedented success in all the Great Lakes and in many landlocked reservoirs throughout the United States.

HABITAT: This fish spawns in gravel in freshwater rivers, either near the sea or far upstream.

SIZE: Cohos reach weights approaching 30 pounds, but they average 6 to 12 pounds.

FOOD: A coho's diet is mainly baitfish, squid, crustaceans, and crab larvae.

Kokanee Salmon
(Oncorhynchus nerka kennerlyi)

COMMON NAMES: Kokanee salmon, silver trout, blueback, little redfish, Kennerly's salmon, landlocked sockeye, redfish, and silversides

DESCRIPTION: The kokanee is a landlocked strain of the anadromous sockeye salmon. Biologically identical with the true sockeye (though much smaller), the kokanee is silvery on its sides and belly, but during spawning the males have reddish sides and the females have slate-gray sides. Kokanees resemble some trout, but differ from all trout in that they have more than 12 rays in the anal fin. The kokanee is the only Pacific salmon that matures in fresh water. It is much prized by fishermen.

RANGE: The kokanee's original range extended from Idaho and Oregon north to Alaska, but it has been introduced in recent years in lakes as far south as New Mexico and as far east as New England.

HABITAT: The kokanee spawns in gravel, both in lakes and in tributary streams, and ranges throughout lakes at other times.

SIZE: Much smaller than the true sockeye salmon, the kokanee reaches a maximum weight of about 4 pounds. The average length varies greatly, depending upon water and food conditions. In some places they never exceed 10 inches, while in other places—California's Donner Lake, for example—their average length is more than 18 inches.

FOOD: Kokanees feed almost exclusively on tiny forage—minute crustaceans and other plankton.

■ Arctic Char *(Salvelinus alpinus)*

COMMON NAMES: Arctic char, Arctic trout, alpine trout, and Quebec red trout

DESCRIPTION: The Arctic char is a far-north salmonid whose colors vary greatly. Sea-run char are quite silvery as they enter freshwater rivers, but their freshwater colors soon predominate, turning the char into a stunning fish with sides ranging in color from pale to very bright orange and red. Char are usually spotted in red, pink, or cream, and have the white-edged fins of brook trout, but they lack the brook trout's vermiculations (wormlike markings) on the back. There are both anadromous and landlocked strains of Arctic char.

RANGE: Arctic char are found in northern Canada, Alaska, Iceland, Greenland, Scandinavia, England, Ireland, Scotland, Europe, and the Soviet Union.

HABITAT: As its range indicates, the char thrives in very cold, clean water, preferring fast, shallow river water near the mouths of tributary streams. Relatively little is known about the nomadic movements of anadromous char, but they apparently spend the summer near the mouths of rivers, where they feed heavily before moving inland.

SIZE: Arctic char reach weights of nearly 30 pounds, but the average weight is 2 to 8 pounds.

FOOD: Char feed on a species of smelt called capelin and on sand eels, various baitfish, some crustaceans, and occasionally on insects.

■ Brook Trout *(Salvelinus fontinalis)*

COMMON NAMES: Brook trout, speckled trout, speck, and squaretail

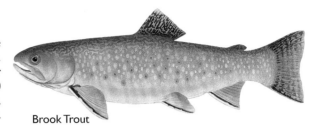

Brook Trout

DESCRIPTION: This best-loved American native fish is not a true trout but actually a member of the char family. It is a beautiful fish, having a dark back with distinctive vermiculations (wormlike markings), sides marked with yellow spots and with red spots encircled in blue, a light-colored belly (bright orange during spawning), and pink or red lower fins edged in white. Wherever they are found, brook trout willingly take the offerings of fly, bait, and lure fishermen alike, a fact that has contributed to their decrease in many areas, though pollution has done far more to decimate populations of native brookies.

RANGE: Originally native only to northeastern North America from Georgia to the Arctic, the brook trout is now found in suitable waters throughout the United States, Canada, South America, and Europe. Stocking maintains brook trout in many waters, but true native brookies are becoming rare.

HABITAT: Brook trout must have clean, cold water, seldom being found in water warmer than 65°F. They spawn both in lakes and in streams, preferring small, spring-fed brooks.

SIZE: Though the rod-and-reel record for brook trout is 14½ pounds, fish half that size are a rarity today. In fact, a 5-pounder is an exceptional brook trout, and fish of that size are seldom found anywhere but in Labrador, northern Quebec and Manitoba, and Argentina. Native brook trout caught in streams average about 6 to 12 inches in length.

FOOD: Brook trout eat worms, insects, crustaceans, and various kinds of baitfish.

■ Sunapee Trout *(Salvelinus aureolus)*

COMMON NAMES: Sunapee trout and Sunapee golden

DESCRIPTION: This attractive fish—which may be a member of the char family or a distinct species of trout (there is some disagreement on the subject)—has a dark-bluish back that lacks the wormlike markings of the brook trout. Its sides have spots of pinkish white, yellow, or red, and the yellowish or orange fins are edged in white.

RANGE: Originating in New Hampshire, principally in Sunapee Lake, the Sunapee trout is exceedingly rare, being found only in Sunapee Lake and in a few lakes and ponds in northern New England. The introduction of lake trout in Sunapee and other lakes has had a deteriorating effect on populations of Sunapee trout.

HABITAT: Little is known about the wanderings of this attractive fish, but it is known that in Sunapee Lake these trout move into the shallows in spring and fall, while in summer they are found in the deepest parts of the lake—way down to 60 to 100 feet, where the water is quite cold.

SIZE: Many years ago, 10- and 12-pound Sunapees were taken in the lake from which they derive their name, but today a fisherman is lucky to catch a 15-incher.

FOOD: Smelt makes up the majority of the Sunapee trout's diet.

Dolly Varden Trout
(Salvelinus malma)

COMMON NAMES: Dolly Varden trout, Dolly, western char, bull trout, salmon trout, and red-spotted trout

DESCRIPTION: This member of the char family somewhat resembles the brook trout, but it lacks the brookie's wormlike back markings and is usually more slender. It has red and yellow side spots and the white-edged fins typical of all chars. In salt water, the Dolly is quite silvery. The Dolly, said to have been named after a Charles Dickens character, is not as popular in some parts of its range as other trout species, possibly because it is not as strong a fighter.

RANGE: Occurring from northern California to Alaska and as far from the United States as Japan, the Dolly is found in both fresh water and, in the northern part of its range, in salt water.

HABITAT: Dolly Vardens spawn in gravel in streams. At other times of the year, stream fish are likely to be found in places similar to those preferred by brook trout, such as under rocks, logs, and other debris and lying in deep holes. In lakes, they are likely to be found near the bottom near reefs and drop-offs. They are seldom found near the surface.

SIZE: Dolly Vardens reach weights of upwards of 30 pounds. The average size is 8 to 18 inches in some places (usually streams), and 3 to 6 pounds in other places (usually lakes).

FOOD: These fish are primarily bottom-feeders, though in streams they feed heavily on insects and may be taken on flies. Large fish feed heavily on baitfish, including the young of trout and salmon. It has been said that these trout will eat anything, which may be true considering that in some areas fishermen shoot ground squirrels, remove the legs and skin them, and use the legs for Dolly Varden bait!

Lake Trout *(Salvelinus namaycush)*

COMMON NAMES: Lake trout, togue, mackinaw, gray trout, salmon trout, forktail, and laker

DESCRIPTION: More somberly hued than most other trout, the laker is usually a fairly uniform gray or bluish gray, though in some areas it is a bronze green. It has irregular, pale spots over its head, back, and sides and also has the white-edged fins that mark it as a char.

RANGE: The lake trout is distributed throughout Canada and in the northern United States, principally in New England, and New York's Finger Lakes, the Great Lakes, and many large western lakes. Stockings have widened the laker's range considerably and have restored the species to portions of the Great Lakes where an incursion of lamprey eels decimated the laker populations in the 1950s and early 1960s.

Lake Trout

HABITAT: Lake trout are fish of deep, cold, clear lakes, though in the northern part of their range they are also found in large streams. Lakers prefer water temperatures of about 45°F and are rarely found where water rises above 70°F. In the southern part of their range, they are usually found only in lakes that have an adequate oxygen supply in the deeper spots.

SIZE: The lake trout is the largest of the trout species, reaching weights of more than 100 pounds. Their average size often depends on the size, depth, and water quality of a given lake.

FOOD: Though the young feed on insects and crustaceans, adult lake trout eat primarily fish, such as smelt, small kokanee salmon, ciscoes, whitefish, and sculpin.

■ Rainbow Trout
(Oncorhynchus mykiss)

COMMON NAMES: Rainbow trout, steelhead, Kamloops rainbow, Kamloops trout, and redsides

DESCRIPTION: This native American trout takes three basic forms: the nonmigratory rainbow, which lives its entire life in streams or lakes; the steelhead, which is spawned in freshwater rivers, migrates to the sea, and returns to the rivers to spawn itself (large rainbows that live in the Great Lakes and elsewhere in the eastern United States also are called steelheads but are not true members of the steelhead clan); and the Kamloops rainbow, a large subspecies found mostly in interior British Columbia. Though the rainbow's colors vary greatly depending upon where it is found, the fish generally has an olive or lighter-green back shading to silvery or white on the lower sides and belly. There are numerous black spots on the upper body from head to tail and a distinctive red stripe along the middle of each side. Sea-run and lake-run rainbows are usually quite silver, with a faint or nonexistent red stripe and few spots. The rainbow is an extremely important sport fish and will take flies, lures, and bait willingly. It usually strikes hard and is noted for its wild leaps.

RANGE: The natural range of the rainbow trout is from northern Mexico to Alaska and the Aleutian Islands, but stocking programs have greatly widened that range so that it now includes most of Canada, all of the northern and central states of the United States, and some of the colder waters in such southern states as Georgia, Tennessee, Arkansas, and Texas.

HABITAT: The rainbow, like all trout, must have cold, clean water, though it does fairly well under marginal conditions. It is found in shallow lakes and deep lakes, in small streams and large ones. It may be found at the surface one day, and feeding on the bottom the next. The rainbow's universality is due partly to the fact that it can do well in a wide variety of environments.

SIZE: The average nonmigratory stream rainbow runs from 6 to 18 inches in length, though some much larger specimens are occasionally taken. Nonmigratory lake fish tend to run considerably larger—up to 50 pounds or more. An average migratory steelhead runs from 8 to 12 pounds, but this strain reaches 35 pounds or so.

FOOD: Rainbows feed heavily on insect life, but they also eat baitfish, crustaceans, worms, and the roe of salmon and trout. The diet of the Kamloops rainbow is mainly kokanee salmon.

■ Cutthroat Trout (Salmo clarki)

COMMON NAMES: Cutthroat trout, cut, native trout, mountain trout, Rocky Mountain trout, black-spotted trout, harvest trout, Montana black-spotted trout, Tahoe cutthroat, and Yellowstone cutthroat

DESCRIPTION: Occurring in both nonmigratory and anadromous forms, the cutthroat trout gets its common name from the two slashes of crimson on the underside of its lower jaw. Its scientific name honors William Clark of the famed Lewis and Clark expedition. The cutthroat is often mistaken for the rainbow, but it lacks the rainbow's bright-red side stripe, and its entire body is usually covered with black spots, while the rainbow's spots are usually limited to the upper half of the body. The cut-

Rainbow Trout

Brown Trout

throat usually has a greenish back, colorful gill plates, sides of yellow or pink, and a white belly. Coastal cutthroats are greenish blue with a silvery sheen on the sides and heavy black spots. The cutthroat is a fine sport fish, taking flies—particularly wet flies—readily and showing an inordinate liking for flashy spoons.

RANGE: The cutthroat is found from northern California north to Prince William Sound, Alaska, and inland throughout the western United States and Canada.

HABITAT: A fish of clean, cold water, the cutthroat frequents places like those preferred by the brook trout—undercut banks, deep holes, logs, and other debris. They prefer quiet water, generally, in streams. Unlike other trout that go to sea, anadromous cutthroats do not range widely in the ocean depths. Instead, they remain in bays at the mouths of their home streams or along the nearby ocean shores.

SIZE: Though cutthroats of up to 41 pounds have been caught by anglers, they seldom exceed 5 pounds and average 2 to 3 pounds. A fish weighing 4 pounds is considered large for a sea-run cutthroat.

FOOD: Young cutthroats feed mainly on insect life, while adults eat insects, baitfish, crayfish, and worms.

Golden Trout *(Salmo aquabonita)*

COMMON NAMES: Golden trout, Volcano trout, and Sierra trout

DESCRIPTION: This rare jewel of the western high country is the most beautiful of all trout. The golden trout has an olive back and crimson gill covers and side stripes, while the remainder of the body ranges from orangish yellow to gold. The dorsal fin has orange tips, and the anal and ventral fins have white edges. Each side contains about 10 black parr markings. The coloring differs from lake to lake. The golden is a rarely caught but highly prized sport fish.

RANGE: Originally found only in the headwaters of California's Kern River, the golden is now present in high-mountain lakes in many western states, including California, Wyoming, Idaho, and Washington. Modern fish-breeding and stocking techniques have extended the range of the golden—or, rather, a golden-rainbow

trout cross—to the eastern states, including West Virginia and New Jersey.

HABITAT: The true golden trout is found in small, high lakes and their tributary streams at elevations of 9,000 to 12,000 feet. The water in these lakes is extremely cold, and weed growth is minimal or nonexistent. Because of the golden's spartan habitat, it can be extremely moody and difficult to catch.

SIZE: Golden trout are not large, a 2-pounder being a very good one, though some lakes hold fair numbers of fish up to 5 pounds. The maximum size is 11 pounds.

FOOD: Golden trout feed almost exclusively on minute insects, including terrestrial insects, but also eat tiny crustaceans and are sometimes caught by bait fishermen using worms, salmon eggs, and grubs.

Brown Trout *(Salmo trutta)*

COMMON NAMES: Brown trout, German brown trout, and Loch Leven trout

DESCRIPTION: Introduced in North America in the 1880s, the brown trout is a top-notch dry-fly fish, and yet its daytime wariness and whimsy can drive fishermen to the nearest bar. The brown trout is generally brownish to olive brown, shading from dark brown on the back to dusky yellow or creamy white on the belly. The sides, back, and dorsal fin have prominent black or brown spots, usually surrounded by faint halos of gray or white. Some haloed red or orange spots are also present. Sea-run browns and those in large lakes are often silvery and resemble landlocked salmon.

RANGE: The brown is the native trout of Europe and is also found in New Zealand, parts of Asia, South America, and Africa. It is found in the United States from coast to coast and as far south as New Mexico, Arkansas, and Georgia.

Rocky Mountain Whitefish

HABITAT: The brown trout can tolerate warmer water and other marginal conditions better than other trout species can. It is found in both streams and lakes, preferring hiding and feeding spots similar to those of the brook trout. It often feeds on the bottom in deep holes, coming to the surface at night.

SIZE: Brown trout have been known to exceed 40 pounds, though one of more than 10 pounds is exceptional. Most browns caught by sport fishermen weigh ½ to 1½ pounds.

FOOD: Brown trout feed on aquatic and terrestrial insects as well as worms, crayfish, baitfish, and fish roe. Large specimens will eat such tidbits as mice, frogs, and small birds.

■ Grayling *(Thymallus arcticus)*

COMMON NAMES: Grayling, Montana grayling, and Arctic grayling

DESCRIPTION: Closely related to trout and whitefishes, the grayling's most distinctive feature is its high, wide dorsal fin, which is gray to purple and has rows of blue or lighter dots. Its back is dark blue to gray, and the sides range from gray to brown to silvery, depending upon where the fish lives. The forepart of the body usually has irregularly shaped dark spots. The grayling is a strikingly handsome fish and a fly fisherman's dream.

RANGE: The grayling is abundant in Alaska, throughout northern Canada from northern Saskatchewan westward, and northward through the Northwest Territories. It is less common in the United States, ranging in high areas of Montana, Wyoming, and Utah. Recently developed grayling-breeding procedures are extending the range of this fish into Idaho, California, Oregon, and other mountain states.

HABITAT: The grayling is found in both lakes and rivers, but is particularly at home in high and isolated timberline lakes. In lakes, schools of grayling often cruise near the shore. In rivers, the fish are likely to be found anywhere, but they usually favor one type of water in any given stream.

SIZE: The maximum weight of the grayling is 20 pounds or a bit heavier, but in most waters, even in the Arctic,

a 2-pounder is a good fish. In U.S. waters, grayling seldom top 1½ pounds.

FOOD: The grayling's diet is made up almost entirely of nymphs and other insects and aquatic larvae. However, this northern fish will also readily eat worms and crustaceans.

■ Rocky Mountain Whitefish *(Prosopium williamsoni)*

COMMON NAMES: Rocky Mountain whitefish, mountain whitefish, and Montana whitefish

DESCRIPTION: The Rocky Mountain whitefish resembles the lake whitefish, though its body is more cylindrical. Coloration shades from brown on the back to silver on the sides to white on the belly. The dorsal fin is large, but not nearly as large as that of the grayling. Where it competes with trout in a stream, the Rocky Mountain whitefish is considered a nuisance by many anglers, though it fights well and will take dry and wet flies, spinning lures, and bait.

RANGE: The Rocky Mountain whitefish is endemic to the western slope of the Rocky Mountains from northern California to southern British Columbia.

HABITAT: Found in cold, swift streams and in clear, deep lakes, these whitefish school up in deep pools after spawning in the fall and feed mostly on the bottom. In spring, the fish move to the riffles in streams and the shallows in lakes.

SIZE: Rocky Mountain whitefish reach 5 pounds, but a 3-pounder is an exceptional one. The average length is 11 to 14 inches and the weight is 1 pound.

FOOD: These fish feed almost entirely on such insects as caddis and midge larvae and stone fly nymphs. They also eat fish eggs, their own included.

Lake Whitefish
(Coregonus clupeaformis)

COMMON NAMES: Lake whitefish, common whitefish, Great Lakes whitefish, Labrador whitefish, and Otsego bass

DESCRIPTION: Similar in appearance—though only distantly related—to the Rocky Mountain whitefish, the lake whitefish has bronze or olive shading on the back, with the rest of the body being silvery white. It has rather large scales, a small head and mouth, and a blunt snout. Large specimens appear humpbacked. Lake whitefish, because they spend much of the year in very deep water, are not important sport fish.

RANGE: Lake whitefish are found from New England west through the Great Lakes area and throughout much of Canada.

HABITAT: These fish inhabit large, deep, cold, clear lakes and are usually found in water from 60 to 100 feet deep, though they will enter tributary streams in spring and fall. In the northern part of their range, however, lake whitefish are often found foraging in shallow water, and they will feed on the surface when mayflies are hatching.

SIZE: Lake whitefish reach weights of a bit more than 20 pounds, but their average size is less than 4 pounds.

FOOD: Lake whitefish feed primarily on small crustaceans and aquatic insects, but they will also eat baitfish.

Cisco (Coregonus artedii)

COMMON NAMES: Cisco, herring, lake herring, common cisco, lake cisco, bluefin, Lake Erie cisco, tullibee, short-jaw chub, and grayback

DESCRIPTION: Though the cisco superficially resembles members of the herring family, it is not a herring but rather a member of the whitefish family. The cisco has a darker back (usually bluish or greenish) than the true whitefish. The body is silvery with large scales. There are more than 30 species and subspecies of ciscoes in the Great Lakes area alone, and all of them look and act alike. Ciscoes occasionally provide good sport fishing, particularly on dry flies, but they are more important commercially.

RANGE: The various strains of ciscoes occur from New England and New York west through the Great Lakes area and range widely through Canada. Their center of concentration seems to be the Great Lakes area.

HABITAT: Ciscoes prefer large, cold, clear lakes, usually those having considerable depth. Little is known of the wanderings of these fish; some species are found from the surface to several hundred feet down. They spawn in July and August over hard bottoms. In summer, ciscoes often come to the surface to feed on hatching insects, usually at sundown.

SIZE: The size of a cisco depends on its species. Some average only a few ounces in weight, while the largest attain a maximum weight of about 7 pounds. The average length is about 6 to 20 inches.

FOOD: Insect life—mainly bottom-dwelling types—is the blue-plate special of the cisco, though it sometimes feeds on surface insects and on minute crustaceans and worms as well.

American Shad (Alosa sapidissima)

DESCRIPTION: The American shad is an anadromous fish—meaning one that ascends coastal rivers to spawn but spends much of its life in salt water. A member of the herring family, the shad has a greenish back, with the remainder of the body being silvery. There are usually a few indistinct markings on the forebody. Shad put up a no-holds-barred battle on hook and line and are important sport and commercial fish, though pollution is putting a dent in their population in some areas.

RANGE: American shad were originally native only to the Atlantic, but they were introduced in the Pacific in the 1870s. On the Atlantic coast, they are found from Florida to the Gulf of St. Lawrence, while on the Pacific

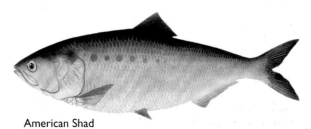

American Shad

Largemouth Bass

coast, they range from San Diego, California, to southern Alaska. They are also found in Scandinavia, France, Italy, Germany, Russia, and elsewhere.

HABITAT: American shad swarm up large, coastal rivers to spawn in the spring—from March to May, depending upon the location of the river. They are particularly susceptible to anglers below dams and in holes and slow runs just upstream of riffles, where they tend to rest before continuing upriver. They generally spawn in the main river.

SIZE: The average weight of an American shad is 3 to 5 pounds, while the maximum weight is 12 to 13 pounds. Egg-laden females are usually heavier than males.

FOOD: While in the ocean, American shad feed almost exclusively on plankton, so far as is known. After they enter fresh water on the spawning runs, these fish apparently do not feed at all. Curiously, however, they will strike at a small variety of artificial lures, including small, sparsely dressed wet flies and leadhead jigs tied on a gold hook and having a wisp of bucktail at the tail.

◾ Largemouth Bass
(*Micropterus salmoides*)

COMMON NAMES: Largemouth bass, bigmouth bass, black bass, green trout, Oswego bass, and green bass

DESCRIPTION: The largemouth bass is among the most important of this continent's freshwater game fish. In physical makeup it is a chunky fish, with coloration ranging from nearly black or dark green on the back, through varying shades of green or brownish green on the sides, to an off-white belly. The largemouth's most distinctive marking, however, is a horizontal, dark band running along its side from head to tail. In large, old bass particularly, the band may be almost invisible. There are two reliable ways to distinguish the largemouth from its close relative and look-alike, the smallmouth bass: the largemouth's upper

jaw (maxillary) extends back behind the eye, while the smallmouth's does not; and the spiny part of the largemouth's dorsal fin is almost completely separated from the softer rear portion, while in the smallmouth the two fin sections are connected in one continuous fin.

RANGE: The largemouth is native to or stocked in every state in the Lower 48 and is found as far south as Mexico and as far north as southern Canada.

HABITAT: Largemouths are found in slow-moving streams large and small and in nonflowing waters ranging in size from little more than puddles to vast impoundments. They thrive best in shallow, weedy lakes and in river backwaters. They are warm-water fish, preferring water temperatures of 70°F to 75°F. Largemouths never venture too far from such areas as weed beds, logs, stumps, and other sunken debris, which provide both cover and food. They are usually found in water no deeper than 20 feet.

SIZE: Largemouth bass grow biggest in the southern United States, where they reach a maximum weight of a little more than 20 pounds and an 8- to 10-pounder is not a rarity. In the north, largemouths rarely exceed 10 pounds and a 3-pounder is considered a good catch.

FOOD: The largemouth's diet is as ubiquitous as the fish itself. These bass eat minnows and any other available baitfish, worms, crustaceans, a wide variety of insect life, frogs, mice, and ducklings.

◾ Smallmouth Bass
(*Micropterus dolomieui*)

COMMON NAMES: Smallmouth bass, black bass, and bronzeback

DESCRIPTION: A top game fish and a flashy fighter, the smallmouth bass is brownish, bronze, or greenish

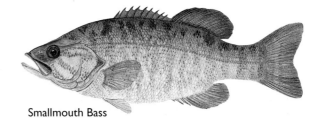

Smallmouth Bass

brown in coloration, with the back being darker and the belly being off-white. The sides are marked with dark, vertical bars, which may be indistinguishable in young fish. (For physical differences between the smallmouth bass and its look-alike relative, the largemouth bass, see Largemouth Bass.) The smallmouth is not as common as, and is a wilder fighter than, the largemouth.

RANGE: The smallmouth's original range was throughout New England, southern Canada, and the Great Lakes area, and in large rivers of Tennessee, Arkansas, and Oklahoma. However, stocking has greatly widened this range so that it now includes states in northern and moderate climates from coast to coast.

HABITAT: Unlike the largemouth bass, the smallmouth is a fish of cold, clear waters (preferring water temperatures of no higher than 65°F or so). Large, deep lakes and sizable rivers are the smallmouth's domain, though it is often found in streams that look like good trout water—that is, those with numerous riffles flowing over gravel, boulders, or bedrock. In lakes, smallmouths are likely to be found over gravel bars, between submerged weed beds in water 10 to 20 feet deep, along drop-offs near shale banks, on gravel points running out from shore, and near midlake reefs or shoals. In streams, they often hold at the head of a pool where the water fans out, and in pockets having moderate current and nearby cover.

SIZE: The maximum weight attained by smallmouth bass is about 12 pounds. In most waters, however, a 4- or 5-pounder is a very good fish, and the average weight is probably 1½ to 3 pounds.

FOOD: Smallmouths eat baitfish and crayfish mainly, though they also feed on hellgrammites and other insect life, worms, small frogs, and leeches.

Redeye Bass *(Micropterus coosae)*

COMMON NAMES: Redeye bass, Coosa bass, shoal bass, and Chipola bass

DESCRIPTION: Given full status as a distinct species in about 1940, the redeye bass is a relative of the smallmouth. Though this fish is often difficult to identify positively, especially in adult form, the redeye young have dark, vertical bars that become indistinct with age and brick-red dorsal, anal, and caudal fins. This fin color and

the red of its eyes are the redeye's most distinctive physical traits. The redeye is a good fighter and is good eating.

RANGE: An inhabitant of the southeastern states, the redeye bass is found mainly in Alabama, Georgia, and South Carolina. It is also found in the Chipola River system in Florida.

HABITAT: The redeye bass is mainly a stream fish, usually inhabiting upland parts of drainage systems. It often feeds at the surface.

SIZE: The maximum weight of the redeye bass is 6 pounds, but, in Alabama at least, the average weight is about 12 ounces.

FOOD: A large portion of the redeye's diet is insects, but it also feeds on worms, crickets, and various baitfish.

Spotted Bass *(Micropterus punctulatus)*

COMMON NAMES: Spotted bass, Kentucky bass, and Kentucky spotted bass

DESCRIPTION: The spotted bass, recognized as a distinct species only since 1927, is quite similar in appearance to the largemouth bass and has characteristics of both the largemouth and the smallmouth. The spotted bass is olive green on the back with many dark blotches, most of which are diamond shaped. A series of short blotches form a horizontal, dark band along the sides that is somewhat more irregular than that of the largemouth. Spots below the lateral line distinguish the spotted bass from the largemouth, and that spotting, plus the lack of vertical side bars, distinguishes it from the smallmouth bass.

RANGE: The spotted bass is found in the Ohio-Mississippi drainage from Ohio south to the states bordering the Gulf of Mexico and western Florida, and west to Texas, Oklahoma, and Kansas.

HABITAT: In the northern part of its range, the spotted bass prefers large, deep pools in sluggish waters. Its preferred habitat in the southern part of its range is quite different, consisting of cool streams with gravel bottoms and clear spring-fed lakes. In lakes, spotted bass are sometimes found in water as deep as 100 feet.

SIZE: The maximum weight of spotted bass is 8 pounds, but few specimens top 4 or 5 pounds.

FOOD: Spotted bass, like most other members of the bass family, feed on various baitfish and insects, frogs, worms, crustaceans, grubs, and the like.

■ Bluegill *(Lepomis macrochirus)*

COMMON NAMES: Bluegill, bluegill sunfish, bream, sun perch, blue perch, blue sunfish, copperbelly, red-breasted bream, copperhead bream, and blue bream

DESCRIPTION: Many fishermen cut their angling teeth on the bluegill, the most widely distributed and most popular of the large sunfish family. The color of the bluegill varies probably more than that of any other sunfish, ranging in basic body color from yellow or orange to dark blue. The shading goes from dark on the back to light on the forward part of the belly. The sides of a bluegill are usually marked by six to eight irregular, vertical bars of a dark color. A bluegill's prominent features are a broad, black gill flap, and long, pointed pectoral fins. Bluegills are excellent fighters, and if they grew to largemouth-bass size, they would break a lot of tackle.

RANGE: The bluegill's range just about blankets the entire 48 contiguous states.

HABITAT: The bluegill prefers habitat very much like that of the largemouth bass—that is, quiet, weedy waters, in both lakes and streams, where it can find both cover and food. In daytime, the smaller bluegills are usually close to shore in coves, under overhanging trees, and around docks. The larger ones are usually nearby but in deeper water, moving into the shallows early and late in the day.

SIZE: The maximum size of bluegills is about 4½ pounds

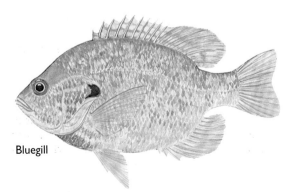

Bluegill

in weight and 15 inches in length, but the average length is 4 to 8 inches.

FOOD: A bluegill's food consists chiefly of insect life and vegetation. Other items on the menu include worms, grubs, small baitfish, crustaceans, small frogs, grasshoppers, and the like.

■ Redear Sunfish *(Lepomis microlophus)*

COMMON NAMES: Redear sunfish, redear, shellcracker, stumpknocker, yellow bream, and chinquapin

DESCRIPTION: A large and very popular sunfish in the South, the redear has a small mouth, large and pointed pectoral fins, and a black gill flap with a whitish border (the bluegill lacks the white gill-flap border). The body color is olive with darker olive spots, and the sides have five to 10 dusky vertical bars. The redear is distinguishable from the pumpkinseed—the member of the sunfish family it most closely resembles—by the lack of spots on the dorsal fin.

RANGE: The redear sunfish ranges from southern Illinois and southern Indiana south to Florida and the other Gulf states and westward to Texas and New Mexico. Its heaviest concentration is in Florida.

HABITAT: The redear sunfish shows a definite liking for large, quiet waters, congregating around logs, stumps, and roots. It will, however, frequent open waters and seems to require less vegetation than other sunfish.

SIZE: The redear is more likely to run to a large size than most any other sunfish. The maximum weight seems to be 3 pounds, but 2-pounders are not uncommon.

FOOD: Redears depend mainly on snails for food, but will eat other mollusks, crustaceans, worms, and insects.

■ White Crappie *(Pomoxis annularis)*

COMMON NAMES: White crappie, papermouth, bachelor perch, papermouth perch, strawberry bass, calico, calico bass, sago, and grass bass

DESCRIPTION: This popular freshwater panfish is a cousin to the true sunfish. In coloration, its back is olive

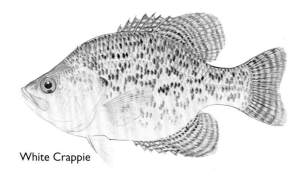

White Crappie

green and its sides silvery olive with seven to nine dark vertical bands, while the sides of the very similar black crappie have irregular dark mottling. Another, more reliable way to tell the white crappie from the black is the number of spines in the dorsal fin: the white has six while the black has seven or eight. The white is more elongated in general shape, while the black, by comparison, has a high, rather arched back.

RANGE: The original range of the white crappie extended from Nebraska east to the Great Lakes, south through the Mississippi and Ohio River systems, and throughout most of the South as far north as North Carolina. Stocking has greatly extended that range, though the white crappie is still predominantly a southern species.

HABITAT: The white crappie can live under more turbid conditions than the black crappie—in fact, it prefers silty rivers and lakes to clear water and is common in southern impoundments and cypress bayous, warm and weedy ponds, and slow streams. The ideal home for these schooling fish is a pile of sunken brush or a submerged treetop. In summer, crappies often seek such a spot in deep holes, moving into the shallows in the evening to feed.

SIZE: White crappies average 6 to 10 inches in length and less than a pound in weight. However, individuals of more than 5 pounds have been caught by sport fishermen, and 2- or 3-pounders are not rare.

FOOD: White crappies eat baitfish for the most part—gizzard shad is their blue-plate special in southern lakes—but also feed on worms, shrimp, plankton, snails, crayfish, and insects.

■ Black Crappie
(Pomoxis nigromaculatus)

COMMON NAMES: Black crappie, calico bass, papermouth, and grass bass

DESCRIPTION: This near-identical twin of the white crappie is dark olive or black on the back. Its silvery sides and its dorsal, anal, and caudel fins contain dark and irregular blotches scattered in no special pattern. (For physical differences between the black and white crappie, see White Crappie.) Though it is a school fish like the white crappie, the black crappie does not seem to populate a lake or stream so thickly as does the white.

RANGE: The black crappie, though predominantly a northern United States fish, is found from southern Manitoba to southern Quebec, and from Nebraska to the East Coast and south to Texas and Florida. However, stocking has widened this range to include such places as British Columbia and California.

HABITAT: The black crappie prefers rather cool, clear, weedy lakes and rivers, though it often shares the same waters as the white crappie. The black is a brush lover, tending to school up among submerged weed beds and the like. It occasionally feeds at the surface, particularly near nightfall.

SIZE: See White Crappie.

FOOD: See White Crappie.

■ White Bass *(Morone chrysops)*

COMMON NAMES: White bass, barfish, striped bass, and streak

DESCRIPTION: This freshwater member of the ocean-going sea-bass family has boomed in popularity among sport fishermen in recent years, thanks to its schooling habits, eagerness to bite, tastiness of its flesh, and increase in its range. The white bass is a silvery fish

White Bass

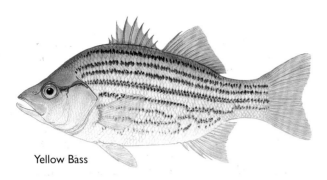

Yellow Bass

tinged with yellow toward the belly. The sides have about 10 narrow dark stripes, the body is moderately compressed, and the mouth is bass-like. The white bass may be distinguished from the look-alike yellow bass by its unbroken side stripes (those of the yellow bass are broken) and by its projecting lower jaw (the upper and lower jaws of the yellow are about even). The white bass is astonishingly prolific.

RANGE: White bass are found in the St. Lawrence River area and throughout the Mississippi and Missouri River systems, west into Texas, and in most of the other southern and southwestern states.

HABITAT: The white bass lives in large lakes and rivers, but it appears to prefer large lakes containing relatively clear water. The burgeoning number of large, deep reservoirs constructed recently in the South and Southwest are tailor-made for the white bass. These fish like large areas of deep water and need gravel or bottom rubble for spawning. Schools of whites can often be seen feeding voraciously on or near the surface, particularly in the evening.

SIZE: The maximum size of the white bass is about 6 pounds, but the average size is ½ to 2 pounds. A 3- or 4-pounder is an excellent specimen.

FOOD: Baitfish, particularly gizzard shad, form the main part of the white bass's diet, though it will also eat crustaceans, worms, and insect life.

■ Yellow Bass *(Morone mississippiensis)*

COMMON NAMES: Yellow bass, barfish, brassy bass, stripe, striped bass, and streaker

DESCRIPTION: Quite similar in appearance to the white bass (for physical differences, see White Bass), the yellow bass has an olive-green back, silvery to golden-yellow sides with six or seven dark, horizontal, broken stripes, and a white belly. Like the white bass, the yellow bass is a member of the seabass family. It is a school fish, but its population levels tend to fluctuate drastically from year to year.

RANGE: The range of the yellow bass is quite restricted, being mainly the Mississippi River drainage from Minnesota to Louisiana and eastern Texas, plus the Tennessee River drainage, and Iowa. Even within its range, the yellow bass is found only in scattered lakes and streams.

HABITAT: One of the yellow's primary habitat requirements is wide, shallow, gravelly areas and rocky reefs. This fish prefers large lakes and large rivers, especially those with clear water. Yellow-bass schools tend to roam in deep water in daytime, coming into the shallows to feed late and very early.

SIZE: Most yellow bass caught by sport fishermen range from 8 to 11 inches, and ¼ to ¾ pound. The maximum size is probably about 3 pounds.

FOOD: Yellow bass feed almost exclusively on baitfish, but occasionally take crustaceans and insects.

■ White Perch *(Morone americanus)*

COMMON NAMES: White perch, silver perch, and sea perch

DESCRIPTION: This fish is not a perch but rather a bass. And though it is often found in fresh water, it is not a freshwater bass. It is a member of the sea-bass family and superficially resembles one other member of that family—the saltwater striped bass—though it is much

White Perch

smaller. The white perch is greenish to blackish green on the back and silvery on the sides, particularly when living in salt water (freshwater individuals are usually darker). Young white perch have indistinct stripes on the sides, but adult fish lack them.

RANGE: In salt water, white perch range along the Atlantic coast from Nova Scotia to North Carolina. They are found inland as far as the Great Lakes and are especially abundant in New York State and New England.

HABITAT: In salt water, white perch are most likely to be found in brackish ponds and backwaters formed by coastal sandbars. Anadromous members of the clan run upriver to spawn. In inland lakes, these fish usually lie in deep water over a sand or gravel bottom during the day, sometimes at 50 feet or deeper, but often come into shoreside shallows in the evening and at night to feed. At those times, and on dark days, schools of white perch may be seen breaking the surface.

SIZE: White perch seem to run larger in salt and brackish water than in fresh water. The average size, generally, is 8 to 10 inches. As for the weight, 2-pounders are not rare, but white perch seldom exceed 4 pounds.

FOOD: In salt water, white perch forage on small fish, shrimp, squid, crabs, and the like. In fresh water, their diet includes larval and other insect forms, crustaceans, baitfish, and worms.

Yellow Perch *(Perca flavescens)*

COMMON NAMES: Yellow perch, ringed perch, striped perch, coon perch, and jack perch

DESCRIPTION: The yellow perch, in no way related to the white perch, is an extremely popular freshwater panfish. Though its colors may vary, the back is generally olive, shading to golden yellow on the sides and white on the belly. Six to eight rather wide, dark, vertical bands run from the back to below the lateral line. Though the body is fairly elongated, the fish has a somewhat humpbacked appearance.

RANGE: The yellow perch is a ubiquitous species, being found in most areas of the United States. It is most common from southern Canada south through the Dakotas and Great Lakes states into Kansas and Missouri, and in

the East from New England to the Carolinas. Stockings have also established it in such places as Montana and the Pacific slope.

HABITAT: The yellow perch is predominantly a fish of lakes large and small, though it is also found in rivers. It prefers cool, clean water with plenty of sandy or rocky-bottomed areas, though it does well in a wide variety of conditions. As a very general rule, the best perch lakes are large and have only moderate weed growth. These fish feed at various levels, and the fisherman must experiment until he finds them.

SIZE: The average yellow perch weighs a good deal less than a pound, though 2-pounders aren't uncommon. The maximum weight is about 4½ pounds.

FOOD: Yellow perch eat such tidbits as baitfish (including their own young), worms, large plankton, insects in various forms, crayfish, snails, and small frogs.

Walleye *(Stizostedion vitreum)*

COMMON NAMES: Walleye, walleyed pike, pike, jack, jackfish, pickerel, yellow pickerel, blue pickerel, dore, and pikeperch

DESCRIPTION: The walleye is not a pike or pickerel, as its nicknames might indicate, but rather the largest member of the perch family. Its most striking physical characteristic is its large, almost opaque eyes, which appear to be made of glass and which reflect light eerily. The walleye's colors range from dark olive or olive brown on the back to a lighter olive on the sides and white on the belly. Here's how to tell the walleye from its look-alike relative, the sauger: the lower fork of the walleye's tail has a milky-white tip, absent in the sauger; and the walleye's dorsal-fin foresection has irregular blotches or streaks, unlike the definite rows of spots found on the sauger's dorsal. The walleye isn't the best fighter among game

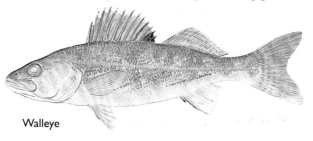

Walleye

fish, but it makes up for that shortcoming by providing delectable eating.

RANGE: The walleye is found in most of Canada as far north as Great Slave Lake and Labrador. Its original U.S. range was pretty much limited to the northern states, but stocking has greatly widened this range to include all of the East and most of the Far West and southern states.

HABITAT: The walleye loves clear, deep, cold, and large waters, both lakes and rivers, and prefers a sand, gravel, or rock bottom. It is almost always found on or near the bottom, though during evening and night hours it may move into shallow water to feed. Once you find a walleye hole, you should catch fish there consistently, for walleyes are schooling fish and are unlikely to move their places of residence.

SIZE: The top weight of walleyes is about 25 pounds, but a 6- to 8-pounder is a brag fish. Most walleyes that end up on fishermen's stringers weigh 1 to 3 pounds.

FOOD: Walleyes feed primarily on small fish and crayfish. Strangely enough, though they don't often eat worms, night crawlers are a real walleye killer, especially when combined with a spinner.

■ Sauger *(Stizostedion canadense)*

COMMON NAMES: Sauger, sand pike, gray pike, river pike, spotfin pike, and jack fish

DESCRIPTION: The sauger is very much like the walleye in all important respects, except that it is quite a bit smaller. It is olive or olive gray on its back and sides and has a white belly. Its large, glassy eyes are very much like those of the walleye. (For physical differences between the sauger and the walleye, see Walleye.)

RANGE: The sauger's range is generally a blueprint of the walleye's. However, sauger are most common in the Great Lakes, other very large lakes in the northern United States and southern Canada, and in the large rivers (and their tributaries), such as the Mississippi, Missouri, Ohio, and Tennessee.

HABITAT: In this category, too, the sauger is much like the walleye, though the sauger can tolerate siltier or murkier water than the walleye and tends to stick to deeper waters. A good place to look for sauger is in tailwaters below dams.

SIZE: The sauger's maximum weight is about 8 pounds. Its average size is 1 to 2 pounds.

FOOD: See Walleye.

■ White Sturgeon *(Acipenser transmontanus)*

DESCRIPTION: This huge, primitive throwback to geological history is one of 16 species of sturgeon in the world, seven of which occur in the United States. It is the largest fish found in this country's inland waters and the only member of the sturgeon family that is considered a game fish. The white sturgeon does not have scales but rather five rows of bony plates along the body. It has a large, underslung, sucking mouth, and its skeleton is cartilage rather than true bone. Sturgeon roe is better known as caviar. Though relatively few anglers fish for these behemoths, careful regulation of the fishery is necessary to prevent depletion of the populations of white sturgeon.

RANGE: The white sturgeon is found along the Pacific coast from Monterey, California, to Alaska. They are also found inland in the largest of rivers, including the Columbia and Snake.

HABITAT: Some white sturgeon are entirely landlocked, but many spend much of their lives at sea and ascend large West Coast rivers to spawn. In large rivers, they lie on the bottom in deep holes.

SIZE: The largest white sturgeon reported taken pulled the scales down to 1,800 pounds. The average size is difficult to determine.

FOOD: In fresh water, the white sturgeon uses its vacuum-cleaner mouth to inhale crustaceans, mollusks, insect larvae, and all manner of other bottom-dwelling organisms. Bait used by sturgeon anglers includes night crawlers, lamprey eels, cut bait, and even dried river moss.

■ Channel Catfish *(Ictalurus punctatus)*

COMMON NAMES: Channel catfish and fiddler

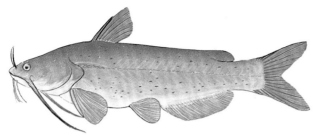

Channel Catfish

DESCRIPTION: This sizable member of the large catfish family (which includes bullheads) is undoubtedly the most streamlined, gamest, and most agile of the whole clan. In coloration, the channel cat is steely blue on top and shades to white on the belly, though young ones may be silvery even along the back. It is the only spotted catfish (it has dark speckles on the sides, though these spots may be missing in large specimens) with a deeply forked tail.

RANGE: The channel catfish occurs from the Saskatchewan River and entire Great Lakes area southward into Mexico. Stocking has transplanted this fish far west and east of its natural range.

HABITAT: Channel catfish are found in lakes, but they are more common to rivers, especially large ones. They are likely to be found in faster, cleaner water than other catfish and seem to prefer a bottom composition of sand, gravel, or rock. Like all other catfish, they are bottom-feeders and are especially active at night.

SIZE: Channel cats are among the larger members of the catfish family, attaining weights of up to 60 pounds. The average size is 1 to 5 pounds.

FOOD: The channel cat's varied menu includes just about anything it can get its jaws around—small fish, insects, crustaceans, worms, grubs, frogs, and many other aquatic food forms.

■ **Blue Catfish** *(Ictalurus furcatus)*

DESCRIPTION: The blue is the largest member of the catfish clan. It has a deeply forked tail, but lacks the spots of the channel catfish. In color, the blue catfish is pale blue on the back, a lighter silvery blue on the sides, and white on the belly. The most reliable way to tell the blue from other catfish is by the number of rays on its straight-edged anal fin (there are 30 to 36 rays).

RANGE: The blue catfish is found mainly in the Mississippi River system, but it occurs south into Mexico and has been introduced into some rivers on the Atlantic coast.

HABITAT: The blue is a catfish of large rivers and is likely to be found below the dams creating large impoundments, especially in the southern United States. It prefers less-turbid waters than do most other catfish and seems to do best over bottoms of rock, gravel, or sand. It feeds in rapids or fast chutes.

SIZE: This heavyweight grows to well more than 100 pounds. The average size, however, is 2 to 15 pounds.

FOOD: The blue catfish feeds primarily on small fish and crayfish. A favorite bait in some areas is a whole golden shad.

■ **Brown Bullhead** *(Ictalurus nebulosus)*

COMMON NAMES: Brown bullhead, horned pout, and speckled bullhead

DESCRIPTION: Probably the most popular of the catfish—at least, it's the most often caught—the brown bullhead is a rather slender catfish with typical catfish features: sharp dorsal spine and sensitive barbels (the "feelers" projecting from the mouth area). The brown bullhead's chin barbels are dark brown or black. The tail has almost no fork, and the anal fin has 22 or 23 rays. The back is yellowish brown to light chocolate brown and has vague dark mottling, the sides are lighter, and the belly is yellow to milky white.

RANGE: Brown bullheads occur from Maine and the Great Lakes south to Mexico and Florida, but stocking has greatly expanded this range.

Brown Bullhead

HABITAT: Brown bullheads prefer relatively deep, weedy waters in lakes and slow-moving streams. They may be found over sand and gravel bottoms and also over mud. They are almost exclusively bottom-feeders.

SIZE: The brown bullhead seldom weighs more than 3 pounds, with its average length being 6 to 16 inches.

FOOD: Insect larvae and mollusks constitute the majority of the brown bullhead's menu, but it will eat almost anything, from worms, small fish, and frogs to plant material and even chicken livers (a favorite catfisherman's bait).

■ Black Bullhead *(Ictalurus melas)*

COMMON NAMES: Black bullhead and horned pout

DESCRIPTION: Quite similar in appearance to the brown bullhead, the black bullhead is black to yellow green on the back, yellowish or whitish on the sides, and bright yellow, yellow, or milky on the belly. Its chin barbels are dark or spotted, and its pectoral spines have no serrations. The body is chunky.

RANGE: The areas in which the black bullhead is most numerous are New York, west to the Dakotas, and south to Texas. However, the fish has been introduced into most other areas of the United States.

HABITAT: The black bullhead is a fish of muddy, sluggish, turbid streams and lakes. It seems to do well, in fact, in any kind of environment except cool, clear, deep water. It is a bottom-feeder.

SIZE: The largest black bullhead taken by sport fishing weighed 8 pounds, but this catfish seldom weighs more than 2 pounds.

FOOD: See Brown Bullhead.

■ Carp *(Cyprinus carpio)*

COMMON NAMES: Carp and common carp

DESCRIPTION: This big, coarse, much maligned rough fish belongs to the minnow family and is related to the goldfish. In color, the carp is olive to light brown on the back, golden yellow on the sides, and yellowish white on the belly. At the base of each of its large scales is a dark spot. On each side of the upper jaw are a pair of fleshy barbels, and the dorsal fin has a serrated spine. Though the carp is cussed out by most sport fishermen and often poisoned out of lakes and streams, it is taken by rod and line, bow and arrow, spear, ice gig, and set line, and it can put up a whale of a battle.

RANGE: Introduced into the United States in 1876, the carp has found its way into just about every area in the nation. It is also widely distributed throughout Europe and Asia.

HABITAT: The carp can live almost anywhere and under almost any conditions—except cold, clear waters. It is almost always found on the bottom, except during spawning, when schools of carp are often seen slashing around on the surface.

SIZE: Carp reach a maximum size of about 60 pounds, but the average weight is 8 to 15 pounds.

FOOD: Carp are mainly vegetarians, feeding on aquatic plant life and plankton, though they also eat insects and are often caught by anglers on doughballs, cornmeal, and such.

■ Alligator Gar *(Lepisosteus spatula)*

DESCRIPTION: Exceeded in size in fresh water only by the western sturgeons, the alligator gar is the largest of the ancient gar family. It can be distinguished from its relatives by an examination of the teeth. Young alligator gars have two rows of large teeth on each side of the upper jaw; other gars have only a single row. The alligator gar has a long, cylindrical body that is olive green or brownish green along the back and lighter below. The sides and rear fins have mottling or large, dark spots. Gars are of minor importance as sport fish, though they wage a wild, no-holds-barred battle when taken on rod and line.

RANGE: The alligator gar is found mainly in the Mississippi and Ohio River systems as far north as Louisville, Kentucky, and St. Louis, Missouri, and as far south as northeastern Mexico.

HABITAT: Alligator gars prefer sluggish rivers, lakes, and backwaters over muddy, weedy bottoms. They often congregate in loose schools, usually near the surface, where they roll around.

SIZE: The largest reported alligator gar was 10 feet long and weighed 302 pounds. The average size, however, is undetermined.

FOOD: Various kinds of fish, notably the freshwater drum (or gaspergou), are the principal food of alligator gars, though anglers catch them on wire nooses baited with minnows and on bunches of floss-like material that tangle tenaciously in the gar's teeth.

Longnose Gar *(Lepisosteus osseus)*

DESCRIPTION: The longnose gar is the most common and most widely distributed of the entire gar family. Its name derives from its long, slender beak (nose). Other distinguishing characteristics are its overlapping diamond-shaped scales and the unusual position of its dorsal fin—far back near the tail and almost directly above the anal fin. The coloration is similar to that of the alligator gar.

RANGE: The longnose gar occurs from Quebec's St. Lawrence drainage west to the Great Lakes (excluding Lake Superior) and as far as Montana, south along the Mississippi River system, and down into Mexico.

HABITAT: The longnose lives in much the same habitat as the alligator gar, though it is more likely to be found swimming and feeding in flowing water—that is, where there is a moderate current.

SIZE: Smaller by far than the alligator gar, the longnose reaches a length of 4 to 5 feet.

FOOD: The longnose, like the alligator gar, feeds mostly on other fish, though it also eats plankton and insect larvae when young.

Muskellunge *(Esox masquinongy)*

COMMON NAMES: Muskellunge, maskinonge (and a variety of other spellings), muskie, pike, blue pike, great pike, jack, spotted muskellunge, barred muskellunge, and tiger muskellunge

DESCRIPTION: Moody, voracious, and predaceous, the muskellunge, the largest member of the pike family, presents one of the greatest challenges of any freshwater fish. Its adherents probably catch fewer fish per hour than do those who fish for any other freshwater species, and yet muskie fishermen are legion—and growing in number. The muskellunge—whose name means "ugly fish" in Ojibway dialect—is green to brown to gray in overall color, depending upon its geographical location. Side markings are usually vertical bars, though the fish may be blotched or spotted or lack any distinctive markings. The muskie has no scales on the lower part of its cheek and gill covers; other members of the pike family have scales in those areas. There are three subspecies of the muskellunge: the Great Lakes muskie, the Ohio (or Chautauqua) muskie, and the tiger (or northern) muskie.

RANGE: The Great Lakes muskie is generally a fish of the Great Lakes basin area. The Ohio (Chautauqua) muskie occurs in New York's Chautauqua Lake and through the Ohio River drainage. The tiger (northern) muskie is common in Wisconsin, Minnesota, and western Michigan. In overall distribution, the muskellunge is found as far north as the James Bay and Hudson Bay drainages in northern Canada, across the northern United States, from Wisconsin east to New York and Pennsylvania, and south into Tennessee, North Carolina, Georgia, and in much of the northern Mississippi drainage. Stocking and propagation methods are greatly widening the muskie's range.

HABITAT: Muskies live in rivers, streams, and lakes, usually only in clear waters, though they may inhabit discolored water in the southern part of their range. They prefer cold waters, but they can tolerate water as warm as 70°F to 75°F. Favorite hangouts for adult muskies are shoreline weed beds, particularly near deep water, and such items of cover as logs, stumps, and rocks. They are usually found in water shallower than 15 feet, though midsummer may find them as deep as 50 feet.

Muskellunge

SIZE: Muskies can reach weights of more than 100 pounds. However, the biggest rod-caught specimen weighed just shy of 70 pounds, and the average is 10 to 20 pounds.

FOOD: Muskies feed mainly on fish, including their own young, as well as suckers, yellow perch, bass, and panfish. They also eat crayfish, snakes, muskrats, worms, frogs, ducklings, squirrels, and just about anything else they can sink their ample teeth into.

◾ Northern Pike
(Esox lucius)

COMMON NAMES: Northern pike, pike, northern, snake, great northern, jackfish, and jack

DESCRIPTION: This baleful-looking predator of the weed bed is of great importance as a sport fish. In color, it is dark green on the back, shading to lighter green on the sides to whitish on the belly. Its distinctive side markings are bean-shaped light spots, and it has dark-spotted fins. The entire cheek is scaled, but only the upper half of the gill cover contains scales. The dorsal fin, as in all members of its family, is far to the rear of the body, almost directly above the anal fin.

RANGE: The pike is found in northern waters all around the globe. In North America, it occurs from Alaska east to Labrador, and south from the Dakotas and the St. Lawrence River to Nebraska and Pennsylvania. Stockings have extended this range to such states as Montana, Colorado, North Carolina, and Maryland.

HABITAT: Over its entire range, the pike's preferred living conditions are shallow, weedy lakes (large and small); shallow areas of large, deep lakes; and rivers of moderate current. In summer, pike are normally found in about 4 feet of water near cover; in fall, they are found along steep, stormy shores.

SIZE: In the best Canadian pike lakes, rod-caught pike average 5 to 25 pounds, but in most waters, a 10- to 15-pounder is a very good pike. The maximum weight is a little more than 50 pounds.

FOOD: Pike are almost entirely fish eaters, but they are as voracious and predacious as the muskie and will eat anything that won't eat them first.

Chain Pickerel

◾ Chain Pickerel *(Esox niger)*

COMMON NAMES: Chain pickerel, jack, and chainsides

DESCRIPTION: This attractive pike-like fish with chainlink markings is the largest of the true pickerels. Its body color ranges from green to bronze, darker on the back and lighter on the belly. Its distinctive dark, chain-like side markings and larger size make the chain pickerel hard to confuse with the other, less common pickerel (mud or grass pickerel and barred or redfin pickerel).

RANGE: The chain pickerel originally was found only east and south of the Alleghenies, but its range now extends from Maine to the Great Lakes in the north and from Texas to Florida in the south.

HABITAT: The pickerel is almost invariably a fish of the weeds. It lurks in or around weed beds and lily pads, waiting to pounce on unsuspecting morsels. It is usually found in water no deeper than 10 feet, although in hot weather it may retreat to depths of as much as 25 feet.

SIZE: Chain pickerel attain a maximum weight of about 10 pounds, but one of 4 pounds is bragging size. The average weight is 1 to 2½ pounds.

FOOD: Chain pickerel eat fish for the most part, although they will also readily dine on frogs, worms, crayfish, mice, and insects.

◾ Redhorse Sucker
(Maxostoma macrolepidotum)

COMMON NAMES: Redhorse sucker, redhorse, northern redhorse, redfin, redfin sucker, and bigscale sucker

DESCRIPTION: Many anglers look at the entire sucker clan—of which the redhorse is probably the best known and most widely fished for—as pests or worse. And yet countless suckers are caught on hooks, netted, trapped, and speared every year, particularly in the spring, when their flesh is firm and most palatable. The redhorse, like all other suckers, has a large-lipped, tubelike, sucking mouth on the underside of its snout. Its overall color is silver, with the back somewhat darker. The mouth has no teeth, and the fins lack spines.

RANGE: The redhorse is found east of the Rocky Mountains from the midsouth of the United States north to central and eastern Canada.

HABITAT: Unlike some of its relatives, the redhorse prefers clean, clear waters and is at home in large and medium-size rivers, even swift-flowing ones, and in lakes. These fish seem to prefer sandy shallows in lakes, and deep holes in streams. As spawning runs begin in the spring, the redhorse congregates at the mouths of streams.

SIZE: The redhorse sucker's maximum weight is about 12 pounds. Most of the redhorses taken by anglers weigh 2 to 4 pounds.

FOOD: This bottom-feeding species eats various small fish, worms, frogs, crayfish, various insects (both aquatic and terrestrial), and insect larvae.

Splake
(Salvelinus namaycush x S. fontinalis)

DESCRIPTION: The splake is a trout hybrid created by crossing lake trout with brook trout. The name is a combination of *speckled* (brook) trout and *lake* trout. The first important crossing of these two trout species was done in British Columbia in 1946, and some of the new strain was stocked in lakes in Banff National Park in Alberta. The body shape of the splake is midway between that of the brook trout and lake trout—heavier than the laker, slimmer than the brookie. Like the true lake trout, the splake's spots are yellow, but its belly develops the deep orange or red of the true brook trout (see Brook Trout and Lake Trout). Splake mature and grow faster than lake trout. Unlike many other hybrids, the splake is capable of reproducing.

RANGE: The splake's range is quite spotty, including a number of western-Canada lakes, at least one of the Great Lakes, and a few lakes in the northern United States. Stockings are slowly increasing this range.

HABITAT: See Lake Trout.

SIZE: The world-record splake, caught in Georgian Bay, Ontario, Canada, was 20 pounds, 11 ounces.

FOOD: See Lake Trout.

Tiger Trout
(Salmo trutta x Salvelinus fontinalis)

DESCRIPTION: This hybrid is a cross between the female brown trout and the male brook trout. The tiger's most prominent physical characteristic is the well-defined vermiculations (wormlike markings) on its back and sides. Its lower fins have the white edges of the true brook trout. The tiger is an avid surface-feeder and is considerably more aggressive than either of its parent species. Under hatchery conditions, only 35 percent of the tiger's offspring develop. The tiger occasionally occurs under natural conditions, but it does not reproduce.

RANGE: The tiger, being a hybrid, has no natural range, but stockings have introduced it into a few streams in the United States. At least one state, New Jersey, has stocked this trout in its waters on an experimental basis.

HABITAT: The tiger's habitat is undetermined, but it is probably similar to that of the brook trout.

SIZE: The world-record tiger trout, caught in Lake Michigan, Wisconsin, was 20 pounds, 13 ounces.

FOOD: The tiger's food is undetermined, but it is probably similar to that of the brook trout.

Rock Bass
(Ambloplites rupestris)

COMMON NAMES: Rock bass, goggle eye, redeye, rock sunfish, black perch, and goggle-eye perch

DESCRIPTION: The rock bass isn't a bass—it's one of the sunfishes. And though it isn't much of a fighter, it is fun to catch and is sometimes unbelievably willing to gobble any lure, bait, or fly it can get its jaws around. The basic color of the rock bass is dark olive to greenish bronze, with a lighter belly. The sides contain brownish or yellowish blotches, and a dark spot at the base of each scale produces broken horizontal streaks. The mouth is much larger than that of most other sunfishes, and the anal fin has six spines, while the anal fin of most other sunfishes has only three spines. There is a dark blotch on the gill flap.

RANGE: The rock bass occurs from southern Manitoba east to New England, and south to the Gulf states. Stockings have somewhat widened this range in recent years.

HABITAT: Rock bass prefer large, clear streams and lakes and are often found in the same waters as smallmouth bass. As their name suggests, the more rocks and stones on the bottom of the stream or lake, the better a fisherman's chances of finding rock bass. The species seems to prefer pools or protected waters to fast current or open waters.

SIZE: The top weight of rock bass is a bit more than 2 pounds. Most of those caught by fishermen are 6 to 10 inches long and weigh about ½ pound.

FOOD: A voracious eater, the rock bass eats crawfish, minnows and other baitfish, worms, adult and larval insect life, and the like.

Hickory Shad
(Alosa mediocris or Pomolobus mediocris)

DESCRIPTION: The hickory shad—like its larger relative, the American shad—is a herring. In color, it is gray green above, with silvery sides and underparts. Behind the upper part of the gill cover is a horizontal row of dark spots, usually numbering about six. Spots on the upper rows of scales form faint horizontal lines. It has a shallow-notched upper jaw, and the lower jaw projects prominently. The hickory shad is not so important a food or sport fish as is the American shad.

RANGE: The hickory shad is found along the Atlantic coast from the Bay of Fundy south to Florida.

HABITAT: An anadromous species (it lives in salt water but ascends freshwater rivers to spawn), the hickory shad's movements in the ocean are little known. But in the spring, it goes up the rivers, often the same rivers in which American shad spawn, though its runs usually precede those of the American shad.

SIZE: Though 5-pounders have been reported, the hickory shad seldom tops 2½ pounds in weight or 24 inches in length.

FOOD: The hickory shad feeds more on fish than does the American shad, and it is often caught by anglers using artificial flies and small spoons.

Freshwater Drum
(Aplodinotus grunniens)

COMMON NAMES: Freshwater drum, sheepshead, gray bass, gaspergou, white perch, croaker, crocus, jewelhead, and grunter

DESCRIPTION: This species is the only freshwater member of the drum (croaker) family, which has about three dozen saltwater members. The freshwater drum has a blunt head, rounded tail, long dorsal fin, and a humped back. Colors are pearly gray on the back and upper sides, silver on the remainder of sides, and milky white on the belly. A rather faint lateral line runs all the way into the tail. These fish make a weird "drumming" noise that, when they feed near the surface on calm evenings, seems to come from everywhere. It is caused by repeated contractions of an abdominal muscle against the swim bladder. Another oddity: the otoliths, or ear bones, of freshwater drum were used by Indians as wampum, as lucky pieces, and to prevent sicknesses.

RANGE: Freshwater drum are found from Guatemala north through eastern Mexico and the Gulf states to Manitoba, northern Ontario, Quebec, and the Lake Champlain area. East to west, they range from the Atlantic coast to the Missouri River drainage.

HABITAT: Found principally in large lakes and large, slow rivers, this species prefers modest depths (10 to 40 feet) and silty or muddy bottoms. It is a school fish, often congregating below large dams.

SIZE: Freshwater drum attain a maximum weight of about 60 pounds, but the average size is 1 to 5 pounds.

FOOD: Primarily a bottom-feeder, this species feeds almost entirely on mollusks—clams, mussels, and snails—which it "shells" with its large, strong teeth. Other foods include crawfish and some baitfish.

SALTWATER SPECIES

■ Blue Shark
(Prionace glauca)

DESCRIPTION: This large shark species, which has a reputation as a man-eater, is distinguished by its abnormally long pectoral fins and by its bright-cobalt color (the belly is white). It has the long snout of many members of the large shark family, and the dorsal fin is set well back on the back, nearly at the midpoint.

RANGE: Blue sharks are found throughout the tropical and temperate waters of the world.

HABITAT: Though often seen in shallow waters on the Pacific coast of the United States and on the surface in other northern areas, the blue shark is usually caught in deep water. It often roams in packs, while at other times it is found singly or in pairs.

SIZE: Blue sharks average less than 10 feet in length, but have been reported to attain lengths of more than 20 feet. The largest rod-caught blue shark weighed 410 pounds.

FOOD: Blue sharks eat mainly mackerel, herring, squid, other sharks, flying fish, anchovies, and even such tidbits as seagulls and garbage deep-sixed from ships.

■ Mako Shark (Isurus oxyrinchus)

COMMON NAMES: Mako shark and mackerel shark

DESCRIPTION: This huge, dangerous, fast-swimming, hard-fighting shark is closely related to the white shark. It differs from the white mainly in the dorsal and pectoral fins, the tips of which are rounded in the mako, rather than pointed in the white. In color, the mako is dark blue to bluish gray above, shading to silver on the belly. The mako differs from the porbeagle shark in that its second dorsal fin is positioned a bit forward of the anal fin, while the porbeagle's second dorsal is directly above the anal fin.

RANGE: The mako is an inhabitant of the tropical oceans and the warmer areas of the Atlantic Ocean. In

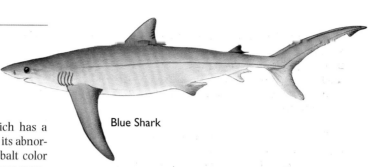

Blue Shark

U.S. waters, it is found as far north as Cape Cod. It seems to be most numerous around New Zealand.

HABITAT: Makos tend to stay near the surface in open-ocean areas.

SIZE: Makos reach lengths of more than 12 feet and weights of more than 1,000 pounds.

FOOD: Staples of the mako's diet include tuna, mackerel, and herring. For some reason, it often attacks, but seldom kills, swordfish.

■ White Shark (Carcharodon carcharias)

COMMON NAMES: White shark, great white shark, and man-eater

DESCRIPTION: The white shark—enormous, vicious, and incredibly powerful—is one of the largest of all fish. Its usual colors are grayish brown, slate blue, or gray, while the belly is off-white. Large specimens are sometimes a general off-white. The white shark is built blockier than the look-alike mako, having a much deeper body. The white has a pointed snout, triangular serrated teeth, and a crescent-shaped caudal fin.

Mako Shark

RANGE: The white shark is found throughout the world in tropical and temperate waters, though it seems to prefer warm to temperate regions over tropics. It is not numerous anywhere.

HABITAT: White sharks generally stay well offshore and seem to prefer relatively cool waters.

SIZE: The white shark is a true behemoth; one specimen 36½ feet long has been captured. The weight of that fish must have been astronomical, considering that a white shark just 13 feet long weighed 2,100 pounds! Whites that are 20 feet long are not at all uncommon.

FOOD: White sharks eat such things as other sharks 4 to 7 feet long, sea lions, seals, sturgeon, tuna, sea turtles, squid, and refuse.

Porbeagle Shark *(Lamna nasus)*

COMMON NAMES: Porbeagle shark and mackerel shark

DESCRIPTION: The porbeagle is a blocky-bodied shark that closely resembles the mako, though it is much less game. The best way to distinguish the porbeagle from both the mako and the white shark is the location of the second dorsal fin—the porbeagle is the only one whose second dorsal is directly above the anal fin. In color, the porbeagle shades from black to bluish gray on the back to white on the belly. Its anal fin is white or dusky.

RANGE: The porbeagle is found on both sides of the Atlantic as far south as the Mediterranean and Africa. On the Atlantic coast of the United States, it has been taken from South Carolina to the St. Lawrence Gulf. It is also found along most of the Pacific coast.

HABITAT: The porbeagle is a fish of temperate waters. In warm waters, it is found closer to shore and nearer to the surface, but when the water cools it may head for depths as great as 80 fathoms.

SIZE: The porbeagle apparently reaches a maximum length of about 12 feet, though the largest definitely recorded stretched 10 feet. The largest rod-caught porbeagle weighed 465 pounds.

FOOD: Porbeagles thrive on school-type fish such as mackerel and herring and on bottom-dwelling fish including cod, hake, and flounders.

Thresher Shark *(Alopias vulpinus)*

DESCRIPTION: The thresher shark is nearly as large as the mako and is an excellent fighter, making breathtaking jumps and long runs. The thresher has one unique physical characteristic—its inordinately long upper lobe of the tail, or caudal fin, which is at least as long as the body. The thresher shark is dark gray, bluish, brown, or even black on the back and sides, while the belly is white, sometimes with a gray mottling.

RANGE: Threshers are found from Nova Scotia to Argentina and from Ireland to the Cape of Good Hope. They occur throughout the Mediterranean, in the Pacific from Oregon to Chile, and as far from the continental United States as Hawaii, Japan, and Australia.

HABITAT: The thresher is most at home at or near the surface in subtropical to temperate waters.

SIZE: Threshers reach lengths of 20 feet and weights of half a ton.

FOOD: The thresher shark uses its long tail to herd and injure such schooling fish as mackerel, menhaden, and bluefish.

Tiger Shark *(Galeocerdo cuvieri)*

DESCRIPTION: One of the so-called requiem sharks, the aptly named tiger is often the culprit in attacks on swimmers. In color, it is usually a general steel gray or brownish gray with a white belly, though the young have bars and spots on the back and upper sides. The upper lobe of the tail is long and slender, and it has a short and sharp-pointed snout.

RANGE: Tiger sharks are found throughout the world's tropical and subtropical regions.

HABITAT: Though sometimes caught offshore, the tiger seems to be largely a coastal fish, and it occasionally comes into quite shallow waters. It stays near the surface.

Tiger Shark

SIZE: Tigers are reported to reach lengths of 30 feet. The maximum weight is unknown, but 13- to 14-footers tip the scales at 1,000 to 1,500 pounds.

FOOD: Tiger sharks are omnivorous and cannibalistic. They eat their own kind, as well as fish of most species, crabs, lobsters, and even sea lions and turtles. Examinations of their stomachs have revealed such things as tin cans, parts of crocodiles, and even human remains.

Hammerhead Shark
(Sphyrna mokarran)

COMMON NAMES: Hammerhead shark, hammerhead, and great hammerhead

DESCRIPTION: There's no mistaking the hammerhead shark. Its small eyes are located at each end of its unique and grotesque head, which looks as if it had been modeled after the head of a huge mallet that had been pounded nearly flat. Gray or sometimes brownish gray on its back and sides and off-white on its underparts, the hammerhead's dorsal fin is less erect than that of any of its Atlantic relatives. Though not officially classified as a game fish, the hammerhead is a large and powerful adversary. Its hide makes fine leather, and its liver contains a high-grade oil.

RANGE: In the western Atlantic, the hammerhead occurs from North Carolina to Argentina. It is found elsewhere in the tropical and subtropical areas of the Atlantic, as well as in the eastern Pacific and the Indo-Pacific.

HABITAT: Hammerheads often travel in schools and may be found both near shore and far offshore.

SIZE: The average size is difficult to determine, but hammerheads apparently reach a maximum length of about 18 feet and a maximum weight of considerably more than 1,600 pounds.

FOOD: Voracious and cannibalistic, the hammerhead eats just about anything unlucky enough to get in its way, including big tuna, tarpon, and other sharks.

Swordfish (Xiphias gladius)

COMMON NAMES: Swordfish, broadbill, and broadbill swordfish

DESCRIPTION: The swordfish is one of the elite saltwater fish, much sought by both commercial and sport fishermen. It is distinguished from the other billfish (sailfish and marlin) by its much longer, flat bill (sword) and by its lack of scales and pelvic fins (the other billfish have both). The swordfish's dorsal and anal fins are sickle shaped. Its color is usually dark brown or bronze, but variations of black to grayish blue are common. The belly is usually white, but the dark colors sometimes extend right down to the fish's undersides.

RANGE: Swordfish are migratory and are found worldwide in warm and temperate waters. Their occurrence in the United States and adjacent waters extends in the Atlantic from Newfoundland to Cuba and in the Pacific from California to Chile.

HABITAT: Swordfish are open-ocean fish, usually feeding in the depths but often seen "sunning" on the surface.

SIZE: The maximum size of swordfish is a matter of some uncertainty, but specimens of nearly 1,200 pounds have been taken on rod and line. The average size is probably 150 to 300 pounds.

FOOD: Swordfish use their greatest weapon, the sword, to stun and capture such food as dolphins, menhaden, mackerel, bonito, bluefish, and squid.

Blue Marlin (Makaira nigricans)

DESCRIPTION: This king of the blue water is probably the most highly prized of the big-game fish, mainly because of its mammoth size and spectacular fighting abilities. In general coloration, the blue marlin is steel blue on the back, shading to silvery white on the belly. In most specimens, the sides contain light, vertical bars, which are not nearly so prominent as those of the white marlin. The dorsal and anal fins are bluish purple and

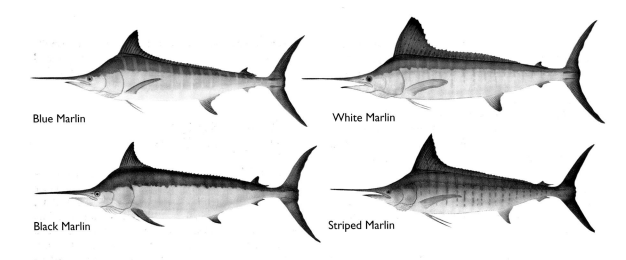

Blue Marlin

White Marlin

Black Marlin

Striped Marlin

sometimes have dark blotches. The blue marlin's distinguishing physical traits include a relatively short dorsal fin and a relatively long anal fin, and a body shape that is considerably rounder than other billfish.

RANGE: Blue marlin are found in warm and temperate seas throughout the world. In the United States and nearby waters, they occur from the Gulf of Maine to Uruguay in the Atlantic, and from Mexico to Peru in the Pacific.

HABITAT: Blue marlin are deep-water fish almost exclusively, and they are often seen cruising and feeding on the surface.

SIZE: The maximum size of the blue marlin is something more than 2,000 pounds, with the average being 200 to 500 pounds. Males seldom exceed 300 pounds, so those monsters often referred to as "Big Daddy" should really be called "Big Mama." Because the biggest blue marlin are thought to be in the Pacific, the International Game Fish Association separates these fish into two categories—Atlantic and Pacific.

FOOD: Blue marlin eat a broad range of fish life, including bluefish, mackerel, tuna, and bonito, as well as squid and octopus.

■ White Marlin
(*Makaira albida* or *Tetrapturus albidus*)

DESCRIPTION: The white marlin is considerably smaller and less universal than the blue marlin. Its colors are

a brilliant greenish blue on the back and upper sides, changing abruptly to white at the lateral line. The sides have an irregular number of vertical bands of light blue or lavender. A unique feature of the white marlin is the rounded tips of its dorsal and anal fins. The relatively flat-sided body is slender.

RANGE: The white marlin is limited to the Atlantic, occurring from Nova Scotia to Brazil and from the Azores to St. Helena Island and South Africa. Centers of concentration at differing times of year seem to be off the coast of Ocean City, Maryland, and near Venezuela.

HABITAT: Like the blue marlin, the white marlin is a fish of warm and temperate waters and is a migrant.

SIZE: Most white marlins caught by fishermen weigh 40 to 60 pounds, but the species apparently can reach 160 pounds.

FOOD: The white is mainly a fish eater, but it will dine on anything it can capture.

■ Black Marlin
(*Makaira indica* or *Istiompax indicus*)

DESCRIPTION: Possibly the largest of the marlins, the black is an ocean giant that is most easily distinguished from other marlins by the fact that its pectoral fins stick out at right angles from the body and are held rigidly in that position. The pelvic fins of the black marlin are shorter than those of other marlins, usually less than

1 foot long. The black marlin is seldom truly black, though its color varies greatly. Most are slate blue on the back and upper sides, shading to silvery white on the underparts. The sides occasionally exhibit pale-blue stripes.

RANGE: Black marlin seem to be found almost exclusively in the Pacific and Indian Oceans, being found as far north as southern California and Mexico. One area of abundance seems to be off the coast of Peru.

HABITAT: Little is known of the movements of the black marlin, though it is certainly a fish of the open oceans, and evidence indicates that it migrates only short distances if at all.

SIZE: The record rod-caught black marlin weighed 1,560 pounds, but specimens of up to 2,000 pounds have been taken commercially. The average size is probably 300 to 500 pounds.

FOOD: Various fish species (a tuna of 158 pounds was found in a black marlin's stomach) and squid are the main items in the black marlin's diet.

Striped Marlin
(Makaira audax or Tetrapturus audax)

DESCRIPTION: Smaller than the blue and black marlins, the striped marlin, as its name suggests, is most easily distinguished by the stripes on its sides. These stripes vary both in number and in color, which ranges from pale blue to lavender to white. Body colors are steel blue on the back and upper sides, shading to white on the bottom areas. The striped marlin also has a high, pointed dorsal fin, which is usually taller than the greatest depth of its body. Like all other marlins, the striped variety puts up a breathtaking battle.

RANGE: Striped marlin are found in the Indian Ocean and in the Pacific from southern California to Chile.

HABITAT: Striped marlin are open-ocean fish. The fairly well-defined local populations seem to make short north-to-south migrations. Like all the other marlins, they are often seen feeding on the surface.

SIZE: The average rod-caught striped marlin weighs about 200 to 250 pounds, but the species grows to more than 500 pounds.

FOOD: Striped marlin feed on a wide variety of fish life (anchovies, bonito, mackerel, and many others), and on squid, crustaceans, octopus, and anything else that might get in their way.

Atlantic Sailfish
(Istiophorus albicans)

DESCRIPTION: The uncommonly beautiful sailfish probably adorns more den and living-room walls than any other marine game fish. Sailfish are spectacular fighters, hurling themselves high out of the water time and time again. You can't mistake the sailfish for anything else that swims—thanks to its enormous purple (or cobalt-blue) dorsal fin, which it often seems to flaunt at fishermen. Body colors range from striking blue on the back and upper sides to silver white below the well-defined lateral line. Side markings usually consist of a variable number of pale, vertical bars or vertical rows of pale spots. The dorsal fin usually is marked with numerous black spots. A sailfish's pelvic fins are longer than those of other billfish.

RANGE: The Atlantic sailfish is commonly found in the Atlantic Ocean from Cape Hatteras to Venezuela, with winter concentrations off the east coast of Florida. This species is also found off England, France, Africa, and in the Mediterranean.

HABITAT: Sailfish are most often seen—and are almost always caught—on or near the surface. However, studies of their preferred diet indicate that they do much of their feeding in middle depths, along reefs, and even on the bottom.

SIZE: Most Atlantic sailfish caught by sport fishermen weigh 30 to 50 pounds, but the maximum size is probably a bit larger than the rod-and-reel record of 128 pounds, 1 ounce.

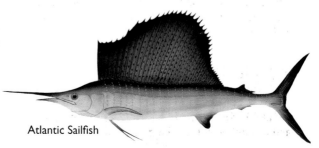

Atlantic Sailfish

FOOD: According to studies made of the feeding habits of Atlantic sailfish in Florida waters, these fish feed mainly on a wide variety of fish life (tuna, mackerel, jacks, balao, needlefish, herring, and a few other species make up 83 percent of the Atlantic sailfish's diet). They also feed on squid and octopus.

Bluefin Tuna

■ Pacific Sailfish *(Istiophorus greyi)*

DESCRIPTION: It is not known for certain whether the Pacific sailfish is truly a distinct species from the Atlantic sailfish, though it does grow considerably larger than the Atlantic variety. In most other important respects, the two fish are exactly alike. The only physical difference is that the Pacific sailfish's body colors tend to be somewhat more muted. It should be noted that in sport fishing for sailfish, marlin, and all other large pelagic game fish, the trend today is toward releasing all fish.

RANGE: Pacific sailfish are found in the Pacific Ocean from about Monterey, California, south to Ecuador, and also in the vicinity of the Hawaiian Islands and elsewhere in the South Pacific.

HABITAT: See Atlantic Sailfish.

SIZE: Pacific sailfish put on a good deal more weight than their relatives in the Atlantic. The maximum weight is about 240 pounds, but the average rod-caught Pacific sailfish weighs from 60 to 100 pounds.

FOOD: See Atlantic Sailfish.

■ Bluefin Tuna *(Thunnus thynnus)*

COMMON NAMES: Bluefin tuna, bluefin, and horse mackerel

DESCRIPTION: The bluefin is the king of the tunas, all of which are members of the mackerel family. Bluefins—from those of school size (15 to 100 pounds) to giants of nearly half a ton—have incredible strength and tenacity, and they are much sought by both sport and commercial fishermen. The bluefin has the blocky, robust body of a typical heavyweight. The head is rather small, and the snout is pointed. The bluefin has shorter pectoral fins than any of the American tunas. It has two

dorsal fins—the forward one retractable and the rearward one fixed—and a sickle-shaped tail. In color, the bluefin is steel blue on its back and upper sides, shading to light gray or creamy white on its lower parts. In small bluefins, the lower sides have vertical white lines.

RANGE: Bluefin tuna are found throughout the world, mostly in temperate and subtropical waters. In the western Atlantic, they occur in abundance from the Bahamas north to the Labrador Current. In the Pacific, they seem to be less abundant, being found in greatest numbers in the general area of Catalina Island.

HABITAT: The bluefin is generally a fish of the open ocean, though school-size bluefins occasionally come quite close to shore. In summer, bluefins show up in large numbers from New Jersey to Nova Scotia, the smaller fish showing up first and closer to shore. Atlantic areas where bluefins tend to congregate and provide good fishing include the New York Bight, New Jersey, Block Island to Rhode Island, Cape Cod Bay, Wedgeport and St. Margaret's Bay in Nova Scotia, and Conception Bay in Newfoundland.

SIZE: For all practical fishing purposes, bluefins can be grouped into two size categories: school fish (those weighing 15 to 100 pounds) and adult fish (those weighing more than 100 pounds). The average schoolie weighs 30 to 50 pounds, while the giant bluefins attain maximum weights estimated to be 1,500 pounds or more. The rod-and-reel record is 1,496 pounds.

FOOD: Bluefin tuna feed on whatever is available, including a wide variety of fish (including herring, sand lance, hake, and even dolphin), as well as squid and crustaceans.

■ Yellowfin Tuna *(Thunnus albacares)*

COMMON NAMES: Yellowfin tuna and allison tuna

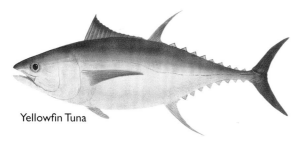

Yellowfin Tuna

Blackfin Tuna

DESCRIPTION: Considerably smaller than the bluefin, the yellowfin tuna is a top sport and commercial fish, particularly in the Pacific. In color, the yellowfin is steel blue or nearly black on the back and upper sides, silvery white on the lower parts. Characteristics that distinguish it from the bluefin are its much longer pectoral fins and the generous amount of the color yellow in most of the fins. The yellowfin is difficult to distinguish from some of the other tunas, but in large specimens the second dorsal fin and anal fin are much longer than those of any other tuna. The side markings of the yellowfin include a sometimes indistinct golden-yellow horizontal streak and white spots and vertical stripes on the lower sides.

RANGE: Yellowfins are found worldwide in tropical and subtropical waters. They are most numerous in the Pacific, where they are found widely off the coast of southern California and Baja California. They also range from the Gulf of Mexico north to New Jersey.

HABITAT: Yellowfin tuna are more southerly in general range than are bluefins. They are open-ocean fish, though there is some evidence that they do not make such long-range migrations as bluefins do.

SIZE: Yellowfins are thought to reach a maximum size of some 500 pounds. However, the rod-and-reel record is 405 pounds, and the average size is less than 100 pounds.

FOOD: See Bluefin Tuna.

Bigeye Tuna *(Thunnus obesus)*

COMMON NAMES: Bigeye tuna, Pacific bigeye tuna, and Atlantic bigeye tuna

DESCRIPTION: Its eyes are not abnormally large, so it's difficult to determine how the bigeye tuna got its name. Its coloration is similar to that of its big brother, the bluefin, though its pectoral fins are longer. It is often hard to

distinguish the bigeye from some of the other tunas. Its dorsal and anal fins are never greatly elongated (as in the large yellowfins), and the finlets running along the back and belly from the dorsal and anal fins to the tail are yellow with black margins. Though Atlantic and Pacific bigeyes are the same species, the International Game Fish Association separates them for record-keeping purposes.

RANGE: Bigeye tuna range throughout the world in tropical and subtropical waters.

HABITAT: Bigeyes are fish of the open oceans and deep water, as evidenced by the fact that many are caught by commercial longline fishermen.

SIZE: Bigeyes probably reach weights of 500 pounds and seem to grow somewhat bigger in the Pacific than in the Atlantic. The average size is about 100 pounds.

FOOD: See Bluefin Tuna.

Blackfin Tuna *(Thunnus atlanticus)*

DESCRIPTION: Far more restricted in range than any of the other popular tunas, the blackfin is also one of the smallest members of the family. It is darker in color than the other tunas and has fewer gill rakers. The finlets behind the dorsal and anal fins are totally dark—not marked with yellow like most of the other tunas.

RANGE: Blackfin tuna are found only in the western Atlantic Ocean, ranging from Cape Cod south to Brazil.

HABITAT: Blackfins are open-ocean, deep-water fish, like almost all the other members of the tuna family.

SIZE: The blackfin's top weight is probably not much more than 40 pounds or so. Most average 10 to 15 pounds. The world-record, rod-caught blackfin weighing 49 pounds, 6 ounces, is an exceptionally big tuna for this species.

FOOD: The blackfin's diet is about the same as that of the other tunas, except that its prey is properly smaller.

Albacore *(Thunnus alalunga)*

COMMON NAMES: Albacore and longfin tuna

DESCRIPTION: The albacore is what you are likely to get when you buy a can of "all-white-meat tuna." It is one of the tunas, and thus a member of the mackerel family. The albacore's most outstanding physical trait is its abnormally long pectoral (side) fins, which extend from behind the gills well past the second dorsal fin, ending about even with the third dorsal finlet. The coloring is an iridescent steel blue above, shading to silvery white on the belly. The fins are generally blue and bright yellow.

RANGE: Albacore are found in tropical, subtropical, and temperate waters in most parts of the world. In U.S. and adjacent waters, they are primarily a Pacific species, being plentiful from southern British Columbia to southern California and Baja. In the Atlantic, quite a few are caught off Florida, and they are occasionally found as far north as Massachusetts.

HABITAT: Albacore almost never come close to shore. They haunt deep, open waters and often feed near or on the surface. When on top, they can be seen smashing wildly into schools of frenzied baitfish.

SIZE: Albacore of up to 90 pounds have been taken in nets, and the record rod-caught fish was 88 pounds, 2 ounces. The average weight is 5 to 25 pounds.

FOOD: Albacore feed on a wide variety of fish, as well as squid and crustaceans.

Oceanic Bonito
(Euthynnus pelamis or *Katsuwonus pelamis)*

COMMON NAMES: Oceanic bonito, bonito, skipjack, skipjack tuna, oceanic skipjack, and striped tuna

DESCRIPTION: The oceanic bonito is the most impor-

tant member of the bonito group (which also includes the common, or Atlantic, bonito and the striped bonito, among others) and is the only bonito classified as a game fish by the International Game Fish Association. The oceanic bonito is striking blue above and silvery below, with some shadings of yellow and red. It is unique in having four or more well-defined dark stripes running from the area of the pectoral fin to the tail along the lower part of the body.

RANGE: Oceanic bonito are found in tropical and subtropical waters throughout the world. In U.S. and adjacent waters, they are most common off the southern coasts.

HABITAT: All the bonitos are fish of offshore waters, though they come relatively close to shore if that is where their favorite food is. They are school fish and generally feed on or near the surface.

SIZE: The average weight of the oceanic bonito is probably 10 to 18 pounds. The maximum is about 40 pounds.

FOOD: All the bonitos feed on a wide variety of fish, plus squid and crustaceans.

King Mackerel
(Scomberomorus cavalla)

COMMON NAMES: King mackerel, kingfish, cavalla, and cero

DESCRIPTION: Fast, strong, and good to eat is the king mackerel, the largest member of the Spanish-mackerel family in U.S. waters. Its streamlined body—colored in iridescent bluish green above and shading to platinum below—seems built for speed, which the fish exhibits both in the water and above in soaring leaps. The king's meandering lateral line and its lack of other side markings set it apart from most other fish. The lack of black in the rear part of the first dorsal fin distinguishes the king mackerel from other Spanish mackerels.

RANGE: Generally found from Brazil north to North Carolina and occasionally up to Cape Cod, the king mackerel is most numerous in the Gulf of Mexico and southern Atlantic Ocean.

HABITAT: King mackerel range in schools and usually stick to open water, though they sometimes hover near

Cobia

the outer reaches of bays, feeding on baitfish. March is the peak of the king-mackerel season for Florida anglers, while in the Gulf the fishing runs from spring into September.

SIZE: The average rod-caught king mackerel weighs 5 to 15 pounds, but the species apparently reaches a length of 5 feet and a weight of 100 pounds.

FOOD: King mackerel feed mostly on smaller fish.

Wahoo *(Acanthocybium solandri)*

COMMON NAMES: Wahoo, queenfish, peto, and ocean barracuda

DESCRIPTION: It is probably good that wahoo are neither as numerous as striped bass nor as large as bluefin tuna, for they are one of the wildest things with fins. They smash a trolled lure or bait with incredible force, make blitzing runs, and hurl themselves far out of the water (reports have it that wahoo have leaped over a fishing boat lengthwise!). The wahoo resembles no other fish, though it is shaped generally like the king mackerel. Its iridescent colors include blue or blue green above, shading through coppery tints to silver below. The sides have narrow, wavy, dark, vertical bars. Older fish may lack the side markings.

RANGE: Wahoo range throughout the world in tropical and subtropical waters. In the Atlantic, they stray as far north as the Carolinas, but they are most often caught off the Florida Keys, Mexico, and the West Indies.

HABITAT: Unlike most other mackerel-like fish, wahoos are loners—that is, they do not range in schools. They live in deep water, often staying near the edges of deep drop-offs or along reefs.

SIZE: The average wahoo caught by anglers weighs 10 to 25 pounds, but the species is reported to hit 150 pounds.

FOOD: Wahoos eat various fish, including flying fish, mackerel, mullet, and squid.

Wahoo

Cobia *(Rachycentron canadum)*

COMMON NAMES: Cobia, crabeater, ling, coalfish, black salmon, lemonfish, black bonito, cabio, and cobio

DESCRIPTION: The cobia is something of a mystery. Little is known of its wanderings or life history, and the species has no close relatives. In color, the cobia is dark brown on the back and lighter brown on the sides and belly. A wide, black, lateral band extends from its snout to the base of its tail. Less distinct dark bands are found above and below the lateral. The first dorsal fin is actually a series of quite short, stiff, wide spines that look nothing at all like a standard dorsal.

RANGE: The cobia is found in many of the world's tropical and warm, temperate waters. It occurs in the western Atlantic from Massachusetts to Argentina, but its greatest abundance is from Chesapeake Bay southeast to Bermuda and in the Gulf of Mexico.

HABITAT: Young cobia are often caught in inlets and bays, but older fish seem to prefer shallower areas of the open sea. Cobias are almost invariably found around some kind of cover—over rocks, around pilings or bottom debris, and particularly under floating objects such as buoys, weeds, and other flotsam.

SIZE: Cobia reach top weights of more than 100 pounds. The average size is 5 to 10 pounds in some areas, though in other areas, notably the Florida Keys and Gulf of Mexico waters, 25- to 50-pounders are not uncommon.

FOOD: Cobias feed largely on crabs, though they also eat shrimp and small fish of all kinds.

Amberjack *(Seriola dumerili)*

COMMON NAMES: Amberjack, greater amberjack, and horse-eye bonito

DESCRIPTION: Amberjacks are related to pompanos and jacks, and more distantly to tunas and mackerels. The amberjack is a stocky, heavy-bodied fish with a deeply forked tail, the lobes of which are quite slender. Its body colors are blue green or blue on the back, shading to silvery on the underparts. The fins have some yellow in them. A well-defined dark band runs upward from the snout to a point behind the eye. Mostly a solitary wanderer, the amberjack sometimes gathers in small groups in preferred feeding areas.

RANGE: Though occasionally found as far north as New England, the amberjack is primarily a fish of southern Atlantic waters from the Carolinas south to Florida and nearby islands. In the Pacific, it is abundant from southern Mexico southward.

HABITAT: Reefs are the favorite habitat of amberjacks, though these fish often cruise for food at moderate depths—approximately 20 to 40 feet.

SIZE: The average rod-caught amberjack probably weighs 12 to 20 pounds, though ambers of up to 50 pounds are far from rare. The maximum size is about 150 pounds.

FOOD: Amberjacks prey on many smaller fish, as well as on crabs, shrimp, and crustaceans.

■ Pacific Yellowtail *(Seriola dorsalis)*

COMMON NAMES: Pacific yellowtail, yellowtail, and California yellowtail

DESCRIPTION: A member of the amberjack family, the Pacific yellowtail is probably the most popular sport fish on the Pacific coast. It is not, however, of great commercial value. The yellowtail has a horizontal swath, ranging in color from brassy to rather bright yellow, running from its eye to its tail. Above the stripe, the color is blue green to green; below it, the color is silvery. The fins are dusky yellow, except the caudal fin (tail), which is bright yellow. The yellowtail is a tremendously powerful fighter.

RANGE: Yellowtails have been caught from Mazatlan, Mexico, through waters of Baja California, and north to the southern Washington coast. The world-record yellowtail was taken off the coast of New Zealand, but it is not known for sure whether it was of the same species as the Pacific yellowtail.

HABITAT: Yellowtails are fish of the mid-depths for the most part and are migratory. A preferred hangout is a kelp bed, and rocks often harbor yellowtails. Concentrations of yellowtails are around the Coronado Islands, Catalina Island, and off San Clemente, California.

SIZE: Yellowtails reach weights of more than 100 pounds, but the average size is 8 to 25 pounds.

FOOD: Like many other voracious marine species, the yellowtail usually feeds on whatever is available. It seems to prefer sardines, anchovies, mackerel, squid, and crabs.

■ Jack Crevalle *(Caranx hippos)*

COMMON NAMES: Jack crevalle, jack, cavally, cavalla, common jack, horse crevalle, and toro

DESCRIPTION: Probably the best-known member of a very large family, the jack crevalle is considered a fine game fish by some anglers but a pest by others. The crevalle is short, husky, and slab sided. It is yellow green on the back and the upper sides, yellow and silvery on the lower areas. There is a dark mark on the rear edge of the gill cover, and the breast is without scales except for a scaled patch just forward of the ventral fins.

RANGE: The jack crevalle is found from Uruguay to Nova Scotia in the western Atlantic, and from Peru to Baja California in the eastern Pacific. It is most numerous from Florida to Texas.

HABITAT: The crevalle seems to prefer shallow flats, though large, solitary specimens are often taken in deep offshore waters. It is a schooling species.

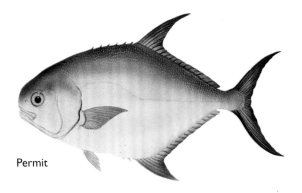

Permit

SIZE: Jack crevalles of more than 70 pounds have been caught, and 45-pounders are not uncommon in Florida waters. The average size is probably 2 to 8 pounds.

FOOD: Smaller fish are the main course of the jack crevalle, but shrimp and other invertebrates are also occasionally on the menu.

Rainbow Runner
(Elagatis bipinnulatus)

COMMON NAMES: Rainbow runner, rainbow yellowtail, runner, skipjack, and shoemaker

DESCRIPTION. The rainbow runner, an excellent game fish, is a member of the jack family, but it doesn't look like most of the others. It is streamlined, not deep bodied and chunky, and its coloration is striking. The back is a vivid blue or green blue, while the lower areas and the tail are yellow. Along the upper sides is a broad dark-blue stripe, and below that are other, less prominent blue stripes. The fins are greenish yellow. Finlets at the rear end of the dorsal and anal fins distinguish the rainbow runner from the amberjack, which it somewhat resembles.

RANGE: Occurring in tropical waters worldwide, the rainbow runner is found in the Atlantic from Colombia to Massachusetts; in the Pacific, it has been recorded from Peru and the Galapagos Islands to Baja California.

HABITAT: The wanderings of this fish, which are nowhere numerous, are little known. Trollers catch rainbow runners off the east coast of Florida and in the Gulf of Mexico.

SIZE: The maximum size is about 30 pounds. Most caught rainbow runners are about 15 inches in length.

FOOD: Rainbow runners feed on smaller fish.

Permit *(Trachinotus falcatus or Trachinotus kennedyi)*

COMMON NAMES: Permit, great pompano, round pompano, and palometa

DESCRIPTION: The shy and wary permit, a much-prized game fish, is the largest of the pompanos. Blocky and very deep bodied (sometimes nearly half as deep as total body length), the permit's coloration varies greatly, especially in the young. Adults are generally bluish or gray on back, with the rest of the body being silvery. Very large ones may be almost entirely silvery with a green-blue tinge. Permit are far more numerous than many anglers think, but while they are often seen, they are much less often hooked and boated, for they put up a fight that is much more powerful than that of a bonefish. It usually takes at least a half hour to tire a big permit.

RANGE: In the Atlantic, permit are found from Brazil to Massachusetts, in the West Indies, and in Bermuda. A Pacific variety is found from Ecuador to southern California. It is most abundant off southern Florida.

HABITAT: Permit are found from the surf out to deep water. They tend to stay in channels and deep holes, but they often come onto shallow tidal flats to feed, at which time their tails and backs can be seen above the surface.

SIZE: Permit reach weights of 50 pounds, but those caught by anglers probably average 15 to 25 pounds.

FOOD: Mainly bottom-feeders, permits prefer crabs and other invertebrates, plus small fish.

Bluefish *(Pomatomus saltatrix)*

COMMON NAMES: Bluefish, chopper, tailor, snapper, and jumbo

DESCRIPTION: Savage, cannibalistic, delicious, abundant, willing—all these adjectives fit the bluefish, the only member of the family *Pomatomidae*. In coloration, the bluefish is a rather dark blue on the back, shading through blue gray and gray silver to silvery on the belly. A fisherman getting his first look at a pack of blues attacking a horde of baitfish finds the sight hard to believe. The water boils white and then turns red and brown with the blood of the frenzied baitfish and the regurgitated stomach contents of the savage blues. Once

Bluefish

hooked, the bluefish makes the angler fervently thankful that these fish don't reach the size of tuna, for blues are among the most powerful fighters in the sea.

RANGE: Blues are found in the western Atlantic from Massachusetts to Argentina, off the northwest coast of Africa, the Azores, Portugal, and Spain, and in the Mediterranean and Black Seas. They are also found in the eastern Indian Ocean, the Malay Peninsula, Australia, and New Zealand.

HABITAT: Though primarily a deep-water species, particularly the large ones, bluefish often come right into the surf and sometimes go quite a distance up brackish-water rivers. Blues are rather erratic wanderers, though their general migration routes are fairly constant. They usually travel in large schools. In winter, they are most numerous in Florida. As the waters warm, they head north to such bluefishing hotspots as the Carolinas, New Jersey, and New England. Tidal rips are top spots to look for blues.

SIZE: Bluefish average 2 to 5 pounds, though 15- to 20-pounders are not uncommon, and there was a 45-pounder taken off the coast of North Africa.

FOOD: Bluefish will eat anything they can handle—and some things they can't, as many fishermen who have been bitten by a just-boated blue will attest. Menhaden is a bluefish's blue-plate special, and other preferred foods are mullet, squid, and eels.

■ Dolphin (*Coryphaena hippurus*)

COMMON NAMES: Dolphin, bull dolphin, dorado, and mahimahi

DESCRIPTION: The dolphin (a cold-blooded species that should not be confused with the warm-blooded dolphin, which is a mammal and a member of the porpoise family) is spectacular in both coloration and fighting ability. Purple and blue on the dorsal surface, and iridescent green and yellow on the sides and lower body, the dolphin's merging colors are enhanced by scattered blue dots. The head is extremely blunt, being almost vertical in large specimens (called bulls, though they may be either male or female). The dorsal fin extends from the head nearly to the tail. The dolphin is an explosive battler and an acrobatic leaper.

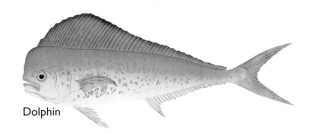
Dolphin

RANGE: Dolphins range widely in tropical and subtropical seas. In the western Atlantic, they are found in relative abundance from North Carolina (particularly in or near the Gulf Stream) south into the Gulf of Mexico as far west as Texas. In the Pacific, they range as far north as Oregon, but they are most numerous off the coast of southern California.

HABITAT: Dolphins are usually school fish, though large ones are often loners. They are fish of the open oceans, however, they lie under and cavort near various patches or bits of flotsam—floating grass, pieces of driftwood, and the like.

SIZE: The largest dolphin on record weighed 87 pounds. However, most rod-caught dolphins are 5 to 15 pounds.

FOOD: The food of dolphins includes a wide variety of smaller fish, squid, and crustaceans. In many parts of the dolphin's range, the flying fish forms a large portion of its diet, and the dolphin can often be seen soaring far out of the water in pursuit of a flying fish.

■ Tarpon (*Megalops atlantica*)

COMMON NAMES: Tarpon, silver king, and sabalo

DESCRIPTION: The tarpon, considered the king of game fish by the majority of those who have caught it, is a leaper to end all leapers. Tarpon jumps of 8 feet above the surface and 20 feet long have been measured. Tarpon are related to herring and shad, and, oddly enough, to smelt and salmon. Usually blue or greenish black on

Tarpon

Bonefish

the back, the tarpon's sides and underparts are sparkling silver. The scales are very large, and there is a bony plate between the branches of the bottom jaw. The dorsal fin has no spines, but its last (rear) ray is abnormally extended and whiplike. The pectoral fins are quite low on the body. The tarpon's spectacular fighting tactics and hard, bony mouth make it difficult to subdue—one fish boated out of 20 strikes is about average success for a tarpon fisherman. The tarpon's only shortcoming is that it isn't much on the table. Most rod-caught tarpon are released.

RANGE: Tarpon are found on both sides of the Atlantic in tropical and subtropical waters. In the western Atlantic, they stray as far north as Nova Scotia and range well south in the Gulf of Mexico. Main concentrations seem to be off southern Florida, Texas, and eastern Mexico.

HABITAT: Except in winter, when they apparently retreat to deeper water, tarpon are schooling fish of shallow waters. They frequent such places as mangrove flats, shoals, brackish bayous, cuts, inlets, and the lower reaches of coastal rivers. Sometimes they travel many miles upriver into fresh water. They are seldom far from the shore in summer.

SIZE: Though the rod-and-reel record is 286 pounds, 9 ounces, tarpon reportedly attain weights in excess of 300 pounds. The average size of an adult tarpon is probably 30 to 100 pounds. Tarpon of more than 100 pounds are subdued each year on fly rods!

FOOD: Tarpon feed on a variety of marine life, including pinfish, mullet, needlefish, and other small fish, plus crabs and shrimp.

Bonefish *(Albula vulpes)*

COMMON NAMES: Bonefish, ratfish, and banana

DESCRIPTION: What the tarpon is to leaping, the bonefish is to running. No one using sporting tackle can stop the blazing initial run of a hooked bonefish, which may tear 150 yards or more of line from a reel. The bonefish's body, built for speed, is shaped like a torpedo. The colors are bronze or blue green on the back, shading through bright silver on the sides to white on the belly. The sides occasionally have some dark mottling. The bonefish is sometimes confused with the ladyfish, but telling them apart requires only a look at the mouth. The bonefish's upper jaw—a snout, really—is far longer than the lower, giving the fish a sucker-like look. The ladyfish has jaws of about equal length. Bonefish are related to tarpon.

RANGE: Bonefish are found in all tropical marine waters, being caught in such widely separated places as South Africa, Brazil, and Hawaii, where the biggest ones are found. By far the largest concentrations of bonefish in North America are around the Florida Keys and in the Bahamas.

HABITAT: Bonefish are a shallow-water species. They move onto very shallow tidal flats, sometimes in water only 6 inches deep, with the high tide to feed and then drop back into deeper water as the tide ebbs. On the flats is where fishermen—particularly fly fishermen—seek this ultrawary quarry.

SIZE: Bonefish probably reach a maximum weight of about 20 pounds or a bit more, but one of more than 8 pounds is worth bragging about. The average size is about 4 to 6 pounds.

FOOD: Bonefish are primarily bottom-feeders, preying on crabs (particularly the hermit crab), shrimp, squid, sand fleas, and other crustaceans and mollusks.

Striped Bass *(Morone saxatilis)*

COMMON NAMES: Striped bass, striper, linesides, rock, rockfish, squidhound, and greenhead

DESCRIPTION: The striped bass is one of the most popular coastal game fish. It fights well, and it "eats well." It is not likely to be mistaken for any other game fish in its range, primarily because of its general shape, side stripes (there are seven or eight horizontal dark stripes on each side), and the separation between the front and rear dorsal fin. The coloration is dark green to almost black on the back, silver on the sides, and white on the underparts. The striper is anadromous, living in the sea but ascending rivers to spawn.

Striped Bass

RANGE: On the Atlantic coast, the striped bass is found from the Gulf of St. Lawrence south to the St. Johns River in Florida and in the Gulf of Mexico from western Florida to Louisiana. Introduced on the Pacific coast in the 1880s, the striper is found there from the Columbia River south to Los Angeles, California. The center of the striper's range in the Atlantic is Massachusetts to South Carolina; in the Pacific, it is in the San Francisco Bay area. Efforts to establish the striped bass in fresh water have been successful in such spots as the Santee-Cooper impoundment in South Carolina, Kerr Reservoir in North Carolina, some stretches of the Colorado River, and elsewhere.

HABITAT: Striped bass are almost exclusively coastal fish, seldom ranging more than a few miles offshore. Among the striper's favorite haunts are tidal rips, reefs, rocky headlands, jetties, bays, inlets, channels, canals, and reedy flats in tidal marshes.

SIZE: Most striped bass caught by anglers probably fall between 3 and 15 pounds, but many fish of 40 to 60 pounds are caught each year, most of them by trollers in the Cape Cod to Delaware range. The rod-and-reel record is an 81-pound, 14-ounce fish caught in Long Island Sound, Connecticut, but there are reliable records of a 125-pounder having been caught off North Carolina in 1891.

FOOD: The striper is a voracious feeder that preys on a wide variety of fish and invertebrates. The list includes herring, mullet, menhaden, anchovies, flounders, shad, silver hake, eels, lobsters, crabs, shrimp, sea worms, squid, clams, and mussels.

■ Snook *(Centropomus undecimalis)*

COMMON NAMES: Snook and robalo

DESCRIPTION: A fine fighter and excellent table fare, the snook is a much-sought prize of southern waters. In color, the snook is brown, green, or brownish gold on the dorsal surface (back), shading to greenish silver on the sides, and becoming lighter on the belly. Distinctive traits include a depressed upper jaw and a jutting lower jaw, a somewhat humped back, and, probably most distinctive of all, a prominent dark lateral line that usually extends to and into the tail. The snook strikes a fisherman's offering with a startling smash, but it is an unpredictable feeder.

RANGE: Snook are found throughout tropical waters on the Atlantic and Pacific coasts, though they have been known to stray as far north as Delaware. They are plentiful along the Florida coasts and along the Gulf Coast in the United States and Mexico.

HABITAT: Snook are shallow-water fish that frequent such spots as sandy shores, mangrove banks, tidal bayous and canals, flats, bays, bridges, and pilings, and sometimes go upstream into fresh water. In cold weather, they lie in deep holes.

SIZE: Snook probably average 2 to 5 pounds, but 10-pounders are not rare, and the top weight is more than 50 pounds.

FOOD: The voracious snook feeds on many varieties of fish, particularly mullet, but also eats crabs, shrimp, and crustaceans.

■ Great Barracuda *(Sphyraena barracuda)*

COMMON NAMES: Great barracuda, barracuda, and cuda

DESCRIPTION: This toothy warrior is the subject of misunderstanding by both anglers and swimmers. Proven records of barracuda attacks on swimmers are relatively rare, though this fish, apparently out of curiosity, often approaches quite close to swimmers. Many fishermen write the cuda off as a poor fighter, but it usually puts on a powerful, acrobatic battle when hooked

Great Barracuda

on sporting tackle. Shaped much like the freshwater pikes, the great barracuda is bluish gray or greenish gray on the back, silvery on the sides, and whitish on the belly. Dark, irregularly shaped blotches mark the sides, particularly toward the rear. The teeth are large and pointed. The cuda is a poor food fish and, in fact, may be poisonous.

RANGE: The great barracuda occurs in the American Atlantic from Brazil as far north as the Carolinas, though it occasionally strays north to Massachusetts. Centers of abundance are in Florida waters and in the West Indies.

HABITAT: Though barracuda are found in depths ranging from a couple of feet to 200 feet, they are mainly a shallow-water species. Preferred hangouts are reefs, flats, and around mangrove islands. The largest are usually found near offshore reefs.

SIZE: Known to reach a weight of more than 100 pounds and a length of 6 feet, the great barracuda probably averages 5 to 25 pounds. However, 50-pounders are not uncommon.

FOOD: Voracious in appetite, the barracuda feeds on a wide variety of smaller fish, preying largely on whatever is most numerous in any given area. A favorite prey is mullet, though it will eat everything from puffers to small tuna.

Channel Bass *(Sciaenops ocellata)*

COMMON NAMES: Channel bass, red drum, and redfish

DESCRIPTION: The name channel bass is actually a misnomer, for this species isn't a bass at all but rather a member of the croaker family. An important East and Gulf Coast game fish, the channel bass is copper or bronze in overall body coloration. It can be distinguished from the black drum, which it resembles, by its lack of chin barbels and the presence, at the base of the upper part of the tail, of at least one large, black spot. Food value of the channel bass varies with size. Small ones—often called puppy drum or rat reds—are fine eating, but large specimens have coarse flesh and are only fair eating.

RANGE: Channel bass are found along the Atlantic and Gulf coasts from Massachusetts to Texas.

HABITAT: These coastal fish are found off sandy beaches for the most part, moving shoreward as the tide rises to feed in holes, behind sand bars, and on flats. They are also found in such spots as the lee of mangrove islands, sloughs, channels, and bayous.

SIZE: Channel bass reach weights of well more than 80 pounds, though those of 50 pounds or more are relatively rare.

FOOD: Channel bass are bottom-feeders, eating mainly crustaceans, mollusks, and sea worms, though they sometimes prey on smaller fish, particularly mullet and mossbunker.

Weakfish *(Cynoscion regalis)*

COMMON NAMES: Weakfish, common weakfish, gray weakfish, squeteague, yellowfin, and tiderunner

DESCRIPTION: The weakfish gets its name not from its fighting qualities, which are excellent, but rather from its quite delicate mouth, which is easily torn by a hook. This popular, streamlined game fish is olive, green, or green blue on the back and silver or white on the belly. The sides are quite colorful, having tinges of purple, lavender, blue, and green, with a golden sheen. The back and upper sides contain numerous spots of various dark colors. The lower edge of the tail is sometimes yellow, as are the ventral, pectoral, and anal fins. The weakfish is excellent table fare.

RANGE: The weakfish occurs along the Atlantic coast of the United States from Massachusetts south to the east coast of Florida. Populations of the fish center around the Chesapeake and Delaware Bays, New Jersey, and Long Island.

HABITAT: Basically a school fish (though large ones are often lone wolves), weakfish are a coastal species, being

Weakfish

found in the surf and in inlets, bays, channels, and saltwater creeks. They prefer shallow areas with a sandy bottom. They feed mostly near the surface, but they may go deep if that is where the food is.

SIZE: The average size of a weakfish seems to be declining. Today, most rod-caught fish are 1 to 4 pounds. Those early fall "tiderunners" of past decades, fish of up to a dozen pounds, are seldom seen nowadays. The biggest rod-caught weakfish was 19½ pounds.

FOOD: Weakfish eat sea worms, shrimp, squid, sand lance, crabs, and such small fish as silversides, killies, and butterfish.

Spotted Weakfish
(Cynoscion nebulosus)

COMMON NAMES: Spotted weakfish, spotted sea trout, speckled trout, trout, and speck

DESCRIPTION: This species is a southern variety of the common weakfish (see Weakfish), which it resembles. As its name might suggest, its markings (many large, dark, round spots found on the sides and back and extending onto the dorsal fin and tail) are far more prominent than those of the common weakfish. In general, body coloration of the spotted weakfish is dark gray on the back and upper sides, shading to silver below. Like the common weakfish, the spotted variety has a projecting lower jaw and two large canine teeth at the tip of the upper jaw. It is a top food fish.

RANGE: The spotted weakfish occurs throughout the Gulf of Mexico, in Florida waters, and north to Virginia, though it is found as a stray as far north as New York. It is most abundant in the Gulf of Mexico and in Florida.

HABITAT: See Weakfish.

SIZE: The average size of a spotted weakfish is somewhat smaller than that of a common weakfish. Most rod-caught spotted weaks fall in the 1- to 3-pound range. The maximum size is about 15 pounds.

FOOD: In many areas, spotted weakfish feed almost exclusively on shrimp. They may also eat various smaller fish, particularly mullet, menhaden, and silversides, as well as crabs and sea worms.

California White Sea Bass
(Cynoscion nobilis)

COMMON NAMES: California white sea bass, sea bass, white sea bass, croaker, and white corvina

DESCRIPTION: Not a true sea bass, the California white sea bass is a relative of the weakfish of the Atlantic. It is a rather streamlined fish with front and rear dorsal fins that are connected. The body colors are gray to blue on the back, silvery on the sides, and white on the belly. The tail is yellow. The belly is somewhat indented from pelvic fins to vent. There is a dark area at the base of the pectoral fins.

RANGE: The California white sea bass has an extreme range of Alaska to Chile, but it is not often found north of San Francisco. The population center seems to be from Santa Barbara, California, south into Mexico.

HABITAT: The white sea bass seldom strays far offshore and is most often found in or near beds of kelp. Night fishing is often very productive.

SIZE: The white sea bass averages about 15 to possibly 25 pounds, though specimens of more than 40 pounds are not uncommon. The maximum weight is a bit more than 80 pounds.

FOOD: White sea bass feed on a variety of small fish, as well as squid, crabs, shrimp, and other mollusks and crustaceans.

California Black Sea Bass
(Stereolepis gigas)

COMMON NAMES: California black sea bass, giant black sea bass, and giant sea bass

DESCRIPTION: This large, blocky fish is a Pacific version of the eastern sea bass. It is black or brownish black in general coloration, lighter on the underparts. Because of its size and color, the California black sea bass cannot be confused with any other species in its somewhat limited range.

RANGE: The California black sea bass is most numerous off Baja California and southern California, though it also ranges north to central California.

HABITAT: The California black sea bass is strictly a bottom-feeder, being found in deep water, usually over rocks and around reefs.

SIZE: The rod-and-reel record California black sea bass weighed 563 pounds, 8 ounces, which is probably about the maximum for the species. The average size is 100 to 200 pounds.

FOOD: California black sea bass feed on a variety of fish, including sheepsheads, and on crabs and other mollusks.

Black Drum *(Pogonias cromis)*

COMMON NAMES: Black drum, drum, and sea drum

DESCRIPTION: A member of the croaker family, the black drum is not as popular a game fish as the red drum. It is most easily distinguished from the red drum (channel bass) by the lack of a prominent dark spot near the base of the tail. The overall color of the black drum ranges from gray to almost silvery, usually with a coppery sheen. Young specimens usually have broad, vertical bands of a dark color. The body shape is short and deep, the back is arched, and the undersurface is somewhat flat. There are barbels on the chin.

RANGE: Black drums are an Atlantic species found from southern New England to Argentina, though they are rare north of New York. Centers of abundance include North Carolina, Florida, Louisiana, and Texas.

HABITAT: Usually found in schools, black drum prefer inshore sandy areas such as bays, lagoons, channels, and ocean surfs, and are also often found near wharves and bridges.

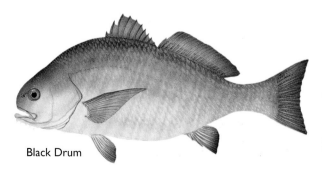

Black Drum

SIZE: The black drum is known to reach a maximum weight of nearly 150 pounds. However, the average size is 20 to 30 pounds.

FOOD: Black drum are bottom-feeders, preferring clams, mussels, crabs, shrimp, and other mollusks.

Goliath Grouper *(Epinephelus itajara* or *Promicrops itajara)*

COMMON NAMES: Goliath grouper, giant sea bass, spotted jewfish, jewfish, spotted grouper, and guasa

DESCRIPTION. Probably the largest of the groupers, the goliath grouper is not the gamest of fighters, but its weight alone makes up for that shortcoming. The overall color ranges from black to grayish brown, and the back and sides are mottled. The upper sides contain dark spots. The tail is convex along the rear margin. The flesh of the goliath grouper is quite tasty. During World War II, it was sold as "imported salt cod."

RANGE: The precise range of the goliath grouper seems uncertain. However, it is found in warmer waters of both the Atlantic and the Pacific and is most abundant in Florida waters and off the coast of Texas.

HABITAT: Despite its large size, the goliath grouper is most often found in relatively shallow water along the coast. It is at home under ledges and in reefs, in rocky holes, around bridges, and in deep channels.

SIZE: Though the rod-and-reel record is a 680-pounder, goliath groupers reach weights of at least 750 pounds. The average is probably 100 to 250 pounds.

FOOD: Goliath groupers feed on a great variety of small reef fish, including sheepshead, and also feed on crabs and squid.

Blackfish *(Tautoga onitis)*

COMMON NAMES: Blackfish, tautog, and oysterfish

DESCRIPTION: The blackfish is a member of the wrasse family, most of which are very brightly colored. The blackfish, however, is a drab gray or gray brown with irregular black mottling. Its body shape is relatively long and quite plump. The snout is blunt, lips are thick, and the jaws hold powerful crushing teeth. The edge of the tail is straight. The dorsal fin is quite long and spiny. The blackfish's flesh is very tasty, but for some reason it is not much used. The blackfish is an accomplished bait stealer.

RANGE: The blackfish is an Atlantic species found from Nova Scotia to South Carolina. It is most numerous from Cape Cod to Delaware Bay.

HABITAT: Blackfish are a coastal bottom-feeding species, preferring such lies as mussel beds, rocky areas both inshore and offshore, the outer edges of jetties and piers, and old wrecks. They are seldom found in water deeper than 60 feet.

SIZE: The average rod-caught blackfish weighs about 3 pounds, but 6- to 8-pounders are far from unusual, and the species can reach a maximum weight of about 25 pounds.

FOOD: Blackfish are bottom-feeders that eat such items as barnacles, mussels, crabs, snails, sea worms, shrimp, and even lobsters.

Sea Bass *(Centropristes striatus)*

COMMON NAMES: Sea bass, black sea bass, blackfish, humpback, and black will

DESCRIPTION: The sea bass, though small, is one of the most popular game fish in its somewhat restricted range. It has a rather stout body shape, with a high back and a moderately pointed snout. The apex of each gill cover holds a sharp spine. The overall color is gray to brownish gray to blue black, lighter on the fish's underparts. The sides are sometimes mottled and at other times appear to have light, horizontal stripes formed by rows of spots. The dorsal fin also has rows of spots. The most distinctive trait of the sea bass is the elongated ray on the upper edge of the tail—it sticks out far to the rear of the rest of the tail. Sea bass are fine eating.

RANGE: Sea bass are found from Maine to northern Florida, but they are most common from Cape Hatteras to Cape Cod.

HABITAT: Sea bass are bottom-dwellers of coastal areas.

Their preferred depths seem to be 20 to 50 feet, though large sea bass are often found at depths of up to 100 feet, especially in winter. Sea bass like such spots as mussel beds, rocky areas, wrecks, pilings, bridges, offshore reefs and ledges, and rocky heads.

SIZE: Sea bass hit about 8 pounds maximum. The average weight is 1 to 3 pounds.

FOOD: Sea bass feed on smaller fish, but they prefer clams, mussels, crabs, shrimp, sea worms, and squid.

Atlantic Codfish
(Gadus morhua)

COMMON NAMES: Atlantic codfish, codfish, and cod

DESCRIPTION: This pot-bellied heavyweight of the northern Atlantic is the cause of many a runny nose among sport and commercial fishermen in the cold-weather months. The thick-bodied Atlantic cod seems to have two color phases: red and gray. In the red phase, the fish may vary from orange to reddish brown. The gray phase ranges from black to greenish to brownish gray. The underparts are lighter, and the sides have many dark spots. The pale lateral line distinguishes the Atlantic cod from the haddock. The cod differs from the look-alike pollock in its longer chin barbel and the fact that its upper jaw projects past the lower (the opposite is true of the pollock). The cod's dorsal fin is in three spineless sections, and the anal fin, also spineless, has two sections—an unusual fin makeup.

RANGE: In the western Atlantic, the cod is found from Greenland south to North Carolina. In the eastern Atlantic, it ranges throughout the Baltic Sea, from northern Scandinavia east to some parts of Russia, and south to the Bay of Biscay.

HABITAT: Atlantic cod are schooling fish for the most part, bottom-feeders, and lovers of cold water. Though the young may be found in shallow water, cod generally prefer depths of 60 feet or more and are sometimes found down to 1,500 feet. Sport fishermen usually catch cod at the 50- to 300-foot levels. Cod migrate north and south to some extent, but most movement is from relatively shallow water, where they are likely to be found in winter, to the deeps, where they go in summer.

Cod seem to prefer areas with a rocky or broken bottom and such places as wrecks.

SIZE: The average Atlantic cod taken by sport fishermen probably falls into the 6- to 12-pound category, but the rod-and-reel record is more than 80 pounds, and the species is known to exceed 200 pounds. Cod of up to 60 pounds are not unusual in the New Jersey to southern New England area.

FOOD: Atlantic cod feed on a variety of bottom life, including various small fish (notably herring), crabs, clams, squid, mussels, snails, sea worms, and lobsters.

Pollock *(Pollachius virens)*

COMMON NAMES: Pollock, Boston bluefish, green cod, and coalfish

DESCRIPTION: The pollock, in effect, lives under the shadow of its famous relative, the Atlantic cod. A better fighter than the cod (probably because it is generally taken from shallower water), it has a shorter chin barbel than its relative, and its lower jaw projects beyond the upper (the cod's upper jaw projects farther than the lower). The pollock is not spotted, as is the cod, and its tail is more severely forked. A pollock's colors range from dark-olive green to brownish on the upper parts, yellowish to gray on the lower sides, to silvery on the belly. Like the cod, its flesh is excellent eating.

RANGE: Pollock range in the western Atlantic from the Gulf of St. Lawrence to Chesapeake Bay and in the eastern Atlantic from Iceland south to the Bay of Biscay.

HABITAT: In general, pollock are found in somewhat shallower water than are cod, and they are often caught at intermediate depths. Occasionally, usually during May at such points as Cape Cod's Race Point Rip, pollock come into shallow water near shore and can be taken on or near the surface.

SIZE: Most pollock caught by sport anglers weigh 4 to 12 pounds. However, the species has a maximum weight of some 45 pounds.

FOOD: Pollock feed on a variety of fish—including herring and small cod—and on shrimp and some crustaceans and mollusks, as well as sea worms.

Summer Flounder *(Paralichthys dentatus)*

COMMON NAMES: Summer flounder, fluke, and flatfish

DESCRIPTION: The summer flounder is one of about 500 members of the flatfish family, a curious group. They begin life in an upright position and have an eye on each side of the head. As they grow, however, the body begins to "tilt," in some species to the right, in others to the left, and the eye on the downward-facing surface begins to travel to the upward-facing surface. Finally, the transformation is complete, and the fish spends the rest of its life on its side, with both eyes on the same side of the head (above and just to the rear of the point of the jaw). The summer flounder is white on the side that comes in contact with the ocean floor. The color of the upper surface depends on the physical makeup of the ocean floor, but is usually olive, brown, or gray, with prominent dark spots and some mottling. The body is flat and quite deep. The dorsal and anal fins are extremely long.

RANGE: The summer flounder occurs in the United States from Maine to South Carolina.

HABITAT: The summer flounder lives on the bottom, often buried in sand or mud. In summer, it is found in shallow water, sometimes in depths of only a few feet, while in winter, it moves offshore into as much as 50 fathoms of water. It frequents bays and harbors, the mouths of estuaries, and is often found around bottom obstructions such as wrecked ships.

SIZE: Most summer flounders caught by sport fishermen weigh 1 to 4 pounds, but the maximum size is probably close to 30 pounds.

FOOD: Summer flounders eat a wide variety of small fish, as well as sea worms, crabs, clams, squid, and shrimp.

Winter Flounder *(Psuedopleuronectes americanus)*

COMMON NAMES: Winter flounder, flatfish, blueback, blackback, black flounder, and mud dab

DESCRIPTION: One of the smaller members of the vast flatfish family, the winter flounder differs from the summer flounder in its smaller size and weight and in the fact that it is "right-eyed" (that is, it has both eyes and the skin pigmentation on the right side of its head) while the summer flounder is "left-eyed." The winter flounder is white on the underside (the side on which it lies on the ocean floor), while on the other side the colors range from reddish brown to slate gray, usually with some dark spots. The mouth is small, and the lateral line is relatively straight. The winter flounder is widely sought for food by both sport and commercial fishermen.

RANGE: The winter flounder has an extreme range of Labrador south to Georgia, but it is most common from the Gulf of St. Lawrence to Chesapeake Bay.

HABITAT: The winter flounder is found mostly in shallow water—as shallow as 1 foot, in fact—but is occasionally found at depths of up to 400 feet. It lies on the bottom, preferring sand or mud, but accepting clay, gravel, or even a hard bottom. In the fall, this species tends to move toward the shallows, while in spring the movement is toward deeper water.

SIZE: Winter flounders average from ½ to 1½ pounds in weight and 8 to 15 inches in length. The maximum size is about 8 pounds, and such heavyweights are often called snowshoes.

FOOD: Winter flounders eat such items as sea worms, crabs, shrimp, and minute crustaceans, as well as small fish and fish larvae.

Roosterfish
(Nematistius pectoralis)

COMMON NAMES: Roosterfish, papagallo, gallo, and pez de gallo

DESCRIPTION: The roosterfish—a relative of the jacks and pompanos, which it resembles at least in body shape—gets its name from the seven extremely long (far longer than the greatest body depth) spines of the forward dorsal fin, which vaguely resemble a rooster's comb. Its body colors are green to gray blue on the upper areas, white to gold below. Two black stripes curve downward and then rearward from the forward dorsal fin, which itself has a white, horizontal stripe. The roosterfish is a furious fighter and a fine table fish.

RANGE: Roosterfish are a Pacific species occurring from

Roosterfish

Peru as far north as southern California. They are particularly abundant in the Gulf of California.

HABITAT: Little is known of the movements and life history of the roosterfish. However, fishermen often catch them in sandy inshore bays and by trolling in open water. The fish are sometimes seen swimming on the surface, their dorsals erect and waving above the surface.

SIZE: The average size of a roosterfish is estimated at around 5 to 20 pounds. The maximum size is probably about 130 pounds.

FOOD: The dietary preferences of the roosterfish aren't known in detail, but these fish certainly feed on almost any small fish that is available. They strike artificial lures and plugs willingly.

Porgy (Stenotomus chrysops)

COMMON NAMES: Porgy, northern porgy, and scup

DESCRIPTION: The porgy (most often called scup in some areas of its range) is what might be called a saltwater panfish. It has a somewhat ovate, high-backed body with a small mouth and strong teeth. The basic body color ranges from silvery to brown, and there are usually three or four dark, vertical bars on the sides. The dorsal fin is quite spiny. The porgy's flesh is highly palatable, and it is caught by both sport and commercial anglers, though in some areas rod fishermen consider the porgy a nuisance.

RANGE: The porgy (northern porgy) is found from Nova Scotia south to the Atlantic coast of Florida. In summer and fall, it is quite abundant off the coasts of New England, New York, and New Jersey.

HABITAT: Porgies seem to prefer some bottom debris, such as mussel beds. They live on or near the bottom in the middle depths of the continental shelf.

SIZE: Porgies average ½ to 2 pounds. The maximum size is about 4 pounds, and such individuals are often called humpbacks.

FOOD: Porgies feed mainly on small crustaceans, worms, mollusks, and occasionally on vegetable matter.

Spanish Mackerel
(Scomberomorus maculatus)

DESCRIPTION: This beautiful, streamlined fish though of modest size as mackerels go—is a magnificent fighter, making sizzling runs and soaring leaps. Its body shape is rather compressed, and its colors range from an iridescent steel blue or occasionally greenish on the dorsal surface to a silvery blue below. The side markings are mustard or bronze spots, and are quite large. The dorsal fin is in two sections, and there are dorsal and anal finlets. Its side spots, lack of stripes, and absence of scales on the pectoral fins distinguish the Spanish mackerel from the king mackerel and the cero.

RANGE: Spanish mackerel occur from Cape Cod south to Brazil, but they are never numerous in the northern part of their range. They are most plentiful from the Carolinas into the Gulf of Mexico.

HABITAT: This warm-water species is usually found in open waters, cruising near the surface and slashing into schools of baitfish. They do, however, make occasional forays into the surf and into bays and channels in search of food sources.

SIZE: Spanish mackerel average 1½ to 4 pounds but reach a maximum weight of about 20 pounds. A 10-pounder is a very good one.

Spanish Mackerel

FOOD: Spanish mackerel feed primarily on a wide variety of small baitfish and on shrimp. A favorite bait in some areas, particularly Florida waters, is a very small baitfish called a glass minnow.

Sheepshead
(Archosargus probatocephalus)

COMMON NAMES: Sheepshead and convict fish

DESCRIPTION: Similar in shape and appearance to the porgy, the sheepshead is a high-backed, blunt-headed species whose bait-stealing abilities have frustrated countless fishermen. Its small mouth has a formidable set of rock-hard, close coupled teeth that are capable of demolishing a crab and biting through a light-wire hook. The basic color is silvery, though the dorsal surface's color is closer to gray. The sides have five to seven dark, vertical bands, and the spines of the dorsal fin are large and coarse. Sheepsheads fight well and are excellent on the table.

RANGE: The sheepshead is found from Nova Scotia south to the northeastern Gulf of Mexico. It is far more numerous in the southern part of its range, particularly in Florida waters.

HABITAT: The sheepshead is a gregarious species that moves with the tides to wherever the food is plentiful. It is an inshore fish, taking up residence in bays and channels and around bridges, piers, pilings, and the like.

SIZE: The sheepshead averages about 1 to 5 pounds, but it may attain weights in excess of 20 pounds.

FOOD: Its teeth are a dead giveaway to the sheepheads's dietary preferences, which include crabs, mollusks, barnacles, and the like, as well as shrimp.

African Pompano
(Alectis crinitus)

COMMON NAMES: African pompano, threadfish, Cuban jack, and flechudo

DESCRIPTION: The head profile in adult fish is slanted and almost vertical and the eyes are large. The body is flat with silver sides with an almost iridescent sheen. The forward rays of the dorsal and anal fins are long.

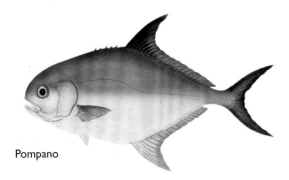

Pompano

RANGE: The African pompano's range is from Brazil to Massachusetts. It is commonly caught in Florida waters.

HABITAT: Young African pompano like shallow reefs. As the young Africans mature and become adults, they seek deeper reefs and wrecks.

SIZE: Adults can grow to lengths of 3 feet and weights of 30 to 35 pounds are common. They are tough fighters, especially on light tackle. The record fish in Florida weighed 50 pounds, 8 ounces.

FOOD: Not a true pompano, the African feeds on small baitfish and can be caught by chumming over reefs. Drifting or trolling a rigged bait is the most common technique.

■ Pompano *(Trachinotus carolinus)*

COMMON NAMES: Pompano, common pompano, and sunfish

DESCRIPTION: This high-strung, slab-sided character is the most abundant and most important member of the pompano family, which includes such fish as the much-prized permit. It has a small mouth, blunt head, and a relatively shallow body (its body depth decreases proportionally with growth). Dorsal-surface colors range from gray, silver, or blue to blue green, and the sides and underparts are silvery. The ventral surfaces are flecked with yellow. The dorsal fin is bluish, and most of the other fins are yellowish. The pompano is an epicurean's delight.

RANGE: The pompano is found from Brazil north to Massachusetts, and also in the West Indies and in Bermuda waters. It is particularly numerous in Florida and the Gulf of Mexico.

HABITAT: Pompano are inshore school fish, feeding on the bottom in shallow water in the surf, in channels and inlets and bays, and around bridges. They occasionally range well up into rivers with the tide.

SIZE: Pompano average about 2 pounds in weight, and the maximum size is thought to be about 8 pounds.

FOOD: Pompano feed mostly on bivalve mollusks and on small crustaceans, notably a small beetle-like crustacean called the sand flea.

■ California Corbina
(Menticirrhus undulatus)

COMMON NAMES: California corbina, corbina, corvina, whiting, and sea trout

DESCRIPTION: The wary and unpredictable corbina, a member of the whiting group, is among the most popular fish caught in inshore waters of the Pacific. The basic color is some shade of blue gray, and identifying characteristics include a blunt snout; a short, high forward dorsal fin and a long, lower rear dorsal fin; and small barbels at the tip of the lower jaw. The corbina is a strong underwater fighter and an excellent food fish.

RANGE: The corbina is found from the Gulf of California north to Point Conception.

HABITAT: Primarily a target of surf fishermen, the corbina is an inshore species found primarily along sandy beaches and in shallow bays, moving into the surf line on the incoming tide.

SIZE: Corbina reach a maximum weight of about 8 pounds. The average size is 2 to 3 pounds.

FOOD: Crabs of various kinds are the favorite food of the corbina, but it also feeds on clams and sea worms.

■ Atlantic Croaker
(Micropogon undulatus)

COMMON NAMES: Atlantic croaker, croaker, hardhead, and golden croaker

DESCRIPTION: The most common and most prized of the eastern U.S. members of the huge croaker family, the Atlantic croaker is a strong fighter and makes for delicious eating. The croaker family gets its name from the sound it makes—audible for quite a distance—by repeated contractions of its swim bladder and a unique "drumming muscle." The Atlantic croaker has a small, tapered body; a short, high forward dorsal fin and a long, lower rear dorsal fin; and small barbels on the chin. The colors are brassy gold and silver, and the upper parts of the body contain numerous dark spots that sometimes form slanting bars.

RANGE: The Atlantic croaker is found from Massachusetts south to Florida and west to Texas and eastern Mexico. In recent years, however, its numbers have declined in the northern part of the range. The center of abundance seems to be from the Carolinas to Florida and in the northern Gulf of Mexico.

HABITAT: Atlantic croakers are seldom found far from estuaries, preferring sandy shallows, shallow shell beds, sloughs, lagoons, and weedy flats. However, cold weather often sends the fish into deeper water.

SIZE: Atlantic croakers average ½ to about 2½ pounds and attain a maximum size of about 5 pounds.

FOOD: Predominantly bottom-feeders, Atlantic croakers feed on clams, crabs, sea worms, shrimp, snails, mussels, and sand fleas.

Red Snapper *(Lutjanus blackfordi)*

DESCRIPTION: Most widely known for its eating qualities, the red snapper is among the best known of the more than 200 species of snappers found in the world's warm seas. The red snapper's color pattern (rose red overall, though paler red on the underparts, with red fins and eyes, and a black spot on each side), long pectoral fin, and more numerous anal-fin rays distinguish this species from other snappers.

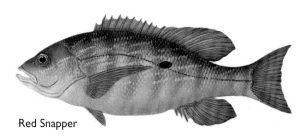

Red Snapper

RANGE: The red snapper occurs from the Middle Atlantic and Gulf Coast of the United States southward throughout the tropical American Atlantic.

HABITAT: The red snapper's preference for deep waters—it is sometimes found as deep as 100 fathoms and seems most prevalent at 20 to 60 fathoms—detracts from its importance as a sport fish. It usually is found a few feet above a hard bottom.

SIZE: Most red snappers caught commercially run from 5 to about 30 pounds. The maximum size seems to be about 35 pounds.

FOOD: Red snappers eat baitfish and various deep-water mollusks and crustaceans.

Northern Whiting *(Menticirrhus saxatilis)*

COMMON NAMES: Northern whiting, whiting, northern kingfish, and kingfish

DESCRIPTION: The northern whiting is one of four whitings (all members of the large croaker family) that inhabit the Atlantic and Gulf coasts of the United States. The basic color is silver gray or silver brown, and the upper part of the body contains rather indistinct dark, vertical bands. The mouth is small, and there is a single chin barbel. The northern whiting is the only one of the four U.S. whitings in which the third and largest spine of the forward dorsal fin, when laid flat, reaches well past the beginning of the long and soft rear dorsal fin. The northern whiting is an excellent food fish.

RANGE: The northern whiting is found on the Atlantic coast of the United States from Maine to Florida.

HABITAT: Northern whiting are usually found over a sandy bottom in the surf, shallow sloughs and bays, and, as the water temperature cools, in depths as great as 100 feet or more.

SIZE: Averaging about 1 pound, the northern whiting reaches a maximum size of about 3 pounds and 18 inches in length.

FOOD: The northern whiting feeds mainly on small baitfish, sea worms, and small crustaceans.

TENTS

Tents are manufactured in a variety of shapes and sizes, so whether you're just doing some backyard camping or heading for a couple of weeks in the mountains, there's probably a tent made for you and your family. Manufacturers frequently use different names to describe their tent models. The tent designs and names illustrated here are generally accepted to describe traditional tent designs and their features.

▉ Wall Tents

Many campers, particularly those who have spent time in the Army, are familiar with the traditional wall tent. Its main advantages are that it has ample headspace, that it can house a wood-burning stove in cold weather, and that it readily sheds water off its inverted-V roof.

A psychological benefit of the wall tent is that it somewhat resembles a small house in design, but upon closer examination, you'll see it is not quite as comfortable as it looks, nor is it very stable in wind.

There usually are no floors or windows, nor netting at the flap doors. Moreover, the walls tend to be so low that the only walking space is directly below the ridgepole. The large end pole that stands in the center of the doorway is another nuisance.

A wall tent is inexpensive and to erect it you only need two upright poles, a ridgepole, guy ropes, and pegs. Ventilation is poor in rainy weather, and the tent offers little resistance to the wind. The door flaps leave myriad openings for insects and, if closed, make the tent's interior quite dark and warm. Automobile campers appreciate the heavy wall tent, as it can be pitched right next to their cars, but for those who wish to travel light, it is a poor choice.

The wall tent is generally available in sizes ranging from 6½ by 6½ feet to 16 by 20 feet, although larger sizes are available from custom tent makers. The wall tent in these bigger custom sizes is favored by many big-game outfitters and guides. These tents are fitted with wood-burning stoves and chimneys. On average wall tents, however, the side walls run from 2 to 4 feet in height, but 3 feet is standard. Heights at the center are usually 7 to 7½ feet, adequate for the average adult.

This type of tent with a 7-by-9-foot floor space will provide sufficient room for two campers with gear. A trio of hunters will require at least a 9-by-12-foot wall tent for comfort.

▉ Cottage or Cabin Tents

If you're planning a long stay in an area and need plenty of space, the cottage or cabin tent just might be the answer.

This style of tent features vertical sides that give you more space for your gear than tents with short side walls. The eaves are high and there are large windows with storm flaps. You've also got walking room to spare and sewn-in floors. Though the number of poles required to pitch it may approach 10, modern cottage tents generally employ light aluminum telescoping poles that are not difficult to handle. Guy lines are not required with most cottage or cabin tents, though the outside edges of the tent floor should be staked down. A large area of level ground is needed to put up the tent. An 8-by-10-foot tent can sleep four persons; a 9-by-12-foot tent can sleep five to six persons.

▉ Umbrella Tents

The umbrella tent is best designed for the motorist who goes touring with his own shelter. A pyramid-shaped roof and straight sides distinguish this unit.

TENT TYPES

▲ Wall Tent

◄ Cottage Tent

▲ Umbrella Tent

▼ Wedge Tent

▲ Pyramid Tent

▶ Forester Tent

▶ Baker Tent

Pop Tent

Canvas Lean-To Tarp

Mountain Tent

Explorer Tent

Tepee Tent

Geodesic Tent

Wind resistance is exceptional and the vertical walls offer plenty of space for storing gear. The ample headroom lets you walk around without stooping, and, save for the door awning, there aren't any large, flat surfaces that will hold rain or catch snow. A big door and one or more windows in the sides give good ventilation on warm evenings.

A sewn-in, waterproof floor keeps out drafts, bugs, and surface moisture, while a 4- to 6-inch doorsill strip in some models wards off snakes and small animals. With assembly time ranging from four to five minutes, this is a fine tent to have when a storm is approaching.

One of the main faults of the umbrella tent, however, is its pole arrangement. If it has but one pole (rare nowadays), you will need a small umbrella frame to hold the cloth straight. The center pole takes up entirely too much room inside, and its sole advantages are that you can reach up and slacken the umbrella to loosen the stakes, and that useful shelves can be attached to the pole. Most current umbrella tents feature four aluminum poles, so if you're backpacking or canoeing, ignore this one.

Models come in interior- and exterior-pole styles. The former type can cause wear and capillary leaks due to metal rubbing against canvas. The latter is preferable, as there is no center pole. Thus, there is more room inside. The exterior-pole setup is somewhat heavier and more expensive, however.

Another drawback is weight—it weighs 30 to 65 pounds, depending on its size and method of pole support.

A couple can be accommodated by a 7-by-8-foot or an 8-by-8-foot model. Four persons would be better off in a 9½-by-9½-foot or 10-by-10-foot model. Don't get anything bigger, as it will be unwieldy to pitch. You're better off with two small umbrella tents if the crew is large.

Wedge Tents

Although the Boy Scouts and the U.S. Army have taken a fancy to the wedge tent (also called the pup tent, A tent, Hudson Bay tent, or snow tent), it's not recommended if you're thinking of camping in any comfort. The wedge tent has no place to stand upright.

But there are several factors in this tent's favor: it's inexpensive, quite simple to erect, lightweight, sheds rain and snow rather well, and is quite stable (if properly pitched) on a windy day.

Heating this type of tent in cold weather is difficult, as a campfire inside is out of the question and a small heater can lead to asphyxiation if enough fresh air is not allowed in the tent.

A 5-by-7-foot tent of this style can sleep two persons. The weight with stakes and poles is approximately 6 pounds.

Pyramid Tents

For shedding rain and snow, the pyramid, or miner, tent is the best designed for the purpose. Also, when well pitched at the base and supported by an outside tripod of poles or a strong center pole, this tent can brave almost any windstorm.

A 7-by-7-foot tent of this style is adequate for sleeping and shelter, but buy the zipper-door type rather than the one with tie tapes, as there will be less chance of leakage at the door.

Keep the doors open on hot days and use a reflector fire when the weather is brisk; wood stoves are not suitable for these small tents. Another flaw is that they are somewhat cramped, and an alcohol, gas, or oil stove can make the air stuffy.

Baker Tents

Similar to the wall tent except for one wall that is raised to form a front awning, the baker tent is quite roomy and is exceptional as a campfire tent. Temperatures can be far below the freezing point, but this tent, provided it has a good fire in front of it, will keep you warm. Green logs or rocks can be stacked up behind the fire to reflect heat into the open tent.

Important: A waterproofing solution with fire-resistant chemicals should be used to treat the baker tent. Also, keep the fire at a reasonable level and the awning pitched high enough so that the two do not meet to create a hazard. As the roof is flat, a tight-woven fabric or a fine waterproofing is essential to help shed rain.

If you're looking for privacy, this tent is not for you. As the accompanying illustration shows, the front is wide open and, if the porch is dropped down, ventilation is minimal. In addition, in a driving rain the tent may have to be repositioned so as not to get the occupants wet.

Wind can be more harmful to a baker tent than it can to a wedge, pyramid, or wall tent. Therefore, face the tent away from prevailing winds and, if a storm is in the offing, anchor the tent with long stakes.

The open baker tent is poor protection from mosquitoes and other biting flies. Cheesecloth or netting placed over the entrance can be helpful, but bed nets for each individual are more convenient and effective.

A 6-by-8-foot baker tent will sleep two campers comfortably, and perhaps three with a tight fit. A baker larger than 8 by 10 feet will render your fire virtually useless.

Forester Tents

When there is a question of light weight and optimum warmth in cold weather, the forester tent is the best choice. The interior is so designed that the heat of a campfire will be well reflected throughout the entire unit. Pitching time is short, and the tent is stable if correctly pitched. It also sheds heavy rain and withstands high winds. The tent is small—typically 6 feet wide at the front and 8 feet deep. The shape of the interior is triangular, narrowing to a point at the back. Two campers will have sufficient sleeping room in this tent, but it is best for a lone camper who will have enough space for food and gear. During seasons when insects are a problem, individual bed nets are recommended for protection.

Lean-To Shelters

This shelter is not only the simplest one, but also the lightest and cheapest. It is merely a square sheet of fabric hemmed at the edges and provided with eyelets or loops through which supporting ropes are placed.

In the dry southwestern sections of the United States, outdoor enthusiasts have learned that a tent is rarely necessary from July through September; thus, the popularity of the lean-to.

An 8-by-10-foot shelter, preferably waterproofed, can be set up in a variety of ways: draped over a pole to resemble a pup tent, angled higher to create a baker-tent type of shelter roof plus an awning, raised as a flat roof, etc.

If the fabric is untreated, it could leak at once—and badly, too. Also, the fabric may wilt or burn if placed too close to a fire. Other disadvantages are deterioration from intense sunlight and the tendency of some material to tear.

Pop Tents

The canvas igloo or dome tent can be assembled in a short time. Commercial models are usually waterproof and mildew resistant, with an exterior rib setup to aid in pitching. One model, 7 feet in diameter, will sleep two adults. But if you're a trio, a 9-foot diameter would prove more satisfactory. Not all styles permit you to stand upright, so sweeping out the sewn-in floor could prove to be a problem.

There appears to be some controversy as to this unit's stability in high winds. Some experts say it can be set up in sand without stakes and remain sturdy; others assert that unless the individual or his gear is present inside, the pop tent may blow over.

Zippered storm flaps on some models will keep out wind and insects, and a window assists in cross ventilation. A few models also feature an awning.

Explorer Tents

The explorer tent has a number of advantages: it is lightweight, wind resistant, has adequate floor space, and, when checked thoroughly, is bug free.

This unit features a sewn-in floor as well as a large, netted front door that is shaped somewhat like a huge porthole.

In Canada and Alaska, mosquitoes can be a problem. For this reason, many outdoors enthusiasts turn to the explorer tent when they're northward bound. Once the netting sleeve has been tied shut—after shooing away any tiny stragglers—you're in for a comfortable evening. The steep walls are designed to readily shed rain and to provide additional storage space. A 7-by-7-foot explorer tent sleeps one or two campers, and weighs a mere 10 to 12 pounds.

Mountain or Backpack Tents

In any weather except a very hot summer's day, the mountain tent (a form of backpacking tent) is a feasible proposition. But wintertime is the season when this tent really shows its stuff.

A stove—never an open wood fire—placed in the forepart of the tent will keep you warm in the coldest times. The vent at the peak of the tent must be opened before you light your stove, as the fumes can be lethal.

It is advisable with some models to take along one or two telescopic poles if the area you're camping in has no timber. This tent should be anchored to a point a minimum of 5 feet off the ground. Other styles, however, feature an exterior frame, and a center pole or guy ropes that attach to pegs. The floor is sewn-in on most models.

Front flaps are somewhat standard, and there usually is adequate screening to keep out insects.

Geodesic or Dome Tents

The geodesic simply means a domed framework of polygons in tension. There are no poles or structures inside the tent. The dome design is highly wind resistant and sheds rain and snow well. The tents are freestanding with minimal outside staking and pegging. Many of these new tents are made of breathable nylon taffeta with water-repellent, polyurethane-coated nylon floors. Setup is fast with the continuous shock-corded fiberglass frame-pole system.

A typical geodesic dome tent that measures 8 by 7 feet has about 43 square feet of usable space, will sleep two or three persons, and weighs 10 to 11 pounds.

Tepee Tents

If you're staying in one spot for a long while, the tepee is a good choice. Unfortunately, marketed models are not as well designed as the original Native American tepees. Some do feature smoke flaps, but they are smaller than those of the true tepee. The smoke leaves the tent at the point where the poles come together, rather than directly above the fire as in the early tepees. Tepees of old had several advantages. A weathertight seal would be created at the apex of the tent when the smoke flaps were closed. Contemporary tepees do not feature this.

The floor is oval shaped, and it is possible to stand upright within 3 feet of the front and 2 feet of the rear. As many as 15 people can be housed in an 18-by-21-foot tepee, but they would be rather uncomfortable. Wind resistance is high despite the extensive wall area. The tepee is primarily for permanence, so the heaviness of the total unit (300 pounds including cover, lining, poles, and pegs), plus the extensive time needed for its erection, rule it out if you're constantly on the move.

Tent Poles

Since most economy-minded campers are do-it-yourselfers, homemade tent poles are a good place to save money. Obtain a 2-by-2-inch board the same height as your tent. With a saw, cut the wood at a sharp angle into two equal pieces. Then, affix a metal bracket to the angled end of each piece. The two halves will lock together firmly when necessary.

One commercial model features a metal sleeve that slides to lock the joint. Another factory-made tent pole is the adjustable Safetite aluminum upright that has a metal clamp instead of set screws or nuts. If this pole is lost, you can substitute a wooden or steel pole in its place. Even a broomstick will work in an emergency. Both styles are available in several sizes to suit your tenting needs. For ultimate ease of use, look for tent poles that are shock corded together.

Tent Pegs

Just as tent poles can be homemade or purchased over the counter, the same goes for tent pegs, also known as tent stakes. The array available is large enough to satisfy any camper, as the following list of types indicates:

- Aluminum
- Plastic
- Steel
- Wood
- Metal spike
- Workshop wood
- Whittled branch

The automobile camper can buy iron or aluminum tent pegs, as weight makes little difference. The

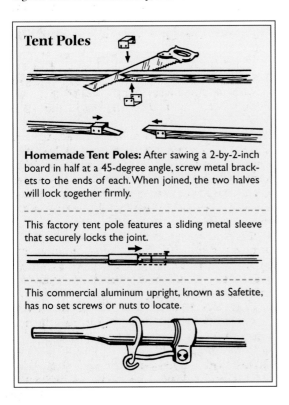

Tent Poles

Homemade Tent Poles: After sawing a 2-by-2-inch board in half at a 45-degree angle, screw metal brackets to the ends of each. When joined, the two halves will lock together firmly.

This factory tent pole features a sliding metal sleeve that securely locks the joint.

This commercial aluminum upright, known as Safetite, has no set screws or nuts to locate.

Tent Pegs

These tent pegs range from field-made (wood) styles to store-bought styles of steel, iron, and lightweight aluminum.

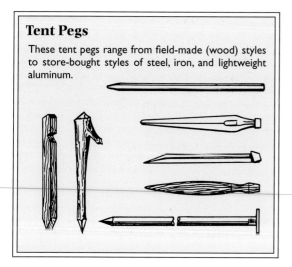

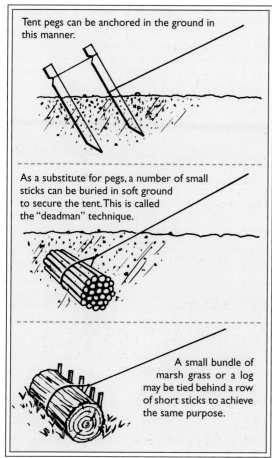

Tent pegs can be anchored in the ground in this manner.

As a substitute for pegs, a number of small sticks can be buried in soft ground to secure the tent. This is called the "deadman" technique.

A small bundle of marsh grass or a log may be tied behind a row of short sticks to achieve the same purpose.

backpacker, on the other hand, must keep pack weight in mind. Therefore, he may resort to cutting his own wooden stakes. The softer the ground, the deeper the stakes must be buried. As a substitute for tent stakes, you can bury a bundle of stiff marsh grass, brush, or sticks in sand or dirt. In winter, blocks of ice or frozen snow will also make for a more rigid tent when you're out of pegs.

■ Tent Fabrics

COTTON: You may have heard the terms "canvas," "duck," and "balloon silk" mentioned when you were looking for a cotton tent. All three are various forms of cotton used in the manufacture of tents. Canvas and duck are a bit heavier than balloon silk—a long-fibered, high-quality cotton. Until World War II, practically every tent was made of cotton. Today, nylon, Dacron, and other synthetic fibers, which have proven to be very lightweight, are replacing cotton in tent manufacturing.

Duck and canvas, if properly waterproofed, will shed water well, but are relatively heavy. The heavier the fabric, however, the stronger the tent. Conventional cotton tents are made in grades of 8, 10, and 12 ounces. The 8-ounce type is more fit for a hiking tent, while the 12-ounce type would be required for a wall tent and the like. Another advantage is that cotton "breathes" well. Thus, there's no stuffiness.

The disadvantages of a mediocre cotton tent are several: It weighs more than the synthetic tents, and it may leak water and tear readily. Also, this material can only be dry-cleaned, as machine washing would destroy it.

NYLON: This synthetic has two prime advantages for the camper—it is relatively lightweight and is far less bulky to pack. Its disadvantages are that condensation forms in humid weather and, when the fabric is wet, the seams do not swell. This can lead to a clammy tent. Mountain tents and other styles valuable to the backpacker are often made of nylon.

Some nylon tents are waterproof, and some of the newer ones do breathe, as cotton does, but this material cannot be "breathable" and waterproof at the same time. Most of the nylon tents that breathe therefore come equipped with waterproof overhead flies (a cover suspended over the roof). Some nylon tents have cotton roofs—another solution to the same problem—and some are a blend of nylon and cotton.

DACRON: Like nylon, this synthetic is lightweight. It also stretches and shrinks much less than nylon and is more resistant to the effects of the sun. In addition, it can be either dry-cleaned or machine washed. Unfortunately, it tends to be bulky when rolled up, and also is somewhat water retentive.

POLYESTER: This tent fabric is spun polyester. It has nylon's strength, is lightweight, and breathes and repels water pretty much like cotton does. Like the other synthetics, polyester can be blended with cotton to achieve the desirable qualities of both fabrics.

Tents featuring blends of synthetic fibers and cotton are the most excellent of all for camping. They're highly water repellent, strong, lightweight, and porous enough to provide maximum comfort. Probably the best way to locate these models is to look for the ultrahigh price tags.

FLAME-RESISTANT TENTS: Regardless of fabric, more and more tents are now treated to be flame resistant— sometimes called fire retardant. It should be stressed that this treatment, though it is an excellent safety precaution, does not make the tents fireproof. A flame-resistant tent bears a label with wording that may vary slightly but with a clear message: "Warning. Keep all flame and heat sources away from this tent fabric. This tent is made with flame-resistant fabric . . . It is not fireproof. The fabric will burn if left in continuous contact with any flame source. The application of any foreign substance to the fabric may render the flame-resistant properties ineffective."

■ Pitching a Tent

A tent is not a house. It's not even a small cabin. Pitch your tent in the wrong place and you could be in for a cold, wet night. Once you have selected a level site free of rocks and vegetation that might damage the tent floor or poke you in the back, you will have to deal with the two biggest campsite enemies: wind and water. In cold

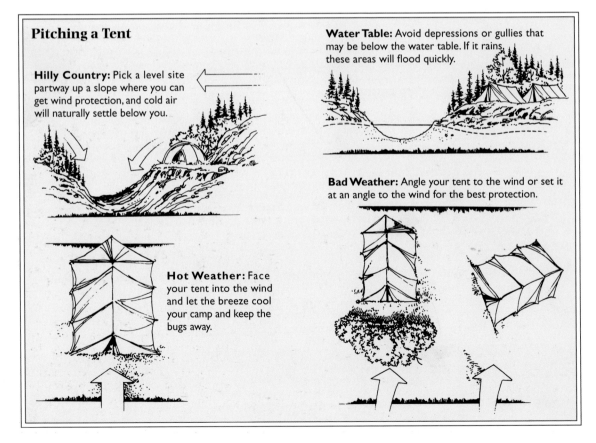

Pitching a Tent

Hilly Country: Pick a level site partway up a slope where you can get wind protection, and cold air will naturally settle below you.

Hot Weather: Face your tent into the wind and let the breeze cool your camp and keep the bugs away.

Water Table: Avoid depressions or gullies that may be below the water table. If it rains, these areas will flood quickly.

Bad Weather: Angle your tent to the wind or set it at an angle to the wind for the best protection.

Tent Makes and Models

L.L. Bean's Big Woods Dome Tent is a three-room family tent that measures 18 feet by 8 feet with a peak height of nearly 7 feet. The maximum capacity is eight persons. The packed size is 34 inches by 14 inches. Four waterproof double doors are equipped with mesh panels for maximum ventilation.

The L.L. Bean Vector XL Dome Tent is a tough family tent designed to handle wind and storms. It comes in two versions, with a vestibule area of nearly 22 square feet or 29 square feet. A three-pole design provides a streamlined shape to minimize the effect of wind. Aluminum poles are shock corded for easy handling.

The L.L. Bean Northwoods Cabin Tent has floor dimensions of nearly 10 by 10 feet with a tent height of close to 7 feet. It has a weight of 23 pounds, 11 ounces, and a capacity of six persons. The walls are made of ripstop polyester. With its polyurethane waterproof coating, this model would be a good choice as a weekend tent for a small family.

Typical of backpacking tents is L.L. Bean's Mountain Light XT Tent, which weighs only 4 pounds, 12 ounces, with a capacity of two campers. The floor dimensions are 7½ by 4½ feet. The user-friendly, two-door design allows campers to get out without climbing over gear. The aluminum frame is lightweight and easy to set up. No-see-um mesh will keep out the smallest bugs without restricting air flow.

The Coleman Evanston is a fully screened and roomy six-person tent with a screened front porch that will allow you to enjoy camping with maximum protection from bugs. This tent's waterproof floor, four large windows, and one-room interior make it a good choice for family camping in spring and summer.

Tent Makes and Models (continued)

Cabela's Ultimate Alaknak Tent is a hunting-camp design constructed of waterproof 250-denier polyester, which weighs a fraction of the amount of traditional canvas. All models are designed for stove heating with roof panel protection for a hot stovepipe. Models are available in three sizes: 12 by 12 feet, 12 by 20 feet, and 13 by 27 feet. The center height is nearly 10 feet. A floor liner is optional.

The Sportz Truck Tent is designed to make camping in the bed of your truck more comfortable. It weighs only 24 pounds and sleeps two persons. It features a sewn-in nylon floor and a 4-by-4-foot awning. Shock-corded and color-coded fiberglass poles make setup simple. Models vary with truck-bed lengths.

weather, you should find an area sheltered from the wind, but not at the bottom of a steep hill where you may get hit with frost-heaved rocks. If practical, pitch your tent facing east, so you can catch the morning sun.

It may be easier to drive a tent peg into soft ground, but that's also the type of terrain that holds moisture and dampness. Hard ground is better. Stay clear of dried riverbeds and gullies. In a sudden rainstorm, they can quickly fill with water.

In bad weather, look for a site in the lee of a fallen tree or huge boulder. Don't ditch (dig a rain trench around your tent) unless you own the land. Most tents have sewn-in waterproof floors, so there is no need to destroy vegetation with a trench.

■ Care of Tents

Many tents have been in constant use for more than 20 years. Others have been inadvertently destroyed by campers in a matter of days. There is no reason why your tent, often the most expensive item of camping gear you own, cannot live a normal existence if you give it the proper care.

When you buy a tent, it is advisable to condition the canvas by pitching it for several days in the open air and spraying it lightly with your garden hose to get it used to moisture.

A campfire should be kept safely away from your tent as well as downwind from it, as canvas is far from fireproof.

Canvas is vulnerable to mildew—a parasitic growth that develops in dampness. To prevent mildew from forming, your tent should be as dry as possible before you pack it. If you get caught in a heavy shower and must roll up a wet tent, you had better unroll it within three or four hours for a thorough drying. If you have D-rings on the outside of your pack, lash the tent to these rings and let it hang in a loose pike to dry. Occasionally change the tent's position to obtain as complete a drying as possible. Check seams, edges, reinforcements, and sod cloth for dampness, as the entire tent should be dry.

Needless to say, moisture is but one of the adversaries your tent faces. Trees, particularly in late spring, drop blossoms, along with an assortment of leaves, twigs, and sap. All can be damaging to the tent fabric, the waterproofing, and the dyes. Bombardment by birds is another hazard.

For these reasons, your tent should be kept as clean as possible. When you're finished tenting, spread out the material and brush it well on every side, particularly at wrinkles, seams, and the section of the floor by the door, where the most dirt accumulates. When you wash the tent, use soap and water.

Bird droppings shouldn't be allowed to harden, but if you're too late, you can work them loose and brush them off with a stiff brush. If you use a knife to remove droppings or dried pitch from the canvas, be sure the blade is dull and that you don't cut into the fabric. Any discolorations left behind can be removed with lighter fluid, but if the fabric has undergone wax treatment, forget about it. The lighter fluid will remove the foreign matter and the wax as well. The use of brown soap and water is a less effective, but safer, method of treating discolorations.

Poles and stakes should be kept separate from the fabric when packing. Otherwise, you may be in for some damage. Guy ropes, however, can be placed inside the fabric when you're rolling it up, except for one rope. That piece should be used to tie up the completed roll. Rolling is more feasible than folding for your tent, as the latter causes the fibers in the cloth to break.

Never dry a tent on the ground or let it hang outside until sundown. Absorbed moisture could cause mildew to begin. Optimum times to take down the tent are late morning or early afternoon, after the sun has done its work.

After a trip is completed and you're home again, pitch the tent and thoroughly hose it down. Then let it dry overnight, loosely packed.

When possible, try to open the tent frequently to permit the air to circulate through it. This will dry up any moisture. If you store your tent, keep it in a dry, cool area, and keep it loosely rolled to permit maximum circulation of air.

Avoid bumps and pressures against a pitched tent during rain. Such objects can cause slow leaks to spring in the material.

Temporary repairs on your tent can be made with small patches and patching cement. Adhesive tape can mend small tears for a while, but a sewing machine designed for canvas can do the repair work so it will last for the lifetime of the tent.

RECREATIONAL VEHICLES

Recreational vehicles today are designed with America's economy-oriented society in mind, and statistics indicate that an RV owner no longer need be a person with money to burn, though there are models for this type of person, too.

■ Folding Camping Trailers

Folding tent or camp trailers are collapsible tents on wheels that are towed by a car. The trailer usually opens up to form beds with foam mattresses on opposite sides of a camping or living area a foot or more off the ground. Erection of some models has been simplified through hydraulic or electric crank-up systems that work by merely pushing a button.

Tent trailers range in body length from 6 to 26 feet, and the standard width is 6½ or 7 feet. A 17-foot camp trailer, for example, can open up to a campsite length of 26 feet. The lightweights weigh 500 pounds, but the heavyweights may register nearly 3,000 pounds or perhaps more when the load is full. The low price is the big draw for this RV.

Depending on how much you care to spend for a tent trailer, there is a wide array of equipment, both standard and optional. Current styles usually feature huge, screened windows to protect campers from insects; built-in refrigerators and kitchens; plastic tops; screen doors rather than zippered flaps; and wardrobes, toilets, and lighting arrangements. Optional gear on many models includes 12-inch

Tent trailers range in body length from 6 to 26 feet and can weigh from 500 to 2,500 pounds. The rig's low profile when collapsed permits easy towing with complete visibility through the rearview mirror and easy parking.

rather than 8-inch wheels, electric brakes, road covers for added protection, and carrying racks for a boat or canoe. Although camping trailers come equipped with brake lights, directional signals, standard clearance, and leveling jacks (all), use two safety chains rather than one, as this prevents the unit from swaying, or "fishtailing," to a dangerous degree.

It is wise to remember that you'll save money by having the optional equipment put on prior to delivery rather than deciding on it several weeks afterward.

The rig has a low profile, permitting the driver a rear view through his center-mounted mirror that is very similar to what he would see if he were towing no rig at all. This same low profile lends itself to a reduction in wind resistance, simplifying the tasks of the driver.

The fact that the open rig is shaped like a tent is psychologically satisfying to a number of campers, as they can realistically enjoy the outdoor life under canvas, yet be far enough above the ground that crawlers, creepers, and dampness aren't too close for comfort.

The light weight of the unit permits it to follow along rather inconspicuously, and it's simpler to park or back into a tight place than other RVs. Also, it can be used in numerous far-off and unpaved regions where a motor home or travel trailer might not successfully travel. In addition, higher speeds are attainable and the effect on gasoline mileage is slight.

■ Truck Campers

Truck campers fall into three categories. The big seller is the unit that can be installed in and readily removed from the bed of a pickup, leaving the truck free for countless other outdoor chores. The second-most popular is the rig that is permanently installed on the chassis of the truck. The third is a basic roof or shell that clamps onto the truck bed. This unit will suffice if you only need one or two bunks and an area to sit down. The shell is adequate for two campers.

The first model mentioned slides onto the truck when you're ready to use it. (The tailgate is either lowered or completely removed.) Other times, the camper can rest on tripods or jacks. The interior has standing room; a kitchen with a sink, stove, and refrigerator; a dinette that converts to a bed; and space for storing groceries and clothing. The majority of these units also have an extended area over the cab to serve as sleeping quarters by night and storage space by day. The larger rigs may include a shower and toilet. Optionals include

Truck campers can have a unit mounted permanently to the bed of a truck or choose a unit that can be removed from the bed, leaving the truck free for other outdoor chores. A big advantage for pickup campers, especially those with four-wheel-drive trucks, is that they can negotiate roads that a motor home or travel trailer couldn't begin to navigate.

a radio, air conditioning, trailer hitch, step bumper, and auxiliary gas tank. One model even boasts an expanded rear door plus a ramp so that you can ride your ATV or snowmobile right up into the vehicle and tote it with you.

The camper—minus the truck—may weigh from 800 pounds to more than a ton. The length ranges from 6 to 15 feet or more.

The permanently mounted campers are often wider and longer than the other two styles because the bed of the truck is eliminated, and they're also superior in regard to self-containment. The chassis mounts vary between 10 and 18 feet and weigh from 1,500 to 2,700 pounds. The legal maximum width is 8 feet, and these beauties often have that expanse. Formerly, most units were 6 feet wide.

The chassis mounts are said to have better roadability and easier driving over lengthy hauls than the non-permanent campers, but campers as a whole have some advantages over the other RVs.

Since the vehicle is basically a truck—perhaps four-wheel drive—it can negotiate roads that a motor home or a travel trailer couldn't begin to navigate. The non-permanent pickup camper leaves the truck free for numerous other purposes.

If it's pouring outside, you can merely park the vehicle and proceed to prepare supper or simply relax. There are no problems with firewood or tent stakes.

Riding in the camper coach is permissible while on the road, so the cab needn't be overcrowded. An intercom can even be installed to aid communication between the rear and the cab.

Now for the disadvantages:

Whenever you want to travel, you must take the entire camp with you. This necessitates securing gear and putting away all the utensils and dishes.

Highway driving can occasionally be frightening. A gusty headwind or strong crosswinds can turn the rig into a huge sail, making the driver's job a difficult one—power steering or no!

When the time comes to store this vehicle, you might be in for some trouble. Several suburban regions prohibit parking on driveways, necessitating the rental of space or the use of your garage. With the unit measuring from 8½ to 10 feet in height when it is high enough on the jacks to be loaded, or on the pickup itself, you'll probably find that the ceiling of your garage isn't quite high enough. Take this into account before buying.

Travel Trailers

The travel trailer is a permanent living area that features one or more rooms, and is mounted on two or four wheels, depending on its weight and size. Travel trailers range in length from 12 to 35 feet, with the 22-footer apparently the most popular according to sales figures. The array of vehicles is extensive, and there is a comparably wide range of prices. The interiors are usually plywood, while the exteriors are aluminum. Foam insulation resides between the two, and the entire unit sits on a welded chassis of steel.

A 6-footer could stand up easily in the average trailer, as the overall distance from floor to roof is 7 to 8 feet. The unit is rarely less than 7 feet wide, and often closer to the maximum of 8 feet.

With the accent on compact and subcompact automobiles in recent years, the trailer industry has followed the trend and produced a large selection of mini travel trailers.

To be self-contained, a vehicle must be able to supply sewage disposal, water, and power. To do this, it must hold a minimum of 30 gallons of water, a holding tank for waste, and enough bottled gas to take care of the stove, heater, and refrigerator. The average travel trailer is conveniently self-contained, with a sleeping space, heater, toilet, and shower. When it comes to optionals, you can have air conditioning, television, stereo, and even a bathtub. With all of these comforts just behind the towing vehicle, it's easy to see why this RV is so popular.

The travel trailer also holds the upper hand over the pickup camper and the motor home in that you can park it and use the car or truck exclusively. With the other two options, you have to drag your kitchen sink along wherever you go.

But there is less of an area where you can go if you want to take the trailer. It won't negotiate the same roads that a pickup camper will, particularly if the latter is equipped with four-wheel drive. And also on the negative side, unless the trailer can be adjusted to a low silhouette to somewhat resemble a tent trailer, you may have some trouble driving it at first. Sway is a problem, often caused by poor distribution of weight over the axle of the trailer. To prevent it, try to place the bulk of the weight forward of the trailer's wheels. Also, decrease front-tire pressure prior to your trip. It can speed up tire wear, but it may save your life. Use an equalizer hitch if the trailer weighs more than a half ton to shift more weight to the car's front wheels. Power steering seems to be the culprit in many trailer accidents, as the inexperienced driver tends to oversteer once swaying begins.

As mentioned earlier in this section, you would be smart to have the correct options put on your vehicle during assembly. Such items as oversize radiators, extra blade fans, heavy-duty springs and shock absorbers, heavy-duty batteries and alternators, fade-resistant brake linings, etc., will cost you far more to put in after you've had the vehicle for a while.

Conventional travel trailers can range from 17 to 35 feet in length and can be a permanent living area with one or more rooms. The biggest advantage of a travel trailer over a pickup camper and motor home is that you can park it and use the car or truck without dragging the trailer wherever you go.

Fifth-wheel trailers are designed to be hitch mounted to the bed of a pickup truck. Sizes can range from 26 to about 32 feet. The master bedroom is usually located in the overhang over the bed of the truck. Most fifth-wheel trailers require a three-quarter-ton or one-ton pickup truck.

Trailers can be used in winter, but you may want to store your own. If so, remember to do the following: Drain the complete water system, septic holding tank, and the water heater. Also, drain traps or pour alcohol into them. Remove the tires to prevent deterioration. If you want to leave the tires on, jack up the trailer to relieve the tires of weight. Also take the hubcaps off, as they tend to rust quickly. When snow accumulates to more than a few inches on the trailer roof, clear it off—but not with a shovel. A broom will do.

Fifth-Wheel Trailers

Fifth-wheel trailers—often just called fifth-wheelers—are the newest type of RV. The fifth wheel is the hitch, a modification of the fifth-wheel hitch used on tractor-trailer rigs. It goes over the axle of a pickup truck and is bolted to the frame, not just to the floor of the truck bed. The trailer itself has a cutout so that it can hang over the pickup's bed by about 7 feet, reducing the combined length of towing vehicle and trailer. A 29-foot fifth-wheeler, for example, extends only about 22 feet from the rear of the truck when it's hitched.

This design has several purposes. Most obviously, it provides extra interior trailer space in proportion to the rig's overall length. The objective is spacious luxury. The type of hitch also reduces the trailer sway, helps protect against jackknifing, and makes for an extremely secure, safe coupling. In addition, hitching is easier. A big king-pin hangs down and couples to the hitch in the pickup bed. As you back the truck toward the kingpin, you can see it clearly, and this makes the connection easier than positioning a conventional coupler over a ball.

Fifth-wheelers come in a variety of lengths, from compact 18-footers to models as long as 35 feet. Most are in the 26- to 32-foot range. Some of the smaller ones can be towed by a half-ton pickup, but most need a three-quarter-ton or one-ton pickup truck.

Although the construction techniques are pretty much the same as for travel trailers, the insulation tends to be better, the appliances bigger. Many fifth-wheelers are more like motor homes than travel trailers. The master bedroom, built into the overhang, may be big enough for a large double bed or twin beds. Some models have sliding glass patio doors and very spacious, open-looking interiors. And some have "tip-out" alcoves that crank out when parked at a campsite. Small couches or lounges fit to make the main floor less cluttered. Depending on size and interior features, fifth-wheelers sleep from four to eight persons. Like motor homes, they are, of course, expensive.

Motor Homes

The motor home is a self-contained home on wheels, and the driver sits near facilities for dining, cooking, sleeping, sanitation, water supply, and usually air conditioning.

One manufacturer's standard equipment includes wall-to-wall foam-padded nylon carpet, storage drawers, a four-burner stove with an automatic oven, a

The motor home is literally a self-contained drivable home on wheels featuring facilities for dining, cooking, sleeping, sanitation, water supply, and air conditioning. Models can be up to 40 feet, but the most popular sizes are 20 to 24 feet. Parking, depending on size, can sometimes be a problem.

dinette that converts into a bed, tinted windows, two skylight roof vents, a fire extinguisher, a bedroom privacy curtain, four adjustable defroster vents, and many other worthwhile items. Optionals are quite numerous in many models. For the extra cost, you can include a home theater sound system, high-definition television, satellite system, trailer hitch, dash-mounted water-tank gauge, wraparound windshield curtains, headrests and armrests for driver and copilot, and many other conveniences to make for a safer and more enjoyable excursion in your motor home.

The rigs measure from 17 to 42 feet in length. The interior of most units is plywood with the outside constructed of molded fiberglass or aluminum. The counter and tabletops are made of material that can readily withstand any punishment.

Owing to the vehicle's enormous size and its overhang, you must travel on good roads. Parking also may be a problem, but this is not true in all cases. That same overhang, though, can come in very handy when you're launching a boat. And motor homes are excellent vehicles to tow such craft behind.

One drawback of the motor home is its shoebox shape, but some new models are being aerodynamically designed to cut down on the hazards of wind.

If you store your motor home during the winter, remove water from every pipe in the system and leave valves in the open position. Also make certain that water is drained from the toilet and toilet holding tank, and follow this up with a thorough cleansing and deodorizing. LP gas-tank valves should be closed securely, as well as all windows and roof vents. The refrigerator should also be cleaned and emptied, and the door left open. Take out all food from the vehicle, as well as such items as fishing tackle, which may leave undesirable odors. Give the vehicle a walk-through check on occasion, airing it out when possible. As tires are usually left fully inflated on the motor home, move the unit a couple of feet each week or so to avoid continuous stress on one section of the tire due to the total weight of the home being on it and the three to five other tires. Otherwise, jack up each wheel on occasion and slightly rotate it.

Van Conversions

Van conversions, also called van campers, have become extremely popular. One reason is that some models cost little more than a full-size station wagon. Another is that they're easier to handle and park than some of the bigger camping rigs, and they can be used for everyday purposes around home, like an ordinary van or station wagon. Thus, they combine the advantages of a super station wagon and "pocket" motor home. Many models provide not only sleeping bunks, but also a galley and even a shower and toilet, making them completely self-contained camping rigs.

The RV manufacturers convert all the standard van models—Chevrolet, Dodge, Ford, and GMC—using vans with both short and long wheelbases. Some RV companies stretch the width or length to provide jumbo interiors.

You can't stand up inside a standard van, so headroom is an important part of conversion. Most often, the roof is cut off and a raised fiberglass structure is substituted, resulting in more than 6 feet of interior height. However, the added frontal area can cause extra drag, and the increased height may make the vehicle slightly more susceptible to wind sway. Another approach is to increase headroom only in the galley area by building a dropped floor well. The disadvantage here is that you can stand straight only in that area—when preparing meals. Also, the floor well reduces ground clearance, which can be important on rough roads. A third way is to install an expandable top that lies almost flat (adding only about 4 inches to the van's height while driving) and can be popped up when parked to provide headroom.

A typical interior might have a dinette that can be turned into a double bunk, plus another double bunk over the driver's cockpit. The galley generally contains a sink, range, and refrigerator or cooler. Models with a lavatory contain a chemical toilet, wash basin, and shower.

This van camper from Classic Vans is a typical conversion van that offers most of the benefits of a motor home, but is easier to handle and park. Van campers can also be used as a second car for everyday chores. Interiors can include bunks, a galley, and even a shower and toilet.

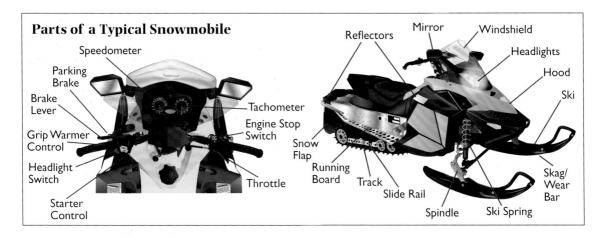

Parts of a Typical Snowmobile

Speedometer

Parking Brake

Brake Lever

Grip Warmer Control

Headlight Switch

Starter Control

Tachometer

Engine Stop Switch

Throttle

Snow Flap

Running Board

Track

Slide Rail

Spindle

Reflectors

Mirror

Windshield

Headlights

Hood

Ski

Skag/ Wear Bar

Ski Spring

■ Snowmobiles

The snowmobile is the only vehicle available for traveling in remote, snow-covered regions. It's steered by ski-type runners up front and is propelled by a continuously running belt or track below the vehicle that grips the surface of the snow and sends the sled flying over it.

Low-priced models are compacts with engines averaging 225 cubic centimeters, but the big ones are known in the snowmobiler's lingo as "class 5 modifieds." The latter is one of the largest on the market, featuring a 350-pound toboggan with an 85-horsepower, 800-cubic-centimeter engine. These machines hit 90 miles per hour and beyond with little effort.

The track on the typical snowmobile measures 15 inches in width, and permits you to steer the vehicle by shifting your weight. Tracks, however, sometimes reach 30½ inches.

Snowmobiles can get into many areas where a car or an RV wouldn't stand a chance. Before the age of the snowmobile, conservation officers had to don their snowshoes. In times of accident or disaster in snowbound areas, help can get there quickly with a snowmobile to provide rapid medical assistance and transportation to a hospital. For the outdoors enthusiast, the snowmobile offers enjoyment. He can go hunting, ice fishing, racing, or skijoring (skiing behind a snowmobile) with the rig.

Unfortunately, some people chase deer and other game animals with their snowmobiles. This practice, of course, is against the law.

Though a few snowmobiles on the market feature reverse transmission on an optional basis, most do not have standard reverse, making them somewhat dangerous. Accidents such as fatal or maiming collisions with automobiles, trains, pipes, fences, and the like also show the hazards of driving the vehicle.

Other disadvantages include its heavy weight, its often low, cramped size, and narrow cleats that often don't adhere to the ice and snow.

The heavier snowmobiles cannot negotiate all types of snow, but there are relatively new, lightweight models designed for better flotation on soft snow. Be careful with a heavier one, which may bog down. Also, be sure to wear appropriate clothing for safety and warmth. Insulated snowmobile suits are recommended, as are helmets, goggles, and face masks. Some of the snowmobiles themselves have built-in safety features, such as padded handlebars and breakaway windshields—excellent improvements.

In addition, the noise has been substantially reduced in recent years. Machines built since June 30, 1976, and certified by the Snowmobile Safety and Certification Committee of the International Snowmobile Manufacturers Association, emit no more than 73 decibels at 50 feet when traveling at 15 miles per hour, and similarly certified machines produced since February 1, 1975, emit no more than 78 decibels at 50 feet when traveling at full throttle. By comparison, snowmobiles built before 1969 produced 102 decibels.

Snowmobiling has become more than a mechanized means of traveling over snow; it has become a sport (and almost a way of life in some regions). Trail systems have been developed in forest lands to accommodate snowmobilers without interfering with skiers or other winter-sports enthusiasts. Regulations have been established by states—and in some cases by the snowmobil-

Depending on snow conditions, here are the recommended riding positions for snowmobilers.

Kneeling

Posting

Sitting

Standing

Obviously, the snowmobile season is rather short. Therefore, correct storage of your vehicle is essential. Store it in a dry place, and block it off the ground to take the weight off the skis and track. Loosen the track tensioner. Drain the fuel tank and pour a quart of SAE 30 oil into the oil tank. Then, roll the machine from side to side so the fuel-tank walls are well lubricated. Drain the carburetor. Take out the spark plug and pour a tablespoon of SAE 30 through the spark-plug hole. Turn the engine over four times by pulling the starter rope. Then, replace the spark plug. Clean the outside of the engine and spread a thin film of oil over any of its exposed surfaces that could corrode.

▓ All-Terrain Vehicles

The snowmobile's counterparts are the two- and four-wheel-drive all-terrain vehicles (ATVs)—tough, knobby-tired vehicles designed to take sportsmen nearly everywhere off-road. Used properly, an ATV can safely take you into remote areas to hunt, fish, and camp.

If you are a farmer, guide, or outfitter, an ATV can haul people and a trailer full of gear into a backcountry camp. It can also get downed game back to your cabin or rescue a lost hunter or hiker.

ATVs are available in a variety of sizes with options ranging from front-load racks to rear cargo boxes and rifle scabbards. Most ATVs will carry loads up to 100 pounds on a front rack and up to 250 pounds on a rear-load carrier and will tow 1,000 pounds or more.

The Kawasaki Bruce Force 750 is typical of ATVs built for sportsmen who want to get into the backcountry. Powered by a liquid-cooled, four-stroke engine, the ATV has a 10-foot turning radius, weighs 695 pounds, and will carry up to 242 pounds on the front and rear racks.

ers themselves—to promote safety. Some trails have stop signs, yield signs, and even information kiosks at strategic locations. Perhaps the most important improvements have come from the snowmobiling clubs, which have promoted responsible snowmobiling—not only in terms of safety, but also in terms of concern for wild animals and forest vegetation. When carried on in such a responsible manner, the sport is harmless to wildlife.

Built for several sportsmen traveling to remote grounds, the Kawasaki Mule 4010 can seat four people and their gear. The ATV can carry a payload from 400 pounds with four passengers to 800 pounds with two passengers. Selectable four-wheel drive to two-wheel drive gives the driver traction options.

Many are two-wheel drives with a button to engage the four-wheel drive. An ATV can weigh from 400 to 800 pounds, depending on its power and utility. A typical sportsman's model will have a four-stroke, liquid-cooled 500 engine, a DC outlet, disc brakes, and full steel skid plates to protect the bottom.

As with snowmobiles, ATVs sometimes suffer from a bad reputation because of the reckless antics of a few. ATVs, improperly used, can damage the environment by tearing up wet trails and by being ridden across streambeds and creeks. ATVs should also avoid livestock and wild game. Stressing game animals by driving too close can seriously sap their energy reserves when they may need it the most.

Ideally, ATV operators should not be under 18 years old. ATVs should be ridden only on designated roads and trails, and operators should wear helmets and hemmed and protective clothing. And, above all, operators should resist the urge to pioneer a new road or trail with an ATV.

CAMP BEDDING

▓ Sleeping Bag Insulation

The warmest and lightest insulation used in today's sleeping bags is down, the breast feathers of a goose or a duck. Besides being quite soft and warm, down holds the heat generated by the body. It does not, fortunately, hold body moisture. This throwing-off process is known as "breathing," and prevents the bag from becoming uncomfortably clammy.

"Loft"—the height of a sleeping bag when fully fluffed and unrolled—is a good indication of the bag's insulating ability. A couple of synthetic fillers, Polarguard and Hollofil, exhibit good loft and offer about two-thirds as much insulating efficiency as down per pound. Quallofil, a DuPont synthetic, has excellent loft, comes close to down in its insulating efficiency (and far surpasses down under wet conditions), and is almost as compactable as the finest goose feathers. There are 3-pound mummy-type sleeping bags with Quallofil insulation that have a temperature rating down to 5°F below zero. For certain purposes—canoe or boat camping, wet-weather camping, or camping from spring through fall, when the temperature isn't extremely cold—the synthetics have several advantages over down.

For one thing, down becomes almost useless as an insulator when it gets wet, and it dries slowly. Polyester provides warmth even when wet, and it dries quickly. For another thing, down tends to shift around in a bag, making lumps and thin, cold spots unless extensive sewing "quilts" it in place. Polarguard is batting-like and so doesn't shift and needs little quilting. Hollofil needs almost as much quilting as down, while Quallofil seems to need a bit less. Finally, the synthetics cost less, primarily because the raw materials are cheaper than down.

Even some of the polyester-and-acrylic combination fillers provide some warmth when wet, assuming that outside temperatures aren't extremely cold. And, like down, the newer polyesters retain body heat while allowing body moisture to escape and evaporate. Some synthetic-filled bags are more compressible than down—in spite of their good loft when fluffed out—and this can be another advantage when gear space is limited.

Other filler materials include wool, cotton (poplin), kapok, and Dacron. Except for Dacron, these insulators mat easily and aren't very resilient. Yet they may suffice in relatively thin, warm-weather bags, and such bags are relatively inexpensive.

The label or packaging of a good sleeping bag usually states the weight of the filler and the temperature range or minimum temperature at which the bag will keep you comfortable. Of course, with a bag that doesn't provide much insulation, you can wear extra sleeping clothes to add 20°F to 30°F effectiveness to the bag. But it pays to buy a bag of good quality—both for warmth and durability—and to compare weights and comfort ranges before deciding which one to buy. About 3 pounds of one synthetic filler, for example, may keep you comfortable when the temperature dips to 30°F, while you'll need only about 2 pounds of down at that temperature. Consider the kind of camping you'll be doing and the price you can afford—and then shop aggressively.

Styles

Sleeping bags come in two basic configurations—the rectangular bag and the mummy bag. A variation, designed for recreational vehicles, is called the station-wagon bag, but this is simply an oversize rectangular bag. The rectangular type is basically a three-season bag, but it is available in grades from summer weight to heavy winter weight. The mummy bag is intended primarily for cold weather and backpacking; it fits more closely and cinches tight around the head and shoulders, impeding exchange of inside and outside air.

Except for a few huge station-wagon bags, the rectangular style is usually offered in a choice of sizes. The youth size often measures about 26 inches by 66 inches. Most common is the adult or full size, which is 33 inches by 75 inches. The third size is king size, which usually measures 39 inches by 79 inches. Some companies also offer a tall size for people taller than 6 feet.

Two sleeping bags may be paired together by opening and completely unzipping both. One should be placed atop the other so that the bottoms of both zippers meet. Then, simply connect each zipper at the point where the two meet. Double bags when used by two persons tend to be warmer than they are when used individually.

A junior bag is a waste of money; get an adult bag for your youngster as, with proper care, it will last him for several years.

Rectangular bags in general are fine for car, canoe, and recreational-vehicle camping. But if you're backpacking, you'll probably have to put your faith in the mummy bag. You won't be making the wrong move, though.

As mentioned, weight is an important consider-

Sleeping Bag Styles

A typical mummy bag for extreme cold is the Ascend Mummy Sleeping Bag rated for 40°F below zero. It has a double-layered quilt construction with four-chamber, hollow insulation, a polyester ripstop shell, and a poly-taffeta lining. The Ascend also has a chest baffle, hood, and a compression stuff sack. The weight is about 6 pounds.

The Bass Pro Rectangular Sleeping Bag, rated for zero degrees to 20°F below zero, is designed for big campers and hunters. The bag measures 40 inches by 94 inches. If you are looking for roomy comfort in a hunting camp, a bag of this size would be a good choice. At weights of 8 or 9 pounds, depending on ratings, this bag is too heavy for backpacking.

The L.L. Bean Adventure 20/40 Sleeping Bag is designed for multiseason camping. Sleep with the 40-degree side up for warmer nights. If it cools off, flip it over to the 20-degree side. It's filled with Climashield synthetic insulation with overlapping baffles to eliminate cold spots. It is a good, versatile choice except in extremely cold temperatures.

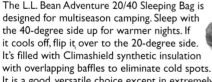
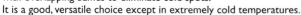

ation to the backpacker, and the mummy bag is designed with this in mind. It is widest at the shoulders—usually 33 inches—and tapers to about 19 inches at the feet. This tapering makes the bag fit like a robe, and that means additional warmth. Some mummy bags can keep the sleeper comfortable at zero degrees and weigh only 3 or 4 pounds, half the weight of comparably warm rectangular bags. Mummy bags are usually filled with down and have nylon covers.

Another valuable item for the backpacker is the stuff bag, into which he actually stuffs his sleeping bag. This method of storage saves wear on the bag through compression fatigue, and helps to fluff it up when you're extracting it for use. Stuff bags usually are waterproof.

Liners

Although a majority of sleeping bags on the market have an inner lining made of flannel, it is worthwhile to purchase an additional flannel or silk liner. If you can carry the extra weight, an extra liner helps to regulate warmth during the night. Should it be warm when you fall asleep, you can take out the lining completely or use it folded underneath as a mattress pad. If the temperature drops substantially later on, the liner can be readily shifted so that you sleep between the layers or under both of them. This separate liner will stop drafts where the sleeper's head protrudes and will provide further insulation near the areas of the zipper or snap fasteners, where cold air may enter.

By purchasing a variety of liners, you can adjust your sleeping bag for practically any weather. That's the reason why a four-season camper usually relies on liners.

An advantage of the removable liner is that cleaning will be no problem, and the bag itself will remain unsoiled within. Tie tabs on your sleeping bag are good for quickly attaching or removing such liners.

Liners are also made of synthetics and fleece. One manufacturer claims that a 3-pound liner consisting of 2 pounds of polyester fibers will add approximately 20 degrees to the minimum comfort range.

Shells for Sleeping Bags

It is important that sleeping bags breathe, letting body moisture escape. Otherwise, you wind up with a sauna effect.

Beware of any bag—especially a cheap one—advertised as waterproof. Such shells may be coated so they won't allow body vapors to pass through. On the other hand, some excellent waterproof shells, such as those made of a nylon and Gore-Tex laminate, do breathe while being impermeable to rain.

Economical station-wagon bags often have an inner shell of cotton flannel and an outer shell of heavy cotton. These bags are practical for warm-weather car camping or for use in a recreational vehicle. But since they are heavy, bulky, and highly moisture-absorbent in relation to the warmth they provide, they are not suitable for backpacking or canoe camping.

Better bags filled with down or polyester usually have inner and outer shells made of nylon in ripstop or taffeta weaves. Both fabrics breathe. They also feel good next to the skin, wear well, resist mildew and fading, and are unaffected by machine washing.

There are also bivouac covers, which serve as minitents but drape over you and your sleeping bag like a sock—complete with mosquito netting. These covers normally have an airtight and waterproof underside and a waterproof (though breathable) topside made of materials such as Gore-Tex. Larger bivouac covers can house a couple of sleepers and their gear. Though more restrictive than tents, these covers are lighter and so get the nod from weight-conscious backpackers.

Zippers

Zippers on mummy bags typically run three-quarter length or full length down one side. A rectangular sleeping bag should be equipped with a heavy-duty zipper that runs completely down one side and across the bottom. This type of zipper permits you to open the bag completely for a thorough airing, and lets you zip together two matching sleeping bags. Two bags zipped together will accommodate two adults or up to four youngsters.

For both mummy and rectangular bags, zippers should have slides at both ends that allow you to ventilate the head and foot ends independently. Both slides should have finger tabs inside and out.

Zippers themselves may be made of metal, nylon, or other synthetics. Metal tends to feel colder in cold weather, work harder in all weather, and frost up in winter. A sleeping-bag zipper should be large, whether it be of the conventional ladder design of most metal zippers or of the toothed-interlock or continuous-coil designs used for synthetic zippers. Large zippers don't catch and abrade shell fabrics as readily as smaller, toothed zippers do—especially smaller metal-toothed zippers. Of all zippers, the continuous coil is easiest on fabric.

Most sleeping bags have a baffle panel—weather stripping made of insulated material to prevent air from traveling through the zipper. This strip lies along the inner surface of the zipper, and, in better bags, may be from 1 to 1½ inches thick and from 3 to 4 inches wide. A cheaply made bag, needless to say, would have little or no weather stripping or a short (30- to 36-inch) zipper that may tend to drag when the bag is closed or opened.

Dry-Cleaned Bags

Proper airing of the sleeping bag is important, particularly when it has been dry-cleaned. An oft-told tale that bears repeating now deals with a teenager who slept in a bag that had only recently been dry-cleaned and then left for one and a half days in a car trunk. The boy's parents found him in a coma after the first night. Eleven days later, he was dead. The hospital reports said the cause of death was due to the inhaling of perchloroethylene fumes that had been trapped within the insulation. The solvents used in dry-cleaning may leave behind long-lasting lethal fumes. A thorough airing is a must.

Air Mattresses

An air mattress is not essential for sleeping in the outdoors, but it does add comfort. Most are made of nylon, which is lightweight enough for backpacking.

The chief drawback is that an air mattress can be used only at temperatures of about 45°F and higher unless you lay some insulation over the mattress. Otherwise, cold air in the mattress will convect body heat away. Another disadvantage is that air mattresses are subject to punctures as well as leakage from seams and valves, so a special patching kit should always accompany you on your travels.

Catalog listings of air mattresses often give both the deflated size and the inflated size. The latter is the one you should pay attention to, as that is what you will be sleeping on.

The average adult can be comfortably accommodated on a mattress measuring between 70 and 74 inches. A 6-footer would require the longest standard length—75 inches. A stout camper might need 32 inches of mattress across his back, but most people can fit comfortably on 28- to 30-inchers with adequate elbow room.

There are two designs of air mattress—the I-beam style and the tufted. The I-beam typically consists of five tubes that resemble steel construction beams when

Air mattresses can range from poor to excellent in durability. For sheer comfort, this Aerobed features a built-in pillow and an internal pump powered by four D batteries. At the other end of the range, there are some models that have an I-beam or waffle design, which may not be as comfortable but are less expensive.

viewed from one end. The tufted design is waffle-like in appearance, and provides the sleeper with full support. It's more comfortable than the I-beam style, but is the more expensive of the two. When buying an air mattress, either I-beam or tufted, choose one with a metal valve, never the rubber or plastic type. The metal valves have screw tops.

If you sleep with a pillow, there's no need for you to do without one outdoors. Many sleeping bags come with built-in air pillows, or else the pillows—either filled with down, synthetic fibers, or air—can be bought separately.

There are many air mattresses made solely of plastic or rubber. Avoid them. Although plastic or rubber air mattresses are lighter than the recommended fabric-rubber combinations, they are delicate and tear easily.

There are four ways to inflate an air mattress: a hand pump, a foot pump, a 12-volt or 120-volt pump, or your own lungs. You also have the option of choosing a self-inflating mattress. If yours doesn't inflate itself, using your own lung power isn't very difficult, but the resulting moist vapor can condense and freeze in cold weather. A hand pump adds weight to your gear. Lightweight plastic foot pumps are popular; although they are bulky, they provide dry air quickly.

When you inflate an air mattress, keep it out of the sun. Otherwise, the heat will cause the air to expand, possibly breaking the mattress. Also, never use a gas-station air-pressure pump to inflate a mattress.

To deflate an air mattress, unscrew the metal cap, leaving the valve completely open. Then, put a heavy object on the mattress to force air to escape more quickly. The last step is to slowly roll the mattress, beginning with the end opposite the valve, until all the air has been expelled.

When not in use, an air mattress should be blown up slightly and kept away from heat. Use it only for sleeping; it is not meant to be a surfboard. If the mattress does get wet, though, stand it up in an airy, shady place.

■ Foam Pads

Sleeping pads are of two basic types: hard, closed-cell foams and soft, open-cell foams. The hard pads contain sealed bubbles that resist compression. The soft pads contain bubbles and a network of passages that allow air to escape when compressed.

Hard-foam pads are sold in thicknesses ranging from ⅜ inch to 1 inch and provide almost as much insulating loft as the pad's thickness. Soft-foam or open-celled pads must be purchased four to five times as thick (usually 3½ inches) as hard foams to provide as much insulating loft when compressed under your body. Though more comfortable, soft-foam pads are bulkier to carry, and they absorb ground and body moisture, adding inconvenience and weight.

Both hard- and soft-foam pads can be purchased in various lengths and widths. To capitalize on the advantages of each type of pad, some manufacturers laminate them together. Here, the top layer is soft foam for comfort, and the bottom layer is hard foam for insulation and watertightness. Or you may see a soft-foam pad enclosed in a fabric cover. Better covers have a cotton upper surface so that body moisture won't be trapped on top, and a lower surface of waterproof nylon.

Tough, young backpackers use hard foams almost exclusively. But age and desire for comfort usually lead even the toughest backpackers to combine the use of hard foam with either soft foam or an air mattress.

■ Canvas Cots

A cot can waste floor space if you have a sloping wall tent. Also, it's quite a task to set up alone. Canvas cots also tend to let cold air circulate beneath them, but some 6-inch-high models come equipped with down or Dacron batting. This insulation isn't compressed by the camper's weight while he sleeps, so it remains at peak efficiency.

On the other hand, cots are comfortable, if weight and bulk are unimportant. If you decide on a canvas cot, get a model that is about 12 or 14 inches off the ground so it can double as a tent seat.

FOOTGEAR

■ Leather Boots

The sturdiest boots are those constructed totally of leather, the best all-around material for four-season wear. Leather boots permit the feet to "breathe," giving off moisture that would otherwise tend to make the camper's feet hot and uncomfortable and cause blisters. Some manufacturers have treated boots with waterproofing compounds, but leather so treated seals in body heat and moisture.

The proper height for a boot is about 8 inches. A higher boot may constrict your leg muscles as well as restrict free circulation. Also, high boots are hot and heavy in summertime. The boot should also be uninsulated, for reasons to be discussed shortly.

Avoid boots with leather soles and heels; they are not very water resistant. Leather soles wear quickly and slip on smooth rocks, pine needles, dry grass, and the like. Get boots with soles and heels of rubber or one of the tough synthetics. Rubber soles provide a good grip, and are flexible, long lasting, and tough.

Many campers like boots with a platform, or straight-bottom, sole that has no heel. These soles are not recommended for mountain climbing. A heel permits you to hold back when you're descending a slope. Cleat-like treads (Vibram) are good if you hike on rocky trails.

Be certain that the tops of the boots are made of soft leather so that enough insulation is provided. The air space between the sock and the boot and the area around your foot should permit free, comfortable movement. In winter, a boot should keep cold air out and warm air in; that air space, if sufficient, will help achieve this dual purpose. The toe and heel should be hard to give your feet the protection they need.

Some styles of leather boots are insulated. If the temperature is below freezing, and dry, such boots may be suitable for casual walking. But for all-around use, they are a poor choice. They become stuffy, heavy, and hot during strenuous activity, and when wet take a long time to dry. In cold weather, you are better off with plain leather boots and several pairs of socks of varied weights, which you can change if a pair becomes wet.

Before you try out your new boots on a hike, a thorough breaking in is in order. That's why shoe grease should be applied, but not to any particular excess. Otherwise, your boots will become overly soft and all but worthless. Also, try short hikes at regular intervals with the new boots so that your feet will get accustomed to them. Bend your feet frequently to make each boot more pliable. Old-timers used to break in their boots by standing in a bucket of water until the boots were saturated, and then walking around in them until they were dry. Fortunately, this is no longer necessary.

Through proper care, you can add substantial life to your boots. When you're finished for the day and your boots are coated with mud, wash them off thoroughly. Then, fill them with wads of newspaper and place them in a warm, dry area (not above 100°F). When they're dry, rub some shoe grease into the leather to soften and waterproof it.

Another simple way to waterproof leather boots is to treat them with paraffin or a silicone-dressing spray. The method of waterproofing preferred by some outdoors enthusiasts is to use neat's-foot oil. (Keep the oil off rubber heels and soles, as it may prove harmful to them.) Prior to application, wash the leather with warm water and mild soap. The purpose of this measure is to open the leather's pores for better absorption of the oil. Be sure the leather is still wet when you rub on the oil. A handy applicator is an old toothbrush, as its bristles help get the oil deep into the seams.

For securing the boot to the foot, rawhide laces and eyelets have proved the best, with nylon strings running a close second. Some hikers prefer the quicker hooks, but they are not quite as reliable as laces. And if you get a cheap set of hooks, they'll break, rust, or bend in no time. Also, hooks often catch on twigs.

Rubber and Leather Boots

Though the all-leather boot is the best all-around boot for hiking, for wet weather many people prefer shoepacs. These boots have a leather top and a rubber bottom and are the perfect choice for hiking in rain, swamplands, and wet snow. The classic Bean Boot by L.L. Bean is a good example of a shoepac. The leather tops shed moisture well if they're properly oiled or greased, and are flexible. As these tops aren't as airtight as they would be if they were of rubber composition, they provide good ankle support and a wide, roomy area for the foot. This air space lets you wear two pairs of socks—woolen over thermal—to withstand the cold down to zero degrees. The rubber bot-

toms of shoepacs perform the all-important function of keeping the feet dry.

As noted, shoepacs are designed for the wet-weather enthusiast. That's why the neat's-foot oil treatment described earlier should be used to waterproof the boots. But be careful not to harm the rubber bottoms when applying the oil.

Manufacturers have developed shoepacs up to 18 inches in height, but a model from 8 to 12 inches should prove adequate. The extra inches will just hinder the circulation in your leg, and will add extra lacing and unlacing time to your chores outdoors.

Rubber Boots (Uninsulated)

The camper who fishes on his outings often finds himself pushing boats off beaches, and sloshing in water in his small craft. The top choice in footgear for this person is the uninsulated rubber boot.

The optimum choice is a boot about 12 or 13 inches high with no more than three eyelets at the top. The remainder of the boot is totally enclosed, protecting the feet from water.

In extreme cold, two pairs of socks—heavy woolen ones over thermal or athletic-type socks—are warmer than a single pair of heavy socks, and keep your feet dry and comfortable for quite a while.

When you shop for footgear, take along two pairs of socks to ensure that you're getting the proper size. You're better off learning about a too-snug fit in the store than when your feet begin to hurt on a cold day outside.

Composition Boots

The best news in outdoor footwear is the constant improvement in boots that combine developments in modern technology, such as tough Cordura nylon and the waterproofing properties of Gore-Tex, a microporous membrane. The most popular boot of this type has a lug sole with a leather toe and heel. The rest of the boot, however, is made of light Cordura nylon. The entire boot is lined with Gore-Tex, which makes it virtually waterproof. The resulting boot is frequently half the weight of a full leather boot. It requires very little breaking in because the nylon sides mold more quickly to the foot than new leather. And the wearer can literally stand in water without getting wet.

For warm weather or early fall hunting and hiking, these boots are an excellent choice. If you expect to

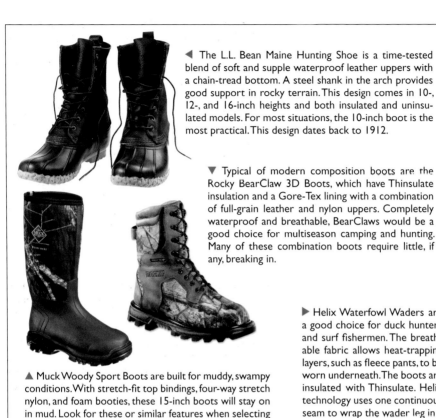

◄ The L.L. Bean Maine Hunting Shoe is a time-tested blend of soft and supple waterproof leather uppers with a chain-tread bottom. A steel shank in the arch provides good support in rocky terrain. This design comes in 10-, 12-, and 16-inch heights and both insulated and uninsulated models. For most situations, the 10-inch boot is the most practical. This design dates back to 1912.

▼ Typical of modern composition boots are the Rocky BearClaw 3D Boots, which have Thinsulate insulation and a Gore-Tex lining with a combination of full-grain leather and nylon uppers. Completely waterproof and breathable, BearClaws would be a good choice for multiseason camping and hunting. Many of these combination boots require little, if any, breaking in.

▲ Muck Woody Sport Boots are built for muddy, swampy conditions. With stretch-fit top bindings, four-way stretch nylon, and foam booties, these 15-inch boots will stay on in mud. Look for these or similar features when selecting a boot for hunting in swampy woods.

► Helix Waterfowl Waders are a good choice for duck hunters and surf fishermen. The breathable fabric allows heat-trapping layers, such as fleece pants, to be worn underneath. The boots are insulated with Thinsulate. Helix technology uses one continuous seam to wrap the wader leg in a spiral or helix pattern.

encounter colder temperatures, the same composition boots are also available insulated. Modern synthetic insulating materials such as Thinsulate and Insolite make them warmer per ounce of boot weight than any older type of insulation, yet they seem to "wick" away moisture. With proper socks, therefore, they don't tend to hold perspiration and make your feet uncomfortably clammy.

■ Rubber Boots (Insulated)

Insulated rubber boots are a good choice for ice fishing or sitting on a deer stand for lengthy periods—both of which are done in bone-chilling temperatures. These boots are much too heavy for conventional hiking, and even a lengthy walk will cause your feet to become clammy and sweaty.

Another disadvantage is that if you should snag the outside layer, water may seep into the insulated lin-

ing. The proper procedure at that point is to squeeze out the moisture toward the area of the punctures until it is completely outside. Then, prop open the tear with a twig or toothpick to let the insulation air out. Wait until all the moisture is removed before repairing the tear with a rubber-tube patch.

Many campers wear boot liners inside waterproof boots. These add to the warmth and reduce clamminess. Most liners have an outer layer of cotton tricot to act as a blotter and an inner layer of insulating, moisture-resistant acrylic fiber. For a comfortable fit with liners, you may need slightly larger boots than you'd otherwise wear. When buying new boots, therefore, it's best to try them on over the liners.

A final word on the insulated rubber boot: As mentioned, it can become clammy inside. By merely sprinkling talcum in the boot at night, you'll find that the clamminess will disappear, and your feet will slide in easier and not bunch up your socks uncomfortably.

Leather Boots (Insulated)

Though not quite as waterproof as the insulated rubber boot, the insulated leather boot has some virtues. It generally gives a more comfortable fit and provides better ankle support.

You can't remove the insulation for cleaning and drying, and you can't adjust the boot to rising temperatures. Thus, the boots tend to become hot, stuffy, and heavy in warmer weather.

Most insulated leather boots are quite waterproof, but in wet weather over an extended period some moisture will seep inside. To further waterproof your boots, try silicone-dressing sprays, paraffin, or the neat's-foot oil method described earlier.

Hipboots and Waders

Duck hunters and fishermen find themselves up to their knees—and often higher—in water. Hipboots or waders are an essential part of their equipment.

When the water is no more than knee-deep and a substantial amount of walking is required, hipboots will suffice. For the fisherman or marshland hunter, the uninsulated hipboot is best. It features the standard, heavy-rubber foot that is welded to a top of strong fabric—usually a laminated nylon-rubber-nylon sandwich—with a thin inner bond of waterproof rubber. Although some models are manufactured with uppers of rubber-coated fabric, the welded ones are recommended. Though the price is just a bit higher, they're more flexible and far lighter.

The winter steelheader, fall surf fisherman, or duck hunter will find the insulated hipboot to be the best buy.

The weather is usually bitter, and the core of insulation built into the shoe and ankle of the hipboot will keep him warm.

If you are a stream fisherman who wades on slick rocks, felt-soled hipboots are required. They provide sure-footed, quiet movement. The soles wear quickly, but can be replaced with special felt-sole kits available in sporting-goods stores. These kits also can be used to apply felt soles to rubber-soled boots.

Waders are simply hipboots with waterproof tops that extend to the waist, or even to the chest. Some have stocking feet of thin rubber or a rubberized fabric, over which wading shoes are worn. Others have boot feet with waterproof uppers. The boot-foot style is simpler to put on, carry, and store; it is also less apt to develop leaks.

Snowshoes

When snow depths reach a foot or more, conventional boots are rendered virtually ineffectual. At such times, snowshoes must be worn on outdoor treks. The purpose of the snowshoe is to distribute the weight of the body over a greater surface of snow than the shoe sole alone, thereby increasing support.

Snowshoes come in three basic styles—the Alaskan, the Michigan, and the bearpaw—plus several modifications of each of these styles.

The Alaskan is also known as the Yukon, pickerel, trial, or racing snowshoe. It's good for long-distance walking, even with a heavy load. Long and narrow, it has a conspicuous upward curl at the toe and a tail at the rear—a design suited to open country and powder snow with little timber or brush.

The "classic" style, the one that conforms to most

Snowshoes

Left: For relatively open country with just traces of brush or timber, the Alaskan snowshoe will suffice. **Middle:** In areas of heavy brush, use the Michigan snowshoe. **Right:** When you need to make frequent turns, such as on hills or mountains, your best bet is to strap on a pair of bearpaws.

Types of Snowshoes

Body Weight (pounds)	Michigan	Alaskan	Bearpaw
35 to 50	9 x 30"	——	——
50 to 60	10 x 36"	——	——
60 to 90	11 x 40"	——	——
100 to 125	12 x 42"	——	——
125 to 150	12 x 48"	10 x 48"	——
150 to 175	13 x 48"	10 x 56"	14 x 30"
175 to 200	14 x 48"	12 x 60"	13 x 33"
200 to 250	14 x 52"	——	14 x 36"

pictures, is the Michigan, also known as the Maine or Algonquin snowshoe. It, too, has a tail, but tends to be wider and shorter than the Alaskan, and with less front curl—usually 2 inches or under—making it suitable for brushy country.

The bearpaw has no tail and little (or occasionally no) front curl. Its shape is more or less oval, but the forepart is often slightly wider than the rear. Shorter than the other types, it's good for hilly, brushy terrain, especially where abrupt turns are common. This is believed to be the most ancient of all snowshoe designs.

One modification, sometimes called the Green Mountain snowshoe, is narrower than the usual bearpaw and almost uniform in width. One advantage is that it's easy to learn to walk on and is very maneuverable. Another is that it's compact. Green Mountain snowshoes and more or less similar models are popular with snowmobilers and, indeed, are sometimes called snowmobile snowshoes.

Another variation, known simply as a modified bearpaw, has a short tail, which helps to prevent twisting. Still another, usually called the cross-country snowshoe, is a narrow, slightly elongated bearpaw (like the Green Mountain) with a tail that helps prevent twisting but isn't long enough to snag. Good for relatively even but somewhat brushy terrain, it's essentially a cross between the bearpaw and the Alaskan.

Traditionally, snowshoes are composed of frames made of ash—a tough and flexible wood—and rawhide webbing. The webbing must remain taut to perform properly, and freezing weather does the trick. Thus, keep snowshoes far from the campfire and warm cabins. Moisture can dangerously stretch the webbing. Using spar varnish or polyurethane, you can give your webbing a protective, waterproof coat. Additional wrap-

pings of rawhide near the snowshoe's toe can add to its life. As crusted snow usually affects the toe area first, this precaution should prove useful.

The size of the snowshoe depends on the weight of the snowshoer. The accompanying chart will help you determine the correct size for your boot.

Between seasons, remove and replace all broken, weak, or frayed webbing. Clean the entire snowshoe rapidly with soap and water to prevent any unnecessary stretch. Dry the pair a minimum of 36 hours if some or all of the rawhide has been replaced.

In recent years, several new materials for snowshoe frames have come into use, as have two new kinds of webbing. In addition to fine-grain ash, frames are now made of aluminum, magnesium, or synthetics. Frames of metal or plastic are durable, won't warp, and require no maintenance. On the other hand, wood has more aesthetic appeal, won't usually crack in extreme cold, and doesn't readily cake with heavy snow.

Instead of naked or varnished rawhide webbing, leading snowshoe makers now offer rawhide coated with polyurethane, which has superior moisture resistance. Most modern of all is nylon-coated neoprene lacing, which is very strong, doesn't stretch or absorb water, doesn't attract gnawing animals, and needs no seasonal varnishing or any other maintenance. With use, however, it does become abraded and hairy looking, so a great many snowshoers prefer the tradition of rawhide combined with the protection of polyurethane.

As you may suspect, a device is needed to hold the snowshoe to your boot. The harness is a leather or leather-and-nylon strap arrangement that permits the toe to tilt downward and the heel to rise.

The Pathfinder Showshoes are designed for hikers traveling in all kinds of terrain. Carbon-steel crampons easily bite into snow and ice for solid traction. Duralight material is waterproof and rugged. The anodized aluminum frame is 25 inches long and the snowshoe will handle people weighing 120 to 200 pounds. A 36-inch model is rated up to 300 pounds. The Pathfinder is made exclusively for L.L. Bean.

CAMP CLOTHING

■ Warm Weather

UNDERWEAR: The underclothing you wear at home or at work will suffice, although cotton boxer-type shorts, which cling less to your skin, are more comfortable than the jockey style. Two pairs of shorts and two T-shirts will last for a hike of less than a week, one set for wearing and one for washing. Drying in the sun ordinarily takes about two hours.

Though underwear can go for two days without a wash, the same does not go for your socks. A daily change and washing are necessary for health and comfort. Cotton wash-and-wear socks are recommended; wool may be too warm and scratchy. Light wool sweat socks with low boots are fine only in mountainous areas. In coastal regions that are flat and sandy, you may not need socks but simply sneakers. Prior to a day's hike, cut down on perspiration with a healthy sprinkle of foot powder or baby powder in your boots.

Waffle-weave underwear is intended for cooler temperatures, but the top part worn under a thin cotton shirt will keep you warm in an early morning chill.

OUTERWEAR: Khaki (cotton) pants are appropriately light and durable. Look for cuffless models that are an inch or so shorter than your regular pants, because cuffs tend to catch mud, water, stones, and twigs. Denim pants are also sturdy, but should be loose fitting for the active camper.

Allow extra room between your crotch and the top of your trousers for bending and taking lengthy steps. Roomy pockets are important, but don't overfill them. Make sure the seams have been reinforced for longer wear.

Shorts are acceptable in hot areas, but they don't guard against underbrush and sunburn. A short-sleeved cotton shirt during the day is fine, but be careful of too much sun on your forearms. At night, when mosquitoes and other insects appear, you will need a long-sleeved cotton shirt. Shirttails that fall well below the waist are advisable. Have a sweater or sweatshirt on hand for the evenings.

As mentioned in the Camp Bedding section, water fowl down is the prime insulating material, but synthetics, such as Thinsulate, are acceptable and less expensive. A lightweight, quilted, insulated jacket that uses a good synthetic will keep the early morning fisherman comfortably warm and dry all summer.

HEADGEAR: A cotton hat like baseball players wear screens your head from the sun. Though the bill in the front shields your face from rain, you may need the additional protection of a light nylon, hooded jacket to cover your neck in a downpour.

■ Cool Weather

UNDERWEAR: On cool days, when the temperature hovers around 40°F, leave on the warm-weather shorts and T-shirt, but add a one- or two-piece suit of cotton underwear with full sleeves and legs. Thermal-weave or waffle-weave underwear supplies greater warmth and more ventilation than the flat design. The weaving pattern consists of protrusions and hollow pockets close to the skin that trap body heat.

Two-layer underwear—often labeled Duofold—is another reliable insulated model. The smooth cotton layer facing the skin absorbs perspiration and passes it through the insulating air space to the outer layer of cotton, nylon, and wool. Moisture evaporates from the outer layer.

Wool socks are unparalleled for warmth. Make sure they extend a couple of inches over your boot tops. To prevent blisters on your feet, wear a thin pair of cotton socks underneath. The combination keeps your feet comfortable and free of moisture.

OUTERWEAR: A good choice for cool weather are the heavy-duty work khakis simply called "work clothes" by most stores. As with summer outdoor pants, cuffless styles are best. Wear the inseam a few inches shorter than usual and look for reinforced seams. The cut of the pants should be full rather than ivy-league trim to facilitate climbing, bending, and the like. An extra inch between the crotch and belt is also helpful.

If you prefer wool pants, get a lightweight pair. Twill fabric, which frequently consists of 65 percent Dacron polyester and 35 percent cotton, is a sturdy and less expensive alternative.

Loose-fitting trousers are important. A size larger at the waist may not be flattering, but with a heavy shirt, thicker undergarments, and a sweater to tuck in, it is a wise idea. A belt or suspenders are fine, and deep pockets on the trousers are also convenient.

Fall is a good time for lightweight wool or flannel shirts. These too should allow freedom of movement. Wool is warmer, and with a waffle-weave turtleneck worn underneath, you're ready for real cold. The shirt-tail should extend several inches below the waist so it doesn't slip out while you're moving. The buttons should be big so they are easy to handle with cold fingers.

A quilted, insulated jacket ensures warmth if the insulating agent is down or a good-quality synthetic. The quilting prevents the insulation from bunching up. Excess moisture is absorbed and expelled through the insulation and fabric. Slip the jacket on whenever a shirt alone won't be enough. The jacket should have pockets and a strong, trustworthy zipper.

Down jackets are matchless for warmth and insulation, but prices are high. In cool weather, synthetics such as Thinsulate, Polarguard, and Thermoloft are quite adequate. When available, choose garments with Gore's Windstopper fabric, which stops cold wind from penetrating, yet remains breathable.

HEADGEAR: A billed cap of wool, cotton, or leather is the first choice.

The beret and the tam-o-shanter are underrated as hats in the United States, but either one supplies a large amount of heat to your head and body. Both styles can be pulled down to protect your ears, and each is compact, inexpensive, and long lasting.

A watch cap—the type worn by merchant seamen—or a ski hat is acceptable. If it isn't too cool, they can be worn with the cuff doubled up, and in harsh cold, both can be pulled down to cover the neck, ears, and forehead.

■ Cold Weather

When temperatures drop to zero degrees and below, your life may depend on the clothing you wear.

UNDERWEAR: The T-shirt and boxer shorts you wore in summer and fall should be the first clothes you put on. Follow with a full set of waffle-weave, quilted, or polypropylene underwear. The waffle-weave design traps body heat and permits moisture to escape at the neck, a more rapid exit point than the underwear itself. The quilted underwear gives warmth by stopping the circulation of air inside your clothing. Polypropylene is a synthetic fiber

with the softness of cotton and the wicking ability to pull moisture away from the body for evaporation.

A properly fitted sock is snug enough not to bunch around the toe or heel, but is not so tight it causes discomfort.

Top-grade wool socks provide superior warmth and durability through many hard months and washings. Avoid colored wool, which may cause an allergic reaction, infect a blister, or discolor other clothing you may have thrown in your laundry pail.

Wool socks reinforced with a strong synthetic such as Dacron or nylon last longer and are less expensive in the long run, but lose some advantage in ventilation, softness, and warmth. Socks made totally of nylon, Dacron, Orlon, or another synthetic are also not on par with wool when it comes to softness and getting rid of moisture. Cotton socks are comfortable only until they're soaked with water or perspiration.

The wisest choice, however, is a pair of good-quality, wool hunting socks worn over a pair of cotton socks. Whatever the height of your boots, select socks that are 3 inches higher. Lap the extra material over the boot.

OUTERWEAR: Cuffless wool pants and a lightweight wool shirt—with large buttons for ease of handling—furnish ample warmth when worn over the proper underwear. The advantage of wool to the camper who also hunts is that it is noiseless. Wool also does a fine job of shedding and repelling water. Similar fabrics include Polartec and fleece.

Take along a quilted jacket insulated with down or one of the better synthetics. The camper who feels too restricted in a quilted jacket might choose a less cumbersome vest insulated with down or a good synthetic. A vest with a good zipper front, a button-down collar, and a flap pocket on either side is a treasure; more so when it is low enough in the rear to cover the kidneys. In extreme cold, the topmost outer garment can also be an oversize wool hunting shirt or jacket.

Heavy wool or leather gloves worn over a pair of cotton work gloves protect the hands. Although mittens may keep you somewhat warmer, they inhibit your ability to grasp triggers, utensils, and the like, so gloves are a better choice.

HEADGEAR: A wool hunting cap with earflaps along with a wool or cotton scarf is suitable. On a deer stand in a windy area, this combo is perfect. Place the scarf around the neck or over your head under the cap. Hoods tend to restrict head movement and muffle sounds coming from the sides and back, but a scarf can be quickly loosened when necessary.

The watch cap and ski hat tend to hamper peripheral vision. They are acceptable substitutes for the wool hunting cap, however, because they pull down completely to protect almost everything from the top of the head to the neck, revealing only the eyes, nose, and mouth.

■ Raingear

There are two styles of raingear: the rainsuit and the poncho. The rainsuit is a waterproof jacket and pants, while the poncho is a square of waterproof fabric with a hole for the head. The poncho does little to restrict the arms, but flares enough to protect the legs—when you are standing—and let in cooling air. It is a poor choice for the shotgunner because it tends to be clumsy and dangerous.

For sitting in a duck blind or boat most of the day, take a rainsuit. It keeps your entire body dry whether you are standing or sitting. It should have drawstring pants and a hooded zipper jacket with elastic or snap-fastener wrists. These features will also keep out wind.

Though somewhat expensive, Nylon shell fabric with waterproof Gore-Tex is a good buy in rainsuits. It's durable, waterproof, and lightweight, and doesn't stiffen as much in cold weather as the popular and less expensive rubberized cotton suits. The inexpensive vinyl or plastic suits are worthless because they rip. Easily split seams, snagged material, and stiffness in cold weather are further drawbacks.

The backpacker, however, may find the poncho preferable to the rainsuit because of its lighter weight.

A poncho with a rear flap will protect the pack as well. Don't buy a cheap poncho. A good one slips on easily and doubles as a ground tarp, makeshift lean-to, or tent. Most serious outdoors enthusiasts own both a rainsuit and poncho.

No discussion of raingear would be complete without a special look at Gore-Tex, a form-fitting stretch material that keeps the wearer from getting wet. What is Gore-Tex? The key to the unique, waterproof, windproof, breathable performance characteristics of Gore-Tex fabric lies in the patented microporous membrane that is laminated to outer shell fabrics. The Gore-Tex membrane is composed of 100 percent expanded polytetrafluoroethylene. This is the same resin that composes DuPont's Teflon. The Gore-Tex membrane contains 9 billion pores per square inch, each 20,000 times smaller than a water drop, but 700 times larger than a water vapor molecule. The membrane, therefore, effectively blocks wind and wet weather but lets perspiration vapor pass through.

In two-layer Gore-Tex fabric, the Gore-Tex membrane is laminated to one side of an outer shell fabric. In three-layer Gore-Tex fabric (for heavier uses), the membrane is sandwiched between a shell fabric and a tricot knit fabric. Because the Gore-Tex membrane is permanently bonded to fabrics, it does not peel off or degrade after washing like most "waterproof" coatings or treatments. It is also not subject to contamination by body oils.

Today, outdoors enthusiasts will find Gore-Tex fabric in everything from rainwear, hunting gear, cycling gear, and dress outerwear to accessories such as waterproof boots, gloves, socks, and hats.

CAMP STOVES AND HEATERS

An open wood fire in a public campground is becoming a rare sight. For too long, careless campers haphazardly cut down trees for fuel and left their fires unattended, causing costly forest fires that destroyed thousands of acres of woodland every year. As a result, most campgrounds today prohibit open fires. Even if they didn't, the lack of available wood would be a prohibition in itself.

Thus, the modern camper has been compelled to carry a stove on his camping trips, and in some ways has improved his lot. Certainly people who like to cook are more at home with a stove than a wood fire. A stove does away with blackened cooking utensils, hot sparks, and eye-watering smoke.

■ Wood Stoves

The sheepherder's stove is the best known of this type, but due to their weight and awkwardness, wood stoves in general are fading from the camping scene. The sheepherder's stove is constructed of sheet metal and often features a small oven for baking, as well as several sections of piping to carry smoke outside the tent. An asbestos collar around the pipe where it passes through the tent is a necessity. Some models fold flat and have telescoping piping. Nevertheless, the wood stove is impractical for the average camper, particularly because modern tents are not equipped to handle stovepipes.

■ Gasoline Stoves

With white, unleaded gasoline a readily available commodity these days, the gasoline stove has become the leader among camp stoves. It's fine for year-round use, as bitter-cold weather has little or no effect on gasoline.

The typical gasoline stove with just one burner weighs 2½ pounds and has a tank capacity of 2 pints of fuel, which should keep it burning approximately 3½ hours. For large families, there are two- and three-burner gasoline models that weigh up to 25 pounds.

The two-burner stove is the best choice for general camping. For large families on a short outing, one two-burner and one single-burner stove are better than one bulky three-burner stove. But for cabin or long-term camping, choose the three-burner model. The backpacker can get along with just one burner. Some backpacker models tip the scales at a mere 20 ounces and can fit in a large coat pocket. Hunters and fishermen who just want a quick pot of coffee or hot soup during the day appreciate the lightweight, one-burner stoves.

■ Propane Stoves

Highly popular among warm-weather campers is the stove that runs on propane gas, also known as LP, or liquefied petroleum. In winter, propane stoves do not work well because the cold tends to reduce the temperature of gas, thereby diminishing volatility and ultimately the vital heat output.

A 5-pound, single-burner stove is typical, with a usually disposable 14.1- or 16.4-ounce cylinder of gas. A double-burner stove weighs about 12 pounds and often uses a separate cylinder for each burner. For extended stays in camp, many manufacturers make large-capacity, refillable tanks of propane that can be carried aboard a plane or packhorse.

As with gasoline stoves, a two-burner stove is recommended for general camping, and one single-burner and one double-burner model for larger families.

The advantages of propane gas over white gasoline are the ease with which it lights and its carrying convenience. Also, no pumping, priming, and pouring are necessary because the sealed containers of propane readily attach to the stove.

On the other hand, propane is not as easily available throughout the country as is gasoline. Before leaving home, take into account the length of your trip, whether or not you are carrying an ample supply of propane gas, and the proximity along your route of stores stocking propane. Another problem with propane is that you're never quite sure if you are running low. Thus, it's a good idea to have two cylinders.

Getting down to economics, studies have shown that the average camp meal costs a few cents to cook with gasoline, but approaches 50 cents when propane is used. With the advantages that propane stoves have in summer, many campers care little about the added expense. Another featherweight gas used in contemporary stoves is butane, also a liquefied petroleum.

■ Canned Heat

Known commercially as Sterno, this is a solid, non-melting fuel that's odorless and safe, and burns clearly and steadily until totally consumed. You can extinguish it as many times as you like by simply replacing the pry-off top. The touch of a match will quickly re-light it. Sterno is sold in several sizes. The 7-ounce can, for example, will burn for 1½ hours. A pint of water can be brought to a boil with Sterno in just 15 minutes, but canned heat is not intended for much else.

Stoves designed specifically for cans of Sterno can be purchased, ranging from inexpensive stamped-metal racks to two-burner models.

■ Reflector Oven

This device is used for baking bread, rolls, pies, muffins, cake, fish, and meat at your campsite. It is a simple, collapsible, lightweight (about 3 pounds) contraption made of sheet aluminum that reflects the heat of a stove or campfire onto the food. A stainless-steel shelf provides more even heating, but an aluminum shelf will suffice. A good shelf can handle up to 10 pounds of food.

■ Dutch Oven

If you could take only one pot on a camping trip, it would have to be the Dutch oven. Why? Because it does everything! In addition to helping create great one-pot

Propane Stoves

A Bass Pro single-burner propane stove turns any standard 16.4-ounce propane cylinder into a stand-up camp stove that will produce 16,000 BTUs of power. It is designed with a 7½-inch grid and four folding feet for extra stability.

Two stainless-steel burners produce 25,000 BTUs of propane heat on the Bass Pro Outfitter Stove. It uses any standard 16.4-ounce propane cylinder. It features a high-altitude regulator, electronic ignition, and a heavy-duty steel frame built to handle heavy pots. The stove measures about 24 inches by 13 inches and is about 6 inches high.

The Camp Chef Outdoorsman Stove is designed for people who plan to camp for more than a couple of days. Two cast burners produce 90,000 BTUs from a 20-pound propane tank for up to 15 hours of cooking time. The stove weighs 41 pounds and stands 31 inches high. It is a good choice for a deer camp or tailgating.

dinners that require very little attention, it can also be used to bake, grill, and stir-fry. Introduced to the Americans by Dutch traders, it was improved by Paul Revere, who added a flat top with a turned-up edge (to hold coals) and three stubby legs (to sit over coals). It was the most important cooking pot for pioneers as they moved westward, and today it's an essential piece of gear for

sportsmen, outfitters, camp cooks, and anyone else who enjoys preparing meals in the outdoors.

In fact, there's only one drawback to a good Dutch oven. It's heavy. An 8-quart pot may weigh nearly 20 pounds—it's obviously not for backpackers.

When buying a Dutch oven, avoid aluminum, steel, and glass-lined versions, since they don't distribute heat evenly and can cause your food to scorch. Instead, look for a cast-iron pot, which retains heat and distributes it equally throughout. And stick to the traditional oven, with the flanged lid and legs.

All cast-iron Dutch ovens must be "seasoned" before being used for the first time. Wash the pot thoroughly with a mild dishwashing detergent to remove the wax coating used for protection in shipping. Rinse with hot water and dry with a paper towel. Grease the inside of the pot and the lid with pure vegetable shortening (do not use margarine or butter), and then place in a 250°F to 300°F oven for 15 minutes. Remove the pot, carefully drain off any excess oil, and return to the oven for another hour. Allow the pot to cool at room temperature. Your Dutch oven is now ready for use.

Your first step in cooking with it is to get some hot coals. You can get them in the traditional way from a campfire (a keyhole campfire is best) or you can cheat

This Lodge Logic 5-Quart Dutch Oven is pre-seasoned by an electrostatic spray system that applies just the right amount of vegetable oil that deeply penetrates the pores of the cast iron. Dutch ovens are popular with camp cooks because they do everything and excel at one-pot meals that require little attention.

Dutch Oven Venison Recipe

Taken from *Backcountry Cooking* by Wayne Fears

INGREDIENTS:

6-pound venison roast	Hot water
Salt and pepper to taste	Dry onion soup mix
Meat tenderizer	Worcestershire sauce
	Cold water

INSTRUCTIONS:

Put salt, pepper, and meat tenderizer on the venison roast. Make a thick paste with the hot water and dry onion soup mix, and coat the entire roast. Sprinkle Worcestershire sauce over the roast. Add a cup of cold water to the Dutch oven, place the roast in the oven, and cover. Place in hot coals, adding coals to the lid for approximately four to five hours. Serves 12.

by using charcoal briquettes. In fact, many Dutch-oven recipes now specify the number of briquettes you'll need for the lid and beneath the pot.

With a Dutch oven, you can cook either above ground or below ground. It may take some practice, but you can prepare a venison stew in a Dutch oven in the morning, bury it in hot coals, and it will be ready for dinner when you return to camp in the evening. You can also use your Dutch oven to bake a batch of biscuits or an apple pie.

▨ Box Oven

Coleman manufactures a collapsible oven—the box oven—which has about the same capacity as a typical Dutch oven, and can be used with a gasoline stove for baking pies, biscuits, etc. This oven may be used on wood fires after some modifications have been made, provided it is always placed over the coals, never over the flame. Otherwise, your food will become smoked.

▨ Camp Heaters

Called catalytic heaters because they use a catalyst—usually platinum—that burns the fuel (gasoline, propane, etc.), these heaters do not produce any flame, odor, or carbon monoxide. The catalytic heater provides an effective heat that can be regulated according to your needs. The heat output is measured in BTUs—British Thermal Units. Because of its safety, the catalytic heater is well ahead of other types on the market.

The Mr. Heater Base Camp Buddy puts out 3,800 BTUs and will heat up to 100 square feet. The unit runs on a 16.4-ounce propane cylinder and has a safety shut-off. It is certified for indoor and outdoor use, and it is especially effective for campsites and deer and duck blinds.

CAMP LIGHTING

▨ Gasoline Lanterns

For all-around use, the gasoline lantern is the most practical camp light. The fuel employed is white or unleaded gasoline (readily available throughout the United States) or kerosene, and it is fed from a pressure tank to relatively fragile mantles made of ash. A vapor given off by the gasoline collects in one or two mantles, and is ignited with a match. Should the lantern flare at this point,

check for a generator leak. A wise move is to bring along a spare generator—they also tend to clog—and one or two extra mantles. They do add weight to the total unit, but you'll be in the dark without them should something go wrong.

Pumping a built-in tank device before lighting and at intervals during the burning should inspire adequate candlepower. If the pressure drops and the light seems

Coleman Powerhouse technology enables this lantern to burn both Coleman liquid fuel and unleaded gasoline. Light comes from two mantles and will run for seven hours on high on one tank of fuel. It produces 1,107 lumens on high. It also lights easily with matches.

to dim or pulsate at times, bring the pump into play to correct the pressure.

The typical gasoline lantern is constructed of stainless steel and brass with a porcelain reflector (also called a deflector) to provide ventilation and help direct the light in a wide circle or in one particular spot. A globe of clear Pyrex glass encircling the lit mantles is durable enough to withstand heat. The capacity of the fuel tank is normally 2 pints, enough for 10 to 12 hours of intense light. Before bedtime, turn off the fuel valve. The minute amount of vapor remaining in the mantles will give you enough light to get into your sleeping bag. The gasoline lantern is unaffected by wind, rain, and cold. It is a valuable piece of camp equipment, but its weight—often close to 10 pounds when you add in fuel—rules it out for the backpacker.

▪ Propane Lanterns

If your camping is usually confined to summer weekends, the propane-gas lantern is for you. There is no generator to clog and replace or liquid fuel to spill and perhaps taint your food. Working off lightweight propane gas that is sold in a 16.4-ounce (usually disposable) cylinder, this lantern can give you anything from a soft glow to a bright beam. Large-capacity propane tanks are also sold.

As with gasoline lanterns, one or more mantles are used to catch the gas vapors, but no pumping and priming are required. Porcelain reflectors are also featured to place the light where you want it. One propane cylinder can last from eight to 12 hours, depending on how intense a light you require.

Since you never know how much gas remains in

the cylinder, it is a necessity to take along a pair of cylinders, as well as extra mantles.

Weight is a problem with propane lanterns and backpackers should avoid them. But if you are traveling by automobile, propane lanterns are suitable, provided the weather isn't too cold. Otherwise, the pressure in the tank drops and you're lucky if you even get a dim glow.

▪ Battery-Powered Lights

Flashlights are available in all stores stocking camp gear, but get the right kind. There are three- and four-cell models that throw a lot of light, but a two-cell flashlight is adequate, especially if it's a super-bright, long-lasting LED flashlight. Also, anything larger than two cells means surplus weight. Choose a model with an angled head so that it can be hung on your belt or stood on end, leaving both hands free.

Besides being durable and water resistant, the flashlight should have a shiny or bright finish—perhaps with a luminous stripe painted on it—so it can be located easily. A hang-up ring is also helpful, and a slightly recessed glass lens is close to shatterproof because of the protective lip. Some of the new LED flashlights are ultrabright with bulbs that last up to 100,000 hours and some never need replacing. LED lights are brighter, with more than 500 lumens of bright beam.

Dry-cell batteries aren't too efficient when the weather turns cold; they'll throw a rather dim light. Your best bet is to warm them in your hands or place them under your sleeping bag at night.

When carrying your flashlight in your pack, tape the switch in the off position or reverse one of the

Coleman technology has produced the Coleman CPX 6 Classic LED Lantern, which will put out 200 lumens for up to 25 hours. It will run on four D batteries or an optional CPX 6 rechargeable power cartridge. It will hang in any position, including sideways. It is a good choice where safety is a factor.

batteries in the tube. This will prevent you from accidentally turning on the flashlight. Also, keep in mind that batteries last longer when they are burned for only short periods of time.

If you prefer a battery-powered lantern to a flashlight, you can get up to 50 hours of intense light if the weather is mild. These lanterns work on 6-volt batteries and generally weigh about 5 pounds. If weight is not important, get the widebeam rather than the searchlight model.

■ Candles

Primitive is the word for the candle as a light source, but it's 100 percent reliable and multipurpose. It can be used to boil a pot of water, start a fire, or mend a leaky spot in your tent.

No matter what kind of camper you are—backpacker through RVer—a few handy candles are a worthwhile investment. It must be stressed that the proper kind is the stearic-acid plumber's candle, made of animal fat. Paraffin candles that you may have at home for decorative purposes or for maneuvering when a fuse blows are useless in camp. Paraffin will melt in a warm pack.

Never leave your tent unattended with a burning candle inside, even if it is in a candle lantern—as it should be.

And a final note of caution on the use of candles: Some modern waterproofing mixtures have proven to be flammable. If you are a backpacker and recently have waterproofed your small tent with a commercial product, carefully check the ingredients. Should any one of them be flammable, do **not** use a candle in your tent.

CAMP COOK KITS

For a party of four campers willing to accept the fact that filet mignon will not be on the menu, the most practical cook kit—in automobile, tent, or trailer camping—is a nesting set in which the pots, pans, plates, and cups fit inside one another. A typical aluminum cook kit for four campers should include:

- one 8-quart kettle
- one 4-quart stewpot
- one 2-quart stewpot
- two frying pans with handles
- one spouted pot
- four plates
- four plastic cups

Extra plates and cups can be purchased for a group of more than four. Cups should be plastic rather than aluminum, since aluminum gets too hot to hold or drink from. Aluminum also lets liquids cool too quickly.

If you don't mind some additional weight, there are commercial kits made of stainless steel. Much more durable than aluminum and simpler to clean, stainless steel is also more expensive. Make sure that the plates, frying pans, and cups are not too thin, as they too will become too hot or cold to handle.

Teflon keeps food from sticking and makes cleaning easier. Teflon-coated utensils require special tools to protect the thin coating from scratching, but if the added weight and bulk are no problem, these are excellent items.

In addition to knife, fork, and spoon sets for each camper, the cook needs a tool kit and it should include:

- one carving knife
- one paring knife
- one potato peeler
- one long fork
- one spoon
- one ladle
- one turner
- one bottle/can opener

The backpacker, who must limit his supplies to a minimum, may be inclined toward a more compact unit, which should include:

- one 1-quart pot
- one 5½-inch frying pan
- one 1-pint bowl
- one 1-cup mug

Coleman's Camp Oven is made of aluminized steel and can be used on any camp stove to trap heat for baking and warming. It features a thermostat to control heat and folds flat for easy packing.

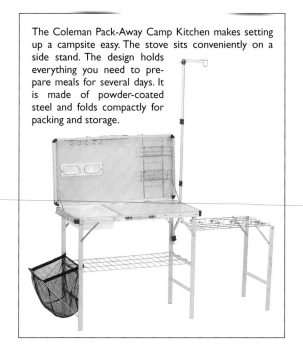

The Coleman Pack-Away Camp Kitchen makes setting up a campsite easy. The stove sits conveniently on a side stand. The design holds everything you need to prepare meals for several days. It is made of powder-coated steel and folds compactly for packing and storage.

Examine any mess kit before buying it. It is best to discover a missing utensil in the store. Avoid gadgets—from folding toasters to corn poppers to immersion heaters, advertised to simplify camp meals—until you are certain you need them. Begin with the basics and experiment.

To make cleaning easier, use all-purpose paper (toilet paper, for example) to wipe excess food out of your plate immediately after eating. Beware of slipshod washing, which can produce gastric upsets such as dysentery the next meal around.

A pair of lightweight cotton gloves may save the cook from getting burned, cut, or grimy. And while soap, towels, dishrags, and scouring pads (plastic, steel wool, or copper wire) add ounces to your gear, they also speed up the cleaning and drying process.

Aluminum foil, though not recommended as a cook kit in itself, proves quite useful as a supplementary item. As a pot liner, foil keeps food from gumming up the pot. Wrapped around the bottom of the pot, it stops blackening from the fire. The same result can also be achieved by rubbing the pot's exterior with a bar of soap.

Paper plates and cups save time in cleaning up, but the choice is up to you.

The travel kitchen or chuckbox is recommended if you're camping in a motorized vehicle. Available assembled or in kits, these kitchens have five or six compartments to separately store items such as utensil kits, cleanup kits, nonperishable foods, and the like. Because of weight and bulk, the kitchen is inappropriate for horsepacking, canoeing (with portages), and backpacking trips. Many campers make wood-box arrangements with their own modifications after several years of camping.

Canteens come in various styles—round, oval, and a flask-shaped model that clips to the belt. All can be filled with practically any liquid and, if you care to, you can freeze the entire contents. Aluminum models are more rugged than plastic ones. Some feature a chained screw cap and most have a shoulder strap. Canvas covers ward off dirt and dents.

The main concern in purchasing a canteen is proper size. Many tenderfoot campers make the mistake of hauling along a canteen with a 4-quart capacity. That's a gallon, and awfully heavy to carry. For most daylong outings, a 1-quart model is sufficient. For weekends, a 2-quart canteen is advisable, particularly if potable water is a rarity in the area you are in. Water-purification tablets are inexpensive and valuable if you're not sure how drinkable the water is.

CAMP TOOLS

◼ Hatchets

Way back when trees were plentiful, many campers wielded a full-length ax, relegating the smaller hatchet to novice woodchoppers. Nowadays, when wood is an all-too-precious resource, the hatchet has become the most common woodcutting tool at the campsite.

Invest extra money in a premium-quality hatchet. The one-piece styles are the best, with all-steel construction from the head to the bottom of the handle. A cheap hatchet, which may have loose headwork, might injure a nearby camper or shatter after several sessions of chopping. As perspiration can make a handle slippery,

Hatchet Know-How

Once a tree has been felled, strip the branches by always cutting with the slant of the branch.

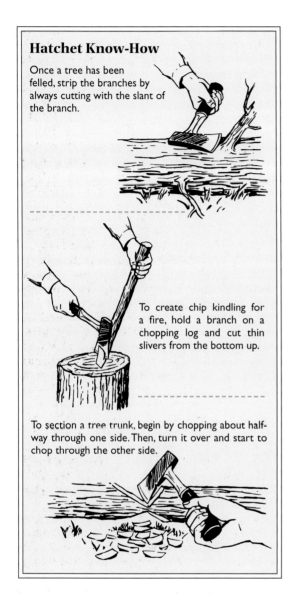

To create chip kindling for a fire, hold a branch on a chopping log and cut thin slivers from the bottom up.

To section a tree trunk, begin by chopping about halfway through one side. Then, turn it over and start to chop through the other side.

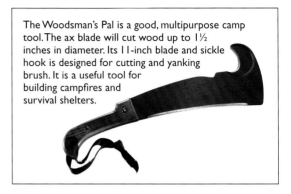

The Woodsman's Pal is a good, multipurpose camp tool. The ax blade will cut wood up to 1½ inches in diameter. Its 11-inch blade and sickle hook is designed for cutting and yanking brush. It is a useful tool for building campfires and survival shelters.

Some hatchets feature neither the one-piece construction nor the bonded head. These models frequently use a wedge to secure the head to the handle. As this is far from safe, check this type of hatchet frequently during chopping.

Hatchets—also known as belt axes—come in a number of sizes and weights. The right choice obviously depends on your own needs. For all-around use, however, a hatchet with a 1-pound head and handle about a foot long is an excellent choice. Slightly larger ones are preferred by some campers, and manufacturers have recently offered much smaller ones as well. The light, very short-handled models, sometimes called backpacker's axes or hunter's axes, are fine for chopping kindling or the wood for a small campfire, and they can also be used to fashion wooden tent stakes (but then, so can a knife). They're useless for heavier work, though adequate for their intended purpose.

Despite its smaller size when compared to the ax, the hatchet is an important tool that needs special care. Never throw a hatchet. Besides ruining the bit and other important parts, you may injure someone. Only use a hatchet to hammer metal stakes or nails if it is a half-hatchet, which features a regular hatchet blade at one end of the head and a tempered hammer head on the other end. A conventional hatchet used for such purposes soon becomes worthless.

A durable leather sheath with a sturdy leather buffer strip or rivets facing the cutting edge should be used to carry the hatchet. If you don't have a sheath handy, drive the blade into a stump or log so it is not dangerously exposed. (Avoid the double-bitted hatchet on the market featuring blades at both ends of the head. It is dangerous except in the hands of a skilled chopper.)

To cut a piece of wood, use the contact method. Place the edge of the hatchet on the stick. Lift the two and then bring them down together hard on the chop-

get a hatchet with a handle of rubber, wood, or leather lamination, which will provide a secure grip.

Should you prefer a hatchet with a wood handle, make sure the handle is chemically bonded to the head. This process ensures that it will rarely, if ever, come loose. Some choppers prefer wood handles because there isn't as much cushioning in them. Though the resultant shocks may be uncomfortable, they signify that you are chopping ineffectively. When the shocks cease, you will know you are handling your hatchet correctly.

ping block. To split the wood, place the hatchet edge in a crack. Again, lift the two and bring the hatchet and stick down hard on the log or stump. Once contact has been made, slightly twist the hatchet hand to separate the pieces.

On a cold day, heat the hatchet slightly before putting it to work so it won't become brittle and crack.

To pass a hatchet to another person, hold it vertically, head down, with the blade facing away from the two of you. Give the receiver more than enough room to grasp the top of the hatchet handle. When you are carrying it in camp, hold the hatchet firmly by its head, keeping the cutting edge away from you.

If not inside your pack while hiking, the hatchet should be strapped to the outside and sheathed. When the hike is a short one, sheath the hatchet and carry it on your belt on your right hip. Never strap it near the groin or kidney area. Another useful tool in camp is the Woodman's Pal, a unique combination tool with an 11-inch carbon-steel blade that will cut branches up to 1½ inches with a single stroke.

Axes

Some chopping chores call for an ax. A camping trip, in this case, is usually for a week or more, and the work might include felling a tree or cutting firewood.

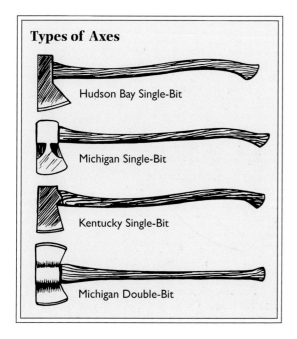

Types of Axes

Hudson Bay Single-Bit

Michigan Single-Bit

Kentucky Single-Bit

Michigan Double-Bit

Among the many types of axes available, there are four common ones—the Hudson Bay single-bit, the Michigan single-bit, the Kentucky single-bit, and the Michigan double-bit.

Experienced choppers agree that a head that provides maximum steel-to-wood contact is best. This means the squarish Michigan-style head is preferred to the Hudson Bay or tomahawk-type head, which has little steel-to-wood contact in proportion to the size of the bit. The tomahawk head has a lot of eye appeal and was popular with French Canadian trappers when weight was a big factor, but it's a poor design when compared to a Michigan head.

If you're selecting an ax for a permanent camp, your best bet is a full-size cabin ax, which usually has a 36-inch handle and a 3½- to 4-pound head. Stick with the Michigan head, which is the best design for nearly all situations. Avoid double-bit axes unless you're an experienced woodcutter. The dangers of using a double-bit ax far outweigh the advantages.

Fancy burl may be desirable in a shotgun stock, but not in an ax handle. You can, however, learn how to pick the best handle in your sports shop. Nearly all wood ax handles, incidentally, are made from hickory. First, eliminate handles with obvious flaws, such as knots in the wood. Next, narrow your selection down to handles that have straight grains running the entire length. Then, look at the cross-sectioned area of the handle butt. Make a quick count of the number of grains running across the butt and apply this rule: the fewer the grains, the stronger the handle. And grain should run roughly parallel to the long axis of the oval cross section. Avoid axes with painted wood handles. There's no telling how many flaws lie hidden under a coat of paint.

Handles are varnished for two reasons: eye appeal or protection from moisture during shipping and storage. Bare wood, however, affords a better grip. Your ax will be more comfortable to use if you remove the varnish from the handle.

Apply bright-yellow, red, or bright-blue paint to the ax head once you buy it. The paint will help you locate the ax in weeds or brush if it is lost. The paint also assists in bonding the handle and head together. Last, if the paint cracks over the eye, it is a clear danger signal that the handle is loosening inside and may come off at any time.

The handle of an ax, no matter what the size, should be made of seasoned hardwood with a grain that is both fine and straight. The handle itself should also be straight. Check to see that the "hang" of the ax is proper.

How to Sharpen a Double-Bit Ax

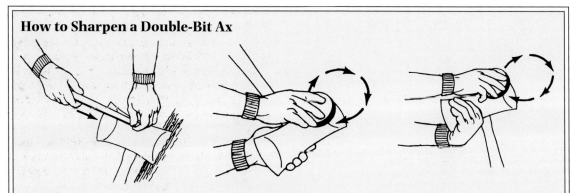

Left: To sharpen a double-bit ax, embed one edge in a log and file the other edge, using downward strokes only. File far back from the edge, gradually thinning down the blade until a fanlike pattern appears. **Middle:** Then, take the ax in your hand and, with a whetstone, use circular strokes on one side. **Right:** Sharpen the other side by letting the head twist so the handle points downward.

Hang is determined by holding the ax in front of you and sighting down as if it were a rifle. If the center of the handle is in line with the cutting edge of the blade, the hang is correct.

Inspect the point where the handle fits the eye of the steel head, unless you have a one-piece model. If even the slightest gap shows there, look for another ax. An imperfect fit means the handle may work loose soon after continued chopping or pounding.

Several manufacturers use a chemical bond to anchor the ax handle to the head. This holds more securely than the wedges—either wood or steel—that conveniently attach the two parts. Wedges, however, are efficient.

If you want to avoid wood handles, pick one of the all-steel one-piece axes. With some cheap models, you'll experience a shock to the hands when chopping, but one manufacturer solved the problem with a nylon-vinyl grip.

There a few important safety factors to keep in mind when you chop wood. First, check your ax for a loose head or a damaged handle. If the head continually comes loose, replace the handle. If you're on a trip, you can temporarily solve the problem by soaking the head in a bucket of water. The wood will swell and tighten against the head.

Before you start cutting, hold your ax at arm's length and turn a complete circle. Then, move the ax slowly overhead in an arc. Clear away any limbs or brush that will be in your way and could deflect your ax during a swing. Also, no one should be within 30 feet of the person with the ax. Check the cutting edge. A dull ax

is a dangerous tool. A sharp ax will dig into wood, but a dull blade can bounce off and strike your leg.

Sharpening an ax is a two-stage job. You'll need a file, such as a Nicholson Black Diamond, and a round whetstone. (If there's any paint on the metal where you'll be filing, first remove it with sandpaper. Otherwise, the paint will clog the file and the whetstone.)

Anchor the ax blade securely. If you're in the field, where there is no vise, drive a wood peg into the ground and brace the single-bit head against it. A double-bit can be driven into a log to hold it in position. When sharpening, wear gloves to protect your hands.

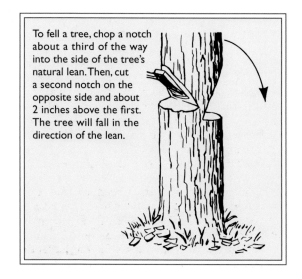

To fell a tree, chop a notch about a third of the way into the side of the tree's natural lean. Then, cut a second notch on the opposite side and about 2 inches above the first. The tree will fall in the direction of the lean.

Ax Care and Safety Tips

Here are some final bits of advice to remember when using an ax:

1 • Always wear gloves when using and sharpening your ax.

2 • Never carry an ax over your shoulder. Hold it close to the ax head, blade pointed downward and at your side. If you trip, hold it or throw it away from you.

3 • Between cutting sessions, bury the blade of your ax in a log or lay it under a log so that no one can blunder into the blade.

4 • Use a wood chopping block. Never cut on rock and other hard surfaces.

5 • Never use the butt end of the ax head to drive anything heavier than a tent peg. Using it as a wedge or to drive wedges will weaken and perhaps crack the eye.

6 • A split handle is best removed by sawing it off below the head and driving the rest of it out of the top with a steel bar. You can also burn it out if you bury the blade in wet earth to protect the heat-tempered edge.

7 • Logs will split more easily if you aim for the cracks in the top of the log you're about to split. They indicate weak sections. Avoid the knots; split around them.

Start with the file, pushing it from toe to heel (top to bottom) of the blade, about 1 inch back from the edge. The purpose of this step is to cut some of the metal away from the blade so that the taper is uniform. Nearly all new axes have a blade that is too thick. When a good taper is achieved, a fine edge can be easily put on the bit with a round whetstone.

Don't tackle the entire job with only a whetstone. A whetstone is fine for honing a knife, but it is not designed to cut enough metal from an ax head. The whetstone is only used for honing the bit after the blade has been taken down with a file. Don't use the file directly on the cutting edge; that's a job for the whetstone.

Perhaps the most common woodcutting job for the average camper is trimming limbs off downed trees and then chopping the limbs into firewood. Trimming limbs is safe and easy if you follow this advice.

First, always trim toward the top of the tree, which will point the limbs away from your body. Keep the trunk between you and the limbs you're trimming. For example, stand on one side of the log and trim the far side first, then change position. There's almost no chance of hitting your legs if there's a tree trunk between you and the blade.

If this is not possible and you have to stand on the same side as the ax, stand slightly forward of the limb you're trimming and swing the ax so that the blade strikes the limb behind your legs.

To cut a limb into campfire lengths, hold it firmly against a stump or log and chop it away from you at about a 45 degree angle. Using a three quarter length ax, you should have no trouble cutting limbs up to 1 inch in diameter with a single blow.

■ Camp Saws

To cut wood neatly into particular sizes, the saw is the proper tool. An ax or a hatchet wastes a lot of wood, can't be too exact, and stands the chance of causing injury with flying chips or the blades themselves. Saws are precise, much faster than either ax or hatchet, and a camper can get the knack of using them with just a couple of minutes of instruction.

Lighter saws are suitable for camping, as the heavier models are impractical to carry along. There are three saws used by backpackers and other campers who must limit the bulk and weight of their packs: the bow saw, the folding saw, and the cable saw.

The collapsible bow-type saw, also known as the Swede saw, features a thin, narrow blade of flexible steel. This blade is held taut by a tubelike, jointed metal frame, which can be taken apart and slipped into a case up to 1½ feet long. Several models are designed to carry spare blades.

A blade from 20 to 24 inches in length handles wood from 8 to 10 inches in thickness. Larger-diameter logs, however, require the use of a 30- or 36-inch blade.

Bow-saw frames come in U shapes and L shapes, but the former is recommended. The L-shaped models, though more compact, diminish the amount of blade that may be applied on the wood.

The folding saw is even more compact than most bow saws and will still do the same job. The safest camp saws will either fold or have a case, protecting the

Camp Saws

Basic camp tools should include a hand saw. These handy camp saws are available at any well-equipped outdoors stores. These saws will handle most jobs, from gathering firewood to building a tree stand to quartering an elk.

camper from exposed teeth. The cable saw is the most compact of all, but it requires two hands and is sometimes difficult to use.

■ Knives

Selecting a quality hunting knife, never an easy task, is no longer quite so difficult. Even though a growing emphasis on knives in recent years has resulted in many fine models on the market, you can narrow down the selection by following a few simple rules.

First, there is no need for a hunting knife with a blade longer than 5 inches. I've found that a straight blade or a slight drop-point design works best for most field chores. Remember that hunting knives frequently are used more for camp jobs than for dressing and skinning game.

Second, on a sheath knife, check the tang (the blade extension around which the handle is attached) and make sure it extends well up into or through the handle. This is the strongest design.

Grip the knife in your hand. Does the handle extend ¼ inch or so beyond each side of your hand? If so, it fits your hand properly. If not, it doesn't fit properly and will probably be uncomfortable to use for extended periods.

Selection of blade steel is another consideration. Stainless steel is very hard, and will not sharpen easily with just a few quick strokes, but it is easy to maintain because it won't rust. Carbon steel, on the other hand, is easier to sharpen and will take an edge faster, but it generally requires more care than stainless does.

The choice of sheath-type or folding knife is pretty much a matter of personal preference. Many hunters prefer a folding knife. The reason is simple. A Buck Folding Hunter, for example, has a 3¾-inch blade, but it's still only 4⅞ inches long when carried folded on a belt or in a pocket. For big skinning jobs at camp or home, though, most hunters like a sheath knife, also with a 4- or 5-inch blade.

What about sharpening a knife? A dull knife is both annoying and dangerous, especially in the woods where you may be rushing a field-dressing or skinning job. It's a good idea to carry a sharpening steel and a pocket-size whetstone to touch up the blade when it begins to dull. Many steels have two sharpening surfaces: a grooved side to put a uniform cutting edge on the blade and a smooth surface for final honing.

These steels are not designed to take an appreciable amount of metal from the edge, so on knives that are quite dull a stone must be used. For this job, you should carry a double-sided whetstone to get the edge back on your knife if it's badly dulled on bone or wood. Use a whetstone with a coarse 100 grit on one side and a medium-fine 240 grit on the other. Usually about 10 strokes per side on the medium-fine grit and 10 on the steel will sharpen a knife well enough to dress and skin a couple of deer.

A dirty stone will make sharpening a tough job. If a stone is glazed smooth with dirt, wash and scrub it with kerosene or a detergent, then let it dry out thoroughly. Whetstones should never be used dry, however. If you're using the stone in the field, wet it with snow, spit on it, or even put carcass fat on it. The idea is to float steel filings above the surface of the stone, so that the stone's pores are not clogged. Some manufacturers produce stones that are already oil-filled, but for stones that do not have this feature it's important to use a generous amount of honing oil, and to bear down hard as you move the edge of the blade across the stone. The oil, in addition to floating the steel filings, allows the blade to move smoothly.

Knife Designs

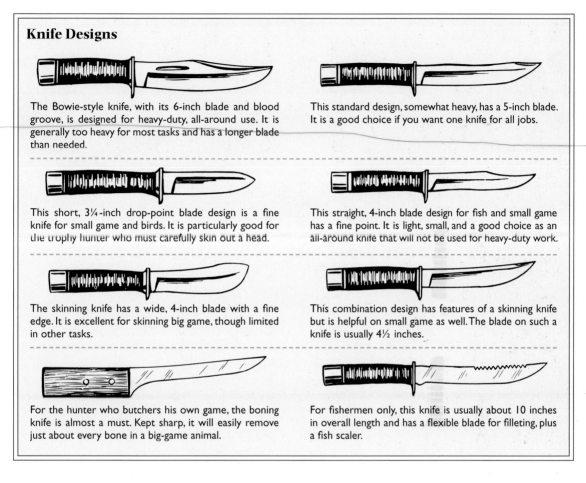

The Bowie-style knife, with its 6-inch blade and blood groove, is designed for heavy-duty, all-around use. It is generally too heavy for most tasks and has a longer blade than needed.

This standard design, somewhat heavy, has a 5-inch blade. It is a good choice if you want one knife for all jobs.

This short, 3¼-inch drop-point blade design is a fine knife for small game and birds. It is particularly good for the trophy hunter who must carefully skin out a head.

This straight, 4-inch blade design for fish and small game has a fine point. It is light, small, and a good choice as an all-around knife that will not be used for heavy-duty work.

The skinning knife has a wide, 4-inch blade with a fine edge. It is excellent for skinning big game, though limited in other tasks.

This combination design has features of a skinning knife but is helpful on small game as well. The blade on such a knife is usually 4½ inches.

For the hunter who butchers his own game, the boning knife is almost a must. Kept sharp, it will easily remove just about every bone in a big-game animal.

For fishermen only, this knife is usually about 10 inches in overall length and has a flexible blade for filleting, plus a fish scaler.

Your stone will stay cleaner longer if you wash your knife completely before you sharpen it.

Keep in mind that any field sharpening steels or small whetstones are designed to put a quick edge on a knife. They will get you out of a tight spot, but don't expect them to put a lasting edge on your knife. For that final edge, you'll have to use better, mounted stones such as a Washita for sharpening and perhaps a Hard Arkansas for final honing.

The accompanying sidebar shows how to sharpen a knife correctly. Once you have cleaned both the knife and the stone, oil the stone generously and spread the oil over the entire surface of it. A hard, steady pressure will be necessary as you begin to draw the edge of the knife across the stone, starting at the heel of the blade and ending each stroke by lifting the handle to sharpen the point. Alternate sides of the blade until you have made 10 to 15 strokes on each side. A fine, hard honing stone will give a keen edge if you draw the knife as if you were taking a thin slice off the top of the stone.

A key factor in putting a good edge on any knife is maintaining a constant angle, usually 15 degrees, between the back of the blade and the stone. You can keep the angle constant for 30 or 40 strokes and then ruin all this work by changing the angle for the last six strokes. If this is your problem, pick up a device that will maintain this critical angle. Most devices are nothing more than a combination clamp and guide bar. Fit this onto your blade, hold the guide bar flat against the stone, and you can be sure of a constant angle.

The last step is stropping the knife against a piece of leather or cardboard. This is the only step in which you draw the edge backward with each stroke, instead of moving it forward as you did on the whetstone.

Typical Knives

The Buck Folding Hunter and Pathfinder knives are traditional and successful designs that continue to handle nearly all chores for generations of campers, hunters, and fishermen. The Buck knife has a 4-inch stainless-steel clip blade. The Pathfinder has a leather handle and a 5-inch blade.

A tough, high-tech, multi-purpose knife is the Gerber Bear Grylls, which will do double duty as a camp tool and a survival knife. It's available with a serrated blade or a fine edge. The high-carbon steel blade measures 4.8 inches. The survival model comes with an emergency whistle, diamond sharpener, fire starter, and nylon sheath.

The DMT knife sharpeners use micron-sized diamonds bonded to precision-ground steel. Used properly, the surface will put an edge on a knife faster than a stone.

Stropping lays down any roughness and "sets" the edge. You can check the sharpness by carefully pulling the edge toward you across your thumbnail. A well-sharpened knife will grab and stop. If it slips, it needs more strokes on the stone.

After getting a final edge on your knife, don't jam it back into its sheath unless you're going back in the field. Leather sheaths collect and hold moisture, which will rust a knife. The best way to store a knife is to oil it lightly, wrap it in waxed paper, and store it where no one will accidentally blunder against the edge or point.

Folding Knife Blade Designs

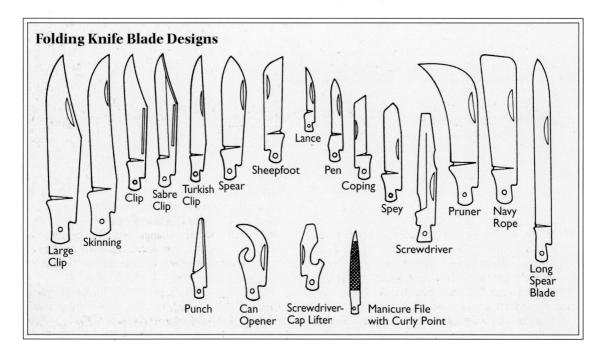

Large Clip, Skinning, Clip, Sabre Clip, Turkish Clip, Spear, Sheepfoot, Lance, Pen, Coping, Spey, Screwdriver, Pruner, Navy Rope, Long Spear Blade, Punch, Can Opener, Screwdriver-Cap Lifter, Manicure File with Curly Point

How to Sharpen a Knife

Step 1 • A good stone will last a lifetime with some care. Never use it dry. Oil the stone generously, spreading the oil over the entire surface of the stone. After the job is done, apply more oil and wipe the stone clean. Oil floats steel particles above the stone, so that they do not clog it.

Step 2 • Grip the knife as shown, maintaining an angle of 15 degrees between the back of the blade and the stone. Applying hard, steady pressure, draw the knife across the stone, beginning at the knife heel. Draw the knife across the stone as if you were taking a slice off the top of the stone.

Step 3 • As you come to the edge of the stone, lift the handle and sharpen the point. Repeat these strokes 10 to 15 times on each side of the blade. Do not alternate strokes. Sharpen one side, then the other. A very dull knife may need more than 15 strokes.

Step 4 • You can check the sharpness by drawing the blade across your fingernail. A well-sharpened blade will bite in and not slide across your fingernail.

BACKPACKS

Throughout this section on camping, there have been references to the backpacker, the camper who takes to the open air with all he needs on his back.

The backpacker is a keen weight watcher. He keeps in mind at all times that he should have with him the barest of essentials, and not one ounce more.

There are five basic pack designs. The type the individual camper needs depends upon the load he expects to carry as well as the distance he must carry it. The five designs are: daypack, rucksack, backpack and frame, packbasket, and hip or waist pack.

■ Daypack

The daypack, known to most campers as the knapsack, is pretty much what its name indicates—a pack that is useful on a daytime outing. It is little more than a rectangular canvas or nylon pack with shoulder straps that may or may not have side pockets, but never a metal frame.

When filling the daypack, place soft items—a poncho or a sweater—against the part of the pack that will press against your back. Also, don't load this pack too heavily, as the total weight of the full pack will pull down uncomfortably on your shoulders and against your back.

For pack material, nylon is recommended for the adult camper, as it is lightweight and waterproof. However, for youthful campers, who may carelessly toss their packs around, a canvas daypack can take more punishment and is less expensive. Some daypacks have waist straps as well as shoulder straps to take some weight off the shoulders.

▪ Rucksack

The rucksack seems to fall midway between the daypack and the larger packs for carrying big loads on long outings. The backpacker who uses the rucksack is usu-

A typical rucksack, which sometimes comes with a small frame, can carry gear and food for a full day. When packing a rucksack, keep heavy gear next to your lower back to minimize sagging.

The combined weight of the pack and frame should be about 5 pounds. When backpacking in flat country or rolling terrain, keep the weight in your backpack high, so that the center of gravity is on or above your shoulders (see Pack A). When packing a load in rocky or steep country, load your pack low so that the center of gravity is at the middle of your back (see Pack B).

Pack A   Pack B

◀ L.L. Bean's Rucksack is typical of this Continental design. With a 2,000-cubic-inch capacity, the rucksack will hold enough gear for a full day of hiking and camping and possibly an overnight spike camp for a hunter or fisherman.

▶ The L.L. Bean Daypack will store all the gear you need for a day in the field. The fleece-lined pockets will protect optics and GPS units. The capacity of the pack is 1,500 cubic inches. It is a good choice for hikers, hunters, and fishermen.

ally out for a full day and must cook a couple of meals in the field.

Unlike the daypack, the rucksack features one or two outside pockets as well as an inside or outside metal frame. This frame prevents the pack from sagging, and puts less tension on the back. These features make it preferable to the daypack in numerous ways. Many rucksacks, however, do not have metal frames.

A sleeping bag is too bulky to put inside a rucksack, but it can be rolled short and lashed to the top or rolled long into a horseshoe shape and lashed to the top and sides. This pack is ill suited for backpacking canned goods, steel traps, and other hardware that can bite into your back.

The rucksack should have web or leather shoulder straps that are a minimum of 2 inches wide and thick enough so as not to curl into narrow bands from a heavy pack. These bands can cut mercilessly into your shoulders.

Strong buckles, snaps, and rings of bronze, brass, or rustproof steel are essential. Beware of an overabundance of tricky snaps, zippers, and buckles. They add to the cost, and usually just bring trouble.

Although such synthetics as nylon and Dacron are being used widely for rucksacks, a good choice is heavy

▶ The RedHead Hybrid Pack is actually a two-in-one pack. The lower detachable section is a waist pack that can be used for hands-free hiking and hunting. When attached to the large compartment, the total pack has a capacity of 2,625 cubic inches. It is a good combination pack for all field activities.

◀ Cabela's Alaskan Outfitter Pack and Frame is a good choice for the serious hunter and hiker who intends to spend several days in the field. The main compartment has a 5,300-cubic-inch capacity, and there are several outside pockets. The pack can be removed and the frame used to pack quartered game and bulky gear, such as a small outboard motor. The pack and frame weigh about 12 pounds.

▶ The RedHead Enduroflex Field Frame can handle most heavy, bulky gear that can't be comfortably carried in a conventional pack. Small outboard motors, quartered game animals, camp stoves, and even a tent can be lashed to this frame. A padded waist belt and suspended back allows air to flow between the frame and the carrier.

canvas. The extra weight will seem inconspicuous, considering the padding to your back that canvas provides. Incidentally, a canvas pack is also simpler to waterproof and keep waterproofed than one made of synthetic fibers.

■ External and Internal Framed Backpacks

For the serious backpacker whose trips last from one to two weeks, the backpack and frame is the best choice. In the 1980s, most backpacks of this type consisted of an external frame constructed of a light metal alloy, and a backpack with both shoulder straps and back supports. The frame is attached to the backpack.

Of all the frames, those made of magnesium are the best. They are lightweight and sturdy, but they are expensive. A practical choice is a frame of an aluminum alloy. It will have shoulder and waist straps, and on some models nylon mesh to keep the load away from the back. This mesh allows air to circulate between pack and back.

Since you need roominess for all of your equipment, a good backpack has five or six outside pockets for smaller, oft-used items. Inside the pack itself are

two large compartments for larger items. Below the pack, on the frame, there is room to strap on a sleeping bag. Gear that won't fit inside the pack can be safely lashed to the frame.

External-framed backpacks are still in wide use today and offer some definite advantages. Remember that the backpack and frame can be removed from one another, permitting the packer to lash such bulky objects as an outboard motor or game to the frame for easy transportation.

In the 1990s, backpacks with internal frames, usually aluminum stays, were developed. Internal-framed backpacks are designed to conform more closely to the body. One manufacturer, REI, went one step further and developed a hybrid it calls perimeter-frame packs. It routes a small-diameter aluminum tube around the periphery of the pack and the design gives the pack the load capacity of an external design. There is a wide range of backpack designs available today and choice pretty much becomes a matter of personal preference.

There are certain things to look for in choosing a framed backpack. The best choice for lightness is a waterproof nylon backpack, as it will keep the rain off your gear. Look for a top flap on the pack that is long enough to cover the top of the bag when it is full; heavy-duty, corrosion-proof zippers on the exterior side and back pockets that won't jam and will keep out dirt and rain; seams and pockets that can withstand rugged use; and shoulder and waist straps that are at least 2 inches wide so they won't curl up and cut you. Also, shoulder straps and harnesses for back support should be adjustable to allow for tightening and taking up slack as the load is increased or decreased.

Don't buy a pack just because it fulfills these requirements, though. Try on various models. Internal and external framed packs should permit the load to be carried vertically with its center of gravity close to your back. In this manner, the weight will be transferred to the legs, the most powerful part of the human body.

The backpack should weigh approximately 2 pounds, the pack frame 3 to 4 pounds. That means the frame and pack together should weigh close to 5 pounds.

The total amount of gear and food carried depends on the individual. An average man can camp on his own for three days, using a good pack and frame, with carefully selected equipment and freeze-dried food weighing a total of 20 to 25 pounds. That same man can stay in the bush for up to two weeks if he carries a pack with 40 pounds of sustenance.

Pack Basket

The pack basket is an old-time favorite that seems to retain limited popularity because of tradition rather than utility.

Made of thin strips of wood from willow or ash logs, the pack basket is light and rigid. The construction protects the contents from breakage and the packer's back from rough or sharp objects inside. Trappers appreciate

The Allagash Pack Basket is typical of this classic design. A pack basket is one of the safest means of carrying breakable goods. This model is made of handwoven maple. It has adjustable straps, and is a good choice for carrying odd-shaped objects.

The RedHead Dry Creek Waist Pack is ideal for the day hiker or hunter who wants to carry only essential gear and still keep both arms free to hold a rifle, bow, fishing tackle, or camera. The pack weighs about 1 pound, has a capacity of 850 cubic inches, and has side and front pockets.

the basket for packing tools, axes, and traps. Canoeists favor it for packing odd-size canned goods and gear. Nevertheless, the basket is not recommended for general backpacking.

Hip or Fanny Pack

This pack provides an ideal alternative for the person who doesn't like to carry a pack by means of shoulder straps. As the name implies, the pack rests on the hips and lower back, and easily carries whatever small gear a hunter, fisherman, or camper might bring along on a one-day trip.

How to Pack a Backpack

How you load your pack is critical. A 50-pound pack may seem manageable when you start out, but it will wear you down quickly after a mile or so. Learn to trim your load. Get rid of those food boxes and cans. Repack everything in leakproof, sealable, plastic bags. When you shop, look for dehydrated or freeze-dried foods.

How much weight you can carry depends on your size, strength, and appetite. There is a limit to how much a person can comfortably carry over a certain period of time. With carefully selected gear and food, an average man can camp for about three days with a backpack that will weigh 30 pounds. Here are some safe limits for maximum backpack weights:

Men: 35–40 pounds
Women: 20–30 pounds
Children: 15 pounds

Stray from these weight limits and you'll find backpacking a chore rather than a pleasure. Take a few backpack trips and you will soon discover how little you actually need to camp in the woods.

ROPES AND KNOTS

Ropes for camp use are made of either natural or synthetic materials. The natural fibers come in hemp, available in such types as manila and sisal, and in cotton strands of everyday cotton fiber that has been specially treated.

Synthetic fibers such as Dacron, nylon, and polypropylene often prove to be from 50 to 100 percent stronger than hemp or cotton rope of equal diameter. These waterproof synthetics do not swell or kink when they are wet. They are likewise unaffected by such hemp maladies as fungus, mildew, and dry rot.

A disadvantage of synthetics is the price. Cotton rope typically costs one-tenth the amount of most synthetic rope of the same diameter. Hemp costs are usually one-third the amount of synthetics. And knots made with synthetic rope do not hold as well as those made with hemp or cotton. In the case of nylon rope, the stretch range may be up to 20 percent of the total length.

The accompanying chart shows the approximate breaking strengths in pounds of dead weight of the various types of ropes.

The safe working load for a brand-new rope is one-quarter the breaking strength. If the rope has been through average use, figure one-sixth of the breaking strength. Dropping the load or jerking the rope doubles the strain, and knots and splices diminish its strength, sometimes drastically.

To care for a hemp rope, remember that moisture causes damage. Keep this rope as dry as possible, whether you are storing it or using it. By hanging hemp or cotton rope in a dry, high, cool place, you protect it from harmful rodents. The sweat-salt traces left on a rope by human hands attract mice and rats with their ever-sharp teeth.

Synthetics need little protection from water, but they can be substantially weakened by acids, oils, and intense heat.

▪ WHIPPING

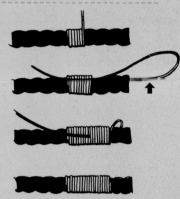

The purpose of whipping, using several turns of a strong thread, is to prevent the end of a rope from unraveling. Hold the thread taut during the wrapping turns. The section of the thread where the arrow points is given a half dozen turns once the pull-through loop has been formed. The loop should be pulled snug and the end trimmed. If the rope is synthetic, melt it with a cigarette lighter for a tighter seal. Hemp and cotton also seal more securely if dipped in a quick-setting glue.

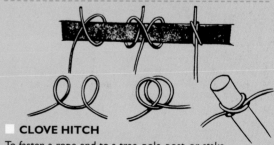

▪ CLOVE HITCH

To fasten a rope end to a tree, pole, post, or stake, use the clove hitch.

▪ SQUARE KNOT

Also known as the reef knot, the square knot attaches two ends of the same rope, or joins two similar-size ropes or lines. The chances of this knot slipping are nil.

Approximate Breaking Strength of Ropes (pounds)

Diameter (inches)	Sisal	Manila	Poly-propylene	Dacron	Nylon
¼	480	600	1,050	1,600	1,800
⅜	1,080	1,350	2,200	3,300	4,000
½	2,120	2,650	3,800	5,500	7,100
¾	4,320	5,400	8,100	11,000	14,200
1	7,200	9,000	14,000	18,500	24,600

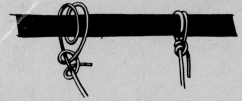

■ TURNS WITH HALF HITCHES

To make a simple knot for tying a rope end to a pole or ring, make two turns around the object, followed by a pair of half hitches. For additional strength, use more of each.

■ BOWLINE

Easy to tie and untie, the bowline is best for such tasks as leading or hitching a horse with a rope around its neck. When you need to tie a loop around an object, the bowline will not slip.

■ GUY-LINE HITCH

The guy-line hitch tightens tent and other guy ropes that need adjustment. Begin with two basic overhand knots, with the rope running through the top one. The bottom overhand knot will slide up or down to give or take slack on the guy line or tent rope. You needn't worry about tearing the tent fabric with this hitch.

■ DOUBLE-SHEET BEND

When you are linking up a pair of ropes of varied diameters, try the double-sheet bend. Make the simple loop in the thicker of the two ropes, using the thinner one for the turns. The double-sheet bend is preferable to the single style because it is safer and takes perhaps a second longer to finish up.

■ CARRICK BEND

The carrick bend will join ropes to tow or support hefty loads. It doesn't jam and can be easily untied.

■ TIMBER HITCH

For towing logs or hitching to a pole or tree with a rope that must sustain constant, strong pressure, the proper knot is the timber hitch. It ties in seconds and will not jam.

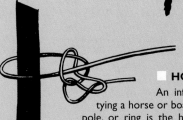

■ HORSE HITCH

An infallible knot for tying a horse or boat line to a tree, pole, or ring is the horse hitch. The running end of the rope passed through a broad loop at the completion of the hitch will make it more secure.

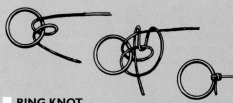

■ RING KNOT

This knot works best when tied to a ring, such as a swivel end or a metal loop in a lure. If you are using slick monofilament fishing line, do not trim the loose end too closely or it may slip.

■ SLIP KNOT

The slip knot is simple and won't untie very quickly. A half hitch or two around the standing part of the rope or line will further bind this knot.

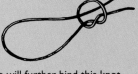

WATER KNOT

Any fisherman should be familiar with the water knot. Adequate for joining fishing lines, leaders, ropes, or small cords, the water knot begins with an overhand knot made loosely in the end of either line. Put the running end of the other line through it, and secure it using an overhand knot around the first line's standing part. Next, pull both overhand knots together. Half hitches on either side will tighten the knot. Trim the water knot carefully to prevent it from catching in your rod guides.

FIGURE-EIGHT KNOT

Tie the figure-eight knot just like the overhand knot, but give the loop a half twist before the running end is passed through. Also an end knot, the figure eight is slightly less compact than the overhand but significantly stronger.

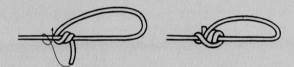

TAUT-LINE HITCH

Primarily for tightening tent ropes, the taut-line hitch is actually a running loop that holds under strain.

Form a loop around the anchor. Then, with the running end, make a pair of small turns around the standing part, spiraling it in the direction of the inside of the loop. A half hitch tied around the standing part, outside of the big loop, completes the loop knot.

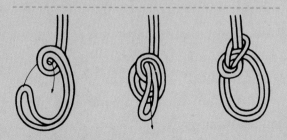

BOWLINE ON A BIGHT

The bowline mentioned earlier has a variation called bowline on a bight, which is especially useful for climbing.

Make an overhand loop and place the bight through it. Pull the bight downward to the end of the big loop formed by the running end. Then, separate the bight, putting the big loop through it. Slide the running-end bight upward so it goes around the standing part. Pull it tight, and the knot is ready.

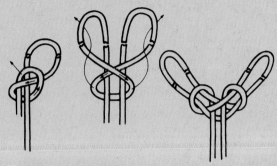

SPANISH BOWLINE

Different from the bowline on a bight in that its two loops are separated, the Spanish bowline is another variation. It functions as an improvised seat and backrest.

A slip knot about twice the size of either of the completed loops is the first step. Give the loop a half twist so the standing part crosses in the rear. Keep the running end of the slip knot tight against the standing part where they form parallel lines. At the same time, hold the turn at the back of the knot, and immediately slide the bight next to the running end outward. Stop when it forms a loop equal in size to the original slip knot.

The resulting X pattern should now be slid up the loops until both are rather small. Reach through the pair from the back, taking the bight below the X and pulling it through. You will now have both loops and an X pattern between the two.

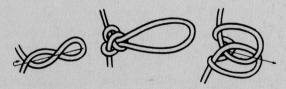

BUTTERFLY LOOP

When three persons are climbing, the person in the middle should be held with a fixed or butterfly loop. This loop also makes an excellent harness for dragging weighty loads.

Make a bight as big as you want the loop to be. Twist it one complete turn, forming a loose figure eight. Fold this double loop over the standing part to produce a pair of intertwined loops. Pass the tip of the original bight through the two loops where the overlapping takes place. Pull on the bight to tighten.

CAMPFIRES

To start a campfire, clear a site—always on rock or dirt—by removing all ground debris for at least 3 feet on all sides. This prevents any combustible material such as rubbish and underground roots from igniting and causing a possible forest fire. When using the top of a ledge for your fire, beware of small cracks through which hot coals might tumble into flammable material.

A good fire for cooking, lighting, or heat starts with tinder, thin sticks of kindling, and medium-size sticks of firewood. Stack them loosely or in pyramid fashion in that order. Then stand on the upwind side and light the tinder from there. This directs the flame upward and into the mass of tinder. Lighting from the downwind side leaves you little opportunity to direct the flame.

Once the tinder is well ignited, blow on it or fan the fire gently with your hat. The tinder will light the slim sticks, which in turn will set the medium-size sticks ablaze. Tinder, which forms the bottom layer of the fire, is any small-size fuel that ignites readily. Any scrap of dry paper will do, especially waxed paper and the like.

Firewood Characteristics

Species	Heat Value	Ease of Splitting	Ease of Starting	Sparks
Alder	Medium/Low	Easy	Fair	Moderate
Apple	Medium/High	Difficult	Difficult	Few
Ash	High	Easy/Moderate	Fair/Difficult	Few
Aspen	Low	Easy	Easy	Few
Beech	High	Difficult	Moderate	Few
Birch	Medium	Moderate	Easy	Moderate
Cedar	Medium/Low	Easy	Easy	Many
Cherry	Medium	Easy	Difficult	Few
Cottonwood	Low	Easy	Easy	Moderate
Cypress	Low	Easy	Easy	Few
Dogwood	High	Difficult	Easy	Few
Douglas Fir	Medium	Easy	Moderate	Moderate
Elm	Medium	Difficult	Moderate	Few
Fir, Grand Noble	Medium/Low	Easy	Easy	Moderate
Gum	Medium	Difficult	Moderate	Few
Hemlock	Medium/Low	Easy	Easy	Many
Hickory	Medium/High	Difficult	Difficult	Few
Juniper	Medium	Difficult	Fair	Many
Larch	Medium/High	Easy/Moderate	Easy	Many
Locust	Very High	Very Difficult	Difficult	Very Few
Madrone	High	Difficult	Difficult	Very Few
Maple, Hard	High	Easy	Difficult	Few
Maple, Soft	Medium	Easy	Fair	Few
Oak	Very High	Moderate	Difficult	Few
Pecan	High	Easy	Difficult	Few
Pine, Lodgepole	Low	Easy	Easy	Moderate
Pine, Ponderosa, White, Yellow	Medium/Low	Easy	Easy	Moderate
Pinyon	Medium	Easy	Easy	Few
Redwood	Low	Easy	Easy	Few
Spruce	Low	Easy/Moderate	Easy	Moderate
Sycamore	Medium	Difficult	Moderate	Few
Walnut	Medium/High	Easy/Moderate	Fair	Few
Willow	Low	Easy	Fair	Moderate

There are also wood sources of tinder. Birch bark that is stripped and wadded loosely, and dry cedar bark both perform well. Sagebrush bark, dead evergreen twigs still on the tree with brown needles intact, and dry, dead grass or weeds that are crushed into a ball are also effective.

Pitch is a primary burning agent that is found in the decayed trunks and upturned roots of woods such as spruce, pines, and fir. It also works efficiently as tinder when sliced up with the wood still attached. To tell if a wood contains pitch, alert yourself to the resinous odor and weighty heft of the wood. Even heavy rains don't change the quality of pitch slabs as excellent tinder.

If you are handy with a knife and adept at whittling, you can make fuzz sticks (also known as fire sticks). Shave lengthy splinters from almost any dry, soft stick, leaving as many splinters attached as possible. When you have what resembles a tiny pine tree, thrust it upright into the ground and place some tinder around it. Set a match to the lower slivers, and you have a fine fire starter.

You can squirt a little kerosene, stove gasoline, or lighter fluid on the kindling as an alternative to gathering tinder. Be sure, however, to use these liquid fuels prior to striking your match to prevent an explosion. Kindling, which consists of thin, dry sticks, is ordinarily placed loosely in a tepee shape above the tinder, or crisscrossed on top of it.

The basic firewood is not added until both tinder and kindling are in place. This wood is necessarily heavier than the kindling, usually longer, and from 3 to 4 inches, or possibly even 6 inches, in thickness. Small logs or thick branches are prime sources of this firewood, which catches from the combustible material beneath to provide a strong and stable fire.

Woods vary in burning qualities. They catch fire primarily in relation to their dryness, cut size, and resin content. They give heat and good cooking coals primarily in relation to their density—the denser the wood, the more mass available for combustion.

Any dry (seasoned) wood will be good kindling if cut to finger thickness. Wood of conifers tends to catch fire more easily than that of deciduous trees because their high amounts of resin ignite at lower temperatures than the gases generated from wood fibers alone. But conifers tend to be smokier, and their resin pockets cause more popping and sparks.

If you are forced to burn unseasoned wood, as in a survival predicament, ash is one of the best because of its low moisture content "on the stump." For cooking, if very dry, the densest deciduous woods are best. These include the oaks, hickories, locusts, beech, birches, ashes, and hawthorns. Yet in parts of western states, you may find that conifers are the only woods available. In northwestern Canada and Alaska, birch and alder are about the only abundant, dense deciduous woods.

Oak and hickory rate as good wood, but remember that these hardwoods will quickly take the edge off an ax or saw—something you may want to keep in mind if you're on an extended trip. And if sparks and smoke bother you, avoid the pines and spruces, tamarack, basswood, and chestnut.

■ Hunter's Fire

Among the many possible arrangements of the basic campfire, the hunter's fire is a simple, dual-purpose one that provides hot coals for cooking along with heat and light.

Start your fire as described earlier and wait for a bed of hot coals to form. At that point, place two green logs on either side of the fire to resemble a corridor. If this is done before the coals form, the fire will eventually eat right into the logs. Rocks can also be used to form a corridor. The camper out for a brief time or on a string of one-night stands on a pack trail or canoe route benefits most from this type of fire.

If the fire dies down, place a support under the ends of the logs to let more air in through the sides.

Two Types of Hunter's Fire

Keyhole Fire

Like the hunter's fire, the keyhole fire supplies heat and light, and a place for cooking chores. Also for short-term use, this campfire consists of flat, small rocks arranged in a keyhole shape. It features a corridor 3 to 6 feet long and 1 foot wide, and a circle adjacent to the rectangle.

Begin the fire in the center of the corridor, and wait until you see that the surrounding rocks are hot and the trench is lined with a bed of coals. Using a piece of dry firewood, push the blazing wood to one end of the trench. The remainder stays at the other end for cooking. When the cooking coals seem to be losing their vigor, move some of the other coals to the cooking area.

Some campers prefer two keyhole fires rather than one, particularly for large groups of campers, so there is always a substantial amount of hot coals to work with.

Trench Fire

When stoves and wood are nowhere to be found, and the pots you are using have no bails, set up a trench fire.

Dig a trench as deep as you need, parallel to the direction of the prevailing wind. Leave the upwind end open to provide an effective draft. If the trench is very narrow, its sides may support the pots. Otherwise, you may need to use green sticks to hold up your cooking gear.

Indian Fire

When wood fuel is at a premium and it is necessary to conserve what you have, try the Indian fire. Note that five thick logs radiate outward from the center. Tinder should be placed at this midpoint. As the logs burn, push them gradually into the middle.

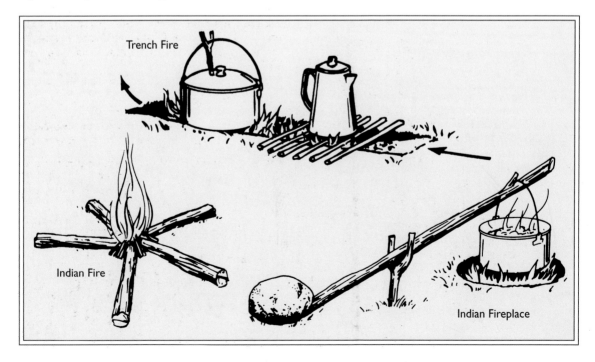

Dingle Sticks

Indian Fireplace

If you have to contend with strong winds, the Indian fireplace is appropriate. Dig a hole that is a bit larger than your kettle, and build a small fire at the bottom. Using a fork-shaped stick to support a straight stick with one end secured in the ground, hang the kettle over the hole. If you have enough fuel, set the pot in the hole itself, but be sure there is adequate space at the bottom for air to circulate.

The lower end of the stick for hanging the kettle doesn't have to be buried or driven into the ground if a heavy enough rock or log is handy. Just lay this weight on the end of the stick, or wedge the stick under it securely.

Reflector Fire

The reflector fire provides heat to a tent or an oven. A small raft of 1-inch-thick logs, rocks or sod, or aluminum foil will direct heat to the desired spot. A conventional fire built in front of the reflector safely warms up a baker tent or practically any other type of tent. The reflector oven using this fire lets you bake biscuits and such.

The reflector fire requires flames to project enough heat to a selected spot. Coals alone unfortunately radiate in all directions, making cooking more difficult.

Dingle Stick

One of the simplest and most practical campfires uses the dingle stick, a device that holds a pot securely over a fire. The accompanying illustrations show two arrangements of the dingle stick. Be sure to choose a durable stick for either one.

Swedish Fire Lay

An efficient fire for heating a single kettle, pot, coffee-pot, or frying pan is the Swedish fire lay. It's especially

Reflector Fire

Swedish Fire Lay

Nutrition Information for Freeze-Dried Foods

Several companies produce complete lines of freeze-dried food for campers, hikers, survivalists, and anyone interested in these lightweight packaged foods. Here, courtesy of Mountain House, is a nutritional chart of its line of entrees. The data here is a typical example of the nutritional values of foods from other companies.

Product				Calories		Fat/Grams		Milligrams
Product Name	Pkg. Net Wt. (ounces)	Servings per Pkg.	Serving Size	Total	From Fat	Total	Saturated	Cholesterol
Beef Stew	4.30	2.5	I cup	150	40	4.5	I	20
Beef Stroganoff with Noodles	4.80	2.5	I cup	250	100	II	4	40
Beef Teriyaki with Rice	5.75	2.5	I cup	260	25	2.5	.5	10
Chicken a la King with Noodles	6.35	3	I cup	260	80	9	2.5	50
Chicken Breasts with Rib Meat and Mashed Potatoes	3.70	2	½ pkg.	210	30	3	1.5	55
Chicken Teriyaki with Rice	5.01	2.5	I cup	230	20	2	0.5	20
Chili Mac with Beef	4.80	2.5	I cup	240	60	7	2.5	30
Lasagna with Meat Sauce	4.8	2.5	I cup	240	70	8	3.5	25
Long Grain and Wild Rice Pilaf	5.08	2.5	I cup	220	35	4	2	10
Macaroni and Cheese	6.81	3	I cup	310	130	15	7	35
Mexican Style Rice and Chicken	5.40	3	I cup	220	45	5	2	20
Noodles and Chicken	4.73	2.5	I cup	220	45	4.5	0.5	40
Pasta Primavera	4.80	2.5	I cup	170	30	3.5	2	10
Potatoes and Cheese with Broccoli	4.37	2.5	I cup	200	40	4.5	2.5	15
Rice and Chicken	6.38	3	I cup	270	80	10	1.5	10
Seafood Chowder	4.44	2.5	I cup	230	90	10	6	60
Spaghetti with Meat Sauce	4.51	2.5	I cup	230	45	5	2	20
Sweet and Sour Pork with Rice	6.10	2.5	I cup	280	45	5	1.5	40
Turkey Tetrazzini	4.27	2.5	I cup	230	70	8	1.5	30

convenient in confined spaces. Its foundation is a small fire with the sticks arranged in a star shape, like the basic Indian fire. Around this foundation, three split chunks of log, each about a foot long, are stood on end. Tilt the split logs in at the top, propping them against one another to form a pyramid. The heat travels up the logs to the top, and eventually they'll begin to burn. But even before they do, the top will be hot, and it serves as a base for the cooking utensil.

■ Rain or Snow

Starting a fire in driving rain or snow is usually possible, and often easy. On rain-soaked ground, you can construct a foundation for the fire using slabs of bark,

rocks, or broken limbs. On snow, build the foundation from thick pieces of green or punky and wet downfall. Avoid all fires beneath trees capped with snow, as the rising heat will melt the snow and possibly extinguish your fire.

The optimum wood under these conditions comes from standing dead trees. Most of the wood chopped from their insides will be dry enough to burn. Birch bark, pitch-saturated evergreen, and white ash are excellent choices, even when moist.

When you have gathered tinder, kindling, and firewood, look for a natural overhang—a rock ledge, for example. If none is available, improvise with a flat rock, a slab of bark, or a log propped up at an angle. A poncho, a canvas tarp, or a tent awning is even better.

	Grams			
Sodium	Carbs	Dietary Fiber	Sugars	Protein
620	16	2	2	12
820	29	1	3	10
760	48	2	13	11
750	29	2	2	16
800	21	2	2	24
700	41	2	13	10
650	31	3	3	12
330	28	3	7	14
660	44	2	3	6
640	31	1	1	14
620	32	6	3	13
870	34	1	2	9
330	28	1	4	6
370	31	5	7	9
740	41	1	1	7
840	23	1	7	13
560	32	3	6	12
950	47	1	16	12
700	22	1	5	14

CAMP FOODS AND MENUS

To plan nutritious camp menus, consider these four basic questions:

1. How many meals of each type (breakfast, lunch, etc.) will there be?
2. Where will the meals be prepared (in a blind, on a mountainside, etc.)?
3. How will the supplies be transported (backpack, RV, etc.)?
4. How many people are in the group and what kind of appetites do they have?

Apply the answers to the three main groups of food—carbohydrates, proteins, and fats—and determine the necessary amount of calories.

Calories supply energy. How many calories you need depends on your weight, your rate of metabolism, and how much work you are doing. Everyday camping chores use up about 3,000 calories per day, while backpacking requires 4,000 calories for the same period. Cold weather and a steep climb may call for as many as 5,000 calories. When your intake of calories is less than your output, fat already stored by your body will be burned off. To prevent weight loss, it is necessary to consume a sufficient amount of calories daily.

The protein requirement depends primarily on body weight. A man weighing 130 pounds needs 60 grams of protein per day, while a 175-pound man needs 80 grams. Protein is essential because it builds and repairs body tissues. Good sources are cheese, meat, milk, eggs, and fish.

A wide variety of dehydrated or freeze-dried foods is available through sporting-goods stores, camp-equipment dealers, and even supermarkets. Both processes take as much water out of the food as possible to permit lightweight packing and simple preparation.

Straight dehydration is an air-drying process wherein heat dries the food but leaves it flexible. Once the food is cooked, the water returns. Freeze drying, on the other hand, removes water by quick-freezing and placing of the food in a vacuum chamber. The pressure drops in the chamber and heat is added. The ice then sublimates slowly, meaning it goes directly from solid to gaseous form with no intermediate liquid state. The resultant food is the same size, slightly paler, and far lighter. Soaking the food from 10 to 30 minutes brings on the flavor. Besides being odor-free, the freeze-drying

Prepare the firewood, and search out a dry area to strike a match on. Your match case will probably be dry, and zippers and buttons on the inside of clothing will work in a pinch. Try scraping the match against your thumbnail, or even on the edge of your teeth as a last resort. Then, shield the initial fire until the heavy firewood is securely aflame. At that point, the fire stands little chance of being put out by the elements.

Make certain to carefully douse any fire you build with bucketful after bucketful of water when you are finished with it. Don't stop until every piece of wood and all coals are drenched. Then, stir the coals until all sparks and steam are gone. A healthy mound of wet mineral soil guarantees that the fire is completely and safely extinguished.

process leads to finer taste and quality than standard dehydration.

The outdoor cook should stress simplicity, but variety is possible. Have cereal with dried fruit one day and pancakes with syrup the next. Lunches can go from cheese to sausage to peanut butter. Suppers can be more elaborate if you'd like, and precooked items are worthwhile in that respect. By adding water to certain foods, the camp chef can prepare delicious chicken or beef stew. And water is always available if you are near a stream or lake.

Consider prepackaging such foods as sugar, salt, bacon, and flour. There's no need to lug along much more than a quarter of the contents. Premeasure this food, and then pack and label it, specifying for which meal and which day it is intended.

Remember to include supplementary or trail foods. They are not a part of any set meal, but they may increase flavor (condiments, for example), add flexibility to the menu, or give rapid-fire energy. Supplementary foods should be high in protein. Trail foods can substitute as lunch or emergency food when cooking a full meal is impractical. Often high in calories, fat, and carbohydrates, foods such as raisins, nuts, chocolate, bacon,

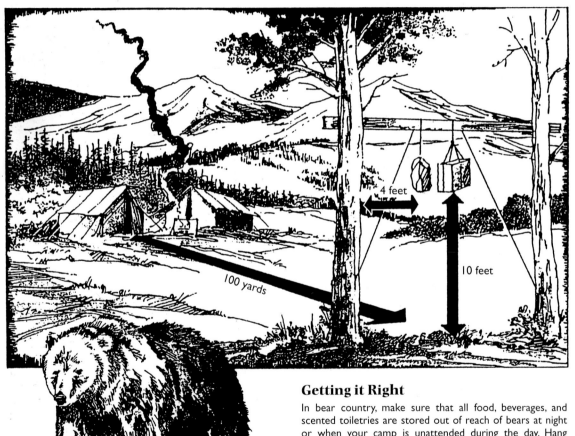

4 feet

10 feet

100 yards

Getting it Right

In bear country, make sure that all food, beverages, and scented toiletries are stored out of reach of bears at night or when your camp is unattended during the day. Hang your food 10 feet off the ground and 4 feet from any vertical post, or store it inside a bear-resistant container, such as a car, pickup cab, or hard-sided container. Coolers, pop-up campers, and tents are **not** bear-resistant containers.

The traditional shore lunch of fried fish, especially if it's walleye fillets, frequently becomes the highlight of any fishing or camping trip. Don't forget the potatoes, beans, and onions.

candy bars, and hard candy provide instant energy and keep the saliva flowing in your mouth so it doesn't become uncomfortably dry.

Keep in mind that fresh food is fine the first day out, but thereafter stick to foods that will not spoil quickly, if at all, on what might be a humid trail.

■ Animal-Proof Your Camp

If you're a hunter, fisherman, or camper, there is always the chance that you will encounter bears or other wild animals. How you behave may determine the outcome. Most advice on bears focuses on grizzlies, but the information can just as easily be applied to black bears and other wild animals. Most animals will avoid you, but there will always be the one that will break the rules.

If you're at a designated campsite, take all garbage with you. Don't leave it in a trash barrel to attract animals.

If you're a hunter, animal carcasses or parts of carcasses should be stored at least 100 yards from any campsite or trail. In bear country, never sleep within 100 yards of any animal carcass.

If you encounter a grizzly, your behavior can affect the situation. The Wyoming Fish and Game Department advises that you should first try to slowly leave the area. Keep calm, avoid direct eye contact, back up slowly, and speak in a soft monotone. Never run and do not try to climb a tree unless you are sure that you have time and ability to climb at least 10 feet before the bear reaches you. Grizzlies can run faster than you can.

If a grizzly charges, stand your ground. Bears will often mock charge or run past you. If you're unarmed and a bear overpowers you, assume a cannonball position, covering your head and neck with your hands and arms. Stay in this position until you are sure that the bear is gone.

Section Six
SURVIVAL

Survival is the art of making efficient use of any available resource that can help sustain an individual. If a person is able to think clearly and objectively about an emergency situation—because he has prepared for it—he is far more likely to survive than someone who panics and is unable to take full advantage of the resources that may be at hand.

To survive, five basic needs—sustenance, medical, fire, shelter, and rescue—must be met. Few survival situations are identical, and not all of the needs must be met in every case. However, when thinking about and planning for survival, it is important to prepare for emergencies in which all of these needs must be met.

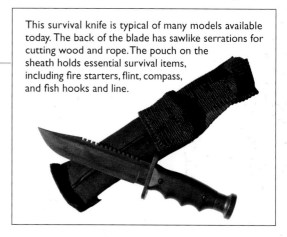

This survival knife is typical of many models available today. The back of the blade has sawlike serrations for cutting wood and rope. The pouch on the sheath holds essential survival items, including fire starters, flint, compass, and fish hooks and line.

PLANNING AHEAD

It is ironic that many survival situations often strike the ill prepared. The day hiker, who is wearing nothing but shorts and a T-shirt, invariably is the one caught in an unexpected late-spring snowstorm. Likewise, boats never seem to sink when there are enough life jackets to go around.

Planning and preparing for emergencies is more than carrying a survival knife into the woods with a compass on the end and three matches inside. Preparation requires investing time to be physically and mentally fit, and thoughtful planning and intelligent selection of resources that will be available when you need them.

Mental preparation starts with the belief that it can happen to you. Nobody buckles their seat belt with the intention of getting into an accident. Likewise, it is foolhardy to head into the woods without enough gear to

help you get through a day when Mother Nature throws you a curveball.

The will to survive is influenced by skill, faith, and courage. The more practice, the more skill. The more skill, the greater the faith. The greater the faith, the more confident you are, and the more enjoyable your outdoor experience can be.

PREPARING A SURVIVAL KIT

Preparation is the key. Far more is involved than simply buying a prepackaged survival kit. It is unlikely that any single kit will meet your specific needs. As

a reminder, sustenance, medical care, fire, shelter, and rescue are the major categories of needs a survivor may have. Equally important, however, is thinking about these needs in the context of the environment that you will be in. A midsummer hike in the Grand Canyon requires different gear than a December snowshoe trip in the Rockies. As an example, carrying water to meet a sustenance need in the desert may make more sense than carrying water-purification tablets, a logical choice when hiking in an area where water is plentiful. The need for water does not change, but how an individual prepares to meet that need does.

Select the items for your survival kit based on their versatility, multifunctionality, and practicality. While improvising is not one of the five basic needs for survival, it is an important process in bringing all of these needs together. For example, surgical tubing, selected as a tourniquet for a first-aid kit, can be used for collecting water from an improvised solar still, drinking water from your water-collection containers, or making a slingshot.

Daypack or Hiker Survival Kit

The following items are recommended for a complete, quality daypack or hiker survival kit. These items have been selected for their versatility for all survival-related emergencies. No kit, however, can be entirely right for every situation. These items form the basic foundation on which you should build after taking into account your activity and the environment. While the list may seem long, consider that many of these items are small and light, and a number of the items (such as knives and saws) are tools you will want to take with you anyway for everyday use. The daypack survival kit includes:

- Fully charged cell phone
- GPS (global positioning system)
- 1-gallon water bag or container (collapsible or folded)
- Water-purification tablets
- 3,600-calorie, nonperishable food ration (Datrex, MRE, etc.)
- Hard candy
- Container for boiling water
- Large, fixed-blade knife
- Pocket knife with locking blade
- Flint and steel fire starter
- Fire-lighting tinder
- Windproof and waterproof matches (strike-anywhere versions are best)
- Waterproof match case
- Lighter
- Flashlight with spare batteries
- Three 12-hour, high-intensity Cyalume snap lights

- Signal mirror
- Whistle
- Compass
- Compact strobe light
- First-aid kit (should include prescription medicines and large compresses, and should be adequate for the environment)
- Saw
- Multiperson emergency tube shelter
- Survival bag
- Mylar space blanket sleeping bag
- Space blanket
- Wool gloves
- Wool hat
- Dry socks
- Emergency poncho or rain jacket
- Cord or rope
- Sewing kit
- Multitool (Leatherman, etc.)
- Sharpening stone
- Carry/storage bag (sealed for pilfer resistance)

Optional items:
- Fishing kit
- Snare wire
- Surgical tubing

Vehicle Survival Kit

The following items are recommended for a complete, quality vehicle survival kit. While items like jumper cables, tire chains, and road flares are not normally considered part of a vehicle survival kit, but rather safety items, far too many survival situations have started along the side of the road because they were not present. Be ready to improvise! For example, if your car overheats because of a ruptured hose, wait for the car to cool and fix the rupture with duct tape. This may not be the perfect fix, but it can get you to the next town or nearest phone.

Remember also that your vehicle is poorly insulated and that as soon as you lose your power to run the heater or air conditioner, the car will become an icebox or an oven. If you are using part of the car as shade, shelter, or a wind block, don't forget to keep your fire well away from the vehicle. Getting outside the vehicle can greatly improve your survivability, but do not leave your vehicle or fail to cannibalize all of the resources it may offer. The thought of cannibalizing your car can be disheartening when you think about its cost, but any vehicle can be replaced, so don't fret too long. The mirrors make great signals; the hubcaps can boil water; the tires can make a dark black, smoky signal fire; and the insulation in the seats can insulate you outside as well. A good vehicle survival kit includes:

- Cell phone (a good recommendation for any traveler)
- GPS
- Spare tire
- Flashlight
- Jack
- Gas can
- Spool of 20-gauge wire
- Tire chains
- Flat tire repair kit
- Ground tarp
- Jumper cables
- Tool kit
- Tow rope
- Road flares (red Cyalume 12-hour snap lights also work well)
- Shovel
- Duct tape
- 1 gallon of water
- Blanket
- Saw
- Emergency poncho or rain jacket
- Wool gloves
- Wool hat

- Multitool (Leatherman, etc.)
- Cord or rope
- Large emergency tube shelter or tarp
- Mylar emergency space blanket
- Sleeping bags (during certain weather conditions)
- Water-storage container
- Water-purification tablets
- Six red, 12-hour Cyalume lights
- Six yellow, 12-hour, high-intensity Cyalume lights
- 3,600-calorie, nonperishable ration (Datrex, MRE, etc.)
- Signal mirror
- Whistle
- Compact strobe light
- First-aid kit (should include prescription medicines, trauma dressings, and other large bandages)
- Surgical tubing
- Large, fixed-blade survival knife
- Pocket knife with locking blade
- Flint and steel fire starter
- Fire-lighting tinder
- Windproof and waterproof matches (strike-anywhere versions are best)
- Waterproof match case
- Lighter
- Compact sewing kit
- Holding container (sealed for pilfer resistance)

SUSTENANCE

Sustenance is the need for food and water, which supplies your energy, increases your metabolism, regulates your temperature, and allows your mind to work rationally. Most healthy adults can miss a few meals without significant distress. However, even the healthiest adults can go no longer than a few days without water before they become delirious and lose vital body functions. While ready-to-eat, low-water rations make excellent additions to many survival kits, far too much emphasis is placed on food and not nearly enough on water, water storage, and water purification.

▨ Making Potable Water

Rainwater collected in clean containers or in plants is generally safe for drinking. However, you must purify water from lakes, ponds, swamps, springs, or streams, especially those near human habitation. When at all possible, you must disinfect all water by using iodine or chlorine or by boiling. You can purify water by:

- Using water-purification tablets.

- Pouring five drops of 2 percent tincture of iodine in a canteen full of clean water, and 10 drops in a canteen of cloudy or cold water. (Let the canteen stand for 30 minutes before drinking.)

- Boiling water for one minute at sea level, adding one minute for each additional 1,000 feet above sea level, or boiling for 10 minutes no matter where you are.

- Using a commercial water-purification device.

POTABLE DRINKING-WATER SYSTEM DEVICES: Having to purify water is a bother. The only reason to carry any drinking-water purifier at all is to protect your health against microbiological and chemical contaminants. Water-related health threats can occur any time you are in contact with water: drinking water directly, using water as a food or beverage ingredient, using water for washing or brushing your teeth, or using water to clean cookware.

Primary exposure to drinking-water contaminants occurs at the following times:

- When collecting raw water for purification. To avoid this threat, use a separate container for your raw water supply whenever possible. Be selective when possible. Choose a source least likely to be badly polluted.

- During purification. Be careful to prevent dirty water from dripping or flowing into purified water.

- When storing your purifier either at meal sites or campsites or in your carry pack.

- Especially when handling the purifier during storage, back washing, brushing, scraping, or other maintenance functions.

Remember, the primary microorganisms of concern in most wilderness recreation areas are tough, hardy cystic parasites that resist heat and cold (even freezing temperatures), drought, chlorine, iodine, and just about everything else. And while bacteria are relatively fragile and have very short life cycles, often less than a day, cysts can exist for months. All microorganisms of chief concern are invisibly small and cannot be seen, smelled, or detected in any quick and easy manner. Accordingly, you must rely on knowledge of your area and on common sense.

It is widely known today that *Giardia* or *Cryptosporidium* have been found in water supplies essentially in every country in the world. Therefore, you should always protect against parasitic cysts and insist on 100 percent reduction. Where one cyst can infect, a 99.9 percent reduction may not be good enough, especially when there is no known treatment for some cysts.

There have been essentially no waterborne typhoid, cholera, or Hepatitis A epidemics in the United States for the last 50 years, so the likelihood of their occurrence from a U.S. wilderness water source is very low.

Pesticides, herbicides, and other chemicals can be present anywhere downwind or downstream from major agricultural and industrial areas even hundreds of miles away. These contaminants concentrate in streams, rivers, and lakes.

Asbestos fibers can be found in very high numbers of more than a million fibers per liter in most western and some eastern wilderness waters. Even though trace amounts of these chemicals won't make you ill today, no one wants to drink asbestos fibers if they can easily be avoided.

Micron ratings must be absolute to be meaningful, and precise measurements are essentially impossible to make. Micron ratings pertain only to the physical removal or straining of particles, so absolute micron ratings are only one means of evaluation for removal effectiveness. Removal of pesticides, herbicides, tastes, odors, and most colors and solvents require other purification (separation) mechanisms. Many units, even those with very low micron ratings, have little or no ability to remove anything other than particles.

According to federal regulations, all water-purification devices are defined as being either pesticide or device products. Pesticide products rely on chemically poisoning organisms (pests), while devices rely on physically removing them. It's easy to tell whether a product is categorized as a pesticide or a device. All products must carry an Environmental Protection Agency (EPA) establishment number. Pesticide products, however, must carry two EPA numbers, one for the manufacturing establishment and one for the pesticide being used. So, decide if you want to use a device or a pesticide for your water-purification needs, and be sure to check the label to choose the right type. In certain applications, it may be desirable to use a pesticide to purify water, but complete removal of the pesticide is very desirable after enough kill time is allowed.

It is important to note that iodine resins are not effective against cysts.

All products being marketed today that carry an EPA establishment number are deemed to meet all current, pertinent EPA and other federal regulations. Otherwise, they would not be permitted on the market.

▓ Wild Plants for Food

After water, food is your most urgent need. In a survival situation, you should always be on the lookout for wild foods and live off the land whenever possible. Plants are a valuable food source. Although they may not provide a balanced diet, they will sustain you, even in arctic areas, where the heat-producing qualities of meat are normally essential. Many plant foods such as nuts and seeds will give you enough protein for normal efficiency. Roots, green vegetables, and plant foods containing natural sugar will provide calories and carbohydrates that will give your body energy.

Solar Still for Safe Water

No matter how fresh and clean water may appear to be in that mountain stream or creek, you can never be sure that it isn't contaminated with chemicals and bacteria that make it unsafe for drinking. It is common sense to always carry a container of water with your gear, especially in warm climates where dehydration is a danger. In a survival situation, a sportsman can get safe drinking water by building a solar still, which will usually provide at least a pint of water every 24 hours. Here's how to use the sun to get safe drinking water:

Step 1 • Dig a hole in the ground about 2 feet deep and 3 feet across.

Step 2 • Place a clean bucket or pan at the bottom of the hole.

Step 3 • Set a plastic sheet over the hole and hold it in place by piling stones or dirt around the edges.

Step 4 • Place a small stone in the center of the plastic sheet so that the water formed by condensation on the sheet's sides is funneled down into the catch container.

The sun causes condensation to form on the sides of the plastic sheet. As the water collects at the bottom of the sheet, it drips into the bucket. As an extra precaution, boil the water for 10 minutes or add a commercial water-treatment tablet.

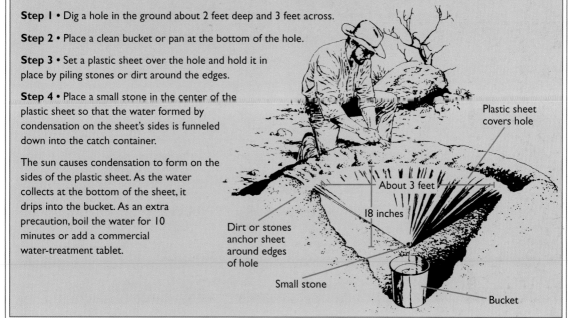

Plastic sheet covers hole

About 3 feet

18 inches

Dirt or stones anchor sheet around edges of hole

Small stone

Bucket

EDIBILITY OF PLANTS: Being able to recognize wild edible plants is important in a survival situation. There are certain factors you should keep in mind when collecting edible plants:

- Cultivated plants and wild plants growing in or near cultivated plants may have been sprayed with pesticides, so thoroughly wash whatever plants you collect.

- The surface of any plant food that grows in or is washed in contaminated water is also contaminated. If you are going to eat the plant raw, wash it in water suitable for drinking.

- Some plants may have fungal toxins that are extremely poisonous. To lessen the chances that these toxins are present, collect fresh seeds, fruits, or leaves—not those that have fallen to the ground.

- Plants of the same species may differ in the amount of toxic or subtoxic compounds they contain because of different environmental and genetic factors. One example of this is the foliage of the common choke-berry. Some chokeberry plants have high concentrations of cyanide compounds, while others have low concentrations.

- Some people are more susceptible than others to gastric upsets from plants. If you are sensitive this way, avoid unknown wild plants. If you are extremely sensitive to poison ivy, avoid products from this family of plants, including drinks made from sumacs, mangos, and cashews.

- There are some edible wild plants, such as acorns and water lily rhizomes, that are bitter. These bitter substances (usually tannin compounds) make them unpalatable. Boiling in several changes of water will help remove these substances.

- There are many valuable wild plants that have high concentrations of oxalate compounds. Oxalates usually produce a sharp burning sensation in your mouth. And they are bad for the kidneys. Boiling usually destroys these oxalates.

- The only way to tell if a mushroom is edible is by proper determination. Even then, some species are questionable, so do not eat mushrooms.

There are many, many plants throughout the world. Tasting or swallowing even a small portion of some can cause severe discomfort, extreme internal disorders, or death. Therefore, if you have the slightest doubt as to the edibility of a plant, apply the Universal Edibility Test before eating any part of it.

Before testing a plant for edibility, make sure that there are a sufficient number of the plants to make testing worth your time and effort. You need more than 24 hours to apply the edibility test.

Keep in mind that eating large amounts of plant food on an empty stomach may cause diarrhea or cramps. Two good examples of familiar foods that cause this problem are green apples and too many fresh berries. Even if you have tested plant food and found it safe, eat it in moderation with other foods.

UNIVERSAL EDIBILITY TEST: You can see from the steps and time involved in testing edibility just how important it is to be able to identify edible plants.

1. Test only one part of a potential food plant at a time.

2. Break the plant into its basic components—leaves, stem, roots, buds, and flowers.

3. Smell the food for strong or acrid odors. Keep in mind that smell alone does not indicate whether or not a plant is inedible.

4. Do not eat for eight hours before starting the test.

5. During the eight hours you are abstaining from eating, test for contact poisoning by placing a piece of the plant part you are testing on the inside of your elbow or wrist. Usually 15 minutes is enough time to allow for a reaction.

6. During the test period, take nothing by mouth except purified water and the plant part being tested.

Preparation of Plant Food

Although some plants or plant parts are edible raw, others must be cooked to be edible or palatable. Some methods of improving the taste of plant food are soaking, parboiling, cooking, or leaching. (Leaching is done by crushing food, placing it in some sort of strainer, and pouring boiling water through it.)

Leaves, Stems, and Buds: Boil until tender. Several changes of water help to eliminate the bitterness.

Roots and Tubers: Boil, bake, or roast. Boiling removes harmful substances such as oxalic-acid crystals.

Nuts: Leach or soak acorns in water to remove the bitterness. Although chestnuts are edible raw, they are tastier roasted or steamed.

Grains and Seeds: Parch to improve the taste, or grind into meal to use as a thickener with soups or stews or as flour to make bread.

Sap: If the sap contains sugar, dehydrate it by boiling until the water is gone.

Fruit: Bake or roast tough, heavy-skinned fruit. Boil juicy fruit.

7. Select a small portion of a single component and prepare it the way you plan to eat it.

8. Before putting the prepared part in your mouth, touch a small portion (a pinch) to the outer surface of your lip to test for burning or itching.

9. If after three minutes there is no reaction on your lip, place the plant part on your tongue, holding it there for 15 minutes.

10. If there is no reaction, thoroughly chew a pinch and hold it in your mouth for 15 minutes. Do **not** swallow.

11. If no burning, itching, numbing, stinging, or other irritation occurs during the 15 minutes, swallow the food.

12. Wait eight hours. If any ill effects occur during this period, induce vomiting and drink a lot of water.

13. If no ill effects occur, eat ½ cup of the same plant part prepared the same way. Wait another eight hours. If no ill effects occur, the plant part as prepared is safe for eating.

Caution: Make sure to test all parts of the plant for edibility, as some plants have both edible and inedible parts. Do not assume that a part that proved edible when cooked is also edible when raw. Test the part raw to ensure edibility before eating it raw. Do **not** eat unknown plants that:

- Have a milky sap or a sap that turns black when exposed to air.
- Are mushroom-like.
- Resemble onion or garlic.
- Resemble parsley, parsnip, or dill.
- Have carrot-like leaves, roots, or tubers.

MEDICAL CARE

The second basic need is medical care. One need not be a doctor to be prepared to meet basic medical and health needs. While there are good outdoor first-aid kits available, make sure to take your circumstances into account and supplement any kit with items you will need. This means taking sufficient quantities of any prescribed medicines, bringing extra contact lenses or pairs of glasses, and taking additional supplies (bug spray, antivenin, seasickness medication, etc.) that are appropriate for the environment. (For medical treatment of any field emergencies and a detailed list of what a first-aid kit should contain, see Section Ten: First Aid.)

FIRE

It is often said that the presence of a fire means the survivor is going to make it. Although not an absolute truth, it certainly is the case that nothing can warm the soul, calm fear, and bring hope to a survivor more than a warm fire. In addition, fire is a resource that helps the survivor meet other needs—from purifying water to sterilizing bandages to day and night signaling. Fire is a versatile and often essential survival resource. Cold weather, wind, and moisture are three enemies of the survivor. A good fire can help fight and prevail against them all. Unfortunately, most survival kits offer at best only mediocre fire-making implements, and firecraft seldom is given the attention it deserves in survival guides.

It takes skill to build a warming fire in the pouring rain, and for a small investment of time, learning this skill can help save your life. First, use good judgment when selecting fire-making implements for a survival kit, and think about how the tools you are selecting might fail under various conditions. For example, most lighters work poorly in extremely cold temperatures, can blow out in the wind, and last only as long as the butane fuel source. Most waterproof matches are waterproof only at the striking head and will stay lit for only four to five seconds.

In the hands of someone who has practiced with it, there is no better all-purpose fire-starting device than a large piece of flint and something to scrape it. Flints work effectively in the wind or rain and last a long time. Major outdoor retailers, such as REI, are excellent sources for flint-based fire-starter tools, as well as other survival gear.

Fibrous fire sticks, broken in half and inserted under loosely stacked wood, will start a campfire even if wet. You can also burn a single stick in a can for light and warmth. The magnesium fire starter is a good backup if your matches are damp or wet.

Commercial fire starters or fuels, likewise, should be chosen with care to ensure that they will work in wet weather. For those wanting to save a few pennies, a good homemade tinder is a 100 percent cotton ball saturated with Vaseline. About 10 to 20 of these can be crammed into a waterproof match case or small plastic canister.

Building a campfire for warmth or cooking in bad weather will be a lot easier with a good supply of waterproof matches in a watertight case. This match case has added features of a compass, whistle, and fire-starter flint on the case.

Good cutting tools can help immeasurably when you are preparing to make a fire. First, it makes sense to carry both a fixed-blade and a folding knife. A large, fixed-blade knife is great for cutting into the heart of dry wood. A smaller folding, locking-blade knife is good for preparing shavings and fire-starting materials. You should also always carry a good lightweight saw. Nothing works like a saw for quickly collecting dead, dry standing materials for fuel. The Ultimate Survival SaberCut pocket chain saw is flexible and comes packed in a floating case. Good fixed-blade saws include the Sven Saw and the Sawvivor.

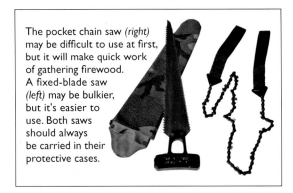

The pocket chain saw (right) may be difficult to use at first, but it will make quick work of gathering firewood. A fixed-blade saw (left) may be bulkier, but it's easier to use. Both saws should always be carried in their protective cases.

SHELTER AND PERSONAL PROTECTION

Shelter starts at the human body and works its way to protection overhead. Insect repellent falls within this category because protection from the elements means all of them: insects, wind, sun, heat, rain, snow, snakebite, cold, and others. Clothing should be worn for the weather, workload, and activity, taking into account possible extremes and worst-case scenarios. Would these clothes be sufficient to spend the night in, if you couldn't get back to camp or your vehicle? This is the question you should be asking yourself as you prepare to set out.

Personal survival protection items like space blankets, emergency tube shelters, and others lead far too many people down the road to false security. Most space blankets come with the statement that they reflect up to 90 percent of your body heat back to you. This might be true when used in perfect conditions, but these blankets can tear in the wind and are open at the end. The best of the lightweight shelters are the Mylar (or equivalent) film sleeping bags. This is because you can get inside of them and trap the heat while minimizing the loss of

heat through convection. Heat transfer in cold weather from the body is done by evaporation, radiation, convection, conduction, and respiration. Up to 50 percent of all body heat can be lost through the head alone. The better reflective-type blankets are reinforced by polyethylene or polypropylene materials. These resist tearing and damage. Survival bags (oversize and double-strength garbage bags that go from head to toe) are widely available. This item in the survival kit makes an excellent emergency shelter to climb into, especially when used in conjunction with a Mylar space blanket sleeping bag. It is important to recognize, however, that these emergency shelters are not self-regulating and that they can become exceptionally hot and wet inside when moisture is not allowed to escape.

Sheltering not only affects the body directly, but it is important in meeting other survival needs as well. It is very difficult to build a fire in the pouring rain if you cannot keep the material you are preparing dry, including your hands.

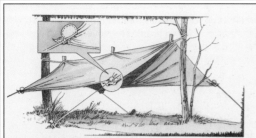

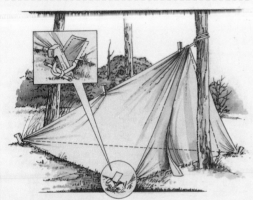

A simple shelter provides protection in rainy weather. It can be set at any height, allowing campers to sit, stand, or sleep. Clothespins will keep the tarp taut on the ridgepole. Use pebble tie-downs and pegs on corners.

A modified mountain shelter is ideal for hunters faced with a night in the woods. It's easy to set up and will totally enclose and protect a camper from foul weather. Always carry enough line to make a rope ridgepole.

A lean-to is a quick and easy shelter for warm weather. If it gets chilly, a lean-to will reflect the warmth from a campfire built in front of it.

▮ Emergency Tarp Shelters

Only your imagination limits the use of tarps. They can protect you from foul weather, keep your sleeping bag dry on wet ground, make an emergency stretcher, and a lot more. Tarps are most useful, however, when made into shelters or makeshift tents. The most practical tarp size is 12 by 8 feet. When setting up any of the shelters shown here, you will have to make strong tie-down points without puncturing the tarp. Place a small rock or pebble an inch or so from the edge, bunch the plastic tarp around it, and tie your line around the neck. You can also use duct tape. Make small loops of line, pass the duct tape through the loop, and tape it to both sides of the tarp.

RESCUE

The survivor can dramatically improve his chances of being rescued if he knows, and can use, some basic signaling skills. Being seen or heard is the key. No person should ever venture off into the woods, go anywhere in their car, boat, or plane, or engage in any other outdoor activity without a signal mirror and a whistle. You can't out-scream the best whistles, and even if you could, you could not sustain the effort.

The signal mirror is second only to the radio or telephone for communicating your need for help. Unfor-

An emergency strobe is a hand-sized, battery-powered personal strobe light that emits pulsing beacons of light 50 to 70 times a minute for up to 16 hours. The light is visible up to 3 miles. The value of a signal mirror is often underrated. Used properly, the signal can be detected more than 11 miles away.

tunately, outside of the military, which uses signal mirrors religiously (including them in every survival kit), the general public has only limited knowledge of the value of the signal mirror. A targetable signal mirror—such as the official Air Force Star Flash, which enables the survivor to aim the signal flash—is the key.

Other widely available signaling devices include flashlights, strobe lights, and chemical lights. High-intensity, 12-hour chemical lights are a better choice in most instances than a flashlight, because they are lighter in weight and do not require batteries. A small string tied to the end of a chemical light and spun in a circle over your head makes an excellent night signal that can be seen from a great distance. Moreover, when considering items to place in your home disaster kit, take into account that the spark from the switch of a flashlight can trigger an explosion in a gas-filled room, while a chemical light poses no such danger.

With signaling and rescue devices, the key is to be seen. Bigger, louder, and more is better. A recognized international symbol of distress is a series of three signals. Three blasts of your whistle, three long honks of your car horn, three small fires (smoke or flame), or three shots from your rifle or shotgun are examples.

SURVIVING THE COLD

There is no way to beat the cold, but you can learn how to survive in it. High-tech manufacturing now offers clothing that is insulated, waterproof, and windproof, but even with all of these advantages, there will always be someone who will get into trouble. Hypothermia is the cold-weather killer, and it is caused by exposure to wind, rain, snow, or wet clothing. (For treatment of hypothermia, see Section Ten: First Aid.) Allow your body's core temperature to drop below the normal 98.6°F, and you will start to shiver and stamp your feet to keep warm. If these early signs are ignored, the next symptoms will be slurred speech, memory lapses, fumbling hands, and drowsiness. If not treated quickly, hypothermia can kill its victim when body temperature drops below 78°F, and this can happen within 90 minutes after shivering begins.

If you detect these symptoms in yourself or a friend, start treatment immediately. Get to shelter and warmth as soon as possible. If no shelter is available, build a fire. Get out of wet clothing and apply heat to the head, neck, chest, and groin. Use body heat from another person. Give the victim warm liquids, chocolate, or any food with a high sugar content. Never give a victim alcohol. It will impair judgment, dilate blood vessels, and prevent shivering, which is the body's way of producing needed heat.

You can also survive the cold by staying in shape and getting a good night's sleep before going outdoors. Carry candy, mixed nuts, raisins, and any other high-energy food. Stay as dry as possible and avoid overheating. Most important, dress properly. This means several

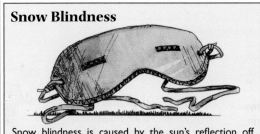

Snow Blindness

Snow blindness is caused by the sun's reflection off snow, ice, or sand burning the corneas of the eyes. It is temporary, usually lasting 24 hours. Symptoms include red, watery, and itchy eyes and pain when eyelids move. Snow blindness can be prevented by wearing sunglasses designed to cut ultraviolet radiation (UVR). If sunglasses are not available, make a snow mask by cutting narrow slits in cardboard and tying it to your head with string.

layers of clothing and rain gear. And wear a wool hat with ear protection. An uncovered head can lose up to 50 percent of the body's heat.

■ Surviving a Snowstorm

If you're a winter sportsman, you should know how to survive a snowstorm. First, always travel with a daypack stocked with survival gear, such as a cell phone, handheld GPS, knife, compass, map, waterproof matches, whistle, space blanket, water, high-energy food, flashlight, spare socks, and gloves.

Cooling Power of Wind Expressed as Equivalent Chill Temperature

Wind Speed		Temperature (°F)																				
Calm	Calm	40	35	30	25	20	15	10	5	0	-5	-10	-15	-20	-25	-30	-35	-40	-45	-50	-55	-60
Knots	MPH	Equivalent Chill Temperature (°F)																				
3–6	5	35	30	25	20	15	10	5	0	-5	-10	-15	-20	-25	-30	-35	-40	-45	-50	-55	-65	-70
7–10	10	30	20	15	10	5	0	-10	-15	-20	-25	-35	-40	-45	-50	-60	-65	-70	-75	-80	-90	-95
11–15	15	25	15	10	0	-5	-10	-20	-25	-30	-40	-45	-50	-60	-65	-70	-80	-85	-90	-100	-105	-110
16–19	20	20	10	5	0	-10	-15	-25	-30	-35	-45	-50	-60	-65	-75	-80	-85	-95	-100	-110	-115	-120
20–23	25	15	10	0	-5	-15	-20	-30	-35	-45	-50	-60	-65	-75	-80	-90	-95	-105	-110	-120	-125	-135
24–28	30	10	5	0	-10	-20	-25	-30	-40	-50	-55	-65	-70	-80	-85	-95	-100	-110	-115	-125	-130	-140
29–32	35	10	5	5	-10	-20	-30	-35	-40	-50	-60	-65	-75	-80	-90	-100	-105	-115	-120	-130	-135	-145
33–36	40	10	0	-5	-15	-20	-30	-35	-45	-55	-60	-70	-75	-85	-95	-100	-110	-115	-125	-130	-140	-150

		Little Danger				Increasing Danger (flesh may freeze within one minute)					Great Danger (flesh may freeze within 30 seconds)											
		Danger of Freezing Exposed Flesh for Properly Clothed Persons																				

Note: Winds above 40 miles per hour have few additional effects.

Shelters

▼ **If you're stuck in a snowstorm with huge drifts,** you can build a snow cave. Snow is effective insulation and will keep you warm in zero temperatures. Make sure your snow cave is air-vented.

◄ **If you have a knife or small ax,** make the familiar lean-to. The big advantage is that you can build a fire in front of it. Pine boughs will break the wind.

▶ **A tree pit is the easiest snow shelter to build.** Find a tree and dig a hole in the snow next to it, then cover yourself with a piece of plastic or your space blanket draped over a small limb.

During the winter, never hunt alone. It's also important to tell a friend where you are hunting and when you expect to return.

If travel in a snowstorm is hazardous, find shelter and don't venture far from a trail. Next, build a fire. It will give you light, warmth, dry clothing, a signal, hot food, and even drinking water from melted snow.

If you're driving off-road, don't leave your vehicle. It will provide shelter. To keep warm, use seat covers and carpeting. The stuffing from car seats makes good tinder for a fire. Unhook the carburetor hose and you will be able to drain enough gasoline to start a fire.

SURVIVING THE HEAT

To survive in a hot area, you must know about and be prepared for the environmental conditions you will face. You must determine the equipment you will need, the tactics you will use, and how the environment will impact them and you.

■ Low Rainfall

Low rainfall is the most obvious environmental factor in a hot, arid area. Some desert areas receive less than 4 inches of rain annually, and this comes in brief torrents that quickly run off the ground surface. With the high desert-air temperatures, you cannot survive long without water. So in a desert survival situation, you must first consider these questions: "How much water do I have?" and "Where are other sources of water?"

A key factor in arid area survival is understanding the relationship between physical activity, air temperature, and water consumption. The body requires a certain amount of water for a certain level of activity at a certain temperature. For example, a man performing hard work in the sun at 110°F requires 5 gallons of water a day. Lack of the required amount of water causes a rapid decline in a person's ability to make decisions and to perform tasks efficiently.

Your body's normal temperature is 98.6°F. Your body gets rid of excess heat by sweating. The warmer your body becomes, whether caused by work, exercise, or air temperature, the more you sweat. The more you sweat, the more moisture you lose. Sweating is the principle cause of water loss. If a man stops sweating during periods of high air temperature and heavy work or exercise, he will have a heat stroke. This is an emergency that requires immediate medical attention.

Understanding how the air temperature and your physical activity affect your water requirements allows you to take measures to get the most from your water supply. These measures are:

- Find shade. Get out of the sun. Place something between you and the ground. Limit your movements.

- Conserve your sweat. Wear all your clothes, including a T-shirt. Roll the sleeves down, cover your head, and protect your neck with a scarf or similar item. This will protect your body from hot-blowing, sand-laden winds and the direct rays of the sun. Your clothing will absorb your sweat, keeping it against your skin so that you gain its full cooling effect. By staying in the shade quietly and fully clothed, not talking, keeping your mouth closed, and breathing through your nose, your water requirement for survival drops dramatically.

- If water is scarce, do not eat any food. Food requires water for digestion. Eating food will use water that you need for cooling.

Thirst is not a reliable guide for your need for water. A person who uses thirst as a guide will only drink two-thirds of his daily requirement. To prevent this "voluntary" dehydration, use this guide:

- At temperatures below 100°F, drink 1 pint of water every hour.

- At temperatures above 100°F, drink 1 quart of water every hour.

Drinking water at regular intervals helps your body to remain cool, decreasing sweating. Even when your water supply is low, sipping water constantly will keep your body cooler and reduce water loss through sweating. Conserve your sweat by reducing activity during the heat of the day. Do **not** ration your water. If you attempt to ration your water, you stand a good chance of becoming a heat casualty.

Intense Sunlight and Heat

Intense sunlight and heat are present in all arid areas. Air temperature can rise as high as 140°F during the day. Heat gain results from direct sunlight, hot, blowing winds, reflective heat (the sun's rays bouncing off the sand), and conductive heat from direct contact with the desert sand and rock. The temperature of desert sand and rock averages 30 to 40 degrees more than that of the air. For instance, when the air temperature is 110°F, the sand temperature may be 140°F.

Intense sunlight and heat increase the body's need for water. To conserve your body sweat and energy, you need a shelter to reduce your exposure to the heat of the day. Travel at night to minimize the use of water. You can survey the area at dawn, dusk, or by moonlight when there is little likelihood of a mirage.

Temperatures may get as high as 140°F during the day and as low as 50°F at night in arid areas. The drop in temperature at night occurs rapidly and will chill a person who lacks warm clothing and is unable to move around. The cool evenings and nights are the best times to work or travel. If you plan to rest at night, you will find a wool sweater, long underwear, and a wool stocking cap extremely helpful.

Sunburn results from overexposing your skin to the sun's rays. Keep your body completely clothed, including gloves on your hands and a scarf around your neck. Use sunscreen liberally on any exposed areas of skin. Sun poisoning equals nausea and dehydration. In addition, burns may become infected, causing more problems. Remember the following:

- There is as much danger of sunburn on cloudy days as on sunny days, especially at high altitudes.

- Most sunscreens do not give complete protection against excessive exposure.

- The glare on the sand causes eyestrain, and wind-blown, fine sand particles can irritate the eyes and cause inflammation. Wear goggles and use eye ointments to protect your eyes.

- The combination of wind, sand, or dust can cause your lips and other exposed skin to chap. Use lip balm and skin ointments to prevent or overcome this problem.

- Rest is essential in this environment. You need 20 minutes of rest for each hour in the heat and you need six hours of sleep each day.

Sparse Vegetation

Vegetation is sparse in arid areas. You will therefore have difficulty finding shelter. Seek shelter in dry washes or riverbeds with a thicker growth of vegetation. Use the shadows cast from brush, rocks, or outcroppings. The temperature in shaded areas will be 20 to 30 degrees cooler than the air temperature. Finally, cover objects that will reflect light from the sun.

Prior to moving, survey the area for sites that provide cover. A problem you will have is estimating distance. The emptiness of a desert terrain causes most people to underestimate distance by three: what appears to be 1 mile away is really 3 miles away.

DEALING WITH DANGEROUS WATER

When you are in a survival situation in any area except the desert, you are likely to encounter a water obstacle. It may be in the form of a river, stream, lake, bog, quicksand, quagmire, or muskeg. Whatever it is, you need to know how to cross it safely.

Rivers and Streams

A river or stream may be narrow or wide, shallow or deep, slow moving or fast moving. It may be snow-fed or ice-fed. Your first step is to find a place where the river is basically safe for crossing. (For more information on how to wade a river, see Section Three: Fishing.) Look for a high place from which you can get a good view of the river. If there is no high place, climb a tree. Check the river carefully for the following areas:

- A level stretch where the river breaks into a number of channels. Two or three narrow channels are usually easier to cross than a wide river.

- Obstacles on the opposite side of the river that might hinder your travel. Try to select the spot from which travel will be safest and easiest.

- A ledge of rocks that crosses the river. This often indicates dangerous rapids or canyons.

- A deep or rapid waterfall or a deep channel. Never attempt to ford a stream directly above or even close to such spots.

- Rocky places. Avoid such places; you can be seriously injured from falling on rocks. An occasional rock that breaks the current, however, may assist you.

- A shallow bank or sandbar. If possible, select a point upstream from a bank or sandbar so that the current will carry you to it if you lose your footing.

- A course across the river that leads downstream. This will help you will cross the current at about a 45-degree angle.

■ Rapids

Crossing a deep, swift river or rapids is not as dangerous as it looks. If you are swimming across, swim with the current—never fight it—and try to keep your body horizontal to the water. This will reduce the danger of being pulled under.

In fast, shallow rapids, go on your back, feetfirst; fin your hands alongside your hips to add buoyancy and to fend off submerged rocks. Keep your feet up to avoid getting them bruised or caught by rocks.

In deep rapids, go on your belly, headfirst; angle toward the shore whenever you can. Breathe between wave troughs. Be careful of backwater eddies and converging currents, as they often contain dangerous swirls. Avoid bubbly water under falls; it has little buoyancy. If you are going to ford a swift, treacherous stream, remove your pants and underpants so that the water will have less grip on your legs. Keep your shoes on to protect your feet and ankles from rocks and to give you firmer footing.

Tie your pants and important items securely to the top of your pack. This way, if you have to release your pack, all your items will be together. It is easier to find one large pack than to find several small items.

Carry your pack well up on your shoulders so you can release it quickly if you are swept off your feet. Not being able to get a pack off quickly enough can drag even the strongest of swimmers under.

Find a strong pole about 5 inches in diameter and 7 to 8 feet long to help you ford the stream. Grasp the pole and plant it firmly on your upstream side to break

the current. Plant your feet firmly with each step, and move the pole forward a little downstream from its previous position, but still upstream from you. With your next step, place your foot below the pole. Keep the pole well slanted so that the force of the current keeps the pole against your shoulder.

If there are other people with you, cross the stream together. Make sure that everyone has prepared their

Cold Water Survival

Solo Survival: H.E.L.P. (Heat Escape Lessening Posture) is the body position that will minimize heat loss if you are alone. If you are wearing waders, keep them on, and assume a sitting position. The trapped air in your waders will help keep you afloat. Cover your head and neck if possible.

Group Huddle: Two or more persons in cold water should huddle together to conserve body heat. A small group in this position can extend survival time 50 percent longer than if they were swimming.

pack and clothing as described above. Have the heaviest person get on the downstream end of the pole and the lightest person on the upstream end. This way, the upstream person will break the current, and the people below can move with comparative ease in the eddy formed by the upstream person. If the upstream person is temporarily swept off his feet, the others can hold steady while he regains his footing.

As in all fording, cross the downstream current at a 45-degree angle. Currents too strong for one person to stand against can usually be crossed safely in this manner.

Do not be concerned about the weight of your pack, as the weight will help rather than hinder you in fording the stream. Just make sure you can release the pack quickly if necessary.

■ Surviving in Cold Water

Spring and fall are traditional times for trout fishing and waterfowl hunting, and this means greater chances of accidentally finding yourself in cold water. If you are suddenly the victim of a capsizing, you can survive a cold-water dunking if you follow a few survival rules.

First, don't panic. Clothing will trap body heat, so don't remove your clothes. If you are wearing a life jacket, restrict your body movements and draw your knees up to your body, a position that will reduce heat loss.

Don't try to swim or tread water. That will just pump out warm water between your body and clothing. Instead, get into a protective posture and wait for rescue. See the accompanying illustrations for the body positions that will minimize heat loss and increase your chances of survival.

PATHFINDING THE EASY WAY

There is nothing difficult about using a compass and map. If you're a sportsman, you need these tools to reach hot spots and to get in and out of the woods safely. Basic orienteering is quite easy to learn.

You should start with a topographic map, as it will contain a wealth of information. Topo maps have a scale of 1:24,000, which means that 1 inch on the map equals 24,000 inches (or 2,000 feet) in the field. It may be easier to visualize the area covered by such a map if the scale is translated as 2⅝ inches equals 1 mile.

The topo maps shown in the accompanying illustrations have a scale of 1:24,000. They show four important features: man-made structures, water, vegetation, and elevation. Though the maps here are reproduced in black and white, these four symbols usually have distinct colors. Man-made features include roads, trails, and buildings. All are in black except some major

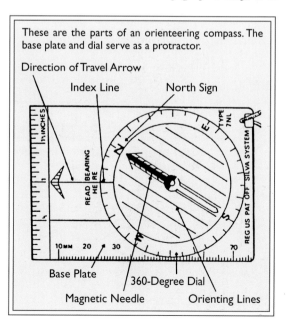

These are the parts of an orienteering compass. The base plate and dial serve as a protractor.

Direction of Travel Arrow
Index Line
North Sign
1½ INCHES
READ BEARING HERE
E
N
TYPE 7NL
REG US PAT OFF SILVA SYSTEM
10MM 20 30 70
Base Plate
360-Degree Dial
Magnetic Needle
Orienting Lines

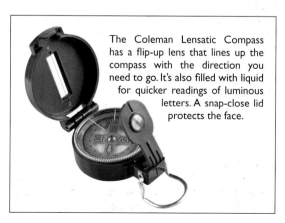

The Coleman Lensatic Compass has a flip-up lens that lines up the compass with the direction you need to go. It's also filled with liquid for quicker readings of luminous letters. A snap-close lid protects the face.

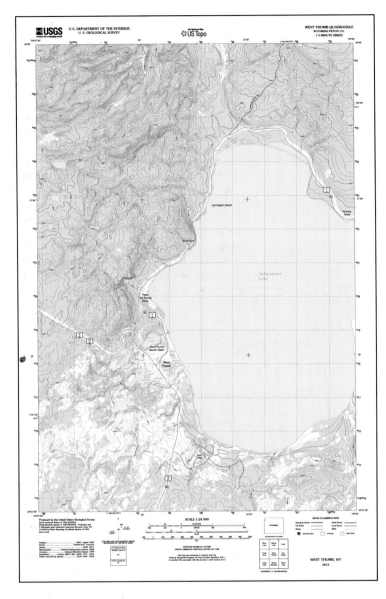

This topographical map is an example of the type you can download for free from the USGS website.

of 100 feet. (Generally, the contour interval is 20 feet.) This information is noted at the bottom of topographical maps. These maps are easy to get. Visit the U.S. Geological Survey website (www.usgs.gov/pubprod) to download free topographical maps.

Now let's talk about compasses. A compass contains a magnetized steel needle that points toward magnetic north. The end of this needle will be black or red, stamped with the letter N, or shaped like an arrow.

The force that attracts this magnetized needle is the earth's magnetism. The earth is similar to a tremendous magnet, with one pole in the north, the other in the south. Compass needles always point toward magnetic north when at rest. The magnetic North Pole is about 1,400 miles south of the true North Pole. That means you have two north directions to deal with—true north as it is shown on your map, and magnetic north as you find it with the compass.

Most compasses fall into one of two categories: conventional, which can be of watchcase, pin-on, or wristwatch design, or orienteering, which combines a compass, protractor, and ruler. The latter has a magnetic needle, a revolving compass housing, and a transparent base plate. Carry two compasses in the field: a pin-on model for quick reference and an orienteering compass for cross-country traveling when map work is involved.

highways, which may be in red. Water features are printed in blue, and vegetation in green.

Elevation is represented by thin, brown contour lines. A contour line is an imaginary line on the ground along which every point is at the same height above sea level. Follow a brown line on the map, and you'll find a number—for example, 100. Everything on that line is 100 feet above sea level. If the line next to it reads 200, then you have a rise of 100 feet and a contour interval

■ Finding a Bearing

To find a bearing with an orienteering compass, face the distant point toward which you want to know the direction. Hold the orienteering compass level before you,

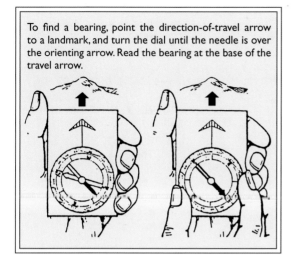

To find a bearing, point the direction-of-travel arrow to a landmark, and turn the dial until the needle is over the orienting arrow. Read the bearing at the base of the travel arrow.

at waist height, with the direction-of-travel arrowhead pointing straight ahead.

Orient your compass by twisting the housing (without moving the base plate) until the needle lies over the orienting arrow on the inside bottom of the compass housing, with its north part pointing to the letter N on the top of the housing. What you've done is made your compass show actual field directions.

Read the degrees of your desired direction—the bearing—on the outside rim of the compass housing at the spot where the direction line, as an index pointer, touches the housing. It's as easy as that with an orienteering compass.

Following a Bearing

Suppose you're standing in a field and have decided to travel cross-country to a distant hilltop. Set your orienteering compass for the direction of the hilltop by holding your compass in your hand with the direction-of-travel arrowhead pointing to your destination. Twist the compass housing until the north part of the compass needle points to the letter N on the housing rim. Proceed in the direction in which the direction-of-travel arrowhead points.

If you lose sight of the distant hilltop, hold the compass in front of you, orient it, and sight a nearby landmark in the direction in which the arrowhead points. Walk to that point, then take a similar reading to another landmark, and so on until you reach the destination.

You can forget about degrees and figures when you use an orienteering compass. Your compass is set. Just orient it and proceed.

Returning to Original Location

You have reached your destination and want to return home. How? Your orienteering compass is already set for your return journey.

When you went out, you held the compass with the direction-of-travel arrowhead at the front of the base plate pointing away from you toward your destination. The back of the base plate was in the opposite direction, pointing backward toward the spot from which you came. Make use of this fact.

Hold the compass level in your hand, but with the direction-of-travel arrow pointing toward you instead of away from you. Orient the compass by turning your body (don't touch the compass housing) until the north end of the compass needle points to the N on the compass housing. Locate a landmark, and head for home. Your compass is set—simply use it backward.

Using a Map and Compass Together

Let's take a look at how to use a compass and map together. The difference or angle between magnetic north and true north is called declination, and it varies according to your geographic location. The degree of declination is indicated on topo maps. Fortunately, magnetic north is also indicated on topo maps, and you can use it to avoid the whole problem of declination and adjusting map bearings.

Instead of compensating for declination, simply draw magnetic-north lines on your topo map. By using these lines instead of the true-north lines of the regular meridians, you make your map speak the same language as your compass. The settings you take on your compass using these lines do not require resetting to compensate for declination. The declination has already been addressed. To provide your map with magnetic-north lines, draw a line up through the map on an angle to one of the meridian lines corresponding to the degrees of declination given on the map. Then, draw other lines parallel to this line, 1 to 2 inches apart.

With your combined knowledge of map and compass, you can now travel from point to point: cabin to lake, camp to deer stand, and so on. It's done with three easy steps.

Step 1 • On the map, line up your compass with your route. Place the orienteering compass on the map with one long edge of its base plate touching both your starting point and your destination, and with the base plate's direction-of-travel arrow pointing in the direction you want to go. Disregard the compass needle.

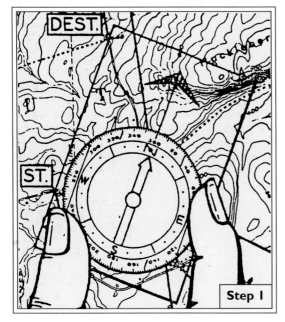

Step 2 • On the compass, set the housing to the direction of your route. Hold the plate firmly against the map. With your free hand, turn the compass housing until the orienting arrow on the bottom of the housing lies parallel to the nearest magnetic-north line drawn on your map, with the arrow pointing to the top. Disregard the compass needle. The compass is now set for the direction of your destination. By using the drawn-in magnetic-north line, you have compensated for any compass declination in the territory covered by your map.

Step 3 • In the field, follow the direction set on the compass. Hold the compass in front of you, at waist height, with the direction-of-travel arrow pointing straight ahead. Turn yourself, while watching the compass needle, until the needle lies directly over the orienting arrow on the bottom of the compass housing, with the north end of the needle pointing to the letter N on the housing. The direction-of-travel arrow now points to your des-

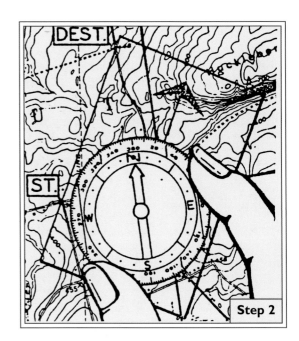

tination. Raise your head, pick a landmark, and walk to it. When you have reached it, again check the direction with your compass, on which you have been careful not to change the setting. Ahead is another landmark, and still another, until you reach your destination. When it's time to return to your starting point, repeat Step 3, but keep the direction-of-travel arrow pointing toward you. Your compass is already set—simply use it backward to return home.

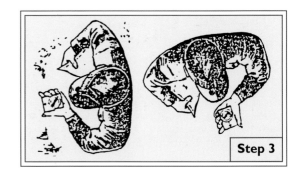

Applying what you've learned to hunting and fishing situations is not difficult. If you can follow a bearing, you can easily travel across strange country to a remote lake that you've found on a topo map. You can hunt in any direction from camp and be confident about finding

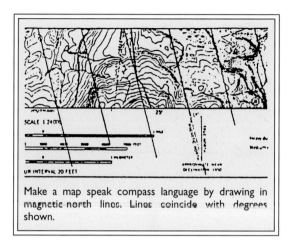

Make a map speak compass language by drawing in magnetic north lines. Lines coincide with degrees shown.

Handheld Global Positioning System (GPS)

Learning to master a compass and map may sound easy, but it can be confusing to many sportsmen. If you fall into this group, select one of the many handheld GPS units available today. These units offer a range of sophisticated features that will easily track your travel in remote areas and guide you back to your camp at the end of the day. For example, the Garmin Montana 650 is a rugged navigator with a 4-inch touchscreen and a five-megapixel camera. The unit weighs only 10 ounces and is powered by a rechargeable lithium battery or three AA batteries, which will run the unit up to 22 hours. Handheld GPS models also serve double-duty in automobiles, boats, and ATVs. They are not expensive and will free you of worry about traveling off trails and possibly getting lost. Garmin, Magellan, and Lowrance are major manufacturers of handheld GPS units. If you venture far off the beaten path, it's also good advice to pair a GPS with a fully charged cell phone.

camp again. When it's time to head back, simply let your compass lead you safely back to camp. With a little practice, you'll be able to travel in the woods with complete confidence.

The Garmin Oregon 450t, a waterproof GPS with touchscreen navigation, is preloaded with U.S. topographical maps. It will show shoreline detail, highways, roads, and hiking and snowmobile trails. This unit has a 3-inch color display and runs up to 16 hours on two AA batteries. It is a good option for those who have difficulty with compasses.

The Garmin Montana 600 GPS features a 4-inch sunlight-readable color touchscreen. This Wide Area Augmentation System (WAAS)-enabled GPS receiver with HotFix satellite prediction will wirelessly share routes, tracks, waypoints, and geocaches between compatible units.

Section Seven
BOATING

• FISHING BOATS • HUNTING BOATS •
• CAMPING BOATS • BOATING ELECTRONICS •
• PREPARING FOR STORAGE AND LAUNCHING •
• BOATING SAFETY • PERSONAL WATERCRAFT •

HULL DESIGN

The shape of a boat's hull is the biggest factor in how it will do its job for you. Hull design has always been the most intriguing subject among people who know boats and keep up with new developments, for changes in hull lines—skillfully conceived—have brought about some dramatic developments in how boats perform.

There are really just two types—displacement and planing hulls—but boat hulls in common use today are far from simple. In some, characteristics of the two types have been combined in order to get the best of both. Also, a variety of specific shapes have been designed to do certain things well that another shape cannot do. And there remain several traditional hull shapes that have changed little in the midst of a marine-design revolution, continuing to do a modest job well, and often at minimum cost.

■ Displacement Hulls

Displacement hulls push through the water rather than planing on top of it, and therefore speed is limited. A round-bottomed, full-keeled displacement hull rides comfortably down in the water where wave and wind action have relatively little effect. The Indian canoe, the Viking ship, and the Great Banks fishing dory (a flat-bottomed boat) were all displacement-type hulls. They were narrow beamed and pointed at both ends—for excellent reasons. They could be moved through the water more easily with only oars or a sail for power; they could be maneuvered in either direction; following seas had much less effect on them than on a flat stern; and a pointed trailing end dissipated suction created by the water displacement. Today, there are squared-off sterns

to provide useful space for the motors and deck, but the displacement hull is probably tapered back from a wide point amidships.

The sea-kindliness of a displacement hull is due principally to its low center of gravity. It rises with the swells, and a surface chop has little effect. A full-displacement hull with round quarters is less affected by beam seas (waves rolling in from one side or the other), while its full keel gives a good bite in the water, helping you hold a course through winds and current. Because weight in a displacement hull is much less critical than in a planing hull, it can be sturdily, even heavily, built to take the worst punishment. Good examples of displacement hulls are present-day trawlers.

Small displacement hulls are excellent for passing rocky river rapids and surviving the worst chop on a lake. In large boats, cabin space is lower in the water, where it is more comfortable and feels more secure, especially on long cruises. On big water, you might be annoyed

The 38-foot Sabre Salon Express is a classic example of a seaworthy displacement hull. With a 13-foot beam, it is powered by a Volvo Penta pod propulsion drivetrain.

Boat Hulls

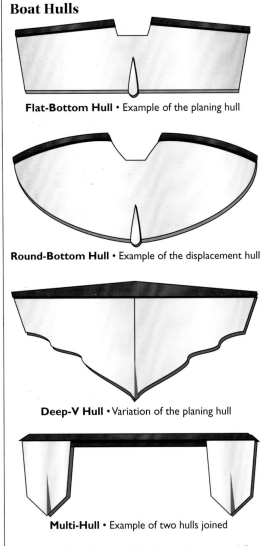

Flat-Bottom Hull • Example of the planing hull

Round-Bottom Hull • Example of the displacement hull

Deep-V Hull • Variation of the planing hull

Multi-Hull • Example of two hulls joined

A boat's hull may be one of four basic shapes: round, flat, V, or multi-hull. Some designs may also be a combination of these hull shapes and each shape has its advantages and disadvantages. For example, the flat hull has a shallow draft and is stable. It is good for fishing small waters, but a flat hull also means a rough ride, and it will pound in choppy water. A deep-V hull is stable and will not pound, but it may roll or bank in sharp turns. A round-bottom hull offers a slow but comfortable ride. Unfortunately, it has a tendency to roll. A multi-hull has great stability because of its beam, but needs more room to turn and maneuver.

at first by the constant roll, but the roll period is slower than the chop-chop surface banging of a planing hull on the same water and never as sharp. What's more, the displacement hull will keep you dry in wave action that would soak you continually in a planing hull.

Just how limited is a displacement hull's speed? There is an actual formula. The square root of the waterline length times 1.5 equals possible speed. For example, an 11-foot lake fishing boat might measure 9 feet at the waterline. Thus, the square root of 9 is 3, which is then multiplied by 1.5, and then you get 4.5. That boat's probable maximum speed is 4.5 miles per hour. Load it deeper so the waterline is extended and you increase the possible top speed slightly. But there's no point in loading it down with more power, for you won't increase the speed significantly above the formula figure. How narrow is the hull width? Designers work on ratios from 3.5:1 up to 5:1, length to width. To some, this describes a "tippy" boat, tender when you step in or lean over.

While a small displacement hull, such as a canoe, can dump you and then skitter away high and dry on top of the water while you try to grab it, a bigger displacement hull, say from 18 feet up, is as safe, even for novices, as anything in the water. And since speed is inherently limited, a small motor is in order. This makes for a safe, economical way to cruise or fish all day. You just move along at a modest, steady rate, dry and comfortable in big water (though not as comfortable in a small displacement-type boat on calm water, where tippiness is tiresome). You conserve your resources and enjoy the boat's natural action, and the boat is always under control. That's the portrait of boating with a displacement hull.

Modified displacement hulls and semi-planing hulls are made so that the after-third or more of the bottom is flattened. A flat bottom toward the stern rides higher as speed is applied, instead of digging in and pushing the bow up, as will happen in a full-displacement hull. The flat section aft also reduces the tendency to roll. These boats have wider transoms, and can use bigger motors and run faster. You'll find modified round-bottomed hulls in small aluminum fishing boats, as well as in offshore fishing boats, with a wide range of variations in design.

ROUND-BOTTOMED CARTOPPERS: Small aluminum fishing boats and fiberglass dinghies are often modified hulls that have round-bottom characteristics, yet they can move at high speed. You need a displacement hull for sitting on a choppy lake all day; nothing else will do. Using a motor of up to 25 horsepower, put the boat in the

Cruisers

Cruisers are generally more seaworthy and comfortable than runabouts. Size can range from 20 to more than 100 feet. Cruisers usually have overnight accommodations.

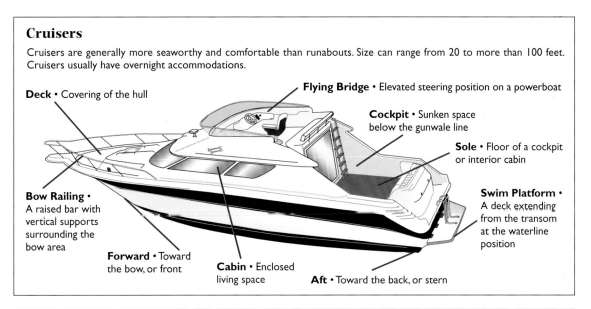

Deck • Covering of the hull

Flying Bridge • Elevated steering position on a powerboat

Cockpit • Sunken space below the gunwale line

Sole • Floor of a cockpit or interior cabin

Bow Railing • A raised bar with vertical supports surrounding the bow area

Swim Platform • A deck extending from the transom at the waterline position

Forward • Toward the bow, or front

Cabin • Enclosed living space

Aft • Toward the back, or stern

Runabouts

Most runabouts range in size from 16 to 25 feet and can be either outboard or inboard powered.

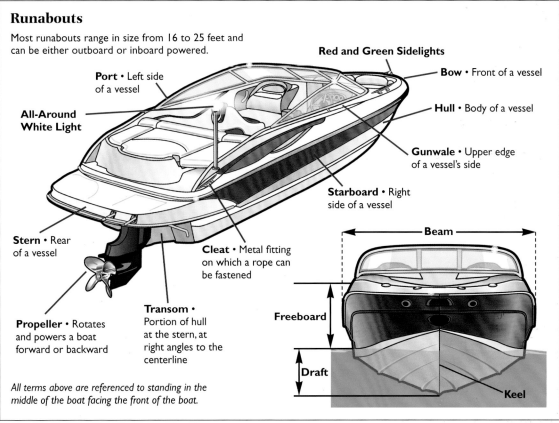

Red and Green Sidelights

Port • Left side of a vessel

Bow • Front of a vessel

All-Around White Light

Hull • Body of a vessel

Gunwale • Upper edge of a vessel's side

Starboard • Right side of a vessel

Stern • Rear of a vessel

Cleat • Metal fitting on which a rope can be fastened

Beam

Freeboard

Propeller • Rotates and powers a boat forward or backward

Transom • Portion of hull at the stern, at right angles to the centerline

Draft

Keel

All terms above are referenced to standing in the middle of the boat facing the front of the boat.

water and give it full speed. If the bow goes up and the stern digs in until you are depressed in a bowl the prop action makes in the water, reduce speed; it's a displacement hull, and your power is beyond the safe hull speed.

These boats have a rather full bow entry in relation to the beam, and there is a small keel. The middle and aft sections will be distinctly rounded, in contrast to the V-shaped cartop hull. If the sides taper toward the stern, you will find it better for rowing.

PUNT, PRAM, JOHNBOAT: Anyone can build and care for a flat-bottomed boat. This is the least complicated and least costly hull shape, and the amateur can build a large craft on simple lines at low cost. Flat-bottomed hulls pound more than others, but while newcomers dislike their clumsy appearance and strictly functional design, serious boaters continue to choose them for hunting and fishing on quiet waters, for they make an excellent platform.

The punt, pram, and johnboat are often indistinguishable except in name. What might be called a pram Down East and a punt on England's Thames River could be called a johnboat in Missouri. These square-ended, flat-bottomed hulls are the most stable and best load carriers of all little boats. They are rather heavy handling, and are designed for use in quiet water, where their low sides and flat bottoms come into their own.

The true punt is made to be poled. The sides are straight, and both ends are identical, rising flat at about 45 degrees. The bottom slopes up slightly toward the ends. The pram has bowed sides, tapering forward, and the bottom rises toward the bow. The bow end rises at a rather shallow angle, and the stern end is broader. The pram is usually rowed or sailed, but may be powered with a small outboard or electric motor.

The johnboat, the most popular with sportsmen, is made by a number of aluminum and fiberglass boat manufacturers. The hull figure has nearly as many variations within the basic plan as the number of regions in which it has been built and used. For instance, in marshy country, a coffin-shaped johnboat was built with a stern wide enough only for one person; it tapered toward a slight flare forward, then in again toward a narrow bow. Sometimes the bow was decked over to cover gear. The bottom sloped up from the flare both fore and aft, easing the push through vegetation and making it easy to maneuver in open water. This version continues to be a useful fishing boat in marshland and bayous.

Modern aluminum johnboats have riveted or welded hulls and range from 12 to 20 feet long. The bottom slopes up a bit forward from a low point directly in the midsection, and is rockered aft. The sides may be bowed somewhat forward and slope in toward the bottom. Three or four seats, with a wide bow seat, provide reinforcement in a broad-beamed hull that can carry a big load. Johnboats are rowed, poled, or powered.

Fiberglass johnboats are a better choice for saltwater fishermen. Saltwater corrosion will eventually take its toll on riveted aluminum hulls. Fiberglass johnboats can be molded in a variety of designs and are virtually maintenance free. Some manufacturers, such as Carolina Skiff, will custom design the interior, starting with the basic hull. These skiffs are also unsinkable and can be left in the water indefinitely with the scuppers open.

FLAT-BOTTOMED SKIFF: Put a pointed bow on a flat-bottomed shape and you have a hull that gives sharper entry to oncoming waves and reduces the tendency to pound that is characteristic of the square-ended johnboat or pram. It does, however, reduce stability.

For good rowing qualities, a skiff is built with a relatively narrow stern; the sides curve upward both fore and aft so that the tip of the bow and stern both clear the water slightly. The "active" bottom is the broad midsection. Such a boat is relatively easy to control and safe. For outboard power, the stern is built wider and lower. Flat-bottomed skiffs 12 to 16 feet long are common in all parts of the country. In shorter lengths, this hull is unstable, for the bow is too light.

THE DORY: This hull is fun to handle and is also very competent. You can take it through the surf or into fast, shallow rivers, for its two pointed ends and narrow bottom make it easy to row and control. Flaring, tall sides keep it dry inside, but this shape is somewhat tender, especially in small sizes. For use with an outboard, the design is modified by squaring off the stern. This presents a V-shaped transom, far from ideal for handling an outboard. Modern dory hulls have wider and lower sterns to improve handling with a motor. Mounting a small inboard engine amidships is the solution to powering the traditional double-end dory.

Planing Hulls

Planing hulls are built for speed. Given enough acceleration (called planing speed), the hull rises to the water's surface, levels off, and planes along the top. Design efficiency and possible power impose the only limits on its speed. The objective is to reduce wetted surface

Planing-Hull Designs

▲ The MAKO Pro Skiff is a 17-footer with an inverted-V hull. Rated for outboards up to 60 horsepower and with a weight capacity of 1,400 pounds, this is an ideal utility craft for sportsmen.

▲ The G3 Angler V172C is a typical side-console planing hull runabout. It's a 17-footer with a 92-inch beam and a 115-horsepower rating. The double-plated bow makes it a good choice for shoreline fishing.

▲ The Yellowfin 42, a 42-footer, is a good example of progress made in center consoles built to get offshore quickly with four 300-horsepower outboards totaling 1,200 horsepower.

▲ The G3 Eagle 166 SE is a 16½-foot rigged johnboat with a welded hull. Rated for a maximum of 60 horsepower, this model is ideal for most freshwater fishing. It comes with a 19-gallon livewell.

▲ The Viking 82 Convertible represents the ultimate in offshore fishing. The overall length is 87 feet and the beam measures 22 feet. With fuel options, it holds 6,750 gallons of fuel and 450 gallons of water. It is capable of bluewater big-game fishing all around the world.

▲ The MAKO 284 CC, a 28-footer with a 10-foot beam and deep-V hull, will handle nearly all offshore waters. This center console is rated for 600 horsepower with a fuel capacity of 228 gallons.

◄ Maverick's Mirage 18 HPX-V is a typical well-equipped flats boat. This 18-footer has a 150-horsepower rating, draws only 9 inches, and has both a poling tower and a bow casting platform.

(friction) and the weight of the bow wave that a nonplaning hull pushes before it. To achieve this, a lightweight hull is important, but weight is related to power. A planing hull can have a wider beam, with length-to-width ratios ranging from 2.5:1 to 3.5:1. A wider beam, especially in the aft section, makes more space for the power plant. In relation to power carried, the hull is lightweight.

On plane, this hull is more nimble in handling, since a substantial part of it is airborne and steering action is quicker. The wider beam and hard chines (where the bottom and sides meet) make for a more stable boat in calm water, though less so in a big roll.

But advantages in speed and handling bring penalties. A planing hull is more subject to wind and wave action—a surface chop can sometimes feel like a rock-strewn road at high speed. The lack of a useful keel on some planing hulls makes it hard to hold a course in heavy going. Aggravating these effects is the tendency of the bow to lift as more power is applied; the "active" hull on plane is aft, where the greatest weight is located in the broad beam and power plant. Power trimming the outboard engine may adjust the planing angle to level. Or, trim tabs may be added at the stern. These are metal power-operated tabs installed at the bottom of the hull at the transom that adjust the stern and bow up and down at planing speeds. Trim tabs are also used to adjust the boat's ride to compensate for passengers and gear that may be off center or when running in a rough sea to avoid spray and a wet ride. When a planing boat holds a horizontal angle at plane, it is easier to steer, gives a drier ride, and rides better.

But it goes without saying that much boating is on quiet water, where the planing hull has few if any serious problems. In any case, not many planing hulls now made are the pure type—flat bottoms or simple Vs. Manufacturers have adapted planing advantages to practical conditions, and come up with combinations that are safe, fast, comfortable, and still easy to handle.

CABIN DORY: This is one flat-bottomed boat that is still being made in sizes of 20 feet or more. The explanation is that the dory hull's sloping sides and narrow bottom give it some of the features of a deep-V hull in handling rough water. On the Gulf and the northwestern and northeastern coasts, you will see cabin boats with dory hulls made locally that have high bows running back to a flat, low stern, which is also wider than the stern of a displacement dory hull. The wide, flat section of the bottom aft makes this a planing hull. But even at low speed, it draws less water than a V-shaped hull and can be run

in rough surf and shoal water where no other boats of this size would be safe.

V-BOTTOMED SKIFF: The first design aimed to combine planing ability with the kinder qualities of the displacement hull was the simple V bottom, with flat planes rising from the keel to hard chines. V-bottomed skiffs under 20 feet have slightly rounded chines to improve turning and reduce the slap of beam waves; the bottom aft is flattened; and the bow is deeper, with a sharp forefoot section. This makes a hull that is comfortable for all-day use on big lakes and bays, and can still plane off for a fast trip there and back. The bow deck line often has a wide flare overhanging the fine pointed bow. As the bow cuts the waves, the flare casts the spray aside, keeping passengers dry in moderate waves.

V-BOTTOMED CARTOPPER: Most cartop boats have planing hulls. To be light enough to qualify as a cartop boat, construction must be so light that you can lift it to a rack on top of a car. A planing hull is the logical type. Cartoppers that plane are usually modified-V hulls, though they may look round bottomed at a glance. The bow is sharp, molding to a flat aft bottom with rounded chines and a broad stern. If the shape tapers back to a narrower stern for easy rowing, you'll pay for it in reduced planing ability. Depending on the physical strength of the fisherman, 100 pounds seems to be the upper limit for a manageable cartop boat. There are racks designed for one-man loading and unloading.

DEEP-V BOTTOM AND CENTER CONSOLES: From a performance standpoint—when big demands are put on a hull—the best combination of displacement- and planing-hull traits is the deep V. Invented by designer Ray Hunt, the deep-V bottom extends from a slightly rounded forefoot all the way to the stern. The V shape at the stern works well with single or multiple outboards.

In a well-designed deep-V hull, the rounded, deep forefoot and full keel enable it to perform well in big waters, rising with the seas and rounding off a chop even at high speed. But how does such a hull rise on plane? With the help of longitudinal strakes, or steps in the bottom. As power is poured on, the strakes help the hull step up onto plane, while the V shape and flared bow part the wave tops and keep you reasonably dry. World ocean-racing records have been broken again and again with deep-V hulls.

Tough seagoing center-console boats ranging up to 42 feet with multiple outboard motors have created a brand-new category of offshore boats. It is not unusual to see these tough offshore boats with three and even four 300-horsepower outboard engines totaling up to 1,200 horsepower mounted on their transoms. In some respects, this breed of boat is safer than the big inboard-powered sportfisherman. It can run faster with less horsepower to offshore grounds on less fuel and get back to port more quickly in case of bad weather. It is exceptionally seaworthy in all but extremely rough and dangerous waters. These center consoles are also excellent fishing machines, giving fishermen 360 degrees of space to fight big fish. Smaller center consoles, say up to 26 feet, are trailerable with 8-foot beams. Bigger models, up to 42 feet, feature beams of nearly 12 feet, creating huge cockpit space for fishermen, tackle, and gear. Added advantages are that the engines can be replaced and there are no smelly and oily bilges to worry about. If an outboard-powered boat runs aground or hits underwater debris, it is less likely to incur serious damage, whereas an inboard risks damaging rudders and shafts.

FLATS AND BAY BOATS: There was a time when flats boats were made by a handful of local builders. The boats weren't big and the hulls weren't very user-friendly in rough water. Those early boats just didn't perform well north of the bonefish flats. A lot has happened since those early years, and constantly evolving flats-boat designs have now migrated north and west of the Florida flats.

What is a flats boat? Essentially, it's a boat designed for shallow-water fishing, usually for bonefish, permit, and tarpon. It also has low freeboard, which means the wind won't blow it around and the low profile won't spook fish. A flats boat has a wide beam, which makes it exceptionally stable for two standing fishermen. The casting decks are flat fore and aft. The decks are also uncluttered, as gear is stored out of sight in hatches. Boat cleats and hardware are minimal to avoid line snagging. A poling platform is usually mounted over the outboard engine. Before the time of poling platforms at the stern, guides poled their boats from the bow, which proved a tiring task.

Flats boats are also fast. Some 18-footers are rated for outboards up to 150 horsepower. Flats boats can run at speeds of 50 miles per hour or more and maneuver like sport cars. Typical sizes range from 16 to 18 feet.

Take a close look at a flats boat and its special features, and you'll suddenly realize that it could also make an acceptable bass boat. But a flats boat is perfectly designed for saltwater anglers stalking tidal flats, rivers, and barrier islands for striped bass, bluefish, weakfish, bonefish, and tarpon.

Bay boats are designed for fishermen who prefer to fish inshore waters, including bays, rivers, and sounds. Most bay boats are built to handle bigger waters than a flats boat. Bay boats are also bigger, ranging up to 25 feet with 8½-foot beams, and are powered with outboards up to 250 horsepower. Even the bigger models will have a draft of only 11 inches. On good weather days, some bay boats can also handle inshore waters. Typical bay boats are center consoles, though dual-console designs are becoming more popular and practical as family boats.

SEA SKIFF: This boat is often described as round bottomed, but in fact it is usually a combination of a V-hull and displacement-hull design. Forward, a rounded bilge helps it rise with waves and pound less in a chop. The bottom, with rounded chines, slants to a shallow V to form a keel, and flattens aft. The Jersey sea skiff, a remarkably practical and able hull for fishing in bigger waters, will taper to a narrower stern than many planing hulls. This raises the planing speed, but makes it a safer boat for getting home and running inlets when following seas may present the most trouble. Sea skiffs are usually planked with lapstrake. The strakes help lift the hull to reach plane when power is applied, and reduce roll in big water. But this also increases the total wetted surface or drag on the hull. Wood lapstrake hulls have great pliability and shock resistance, which admirably suits fishing the coasts. Today, nearly all wood skiffs of this design are custom built.

■ Multiple Hulls

You've heard them called tri-hulls, cathedral, trihedral, gullwing, and more. The basic principle is the catamaran, adding stability to a hull by means of a secondary hull. In the catamaran, the secondary hull is called an outrigger. A trimaran has two outriggers—one on each side of the load-bearing hull.

This idea, applied to modern fiberglass and aluminum boat design, has just about taken over boat manufacturing in the 15- to 35-foot class. First, it has brought unbelievable stability to small boats, even in rough water. Second, it has made the entire deck usable; you can fight a big fish standing on the gunwale or bow of such a boat without rocking it dangerously. The deck area is actually increased up to 100 percent, since a much wider beam in the same length is possible, with a bowline topside that is more square than pointed. This makes a boat that is useful all over. For families and fishermen and hunters who tend to concentrate on

Multiple-Hull Designs

▲ The G3 LX 22, a 22-foot pontoon boat with a beam of 8½ feet, has a horsepower range from 40 to 115. Pontoon boats are a good choice for a variety of water sports. Under most water conditions, they are stable, safe, and easy to operate.

▲ The Boston Whaler 19-foot Montauk is a good example of a multiple-hull design. This popular unsinkable Montauk design is also available in 15-, 17-, and 21-foot models. With a 96-inch beam and a 115-horsepower outboard, this Montauk is a good choice for lakes, bays, and inshore waters.

▲ The World Cat 330TE is a 34-foot center-console catamaran built for offshore waters. A 10½-foot beam makes it a stable fishing platform. This World Cat is rated for twin 300-horsepower outboards. The twin-hull design affords stability and handles rough water very well.

matters other than boat handling when the fun and action warms up, it has great value.

You can see why the multiple-hull design has brought about a revolution in small boats. Naturally, the hulls are unified—built in a single structure—while the Polynesian and East Indian catamaran and trimaran boats had hulls joined with wood poles bound at each hull. Between keel points are sculptured hollow spaces, where air is trapped when the boat is on plane, making a cushion against the chop and providing a lifting effect. In a tri-hull design, the middle hull is deepest (often with a deep-V bow and forefoot line), and the side hulls are minor points interrupting the rise of the V toward the waterline, sometimes acting as deep chines.

This hull is slower to plane than the other V hulls, for the multiple points tend to push a bow wave ahead of the boat until planing speed is reached. Also, the wetted area is greater, holding the hull off plane until considerable power pushes it up. It's also a heavy hull compared to others of the same length. Obviously, it takes more gas to operate. You have to reckon the greatly increased useful deck area and stability against these drawbacks.

A second revolution that has become as big as the multiple-hull takeover is the continuous boom in bass boats with multiple-hull characteristics. These bass boats, made of fiberglass, aluminum, or Kevlar, are mostly 14- to 20-foot boats with two- or three-point molded hulls. The difference is that the beam is narrow, requiring less power and making them practical in weedy waters and in the brush-filled shorelines of reservoir lakes. This hull is potentially very fast, but that's hardly the purpose in a bass boat.

■ Canoes and Kayaks

A camper or a fisherman who has never used a canoe or kayak to reach backwater havens is missing a rare wilderness experience. These silent boats can take you deep into remote areas that are hardly ever reached by most people.

Most canoes in the 16- to 17-foot range will work fine. Aluminum canoes are noisy, but they are also tough. Some space-age canoes made of Kevlar or Royalex ABS material are so tough that they can take as much abuse as aluminum.

For most canoe camping and fishing, pick out a 17-footer. It will weigh 60 to 80 pounds and hold roughly 1,000 pounds of gear and people. Don't plan on putting more than two passengers in a canoe this size.

If you're new to canoeing, pick a model with a keel, which will make it easier to paddle in a straight line for

Canoes and Kayaks

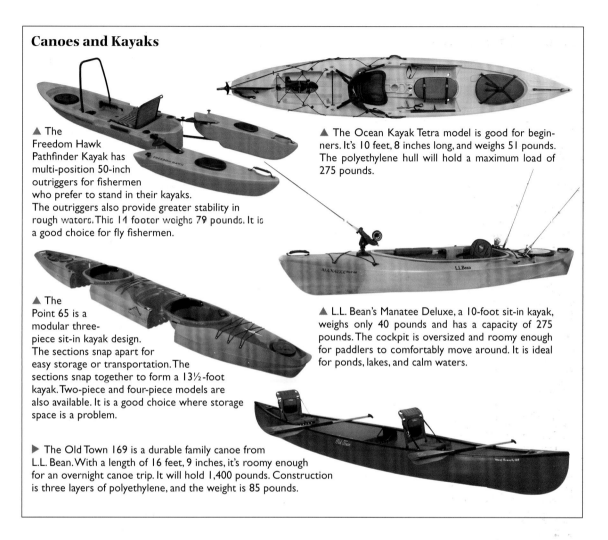

▲ The Freedom Hawk Pathfinder Kayak has multi-position 50-inch outriggers for fishermen who prefer to stand in their kayaks. The outriggers also provide greater stability in rough waters. This 14 footer weighs 79 pounds. It is a good choice for fly fishermen.

▲ The Ocean Kayak Tetra model is good for beginners. It's 10 feet, 8 inches long, and weighs 51 pounds. The polyethylene hull will hold a maximum load of 275 pounds.

▲ The Point 65 is a modular three-piece sit-in kayak design. The sections snap apart for easy storage or transportation. The sections snap together to form a 13½-foot kayak. Two-piece and four-piece models are also available. It is a good choice where storage space is a problem.

▲ L.L. Bean's Manatee Deluxe, a 10-foot sit-in kayak, weighs only 40 pounds and has a capacity of 275 pounds. The cockpit is oversized and roomy enough for paddlers to comfortably move around. It is ideal for ponds, lakes, and calm waters.

▶ The Old Town 169 is a durable family canoe from L.L. Bean. With a length of 16 feet, 9 inches, it's roomy enough for an overnight canoe trip. It will hold 1,400 pounds. Construction is three layers of polyethylene, and the weight is 85 pounds.

long distances. White-water models that have no keel (or a very shallow keel) are designed for fast maneuverability and not suitable for cruising. A good cruising canoe should have a beam of at least 36 inches and a center depth of 12 to 14 inches. The beam should be carried well into the bow and stern, so it can carry the maximum amount of gear and food.

Wood canoe paddles may look pretty, but you're better off with tough resilient fiberglass paddles. If you insist on wood, always carry a spare. For both the bow and stern paddler, pick a paddle that reaches between your chin and eyes.

The kayak is a direct descendant of the seagoing kayaks of the Eskimos of the Far North. The basic kayak is a slender, closed-decked craft with a body-fitting cockpit and a waterproof skirt that seals the hatch around the paddler, who feels that he is "wearing the boat."

A two-bladed paddle propels the boat and a small rudder at the stern assists in steering, making the kayak track straight, or holding the craft in position. The kayak is light, fast, and easy to handle in nearly all types of water.

Various models are designed for touring, fishing, white-water, and sea kayaking. White-water kayaks are nearly always single-cockpit crafts designed for high maneuverability and minimal effort in paddling upriver or downriver. White-water models are usually 13 to 15 feet long with beams of 23 inches or so. Skilled paddlers

The Ocean Kayak Hands-Free model is motorized with a Minn Kota 36-pound thrust electric motor. It measures 14 feet and weighs 86 pounds with the motor.

can run white water forward, backward, or even broadside in a kayak.

Touring kayaks, sometimes called expedition kayaks, are designed to carry one or two paddlers and range from 16 to 18 feet. Sea kayaks are bigger crafts with exceptional load capacities, as much as 900 pounds, and range from 18 to 22 feet in length with 30-inch beams. Some sea kayaks can accommodate three paddlers, and several manufacturers build collapsible and inflatable kayaks for ease of storage for traveling kayakers. Some inflatables feature multi-chambered bodies and aluminum-frame reinforcements. One touring model for two paddlers measures 12 feet with a beam of 34 inches. It weighs only 37 pounds and has a capacity of 350 pounds. It will store into a package that measures 35 by 19 by 7 inches.

FISHING KAYAKS: Almost any kayak can be used for fishing, but beginning around 2010, kayaks designed specifically for fishing literally stormed the outdoor market. Today, kayaks are used to fish all waters, from farm ponds to offshore waters for billfish. Kayaks can now take anglers into remote backwaters of fresh and salt water that were previously inaccessible.

There are at least a dozen kayak manufacturers producing models suitable for fishermen. First, a fisherman must decide whether he wants a sit-in or a sit-on model. Sit-in kayaks have a cockpit in which you sit, which is the traditional kayak design. Sit-on models have no cockpit, but are molded with exposed seat arrangements on top of the kayak, a design most fishermen seem to prefer. The sit-in models may be drier and warmer in some waters and allow you to keep more gear covered and dry, but the sit-on kayaks are easier to get on and off, an important factor for fishermen who also like to wade.

There are additional advantages to sit-on models. Some newcomers to kayaking harbor a fear of capsizing and getting trapped upside down underwater. If you capsize with a sit-on kayak, you simply roll the kayak over and climb back on. Sit-on kayaks are also more comfortable if you are big with long legs. Most sit-on models have watertight hatches, which make them a good choice for divers and photographers. Sit-on kayaks also tend to be more stable than the traditional sit-in models.

Good fishing kayaks should measure 12 to 14 feet with a beam of about 30 inches and weigh 60 to 80 pounds. Stability in a fishing kayak is a key factor. Those long, slender kayaks may be faster, but short, beamier models will be more stable and a better choice for fishing. For extra stability, some models offer removable outriggers.

INS AND OUTS OF CANOES: The cardinal rule for fishermen who use canoes is don't stand! Learn to cast, fight fish, and haul an anchor from a sitting position. Standing is one of the most common causes of people falling out of, or capsizing, canoes. Rule No. 2 is never swim away from your canoe if you get dumped. Most canoes have enough flotation to keep afloat until help arrives. Never be afraid of your canoe. I did some testing several years ago and I was amazed at how difficult it was to intentionally capsize or tip a canoe over from a sitting position. Getting in and out of a canoe, however, can be tricky unless you follow some basic procedures (see accompanying illustrations on the next page).

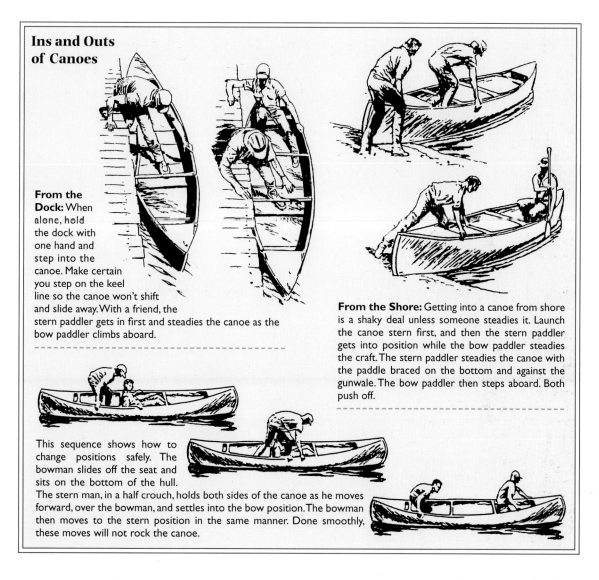

Ins and Outs of Canoes

From the Dock: When alone, hold the dock with one hand and step into the canoe. Make certain you step on the keel line so the canoe won't shift and slide away. With a friend, the stern paddler gets in first and steadies the canoe as the bow paddler climbs aboard.

From the Shore: Getting into a canoe from shore is a shaky deal unless someone steadies it. Launch the canoe stern first, and then the stern paddler gets into position while the bow paddler steadies the craft. The stern paddler steadies the canoe with the paddle braced on the bottom and against the gunwale. The bow paddler then steps aboard. Both push off.

This sequence shows how to change positions safely. The bowman slides off the seat and sits on the bottom of the hull. The stern man, in a half crouch, holds both sides of the canoe as he moves forward, over the bowman, and settles into the bow position. The bowman then moves to the stern position in the same manner. Done smoothly, these moves will not rock the canoe.

UNSWAMPING A CANOE: As mentioned, the most important rule in canoeing is don't stand! Standing is the most common cause of people falling out of canoes, but the rule is often violated by sportsmen who are casting, fighting fish, or hauling an anchor. Equally important, if your canoe swamps, is to never leave it to try to swim toward shore. Most modern canoes will keep you afloat, even when full of water. In fact, you can sometimes paddle a swamped canoe to shore with only your hands.

If another canoe swamps, you can use your canoe as a rescue craft to get the swamped canoe back into service without having to beach it (see illustrations on the next page).

Paddleboarding

Sportsmen who are interested in kayaks and canoes are also likely to be interested in paddleboarding, a water sport dating back to 1926 when some boards were made of redwood. The big comeback of paddleboarding started around 1996 and this water sport is still growing. Paddleboarders can lie down or kneel on a

Unswamping a Canoe

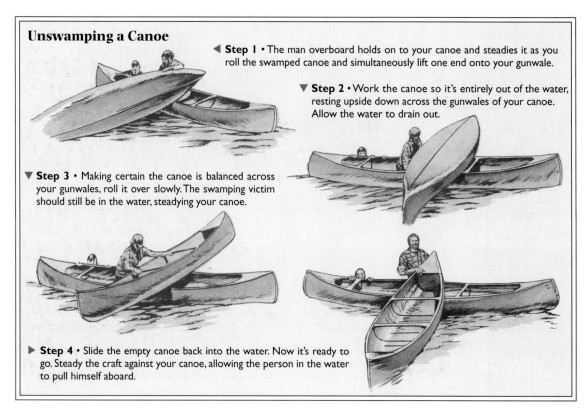

Step 1 • The man overboard holds on to your canoe and steadies it as you roll the swamped canoe and simultaneously lift one end onto your gunwale.

Step 2 • Work the canoe so it's entirely out of the water, resting upside down across the gunwales of your canoe. Allow the water to drain out.

Step 3 • Making certain the canoe is balanced across your gunwales, roll it over slowly. The swamping victim should still be in the water, steadying your canoe.

Step 4 • Slide the empty canoe back into the water. Now it's ready to go. Steady the craft against your canoe, allowing the person in the water to pull himself aboard.

paddleboard, but standing has become the new norm. Manufacturers recommend paddleboards roughly 10 to 12 feet long with a fixed rudder and a weight capacity of about 250 pounds. The boards, which look like surfboards, are usually constructed of a polyethylene outer shell over a watertight polyurethane inner core. Paddles should be 8 to 10 inches taller than the paddler. Some paddles have an angle built in for better efficiency.

Paddleboards are designed for use in calm water or light surf conditions. As a beginner, you should start out by kneeling on paddleboards first. When you feel comfortable with the balance and stability, place your hands on the sides of the paddleboard and try to stand up, placing your feet where your knees were. Falling is part of the learning process. If you fall, aim for the side of the board and fall into the water. Never fall on the board, which could cause injury.

The BIC ACE-TEC Stand-Up Paddleboard is 11 feet, 6 inches long, and will support paddlers up to 260 pounds. The construction is multiple layers of styrene polymer and fiberglass with a foam core. It's designed for ponds, lakes, bays, and calm ocean waters.

The Pelican Surge Stand-Up Paddleboard is 10 feet, 4 inches long, and weighs 33 pounds. It's made of a polyethylene outer shell over a polyurethane inner core. The EVA deck is skidproof. A removable fiberglass fin helps tracking.

Sailboats

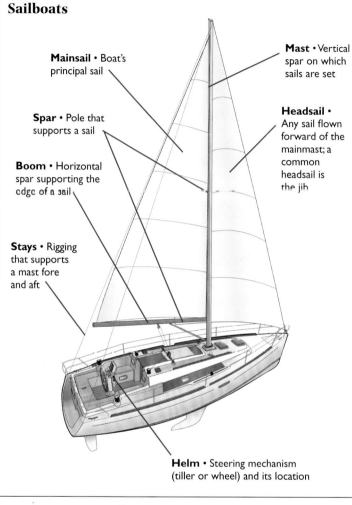

Mainsail • Boat's principal sail

Spar • Pole that supports a sail

Boom • Horizontal spar supporting the edge of a sail

Stays • Rigging that supports a mast fore and aft

Mast • Vertical spar on which sails are set

Headsail • Any sail flown forward of the mainmast; a common headsail is the jib

Helm • Steering mechanism (tiller or wheel) and its location

Wind is the oldest form of power for boats. There are many types and sizes of sailboats, but most of the components are the same. Regardless of size, all sailboats use a rudder to steer and wind for power. Here are the parts and types of popular sailboats.

Sloop • A single-masted sailboat with the mast less than 40 percent of the boat length aft of the bow with a mainsail and normally one headsail

Cutter • A single-masted sailboat with a mainsail and usually two headsails, with the mast closer to amidships than for a sloop

Catboat • A sailboat with a mast near the bow, and no headsail

Yawl • A two-masted sailboat with the rear mast aft of the rudderpost

Ketch • A two-masted sailboat with the after mast forward of the rudderpost

BOAT CONSTRUCTION

The material of which a boat is made and the way that material is used in building a boat has a direct effect on its cost, strength, weight, buoyancy, and durability. Commercial builders have turned mostly to fiberglass and aluminum hulls because they are easier to mass-produce. And people are buying them because the man-made materials require less upkeep than wood. But there are still wood-boat builders in business today, and some of the woodworking techniques are worth noting.

Wood

It's hard to appreciate the work and time needed to keep a wood boat in good shape until you have stripped a hull down to clean, bare board, repaired rot and loose fastenings, filled and sanded it all smooth, and then fiberglassed, repainted, and refinished it inside and out.

Wood is a natural material. It feels good, absorbs sound and shock, and can be worked and repaired by anyone. An important advantage over fiberglass and aluminum is that wood is naturally buoyant. Wood burns, but it's less flammable—especially the hardwoods—than most people think.

Generally, round-bottomed, wood displacement hulls are built on temporary molds with ribbands connecting to delineate the shape. Structural members are bent to the molds. Planking is lined up and secured by the structure. V-bottomed, planing hulls are generally built on sawn frames (sawn lumber firmly jointed at angles where the contour changes). Here, the frames make permanent molds to which the planks or plywood are attached.

But wood boats take their characteristics from the way the hull is covered as well as from the hull shape. Structural features, weight, strength, and, to an extent,

Kinds of Planking

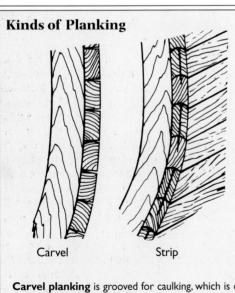

Carvel   Strip

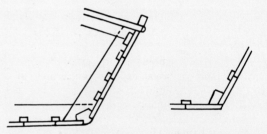

In batten-seam construction, battens are notched into frames and seal planking seams from inside. The left illustration shows construction for bigger boats, while the right illustration shows simpler work often seen in home-made rowboats.

Carvel planking is grooved for caulking, which is driven between planks. In larger boats, screw holes may be counter bored and wood plugged, keeping the smooth carvel look and keeping the fasteners tightly seated as well.

In strip planking, tight, strong seams have concave-convex edges. The edges are glued as the planks are clamped in place. Then, the planks are edge-nailed. The frames are fastened from the inside.

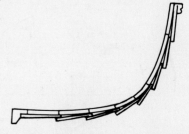

Lapstrake (clinker) planking may be as simple or as detailed as you desire. Strakes are fitted from the garboard at the keel upward.

water characteristics go hand in hand with the planking method. Some of the methods have been almost abandoned in favor of simpler and cheaper ones, but they are described here because valuable older hulls made with great skill are still available.

PLYWOOD: The advantages of building with marine-grade plywood are economy, simplicity, and availability of the material. Most amateur boat builders, especially those who build from kit plans, use plywood. There are fewer fastenings, and the tricky work of fitting plank lines into a pleasing boat shape is largely avoided. Of course, plywood works best in boats with a rather simple design, since it won't take compound bends. The dory, with a flat bottom and flat-curved sides, is a good example. In bigger boats, plywood is used with hard chines and flat bottoms for flat-V designs.

One big-boat builder starts with a frame of white oak ribs, over which sheets of plywood are laid from sheer to sheer as a tough and tight inner hull. Over the inner hull, another of solid mahogany planks is built in carvel fashion.

Don't be alarmed when you see fist-size patches in marine plywood: voids in the core have been filled. When used in exterior hull covering, the seams, which expose the laminations, must be thoroughly treated and sealed, and the surface must be fiberglassed to protect the end-grain exposed in all plywood. Repair is simpler than in any other wood boat. Maintenance is relatively easy, but must be regular. Delamination of the wood plies can result from spray collecting in the bilges, as well as from outside the hull, so many plywood boats are fiberglassed both inside and out.

Plywood is also used in sawn strips for other planking methods.

CARVEL: This is a tighter and stronger form of carvel planking, originated thousands of years ago. Planks are laid edge to edge to form a smooth hull. Simple carvel planking is fastened only to ribs or frames, which must be closely spaced and therefore make a boat heavier. Caulking is put between planks, the exterior edges of which are grooved slightly to hold the caulk. In water, planks swell into the caulk for tightness; out of water (and this goes for planks above the waterline as well), drying tends to open seams. A simple carvel-built boat is not a very dry one, and requires seasonal work to keep shipshape.

BATTEN-SEAM: This is another tighter and stronger form of carvel planking. Staunch battens are notched into the frames, and planks are laid so that the seams fall at the centers of the battens. This closes the seams from behind, and planks are shaped so that the seams are tight when laid, without caulking on the exterior. Pliable batten compound is spread on the battens and plank edges, and planks are screwed along the edges through the battens into the frames.

LAPSTRAKE: A favorite method for building boats that are very light and strong, lapstrake is also referred to as clinker-built or clinch, referring to clinched nails traditionally used in fastening. Planks are overlapped, resembling clapboard on a house. The effect looks "boaty." Relatively thin, wider planks can be used, and are fastened to each other along the overlap and also through frames where they occur. Frames can be wider spaced than in most other construction. Seam compound is applied to the overlap before fastening.

Lapstrake building is an expert's job; planking must be painstakingly lined up with the boat's shape, without stealers (which are cut to fit awkward places in carvel construction, where their use in the flat skin does not destroy the appearance). Repairing damage to lapstrake is also an expert's job.

STRIP PLANKING: This is a popular and successful way for amateurs to build wood boats, but it requires too many fastenings to be the choice of professional builders. Narrow strips (about 1¼ inches for a 20-foot boat) are used in planking. Another variation of carvel, it combines light weight with great strength, long life, and minimum maintenance compared to ordinary carvel planking. The narrow planks will not often warp or lift, which happens even with professionally built carvel boats when planking that is too wide and thin has been used.

Tight, strong seams are achieved by shaping the edges, one side concave, and the other convex. The edges are covered with marine glue as a plank is laid, and then the plank is clamped tight in place and edge-nailed through the width of two planks and into a third. Only each third or fourth plank is fastened through frames. Fewer and lighter frames reduce weight and save interior space, as in lapstrake planking. All the fastenings in strip planking make it hard to repair; the job should be turned over to a skilled worker.

DIAGONAL PLANKING: Strong, true, and trim boats are produced this way. An amateur can handle it successfully in its simpler forms. For instance, a single layer of ¼-inch diagonal strips can be applied to plywood transverse frames for very small and light boats, such as a shallow duckboat. Strips are laid at 45-degree angles to the centerline, glued and fastened to each frame at the crossing point. The edge of each strip is glued before the next is laid, and clamped in place for fastening to the frames. In this lightweight construction, fiberglassing the hull both inside and out is imperative for watertightness and strength.

In larger and heavier boats, planks are laid tight in two layers and overlapped. This is an easy way for an amateur to build a dinghy-shaped boat. The keel, sheer, and longitudinal frames make the bones in this construction without transverse framing, except in offshore boats. Double-planking compound, available in marine stores, is laid between the layers of planks. An unusually strong, lightweight hull results.

Professionals build double-diagonal hulls. One method is to plank in two layers laid at opposite 45-degree angles. Another is to lay the first layer at the angle, and the second straight fore and aft as in strip planking. The first layer is fiberglassed. You will find older boats with a first layer that has been covered with construction canvas and glued before laying the second layer of planking.

■ Aluminum

Light weight, low cost, and low maintenance make aluminum a popular and useful material, especially in small boats such as cartoppers. Another important quality often overlooked: it won't burn. These boats can be noisy, and poorly made aluminum hulls will "pong" as panels flex under pressure and temperature change. Some makers use sound-deadening rubber-based paints and other coatings on the inside. In larger hulls, a layer of flotation is sandwiched between two aluminum skins, providing safety and quiet operation, too. It may surprise you, but an unpainted and uninsulated aluminum boat is not hot, but cool. Sun rays are radiated through the metal into the water.

Aluminum boat building came of age with the development of the 5000 and 6000 series of marine aluminum, which contain no copper. The 5000 is alloyed with magnesium and manganese, the 6000 with magnesium and silicon. Corrosion is not a problem, even in salt water, if the boat is built with marine aluminum. A reputable maker will declare this in a label on the boat.

Electrolysis presents a real danger to aluminum hulls in salt water, however. Copper, steel, nickel, or chromium, for instance, will cause electrolytic decay in aluminum in the presence of an electrical current in salt water. Motor ignitions and electronic gear and lighting systems must be properly grounded by a qualified technician to avoid this danger. For this reason, aluminum boats sell better in freshwater areas.

Aluminum hulls may be welded or riveted, and frequently both fastening methods are used. Stretch-forming presses make almost any hull form possible. Smooth, structurally sound extrusions provide strength needed

Aluminum boats are tough and easier to maintain than fiberglass boats. They are a good choice for fishermen and hunters, who frequently take their boats in shallow or timbered shoreline waters.

in keels, stringers and ribbing, transom, and gunwales. You will dent an aluminum hull more often than you will crack and rip it open, but even at the worst, it is surprisingly easy to repair.

Fiberglass

Seamless and impervious to marine parasites, rot, or electrolysis, fiberglass is popular because it needs little maintenance or caution in use in either fresh or salt water. Laminated fiberglass has great strength and versatility. Because it can be molded in any shape, it has aided development of hull shapes that are more useful and popular, such as cathedral hulls. If made with a good gel coat, the slick surface is faster in the water.

A well-made fiberglass boat will be totally free of leaks, but it's a common misconception that fiberglass can't leak and that therefore any fiberglass boat will be securely dry. In careless production, pinhole leaks will occur because resin has been unevenly applied to the glass cloth and mat, resulting in dry patches in the glass where water can enter. These patches are also weak.

Fiberglass boats are production boats now; the cost and complexity of molds, skills, and technology have made custom- or amateur-built boats rather rare. Building methods are by contact or hand layup or matched-die molding.

CONTACT OR HAND LAYUP: Improvements and techniques in fiberglass boat construction continue to produce better boats. Typically, quality construction of larger and more valuable boats is by the hand-layup method. A male mold is carefully made of wood, the details complete. On this, a female mold is formed of plastic materials. Laminations are laid, outside in. First, the gel coat: this is the outside surface of the boat and is an epoxy or polyester resin in which desired color is mixed, but without fiberglass body. Next comes a layer of fiberglass mat made of random fibers woven together, very porous but a suitable base for the finish just laid. Into this is laid polyester resin with a mohair or nylon roller, binding the fibers and creating a bond to the gel coat. Depending on required strength and weight of the hull, additional layers of fiberglass cloth and woven rovings (cord-twisted fiberglass for strength) are laid, and then the reverse order—cloth, mat, and inside gel coat. All layers are rolled or painted with resin to bond them together and to the next layer. The exact composition and number of laminations may vary to suit design requirements. When layup is complete, the laminate is cured at atmospheric temperature. When the resin hardens, it permanently bonds the fiberglass in a tough sheet.

The roller or brush work with resin is most important. Too much laid on will result in weakness in any lamination because a bulk of resin will be unstructured—without fiberglass. Too little anywhere will result in a dry patch that may become porous, delaminate, and leak, as noted above.

Foam planks, balsa wood, or plywood can be laid at the core to add strength and built-in flotation, and these cores also help to reduce noise and vibration. In bigger boats, the core is laid with resin I-beams joining laminations on either side at intervals to give structure to the sandwich construction. Some builders avoid any wood in the construction to dispel fear of rot and parasites. Others swear by the shock resistance and flex of wood in the core.

The big advantage of contact or hand layup is that the whole hull or deck is visible at one time. Defects such as air bubbles or dry patches can be seen and remedied before proceeding. Sometimes a hull mold is made in halves to aid this; a large wheel is often built into the mold platform to roll the lamination into accessible positions as it proceeds.

Extra layers of lamination needed at the chines, keel, stem, and transom are applied according to design needs. Stringers and stiffening of fiberglass or plywood may be bonded in place as the schedule proceeds, and bulkheads and motor mounts in larger craft laid after the glass hull is complete. Even hardware may be fastened and bedded in during glassing.

MATCHED-DIE MOLDING: This method is used in large-volume production of fiberglass hulls under 20 feet. A fiberglass preform is made on a shaped vacuum screen placed over a metal male mold. The female mold is pressed onto it, heat is applied, and the hull (including any core and ribs) is quickly fused into a unit. Voids and flaws cannot be seen during fabrication, but techniques of reputable builders are advanced and there are few rejects.

In some production lines, fiberglass fibers and catalyzed resin are shot with a chopper gun into a female mold and cured at atmospheric temperature.

Fabric

WOOD-CANVAS: Making a wood-canvas canoe is started by shaping white cedar ribs around a canoe form. Red cedar planking is clinch-nailed to these, and then

The Old Town 100th Anniversary Canoe features beautiful wood-and-canvas construction. It is a good example of the canoes Old Town originally built in 1908. The process consists of bending wood ribs on a form, and then stretching canvas over the ribs. This classic 16-foot canoe is available as a limited edition through L.L. Bean.

mahogany gunwales are attached. Seamless canvas, Dacron, or a reinforced plastic is used for the outside skin. Seats are framed with ash; seat bottoms are cane. Thwarts are separate, not embodied in the seats. A small keel may extend the entire bottom length for directional stability, or may be omitted on white-water canoes. Coats of waterproof varnish are laid on exposed wood surfaces, and the entire exterior is brushed with a high-gloss enamel to reduce water friction. Such a canvas canoe will stand many years of hard use.

Duckboats, kayaks, and portable canvas-covered rowboats are made by similar methods.

INFLATABLES: Serviceable inflatables are made by laminating nylon on both sides with neoprene or Hypalon, which toughens the fabric, resists aging, and withstands petroleum and sun, as well as abrasion. Thick patches reinforce wear and chafing points. The neoprene-nylon ply is tremendously strong for its weight, and a boat made of it can take collision and grounding on rocks better than any other hull.

The secret to the serviceability of a quality inflatable is its low air pressure—only 2 or 3 pounds. It inflates quickly, but leaks, if any, are slow—usually very small breaks that are easy to repair. A good inflatable is made with at least three buoyancy chambers, any of which will keep the boat afloat.

In the bigger sizes, longer than 20 feet, these inflatables are extremely tough and rigid. Some models, rigged with twin outboard motors, are used for rescue work by the Coast Guard in coastal offshore waters.

Serviceability, almost no maintenance, and portability are the main reasons for the popularity of most of these inflatables.

The Sea Eagle 14 SR is a good example of a rugged inflatable capable of handling lakes, bays, or oceans. This 14-footer has a fiberglass-reinforced transom and plastic floorboards. With a capacity of 2,000 pounds, this model weighs 187 pounds. Sea Eagle sport/runabouts are also available in 10.6- and 12.6-foot models.

Lightning and Your Boat

No other kind of foul weather will make a person feel as helpless as lightning. And there's good reason to be scared. Lightning is deadly, but there are certain precautions to take to minimize the risk of being struck.

Lightning is a discharge of static electricity from a charged cloud to earth or from one cloud to another. The electric charge is created when a cumulus cloud is formed in an updraft of warm, moist air. This combination results in a huge build-up of static electricity in a big cumulonimbus cloud. The top part of the cloud holds a positive charge and the bottom part holds a negative charge from the friction of the updraft. When a thundercloud passes overhead, the negative charge induces the earth to take on a positive charge, usually at the highest points, such as tall buildings, poles, or even humans. These charges in clouds and ground are normally kept apart by air, which acts as an insulator. When the static charge becomes strong enough, however, it overcomes the resistance of the air, and lightning occurs.

When a lightning bolt with a current of more than 100,000 amps passes through the atmosphere, the air is heated and expanded, creating a strong vacuum. It's this rapid expansion and collapse of air that creates the loud shock wave known as "thunder."

Thunder can also tell you how far you are from lightning. Count the seconds between lightning and thunder, and then divide by five. The answer is the distance between you and the lightning in miles. If there's a five-second lapse between lightning and thunder, for example, the lightning is a mile or so away.

If you're in a boat on a lake or offshore, lay fishing rods down and head for cover. If you're in a cabin boat and can't reach land ahead of the storm, stay in the cabin and close all the hatches. If you're running the boat, stay as low as possible at the controls. Lower all fishing rods, antennas, and outriggers. Don't hold any gear connected with the grounding system, and don't hold lifelines or rigging. Avoid acting as a bridge between conductive objects. Never touch outriggers, radio antennas, or electrical appliances until the storm has passed. Keep the boat's bow in the wind as much as possible and head for shore. Passengers should wear life jackets and stay in the cabin or as low as possible in the boat.

MARINE MOTORS

Naturally, your choice of power should be matched to the boat you select. Don't feel limited, however, to what you see already mounted. The great variety of motor designs and horsepower ratings available, and the versatility of these motors, give you options that boaters have never had before. You can customize your boat-motor rig precisely to your own preferences—if you inform yourself before you buy.

An offshore fishing boat up to 40 feet and longer, for instance, doesn't have to be powered by inboard engines. It's common now to see unusually seaworthy deep-V hulls in the 25- to 42-foot range heading off-shore with two, three, or four outboard engines totaling up to 1,200 horsepower.

Similarly, a 14-foot bass boat doesn't necessarily "take" a 10-horsepower trolling motor; depending on the boat's power rating, you can mount a much bigger outboard for covering distance, plus a small electric trolling motor. And for that matter, you don't have to paddle your own canoe; a 2-horsepower gas or electric motor will do it for you handsomely.

The motor to buy is the one that you particularly want and that is safe and sensible for your use. Power your boat adequately, but take care not to overpower it. Check the Boating Industry Association (BIA) plate and the maker's specs for the recommended and maximum power rating for that boat.

Outboard

The outboard is a self-contained power unit that, happily, does not require through-hull fittings. It is light-weight in relation to the horsepower produced and it can be installed or removed quickly and inexpensively.

Mounted outside the boat, its fuel and vapor can be kept safely out of bilges and the cabin; deck space is clear of engine boxes or hatches. You have positive steering with outboard power—the whole motor turns, and the propeller thrust is in the direction that will help turn the boat, instead of at an angle to a rudder. The outboard tilts up for shallow running, beaching, or trailering. There are no underhull fittings that have to be protected at all costs.

A large outboard presents something of an obstacle to fishing lines, and the propeller, out from the hull, can be a hazard to divers and skiers. Mounted on the transom, the outboard is an unbalanced weight that is

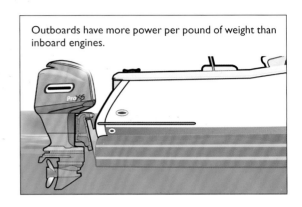

Outboards have more power per pound of weight than inboard engines.

trimmed by adjusting the position of its thrust relative to the plane on which the boat is moving—but it can be trimmed, whereas an inboard-powered boat must have its load trimmed instead.

Trim is easy to understand if boaters remember that at normal running speeds the outboard propeller shaft should be parallel to the surface. Some boats, however, obtain optimum planing attitude with the motor trimmed out slightly past this point. When trimmed out too far, the boat will not operate efficiently. The bow may plane too high or too low.

Boaters should have their outboards "tucked" under (trimmed in) when starting. This forces the bow down and the stern up, and the boat pops up on plane much quicker. As the engine is trimmed out, the bow rises and more of the boat clears the surface. With reduced drag (less friction between the boat and water), the boat gains speed. Once on plane at wide-open throttle, the outboard should be running in the middle of the recommended revolutions-per-minute range.

On bigger outboards, the power trim control button is on the end of the throttle control. With one finger, the boater can trim the engine for the best performance. The operator can easily adjust the engine for optimum boat attitude as boat load or water conditions change. Power trim improves acceleration and helps get a boat on plane quicker. It also means top-end speed advantages.

Outboard manufacturers now produce four-stroke engines up to 350 horsepower. Surprisingly enough, these big outboards with V6 engines are more fuel efficient per horsepower than smaller motors. A 250-horsepower outboard, for example, burns less gas at cruising speed than twin 150s. Some manufacturers used to

Outboard Motors

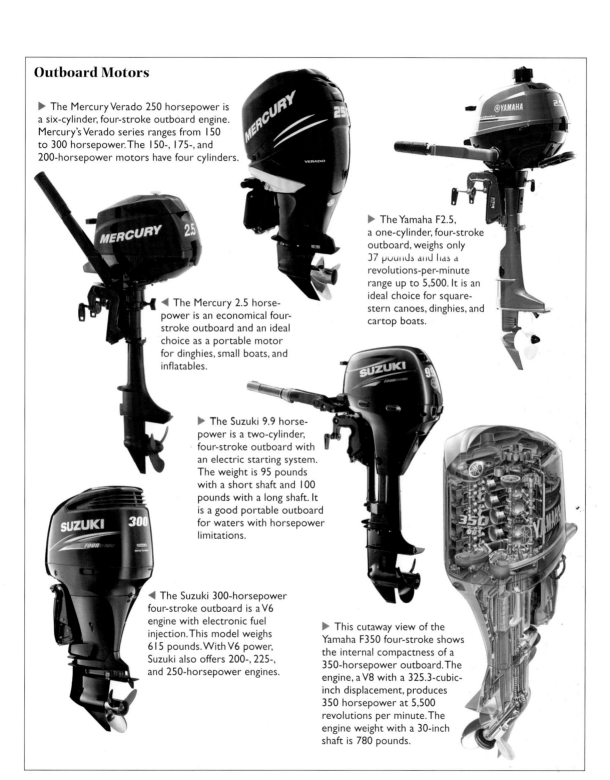

▶ The Mercury Verado 250 horsepower is a six-cylinder, four-stroke outboard engine. Mercury's Verado series ranges from 150 to 300 horsepower. The 150-, 175-, and 200-horsepower motors have four cylinders.

◀ The Mercury 2.5 horse-power is an economical four-stroke outboard and an ideal choice as a portable motor for dinghies, small boats, and inflatables.

▶ The Yamaha F2.5, a one-cylinder, four-stroke outboard, weighs only 37 pounds and has a revolutions-per-minute range up to 5,500. It is an ideal choice for square-stern canoes, dinghies, and cartop boats.

▶ The Suzuki 9.9 horse-power is a two-cylinder, four-stroke outboard with an electric starting system. The weight is 95 pounds with a short shaft and 100 pounds with a long shaft. It is a good portable outboard for waters with horsepower limitations.

◀ The Suzuki 300-horsepower four-stroke outboard is a V6 engine with electronic fuel injection. This model weighs 615 pounds. With V6 power, Suzuki also offers 200-, 225-, and 250-horsepower engines.

▶ This cutaway view of the Yamaha F350 four-stroke shows the internal compactness of a 350-horsepower outboard. The engine, a V8 with a 325.3-cubic-inch displacement, produces 350 horsepower at 5,500 revolutions per minute. The engine weight with a 30-inch shaft is 780 pounds.

Trimming In (Down)
- Lowers the bow
- Results in quicker planing, especially with a heavy load
- Improves the ride in choppy water
- Increases steering torque or pull to the right

Neutral Trimming
- Levels the bow
- Normally results in greater efficiency

Note that the propeller shaft, which connects the propeller to the drive shaft, is parallel to the surface of the water.

Trimming Out
- Lifts the bow
- Increases top speed
- Increases clearance in shallow waters
- Increases steering torque or pull to the left
- In excess, causes the boat to bounce

How Outboard Trim Affects Planing

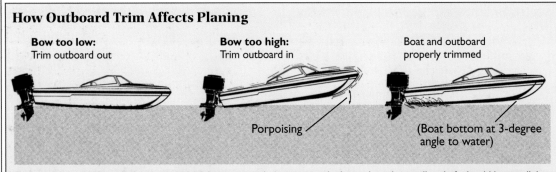

Bow too low:
Trim outboard out

Bow too high:
Trim outboard in

Boat and outboard properly trimmed

Porpoising

(Boat bottom at 3-degree angle to water)

Trim is easy to understand if you remember that at normal running speeds the outboard propeller shaft should be parallel to the surface. Some boats, however, obtain optimum planing attitude with the motor trimmed out slightly past this point. When trimmed out too far, the boat will not operate efficiently.

produce special outboard engines for saltwater use. Today, however, nearly all outboard motor manufacturers build engines up to 350 horsepower that handle salt water and its corrosion problems.

▪ Electrics

The small, silent electric trolling motor purred along unnoticed by all but the most devoted fishermen and hunters until a decade ago, when it took off. Why? Better designs have made electric motors more versatile, there are more models to match boats that people buy, and the new motors are more efficient—that is, they run longer on a battery charge. These motors are also slimmer, more powerful, saltwaterproof, and they pass through water and weeds with less resistance.

Because models and characteristics are changing rapidly, partly due to the developing popularity, a detailed discussion about how they work and what features are important is included here. All electrics are easy to start

Electric Motors

▶ The MotorGuide Digital Tour Electric has a bow mount with a foot control and thrust ratings up to 109 pounds. Some models have a bow mount with a transducer. Digital variable-speed control also maximizes fishing time.

▶ A bow-mounted electric outboard allows two anglers hands-free casting along a shoreline. New electric motors with sealed lower units are equally at home in salt water.

and operate. Endearing traits include low cost, light weight, and near-silent running. Electric is the ideal power for quiet waters, where silence and small movement are important to the careful fisherman and hunter.

Electric motors are powered with one of three systems. Motors listed as 12-volt models are powered with one 12-volt battery; 24-volt motors require two batteries; and 36-volt motors require three batteries. It's also best to use deep-cycle marine batteries. Obviously, the bigger electrics will provide more power (thrust) and will allow you to stay out on the water longer. Always use a model with a built-in battery gauge.

Nearly all electric motors are rated in pounds of thrust ranging from 8 to 109 pounds. If you have a 14-foot aluminum boat, motors with 30 to 40 pounds of thrust will be adequate. Bigger and heavier bass boats and flats boats, however, might need 75 to 100 pounds of thrust to handle the weight and bigger waters.

The penalty of electric motors? Slow speed (about 3.5 miles per hour with a canoe and one man and gear, 2.5 miles per hour with a cartop boat), and the storage battery, which gives you about four hours of continuous trolling time on one charge. But it's unlikely that you'll ever run an electric continuously for that long. In the careful sport it suits, your electric will be turned off frequently, and with experience, you'll learn how to conserve a battery charge. If you are casting or staked out with decoys, it's not hard to get a full day's use from one battery with a full charge. Trolling is another

matter; then, a second battery and your own battery charger are good investments.

How much current a motor draws, of course, determines how many hours of running time you can get on a battery charge. Several things affect this. First, always use a deep-cycle marine battery; some are specially designed for electric motors. Speed is also a big factor in current draw—electrics are most efficient at low speed settings. If your motor draws six amps to move your boat at 1.5 miles per hour, it might draw 16 to 18 amps to go 2.5 miles per hour. Also, some motors are designed with a higher speed range than others and will take more from your battery throughout the range.

Most models house the motor in a pod underwater, connected to the propeller by direct drive. A sturdy control shaft from 20 to 50 inches long mounts to the boat's transom or bow, and the controls are located at the top. This motor position eliminates transmission gears, gives quieter operation, and leaves only the control head at the top to get in the way of action. Waterproof shaft seals and tough motor housings take care of the once-important problem of a wet motor resulting from hitting rocks and logs.

For regular use in water that is filled with weeds and obstructions, some boaters prefer electrics that have the motor on top of the shaft, with the tiller and controls attached to the motor housing.

The ultimate convenience is a remote foot-pedal control that's available with many top-of-the-line models. All remotes give you no-hands steering and an on-off motor. Depress the pedal and the motor goes. Roll the ball of your foot over the pedal and three switches can activate a servomotor on the shaft that will give you right, middle, or left "rudder." A variable-speed control, which comes with remote-controlled models, is realized to full advantage only if you can control it from a remote box placed on the seat beside you.

Remote controls radically change the weight and cost features of electrics, however. Weight is increased by two or three times; price is increased drastically. Plug-in remotes, which let you detach the controls from the mounted motor unit, keep it a manageable package to tote to the car. Remote digital controls are also available for some models, as well as GPS control systems.

Most electrics can be mounted on the transom, on either side of the boat, or at the bow. Canoes give you an even choice, but most boats handle best with the electric attached to the transom. It's hard to hold a true course when it's attached on a midship gunwale, and at the bow—unless you have a remote control—you have to sit in the most uncomfortable place in the boat in order to run it. Many experienced hands prefer bow mounting because they can see the direction of steering while looking ahead, and because this gives them more exact steering since the motor leads the boat. With a foot control, it also leaves both hands free for casting.

Other things to look for on electrics: Make sure the shaft length fits the freeboard of your boat, especially at the bow. The prop should be 6 inches down in the water for its best bite. Brackets and tilt-control hardware must be well designed, so that the unit does not wobble or shift. Also, it should permit you to swing or bring the motor inside the boat readily for moving out fast with your regular outboard power.

■ Inboard (Gasoline)

The typical inboard engine's similarity to an auto engine brought it to popularity and keeps it there. Inboard engine blocks are manufactured by car or truck engine makers, and then are converted to marine use. It is always possible to make repairs locally because it's the most common type of engine available.

The four-cycle inboard is heavier than a comparable outboard, requires permanent installation, and keeps fuel and vapor inside the boat. It also occupies a lot of space. But it's lighter on gas and oil, the lubricating oil system puts out less smog and takes less maintenance, and muffling and insulation can control its noise.

A major advantage is the inboard motor's location amidships, where the hull is capacious and weight is best handled. With a fixed, through-hull propeller shaft and separate rudder, however, an inboard installation presents rather delicate bottom gear that must always be protected. Since the shaft runs at a downward angle to clear the prop action, its thrust is less efficient, pushing at an upward angle.

The V drive helps to beat these drawbacks. It may also permit a lower engine location right against the stern, an advantage on some smaller inboard boats. Penn Yan boats, no longer in production, had improved this design with its tunnel drive section in the hull to protect the propeller. The Shamrock boat company features models with a pocket drive system in its hull. Another solution is the popular stern drive or inboard/outboard.

The first and last word about inboards is to the skipper: keep critical attention on good ventilation and fuel fixtures, and on the quality and condition of fuel lines.

■ Diesel

You'll see diesels now in many sport-fishing boats under 50 feet that could not have accommodated this heavy machinery years ago. Compact designs and lighter metals in the high-compression cylinder walls have put them in hearty competition with gasoline engines in some categories.

Diesel Engine

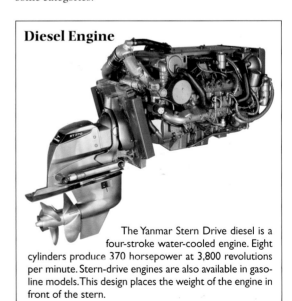

The Yanmar Stern Drive diesel is a four-stroke water-cooled engine. Eight cylinders produce 370 horsepower at 3,800 revolutions per minute. Stern-drive engines are also available in gasoline models. This design places the weight of the engine in front of the stern.

While the diesel burns only half as much fuel as its gasoline counterpart, the diesel doing the same job weighs a third more, and the initial cost is twice as much. But with a diesel, you can increase your cruising range with the same gallons, or reduce the fuel carried to save weight. Because this fuel is less volatile, you have a safer boat. On a still day, however, diesel exhaust odor will not be pleasant. This engine makes sense if you use your boat hundreds of hours each year for extended cruising, chartering, and chasing game fish.

■ Stern Drive

The stern drive, or inboard/outboard, as you might know it, is an inboard four-cycle engine mounted at the stern with an outboard drive. The propeller of a stern drive drives parallel with the boat, and the lower unit of the outdrive turns, giving positive prop steering as with an outboard motor. There is no separate rudder. A power lift is much favored, as is an automatic kickup release that may save the lower unit when it hits an obstacle.

A stern drive is popular on smaller cruisers and open boats, for it is a compact inboard power arrangement that is feasible even where there is insufficient space for underdeck installation. The stern drive is a heavy machine to be located at the transom on small boats. It is a successful match with fast, deep-V hulls, for the point of the V helps to protect the propeller, and prop

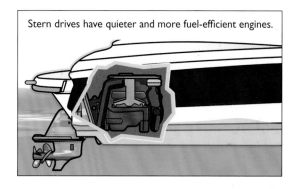
Stern drives have quieter and more fuel-efficient engines.

steering combines with the keel action of the V bottom to reduce sideslip in turns and maneuvers. It is more expensive than a straight inboard engine, but obviously more versatile. It is also the choice power for most racing boats.

■ Jet Drive

The jet drive is another exciting design that is a practical buy for some boaters. Water-jet propulsion is most efficient at high speeds, and it's an attractive choice for water skiers and personal watercraft (PWCs), also called jet skis.

Any inboard engine can be used with a jet pump. The engine is linked by direct drive to a high-speed impeller, and a water jet is forced out a nozzle to propel the boat. With the nozzle gate raised, the jet pushes the

Stern-Drive Engine

The Mercury MerCruiser 4.3L stern-drive package shows typical stern-drive construction. These engines are typically water cooled.

Jet-Drive Engine

The Yamaha F90 is a 90-horsepower, four-stroke, propeller-free jet drive. With no gear case or propeller below the hull, a jet-drive outboard allows boaters to pass over obstructions that would not be possible with a conventional outboard motor. Models are also available from 40 to 150 horsepower.

boat forward. With the gate down, the jet is deflected downward and forward to reverse the boat.

Jet boats used to spin out at high speeds. To improve directional stability, manufacturers have put a small rudder under the jet nozzle and keels 1 inch deep on either side of the impeller screen on the boat's bottom.

Any jet intake can be clogged eventually by thick weeds, but the impeller shrugs off sand, and passes small gravel without harm. One innovation incorporates water-jet drives into conventional outboard fish-

ing motors to permit operation in water too shallow for a prop. Initially, a jet-conversion unit had to be purchased, but now it's a standard propulsion system in most models. A crankshaft-driven impeller draws water through an intake grill, and the water is jetted rearward at high pressure, like the compressed air in a jet aircraft engine. When the motor is put in reverse, a cup swings over the jet stream, channeling it in the opposite direction. The throttle, shift, and, of course, steering are conventional.

BOATS FOR FISHING

You'll catch more fish and enjoy it more if you suit your boat and motor combination to the type of fishing you do. A good rule is small boats for sheltered waters and big, beamy boats for big waters. But that is only the beginning. Most people want a boat that will handle more than one type of fishing, so they look for the best combination of qualities. If you analyze your needs and preferences and decide what is really important, you'll be able to select a boat-motor combination with confidence.

■ Boats for Sheltered Waters

Trout ponds, little bass lakes, and such are not called quiet waters because nothing happens there. They are truly quiet, and the noise you make there will be the loudest heard all day unless it's moose country. Therefore, it is sensible to use the quietest boat you can find. If you stay within the 12- to 14-foot range, the size of your shadow will be reduced, and boat action will be in scale with the surroundings. Inflatables, canoes, kayaks, and

12-foot cartop boats fit quiet waters perfectly. You can launch these boats into the water soundlessly, with little more than a ripple. If you want to catch fish and keep the fishing good, make your outfit as simple as possible. Leave the outboard at home, bring only a paddle or pole, and be proud of your inexpensive rig. You've matched nature, and that is the sportsman's art.

For small rivers and streams, canoes, kayaks, lightweight johnboats, or cartop boats are time-honored choices and cannot be beat. They move easily against the current. Add a small outboard and you're in clover. The johnboat is probably more comfortable for two fishermen and gear when casting and moving for long hours, but experience with a canoe or kayak will win you over with its easy movement, light weight, and silence. A length of 15 feet or more offers enough space for two fishermen.

When you fish lakes only a few miles across, many types of boats will do the job. First, observe the wave action, wind, and depth; then, take a good look at the boats commonly used there. They probably suit those conditions remarkably well.

Small aluminum boats in the 12- to 14-foot range are ideal for ponds, lakes, and rivers. In the 12-foot length, they can be cartoppers.

Bass Boats

The Nitro ZV 21 is a classic bass-boat design. At 21 feet, 7 inches, with a 100-inch beam, the Nitro has a maximum rating of 350 horsepower. The maximum weight capacity is 2,500 pounds. The dual console and deep-V hull are designed for rough-water running.

The Ranger RT188C is an 18-foot crappie/bass boat rated for 115 horsepower. Built with a 92-inch beam, this aluminum model has an all-fiberglass console and comes with a custom-fitted trailer. This model is also available in camo for waterfowl hunters.

The Stratos 186 VLO, a fiberglass bass boat, measures 18 feet, 9 inches, and is rated for 115 horsepower. The bow is rigged with a Minn Kota trolling motor and foot pedal. Stratos offers this model factory rigged with its own custom-built trailer.

If the surface is usually quiet, consider a boat that will give you platform space with shallow draft, such as the johnboat or pontoon boat. If your sport is fishing for bass and crappies in brush and weeds, look for a boat that is easy to push and pry loose; the canoe, kayak, or johnboat works well.

The most popular boat in America today may well be the bass boat. The phenomenal boom in this new breed is well deserved because it fits the sport so well. The hull, developed on southern lakes, is a cross between the johnboat and tri-hull. Forrest L. Wood, founder of Ranger Boats, is credited with the creation of the first bass boat. It is very stable, yet rises quickly to the top of the water and moves fast when you want to cross the lake. With its shallow draft, you can get in almost anywhere there is water that holds fish. The seats are designed for all-day fishing, rod holders are located where you want them—it's all thought out. The typical bass boat today is built of fiberglass or Kevlar or a combination of both materials. These boats can range from 15 to 21 feet and can handle outboard motors up to 300 horsepower. The hulls are designed to handle almost any

kind of water and speeds. There are only two drawbacks: weight and price. Both are big. You'll also need a trailer for these rigs.

The favorite all-arounder, however, is the aluminum fishing boat. Successful makes are designed to adapt to the widest variety of conditions. With flotation built in, they are good in fairly rough water, are lightweight and easy to handle, can be stored anywhere, and certainly cost little for the service they give. You see them on all inland waters, whatever the area and fishing sport. They come in sizes from 12 feet up; probably the most serviceable length is 14 feet. A 10-horsepower outboard is the common power match, but they will take huskier pushers if that's what you need.

For remote waters where the approach is on foot, check out inflatables. You can backpack in, and then inflate at the water's edge with a CO_2 cartridge or foot pump. Inflatables handle rather badly, but they are very stable and surprisingly tough, and are a lot of fun. They can also handle small outboard motors and electrics. Other candidates for these backwaters are canoes and kayaks, but most of those take two persons to tote.

■ Float-Trip Boats

Several schools of thought about boats for float trips are all cogent and tend to follow regional custom—not for custom's sake, but because water conditions vary considerably. A broad, fairly slow river without rapids will usually see shallow-draft boats that maneuver slowly but offer comfort and convenience in their broad-beamed stability. Johnboats, large inflatables, pontoon boats, and river-style houseboats fit these conditions. Such boats have broad front ends that are inefficient in meeting waves or cutting much speed, but those aren't the needs. All you need is enough power to push a heavy bow wave upstream when you return. Knowing your stream, the weight and size of the boat will help you determine how much power you need.

For fast rivers with rapids and white water, the needs are more demanding. First, you need a hull that will withstand a lot of punishment; it must be built strong to survive bumping hard into rocks, logs, and gravel bottoms without damage. Flotation must be positive—sufficient to support the craft, occupants, and load if swamped. Maneuverability is very important, as is a bow design that will lift and throw off white water. Light weight is necessary so that portages will be easy. The choice is usually a canoe or kayak for rivers where narrow bends and fast water between rocks make maneuverability essential. Expert white-water canoeists prefer craft under 15 feet, with round bottoms and no keel for quicker handling. However, since a canoe of this design won't hold much, the choice for float trips is usually a bigger canoe with high ends. Kayaks are another excellent choice when you will encounter some white water. Kayaks in the 12- to 14-foot range designed for fishing are more than adequate for float trips.

Open boats are good equipment carriers for extended float trips. Some can even be rigged to carry a couple of kayaks for exploring backwaters.

Inflatables are usually chosen for big, fast rivers. A big inflatable has great stability and is forgiving when you bounce it off banks and obstructions, and it's roomy enough to let you relax when the going is straight. But maneuvering a big inflatable is a real problem. Some experienced float men add a broad, shallow tiller for steering. On some rivers, this is essential. Don't plan on powering your boat on fast streams, but arrange for transport at the lower end of your float trip.

■ Boats for Open Waters

On big lakes, river estuaries, coastal bays, inlets, and inshore waters, size and seaworthiness are absolutely essential. The bigger the water, the greater the potential dangers—and the need for a capable hull that will bring you safely back through all weather yet serve you comfortably in routine use and help you catch more fish. Open waters are not the places for a flat-bottomed, 12-foot skiff. Look at what is being used. You will see deep-V bow points, rounded chines on smaller boats, probably with flat planing surface aft, and enough freeboard to keep dry when the wind comes up. If your waters commonly have a sharp chop, as in many Great Lakes locations, you will need more freeboard, and the hull shape should ride comfortably in those conditions. Too much freeboard can be a curse, however, making fish handling difficult and presenting a big profile to the wind, causing eternal drifting.

Fishermen who run out to the reefs on the Great Lakes to anchor and drop a line for perch want a boat that gives a comfortable seat for hours on end, riding the waves without slapping and shipping water. The man who trolls for lake trout or coho salmon prefers a competent running boat that also provides a good platform for fighting and landing the fish, with a bow shape that will handle the waves when they rise, and that can move off fast to change locations and make the run home.

Calm days on open waters—and many big lakes a fraction of the size of the Great Lakes fit the case—are deceptive. The water looks calm when you start out in the morning. By noon, you are occupied with sunburn and poor fishing, so that when the wind and big waves come up at 3:00 p.m., you're taken by surprise. Getting back to shore can be dangerous if you are out in a 12- or 14-footer with a 10-horsepower motor. Think in terms of 16 feet or more length, with plenty of beam in relation to length. For big inland lakes and coastal bays, you will need a motor of 25 horsepower and up. For trolling the ocean beaches, a motor or twin motors from 100

The Boston Whaler 345 Conquest is designed for offshore waters. The length is 34 feet with a beam of nearly 12 feet. The Conquest has a maximum horsepower rating of 900. The fuel capacity is 391 gallons. A big, comfortable cabin makes this a good choice when fishing in unpredictable ocean waters.

The World Cat 330TE, a catamaran-hulled offshore boat, will handle twin outboards totaling 600 horsepower. A 34-footer with a beam of nearly 11 feet, the hull is designed to cushion impact when running in a rough ocean. The fuel capacity is 300 galloons.

horsepower up are necessary. If you plan to troll, choose a boat with a broad, clear stern for handling the lines. For casting, you should consider a boat that also provides a good casting platform both fore and aft.

▪ Offshore Outboard-Powered Boats

Perhaps the most versatile boats available are the center-console, deep-V boats. A deep bow permits them to handle the seas, but this slopes into a moderately flat mid and stern bottom that permits them to plane easily and ride over the flats without scraping. This design is also very stable for its seaworthiness. These boats are best described as inshore-offshore boats, great for fishing coastal bays and reefs, for running the inlets, and for going offshore—weather permitting—into really big-water country.

It is increasingly common to see these boats, some of them powered with up to three and four outboard engines, running to far offshore waters. Typical rigs are in the 28- to 40-foot range and are usually powered by twin 300- to 350-horsepower four-stroke outboard engines. Some boats, however, can range up to 45 feet with four 300-horsepower outboard engines for power. Some of these boats have beams exceeding 12 feet, weigh 24,000 pounds, and can carry about 500 gallons of fuel. Digital technology makes synchronizing revolutions per minute and trimming multiple outboard engines easy. With the right preparations, these boats are canyon ready.

▪ The Sportfisherman

The sportfisherman is a well-designed fishing machine with all the comforts of home that can sail in nearly all kinds of weather and offshore seas. It is, indeed, a breed apart from all other fishing boats. Until you have handled a boat on the ocean, following fish on really big water, it's hard to imagine what is required of a boat in these conditions. Not only are these boats bigger (typically 35 to 82 feet), with deeper hulls and more beam, but they are built to take tremendous force. Big power is needed, as well as great reliability and fuel economy, and a frequent choice is twin diesels. For example, an 82-foot sportfisherman has a 22-foot beam and a fuel capacity of 3,000 gallons. Cockpit space measures a huge 255 square feet. This boat would likely be powered by twin diesel engines putting out more than 2,000 horsepower each.

Fortunately, there are more economical choices if a fisherman is interested in a sportfisherman. Much more common and affordable to serious bluewater fishermen are sportfisherman boats in the 38- to 54-foot range. Regardless of size, in any sportfisherman, layout and cockpit space is critical. Captains, mates, and fishermen must be able to handle the boat efficiently when baiting and hooking a big fish, so that it is not broken off or lost due to a slack line or pulled hook. With an inadequate boat or inept skipper, it can take hours to boat a good billfish. In that time, tackle and equipment break down, people have accidents brought about by fatigue, and the boat itself can be endangered. The steering station, whether it is from the bridge or tuna tower, should give the captain a clear view of the cockpit and stern as well as forward. The cockpit should be clear of all equipment except the fighting chair and tackle with a clean and unobstructed transom. The sportfisherman

should be built with engine hatches under the cabin floor for easy access. Several staterooms, a galley, air-conditioned salon, extensive electronics, a generator, bait wells, and refrigerated fish boxes are typical features on most sportfisherman models.

BOATS FOR HUNTING

Any boat is potentially a hunting boat. If you have a fishing boat, it will probably serve your hunting needs well. Every boat discussed in the previous section has been used successfully in hunting, even the big sportfisherman.

If hunting is your sole game, you may want a specialized boat, such as a duckboat. There are good reasons, however, for having a boat that will do several things well. If you must travel far on water to reach your hunting ground, you need outboard speed to save time. If you usually hunt in protected waters, you may still want to go to the big lakes or the shore to hunt. You may want to spend the night in your boat on some trips. You may like more than one kind of boat hunting—float hunting for deer, for small game, or waterfowling.

If you already own a good-size fishing boat and trailer, a good solution for the all-around hunter is to get an additional, specialized hunting boat. On the water, you can use the big boat to cover distance, then use it as your "lodge," where you make your meals, keep supplies, and bed down overnight. Towing the small hunting boat behind, you can hop in when you're ready to hunt and have a small, maneuverable boat that is quiet, easy to handle, and able to get in close and keep a low profile.

■ Float Hunting

Any of the flat-bottomed, low-sided boats, such as the johnboat, make practical float hunters. These boats have tremendous load-carrying capacities for their size, so that two hunters and their gear, including camping equipment and a tent, are no problem at all to fit. And I have seen two deer laid across the gunwales of a johnboat in addition to everything else, and there was still enough freeboard to run slowly back upstream to the car.

The stability and broad beams of these boats is another reason for their popularity with float hunters. You can stand to shoot with confidence, take a wide stance, and move around easily. Besides, bird dogs and

retrievers like them, while they dislike tippy and confining boats.

The flat bottom is ideal for setting up the frame of a blind, and you can pop up a small aluminum-framed tent there for overnight shelter if you're in marshland. Waiting hour after hour in cold, cramped quarters doesn't describe the experience of hunters in a johnboat. There's plenty of room for sleeping bags and a heater to keep you warm.

Big inflatables are also popular with float hunters. They are comfortable to lounge around in while floating or waiting it out. But the flexible construction means that you should kneel or sit to shoot. A big plus is the light weight of an inflatable, making portages easy, and you can turn it over on shore for a blind, propping up one side for gunning while you stay in the shadow.

An outboard of 10 to 20 horsepower is suitable for either of these types. You have to be guided by the boat's size, the load you carry, the distance you have to motor upstream and the strength of the current, and, of course, the maximum-horsepower rating of the boat.

Important: Check out your state's hunting laws before you shoot from a boat. Some states require that you have the outboard tilted up and not operating when you shoot. Others will not permit shooting from a boat equipped with a motor.

■ Duckboats

Duckboats suit any hunting for shy game, especially in small hunting grounds such as island country, where you need something stealthy to succeed. Double-enders are the most popular: a small duckboat, canoe, or kayak. If you can, leave the motor at home and use paddles or oars; work around your base, and move your base often. If you need a motor to cover distance and reach fallen game before the current takes it, think of a really small outboard. An electric trolling motor is preferred by some hunters because it's quiet.

The decked-over double-ender will keep you dry and snug, but the limitation is tight space. There is room for only one hunter and little else. A classic example of this

Tough aluminum johnboats with a shallow draft are ideal for waterfowl hunting. Johnboats can be camouflage painted, built into duck blinds, and can safely be dragged up on sandbars and gravel beaches. Most johnboats are also extremely stable.

type of hunting boat is the Barnegat sneakbox, which was designed by Captain Hazelton Seaman in 1836 in West Creek, New Jersey. The sneakbox was designed for hunting waterfowl and marsh birds. Originally built with white cedar, it will float in 4 to 6 inches of water and can be sailed, rowed, poled, or sculled. There are a limited number of builders in the Barnegat area of New Jersey still building the sneakbox.

Small canoes afford more space. If you use a canoe, treat yourself to detachable buoyant pontoons. This makes shooting more secure and the whole platform more relaxed. A well-made aluminum canoe is great for beaching in a marsh, and also for breaking through the thin sheet of ice in late fall. You would wreck a wooden or canvas canoe doing this unless you cover the ends with aluminum.

Take the trouble to paint your aluminum canoe before you go hunting. There's nothing more alarming to waterfowl than sun rays reflected from the mirror finish of unpainted aluminum. Camouflage paint colors should be chosen to suit the seasonal color of your hunting grounds.

BOATS FOR CAMPING

Boat camping is a natural way to extend your enjoyment of fishing, hunting, and life in the outdoors. Instead of having to backtrack to your starting point toward the end of the day, just when things are going well, you can put ashore at the first suitable site if you are prepared for camping. If your boat is big enough, you can anchor and camp aboard. Still another version of boat camping is to trailer or cartop a boat to your base camp and extend your range from there by means of the boat.

For those whose primary pleasure is camping, a boat gets you away from crowded, metropolis-like campgrounds. Going camping by boat gives you a private preserve in the outdoors, brings you closer to unspoiled nature, and increases your alternatives for camping locations tenfold.

■ Camping with Small Boats

When you camp with a canoe, kayak, cartopper, inflatable, johnboat, or other really small boat, you can pack your supplies and tent or sleeping bags in the boat, travel through the wilderness on water, and then make your camp ashore. This style suits many lake chains and small rivers. With careful packing, there is room for your supplies and gear, two adults, or a couple and a small child in this size of boat.

When you plan your trip, make a list based on roughing it, with the minimum of equipment, only one change of clothing, backpack-style tents, concentrated and freeze-dried foods, and a streamlined fishing or hunting outfit. There is a distinct pleasure in traveling light, and as the experience progresses, you'll be glad to have discovered a simple way to camp. Portages will be light, and if you get a dunking the damage will not be irreparable.

A canoe for camping should be from 16 to 18 feet long. If you are going to camp on a lake, use a canoe with a keel. This will help you hold your course easily in a wind. With canoe ends slightly rockered, you can adjust course fairly easily even with a heavy load. For canoe camping on a river, avoid a canoe with much of a keel, and stick to the camping length. Loaded with gear, a canoe with a keel will catch rocks and snags too often for comfort. The camping length, as opposed to shorter white-water canoes, will keep handling easy. There is a lot in favor of using a small motor on a canoe for camping. In that case, choose a canoe with full rather than fine ends so the motor will not cause the ends to dig in.

Kayaks also make excellent boats for camping. Select a touring or expedition model with a sit-in cockpit. This design will allow you to store gear where it will be safe and dry. A 14-foot kayak might be adequate, but a 16- or 17-footer will give you more space for gear.

A cartop boat will increase your load capacity, and by using an outboard you will extend your range considerably compared to paddling or drifting. Don't forget that you will have to carry enough gas to make it between refueling points. Determine gas-pump locations in advance, and make sure you can get to them from the water's edge. Cartop fishing boats are ideal for light camping.

Inflatable boats are excellent for drift camping on a large river. Four passengers can camp with a 16-foot inflatable. An inflatable of this size can carry big loads, and the relatively wide beam makes it easy to load and stay aboard for long hours without getting cramped. At night, you can use an inflatable as a lean-to over your sleeping bags and avoid carrying a large tent.

A full-size johnboat of 16 feet or so is too big and heavy to cartop, but it's a good candidate for trailering or loading in the back of a truck with your gear already packed in the boat. The johnboat design is excellent for boat camping, as it can carry great loads for its size. Depending on the number of campers, you may prefer a smaller johnboat that can be cartopped. It's always easier to drive with your boat on top of your car than trailering it behind the vehicle.

Another option for on-water camping is a pontoon boat, which can be beached or anchored near shorelines. For a bigger group, a pontoon boat makes sense. Depending on the size, a tent can even be pitched on the deck and, with safety precautions, food can be cooked on a grill.

■ Family Runabouts

When a family with a new runabout gets over its novelty and has learned to water ski, going camping with the boat is an interesting next stage. This is an imaginative and ambitious way to use the family's recreational resources.

Since runabouts have more beam and weight capacity than a fishing boat or canoe of the same length, you are not quite so limited in the amount of gear and supplies aboard. Often there is enough space to do simple cooking and bed down. Runabouts from 16 to 19 feet suit camping best. You can use the runabout to go greater distances at faster speeds with its greater horsepower capacity. If the boat is not big enough to eat and sleep aboard, use its range to reach choice campsites with more variety.

A family boat of 18 or 19 feet is generally big enough for four passengers, if they are good organizers. Boats of this size have several advantages. You can travel on large, open waters such as the Great Lakes, large river estuaries, and the Inland Waterway, moving in close along shore on bad-weather days or to camp for the night, and also pass through fairly shallow places when necessary. Many families enjoy camping vacations in the Florida Keys aboard large runabouts. These boats are a size that can be trailered at fair highway speeds, so that reaching a distant vacation area is not a big problem.

Many makers offer camper tops as options for family runabouts. These vary considerably in quality of materials, workmanship, and design. Shop with your eyes open when buying a runabout if you think you will use it for camping. A good camper top is made of high-grade nylon with double seams, double zippers, tough plastic windows, and nylon-mesh screening. Designs that have at least one large area with stand-up height are the most useful. A tight closure all around is usually achieved with a plastic rubber channel that presses together, and strong grommets and double-reinforced

The Sun Tracker Fishin' Barge 20 DLX, a 20-foot pontoon boat, is a good choice for overnight fishing and camping on big lakes and bays. With an economical 40-horsepower four-stroke outboard, this pontoon boat can easily hold anglers and camping gear.

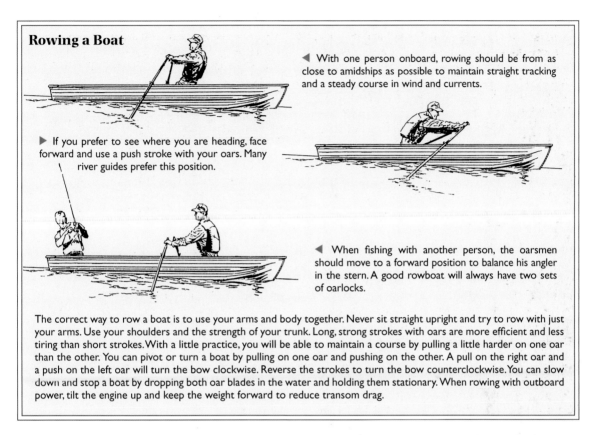

Rowing a Boat

◀ With one person onboard, rowing should be from as close to amidships as possible to maintain straight tracking and a steady course in wind and currents.

▶ If you prefer to see where you are heading, face forward and use a push stroke with your oars. Many river guides prefer this position.

◀ When fishing with another person, the oarsmen should move to a forward position to balance his angler in the stern. A good rowboat will always have two sets of oarlocks.

The correct way to row a boat is to use your arms and body together. Never sit straight upright and try to row with just your arms. Use your shoulders and the strength of your trunk. Long, strong strokes with oars are more efficient and less tiring than short strokes. With a little practice, you will be able to maintain a course by pulling a little harder on one oar than the other. You can pivot or turn a boat by pulling on one oar and pushing on the other. A pull on the right oar and a push on the left oar will turn the bow clockwise. Reverse the strokes to turn the bow counterclockwise. You can slow down and stop a boat by dropping both oar blades in the water and holding them stationary. When rowing with outboard power, tilt the engine up and keep the weight forward to reduce transom drag.

eyelets anchor the camper top to the boat. If you cannot get a camper top to suit you with the boat you want to buy, shop around for a good tent maker who will make the top to your specifications.

Optional camper built-ins are a good investment if they are efficiently designed and well made. Choose your gear and boat options carefully, such as a fold-up alcohol stove or a portable propane stove that stows out of the way in a side storage space under the gunwales. Deluxe double lounge seats with comfortable padding and vinyl covering are made to fold down to make a bed for one person. Removable seats can be lifted out to make more space on deck for sleeping bags.

Houseboats and Cruisers

Whether this should be called camping depends on your own point of view and how you go about it. If you want to camp, you'll do so, and some families are inveterate campers even in a 50-foot houseboat with automatic laundry and an electric stove. The lure of

building a campfire ashore, and tenting along the way, is very attractive when you have a boat with shallow draft that can be beached. With a small houseboat or pontoon boat, camping is still a natural extension of what you can do with such a boat. Planning is more relaxed because you can keep more aboard. People who like camping in a travel trailer or motor home will find houseboats to their taste.

Houseboats and small cruisers are used extensively on big rivers, along the shores of the Great Lakes, and on other open waters where you can keep in touch with shore and duck in if the weather blows up. These hulls usually have fairly shallow drafts, so you have many options in where you go.

One pleasure with a houseboat or small cruiser is to nose up to a riverbank or anchor near shore, and then have a barbecue ashore, follow deer tracks, explore islands, or walk the beaches. You can tow a small dinghy or stow it on the cabin roof for fishing and going ashore. Some houseboats and cruisers carry a bicycle to run into towns along the way for groceries, laundry, and mail.

BOATING ELECTRONICS

Once you have selected your boat, you will need to rig it. And this means learning the basics of marine electronics. Basic electronic gear ensures the safety of your boat and passengers. A radio will summon help in case of an accident, and a depthsounder will help keep you out of trouble in unfamiliar waters. Once you've met the basic safety requirements, however, you'll quickly discover that electronics can be interesting and useful—whether cruising or fishing.

It's easy to pick out rod holders and similar accessories, but electronic equipment is a different story. If you make the wrong choice there, you could be out hundreds of dollars and stuck with something that doesn't perform as needed. Let's look at some of the electronics to consider.

■ Depthsounders

How does a sounder work? The word "sonar" is an acronym for SOund, NAvigation, and Ranging. It was developed during World War II as a means of tracking enemy submarines.

With sonar, an electrical impulse is converted to a sound wave and transmitted into the water. When this sound wave strikes an obstacle, it rebounds. Sound transmitted through water travels at approximately 4,800 feet per second, compared with 1,100 feet per second through air. And since the speed of sound in water is a known constant, the time lapse between the transmitted signal and the received echo can be measured and the distance to the obstacle determined. An electronic sonar unit can both send and receive sound waves, as well as time, measure, and record them.

A depthsounder's transducer sends a high-frequency sound wave through the water. This sound wave is inaudible to fish as well as humans. When the echo returns, the transducer picks it up and reconverts it to electrical energy. The unit times the interval and puts a signal on the screen of your depthsounder. The signal identifies the distance between the transducer and the obstacle that returned the echo.

Some of the early depthsounders were called flashers and used a dial with a high-intensity neon bulb whiling at a constant speed. The biggest disadvantage of these early flashers was that they had no recording features. If a fisherman did not constantly monitor his flasher, he could pass over fish and not see them.

TYPES OF DEPTHSOUNDERS: There are three main types of depthsounders: chart recorder, liquid-crystal recorder, and video sonar.

- **The Chart-Recorder Depthsounder:** When a chart recorder is operating, an electronically regulated motor drives a lightweight belt at the edge of the recording paper. A stylus is attached to this belt. When the stylus is at the top of the paper, a small mark is burned onto the paper. This is called the zero mark, and represents the water surface. The stylus continues to move down the edge of the paper while the second pulse is traveling through the water. When an echo is detected, the stylus burns another mark on the paper. The depth of the object that reflected the echo can be read in feet by comparing its location on the paper to the depth scale printed on the paper.

  The paper speed is controlled by a variable-speed motor. During one revolution of the stylus belt, a very narrow mark will be made by the flexible stylus, but the paper will move a small amount before the next revolution. Each mark will blend into the one before so that a composite "picture" of the target will be made, one tiny mark at a time.

- **The Liquid-Crystal-Recorder Depthsounder:** In principle, the liquid-crystal recorder, or graph, works like a paper recorder, except that these "paperless recorders" use liquid-crystal squares, called pixels, on a display screen. When an impulse or electronic signal

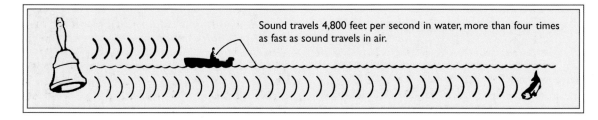

Sound travels 4,800 feet per second in water, more than four times as fast as sound travels in air.

Depthsounders

The Hummingbird 1158c DI Combo will show detailed views of the bottom and structures below your boat on a 10.4-inch color screen. This unit has chart-plotting capabilities and readings down to 1,500 feet.

The Hummingbird DI has a 5-inch grayscale display and is a good basic affordable unit that will give readings down to 500 feet.

The Lowrance HDS-12 Gen2 is a touch-screen fish finder and chart plotter. With its 12-inch widescreen color display, this unit has built-in Insight USA mapping, Broadband Sounder, and StructureScan high-definition imaging. It is a good choice for an all-in-one electronics package.

---

is sent to the screen, it hits the liquid and turns it so the tiny square shows black on the screen. A continuing series of signals will literally draw a picture of the bottom or any object or fish between the bottom and the boat. Some of the latest liquid-crystal recorders, or graphs, have features that border on the amazing. Some have memories with playback. Others have a split screen that shows two segments of the water. And many have optional fish alarms and water-temperature readouts.

- **The Video-Sonar Depthsounder:** Instead of using chart paper or liquid-crystal squares, an underwater video sonar produces a sharp clear black-and-white or color picture on a cathode ray tube (CRT) screen. The imaging principle is the same as that of a television picture. With color video sonar, the screen shows signal intensity by color difference, making it easier to distinguish individual fish from structures and the bottom. With black-and-white video sonar, the unit provides a constant view of the bottom, underwater structures, drop-offs, schools of fish, and even single fish in distinct, easy-to-identify shades of gray.

USES FOR DEPTHSOUNDERS: Though most fishermen believe the primary use for a depthsounder is to find fish, there are many other uses. Since a depthsounder tells depth accurately, it can be used for making contour maps of lakes, bays, saltwater areas, or large streams. It is useful in navigation because it warns you when you are approaching shallow water. It will find the deep holes in rivers. It is useful in salvage operations because

it will accurately show a sunken boat on the bottom. It even tells what kind of bottom your boat is passing over. Divers use it to study the depths before descending.

It tells the depth of the water accurately, but since everything it reports is shown by signals on a screen, the amount it can tell is limited by your ability to interpret the signals. The more skillful you become at reading the signals, the more your depthsounder will tell you about the mysterious world beneath the surface.

Marine Radios

In times of serious boating emergencies, the ability to summon help quickly can make the difference between life and death. If you don't already own one, consider purchasing a Very High Frequency (VHF) marine radio. VHF radios have channels that are reserved for distress calls and are continuously monitored by the U.S. Coast Guard. You may legally use your VHF radio for distress, safety, operational, and public correspondence communications. Distress and safety communications include calls relating to danger to life and property, safety bulletins, weather warnings, and talking with other boats to avoid a collision.

If you have a life-threatening emergency, issue a MAYDAY signal on Channel 16 (the calling and distress channel). This is a call to ask for assistance if there is immediate danger to life or property. A MAYDAY call has priority over all other radio calls. Use a MAYDAY call only for life-threatening medical emergencies or if your boat is sinking or on fire.

Marine Radios

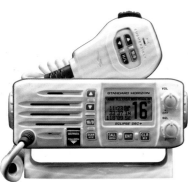

◀ The Standard Horizon HX851 Floating VHF is a 12-channel VHF radio with a built-in GPS with waypoint navigation and compass distress calling. It receives all channels and NOAA weather alerts. It operates more than seven hours on a rechargeable lithium-ion battery. It is a good handheld choice for a marine radio and GPS.

▲ The Standard Horizon Eclipse GX1150 VHF marine radio will pick up all NOAA channels and U.S. and Canadian marine channels. It also includes a time and GPS display. For boaters who prefer a permanently mounted marine radio, this would be a good choice.

▶ The Uniden Atlantis 250 Handheld VHF radio will handle U.S., Canadian, and international channels, including 10 NOAA weather channels. This compact unit has a 10-hour battery life on a rechargeable NiMH battery pack. VHF handheld units are a must-have investment for all boaters.

If you hear a MAYDAY call, remain silent, listen, and write down the information being given by the boat in distress. If the U.S. Coast Guard or other rescue authority does not respond, try to reach the Coast Guard while traveling toward the boat. If you cannot reach the Coast Guard, try to assist the other boat to the best of your ability while not placing yourself or your passengers in danger.

Channel 16 is a calling and distress channel only. It is not to be used for conversation or radio checks. Penalties exist for misuse of a radio; hoax MAYDAY calls are felonies.

Be aware that the distance of sending and receiving messages is limited by the height of the antenna and the power of the radio.

■ Global Positioning System (GPS)

The Global Positioning System (GPS) is a constellation of satellites that orbit the earth twice a day, transmitting precise time and position (latitude, longitude, and altitude) information. With a GPS receiver, users can determine their location anywhere on earth. Position and navigation information is vital to a broad range of professional and personal activities, including boating,

fishing, surveying, aviation, vehicle tracking and navigation, and more.

The complete system consists of 24 satellites orbiting about 12,000 miles above the earth, and five ground stations to monitor and manage the satellite constellation. These satellites provide 24-hour-a-day coverage for both two- and three-dimensional positioning anywhere on earth.

Development of the GPS satellite navigation system began in the 1970s by the U.S. Department of Defense,

The Garmin GPS-MAP 546s is a GPS/digital sonar with a 5-inch color screen. Sonar readings can go to depths of 2,000 feet. This unit is preloaded with U.S. coastal marine charts. It also has split-screen options.

which continues to manage the system to provide continuous, worldwide positioning and navigation data to U.S. military forces around the globe. However, GPS now has an even broader civilian and commercial application. The GPS signals are available to an unlimited number of users simultaneously.

HOW GPS WORKS: The basis of GPS technology is precise time and position information. Using atomic clocks (accurate to within one second every 70,000 years) and location data, each satellite continuously broadcasts the time and its position. A GPS receiver receives these signals to determine the user's position on earth.

By measuring the time interval between the transmission and the reception of a satellite signal, the GPS receiver calculates the distance between the user and each satellite. Using the distance measurements of at least three satellites in an algorithm computation, the GPS receiver arrives at an accurate position fix.

The position information in a GPS receiver may be displayed as longitude and latitude, military grid, or other system coordinates. Information must be received from three satellites in order to obtain two-dimensional (latitude and longitude) fixes, and from four satellites for three-dimensional (latitude, longitude, and altitude) positioning.

Newer GPS units are now also equipped with either Differential Global Positioning System (DGPS) or Wide Area Augmentation System (WAAS) capabilities, which simply means a fisherman can return to a fishing hotspot with 3-meter accuracy.

GPS receivers provide positioning, velocity, and navigation information for a variety of purposes. Anyone who needs to know the precise time or the exact location of people or objects will benefit from a GPS. In turn, this information can be used in charting and mapping, plotting a course, navigating from point to point, tracking vehicle movement, locating previously identified sites, or any number of similar functions.

GPS/PLOTTER/SOUNDER: GPS/plotters/sounders are the ultimate in boating electronics for recreational boaters and fishermen. These combination split-screen units allow you to chart courses, mark waypoints, and record fishing hotspots while giving you a detailed picture of the depth, bottom structures, and the fish under your boat. With a GPS/plotter/sounder, you can return to a wreck or reef with an accuracy of 3 meters. These sophisticated units can cost several thousand dollars, depending on the features. They will help you find and catch fish, but bear in mind that GPS/plotter/sounders will also keep you and your boat safe in unfamiliar waters.

■ Radar

RADAR means RAdio Detection And Ranging. Basically, it's an electronic device that provides ranges and bearings as well as visual pictures of boats, planes, land, and so on. Radar is extremely valuable to boaters on the water in times of low visibility, such as fog and night.

Radar operates much the way a depthsounder does, except that the transmission is through air rather than water. A radar unit transmits pulses of super-high frequency radio waves that are reflected by objects in the distance. The time it takes for the radio wave to go out and the echo to return is the measure of the distance to the object.

There are four components to a radar set:

1. The transmitter, which transmits radio waves in brief impulses.

2. The antenna, which radiates the impulses and collects the returning echoes.

3. The receiver, which picks up the returning echoes.

4. The screen, which produces a visual display of the objects in the path of the radar signals.

Makers of modern radar units for small boats have managed to combine these four components into two units: the transmitter and antenna in one unit, and the receiver and screen in another.

The Furuno Radar is available in three models: the 1834, 1935, and 1945. Depending on the antenna used, these units have a range from 36 to 64 nautical miles. All units have a 10.4-inch color LCD display with crystal-clear presentation and automatic gain/sea/rain controls for noise-free radar. The radar allows you to see other boats and targets both at short and long range in the dark, fog, or any weather condition.

As with other marine electronics, stiff competition has driven down the price of radar. Radar, at one time, was found only on big private yachts or commercial vessels. Today, it is not uncommon to see radar on small fishing boats in the 25-foot range. There's no doubt that radar can give you a much greater edge of safety.

▮ EPIRB

EPIRBs (Emergency Position Indicating Radio Beacons) are electronic devices that transmit signals that can guide rescuers to your disabled boat. If you regularly go far offshore, especially beyond 20 miles or so, where you will be stretching the range of your Very High Frequency (VHF) radio, it's wise to carry an EPIRB. In an emergency, this device will transmit a continuous international distress signal on 406 megahertz (MHz). High-flying aircraft can pick up these signals as far away as 200 miles. More important, Coast Guard planes are equipped with automatic direction finders for EPIRB frequencies. EPIRBs are classified as Category 1 or Category 2. Category 1 EPIRBs are automatically activated when the unit hits the water and the signal can be detected anywhere in the world. Category 2 EPIRBs are similar to Category 1, except some models have to be manually activated. EPIRBs use a special lithium battery for long-term low consumption. EPIRBs must also be properly registered with the Federal Communications Commission (FCC) and Coast Guard.

The ResQLink Personal Locator Beacon is for use when all other rescue means have failed. Deploy the antenna and press the on button and the unit will relay your position to a worldwide network of satellites to help lead rescue teams right to you. The unit is also waterproof with a built-in strobe light. It is a must-have unit for boaters offshore and on remote waters.

ANCHORS, MOORINGS, AND ROPES

An anchor is essential to safe boat operation, yet some boat liveries where small fishing boats are rented put their boats out without either an anchor or lines. When you know the importance of having an anchor, you will insist on having an effective one aboard even on a normally calm lake, and enough anchor line to give safe scope. In addition to safety, an anchor is necessary to hold position in a breeze or current when fishing and hunting. For a boater, a boat is half useless without a good anchor.

The major misconception about anchors is that the heavier the anchor, the more it will hold. This is not the case. The key is the meaning of hold. An anchor does not function by weighing down, but by holding on to the bottom effectively. A concrete block weighing 20 pounds may roll on a sloping bottom and slide on a hard bottom as the wind tugs at the boat. In the same situation, a Danforth anchor weighing only 3 pounds will probably hold the boat fast after kedging only several feet until its sharp flukes find a grip on the bottom.

Many small boats are equipped with mushroom-type anchors. These have a solid, weighty feel—even the small ones. Regardless of the direction in which they are pulled, the lip of the cup will drag in contact with the bottom and possibly hold. But when they hook a bottom snag or settle in mud, the weight of the cast-iron mushroom plus the weight of the bottom becomes a formidable load to haul up through the water.

A mushroom anchor may be adequate on a protected lake with a firm bottom, but on a fast-moving stream this anchor will be ineffective. On big open water, a concrete block or any other simple, heavy anchor can be a hazard. When the wind blows, the anchor will roll until the boat is in water deeper than the length of the anchor rope. The anchor then becomes a load on the bow, dipping deeper in the trough of waves than it should.

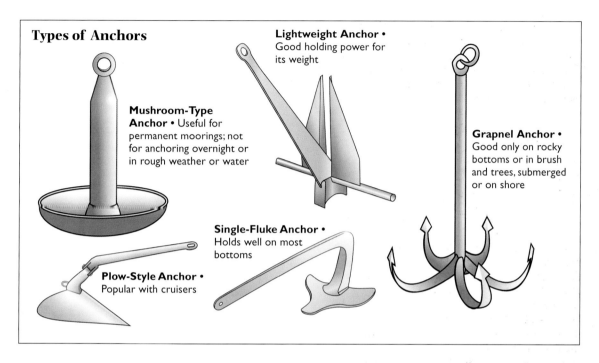

Types of Anchors

Lightweight Anchor • Good holding power for its weight

Mushroom-Type Anchor • Useful for permanent moorings; not for anchoring overnight or in rough weather or water

Grapnel Anchor • Good only on rocky bottoms or in brush and trees, submerged or on shore

Single-Fluke Anchor • Holds well on most bottoms

Plow-Style Anchor • Popular with cruisers

A number of anchor designs for pleasure boats have been developed that are effective by application rather than weight. One of the best is the Danforth. This anchor will hold on a hard bottom and can be retrieved on a rock-filled bottom. Most have trip features for releasing the anchor when it gets caught on the bottom.

Since anchor weight and size suitable for a boat of a given size vary widely according to the anchor design and to local conditions, no guidelines can be given that apply to all anchor types in common use. (Remember that concrete blocks and cans filled with concrete are among the most common small-boat anchors.) However, guidelines for mushroom-type and Danforth anchors are provided in the accompanying charts on the next page.

▶ If you fish in shallow water, you may never have to touch a rope or a muddy anchor again if you have a shallow-water anchoring system. These anchor systems, mounted on a boat's transom, can anchor your boat in waters up to 10 feet deep. Minn Kota's Talon Shallow Water Anchor is typical of these anchoring systems. Powered by a boat's battery, an anchoring spike is slightly driven into the bottom. These anchors can be lowered by a dash or foot switch. Protected from saltwater corrosion, these shallow-water anchors are ideal for flats boats and freshwater lakes and ponds where deep water is rarely encountered.

Mushroom Anchor Weights

Length of Boat (feet)	Power (pounds)	Sail: Racing (pounds)	Sail: Cruising (pounds)
25	225	125	175
35	300	200	250
45	400	325	400
55	500	450	550

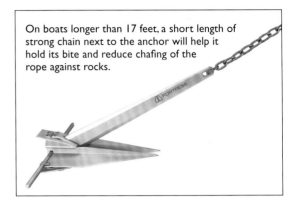

On boats longer than 17 feet, a short length of strong chain next to the anchor will help it hold its bite and reduce chafing of the rope against rocks.

The length of the anchor line is an important factor in effective anchoring. In calm waters, twice the depth of the water is enough line. This assumes you are in the boat and can bring it easily to shore if a sudden storm comes up or your motor gives out. In open waters, your anchor line should be three to five times the depth of the water. For riding overnight or when the boat is unattended, you need seven times the depth. Obviously the reason is holding power. If the length of the line plus the anchor design permit the pull to be applied horizontally against the anchor's purchase on the bottom, it will help it to hold. On boats 17 feet and longer, a short length of strong chain next to the anchor will help it hold its bite and reduce chafing of the rope against rocks and the anchor itself.

The best way to free most anchors that are stuck in the bottom is by pulling straight up. If you find you cannot do this, try snubbing the line until it runs vertically down to the snagged anchor. Take a bit around the cleat to hold the line tight, and then rock the boat fore and aft, or let the wave action do this until the anchor is worked free. The force of the boat's motion is greater than the force you can apply by hand.

When anchoring on large or windy waters, check the direction of the wind and wave action before setting anchor. If you have a choice of anchoring on a lee or windward shore, choose the lee. Then your boat won't be blown or washed onto the rocks by morning. In a popular mooring place, set your anchor so that you have several boat lengths between you and any other craft. Then, if a storm arises, even the worst fury won't cause damage.

Some fishermen like to drag or tow their anchor when drift fishing in windy, deep waters. This is a hazard to the anchor and line, and the anchor must be fully hauled to start the motor again to regain the best position. You might prefer instead to store a sea anchor or two for this purpose. This is a canvas bucket that acts as a drag. It is attached with a halter to a light nylon line that can be hauled in easily.

Suggested Danforth Anchor Sizes

Length of Boat (feet)	Beam		Standard Sizes		Hi-Tensile Sizes		
	Sail	Power	Working	Storm	Lunch	Working	Storm
10	4	4	2½	4	Hook	5	5
20	6	6	8	13	—	5	12
25	6½	7	8	13	5	12	12
30	7	9	13	22	5	12	18
35	8	10	22	22	5	18	18
40	9	11	22	40	5	18	28
50	11	13	40	65	12	28	60
60	12	14	65	85	12	60	90

Moorings

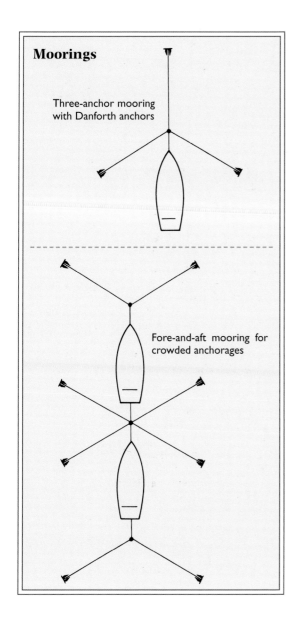

Three-anchor mooring
with Danforth anchors

Fore-and-aft mooring for
crowded anchorages

■ How to Set a Mooring

An anchored mooring is cheaper than a dock, and in many crowded public facilities it is the only choice. The authorities may stipulate the minimum mooring that is acceptable. You may want to improve on this, particularly if you have a valuable boat. In any case, remember that your boat might do damage if it drags its mooring or breaks loose—and the responsibility is yours.

The Elusive Green Flash

Consider yourself very lucky if you witness the green flash. Not many boaters are so fortunate and some don't even believe it actually happens. The green flash is an amazing sunset phenomenon. Watch the red ball of the sun descend at sunset when you're on the water, especially if you're offshore in the southern half of the country. When the sun touches the horizon, it will turn orange, and then yellow. When the sun drops out of sight, you may instantly see a brilliant green flash. The color change is caused by the refraction of the sun's rays passing through layers of atmosphere. Your best chance of seeing the green flash is on a calm ocean with a clear view of the horizon. Look for this phenomenon when conditions are right. If you see the green flash, you are one of the lucky ones to witness this amazing end-of-day display.

As sunset approaches, these Florida Keys anglers might see the green flash.

On soft bottoms, heavy iron mushroom-type moorings are often used successfully. A chain is attached from the mooring anchor to a floating buoy, where the boat is tied, usually with a snap hook on a short line from the bow. Even a big mushroom mooring can be pulled through the mud if a really hard storm or hurricane blows, however, and it is for this occasional danger that you must prepare when setting a permanent mooring. A single mooring anchor assumes adequate scope on the line to hold in a blow, but scope of this length is impossible in crowded anchorages. Therefore, three anchors are sometimes used, set in an equilateral triangle with only one boat length of extra scope to the buoy (see accompanying illustrations). An alternative in the most crowded

BOAT KNOTS

Part of the fun of owning a boat is in learning and using boat knots. Most of the knots commonly used in boating are illustrated in Section Five: Camping. Here are ways to make knots and splices needed for anchoring and mooring your boat.

◼ SHORT SPLICE

This is the strongest of splices for joining ends of two pieces of rope, but it cannot be used to run through a pulley due to the bulk of the splice. This procedure also applies to splicing nylon and other synthetic ropes, but one additional full tuck should be used.

1 • Lash rope about 12 diameters from each end (A). Unlay the strands up to the lashings. Whip the strands to prevent untwisting and then put together as in illustration, alternating the strands from each end. Pull it up taut.

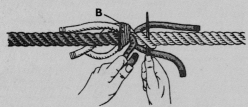

2 • Now, tie down all the strands temporarily (B). Take off the lashing from one side of the rope and raise one strand on this side, using a fid. Take the middle strand of the opposite side, and tuck it over one strand and under the raised strand. Pull it up taut.

3 • Tuck against the twist or "lay" of the rope. What happens is that the tuck goes over one strand, under the second, and out between the second and third.

4 • Roll the rope toward you. Pick up the second strand, and repeat the same operation. Then, do it again with the third strand. You have now made one full tuck.

5 • Take both lashings (which were applied in Steps 1 and 2) off the other side of the rope. Repeat the above operations.

6 • To finish, cut off the ends of the strands, leaving about 1 or 2 inches protruding.

Note • To taper the splice, first make one more tuck just like the first one. Then, make the third tuck the same way, but first cut off one-third of the yarn from the strands. For the fourth tuck, cut off half of the remaining yarn. For the untapered short splice, you do not cut the strands. You just make three more tucks, exactly like the first one.

◼ LONG SPLICE

This knot is slightly weaker than the short splice, but it allows the rope to run freely through a properly sized pulley and causes less wear at the point of splicing.

1 • Unlay the end of each rope about 15 turns and place the ropes together, alternating strands from each end as shown.

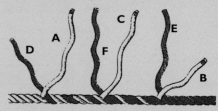

2 • Start with any opposite pair, unlay one strand, and replace it with a strand from the other part. Repeat the

operation with another pair of strands in the opposite direction as shown.

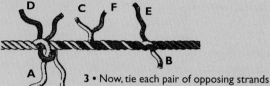

3 • Now, tie each pair of opposing strands (see B and E) with an overhand knot, tuck each strand twice, as in the short splice, and then twice more. Or, halve each strand (see A and D) and tie with an overhand knot before tucking. With this latter method, a smaller splice results—but at a considerable sacrifice of strength.

4 • Roll and pound well before cutting the strands off close to the rope.

■ EYE OR SIDE SPLICE

The side splice is also called the eye splice because it is used to form an eye or loop in the end of a rope by splicing the end back into its own side.

▶ **1 •** Start by seizing the working end of the rope. Unlay the three strands—A, B, and C—to the seizing and whip the end of each strand. Then, twist the rope slightly to open up strands D, E, and F of the standing part of the rope as shown.

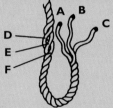

◀ **2 •** The first tuck is shown. The middle strand is always tucked first, so strand B is tucked under strand E, the middle strand of the standing part.

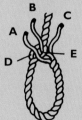

▶ **3 •** The second tuck is now made as shown. The left strand A of the working end is tucked under strand D, passing over strand E.

 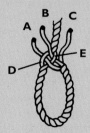

◀ **4 •** This illustration shows how the third tuck is made. In order to make strand F easy to grab,

the rope is turned over. Strand C now appears on the left side.

▶ **5 •** Strand C is then passed to the right of and tucked under strand F as shown. This completes the first round of tucks.

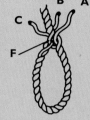

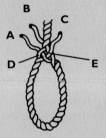

▼ **6 •** This illustration shows the second round of tucks started, with the rope reversed again for ease in handling. Strand B is passed over strand D and tucked under the next strand to the left. Continue with strands A and C, tucking over one strand and then under one to the left. To complete the splice, tuck each strand in once more.

▶ **7 •** The finished eye splice is shown. Remove the temporary seizing and cut off the strand ends, leaving at least ½ inch on each end. Roll the splice back and forth under your foot to even up and smooth out the strands.

■ FIGURE-EIGHT KNOT

This knot can be tied simply and quickly. Used in the end of a rope to temporarily prevent the strands from unlaying, it does not jam as easily as the overhand knot and is therefore useful in preventing the end of a rope from slipping through a block or an eye.

■ BOWLINE

The bowline is often used for temporary anchor knots. It never jams or slips if properly tied.

DOUBLE BOWLINE

Make an overhand loop with the end held toward you, exactly as in the ordinary bowline. The difference is that you pass the end through the loop twice—making two lower loops, A and B. The end is then passed behind the standing part and down through the first loop again as in the ordinary bowline. Pull tight. Used as a seat sling, the outside loop B goes under the person's arms, and the inside loop A forms the seat.

BOWLINE IN BIGHT

Here's a useful knot to know when you want to attach tackle to, say, the middle of a line when both ends of it are made fast. Grasp the rope where you want the new knot, shape it into a loop in one hand, and strike this against the two lines leading to the loop held in the other hand. Next, complete the first bight used in tying a regular bowline. Then, open up the loop after it has passed through the bight and bring the whole knot through it. Pull the loop tight over the standing part.

RUNNING BOWLINE

Tie the regular bowline around a loop of its own standing part. This makes an excellent slipknot, commonly used to retrieve spars, rigging, etc. And with lighter rope or twine, it's good for tightening to begin package tying.

SURGEON'S KNOT

This knot is usually tied with twine. It is a modified form of the reef knot, and the extra turn taken in the first tie prevents slipping before the knot is completed.

FISHERMAN'S BEND

An important knot because of its strength and simplicity, it is used for making the end of a rope fast to a ring, spar, or anchor, or for a line to a bucket. It is more secure when the end is tied as shown.

REEF KNOT

Probably the most useful and popular of all knots, this is also known as the square knot. Used to join two ropes or lines of the same size, it holds firmly and is easily untied.

TIMBER HITCH

This knot is very useful for hoisting spars, boards, or logs. It is also handy for making a towline fast to a wet spar or timber. It holds without slipping and does not jam.

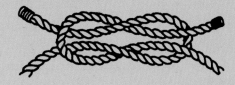

SHEET BEND

Used aboard a boat for joining small or medium-sized ropes, this knot is sometimes used for attaching the end of a rope to an eye splice.

FISHERMAN'S KNOT

This is probably the strongest known method of joining fine lines such as fishing lines. It is simple to tie and untie.

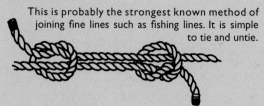

CLOVE HITCH

This is the most effective and quick way to tie a boat line to a mooring post. It can be tied in the middle or end of a rope, but it is apt to slip if tied at the end. To prevent slipping, make a half hitch in the end to the standing part.

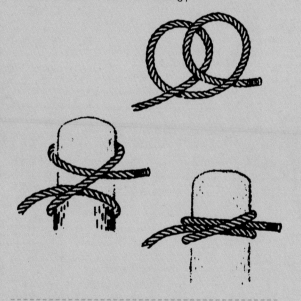

TYING LINE TO A CLEAT

This is the correct method for tying line to a cleat. The half hitch that completes the fastening is taken with the free part of the line. The line can then be freed without taking up slack in the standing part.

KNOTS FOR POLYPROPYLENE CORD

These are the knots to use for polypropylene cord.

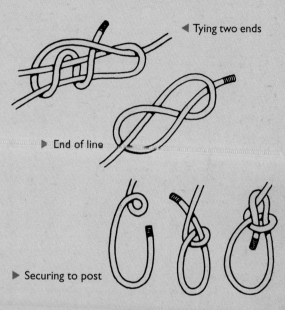

◄ Tying two ends

▶ End of line

▶ Securing to post

TO PREVENT TWISTED ROPE FROM UNRAVELING WHEN CUT

For nylon, polyester, and polypropylene, tape the rope around the circumference as shown. Cut in the middle, leaving tape intact on either side. When cutting these synthetic fibers with a pocketknife or scissors, fuse the cut ends by match flame to prevent untwisting. Tape is unnecessary if a "hot knife" is used. Heat will melt and fuse the cut ends.

For manila and sisal, tape the rope as shown. Cut in the middle so that each end remains permanently taped. Natural fibers do not fuse with heat.

Ropes: Minimum Tensile Strength (pounds)*

Circumference (inches)	Diameter (inches)	Ship Brand Manila	Yacht Manila	Linen Yacht	Nylon and Gold Line	Dacron	Poly-ethylene	Poly-propylene
9/16	3/16	450	525	600	1,100	1,050	690	1,050
3/4	1/4	600	688	1,020	1,850	1,750	1,150	1,700
1	5/16	1,000	1,190	1,520	2,850	2,650	1,730	2,450
1 1/8	3/8	1,350	1,590	2,090	4,000	3,600	2,400	3,400
1 1/4	7/16	1,750	1,930	2,700	5,500	4,800	3,260	4,300
1 1/2	1/2	2,650	2,920	3,500	7,100	6,100	4,050	5,300
1 3/4	9/16	3,450	3,800	4,350	8,350	7,400	5,000	6,400
2	5/8	4,400	4,840	5,150	10,500	9,000	6,050	7,600
2 1/4	3/4	5,400	5,940	7,100	14,200	12,500	9,000	10,000
2 3/4	7/8	7,700	8,450	9,400	19,000	16,000	12,000	13,000
3	1	9,000	9,900	12,000	24,600	20,000	15,000	16,500
3 1/2	1 1/8	12,000	13,200	——	34,000	21,500	18,500	19,500
3 3/4	1 1/4	13,500	14,850	——	38,000	24,500	21,000	22,000
4 1/2	1 1/2	18,500	——	——	55,000	36,000	29,000	31,500

*For the approximate average tensile strength, add 20 percent for Ship Brand, Yacht Manila, and Linen Yacht ropes.

Recommended Anchor Lines for Power Craft

	Anchor	Overall Length of Boat					
		Under 20 Feet	20–25 Feet	25–30 Feet	30–40 Feet	40–50 Feet	50–65 Feet
Length of anchor lines	Light	100 feet	100 feet	100 feet	125 feet	150 feet	180 feet
	Heavy		150 feet	180 feet	200 feet	250 feet	300 feet
Diameter if nylon	Light	3/8 inch	3/8 inch	1/2 inch	9/16 inch	3/4 inch	7/8 inch
	Heavy		1/2 inch	9/16 inch	3/4 inch	1 inch	1 1/8 inches
Diameter if first-class manila	Light	1/2 inch	1/2 inch	5/8 inch	3/4 inch	1 inch	1 1/4 inches
	Heavy		5/8 inch	3/4 inch	1 inch	1 3/8 inches	1 1/2 inches
Diameter if Plymouth bolt manila	Light	7/16 inch	7/16 inch	9/16 inch	5/8 inch	7/8 inch	1 inch
	Heavy		9/16 inch	5/8 inch	7/8 inch	1 1/8 inches	1 1/4 inches

locations is fore-and-aft anchoring, with two anchors to each buoy, and each boat tied to the buoy both fore and aft of it.

■ Anchor Lines and Strength

Synthetic fibers have produced ropes that are a blessing to boatmen. The new ropes are somewhat more expensive than manila, but they are stronger for their size, lighter, and more comfortable to handle. They also won't rot or mildew, and are easy to work with. One drawback is that they resist bite in tying; therefore, knots must be positive. Granny knots and loose knots are out.

Elasticity is always a factor to be considered when using any line for anchoring or tying a boat at a dock. Nylon rope is more than four times as elastic as manila when loaded repeatedly; Dacron is about 50 percent more elastic than manila, but it is more sensitive than nylon to abrasion.

Easy Anchor Retrieval

This simple-and-easy method of pulling up your anchor is a boon to bad backs and big boats. Learn this technique and the hard work is done by an inflated net ball, the kind usually found on commercial fishing boats. The only equipment you will need is a stainless-steel anchor ring, heavy-duty stainless snap, 5 or 6 feet of nylon, and the net ball. The accompanying illustration shows all of the elements of an anchor-retrieval system properly rigged. This anchor-retrieval rig is available at all marina stores. The accompanying chart shows the suggested ball sizes.

Ball	Anchor/Chain
NB-40	40 pounds
NB-50	75 pounds
NB-60	130 pounds
NB-75	240 pounds

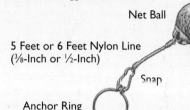

Net Ball

5 Feet or 6 Feet Nylon Line
($\frac{3}{8}$-Inch or $\frac{1}{2}$-Inch)

Snap

Anchor Ring

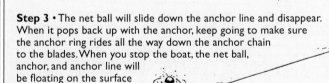

Step 1 • When you are ready to haul your anchor, take the anchor-retrieval rig and snap the ring on your anchor line. Start your boat.

Step 2 • Run your boat at a slow speed in a direction slightly to either side of the anchor line. Watch your anchor line so you do not run over it. When the anchor line comes alongside, fasten the line to a rear cleat and keep the boat moving in the same direction.

Step 3 • The net ball will slide down the anchor line and disappear. When it pops back up with the anchor, keep going to make sure the anchor ring rides all the way down the anchor chain to the blades. When you stop the boat, the net ball, anchor, and anchor line will be floating on the surface for an easy pickup.

PREPARING FOR WINTER STORAGE

This work is necessary to keep your boat serviceable and to protect your investment in it. If you live where you can enjoy year-round boating, there are important semi-annual maintenance jobs that you will recognize. If you can store your boat at home, the job will be greatly simplified, but if you store it in a boatyard, you may have to work within the yard's schedule.

In deciding whether to store your boat outside or in a heated garage, for instance, there are two dangers that must be avoided: formation of ice on the boat and continual dry heat. Small aluminum boats are affected less than wood, fiberglass, or fabric ones. Hard freezing and ice can pop fastenings, open seams, split and check the surface, and cause permanent warp in straight lines.

Dry heat for long periods can destroy the resins in woods (including wood stringers and fittings in all boats) and dry out caulking and seam compounds. If you store your boat outdoors in natural humidity conditions, keep it covered so that water cannot collect and form ice. Indoors or out, free ventilation is essential so that condensation can evaporate. Here are the steps to preparing your boat for winter storage:

1. First, make sure your boat is properly cradled for storage. If you have a trailer that fits your boat, you have no problem. Level the trailer on chocks, wheels off the ground. If you own a small aluminum boat, it will store well turned facedown, resting on the strongly built gunwales. If you must build a cradle for a larger boat, make accurate templates and cut cradle supports for the transom, engine bed, construction center, and stem at least.

2. Clean the bottom and outside hull entirely of algae, fungi, and barnacles. This must be done immediately, before they harden and dry fast. At this time, you'll get a good look at the condition and know what repairs have to be made before spring launching.

3. Scrub down the entire boat inside, starting at the top. Flush and clean out bilges with bilge cleaner. Flush out freshwater tanks, fish and bait boxes, and freshwater lines with disinfectant solution and let them dry. Remove all traces of salt water, polish, clean, and spray with preservative.

4. Wash canvas tops, curtains, and rope lines with mild soap and rinse with fresh water. Spray with preservative before storing in a dry place. Whenever possible, have your boat entirely shrink wrapped for maximum protection. Make certain that several vent openings are in the shrink wrap to allow plenty of ventilation.

5. Treat serious rust at once. Clean down to the bare metal or remove and replace. Re-putty the fastenings, and spray fixed and moving hardware with light machine oil or WD-40.

6. Make sure every corner of the boat, every fitting and joint, is dry, clean, and free of fungi. Put desiccants wherever needed. Air the boat by opening all the hatches on a dry, bright day.

Follow motor-storage procedures in the owner's manual. Cover these points particularly:

1. Flush the cooling system with fresh water and a rust inhibitor, and then drain the system well.

2. Disconnect fuel lines and run idle until out of fuel.

3. Disconnect the battery, wipe the connectors and terminals clean, and then follow the maker's battery-storage procedures.

4. Clean the carburetor bowl with automotive carburetor cleaner or lacquer thinner. Slosh the cleaner fluid around in a portable gas tank and pour out through the fuel lines and drain it well. This removes the gummy substance left by fuel.

5. Remove the spark plugs with a spark-plug wrench, squirt lubricating oil into each cylinder, and then turn the crankshaft by hand to distribute the oil. Replace the spark plugs.

6. Leave the motor head and lower unit clean of heavy dirt, rust, and grease deposits. Wipe the head and lower unit with an oily cloth.

7. Make sure the lower unit grease reservoir is left full.

PREPARING FOR SPRING LAUNCHING

Most owners start too late, missing a month or two of good boating before they are ready to launch. Use the post-holiday season to do inside work you want to accomplish: build cabinets, a fish box, circulating baitwell, or do other basement or garage jobs. Keep your eye on the boat throughout the winter if it's stored outside. If the boat is stored at a marina, check the boat often head to foot. Make an estimate of jobs, tools, and materials you'll need. First, do the outside hull—everything it needs to give you a safe and trouble-free season. If you have a wood boat, the hull should be sanded down to clean, bare wood, whether you are restoring a few spots where needed or refinishing the complete hull. Peeling and cracking on top indicates trouble underneath. Down to bare wood, you may discover the source. Sand the wood smooth, fill in cracks and holes and over fastenings, replace damaged boards, and dust clean before starting to paint.

Proceed carefully until you know what to do. Get paint maker's recommendations and specifications for your hull. Polyester paints will give you an amazingly tough coat when properly applied, but you will probably do better with an epoxy-based paint over fiberglass. Talk to your dealer and other owners. If you want to paint an originally unpainted aluminum boat, get the boat maker's specifications; certain paints can't be used.

Before you paint a bare fiberglass hull or cabin, think twice. You will not be able to sand and strip as you would with a wood hull. To repaint, you have to leave the first coat of paint on or risk damaging the gel coat. Most owners for this reason try to bleach out discolorations and stains. Spots can be scoured and buffed. Ask for recommended materials at a marine store. Damaged spots can be patched with fiberglass. The best overall treatment is to wax well with a marine-grade wax and sail on. If you must paint, use steel wool, which will give tooth for the paint, and use paints recommended by the manufacturers. Any surface must be absolutely clean before repainting.

On cabin woods, spar varnish is usually used; it's tough and looks good. Whatever your choice, on high-wear areas that scuff and go bare quickly, use a good grade of marine spar varnish, preferably every season.

If you find mildew or water inside, note how they got in and repair the damage. Next fall, use more desiccants in some corners, buy a better tarp, or add weather stripping to your windows. Neutralize foul odors before you launch. It's easy; try the supermarket.

Flush out all freshwater systems again with disinfectant, fill the tanks, and turn on the pressure. A drip is a leak. Fix it before you sail and you'll have a drier, safer boat. Check all through-hull fittings. If you find any signs of leaking or rot, restore the watertight fit and get the best advice you can to make it permanent.

Here, from service experts, are some important steps to follow to get your outboard motor ready to go after winter storage:

1. Check the level of lubricant in the lower unit and make sure it's filled to the proper level. If it appears oil has been leaking, have a service expert check it out since it could indicate the lower seals and gaskets need replacing. And if you didn't do this before off-season storage, drain the gear case and refill it with the manufacturer's recommended lubricant.

2. If your motor has a power trim or power tilt unit, check the level of fluid in the system's reservoir, and refill it with the recommended fluid as needed.

3. Check your spark plugs. Your outboard can't start quickly and run efficiently if the plugs aren't sparking. Remove them, clean them, and make sure they are gapped to specification. Also make sure the spark-plug terminal connections and wiring are clean, unfrayed, and snug-fitting.

4. Check the boat's battery. Make sure it's fully charged. Clean the terminal posts and connectors so they are free of corrosion.

5. If there was unused fuel left in the tank and engine over the winter, it should have been treated with a fuel conditioner before storage. If the fuel was conditioned, all you need to do in the spring is make sure the fuel-system clamps and fittings are tight and not leaking. Also check for cracked, worn, or aged fuel lines and replace as necessary. However, if no fuel conditioner was added before storage, clean the fuel-pump filter before adding fresh fuel. Although they vary from brand to brand, most outboard fuel filters are designed for easy cleaning. Check your owner's manual for instructions. Of course, all the old, untreated fuel should be drained from the tank and disposed of properly before new, fresh fuel is added. If you have an outboard with an oil-injection system, check to make sure the oil tank is filled. Also, check your owner's manual for any special maintenance the oil-injection system might require.

6. Many boaters use a fuel conditioner for winter storage, but then neglect its in-season use. Used in much smaller quantities during the boating season, outboard fuel conditioners help keep the carburetor clean, reduce plug fouling, and reduce moisture in the fuel system. A note of caution: use only fuel conditioners designed for marine use in your boat, not automotive additives or conditioners, which can do your motor more harm than good.

7. Check your propeller. A little ding in the prop can make a big dent in your boat's performance. If the propeller is nicked, gouged, or bent, take it to your dealer or a prop shop for repair. If the prop is too far gone, invest in a new one. Stainless propellers offer much greater durability than most aluminum props. Here's a safety tip: before removing your propeller, always shift your motor to neutral and remove the key from the ignition switch to prevent the motor from accidentally starting. If you have trouble loosening the propeller nut, try wedging a piece of two-by-four between the prop blade and the antiventilation plate

to keep the prop from turning. Before replacing the propeller, lube the prop shaft with grease as specified in your owner's manual. Also, check around the base of the prop shaft for monofilament fishing line that may have become wrapped around the shaft. Look closely—old monofilament might look like a plastic washer. Be sure to check your owner's manual for any special instructions and torque specifications before installing the propeller.

8. While you're checking the prop, also check the bottom of the boat. For clean, efficient running, the hull must be clean and efficient, too. Now's the time to remove any leftover barnacles or dried-up marine algae or weeds.

9. Spring is also a good time to touch up any scrapes or scratches in your motor's paint job. Most manufacturers offer factory-matched colors in easy-to-use spray-paint cans. If you're touching up the lower unit, be careful not to clog the water intake screen with paint. This could lead to the motor overheating. Also, don't make the mistake of painting over the sacrificial zinc anodes on your motor. They won't work if they're covered with paint. While you're inspecting the motor, check the anodes. If they are more than 50 percent destroyed, replace them with new ones. If you boat in salt water or brackish water, the anodes are supposed to dissipate as they protect your motor.

10. After the mechanical work is done, give your motor (and boat) a good cleaning. Remove all the dirt and grime collected over the winter. Use an engine degreaser to clean up your outboard's power head. As a final touch, give the motor a coat of automotive wax or polish. This will help it sparkle and protect the finish from the sun and water.

11. After the motor's all cleaned up, consult the lubrication section of your owner's manual. Most motors require a shot of lubricant on the throttle linkage or other moving parts on the engine. On motors with remote steering, the steering cable ram should be greased before the start of each season and periodically thereafter. Once again, check the owner's manual for detailed instructions.

BOAT TRAILERS

What size boat is trailerable? That is really a conundrum. The answer depends on how much you are willing to put into trailering. Each year's new-boat announcements include a large cabin cruiser with the claim " . . . and it can be trailered!" The fact is that it actually can be trailered, but it may be a professional transport job. You will need a heavy-duty, custom-built trailer, and should have a heavy-duty truck to make it go. And then it might do the boat no good. It's not a consumer proposition.

Common boat sizes for regular trailering are 14 to 26 feet. It is true that some 12-footers weigh more than 120 or 130 pounds, more weight than can be lifted to the top of a car by two persons. On the other end of the range, boats longer than 20 feet commonly have a deep bow, broad beam, and big weight that cause all sorts of problems in trailering. For a start, most state and all federal highways have a width limit of 8 feet; beyond that, you'll need a special permit and arrangements to travel.

If you are going to buy a boat in the prime size range for trailering, should you get a trailer at the same time? You will probably get a better fit for your boat if you do. The maker can supply information about trailer specifications for current-model hulls, and the dealer will probably carry trailers that suit.

But if you live near the water, why have a trailer? First, you save on mooring fees and winter storage. Second, your boat will be a much bigger asset if you can take it along on vacations, trailering it to another water when you want to fish and hunt or camp away from home. Keeping a boat on its trailer in your yard, you can keep bottom fouling cleaned off instead of facing a big job once or twice a year. Make it part of your routine when washing and waxing the car, and you will have a hull that is always in good shape. Keep a tarp over the boat and motor when it's idle on the trailer. When it sits in your own yard, there's no worry about vandalism at a mooring or a marina dock.

▪ Choosing a Trailer

The best advice is to get a trailer one size bigger than your present boat requires. This will accommodate the occasional extra-heavy load you will pack in it. If you

The best advice is to get a trailer one size bigger than your boat requires. This will allow for the extra weight of the gear you pack in the boat.

get a trailer larger than that, your boat will not be properly supported and the trailer will be awkward to tow, bouncing around because the boat is not heavy enough to hold it on the road.

Proper hull support is essential in a trailer. This is where the boat maker's advice is important. Three critical points are: full support at the transom, at the bottom forefoot, and at the construction center, either where the greatest weight is built in amidships or under the engine stringers in an inboard boat. You must avoid a trailer mismatch that will, over a period of time, cause the hull to hook or rocker. A well-engineered trailer for a boat of 500 pounds or more will have pairs of strong, securely set rollers on good bearings at frequent intervals for the entire bottom length.

Regardless of size, the trailer must enable you to back down to the water and launch your boat efficiently without getting the trailer-wheel hubs in the water. Winch quality is important for heavier boats. A wobbly or ill-fitting crank, wheel, and ratchet won't do. For a boat of 1,500 pounds or more, you might consider adding an electric winch. It saves a lot of knuckle busting.

Trailer suspension, wheel mounts, and general construction should be spelled out by the trailer maker. Study these and get full information from the dealer about use and maintenance. Leaf springs are good on a heavy trailer; a soft ride is not important, while good support is. If you trailer 3,500 pounds or more, tandem wheels are needed.

You will have to look up state laws on trailers for your region, and then equip your trailer and the tow vehicle according to those laws. The laws specify over what weights trailer brakes are required, but you may decide you want brakes even if your trailer is below the limit. In that case, look into brakes that operate in tandem with your car's foot pedal. Quality trailer brakes are practically foolproof, make driving safer and easier, and they reduce wear on the tow vehicle's rear suspension and tires.

Insist on a frame-mounted hitch, even though the salesman may try to give you a shallow hitch bolted to the body pan when you buy that new wagon. As for bumper-mounted hitches, they are dangerous. With a frame-mounted hitch, you will be able to step up in weight over a big range without additional expense, and you'll be able to trailer your present boat without worry. You will need an umbilical electric hookup to your car's electrical system for trailer lights and brakes and other accessories. The cable, clamps, and plugs come in a package at a reasonable price. On your car you'll need western-type rearview mirrors—big, rectangular ones mounted on arms on each side that let you see around the trailer. For a trailer load of 3,000 pounds or more, you should have an equalizing hitch that compensates for a big load in normal travel and substantially reduces danger in a crash stop.

■ Loading Your Boat and Trailer

Most makers recommend loading with 5 to 7 percent more weight ahead of the trailer axle. This prevents fishtailing and gives you good load control. If you are going on an extended trip with camping gear loaded inside the boat, watch the weight distribution. Weigh big items as they are loaded, and don't under any circumstances exceed the maker's maximum weight limit. Your trailer will be designed to haul your boat and motor with the correct load in front of the axle. Additional weight inside the boat should maintain this distribution, or the position of the boat on the trailer bed should be adjusted accordingly. A well-made trailer will let you do this.

■ Trailer Maintenance

Wheel bearings are the critical point. When traveling, stop every few hours to feel for excessive heat at the hubs. If the hubs are hot, let them cool off, and then drive slowly to the nearest service station and have them repack the wheel bearings. Have the bearings inspected before each trip, and have them repacked at the start of each season.

Keep the hitch and mount free of rust, repaint each season with metal paint on clean metal, and grease moving joints on an equalizing hitch only as the maker specifies. You'll find that a well-made boat trailer will last at least as long as the boat if it's well maintained. And you will be delighted when you learn how much extra gear you can take along in the boat.

■ On the Road and Launching

The U.S. Coast Guard makes the following recommendations for trailering a boat. Heeding their advice will ensure your safety on the road and also at the launch ramp.

Pre-Departure Checks

Make a complete check of the trailer and towing vehicle. Inspect tires for tread wear, inflation, and condition. Examine the hitch and associated safety devices, and check brakes on both vehicles.

- Check the tightness of the wheel lugs. Repeat this periodically during the trip.
- Equip the towing vehicle with large rearview mirrors on both sides. Check the inside rearview mirror. The boat and the load should be low enough so that it does not obstruct the view.
- Check shocks and springs on both vehicles.
- Load tools, emergency equipment, and foul-weather gear in a readily accessible location in the towing vehicle.
- Check the load on the trailer. It must be loaded correctly from front to rear, and from side to side for the best balance.
- Couple the trailer to the tow vehicle and observe the attitude of it. Check the trailer lights.
- Check the wheel bearings on the trailer.
- Check all tie-down straps.

UNDERWAY: Once underway, never forget that you have a boat behind you. This sounds foolish, but when you're wheeling along at highway speeds it is all too easy to lose a feel for the tow—until you have to pass, turn, or brake. Always start slowly, in low gear, and take the car up through the gears gently. Think twice about passing other vehicles—but if you decide to pass, don't delay. Be alert for signs restricting trailers. Remain sensitive to unusual sounds or handling factors, and if there's anything that seems at all strange, pull over immediately and check. In fact, you should pull over and check the entire rig every hour or so—check for high temperatures in the wheel bearings and slackening tie-downs, and make sure the lights, tire pressure, and car-engine temperature are OK. Here are some other safety tips to keep in mind when towing a trailer:

- Never let anyone ride in the trailer while moving. It is dangerous, and illegal in many states.
- Observe speed limits. In many states, the speed limit for a car towing a trailer is lower than for a car traveling by itself.
- Maintain a greater following distance between your vehicle and the one in front of you. With the trailer, you need much more room to stop.
- When traveling over bumpy roads or crossing railroad tracks, slow down. Going too fast may cause the tow vehicle to bottom out and the hitch to scrape, causing damage to both the car and the trailer.
- Large trucks and buses create considerable turbulence, which may cause the trailer to fishtail. Keep a firm grip on the steering wheel and tension on the hitch ball. If there is a manual lever that will operate the trailer brakes separately from those on the car, a quick application of the trailer brakes may slow the trailer sufficiently to eliminate sway.

LAUNCHING: Launching will be the critical part of your trailer-boating expedition. It's embarrassing, as well as expensive, to safely travel many highway miles just to do something dumb at the moment of truth. Before going to the ramp, check with the marina operator or others to determine if there are any unusual hazards, such as a drop-off at the end of the ramp. You should prepare your boat for launching away from the ramp so that you don't hold up other boaters. This is known as "ramp courtesy." Preparations for launching should include raising the lower unit to avoid scraping, installing the drain plug,

When launching or recovering, never turn off the car's engine, and keep the parking brake set while you work the boat off the trailer.

releasing the tie-downs, and disconnecting or removing the trailer's stop and directional lights.

When launching or recovering, never turn the car's engine off, and keep the parking brake set while you work the boat off the trailer. Only the driver should be in the towing vehicle during launching and recovering. One or two observers can help the driver watch the trailer and traffic. Keep everyone else away from the launching ramp. It is also prudent to use a tire stop to avoid an unexpected dunking of trailer and car.

Many trailer-boat owners' worst moments have occurred at busy launching ramps because they have not practiced backing their rig. Before you attempt a launching, you should put in a couple of hours in a deserted parking lot learning how to back your rig through a maze of cardboard boxes. A helpful hint when backing is to place your hand on the bottom of the steering wheel and move the wheel in the direction you want the trailer to go. Do **not** oversteer.

If you have an unwieldy trailer, you may want to get an auxiliary front bumper hitch, which will make close-quarters maneuvering much simpler, as well as keep the drive wheels of the towing vehicle on higher, drier ground.

Make sure you **never, ever** cast off all the lines from the boat before launching. Someone on shore must have a line that is made fast to the boat. The line makes it easy to shove the boat off the trailer and then pull the boat to a dock or boarding platform or back to the trailer at a wide, busy launching ramp. Above all, take the time necessary to launch safely, but as soon as the boat is afloat, move the vehicle and the trailer to the parking lot and the boat to the dock for loading. Don't loiter.

Always try to avoid getting the trailer hubs in the water. If you cannot avoid dunking them, at least let

them cool first. If you don't, the sudden cooling may crack or chip the bearings or suck them full of water. One way to pass the time, if you are a sailor, is to step the mast in the parking lot while waiting to launch. However, make sure that there are no low power lines or other overhead obstructions between you and the launching ramp. Unfortunately, a few boaters are electrocuted every year because their rigging comes in contact with overhead electrical wires.

BACKING A TRAILER: Backing a boat trailer down a tight, slick launch ramp can be tricky, and a busy ramp is not the place to learn. Practice in an empty parking lot on a Sunday morning. You'll be able to go at your own pace without an impatient audience.

When backing the trailer, keep in mind that you're pushing it, not pulling it. No big deal when you back straight up—you just have to keep the wheels of the tow vehicle perfectly straight. But when it's time to turn, everything is reversed: turning the steering wheel to the right will turn the rear end of the tow vehicle to the right, causing the trailer to turn left, and vice versa.

Steering Tip

Placing your hand on the bottom of the steering wheel simplifies the process of backing up. Pull the wheel to the right, the trailer heads right, and vice versa.

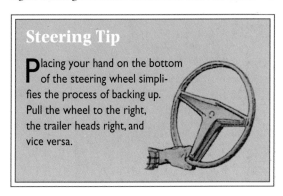

Backing a Trailer

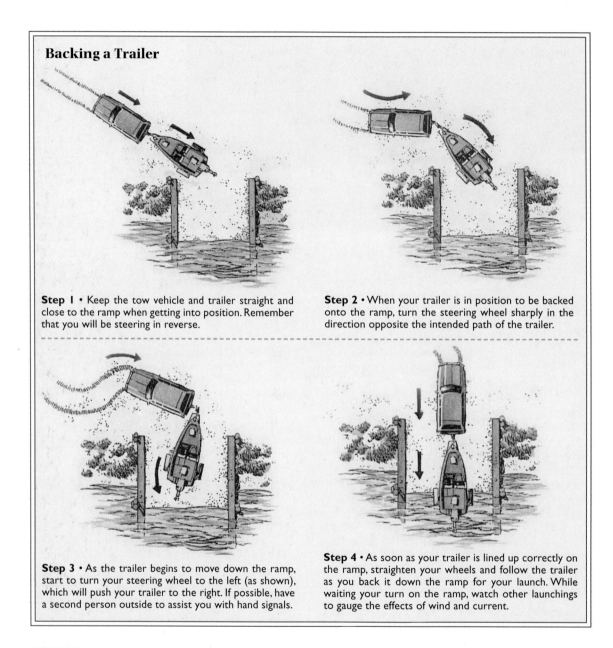

Step 1 • Keep the tow vehicle and trailer straight and close to the ramp when getting into position. Remember that you will be steering in reverse.

Step 2 • When your trailer is in position to be backed onto the ramp, turn the steering wheel sharply in the direction opposite the intended path of the trailer.

Step 3 • As the trailer begins to move down the ramp, start to turn your steering wheel to the left (as shown), which will push your trailer to the right. If possible, have a second person outside to assist you with hand signals.

Step 4 • As soon as your trailer is lined up correctly on the ramp, straighten your wheels and follow the trailer as you back it down the ramp for your launch. While waiting your turn on the ramp, watch other launchings to gauge the effects of wind and current.

RETRIEVAL: Retrieving your boat is similar to launching and should be done with the same courtesy by reversing the procedures. Unload your boat at the dock and keep it there until the trailer is ready to move down the ramp. Move the boat to the trailer and raise the lower unit. Winch the boat on to the trailer and secure it. Finally, move the towing vehicle and trailer with the boat to the parking area for loading, housekeeping, and other general maintenance chores.

STORAGE: To prevent water from accumulating in the boat, remove the drain plug and tilt the trailer and the boat enough to allow drainage. This should be done for even short-term storage.

When storing the boat on its trailer for any length of time, get the weight off the wheels. Cinder blocks under the tongue and four corners of the frame of the trailer should be adequate support, shimmed up if necessary by boards. Once the trailer frame is jacked up, you should check to be sure that the boat itself is evenly supported. Be forewarned: the frame itself can easily be bent out of its normal shape by excessive jacking at a corner.

SAFE BOATING

Boaters don't have a clean record when it comes to accidents afloat. It has little to do with the perquisites of fishing and hunting, but much to do with neglecting to control the boat and guard personal safety aboard. A sportsman who has not schooled himself in basic boating safety and safe habits will forget about them in an emergency. Here's your chance to start right.

Basic Tool Kit

Every boat must be equipped to get home on its own. The exact selection of tools, spare parts, and supplies necessary must be suited to your boat and motor and to problems you are most likely to encounter. Here are the items that should be in a basic tool kit:

- Ordinary pliers
- Vise-grip pliers
- Diagonal-cutting pliers
- Long-nose electrician's pliers
- Screwdrivers
- Spark-plug wrench to fit
- Combination open-end and box wrenches in sizes ⅜ to ¾ inch
- Sharp knife

Spare Parts

Keep these spare parts on hand:

- Spark plugs of correct specifications
- Distributor cap, rotor, condenser, and point set
- Fuel pump and filter
- Oil filter
- Water-pump impeller
- V-belts to match each size used
- Spare fuel lines, cocks, and fittings
- Gaskets and hoses
- Bailing-pump diaphragm
- Fuses and bulbs to double for each used

All-Purpose Kit

For an all-purpose kit, include the following:

- 50-foot chalk line
- Nails, screws, bolts and nuts, and washers
- Hose clamps
- Electrical tape
- Insulated wire
- Cotter pins
- Elastic plastic bandage material and duct tape
- Machine oil

Outboard Motor Troubleshooting Checklist

Follow these steps to check the condition of your outboard motor:

- Check gas supply and tank pressure; squeeze the bulb several times.
- Check to be sure the propeller is not wrapped in weeds, line, or net. If line is wrapped around the prop, try to slow reverse to loosen it. Then, cut off pieces until you can pull the rest free.
- Look for loose wires and clamps at battery terminals.
- Remove ignition wire from any spark plug and crank the motor. A spark should jump from the wire end to the engine head; if there is no spark, check back to the ignition switch.
- If you have a hot spark, look into the fuel feed, pull the gas feed line off from the side of the outboard, and blow through the line until you hear bubbles in the tank.
- Clean the carburetor bowl and fuel filter.

Quartering a Following Sea

Quartering may be the only solution to crossing a following sea. Your speed, however, must be faster than the waves running at your stern. You'll have to make corrections with each wave you meet. As you cross the crest, wave action tries to turn a quartering boat broadside by pushing its stern into the trough between it and the next wave crest. You must power your boat into the direction of the trough to properly point your bow toward the next crest. (Note the direction of the outboard and prop in illustration.) Never allow wave action to push your boat parallel to the trough.

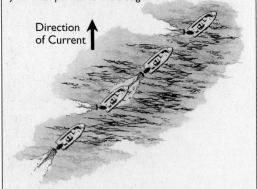

Direction of Current

Mouth of River or Inlet

Wherever a current enters a body of water—this is true for river mouths as well as ocean inlets—you can expect to find relatively calm water at the edge of the intruding flow. Usually this calm transition zone is marked by surface wave action. When running any inlet, always ride the back of the wave in front of you. Never power over its crest, or drift far enough back to be picked up by the crest of the following wave.

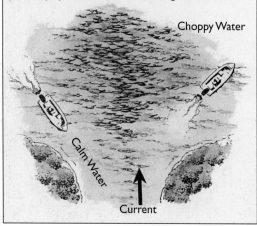

Choppy Water

Calm Water

Current

◼ Safe Boating Procedures

First, it is important to know your boat. Get familiar with its equipment and discover its limitations. If it's a livery rental, check it over completely before you push off.

Make a habit of checking off safety equipment aboard. First, locate the safety items required by law. Then, compare your optional equipment with the Coast Guard's list of recommended equipment. Count the life preservers, and make sure that each passenger has one that will keep him afloat in the water.

Carry a proper chart, GPS, compass, VHF, and a fully charged cell phone.

Put tackle, guns, decoys, nets, and other gear where they are secure and won't clutter walkways and footing.

Check the fuel supply, and the condition of the tank and feed line. Make sure the spark is strong and regular. Take along at least 1½ times as much fuel as you estimate you will need. If you run into heavy waves, your boat will take more fuel to go the same distance.

Gasoline vapors are explosive and will settle in the low areas of a boat. During fueling, keep doors, hatches, ports, and chests closed, stoves and pilot lights off, electrical circuits off, and absolutely no smoking! Keep the fill nozzle in firm contact with the fill neck to prevent static spark. Don't spill, for you'll have to dry it up before starting the engine. Do not use gasoline appliances aboard—they're lethal risks. Use alcohol and other less volatile fuels.

After fueling, ventilate thoroughly before pressing the starter. One minute is the minimum safe ventilation time. Big boats should be ventilated longer, with effective blowers operating and all ports opened. Keep your fuel lines in perfect condition and the boat's bilges clean.

Electrical equipment, switches, and wiring are some prime sources of boat fires and explosions. Keep batteries clean and ventilated.

Do not overload your boat. Make sure you have safely adequate freeboard before casting off. Look ahead to water conditions and weather changes you may encounter.

Keep an alert lookout. If you have a boat longer than 20 feet, name your mate and agree that he'll keep lookout any time you can't. You have more to watch out for than other boats and shallow water. Watch for obstructions such as rocks and floating logs.

Swimmers are hard to see in the water. Running through swimmers or a swimming area is the most sensitive violation a boat can make. If in doubt, give beaches and rafts a wide swing.

Buoys

Buoys are traffic signals that guide boaters safely along waterways. They can also identify dangerous areas, as well as give directions and information. The colors and numbers on buoys mean the same thing regardless of what kind of buoy on which they appear.

Red colors, red lights, and even numbers • These indicate the right side of the channel as a boater enters from the open sea or heads upstream. Numbers usually increase consecutively as you return from the open sea or head upstream.

Green colors, green lights, and odd numbers • These indicate the left side of the channel as a boater enters from the open sea and heads upstream. Numbers will usually increase consecutively as you return from the open sea or head upstream.

Red and green horizontal stripes • These are placed at the junction of two channels to indicate the preferred (primary) channel when a channel splits. If green is on top,

the preferred channel is to the right. If red is on top, the preferred channel is to the left. The light color matches the top stripe. These are also sometimes referred to as junction buoys.

Nun buoys • These cone-shaped buoys are always marked with red markings and even numbers. They mark the right side of the channel as a boater enters from the open sea or heads upstream.

Can buoys • These cylindrical-shaped buoys are always marked with green markings and odd numbers. They mark the left side of the channel as a boater enters from the open sea or heads upstream.

1 • Red Colors and Lights

2 • Green Colors and Lights

3 • Red/Green Horizontally Striped Buoy

4 • Green/Red Horizontally Striped Buoy

5 • Nun Buoy (Red with Even Numbers)

6 • Can Buoy (Green with Odd Numbers)

Your wake is potent. You can swamp small craft such as canoes or rowboats, damage shorelines and shore property, disturb sleepers, and ruin fish and wildlife sport for hours by running fast through small passages and shallows. You are always responsible for any damage caused by your wake.

Learn the Coast Guard navigation rules and obey them at all times. Copies are available to download free on the Coast Guard website. Most collisions are caused by one-time violations.

Make sure at least one other person aboard knows how to operate the boat and motor in case you are disabled or fall overboard. Know a plan of action you will take in emergencies such as a man overboard, bad leak, motor that won't run, collision, bad storm, or troublesome passenger.

Storm signals and danger signs are often informal. Learn to read the weather, and keep alert to what passing boats are trying to tell you.

Wear your life preserver and make all your passengers, especially children, wear life preservers at all times. In a capsizing, remember that you are safer if you stay with the boat, where you can be seen. It will also help you stay afloat until help arrives.

Under Coast Guard legislation, it is illegal for anyone to build, sell, or use a craft that does not conform to safety regulations. Check with your dealer, and check yourself to make sure your boat measures up.

Small Boat, Big Water

The best way to stay out of trouble on open water is to learn how to read the wind and weather. The National Oceanic and Atmospheric Administration (NOAA) issues marine weather forecasts every hour with details of winds and seas. If you have a VHF-FM radio, NOAA weather radio broadcasts weather and warnings continuously on these frequencies: 162.400 MHz, 162.425 MHz, 162.450 MHz, 162.475 MHz, 162.500 MHz, 162.525 MHz, and 162.550 MHz. Matching the wind forecast with the accompanying chart will give you a good idea of the seas you can expect to encounter.

But such forecasts are regional, and local conditions can be radically different—thunderstorms, for instance. You can determine the distance in miles of an approaching thunderstorm by counting the interval between seeing a lightning flash and hearing its accompanying thunder in seconds, and then dividing by five. For example, if it takes 10 seconds to hear the thunder, the storm is 2 miles away.

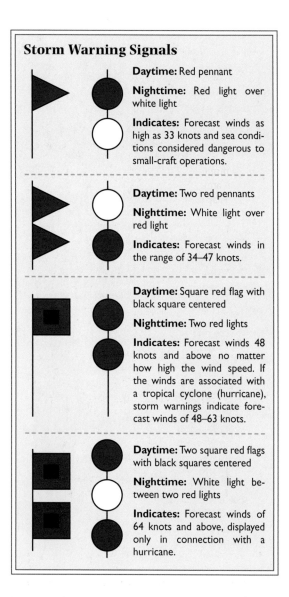

Storm Warning Signals

Daytime: Red pennant

Nighttime: Red light over white light

Indicates: Forecast winds as high as 33 knots and sea conditions considered dangerous to small-craft operations.

Daytime: Two red pennants

Nighttime: White light over red light

Indicates: Forecast winds in the range of 34–47 knots.

Daytime: Square red flag with black square centered

Nighttime: Two red lights

Indicates: Forecast winds 48 knots and above no matter how high the wind speed. If the winds are associated with a tropical cyclone (hurricane), storm warnings indicate forecast winds of 48–63 knots.

Daytime: Two square red flags with black squares centered

Nighttime: White light between two red lights

Indicates: Forecast winds of 64 knots and above, displayed only in connection with a hurricane.

But that knowledge won't help much if you don't have time to get to safety. Odds are you're going to get caught on the water eventually. Knowing how to handle difficult seas in a small boat is insurance all sportsmen should have.

Coast Guard–Approved Equipment

For safe boating under most conditions, you are required by federal law to carry Coast Guard–approved equip-

Wind/Sea Relationships

	Velocity (knots)	Conditions
Calm Conditions	0–3	Sea like a mirror
	4–6	Ripples, less than 1 foot
	7–10	Smooth wavelets, 1 to 2 feet
	11–16	Small waves, 2 to 4 feet
Small Craft Warning	17–21	Moderate waves, 4 to 8 feet, whitecaps
	22–27	Large waves, 8 to 13 feet, spray
	28–33	High waves, 13 to 20 feet, heaped seas, foam from breaking waves
Gale Warning	34–40	High waves, 13 to 20 feet, foam blown in well-marked streaks
	41–47	Seas rolling, reduced visibility from spray, waves 13 to 20 feet
Storm Warning	48–55	White seas, very high waves, 20 to 30 feet, overhanging crests
	56–63	Exceptionally high waves, 30 to 45 feet
Hurricane Warning	More than 63	Air filled with foam, sea white, waves over 45 feet

ment aboard your craft. Coast Guard–approved equipment simply means that it has been approved by the Commandant of the U.S. Coast Guard and has been determined to be in compliance with U.S. Coast Guard specifications and regulations relating to materials, construction, and performance.

Here are the Coast Guard recommendations for the most essential lifesaving equipment you must have onboard under federal law.

FIRE EXTINGUISHERS: Each approved fire extinguisher is classified by a letter and a Roman numeral according to the type of fire it is designed to extinguish and its size. The letter indicates the type of fire:

A: Fires of ordinary combustible materials

B: Gasoline, oil, and grease fires

C: Electrical fires

Fire extinguishers must be carried on **all** motorboats that meet one or more of the following conditions:

- Inboard engines
- Closed compartments under thwarts and seats where portable fuel tanks may be stored
- Double bottoms not sealed to the hull or not completely filled with flotation materials
- Closed living spaces
- Closed stowage compartments in which combustible or flammable materials are stored
- Permanently installed fuel tanks

There is no gallon capacity to determine if a fuel tank is portable. However, if the fuel tank is secured so it cannot be moved in case of a fire or other emergency, or if the weight of the fuel tank is such that people onboard cannot move it in case of a fire or other emergency, then the Coast Guard considers the tank permanently installed.

Dry chemical fire extinguishers without gauges or indicating devices must be inspected every six months. If the gross weight of a carbon dioxide (CO_2) fire extinguisher is reduced by more than 10 percent of the net weight, the extinguisher is not acceptable and must be recharged. Check extinguishers regularly to be sure that the gauges are free and nozzles clear.

Fire-extinguisher requirements are classified by the size of the vessel:

1. Boats less than 26 feet in length with **no** fixed fire-extinguishing system installed in machinery spaces must have at least one approved Type B-I hand-portable fire extinguisher. When an approved fixed fire-extinguishing system is installed in machinery spaces, no Type B-I extinguisher is required. If the construction of the boat does not permit the entrapment of explosive or flammable gases or vapors, no fire extinguisher is required.

2. Boats 26 feet to less than 40 feet in length must have at least two approved Type B-I or at least one Type B-II hand-portable fire extinguishers. When an approved fixed fire-extinguishing system is installed, only one Type B-I extinguisher is required.

3. Boats 40 feet to not more than 65 feet in length must have at least three approved Type B-I or at least one Type B-I and one Type B-II hand-portable fire extinguisher. When an approved fixed fire-extinguishing system is installed, one fewer Type B-I or one Type B-II extinguisher is required.

Note: Coast Guard–approved extinguishers carry the following label: Marine Type USCG Approved, Size —, Type —, 162.208/, etc. UL-listed extinguishers not displaying this marking are also acceptable, provided they are of the above sizes and types and carry a minimum UL rating of 5-B:C.

Fire Extinguishers

Extinguishers approved for motorboats are hand portable, of either B-I or B-II classification or their UL equivalents, and have the following characteristics:

Coast Guard Classes	UL Listing	Foam (gallons)	CO_2 (pounds)	Dry Chemical (pounds)	Halon (pounds)
B–I	5B	1¼	4	2	2½
B–II	—	2½	15	10	10
—	10B	—	10	2½	5

PERSONAL FLOTATION DEVICES (PFDS): All boats must be equipped with U.S. Coast Guard–approved life jackets called personal flotation devices, or PFDs. The quantity and type depends on the length of the boat and the number of people onboard or being towed. Each PFD must be in good condition, the proper size for the intended wearer, and, very important, must be readily accessible.

▪ Type I: Offshore Life Jacket
These PFDs provide the most buoyancy. They are effective for all waters, especially open, rough, or remote waters where rescue may be delayed. They are designed to turn most unconscious wearers to a face-up position.

▪ Type II: Near-Shore Vest
These vests are intended for calm, inland waters or where there is a good chance of quick rescue. This type will turn some unconscious wearers to a face-up position, but will not turn as many people to a face-up position as a Type I.

▪ Type III: Flotation Aid
These vests are good for calm, inland waters, or where there is a good chance of quick rescue. They are designed so wearers can place themselves in a face-up position. The wearer may have to tilt his head back to avoid turning facedown in the water. It is generally the most comfortable type for continuous wear.

▪ Type IV: Throwable Device
These cushions or ring buoys are intended for calm, inland waters where help is always present. They are not designed to be worn, but to be thrown to a person in the water and held by the victim until they are rescued.

▪ Type V: Special-Use Device
These PFDs are intended for specific activities and may be carried instead of another PFD only if used according to the label. Some Type V devices provide significant hypothermia protection. Type V PFDs must be used in accordance with their labels to be acceptable.

Note: U.S. Coast Guard–approved inflatable life jackets are authorized for use by people over 16 years of age. They must have a full cylinder and all status indicators on the inflator must be green or the device does not meet the legal requirements. Inflatable life jackets are more comfortable, which encourages regular wear.

VISUAL DISTRESS SIGNALS: All recreational boats, when used on coastal waters, the Great Lakes, territorial seas, and those waters connected directly to the Great Lakes and territorial seas, up to a point where a body of water is less than 2 miles wide, must be equipped with visual distress signals. Boats owned in the United States operating on the high seas must also be equipped with visual distress signals. The following are exempted from the requirements for day signals and only need to carry night signals:

- Recreational boats less than 16 feet in length

- Boats participating in organized events, such as races, regattas, or marine parades

- Open sailboats less than 26 feet in length not equipped with propulsion machinery

- Manually propelled boats

Pyrotechnic visual distress signals must be Coast Guard–approved, in serviceable condition, and stowed to be readily accessible. They are marked with a date showing the serviceable life, and this date must not have passed.

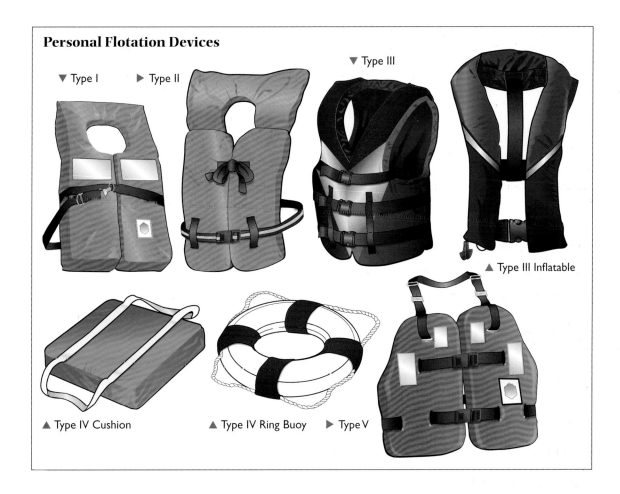

Personal Flotation Devices

▼ Type I   ► Type II   ▼ Type III   ▲ Type III Inflatable

▲ Type IV Cushion   ▲ Type IV Ring Buoy   ► Type V

Coast Guard–approved pyrotechnic visual distress signals and associated devices include:

- Pyrotechnic red flares, handheld or aerial
- Pyrotechnic orange smoke, handheld or floating
- Launchers for aerial red meteors or parachute flares

Non-pyrotechnic visual distress signaling devices must carry the manufacturer's certification that they meet Coast Guard requirements. They must be in serviceable condition and stowed to be readily accessible. This group includes:

- Orange distress flags
- Electric distress flags

No single signaling device is ideal under all conditions and for all purposes. Consideration should there-fore be given to carrying several types. For example, an aerial flare can be seen over a long distance on a clear night, but for closer work, a handheld flare may be more useful.

HANDLING AND STORAGE OF PYROTECHNIC DEVICES:
Pyrotechnic devices should be stored in a cool, dry location and must be readily accessible in case of an emergency. Care should be taken to prevent puncturing or otherwise damaging their coverings. A watertight container, such as a surplus ammunition box, painted red or orange and prominently marked "distress signals" is recommended.

If young children are frequently aboard your boat, careful selection and proper stowage of visual distress signals becomes especially important. If you elect to carry pyrotechnic devices, select devices that are in tough packaging and that would be difficult to ignite accidentally.

Coast Guard–approved pyrotechnic devices carry an expiration date. This date cannot exceed 42 months from the date of manufacture and at such time the device can no longer be counted toward the minimum requirements.

A wide variety of signaling devices, both pyrotechnic and nonpyrotechnic, can be carried to meet the requirements of the regulation.

Boats less than 16 feet long operating in coastal waters, and certain other exempted boats listed in the previous section, need only carry signaling devices when operating at night. All other recreational boats must carry both night and day signaling devices.

The following is an example of the variety and combinations of devices that can be carried in order to meet the requirements:

- Three handheld red flares (day and night)

- One electric distress light (night)

- One handheld red flare and two parachute flares (day and night)

- One handheld orange smoke signal, two floating orange smoke signals, and one electric distress light (day and night)

All distress-signaling devices have both advantages and disadvantages. The most popular, because of cost, are probably the smaller pyrotechnic devices. Pyrotechnics make excellent distress signals, universally recognized as such, but they have the drawback that they can be used only once. Additionally, there is the potential for both injury and property damage if pyrotechnics are not properly handled. Pyrotechnic devices have a very hot flame and the ash and slag can cause burns and ignite materials that burn easily. Projected devices, such as pistol-launched and handheld parachute flares and meteors, have many of the same characteristics of a firearm and must be handled with the same caution and respect.

Under the Inland Navigational Rules, a high-intensity white light flashing at regular intervals from 50–70 times per minute is considered a distress signal. Therefore, a strobe light used in inland waters should only be used as a distress signal.

The handheld and the floating orange smoke signaling devices are good day signals, especially on clear days. Both signals are most effective with light to moderate winds because higher winds tend to keep the smoke close to the water and disperse it, which makes it hard to see.

> ## Sound-Signaling Devices for Vessels Less than 20 Meters (65.6 Feet) in Length
>
> **1 •** Vessels 12 meters (39.4 feet) or more in length, but less than 20 meters (65.6 feet), must carry onboard a power whistle or power horn and a bell.
>
> **2 •** Vessels less than 12 meters (39.4 feet) need not carry a whistle, horn, or bell. However, the navigation rules require signals to be made under certain circumstances, and you should carry some means for making an efficient signal when necessary.

The distress flag must be at least 3 by 3 feet with a black square and ball on an orange background. It is accepted as a day signal only and is especially effective in bright sunlight. The flag is most distinctive when waved on something such as a paddle or boat hook or flown from a mast.

The electric distress light is accepted for night use only and must automatically flash the international SOS distress signal (• • • – – – • • •). Flashed four to six times each minute, this is an unmistakable distress signal, well known to most boaters. The device can be checked anytime for serviceability if shielded from view.

Red handheld flares can be used by day, but are most effective at night or in restricted visibility, such as fog or haze. When selecting such flares, look for the Coast Guard approval number and date of manufacture. Make sure that the device does not carry the marking, "Not approved for use on recreational boats."

▪ Navigation Lights

REQUIRED ON BOATS BETWEEN SUNSET AND SUNRISE: Recreational boats operating at night are required to display navigation lights between sunset and sunrise. Although most recreational boats in the United States operate in waters governed by the Inland Navigational Rules, changes to the rules have made the general lighting requirements for both the Inland and International rules basically the same. The differences between them are primarily in the options available.

1. A power-driven vessel less than 20 meters (65.6 feet) in length shall exhibit navigation lights as shown in

Range and Arc of Visibility of Lights

For Vessels Less than 20 Meters (65.6 Feet) in Length

Light	Visible Range in Miles		Arc in Degrees
	Less than 12 Meters	12 Meters or More	
Masthead light	2	3	225
All-around light	2	2	360
Side lights	1	2	112.5
Stern light	2	2	135

Figure 1. If the vessel is less than 12 meters (39.4 feet) in length, it may show the lights as shown in either Figure 1 or Figure 2.

2. On a vessel less than 12 meters (39.4 feet) in length, the masthead light must be 1 meter (3.3 feet) higher than the sidelights. If the vessel is 12 meters or more in length but less than 20 meters (65.6 feet), the masthead light must not be less than 2.5 meters (8.2 feet) above the gunwale.

3. A power-driven vessel less than 50 meters in length may also, but is not obligated to, carry a second masthead light abaft of and higher than the forward one.

4. A power-driven vessel less than 7 meters (23 feet) in length and whose maximum speed cannot exceed 7 knots may, in international waters **only**, in lieu of the lights prescribed above, exhibit an all-around white light, and shall, if practicable, also exhibit sidelights.

SAILING VESSELS AND VESSELS UNDER OARS:

1. A sailing vessel less than 20 meters (65.6 feet) in length shall exhibit navigation lights as shown in either Figure 3 or Figure 4. The lights may be combined in a single lantern carried at the top of the mast as shown in Figure 5.

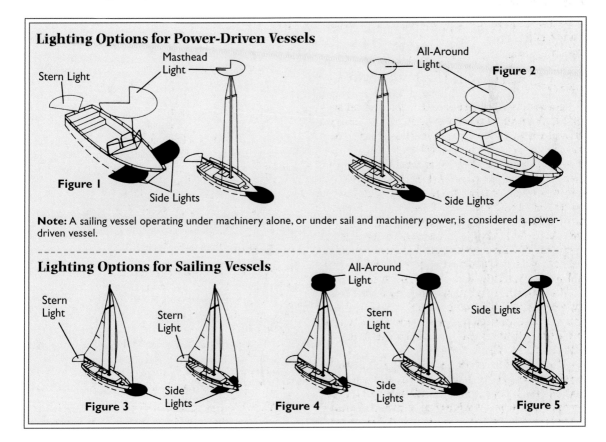

Lighting Options for Power-Driven Vessels

Stern Light

Masthead Light

All-Around Light

Figure 2

Figure 1

Side Lights

Side Lights

Note: A sailing vessel operating under machinery alone, or under sail and machinery power, is considered a power-driven vessel.

Lighting Options for Sailing Vessels

Stern Light

Stern Light

All-Around Light

Stern Light

Side Lights

Figure 3

Side Lights

Figure 4

Side Lights

Side Lights

Figure 5

Lighting Options for Vessels under Oars

Figure 6

Electric Torch or Lantern

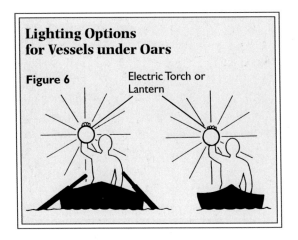

Day Shapes

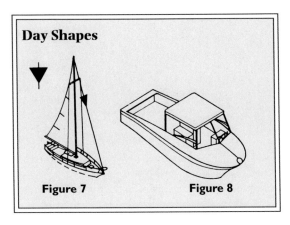

Figure 7   Figure 8

2. A sailing vessel less than 7 meters (23 feet) in length shall, if practicable, exhibit those lights prescribed for sailing vessels less than 20 meters in length, but if it does not, it shall have ready at hand an electric torch or lighted lantern showing a white light that shall be exhibited in sufficient time to prevent collision (see Figure 6).

3. A vessel under oars may display those lights prescribed for sailing vessels, but if it does not, it shall have ready at hand an electric torch or lighted lantern showing a white light that shall be exhibited in sufficient time to prevent collision (see Figure 6).

LIGHTS USED WHEN ANCHORED: Power-driven vessels and sailing vessels at anchor must display anchor lights. However, vessels less than 7 meters (23 feet) in length are not required to display anchor lights unless anchored in or near a narrow channel, fairway, or anchorage, or where other vessels normally navigate.

An anchor light for a vessel less than 20 meters (65.6 feet) in length is an all-around white light visible for 2 miles exhibited where it can best be seen. A vessel less than 20 meters in length in inland waters, when at anchor in a special anchorage area designated by the Secretary of Transportation, does not require an anchor light.

DAY SHAPES: A vessel proceeding under sail when also being propelled by machinery shall exhibit forward, where it can best be seen, a conical shape, apex downward (see Figure 7), except that for Inland Rules, a vessel less than 12 meters in length is not required to exhibit the day shape (see Figure 8).

◾ Loading Your Boat

There are several things to remember when loading a boat: distribute the load evenly, keep the load low, don't overload, don't stand up in a small boat, and consult the U.S. Coast Guard maximum capacities plate. On boats with no capacity plate, use the accompanying formula to determine the maximum number of people your boat can safely carry in calm weather.

The length of your vessel is measured in a straight line from the foremost part of the vessel to the aftermost part of the vessel, parallel to the centerline, exclusive of sheer. Bowsprits, bumpkins, rudders, outboard motors, brackets, and similar fittings are not included in the measurement.

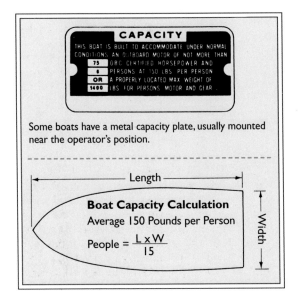

Some boats have a metal capacity plate, usually mounted near the operator's position.

Boat Capacity Calculation
Average 150 Pounds per Person

$$\text{People} = \frac{L \times W}{15}$$

Float Plan

File a float plan. Tell someone where you are going and when you plan to return. Tell them what your boat looks like and other information that will make identifying it easier should the need arise. Print a copy of the float plan from the Coast Guard website (www.uscgboating. org/safety/float_planning.aspx), fill it out, and leave it with a reliable person who can be depended upon to notify the Coast Guard, or another rescue organization, should you not return as scheduled. Do not, however, file float plans with the Coast Guard.

A PDF version of this form can be downloaded from the U.S. Coast Guard website.

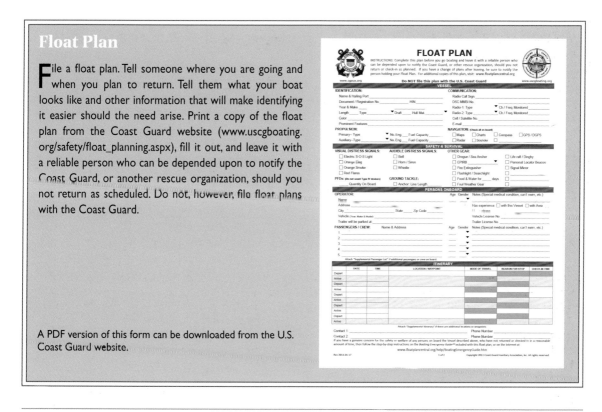

PERSONAL WATERCRAFT

All personal watercraft are officially considered powerboats by the U.S. Coast Guard. No matter how simple they are to ride, under the law, they have the same requirements for registration and regulation, and come under the same laws as other powerboats. Technically, personal watercraft are termed "Class A Inboard Boats" (boats less than 16 feet in length) by the U.S. Coast Guard.

What makes personal watercraft different from other boats on the water? The main difference is the innovative jet-drive propulsion system. With this drive system, a personal watercraft does not have an exposed propeller like most powerboats on the water today. Personal watercraft are smaller boats powered by an inboard engine and a jet-pump mechanism—but they are still boats. Their capabilities and limitations are a little bit different from other boats on the water. They can operate in shallower water and are quickly and easily maneuvered. They can accelerate quickly, but they may be more affected by waves, turbulence, and obstructions than larger craft.

There are several types of personal watercraft on the market. They vary in performance, stability, and the amount of skill necessary to operate them. Some are ridden in a sitting position, while others are ridden while kneeling or standing. Some have the capacity for one person, while others can carry up to three persons. One thing all personal watercraft have in common is that they are designed to allow the operator to fall safely overboard and reboard the boat with little risk if safety guidelines are followed. This reduced risk is because the jet-propulsion system in personal watercraft replaces the rudder and propeller on the outside of the hull.

The jet drive used in a personal watercraft is somewhat similar to the jet drive on modern aircraft. The unit is pushed through the water by the action of a jet pump driven by the engine. To give you an idea of how the jet drive in your personal watercraft works, think about a balloon. Just as the air exiting a released balloon pushes the balloon in the opposite direction around the room,

Stern • Rear of a Vessel   Steering Nozzle

Jet Pump Intake Grate   Impeller   Drive Shaft

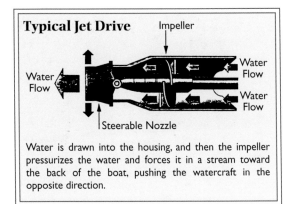

Typical Jet Drive   Impeller

Water Flow

Water Flow

Water Flow

Steerable Nozzle

Water is drawn into the housing, and then the impeller pressurizes the water and forces it in a stream toward the back of the boat, pushing the watercraft in the opposite direction.

the water leaving the jet pump pushes the personal watercraft through the water.

The pump works by drawing water into the housing ahead of the impeller. The impeller (a type of precision propeller contained within the housing) pressurizes the water and forces it in a stream toward the back of the personal watercraft. The force of the exiting water pushes the boat in the opposite direction.

Although you will not have to worry about hurting yourself from an exposed propeller, there are some

precautions you should take with the jet pump on your personal watercraft:

- Keep your hands and feet, as well as hair and clothing, away from the pump intake.

- When checking the pump intake for possible obstructions, make sure the engine is off.

- Don't operate your boat in shallow water (less than 24 inches deep).

- Anything stirred up from the bottom, such as sand or vegetation, can be sucked into the jet pump and damage your personal watercraft, as well as possibly injuring someone if particles are expelled out of the pump.

Most personal watercraft have a steerable nozzle at the rear of the pump housing that is controlled by the

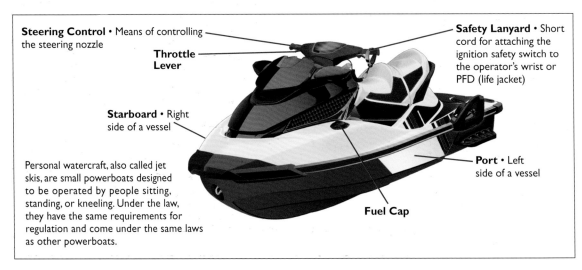

Steering Control • Means of controlling the steering nozzle

Throttle Lever

Safety Lanyard • Short cord for attaching the ignition safety switch to the operator's wrist or PFD (life jacket)

Starboard • Right side of a vessel

Port • Left side of a vessel

Personal watercraft, also called jet skis, are small powerboats designed to be operated by people sitting, standing, or kneeling. Under the law, they have the same requirements for regulation and come under the same laws as other powerboats.

Fuel Cap

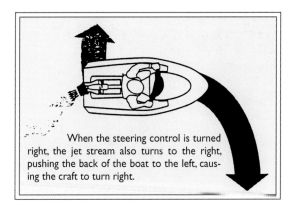

When the steering control is turned right, the jet stream also turns to the right, pushing the back of the boat to the left, causing the craft to turn right.

handlebars. The steering control directs the stream of water to the left or right. When the steering control is turned to the right, the steerable nozzle also turns to the right. As throttle is applied, the force of the water stream, pointed right, then pushes the back of the boat to the left, which causes the craft to turn to the right.

For safety purposes, the most important thing to remember about steering is that you must have power to the pump in order to maintain steering control. If you allow the engine to return to idle or shut off during a turn, the craft will continue in the same direction as it was moving at the point the power was cut, regardless of the steering input from the operator.

Reverse is available on some types of personal watercraft. This is accomplished by a clamshell-type device that moves over the directional nozzle and reverses the water flow, allowing the personal watercraft to "back up." This mechanism is not a brake and should not be regarded as such.

If you take a spill, most personal watercraft have one of the following options:

- The engine will run at idle speed while the boat circles slowly so that the operator can board as it circles past. It is important that the idling speed be properly set.

- An engine-stop lanyard is attached to the operator's wrist or personal flotation device and shuts off the engine when the operator falls off. For this reason, it is essential that the lanyard is always properly attached to the watercraft and the operator.

Swim to your personal watercraft, reboard carefully, reattach the lanyard (if applicable), restart your engine, and continue your ride. If the watercraft has turned upside down, follow the instructions in your owner's manual and turn the watercraft upright. If your personal watercraft has stalled or will not restart, do not attempt to swim to shore. Stay with your vessel and continue to wear your personal flotation device.

The Yamaha WaveRunner VX Deluxe will seat one to three persons. This WaveRunner weighs 681 pounds, has a fuel capacity of 18½ gallons, and is powered by a four-cylinder, four-stroke Yamaha engine. It is a good choice for a multiuse personal watercraft.

All personal watercraft (PWCs) are inboard-powered boats and fall under the same Coast Guard rules and regulations as other powerboats. In addition to recreational use, PWCs have proven effective in rescue operations.

Section Eight
ARCHERY AND BOWHUNTING

TYPES OF BOWS

Archery and bowhunting as sports today are practiced in a variety of ways. There are archers who prefer to shoot at conventional targets; roving archers who ramble through woodlands testing their skill on tree stumps and other natural targets; and field archers who roam a course shooting at targets that simulate hunting conditions. Then there are bowhunters, some of whom have taken every game animal from the groundhog to the bull elephant with well-placed arrows.

An interesting offshoot of bowhunting is bowfishing, in which a harpoon-type rig is used to shoot coarse fish.

Like the hunter who uses various types of guns designed for different species of game, the bowhunter also uses various types of bows according to his sport. While there are differences among bows—some are designed for championship performance on the target range, others for plinking and roving, and still others for hunting big-game animals—foremost to remember

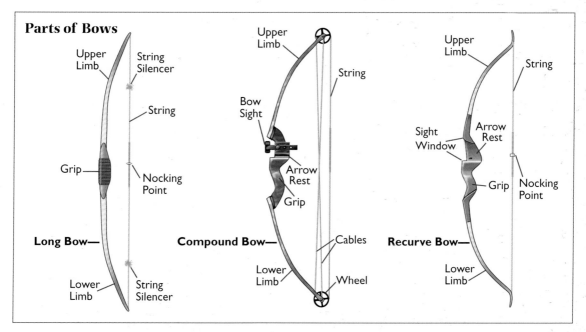

Parts of Bows

Long Bow— : Upper Limb, String Silencer, String, Grip, Nocking Point, Lower Limb, String Silencer

Compound Bow— : Upper Limb, String, Bow Sight, Arrow Rest, Grip, Cables, Lower Limb, Wheel

Recurve Bow— : Upper Limb, String, Sight Window, Arrow Rest, Grip, Nocking Point, Lower Limb

when purchasing any bow is its draw or pull weight, that is, the amount of strength required to pull the string back to full draw. "Overbowing" is the cardinal sin of the beginner.

Compound Bows

The acceptance of compound bows—especially for hunting deer and other good-size game—has been so pronounced that some manufacturers make no other type or else make only a few recurve models. This newest concept in archery was invented by H. W. Allen of Billings, Missouri, and most compounds are manufactured under license from him. A compound bow looks a bit strange but is simple in operation. Attached to its relatively short, stout limbs is a small pulley system. A conventional bowstring is connected to two strands of cable that run over the wheels—an idler pulley, plus an eccentric pulley at each end of the limbs—in the manner of a block and tackle. This device solves bow-weight problems, vastly increases the power and accuracy of an arrow, and eases the draw and release.

To understand some of the reasons this type of bow is so popular, consider how energy is applied in a firearm. A rifle produces greater bullet velocity than a handgun because the rifle's longer barrel applies gas pressure for a longer distance, thus increasing the foot-pounds of energy exerted on the projectile. The eccentric pulleys on a compound's limb tips accomplish the same thing by applying maximum pull weight for a greater number of inches. With an ordinary recurve bow, the pressure decreases steadily from the instant of release as the bowstring moves forward. With a compound, the peak pull-weight poundage is about at mid-draw. Thus, as the bowstring moves forward, the pressure increases to a peak before decreasing. This substantially raises the foot-pounds of energy applied to the arrow.

Also, with a conventional bow the release pressure must overcome the inertia not only of the arrow but also of the bowstring and the moving part of each limb. In a compound bow, limb-tip travel is reduced from about 8 to 3 inches and inertia is greatly reduced. In a conventional bow with a 50-pound pull weight, 50 pounds must propel the weight of the limbs 8 inches while also propelling the arrow and center of the string 20 inches to the string-rest position. With the pulleys and three strands (bowstring plus two strands of cable), the same pull results in three times the power—150 pounds.

Due to the action of the eccentric pulleys, the pull weight reaches a maximum and then relaxes somewhat—

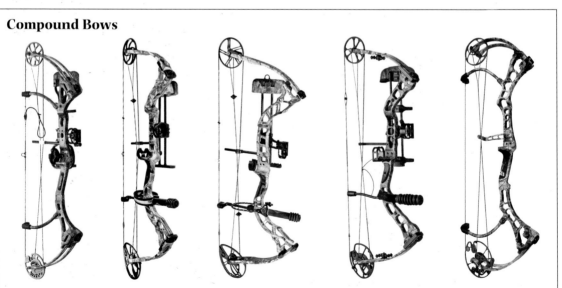

Compound Bows

Typical compound bows (*from left*): Bear Siren RTH (designed for women bowhunters), BowTech Diamond Outlaw, RedHead Blackout, Quest by G5 Torrent, and Bear Carnage. In a compound bow, a pulley system, similar to a block and tackle, is attached to the limb. The system solves weight problems, increases arrow power and accuracy, and eases draw and release. Most modern compound bows will launch arrows up to 345 feet per second.

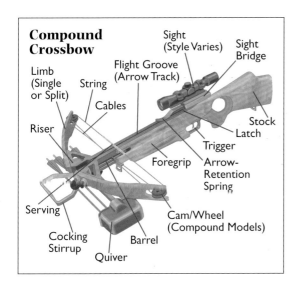

Compound Crossbow

Limb (Single or Split)
String
Cables
Riser
Serving
Cocking Stirrup
Quiver
Barrel
Foregrip
Flight Groove (Arrow Track)
Sight (Style Varies)
Sight Bridge
Stock
Latch
Trigger
Arrow-Retention Spring
Cam/Wheel (Compound Models)

eases off—before full draw is reached. This reduces finger strain and muscle fatigue at full draw, making a compound bow easier to shoot well. The same principle also permits the use of lighter arrows. A compound with a 50-pound peak setting will hold at full draw at approximately 40 pounds, so an arrow spined for a 40-pound pull is about right. (Manufacturers include arrow-matching instructions with their bows, and these instructions should be

Typical modern crossbows are the StrykeZone 350 (*top*) and the Parker Gale Force (*bottom*). Both are capable of launching bolts (arrows) up to 350 feet per second. Most crossbows are extremely accurate, weigh less than 7 pounds, and use scope sights.

followed.) The lighter arrows, released in the compound manner, have a flatter trajectory—a bonus advantage.

In many compound bows, draw lengths can be adjusted somewhat, and peak weight can be adjusted within a 10-pound range. Target compounds are usually 56 to 58 inches long. Hunting models generally range from 38 to 50 inches, and bows to be used for both purposes are about 50 inches long. The weight of these bows ranges from about 3½ to 4¼ pounds. They're made in either a one-piece style or in the takedown style. The cables are steel. The handle risers may be magnesium or hardwood. In top-quality bows, the limbs are laminated wood and fiberglass. Less expensive models may be solid fiberglass. Even those, however, are more costly than high-quality bows of conventional design.

▨ Crossbows

The basic design of the crossbow is centuries old, but a major change has been made in recent years. There are now recurve crossbows and compound crossbows that incorporate the pulley system of the conventional compound bow. Older crossbows were impossible to draw manually and employed a crank for cocking them. The modern compound crossbow, however, has draw weights up to 175 pounds and can be drawn by hand. It has either a stirrup or bipod stand at the front end. The archer plants his feet on this and pulls the bowstring up into the cocking position.

Nearly all modern crossbows have many features in common: they have shoulder stocks, mechanical

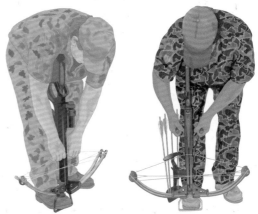

As draw weights for modern crossbows have become heavier, the need for cocking aids has become more important. Although it is still possible to cock a crossbow manually (*left*), bowhunters are advised to use cocking devices (*right*).

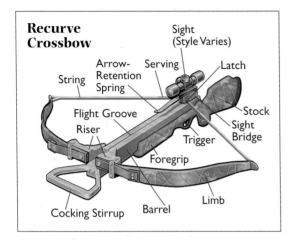

Recurve Crossbow

Sight (Style Varies)

Arrow-Retention Spring

Serving

Latch

String

Flight Groove

Riser

Trigger

Foregrip

Stock

Sight Bridge

Cocking Stirrup

Barrel

Limb

The Bear Super Kodiak recurve bow (*left*) will cast an arrow at greater speeds with less draw weight than older models. The Montana Longbow (*right*) is for archers who enjoy the ancient and classic style of a straight-limbed bow.

"trigger" releases, and telescopic and electronic sights. Modern crossbows will shoot a bolt (arrow) at speeds up to 350 feet per second. Crossbows are also drawn and cocked in advance. They are easier to master than conventional bows because all functions are mechanical.

Recurve Bows and Straight Bows

Conventional bows are of two basic types—straight or long bow and recurve. The straight bow, as its name implies, has straight limbs. Such bows were once standard. Today, few are sold, but there are archers who enjoy the ancient and classic style, and some of these people make their own straight bows. The limbs of a recurve bow curve back, and then, near the tips, curve forward.

The modern recurve bow is popular because it casts an arrow at greater speed with less draw weight than older styles. A relatively short recurve bow has excellent cast and is also maneuverable in brush, so models measuring 50 to 60 inches are popular for hunting. Longer bows—some of them 64 to 70 inches—are more stable, easier to draw, and smoother to release, so long models are usually preferred for target shooting. A bow for both purposes will have a compromise length.

Wood alone is still used in making some bows, primarily inexpensive models. Lemon and hickory are the most common woods. Hickory withstands cold better than lemonwood, but neither material produces the best cast. Various metals (especially tubular aluminum) have also been used by bowyers. Aluminum bows are unaffected by temperature changes, but, again, the cast is poor. Solid fiberglass is also used. It's impervious to weather but lacks the shooting qualities of composite bows, which are now the most common. These are laminations of two or more different materials—metal, wood, fiberglass, and various synthetics. The laminated composite bows produce excellent cast and are, in general, better than any other type.

BOW SELECTION AND CARE

Draw Weight

For tournament shooting (as well as plinking), select a bow that you can easily bring to full draw and hold for 10 seconds without shaking unduly. A little tremor is all right, but if you are forcing yourself to hold the

bow at full draw, it is too heavy for you. The accompanying charts show recommended draw weights for men, women, and youngsters.

A hunter should use a bow with as much draw weight as he can shoot comfortably. This will give an

Draw Weight

This illustration shows why the compound bow is easy to hold at full draw and release smoothly. Peak draw weight is reached when the archer has drawn the bowstring only partway back. Weight then eases down as the string comes back to the let-off point, so less strength is needed to pull it back and hold it steady.

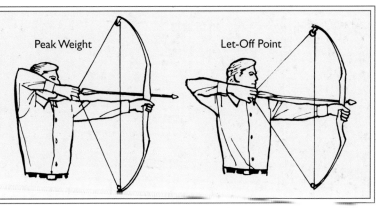

Peak Weight   Let-Off Point

arrow the speed needed for penetration on game. It will also produce a flatter trajectory—hence, more hits on game at unknown distances. Moreover, the faster an arrow arrives, the less chance a game animal has to "jump string" (dodge the arrow). For hunting deer, a recurve bow should have a minimum draw weight of

about 50 pounds, even if your state's game laws set a somewhat lower minimum, and a compound bow should have a minimum peak weight of 50 to 55 pounds. With a little practice, an average man can usually shoot a bow 5 or 10 pounds heavier than that with ease.

Of course, a lighter draw weight is adequate for smaller game, and a heavier draw weight is required for game larger than deer. With a compound bow, the draw weight is the peak weight—the amount you must pull through before the weight decreases at full draw. With a recurve bow, the draw weight is the number of pounds it takes to draw the bowstring back to 28 inches. For each inch of draw above or below 28 inches, add or subtract 2 pounds to determine the approximate weight of your personal draw length.

Recommended Draw Weights for Target Shooting (pounds)

	20 and under	20	25	30	35	40
Children 6–12	X	X				
Teen (Girl)		X	X			
Teen (Boy)		X	X	X		
Women			X	X	X	
Men				X	X	X

Recommended Draw Weights for Hunting (pounds)

	Rabbit and Squirrel	Coyote and Fox	Deer and Bear	Elk	Moose
30–40	X				
40–50	X	X			
50–60	X	X	X		
60–70	X	X	X	X	X
70–80	X	X	X	X	X

▪ Bow Handling

There are a few "don'ts" to remember when handling a bow. A bow at full draw, according to the manufacturer's specifications, is usually considered to be eight-tenths broken. For example, if you have a bow that is designed for 30-inch arrows and pulls 50 pounds at full draw, at that particular point it is eight-tenths broken. If you draw the bow past the 30-inch mark, you will subject it to serious stress that could cause it to break.

Another way to shatter a bow is to pull to full draw without an arrow and release the string. Under no circumstances should you release a bowstring without an arrow in the bow or attempt to overdraw the bow.

Quality bows can also be broken or have limbs twisted by incorrect stringing techniques. String a bow carefully and you'll have it for years. Perhaps the most efficient way to string a bow is with a bow stringer, a

How to String a Recurve Bow

Left: A bow stringer places identical stress on both limbs. Slip leather pockets over the bow tips, place your foot over the center of the cord, and pull up. The bowstring will slip into the nock. **Center:** Lacking a bow stringer, one way to string a bow is to brace the tip against your instep, holding the bow as shown, and flex it by applying opposite pressure with each hand. Then, slide the bowstring into the nock. **Right:** The third method of stringing a bow is to insert your right leg between the string and bow, hooking the tip over your shoe, and use your thigh as a fulcrum to flex the bow as you slip the string into the nock.

device designed to place identical stress on both limbs as in actual shooting. It also eliminates the possibility of the bow accidentally jumping out of your hands and causing injury to yourself or bystanders. The bow stringer is a stout length of nylon cord with leather pockets fitted at both ends that are slipped over the bow tips. By placing your foot over the center of the cord, the bow is readily raised and the limbs bent, permitting the string to be slipped into the nock. To prevent the bowstring from slipping off the opposite nock when stringing, place an elastic band or bow-tip protector over the lower nock and secure the string in place.

There are special bow stringers available for compound bows, but restringing a compound bow, especially if the cables have come off the wheels, is usually a job for an archery pro shop.

Without the assistance of a bow stringer, there are two acceptable ways to string your bow (shown in the accompanying illustrations).

Once the bow has been strung, brace height is the distance from the bowstring to the deepest cut in the handle on the face of the bow, below the arrow shelf. Proper brace height for a particular bow is given in the manufacturer's specifications, but this is not a rigid figure, and by altering it slightly some archers find that they shoot better. Brace height can be altered by twisting the bowstring to shorten it or by untwisting it to lengthen it. However, care should be taken not to twist the string excessively, for this will damage it and ultimately the bow.

The proper brace height for your bow depends entirely on your shooting style and the conditions under which you are shooting. There is no brace height that will give you maximum performance every time. For example, as your bow "warms up" during a sustained shooting session, the string will have a tendency to stretch. Conversely, after a period of idleness, the string will return to its original length. For this reason, it is important that you "tune" your bowstring before and during every shooting session. Proper brace height for your bow and your individual shooting style will give you the least amount of wrist slap, string noise, and vibration, and an arrow that does not wobble in flight.

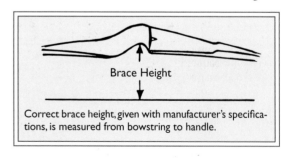

Correct brace height, given with manufacturer's specifications, is measured from bowstring to handle.

■ Bow Care

When not shooting a recurve bow, always keep your bow unstrung and hang it vertically or lay it across pegs supporting both limbs. Keep your bow in a case when transporting it to protect it from damage. When using a bow during rain or snow, coat it generously with high-grade automobile or furniture wax to protect its finish, and wipe it dry after a day afield in bad weather. Prior to sustained periods of storage, apply a generous coat of wax to protect the bow's finish. In cold weather, flex the bow several times to warm it up before shooting.

Another important consideration is the nocking point that is added to the bowstring serving. A nocking point is nothing more than a small piece of tape attached to the bowstring at right angles to the bow to prevent the arrow from slipping up and down or off the bowstring. It aids in consistent shooting. To locate the nocking point, place an arrow on the bowstring as you would when actually shooting the bow, and add the nocking point above, below, or on both sides of the arrow on the string serving. This is essential for the bowhunter, who does not have time to position his arrow correctly on the string when he sights game. With a nocking point, he can quickly feel and place his arrow in the exact position every time.

Most bows manufactured today are weighed in at a given draw length. For example, a bow will be marked 55 pounds at 28 inches. This simply means that manufacturer has weighed the bow when it has been drawn back to 28 inches, the standard length of most arrows. But if the bow is drawn less than or more than 28 inches, its pull decreases and increases accordingly. If you use a 28-inch arrow and desire a 55-pound bow, then the bow marked 55 pounds at 28 inches is for you. On the other hand, if you draw a 26-inch arrow, a bow measured and weighed for a 28-inch draw will lose 2 pounds per inch. Hence, despite the fact that the bow is marked 55 pounds, at your 26-inch draw it will only pull some 51 pounds. Conversely, if you use a 29-inch arrow, the pull will be increased by 2 pounds to 57 pounds.

Proper arrow measurement for your individual requirements varies greatly with every archer. Proper arrow-measurement techniques are shown in the accompanying illustrations.

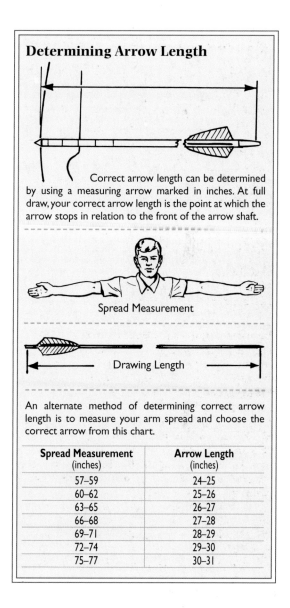

Determining Arrow Length

Correct arrow length can be determined by using a measuring arrow marked in inches. At full draw, your correct arrow length is the point at which the arrow stops in relation to the front of the arrow shaft.

Spread Measurement

Drawing Length

An alternate method of determining correct arrow length is to measure your arm spread and choose the correct arrow from this chart.

Spread Measurement (inches)	Arrow Length (inches)
57–59	24–25
60–62	25–26
63–65	26–27
66–68	27–28
69–71	28–29
72–74	29–30
75–77	30–31

ARROWS

The single most important piece of archer's equipment is the arrow. Any bow of a reputed manufacturer will probably perform well, but not so with an arrow. Purchase a bow within your price range, but under no circumstances should you buy the least expensive arrows.

Matched arrows are a set of six, eight, or one dozen, absolutely straight and of identical length. Each is perfectly round and made of the same material. They are fletched exactly alike, and all balance at the same point. All are of equal weight and have the same spine (stiffness) for your particular bow.

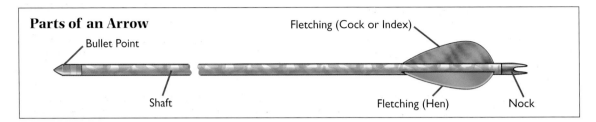

Parts of an Arrow

Bullet Point

Fletching (Cock or Index)

Shaft

Fletching (Hen)

Nock

The parts of an arrow are shown in the accompanying illustration. The arrow is composed of a shaft, nock, fletching, and point. Fiberglass, graphite, and aluminum arrow shafts are beginning to replace the traditional wood in popularity.

Wood arrow shafts come in several varieties. The arrow constructed of a single piece of wood is termed the "self" arrow. The "footed" arrow is a self arrow with a forward segment that has a section of extreme hard wood carefully spliced into it. This design fortifies the foreshaft against weakening and breakage. The diameter of a wood arrow shaft is usually $\frac{9}{32}$ inch, $\frac{5}{16}$ inch, or $\frac{11}{32}$ inch, depending on the draw weight of your bow. Light women's and children's bows ordinarily use the $\frac{9}{32}$-inch shaft. Men's target shafts are $\frac{5}{16}$ inch in diameter. Most hunting arrows constructed of wood are $\frac{11}{32}$ inch in diameter.

The nock is a simple notch in the end of the arrow, or a specially designed plastic contrivance that holds the arrow on the bowstring. It should be deep enough to keep the arrow on the string and wide enough to permit an easy fit on the string without crowding. In former years, nocks were made of such items as horn and fiber, but today cellulose plastic that is easily die-cast and as tough as nails is common nock material. It is readily fitted to the arrow shaft by means of an 11-degree tapered hole inside the nock itself. The nock end of the shaft is tapered and with cellulose cement it is quickly and efficiently glued to the shaft.

Plastic nocks are available in a wide variety of colors and sizes. To replace them, burn them off with a match. The plastic nock burns quickly without damaging the wood. Many plastic nocks contain a small knob

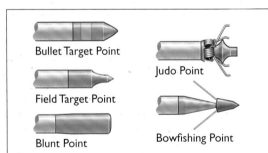

Bullet Target Point

Field Target Point

Blunt Point

Judo Point

Bowfishing Point

The **bullet** and **field target points** are designed to be shot into paper, foam, or grass targets. These points can also be matched to the weight of big-game broadheads that a hunter plans to use during hunting season. **Judo points** are for field practice or while roving under simulated hunting conditions. Springs on the arrow point prevent the arrow from digging into the ground. **Blunt points** are for small-game animals such as rabbits and squirrels, and kill by shock. Most are made from rubber or plastic. **Bowfishing points** are designed to penetrate scales of rough fish, such as carp and gar. Most have retractable barbs to allow removal from the fish.

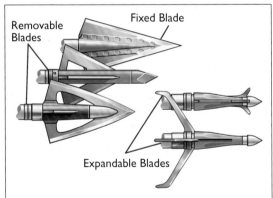

Removable Blades

Fixed Blade

Expandable Blades

Fixed blades are a traditional design for big game. Some are glued onto the arrow shaft and some have screw ferrules to allow sharpening and changing of broadhead weights to match your equipment. **Removable blades** are designed so that the blades can be replaced on the ferrule. There is no need to discard the broadhead if only the blades are damaged. **Expandable blades** retract close to the ferrule before the shot. Upon impact, the blades expand to expose cutting edges. They are recommended for bows rated 50 pounds or more because more mechanical heads require additional energy to open upon penetration. A broadhead wrench is a necessary tool to safely loosen and tighten broadheads.

or marker that is aligned with the cock feather to permit an archer easy reference by feel during rapid shooting. With this marker reference, the archer simply feels for the eruption on the nock and immediately knows the cock feather is in line.

The fletching of feathers on the arrow keeps it stable in flight. "Fletcher" is the old English name for a man who attaches feathers to an arrow; hence, arrow feathers are known by that term. Most feathers are added to the arrow shaft somewhere between ¼ inch and ½ inch below the nock. The size of the feathers is directly proportional to the arrowhead or point used. In target shooting, some use a feather of some 2½ inches in length and not more than ½ inch in height at any given point. Hunting arrows that contain large and heavy broadhead blades have a fletching of some 4 to 6 inches in length.

Standard fletching consists of three individual feathers spaced 120 degrees apart. The cock feather, or odd-colored feather, is the one positioned at right angles to the bow. The odd color tells the archer how to place the arrow to the bow. In addition to the cock feather, there is usually a brace of hen or identically colored feathers. Feathers on one arrow are mainly of turkey right and left wing feathers. It makes no difference which feather is used, right or left, but in constructing a matched set of arrows either all rights or all lefts are used.

Today, many bowhunters prefer all feathers to be the same color. Solid orange, white, or yellow are most often used because they are more easily detected in flight in the early dawn or twilight hours.

There are many methods of arrow fletching. The feathers can be added to the shaft in a straight line, but most archers prefer to add them to the shaft in a slight spiral, as spiral fletching allows the arrow to rotate in flight, creating more stability. Many archers today also prefer four and six fletched arrow shafts—again, for better stability. The basic arrow in wide use today is the three-feather fletched version.

The prime concern with all fletching, however, is uniformity: the feathers must be all right or all left wing, of uniform equal thickness, and carefully fletched to the arrow. Most feathers are not more than ½ inch high at any given point. A feather of greater height retards the flight. On the other hand, an arrow with feathers that are too low will vastly reduce stability and cause wobbling in flight.

In former years, swan and goose wing quills were in common use, and today there are some plastic feathers, but turkey feathers still dominate the field. At one time, arrow feathers were cut to length and attached to the

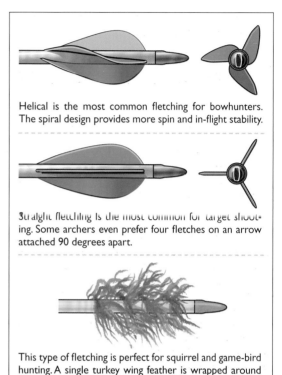

Helical is the most common fletching for bowhunters. The spiral design provides more spin and in-flight stability.

Straight fletching is the most common for target shooting. Some archers even prefer four fletches on an arrow attached 90 degrees apart.

This type of fletching is perfect for squirrel and game-bird hunting. A single turkey wing feather is wrapped around the arrow shaft, glued in place, and picked apart to form a bristlelike appearance. Flu-flu arrows do not fly far because of increased resistance to oversize fletching.

shaft by tying them with sinew, but today a wide variety of fletching jigs perform this task. The feather is "base ground" before it is applied to the shaft. Base grinding means that the quill itself is ground until a mere wisp remains to hold the feather to the quill itself. The feathers are glued to the shaft by means of cellulose cement. A feather burner burns the feather to shape once it is attached to the arrow.

A reliable substitute for feathers is plastic fletching, often called vanes. Vanes are made of soft plastic or vinyl and available in many colors and sizes. Vanes are easily glued onto arrows of any material.

Woods used for the construction of arrow shafts over the years included Norway pine, Douglas fir, birch, and Port Orford cedar. Port Orford cedar comes from the West Coast forests in the United States and from the mountain region north of Palestine, where it is known as the cedars of Lebanon. Port Orford cedar has an extremely straight grain and provides the finest spine of any wood material.

All woods have a tendency to warp, however; hence, the introduction of other materials. Aluminum provides a uniformity that wood cannot equal and it is unaffected by wide temperature changes. Aluminum arrows today are selected by tournament archers for their uniformity and outstanding precision performance.

While some bowhunters choose aluminum shafts for hunting, most prefer the fiberglass shaft that appeared after World War II. The development of quality fiberglass and tubular carbon-fiber arrows followed. Aluminum tends to be too noisy afield and is invariably rendered useless once it strikes an animal, tree, or rock. The fiberglass and carbon arrow shafts lack these drawbacks. They are unaffected by temperature changes, can be produced to exacting specifications, and will not warp or bend out of shape, the most common fault of other materials. The rugged fiberglass and carbon arrows are capable of deep penetration in game animals and are thus most widely used by bowhunters throughout the world.

Although fiberglass and carbon arrows cost about twice as much as high-grade wooden arrows, their quality and durability make them a good buy for many archers. Their shafts are tubular. The fiberglass is wrapped around a metal mandrel that is removed after construction. These arrows are made in suitable sizes for bow weight and draw length. Some glass hunting arrows are available with inserts that allow the use of either broadheads or field points on the same shaft. Solid fiberglass arrows are preferred for bowfishing.

A matched set of arrows must be carefully adjusted in weight and spine to the individual bow and carefully matched in length to your individual draw length. Spine or "stiffness" of an arrow is of utmost importance. An arrow with too soft a spine tends to shoot to the right of the point of aim. Conversely, too stiff a spine deflects the arrow to the left of the point of aim. The spining of arrows is difficult to comprehend. Formerly, archers merely flexed arrow shafts in their hands to determine stiffness. Today, the various arrow-shaft manufacturers have developed formulas that quickly and easily determine arrow spine.

When an arrow is released from a bow, the weight of the bowstring and the friction against the bow handle bend the arrow slightly to the right. As the string moves forward, it violently draws the arrow shaft to the left. As the arrow leaves the string, the shaft recovers stability by straightening, or by bending toward the right, until it has fully corrected itself and assumed a straight course. An arrow must be spined exactly to the individual bow weight if it is to bend uniformly and recover quickly. Too

weak a spine will send the arrow to the right; too stiff a spine will send it to the left.

The weight of individual shafts is important. Although the exact weight of the arrows is not critical, every arrow in a matched set must weigh within a few grains of the others for uniform shooting. The lightest arrows possible are best for tournament shooting, while slightly heavier shafts are more suitable for field and hunting.

The method for determining the correct arrow length for individual requirements was addressed in the Bow Care section. When purchasing arrows, you must know your proper arrow length and obtain a complete set that is matched in weight and spine to your individual bow.

Various types of arrows draw to different lengths. The target arrow with its target point is usually drawn to the end of the pile. Field and broadhead-blade points, however, can be added to an arrow shaft by increasing the shaft length by ¾ inch. This is usually done to prevent the bowhunter with a razor-sharp broadhead blade from mistakenly overdrawing.

Most quality wood, aluminum, graphite, and fiberglass arrows in use today have either tapered ends or some type of insert for the attachment of arrow points. Thus, an archer who purchases one set of matched arrows can quickly add field points to his shaft (which would weigh the same as the broadhead he planned to use during the hunting season) for between-season field practice on the target butt. When hunting seasons open, it is simple to remove the field points and add broadhead blades. Many matched field-hunting arrow sets are often fitted with six arrows using field points and six fitted with broadhead blades. Passing the point over an open flame, being careful not to burn the shaft itself, will remove it easily from the shaft.

Among the many arrow types designed for special purposes, there are only a few the archer should know. These are the target arrow, field or roving arrow, hunting arrow, and flu-flu and fish arrows.

Most high-quality target arrows are now made of lightweight aluminum alloy. They are fletched with small feathers and have light target points. These arrows are intended for shooting into a straw-type mat or target butt.

The field, roving, and hunting arrows are basically the same. They are usually more ruggedly constructed than the target arrow, though of similar materials to withstand great abuse. They are heavier and contain larger fletching to permit more stability in flight. The roving or field arrow uses a point that should weigh the same as the broadhead blade the hunter anticipates using during the hunting season. The field or roving arrow, then, is primarily a practice arrow for the bowhunter since it weighs exactly the same as the hunting arrow. Roving or field arrows become hunting arrows merely by changing the points to broadheads and vice versa.

The flu-flu arrow is used for hunting or wing shooting where the archer is required to shoot his arrow skyward. The flu-flu arrow has abnormally high fletching to retard its flight. The high feathers prevent the arrow from traveling more than 30 to 50 yards. The point is usually a blunt or small-game type and is ideal where small-game and especially squirrel hunting are legal with the bow and arrow. Flu-flus are also used by enterprising bird hunters who have the courage to attempt wing shooting for upland game birds. Blunt points are far superior to all other types of points for small-game hunting. Broadhead blades used so efficiently by bowhunters on big-game animals will not stop the small game birds and animals as well as the blunt. The blunt stuns the small bird or animal, allowing the archer quick recovery of his quarry.

Another arrow type in wide use today is the fish or harpoon arrow. Bowfishing for coarse fish, such as carp and suckers, is a challenging sport. The fish arrow must be heavy in order to penetrate the water's depths; hence, heavy, solid fiberglass arrows are appropriate. The conventional turkey feathers must also be replaced, and today rubber-type arrow fletching appears on most fishing arrows. The fish arrow contains a removable barbed fish point. For further details on this sport, see the Bowfishing section.

All arrows require some care in use and storage. Most arrows are best stored in the boxes they came in. Never stack wood arrows haphazardly in an inaccessible corner of the closet, as they will warp. Keeping arrows in a quiver is fine with fiberglass or aluminum, but wood arrows must be stored to avoid warpage.

During sustained periods of storage, watch arrow fletching carefully to prevent moth damage. It is also a good idea to lightly oil field, blunt, broadhead, and fish points. Wood arrow shafts should be waxed with a good-grade automobile wax before use in the field. Fiberglass and aluminum require no other care. In extremely damp or rainy weather, coat the arrow fletching with a silicote-based liquid or spray to keep it from becoming matted to the shaft.

BOWSTRINGS

One of the least expensive items in the archer's kit, yet one of the most important, is the bowstring. A string that is too long or constructed of fewer strands than required to sustain the pull weight can cause severe damage to a quality bow.

The bowstring is subjected to extreme wear at three points—the nocking position of the arrow and the nocking point at the two bow tips. A bowstring should be checked carefully prior to each shooting stint for any signs of fraying or excessive wear. At the slightest indication of wear, the string should be immediately replaced.

Through the years, bowstrings have been made from a wide variety of materials, including rawhide, sinew, linen or flax, hemp, fortisan (a synthetic rayon yarn), Dacron, and Kevlar. Dacron is most universally accepted by modern archers. Bowstrings are composed of a number of strands in accord with bow weight.

Inexpensive bowstrings used for children's lightweight target bows are made of hemp and have a single loop. The single loop string has the one advantage of being suited to any bow length since it can be tied to one nock of the bow at any length desired. However, quality bowstrings are made of top-grade Dacron, with double loops, and are manufactured to exact dimensions.

Although some archers make their own strings to suit their bows, top-grade bowstrings can be purchased so inexpensively today that it is hardly worth the time or effort required to make a string.

The double-loop Dacron bowstring is composed of a varied number of strands for varied pull weights and averages some 3 inches shorter than the bow for which it was constructed. Hence, the pull and length of the bow are important numbers to remember when purchasing bowstrings. Most quality bows manufactured today are marked with the draw weight at a particular arrow length, as well as its overall length.

For example, a bow marked 50 pounds at 28–60 inches simply means that it will draw 50 pounds at a 28-inch draw length and measures 60 inches in overall length. Therefore, when purchasing a bowstring for this bow, simply remember its draw weight of 50 pounds and the bow's overall length—60 inches. Manufacturers invariably build into the bowstring the necessary compensation for overall length, and the bowstring marked 60 inches is not actually 60 inches, but some 3 inches shorter.

A new bowstring has a tendency to stretch and can stretch almost an inch after hard use. Keep this point in mind, for after a day spent shooting with a new string it will have stretched enough to reduce the brace height of your bow. If you find the string has stretched to a point where your bow's brace height is too low, the bowstring can be shortened by merely twisting it several turns. However, be careful not to twist the string excessively or you could cause wear and damage to the string itself. Usually several turns is sufficient to bring the new string back to brace height.

After sustained periods of shooting, the bowstring should be rewaxed. Apply gently an additional layer of wax and briskly rub into the string with a piece of brown wrapping paper. The paper, quickly moved over the surface of the string, tends to melt the wax and permit it to penetrate into the individual strands.

To prevent excess wear to the string, a serving, consisting of cotton thread, is added to the string at both nocking points and where the arrow is fitted to the string. The serving at the arrow nock position is of such a length to cover the string where the arrow is fitted and where the archer places his fingertips. String serving, especially at the arrow nock position, takes severe wear. At any sign of fraying, the serving should be renewed with the aid of a string-serving tool.

It is of prime importance that every bowstring has an arrow nocking point to permit the arrow to be placed on the bowstring in exactly the same location every time and to prevent the arrow from sliding off, or up and down, the string.

Remember, however, that the nocking point should not be positioned on the bowstring until after the string has been used several times to eliminate all possible stretch. There are numerous commercially produced nocking points in use today, but a suitable nocking point can be quickly made by simply wrapping the nocking point location with a piece of tape or several turns of serving thread.

There are several other necessary items that can and should be fitted to the bowstring, especially when in the hunting field. The bowstring should be fitted with brush buttons and string silencers (see the Archery Accessories section). Brush buttons are fitted to the bowstring at the bow's nocking points to prevent brush and leaves from catching between the string and bow. String silencers, usually constructed of pieces of rubber and attached to the bowstring at the midpoint between the serving and nocking areas, are also added to eliminate excessive string noise that can spook game in the field.

In conclusion, remember that bowstrings are cheap insurance and can easily mean the difference between success and failure in the field or on the range. Always carry a few extra strings with you whenever you are shooting.

ARCHERY ACCESSORIES

■ Shooting Gloves

To prevent the string from irritating the drawing fingers and to assist in releasing it smoothly and without creep, some sort of leather protection is required. Fitted on the three fingers of the archer's drawing hand, this protection is available either as a three-finger shooting glove or a tab. Most shooting gloves are of the skeleton type, with leather finger stalls or tips that fit over the three drawing fingers. These are available in various sizes in either right- or left-handed models.

The shooting glove provides ample all-around protection to the archer's drawing hand and is widely accepted among archers in both the hunting and target fields. However, there is another group of archers who prefer the three-finger tab to the glove simply because they have better "feel" of the bowstring when using the tab.

The tab is cheaper than the glove. Constructed of cordovan leather, tabs are available to fit one or two fingers of the shooting hand. They are slotted to permit the arrow nock to pass through. The tab affords excellent protection for the balls of the fingers, but not for the inside of the fingers. In recent years, tabs have been made with finger separators. In any case, archers require some sort of finger protection for the bowstring drawing hand. The choice is up to the individual. You can also choose a mechanical release, which will allow you to pull, hold, and release the string more smoothly without chafing your fingers.

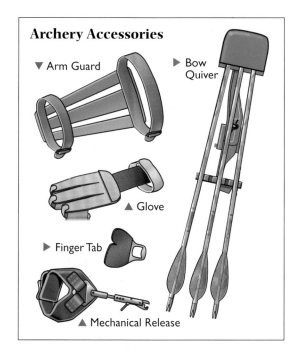

Archery Accessories

▼ Arm Guard

▶ Bow Quiver

▲ Glove

▶ Finger Tab

▲ Mechanical Release

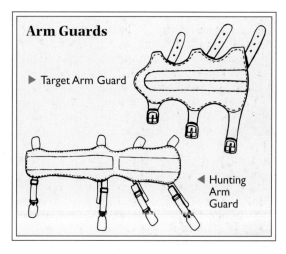

Arm Guards

▶ Target Arm Guard

◀ Hunting Arm Guard

■ Arm Guards

The next item of importance so essential for the archer is some sort of protection for the wrist and lower forearm of the bow arm. When a bowstring is released, it may strike the inside of the archer's forearm, and without some sort of protection for this tender portion of the anatomy, the arm can become severely and dangerously bruised.

The arm guard buckles or snaps around the wrist of the bow arm. It is usually made of cordovan leather, with a few steel stays sewed between the leather and lining for added protection.

■ Quivers

Aside from the shooting glove or tab and the arm guard, the archer needs something to carry his arrows afield or to the target range—a quiver. Quivers that hold anywhere from a half dozen to a few dozen arrows are available in many styles, each designed for a specific purpose.

The ground quiver, a metal stake with an attached metal ring, is stuck in the ground to hold arrows when shooting from a stationary position on the target field. The ground quiver is popular with target archers. Center-back and shoulder quivers are used by bowhunters. Belt, hip, and pocket quivers are used by both

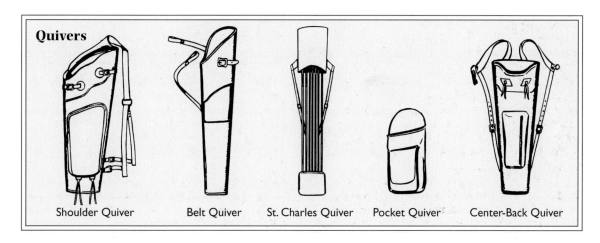

Quivers

Shoulder Quiver   Belt Quiver   St. Charles Quiver   Pocket Quiver   Center-Back Quiver

tournament and field archers. Most bowhunters have adopted the bow quiver, which attaches directly to the bow itself.

The shoulder quiver is the traditional bowhunter's quiver. It is available in either right- or left-handed models, permitting the archer to reach back with his bowstring hand, grasp the nock end of the arrow, and, with a forward swing, draw the arrow from the quiver. The only drawbacks to the shoulder quiver are that, in the hunting field, the arrows projecting from the quiver tend to catch on tree limbs or rattle freely and spook game.

The center-back quiver was developed to help eliminate the problem of arrows getting caught in brush. The quiver fits the center of the archer's back, the protruding arrows nesting neatly behind his head.

Used widely by target archers, belt and pocket quivers are smaller than back and shoulder models, holding at most a half-dozen arrows.

The bow quiver, attached directly to the bow, provides the fastest delivery and also ample protection for the arrows. Most quality quivers are equipped with some sort of metal shield to cover the broadhead blades. Without a shield to protect the blades, a bow quiver can be a dangerous piece of equipment with exposed razor-sharp broadheads. Bow quivers are constructed to hold four to six arrows; some hold as many as eight.

Bow Sights and Bow Scopes

Bow sights, especially bow scopes, are relative newcomers to archery. The early archer used no mechanical sighting aids—he aimed instinctively. The modern archer and bowhunter, however, has a wide variety of bow sights and bow scopes from which to choose. Archery tournaments are divided into two divisions, the instinctive and the freestyle. It is the freestyle group that uses the bow sight.

Bow sights and scopes are highly sophisticated, and many have micrometer windage and elevation adjustment knobs, prisms, and aperture inserts, as well as a variety of post sighting points for shooting at varied yardages.

It is interesting to note that both schools—freestyle and instinctive—have turned in equally creditable scores in the hunting field. The bow sight used for hunting is usually made with a number of sighting posts; each post is sighted for a given or known range for a particular bow.

Bow Sights and Bow Scopes

The Truglo Red-Dot Crossbow Sight has an 11-position brightness control, a three-dot reticule, and a see-through, flip-up lens cap.

The RedHead Kryptik Bow Sight is a typical modern lightweight three-pin bow-sight design with windage and elevation adjustments. Fiber-optic pins stand out brilliantly.

The Cobra Buckhead is a camouflaged bow sight with five fiber-optic adjustable pins for windage and elevation. It also features a rheostat light.

The Redfield Revenge is a modern crossbow scope with 1/4-MOA windage/elevation and a crossbow reticle with five aiming points. Nitrogen-filled, this scope is waterproof and fogproof.

Stabilizers

The torque stabilizer has become a standard and accepted innovation in the field of tournament or target archery, and has also gained popularity in the hunting field. The torque stabilizer does exactly what its name implies—it stabilizes the bow when the string is released. Miniature torque-stabilizing inserts are fitted into tourney bows to absorb the forward shock and thrust of the bowstring.

Torque stabilizers are fitted to the bow face just below the bow handle and vary in length according to the archer's preference. This stabilizing unit quickly dampens vibration. It further provides the tournament archer with additional weight for added stability, permitting a far more steady hold and smoother follow-through after the arrow has been released. But, above

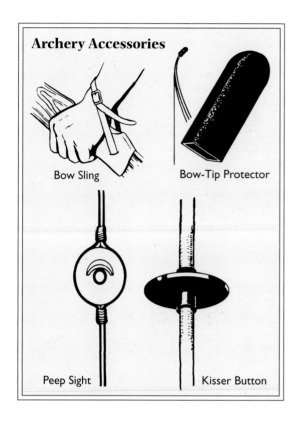

Archery Accessories

Bow Sling

Bow-Tip Protector

Peep Sight

Kisser Button

MECHANICAL RELEASE: This is a trigger device that releases the bowstring cleanly and exactly the same way every shot. There are a variety of designs, but all operate pretty much the same way. The archer holds the release in his string hand and clips it to his string. At full draw, he "pulls" a trigger, usually a button, and the string is released. His finger never touches the string.

CAMOUFLAGE: The sheen and sparkle of a highly polished bow can readily startle game. The glitter can be eliminated by the addition of some sort of camouflage, such as a cloth sock slipped over the limbs of the bow. Camouflage tape is also available, but if you use it remember to wax your bow well to prevent damage to the finish when the tape is removed. Nearly all hunting bows are available with a camouflage finish.

BOW STRINGER: The bow stringer is another important piece of equipment. A quality bow that is not strung properly will wear quickly and warp, eventually even break. However, the bow stringer eliminates this problem. Made of a stout length of nylon rope and a pair of leather bow-tip protectors, the stringer quickly, efficiently, and safely strings the bow. With compound bows and crossbows, stringing should only be done by an archery pro shop.

BOWSTRING NOCKING POINTS: These are added to the bowstring to permit positioning the arrow in the same spot each time and to prevent the arrow from slipping off the string when afield. A number of archery manufacturers produce varied nocking points at a nominal price.

BOW-TIP PROTECTORS: Made of soft rubber, the bow-tip protector prevents scuffing the bow when stringing, keeps bow tips in good condition, and holds the bowstring in place when stringing.

BOW SLING: Used primarily by tournament archers, the bow sling provides perfect balance and holds the bow in shooting position, giving the archer confidence that his bow cannot fall.

PEEP SIGHT: This is a disc device with a small hole in the center. It is mounted on the bowstring and used to help the shooter line up sights on his bow more accurately.

KISSER BUTTON: This device is used primarily by target archers to ensure consistency of draw. Attached to the

all, the stabilizer absorbs the bow's recoil energy and greatly assists the archer in achieving accuracy.

■ Other Equipment

BRUSH BUTTONS: Although not required by the target archer, the bowhunter and field archer should add brush buttons to their bowstrings to prevent snagging the bow in brush and undergrowth when afield. The brush button is made of soft rubber and is quickly added to the bowstring at both nocking points on the bow.

SILENCERS: Bowstring silencers are also a requisite for the bowhunter. Bowstrings have an uncanny ability to "twang" when released, which can quickly spook game. The string silencers, fitted to the bowstring midway between the string serving and the nocking points, reduce such noise. A simple pair of string silencers can be made by attaching a portion of a rubber band to the string. However, quality string silencers are available at a nominal price.

bowstring, it touches the archer's lip when at full draw to signal he is at proper draw.

ARCHERY TARGETS: Available in 24-inch, 36-inch, and 48-inch sizes, archery target mats are often made of Indian cord grass covered with burlap. Conventional "ringed" target faces, as well as animal faces, are available. Using a proper archery target is essential for the preservation of your arrows. Shooting quality arrows into a rock-studded field can quickly ruin them. On the other hand, broadhead hunting arrows should not be used when shooting at a conventional archery mat since a few well-placed broadheads can quickly destroy the target. A better choice would be compressed foam targets, which will withstand many hits from field points as well as broadheads.

HOW TO SHOOT

Shooting the modern bow and arrow, as with all other forms of shooting sports, requires patience and endless practice for the basic techniques required to strike a target consistently to become instinctive. No shooter can expect to pick up a trap or skeet gun for the first time and break 25 straight targets on the claybird layouts. Neither can the neophyte archer expect to place all his arrows in the gold or drop a deer as it approaches his stand in the twilight hours without acquiring the fundamentals of shooting: stance, nocking, drawing, aiming, release, and follow-through.

Stance

Proper stance is essential in archery. Shooting a bow and arrow differs from other forms of shooting in that considerable strength and effort are required. Hence,

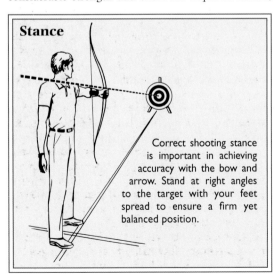

Stance

Correct shooting stance is important in achieving accuracy with the bow and arrow. Stand at right angles to the target with your feet spread to ensure a firm yet balanced position.

the shooting stance must not only be comfortable, but the feet must also be correctly positioned so the body is properly braced.

Stand with your feet about 15 inches apart and at right angles to the target. You must be comfortable, and if you feel more comfortable with a slightly wider stance, take it. But remember not to stand with your feet too close together since such a stance creates strain and invariably results in poor aiming techniques and sloppy shooting.

After finding the best shooting stance for yourself, remember it well and stick to it; do not vary the position. Consistency is the key to success.

Nocking

Nocking simply means placing the arrow on the bowstring. Foremost to remember is that the arrow must be fitted to the bowstring in exactly the same place each time; hence, the use of a string nocking point, which assures the archer of the correct position.

Before the introduction of center-shot bows and those with built-in arrow rests, the archer used his hands as an arrow rest, but this made for inconsistent shooting since he could not place his hand exactly in the same position every time. The arrow rest on most modern bows eliminates this age-old problem.

Once you have correctly positioned the string nocking point on the bowstring, you are ready to place (nock) the arrow. With the bow firmly, but not tightly, held in the left hand at the left side, grasp an arrow in the quiver with the thumb and forefinger of your right hand. (All instructions assume a right-handed archer.) With one motion, as you remove the arrow from the quiver, bring the bow to waist height in a horizontal position, and place the arrow across the bow. Center the arrow on the bowstring at the predetermined nocking point with

Nocking

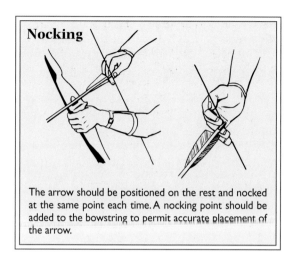

The arrow should be positioned on the rest and nocked at the same point each time. A nocking point should be added to the bowstring to permit accurate placement of the arrow.

the fingers of your right hand, holding the arrow firmly at the bow handle with the forefinger of your left hand. Place the first three fingers of your right hand on the bowstring, one finger above the arrow nock, the second two fingers below. You need not grasp the nock tightly.

◼ Drawing

Prior to starting the draw, cock your head toward the target, breathe deeply, and relax, bringing the bow

Drawing

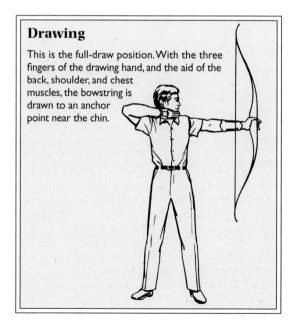

This is the full-draw position. With the three fingers of the drawing hand, and the aid of the back, shoulder, and chest muscles, the bowstring is drawn to an anchor point near the chin.

and fitted arrow into shooting position by extending your left arm forward with your elbow pointing slightly to the left and with the bow vertical or cocked slightly to the right. (The target and tournament archer prefers to keep his bow vertical; the bowhunter tends to cant it to the right.) Be certain that the bow hand, and especially the forearm, is not in the path of the bowstring; otherwise it could be struck as the arrow is released.

Now you are ready to draw back the bowstring to full-draw position. It is at this point that the beginner may encounter the problem of the arrow slipping from the arrow rest. This happens when the archer tries to apply pressure to the bowstring by curling his fingers around it, causing the string to roll to the left and the arrow to slip off the bow handle.

The bowstring should be grasped only with the pads of the three fingers of the drawing hand, with the hand, wrist, and forearm in a straight line. This way, the string will be rolled to the right and will keep the arrow on its shelf.

As you bring the bow to full draw, keep the elbow of the drawing arm at right angles to the body. Such a position will bring the muscles of the shoulder and upper back into play and make drawing the bow much easier. Remember to push with the left shoulder and pull with the right side of the body. The chest, shoulders, and back will do the work.

Bring the bowstring back to full draw to the position near the cheek or chin, being certain the string is anchored at the same point each time. Tournament archers invariably use the low anchor point with the bowstring hand resting just below the chin and the string touching the nose. On the other hand, the bowhunter likes to be closer to his line of sight and usually prefers the high anchor point with the second finger of the drawing hand anchored at the corner of the mouth. Some bowhunters anchor just below the eye as well. Again, the exact anchor point depends primarily on your individual preference and shooting style. But remember, once the anchor point has been established, do not vary it.

If you are a right-handed archer and you have established that your shooting eye is your right eye, then shoot with both eyes open. In all kinds of shooting, most top-notch shooters use both eyes. Closing one eye merely limits your vision. However, if your left eye is your shooting eye, learn to shoot left-handed.

Many tournament archers use a small rubber button, called a kisser, fitted to the bowstring to determine full draw. It is positioned on the string at the correct

Anchor

This is the low anchor position (*left*) and the high anchor position (*right*). The choice of position depends on individual preference.

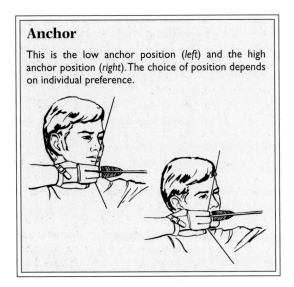

anchor point for the individual archer and centered between the lips. With the anchor point under the chin, the bow should be held vertical. The bowhunter, on the other hand, with his higher anchor point, tilts both his head and his bow.

■ Aiming

You are now at the full-draw position, relaxed, with the bow held firmly and the arrow resting snugly in the anchor position. You are now ready to aim.

There are three basic methods of aiming, each designed for a specific form of shooting. These include the bow-sight method, the point-of-aim, and the instinctive style.

The instinctive style is without doubt the oldest method of aiming a bow and arrow. It is extremely accurate and consistent up to a distance of 40 yards. At ranges of 20 to 25 yards, it is deadly. In instinctive aiming, your foremost attention is directed to the target while you see the arrow shaft indirectly. Concentrating on the target, your indirect vision automatically adjusts and compensates for elevation and windage. Foremost to remember is that everything must be done in exactly the same manner each time you draw, sight, and release an arrow.

Aiming Methods

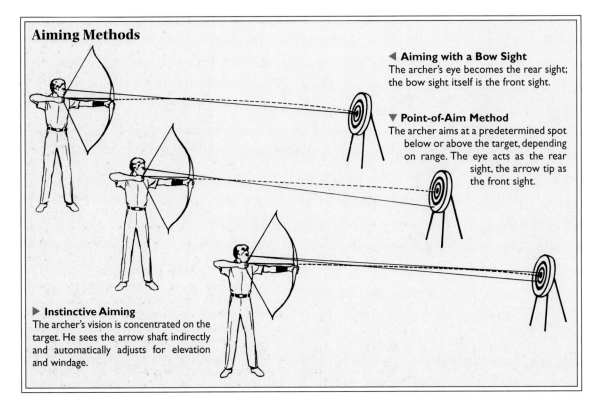

◀ Aiming with a Bow Sight
The archer's eye becomes the rear sight; the bow sight itself is the front sight.

▼ Point-of-Aim Method
The archer aims at a predetermined spot below or above the target, depending on range. The eye acts as the rear sight, the arrow tip as the front sight.

▶ Instinctive Aiming
The archer's vision is concentrated on the target. He sees the arrow shaft indirectly and automatically adjusts for elevation and windage.

Your anchor point must be constant; the arrow must be drawn to its exact full length each time and positioned exactly on the bowstring and on the arrow rest. Uniformity is the key. Instinctive shooting comes from practice and more practice, but once you begin using this method, you will be surprised at how swiftly you become proficient.

The second-most popular method, commonly used by target archers, is the point-of-aim method. As shown in the accompanying illustration, when using the point-of-aim method, the archer does not aim at the center of his target, but at a predetermined location below or above the target depending on range. Unlike instinctive shooting, the anchor point usually is located directly under the chin with the bowstring touching the lips and nose, the bow held in the vertical position.

With the point-of-aim method, the eye acts as the rear sight and the point of the arrow acts as the front sight. Through trial and error, the archer determines the exact trajectory of his arrow for the particular bow he is shooting and adjusts his "sights" accordingly. The average target bow of about 40-pounds draw usually shoots dead-on at a range of 80 yards. At more than 80 yards, the archer sights at an object above the point of intended impact; short of 80 yards, he centers on a point below the target.

Target archers using the point-of-aim technique usually have a small stake that they push into the ground for a point-of-aim when the aim is below the target. The point-of-aim method is widely used by target archers, but it is ineffective for bowhunters since the exact range must be known.

The third method of aiming is with a bow sight or bow scope. When using a bow sight, the archer's eye becomes the rear sight and the bow sight itself becomes the front sight.

The simplest form of sight is nothing more than a pin or marker of sorts attached to the bow just above the handle that is adjusted for windage and elevation by moving it up or down, to the right or left.

The refined bow sight has adjustment knobs for windage and elevation, and is quickly adjusted. Remarkable scores have been compiled by archers using such a sight. However, like the point-of-aim method, the bow sight must be adjusted to a given range before it becomes effective.

■ Release

Hold the bow at full draw just long enough to be certain your aim is correct, and then relax your fingers, permitting the bowstring to slip smoothly away. Any undue movement of the three fingers of the drawing hand will cause "creep," which can greatly affect the accuracy of the release. Another common fault among neophyte archers is what is termed "plucking" the string—pulling or drawing the bow hand away from the string. This is sure to spoil your aim. Again, the exact manner of release rests with the individual archer. Many "release" problems are eliminated with a mechanical release.

■ Follow-Through

Your arrow is away, speeding toward its target. At the moment the arrow is released, the tension in your body created during the draw and sighting is totally relaxed. At this point, you must follow through.

A proper follow-through is just as essential to accuracy as any other step in correct shooting. At the moment of release, the shooting hand and right shoulder move backward slightly. The bow should slip loosely in the bow hand, but the bow arm should be kept extended and the shooting hand held firmly at the anchor point. Follow-through is essential to prevent a relaxation of your shooting stance just before the release of the arrow.

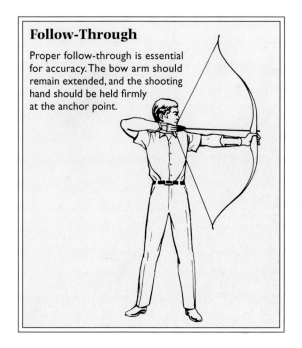

Follow-Through

Proper follow-through is essential for accuracy. The bow arm should remain extended, and the shooting hand should be held firmly at the anchor point.

BOWHUNTING

Within the last several decades, bowhunters in North America have taken moose, deer, and the three species of bears. In Africa, bowhunters have felled rhinos, elephants, Cape buffalos, leopards, and lions. Clearly, bowhunting as a sport has become enormously popular, to the extent that every state has set aside a special game season for bowhunters.

Among all game, deer are still the favorite of the bowhunter—especially whitetails. It has been said that if a bowhunter can successfully bag a whitetail deer, he can easily take any other game animal in the world.

Bowhunting requires more patience and perseverance than firearm hunting. The bowhunter must be within relatively close range to be assured a hit in a vital area. And he must be certain that his arrow has a clear path to its target, for the slightest twig or hidden branch can quickly deflect a shaft.

To be assured of a positive hit in a vital area, the bowhunter would be wise not to shoot at any deer beyond a range of 40 yards. While it's true that deer have been taken with the bow at far greater distances, it is by its very nature a short-range weapon. Limit your distance

No longer uncomfortable, most ladder stands, such as the Next-Gen Stealth DX stand (*left*), have a flip-up foot rest and a padded, removable shooting rail. The seat also flips up and out of the way so the shooters can stand to take a shot. The stand weighs 55 pounds and measures 14 feet to the platform.

There are literally dozens of climbing tree stands for bowhunters. Typical is the Summit Viper Elite SD Climbing Stand (*top right*), which weighs only 16 pounds and will hold hunters weighing up to 250 pounds. It is built of high-tech aluminum. These mechanical climbing stands permit a hunter to climb a tree trunk and also provide a steady platform.

Not all hunters feel comfortable with tree-stand ladders or climbing stands. Recent years have produced many models of ground blinds, which permit a hunter to stay comfortably concealed while still allowing shooting ports. A good example is the camouflaged Ameristep Carnivore (*bottom right*), which measures 74 by 74 inches and weighs only 22 pounds. Folded, this blind measures 9 by 47 inches. The six-window blind will also protect you from insects and the poly-cotton blend is treated to reduce human scent.

before you loose an arrow; your chance of a successful hit and a clean kill will be vastly enhanced.

Trail Watching

The bowhunter after deer employs various hunting methods. Most bowhunters prefer "runway" watching—finding a well-worn deer trail and sitting motionless several yards away to wait for a deer to amble by. Others like to still-hunt, that is, to walk up a deer. Some bowhunters also like to hunt in teams of three or four, and there are others who "drive" deer, emulating the firearm deer hunter in many sections of the East.

Trail watching calls for several preseason trips to your favorite deer area. Deer are creatures of habit, and when not pushed or spooked they prefer to select the easiest route between bedding, watering, and feeding grounds. They move from these areas usually twice a day: at dusk, from ridgetop bedding grounds down to feed and water, and at dawn, returning to the high country along specific runways. Trails used by deer can be easily recognized: they are well worn and often contain tracks and droppings. By carefully selecting a good vantage point several yards off the main trail, with a clear path to the target area, the bowhunter's opportunity for success is greater than in other methods of hunting.

A good location for the bowhunter is near an apple orchard. Whitetails love apples and will travel many miles to find them. If you can find such a spot, especially with fruit-laden trees, you're in luck. Look for well-used trails leading into the orchard and choose a stand that will afford you a good shot as the deer enter the orchard. Better yet, select a good apple tree that will afford a comfortable position and climb into the tree.

Of utmost importance when trail watching is that the archer must remain motionless and be well hidden or camouflaged. This may sound easy, but it's not. Deer are most easily spooked by motion, and a bowhunter who slaps at buzzing insects or squirms restlessly will never see a deer.

One way to avoid detection when trail watching is to use a tree stand or a blind. If a blind is properly constructed with material from the surrounding area, the bowhunter is perfectly concealed and can readily move around without being detected by the deer. The blind can be constructed several yards from a well-used runway at ground level or in a tree. A bowhunter can also choose from the many commercially available camouflaged ground blinds, some of which are constructed of low-sheen and scent-blocking fabric.

Perhaps one of the handiest items for the bowhunter to carry afield, if he anticipates constructing a blind, is a spool of monofilament fishing line. He can wind several yards of line between two trees, and then carefully interweave brush and foliage. Burlap bags are also useful in blind construction. Remember to construct the blind so that it provides good visibility and offers complete freedom of movement when the bow is brought to full draw.

Tree stands include everything from a limb to an elaborately constructed platform. The advocates of the tree stand reason that usually deer do not look up, and if a blind is placed in a tree, often a deer will approach at close range.

The most effective time of day for trail watching is at dawn and late twilight when deer move between feeding and watering and bedding grounds. During the day, when deer are not pushed or spooked, they will simply bed down and refuse to move. However, if there are a number of hunters in the woods, deer will keep moving and the runway method can be effective throughout the midday hours. Usually, however, trail watching is only productive from daybreak to 9:00 a.m. and again from 3:00 p.m. to dark.

Remember to take account of the wind. When you are stationed along a runway, the wind should never be blowing at your back, toward the direction you expect the deer to come. Your scent will be carried to the deer. Keep the wind in your face, and deer approaching you will not detect your presence. You can also use commercial or natural scents to neutralize or mask human scent, or even a buck lure made from glandular secretions.

Still-Hunting and Stalking

While not as effective as trail watching, still-hunting and stalking are more thrilling, steeped as they are in the traditions of the longbow hunters of yesteryear. The still-hunter prowls silently through the woods, hoping to sight a deer. Upon sighting a deer, he then stalks to within bow range. This is often a good tactic during daylight hours when deer are bedded down.

Wind direction plays the most important role in still-hunting. Always hunt with the wind in your face. If you sight a deer, only move when the animal's head is down in feeding position. Never attempt to approach a deer when its head is erect and its ears are cocked—it will immediately spook. But when the deer brings its head down, you can move toward it, instantly freezing again when it snaps its head upward. Make use of every bit of cover. Watch for other deer in the general area, too. You can be stalking one animal only to be startled when another snorts a few yards away.

The Mystery of Deer Scents

Every deer season there will be many bowhunters who will go into the woods and start squirting all sorts of deer scents around their stands, on their boots, or wherever. They will try to mask their human odor with food or animal scents. Or perhaps, they will spray a little sex scent to draw a buck within range. There's no doubt that these deer scents will work, but unless you know what you're doing, you may well scare off a buck before he even gets within a few hundred yards of your stand.

Understanding this whole business of deer scents is not difficult if you think about it logically. You can start by learning the three classifications of deer scents: cover or masking scents, attracting scents, and food lures or scents. Let's take them one by one. You will see why all of them will not work all of the time.

The cover scents are designed to mask human odor, and they can be used any time around your tree stand or hunting area. These cover or masking scents include skunk essence, cattle scent, earth, pine, cedar, fox urine, and interdigital gland scent. There may be more cover scents available, but these are the most common.

The major cover or masking scents are fox and skunk, but even these should be selected carefully. Skunk essence may not be the best choice because it is an alarm scent and could alert deer that something is wrong. Fox scent is good, but you will still have to choose between red fox and gray fox. Use red-fox scent in farm land, where they are most common. In mature timber, however, go with the gray fox, an animal that you will rarely see in farm fields or hedgerows.

Regardless of what cover scent you choose, it is very important that you use it sparingly. A deer will pick up the scent hundreds of yards away. Use too much scent and you risk the chance of spooking a deer.

Attracting scents make up the next major classification. There are only three types of attracting scents that you should know about. The first is estrus, which is the scent of a doe in heat. This, obviously, cannot be used all the time. Hunters should use it only during the rut (mating season). You can get approximate dates of the rut in your region from your state wildlife biologists. The dates, however, are never exact. In the East, for example, from southern Canada to Georgia, the rut

will run from November 1 to December 10, with the peak from November 1 to November 5. Use estrus scent around your stand or on your boot pad. With this scent, you are trying to attract a buck within range.

The next attractant is called interdigital gland scent, which comes from the bottom of a deer's foot or between the hooves. A deer leaves this scent in its tracks, and it is how one deer locates another or how a doe finds its fawn. This is the ideal scent for the hunter who prefers to move quietly through the woods. Put it on your boot pad when you're still-hunting and walking to your tree stand. Interdigital gland scent also works well as a cover or masking scent. It's critical that you use only three or four drops of this scent and never use any of it on your body. A felt boot pad tied to your laces is ideal.

The last attractant is buck urine, which is used to draw bucks by making them think another buck has moved into their territory. It is also the scent to use when making a mock scrape, which is a buck's way of leaving his calling card in his area.

Finally, there are food lures. These include such scents as apple, acorn, corn, and grape, to name a few. The most common mistake with food lures is using them in areas where the food and scent may be completely foreign to deer. You would not, for example, use corn scent in a swamp or acorn scent in an orchard. Food lures should be used in areas where deer will be able to identify the scent, and seek it out as a food source.

Always remember that a deer's sense of smell is its key to survival. Therefore, the most common human scents should be avoided. If you're deer hunting, don't use scented soaps, shampoos, laundry detergents, or aftershave lotions. Never wear your hunting boots in your house, garage, or gas station, where they will pick up odors that don't belong in the woods. There are plenty of soaps and chemicals specially designed to neutralize human scent. This may all seem like a lot of work, but it will be worth it when a buck walks up to your stand.

Driving

Another effective way of hunting deer is by driving. Though not one of the more popular methods of bowhunting, deer driving is productive during the midday hours. For a drive to be successful, several hunters must work in close agreement with one another and be intimately familiar with the territory they plan to hunt.

In a properly organized deer drive, several bowhunters take stands along varied known escape routes of deer in a particular piece of woodlot, while several

Archery and Bowhunting Organizations

There are numerous archery organizations in the United States whose purpose is to regulate competition and bring together archers from all parts of the world. Visit these websites for more information.

National Archery Association
www.teamusa.org/USA-Archery

National Field Archery Association
www.nfaa-archery.org

World Archery Federation
www.worldarchery.org

Pope and Young Club
www.pope-young.org

National Bowhunter Education Foundation
www.nbef.org

others move through the woodlands "pushing" any deer that are in the cover to the waiting hunters. Successful drives have been managed with only five or six hunters, but eight bowhunters make an ideal group.

In a successful deer drive, the elected drivers move toward the standers as silently as possible. In this way even the drivers have an occasional opportunity of getting a good shot. Often a wary old buck won't move ahead of the driver, but instead will quarter and cut back through the drive, and the alert driver will then have an opportunity for a shot. When posting standers, remember to place one or two hunters on the flanks, since a wary whitetail will often attempt to slip through or out the flank of a drive. With flank standers, this possibility is eliminated and will usually produce a shot for the hunter.

The successful deer drive should be planned with extreme care. A captain of the hunt should be elected. He is the one who should know the area most intimately. Standers should be spaced sufficiently far apart so that they will not interfere with each other. Drivers should also be placed sufficiently far apart, but in as parallel a line as possible to the standers. They should be extremely cautious and aware of the other hunters in the area. When possible, deer should be driven crosswind.

Driving deer does have one disadvantage. Often a driven deer will come bounding through the forest at top speed, an almost impossible target for the bowhunter. A whitetail deer at top speed is moving at about 40 miles per hour. To hit such a rapidly moving target, the bowhunter would have to lead his target by 12 feet at 10 yards, 24 feet at 20 yards, and 35 feet at 30 yards. Such a running target should not be taken, for it is almost impossible to strike the vital area of a running deer under such conditions. Unless you are extremely close to a moving deer, do not attempt a shot; invariably the deer will be struck far back and will escape.

At some point during your bowhunting days, you're going to release an arrow at an animal only to have it "jump the string." How many times have you heard a bowhunter remark that his arrow was flying directly at the deer's chest area, but it jumped aside and the arrow flew harmlessly by?

While it is doubtful that the deer saw the arrow coming toward it, jumping the string is nothing more than an instinctive reflex action. Compared with a rifle bullet, an arrow is comparatively slow in flight, and the twang of a bowstring, or the whispering of the arrow as it moves in flight, is sufficient to cause a deer to jump.

■ Small Game

Although bowhunters have hunted the world for trophy big-game animals, small-game and varmint hunting is also popular. It's a year-round sport; during the legal hunting season the bowhunter can seek small game, while the remainder of the year he can devote to varmints.

The woodchuck is the ideal bowhunter's game since it requires the utmost stalking skill to approach the wary animal and considerable shooting finesse to bring it to bag. While most small-game targets should be hunted with blunt field arrows, the woodchuck requires broadheads.

Woodchucks venture out during the early morning and late evening hours, spending the remainder of the day comfortably snoozing in the cooling depths of their dens. Consequently, the bowman must be afield during the early morning and late twilight hours. Some hunters prefer to wait motionlessly within a few yards of a den for the woodchuck to appear. Others prefer to stalk the woodchuck, attempting to get as close as possible before loosing an arrow. Both methods are successful, although the hunter who stalks his game will undoubtedly sight more animals.

Woodchucks emerge from their dens in early spring and spend the remainder of the summer stuffing themselves with clover in preparation for their long winter's sleep, giving the hunter several months of the year to stalk his quarry. The successful woodchuck hunter can be assured that come deer season he won't miss too many bucks.

Other small game eagerly sought by bowhunters include rabbits and squirrels, quail, ringneck pheasants, turkeys, and grouse. While a few professionals have had success with wing shooting, the average hunter would find it difficult to hit birds on the wing.

The flu-flu arrow must be used when hunting squirrels in trees. This is an arrow shaft fletched with sufficient feathers to retard its flight. Such shafts will not travel much beyond 50 yards and can be readily recovered. The broadhead blade, while perfect for big-game animals, does not work as well on small game. The blunt point or field point should be used when hunting small game. There are a number of small-game points

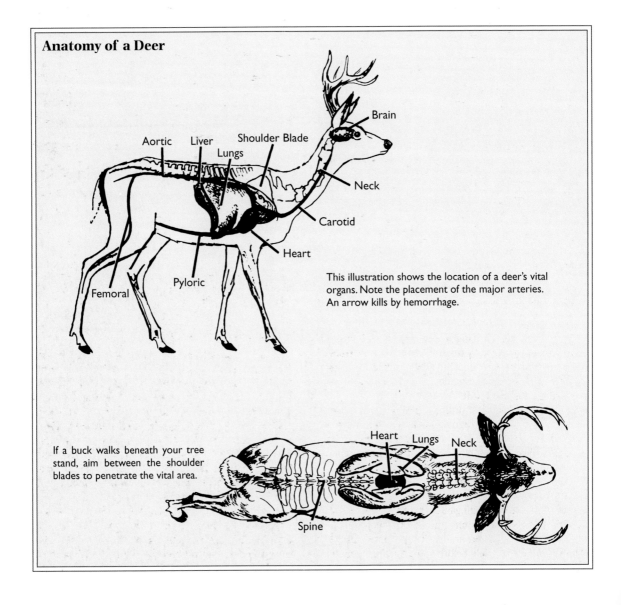

Anatomy of a Deer

Aortic
Liver
Shoulder Blade
Lungs
Brain
Neck
Carotid
Heart
Femoral
Pyloric

This illustration shows the location of a deer's vital organs. Note the placement of the major arteries. An arrow kills by hemorrhage.

If a buck walks beneath your tree stand, aim between the shoulder blades to penetrate the vital area.

Heart
Lungs
Neck
Spine

Still-hunting and stalking, while not as productive as trail watching, can sometimes be more rewarding. The bowhunter moves silently through the woods, stalking within bow range of a deer. It is a good technique during daylight hours when deer are bedded down.

currently available, ranging from empty rifle or pistol cartridge cases to specially manufactured blunts, which produce a great deal of shocking power. A fine commercially manufactured small-game point in wide use today is termed the "rubber blunt."

Since small-game hunting seasons vary from state to state, as well as regulations pertaining to legal weapons, be sure to check your local game laws before venturing afield with a bow and arrow. For example, in most states the prospective bowhunter must compete with the firearm hunter since there are few states that offer special small-game seasons specifically for archers. But hunting small game with a bow and arrow is a keenly satisfying pastime and in the long run will enhance your skills as an archer and provide hours of relaxing enjoyment afield before and after the big-game hunting seasons.

■ Where to Hit Big Game

The most important factor in killing big game quickly and cleanly is arrow (or bullet) placement. You'll minimize the chance of losing wounded game if you take time to study the animals you hunt and learn the location of vital organs, as well as where to aim in order to hit those vital organs when the animal is seen at different angles.

The accompanying illustrations show the anatomy of a deer—the most popular game for bowhunters—and the aiming points that are important. Remember that an arrow kills by hemorrhage. A bowhunter should note especially the location of main arteries.

A neck shot should not be attempted except at close range, and even then it's only a fair choice. An arrow in the neck may possibly damage the spinal column and cause the deer to drop quickly, but you don't want to gamble on that. If you hit a big artery such as the carotid, bleeding will be profuse and you may not have to track the deer far. However, your chance of causing major hemorrhaging is better if you can place the arrow low in the neck (in the brisket area) or in the chest cavity.

The best shots should really be described in terms of vital areas rather than vital organs. The forward one-third of a deer's body is a vital area since it houses the heart, lungs, several major arteries, spine, and shoulder. An arrow penetrating one of the organs will bring down a deer (though not as quickly as a bullet). When possible, try for the heart. If you miss, the arrow has a good chance of hitting one of the other vital organs—particularly the lungs. Even though a lung-shot deer may not drop because of shock (since an arrow produces little shock in comparison to a bullet), the animal will die through hemorrhaging.

In this case, however, the deer may travel a good distance, so tracking is even more important for the bowhunter than for the rifle hunter. If you're not sure

where your arrow struck, the blood may tell you. If you spot blood on brush a few feet off the ground and to the side of the tracks, it's coming from the side of the deer—a good indication of a lung hit. Frothy blood also signifies a lung hit. Bright-red blood usually means a heart or lung shot. Brownish-yellow blood, particularly if you see white hair in it, means the deer is gutshot. This is unfortunate. A gutshot deer can travel a long way, and you'll just have to stick with the track.

If you're in a tree stand shooting down as a buck walks below, less of the vital area will be exposed than when you have a broadside shot. The best place to aim then is between the shoulder blades. An arrow there may penetrate the heart, lungs, or arteries. A shot at a quartering animal should not be quite the same as a broadside shot, either. When a deer is quartering away, your point of aim should be somewhat farther back on the body. A straight-traveling broadhead will penetrate from that rearward point forward into the vital area.

BOWFISHING

Most bowhunters have learned that the hunting seasons are brief and that they must either turn to target archery or to the sport of bowfishing.

In fresh water, the most popular species sought by bowhunters is the carp, which can attain heavyweight proportions. Other species hunted are suckers, buffalofish, squawfish, dogfish, and gar. In salt water, stingrays, skates, barracuda, and sharks all offer sport.

The tackle required to convert to bowfishing consists of a few inexpensive items—a bow reel, some line, and a few bowfishing arrows.

A bow reel is nothing more than a special large spool to which at least 50 feet of stout nylon line is attached. The bow reel itself is easily and quickly fastened to the bow with tape and can be easily removed when the big-game hunting season arrives. Some bow reels manufactured today do not require taping to the bow, but have a bracket that can be instantly attached or removed from the bow. Most bow reels contain a small catch built into the reel spool to keep the line from peeling off when making shots at extreme angles. Some bows are mounted with conventional spincast reels.

For most freshwater fishing, 36-pound-test nylon line can handle most fish bowhunters will encounter, but for those enterprising bowhunters who take to salt

Bowfishing gear can be simple and inexpensive: a bow reel, line, and a few arrows. Bow reels usually hold 50 or more feet of stout nylon line. The reel is typically taped to the bow and can easily be removed when big-game season arrives. A typical bowfishing rig is the PSE Kingfisher Bow with a front-mounted reel, 50 yards of 80-pound-test line, and a 31-inch solid fiberglass arrow. It has bow weights of 40, 45, and 50 pounds.

Carp are the usual freshwater targets for bowfishing during spring and summer. In salt water, bowhunters search the flats for skates and stingrays. A big ray can actually tow your boat, so make sure you have enough 100-pound-test line for those surging runs.

water seeking larger species, 100-pound-test nylon line is in order. Any bow you use for big game hunting will suffice for bowfishing.

Arrows must be made of solid fiberglass for durability. A fish weighing more than several pounds can easily roll on an arrow once it is struck and snap a wood shaft or bend an aluminum one. The solid, fiberglass arrow also has the extra weight required to drive it into the water. From a husky hunting bow, a solid fiberglass arrow can often be driven to depths of 10 feet or more.

Conventional feather fletching is out for the bowhunter since feathers can quickly be ruined in water. The bowfishing arrow is therefore manufactured with rubber fletching, and if you are shooting at extremely close range, even this can be eliminated. However, since most bowfishing arrows are equipped with rubber fletching, the bowfisherman should use them.

The solid fiberglass fishing arrow is equipped with some sort of barbed or harpoon head, which is not permanently fastened to the arrow shaft. Instead, the head slips over the end of the arrow and is attached to a line that runs through a small hole in the shaft just above the nock, then down the length of the shaft, and is tied to the hole in the harpoon head itself.

Once a fish is struck, it is easy to handline it in. However, when seeking large, heavy fish, some bowhunters prefer to eliminate the bow reel and attach the line directly to a fishing rod and reel. When using the rod and reel, strip some 20 yards of line through the rod guides and carefully coil it on the bottom of the boat or in a small tub or bucket, and attach the forward end of the line to the arrow.

Arrow points or harpoon heads vary widely. For greatest penetration, the single barbed point is best, but the double-barbed rig is needed for big fish, especially in salt water.

Foremost to remember when shooting fish underwater is to aim low. Your view underwater is affected by light refraction, and when fish are working under the water's surface and viewed at an angle, your quarry is always lower than it appears to be. A few shots taken at such targets will quickly show the bowhunter where he should aim his arrow.

Polaroid sunglasses should be worn when bowfishing to help you see the quarry. The best time for bowfishing is midday, when the sun warms the surface and brings the fish up within easy view. Without polarizing sunglasses, you will be at a loss to spot fish.

Carp provide outstanding sport for the bowhunter, especially during early spring and summer when, heavy with roe, they move into the shallows of rivers and lakes to spawn. Many southern bowhunters also find action hunting garfish—including the shortnose gar, which rarely exceeds 3 feet in length; the longnose gar, which usually attains a length of 5 feet; and the giant alligator gar, which can attain a length of 8 feet and a weight in excess of 300 pounds. Hot summer evenings are best for hunting large garfish. Bowhunters paddle slowly through the water searching with a flashlight for these prehistoric giants. They always use a wire leader between the harpoon head and line.

In salt water, the bowhunter can choose from a wide variety of fish. Fast and furious action can be found by searching the flats in back-bay country for skates and stingrays. Rays are powerful and once harpooned can tow a boat with ease. When seeking large rays, remember to add additional line to the bow reel to allow for their powerful, surging run.

Bowfishing has become so popular in recent years that most states now have special seasons for taking rough fishes. Check local regulations, as most states require bowmen to have fishing licenses.

POINTERS

▓ Pointer

HISTORY: The pointer (formerly known as the English pointer) dates back as far as the 14th or 15th century. Its exact origins are not known, though many fanciers of the breed believe that the first pointers came from Spain. However, equally reliable records indicate that dogs of similar conformation and traits existed at about the same time in France, Belgium, Portugal, and other European countries. The French "Braque"—described as a dog that "stops at scent and hunts with the nose high"—was such an animal.

There can be little doubt, however, that England is the nation most responsible for the breed as it is known today. Among the English nobility whose breeding practices helped the pointer soar in popularity were Thomas Webb Edge, John Legh, Lord Combermere, the Earl of Sefton, Thomas Statter, Lord Derby, and George Moore. The fountainheads of the breed in England were such dogs as Brockton's Bounce, Statter's Major, Whitehouse's Hamlet, and Garth's Drake.

The 19th-century pointer in England was a large, relatively slow, big-boned animal that was ideal for hunting slow-flying, tight-sitting grouse, birds that were raised domestically and freed in rather restricted hunting areas. But such dogs were far from ideal for hunting in the United States, where the birds were wild and scattered.

Since the mid-19th century, the breed has undergone a drastic change, thanks to the efforts of such dog fanciers and breeders as T. H. Scott, S. A. Kaye, U. R. Fishel, C. H. Foust, and A. G. C. Sage. Sage's Alabama plantation, called Sedgefields, has long been famous as a trial grounds.

The pointer today is fast, agile, and wide ranging, able to seek out birds and pin them. Such qualities were passed down from such famous U.S. pointers as Mary Montrose, Becky Broomhill, and Ariel, each of which won the National Championship three times.

Most top hunting pointers are registered with the *Field Dog Stud Book*, while most show-type pointers are on the list of the American Kennel Club.

DESCRIPTION: The pointer is a beautiful animal, the epitome of what a bird dog should look like. Streamlined, and with a build that bespeaks speed and endurance, it carries its head high.

The pointer's skull is long and moderately wide, with the forehead rising well at the brows. The muzzle is long, square, and straight. The ears are thin and silky, long enough to reach just below the throat when hanging normally. The eyes are soft and dark. The neck is long, clean, and firm.

The shoulders are long and oblique, with the tops of the blades close. The chest is deep, and as wide as the

Pointer

shoulders will permit. The ribs are well sprung. The back is strong, with a slight rise to the tops of the shoulders. The tail is straight, strong, and tapered, carried level or just above the line of the back.

The hindquarters are very muscular, the legs moderately short but well boned. The feet are round, deep, and well padded, with well-arched toes.

The coat is short, flat, and firm. Coat colors range from liver and white (the most common) to black and white, lemon and white, or solid white, all of which are highly visible in the field.

SIZE: The pointer is a medium to fairly large animal, as bird dogs go. The average weight is 50 to 65 pounds, though some small specimens, particularly females, may weigh as little as 35 pounds and some large males may hit 80 pounds. Shoulder height is 24 to 25 inches.

HUNTING ABILITY: The pointer is at present the "top dog" among the pointing breeds, both in the field and in trials, and that stature is well earned. This breed is fast, enduring, and has a great nose and sometimes uncanny bird sense (the ability to recognize and home in on birdy-looking cover, anticipate what birds are going to do, and react to it).

The pointer's strong suit is quail, particularly bobwhites, on which it has no peer. There are few sights in the hunting world that can match that of a staunch pointer locked up in a statuesque point over a covey of bobwhites.

But this dog has also proven itself on pheasants, one of the most demanding assignments for any bird-dog breed. It will also work well on any of the western quail and on woodcock and grouse, though closer-working breeds are usually preferred for the latter two species.

The pointer has a deeply engrained and well-defined instinct to hunt and to point. It has a rugged constitution and can withstand long hours in hot weather, a factor that has made it extremely popular in the southern United States. Some other breeds, however, are better able to stand bitter-cold weather.

DISPOSITION: The pointer has a temperament that might be best termed as reserved. Though it is not unresponsive to gentle and kind treatment, it cannot truthfully be called affectionate. It is not much for hand licking. In fact, it sometimes assumes an air of indifference toward people other than its master. That aloofness may be attributed to the fact that the pointer—most individuals, at any rate—just lives to hunt game birds, and unless it

is doing that job it's not happy. Of course, in the pointer, as in any other dog breed, you may find an individual dog that seems to be the rule-proving exception.

The pointer's rugged disposition is an asset, as far as training is concerned. The breed will tolerate a considerable amount of force by a trainer without becoming balky or allowing itself to be made into a "mechanical" dog lacking style and dash.

English Setter

HISTORY: The English setter dates back at least as far as the 16th century. Etchings and other illustrations of that time show a pointing dog that looks very much like the English. The breed in all probability originated in Spain, from a cross between a Spanish pointing dog and one or more spaniel-type dogs. The early setters were known as "setting spaniels" because they "set" (pointed) their game. One of the earliest dog writers called the setter "a spaniel improved."

Many setter strains were developed in England, among them Featherstone, Lovat, Southesk, Naworth Castle, Seafield, and Laverack. Edward Laverack, the first major breeder of the English setter, set the breed's type during a period of some 35 years of demanding inbreeding.

In the 1870s or 1880s, Laverack and R. Purcell Llewellin imported some outstanding setters to North

English Setter

America. The Llewellin strain, established from Laverack stock, became very popular in the United States (see Llewellin Setter section for more information).

During the English setter's early days in this country, the breed was all but untouchable in field trials. In fact, the setter's performance was so superior to that of the pointer (whose ascendancy had not yet begun) that putting the two in head-to-head competition was not considered sporting. The pointer has since, of course, surpassed his longer-haired rival. The first National Bird Dog Championship, held in 1896, was won by a setter—Count Gladstone IV. Other famous English setters include Count Noble (whose name is found in the pedigrees of many of today's setters), Druid, Sport's Peerless, and Florendale Lou's Beau.

DESCRIPTION: The English setter is a graceful and hand-some animal, alert and agile. In general build, it is not so heavily muscled, particularly in the hindquarters, as the pointer, and its chest is not so broad. The following are the standards for the breed:

The head is long and lean, not so broad and square as that of the pointer, and the dome tends more toward an oval shape. The muzzle is long and square, but not so square (particularly in trial dogs) as the pointer's. The ears are set low and well back and are of moderate length, and they are covered with silky hair. The eyes are dark brown and project an intelligent and mild expression.

The neck is long and lean. The shoulder blades stand moderately close at the tops. The chest is deep, but not overly wide. The ribs are well sprung. The back is strong and either straight or sloping upward slightly to the shoulders. The legs are strong, straight, well boned, and muscular. The feet are closely set and strong, with tough pads and well arched toes that are covered with thick, short hair.

The tail is straight and tapers to a fine point, and its feathering is straight and silky but not bushy.

Field and trial English setters should not be overly tall and thin, as are many show setters, for this conformation detracts from the ruggedness needed for field work.

The setter's coat is long and flat and without curl. Colors vary, but they include white and black; white, black, and tan; white and orange; white and chestnut; blue belton; orange belton; and others. Among the most popular color combinations is white with a mixture of black, tan, lemon, and orange.

SIZE: Similar in size and weight to the pointer, the English setter ranges in average weight from 50 to 60 pounds, with some small females weighing as little as 35 pounds and some large males weighing up to 75 pounds. The average height at the shoulders is 24 to 25 inches.

HUNTING ABILITY: The English setter is the only pointing dog that rivals the pointer on drive, speed, nose, and bird sense. Though the setter has not even approached the pointer in field-trial accomplishments, the two are not so far apart in performance for the general hunter.

Though the pointer is the generally acknowledged king of quail country, meaning the southern United States, many quail hunters prefer the English setter because it tends to work a bit closer to the gun.

Just as the pointer, because of its short hair, is better able to withstand hot-weather conditions, the setter, because of its long hair, is unquestionably better than the pointer under the rigors of winter hunting. The setter is also better able to cope with briars and other tough cover, again because of its thick and protective coat. That long hair, on the other hand, can pose a maintenance problem for the setter owner. Burrs and matted hair may take hours to remove. Some setter fanciers suggest that this problem can be reduced by trimming the feathering on a dog's underparts, tail, and ears.

English setters are particularly adept at handling pheasants. A top setter will even circle ahead of a running pheasant to pin it and prevent it from flushing wild. Also, a setter is more apt to keep in touch with the hunter than a pointer.

In midwestern and northern states, the setter does more than a passable job of water work, hauling pheasants and Hungarian partridge out of potholes and performing similar damp duties.

A prospective dog buyer—and this advice applies not only to purchasing English setters but all other hunting-dog breeds—should be certain that any dog in which he is interested comes from ancestors that have proven their worth as hunting dogs.

DISPOSITION: The English setter is not a tough nut, as are many pointers. It literally thrives on attention and affection, and it will dispense those same feelings. The setter is seldom timid, but it is sensitive, and a trainer would do well to keep that fact in mind. Too much force can cow a setter or make it a sulker, and the breed cannot take too much punishment.

The setter takes well to gentle, unhurried training tactics, and it learns its lessons well, being less apt to forget or disregard them than the pointer. It is also more likely to become a one-man dog than a pointer.

It pays for a hunter to make a companion of an English setter. The dog is sure to meet the man more than halfway.

■ Irish Setter

HISTORY: The Irish setter, a product of the British Isles, was not always the solid, mahogany-red animal of today. Most of the original Irish were red and white, though the red predominated.

The development of the Irish setter rather closely paralleled that of its English cousin (see the English Setter section). The Irish dogs, a bit more rough and rugged, were much prized by hunters, for they performed many tasks, ranging from seeking out and pointing such upland game birds as woodcock, grouse, and quail, to the retrieving of waterfowl from the most frigid of waters.

The Irish setter's heyday in the United States began, for all intents and purposes, in 1876, when one of the early imports, an Irish named Erin, won an important stake at the Tennessee State Sportsmen's Association field trials, only the third trial series ever held. The Irish won a surprising number of placements in early trials—surprising because of the small number of Irish setters entered in the competitions.

A dog named Elcho might well be considered the fountainhead of the breed in the United States. Elcho—imported from Dublin by Charles H. Turner of St. Louis, Missouri—won fame in bench shows. Most of today's Irish setters are traceable to Elcho.

The breed's outstanding beauty has led directly to a decline in its field capabilities, and thus to a drop in popularity among hunters. In the early part of the 20th century (and continuing even today), many breeders became

Irish Setter

interested in bench shows and so bred into many Irish setters physical characteristics that improved the breed's already handsome looks but were a handicap in the hunting field. That factor, plus the rapid rise in the popularity of the pointer and other bird-dog breeds, has shunted the Irish into the background of hunter popularity.

DESCRIPTION: The Irish setter is generally hailed as the most beautiful of all the sporting breeds. It should be noted, however, that physical characteristics can vary considerably from hunting to show stock.

The physical standards are of interest mainly to dog fanciers who are concerned with show animals and in many instances do not accurately describe Irish setters from good hunting stock.

In general, the hunting Irish is a dog with a powerful build, being well boned and quite muscular, particularly in the quarters. The head is good and broad. The coat is rather heavy, flat, and silky. The coat color is a deep mahogany, often with white areas on the chest, feet, and face.

Show breeding produces such characteristics as a rather snippy or narrow head, slim hips, weak quarters, long legs, and a lack of roundness in the rib cage, a shortcoming that usually causes a dog to lack endurance.

Basically, the Irish setter is an English setter with a red coat.

SIZE: The Irish setter, being of somewhat slighter build than the English setter or the pointer, will weigh a bit less. On average, an Irish setter of normal height will be about 55 pounds. Shoulder height ranges from 25 to 26 inches.

HUNTING ABILITY: Though field excellence is hard to find in today's Irish setter breed as a whole, there are still a few breeders who concentrate on hunting ability. If you can find a dog from good hunting stock, you might well find yourself stuck on this breed.

A good hunting Irish has a nose that is the equal to that of any other breed. The Irish is rugged, sturdy, and enduring and can handle bitter weather with the best of them. It has a deeply engrained pointing instinct, though many field trialers dislike the Irish's tendency to point with a rather low tail, a factor that takes away from the stylishness of a point.

Few Irish setters display the dash or the wide range of the English setter or pointer, but the Irish generally does its job in a businesslike manner, covering the terrain thoroughly. Above all, the Irish almost always keeps in visual touch with the hunter—that is, it hunts for the gun, not for itself.

The coat is a drawback. The dark red of the Irish is more difficult to see in thick cover than that of the English or the pointer, both of which have some white.

DISPOSITION: The Irish setter is an extremely affectionate animal that thrives on attention. Of all the pointing breeds, it is the most likely to become a one-man dog and may, in fact, hunt only for its master.

The Irish has long carried a reputation for being stubborn and hard to handle. That may have been true of some of the early imports into this country, but it does not apply to the Irish of today.

However, it is true that patience and kindness, rather than force and abuse, should be the bywords of the trainer of an Irish. The breed is eager to please, a factor that can also be used to a trainer's advantage.

■ German Shorthaired Pointer

HISTORY: The basic original stock from which the German shorthair evolved was an early Spanish pointing dog, probably crossed with the Braque, an early French pointing dog. Later a cross with the bloodhound added to the breed's nose, and still later foxhound blood was added to improve the speed and endurance (though this infusion may well have detracted from the dog's bird sense).

A strange mixture? It would be for American hunting conditions, but the German breeders, who followed a rigorous selective-breeding program, knew what they wanted—a multipurpose dog suitable for hunting on German shooting preserves. These preserves held many varieties of game, both feathered and furred, and the ideal dog had to have a good nose and trailing ability for such game as rabbits and foxes; pointing instinct and bird sense for upland game birds such as grouse and woodcock; and the size, strength, and courage to handle such big game as wild boar and deer. The German shorthair filled the bill as well as any dog in existence.

The German Shorthaired Pointer Club of America, with its headquarters in Minneapolis, Minnesota, did much to further the development of the breed in this country. The breed is slowly becoming quite popular in the United States, probably because it is a jack-of-all-trades.

DESCRIPTION: Good individuals of this breed are extremely attractive animals. In general, they are rela-

German Shorthaired Pointer

tively tall and quite strong, slightly lower in the hips than in the shoulders. The legs are straight, and the overall build is powerful.

The German shorthair's head is similar in conformation to that of the pointer, except that it is longer, a bit narrower, and not so squared off at the muzzle. The ears are quite long and often quite hound-like, and they are set lower on the head than a pointer's.

The shoulders are muscular and moderately wide, the chest deep and wide, and the ribs well sprung.

The tail is docked, or cut, to approximately one-third of its original length and is carried almost straight out behind.

The coat is short, flat, and firm. Its texture is somewhat heavier than the pointer's. The color is all liver or different combinations of liver and white that may involve ticking, spotting, or both.

SIZE: German shorthair males weigh 55 to 70 pounds, females 45 to 60 pounds. Shoulder heights range from 23 to 25 inches in males, 21 to 23 inches in females. However, specimens of this breed tend to be taller and heavier than other pointing breeds. For example, a shorthair standing 26 inches at the shoulder is not at all uncommon.

HUNTING ABILITY: The German shorthair as a bird dog has an excellent nose, medium range, and moderate speed. Its head is generally carried rather low, and it tends to crouch while on point (actions that are not stylish), and its somewhat bulky build prevents it from being as fast as the pointer and English setter.

However, while those factors make the shorthair a poor choice for pheasants in big fields or for such open-country birds as sharptailed grouse, they make it eminently practical for the man who hunts woodcock, ruffed grouse, and quail in heavy cover. And the shorthair, despite its relatively thin coat, will retrieve shot waterfowl, even in bitter water.

DISPOSITION: The German shorthair has a mild and even temperament. It is seldom quarrelsome, though it can certainly hold its own in a fight. This dog is tractable and not overly difficult to train—provided it has the natural instincts to begin with.

The shorthair does exhibit a tendency to be possessive, and dogs of that type make very good watchdogs. The Germans prize this quality highly, calling it "sharpness," but some hunters consider it a shortcoming.

Gordon Setter

HISTORY: Tradition has it that some two centuries ago, the Duke of Gordon heard reports of a dog, owned by a shepherd in the highlands of Scotland, that was an accomplished finder of game. The Duke acquired the dog, a Collie-type female named Maddy, and crossed it with the setters that were kept at Gordon Castle. The result was what is known today as the Gordon setter.

But the Gordon may have had even earlier origins. It is possible that the breed was developed from a "black

Gordon Setter

and fallow setting dog" that was described in print as early as the first half of the 1600s.

In 1842, a man named George Blunt brought Rake and Rachel, both bred at Gordon Castle, to the United States. Unlike today's Gordons, these animals were white with black-and-tan markings. The two dogs were bred, and a resulting puppy wound up, via Daniel Webster, in the hands of Henry Clay, who apparently had no great love of dogs but who seemed to have been won over by the beguiling pup.

In the 1880s, a lighter, more streamlined Gordon was brought to the United States. It proved to be a hunting and show animal.

There was a time—the late 1800s—when the Gordon setter knew few peers as a bird-finding hunting dog. But the English setter, pointer, and, to a lesser degree, Irish setter—bred for speed and other qualities needed to handle the decreasing amount of game in this country—soon outstripped the Gordon in popularity.

DESCRIPTION: The Gordon setter is a bird dog of great beauty. Its body symmetry and proportions are similar to those of other setters, except that the Gordon is slightly heavier and often has slightly shorter legs.

The Gordon's beauty is rooted in its heavy coat of smooth, silky hair. The color is jet black, except for mahogany markings above the eyes and on the chops, ear linings, chest, belly, and feathers. The coat should be as free from white hair as possible. Feathering is generous on the legs, underparts, and tail.

The Gordon is wide across the forehead and has a fairly long muzzle. The nose is big and broad. The eyes are dark brown and have a wise look. The chest is deep, and the ribs are well sprung. The forelegs are big boned and straight, the hind legs muscular.

The feet have close-knit, well-arched toes, plenty of hair between the toes, and generous pads. The tail is relatively short (it should not reach below the hocks) and is carried horizontally or nearly so.

SIZE: The Gordon is a bit heavier than the other setters, ranging in weight from 45 to about 75 pounds. Shoulder height ranges from 23 to 27 inches. The official standard for the breed allows considerable range in size to suit sportsmen in various parts of the United States.

HUNTING ABILITY: The Gordon setter is rarely seen today in the hunting fields. Its decline in popularity since the late 19th century can be ascribed to a number of factors, chief among them being that few breeders made any effort to widen the breed's range and increase its speed, as was done with the English setter and the pointer. Good range and speed are qualities that more and more hunters are demanding because of the increasing scarcity of game birds. Also, the Gordon lacks the dash, determination, and stylishness of the English setter and pointer.

The above is not meant to imply that the Gordon is a poor hunter. It has an excellent nose and a good pointing instinct, and its heavy coat enables it to handle the heaviest of cover. (On the other hand, that same coat, because of its black and mahogany coloration, tends to make the dog hard to see in heavy cover.)

Though the Gordon is a slow hunter, it is also a sure hunter and tends to keep in touch with its master. Those factors make the Gordon a good choice for the man who hunts ruffed grouse and woodcock.

The Gordon is quite trainable, and is easily broken to retrieving. It makes a good retriever from land or water.

DISPOSITION: The Gordon setter's most endearing quality is its loyalty. It forms such a strong attachment to its owner or handler that it may not hunt for anyone else. That loyalty, however, should not be allowed to become so pronounced that, for example, the dog finds it impossible to readjust to its owner after spending some time under the whistle of a trainer.

The Gordon is responsive to training, eager to please, and wary of intruders. It jealously guards its human family and is regarded as a "most pettable" dog.

Llewellin Setter

HISTORY: The Llewellin setter is not a distinct breed but rather one of the many strains of the English setter (see English Setter section for more information). But it attained such a high degree of popularity that it once was accorded virtual—if not official—breed status among hunters. The *Field Dog Stud Book* recognizes the Llewellin as a distinct strain of English setter. The American Kennel Club does not distinguish between the various setter strains.

The Llewellin had its beginnings in England in about 1825, when Edward Laverack began a rigorous setter-breeding program. Using a female from a strain said to have been kept pure for 35 years, he produced some noteworthy hunting animals.

In 1871, another Englishman, R. Purcell Llewellin, while attending a field trial, bought a pair of male set-

Llewellin Setter

ters—Dan and Dick, offspring of parents named Field's Duke and Statter's Rhoebe—and later bred them to Laverack females that he already owned. This was the foundation of the Llewellin strain.

Llewellin, aided greatly by his kennel manager, G. Teasdale Buckell, did much to develop and popularize the strain that bears his name.

American sportsmen were greatly impressed with the hunting capabilities of the Llewellin setters and imported many of the animals to this country. (Oddly, the fountainheads of the Llewellin strain, Field's Duke and Statter's Rhoebe, never amounted to much as field dogs.)

Among the early Llewellin imports to the United States was Count Noble, a prepotent dog and a great trial winner. When Noble died, he was mounted, and the mount is now on display at the National Bird Dog Museum in Grand Junction, Tennessee.

Another import was Gladstone, whose work in trials and in the field did much to promote setter popularity in the United States. Gladstone was the loser in a well-publicized, two-day quail hunt in which he was worked against a "native" (American-bred) setter named Joe Jr.

The Llewellin setters took the United States by storm. In the strain's heyday, the ownership of a true Llewellin was a matter of great prestige. But that heyday was short-lived, and the ascendancy of the pointer relegated the Llewellin to the status of an also-ran. Today, very few true Llewellins are found in the hunting fields.

DESCRIPTION: This dog resembles the English setter, with the following exception: some dog fanciers incorrectly assume that any lightly marked, blue-ticked setter is a Llewellin. However, color and physical appearance are invalid criteria. The *Field Dog Stud Book* recognizes as members of the Llewellin strain only those animals that are traceable back, without outcross, to the Duke-Rhoebe-Laverack origins.

SIZE: See English Setter.

HUNTING ABILITY: See English Setter.

DISPOSITION: See English Setter.

▨ Wirehaired Pointing Griffon

HISTORY: In 1874, E. K. Korthals, a young Dutchman living near Haarlem, Holland, became preoccupied with creating a new breed of hunting dog, a dog that would have a keen nose, ability to trail, an instinct to point birds, and the ruggedness to enable it to withstand rigorous conditions. The young man's father, a wealthy banker, apparently became so angered with his son's quest that the younger Korthals was obliged to leave home.

It was in Germany, and later in France, that much of Korthals's breed development took place (in France, the wirehaired pointing griffon is known today as the Korthals griffon). Korthals—using woolly-haired, rough-coated, and short-haired animals as basic stock—came up with a harsh-coated animal. It is generally believed that the blood of the otterhound, setter, pointer, and probably a large spaniel were used. The result was a useful—and unusual—hunting animal.

DESCRIPTION: The wirehaired pointing griffon's most striking physical characteristic is its unique coat, which, though short-haired, is best described as unkempt. It is made up of harsh bristles, a good deal like those of a wild boar. The bristles form on the dog's head a "moustache" and heavy eyebrows. The coat colors are mixed: steel gray, gray white, and chestnut—never black.

The skull is long and narrow, the muzzle square. The large eyes are iris yellow or light brown. Ears are of medium size, and are set rather high. The nose is always brown. The neck is rather long, shoulders long and sloping. The ribs are slightly rounded. The forelegs are straight and muscular and have short, wiry hair, as do the hind legs, which are well developed. The feet are round, firm, and well formed. The tail is bristly and has no plume, and it is usually docked to one-third of its normal length.

SIZE: The wirehaired pointing griffon has an average shoulder height of 19½ to 23½ inches. Its weight averages about 56 pounds.

HUNTING ABILITY: Though the wirehaired pointing griffon has been known in the United States since 1901, it has never acquired even a modicum of popularity with American hunters. It is seldom seen here. The reasons are many. For one, the breed is too slow to be suitable for many game-bird hunting situations in this country. For another, the breed's coat and color fail to appeal to U.S. hunters.

The griffon is not the best choice if the game to be hunted is such open-country birds as quail and Hungarian partridge. It is much better suited to heavy-cover work on such targets as woodcock and ruffed grouse. It is an excellent retriever on both land and water, being a strong swimmer and having a rough coat that affords excellent protection from frigid water and briary cover.

Despite those strong points, however, the wirehaired pointing griffon is unable to compete on even terms with many of the established pointing breeds.

DISPOSITION: Because so few wirehaired pointing griffons exist in the United States today, an accurate rundown on the breed's temperamental and mental makeup is difficult. However, these dogs are known to be quite intelligent. They learn their lessons well and take read-

Wirehaired Pointing Griffon

German Wirehaired Pointer

ily to training. It is safe to say that the breed is highly unlikely to have any behavioral quirks that would make it unsuitable as a hunting companion in the field or as a family pet.

■ German Wirehaired Pointer

HISTORY: Much speculation and assumption is involved in tracing the origins of most dog breeds, and the German wirehair is no exception. It is known, however, that this breed's development began in Germany about 1870, when it was known as the Deutsche Drahthaar.

According to historical accounts, the early wirehairs represented a combination of the wirehaired pointing griffon, the Deutsche Stichelhaar, and the Pudel-Pointer (those dogs being three other wirehaired German pointing breeds), as well as the German shorthaired pointer. It is likely that the German wirehair's makeup also includes the blood of a strain of terrier.

The German wirehair was first brought to the United States in about 1920. It was known as the Drahthaar until the American Kennel Club recognized it in 1959 (the *Field Dog Stud Book* recognized the breed some years earlier).

The first wirehair to win an American Kennel Club–licensed field trial was Haar Baron's Mike, who won the German Pointing Dog National in 1959. However, the individual wirehair that probably had the most to do with publicizing the breed was Herr Schmardt v. Fox River.

Owned by an Illinois couple, Mr. and Mrs. A. H. Gallagher, Schmardt hunted widely in the Midwest, placed in many trials, and took part in numerous hunting-dog demonstrations. A. H. Gallagher was a prime mover in the German Drahthaar Pointer Club of America.

DESCRIPTION: The German wirehaired pointer resembles the German shorthaired pointer except for its coarse coat and whiskered face. Essentially a pointing dog in general type, the wirehair is usually an aristocratic-looking animal of sturdy build, lively manner, and an intelligent, determined expression. That facial expression, on the other hand, can sometimes appear almost monkey-like.

The wirehair's coat is straight, harsh, wiry, and rather flat lying. Its color is best described as grizzle (gray), with sizable patches of liver or brown on the head and body. Rare individuals are self-colored (solid) brown.

The eyebrows are heavy, and there is a short beard and whiskers. The undercoat ranges from dense to quite thin, depending upon the season, and is sometimes absent. The tail is usually docked to one-third of its normal length.

The better wirehairs are trim and agile, rather than blocky, though some individual specimens are heavy boned and plodding.

SIZE: According to the American Kennel Club standard, the German wirehair ranges in shoulder height from 22 to 26 inches. The weight averages 55 to 65 pounds.

HUNTING ABILITY: Like most of the other Continental pointing breeds, the German wirehair is best described as a general-purpose hunting dog that points and retrieves. It is agile, has a fine nose, and will work relatively close to the hunter, though it will move out a fair distance if the situation calls for it. It is essentially taught its manners on game and just as quickly picks up the knack of fetching shot birds, including waterfowl.

What game birds will the breed work best? That depends on the individual dog and on its training. But generally, the breed does best in relatively thick cover on tight-sitting birds. Because of the coat's color, however, the wirehair is a bit hard to see in heavy cover.

In general, the wirehair has a bit more range than the shorthair and a good deal more than the Weimaraner and Brittany spaniel. The wirehair's gait is freer and more flowing than that of the Weimaraner and the shorthair.

For water work and in rugged cover, the wirehair's rough coat gives it an edge over the other German breeds. And it has the drive and stamina to hunt hard all day. The wirehair's coat, however, tends to pick up a great quantity of burrs and dirt.

DISPOSITION: The German wirehair is intelligent, sensitive, and inherently clownish, having quite a sense of humor. It is quick to learn, has a retentive memory, and is eager to please.

Like most intelligent dogs, however, the wirehair requires firm (but not harsh) and consistent discipline. It is easily bored and will become mischievous if left to its own devices.

The wirehair tends to be aloof or suspicious with strangers, but to those humans it knows, it is ingratiatingly affectionate. It makes a good house dog and family companion.

FLUSHING DOGS

English Springer Spaniel

HISTORY: The word "spaniel" has its origins in the Roman term for Spain—Hispania. But there is no concrete proof that this type of dog originated in Spain. It is known, though, that spaniels have been in existence for thousands of years. In New York's Metropolitan Museum of Art there is a figure of a spaniel-like dog that dates back to about 3000 BC.

Starting in about 1800, spaniel-type dogs were classified in three rather loose categories that were based mainly on size. Dogs of less than 14 pounds were called lap (or comforter) spaniels, those of 14 to 28 pounds were called cocker spaniels, and those weighing more than 28 pounds were called springer, English, or field spaniels.

The English springer spaniel of today apparently dates back to about 1812, when the Boughey family of Shropshire, England, began to keep a relatively pure line of these dogs. The first trials for springers, run under the auspices of the sporting Spaniel Club, were held in England in 1895. The larger and faster springers began to dominate the trials, outhunting the cocker, Clumber, and field spaniels, and sportsmen esteem for the springer grew.

The generally agreed-upon date for the introduction of the purebred springer to America is 1907, but the breed did not take hold until a Manitoba dog fancier, Eudore Chevrier, began to import and train large numbers of these dogs in about 1921.

The English Springer Field Trial Association was formed in 1924, and the first trials were held that same year. A standard for the breed was devised, and the American Kennel Club approved it in 1932.

DESCRIPTION: The English springer spaniel is a flushing dog—that is, it hunts the ground ahead of its master, but within shotgun range, and puts game birds into flight, rather than pointing them.

The springer's coat is flat and somewhat wavy (but not curly), of medium length, and dense enough to provide protection against water, weather, and briary vegetation. There is a fringe of wavy hair on the throat, brisket, chest, and bell. Coat colors include liver and white (the most prevalent), liver and tan, black and white, black and tan, tan and white, black and white and tan, and others. Unacceptable color combinations are red and white, and lemon and white.

The ears are long and set at about eye level. The tail is docked. The feet are webbed for swimming and for work in muddy and swampy areas. The toes are well arched, and pads are deep and horny. The body is muscular and relatively heavy boned.

In general, the springer's physical conformation should give it speed, agility, and endurance.

SIZE: The springer is a medium-size hunting dog. Weights range from 45 to 50 pounds for males and from 42 to 47 pounds for females. Shoulder height ranges from 18 to 22 inches.

HUNTING ABILITY: Being a flushing dog rather than a pointing dog, the springer must work within range of its master's gun. The breed has a natural tendency to work close and so is easily taught to flush game birds.

Many springers, given the proper training, also make at least passable retrievers and can learn to mark the spots where shot birds fall. They are top-notch bird finders and fetchers in thick cover and in swamps, and they can handle rough weather well.

The springer will hunt any game bird, but it is far more popular with hunters who seek birds that tend to

English Springer Spaniel

comes from the woodcock, which the cocker spaniels were bred to hunt.

But the cocker spaniel as a distinct breed is generally believed to have originated with a dog named Obo, whelped in England in 1879. Obo, 10 inches tall at the shoulder and weighing 22 pounds, led directly to the separate registration of cockers in the *English Stud Book*, beginning in 1893. The first field trial for cockers was held in 1899.

Many English cockers were imported to America, where a separate strain, the American cocker, was developed. The fountainhead of that strain is said to have been a dog named Braeside Bob.

The first major cocker trial held in the United States was run in 1924 under the auspices of the Cocker Spaniel Field Trial Club of America. Field trials were largely responsible for maintaining the breed's value as hunting dogs, but that value declined markedly, particularly with the onset of World War II, which had the effect of almost entirely eliminating cocker field trials. Trials were resumed after the war, but by then the breed was largely relegated to bench shows and pet status. Very few cockers are seen in the game coverts today.

DESCRIPTION: The cocker, like the springer spaniel, is a breed that flushes, rather than points, game birds.

The modern cocker spaniel is actually two dogs: the American cocker and the English cocker. The American cocker is perhaps the most beautiful of all the spaniels. It has a rounded skull, large and rather prominent eyes, and long ears that are placed at eye level or a bit lower. The leather of the ears reaches to the muzzle when the ears are outstretched.

The American's body is rather short, with a much broader chest than other spaniels. The top line slopes from the withers to the croup. The feet are strong and compact, with thick pads.

The American cocker comes in three varieties, based mainly on color. The three are black, any other solid color (but including black and tan), and parti-colors. The black variety usually has a thicker coat and feathering than the other colors.

The English cocker's muzzle is slightly longer than the American's, and there is not the excess of hair as in the American black variety. Colors vary, including many self colors (all black, all liver, and all red) and parti-colors, as well as roan colors of blue, red, orange, liver, and lemon. The English cocker is leggier than the American.

SIZE: The English cocker is somewhat heavier than the

run rather than fly (such as pheasants and desert quail) than it is with hunters who seek tight-sitting game (bobwhite quail and the like). In fact, the recent upsurge in springer popularity in America is due mainly to the rise of the pheasant as the top game bird in the northern United States. Running birds are right down a springer's alley, while they tend to corrupt the performance of a pointing dog.

DISPOSITION: The springer's temperament is gentle, particularly with children, and friendly. The breed adapts well to various maintenance conditions—that is, it is as much at ease in the home as in the kennel. It takes well to training and discipline.

◾ Cocker Spaniel

HISTORY: At one time, beginning in the early 19th century, all spaniel-type dogs were classified according to size, with the cockers (14 to 28 pounds) ranking between the lap spaniels (under 14 pounds) and the field spaniels (more than 28 pounds). The name "cocker"

Cocker Spaniel

American cocker, ranging from 28 to 34 pounds for the males and 26 to 32 pounds for the females. The American cocker should weigh no less than 22 pounds and no more than 28 pounds.

HUNTING ABILITY: As stated above, the cocker spaniel today is far more popular as a bench-show animal and house pet than as a hunter of game birds. Therein lies the breed's major disadvantage, as far as hunters are concerned—it is difficult to find a good hunting strain of cocker spaniel.

If an interested hunter can find a dog whose recent ancestry contains good hunting and field-trial stock, he is on the right track. The hunter should then try to determine whether the dog has the following desirable characteristics: courage, a well-developed instinct for following bird scent, willingness to work, and tractability. The dog should like the water (particularly if the hunter wants the dog to do some waterfowl retrieving) and should be willing to charge right in to get a bird even though the water may be cold or rough. The dog also should be willing to work all kinds of cover with enthusiasm and fair speed.

In general, the English cocker is a better bet than the American as a hunting dog. That is partly due to the fact that in England cockers are required to prove their worth in a field trial before they can become eligible to qualify as a bench champion, a practice that has

prevented the widespread deterioration of the hunting instinct that has plagued the American cocker.

The cocker, being the smallest of the spaniels, is not so effective in heavy cover or in water work. The cocker is not as fast or as effective a hunter as the springer spaniel. It is, however, faster than the Clumber or Sussex spaniels and so is generally preferred over those breeds.

DISPOSITION: Good cockers—especially those that are to be used for hunting—should have a happy, bubbly type of disposition. In recent years, however, many cockers have been extremely high-strung and nervous, given to urinating on the floor because of excitement and to biting people for little reason. Shyness and hysteria are other character faults, but those, like the others, may well be on the way out, thanks to the efforts of breeders. Cockers from good hunting stock are alert and take correction in stride.

■ American Water Spaniel

HISTORY: The American water spaniel is one of only a few hunting-dog breeds that were developed entirely in the United States. Though it has been in existence as a recognizable type for almost 100 years, the American water spaniel was not recognized officially until 1920, when the United Kennel Club accepted a Wisconsin dog for registration as an American water spaniel. The *Field Dog Stud Book* sanctioned the breed in 1938, and the American Kennel Club followed suit in 1940.

The breed's development was centered in the pheasant belt of the Midwest and in New England. One of the men largely responsible for the development was a Wisconsin physician and surgeon, Dr. F. K. Pfeifer, whose dog Curley Pfeifer was the first American water spaniel registered with the United Kennel Club. Dr. Pfeifer's kennels contained as many as 130 of these dogs at one time.

It was Dr. Pfeifer's opinion that the breed was the result of a cross between the English curly-coated retriever and the field spaniel. In all probability, there was also some Irish water spaniel blood. The breed's original purpose was to retrieve ducks shot by hunters in small skiffs.

DESCRIPTION: Once called the American brown water spaniel because of its rich liver color, this breed's coat is closely curled or deeply waved, but not kinky. The hair is quite dense, which gives the dog protection in water and heavy cover.

The forehead is covered with short, smooth hair and lacks the tuft or topknot that is characteristic of the

Irish water spaniel. The American's tail is covered with hair, while the Irish's tail is almost ratlike with smooth, short hair.

There apparently are two strains within the American water spaniel breed. One type is small, compact, and somewhat bench-legged, while the other is quite a bit larger and longer-legged. The larger strain is preferred by jump shooters.

SIZE: The American water spaniel stands 15 to 18 inches at the shoulder and weighs 25 to 45 pounds. It is compact and built close to the ground.

HUNTING ABILITY: The American water spaniel is a natural hunter and over the years has maintained all the "hunt" that was originally bred into it. That is probably due to the fact that this breed has not attracted the attention of dog-show people.

The American is essentially a flushing dog, though it is occasionally classified as a retriever. It can be trained to quarter in the uplands in front of the hunter, to scent and chase upland game, to drop to shot, and to retrieve upon command. Its main use in the uplands is on birds that tend to run rather than fly, such as pheasants and various western quail.

The American is a fair waterfowl retriever, but it can't compare to the various retriever breeds for that purpose, though it is a tougher water breed than any of the other spaniels.

American Water Spaniel

The American doesn't rank as tops in any facet of hunting-dog work. On the other hand, it is an excellent choice as a multipurpose dog, capable of both flushing game and fetching it and able to perform moderately well in a duck blind. And the American will hunt anything from pheasants, grouse, and woodcock to rabbits and squirrels.

DISPOSITION: The American water spaniel is likable, friendly, intelligent, even tempered, and tractable. It is a natural hunter and a quick learner, and it seldom possesses personality quirks. It takes well to training and discipline and adapts well to varying conditions of terrain and weather. Though it has an appealing way about it, the American, more so than most other spaniels, seems to be distrustful of strangers.

■ Welsh Springer Spaniel

HISTORY: No one knows exactly when the Welsh springer spaniel first came upon the dog scene, though it is known to be an ancient breed indeed. As one might expect, the breed was developed in Wales but found its way to England and Scotland and eventually to America and such far-flung lands as India, Australia, and Thailand. The breed standards were drawn up by the Welsh Springer Spaniel Club of England and later adopted by the American Kennel Club.

DESCRIPTION: The Welsh springer spaniel—in contrast to the cocker and English springer, which may be a wide variety of colors—is red and white only. The coat is flat and thick and silky, and it has a soft understory that provides protection from briary cover and from rugged water and weather conditions.

The ears are quite hairy and set low on the head. The legs are straight and fringed with hair. The tail is plumed.

SIZE: The Welsh springer is a bit smaller than the English springer and a great deal larger than the cocker spaniel. The Welsh ranges in weight from 35 to 45 pounds.

HUNTING ABILITY: The Welsh springer is a flushing dog rather than a pointing dog. Its importance as a hunting breed is limited, however, and very few of these dogs are seen in the game coverts.

Nonetheless, the Welsh springer can be taught to hunt in front of the gun like other flushing spaniels, though its training, particularly obedience training, may be more difficult and time consuming than the training of other spaniels.

If this breed has a strong point, it is probably that it is able to work under temperature extremes, particularly on land (it is not able to stand very cold water, as retrievers can). It is capable of hunting upland game when the weather is quite warm.

The Welsh springer has an acutely tuned nose and is a willing worker. However, its working pace is somewhat slower than that of the English springer.

DISPOSITION: The Welsh springer has a pleasant and even temperament. It is kind and gentle with children, fiercely loyal, and dependable. Its training may take more time than some other breeds, but it takes discipline well.

■ Clumber Spaniel

HISTORY: The first mention in print of the Clumber spaniel was an 1807 article that appeared in a British publication, *Sporting Magazine*. An engraving with the article showed part of a painting in which a number of long, low, heavy-bodied dogs surrounded the gamekeeper of the estate—called Clumber House—of the Duke of Newcastle, Henry Clinton. The spaniel-like dogs, which the article called "springers, or cock-flushers," were said to have been a gift of the Duke of Noailles of France. The gamekeeper, William Mansell, was said to have "studied to increase, unmixed, this peculiar race of flushers."

Clumbers dominated the early field trials held for spaniels, despite the fact that at least one authority—the American dog writer James Watson—thought the breed was of "little use" in the field because of its slowness. But then the cockers and springers became faster, and the Clumbers began to lose favor.

Clumbers never became popular in America, mainly because no specialty club was ever formed to espouse the breed. No field trials are held.

DESCRIPTION: The Clumber might be said to be the basset hound of the bird-dog set. Slow moving, short legged, and heavy bodied, it gives the appearance of being very powerful. The head is large and massive, with relatively short ears. The neck is long and thick, and the shoulders are heavily muscled. The back is long, broad, and straight, free from droop or bow. The legs are short but heavy boned, and the feet are large.

The coat is straight and silky, not too long but very dense, and has long and abundant feathers. White predominates in the coat color, which varies from lemon and white to orange and white. The ears are solid lemon or orange. The muzzle and legs are ticked.

SIZE: Today's Clumber spaniel is somewhat larger than the English springer, standing 17 to 18 inches tall at the shoulder, but weighing 55 to 65 pounds for males and 35 to 50 pounds for females.

HUNTING ABILITY: Clumbers were bred as "retired gentlemen's shooting dogs" and were used in restricted areas, such as turnip patches and truck gardens, and in small-game preserves with large populations of birds. In such places, the slow-moving, close-working Clumber was a major advantage. However, most American conditions of cover, terrain, and game require a dog that works at a much faster pace and covers a good amount of ground. That is the main reason the Clumber has never found wide favor in this country. It is so rare here, in fact, that finding a good one is extremely difficult.

Nonetheless, the Clumber is a top-notch game flusher and will retrieve well if trained properly. Because of its light coat, it is said to be unparalleled as a hot-weather hunter.

DISPOSITION: One of the Clumber spaniel's advantages (perhaps the only advantage, so far as many American hunters are concerned) is that it is about the most easily trained of all the spaniels. It takes training and discipline well, remembers its lessons, and does not have to be retrained. Though some early accounts of the breed's temperament called these dogs "naturally ill-tempered" and said they "would not work for every person," such temperament quirks have apparently been bred out.

■ Brittany Spaniel

HISTORY: The distant ancestors of the Brittany spaniel—and those of all other pointing-dog breeds—lived in Spain, where they were used to "set" (point) upland game. Further development of these breeds took place in France and began more than 1,000 years ago.

Some dog historians believe that the Brittany spaniel as it is known today is distantly related to the red-and-white setter, original ancestor of the Irish setter.

Whether or not that is true, the first tailless ancestor of today's Brittany is a pup that resulted from the crossing of a white-and-lemon woodcock-hunting dog brought to France's Brittany area by an Englishman. The pup developed into a top-notch hunting dog and was much in demand as a stud.

The breed's early development was mainly the result of the efforts of a French breeder and sportsman, Arthur Enaud. He used an Italian pointer and the French Braque (also a pointing dog) as outcrosses, thereby improving the bloodlines. The use of outcrosses was then discontinued, and Enaud adhered closely to selective breeding practices, firmly establishing the breed's type.

It is thought that the first Brittany spaniels brought to the United States arrived here in 1912. However, it was not until 1934 through 1936 that the first sizable importations were made and efforts were intensified to establish the breed here. A prime mover in those efforts was Louis Thebaud.

Since that time, the Brittany has become well known in this country and well respected for its abilities in the hunting field.

DESCRIPTION: The Brittany is unique among spaniels for a number of reasons. For one, it is often called "the spaniel that looks like a setter." For another, it is often born without a tail.

The Brittany's head is much like that of the English setter, except that it is shorter, a bit wider across the dome, shorter and higher set in the ears, and a little lighter in the muzzle. While most of the other pointing breeds have dark-brown eyes, the Brittany's eyes are deep amber. They convey an expression of extreme alertness, intelligence, and tractability.

The coat is a good deal like that of the setter, but is heavier and either quite smooth or slightly wavy. The Brittany's coat is not as heavily feathered or silky as that of the setters. The coat color in the Brittany is liver and white or orange and white, preferably with roan ticking. The white usually predominates.

Overall, the Brittany is small, closely knit, and strong, with well-fringed thighs, muscular shoulders, a deep chest, and broad and strong hindquarters. The tail is naturally short, but docking is occasionally needed to keep it to a length of 4 inches.

SIZE: The Brittany is the smallest of all the pointing-dog breeds. Shoulder height ranges from 17 to 19¾ inches, and weight averages 35 to 45 pounds.

Brittany Spaniel

HUNTING ABILITY: The Brittany is the only spaniel with a highly developed pointing instinct, and it is almost always considered a pointing breed. The Britt is also the widest ranging of all of the spaniels. In fact, its range is only slightly shorter than that of pointers and setters. And the Brittany has the ability to adapt its range to the type of terrain it is hunting, staying close to the gun in thick cover and moving well out there in open country. It is at its best, however, in thick stuff and will keep in touch with the hunter. Thanks to its spaniel ancestry, it can easily be trained to fetch.

As a result of that fine admixture of characteristics, the Britt can be used on woodcock and ruffed grouse; on pheasants and other open-country birds, such as quail and sharptailed grouse; and to retrieve shot game from land or water.

The Brittany has fine bird sense, pointing intensity, and style. It also has good speed. Its coat provides fine protection from brambles and other rugged cover, and because of its coloration it is easily seen.

A good indicator of the Brittany's increasing favor among hunters is the fact that more and more Britts are being entered in field trials today.

DISPOSITION: The Brittany is quite friendly, highly intelligent, extremely alert, and very tractable. It makes a fine companion for the one-dog hunter, as well as an excellent family pet. Though not really timid, the Britt is rather sensitive, so rough handling or harsh treatment should be avoided. Gentle coercion is the ticket during training sessions.

RETRIEVERS

■ Labrador Retriever

HISTORY: There is little doubt that the Labrador originated in the Canadian province of the same name, probably from a strain of dog bred in and around St. John's. The breed's greatest development, however, took place in England and began when the Second Earl of Malmesbury imported some of the dogs from Newfoundland. The Third Earl of Malmesbury is given the credit for giving the breed its name and keeping it relatively pure. It is generally agreed, though, that some early English breeders introduced some blood from other retrievers, notably the flat-coated and curly-coated types.

In 1903, the Labrador was recognized as a breed by the English Kennel Club, and in 1906, Labradors were first entered in English field trials.

Labradors first appeared in the United States in the late 1920s, and the first licensed Labrador field trial in this country was held in 1931, in Orange County, New York. Labradors swept the first three placements in the first all-retriever-breed trial, held in 1934 at East Setauket, New York. Since that time, the Labrador has outdistanced all other retriever breeds in popularity among hunters and field trialers. That popularity is due in large measure to such early breeders as J. F. Carlisle and Averell Harriman. About 65 percent of all retriever registrations today are Labradors.

Labrador Retriever

DESCRIPTION: The Labrador's overall appearance is that of a strongly built, close-coupled, and active animal. In comparison with flat-coated and curly-coated retrievers, the breeds the Lab most resembles, it is wider in the head and through the chest, and wider and more powerful in the loins and hindquarters. Generally, the Lab is shorter of leg than other retrievers and of a more solid build.

The Lab's skull is broad and has a slightly pronounced brow, and the head is clean-cut and free from any fleshiness. The jaws are long and powerful, not snippy. The ears hang rather close to the head and well back, and are set somewhat low. They should not be large and heavy. The eyes are brown, yellow, or black.

The neck is long and powerful, the shoulders long and sloping. The legs are straight from shoulder to ground, and the feet are compact, with well-arched toes and well-developed pads.

The tail, almost totally free of feathering but clothed all around with short, thick hair and having a rounded look, is quite thick near the base but tapers gradually toward the tip.

The coat is short, very dense, and without waviness. The coat color is generally all black, though other solid colors—yellow and chocolate being the most abundant—are permissible, as is a white spot on the chest.

SIZE: The standard for Labrador retrievers calls for shoulder heights as follows: 22½ to 24½ inches for males and 21½ to 23½ inches for females. Average weights of Labs in working condition are 60 to 75 pounds for males and 55 to 70 pounds for females.

HUNTING ABILITY: The Labrador well deserves its position of preeminence among retrievers. It is the No. 1 choice of hunters who want a dog that will fetch birds on both land and water. The Lab takes naturally to water and to the job of retrieving, at which it is at its best. Properly trained—and this breed takes training very well—the Lab will sit or lie quietly in a boat or blind or walk at heel until ordered to retrieve.

The Lab is probably best known for its waterfowl work. Its rugged build and constitution, and its short but protective coat, enable it to withstand extremes of heat or cold. It is second in toughness only to the Chesapeake Bay retriever.

Though retrieving downed game birds is its specialty, the Labrador has phenomenal scenting powers and can also be trained to quarter ahead of the hunter and flush upland game, including pheasants, grouse, quail, woodcock, and the like. When working upland coverts, the Lab is quick, stylish, and aggressive—traits that also endear it to field trialers. It will also trail wounded and running birds such as pheasants.

In addition, Labradors—because of their tractability and trainability—are often used as seeing-eye dogs.

Finally, Labradors have compiled an enviable record in retriever field trials, topping all other breeds in numbers of dogs entered and placements won.

DISPOSITION: Even tempered, likable, friendly—all of these words describe the Labrador. It makes an excellent pet for a hunter's family, though the more aggressive individuals of this breed may be too rough for small children (however, the most aggressive Labs are usually the best hunters). The Lab is very easily trained and quite intelligent, takes discipline without cringing or quitting, and is never mean. Some Labs (like some dogs of any breed) tend to be roamers when left to their own devices.

Golden Retriever

HISTORY: The golden retriever is directly descended from a strain of very large, light-colored dogs known as Russian trackers. These animals were part of a circus troupe touring England in 1860. A certain nobleman, Sir Dudley Majoribanks, saw the dogs and was so impressed that he bought the entire group of eight.

Sir Dudley bred the dogs for 10 years without outcrossing, but in 1870, feeling that the dogs—which weighed as much as 100 pounds—were too large and cumbersome to be hunters, he crossed the Russian trackers with the bloodhound. The outcross reduced the size of the breed, improved its scenting abilities, and gave the coat a somewhat darker color and a finer texture. In 1911, these dogs were recognized as a distinct breed by the English Kennel Club, and about the same time, the Golden Retriever Club of England was formed.

It was about the turn of the century when the first goldens came to North America, brought to Vancouver Island, British Columbia, by British army personnel. The breed spread rapidly on the Pacific coast, even as far as Alaska. One of the breeders most responsible was Bart Armstrong of Winnipeg, Manitoba. The golden

Golden Retriever

was recognized by the Canadian Kennel Club in 1927 and by the American Kennel Club in 1932.

DESCRIPTION: From puppyhood, when it is a round little ball of yellow fluff, through adulthood, the golden retriever is a beautiful animal. The gorgeous coat—rich red overall (it must not be too light, like cream, or as dark as, say, the red of an Irish setter)—and soft, honest facial expression give the golden an attractiveness few other breeds can match.

The standard for the golden retriever calls for a broad skull set on a clean and muscular neck. The muzzle is powerful and wide. The eyes are dark and set well apart, kindly in expression, and have dark rims. The coat may be either flat or wavy, and it is dense and water resistant, with a good undercoat. The ears are small and well set on. The feet are round and catlike, not splayed. The forelegs are well boned and straight, hind legs strong and muscular. The tail is straight, not curled at the tip or carried over the back.

The body in general is well balanced, short-coupled, and deep through the chest. The shoulders are well laid back and long in the blade.

SIZE: Ideal weights for golden retrievers in top working condition are as follows: 65 to 68 pounds for males, 55 to 60 pounds for females. Shoulder heights average 23 to 24 inches for males, 20½ to 22 inches for females.

HUNTING ABILITY: The golden's status as the second-most popular retrieving dog in the United States attests to the breed's ability as a bird finder and fetcher.

The golden ranks behind the Chesapeake and the Labrador as a straight retriever of downed waterfowl, particularly under rigorous conditions. Icy water is easily absorbed by the golden's silky coat, so it does not perform its best under most waterfowling conditions (in warmer climates, however, the golden makes a fine waterfowl retriever).

The golden seems to be at its best on dry land. It hunts well in front of the upland gunner, quartering nicely and hunting an area thoroughly and methodically. It marks downed birds well and, of course, is an accomplished fetcher.

The golden isn't as good as the Labrador in the upland coverts, lacking the Lab's speed, style, and aggressiveness, but it tops the Chesapeake in that department.

The golden, on the other hand, is about the most reliable of all bird fetchers when it comes to nonslip retrieving. (A nonslip retriever is a dog that walks at heel or sits quietly at the handler's side until ordered out to retrieve.)

The golden's coat can be a problem, for it collects burrs in the uplands and mud in the marshes. The coat requires considerable attention.

Chesapeake Bay Retriever

DISPOSITION: There is no more affectionate breed than the golden retriever. It thrives on verbal and physical praise, is wonderfully understanding and gentle with children, and makes the best pet by far of any of the retriever breeds.

The golden is exceptionally intelligent and tractable. It is eminently trainable, too—provided that the trainer uses patience and a soft hand. Too much two-fisted discipline can turn this otherwise docile and biddable animal into an obstinate sulker that will refuse to learn or work.

■ Chesapeake Bay Retriever

HISTORY: It is generally agreed that the Chessie, as this breed is affectionately known, descended at least partly from the Newfoundland dog of some 150 years ago. It therefore shares a common heritage with the Labrador.

It is said that an English brig was wrecked off the shores of Maryland in 1807. Aboard the vessel—and rescued—were two Newfoundland puppies, a dingy red male and a black female, which became the property of local breeders. These dogs were reported to have extraordinary retrieving ability.

Stories vary on the development of the breed from that point. Some say the two Newfoundland dogs were crossed with yellow and tan coonhounds. Another story, amusing but absurd, says that a Chesapeake female was mated to an otter! Still another account, possibly the true one, is that the Newfoundland dogs were crossed with English water poodles.

The Chessie's popularity grew rather rapidly, and by 1918, when the American Chesapeake Club was founded, the breed had become the No. 1 duck dog not only in the Chesapeake area, but also in such places as Manitoba, Minnesota, and along the Mississippi Flyway. The breed was recognized by the American Kennel Club in 1931.

DESCRIPTION: Beauty, it is said, is in the eye of the beholder. Under that premise, the Chesapeake is the apple of the eye of many duck and goose hunters. But actually, the Chessie is a sort of homely animal. Chesapeake breeders have resisted efforts to beautify the breed—an attitude that, from the hunter's standpoint, is very fortunate, since a breed's "beautification" is usually accompanied by a drastic decline in its hunting abilities.

The Chessie's most unusual traits are its dense and oily coat (which enables this dog to be oblivious to the coldest water), yellow eyes, rather long tail, and color, which ranges from a light shade quite reminiscent of dead grass to chocolate brown.

The skull is broad, the muzzle is powerful, and the ears are rather small and set well up on the head. The thick and muscular neck appears to be too short for the body. The shoulders are powerful, and the chest is strong, deep, and wide.

The hindquarters are especially powerful for swimming. The legs are of medium length, well boned, and straight. The feet appear abnormally large.

SIZE: Male Chesapeake Bay retrievers weigh from 65 to 75 pounds on the average, females 55 to 65 pounds. Shoulder heights are 23 to 26 inches for males, 21 to 24 inches for females.

HUNTING ABILITY: The Chesapeake is unparalleled as a water retriever of ducks and geese in rugged, wintry weather. There are a number of reasons for this standing.

First, the Chessie has an unbounded love for the water, the icier the better. It hits the water with abandon, which can be somewhat disquieting to occupants of a floating blind.

Second, the dog's coat—heavy, woolly, and oily—prevents its skin from ever getting wet and accounts for its ability to withstand bitter-cold water. A couple of shakes, and the coat is freed of ice and water.

The Chessie has great strength, stamina, and aggressiveness. These dogs have been known to fetch more than 200 ducks in one day under the most inhuman weather conditions and to swim a mile to retrieve a single bird.

The Chessie is possessed of a fine memory. A well-trained one can mark and recall the falls (locations of downed ducks) of as many as six birds at a time.

If the Chesapeake has a fault in the area of waterfowl retrieving, it is that some individual Chessies tend toward hard mouth, the practice of clamping the teeth so tightly on a bird that the bird's flesh is marked or damaged. Training can overcome that problem.

The Chesapeake does have a place in the uplands, but that place is as a nonslip retriever (a dog that stays at heel until it is ordered out to fetch) rather than as a flusher of game.

DISPOSITION: The Chesapeake's temperament is a good deal less even than the Labrador's. The Chessie does not take to strangers well, and it is something of a rugged individualist. It doesn't make as good a pet as most of the

Irish Water Spaniel

other hunting breeds, and it is inclined to fight when put into a kennel with other dogs. Its enthusiasm can make it difficult to train. But such enthusiasm, when linked with drive and aggressiveness, is what makes for a top-notch hunting dog.

Irish Water Spaniel

HISTORY: In Ireland, in the early part of the 19th century, there existed two distinct strains of water spaniels. In the north of Ireland, the strain was small, particolored, and had a wavy coat. In the south of Ireland, around the River Shannon bogs, was a larger dog with a curly coat. This larger dog is thought to be the progenitor of the dog known today.

The Irish water spaniel as it is presently known is directly traceable to one Justin McCarthy, who in 1850 was actively breeding Irish water spaniels, using the larger strain with the curly coat. His most famous dog was Boatswain, whose name is found in the pedigree of one of the early dogs registered in the *Field Dog Stud Book*.

These dogs apparently first appeared in the United States in the 1860s. However, the first official registrations appeared in 1878 in the stud book of the National American Kennel Club, forerunner of the American Kennel Club. The breed is one of the first retrievers to be imported into this country.

The Irish, bred to work the thick cover and cold waters of Ireland's bogs, came into great favor among U.S. market hunters, especially in the Midwest, and its fame spread to both the East and West Coasts. The Irish's popularity probably was never greater than in the early 1920s, but that popularity began to fall off as that of the other retriever breeds increased, mostly because the Irish could not hold its own in field trials with the other breeds. Today, the Irish is seldom seen in the duck marshes.

DESCRIPTION: The Irish water spaniel is the largest of all the spaniels. It is a rather heavy-boned animal whose solid-liver coat is composed of tight, crisp ringlets. The face, however, is smooth and free of any long or curly hair. The leg hair gives the dog the appearance of wearing pantaloons and does not look like the feathering of a setter.

One of the breed's most noticeable physical characteristics is its almost ratlike tail—the reason this breed is sometimes called the rattail. Actually, the tail isn't hairless. It is covered with short, smooth hair—except near the root, where the hair is much longer and curly.

The head is cleanly chiseled, the skull is rather large with a prominent dome, the eyes are dark hazel and browless. The ears are long, lobular, and set low on the head. The neck is long, the shoulders sloping, and the clean chest is deep but not too wide between the legs. The body overall is of medium length. The feet are large, thick, and well clothed with hair both above and between the toes.

SIZE: Irish water spaniels develop slowly, both physically and mentally. They may not reach physical maturity until the age of two years. Generally, males weigh 55 to 65 pounds and stand 22 to 24 inches at the shoulder. Females weigh 45 to 58 pounds and stand 21 to 23 inches at the shoulder.

HUNTING ABILITY: The Irish has a few things going for it. Its thick, ropy, oily coat enables it to withstand the rigors of a typical duck-shooting situation: frigid water, wind, sleet, mud, and the like. It is leggy enough to work in heavy marsh cover and such. And it loves the water and is a strong swimmer. If it is properly (and patiently) trained, it can become a proficient retriever of waterfowl—particularly in jump-shooting situations in wadable marshes—and a nonslip retriever in the uplands. And, if you're very lucky, it might develop a knack for flushing game ahead of the upland shooter.

It must be said, on the other hand, that the Labrador, the golden, and the Chesapeake can be expected to do the job of retrieving better, faster, and easier than the Irish. The Irish is no great shakes in routing out and flushing upland game. And its coat, though it offers fine protection, is an abomination from the hunter's standpoint, for it seems to form mats and pick up burrs as if by magic. And the comings and goings of an Irish in a duck blind can all but inundate the occupants with water and mud. To top it off, the Irish is far more difficult to train than any of the other retriever breeds.

DISPOSITION: The Irish water spaniel's temperament is an odd but often engaging melange of clownishness, perversity, stubbornness, desire to please, and even theatricality. The Irish tends to be loyal to a master yet suspicious of strangers. It thrives on affection and companionship, but will not stand abuse. Its training calls for an inordinate amount of patience and the ability to coax rather than force. Once the Irish learns a lesson, though, it learns it well and remembers it.

■ Flat-Coated Retriever

HISTORY: The flat-coated retriever derives from the original water dogs of Newfoundland, probably from a cross between the St. John's and the Labrador strains. It is also likely that some blood from the Gordon and Irish setters and possibly even the Russian tracker (fountainhead of the golden retriever) was used to advantage in the development of the flat coat.

The earliest-known flat coat was an animal displayed at a show in Birmingham, England, in 1860 by a man named Braisford. This dog looked a good deal like a Labrador, but was larger and its coat was much heavier and had longer hair. This dog was an excellent water dog and also performed well on upland game birds such as pheasants.

The breed was stabilized and developed under the hand of such breeders as Dr. Bond Moore of Wolverhampton, England. Before the Labrador's popularity began to soar, flat coats served as gamekeepers' dogs over much of England. They are still used on estates and moors, mostly as retrievers.

Though recognized by the American Kennel Club, the flat coat has never gained much popularity in the United States and is seldom seen in field trials. None have become field-trial champions.

DESCRIPTION: The flat-coated retriever is possessed of a distinctive coat that is dense, sleek, and fine-haired (the breed was once called the wavy-coated retriever, but as the breed was developed the hair straightened). The color is either all black or all liver, though a small white spot on the chest is not unusual.

The head is long and nicely molded, while the skull is flat and somewhat broad. The dark-brown or hazel eyes convey an intelligent expression. The ears are relatively small and well set close to the side of the head.

The neck is long, the chest deep and fairly broad, and the back short, square, and well ribbed, with muscular quarters. The forelegs are perfectly straight and well boned down to the feet, which are round and strong. The limbs are well feathered when the animal is in full coat.

SIZE: The flat-coated retriever stands between 21½ and 24 inches tall at the shoulder and weighs between 60 and 75 pounds.

HUNTING ABILITY: Because the flat-coated retriever has never mustered much support in the United States and is far from numerous here, its ability to cope with conditions of cover, terrain, and game common in this country has not really been put to the test. It must be said, however, that the flat coat's work in field trials has never measured up to that of the Labrador, Chesapeake, and golden retrievers.

The flat coat is a fine retriever, particularly of upland game birds. It is a strong swimmer and loves water work, including marking, fetching, and delivering.

Because the flat coat's silky hair absorbs water, this breed is not at its best under cold-water conditions. It is also far from the best at hunting for and rousting out birds in front of the gun.

The breed was once notoriously hard mouthed, but that is no longer true.

DISPOSITION: The flat coat has an even, pleasant disposition; it is unsurpassed as a companion. It is intelligent, tractable, and rugged. Though it may occasionally exhibit a hard-headed or stubborn streak, it takes training and discipline well.

■ Curly-Coated Retriever

HISTORY: Though the precise origin of this animal is beclouded by time, it is known that the curly-coated retriever is the oldest of all breeds that are now called retrievers. It is likely that this breed stemmed from a cross of the St. John's Newfoundland with the Irish (or English) water spaniel, despite the fact that the curly coat lacks the Irish's topknot. Some poodle blood was undoubtedly introduced in order to increase the tightness of the curl.

The curly coat has existed as a true breeding strain since 1855. It was first shown on the bench and run in field trials in 1859, in England, and was acknowledged by the international shows in 1864, when it was given a separate classification.

Beginning in about 1890, curly coats were extensively exported to New Zealand and Australia, where today the curly coat is a very popular breed. The first curly coats were brought to the United States in 1907. The breed is recognized by the American Kennel Club.

DESCRIPTION: The curly-coated retriever is indeed a handsome animal. It is named for the mass of crisp, tight curls that cover its body from the occipital crest of the head to the point of its tail. The color is either black or dark liver, but a bit of white on the chest is not overly unusual.

The head is long and well proportioned, the skull not too flat. The eyes are black or brown and rather large; the ears are rather small and set on low, lying close to the head, and are covered with short curls.

The shoulders are deep and muscular, the chest not too wide but quite deep, and the body rather short, muscular, and well ribbed. The legs are quite long, the forelegs being straight. The feet are compact. The tail is moderately short and carried fairly straight. The curly-coated retriever has the longest legs and lightest build of all the retriever breeds.

SIZE: Height and weight are not vitally important in the curly coat; in fact, the breed standard gives neither maximum nor minimum figures for height or weight. On average, however, the curly coat stands 24 inches at the shoulder and weighs 65 to 75 pounds.

HUNTING ABILITY: It is surprising that the curly coat has never found favor among U.S. hunters, for it is a fine water dog and would make any waterfowler happy with its abilities to mark and remember the locations of shot birds, to fetch them unerringly, and to deliver them.

This breed's love for the water is almost a mania, and its thick coat enables it to swim for hours in the bitterest water. The dog will dive for crippled ducks, which often hold on to submerged vegetation with their bills and would die there and otherwise be lost to the hunter.

The curly coat will also do the job in the uplands, though not so capably as in the marshes. In the uplands, it is best suited as a nonslip retriever—a dog that stays at its master's side until it is sent out to retrieve. The curly coat is seldom used to hunt out in front of the gun.

The thick coat that provides such good protection in rugged weather is also a shortcoming, for it picks up mud, burrs, and the like and requires considerable care from the owner.

The breed once had a reputation for being hard mouthed, but that is no longer true.

DISPOSITION: Eager to please, steady, and affectionate are three adjectives that fit the curly-coated retriever. It is intelligent, has a gentle temperament, and makes a splendid companion. Its field traits include eagerness, endurance, and a good nose. It is easy to train and takes discipline in stride.

■ Weimaraner

HISTORY: The Weimaraner, one of the Continental pointing breeds, originated nearly a century and a half ago in Weimar, Germany, where the Grand Duke Charles Augustus held court. The court was a gathering place for the sporting gentry of Germany.

The demands of those hunters were high. They wanted a dog that would trail land game, fetch from water, and point upland birds—and also be a companion. Toward that end they used a number of dog strains, none of which is known for certain. However, the old German bloodhound was probably one. That bloodhound, called the *Schweisshunde*, was a sort of super-bloodhound and a source of most of that country's hunting breeds.

For many years, Germans guarded the Weimaraner jealously, treating it almost as a national dog. This careful supervision even extended so far as to the passage of a law making it a legal offense for a commoner to own a Weimaraner.

The breed was introduced to the United States in 1929, when a man named Howard Knight of Providence, Rhode Island, imported two of the animals. No breed has ever been given such a welcome or so much publicity. Claims of the Weimaraner's field prowess and high intelligence included "Smartest Dogs in the World." It was even said that they could perform such feats as answering the telephone and taking care of children.

That publicity, unfortunately, proved to be the breed's undoing. It became greatly popular with the general public, and unsound breeding programs, including programs aimed mainly at producing show stock, resulted. Only recently has the Weimaraner shown signs of overcoming the pressures of its early days in the United States. The breed was recognized by the American Kennel Club in 1944.

DESCRIPTION: The Weimaraner has been dubbed the "Gray Ghost" because of its distinctive overall gray color, which may vary from a bright or silvery gray, through a yellowish gray, to a dark or blue gray. The nickname also comes from the dog's silent manner of movement. In texture, the breed's coat is short, flat, and dense, and it gives a sleek or velvety appearance. The woolly undercoat protects the animal from rough weather.

The Weimaraner's back should be firm and level, not sagging—a fault seen in many individuals of the breed some years ago. The body in general is quite large and extremely muscular, and the build is much like that of the German shorthaired pointer.

The tail is docked to about one-third to one-half of its normal length, docked length being about 1½ inches just after birth and about 6 inches at maturity. Docking, incidentally, has a utilitarian purpose—if the tail were left at its normal length, it would whip about in heavy cover and be cut by briars.

The Weimaraner's eyes also are rather distinctive, being blue gray or amber but appearing to change color with varying light conditions.

SIZE: The Weimaraner is a big dog, taller and heavier than the German shorthair. Shoulder height averages 24 to 26 inches for males, 22 to 25 inches for females.

Weimaraner

Average weights are 65 to 85 pounds for males, 55 to 75 pounds for females.

HUNTING ABILITY: The Weimaraner has managed to survive the overpublicity of its first quarter century in the United States, and today serious efforts are being made toward the reestablishment of the breed as a working gundog.

In general, the "Gray Ghost" has a well-developed pointing instinct and is fairly staunch. It has good bird sense and a strong penchant for retrieving. It also loves the water.

The Weimaraner is not a fast worker in the field. It is more of a stalker and, in fact, might even be legitimately called a pussyfooter (a trait due probably to its bloodhound origins). This characteristic makes it a good choice for both pheasants and ruffed grouse and for some of the western and southwestern game birds that like to run rather than fly.

The breed's water work is not outstanding. It will do an acceptable job on short retrieves along waterways, for example, but for ambitious retrieves on open water or mud flats, where it must follow hand signals, the Weimaraner is not the best choice.

It has been said that the Weimaraner tends toward being hard mouthed (holding retrieved game so tightly in its teeth that it marks or pierces the skin). This tendency, too, may be ascribed to the breed's bloodhound ancestry.

DISPOSITION: The Weimaraner is a garrulous, friendly dog. It has a good temperament, being tractable and taking well to training. It is also quite intelligent—one individual, Grafmar's Ador, won his obedience degree at the tender age of six months and was at that time the youngest dog ever to accomplish that feat.

The breed learns its lessons not only early but also well. It also adapts well to the home, making an excellent family pet and a top-notch watchdog.

■ Vizsla

HISTORY: More than 500 years ago, certain Magyar tribes, then the ruling element in Hungary, set about to develop a dog that would hunt all the many varieties of game that abounded in that country. Then (as now in most of Europe) dogs were expected to take game as it came—that is, be capable of trailing hare, wild boar, bears, and deer, as well as pointing and retrieving feathered game.

Vizsla

The result of that development was the vizsla (properly pronounced "veesh-lah"), also known as the Magyar vizsla. Little is known about the early development of this breed, except that a generous amount of hound blood (probably bloodhound) was used. The early vizsla differed only slightly from the other Continental pointing breeds (German shorthair, German wirehair, Brittany spaniel, and Weimaraner).

Though famed in Hungary and elsewhere in Europe, the vizsla was little known until after World War I, when fanciers of the breed formed clubs, held trials, and did much to publicize the breed. Colonel Jeno Dus of the Hungarian Cavalry, genealogy registrar and breed supervisor, also did much to further the cause of the vizsla in the United States.

The vizsla was recognized by the American Kennel Club in 1960. Many vizslas are registered with the *Field Dog Stud Book*.

DESCRIPTION: No conformation standards have been set for this breed, but in general the vizsla is an average-size, short-haired pointing dog with a neat, sleek appearance.

The vizsla is often called the yellow pointer because of its sedge-colored (rich yellow or yellowish brown) coat. The coat is smooth and easily cared for. The tail, like that of all the other Continental breeds, is normally docked to one-third of its standard length. This is to prevent it from being cut and torn by briars and other rough cover.

SIZE: The vizsla is about the same size as other short-haired pointing dogs, standing about 25 inches high at the shoulder and weighing an average of about 70 pounds.

HUNTING ABILITY: The vizsla—and the other Continental pointing breeds—has enjoyed a considerable increase in popularity among U.S. hunters in recent years. The breed's versatility in the field is the principle reason.

In the good old days, when game was plentiful, limits were generous, and hunting country was abundant, hunters sought rather specialized game dogs—a wide-ranging quail dog, an open-country pheasant dog, a close-working grouse dog. But today game is scarcer, hunting country is more restricted, and limits are lower. It's not practical for today's hunter to limit himself to one kind of game. He wants a dog that will help him get pheasants, quail, grouse, and woodcock, and maybe fetch ducks and even run a rabbit. The vizsla is—or at least can be—such a dog.

Nova Scotia Duck Tolling Retriever

The key to the development of any multipurpose dog is its training. Only by positive training in control and field work can a dog be made to handle many varieties of game satisfactorily.

No dog can be expected to excel in all forms of hunting, but the vizsla will, if brought along patiently, find, point, and retrieve game birds. Training procedures should cover one kind of game at a time.

Generally, the vizsla performs better as a close worker in heavy cover than it does as a wide-ranging animal in open country. Consequently, it is better on ruffed grouse and woodcock than on pheasants and quail. It is most popular in the midwestern United States.

Field trials have done much to improve the field work of the vizsla. The parent organization, the Vizsla Club, holds a national vizsla trial each year.

DISPOSITION: The vizsla's temperament is much like that of most of the Continental pointing breeds. It is quietly friendly, intelligent, and alert. It learns its lessons well, but the trainer must be sure that his pupil knows what is expected of it and how it should do it. Many vizslas do not take kindly to strangers, but they are not vicious. The breed makes a good home companion.

■ Nova Scotia Duck Tolling Retriever

HISTORY: The tolling retriever is a medium-size gundog bred for hunting. The breed originated in Little River Harbour in Yarmouth County, Nova Scotia, early in the 19th century. The tolling dog was also known as the Little River duck dog or the Yarmouth toller. Other names include toller, Scotty, Novie, and little red duck dog. Background information seems to indicate that spaniels, setters, and farm collies may have been involved in the breeding of the toller.

The toller was admitted to the Canadian Kennel Club in 1945. In 1955, the breed was declared the provincial dog of Nova Scotia. The breed gained national recognition in 1980, when two Nova Scotia duck tolling retrievers were awarded Best in Show at championship events. In 2001, the dog was approved for admission into the Miscellaneous Class of the American Kennel Club and then it gained full recognition in the Sporting Group in 2003.

DESCRIPTION: Tollers have a medium-length soft coat of various shades of red or orange. Built solidly and compact, tollers give the appearance of being powerful and sturdy. Tollers also have webbed feet and at least one white marking, usually at the tail, feet, or chest. The lack of white is not a fault. However, dogs with white on the shoulders, ears, back of neck, or across the back, or with black areas in the coat, are disqualified from conformation shows. Tollers also shed with the seasons.

SIZE: Tolling retrievers stand between 18 and 29 inches tall. The toller is the smallest of the retrievers and is sometimes mistaken for a small golden retriever. Males weigh between 44 and 51 pounds. Females are slightly smaller, with weights between 37 and 44 pounds. Tollers should be slightly longer than tall. The life span of the toller is 10 to 14 years.

HUNTING ABILITY: Tollers are bred to retrieve from icy waters. They have water-repellent double coats with soft, dense undercoats. The Nova Scotia duck tolling retriever was bred to lure ducks into shotgun range by causing a disturbance near the shore. Typically, a hunter tosses a stick into the water and the toller retrieves the stick. It's this activity that attracts curious ducks into gun range. When the duck is shot, the toller retrieves it. Two traits make this breed a good hunter: endurance and love of water.

DISPOSITION: Nova Scotia tollers are high-energy dogs. They are affectionate with family members and children. Some tollers may be shy in new situations, but shyness in adult dogs is considered a flaw. Duck tollers are working dogs and are happiest when they are hunting ducks. Tollers do not have a loud bark. Some have a unique-sounding bark known as the "toller squeal," a high-pitched, howl-like sound.

HOUNDS

■ Beagle

HISTORY: While the origin of the beagle is not definitely known, this small hound was widely bred in England before it was imported into the United States between 1860 and 1870.

There was a great deal of breeding among the various strains of beagles brought into America to develop a small, strong hound capable of hunting small game in all types of cover. Unfortunately, so much of this breeding took place during the late 1800s that problems arose as to what constituted the perfect beagle. This was finally settled by the founding of the American-English Beagle Club in 1884, an organization that set the standards for the ideal beagle. For the most part, the standards are the same as those presently set forth by the National Beagle Club of America. Today, the beagle is the most popular of all the hound breeds.

DESCRIPTION: The most common color combination of the beagle is black, white, and tan, though many good beagles may show up in any hound color.

Here, briefly, are some of the physical characteristics to look for in a purebred beagle:

The head (skull) is long and domed toward the rear, and the cranium is broad. The eyes are large, set well apart, and brown or hazel in color.

The muzzle is medium in length and straight, with a square cut at the nose. The nostrils are open and large.

The ears are set low, close to the head, and long enough to reach nearly the end of the dog's nose when drawn out. A good beagle's ears are also rounded at the tips, with the forward edges of the ears angling slightly toward the cheeks.

The jaws are level and the throat free of folds of skin. The shoulders are muscular and slope cleanly, and the chest is broad and deep. The shoulders and chest should not be overly muscular, which would interfere with freedom of action when working thick cover or chasing cottontails.

The back is muscular and short. The ribs are well spread, giving the hound plenty of lung room. The legs are short and straight, with feet round and firm. The pads are full and hard. Hindquarters are strong and well muscled, giving the beagle plenty of propelling power.

The tail is set high with a slight curve, but not so curved as to turn forward over the back. The tail has a brush and gives the appearance of being a bit short for the size of the beagle. The coat is of medium length with a close, hard texture.

SIZE: Beagles generally stand 11 to 15 inches tall at the shoulder. A good beagle will not exceed 15 inches.

Beagle

Beagles generally fall into two size categories: 13- or 15-inch class, the measurement referring to the height at the highest point of the shoulder. Choice of size class is generally a matter of personal preference. Weight, depending on size, ranges from 20 to 40 pounds.

HUNTING ABILITY: There is no doubt that the beagle is a born hunter and a good gundog. Its specialty is rabbits, and few breeds, if any, can beat it at routing out its quarry. It has a keen nose, and when it "opens up" on a rabbit, its combination bawl and cry is music to the ears of the hunter.

The beagle is also an enthusiastic and hardy worker and will not hesitate to work through thick briar patches to hunt out small game. It learns its lessons quickly, and generally all the training it needs is exposure to rabbits. When it sees a cottontail, it almost instinctively knows what to do and takes up the chase. This makes the beagle a good choice for the hunter who does not have time for extensive training sessions with his dog.

By no means is the beagle limited to chasing rabbits. It also makes an excellent squirrel dog. When it comes to pheasants, it is second only to the pointing breeds and spaniels. In fact, the beagle is worth its salt on just about every kind of upland game. A beagle from good hunting stock may flush, locate, and retrieve downed birds.

For the hunter whose budget cannot carry the expense of a high-priced professionally trained dog, the beagle is strongly recommended. It does not need much kennel room and is quick to adjust to all climates. The little hound is a faithful companion and top-notch hunter in the field and well worth the low cost of feeding and housing it.

DISPOSITION: In addition to its excellent hunting ability, the friendly little beagle makes a fine family dog and companion for children. A loyal and merry little hound, the beagle will usually lick the hand of a child who pulls its tail or twists its ear. Its happy and affectionate disposition makes the beagle a favorite choice for a family pet.

■ Basset

HISTORY: The basset hound's history is a long one, dating back to medieval times. Originating in France, the breed's ancestry includes the old French bloodhound and the now-extinct St. Hubert hound.

According to legend, the basset resulted from attempts to develop a dog that pursued game surely but very slowly, the only pace that the French aristocracy—terribly debauched and badly out of physical shape—could follow. Bassets were brought to England in the late 1860s and later to America, where they were crossed with other bassets that reached America by way of Russia. From those breedings came the American basset hound.

DESCRIPTION: It has been said that the basset has the coloring of a foxhound, the head of a bloodhound, the legs of a dachshund, and the body of a barnyard bull. There's no mistaking this breed, thanks to its inordinately long ears, heavy folds of skin around the entire head, and deep-set, incredibly sad, brown eyes.

A basset hound should meet the following physical standards:

The head is quite large, the skull narrow and long, with a characteristic point. The head, in short, resembles that of a bloodhound. Folds of skin wrinkle perceptibly when the dog puts its nose to the ground.

The nose is strong and not snippy. The ears are long enough that they can be folded well over the tip of the basset's nose.

The neck is powerful, shoulders sloping, and forelegs short, extremely strong, and heavy boned. The rib cage is well rounded, chest broad and powerful, and hindquarters muscular and heavy boned.

The coat resembles that of the beagle: dense, fairly short, and of medium texture. Any good hound color is permissible, but most bassets have some version of the tricolor combination (black, tan, and white).

SIZE: Bassets, like beagles, stand 10 to 15 inches at the highest point of the shoulder, with the average height about 13 inches. Bassets, however, are much heavier than beagles, some of them weighing as much as 80 pounds. The average weight is probably about 50 pounds. The basset is heavy boned and appears to weigh much less than it actually does.

HUNTING ABILITY: The basset is second only to the beagle as a rabbit and hare hunter, and its nose is as keen as any other hound's with the exception of the bloodhound. Bassets also will run pheasants and grouse, and some have even been taught to retrieve. They can easily be trained to tree game and thus make fine coon, possum, and squirrel dogs.

The basset runs game much slower and more painstakingly than the beagle, and many hunters prefer that kind of chase. Most bassets do not give tongue (bark) so readily on a scent trail as most beagles. The basset's voice is much deeper and more resonant than the smaller hound's.

If the basset has a hunting fault, it is that it will often stay quite close to the hunter until it strikes a scent trail. Most beagles, on the other hand, range well out from the hunter and search widely for scent.

DISPOSITION: As the beagle is merry and affectionate, the basset is sadly dignified and extremely friendly. Though it is not as outwardly affectionate as the beagle, the breed is hard to beat as a family dog, house pet, and hunting companion.

■ Black and Tan

HISTORY: The black and tan—generally recognized as a coonhound, though it can be trained to run everything from possums to cougars—is the oldest of the coonhound breeds. The history of the black and tan (and that of most of the other trail and tree hounds) is cloudy at best, for early breeding records, when they were kept at all, were vague and inaccurate. However, it has been pretty well established that the foundation stock of the modern black and tan came from an old Virginia foxhound strain known as the Virginia black and tan (or Ferguson-Virginia black and tan). As the strain was developed, primarily to run possums and raccoons, record-keeping procedures and breeding practices improved, and the modern black and tan came to be recognized as a breed. It is one of six trail-hound breeds recognized by the United Kennel Club and the only one recognized by the American Kennel Club.

DESCRIPTION: In looks, performance, and voice, the black and tan is the ideal of what a coon hunter is looking for in a dog. It has a hound-like appearance and yet is built for speed and agility.

The body is relatively short but quite powerful, particularly in the hindquarters and broad chest. The back is almost level, the stern long and tapering. The legs are straight, strong, and well boned, and the feet are well knuckled and heavily padded.

The black and tan has probably the most attractive head of any of the trail hounds. It is broad and evenly rounded, the muzzle is deep and squared off, and the dark-brown eyes are large and clear. The ears are quite long (when spread, they should measure tip to tip about the same as the dog's shoulder height) and set low on the head. The coat is a little shorter and the hair somewhat finer than that of the other trail hounds. Colors are jet black over the entire body, except for tan areas over the eyes and on the chest, feet, and stern. Some white on the chest is permitted.

Basset

SIZE: As trail hounds go, the black and tan is of medium size. Males stand 24 to 26 inches at the withers, females 22 to 24 inches. Weight should always be proportionate to an animal's bone structure and height. Males should not exceed 60 pounds; females should not exceed 40 pounds.

HUNTING ABILITY: Born to hunt, the black and tan has a full-choke nose, great determination, and durability. It is versatile, too. Though it is most often used to run raccoons and foxes, the black and tan is often put on the trail of deer, bears, boar, bobcats, lynx, and cougars.

The black and tan, particularly those used exclusively on coons, works almost entirely by foot scent (scent secreted by glands in or near the feet of the animal being pursued). It is fast on the trail—an important factor in getting a predator up a tree. It has a magnificent voice and seems to enjoy using it. The black and tan's treeing instinct is as strong as that of any hound.

DISPOSITION: The black and tan is quite affectionate, though less showily so than the beagle. It is not quarrelsome with other dogs and takes readily to being run in a pack. It is a rather shy breed and reacts with equal sensitiveness to praise and discipline. And yet it is more than willing to engage in a tooth-and-fang battle with coons, bobcats, and even larger game.

■ Bluetick

HISTORY: The bluetick has a relatively short breed history, being recognized as a distinct breed (by the United Kennel Club) only since the 1940s. But its ancestry—though a matter of some conjecture, as with most hounds—is a long one.

Some dog fanciers claim that the bluetick (and all other coonhound breeds except the Plott hound) branches from black and tan stock. Others say it is an offshoot of the English coonhound. However, many authorities are of the opinion that the bluetick's progenitor was the French Gascony bluetick, used widely as a deer and boar hound in France and England as far back as the 13th century. The Gascony hounds were widely acclaimed for their impressive voice, appearance, and performance. The bluetick is one of the six recognized coonhound breeds.

DESCRIPTION: The bluetick's name describes its color, which is unique. The highly attractive coat, in most individuals, is almost solidly ticked with black, which appears to be blue against the white background. The bluetick usually has a black head, some black spots on the body, and some tan trim. The coat is similar in texture to the black and tan's coat, but is somewhat heavier.

The bluetick is quite "houndy" in general appearance. Many blueticks are quite strong and large, powerfully muscled, with a massive head, while others are somewhat smaller and lighter, being bred for speed on the trail.

Often the bluetick's body is longer, in relation to height, than that of the black and tan. The shoulders and chest are broad and powerful, hindquarters are heavily muscled, and legs are straight and substantially boned. The feet are well padded.

Despite its heft and muscle, a bluetick should move gracefully and effortlessly. A good one can leap a 5-foot-high fence almost without breaking stride.

The bluetick's head resembles the black and tan's, but may be a bit heavier and have longer ears.

SIZE: Blueticks exhibit some variance in size. They reach larger maximum sizes than any of the other tree hounds, some of them even exceeding 100 pounds, although the official standard limits a bluetick's weight to between 45 and 80 pounds. Most of those heavyweights are tough old cougar- and bear-hunting bluetick hounds.

The average height ranges from a minimum of 21 inches at the withers for females to a maximum of 26 inches for males.

HUNTING ABILITY: Like the black and tan, the bluetick has an excellent nose and a clear, bawling voice. It is a top cold trailer (that is, it is capable of picking up and following a scent trail that is many hours old) and has a highly refined treeing instinct.

Also like the black and tan, the bluetick is used to pursue a wide variety of game, including raccoons, foxes, bobcats, bears, and cougars. Once it has its quarry up a tree, the bluetick will hold it there for hours or even days, if necessary, until the hunters reach the scene.

Like most hounds, the bluetick needs little formal training, learning most of its lessons on the job.

DISPOSITION: The bluetick in general has the typical hound personality: friendly, affectionate, and even-tempered. Like trail hounds as a whole, however, it can be standoffish with strangers.

▓ English Coonhound

HISTORY: Anyone who tries to pin down the genealogy of any hound breed or strain has cut himself a mighty big slice of trouble. With no other hound breed is this fact truer than with the English coonhound. The breed's actual origins are lost in the mists of antiquity. However, it was first recognized as a distinct breed—and formally registered—in 1900. At that time, the individual members were dogs with heavy blue or red ticking (spotting or dotting). Today, however, the breed will accept registered treeing Walkers and blueticks (the English and the bluetick share common ancestors), grade (unregistered) dogs of those types, and English-type dogs with blue or red ticking into its registry files. In fact, you may even hear English coonhounds called redticks. And you may well have to take an owner's word that his hound is an English coonhound, a bluetick, or a treeing Walker. The English coonhound is one of the six recognized coonhound breeds.

DESCRIPTION: Because of its melting-pot background and present-day registration confusion, it is difficult to categorize the description of the English coonhound. Many individual dogs recognized as bluetick, for example, are nearly identical in conformation to many individuals recognized as English coonhounds.

In general, however, the English standard today calls for a smaller, lighter dog than the bluetick standard.

The ideal English is a medium-size dog with typical hound proportions. It has a broad rib cage and chest and generally appears to be built for speed and stamina.

The head is broad across the skull, the muzzle is square, and the ears are set relatively low and are of medium length. The eyes are large and widely set. The big, flaring nostrils indicate good scenting capabilities.

As for coat color, the English can be any good hound color or combination of colors, including blue ticking, red ticking, black and white, tan and white, and tricolor. Among the members of the breed, those dogs of red ticking and blue ticking are more numerous than English coonhounds of any other color.

SIZE: English coonhounds range in height at the shoulders from 21 inches (for the smallest female) to 25 inches (for the tallest males). Weight depends upon height for the most part; an average English in the 24-inch category would weigh approximately 60 pounds.

HUNTING ABILITY: The English (and all other coon-hounds, for that matter) differs from other trail or predator hounds mainly in its ability to put an animal up a tree. And the English is as good at that as any other coonhound breed.

A hound's working ability is what determines its worth—or lack of it—to a hunter. The English, because of the many different hound types involved in its genealogy and present makeup, may exhibit any of a great number of working characteristics, none of which can be said to be typical of the breed.

For example, some English coonhounds are good cold trailers but work slowly on the trail. Some others are wide-working "drifting" types. Because of this great variety in working traits among members of this breed, it is wise for any prospective buyer to know exactly what he wants and to become thoroughly familiar with the individuals on the dog's pedigree and with the animal's parents.

DISPOSITION: All hounds are good-natured animals, and the English coonhound is no exception. It laps up praise and petting and yet takes discipline well. It is at home either in the house or outside in the roughest of weather.

▓ Redbone

HISTORY: The redbone—one of six coonhound breeds recognized by raccoon hunters everywhere and by such organizations as the United Kennel Club, American Coon Hunters Association, and American Hound Association—originated back in the 19th century, when breeders of the redbone strain of foxhounds began to feel that their dogs were too slow and methodical on the trail. As a result, these dogs were switched from running foxes to running raccoons. Their ability at chasing the smaller and slower game was quickly recognized, and the redbone was recognized as a distinct coonhound breed around 1900 by the United Kennel Club.

Since that time, the redbone has increased in favor among raccoon hunters, mainly because of the work of such well-known breeders as Brooks Magill, R. J. Blakesley, and W. B. Frisbee.

DESCRIPTION: The redbone's most distinctive physical characteristic is its coat, which is a solid, deep red, though some white on the brisket or feet isn't objectionable. Not every red-colored hound is a redbone, but most are.

The redbone's build complements its beautiful coat. The body is large and quite powerful, with long, straight legs, strong hindquarters, and a tail carried smartly. The head is not as typically "houndy" as that of the bluetick and the black and tan. The ears are set somewhat higher on the head; the muzzle and skull are a bit lighter. However, some redbones have extremely long ears and a heavy head—particularly those of R. J. Blakesley's Northern Joe strain.

SIZE: The redbone's size and weight—though perhaps more uniform—are typical of most trail hounds. Shoulder height ranges from 21 inches for females to a maximum of 26 inches for males. Weights are proportionate to shoulder heights, but the maximum is about 90 pounds and the average is 45 to 75 pounds.

HUNTING ABILITY: An excellent voice that might even be described as sweet, a good cold nose, tenaciousness, and an acute treeing ability—these traits describe the redbone as a hunter.

The breed's cold nose (the ability to pick up and follow an old scent trail) has caused some breeders to shy away, reasoning that a dog with a medium nose would waste less time on a bad track. However, the cold-trailing ability is much prized by many breeders and hunters.

In general, redbones bark only occasionally while the trail is cold, but their barking picks up in tempo and intensity as the trail gets warmer. This fact, which makes it easy for the listening hunter to determine the freshness of the track, cannot be said of all trail hounds. Some bluetick and black and tans, for example, will give tongue so often, even on a cold track, that they can be accused of babbling, a fault in a hound. When a redbone pushes a coon or other quarry up a tree, its voice changes from a bawl to a chop.

Redbone

Black and tans and blueticks have sometimes been criticized as being somewhat lacking in fighting ability. Not so the redbone, which is a real scrapper, though that trait, while important if the dog is chasing bears or big cats, is not so important when the quarry is coons.

DISPOSITION: The redbone has a kindly demeanor and, like most hounds, makes a fine family pet and companion. Also like most hounds, when it is on the trail its mind and body are totally committed to the chase, so the hunter is wasting lung power if he attempts to call the dog in. In general, the redbone lives to hunt, is easily taught, and is tractable.

■ Treeing Walker

HISTORY: The treeing Walker, one of the six recognized coonhound breeds, almost certainly is an offshoot of the Walker strain of foxhound, though bluetick blood may also be present. The Walker foxhound is the result of 50 years of careful breeding from the same stock of hounds by two Kentucky sportsmen and neighbors, George Washington Maupin and John W. Walker. Eventually, the Maupin-Walker dogs were outcrossed to the legendary Tennessee Lead (a hound that was said to have been literally stolen from a pack of Tennessee hounds that was in the process of running a deer) and two imports from England—Rifler and Marth. Those three dogs proved to be excellent foxhunters, and their offspring, crossed again with other English imports, eventually came to be known as Walker foxhounds.

It has been theorized that the first treeing Walkers were working Walker foxhounds that, because of advanced age, lack of speed on the trail, and a well-developed treeing instinct, gave up on foxes and took to treeing raccoons.

The treeing Walker was recognized as a distinct breed in the mid-1940s.

DESCRIPTION: The treeing Walker looks much like the Walker foxhound. A wide range of coat colors is permissible, but the most popular and predominant combination is a white background with black spots and tan markings. The saddle is often black. The hair is of medium length and texture.

The head is fairly long, and the skull is slightly domed and broad. The brown or hazel eyes are hound-like and set well apart. The ears are set moderately low, and when stretched out, reach nearly to the tip of the nose.

The neck is of medium length and rises free from muscular shoulders. The throat is free from folds of skin. The chest is deep, ribs well sprung. The back is moderately long, muscular, and strong. The forelegs are straight and well boned, and the pasterns are short and straight.

If there is a notable difference in appearance between the treeing Walker and the Walker foxhound, it is that the treeing Walker is a bit "houndier." Of the other coonhound breeds, the one that most closely approaches the treeing Walker in looks is the English.

SIZE: Weight scales for the treeing Walker run 50 to 75 pounds for males, 40 to 65 pounds for females. Recommended shoulder height for males is 25 inches, for females 21 inches.

HUNTING ABILITY: Due probably to its foxhound ancestry, the treeing Walker's hunting traits include good range, speed, and general aggressiveness. Those characteristics—plus its reputation as a "drifter"—set the treeing Walker apart from most of the other coonhound breeds. A drifter is a dog that doesn't hesitate to range away from the line when the track gets tough, rather than puzzle things out at close quarters. Many hunters don't like this trait in a hound, but there's no quarreling with the fact that it produces game. The opposite of a drifter is a "straddler," a dog that sticks to the track like glue. Black and tans, blueticks, and, to a lesser extent, English coonhounds and redbones are known to be straddlers. Treeing Walkers are not the best at cold trailing, but their treeing instinct is highly developed.

DISPOSITION: The treeing Walker's temperament is much like that of other coonhound breeds; it is not quite so gentle and affectionate as the beagle but more so than, say, the Plott hound. The breed takes discipline well, and training is simply a matter of exposing the animal to the game it is expected to run. Like most hounds, the treeing Walker is quite healthy and does not demand much in the way of living conditions. It must be remembered, however, that any dog worth its salt in the field merits proper care.

■ Plott Hound

HISTORY: In 1750, a man named Jonathan Plott brought to the mountains of North Carolina from his native Germany a pack of hounds, offspring of generations of dogs used to hunt the big and tough German wild boars. These dogs proved to be proficient at hunting black bears, numerous then in the Carolina mountains. For 30 years, Plott kept the strain pure and free from any outcross, selecting his breeding stock carefully.

In 1780, Henry Plott took over the pack from his father and decided to introduce into the strain some blood from a line of Georgia bear hounds called "leopard" or "spotted-leopard" dogs. Only that one cross took place, and the Plott family descendants—who are still breeding Plott hounds today—vehemently deny rumors of subsequent crossings of Plotts with black and tans, bloodhounds, and other breeds.

In 1946, the United Kennel Club recognized the Plott hound as a distinct breed. It is generally recognized as a coonhound breed, though its widest use until recent years had been as a bear and boar hound in the Great Smoky Mountains of Tennessee and North Carolina.

DESCRIPTION: In color, the Plott is brindle (brindle is a mixture of gray and yellowish brown, with darker streaks) with a black saddle and sometimes white points. The coat is thicker, heavier, and provides more protection from the elements than the coat of any of the other trail hounds.

The Plott is of medium height. Its head is rather large and blocky, and the jaws are those of a fighter. The body has a wiry but well-balanced appearance, though it is not so heavily muscled or boned as the bluetick or black and tan. The build is something like that of a husky pointer. Ear length tends to vary (see Hunting Ability section below).

Agility is one of the Plott hound's strong points; it moves with the grace of a cat.

The Plott's voice is not the most attractive of the trail hounds. The chop, in particular, is higher in pitch than the voices of other trail hounds.

SIZE: This breed's standard calls for males to weigh no more than 60 pounds and females to weigh no less than 40 pounds. Despite the standard, the breed's weight is on average somewhat less than that of the other trail hounds. Some individuals, on the other hand, can reach 90 pounds.

The Plott's height ranges from 21 inches at the shoulder for females to 25 inches for males.

HUNTING ABILITY: The Plott is a tough character, as befits a dog bred to battle boars and bears. The breed is also used to hunt wolves, cougars, bobcats, coyotes, deer, and various small game, including raccoons.

The breed's hunting ability seems to depend upon whether an individual dog is of the long-eared or short-eared type, both of which were developed by the Plott family. The short-eared type is generally considered to be faster and a more efficient fighter of dangerous game, and so it is usually preferred by bear and boar hunters. The long-eared type is said to have a better voice, to be a better cold trailer, and to be more "open" on trail. There also seems to be a sort of "happy-medium" type of Plott, which is gaining favor among hunters.

DISPOSITION: Because theirs is a relatively tough life—most of them live in the mountains under rugged conditions and often find themselves within striking distance of an animal that can fight back—the Plott's temperament is less gentle and affectionate than that of most other hounds. In fact, Plotts may be downright quarrelsome, and owners have learned the folly of keeping several in the same pen, for these dogs have a tendency to fight.

American Foxhound

HISTORY: The foxhound is the oldest sporting dog in the United States, dating back to early colonial times. The year 1650 is the date generally accepted as the foxhound's introduction into the United States. That year, a friend of Lord Baltimore's, Robert Brooke, brought to Maryland from England a hound pack used primarily on foxes.

Foxhunting's popularity—and that of the hounds bred for the purpose—spread from Maryland to Virginia, Pennsylvania, New Jersey, New York, New England, and throughout the South in the ensuing 150 years. Among the sport's adherents were George Washington, Thomas Jefferson, Alexander Hamilton, and John Marshall. Washington, in fact, was given seven "staghounds" by the Marquis de Lafayette. Though these large French dogs did not take well to foxhunting, their blood, and to a greater extent the blood of English and Irish hounds imported by foxhunters in the southeastern United States, went into the development of the foxhound known today.

For all intents and purposes, however, the American foxhound was developed within the past 150 years and was largely the result of the breeding practices of a number of families, most of them in the South. Those practices have brought about the recognition by foxhunters of some 20 or so strains of foxhounds (foxhunters are prone to regard these strains as distinct breeds, but they are actually strains, a strain being a line of dogs showing similar characteristics as a result of selective breeding).

The foxhound strains include the Walker, Trigg, and July—by far the most popular—as well as the Brooke, Birdsong, Goodman, Travis, Buckfield, Robinson, Wild Goose, Arkansas Traveler, Avent, Hudspeth, Tucker, Hampton-Watts-Bennett, Shaver, Bywaters, Whitlock Shaggie, Trumbo, Sugar Loaf, Cook, Byron, Gossett, and New England Native.

The history of many of these strains is lost in antiquity, usually because of slipshod or nonexistent record-keeping practices. Among those that are known are the following:

- **Walker:** See treeing Walker section.

- **Trigg:** Dr. T. Y. Henry, a grandson of Patrick Henry, kept at his Virginia home a pack of hounds that had fine reputations as fox chasers. On a trip south for his health, Henry met Colonel George L. F. Birdsong of Georgia. A friendship developed that resulted in Birdsong's acquiring the entire Henry pack when Henry found that in Florida, his new home, the dogs couldn't resist chasing the deer that were abundant there. Birdsong crossed his dogs with a Maryland hound and then began corresponding with Colonel Haiden C. Trigg of Kentucky, who was looking for some new blood with which to put some speed into his pack of slow-moving black and tans. Birdsong sent three of his hounds to Trigg, who then began the breeding process that was to give rise to the strain of foxhounds that today bear his name.

- **July:** Miles G. Harris of Georgia secured a fine hound named July from a hunter in Maryland. This dog, of Irish derivation and believed to be related to dogs bred by Dr. Henry of Virginia, was crossed with Colonel Birdsong's hounds. Hounds tracing back to that breeding and others by Georgia hunters are today known as Julys (or Georgia Julys).

- **Buckfield:** In about 1858, a Canadian peddler is said to have brought to the town of Buckfield, Maine, a red- and blue-mottled female that looked like a cross between a foxhound and an Irish setter. This dog was mated with a black, stump-tailed hound owned by another passer-through described as a tramp. The result of this mating was Bose, a compact, red, shaggy female and a top-notch foxhunter. She is supposedly the fountainhead of the Buckfield strain.

- **Robinson:** A man named B. F. Robinson of Kentucky developed this strain by breeding Irish hounds to hounds from some of the established Maryland packs. The strain that resulted bears his name.

- **Goodman:** W. C. Goodman obtained some of the Robinson dogs and crossed them with some of his own dogs, which were of the Maupin-Walker type. Most individuals of this strain were excellent fox dogs.

- **Wild Goose:** These are Tennessee hounds originally developed in Virginia in the 1830s by John Fuquay and C. S. Lewis and later brought to Tennessee by Lewis.

- **Arkansas Traveler:** Judge C. Floyd Huff of Hot Springs, Arkansas, owned some "Missouri" hounds that were somewhat lacking in size and bone. To build them up, he introduced some blood from English hounds and some from a pack of Kentucky dogs. The result was the Arkansas Traveler strain, dogs that set a fast pace in that state and Louisiana.

- **Avent:** These dogs were the result of a mixture of Ferguson-Virginia black and tans, dogs called "Bachelors," and native hounds that had enjoyed much success around James Monroe Avent's hometown of Hickory Valley, Tennessee. The Avent dogs were hunted widely in South Carolina, in the Mississippi Delta (for bears), in the West (for wolves and coyotes), and even in Africa (for lions and other big game).

DESCRIPTION: Speed, endurance, and toughness are a foxhound's trademarks, and its physical attributes should reflect those trademarks.

Because there are so many strains, it is all but impossible to use specifics in describing the typical foxhound. But since most foxhounds, regardless of strain, are related, a general picture of this breed can be painted.

A foxhound is expected to be sturdily built overall, but the body is not so heavy that the dog's speed or endurance is impeded. The legs are strong and straight, the feet catlike, the chest and hindquarters powerful, the ribs well sprung.

The head is proportionate to the rest of the body—that is, not too large or too small—cleanly formed, and must not have loose skin as in the basset. The ears are of medium length (when extended outward they should reach nearly to the top of the nose) and are set rather low on the head. The eyes are dark brown.

The coat is of typical hound length and hard textured. The predominant foxhound colors are similar to those of beagles and bassets, but there is great variation in colors, which include black and tan, orange and white, solid red, and many others.

SIZE: Because of the great variety in foxhound types, there is considerable variation in the size of these dogs.

In general, however, males should be no taller than 25 inches at the shoulder and no shorter than 22 inches. Females average an inch shorter. Weights range, on the average, from 50 to 65 pounds. Too much weight tends to reduce the dog's speed and stamina.

HUNTING ABILITY: The American foxhound is unsurpassed in speed, courage, endurance, and tenacity. It is far rangier and a better producer of game than its English ancestors.

In effect, the American foxhound's hunting ability is measured by the kind of hunting it is asked to do. There are two major forms of foxhunting practiced in the United States.

In the South, the sport of foxhunting is rooted almost entirely in the chase. The foxes, usually hunted at night, are not shot, but rather are highly valued for their ability to lead hound packs on runs that are fast, merry, loud, and usually long. For this kind of sport, the hound must be inordinately fast, hard driving, and capable of following hot scent that may be floating some distance from the actual track. It must be able to range out well in order to hit the scent of a moving fox (these dogs are expected to find their own foxes).

In the North, foxes are most often hunted on snow during the day, and the object is for the hounds to run the fox around to hunters who station themselves at likely crossings. The foxes are usually shot, for their fur value or for bounty. Dogs for this form of the sport must have cold-trailing ability, for they are seldom put down until a track is found by the hunters, and the track may be an old one. Competition is lacking for the most part, for only one or two dogs are usually put on a track—at least until the fox is up and running, at which time other hounds may be released. Speed is less important than a loud and clear voice in these northern dogs. Such a voice serves to let the owner know the direction of the chase and also prods the fox.

It should be noted that American foxhounds are used to run game animals ranging from rabbits to cougars.

DISPOSITION: The American foxhound's appealing and friendly facial expression is a key to its temperament. It is relatively gentle, takes well to training (though little formal training, other than obedience work, is needed) and discipline, and possesses the common-sense sagacity that all hounds seem to have in one degree or another. It is also greatly adaptable, being able to work out different conditions of terrain, weather, and quarry. And yet it can be cantankerously independent.

EMERGENCY MEDICAL TREATMENT

Let's suppose that you and a companion are well out in the woods on a fishing, hunting, or camping trip and one of the following mishaps occurs:

- Your friend is bitten by a snake that escapes before either of you can identify it. Can you tell from the bite itself whether or not the snake is a poisonous species? If it is, what should you do?

- Your companion suffers a severe fall and begins to act strangely. You fear that he may be going into shock. How do you tell for sure? How do you treat it?

- You've made an ambitious hike on snowshoes on a brilliantly sunny day after a heavy snowfall the night before. Your eyes begin to burn and smart, your forehead aches, and you can't seem to stand the glare from the glistening snow—all symptoms of snow blindness. What do you do?

- A toothache comes on suddenly and savagely. The nearest dentist is hours away by foot and car. Is there anything you can do to ease the pain?

Outdoor sports—as proved by studies made by American insurance companies—are among the safest of pastimes. But accidents do happen, and knowledge of first-aid procedures is especially important to outdoors enthusiasts, whose favorite haunts are seldom down the street from the doctor's office or within an arm's reach of a telephone.

Most accidents or maladies suffered in the outdoors are minor. But if a serious injury should occur, these actions should be taken, in the order given:

1. Give urgently needed first aid immediately: stop severe bleeding, restore breathing, treat for poisoning, or treat for shock. Keep the victim lying down.

2. Examine the victim as carefully—and calmly—as you can, and try to determine the extent of his injuries.

3. Send someone for help if possible. If not, try signaling with a rifle (a widely recognized distress signal is three quick shots) or by building a smoky fire.

4. Take necessary first-aid steps for secondary injuries, making the patient as comfortable as possible and moving him only if absolutely necessary.

This chapter will give detailed step-by-step procedures for every first-aid situation the outdoors person is likely to encounter. It should be remembered, however, that these procedures, though vitally important, aren't the only form of first aid. The victim's mental distress also needs treatment. A reassuring word, a smile, your obvious willingness and ability to help—all will have an encouraging effect. The knowledgeable first-aider also knows what **not** to do and thereby avoids compounding the problem by making errors that could be serious.

The procedures and instructions that follow reflect recommendations of the American Red Cross, the American Medical Association, the U.S. Department of Agriculture, and, of course, respected physicians.

■ Bleeding

EXTERNAL BLEEDING: If a large blood vessel is severed, death from loss of blood can occur in three to five minutes, so it is vital to stop the bleeding at once. Always do so, if possible, by applying pressure directly over the wound.

Use a clean cloth—a handkerchief, an item of clothing, or whatever else is near at hand. Use your

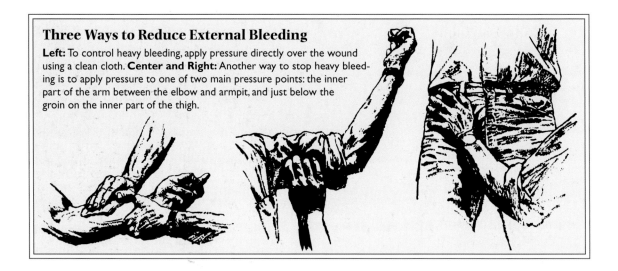

Three Ways to Reduce External Bleeding

Left: To control heavy bleeding, apply pressure directly over the wound using a clean cloth. **Center and Right:** Another way to stop heavy bleeding is to apply pressure to one of two main pressure points: the inner part of the arm between the elbow and armpit, and just below the groin on the inner part of the thigh.

bare hand if nothing else is available, and then, once the bleeding is under control, apply a cloth. Put on additional layers of cloth, and when the covering is substantial, bandage snugly with strips of cloth cut from a bedsheet, neckties, or similar materials. Don't remove the bandage. If it becomes saturated with blood, put on more layers of cloth, and perhaps tighten the dressing directly over the wound.

If you are sure that no bones are broken, try to raise the bleeding area higher than the rest of the body.

If extremely quick action is needed, or if the above method fails to stop the flow of blood, you may be able to diminish the flow by pressing your fingers or the heel of your hand at one of two pressure points. One of these is located on the inner half of the arm midway between the elbow and armpit; pressure applied here will reduce bleeding in the lower area of the arm. Pressure on the other point, located just below the groin on the front, inner half of the thigh, will reduce bleeding on the extremity below that point.

INTERNAL BLEEDING: Often caused by a severe fall or a violent blow, bleeding within the body can be difficult to diagnose, though it may be revealed by bleeding from the nose or mouth when no injury can be detected in those organs. Other symptoms may include restlessness, nausea, anxiety, a weak and rapid pulse, thirst, paleness, and general weakness.

The first treatment procedure is to use pillows, knapsacks, folded clothes, or something similar to raise the victim's head and shoulders if he is having diffi-

culty breathing. Otherwise, place him flat on his back.

Keep him as immobile as possible, and try to have him control the movements caused by vomiting. Turn his head to the side for vomiting.

Do not give the victim stimulants, even if the bleeding seems to stop.

If the victim loses consciousness, turn him on his side, with his head and chest lower than his hips.

Medical care is a must. Get the victim to a doctor or hospital as soon as possible.

NOSEBLEED: Nosebleeds often occur for no reason, while at other times they are caused by an injury. Most of them are more annoying than serious. It occasionally happens, though, that the bleeding is heavy and prolonged and this can be dangerous.

The person should remain quiet, preferably in a sitting position with his head thrown back or lying down with his head and shoulders raised.

Pinch the victim's nostrils together, keeping the pressure on for five to 10 minutes. If the bleeding doesn't stop, pack gauze lightly into the bleeding nostril and then pinch.

Sometimes the application of cold, wet towels to the face will help.

USE OF A TOURNIQUET: According to the American Red Cross, the use of a tourniquet to stop bleeding in an extremity is "justifiable only rarely." Because its use involves a high risk of losing a limb, a tourniquet should be applied only if the bleeding seems sure to cause death.

Applying a Tourniquet

Since a tourniquet can cause the loss of the affected limb, it should be applied only when no other means will reduce blood flow enough to prevent the victim from bleeding to death. **Left:** Wrap strong, wide cloth around the limb above the wound, and tie a simple overhand knot. **Center:** Place a short stick on the knot, tie another overhand knot over the stick, and twist the stick to stem bleeding. **Right:** Bind the stick with the ends of the tourniquet, but be sure to loosen it every 15 minutes.

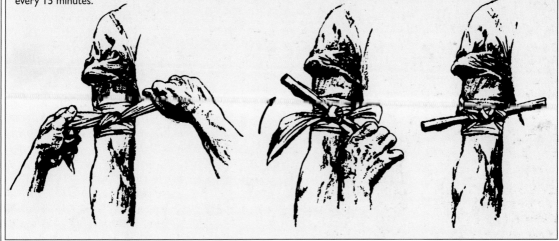

Use only a wide, strong piece of cloth—never a narrow strip of material such as rope or wire. Wrap the cloth around the upper part of the limb above the wound, and tie a simple overhand knot (half a square knot). Place a short stick on the knot, and tie another simple overhand knot (that is, complete the square knot) over the stick. Twist the stick just enough to stop the bleeding. Loosen the binding (untwist the stick) for a few seconds every 15 minutes.

Once the bleeding has been controlled, keep the victim quiet and warm. If he is conscious and can swallow easily, give him some water or maybe some weak tea—no alcoholic drinks. If he is not conscious, or if abdominal or other internal injuries are suspected, do not give him any fluid.

▓ Artificial Respiration

Artificial respiration, now commonly called resuscitation, is the technique of causing air to flow into and out of the lungs of a person whose normal breathing has stopped. Causes of stoppage of normal breathing include inhalation of water, smoke, or gas, electric shock, choking, or drug overdose. In most instances, death will result within six minutes unless artificial respiration is administered.

The treatment may also be needed if breathing does not stop completely but becomes slow and shallow and the victim's lips, tongue, and fingernails turn blue. If you're in doubt, give artificial respiration—it is seldom harmful and can save a life.

Before beginning the artificial-respiration methods described below, check the victim's mouth and throat opening for obstructions; remove any foreign objects or loose dentures.

MOUTH TO MOUTH: Place the victim on his back. Put one hand under the victim's neck. At the same time, place the other hand on his forehead and tilt the head back.

Using the hand that was under the neck, pull the victim's chin up, thereby ensuring a free air passage. Take a deep breath, place your mouth over the victim's mouth, trying to make the seal as airtight as possible, and pinch the victim's nostrils closed. Blow into the victim's mouth until you see his chest rise.

Lift your head from the victim, and take another deep breath while his chest falls, causing him to exhale. Repeat the process. For the first few minutes, do so as

Mouth-to-Mouth Resuscitation for Adults

▶ **Step 1** • Lift the victim's neck with one hand and tilt the head back by holding the top of the head with your other hand.

▼ **Step 2** • Pull the victim's chin up with the hand that was lifting the neck. This ensures a free air passage.

◀ **Step 3** • Take a deep breath, place your mouth over the victim's mouth, and pinch his nostrils. Breathe into his lungs until you see his chest rise. Remove your mouth and let him exhale. Repeat the cycle as rapidly as the victim's lungs empty themselves for the first few minutes, then 15 times per minute.

Mouth-to-Mouth Resuscitation for Children

▶ **Step 1** • Lift the victim's neck with your right hand and with your left lift his lower jaw so that it juts out.

◀ **Step 2** • Place your mouth over the victim's mouth and nose, making a leakproof seal, and force air into his lungs gently until you see the chest rise and you feel the lungs expand.

rapidly as the victim's lungs are emptied. After that, do it about 12 times per minute.

If the victim is an infant or small child, use the same procedure, but place your mouth over both the mouth and nose, and force air into his lungs gently.

HEART STOPPAGE (CPR): If artificial respiration produces no response in an injured person, it may mean that his heart has stopped beating. You can make a fairly certain diagnosis by checking his pulse at the wrist and holding your ear to the victim's chest. If you feel no pulse and hear no heartbeat, you will have to use external heart massage (Cardiopulmonary Resuscitation, or CPR) in addition to artificial respiration.

Here are the warning signs of a heart attack:

- Pressure; feeling of "fullness"; squeezing or pain in the center of the chest lasting more than two minutes

Chest Compressions

For heart stoppage, employ extended chest compressions (CPR) using the weight of the upper part of your body.

- Pain radiating to shoulders, neck, jaw, arms, or back; tingling sensation down left arm
- Dizziness, weakness, sweating, or nausea; pale complexion and shortness of breath

If the victim's heart and breathing have stopped, begin CPR. The technique involves mouth-to-mouth resuscitation, which delivers air to the lungs, and chest compressions, which help circulate the blood.

CHEST COMPRESSIONS: Positioning yourself perpendicular to the victim, place the heel of one hand on the lower third of the victim's sternum (breastbone). Place your other hand on top of the first one. Press down firmly with both hands about 1½ to 2 inches and then lift both hands to let the chest expand. Repeat at a rate of 80 to 100 compressions per minute. The mouth-to-mouth breathing should continue at a rate of two steady lung inflations after every 15 chest compressions.

▓ Choking

More than one person has died from choking on a fish bone, an inadvertently swallowed hard object, a piece of food that went down the "wrong pipe," and the like. Anything that lodges in the throat or air passages must be removed as soon as possible. Here's how to do it.

If the victim is conscious, give him four back blows between the shoulder blades. If the victim is lying down, roll him on his side, facing you with his chest against your knee. If the victim is sitting or standing, you should be behind and to one side of him. If the victim is an

Mouth-to-Mouth Resuscitation

Remember the ABCs: airway, breathing, and circulation, in that order.

Airway. If there are no head, neck, or back injuries, gently tilt the victim's head and raise the chin. This will lift the tongue and ensure a clear air passage. Check for breathing by placing your ear over the victim's mouth and feeling for any exhalation.

Breathing. If the person is not breathing, pinch his nose, take a deep breath, and place your mouth over his. Breathe into his lungs two times slowly—one and a half to two seconds each time. If the victim's chest does not rise, re-tilt the head and repeat the cycle at a rate of 12 times per minute, until the victim can breathe on his own.

Circulation. Check for a pulse. Keeping the victim's head tilted, place your index and middle fingers on the victim's Adam's apple, and then slide your fingers down to the next "ridge" on the neck. This is where you'll find the carotid artery. Press firmly to determine if there's a pulse. If there isn't, proceed with chest compressions.

infant, place him on your forearm, head down. Make sharp blows with the heel of your hand on the spine, directly between his shoulder blades.

If this doesn't remove the object, and the victim is standing or sitting, employ the Heimlich maneuver:

1. Stand behind the victim and wrap your arms around his waist.

2. Place the thumb side of your fist against the victim's upper abdomen, just below the rib cage.

3. Grasp your fist with your other hand and press into the victim's abdomen with two or three quick upward thrusts.

If the victim is in a lying position, do this:

1. Place him on his back and kneel close to his side.

2. Place your hands, one on top of the other, with the heel of the bottom hand in the middle of his abdomen, just below the rib cage.

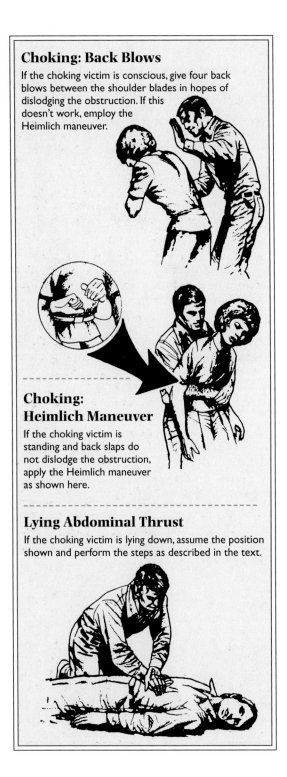

Choking: Back Blows

If the choking victim is conscious, give four back blows between the shoulder blades in hopes of dislodging the obstruction. If this doesn't work, employ the Heimlich maneuver.

Choking: Heimlich Maneuver

If the choking victim is standing and back slaps do not dislodge the obstruction, apply the Heimlich maneuver as shown here.

Lying Abdominal Thrust

If the choking victim is lying down, assume the position shown and perform the steps as described in the text.

3. Rock forward so that your shoulders are directly over the victim's abdomen and press toward the victim's diaphragm with a quick forward thrust.

4. Don't press to either side.

If the victim is unconscious, tilt his head back and attempt to give him artificial respiration. If this fails, give the victim four back blows in rapid succession. If the object has still not been forced out of the air passage, then stand behind the victim, put both of your fists into his abdomen, and give eight upward thrusts.

Finally, if none of these methods work, you should insert your index finger deep into the victim's throat, using a hooking action to try to dislodge the object.

FOR A SMALL CHILD: Put one arm around the youngster's waist from behind, and lift him up so that his head and upper torso are leaning toward the ground. With your free hand, give him several sharp taps between the shoulder blades. When the object has been dislodged, clear his throat with your fingers, and pull the tongue forward.

FOR AN INFANT: Hold him up by the ankles, head hanging straight down. Open his mouth, pull his tongue forward, and the object will likely fall out. If not, give him a tap or two on the back.

■ Shock

Medical (traumatic) shock is a depressed condition of many bodily functions and is usually caused by loss of blood following a serious injury (a burn, wound, fracture, exposure, and the like). However, some degree of shock can result from even minor injuries and from psychological shock.

Prolonged shock can result in death even if the injury causing it would not be fatal otherwise. In every health emergency, the possibility of shock should be considered. Signs of shock include the following: vacant and lackluster eyes and dilated pupils, shallow or irregular breathing, weak or seemingly absent pulse, skin that is pale and moist and cooler than it should be, nausea, perspiration, restlessness, thirst, and unconsciousness.

Symptoms usually develop gradually and may not be apparent at first. Even if a severely injured person exhibits none of the signs, shock is a real danger, and the following steps should be taken:

I. Keep the victim lying down, preferably with his head

How to Treat for Shock

In most cases, treatment for shock includes keeping the victim warm and elevating his feet. But there are exceptions, as described in the accompanying text.

lower than the rest of his body. **Exception:** If there is difficulty in breathing, the head and chest should be elevated.

2. Raise his legs 8 to 12 inches. **Exception:** Do not raise the legs if there is a head injury, if breathing difficulty is thereby increased, or if the patient complains of pain during the raising process. If you are in doubt about the correct position, keep the victim lying flat.

3. Keep the victim warm. If the weather is cold or damp, cover him and put a blanket underneath as well. Do not overheat; keep him just warm enough to prevent his shivering.

Fluids can have value in shock, but don't give the victim liquids unless medical help will be delayed at least an hour. If the victim is conscious and able to swallow, give him water that is neither hot nor cold—a few sips at first and then increasing the amount. If medical help will be considerably delayed, give the victim half-glass doses (at 15-minute intervals) of a solution made by adding 1 teaspoon of salt and ½ teaspoon of baking soda to 1 quart of water. Do not give any fluids if the victim is only partly conscious, if an abdominal injury is suspected, or if he is nauseated.

▪ Oral Poisoning

If the victim has ingested poisonous material and is unconscious or otherwise unable to tell you what it was, you may be able to ascertain the source by the odor on his breath, discoloration on his lips or mouth, or a tell-tale container nearby.

Speed is vital in treating a victim of poisoning. You must take the following steps quickly, before the body has a chance to absorb much of the poison:

1. If you know the antidote (antidotes are printed on containers of almost all potentially dangerous materials) and if it is at hand, give it at once. If not, dilute the poison by giving the victim four or more glasses of milk or water.

2. Call a doctor or hospital if possible.

3. Induce vomiting by sticking your finger into the victim's throat or by making him drink a glass of warm water with 2 tablespoons of salt mixed in.

Exception: Do not induce vomiting if the victim is unconscious, has pain or a burning sensation in the mouth or throat, or has swallowed a petroleum product (gasoline, kerosene, white gas, or the like) or any acid or any alkali (caustic soda, an ammonia solution, or the like).

When the vomiting begins, position the victim face-down, with his head lower than his hips, to prevent the expelled material from getting into his lungs. If you can't identify the poison, save some of the vomitus for subsequent examination by a physician or hospital laboratory.

BITES AND POISONOUS PLANTS

▪ Snakebites

It is doubtful whether any other first-aid situation is more feared and less understood than snakebites, and there is little agreement, even among leading authorities, about their treatment.

About 6,500 people are bitten by poisonous snakes in the United States each year. Of those, only about 350 are hunters or fishermen. And the death rate is very low, an average of 15 persons annually in the entire country. Most of those bites occur south of an imaginary line drawn from North Carolina to Southern California. More than half occur in Texas, North Carolina, Florida, Georgia, Louisiana, and Arkansas.

There are four kinds of poisonous snakes in the United States. Three are of the pit-viper variety: rattlesnakes, copperheads, and cottonmouth moccasins.

North American Poisonous Snakes

Cottonmouth • Eastern cottonmouths as well as Florida and western cottonmouths are frequently confused with non-poisonous water snakes. Cottonmouths have dark blotches on an olive body and broad, flat heads.

Coral Snake • This snake is dangerously poisonous, but its small mouth prevents it from biting most parts of the body. It has red and black rings wider than the interspaced yellow rings. The habitat is open woods in the East and loose soil and rocks in the West.

Timber Rattler and Canebrake Rattler • In the South, there is a dark streak from the canebrake's eye to mouth, and dark chevrons and a rusty stripe along the midline. In the North, the timber rattler has a yellowish body and dark phase in parts of its range. The habitat for the canebrake is lowland brush and stream borders. The timber rattler prefers rocky wooded hills.

Eastern Diamondback • The body has dark diamonds with light borders along a tan or light-brown background. The diamonds gradually change to bands in the tail. The habitat is lowland thickets, palmettos, and flatwoods.

Copperhead • This snake has large, chestnut-brown cross bands on a pale pinkish or reddish-brown surface with a copper tinge on the head. The habitat in the North is wooded mountains and stone walls; in the South, it is lowland swamps and wood suburbs.

Western Diamondback • This snake has light brown to black diamond-shaped blotches along a light gray, tan, and sometimes pink background. It also has black and white bands of about equal width around the tail. The habitat includes woods, rocky hills, deserts, and farmland.

The fourth, the coral snake, is a member of the cobra family. The pit vipers are so named because they have a small, deep depression between the eyes and the nostrils. The coral snake has broad, red and black bands separated by narrow yellow bands, giving rise to the saying, "Red on yellow, kill a fellow."

The bite of a poisonous snake—except for the coral snake, which chews rather than bites—is in the form of fang punctures of the skin. If you are bitten by a snake that leaves two U-shaped rows of tooth marks on your skin, relax—it is almost certainly a nonpoisonous snake. The bite of a nonpoisonous snake produces little pain or swelling.

Symptoms of the bite of a venomous snake include immediate pain, swelling and discoloration in the area of the wound, general weakness, nausea and vomiting, a weak and rapid pulse, dimming of vision, faintness, and eventually unconsciousness.

Most medical authorities now agree that the preferred treatment for a snakebite is antivenin administered as quickly as possible after the bite. If a snakebite victim is within a two-hour drive of a medical facility, get the person there as fast and as calmly as possible. Keep the bite location immobile, even if you have to splint it. Also keep the bitten body part below the level of the heart. A snakebite victim may walk up to a half hour before symptoms start. If the distance is longer to transportation, the victim should be carried. If you are alone, you should still be able to walk for several hours before symptoms start.

Most bites, however, occur in the field, often many miles from a road, so the victim cannot always get antivenin quickly enough. Survival in such cases depends upon the first-aid steps taken by the victim and his companions. And here is where the disagreement among medical authorities is most prevalent.

Proper treatment for a snakebite continues to confuse sportsmen, but the most reliable medical opinions today agree that the old treatments did more damage than good. There are still snakebite kits on the market and they may make you feel better if you have one in your first-aid kit, but the best advice is don't use it. The use of a scalpel and making incisions is no longer recommended and may cause further injury. Suction devices used without incisions are of questionable value. Some tests indicate that such suction devices may only remove about 1 to 2 percent of the venom.

Here's the currently recommended treatment for a snakebite. Call 911 or get to a hospital where you can get antivenin as quickly as possible. Properly treated with antivenin, snakebites are rarely fatal. If you can't get to a hospital within 30 minutes, immobilize the bite and, if possible, keep it lower than the heart. Wrap a bandage 2 to 4 inches above the bite. The bandage should not cut off blood flow from a vein or artery. Make the bandage loose enough so that a finger can slip under it. Do not put ice on the bite. Avoid exertion and excitement. Sit down and try to calm yourself. Panic could bring on shock. Do not eat or drink alcohol. Do not remove any dressings until you reach a hospital. If possible, kill the snake and take the head for identification later. Use caution: The head of a snake can still bite through reflex action up to one hour after it is killed. Get to a hospital or doctor as soon as possible with a minimum of exertion.

Coping with Bugs

The outdoors is a great place, but bugs can turn a pleasant day into a nightmare. You can fight back! There are five bugs that will give you the most trouble: mosquitoes, black flies, no-see-ums, deerflies, and ticks. Mosquitoes, the worst of the bunch, are most active at dawn and dusk. Mosquitoes are attracted to dark colors, so wear light-colored clothing. Black flies draw blood. Male black flies use blood for food, and the female needs blood to complete her breeding cycle. Common throughout Canada and the northern United States, black flies bite as soon as they land and they zero in on the face, hairline, wrists, and ankles. The peak period is spring and early summer. Aside from using a repellent, you should wear a hat, tuck pants into socks, tape cuffs around ankles, and wear long sleeves. No-see-ums are so small you can't see them, but they hurt when they bite. You'll find no-see-ums along lakes, beaches, and marshes. The deerfly is another painful biter and will attack the face, legs, arms, and neck. Once again, wear light-colored clothing. The tick, because of the threat of Lyme disease, is the most dangerous pest. Wear light-colored clothing, tuck pants into socks, avoid wooded areas and high grass, and use a tick repellent. The most effective repellent against these bugs contains DEET.

Bee Stings

Stinging insects are seldom more than an annoyance, even if they hit the target on your hide. Some people, however, are highly allergic to the stings of certain insects. If you or a member of your party has had a

How to Battle the Bugs

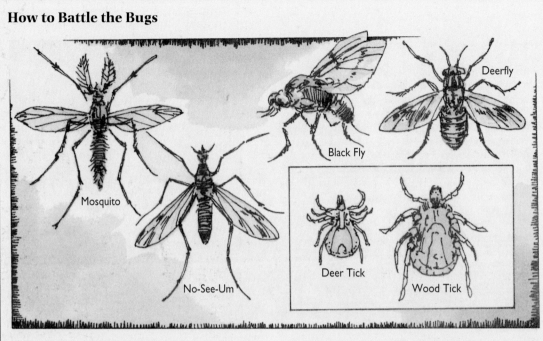

Mosquito · Black Fly · Deerfly · No-See-Um · Deer Tick · Wood Tick

Mosquitoes home in on warmth, carbon dioxide, and the odor of human skin. Your best weapon is a repellant on your skin that will set up a barrier that will confuse the mosquito's sensors.

Black flies are inactive at night but a problem during the day. You will rarely feel the bite. The first thing you may notice is the blood. If you get bitten and begin to itch, coat bites with alcohol or witch hazel.

Deerflies are found anywhere in the northern woods, and both sexes can inflict painful bites. Use a headnet and tape cuffs, but be aware that deerflies can also bite through clothing.

No-See-Ums are troublesome because it is difficult to protect yourself from them. They can fit through headnets, screens, clothing—almost anything. A repellant helps, but the only sure cure is a stiff wind.

Deer ticks pose a Lyme disease threat. They are half the size of the common wood tick and are orangish brown with a black spot near the head. Symptoms of Lyme disease include a red, ring-shaped rash, fever, chills, headache, stiff joints, and fatigue. Learn how to identify ticks and remove them from your body with tweezers. Don't burn, twist, or crush a tick on your body.

---

severe reaction to a bee sting in the past and is stung, take the following steps:

1. Use a tight, constricting band above the sting if it is on the arm or leg. Loosen the band for a few seconds every 15 minutes.

2. Apply an icepack or cold cloths to the sting area.

3. Get the victim to a doctor as soon as possible.

For the average bee-sting victim, these procedures will suffice:

1. Make a paste of baking soda and cold cream (if it is available), and apply it to the sting area.

2. Apply cold cloths to help ease the pain.

3. If there is itching, use calamine lotion.

■ Chigger and Tick Bites

The irritation produced by chiggers, which are the larval stage of a mite, results from fluid the tiny insects

The Deer Hunter and Lyme Disease

Not very long ago, a lucky deer hunter would simply roll up his sleeves and field dress his buck with no concern for his safety. It's a much different story today because of the comparatively new threat of picking up Lyme disease from a deer tick on your buck.

A deer tick is a speck of a bug, but unnoticed on your body its bite can infect you with a spirochete bacteria that produces the crippling Lyme disease. Deer ticks are found on a wide variety of wild and domestic animals, but about 75 percent of deer ticks live on whitetail deer. This means that deer hunters have a greater risk of contracting Lyme disease than most other sportsmen.

Hunters should take certain precautions in the woods. Most hunters will be wearing high boots, but you should start tucking in the bottoms of your pant legs. If you prefer to wear your pants outside your boots, so your pants shed rain and snow outside your boots rather than inside, use masking tape to close off your cuffs. Before you go into the woods, spray yourself with a good tick repellent. There are several on the market that will do the job well, especially if they contain the ingredient DEET.

After a day of deer or small-game hunting, check your body for ticks. The bite of a deer tick is painless, so you may never know you've been bitten unless you look for a tick or signs of a bite. Look wherever you have hair. Check your scalp, and the back of your neck and head. Two favorite spots are your armpits and groin. It's important to check everywhere.

If you find a tick, don't panic. Grab the tick as close to the skin as possible and pull outward slowly and steadily. Don't twist or jerk the tick out, which may break off parts of the tick in your skin. Squeezing it is also risky because you may release bacteria into your body.

It takes at least several hours for a deer tick to release its bacteria into your bloodstream, so it's critical to remove the tick as quickly as possible. When the tick is out, wash and disinfect the bite area thoroughly. If you see signs of redness or a rash, call a doctor immediately.

Many old hunters have field dressed bucks with bare hands and may frown on the idea of wearing surgical gloves, but Lyme disease is a serious threat and can result in headaches, fever, muscle weakness, and an arthritic condition that can persist for years. Surgical gloves can give you a high degree of protection. Sporting-goods stores sell field-dressing kits complete with surgical gloves that cover your entire arms.

There is no doubt that if you're handling a deer carcass you are in a high-risk situation. Deer ticks thrive on warm blood. Once an animal cools, these deer ticks will lose interest and jump on the closest warm body— and that may be you.

Don't load a deer into the back of a van and leave camp with the heater on full blast. This is a high-risk situation. The hunters may well arrive at home with a few ticks in residence on their bodies. Therefore, the best place to transport a deer is on the roof of your vehicle or the open bed of a pickup truck, where it will cool properly and the deer ticks can drop off without finding a warm human body to infect.

Finally, the best solution is to hang the deer outside, whenever possible, for at least 12 hours or overnight. The ticks should have left the carcass by then.

---

inject. Chiggers do not burrow under the skin, as is often suggested.

Since chiggers do not usually attach themselves to the skin until an hour or more after they reach the body, bathing promptly after exposure, using a brush and soapy water, may eliminate them. Once the bites have been inflicted, the application of ice water may help.

The itching and discomfort can be relieved by applying calamine lotion or a paste made of baking soda and a little water.

Ticks—flat, usually brown, and about ¼ inch long—attach themselves to the skin by making a tiny puncture, and they feed by sucking blood. They can thereby transmit the germs of several diseases, including Rocky Mountain spotted fever and Lyme disease. A new strain, granulocytic ehrlichiosis, has flu-like symptoms nearly identical to Lyme disease. Protecting yourself from granulocytic ehrlichiosis is the same as with Lyme disease.

If you have been in a tick-infested area, be sure to examine your clothes and body for the insects, paying particular attention to hairy areas. Removing ticks promptly is insurance against the transmission of any germs they may be carrying since that process seldom begins until six hours or so after the insect attaches itself and begins to feed.

Use tweezers to remove a tick, but don't yank—that may cause the tick's head or mouth parts to break off and remain in the flesh. Pull it gently, taking care not to crush the body, which may be full of germs. If it can't be pulled off gently, cover the entire tick with heavy oil, which closes off its breathing pores and may make it disengage itself.

■ Spider and Scorpion Bites

Scorpions are most common in the southwestern United States and are found in such spots as cool and damp buildings, debris, and under loose banks. Most species of scorpions in the United States are nonpoisonous; few of their stings are dangerous.

The biting spiders in the United States include the black widow, brown widow, and tarantula. The brown widow—its abdomen has a dull-orange hourglass marking against a brown body—is harmless in almost all cases. The tarantula is a large (up to 3 inches long, not including the legs) and hairy spider, but despite its awesome appearance its bite is almost always harmless, though it may cause allergic reactions in sensitive people. The black widow—the female's body is about ½ inch long, shiny black, usually with a red hourglass marking on the underside of the abdomen—has a poisonous bite, but its victims almost always recover.

The symptoms of these bites may include some swelling and redness, immediate pain that may—especially with a black-widow bite—become quite severe and spread throughout the body, much sweating, nausea, and difficulty in breathing and speaking.

First-aid procedures are as follows:

I. Keep the victim warm and calm, lying down.

2. Apply a wide, constricting band above the bite, loosening it every 15 minutes.

3. Apply wrapped-up ice or cold compresses to the area of the bite.

4. Get medical help as quickly as possible.

■ Poison Ivy, Poison Oak, and Poison Sumac

You cannot escape from poison ivy, poison oak, and poison sumac. There are virtually no areas in the United States in which at least one of these plants does not exist. Poison ivy is found throughout the country, with the possible exception of California and Nevada. Poison oak occurs in the southeastern states, and a western variety exists in the West Coast states. Poison sumac grows in most of the states in the eastern third of the country.

If you're lucky, you may be among the 50 percent of the population that is not sensitive to these poisonous plants. If you are not lucky, however, and you've already had a few run-ins with poison ivy, oak, or sumac, you better know how to identify these plants and learn where they grow. Poison ivy grows along streams, lakes, and on sunny hillsides. It can also grow as a shrub, a small tree, or a vine.

If you want to avoid poison ivy and poison oak, beware of low or vine-like three-leaved plants, which in fruit have creamy white berries. Poison sumac has ivory to grayish white berries. Poison sumac likes wet ground, so you are less likely to come in contact with it if you keep your boots dry.

Urushiol is the sticky, colorless oil that comes from the leaves and stems of poison ivy that, when it gets on your skin, causes the irritation. Urushiol in poison ivy is nearly the same in poison oak and poison sumac. If you're sensitive to one, you're sensitive to all of them.

If you don't wash the poison sap off your skin quickly, you will develop a rash within a couple of days. The rash will eventually produce swollen patches with blisters that will break and ooze.

Healing will take about two weeks, no matter what you do, but here is some advice to ease the intense itching and promote healing. The best medicine against poison ivy is cortisone, if given within the first 24 hours. Oral prednisone will also help. If you are sensitive to poison ivy, take a supply of cortisone along on your trips.

Here are other remedies that will at least relieve some of the symptoms:

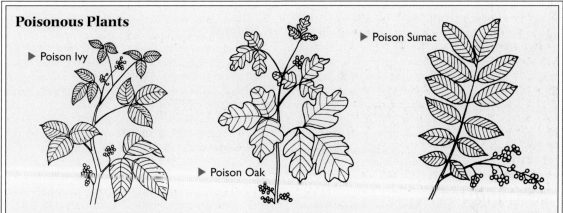

Poisonous Plants

▶ Poison Ivy

▶ Poison Sumac

▶ Poison Oak

For poison ivy and poison oak, beware of low or vine-like three-leaved plants, which in fruit have creamy white berries. Poison sumac has ivory to grayish white berries, but since poison sumac likes wet ground, you'll be less likely to come in contact with it if you keep your boots dry.

1. Cool compresses with Burow's solution will ease itching and speed up the drying process. Apply them for 15 minutes three or four times a day.

2. Calamine lotion will also relieve the itching.

3. Oatmeal baths are helpful. Add a cup of Aveeno oatmeal to the tub and soak in it for 15 minutes two or three times a day.

4. Aloe vera will aid in skin healing. Apply the lotion twice a day.

5. Oral antihistamines will help eliminate the itching, but antihistamine lotions don't help. Don't use anesthetic sprays or lotions, which may actually sensitize the skin and irritate the rash.

6. If you're very sensitive to poison ivy, try Ivy Shield, an organic clay barrier that will give 95 percent protection to the skin.

7. If you come in contact with poison ivy, shower with soap and water immediately.

The best protection is learning how to identify these plants and avoid them. The shiny leaves grow in groups of three, so try to remember the saying, "Leaves of three, beware of me."

BURNS

▮ Thermal Burns

Burns are classified according to degree. In first-degree burns, the skin is reddened. In second-degree burns, blisters develop. Third-degree burns result in destruction of tissue and the cells that form new skin. Another important factor in determining the seriousness of any burn is the extent of the affected area.

The following first-aid procedures have the primary objectives of treating shock (a major hazard that can quickly cause death in severely burned people), relieving pain, and preventing contamination.

Here is how to treat relatively minor first- and second-degree burns:

FIRST-DEGREE BURNS: Medical treatment is usually not required. To relieve pain, apply cold-water applications to the affected area or submerge the burned area in cold water. A dry dressing may be applied, if desired.

MINOR SECOND-DEGREE BURNS: Immerse the burned parts in cold water (not ice water) or apply freshly ironed or laundered cloths that have been wrung out in ice water until the pain subsides. Immediate cooling can reduce the burning effect of heat in the deeper layers of skin. Never add salt to ice water; it lowers the temperature and may produce further injury. Gently blot the area dry with sterile gauze, a clean cloth, a towel, or other household linen. Don't use absorbent cotton. Apply dry, sterile gauze or a clean cloth as a protective dressing. Don't break blisters or remove shreds of tissue, and don't use an antiseptic preparation, ointment, spray, or home remedy on a severe burn.

Because the degree of a burn is often difficult to determine at first, it pays—except with obviously minor burns—to seek medical help.

EXTENSIVE SECOND- AND THIRD-DEGREE BURNS: If a doctor or hospital is within easy reach, cover the burn with a sterile (or at least clean) dressing, treat for shock (see Shock section for procedures), and rush the victim to the doctor or a hospital. If the burn occurs in a remote area, take the following steps:

1. Remove all clothing from the burn area, cutting around any cloth that may adhere to the flesh and leaving it there (trying to remove it may worsen the wound).

2. Apply a sterile, dry dressing to the entire burn area. Do not treat a serious burn with any substance; that is, don't apply ointment, antiseptic, oil, or anything similar. Cover the dressing with at least six more layers of dressing (or clean, tightly woven cloth material). Try not to rupture blisters.

3. Bandage the dressings in place. Make the bandage snug enough to protect the burned area from possible contamination from the air, but not so tight as to cut off circulation.

4. Treat for shock if medical help will be delayed for more than an hour. Give the victim the shock solution: 1 teaspoon of salt and 1 teaspoon of baking soda mixed in 1 quart of water.

5. Arrange for medical help as quickly as possible, notifying authorities that plasma may be needed.

6. Don't try to change the dressing yourself. That is a job for a doctor.

■ Sunburn

Not everyone is aware of the genuine health hazard from the solar system. The National Cancer Institute estimates 600,000 malignancies a year are a direct result of careless exposure to the sun. Of that number, close to 7,000 people will die from malignant melanoma, the most deadly skin cancer.

The sun is the bad guy, causing at least 90 percent of all skin cancers. Fortunately, the sun warns its victims with early symptoms. Those symptoms include those fashionable tans you see around town and usually ignore.

The sun produces two different types of ultraviolet rays, both harmful to the skin. Beta rays (UVB) can cause skin cancer. Alpha rays (UVA) can cause both skin cancer and premature wrinkling of the skin. The easiest and most effective way of protecting yourself from these rays is through the use of a good sunscreen that is rated with an SPF (sun protection factor) of at least 15.

There are sunscreens with ratings of SPF 35 and higher, but in most cases, a rating of SPF 15 is all that is necessary for daily use. With an SPF 15, a person can stay in the sun 15 times longer than without any protection at all. Some doctors claim that regular use of an SPF 15 for the first 18 years of life may reduce the risk of skin cancer by 78 percent. For this reason, it's extremely important for parents to remember to keep small children out of direct sunlight, especially between 10:00 a.m. and 3:00 p.m., when the sun is the strongest and can do the most damage to the skin. Choose a waterproof SPF 15 sunscreen to screen ultraviolet rays. Apply it liberally an hour or two before you go out in the sun, and reapply it every two or three hours, especially after swimming and sweating. Some newer sunscreens are formulated to last all day, even after swimming.

Your skin type is also an important factor. If you're a Type I or II, which means fair skin, blond hair, and blue eyes, you will need more skin protection and a doctor should check you for skin cancer at least once a year. At the other extreme is Type V or VI, which includes people of Middle Eastern and African descent, who will burn only after heavy exposure.

If you spend a lot of time in the sun, you should know about the types of skin cancers and how to detect them early. There are three kinds of skin cancers: basal cell carcinoma, squamous cell carcinoma, and malignant melanoma.

Basal cell carcinoma is the most common skin cancer (about 80 percent) and is seldom deadly. It usually appears on the neck, head, face, and hands. It may be as small as a pinpoint or as large as an inch. It may also crust and bleed.

Squamous-cell carcinoma is the second-most common and looks like a raised pink wart. If left untreated, it can spread to other parts of the body.

Malignant melanoma is the least common, but it is the most deadly skin cancer. It usually appears quickly on the upper back or legs. It can be brown, black, or multicolored. Malignant melanoma grows fast and spreads to other organs.

If you spend a lot of time in the sun, check your skin regularly. Look at the back of your hands and your face. Look for scaly, rough patches of skin. Are there any white spots or red nodules with scales? If you see anything that looks suspicious, see your doctor. Most of the time, skin cancers are easily and successfully removed.

■ Chemical Burns

Chemical burns—from acid, alkali, lime, petroleum products, cleansing agents, and the like—are unusual in the outdoors, but do happen occasionally.

For such burns on exposed skin, the first step is to immediately flush the area with water, thereby lessening the pain and probably reducing the extent of the skin damage. Thereafter, treat as you would a thermal burn.

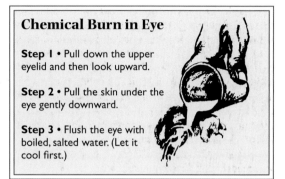

Chemical Burn in Eye

Step 1 • Pull down the upper eyelid and then look upward.

Step 2 • Pull the skin under the eye gently downward.

Step 3 • Flush the eye with boiled, salted water. (Let it cool first.)

If a noxious chemical gets into an eye, flush the eye with water at once. Do so by having the victim lie down with his head tilted slightly to one side. Pour the water in the corner of the eye nearest the nose so that it flows across the entire eye and out the other corner and does not enter the unaffected eye.

Cover the eye with a sterile compress, bandage it in place, and get the victim to medical help as fast as possible.

SURVIVING HEAT AND COLD

■ Sunstroke

Sunstroke is extremely dangerous. Aged people are the most susceptible. The usual symptoms are headache, dry skin, and rapid pulse. Dizziness and nausea may occur, and in severe cases the victim may lapse into unconsciousness. The body temperature soars, sometimes as high as 109°F.

Medical help, as soon as possible, is a must. Until it arrives, do the following:

1. Undress the victim, and sponge the body freely with cool water, or apply cold cloths, the objective being to reduce body temperature to a tolerable level of 103°F or below. If you have no thermometer, check the victim's pulse; a pulse rate of 110 or below usually means a tolerable body temperature.

2. When the body temperature lowers to 103°F, stop the sponging or cool-cloth treatment for about 10 minutes. If the temperature again starts to rise, resume the sponging.

3. If the victim is conscious and can swallow, give him as much as he can drink of a saltwater solution (1 teaspoon of salt to 1 quart of water).

4. Later, cover according to the victim's comfort.

■ Hypothermia

Hypothermia is one of the major causes of death among outdoor people, and it will strike anyone who is not prepared to handle extreme weather conditions. Hypothermia is caused by exposure to high winds, rain, snow, or wet clothing. A person's normal core (inner body) temperature is 98.6°F. When the body begins to lose heat, early stages of hypothermia will be apparent. The person will start to shiver and stamp his feet.

If these early signs of hypothermia are ignored, the next stage of symptoms will be uncontrollable spells of shivering, fumbling hands, and drowsiness. If not treated quickly, hypothermia will likely kill its victim when the body temperature drops below 78°F and this can happen within 90 minutes after shivering begins.

If you're outdoors and detect any of these symptoms

in yourself or a friend, start treatment immediately. First, get to shelter and warmth as soon as possible. If no shelter is available, build a fire. Get out of wet clothing and apply heat to the victim's head, neck, chest, and groin. Use chemical heat packs if you have them. If not, use body heat from another person. If you have a sleeping bag, the victim should be placed in it with another person.

As the victim begins to recover, give him warm liquids, chocolate, or any other high-sugar-content foods. Never give a hypothermia patient alcohol. It will only impair judgment, dilate blood vessels, and impair shivering (the body's way of producing heat).

If you're in a boat and capsize into cold water, don't take off your clothing; it will help trap heat. If you are wearing a life jacket, draw your knees up to your body, which will reduce heat loss. If there are several people in the water, huddle together so you can conserve heat. Survival in cold water depends on the water temperature. If the water temperature is 32.5°F, survival time may be under 15 minutes. If the water is more than 80°F, survival time is indefinite.

Preventing hypothermia is a lot easier than treating it. First, stay in shape and get a good night's sleep before going outdoors. Always carry candy, mixed nuts, raisins, or some other high-energy food. Stay as dry as possible and avoid getting overheated. Wet clothing will lose 90 percent of its insulating qualities and will rob the body of heat.

Stop and rest often, and, most important, dress properly. This means wearing several layers of clothing to form an insulating barrier against the cold. Carry rain gear and use it when the first drops fall. Wear a wool hat with some kind of ear protection. Several manufacturers now make wool knit caps with a Gore-Tex lining, which will keep your head and ears dry in a downpour. It's a fact that an uncovered head can lose up to 50 percent of the body's heat.

You should also carry a survival kit with a change of clothing, waterproof matches, and candy bars or other high-energy snacks.

▪ Frostbite

Frostbite is the freezing of an area of the body, usually the nose, ears, cheeks, fingers, or toes.

Just before the actual onset of frostbite, the skin may appear slightly flushed. Then, as frostbite develops, the skin becomes white or grayish yellow. Blisters may develop later. In the early stages the victim may feel pain, which later subsides. The affected area feels intensely cold and numb, but the victim is often unaware of the problem until someone tells him or he notices the pale, glossy skin. First-aid treatment is as follows:

1. Enclose the frostbitten area with warm hands or warm cloth, using firm pressure. Do not rub with your hands or with snow. If the affected area is on the fingers or hands, have the victim put his hands into his armpits.

2. Cover the area with woolen cloth.

3. Get the victim indoors or into a warm shelter as soon as possible. Immerse the frostbitten area in warm—not hot—water. If that is not possible, wrap the area in warm blankets. Do not use hot-water bottles or heat lamps, and do not place the affected area near fire or a hot stove.

4. When the frostbitten part has been warmed, encourage the victim to move it.

5. Give the victim something warm to drink.

6. If the victim must travel, apply a sterile dressing that widely overlaps the affected area, and be sure that enough clothing covers it to keep it warm.

7. Medical attention is usually necessary.

Hypothermia's Effects on the Body

When extreme cold causes the body to lose its interior heat, these symptoms occur as your temperature drops:

99 to 96 degrees • Shivering becomes intense; ability to perform simple tasks is slowed

95 to 91 degrees • Skin tone pales; shivering turns violent and speech is impaired

90 to 86 degrees • Muscular rigidity replaces shivering; thinking is dulled considerably

85 to 81 degrees • Victim becomes irrational and may drift into a stupor; pulse is slow

80 to 78 degrees • Unconsciousness occurs; reflexes cease to function

Below 78 degrees • Condition may be irreversible; death is likely at this point

Snow Blindness

The symptoms of this winter malady include a burning or smarting sensation in the eyes, pain in the eyes or in the forehead, and extreme sensitivity to light. First-aid steps include the following:

1. Get the victim into a shelter of some kind, or at least out of the sun.

2. Apply cold compresses to the eyes.

3. Apply mild eye drops to the eyes. Mineral oil is a suitable substitute.

4. Have the victim wear dark glasses.

Sun and Eyes

If you're a fisherman or a boater, you are probably already aware of the punishing effects of the sun's glare on your eyes. In fact, the effect of glare on the surface of the water can be 25 times brighter than the light level indoors. For most activities, sunglasses should be able to absorb about 60 percent of the sun's rays. For fishing or boating, however, sunglasses should be darker, absorbing at least 80 percent of the sun's rays. Bausch & Lomb suggests this simple in-store test for lens darkness: Look in a mirror with the sunglasses on. If the lenses are dark enough, you will have some difficulty seeing your eyes. This test does not work for photochromic sunglasses because they would be at their light stage indoors. If you are a fisherman, you should select sunglasses with polarizing lenses, which are usually made by sandwiching polarizing film between layers of dark glass or plastic. They eliminate reflections on the surface of the water and allow fishermen to see beneath the surface. Sunglasses come in a variety of lens colors, but most eye-care professionals recommend green, gray, or brown for outside activities.

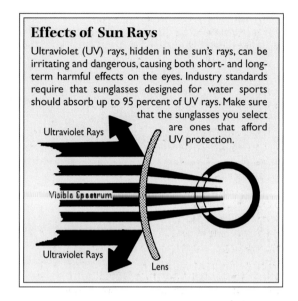

Effects of Sun Rays

Ultraviolet (UV) rays, hidden in the sun's rays, can be irritating and dangerous, causing both short- and long-term harmful effects on the eyes. Industry standards require that sunglasses designed for water sports should absorb up to 95 percent of UV rays. Make sure that the sunglasses you select are ones that afford UV protection.

Ultraviolet Rays

Visible Spectrum

Ultraviolet Rays

Lens

DISLOCATIONS, SPRAINS, AND FRACTURES

Bone Dislocations

A dislocation results when the end of a bone is displaced from its normal position in the joint. The surrounding ligaments and other soft tissue always suffer some damage. The fingers, thumb, and shoulder are the areas most often affected.

Symptoms include severe pain, swelling, and loss of movement. Unless a dislodged bone is properly relocated and cared for, dislocations of the bone may occur repeatedly and eventually cause considerable disability.

Relocating a seriously dislodged bone should be done only by a doctor. The first-aider's primary concerns here are to prevent further injury and to see to the victim's comfort.

The dislocated part of the body should be kept as immobile as possible. Apply cold compresses, and get the victim to a doctor.

If an elbow or shoulder is dislocated, use a loose sling to keep the part immobile during transport. If the dislocation is in the hip, transport the victim on a wide board or on a stretcher that has been made rigid, and use blankets or clothing as a pad to support the leg of the affected side in whatever position the victim finds most comfortable.

If the dislocation is a finger and medical help is far away, you might try pulling—very cautiously—on the finger in an attempt to bring the bone back into place. If a gentle pull does not work, do not persist. And do not

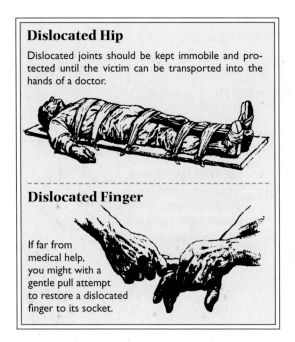

Dislocated Hip

Dislocated joints should be kept immobile and protected until the victim can be transported into the hands of a doctor.

Dislocated Finger

If far from medical help, you might with a gentle pull attempt to restore a dislocated finger to its socket.

try this on a dislocated thumb—the problem is more complicated at this joint, and further injury may result.

■ Bone Fractures

There are two kinds of bone fractures (breaks). In a simple fracture, the broken bone does not push through the skin. In an open fracture, the skin is broken and a wound extends from the skin to the fracture area.

It is often difficult to tell whether or not a bone has been broken. If the first-aider was not there when the injury occurred, he should ask the victim to tell him exactly what happened and then check the injured area for physical evidence.

Symptoms of a break include tenderness to the touch, difficulty or pain in moving the injured part, swelling, skin discoloration, and deformity.

If you're not sure, treat the injury as a break. Never try to reset a broken bone yourself. Your basic objectives are to prevent further injury, treat for shock if necessary, and make the patient as comfortable as possible until medical help arrives.

With any break, handle the victim gently. Careless handling will increase the pain and may also increase the severity of shock and cause jagged bone ends to damage muscle, nerves, blood vessels, and skin.

First-aid procedures for various kinds of breaks are listed below.

ARM OR LEG: If medical help will arrive shortly, don't move either the broken limb or the victim.

If there is bleeding, cut away as much clothing as necessary, place a sterile pad or a piece of clean cloth over the wound, and apply firm pressure. Bandage the pad in place.

If the patient must be moved, position the limb as naturally and comfortably as possible, and put on two splints. Boards, poles, metal rods, or any other firm objects—even a thick layer of newspaper folded to the proper shape and firmness—will do. Splints must be long enough to extend beyond the joints above and below the break. Use soft material as padding between the limb and the splints. Fasten the splints in place with bandage material (or handkerchiefs, cloth strips, etc.) at a minimum of three places: adjacent to the break, near the joint above the break, and near the joint below the break.

Check the splints every 15 minutes or so. If swelling of the limb has caused tightening of the bandaging so that circulation is cut off, loosen the bindings accordingly.

Apply cold packs to the fracture, and get the victim to medical help.

SKULL: Skull fracture symptoms include unconsciousness, mental confusion or dazedness, variation in size of eye pupils, and bleeding from the mouth, ears, or nose.

Keep the victim lying down. If his face has normal color or is flushed, prop up his head and shoulders. If his face is pale, try to position him so that his head is slightly lower than the rest of his body.

If there is an open scalp wound, apply a sterile gauze pad, and bandage it in place.

If the victim must be moved, transport him in a prone position.

Never leave the victim alone, even during transport. If he begins to choke on blood, lower his head and turn it to one side so that the blood can drain from the mouth and throat.

NECK AND BACK: If the victim can't readily open or close his fingers or grip anything firmly, his neck may be broken. If finger movement seems normal but he can't move his feet or toes, his back may be broken. If he is unconscious and you suspect a spinal injury, treat as if the neck was fractured.

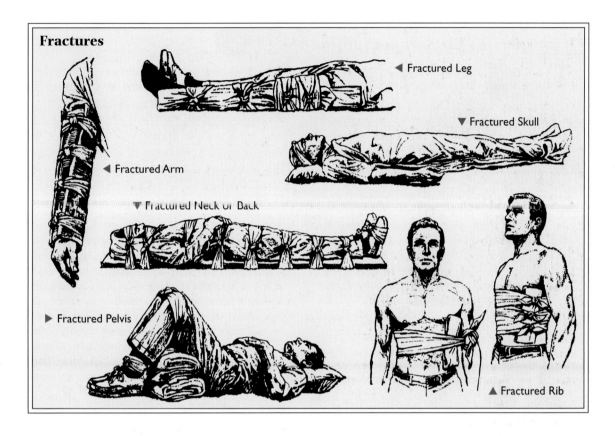

Fractures

◀ Fractured Leg

▼ Fractured Skull

◀ Fractured Arm

▼ Fractured Neck or Back

▶ Fractured Pelvis

▲ Fractured Rib

Do not let the victim move his head.

Cover him with blankets.

Watch his breathing closely. If breathing stops, begin mouth-to-mouth resuscitation, but do not move his head as you do so.

Medical help should be brought to the scene if at all possible. If a move is absolutely necessary, extreme caution is a must, for a slight twist or jerk can be fatal to the victim of a broken neck or spine. Pad the head at the sides to prevent movement. Tie the victim's hands across his chest, and tie his head and body rigidly to the stretcher, which should itself be rigid. Put a pad under the victim's neck.

PELVIS: The pelvis is a basin-shaped bone that connects the spine and legs. It also encloses or protects many important organs; therefore, a fracture of the pelvis is a serious injury that requires careful handling. Evidence of damage to organs or blood vessels includes difficulty in urinating or blood in the urine.

Treat for shock, which may be severe.

Bandage the knees together, and then bandage the ankles together.

Keep the victim lying down, either with the legs flat on the ground or with the knees flexed up and pads positioned under the knees, whichever position is most comfortable for the patient.

If the victim complains of pain when his lower extremities are moved, apply splints to the extremity.

If the victim must be moved, transport him in a prone position on a rigid stretcher.

RIB: Symptoms include pain in the break area and shallow breathing (deep breathing causes pain). A broken rib sometimes punctures a lung, causing the victim to cough up frothy, bright-red blood.

If the broken rib has punctured the skin, it is important to guard against infection. Apply a dressing that is airtight.

Keep the victim lying down and calm.

If the skin is not punctured, apply one or more wide bandages around the chest, thereby restricting rib

Transporting the Seriously Injured

The first-aider's principal objectives in transporting a seriously injured person are to avoid disturbing the victim unnecessarily and to prevent injured body areas from twisting, bending, or shaking.

Transportation is a vital factor, and it requires proper planning by the first-aider and proper preparation of the victim. The rescuers must make every effort to remain calm and mentally alert.

In some situations, however—such as an auto accident, fire, and the like—there is not time for planning or preparation; the victim must be moved from the danger area, or he may suffer further injury.

If such a victim must be pulled to safety, the pull should be along the length of his body (that is, headfirst or feetfirst), not sideways. The danger of compounding the injury during pulling is reduced if a blanket or something similar can be placed beneath him so that he can "ride" the blanket.

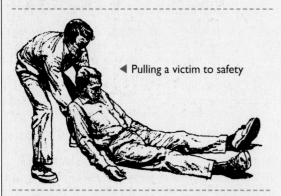

◀ Pulling a victim to safety

If a victim must be lifted to safety, the rescuers should try to protect all parts of his body from the tensions of lifting. The body should be supported at a minimum of three places along its length, not jack-knifed (lifted by head and feet only). Keep the body as straight as possible.

Once a victim is moved to safety, further transportation is inadvisable unless absolutely necessary. The first-aider should make every effort to get medical help to the scene. If the injury occurs deep in the backwoods, it may be possible to arrange for a doctor to come in via floatplane or helicopter.

If there is no way to get medical help to the scene and the victim must be carried to a cabin, farm-house, or road, a stretcher of some sort is a must. A well-padded folding-type cot will serve adequately. If no cot is available, a serviceable stretcher can be made by inserting two sturdy poles inside a buttoned coat or a couple of buttoned heavy-duty shirts, or by wrapping a blanket around two poles as shown in the accompanying illustration.

The victim must be properly prepared for a long carry. In addition to being given the first-aid treatments called for by his particular injury, he may need a period of rest before the ordeal of transportation. Broken bones and other injured areas should be made as immobile as possible. Loosen any tight clothing, and in general make the victim as comfortable as you can.

Care is the watchword when loading a victim onto a stretcher. It is best if at least three persons take part in the loading. The victim should be lying on his back with his feet tied together if feasible. Place the stretcher next to the victim.

The loaders should position themselves facing the victim's uninjured side,

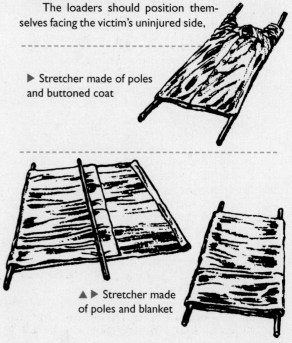

▶ Stretcher made of poles and buttoned coat

▲ ▶ Stretcher made of poles and blanket

one loader at the head, another at the midsection, the third at the feet. Each loader should kneel on the knee nearest the victim's feet. Arms are positioned under the victim as follows: loader at the head cradles the victim's head and shoulders with one arm and puts the other arm under the lower back; loader at the midsection supports the back and area just below the victim's buttocks; and the third loader's arms support the victim's thighs and calves.

One loader gives the command, "Lift," and all three together bring the victim up onto their knees, supporting him there without putting undue strain on the victim's body. One loader pulls the stretcher under the victim, and then all three, again on command, lower the victim down gently.

Provide enough blankets to keep the victim warm during the carry. Place padding wherever it's needed. (If the victim's injury is to the back of the head, he should be positioned on his side.) Tie the victim to the stretcher firmly enough to prevent him from slipping or rolling, but not so tightly as to interfere with blood circulation. Be sure that none of the bindings exert pressure on the injured area.

Ideally, there should be four stretcher-bearers, one at each end and one on each side. It's best to carry the victim so that he can see where he is going. In most cases, the head should be a bit lower than the rest of the body; however, the head should be elevated if there is a head injury or difficulty breathing.

Woods trails can be treacherous, so stretcher bearers should be especially alert for roots and other snags, rocks, slippery mud, and the like. If the carriers should lose their balance, the victim could incur further injury.

Bearers should watch the victim closely for signs of shock, discomfort, breathing difficulties, and other problems. Check the dressings periodically, and change or adjust them if necessary.

Loading a Victim onto a Stretcher

▲ **Step 1** • Loaders should be on the victim's uninjured side, all kneeling nearest the victim's feet.

▲ **Step 2** • At the command "Lift," loaders raise the victim gently to their knees.

▲ **Step 3** • Loader in command moves the stretcher under the victim and the victim is lowered to the stretcher.

▶ **Step 4** • The victim is covered and tied to the stretcher. If possible, there should be a bearer at each end and at each side.

motion. One of the bandages should cross the area of the injury. The knot or knots should be on the side of the chest opposite the break. Put a folded cloth under the knots. If the bandages cause pain, remove them.

If the broken rib seems to be depressed—that is, pushed down into the chest cavity of the victim, do not apply bandages.

If the victim must be moved, transport him in a prone position.

NOSE: Most nose-break victims have a noticeable wound— at least a bruise. There is usually some swelling and discoloration, and sometimes the shape of the nose is altered. Broken nose bones must be treated properly, or permanent deformity and breathing difficulties may result.

If there is bleeding, hold the lower end of the nose between your thumb and forefinger and press the sides of the nose against the septum (middle partition) for about five minutes. Avoid any side-to-side movement.

Release pressure gradually. Apply cold cloths. Have the victim sit up, hold his head back, and breathe through his mouth.

If there is a wound, apply a sterile protective dressing, and tape it into place, or bandage the dressing in place with strips of clean cloth tied around the head.

The nose-break victim should see a doctor as soon as possible.

JAW: In a fracture of the lower jaw, the upper and lower teeth often do not line up properly. There may be mild bleeding of the gum near the break, and jaw movement will cause pain. Speaking and swallowing are usually difficult.

Lift the lower jaw gently so that the lower and upper teeth meet.

Position the middle of a wide strip of clean cloth under the chin, and tie the ends on top of the head, thereby supporting the jaw.

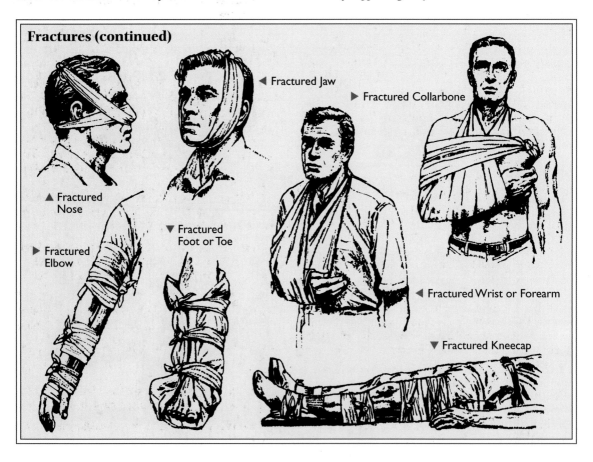

Fractures (continued)

◀ Fractured Jaw

▶ Fractured Collarbone

▲ Fractured Nose

▼ Fractured Foot or Toe

▶ Fractured Elbow

◀ Fractured Wrist or Forearm

▼ Fractured Kneecap

If the victim begins to vomit, remove the cloth bandage at once. Support the jaw with your hand. Replace the bandage when the vomiting stops.

COLLARBONE: A victim of this break will usually assume the following position: shoulder bent forward, elbow flexed, forearm across the chest and supported by the hand on the opposite side. There may be swelling, local tenderness, and possibly some deformity.

Use a sling—wide enough to extend from elbow to wrist—to support the arm on the injured side. Adjust the sling so that the hand is slightly above the level of the elbow.

Tie another bandage, not so wide, so that it encircles the arm on the injured side and the chest, snugging the arm against the side of the body. Don't tie the bandage so tight that it interferes with circulation.

Try to keep the victim's shoulders erect.

ELBOW: One symptom of this fracture is swelling above the elbow joint. Leave the arm in the position in which the victim holds it. Protect the joint from movement.

If the arm is held straight, put on a single splint that extends from fingertips to armpit. Position the splint on the palm side of the arm. Tie it on securely, but do not wrap any of the bindings around the elbow area.

If the arm is bent, put it in a sling, and use an around-the-chest bandage to bind the arm to the side of the body.

WRIST OR FOREARM: A break in one of the two bones in the forearm is quite common. The break is usually near the wrist. A break in one of the eight small wrist bones is sometimes thought to be only a sprain. With a break in either place, the fingers and thumb can be moved freely, though movement may cause some pain.

Put on a padded splint that extends from the victim's palm to elbow.

Put the arm in a sling arranged so that the fingers are about 4 inches higher than the elbow.

The fingers should remain uncovered so that they can be watched for swelling or discoloration. If either of those signs occur, carefully loosen the splint or the sling, or both.

FINGER: Put a splint on the finger, immobilizing it. Support the hand with a sling. Don't treat this injury casually; get the victim to a doctor. Permanent deformity can result if proper treatment isn't given.

KNEECAP: Prompt and proper treatment of this injury is a must, because flexion of the knee can pull apart the pieces of a broken kneecap (patella).

Gently straighten the victim's leg.

Put on a splint on the underside of the leg. The splint should be inflexible, about 6 inches wide, and long enough to reach from the buttocks to just below the heel. Tie the splint in place firmly, but not so tight that circulation is impeded (check the ties every half hour or so). Do not make any of the ties over the kneecap itself.

Transport the victim in a prone position.

FOOT OR TOE: Remove the victim's shoe and sock quickly—swelling may be extremely rapid. Cut away the footwear if necessary.

Apply clean dressings padded with cotton, or tie a small pillow, folded blanket, or something similar around the foot and bottom of the leg.

Caution the victim against movement of the foot, ankle, or toes.

■ Sprains

Sprains are injuries to the soft tissues that surround joints. Ligaments, tendons, and blood vessels are stretched and sometimes torn. Ankles, fingers, wrists, and knees are the areas most often affected.

Symptoms include pain when the area is moved, swelling, and tenderness to the touch. Sometimes a large area of skin becomes discolored because small blood vessels are ruptured.

It is often difficult to tell whether the injury is a sprain or a fracture. If in doubt, treat as a fracture. Otherwise, take the following steps:

1. Elevate the injured joint, using pillows or something similar. A sprained ankle should be raised about 12 inches higher than the torso. For a wrist or elbow sprain, put the arm into a sling.

2. Apply an ice pack or cold cloths to reduce swelling and pain. Continue the cold treatment for a half hour.

3. Always have a sprain X-rayed. There may indeed be a fracture or a bone chip.

If the victim of a sprained ankle is far from help and must walk, make the following preparations:

1. Untie the shoelaces to allow for swelling, but do not take off the shoe.

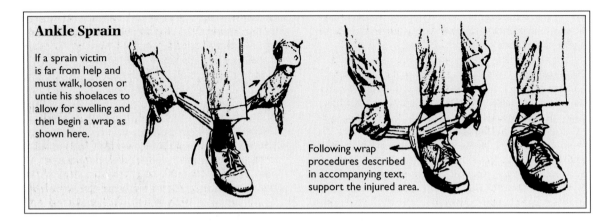

Ankle Sprain

If a sprain victim is far from help and must walk, loosen or untie his shoelaces to allow for swelling and then begin a wrap as shown here.

Following wrap procedures described in accompanying text, support the injured area.

2. Place the middle of a long bandage (a folded triangular bandage is best) under the shoe just forward of the heel.

3. Bring the ends of the bandage up and back, crossing them above (at the back of) the heel.

4. Bring the ends forward around the ankle, and cross them over the instep.

5. Bring the ends downward toward the heel, and slip each end beneath the wrap that comes up from each side of the heel.

6. Bring the ends of the bandage all the way around the ankle again, pull on the ends to produce the desired tension, and then tie a square knot in front.

OTHER INJURIES

■ Eyes Injuries or Foreign Body in Eye

For first-aid purposes, eye injuries fall into three categories: injury to eyelids and soft tissue above the eye, injury to the surface of the eyeball, or injury that extends into the tissue beneath the eyeball surface.

In Category 1, treatment involves putting on a sterile dressing and bandaging it in place. If the injury is in the form of a bruise (the familiar "black eye"), the immediate application of cold cloths or an ice pack should halt any bleeding and prevent some swelling. Later, apply warm, wet towels to reduce discoloration.

Injuries in Category 2 usually occur when a foreign body lodges on the surface of the eyeball. To remove the object, pull the upper eyelid down over the lower one, and hold it there for a moment, instructing the victim to look upward. Tears will flow naturally and may wash out the object.

If that doesn't work, put two fingers of your hand on the skin just below the victim's lower eyelid, and force the skin gently downward, thereby exposing the inner area of the lower lid. Inspect the area closely, and if the object is visible, lift it out carefully, using a corner of a

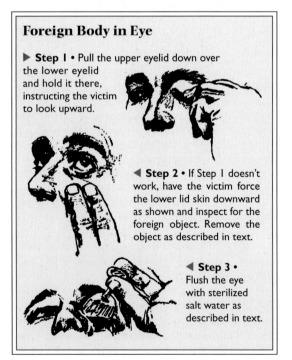

Foreign Body in Eye

▶ **Step 1** • Pull the upper eyelid down over the lower eyelid and hold it there, instructing the victim to look upward.

◀ **Step 2** • If Step 1 doesn't work, have the victim force the lower lid skin downward as shown and inspect for the foreign object. Remove the object as described in text.

◀ **Step 3** • Flush the eye with sterilized salt water as described in text.

clean handkerchief or a small wad of sterile cotton that has been moistened with water and wrapped around the end of a toothpick.

If the foreign object can't be seen, it can sometimes be flushed out. Boil some water, add table salt (¼ teaspoon to an average glassful), and let the salt water cool to about body temperature. With the victim lying down, tilt his head toward the injured side, hold his eyelids open with your fingers, and pour the liquid into the inner corner of his eye so that it runs across the eyeball and drains on the opposite side.

Eye injuries in Category 3 are extremely serious. Never attempt to remove an object that has penetrated the eyeball, no matter how shallow. Apply a sterile compress or clean cloth, cover it with a loose bandage, and get the victim to a doctor at once.

■ Cuts, Abrasions, and Bruises

Minor mishaps frequently involve one of these three injuries. With abrasions (the rubbing or scraping off of skin) and small cuts, the emphasis should be on preventing infection.

Immediately clean the cut or abrasion and the surrounding area with soap and warm water. Don't breathe on the wound or let fingers or soiled cloth contact it.

If there is bleeding, put a sterile pad over the wound and hold it there firmly until the bleeding stops. Then apply an antiseptic, if available, and apply a fresh sterile pad, bandaging it in place loosely.

A bruise results when small blood vessels under the skin are broken, causing discoloration of the skin and swelling, which is often painful.

First aid may be unnecessary if the bruise is minor. If it is more severe, apply an ice pack or cold cloths to reduce the swelling and relieve the pain. Bruises on an extremity can be made less painful if the limb is elevated.

■ Puncture Wounds

A puncture wound results when a sharp object—knife, needle, branch end, or the like—penetrates the skin and the tissue underneath. The first-aider's primary objectives here, and with all other wounds, are to prevent infection and control bleeding.

Puncture wounds are often unusual in that they may be quite deep but the bleeding, because of the small opening in the skin, may be relatively light. The lighter the bleeding, generally, the lesser the chance that germs embedded by the penetrating object will be washed out.

This means that the danger of infection is greater in puncture wounds than in other wounds. The danger of tetanus (lockjaw) infection is also greater in puncture wounds. First-aid procedures are as follows:

1. If the bleeding is limited, try to increase the flow by applying gentle pressure to the areas surrounding the wound. Do not squeeze hard, or you may cause further tissue damage.

2. Do not probe inside the wound. If a large splinter or a piece of glass or metal protrudes from it, try to remove it, but do so with extreme caution. If the sliver cannot be withdrawn with very gentle pressure, leave it where it is, or you may cause further damage and severe bleeding.

3. Wash the wound with soap and water.

4. Apply a sterile pad, and bandage it in place.

5. Get the victim to a doctor for treatment, including a tetanus shot if necessary.

■ Gunshot Wounds

Tetanus is a special problem in gunshot wounds. First-aid steps are as follows:

1. Stop the bleeding (see the Bleeding section for more information).

2. Apply a sterile pad, and bandage it in place.

3. If there is a fracture or a suspected fracture, immobilize the part (see the Bone Fractures section for more information).

4. Treat for shock (see the Shock section for more information).

5. Get the victim to a doctor quickly. A tetanus shot may be needed.

■ Fishhook Removal

A doctor's care—and a tetanus shot, if needed—are recommended for anyone who has had a fishhook embedded past the barb in the flesh. In many cases, however, medical help is not within easy reach. The severity of the injury and the size of the hook determine what action the first-aider should take.

If the hook has penetrated only up as far as the barb or slightly past it—and if it is not in a critical spot such as the eye—you should be able to pull or jerk it out. Then clean the wound, and treat it as you would any other superficial wound (see Cuts, Abrasions, and Bruises section for more information).

If the hook has penetrated well past the barb and is not in a critical area, there are two recommended methods of removal:

1. Force the hook in the direction in which it became embedded so that the point and barb exit through the skin. Try to make the angle of exit as shallow as possible. This can be quite painful, so the victim should anchor the affected part as solidly as possible before beginning the process. Using wire cutters or a similar tool, cut the hook in two at a point on the shank just before the bend. Remove the two pieces.

2. Have the victim anchor the affected part solidly. Take a 12- to 18-inch piece of strong string (30-pound-test fishing line is ideal), and run one end around the bend

Push-Through Hook Removal

▶ **Step 1** • Force the hook in the direction in which it became embedded.

▼ **Step 2** • Cut off the barb with a wire cutter.

▼ **Step 3** • Remove the two pieces of the hook.

Back-Out Hook Removal

Press down

Pull

String Loop

of the hook as if you were threading a needle. Bring the two ends together, and tie them in a sturdy knot. With the thumb and forefinger, push down (toward the affected part) on the shank of the hook at the point where the bend begins. This disengages the barb from the tissue. Maintaining that pressure, grasp the line firmly at the knotted end, and give a strong yank. The finger pressure on the shank should reduce flesh damage to a minimum as the barb comes out the same way it went in. Do not use this method if the hook is large.

If bleeding is minimal after either of these procedures, squeeze the wound gently to encourage blood flow, which has a cleansing effect. Put on a sterile dressing, and get medical help.

If the hook is a large one and is deeply embedded, or if it is in a critical area, do not try to remove it. Cover the wound, hook and all, with a sterile dressing, and get the victim to a doctor.

▉ Boils

A boil—a round, reddened, and usually painful elevation in the skin—is mostly dead tissue and germ-laden pus. Actually, it is an attempt by the body to keep an infection localized.

Do not squeeze a boil, or you may spread the infection. If the boil is very painful or appears to be spreading, apply hot, wet compresses. These may reduce the pain and cause the boil to come to a head more quickly.

When the boil comes to a head and discharges its contents, do not touch the escaping pus. Soak it up thoroughly with a gauze pad or clean cloth, thereby preventing infection of the surrounding skin. Cover the boil with a sterile dressing.

▉ Blisters and Foot Care

There was a time when you were told, "Never take brand-new boots on a hunting trip." That's no longer a hard-and-fast rule. Leather boots still require a break-in period, but composite boots that are synthetic do not require extensive breaking in.

Opinions vary, but most sportsmen prefer 8-inch-high boots for hunting, while 6-inch boots are the favorite for hiking.

Besides boots, there are other ways to protect your feet in the field. You should always wear two pairs of socks. The first pair to go on your feet should be lightweight, preferably polypropylene to wick away perspiration.

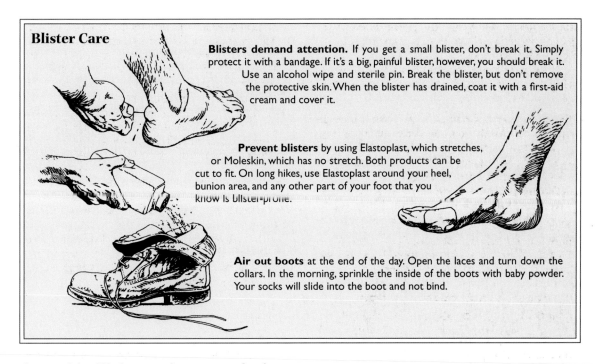

Blister Care

Blisters demand attention. If you get a small blister, don't break it. Simply protect it with a bandage. If it's a big, painful blister, however, you should break it. Use an alcohol wipe and sterile pin. Break the blister, but don't remove the protective skin. When the blister has drained, coat it with a first-aid cream and cover it.

Prevent blisters by using Elastoplast, which stretches, or Moleskin, which has no stretch. Both products can be cut to fit. On long hikes, use Elastoplast around your heel, bunion area, and any other part of your foot that you know is blister-prone.

Air out boots at the end of the day. Open the laces and turn down the collars. In the morning, sprinkle the inside of the boots with baby powder. Your socks will slide into the boot and not bind.

The second should be heavyweight, to warm and cushion your feet. In addition to providing warmth, two pairs of socks rub against each other—not against your feet.

Finally, give your feet a break. On your next trip, occasionally take off your boots and socks and rest your feet on a log.

■ Infected Wounds

One of the primary objectives in any first-aid situation is the prevention of infection, but the first-aider is sometimes called on to treat a wound that has already become infected. Symptoms of infection include swelling, redness (including red streaks emanating out from the wound), throbbing pain, and a "hot" feeling in the infected area.

First-aid steps are as follows:

1. Keep the victim lying down and as comfortable and calm as possible.

2. Apply heat to the area with hot-water bottles, or put warm, moist towels or cloths over the wound dressing. Change the wet packs often enough to keep them warm and cover them with a dry towel wrapped in plastic, aluminum foil, or waxed paper to hold in the warmth and to protect bedclothing.

3. Continue applying the warm packs for 30 minutes. Then remove them and cover the wound with a sterile dressing for another 30 minutes. Apply warm packs again. Repeat the whole process until medical care can be obtained.

ILLNESS

■ Fever

A rise in body temperature is a signal that something is amiss internally. There are many causes of fever, infection being the most common. In fact, fever is one of the body's defense mechanisms against infection. But if the fever reaches 104°F or higher, it may become a danger in itself. Here's what to do:

1. Get the victim into bed, and take his temperature if possible.

2. Send for a doctor.

3. Sponge the victim's body with cool or lukewarm water, treating one part of the body at a time and keeping the other parts covered.

4. Apply an ice bag or cool cloths to his head.

5. If he is conscious and there is no evidence of abdominal injury, give him some cold water to drink.

Epilepsy

In a full-blown epileptic attack, the victim becomes pale, his eyes roll, and he falls down, usually with a hoarse cry. He may turn blue, bite his tongue, and froth at the mouth. His head, arms, and legs jerk violently, and he loses consciousness.

First-aid steps are as follows:

1. Do not try to restrain the victim's convulsions or thrashing; that phase of the attack will pass, usually within a few minutes.

2. Try to protect him against injury by moving away nearby objects.

3. To prevent him from biting his tongue, try to place an appropriate object (wad of cloth, piece of thick rubber, or piece of book cover) between the upper and lower teeth in one side of the mouth. Be sure that the object does not obstruct his breathing.

4. Give the victim no stimulants.

5. When the attack subsides, let the patient rest without being disturbed.

Appendicitis

The principle symptom is pain in the lower right part of the abdomen and sometimes over the entire abdominal region. Nausea and vomiting may be present, as may a mild fever. Constipation often occurs and is sometimes thought to be the cause of the victim's discomfort. Do not give a laxative if appendicitis is suspected—it will increase the danger that the appendix will rupture.

1. Have the patient lie down, and keep him comfortable.

2. Do not give him any food or water.

3. An ice pack placed over the appendix area may relieve pain. Do not apply heat to the appendix area.

4. Get medical help as soon as possible.

Diarrhea

Diarrhea is a common malady among outdoorsmen. Its causes are often associated with change: during an extended hunting or fishing trip, for example, the sportsman's eating and drinking habits are often much different than what they are at home. Attacks of diarrhea usually subside once the body adapts to those changes.

Paregoric is helpful in combating diarrhea, as are many of the products designed for that purpose and sold in drugstores. If you or your companions are particularly prone to attacks of diarrhea, see a doctor and ask him to prescribe a drug, preferably in tablet form, that will combat the problem during trips afield.

Earache

An earache is usually a sign of an infection, so the sufferer should seek medical attention as soon as feasible.

The following first-aid procedures should offer some relief:

1. Treat with either heat or cold. There is no way to predict which will work best, but try cold first, putting an icepack or cold compress over the ear. If that doesn't work, try a hot-water bottle or hot compress.

2. For further relief, put a few drops of warm mineral oil in the affected ear, if it is not ruptured.

3. Caution the sufferer against blowing his nose hard, which probably will increase the pain and may spread the infection.

Toothache

First-aid procedures are as follows:

1. Inspect the sufferer's mouth under the strongest light available.

2. If no cavity is visible, place an ice pack or cold compress against the jaw on the painful side. If that doesn't provide relief, try a hot-water bottle or hot compress.

3. If a cavity can be seen, use a piece of sterile cotton wrapped on the end of a toothpick to clean the cavity as thoroughly as possible.

4. Oil of cloves, if available, can give relief. Pack it gently into the cavity with a toothpick. Do not let the oil touch the tongue or the inside of the mouth—the stuff burns.

FIRST-AID KIT

Improvisation is an ability that most outdoors people seem to develop naturally. But an improvised dressing for a wound, for example, is a poor second-best for a prepackaged, sterile dressing. Any first-aider can function more effectively if he has the proper equipment. A first-aid kit—whether it is bought in a pharmacy or is put together by the individual—should meet the following requirements:

- Its contents should be complete enough for the purposes for which it will be used.
- The contents should be arranged so that any component desired can be located quickly and without removing the other components.
- Each component should be wrapped so that any unused portion can be repacked and thereby prevented from leaking or becoming soiled.
- How and where the kit will be used are the main factors to consider when assembling a first-aid kit. The two kits described below should fill the needs of most outdoor situations.

■ POCKET KIT

Suitable for one-day, overnight, or short-term backpacking trips in areas not far from medical help.

- 1-by-1-inch packaged sterile bandages (2)
- 2-by-2-inch packaged sterile bandages (2)
- 2-by-2-inch packaged sterile gauze pads (2)
- Roll of adhesive tape
- Band-Aids (10)
- Ammonia inhalant (1)
- Tube of antiseptic cream
- Small tin of aspirin (or 12 aspirins wrapped in foil)

■ ALL-PURPOSE OUTDOORS FIRST-AID KIT

Suitable for general outings.

- 4-inch Ace bandages (2)
- 2-inch Ace bandages (2)*
- 2-by-2-inch sterile gauze pads (1 package)*
- 5-by-9-inch combine dressing (3)
- Triangular bandage (1)
- Sterile eye pads (2)
- ½-inch adhesive tape (5 yards)
- Assorted Band-Aids (1 package)*
- Betadine liquid antiseptic
- Yellow mercuric oxide ointment (for eyes)*
- Bacitracin (ointment)

- Tylenol (aspirin substitute)
- Dramamine (for motion sickness)
- Sunscreen
- Insect repellent
- Single-edge razor blade
- Tweezers (flat tip)
- Small scissors
- Eye patch
- Needle
- Matches in waterproof container
- Needle-nose pliers with cutting edge
- First-aid manual

Add these items if going into a remote area for an extended period of time:

- Tylenol with codeine (painkiller)**
- Tetracycline (antibiotic)**
- Lomotil, 2.5 milligrams (for cramps, diarrhea)**
- Antihistamine tablets
- Phillips Milk of Magnesia (antacid, laxative)

* Items, in fewer quantities, are recommended for a small first-aid kit for day trips. ** Requires a prescription.

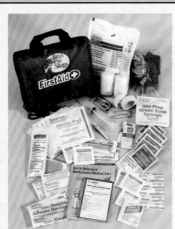

The Bass Pro Family First-Aid Kit is tailored specifically for outdoor activities and includes everything most families would need for a six-day trip. If you're not sure how to assemble a first-aid kit, a professionally packaged kit is a safe and sensible choice.

Index

Acknowledgments

The author would like to thank the following people, companies, organizations, and agencies for their permission, cooperation, and assistance in compiling information and photographs for this new edition:

Andy Anderson • Stu Apte • Joe Arterburn, Cabela's • James Babb • Chris Batin, Alaska Angler • Marilyn Bentz, National Bowhunter Education Foundation • Serio Borders, Classic Vans • Denver Bryan, Images on the Wildside • Dave Chanda, New Jersey Division of Fish and Wildlife • Tim Christie • Dean Corbisier, Suzuki • Chris Corey, L.L. Bean • James Daley, Orvis • Dan Dejkunchorn, Sea Eagle • Bill Dermody, Savage Arms • Daniel D. Dye II, Florida Backyard Snakes • Greg Eck, Yanmar America Corporation • Jim Edlund, Traditions Media • Laura Evans, Crosman • Nathan Figley, New Jersey Division of Fish and Wildlife • Steve Fleming, Mercury Marine • Tim Frampton, Weatherby • Pete Frederickson, Viking Yachts • Elizabeth Friedmann, Lyman Products • Gary Giudice, Blue Heron Communications • Ron Giudice, Blue Heron Communications • Tonya Giudice, Blue Heron Communications • Mary Gladue • Scott Grange, Browning • Jonathan Harling, Chevalier Advertising • William W. Hartley, Hartley Industries • Sheila M. Hassan • Jihan Hill, Rushton Gregory Communications • Kevin Howard, Howard Communications • Jim Hutchinson, Recreational Fishing Alliance • Isaiah James, Windsor Nature Discovery • Andrea Jansen, Mercury Marine • Charlie Johnson, Maverick Boat Company • Ken Jorgensen, Ruger • Jessica Kallam, Remington Arms • Jeff Kauzlaric, Furuno • Karen Kinser, Wright & McGill/Eagle Claw • Greg Lasiewski, Kawasaki • Chip Laughton, Days Afield Photography • Nick Lyons • Linda Martin, Wright & McGill •

Jim Martinson, Sheldon's • Stephen Matt, G3 Boats • Andrew McKean, Outdoor Life • Mac McKeever, L.L. Bean • J. Richard McLaughlin • Tom Mielke, Mercury Marine • Captain Glen Miller, Bud N' Mary's Marina • Stacy Miller, WorldCat • Katie Mitchell, Bass Pro • Gail Morchower, International Game Fish Association • Kellie Mowery, Cabela's • Andy Newman, Florida Keys and Key West Development Council • Wes Owen, Garmin International • Captain Dave Peck, Bud N' Mary's Marina • Martin Peters, Yamaha • Kim Phillips, Bass Pro • Cason Pilliod, Kalkomey • Linda Powell, Mossberg • Greg Proteau, Boating Writers International • Matt Rice, Smith & Wesson • Tom Rosenbauer, Orvis • Len Rue Jr., Len Rue Enterprises • Glenn Sapir, National Shooting Sports Foundation • Tammy Sapp, Bass Pro • Jim Sciascia, New Jersey Division of Fish and Wildlife • Dusan Smetana • Christine Smith, Redbone Coonhound Association of America • Elizabeth Smith • T. J. Stallings, Blakemore Fishing Group • Captain Richard Stanczyk, Bud N' Mary's Marina • Sarah Stern, Sabre Yachts • Mitch Strobl, Kalkomey • Paul Thompson, Browning • Tina Turley-Kocab, Turley Photography • Josh Ward, Ranger and Stratos Boats • Heidi Weber, Yamaha Motor Corporation • Bobby Wheaton, Yamaha Marine Group • Jeff Wieringa, Scientific Anglers • Brittany Williams, Rocky Brands • Tony Williams, Alday Communications • Gregg Wollner, Rapala • Monica Wu • Joan Wulff, Wulff School of Fly Fishing • Leslie Zlotnick, Yamaha Motor Corporation •

Photography Credits

© Andy Anderson: Front Cover, pp. 7 (second from top), and 206.

Courtesy of Bass Pro: pp. 28 (all except second from top), 56 (all except bottom right), 63 (bottom), 72, 92 (top right and bottom right), 208 (all), 213 (all except top right), 222 (all), 223 (all), 224, 228 (left), 230, 232 (all), 252 (all), 253 (all), 254 (all), 255 (all), 256 (top left and middle left), 257 (second from bottom left, bottom left, second from top right, and bottom right), 258 (all), 259 (all except second from bottom right), 262 (bottom left, top right, and bottom right), 389 (bottom), 390 (right), 399 (top and middle), 404 (bottom left and middle), 411 (all), 412, 413 (both), 422 (bottom left), 425 (middle and right), 426 (top), 457 (left), 463 (top left and bottom right), 467 (top left and top right), 470 (right), 481 (both), 485 (top), 490, 493 (left and middle), 494 (top middle, top right, and bottom), 496, 498, 509, 528 (all except right), 529 (bottom left, lower image in box), 540 (all), 546 (all), and 617.

Courtesy of Berkley: p. 262 (top left and middle left).

Courtesy of Boston Whaler: pp. 466 (middle) and 487 (left).

Courtesy of Browning: pp. 15 (bottom), 20 (second from top), 73 (bottom), 74 (second and third from top), and 118 (top right and second from top right).

© Denver Bryan/Images on the Wildside: pp. 7 (third from bottom), 158, 458, 555, 566, 570, and 571.

© Tony Bynum/Images on the Wildside: pp. 7 (top) and 10.

Courtesy of Cabela's: pp. 12 (top), 56 (bottom right), 65, 81 (both), 118 (bottom left and bottom right), 256 (top right), 259 (second from bottom right), 327 (both), 390 (left), 425 (left), 497 (bottom), 528 (right), 529 (bottom left, upper image in box), 530 (both), and 552.

© TimChristiePhoto.com: pp. 159, 160 (top), 161 (both), 162, 163, 164 (both), 165, 166, 167 (both), 168, 169 (top), 172 (bottom), 173, 174 (both), 175, 176 (bottom), 177 (bottom), 178 (both), 179 (bottom), 180, 181, 182 (both), 183, 184, 185, 186, 187 (both), 190, 191 (top), 195 (bottom), 196, 198, 199, 200, 201, and 202.

Courtesy of Classic Vans, California: p. 395.

Courtesy of Coleman: pp. 414, 415, and 453.

Courtesy of Crosman: p. 23 (both).

© Daniel D. Dye II: p. 596 (all).

Courtesy of Eagle Claw: pp. 233, 238 (top left and top right), 249 (all), 256 (bottom left), 257 (top right), 294 (both), and 319 (top).

© John Eriksson/Images on the Wildside: pp. 558, 572, 576, and 578.

Courtesy of Furuno: p. 495.

Courtesy of G3 Boats: pp. 463 (second from top left and top right), 466 (top), 474, 484, 486, 489, 511, and 553.

Courtesy of Garmin: p. 457 (right).

Courtesy of Harrington & Richardson: pp. 22 (bottom), 25 (top), and 73 (top).

© William W. Hartley: pp. 35, 68–71 (all), 116 (both), 120 (both), 123–126 (all), 210–211 (all), 225–226 (all), 228 (right), and 234 (all).

© Sheila Hassan: pp. 215–220 (all).

© John Herr/Images on the Wildside: pp. 7 (bottom), 554, 559, 563, and 577.

© Tim Irwin/Images on the Wildside: p. 560.

© Mark Johnson/Images on the Wildside: pp. 562 and 569.

Courtesy of Kawasaki: pp. 397 (bottom right) and 398.

© Bob Krist Photo/Florida Keys News Bureau: p. 499.

© Chip Laughton/Days Afield Photography: pp. 556, 561, 565, 567, and 580.

Courtesy of L.L. Bean: pp. 319 (bottom), 389 (all except bottom), 399 (bottom), 401, 404 (top left and right), 406, 422 (top left and top right), 424 (both), 426 (bottom), 467 (middle left, middle right, and bottom right), 470 (left), and 476.

Courtesy of Lowrance: p. 493 (right).

Courtesy of Lyman: pp. 28 (second from top), 54 (all), 130, 131 (bottom), 133 (both), 134, 135, 137, 138, 139 (top right and bottom right), 140 (top right and bottom right), 141 (top and bottom right), and 142 (top right and bottom right).

Courtesy of Marlin: pp. 15 (second from bottom) and 20 (third from top).

Courtesy of Maverick: p. 463 (bottom left).

© J. Richard McLaughlin: pp. 31 (all), 32 (all), 420 (all), 423 (all), 439, 445, 446 (both), and 447.

Courtesy of Mepps: pp. 256 (bottom right) and 257 (top left and second from top left).

Courtesy of Mercury: pp. 479 (top left and middle left) and 483 (bottom left).

Courtesy of Mossberg: pp. 77 (second from bottom) and 78 (bottom).

Courtesy of National Shooting Sports Foundation: p. 67.

Courtesy of Ocean Kayak: p. 468.

Courtesy of Orvis: pp. 267 (all) and 270–271 (all).

Courtesy of PARA: p. 118 (second from top left).

Courtesy of Pflueger: p. 213 (top right).

Courtesy of Ranger: p. 485 (middle).

Courtesy of Rapala: p. 238 (bottom left, middle, and bottom right).

Courtesy of Recreation Vehicle Industry Association: pp. 391, 392, 393, and 394 (both).

Courtesy of Redbone Coonhound Association of America: p. 584.

Courtesy of Remington: pp. 12 (bottom), 18 (both), 20 (top and second from bottom), 77 (second from top), 78 (top and second from top), 92 (top left and bottom left), 96, and 97.

© Tom Rosenbauer: pp. 243 and 268.

© Len Rue Enterprises, LLC: pp. 160 (bottom), 169 (bottom), 172 (top), 176 (top), 177 (top), 179 (top), 188 (both), 189, 191 (bottom), 192, 193, 195 (top), 203, and 205.

Courtesy of Ruger: pp. 12 (second from bottom), 20 (bottom), 22 (top), 117 (top left and middle left), and 118 (top left and second from bottom right).

Courtesy of Sabre Yachts: p. 459.

Courtesy of Savage: pp. 12 (third from bottom), 25 (bottom), and 74 (second from bottom).

Courtesy of Sea Eagle: p. 477.

© Dusan Smetana: Back Cover, pp. 2–3, 7 (third from top and second from bottom), 9, 334, 380, 437, 438, 526, 551, 581, 588, 634–635, and 636.

Courtesy of Smith & Wesson: pp. 74 (bottom) and 117 (bottom left, top right, and bottom right).

© Vin Sparano: pp. 63 (top), 236 (bottom), 260 (both), 320 (all), 322–323 (all), and 640.

Courtesy of Standard Horizon: p. 494 (top left).

Courtesy of Stratos: p. 485 (bottom).

Courtesy of Suzuki: p. 479 (bottom left and middle right).

© Turley Photography: p. 573.

Courtesy of Viking: p. 463 (second from top right).

Courtesy of Walther: p. 118 (second from bottom left).

Courtesy of Weatherby: pp. 12 (second from top), 50, and 77 (top).

Courtesy of Winchester: pp. 12 (third from top), 15 (top and second from top), 74 (top), 77 (bottom), 78 (second from bottom), and 98.

Courtesy of Woodsman's Pal: p. 416.

Courtesy of World Cat: pp. 466 (bottom) and 487 (right).

Courtesy of Yamaha: pp. 479 (top right and bottom right), 483 (bottom right), and 525 (both).

Courtesy of Yanmar: p. 482.

Courtesy of Yellowfin: p. 463 (second from bottom left).

ILLUSTRATION CREDITS AND OTHER NOTES

Unless otherwise noted here, all black-and-white line art was picked up from the fourth edition of *Complete Outdoors Encyclopedia*.

© James Daley: pp. 11, 159, 207, 335, 381, 439, 459, 527, 555, and 589 (opener illustrations only).

Courtesy of Kalkomey.com: pp. 396 (both), 397 (all), 460 (all), 461 (all), 471 (all), 478, 480 (all color), 483, 497 (all), 515 (all), 519 (all), 524 (both color), 527 (all), 529 (all), 530, 534 (all), 535 (all), and 539 (all color).

Courtesy of Lyman: pp. 127 (all), 131 (both), 136 (all), 139 (top left and bottom left), 140 (top left and bottom left), 141 (bottom left), and 142 (top left and bottom left).

Courtesy of Scientific Anglers: p. 245 (all).

Courtesy of United States Coast Guard: p. 523.

Courtesy of United States Geological Survey: p. 454.

Courtesy of Windsor Nature Discovery: pp. 335, 337–344 (all), 346–349 (all), 351 (both), 353, 354, 357 (both), 359, 360–363 (all), 365–371 (all), 373, and 376–379 (all).

- All text passages, images, and line art for the Handloading section (pp. 127–143) were provided courtesy of Lyman.

- Photos and portions of the text for the How to Use Fly Tackle section (pp. 215–220) were excerpted from Sheila Hassan's book *Fly Casting: A Systematic Approach* and used with her permission. For more information, visit her website: www.cast90.com.

- Illustrations and information on snowmobiles, boat hulls, sailboats, marine motors, anchors, buoys, personal flotation devices, personal watercraft, and archery were provided courtesy of Kalkomey Enterprises (see page numbers listed above). For more information, visit the company's websites: www.boat-ed.com; www.bowhunter-ed.com; www.hunter-ed.com; and www.snowmobile-ed.com.

About the Author

Vin T. Sparano has been an outdoor editor and writer for more than 50 years. He earned his B.S. degree in journalism in 1960 from New York University. Sparano is editor emeritus of *Outdoor Life* magazine, having served as Editor-in-Chief from 1990 to 1995 and previously as executive editor for more than 10 years.

In addition to his long career with *Outdoor Life*, Sparano was a syndicated features writer for *USA Today* and Gannett Newspapers. He has written and edited 18 books, and has produced electronic software focusing on fishing techniques and hotspots through the use of navigational charts and satellite photos.

Sparano and his wife, Betty, live in Waretown, New Jersey, where he is a familiar sight fishing from his boat, *Betty Boop*. During the fall, his focus is on the great striped bass fishery off Barnegat Inlet. In the winter months, Sparano travels to Florida, where he fishes the famous Islamorada Flats for tarpon and bonefish, as well as the offshore waters for sailfish, tuna, and other bluewater game fish.

A certified NRA rifle, pistol, shotgun, and hunting safety instructor, Sparano has been a member of the Outdoor Writers Association of America, fulfilling a term on its board of directors, and is also a heritage member of the Professional Outdoor Media Association. Sparano was a recipient of a Lifetime Achievement Award from both the New York Metropolitan Outdoor Press Association and the Fisherman's Conservation Association.

In 1996, Sparano was awarded the United States Department of the Interior Conservation Award by Secretary of the Interior Bruce Babbitt for his extraordinary contributions to conservation and outdoor journalism. In 2013, he was enshrined in the Fresh Water Fishing Hall of Fame. Sparano is also listed in *Who's Who in America*.

■ ■ ■